THE
American Tradition
in Literature

VOLUME 1

THE

AMERICAN TRADITION

IN LITERATURE

VOLUME 1

Bradford to Lincoln

VOLUME 2

Whitman to the Present

THE

American Tradition

in Literature

Edited by

Sculley Bradley

UNIVERSITY OF PENNSYLVANIA

Richmond Croom Beatty

VANDERBILT UNIVERSITY

E. Hudson Long

BAYLOR UNIVERSITY

VOLUME

1

Bradford to Lincoln

W · W · NORTON & COMPANY · INC · *New York*

Book design by John Woodlock

PRINTED IN THE UNITED STATES OF AMERICA
FOR THE PUBLISHERS BY THE VAIL-BALLOU PRESS

Contents

DIARISTS AND OBSERVERS

REASON AND REVOLUTION

The New Nation and the House Divided   316

ROMANTIC REDISCOVERY: NATURE, MAN, SOCIETY

SYMBOLIC AND ETHICAL IDEALISM

THE HUMANITARIAN AND CRITICAL TEMPER

Contents · xiii

Preface

In compiling this work we have intended to provide a freshly considered collection of great American writings representing the range and power of our literature as a whole. Our effort has been to represent major authors in the fullness of their stature and variety. Besides the titans, we have included writers of lesser stature whose works endure; but no author was introduced primarily for the purpose of illustrating literary or social history. In the same way, works of popular literature and humor have been admitted as literature, not as social or cultural documents.

While we have made literary merit our final criterion for selection, we have attempted in our critical apparatus to emphasize the relations between the literary work and the general movements in American civilization and intellectual history. In the textual annotations, as in the introductory essays and biographical sketches, we have attempted to secure as much objectivity as possible, to suppress individualistic critical tendencies of our own in favor of the consensus of our professional peers, and to leave the reader free to pursue his own ideas and values without having to contend with ours. Yet we have annotated liberally, believing it our function as editors, while abstaining from the expression of personal prejudice or opinion, to elucidate any substantial obscurity that would handicap a reader lacking immediate access to the appropriate reference books.

During the present century the writings of Americans have become an important influence in the literature of the western world, and our second volume has considerably more than the usual representation of twentieth-century authors. But as early as the age of Jonathan Edwards and Franklin, and even more in that of Poe, Emerson, and Whitman, the voice of our young nation was heard far beyond the shores of our continent. In editing the present collection we have been fully aware of the increasing responsibilities involved in selecting from such a national inheritance the works that would best represent its nature and its values. In performing this task we have become indebted to the rapidly accumulating contributions of American scholars and critics, to whom we have acknowledged our precise obligations in our notes.

The study of American literature can be acceptably organized in several ways; we have therefore attempted to provide a certain flexibility in our sequence of authors and texts. In general we have followed a chronological order, but by a few slight departures we were also able to bring authors together under topical headings which represent the pronounced response of our literature, at one time or another, to regional influences, social forces, dominant ideas, historical events, or aesthetic values.

We have tried to avoid cutting a work. The novelists have been represented by novelettes or short stories where possible; otherwise, as in the case of Wolfe and Dos Passos, the excerpts or works originally published independently in periodicals. These volumes contain four complete novelettes, including Faulkner's *The Bear* (often reprinted in part). In the first volume, Melville's *Billy Budd* appears in a text which has been compared with manuscript sources and is here printed for the first time. The first volume also contains Emerson's *Nature* in its entirety. Obviously it was necessary to make selections from such lengthy works as Franklin's *Autobiography* and Thoreau's *Walden*; in all instances the omission of text has been indicated by three asterisks, and except where printed between square brackets titles are those of the original. Where possible, as in *Leaves of Grass*, we have preserved the original plan of the work.

Since masterpieces endure, many of our selections are, and should be, familiar; but wherever it seemed possible to make a fresh substitution without loss of values, we have done so. For example, besides the less usual selections previously named, we have included Jonathan Edwards' "The Nature of True Virtue," some of the poems of Thoreau, James's *Madame de Mauves*, some less familiar poems of Eliot, and Steinbeck's *The Red Pony*; and we have secured permission to exceed previous limitations upon the amount of material quoted, or the titles available for anthologies, from the works of Dreiser, Cather, and Hemingway.

We have gone to considerable lengths to provide in each case a faithful copy of the text which in our judgment is the best edition of the work. Like the text of *Billy Budd*, that of Emily Dickinson's poems represents a fresh comparison with the original manuscripts, since we were kindly given permission to follow the text newly established by Thomas H. Johnson in *The Poems of Emily Dickinson* (1955). Whether we use the first edition of a work, the last edition supervised by the author, or a later edited text, the source will be obvious in the bibliographical note or is given in a footnote. In editing the difficult texts of colonial writers we have been guided by the condition of the particular texts. Those, like Bradford's *Of Plymouth*

Plantation, in which archaic spelling, punctuation, and abbreviations are a mechanical handicap for many readers, have been normalized in accordance with present practice. But the language has not been altered or "modernized," and the texts of colonial poets are untouched, and like most of the prose, clarified only by annotation. We have dated the works where possible; the date at the lower right margin is the date of first publication in a volume, and this may be immediately preceded by the date of first periodical publication, if significant. If the date of composition is known and is thought to have importance, it also is shown, at the bottom left margin of the selection.

The essays introducing the four periods we deem significant are not intended to constitute a literary history. Most libraries have copies of one or more standard literary histories of the United States, and we have no thought to compete with them. Each essay is designed to introduce the literature we have collected for that period, and to present critical considerations not appropriate for treatment in the individual biographical headnotes. At the end of each volume appears a chronology that includes important American publications, works of foreign literature which then or later became influential in America, significant works in the other arts, events of American political and social history, and such events of world history as had American consequences.

It seems proper to acknowledge the responsibility of each collaborator. Mr. Bradley acted as general editor for the entire work, and wrote the introductory essays for each of the four historical periods. For the first volume Mr. Beatty prepared the texts, Mr. Bradley the headnotes and other critical apparatus. In the second volume, for the period from 1865 to 1914, Mr. Long edited and annotated the texts; the biographical essays for this period represent the collaboration of Mr. Long and Mr. Bradley. Mr. Bradley was responsible for the annotated texts and critical apparatus for the section on the twentieth-century revival after 1914; he prepared the chronology for both volumes.

We have received generous and expert advice from numerous friends and colleagues, to whom we here again extend our thanks. We must particularly acknowledge the assistance of Professor Robert E. Spiller, of the University of Pennsylvania, Professor Leon Howard, of the University of California, and Professor Robert H. Elias, of Cornell University. We are grateful for services rendered by the Vanderbilt University Library and the Baylor University Library. Especially we are indebted to the staff of the Rare Book Collection of the Library of the University of Pennsylvania, who put at our disposal an unusual collection of first editions and other basic texts represented in these volumes, and gave us expert assistance in the

T H E
American Tradition
in Literature

VOLUME 1

The Literature of the Colonies and the Revolution[*]

There was an enormous amount of writing in America during the first century of settlement. The adventurers and settlers wrote descriptions of the country, like those by Captain John Smith of Virginia, the most famous of the scores of chroniclers; they wrote picturesquely of explorations and discoveries, of Indian wars and captivities; they made personal journals of their experiences. They created their instruments of government and law; they recorded the history of their colonies, often for political or economic purposes, but also, in New England especially, to "justify the ways of God to men" in the New Jerusalem. A large number of these works were printed, in England or on the Continent. Most of them were merely timely, although useful for future historians; but with a frequency quite amazing, in view of the physical conditions of life in the New World,

there appeared the writer who was also a great person, who communicated the richness of his spirit or character in writings that time has not tarnished. Our colonial literature became a great reservoir of material and inspiration for that of the nineteenth century; for readers today it still provides an understanding of those bedrock American experiences which developed the national character and our peculiarly American institutions.

Although the people of the colonies derived their language and political institutions from Great Britain, they were to become increasingly indebted, as the British themselves had, to a variety of European cultures. The French, Germans, Swedes, and Dutch—and the Jews from Germany and Portugal, who appeared in the Middle Colonies especially during the eighteenth century—were merely following in the wake of European conti-

[*] This introduction should be read in conjunction with the Chronological Table beginning on page 1332.

nentals as far back as Eric the Red and Leif Ericsson. Also before the British, the Spaniards, in the half century following the voyage of Columbus, had rimmed the Gulf of Mexico and pushed westward to the Pacific. For all their hardihood, the early settlers could only vaguely comprehend the natural immensity that confronted their efforts—an unimaginable empire, between the Isthmus of Panama and the Arctic, of nearly eight million square miles, more than half of it covered by ancient forests of fabulous density. The land stretched before them in majesty and mystery, while the Indians told of wonders yet unseen—vast peaks and mighty rivers, shifting sands and ancient golden cities overrun by ruin.

It is no wonder if the American imagination bears, to this day, the indelible mark of this immeasurable richness, and of those dark people who possessed the land before them. America was El Dorado, the golden western limit of Renaissance energies; and this great tide was still at flood when the Reformation flung out another restless host for whom America became the Promised Land of the human spirit. At the same time that the New World invited the colonial ambitions of rival empires, or lured the adventurer for pelts and pelf, it was also holding out the promise of new freedom and new hope for men of some sober purpose or lofty idealism forbidden in the Old World. The majority of them, and predominantly those who came to rest in New England and the Middle Colonies, were products, in some sort, of the Protestant Reformation, a fact which continues to influence the life and thought of the United States.

VIRGINIA AND THE SOUTH

However, the first permanent English settlement was the result not of religious but of mercantile motives. The Virginia Company promoted the Jamestown colony (1607), expecting that its plantations would provide goods for the British trade and would attract the Englishmen who needed homes and land. Their conception of the new world was so unrealistic that they brought with them to Virginia a perfumer and several tailors. Epidemic fevers and Indian raids during the first few years reduced the colony as fast as new recruits could be brought in on the infrequent supply ships. The Indians, who had been counted on for cheap labor, refused to be enslaved or even to work. Innocent of the European concept of property, they resented the settlers who fenced and cultivated their hunting grounds, and they retaliated with blood and fire. Still, somehow the colony increased, first at Jamestown, then at Williamsburg, the handsome colonial capital where, in 1693, William and Mary was founded as the second college in North America.

During the seventeenth century the South was not a land of large plantations. However, the eventual shift from a yeoman to a slave-holding plantation economy was an inevitable result of British mercantilism, an abusive colonial system to be sure, but one which, for a time, perhaps actually benefited the agricultural colonies of the South. The Navigation Acts of the late seventeenth century were intended to compel the colonists to sell to the mother country all their raw materials and agricultural exports, for which they were to receive in exchange British manufactured products. Since British shipping was given a monopoly of the carriage, at rates fixed in England, the mother country was assured of a credit balance. In the northern colonies, where natural conditions favored manufactures and commerce, this exploitation in time became intolerable, and provided one of the deep-rooted reasons for the Revolution. Although the southern plantation colonies were restless at being confined to the British market, their crops were generally salable there. The southern plantation wealth grew steadily, supporting, in the eighteenth century, a tidewater aristocracy that produced some families of great culture, whose sons enjoyed the advantages of British and continental universities and built up fine private libraries. They ultimately produced such leaders and statesmen as the Byrds, Jefferson, and Madison. Yet, before the period of the Revolution, they added but little to the creative literature of the colonies. This does not seem surprising. The urban centers were small and widely separated; and the population, much dispersed, was composed of a few privileged aristocrats, thousands of slaves, and a white middle class of generally unlet-

tered frontiersmen and small yeoman farmers.

NEW ENGLAND

In the New England colonies, as has been implied, the situation was quite different. At Plymouth (1620), Salem (1628), Massachusetts Bay (1630), and other nearby spots soon settled, more than twenty thousand Englishmen found new homes. A considerable number were learned, especially the Puritan clergymen and governors; and some of them were great men. Even in the seventeenth century they produced a considerable body of writing. Yet they were not literary people in the professional sense, and they were intent upon subduing a wilderness, making homes, and building a new civil society, on which they had staked their lives, and in some instances, their fortunes.

It was not long until the colony at Massachusetts Bay assumed the natural hegemony of New England. Here was the physical situation—a harbor and river—for expansion into a cluster of small towns in close association with each other. The governor of the Massachusetts Bay Company, John Winthrop, a strong Puritan, moved the seat of his company from London to Boston Bay, thus making the chartered company into an overseas colony with limited, but then quite unprecedented, powers of self-government. The Puritans who followed Winthrop were thrifty, and they thrived. They initiated a town-meeting government, popular elections, a bicameral council, and other novelties that were to become parts of the machinery of democracy. They can justly be charged with intolerance, of course, for they soon achieved a consensus on matters of dogma, and they had no such problems of diversity as made toleration inevitable in the Middle Colonies. But in New England such outcasts as Roger Williams and Anne Hutchinson soon founded colonies of their own, thus accelerating the outward flow of forces from Boston into New Hampshire, Connecticut, and Rhode Island. By 1643 there was the beginning of the New England Federation for mutual security and co-operative economic enterprise.

PURITANISM

The earliest English Puritans were devout members of the Church of England and had no desire to produce a schism. By the time of Elizabeth's reign the Church of England was clearly Protestant in respect to its separation from Rome. The Puritans wished the reform to be carried much further, in order to simplify or "purify" the creeds and rituals and to diminish the authority of the bishops, but still no official break was intended. In 1633, however, the elevation of Archbishop Laud put the Church of England in the control of a tyrant who was determined to root out "Calvinist" dissenters, Presbyterian or Puritan, by legal persecution. The consequent soul-searching among Puritans, who were never a "sect" in the sense that the Presbyterians were, carried them closer to certain fundamental tenets of John Calvin (1509–1564); and the most powerful and radical of them, unwilling to submit to the abusive and cruel laws against them, soon formed the core of the New England clergy. It should be emphasized, however, that the Puritans did not regard the word of Calvin as the word of authority. They agreed with him when they thought him reasonable, but there were many aspects of his theology that they found unreasonable and so disregarded.

The ideas of Martin Luther (1483–1546), the earlier leader of the great Reformation, likewise became a permanent influence on both religious and civil institutions of American democracy. Concepts of authority, both civil and ecclesiastical, had been everywhere slowly weakening; they were shattered, wherever Luther's words were received, by his doctrine of the "priesthood of believers." "Neither Pope or Bishop nor any other man," he said, "has a right to impose a single syllable of law upon a Christian man without his consent."

Calvin's *Institutes*, on the other hand, authorized a theological system in certain respects as rigid as that of the Church of Rome, but its ultimate official authority was the consensus of its constituents, and not a hierarchy. In this system the New England "congregational meeting" was inherent from the beginning. In earlier stages of the Reformation it was held that the religion of the ruler should be the religion of the country he dominated, but Calvin, like Catholic thinkers, insisted that the church should be independent. The state should, in fact, be its servant. The result, in early New England during the Puritan period, was that the leading clergymen, powerful and well-trained, were for a time the dominating temporal as well as spiritual authority; but by 1700 their civil powers began to crumble under the weight of new secular influence.

In common with all advocates of strict Christian orthodoxy, American Puritans subscribed to Calvin's insistence that the omnipotent God had created the first man, Adam, in his own perfect image, that Adam in his willfulness had broken God's covenant, and that, as *The New England Primer* put it, "In Adam's fall we sinned all." It was Calvin's dogmas of predestination and grace that set him sharply apart from Luther on the one hand and the Roman Catholic Church on the other. The redemption of the individual came only by regeneration, the work of the spirit of God "in the souls of the elect and of them alone." Calvin and the Puritans put a special emphasis on the doctrine of original depravity. Adam's children were not mere automatons of evil impulse, since they possessed, as Adam had, a limited freedom of the will to make the good or evil choice. Still, nothing in man's personal power could mitigate the original sinfulness of his nature. Hence, redemption must be a free gift of God's saving grace, made to those predestined to receive it. No person could earn grace by good works, since good works, in themselves, could only be the result and

fruition of grace. These doctrines were characteristically reflected in the interpretation of Christ the Redeemer as representing God's New Covenant with mankind, as Adam represented the Old Covenant.

These doctrines, to which Jonathan Edwards gave the classic recapitulation when Puritanism was already waning, have been interpreted by many modern critics as excessively grim and gloomy. A stereotype of the Puritan has been created, depicting him as a dour, thinly ascetic fellow employing censorship and blue laws to impose his prudish standards on others. Most of the Puritans would have voted to put him in the stocks. It is true that extreme zealots among them, overinterpreting their dogmas, despised this mortal life in contrast to the next. The same zealots, during an outbreak of hysterical superstition, persecuted the "witches." Yet the Puritans in general were lovers of life, their clergy were well-educated scholars in whom the Renaissance lamp of humanism still burned. They did not forbid gaily colored clothes if they could get them; they developed a pleasing domestic architecture and good arts and crafts on American soil; they liked the drink even if they despised the drunkard; they feared both ignorance and emotional evangelism, and made of their religious thought a rigorous intellectual discipline. They were the earliest colonists to insist on common schools; they had the first college (Harvard, 1636) and the first printing press in the colonies (Cambridge, 1638); and they were responsible for the most abundant and memorable literature created in the colonies before 1740. In their influence on American life, there is much more to bless them for than to condemn.

THE MIDDLE COLONIES

Lying between New England to the northeast and the sprawling farmlands of the southern colonies stretched the provinces of New York, New Jersey, Delaware, and Pennsylvania. The seed of American toleration was sown in this area, with its diversity of national strains, for here the melting pot that produced Crèvecœur's conception of an American boiled with a briskness unknown elsewhere along the Atlantic seaboard. Dutch and Swedish colonies were established in New York and Pennsylvania before the British came; the tolerance of Pennsylvania attracted large numbers of German and French-Huguenot refugees; and Jewish merchants early appeared in New York and Philadelphia.

Of all the colonies, the Middle Colonies enjoyed the best geographical location, the easiest access to the great inland waterways and stored natural resources of the continent, the largest economic promise, resulting from a fine balance of agricultural, manufacturing, and commercial potentials. By 1750, the Quaker city of Philadelphia had become the unofficial colonial capital by virtue of its location, the size of its population, and the volume of its commercial activity, in which respects it surpassed any city, except London, in the British Empire. The cultural institutions of the Middle Colonies, somewhat different from those of New England, were to prove quite as important in providing those basic conditions and ideas which, during the revolutionary crises of the eighteenth century, were formally welded into a national character and a frame of democratic government then unique among the nations of the world.

Of the many groups present in the Pennsylvania colony, the Quakers were the most homogeneous. Although these Friends, in the beginning, were drawn primarily from the humbler ranks of the English middle classes—they were artisans, tradesmen, and yeoman farmers for the most part—their American leader, William Penn, was one of the best-trained men in the colonies, and one of the greatest. He was a follower of George Fox, the English shepherd and cobbler whose powerful evangelism welded his disciples into the Religious Society of Friends. The early Quaker theology was fundamentally closer to Luther's than to Calvin's. It was less concerned with the original depravity of man than with the abounding grace of God. But Fox and his followers went far beyond Luther's rebellion against the delegated authority of pope or bishop; Fox taught that the ultimate authority for any person was the "inner light," the divine immanence, revealed to his own soul. Thus the Quaker worshiped in quiet, waiting upon the inward revelation of unity with the Eternal.

Penn had inherited from

his father a large financial claim upon the government of Charles II, and in 1681 he secured in settlement the vast colonial estate which the King named Pennsylvania. As Proprietor, Penn exercised great powers, but in writing his famous "Frame of Government" he ordained a free commonwealth, bestowing wide privileges of self-government upon the people. Convinced that "the nations want a precedent," he declared that "any government is free to the people where the laws rule * * * and the people are party to the laws. * * * Liberty without obedience is confusion, and obedience without liberty is slavery." These words, and the precedent which he established by his "Holy Experiment," remained alive in the American colonies, much later to be embodied in the Declaration of Independence of the nation and in its constitutional instrument of government, both written in Penn's city.

Under these favorable conditions the colony thrived. Like the Puritans, the Quakers quickly made provision for education. Four years after Penn's arrival, they had their first press (1686) and a public school chartered by the Proprietor. In 1740 Philadelphians chartered the Charity School, soon called the Academy, and later the University of Pennsylvania, the fourth colonial college (following Harvard, William and Mary, and Yale). During the same period the Middle Colonies founded three other colleges: Princeton (the College of New Jersey, 1746), Columbia (King's College, 1754),

and Rutgers (Queen's College, 1766).

The energies of the inhabitants of these colonies of mixed cultures, centering upon Pennsylvania, fostered the development of science and medicine, technical enterprise and commerce, journalism and government—Penn, for example, made the first proposal for a union of the colonies—but in spite of the remarkable currency of the printed word among them, they produced less than New England of lasting literary value until after the first quarter of the eighteenth century. William Penn, however, proved to be a genuine writer, if on a limited scale. Besides his famous "Frame of Government," two of his works have continued to live: *No Cross No Crown* (1669), a defense of his creed, and *Some Fruits of Solitude* (1693), a collection of essays on the conduct of life and his Christian faith. Many of the early American Friends published journals, but only one, that of John Woolman, survives as great literature. Of the many early colonial travelers and observers, some from the Middle Colonies produced literary records comparable with those of Byrd of Virginia and Madam Knight of Boston. Crèvecœur, perhaps the most gifted of the colonial travelers, settled in Pennsylvania and later in upstate New York. John Bartram and his more famous son, William, established a long tradition of natural history in Philadelphia. Each left an important record of his travels and observations of American natural history, scientifically valuable, and, in William's case, a work of genuine literature. On settling in this country in 1804, the greater naturalist and painter John James Audubon made Philadelphia his home.

THE ENLIGHTENMENT

These Middle Colonies, as a result of their mixed culture and central location, became the natural center for activities of mutual interest, such as the intercolonial convention or congress. A growing sense of unity and independence characterized the second great period of American cultural history, beginning about 1725. Politically, this spirit encouraged the growth of a loose confederation, disturbed by the British colonial wars on the frontier and by "intolerable" British trade and taxation policies. In succession it produced the Revolution, the federal and constitutional union of the states, and the international recognition of the hegemony of the United States on the North American continent by about 1810, roughly the time of Jefferson's retirement as president, when a new national period began in literature and political life. During these years, the frontier moved beyond the Alleghenies, leaving behind it an established seaboard culture, and, in such cities as Philadelphia, Boston, and New York, a growing spirit of metropolitan sophistication.

The Enlightenment and its rationalistic spirit infused the minds and the acts of American leaders. Earlier religious mysticisms, local in character, were now overlaid by larger concerns for general toleration, civil rights, and a more comprehensive democracy in government. The conflict of ideas at the beginning of this period is well represented in a comparison of the contemporaries Jonathan Edwards and Benjamin Franklin, both among the greatest early Americans. Edwards represented the fullest intellectual development of the Calvinistic Puritan; his hard intellect and authoritarian convictions were tempered by human tenderness and spiritual sensitivity. Yet the last member of the Puritan hierarchy, Cotton Mather, had met fundamental and final opposition about the time Edwards was born. The secular spirit, the immigration of a new population, and the development of the urban spirit of enterprise and commerce would have doomed the Puritan commonwealth even if the Puritans themselves had not outgrown it.

The Age of Reason manifested a rationalistic conception of man in his relations with nature and God, suggested the extension of principles of equality and social justice, and encouraged the belief that man might assume greater control of nature without offending the majesty of God. If the universe, as Newton suggested, somewhat resembled a clock of unimaginable size, why might not man, by studying its laws, learn to utilize them for his benefit? The writings of John Locke (1632–1704) had enormous influence, and American readers also knew the writings of Locke's early student, Shaftesbury, and of various other British and French rationalists. Among the French writers, Rousseau and Quesnay, the best known in America, were both influential in their sociological ideas. Rousseau, in emphasizing the social contract as the "natural" basis for government, suggested a consistency between the laws of nature and those of society. Quesnay and his physiocratic followers strengthened this doctrine by asserting that society was based on the resources of nature, on land itself, thus stimulating the agrarian thought that was so attractive to Jefferson. Rationalism applied to theology produced Deism, but the degrees of Deism ranged widely, from the casual to the dialectical severity of Tom Paine. For the confirmed Deist, God was the first cause, but the hand of God was more evident in the mechanism of nature than in scriptural revelation; the Puritan belief in miraculous intervention and supernatural manifestations was regarded as blasphemy against the divine Creator of the immutable harmony and perfection of all things. But most enlightened rationalists confined their logic to practical affairs, or, like Franklin and Jefferson, entertained a mild Deism that diminished as they grew older.

THE BROADENING OF EIGHTEENTH-CENTURY LITERATURE

During this revolutionary end of the eighteenth century, Rationalism, reflected in the neoclassical spirit in literature, began to wane; at the same time a nascent romanticism appeared in life and literature. In England the influence of Pope was quickly superseded by the romanticism of Gray, Chatterton, Goldsmith, and the periodical essayists. Before Tom Paine wrote *The Age of Reason*, the age of revolution was well advanced; and the American and French revolutions advocated rationalistic instruments of government in support of romantic ideals of freedom and individualism. American writers, like the British, responded to these commingled influences, as for example, in the case of Jefferson or Freneau. The latter, an avowed Deist and a neoclassicist in his earliest poems, became in his later nature lyrics a forerunner of the romantic Bryant. This was the pattern of his age, in which the romantic movement, which was to dominate our literature after 1810, was already present in embryo. It was an age of magnificent literary energies, of vast upheaval, spiritual and social; and the rapid growth of publishing provided a forum for contestants of all ranks. The first newspaper to succeed in the colonies, the Boston *News-Letter*, had appeared in 1704; by the time of the Revolution there were nearly fifty. No magazine appeared until 1741, but after that date magazines flourished, and by the time of Washington's inauguration (1789) there had been nearly forty. Periodical publication gave a hearing to scores of essayists, propagandists, and political writers; to such leading authors as Paine and Freneau; and to lesser writers still remembered, such as Francis Hopkinson, whose verse satires plagued the British, and John Dickinson, a lawyer whose *Letters from a*

Farmer in Pennsylvania (1767–1768) skillfully presented the colonial position in various newspapers in the hope of securing British moderation before it was too late. William Smith, Provost of the College of Philadelphia, made his *American Magazine* (1757–1758) a vehicle for a talented coterie of his protégés and students—the short-lived Nathaniel Evans, Francis Hopkinson, and Thomas Godfrey, the first American playwright. Such verse as theirs, both satirical and sentimental, abounded in the periodicals, but although there had been scores of American poets by the time of the Revolution, only Freneau and Taylor have been greatly admired for their literary values. Among still earlier poets, Anne Bradstreet, who died in 1672, is remembered for her small but genuine lyric gift, appearing amid inhospitable conditions in Puritan Massachusetts, and Michael Wigglesworth is remembered for *The Day of Doom* (1662), the most popular Puritan poem, whose lengthy description of the Last Judgment conferred the benison of penance along with the fascinations of melodrama.

Theatrical activity had appeared sporadically ever since the beginning of the century. By 1749 a stock company was established in Philadelphia, and its seasonal migrations encouraged the building of theaters and the growth of other companies of players, in New York, Boston, Williamsburg, and Charleston. The native players, and visiting actors from England, devoted themselves principally to Eliza-bethan revivals and classics of the French theater, but it was an age of great talent on the stage, and the support of the theater, in spite of continuous opposition from religious objectors, illustrates the steady increase of urban sophistication. Thomas Godfrey's *Prince of Parthia*, the first native tragedy to be performed, reached the stage in 1767. During the Revolution, drama survived only as effective political satire. Native authorship revived in 1787, with the appearance of Royall Tyler's *The Contrast*, which still retains an archaic vitality; in its day it established the stereotype of "Brother Jonathan" for the homespun American character. Early native playwrights included two prominent writers of fiction, Susannah Rowson and H. H. Brackenridge. William Dunlap, a portrait painter, among whose many plays *André* (1798) remains a genuine, if now outdated work, lived far into the Knickerbocker period and was the first large-scale producer-playwright of our literature, although he went bankrupt in this enterprise.

Meanwhile, a native fiction had taken root. The great age of British fiction had begun about 1719, and such English novelists as Defoe, Fielding, Richardson, and even Smollett and Sterne were widely read in the colonies. Soon after the Revolution, however, fiction of native authorship appeared, first represented in two domestic novels, *The Power of Sympathy* (1789), by William Hill Brown, and *Charlotte Temple* (1794), by the English-born Susannah H. Rowson, which has been reprinted even in the twentieth century. A really fine picaresque novel, *Modern Chivalry*, by the Pennsylvania jurist H. H. Brackenridge, appeared in five parts between 1792 and 1815. Its author's learning in the classics and his familiarity with the great picaresque tradition of Cervantes were here combined with an acid and clever satire of early American failures in democratic politics. A third European fictional tradition, the Gothic romance of terror, found its American exemplar in Charles Brockden Brown, another Philadelphian, four of whose romances made literary history, if not great literature, between 1798 and 1800.

Freneau is the most important bridge between the classicism of the eighteenth century and the full-fledged romanticism of the nineteenth. Late in the eighteenth century, however, the seven so-called Connecticut Wits, most of them associated with Yale, attracted great attention by devoting themselves to a new national poetic literature. Three of them achieved a considerable distinction in life, but none of them affected the literature of America except in the historical sense. John Trumbull (1750–1831) is best remembered for his satires: *The Progress of Dullness* (1772), an amusing attack on "educators" which makes excellent sense if only passable poetry, and *Mc-*

Fingal (1775–1782), a burlesque epic blasting American Toryism. Timothy Dwight reached distinction as president of Yale, but of his poems only *Greenfield Hill* (1794) rises occasionally above his didactic solemnity. Joel Barlow (1754–1812) was a large-minded liberal and an American patriot, but no one who has been condemned to read his pioneer American epic, *The Vision of Columbus* (1787) or its even longer later version, *The Columbiad* (1807), can quite forgive him. His shorter mock-epic, *The Hasty Pudding* (1796), however, is the very entertaining work of a generous mind.

The literature of America up to the end of the eighteenth century needs no apology. The minor literature was abundant; it was serviceable to its time, and in retrospect it seems no more odd or feeble than the common stock of popular expression of the earlier periods of any nation. What is profoundly important is the wealth of true literature, the inspired expression of great men writing often under conditions unfavorable to literary expression, which appeared from the first, and increasingly through the years, in an abundance entirely out of proportion to the size of the population and the expectations that might be entertained for a country so new, and so wild and sparsely settled during its first century.

The Puritan Culture

WILLIAM BRADFORD
(1590–1657)

William Bradford was one of the greatest of colonial Americans, a man large in spirit and wisdom, wholly consecrated to a mission in which he regarded himself as an instrument of God. The early history of Plymouth Colony was the history of his leadership, and tiny Plymouth occupies a position in history wholly incommensurate with its size.

Like the patriarchs of the Old Testament, William Bradford in his annals recorded God's "choosing" of His people, their exile, and their wanderings. Even after twelve years in Holland, as Bradford wrote in the language of *Hebrews*, "they knew they were pilgrims," and must follow the cloud and fire to a land promised, if at first unpromising, their new Zion. In 1630 Bradford wrote his first ten chapters, dealing with the persecutions of the Separatists in Scrooby, England, their flight to Holland in 1608, and their history until they landed at Plymouth in 1620. His "Second Book," dealing with their history in Plymouth from 1620 until 1647, was written "in pieces," most of it before 1646.

"Of Plimoth Plantation," as Bradford entitled his manuscript, had an unusual history. Although its author was largely self-taught, and without training for literature, the book is a classic among literary annals. Its style is at one with the character and mind of its author; it has the functional propriety of the simple truth, the print of his memory, plain at times, but rising with his spirit to moments of loftiness. Without publication, it became known to the world. Five important colonial historians used and quoted from it before 1730, and Thomas Prince, the latest of them, deposited it in the "New England Library," his treasury of Americana in the "steeple room" of the old South Church in Boston. There Governor Thomas Hutchinson must have consulted it for his *History of Massachusetts Bay* (1767). Then it literally disappeared for nearly a century. In 1855 it appeared in England in the library of the Bishop of Oxford. After forty-two years the British official red tape was finally cut in 1897, when an episcopal court rendered the decision permitting the return to Massachusetts of this precious loot of the Revolution. By this time, the Pilgrim story, retold by historians and by such writers as Hawthorne and Longfellow, had already long ago become an effective part of the American myth, although the first complete edition of the manuscript had not appeared until 1856, 206 years after Bradford wrote his last few words upon it.

Bradford was born of a yeoman farmer and a tradesman's daughter in Yorkshire. Orphaned in his first year by his father's death and trained for farming by relatives, almost without formal education, he was a well-read man who brought a considerable library with him to Plymouth at the age of thirty. When he was twelve he had begun the earnest study of the Bible; at sixteen he joined the Separatist group then forming at nearby Scrooby, an act which taxed both courage and conviction; at eighteen he accompanied the group to Holland to escape persecution, perhaps death. In Holland he lost a small patrimony in business, became a weaver, and achieved relative prosperity. He also read widely in English and Dutch, and somewhat in French, Greek, and Hebrew. At twenty-seven he was a leader of his people in Leyden, a member of the committee which arranged their pilgrimage. On November 11, 1620, just after the *Mayflower* made landfall at Cape Cod, he signed the Mayflower Compact; he was one of the group that explored the unknown shore; he was one of those who, on December 11, entered Plymouth Bay in the teeth of a snowstorm, and stepped ashore—according to legend—on Plymouth Rock. His first wife was lost overboard in his absence, one of the fifty who, out of the 102 Pilgrims who reached Plymouth, were to die within the year. Among these was the first elected governor, John Carver.

Bradford, elected to succeed Governor Carver, probably had already begun to write a sort of history of the colony. The evidence is inconclusive, but it is believed that Bradford and Edward Winslow consolidated their journals and sent them for anonymous publication to George Morton, English agent for the Pilgrims. Morton, as compiler, signed himself "G. Mourt," possibly for political reasons, and the *Relation or Journall of the Beginning and Proceedings of the Plantation Setled at Plimouth*, generally known as *Mourt's Relation*, appeared in London in 1622.

From 1621 until his death, Bradford probably possessed more power than any other colonial governor; yet he refused the opportunity to become sole proprietor, and maintained the democratic principles suggested in the Mayflower Compact. He was re-elected thirty times, for a total term of thirty-three years —in two years no elections were held, and in five terms, "by importunity," he succeeded in passing his authority to another. He persuaded the surviving Pilgrim Fathers to share their original rights with the entire body of

Freemen; at the same time he led the small group of "Old Comers" who controlled the fishing and trading monopolies, not for private gain, but to liquidate the debt to the British investors who had financed their undertaking. He seldom left Plymouth, where he died. His worldly estate was a small house and some orchards and little else, but he was one of his country's first great men.

The first edition of the *History of Plymouth Plantation*, edited by Charles Deane, appeared in Boston, 1856, but it has been superseded. The standard edition is *History of Plymouth Plantation, 1620–1647*, 2 vols., edited, with notes, by W. C. Ford, Boston, Massachusetts Historical Society, 1912; but even this edition is unreliable, there being some twenty-five minor errors in the transcription of the Mayflower Compact alone. For the general reader the best edition is *Of Plymouth Plantation, 1620–1647*, edited by Samuel Eliot Morison, New York, 1952. The selections in this text have been reproduced from this edition, in which spelling and punctuation have been regularized in accordance with modern standards.

Mourt's Relation, first published as *A Relation or Journall of the Beginning and Proceedings of the Plantation Setled at Plimoth*, London, 1622, is available in a new edition, edited by Theodore Besterman, London, 1939.

Good biographical studies are Bradford Smith, *Bradford of Plymouth*, 1951; Samuel Eliot Morison, "Introduction," *Of Plymouth Plantation, 1620–1647*, 1952; and Samuel Eliot Morison, "William Bradford," *Dictionary of American Biography*, 1933.

From Of Plymouth Plantation

Chapter IX: *Of their Voyage, and how they Passed the Sea; and of their Safe Arrival at Cape Cod*

September 6. These troubles[1] being blown over, and now all being compact together in one ship, they put to sea again with a prosperous wind, which continued divers days together, which was some encouragement unto them; yet, according to the usual manner, many were afflicted with seasickness. And I may not omit here a special work of God's providence. There was a proud and very profane young man, one of the seamen, of a lusty, able body, which made him the more haughty; he would alway be contemning the poor people in their sickness and cursing them daily with grievous execrations; and did not let to tell them that he hoped to help to cast half of them overboard before they came to their journey's end, and to make merry with what they had; and if he were by any gently reproved, he would curse and swear most bitterly. But it pleased God before they came half seas over, to smite this young man with a grievous disease, of which he died in a desperate manner, and so was himself the first that was thrown overboard. Thus his curses light on his own head, and it was an astonishment to all his fellows for they noted it to be the just hand of God upon him.

1. The colonists first set sail "about the 5th of August" in two ships: the *Speedwell*, which had brought the original Pilgrims from Holland, and the *Mayflower*, whose passengers were chiefly miscellaneous emigrants. In two attempts, beset by coastal storms, the *Speedwell*, of only sixty tons, proved unseaworthy, and the Pilgrims, along with the hardy remnant of other adventurers, finally left Plymouth, September 16, 1620, on the *Mayflower*, a ship of 180 tons.

After they had enjoyed fair winds and weather for a season, they were encountered many times with cross winds and met with many fierce storms with which the ship was shroudly² shaken, and her upper works made very leaky; and one of the main beams in the midships was bowed and cracked, which put them in some fear that the ship could not be able to perform the voyage. So some of the chief of the company, perceiving the mariners to fear the sufficiency of the ship as appeared by their mutterings, they entered into serious consultation with the master and other officers of the ship, to consider in time of the danger, and rather to return than to cast themselves into a desperate and inevitable peril. And truly there was great distraction and difference of opinion amongst the mariners themselves; fain would they do what could be done for their wages' sake (being now near half the seas over) and on the other hand they were loath to hazard their lives too desperately. But in examining all opinions, the master and others affirmed they knew the ship to be strong and firm under water; and for the buckling of the main beam, there was a great iron screw the passengers brought out of Holland, which would raise the beam into his place; the which being done, the carpenter and master affirmed that with a post put under it, set firm in the lower deck and otherways bound, he would make it sufficient. And as for the decks and upper works, they would caulk them as well as they could, and though with the working of the ship they would not long keep staunch, yet there would otherwise be no great danger, if they did not overpress her with sails. So they committed themselves to the will of God and resolved to proceed.

In sundry of these storms the winds were so fierce and the seas so high, as they could not bear a knot of sail, but were forced to hull³ for divers days together. And in one of them, as they thus lay at hull in a mighty storm, a lusty young man called John Howland, coming upon some occasion above the gratings was, with a seele⁴ of the ship, thrown into sea; but it pleased God that he caught hold of the topsail halyards which hung overboard and ran out at length. Yet he held his hold (though he was sundry fathoms under water) till he was hauled up by the same rope to the brim of the water, and then with a boat hook and other means got into the ship again and his life saved. And though he was something ill with it, yet he lived many years after and became a profitable member both in church and commonwealth. In all this voyage there died but one of the passengers, which was William Butten, a youth, servant to Samuel Fuller, when they drew near the coast.

But to omit other things (that I may be brief) after long beating at sea they fell with that land which is called Cape Cod;⁵ the which

2. *I.e.*, shrewdly, here meaning "bitterly," "severely."
3. To proceed slowly with the wind under very short sail.
4. A roll or lurch.
5. "At daybreak 9/19 Nov. 1620, they

being made and certainly known to be it, they were not a little joyful. After some deliberation had amongst themselves and with the master of the ship, they tacked about and resolved to stand for the southward (the wind and weather being fair) to find some place about Hudson's River for their habitation.[6] But after they had sailed that course about half the day, they fell amongst dangerous shoals and roaring breakers, and they were so far entangled therewith as they conceived themselves in great danger; and the wind shrinking upon them withal, they resolved to bear up again for the Cape and thought themselves happy to get out of those dangers before night overtook them, as by God's good providence they did. And the next day they got into the Cape Harbor[7] where they rid in safety.

A word or two by the way of this cape. It was thus first named by Captain Gosnold and his company,[8] Anno 1602, and after by Captain Smith[9] was called Cape James; but it retains the former name amongst seamen. Also, that point which first showed those dangerous shoals unto them they called Point Care, and Tucker's Terrour; but the French and Dutch to this day call it Malabar by reason of those perilous shoals and the losses they have suffered there.

Being thus arrived in a good harbor, and brought safe to land, they fell upon their knees and blessed the God of Heaven who had brought them over the vast and furious ocean, and delivered them from all the perils and miseries thereof, again to set their feet on the firm and stable earth, their proper element. And no marvel if they were thus joyful, seeing wise Seneca was so affected with sailing a few miles on the coast of his own Italy, as he affirmed, that he had rather remain twenty years on his way by land than pass by sea to any place in a short time, so tedious and dreadful was the same unto him.[1]

But here I cannot but stay and make a pause, and stand half amazed at this poor people's present condition; and so I think will the reader, too, when he well considers the same. Being thus passed the vast ocean, and a sea of troubles before in their preparation (as may be remembered by that which went before), they

---

sighted the Highlands of Cape Cod" [Morison's note]. The dates in Bradford's manuscript are Old Style (following the Julian calendar), ten days earlier than the same dates according to the present (Gregorian) calendar. In these notes, important verifiable dates are given in both forms, as above.

6. Morison's extended note here gives proof that they were indeed bound for the mouth of the Hudson, within the northern limits of the Virginia Company, which had authorized their settlement.

7. Morison notes that this is now Provincetown Harbor, and that they arrived on November 11/21, 1620, the passage from Plymouth having taken 65 days.

8. "Because they took much of that fish there" [Bradford's note]. *I.e.*, cod.

9. Captain John Smith of Virginia made a map of this coast.

1. Bradford cites Epistle LIII. His words, "he had rather remain * * * in a short time," are translated from Seneca, *Epistulae Morales ad Lucilium*, LIII, Section 5.

had now no friends to welcome them nor inns to entertain or refresh their weatherbeaten bodies; no houses or much less towns
to repair to, to seek for succour. It is recorded in Scripture[2] as a
mercy to the Apostle and his shipwrecked company, that the barbarians showed them no small kindness in refreshing them, but
these savage barbarians, when they met with them (as after will
appear) were readier to fill their sides full of arrows than otherwise. And for the season it was winter, and they that know the
winters of that country know them to be sharp and violent, and
subject to cruel and fierce storms, dangerous to travel to known
places, much more to search an unknown coast. Besides, what could
they see but a hideous and desolate wilderness, full of wild beasts
and wild men—and what multitudes there might be of them they
knew not. Neither could they, as it were, go up to the top of Pisgah[3]
to view from this wilderness a more goodly country to feed their
hopes; for which way soever they turned their eyes (save upward
to the heavens) they could have little solace or content in respect
of any outward objects. For summer being done, all things stand
upon them with a weatherbeaten face, and the whole country, full
of woods and thickets, represented a wild and savage hue. If they
looked behind them, there was the mighty ocean which they had
passed and was now as a main bar and gulf to separate them from
all the civil parts of the world. If it be said they had a ship to succour
them, it is true; but what heard they daily from the master and
company? But that with speed they should look out a place (with
their shallop) where they would be, at some near distance; for the
season was such as he would not stir from thence till a safe harbor
was discovered by them, where they would be, and he might go without danger; and that victuals consumed apace but he must and
would keep sufficient for themselves and their return. Yea, it was
muttered by some that if they got not a place in time, they would
turn them and their goods ashore and leave them. Let it also be
considered what weak hopes of supply and succour they left behind
them, that might bear up their minds in this sad condition and
trials they were under; and they could not but be very small. It is
true, indeed, the affections and love of their brethren at Leyden[4]
was cordial and entire towards them, but they had little power to
help them or themselves; and how the case stood between them and
the merchants at their coming away hath already been declared.

What could now sustain them but the Spirit of God and His
grace? May not and ought not the children of these fathers rightly

2. Bradford cites Acts xxviii. Verse 2
refers to the Melitans' kindness to the
shipwrecked Paul.
3. From Mount Pisgah in Palestine
(now Mount Nebo, Transjordan) Moses

saw the Promised Land (Deuteronomy
xxxiv: 1–4).
4. Leyden in Holland, where nearly
half the exiled Separatists remained
when these Pilgrims set out for America
by way of England.

say: "Our fathers were Englishmen which came over this great ocean, and were ready to perish in this wilderness; but they cried unto the Lord, and He heard their voice and looked on their adversity,"[5] etc. "Let them therefore praise the Lord, because He is good: and His mercies endure forever. Yea, let them which have been redeemed of the Lord, shew how He hath delivered them from the hand of the oppressor. When they wandered in the desert wilderness out of the way, and found no city to dwell in, both hungry and thirsty, their soul was overwhelmed in them." "Let them confess before the Lord His lovingkindness and His wonderful works before the sons of men."[6]

Chapter X: Showing How they Sought out a place of Habitation; and What Befell them Thereabout

Being thus arrived at Cape Cod the 11th of November,[7] and necessity calling them to look out a place for habitation (as well as the master's and mariners' importunity); they having brought a large shallop with them out of England, stowed in quarters in the ship, they now got her out and set their carpenters to work to trim her up; but being much bruised and shattered in the ship with foul weather, they saw she would be long in mending. Whereupon a few of them tendered themselves to go by land and discover those nearest places, whilst the shallop was in mending; and the rather because as they went into that harbor there seemed to be an opening some two or three leagues off, which the master judged to be a river.[8] It was conceived there might be some danger in the attempt, yet seeing them resolute, they were permitted to go, being sixteen of them well armed under the conduct of Captain Standish,[9] having such instructions given them as was thought meet.

They set forth the 15th of November;[1] and when they had marched about the space of a mile by the seaside, they espied five or six persons with a dog coming towards them, who were savages; but they fled from them and ran up into the woods, and the English followed them, partly to see if they could speak with them, and partly to discover if there might not be more of them lying in ambush. But the Indians seeing themselves thus followed, they again forsook the woods and ran away on the sands as hard as they could, so as they could not come near them but followed them by the

5. Bradford cites Deuteronomy xxvi: 5–7, referring to God's deliverance of Israel from bondage in Egypt.
6. Bradford cites "107 Psa: v. 1, 2, 4, 5, 8," of which these closing lines, beginning with "Let them therefore praise the Lord . . . ," are a paraphrase.
7. *I.e.*, November 21.
8. Morison notes that the "high land near Plymouth" gives this appearance

from Provincetown Harbor.
9. Captain Myles Standish. *Cf.* Henry Wadsworth Longfellow, *The Courtship of Miles Standish*. Standish, engaged as their military leader, was not a Pilgrim, but became a most dependable supporter.
1. *I.e.*, November 25. The record of these explorations is amplified in *Mourt's Relation*, presumably by Bradford and Winslow.

track of their feet sundry miles and saw that they had come the same way. So, night coming on, they made their rendezvous and set out their sentinels, and rested in quiet that night; and the next morning followed their track till they had headed a great creek and so left the sands, and turned another way into the woods. But they still followed them by guess, hoping to find their dwellings; but they soon lost both them and themselves, falling into such thickets as were ready to tear their clothes and armor in pieces; but were most distressed for want of drink. But at length they found water and refreshed themselves, being the first New England water they drunk of, and was now in great thirst as pleasant unto them as wine or beer had been in foretimes.

Afterwards they directed their course to come to the other shore, for they knew it was a neck of land they were to cross over, and so at length got to the seaside and marched to this supposed river, and by the way found a pond of clear, fresh water, and shortly after a good quantity of clear ground where the Indians had formerly set corn, and some of their graves. And proceeding further they saw new stubble where corn had been set the same year; also they found where lately a house had been, where some planks and a great kettle was remaining, and heaps of sand newly paddled with their hands. Which, they digging up, found in them divers fair Indian baskets filled with corn, and some in ears, fair and good, of divers colours, which seemed to them a very goodly sight (having never seen any such before). This was near the place of that supposed river they came to seek, unto which they went and found it to open itself into two arms with a high cliff of sand in the entrance[2] but more like to be creeks of salt water than any fresh, for aught they saw; and that there was good harborage for their shallop, leaving it further to be discovered by their shallop, when she was ready. So, their time limited them being expired, they returned to the ship lest they should be in fear of their safety; and took with them part of the corn and buried up the rest. And so, like the men from Eshcol, carried with them of the fruits of the land and showed their brethren;[3] of which, and their return, they were marvelously glad and their hearts encouraged.

After this, the shallop being got ready, they set out again for the better discovery of this place, and the master of the ship desired to go himself. So there went some thirty men but found it to be no harbor for ships but only for boats. There was also found two of their houses covered with mats, and sundry of their implements

2. According to Morison, the pond of clear water gives its name to Pond Village; the place where the corn was found is still called Corn Hill; and the river is Pamet River, a salt creek. All three are located in Truro.
3. Numbers xiii: 23–26. From the valley of Eshcol in Canaan, the advance scouts of Moses brought back samples of the fruits of the Promised Land.

in them, but the people were run away and could not be seen. Also
there was found more of their corn and of their beans of various
colours; the corn and beans they brought away, purposing to give
them full satisfaction when they should meet with any of them
as, about some six months afterward they did, to their good content.[4]

And here is to be noted a special providence of God, and a great
mercy to this poor people, that here they got seed to plant them
corn the next year, or else they might have starved, for they had
none nor any likelihood to get any till the season had been past,
as the sequel did manifest. Neither is it likely they had had this,
if the first voyage had not been made, for the ground was now all
covered with snow and hard frozen; but the Lord is never wanting
unto His in their greatest needs; let His holy name have all the
praise. * * *

From hence they departed and coasted all along[5] but discerned
no place likely for harbor; and therefore hasted to a place that their
pilot (one Mr. Coppin who had been in the country before) did
assure them was a good harbor, which he had been in, and they
might fetch it before night; of which they were glad for it began
to be foul weather.

After some hours' sailing it began to snow and rain, and about
the middle of the afternoon the wind increased and the sea became
very rough, and they broke their rudder, and it was as much as
two men could do to steer her with a couple of oars. But their pilot
bade them be of good cheer for he saw the harbor; but the storm
increasing, and night drawing on, they bore what sail they could
to get in, while they could see. But herewith they broke their mast
in three pieces and their sail fell overboard in a very grown sea,
so as they had like to have been cast away. Yet by God's mercy
they recovered themselves, and having the flood[6] with them, struck
into the harbor. But when it came to, the pilot was deceived in
the place, and said the Lord be merciful unto them for his eyes
never saw that place before; and he and the master's mate would
have run her ashore in a cove full of breakers before the wind. But
a lusty seaman which steered bade those which rowed, if they were
men, about with her or else they were all cast away; the which they

4. Morison notes that this second expedition explored the Pamet and Little
Pamet rivers from November 28 to November 30, and that descendants of
these Nauset Indians still survive at
Mashpee, Cape Cod.
5. This is the third exploring expedition, begun on December 6/16, 1620,
after several weeks of confinement on
the *Mayflower* by "foul weather." Ten
men, including Bradford, in their shal-

lop, are to explore as far as Plymouth,
seeking a better ship's harbor than the
Pamet or Ipswich, previously examined.
They have successfully withstood the
first severe Indian attack, and are now
proceeding to Plymouth.
6. "The mean rise and fall of tide
there is about 9 ft. Plymouth Bay
* * * is a bad place to enter in thick
weather with a sea running and night
coming on" [Morison's note].

did with speed. So he bid them be of good cheer and row lustily, for there was a fair sound before them, and he doubted not but they should find one place or other where they might ride in safety. And though it was very dark and rained sore, yet in the end they got under the lee of a small island and remained there all that night in safety.[7] But they knew not this to be an island till morning, but were divided in their minds; some would keep the boat for fear they might be amongst the Indians, others were so wet and cold they could not endure but got ashore, and with much ado got fire (all things being so wet); and the rest were glad to come to them, for after midnight the wind shifted to the northwest and it froze hard.

But though this had been a day and night of much trouble and danger unto them, yet God gave them a morning of comfort and refreshing (as usually He doth to His children) for the next day was a fair, sunshining day, and they found themselves to be on an island secure from the Indians, where they might dry their stuff, fix their pieces and rest themselves; and gave God thanks for His mercies in their manifold deliverances. And this being the last day of the week, they prepared there to keep the Sabbath.

On Monday they sounded the harbor and found it fit for shipping, and marched into the land and found divers cornfields and little running brooks, a place (as they supposed) fit for situation.[8] At least it was the best they could find, and the season and their present necessity made them glad to accept of it. So they returned to their ship again with this news to the rest of their people, which did much comfort their hearts.

On the 15th of December they weighed anchor to go to the place they had discovered, and came within two leagues of it, but were fain to bear up again; but the 16th day, the wind came fair, and they arrived safe in this harbor. And afterwards took better view of the place, and resolved where to pitch their dwelling; and the 25th day began to erect the first house for common use to receive them and their goods.[9]

7. Morison identifies the anchorage as the lee of Saquish Head, and the island there as Clarks Island, where they spent Saturday and Sunday, December 9/19–10/20.

8. "Here is the only contemporary authority for the 'Landing of the Pilgrims on Plymouth Rock' on Monday, 11/21 Dec. 1620. * * * The landing took place from the shallop, not the *Mayflower* * * * Nor is it clear that they landed on * * * Plymouth Rock, [although] it would have been very convenient for that purpose at half tide" [Morison's note].

9. *I.e.*, the *Mayflower* reached Plymouth Harbor on December 16/26, but the Pilgrims did not actually begin to build ashore for nine more days. *Mourt's Relation* shows that the interval was used in exploring for the best possible site.

From Of Plymouth Plantation, Book II

[*The Mayflower Compact* (1620)]

I shall a little return back, and begin with a combination made by them before they came ashore; being the first foundation of their government[1] in this place. Occasioned partly by the discontented and mutinous speeches that some of the strangers amongst them had let fall from them in the ship: That when they came ashore they would use their own liberty, for none had power to command them, the patent they had being for Virginia and not for New England, which belonged to another government, with which the Virginia Company had nothing to do.[2] And partly that such an act by them done, this their condition considered, might be as firm as any patent, and in some respects more sure.

The form was as followeth:[3]

IN THE NAME OF GOD, AMEN.

We whose names are underwritten, the loyal subjects of our dread Sovereign Lord King James, by the Grace of God of Great Britain, France, and Ireland King, Defender of the Faith, etc.

Having undertaken, for the Glory of God and advancement of the Christian Faith and Honour of our King and Country, a Voyage to plant the First Colony in the Northern Parts of Virginia, do by these presents solemnly and mutually in the presence of God and one of another, Covenant and Combine ourselves together into a Civil Body Politic, for our better ordering and preservation and furtherance of the ends aforesaid; and by virtue hereof to enact, constitute and frame such just and equal Laws, Ordinances, Acts, Constitutions and Offices, from time to time, as shall be thought most meet and convenient for the general good of the Colony, unto which we promise all due submission and obedience. In witness whereof we have hereunder subscribed our names at Cape Cod, the 11th of November, in the year of the reign of our Sovereign Lord King James, of England, France and Ireland the eighteenth, and of Scotland the fifty-fourth. Anno Domini 1620.

After this they chose, or rather confirmed, Mr. John Carver (a man godly and well approved amongst them) their Governor for

1. The Mayflower Compact is important as an early American covenant instituting civil government by common consent with reference to the common good. Although it was enacted in an emergency, it followed the precedent of the church covenants already familiar to Puritans and, as Bradford's words suggest, it was the "first foundation" of direct popular government in America, while feudal forms persisted in Europe.
2. The Pilgrims and the "Adventurers" who sailed with them were alike authorized by patent from the Virginia Company, whose territory extended northward only to Manhattan Island.
3. A text differing from this one only in a few insignificant words was published in *Mourt's Relation* in 1622.

that year. And after they had provided a place for their goods, or common store (which were long in unlading for want of boats, foulness of the winter weather and sickness of divers[4]) and begun some small cottages for their habitation; as time would admit, they met and consulted of laws and orders, both for their civil and military government as the necessity of their condition did require, still adding thereunto as urgent occasion in several times, and as cases did require.

In these hard and difficult beginnings they found some discontents and murmurings arise amongst some, and mutinous speeches and carriages in other; but they were soon quelled and overcome by the wisdom, patience, and just and equal carriage of things, by the Governor and better part, which clave faithfully together in the main.

[Compact with the Indians (1621)]

All this while[5] the Indians came skulking about them, and would sometimes show themselves aloof off, but when any approached near them, they would run away; and once they stole away their tools where they had been at work and were gone to dinner. But about the 16th of March, a certain Indian came boldly amongst them and spoke to them in broken English, which they could well understand but marveled at it. At length they understood by discourse with him, that he was not of these parts, but belonged to the eastern parts where some English ships came to fish, with whom he was acquainted and could name sundry of them by their names, amongst whom he had got his language. He became profitable to them in acquainting them with many things concerning the state of the country in the east parts where he lived, which was afterwards profitable unto them; as also of the people here, of their names, number and strength, of their situation and distance from this place, and who was chief amongst them. His name was Samoset. He told them also of another Indian whose name was Squanto, a native of this place, who had been in England and could speak better English than himself.

Being, after some time of entertainment and gifts dismissed, a while after he came again, and five more with him, and they brought again all the tools that were stolen away before, and made way for the coming of their great Sachem, called Massasoit. Who, about four or five days after, came with the chief of his friends and other attendance, with the aforesaid Squanto. With whom, after friendly

4. Several; various persons.
5. That is, the first two months of 1621, "a starving time." The settlers built a large common house and several cottages, and caught a meager quantity of game and fish, while disease took a frightful toll. "Of the 102 *Mayflower* passengers who reached Cape Cod, * * * by the summer of 1621 the total deaths numbered 50 [including] all but a few of the women" [Morison's note].

entertainment and some gifts given him, they made a peace with him (which hath now continued this 24 years)[6] in these terms:

1. That neither he nor any of his should injure or do hurt to any of their people.

2. That if any of his did hurt to any of theirs, he should send the offender, that they might punish him.

3. That if anything were taken away from any of theirs, he should cause it to be restored; and they should do the like to his.

4. If any did unjustly war against him, they would aid him; if any did war against them, he should aid them.

5. He should send to his neighbours confederates to certify them of this, that they might not wrong them, but might be likewise comprised in the conditions of peace.

6. That when their men came to them, they should leave their bows and arrows behind them.

After these things he returned to his place called Sowams,[7] some 40 miles from this place, but Squanto continued with them and was their interpreter and was a special instrument sent of God for their good beyond their expectation. He directed them how to set their corn, where to take fish, and to procure other commodities, and was also their pilot to bring them to unknown places for their profit, and never left them till he died. He was a native of this place, and scarce any left alive besides himself. He was carried away with divers others by one Hunt, a master of a ship, who thought to sell them for slaves in Spain. But he got away for England and was entertained by a merchant in London, and employed to Newfoundland and other parts, and lastly brought hither into these parts by one Mr. Dermer, a gentleman employed by Sir Ferdinando Gorges and others for discovery and other designs in these parts.[8]

[First Thanksgiving (1621)]

They began now to gather in the small harvest they had, and to fit up their houses and dwellings against winter, being all well recovered in health and strength and had all things in good plenty. For as some were thus employed in affairs abroad, others were exercised in fishing, about cod and bass and other fish, of which

6. This first American treaty, with the Wampanoag people, was faithfully kept for fifty-four years, until 1675, when Massasoit's son, Metacomet, or King Philip, began those savage attacks, known as King Philip's War, which included the Deerfield Massacre.
7. Now Barrington, Rhode Island.
8. Squanto, or Tisquantum, had an interesting story. The English slaver, Hunt, kidnaped him in 1614, and it was 1618 before he got back to his native place, probably by escaping from Dermer's ship off Cape Cod. Finding that his entire tribe, the Patuxets, had been destroyed by a pestilence in 1617, he apparently adopted the Pilgrims, in whose service he died of a fever, in September, 1622, while guiding their trading party.

they took good store, of which every family had their portion. All the summer there was no want; and now began to come in store of fowl, as winter approached, of which this place did abound when they came first (but afterward decreased by degrees). And besides waterfowl there was great store of wild turkeys, of which they took many, besides venison, etc. Besides they had about a peck a meal a week to a person, or now since harvest, Indian corn to that proportion. Which made many afterwards write so largely of their plenty here to their friends in England, which were not feigned but true reports.[9]

[Narragansett Challenge (1622)]

Soon after this ship's departure,[1] that great people of the Narragansetts, in a braving manner, sent a messenger unto them with a bundle of arrows tied about with a great snakeskin, which their interpreters told them was a threatening and a challenge. Upon which the Governor, with the advice of others, sent them a round answer that if they had rather have war than peace, they might begin when they would; they had done them no wrong, neither did they fear them or should they find them unprovided. And by another messenger sent the snakeskin back with bullets in it. But they would not receive it, but sent it back again.[2] But these things I do but mention, because they are more at large already put forth in print by Mr. Winslow[3] at the request of some friends. And it is like the reason was their own ambition who (since the death of so many of the Indians) thought to domineer and lord it over the rest, and conceived the English would be a bar in their way, and saw that Massasoit took shelter already under their wings.

But this made them the more carefully to look to themselves,[4] so as they agreed to enclose their dwellings with a good strong pale,[5] and make flankers[6] in convenient places with gates to shut, which were every night locked, and a watch kept; and when need required,

9. The actual date of the "First Thanksgiving" is not recorded, but it was in the autumn of 1621, since Winslow's letter describing it, printed in *Mourt's Relation*, is dated December 11, 1621. He relates that their store of wild meat and produce was such that they were able to entertain Massasoit and "some 90 men" for three days with feasting and competitive games.
1. The ship *Fortune*, which had come unexpectedly in December with settlers for whom there were no provisions, necessitating the reduction to half rations for the entire settlement for the remainder of the winter.
2. "Canonicus, sachem of the Narragansett, sent the challenge; Squanto

did the interpreting. This happened in Jan. 1622" [Morison's note]. Longfellow used the episode dramatically in *The Courtship of Miles Standish*.
3. Edward Winslow, one of the Pilgrims, and probable coauthor with Bradford of *Mourt's Relation*, returned to England as agent for the Pilgrims in 1623 and there published *Good Newes from New England* (London, 1624), to which Bradford here refers.
4. Made the colonists more careful to defend themselves.
5. Palings; poles sunk in the ground for the walls of a fortification.
6. The flanks of a bastion, or a structure extending beyond the wall line of a fortification.

there was also warding[7] in the daytime. And the company was by the Captain's and the Governor's advice divided into four squadrons, and everyone had their quarter appointed them unto which they were to repair upon any sudden alarm. And if there should be any cry of fire, a company were appointed for a guard, with muskets, whilst others quenched the same, to prevent Indian treachery. This was accomplished very cheerfully, and the town impaled round by the beginning of March, in which every family had a pretty garden plot secured.

And herewith I shall end this year. Only I shall remember one passage more, rather of mirth than of weight. On the day called Christmas Day, the Governor called them out to work as was used.[8] But the most of this new company[9] excused themselves and said it went against their consciences to work on that day. So the Governor told them that if they made it matter of conscience, he would spare them till they were better informed; so he led away the rest and left them. But when they came home at noon from their work, he found them in the street at play, openly; some pitching the bar, and some at stool-ball[1] and such like sports. So he went to them and took away their implements and told them that was against his conscience, that they should play and others work. If they made the keeping of it matter of devotion, let them keep their houses; but there should be no gaming or reveling in the streets. Since which time nothing hath been attempted that way, at least openly.

[Thomas Morton of Merrymount (1628)]

About some three or four years before this time, there came over one Captain Wollaston (a man of pretty parts) and with him three or four more of some eminency, who brought with them a great many servants, with provisions and other implements for to begin a plantation. And pitched themselves in a place within the Massachusetts[2] which they called after their Captain's name, Mount Wollaston. Amongst whom was one Mr. Morton,[3] who it should seem had some small adventure of his own or other men's amongst them, but had little respect amongst them, and was slighted by the meanest servants. Having continued there some time, and not finding things to answer their expectations nor profit to arise as they looked for,

7. Guarding.
8. Puritans objected to the celebration of Christmas, both because of its secularization, and because December 25 was not the true date of the birth of Christ.
9. The "new company," those who arrived on the *Fortune*, were "Adventurers," not Puritans.
1. Pitching the bar was a sort of javelin throwing; stool-ball something like cricket.

2. Near Quincy, Massachusetts, on Route 3.
3. Thomas Morton (1590?–1647), like most of Captain Wollaston's settlers, was not a Puritan, but an Anglican, an "Adventurer" who had come to found a plantation and to trade. Naturally the Pilgrims did not like either his "worldly" ways or his commercial rivalry. His side of the resulting feud is told in his amusing *New English Canaan* (London, 1637).

Captain Wollaston takes a great part of the servants and transports them to Virginia, where he puts them off at good rates, selling their time to other men; and writes back to one Mr. Rasdall (one of his chief partners and accounted their merchant) to bring another part of them to Virginia likewise, intending to put them off there as he had done the rest. And he, with the consent of the said Rasdall, appointed one Fitcher to be his Lieutenant and govern the remains of the Plantation till he or Rasdall returned to take further order thereabout. But this Morton abovesaid, having more craft than honesty (who had been a kind of pettifogger of Furnival's Inn)[4] in the others' absence watches an opportunity (commons being but hard amongst them) and got some strong drink and other junkets and made them a feast; and after they were merry, he began to tell them he would give them good counsel. "You see," saith he, "that many of your fellows are carried to Virginia, and if you stay till this Rasdall return, you will also be carried away and sold for slaves with the rest. Therefore I would advise you to thrust out this Lieutenant Fitcher, and I, having a part in the Plantation, will receive you as my partners and consociates; so may you be free from service, and we will converse, plant, trade, and live together as equals and support and protect one another," or to like effect. This counsel was easily received, so they took opportunity and thrust Lieutenant Fitcher out o' doors, and would suffer him to come no more amongst them, but forced him to seek bread to eat and other relief from his neighbours till he could get passage for England.

After this they fell to great licentiousness and led a dissolute life, pouring out themselves into all profaneness. And Morton became Lord of Misrule,[5] and maintained (as it were) a School of Atheism. And after they had got some goods into their hands, and got much by trading with the Indians, they spent it as vainly in quaffing and drinking, both wine and strong waters in great excess (and, as some reported) £10 worth in a morning. They also set up a maypole, drinking and dancing about it many days together, inviting the Indian women for their consorts, dancing and frisking together like so many fairies, or furies, rather; and worse practices. As if they had anew revived and celebrated the feasts of the Roman goddess Flora, or the beastly practices of the mad Bacchanalians. Morton likewise, to show his poetry composed sundry rhymes and verses, some tending to lasciviousness, and others to the detraction and scandal of some persons, which he affixed to this idle or idol maypole. They changed also the name of their place, and instead

---

4. A "pettifogger" was a small-scale lawyer, one dealing in petty cases. Furnival's Inn was one of the London Inns of Court, occupied by lawyers and students.

5. Formerly, in England, a comic master of ceremonies for "revels," masquerades, and other "worldly" celebrations.

of calling it Mount Wollaston they call it Merry-mount, as if this jollity would have lasted ever. But this continued not long, for after Morton was sent for England (as follows to be declared) shortly after came over that worthy gentleman Mr. John Endecott,[6] who brought over a patent under the broad seal for the government of the Massachusetts. Who, visiting those parts, caused that maypole to be cut down and rebuked them for their profaneness and admonished them to look there should be better walking. So they or others now changed the name of their place again and called it Mount Dagon.[7]

Now to maintain this riotous prodigality and profuse excess, Morton, thinking himself lawless, and hearing what gain the French and fishermen made by trading of pieces, powder and shot to the Indians, he as the head of this consortship began the practice of the same in these parts. And first he taught them how to use them, to charge and discharge, and what proportion of powder to give the piece, according to the size or bigness of the same; and what shot to use for fowl and what for deer. And having thus instructed them, he employed some of them to hunt and fowl for him, so as they became far more active in that employment than any of the English, by reason of their swiftness of foot and nimbleness of body, being also quick-sighted and by continual exercise well knowing the haunts of all sorts of game. So as when they saw the execution that a piece would do, and the benefit that might come by the same, they became mad (as it were) after them and would not stick to give any price they could attain to for them; accounting their bows and arrows but baubles in comparison of them. * * *

O, the horribleness of this villainy! How many both Dutch and English have been lately slain by those Indians thus furnished, and no remedy provided; nay, the evil more increased, and the blood of their brethren sold for gain (as is to be feared) and in what danger all these colonies are in is too well known. O that princes and parliaments would take some timely order to prevent this mischief and at length to suppress it by some exemplary punishment upon some of these gain-thirsty murderers, for they deserve no better title, before their colonies in these parts be overthrown by these barbarous savages thus armed with their own weapons, by these evil instruments and traitors to their neighbours and country! But I have forgot myself and have been too long in this digression; but now to return.

This Morton having thus taught them the use of pieces, he sold them all he could spare, and he and his consorts determined to send for many out of England and had by some of the ships sent

6. John Endecott (1589?–1665), several times governor of the Massachusetts Bay Colony, appears in Hawthorne's "The Maypole of Merry Mount" (the present episode), in Hawthorne's "Endicott and the Red Cross," and in Long-

fellow's *New England Tragedies* (as the persecutor of Quakers).

7. Dagon was the pagan god of the Philistines, whose temple Samson destroyed (Judges xvi: 23–31).

for above a score. The which being known, and his neighbours meeting the Indians in the woods armed with guns in this sort, it was a terror unto them who lived stragglingly and were of no strength in any place. And other places (though more remote) saw this mischief would quickly spread over all, if not prevented. Besides, they saw they should keep no servants, for Morton would entertain any, how vile soever, and all the scum of the country or any discontents would flock to him from all places, if this nest was not broken. And they should stand in more fear of their lives and goods in short time from this wicked and debased crew than from the savages themselves.

So sundry of the chief of the straggling plantations, meeting together, agreed by mutual consent to solicit those of Plymouth (who were then of more strength than them all) to join with them to prevent the further growth of this mischief, and suppress Morton and his consorts before they grew to further head and strength. Those that joined in this action, and after contributed to the charge of sending him for England, were from Piscataqua, Naumkeag, Winnisimmet, Wessagusset, Nantasket and other places where any English were seated. Those of Plymouth being thus sought to by their messengers and letters, and weighing both their reasons and the common danger, were willing to afford them their help though themselves had least cause of fear or hurt. So, to be short, they first resolved jointly to write to him, and in a friendly and neighbourly way to admonish him to forbear those courses, and sent a messenger with their letters to bring his answer.

But he was so high as he scorned all advice, and asked who had to do with him, he had and would trade pieces with the Indians, in despite of all, with many other scurrilous terms full of disdain. They sent him a second time and bade him be better advised and more temperate in his terms, for the country could not bear the injury he did. It was against their common safety and against the King's proclamation. He answered in high terms as before; and that the King's proclamation was no law, demanding what penalty was upon it. It was answered, more than he could bear—His Majesty's displeasure. But insolently he persisted and said the King was dead and his displeasure with him, and many the like things. And threatened withal that if any came to molest him, let them look to themselves for he would prepare for them.

Upon which they saw there was no way but to take him by force; and having so far proceeded, now to give over would make him far more haughty and insolent. So they mutually resolved to proceed, and obtained of the Governor of Plymouth to send Captain Standish and some other aid with him, to take Morton by force. The which accordingly was done. But they found him to stand stiffly in his defense, having made fast his doors, armed his consorts, set divers dishes of powder and bullets ready on the table; and if they had not been over-armed with drink, more hurt might have been done. They summoned him to yield, but he kept his house and they could get nothing but scoffs and scorns from him. But at length, fearing they would do some violence to the house, he and some of his crew came out, but not to yield but to shoot; but they were so steeled with drink as their pieces were too heavy for them. Himself with a carbine, overcharged and almost half filled with powder and shot, as was after found, had thought to have shot Captain Standish; but he stepped to him and put by his piece and took him. Neither was there any hurt done to any of either side, save that one was so drunk that he ran his own nose upon the point of a sword that one held before him, as he entered the house; but he lost but a little of his hot blood.[8]

Morton they brought away to Plymouth, where he was kept till a ship went from the Isle of Shoals for England, with which he was sent to the Council of New England, and letters written to give them information of his course and carriage. And also one was sent at their common charge to inform their Honours more particularly and to prosecute against him. But he fooled of the messenger, after he was gone from hence, and though he went for England yet nothing was done to him, not so much as rebuked, for aught was heard, but returned the next year.[9] Some of the worst of the company were dispersed and some of the more modest kept the house till he should be heard from. But I have been too long about so unworthy a person, and bad a cause.

1630–1650   1856

8. Morton, referring to Standish as "Captain Shrimpe," says that they came at him "like a flock of wild geese" to the blind and he simply yielded to prevent bloodshed.
9. He returned in 1629, but in 1630 Endecott arrested him again, confiscated his property, and sent him to England, where again he escaped punishment. Morton returned to America finally in 1643; ordered to leave Massachusetts, he went to Rhode Island and later to Maine, where he died in 1647.

ANNE BRADSTREET
(1612?–1672)

In 1650 a woman poet was a rarity, but Anne Bradstreet's place in literary history is the result not only of her uniqueness but of a genuine if limited inspiration and a force of character which have survived for three hundred years in a few of her poems. This first noteworthy American poet was born in Northampton, England, probably in 1612. Her father, Thomas Dudley, by conviction a sturdy Puritan, had turned from a military career to business; when Anne was born he was steward of the estates of the Earl of Lincoln, a learned and aristocratic Puritan. Thomas Dudley was himself a man of studious character, and his daughter had the advantages of good tutoring, with access to the Earl's considerable library at Sempringham Castle. She was widely read but not learned, drawn chiefly toward the serious and religious writings of the Puritan world, and very little toward those of that other world, just waning, in which there still lived at her birth Shakespeare and Cervantes, Ben Jonson and Bacon.

In 1628, at the age of sixteen, she married Simon Bradstreet, a grave and brilliant young Puritan who had been trained at Cambridge and afterward by her father. Two years later, Bradstreet gave up his position as steward of the Countess of Warwick, and with his young wife embarked upon the *Arabella* for America. Dudley and his family also sailed on that ship, which brought the first settlers to the colony at Massachusetts Bay. One of the most active men in the colony, Dudley served four terms as governor. Simon Bradstreet was governor of the colony for ten years; he served also as judge, and represented Massachusetts at the court of Charles II when curtailment of the charter was threatened in 1661.

Meanwhile, in Cambridge, in Ipswich, and at their permanent home near Andover on the Merrimack, Anne Bradstreet's employments were no less taxing. In a whimsical poem she recorded, as domestic history: "I had eight birds hatcht in one nest, / Four Cocks there were, and Hens the rest." All eight children thrived, and all but one survived her. Among many prominent descendants were the Channings; the R. H. Danas, fa-

ther and son; Holmes the poet and Holmes the jurist; and, collaterally, Edwin Arlington Robinson.

In spite of the hardships of early colonial life and the duties of her household, Anne Bradstreet seems to have turned resolutely to authorship whenever she had the opportunity. Manuscripts of the poems in her first volume bear dates from 1632 to 1643. Whether she intended publication or not, she wrote a dedicatory poem to her father in 1642. In 1647 her sister's husband, John Woodbridge, pastor of the church of Andover, sailed to England and took her manuscript volume with him. Without her consent he had it published in London, in 1650, with the title, *The Tenth Muse Lately Sprung Up in America, * * * By a Gentlewoman of Those Parts.*

It is not this bulky first work, but her less pretentious poems, published later, that have won her a place in literary history. The volume of 1650, consisting chiefly of rhymed discourses and chronicles, was agreeable to the taste of the period, but offers very little for the reader of today. In what the author called "Quaternions," or groups of four, she discussed "The Four Elements," "The Four Humours," "The Four Ages of Man," "The Four Seasons," and "The Four Monarchies." Nathaniel Ward, "the simple cobbler," in a commendatory poem called her "a right *DuBartas* Girle," and she herself admitted that she had attempted to emulate *La Semaine* by the French poet du Bartas, translated by Joshua Sylvester. There are also traces of Raleigh's *History of the World* and Bishop Ussher's *Annales.*

Mrs. Bradstreet's poems in praise of various authors suggest other influences more helpful to her development as a poet. There are traces of Spenser and Sir Philip Sidney, of Donne, Quarles, and Herbert, in her more lyrical poems, and these are given vitality by her observation of the familiar objects of her daily life. Her poems of religious experience and domestic intimacy are genuine, delicate, and charming. Most of them were written after *The Tenth Muse* appeared, one at least as late as 1669. About 1666 she revised all her poems for an authorized edition, which was not published until after her death, and completed the poem "Contemplations," a work of arresting integrity, for which she is best known. Among her surviving prose writings, her "Meditations" deserve to be particularly remembered for their lucid simplicity of style and their wise and generous spirit. The author of the ninth and the eighteenth stanzas of "Contemplations" was a genuine lyrist; there is good craftsmanship in her handling of the extended last line of the "Contemplations" stanza, and of the difficult stanza form of "The Prologue"; but when all has been said, the principal contribution of Anne Bradstreet to posterity is what she revealed, through herself, of the first generation of New Englanders.

The first edition of Anne Bradstreet's writings was *The Tenth Muse Lately Sprung Up in America * * *,* London, 1650, unsigned. The second edition, revised and enlarged by the author, for the first time including the "Contemplations," was posthumously published as *Several Poems Compiled with Great Variety of Wit and Learning,* Boston, 1678. This was reprinted in 1758. The best edition, with biographical and critical comment, is *The Works of Anne Bradstreet in Prose and Verse,* edited by J. H. Ellis, 1867; reprinted 1932. In this edition the prose "Meditations" first appeared. *The Poems of Mrs. Anne Bradstreet, Together with her Prose Remains,* edited by C. E. Norton, 1897, is an accurate text, but does not supersede the Ellis notes. The texts reprinted below are from Ellis' edition, which reproduces those of the 1678 edition. For clarity, the capitalization, spelling, and punctuation have in some cases been normalized, without alteration of the language.

Biographies are Helen S. Campbell, *Anne Bradstreet and Her Time,* 1891; and L. Caldwell, *An Account of Anne Bradstreet,* 1898. Excellent sketches are by Moses C. Tyler, in *A History of American Literature During the Colonial Period,* 1878, revised 1897, 1949; and by Lyon N. Richardson, in the *Dictionary of American Biography,* 1929.

The Prologue[1]

1

To sing of wars, of captains, and of kings,
  Of cities founded, commonwealths begun,
For my mean pen are too superior things;
  Or how they all, or each, their dates have run;
Let poets and historians set these forth;
  My obscure lines shall not so dim their worth.   5

1. Anne Bradstreet apparently intended this poem as a prologue for her lengthy "Quaternions" on the history of mankind and the "four monarchies." In the 1650 edition it stood at the beginning of that work, preceded only by her poem dedicating her poems to her father.

2

But when my wond'ring eyes and envious heart
Great Bartas'[2] sugared lines do but read o'er,
Fool, I do grudge the muses did not part
'Twixt him and me that overfluent store.   10
A Bartas can do what a Bartas will;
But simple I according to my skill.

3

From schoolboy's tongue no rhet'ric we expect,
Nor yet a sweet consort from broken strings,
Nor perfect beauty where's a main defect.   15
My foolish, broken, blemished Muse so sings;
And this to mend, alas, no art is able,
'Cause nature made it so irreparable.

4

Nor can I, like that fluent, sweet-tongued Greek
Who lisped at first, in future times speak plain.   20
By art he gladly found what he did seek;
A full requital of his striving pain.
Art can do much, but this maxim's most sure:
A weak or wounded brain admits no cure.

5

I am obnoxious to each carping tongue   25
Who says my hand a needle better fits;
A poet's pen all scorn I should thus wrong,
For such despite they cast on female wits.
If what I do prove well, it won't advance;
They'll say it's stol'n, or else it was by chance.   30

6

But sure the antique Greeks were far more mild;
Else of our sex why feignèd they those nine,[3]
And Poesy made Calliope's own child?
So 'mongst the rest they placed the arts divine,
But this weak knot they will full soon untie: 35
The Greeks did nought but play the fools and lie.

7

Let Greeks be Greeks, and women what they are;
Men have precedency and still excel.
It is but vain unjustly to wage war;
Men can do best, and women know it well.   40
Pre-eminence in all and each is yours;
Yet grant some small acknowledgement of ours.

2. Guillaume de Salluste du Bartas
(1544–1590), French writer of religious
epics, by whom she was inspired.
3. All nine of the Greek Muses were female deities, each patronizing a different
art. That of Calliope, mentioned in the
following line, was the epic, which Mrs.
Bradstreet was attempting in her
"Quaternions."

8

And O ye high-flown quills[4] that soar the skies,
And ever with your prey still catch your praise,
If e'er you deign these lowly lines your eyes,   45
Give thyme or parsley wreath; I ask no bays.
This mean and unrefinèd ore of mine
Will make your glistering gold but more to shine.

1643?   1650

The Flesh and the Spirit[5]

In secret place where once I stood
Close by the banks of lacrim[6] flood,
I heard two sisters reason on
Things that are past and things to come.
One Flesh was called, who had her eye   5
On worldly wealth and vanity;
The other Spirit, who did rear
Her thoughts unto a higher sphere.
"Sister," quoth Flesh, "what liv'st thou on—
Nothing but meditation?   10
Doth Contemplation feed thee, so
Regardlessly to let earth go?
Can Speculation satisfy
Notion[7] without Reality?
Dost dream of things beyond the moon,   15
And dost thou hope to dwell there soon?
Hast treasures there laid up in store,
That all in th' world thou count'st but poor?
Art fancy sick, or turned a sot,
To catch at shadows which are not?   20
Come, come, I'll show unto thy sense
Industry hath its recompense.
What canst desire but thou mayst see
True substance in variety?
Dost honor like? Acquire the same,   25
As some to their immortal fame;
And trophies to thy name erect
Which wearing time shall ne'er deject.

4. The quill pen, then in general use.
5. This poem seems to be an expansion of St. Paul's conception of the strife between the Flesh and the Spirit (noted in *The Works of Anne Bradstreet* * * * edited by J. H. Ellis, p. 381). See especially Romans viii, *passim*. In medieval poetry, the "debate," especially between body and soul, was an established convention. Various forms of the debate poem reappeared among the Jacobean writers of Mrs. Bradstreet's epoch.
6. *Cf.* the Latin *lacrima*, "a tear."
7. *I.e.*, knowledge; *cf.* the Latin *notio*.

For riches dost thou long full sore?
Behold enough of precious store. 30
Earth hath more silver, pearls, and gold
Than eyes can see or hands can hold.
Affect'st thou pleasure? Take thy fill,
Earth hath enough of what you will.
Then let not go, what thou mayst find, 35
For things unknown, only in mind."
Spirit: "Be still, thou unregenerate part;
Disturb no more my settled heart,
For I have vowed (and so will do)
Thee as a foe, still to pursue, 40
And combat with thee will and must
Until I see thee laid in th' dust.
Sisters we are, yea, twins we be,
Yet deadly feud 'twixt thee and me;
For from one father are we not: 45
Thou by old Adam wast begot,
But my arise is from above,
Whence my dear Father I do love.
Thou speak'st me fair but hat'st me sore;
Thy flattering shows I'll trust no more. 50
How oft thy slave hast thou me made
When I believed what thou hast said,
And never had more cause of woe
Than when I did what thou bad'st do.
I'll stop mine ears at these thy charms 55
And count them for my deadly harms.
Thy sinful pleasures I do hate,
Thy riches are to me no bait,
Thine honors do nor will I love;
For my ambition lies above. 60
My greatest honor it shall be
When I am victor over thee
And triumph shall, with laurel head,
When thou my captive shalt be led.
How I do live thou need'st not scoff, 65
For I have meat thou know'st not of;[8]
The hidden manna[9] I do eat,
The word of life it is my meat.
My thoughts do yield me more content
Than can thy hours in pleasure spent. 70
Nor are they shadows which I catch,

8. See John iv: 32.
9. Manna, or food from heaven, was miraculously sent to sustain the Is- raelites in the wilderness (Exodus xvi: 15); but the mystical "hidden manna" is promised in Revelation ii: 17.

Nor fancies vain at which I snatch;
But reach at things that are so high,
Beyond thy dull capacity,
Eternal substance I do see,   75
With which enriched I would be;
Mine eye doth pierce the heavens, and see
What is invisible to thee.
My garments are not silk nor gold
Nor such like trash which earth doth hold,   80
But royal robes I shall have on
More glorious than the glist'ring sun.[1]
My crown not diamonds, pearls, and gold,
But such as angels' heads infold.[2]
The City[3] where I hope to dwell   85
There's none on earth can parallel;
The stately walls both high and strong
Are made of precious jasper stone;
The gates of pearl both rich and clear;
And angels are for porters there;   90
The streets thereof transparent gold,
Such as no eye did e'er behold;
A crystal river there doth run,
Which doth proceed from the Lamb's throne;
Of life there are the waters sure,   95
Which shall remain forever pure;
Nor sun nor moon they have no need,
For glory doth from God proceed;
No candle there, nor yet torchlight,
For there shall be no darksome night.   100
From sickness and infirmity
For evermore they shall be free,
Nor withering age shall e'er come there,
But beauty shall be bright and clear.
This City pure is not for thee,   105
For things unclean there shall not be.
If I of heaven may have my fill,
Take thou the world, and all that will."

1666?   1678

To My Dear and Loving Husband[4]

If ever two were one, then surely we.
If ever man were loved by wife, then thee;

1. *Cf.* Revelation vi: 11.
2. *Cf.* I Peter v: 4.
3. Ll. 85 to 106, describing the Holy

City of heaven, are based on Revelation
xxi: 10–27 and xxii: 1–5.
4. In the 1678 edition, posthumously

If ever wife was happy in a man,
Compare with me ye women if you can.
I prize thy love more than whole mines of gold,   5
Or all the riches that the East doth hold.
My love is such that rivers cannot quench,
Nor ought but love from thee give recompense.
Thy love is such I can no way repay;
The heavens reward thee manifold, I pray.   10
Then while we live, in love let's so persever,
That when we live no more we may live ever.

1678

Contemplations[5]

1

Some time now past in the autumnal tide,
When Phoebus[6] wanted but one hour to bed,
The trees all richly clad, yet void of pride,
Were gilded o'er by his rich golden head.
Their leaves and fruits seemed painted, but was true,   5
Of green, of red, of yellow, mixed hue;
Rapt were my senses at this delectable view.

2

I wist not what to wish, "Yet sure," thought I,
"If so much excellence abide below,
How excellent is He that dwells on high,   10
Whose power and beauty by His works we know?
Sure He is goodness, wisdom, glory, light,
That hath this under world so richly dight:
More heaven than earth was here, no winter and no night."

3

Then on a stately oak I cast mine eye,   15
Whose ruffling top the clouds seemed to aspire;

published, the anonymous editor included this among "several other poems made by the author upon diverse occasions, * * * found among her papers after her death, which she never meant should come to publick view."
5. "Contemplations" probably was not written before 1666. It is Mrs. Bradstreet's most independent work, and contains a number of her most inspired passages. In spite of its casual tone, this poem is unified. Its subject as a whole is the comparison of the life of mankind with the life of nonhuman nature as the poet observed it among the wild and wooded hills of the Merrimack, where she lived, near Andover, Massachusetts. Stanzas 1–7 recognize the beauty of external nature, and the sun as its generative force; stanzas 8–20 recall man's fall in the midst of this Eden, and the promise of his redemption and immortality; stanzas 21–28 observe the felicity of nonhuman creatures, absolved from the responsibility of moral choice—first the Merrimack and its fish, second the nightingale and other birds, each representing a kind of cycle; finally, stanzas 29–33 return to the plight of man, encumbered in life by wrong choices and insecurity, whose only hope for continuity is to find his name "graved in the white stone" of redemption.
6. In Greek, "the bright one," an epithet for the sun or for the sun god, Apollo.

How long since thou wast in thine infancy?
Thy strength and stature, more thy years admire.
Hath hundred winters passed since thou wast born.
Or thousand since thou brak'st thy shell of horn?   20
If so, all these as nought eternity doth scorn.

4

Then higher on the glistering sun I gazed,
Whose beams was shaded by the leafy tree;
The more I looked the more I grew amazed,
And softly said, "What glory's like to thee?   25
Soul of this world, this universe's eye,
No wonder some made thee a deity;
Had I not better known, alas, the same had I.

5

"Thou as a bridegroom from thy chamber rushes
And as a strong man, joys to run a race,[7]   30
The morn doth usher thee with smiles and blushes,
The earth reflects her glances in thy face.
Birds, insects, animals, with vegetive,[8]
Thy heart from death and dullness doth revive:
And in the darksome womb of fruitful nature dive.   35

6

"Thy swift annual and diurnal course,
Thy daily straight and yearly oblique path,
Thy pleasing fervor and thy scorching force,
All mortals here the feeling knowledge hath.
Thy presence makes it day, thy absence night,   40
Quaternal seasons caused by thy might:
Hail, creature full of sweetness, beauty, and delight!

7

"Art thou so full of glory that no eye
Hath strength thy shining rays once to behold?
And is thy splendid throne erect so high   45
As to approach it can no earthly mould?
How full of glory then must thy Creator be,
Who gave this bright light luster unto thee:
Admired, adored forever, be that majesty!"

8

Silent, alone, where none or saw or heard,   50
In pathless paths I led my wand'ring feet,
My humble eyes to lofty skies I reared,
To sing some song my mazed Muse thought meet.
My great Creator I would magnify,

7. See Psalms xix: 4–5.   8. Vegetable.

That nature had thus decked liberally: 55
But ah, and ah, again, my imbecility!

9

I heard the merry grasshopper then sing,
The black clad cricket bear a second part;
They kept one tune and played on the same string,
Seeming to glory in their little art. 60
Shall creatures abject thus their voices raise,
And in their kind resound their Maker's praise,
Whilst I, as mute, can warble forth no higher lays?

10

When present times look back to ages past,
And men in being fancy those are dead, 65
It makes things gone perpetually to last
And calls back months and years that long since fled;
It makes a man more aged in conceit[9]
Than was Methuselah or 's grandsire[1] great
While of their persons and their acts his mind doth treat. 70

11

Sometimes in Eden fair he seems to be,
Sees glorious Adam there made lord of all,
Fancies the apple dangle on the tree
That turned his sovereign to a naked thrall.
Who like a miscreant's driven from that place 75
To get his bread with pain and sweat of face:
A penalty imposed on his backsliding race.

12

Here sits our grandame in retired place,
And in her lap her bloody Cain[2] new-born;
The weeping imp oft looks her in the face, 80
Bewails his unknown hap and fate forlorn;
His mother sighs to think of paradise,
And how she lost her bliss to be more wise,
Believing him that was, and is, father of lies.

13

Here Cain and Abel came to sacrifice;[3] 85
Fruits of the earth and fatlings each do bring;
On Abel's gift the fire descends from skies,
But no such sign on false Cain's offering;
With sullen hateful looks he goes his ways,
Hath thousand thoughts to end his brother's days, 90
Upon whose blood his future good he hopes to raise.

9. Thought or conception.
1. See Genesis v: 18–27. According to this account, Methuselah lived 969 years; his grandfather, Jared, 962 years.
2. Cain is "bloody" because he was to become the first murderer; see Genesis iv: 8.
3. *Cf.* the source of ll. 85–105 in Genesis iv: 1–16.

14

There Abel keeps his sheep, no ill he thinks,
His brother comes, then acts his fratricide,
The virgin earth of blood her first draught drinks,
But since that time she often hath been cloyed.   95
The wretch with ghastly face and dreadful mind
Thinks each he sees will serve him in his kind,
Though none on earth but kindred near then could he find.

15

Who fancies not his looks now at the bar,
His face like death, his heart with horror fraught?   100
Nor malefactor ever felt like war
When deep despair with wish of life hath fought.
Branded with guilt and crushed with treble woes,
A vagabond to land of Nod he goes;
A city builds, that walls might him secure from foes.   105

16

Who thinks not oft upon the fathers' ages?
Their long descent, how nephews sons they saw,
The starry observations of those sages,
And how their precepts to their sons were law,
How Adam sighed to see his progeny   110
Clothed all in his black sinful livery,
Who neither guilt nor yet the punishment could fly.

17

Our life compare we with their length of days;
Who to the tenth of theirs doth now arrive?
And though thus short we shorten many ways,   115
Living so little while we are alive,
In eating, drinking, sleeping, vain delight.
So unawares comes on perpetual night
And puts all pleasures vain unto eternal flight.

18

When I behold the heavens as in their prime,   120
And then the earth, though old, still clad in green,
The stones and trees insensible of time,
Nor age nor wrinkle on their front are seen;
If winter come, and greenness then do fade,
A spring returns, and they more youthful made.   125
But man grows old, lies down, remains where once he's laid.

19

By birth more noble than those creatures all,
Yet seems by nature and by custom cursed;
No sooner born but grief and care makes fall
That state obliterate he had at first: 130

Nor youth nor strength nor wisdom spring again,
Nor habitations long their names retain,
But in oblivion to the final day remain.

20

Shall I then praise the heavens, the trees, the earth,
Because their beauty and their strength last longer? 135
Shall I wish there or never to had birth,
Because they're bigger and their bodies stronger?
Nay, they shall darken, perish, fade, and die,
And when unmade so ever shall they lie,
But man was made for endless immortality. 140

21

Under the cooling shadow of a stately elm
Close sat I by a goodly river's side,
Where gliding streams the rocks did overwhelm;
A lonely place, with pleasures dignified.
I once that loved the shady woods so well, 145
Now thought the rivers did the trees excel,
And if the sun would ever shine, there would I dwell.

22

While on the stealing stream I fixed mine eye,
Which to the longed-for ocean held its course,
I marked, nor crooks nor rubs[4] that there did lie 150
Could hinder aught, but still augment its force:
"O happy flood," quoth I, "that holds thy race
Till thou arrive at thy belovèd place,
Nor is it rocks or shoals that can obstruct thy pace!

23

"Nor is't enough that thou alone may'st slide, 155
But hundred brooks in thy clear waves do meet;
So hand in hand along with thee they glide
To Thetis'[5] house, where all embrace and greet:
Thou emblem true of what I count the best,
O could I lead my rivulets to rest, 160
So may we press to that vast mansion ever blest.

24

"Ye fish which in this liquid region bide,
That for each season have your habitation,
Now salt, now fresh, where you think best to glide,
To unknown coasts to give a visitation, 165
In lakes and ponds you leave your numerous fry,
So nature taught, and yet you know not why,
You wat'ry folk that know not your felicity.

---

4. Neither bends nor obstructions.   5. A Greek divinity who lived in the
                                         depths of the sea.

25

"Look how the wantons frisk to taste the air,
Then to the colder bottom straight they dive;   170
Eftsoon to Neptune's glassy hall repair
To see what trade they great ones there do drive,
Who forage o'er the spacious sea-green field,
And take the trembling prey before it yield,
Whose armor is their scales, their spreading fins their shield."   175

26

While musing thus with contemplation fed,
And thousand fancies buzzing in my brain,
The sweet-tongued Philomel[6] perched o'er my head,
And chanted forth a most melodious strain,
Which rapt me so with wonder and delight,
I judged my hearing better than my sight,   180
And wished me wings with her a while to take my flight.

27

"O merry bird," said I, "that fears no snares,
That neither toils nor hoards up in thy barn,
Feels no sad thoughts, nor cruciating cares   185
To gain more good or shun what might thee harm;
Thy clothes ne'er wear, thy meat is everywhere,
Thy bed a bough, thy drink the water clear;
Reminds[7] not what is past, nor what's to come doth fear.

28

"The dawning morn with songs thou dost prevent,[8]   190
Sets hundred notes unto thy feathered crew,
So each one tunes his pretty instrument
And warbling out the old, begin anew.
And thus they pass their youth in summer season,
Then follow thee into a better region,   195
Where winter's never felt by that sweet airy legion."

29

Man at the best a creature frail and vain,
In knowledge ignorant, in strength but weak,
Subject to sorrows, losses, sickness, pain,
Each storm his state, his mind, his body break;   200
From some of these he never finds cessation,
But day or night, within, without, vexation,
Troubles from foes, from friends, from dearest, near'st relation.

30

And yet this sinful creature, frail and vain,
This lump of wretchedness, of sin and sorrow,   205

6. The nightingale. Here, as often, the   7. Then signifying "remembers."
allusion is only poetic; the nightingale   8. Then meaning "to anticipate," or "to
was not found in the American colonies.   come before."

This weather-beaten vessel wracked with pain,
Joys not in hope of an eternal morrow;
Nor all his losses, crosses, and vexation,
In weight, in frequency and long duration,
Can make him deeply groan for that divine translation.   210

31

The mariner that on smooth waves doth glide
Sings merrily and steers his bark with ease,
As if he had command of wind and tide,
And now become great master of the seas;
But suddenly a storm spoils all the sport,   215
And makes him long for a more quiet port,
Which 'gainst all adverse winds may serve for fort.

32

So he that faileth in this world of pleasure,
Feeding on sweets, that never bit of th' sour,
That's full of friends, of honor, and of treasure,   220
Fond fool, he takes this earth ev'n for heaven's bower.
But sad affliction comes and makes him see
Here's neither honor, wealth, nor safety;
Only above is found all with security.

33

O Time, the fatal wrack of mortal things,   225
That draws oblivion's curtains over kings,
Their sumptuous monuments, men know them not,
Their names without a record are forgot,
Their parts, their ports, their pomp's all laid in th' dust,
Nor wit nor gold nor buildings 'scape time's rust;   230
But he whose name is graved in the white stone[9]
Shall last and shine when all of these are gone.

1666?   1678

A Letter to Her Husband[1]

Phoebus,[2] make haste, the day's too long, be gone;
The silent night's the fittest time for moan.
But stay this once, unto my suit give ear,
And tell my griefs in either hemisphere;
And if the whirling of thy wheels don't drown'd   5
The woful accents of my doleful sound,

9. Revelation ii: 17.
1. First published in the 1678 edition. There it is simply entitled "Another," following a short poem called "A Letter to Her Husband, Absent upon Publick Employment." These were among the manuscript poems of an intimate nature which Mrs. Bradstreet had apparently not intended to publish.
2. The sun.

If in thy swift carrier[3] thou canst make stay,
I crave this boon, this errand by the way:
Commend me to the man more loved than life,
Shew him the sorrows of his widowed wife,   10
My dumpish thoughts, my groans, my brakish tears,
My sobs, my longing hopes, my doubting fears,
And if he love, how can he there abide?
My interest's more than all the world beside.
He that can tell the stars or ocean sand,   15
Or all the grass that in the meads do stand,
The leaves in the woods, the hail or drops of rain,
Or in a cornfield number every grain,
Or every mote that in the sunshine hops,
May count my sighs and number all my drops.   20
Tell him the countless steps that thou dost trace,
That once a day thy spouse thou mayst embrace;
And when thou canst not treat by loving mouth,
Thy rays afar salute her from the south.
But for one month I see no day, poor soul,   25
Like those far situate under the pole,
Which day by day long wait for thy arise:
O how they joy when thou dost light the skys.
O Phoebus, hadst thou but thus long from thine
Restrained the beams of thy beloved shine,   30
At thy return, if so thou could'st or durst,
Behold a Chaos blacker than the first.
Tell him here's worse than a confused matter—
His little world's a fathom under water;
Nought but the fervor of his ardent beams   35
Hath power to dry the torrent of these streams.
Tell him I would say more, but cannot well:
Oppressed minds abruptest tales do tell.
Now post with double speed, mark what I say;
By all our loves conjure him not to stay.   40

1678

The Author to Her Book[4]

Thou ill-formed offspring of my feeble brain,
Who after birth did'st by my side remain,

3. *I.e.*, "career," or "course."
4. This casual poem is one of Anne Bradstreet's most delightful and genuine. It recounts with humor her feelings at seeing her poems in print in 1650 without her authorization or correction, and her subsequent efforts to improve

them. It appears that she intended this to stand last among her poems when she revised them about 1666 for a proposed second edition. Whoever sent the volume to the printer after her death added a subsequent section of thirteen "Posthumous Poems."

Till snatched from thence by friends, less wise than true,
Who thee abroad exposed to public view;
Made thee in rags, halting, to the press to trudge,   5
Where errors were not lessened, all may judge.
At thy return my blushing was not small,
My rambling brat (in print) should mother call;
I cast thee by as one unfit for light,
Thy visage was so irksome in my sight;   10
Yet being mine own, at length affection would
Thy blemishes amend, if so I could:
I washed thy face, but more defects I saw,
And rubbing off a spot, still made a flaw.
I stretched thy joints to make thee even feet,   15
Yet still thou run'st more hobbling than is meet;
In better dress to trim thee was my mind,
But nought save homespun cloth, in the house I find.
In this array, 'mongst vulgars may'st thou roam;
In criticks hands beware thou dost not come;   20
And take thy way where yet thou are not known.
If for thy Father asked, say thou had'st none;
And for thy Mother, she alas is poor,
Which caused her thus to send thee out of door.

1666?   1678

SAMUEL SEWALL

(1652–1730)

The New England Puritans were closely united by their common faith, but they produced the varied individualism of Bradford, John Eliot, the Mathers, and Jonathan Edwards, among others. Samuel Sewall represents a distinct type of the second and third generations, in which a more secular spirit gradually defeated the waning theocracy. Devoutly religious in private and public life, Sewall resisted an early religious vocation in favor of wealth, public office, and the pursuit of his hobbies. Shortly after his graduation from Har-

vard in 1671, he married Hannah, daughter of John Hull, Master of the Mint and reputed to be the wealthiest person in Massachusetts. His position was soon further strengthened by a small inheritance from his father. Sewall became an early example of the American aristocrat who regards public service as his natural expression. His father, avoiding the consequences of the Restoration of 1660, had brought him at the age of nine to Boston, and he seldom left it afterward. His *Diary*, for which he is best known, is a social history of that city during more than a half century.

Sewall began his public service in his late twenties. He managed the colony's printing press for several years, acting concurrently as deputy of the general court (1683) and later as member of the Council (1684–1686). In England on business in 1688, he assisted Increase Mather, the appointed envoy of the Massachusetts churches, in his unsuccessful efforts to secure the restoration of the charter of the colony. Under the new charter of 1692, Sewall again became a member of the Council, and served for thirty-three years. In the same year, 1692, he achieved his professional objective, being appointed as justice of the Superior Court; and he rose in the judiciary until, from 1718 to 1728, he was chief justice of Massachusetts.

One judicial act above all others is memorable in his life; he was a member of the special court of three which condemned the witches of Salem in 1692. That the blood of these innocents rested heavily on his soul is shown by his public confession of error five years later, and by other acts of contrition recorded in the text of his diary.

Sewall becomes the more interesting, since he represents not only himself but also an epoch. With the rapid influx of new people, the fervid dedication of the Puritan Fathers was doomed. Sewall's *Diary* depicts the resultant secularization, and the daily life of the generation that, within his time, first fully expressed those practical traits that came to be called "Yan-

kee." He was shrewdly aware of the value of money, but wished to earn it honestly; he was ambitious for honors, position, and esteem, but affectionate and neighborly; he was of moderate intelligence, often quaintly obtuse, but he had a quick sense of responsibility, the courage to confess his sins and acknowledge God publicly, and the humanitarian inspiration to become the author of perhaps the first tract published against Negro slavery in this country, *The Selling of Joseph* (1700). Of one of his later arguments concerning slavery, he commented in his *Diary* (June 22, 1716): "I essay'd to prevent Indians and Negroes being rated with horses and hogs; but could not prevail." This was certainly no ordinary man; even his many moments of dullness have a character of their own.

The other writings of Sewall have little intrinsic merit, but certain titles give some idea of the range of his interests. In collaboration with Edward Rawson he wrote *The Revolution in New England Justified* (1691), a defense of the overthrow of the royal governor, Andros, in 1689 in the struggle for a new charter. *Some Few Lines Towards a Description of the New Heaven * * * to Those Who Stand Upon the New Earth* appeared in 1697; later appeared *Proposals Touching the Accomplishment of Prophesies Humbly Offered* (1713), and *A Memorial Relating to the Kennebeck Indians* (1721).

The now famous *Diary* was not published until 1878. His first entries were made in 1673, and the record was copiously continued for most of the years through 1729, a total span of fifty-seven years. In spite of occasional lapses, the style bears the interesting stamp of the man himself, at his best when he portrays with a few suggestive strokes the dramatic essentials of a scene, a conversation, or even a gathering of people.

The Diary of Samuel Sewall was published in the *Collections of the Massachusetts Historical Society*, Fifth Series, Vols. V–VII, 1878–1882, the source of the present text. See also *Samuel Sewall's Diary* [abridged], edited by Mark Van Doren, 1927; and N. H. Chamberlain, *Samuel Sewall and the World He Lived In*, 1897.

From The Diary of Samuel Sewall

[*Customs, Courts, and Courtships*]

April 29, 1695. The morning is very warm and Sunshiny; in the Afternoon there is Thunder and Lightening, and about 2. P.M. a very extraordinary Storm of Hail, so that the ground was made white with it, as with the blossoms when fallen; 'twas as bigg as pistoll and Musquet Bullets; It broke of the Glass of the new House about 480 Quarrels[1] of the Front; of Mr. Sergeant's about as much; Col. Shrimpton, Major General, Govr. Bradstreet, New Meetinghouse, Mr. Willard, &c. Mr. Cotton Mather dined with us, and was with me in the new Kitchen when this was; He had just been mentioning that more Ministers Houses than others proportionably had been smitten with Lightening; enquiring what the meaning of God should be in it. Many Hail-Stones broke throw the Glass and flew to the middle of the Room, or farther: People afterward Gazed upon the House to see its Ruins. I got Mr. Mather to pray with us after this awful Providence; He told God He had broken the brittle part of our house, and prayd that we might be ready for the time when our Clay-Tabernacles should be broken. Twas a sorrowfull thing to me to see the house so far undon again before twas finish'd.

Jan. 13, 1696. When I came in, past 7. at night, my wife met me in the Entry and told me Betty had surprised them. I was surprised with the abruptness of the Relation. It seems Betty Sewall had given some signs of dejection and sorrow; but a little after dinner she burst out into an amazing cry, which caus'd all the family to cry too; Her Mother ask'd the reason; she gave none; at last said she was afraid she should goe to Hell, her Sins were not pardon'd. She was first wounded by my reading a Sermon of Mr. Norton's, about the 5th of Jan. Text, John vii:34. Ye shall seek me and shall not find me. And those words in the Sermon, John viii:21. Ye shall seek me and shall die in your sins, ran in her mind, and terrified her greatly. And staying at home Jan. 12. she read out of Mr. Cotton

1. Squares; panes set diagonally in a window.

Mather—Why hath Satan filled thy heart, which increas'd her Fear. Her Mother ask'd her whether she pray'd. She answer'd, Yes; but feared her prayers were not heard because her Sins not pardon'd. * * * The Lord bring Light and Comfort out of this dark and dreadful Cloud, and Grant that Christ's being formed in my dear child, may be the issue of these painfull pangs.

Dec. 25, 1696. We bury our little daughter. In the chamber, Joseph in course reads Ecclesiastes 3d a time to be born and a time to die—Elisabeth, Rev. 22. Hanah, the 38th Psalm. I speak to each, as God helped, to our mutual comfort I hope. I order'd Sam. to read the 102. Psalm. Elisha Cooke, Edw. Hutchinson, John Baily, and Josia Willard bear my little daughter to the Tomb. * * *

Jan. 14, 1697. Copy of the Bill I put up on the Fast day;[2] giving it to Mr. Willard as he pass'd by, and standing up at the reading of it, and bowing when finished; in the Afternoon.

Samuel Sewall, sensible of the reiterated strokes of God upon himself and family; and being sensible, that as to the Guilt contracted upon the opening of the late commission of Oyer and Terminer at Salem (to which the order for this Day relates) he is, upon many accounts, more concerned than any that he knows of, Desires to take the Blame and shame of it, Asking pardon of men, And especially desiring prayers that God, who has an Unlimited Authority, would pardon that sin and all other his sins; personal and Relative: And according to his infinite Benignity, and Sovereignty, Not Visit the sin of him, or of any other, upon himself or any of his, nor upon the Land: But that He would powerfully defend him against all Temptations to Sin, for the future; and vouchsafe him the efficacious, saving Conduct of his Word and Spirit.

Jan. 14, 1701. Having been certified last night about 10. oclock of the death of my dear Mother at Newbury, Sam. and I set out with John Sewall, the Messenger, for that place. Hired Horses at Charlestown: set out about 10. aclock in a great Fogg. Din'd at Lewis's with Mr. Cushing of Salisbury. Sam. and I kept on in Ipswich Rode, John went to accompany Bror from Salem. About Mr. Hubbard's in Ipswich farms, they overtook us. Sam. and I lodg'd at Cromptons in Ipswich. Bror and John stood on for Newbury by Moon-shine. Jany. 15th Sam. and I set forward. Brother Northend meets us. Visit Aunt Northend, Mr. Payson. With Bror and sister we set forward for Newbury: where we find that day appointed for the Funeral: twas a very pleasant Comfortable day. * * *

Nathan Bricket taking in hand to fill the Grave, I said, Forbear a little, and suffer me to say That amidst our bereaving sorrows We

2. Devout persons often made public confession of sin by posting acknowledgments in the church. Sewall refers to his activity as a judge in 1692 in the Salem witchcraft trials, which condemned nineteen to be hanged and one to be pressed to death, while scores were tortured and publicly disgraced.

have the Comfort of beholding this Saint put into the rightfull possession of that Happiness of Living desir'd and dying Lamented. She liv'd commendably Four and Fifty years with her dear Husband, and my dear Father: And she could not well brook the being divided from him at her death; which is the cause of our taking leave of her in this place. She was a true and constant Lover of Gods Word, Worship, and Saints: And she always, with a patient cheerfullness, submitted to the divine Decree of providing Bread for her self and others in the sweat of her Brows. And now her infinitely Gracious and Bountiful Master has promoted her to the Honor of higher Employments, fully and absolutely discharged from all manner of Toil, and Sweat. My honoured and beloved Friends and Neighbours! My dear Mother never thought much of doing the most frequent and homely offices of Love for me; and lavish'd away many Thousands of Words upon me, before I could return one word in Answer: And therefore I ask and hope that none will be offended that I have now ventured to speak one word in her behalf; when shee her self is become speechless. Made a Motion with my hand for the filling of the Grave. Note, I could hardly speak for passion and Tears.

Jan. 24, 1704. Took 24s in my pocket, and gave my Wife the rest of my cash £4. 3–8, and tell her she shall now keep the Cash; if I want I will borrow of her. She has a better faculty than I at managing Affairs: I will assist her; and will endeavour to live upon my Salary; will see what it will doe. The Lord give his Blessing.

April 3, 1711. I dine with the Court at Pullin's. Mr. Attorney treats us at his house wth excellent Pippins, Anchovas, Olives, Nuts. I said I should be able to make no Judgment on the Pippins without a Review, which made the Company Laugh. Spake much of Negroes; I mention'd the problem, whether [they] should be white after the Resurrection: Mr. Bolt took it up as absurd, because the body should be void of all Colour, spake as if it should be a Spirit. I objected what Christ said to his Disciples after the Resurrection. He said twas not so after his Ascension.

April 11, 1712. I saw Six Swallows together flying and chippering very rapturously.

May 5, 1713. Dr. Cotton Mather makes an Excellent Dedication-Prayer in the New Court-Chamber. Mr. Pain, one of the Overseers of the Work wellcom'd us, as the Judges went up Stairs. Dr. Cotton Mather having ended Prayer, The Clark went on and call'd the Grand-Jury: Giving their Charge, which was to enforce the Queen's Proclamation, and especially against Travailing on the Lord's Day; God having return'd to give us Rest. I said,[3] You ought to be quickened to your Duty, in that you have so Convenient, and August a Chamber prepared for you to doe it in. And what I say to you, I

3. A marginal note reads: "My speech to Grand jury in new Court House."

would say to my self, to the Court, and to all that are concern'd. Seeing the former decay'd Building is consum'd, and a better built in the room, Let us pray, May that Proverb, Golden Chalices and Wooden Priests, never be transfer'd to the Civil order; that God would take away our filthy Garments, and cloath us with Change of Raiment; That our former Sins may be buried in the Ruins and Rubbish of the former House, and not be suffered to follow us into this; That a Lixivium[4] may be made of the Ashes, which we may frequently use in keeping ourselves Clean: Let never any Judge debauch this Bench, by abiding on it when his own Cause comes under Trial; May the Judges always discern the Right, and dispense Justice with a most stable, permanent Impartiality; Let this large, transparent, costly Glass serve to oblige the Attornys alway to set Things in a True Light, And let the Character of none of them be *Impar sibi;*[5] Let them Remember they are to advise the Court, as well as plead for their clients. The Oaths that prescribe our Duty run all upon Truth; God is Truth. Let Him communicat to us of His Light and Truth, in Judgment, and in Righteousness. If we thus improve this House, they that built it, shall inhabit it; the days of this people shall be as the days of a Tree, and they shall long enjoy the work of their hands. The Terrible Illumination[6] that was made, the third of October was Twelve moneths, did plainly shew us that our GOD is a Consuming Fire: but it hath repented Him of the Evil. And since He has declar'd that He takes delight in them that hope in his Mercy, we firmly believe that He will be a Dwelling place to us throughout all Generations.

Saturday, Feb. 6, 1714. * * * My neighbour Colson knocks at our door about 9. or past to tell of the Disorders at the Tavern[7] at the Southend in Mr. Addington's house, kept by John Wallis. He desired me that I would accompany Mr. Bromfield and Constable Howell thither. It was 35. Minutes past Nine at Night before Mr. Bromfield came; then we went. I took Æneas Salter with me. Found much Company. They refus'd to go away. Said were there to drink the Queen's Health, and they had many other Healths to drink. Call'd for more Drink: drank to me, I took notice of the Affront to them. Said must and would stay upon that Solemn occasion. Mr. John Netmaker drank the Queen's Health to me. I told him I drank none; upon that he ceas'd. Mr. Brinley put on his Hat to affront me. I made him take it off. I threaten'd to send some of them to prison; that did not move them. They said they could but pay their Fine, and doing that they might stay. I told them if they had not

---

4. Lye obtained from a solution of wood ashes, used in processing soap.
5. Unequal to his [best] self.
6. An unusual astral or electrical phenomenon of the skies, then regarded as a portent.
7. This event occurred on Queen Anne's birthday, which the worldly would celebrate in a spirited fashion.

a care, they would be guilty of a Riot. Mr. Bromfield spake of raising a number of Men to Quell them, and was in some heat, ready to run into Street. But I did not like that. Not having Pen and Ink, I went to take their Names with my Pensil, and not knowing how to Spell their Names, they themselves of their own accord writ them. Mr. Netmaker, reproaching the Province, said they had not made one good Law.

At last I address'd myself to Mr. Banister. I told him he had been longest an Inhabitant and Freeholder, I expected he should set a good Example in departing thence. Upon this he invited them to his own House, and away they went; and we, after them, went away. The Clock in the room struck a pretty while before they departed. I went directly home, and found it 25. Minutes past Ten at Night when I entred my own House. * * *

Monday, Feb. 8. Mr. Bromfield comes to me, and we give the Names of the Offenders at John Wallis's Tavern last Satterday night, to Henry Howell, Constable, with Direction to take the Fines of as many as would pay; and warn them that refus'd to pay, to appear before us at 3. p.m. that day. Many of them pay'd. The rest appear'd; and Andrew Simpson, Ensign, Alexander Gordon, Chirurgeon, Francis Brinley, Gent. and John Netmaker, Gent., were sentenc'd to pay a Fine of 5s each of them, for their Breach of the Law Entituled, An Act for the better Observation, and Keeping the Lord's Day. They all Appeal'd, and Mr. Thomas Banister was bound with each of them in a Bond of 20s upon Condition that they should prosecute their Appeal to effect.

Capt. John Bromsal, and Mr. Thomas Clark were dismiss'd without being Fined. The first was Master of a Ship just ready to sail, Mr. Clark a stranger of New York, who had carried it very civilly, Mr. Jekyl's Brother-in-Law.

Oct. 18, [1717]. My wife grows worse and exceedingly Restless. Pray'd God to look upon her. Ask'd not after my going to bed. Had the advice of Mr. Williams and Dr. Cutler.

Oct. 19. Call'd Dr. C. Mather to pray, which he did excellently in the Dining Room, having Suggested good Thoughts to my wife before he went down. After, Mr. Wadsworth pray'd in the Chamber when 'twas suppos'd my wife took little notice. About a quarter of an hour past four, my dear Wife expired in the Afternoon, whereby the Chamber was fill'd with a Flood of Tears. God is teaching me a new Lesson; to live a Widower's Life. Lord help me to Learn; and be a Sun and Shield to me, now so much of my Comfort and Defense are taken away.

Oct. 20. I goe to the publick Worship forenoon and Afternoon. My Son has much adoe to read the Note I put up, being overwhelm'd with tears.

Feb. 6, 1718. This morning wandering in my mind whether to live a Single or a Married Life; I had a sweet and very affectionat Meditation Concerning the Lord Jesus; Nothing was to be objected against his Person, Parentage, Relations, Estate, House, Home! Why did I not resolutely, presently close with Him! And I cry'd mightily to God that He would help me so to doe!

March 14, 1718. Deacon Marion comes to me, sits with me a great while in the evening; after a great deal of Discourse about his Courtship—He told [me] the Olivers said they wish'd I would Court their Aunt [Mrs. Winthrop]. I said little, but said twas not five Moneths since I buried my dear Wife. Had said before 'twas hard to know whether best to marry again or no; whom to marry.

June 9, 1718. * * * Mrs. D[eniso]n came in the morning about 9 aclock, and I took her up into my Chamber and discoursed thorowly with her; She desired me to provide another and better Nurse. I gave her the two last News-Letters—told her I intended to visit her at her own house next Lecture-day. She said, 'twould be talked of. I answer'd, In such Cases, persons must run the Gantlet. Gave her Mr. Whiting's Oration[8] for Abijah Walter, who brought her on horseback to Town. I think little or no Notice was taken of it.

June 17, 1718. Went to Roxbury Lecture, visited Mr. Walter. Mr. Webb preach'd. Visited Govr Dudley, Mrs. Denison, gave her Dr. Mather's Sermons very well bound; told her we were in it invited to a Wedding. She gave me very good Curds.

July 25, 1718. I go in the Hackny Coach to Roxbury. Call at Mr. Walter's who is not at home; nor Govr Dudley, nor his Lady. Visit Mrs. Denison: she invites me to eat. I give her two Cases with a knife and fork in each; one Turtle shell tackling; the other long, with Ivory handles, Squar'd, cost 4s 6d; Pound of Raisins with proportionable Almonds.

Oct. 15, 1718. Visit Mrs. Denison on Horseback; present her with a pair of Shoe-buckles, cost 5s 3d.

Nov 1, 1718. My Son from Brooklin being here I took his Horse, and visited Mrs. Denison. Sat in the Chamber next Majr Bowls. I told her 'twas time now to finish our Business: Ask'd her what I should allow her;[9] she not speaking; I told her I was willing to give her Two [Hundred] and Fifty pounds per annum during her life, if it should please God to take me out of the world before her. She answer'd she had better keep as she was, than give a Certainty for an uncertainty; She should pay dear for dwelling at Boston. I desired her to make proposals, but she made none. I had Thoughts of Publishment[1] next Thorsday the 6th. But I now seem to be far from

8. The gift or loan of books, particularly those of a serious character, was a common custom.

9. A marriage agreement customarily involved the legal settlement of a fixed income for the wife.

1. Publishment—the public announce-

it. May God, who has the pity of a Father, Direct and help me!

Nov. 28, 1718. I went this day in the Coach; had a fire made in the Chamber where I spake with her before, November the first: I enquired how she had done these 3 or 4 weeks; Afterwards I told her our Conversation had been such when I was with her last, that it seem'd to be a direction in Providence, not to proceed any further; She said, It must be what I pleas'd, or to that purpose. Afterward she seem'd to blame that I had not told her so November 1. * * * I repeated her words of November 1. She seem'd at first to start at the words of her paying dear, as if she had not spoken them. But she said she thought twas Hard to part with All, and have nothing to bestow on her Kindred. I said, I did not intend any thing of the Movables, I intended all the personal Estate to be to her. She said I seem'd to be in a hurry on Satterday, November 1., which was the reason she gave me no proposals. Whereas I had ask'd her long before to give me proposals in Writing; she upbraided me, That I who had never written her a Letter, should ask her to write. She asked me if I would drink, I told her Yes. She gave me Cider, Apples and a Glass of Wine: gathered together the little things I had given her, and offer'd them to me; but I would take none of them. Told her I wish'd her well, should be glad to hear of her welfare. She seem'd to say she should not again take in hand a thing of this nature. Thank'd me for what I had given her and Desired my Prayers. * * * Mr. Stoddard and his wife came in their Coach to see their Sister which broke off my Visit. Upon their asking me, I dismiss'd my Coach, and went with them to see Mr. Danforth, and came home by Moon-shine. Got home about 9. at night. *Laus Deo.*[2]

My bowels[3] yern towards Mrs. Denison: but I think God directs me in his Providence to desist. * * *

April 1, 1719. In the morning I dehorted Sam. Hirst and Grindal Rawson from playing Idle Tricks because 'twas first of April; They were the greatest fools that did so. N[ew] E[ngland] Men came hither to avoid anniversary days, the keeping of them, such as the 25th of Decr. How displeasing must it be to God, the giver of our Time, to keep anniversary days to play the fool with ourselves and others. * * *

May 26, [1720]. About midnight my dear wife[4] expired to our great astonishment, especially mine. May the Sovereign Lord pardon my Sin, and Sanctify to me this very Extraordinary, awful Dispensation.

ment of an agreement to marry—was required.
2. Praise God!
3. The word then signified a supposed inner organ of compassion or tenderness.
4. Having cooled in his feelings toward the widow Denison in November, 1718,

the undaunted Sewall began, the following August, to court the widow Abigail Tilly. Two months later, in October, 1719, they were married. However, after seven months, Abigail suddenly died in the night, as the diarist records below.

May 29, [1720]. God having in his holy Sovereignty put my Wife out of the Fore-Seat, I aprehended I had Cause to be asham'd of my Sin, and to loath my self for it; and retired to my Pue. * * * I put a Note to this purpose: Samuel Sewall, depriv'd of his Wife by a very sudden and awfull Stroke, desires Prayers that God would sanctify the same to himself, and Children, and family. Writ and sent three; to the South, Old, and Mr. Colman's church.

Sept. 5, 1720. Going to Son Sewall's I there meet with Madam Winthrop, told her I was glad to meet her there, had not seen her a great while; gave her Mr. Homes's Sermon.

Sept. 30, 1720. Mr. Colman's Lecture: Daughter Sewall acquaints Madam Winthrop that if she pleas'd to be within at 3. p.m. I would wait on her. She answer'd she would be at home.

Oct. 1, 1720. Satterday, I dine at Mr. Stoddard's: from thence I went to Madam Winthrop's just at 3. Spake to her, saying, my loving wife died so soon and suddenly, 'twas hardly convenient for me to think of Marrying again; however I came to this Resolution, that I would not make my Court to any person without first Consulting with her. Had a pleasant discourse about 7 Single persons sitting in the Fore-seat[5] September 29th viz. Madm Rebekah Dudley, Catharine Winthrop, Bridget Usher, Deliverance Legg, Rebekah Loyd, Lydia Colman, Elizabeth Bellingham. She propounded one and another for me; but none would do, said Mrs. Loyd was about her Age.

Oct. 3, 1720. Waited on Madam Winthrop again; 'twas a little while before she came in. Her daughter Noyes being there alone with me, I said, I hoped my Waiting on her Mother would not be disagreeable to her. She answer'd she should not be against that that might be for her Comfort. I Saluted her, and told her I perceiv'd I must shortly wish her a good Time; (her mother had told me, she was with Child, and within a Moneth or two of her Time). By and by in came Mr. Airs, Chaplain of the Castle,[6] and hang'd up his Hat, which I was a little startled at, it seeming as if he was to lodge there. At last Madam Winthrop came too. After a considerable time, I went up to her and said, if it might not be inconvenient I desired to speak with her. She assented, and spake of going into another Room; but Mr. Airs and Mrs. Noyes presently rose up, and went out, leaving us there alone. Then I usher'd in Discourse from the names in the Fore-seat; at last I pray'd that Katharine[7] might be the person assign'd for me. She instantly took it up in the way of Denyal, as if she had catch'd at an Opportunity to do it, saying she could not do it before she was asked. Said that was her mind unless she should Change it, which she believed she should not; could

5. It was customary for widows to sit in a pew reserved for them at the front of the church.

6. Castle Island, in Boston Harbor, a small fortress with a garrison.

7. Mrs. Winthrop.

not leave her Children. I express'd my Sorrow that she should do it so Speedily, pray'd her Consideration, and ask'd her when I should wait on her agen. She setting no time, I mention'd that day Sennight.[8] Gave her Mr. Willard's Fountain open'd[9] with the little print and verses; saying, I hop'd if we did well read that book, we should meet together hereafter, if we did not now. She took the Book, and put it in her Pocket. Took Leave.

Oct. 6, 1720. * * * A little after 6. p.m. I went to Madam Winthrop's. She was not within. I gave Sarah Chickering the Maid 2s, Juno, who brought in wood, 1s. Afterward the Nurse came in, I gave her 18d, having no other small Bill. After awhile Dr. Noyes came in with his Mother; and quickly after his wife came in: They sat talking, I think, till eight a-clock. I said I fear'd I might be some Interruption to their Business: Dr. Noyes reply'd pleasantly: He fear'd they might be an Interruption to me, and went away. Madam seem'd to harp upon the same string. Must take care of her Children; could not leave that House and Neighbourhood where she had dwelt so long. I told her she might doe her children as much or more good by bestowing what she laid out in Hous-keeping, upon them. Said her Son would be of Age the 7th of August. I said it might be inconvenient for her to dwell with her Daughter-in-Law, who must be Mistress of the House. I gave her a piece of Mr. Belcher's Cake and Ginger-Bread wrapped up in a clean sheet of Paper; told her of her Father's kindness to me when Treasurer, and I Constable. My Daughter Judith was gon from me and I was more lonesom—might help to forward one another in our Journey to Canaan.[1]—Mr. Eyre came within the door; I saluted him, ask'd how Mr. Clark did, and he went away. I took leave about 9 aclock. * * *

Oct. 10, 1720. In the Evening I visited Madam Winthrop, who treated me with a great deal of Curtesy; Wine, Marmalade. I gave her a News-Letter[2] about the Thanksgiving Proposals, for sake of the verses for David Jeffries. She tells me Dr. Increase Mather visited her this day, in Mr. Hutchinson's Coach.

Oct. 11, 1720. I writ a few Lines to Madam Winthrop to this purpose: "Madam, These wait on you with Mr. Mayhew's[3] Sermon, and Account of the state of the Indians on Martha's Vinyard. I thank you for your Unmerited Favours of yesterday; and hope to have the Happiness of Waiting on you to-morrow before Eight a-clock after Noon. I pray God to keep you, and give you a joyfull entrance upon

8. Seven nights; a week.
9. *The Fountain Opened, or the Great Gospel Privilege of Having Christ Exhibited to Sinful Men * * **, by Samuel Willard (Boston, 1700).
1. Canaan, the Hebrew Promised Land, became synonymous with "Paradise."
2. The *News-Letter*, the first newspaper in the American colonies, was founded

in 1704 in Boston. Sewall refers to the Governor's Proclamation for Thanksgiving Day, 1720, by then an annual custom in Massachusetts. *Cf.* Bradford's *Of Plymouth Plantation*.
3. Experience Mayhew was a well-known Puritan evangelist and Indian missionary of Martha's Vineyard.

the Two Hundred and twenty ninth year of Christopher Columbus his Discovery; and take Leave, who am, Madam, your humble Servt. S.S.

Oct. 12, 1720. Mrs. Anne Cotton came to door (twas before 8.) said Madam Winthrop was within, directed me into the little Room, where she was full of work behind a Stand; Mrs. Cotton came in and stood. Madam Winthrop pointed to her to set me a Chair. Madam Winthrop's Countenance was much changed from what 'twas on Monday, look'd dark and lowering. At last, the work, (black stuff or Silk) was taken away, I got my Chair in place, had some Converse, but very Cold and indifferent to what 'twas before. Ask'd her to acquit me of Rudeness if I drew off her Glove. Enquiring the reason, I told her twas great odds between handling a dead Goat, and a living Lady. Got it off. I told her I had one Petition to ask of her, that was, that she would take off the Negative she laid on me the third of October; She readily answer'd she could not, and enlarg'd upon it; She told me of it so soon as she could; could not leave her house, children, neighbours, business. I told her she might do som Good to help and support me. Mentioning Mrs. Gookin, Nath, the widow Weld was spoken of; said I had visited Mrs. Denison. I told her Yes! Afterward I said, If after a first and second Vagary she would Accept of me returning, Her Victorious Kindness and Good Will would be very Obliging. She thank'd me for my Book, (Mr. Mayhew's Sermon), But said not a word of the Letter. When she insisted on the Negative, I pray'd there might be no more Thunder and Lightening, I should not sleep all night. I gave her Dr. Preston,[4] The Church's Marriage and the Church's Carriage, which cost me 6s at the Sale. The door standing open, Mr. Airs came in, hung up his Hat, and sat down. After awhile, Madam Winthrop moving, he went out. Jno Eyre look'd in, I said How do ye, or, your servant Mr. Eyre: but heard no word from him. Sarah fill'd a Glass of Wine, she drank to me, I to her, She sent Juno home with me with a good Lantern, I gave her 6d and bid her thank her Mistress. In some of our Discourse, I told her I had rather go to the Stone-House[5] adjoining to her, than to come to her against her mind. Told her the reason why I came every other night was lest I should drink too deep draughts of Pleasure. She had talk'd of Canary, her Kisses were to me better than the best Canary. Explain'd the expression Concerning Columbus. * * *

Oct. 13. I tell my Son and daughter Sewall, that the Weather was not so fair as I apprehended.

Oct. 19, 1720. Midweek, Visited Madam Winthrop; Sarah told me she was at Mr. Walley's, would not come home till late. I gave

4. John Preston (1587–1628), English Puritan of Cambridge University, teacher of many early American Puritans.

5. *I.e.,* the prison.

her Hannah 3 oranges with her Duty, not knowing whether I should find her or no. Was ready to go home: but said if I knew she was there, I would go thither. Sarah seem'd to speak with pretty good Courage, She would be there. I went and found her there, with Mr. Walley and his wife in the little Room below. At 7 a-clock I mentioned going home; at 8. I put on my Coat, and quickly waited on her home. She found occasion to speak loud to the servant, as if she had a mind to be known. Was Courteous to me; but took occasion to speak pretty earnestly about my keeping a Coach: I said 'twould cost £100. per annum: she said twould cost but £40. * * * Exit. Came away somewhat late.

Oct. 20, 1720. * * * Madam Winthrop not being at Lecture, I went thither first; found her very Serene with her dâter[6] Noyes, Mrs. Dering, and the widow Shipreev sitting at a little Table, she in her arm'd Chair. She drank to me, and I to Mrs. Noyes. After awhile pray'd the favour to speak with her. She took one of the Candles, and went into the best Room, clos'd the shutters, sat down upon the Couch. She told me Madam Usher had been there, and said the Coach must be set on Wheels, and not by Rusting. She spake somthing of my needing a Wigg. Ask'd me what her Sister said to me. I told her, She said, If her Sister were for it, She would not hinder it. But I told her, she did not say she would be glad to have me for her Brother. Said, I shall keep you in the Cold, and asked her if she would be within to morrow night, for we had had but a running Feat. She said she could not tell whether she should, or no. I took Leave. As were drinking at the Governour's, he said: In England the Ladies minded little more than that they might have Money, and Coaches to ride in. I said, And New-England brooks its Name. At which Mr. Dudley smiled. Govr said they were not quite so bad here.

Oct. 21, 1720. Friday, My Son, the Minister, came to me p.m. by appointment and we pray one for another in the Old Chamber; more especially respecting my Courtship. About 6. a-clock I go to Madam Winthrop's; Sarah told me her Mistress was gon out, but did not tell me whither she went. She presently order'd me a Fire; so I went in, having Dr. Sibb's Bowels[7] with me to read. I read the two first Sermons, still no body came in: at last about 9. a-clock Mr. Jno Eyre came in; I took the opportunity to say to him as I had done to Mrs. Noyes before, that I hoped my Visiting his Mother would not be disagreeable to him; He answered me with much Respect. When twas after 9. a-clock He of himself said he would go and call her, she was but at one of his Brothers: A while after I heard Madam

6. Daughter.
7. Dr. Richard Sibbes, prominent English Puritan, published in 1639 his *Bowels Opened; or Discovery of the Neere and Deere Love of Christ and the Church.* Here again "bowels" denotes a supposed inner organ of compassion.

Winthrop's voice, enquiring something about John. After a good while and Clapping the Garden door twice or thrice, she came in. I mentioned something of the lateness; she banter'd me, and said I was later. She receiv'd me Courteously. I ask'd when our proceedings should be made publick: She said They were like to be no more publick than they were already. Offer'd me no Wine that I remember. I rose up at 11 a-clock to come away, saying I would put on my Coat, She offer'd not to help me. I pray'd her that Juno might light me home, she open'd the Shutter, and said twas pretty light abroad; Juno was weary and gon to bed. So I came hôm by Star-light as well as I could. At my first coming in, I gave Sarah five Shillings. I writ Mr. Eyre his Name in his book with the date Octobr 21. 1720. It cost me 8s. Jehovah jireh![8] Madam told me she had visited M. Mico, Wendell, and Wm Clark of the South [Church].

Oct. 22, 1720. Dâter Cooper visited me before my going out of Town, staid till about Sun set. I brought her going near as far as the Orange Tree.[9] Coming back, near Leg's Corner, Little David Jeffries saw me, and looking upon me very lovingly, ask'd me if I was going to see his Grandmother?[1] I said, Not to-night. Gave him a peny, and bid him present my Service to his Grandmother.

Oct. 24, 1720. I went in the Hackny Coach through the Common, stop'd at Madam Winthrop's (had told her I would take my departure from thence). Sarah came to the door with Katee in her Arms: but I did not think to take notice of the Child. Call'd her Mistress. I told her, being encourag'd by David Jeffries loving eyes, and sweet Words, I was come to enquire whether she could find in her heart to leave that House and Neighbourhood, and go and dwell with me at the Southend; I think she said softly, Not yet. I told her It did not ly in my Lands[2] to keep a Coach. If I should, I should be in danger to be brought to keep company with her Neighbour Brooker, (he was a little before sent to prison for Debt). Told her I had an Antipathy against those who would pretend to give themselves; but nothing of their Estate. I would a proportion of my Estate with my self. And I suppos'd she would do so. As to a Perriwig, My best and greatest Friend, I could not possibly have a greater, began to find me with Hair before I was born, and had continued to do so ever since; and I could not find in my heart to go to another. She commended the book I gave her, Dr. Preston, the Church Marriage; quoted him saying 'twas inconvenient keeping out of a Fashion commonly used. I said the Time and Tide did circumscribe my Visit. She gave me a Dram of Black-Cherry Brandy, and gave me a lump

8. God will provide. See Genesis xxii: 14. These were Abraham's words when God provided him with a ram to use for the sacrifice instead of his son, Isaac.

9. That is, "I accompanied her nearly to the Orange Tree" (an inn on the road).
1. Madam Winthrop.
2. *I.e.*, "It did not accord with my income."

of the Sugar that was in it. She wish'd me a good Journy. I pray'd God to keep her, and came away. Had a very pleasant Journy to Salem.

Nov. 1, 1720. I was so taken up that I could not go if I would.

Nov. 2, 1720. Midweek, went again, and found Mrs. Alden there, who quickly went out. Gave her about ½ pound of Sugar Almonds, cost 3s per £. Carried them on Monday. She seem'd pleas'd with them, ask'd what they cost. Spake of giving her a Hundred pounds per anum if I dy'd before her. Ask'd her what sum she would give me, if she should dy first? Said I would give her time to Consider of it. She said she heard as if I had given all to my Children by Deeds of Gift. I told her 'twas a mistake, Point-Judith was mine &c. That in England, I own'd, my Father's desire was that it should go to my eldest Son; 'twas 20£ per anum; she thought 'twas forty. I think when I seem'd to excuse pressing this, she seem'd to think twas best to speak of it; a long winter was coming on. Gave me a Glass or two of Canary.

Nov. 4, 1720. Friday, Went again about 7. a-clock; found there Mr. John Walley and his wife: sat discoursing pleasantly. I shew'd them Isaac Moses's [an Indian] Writing. Madam W. serv'd Comfeits to us. After awhile a Table was spread, and Supper was set. I urg'd Mr. Walley to Crave a Blessing; but he put it upon me. About 9. they went away. I ask'd Madam what fashioned Neck-lace I should present her with, She said, None at all. I ask'd her Whereabout we left off last time; mention'd what I had offer'd to give her; Ask'd her what she would give me; She said she could not Change her Condition: She had said so from the beginning; could not be so far from her Children, the Lecture. Quoted the Apostle Paul affirming that a single Life was better than a Married. I answer'd That was for the present Distress. Said she had not pleasure in things of that nature as formerly: I said, you are the fitter to make me a Wife. If she hald in that mind, I must go home and bewail my Rashness in making more haste than good Speed. However, considering the Supper, I desired her to be within next Monday night, if we liv'd so long. Assented. * * *

Nov. 7, 1720. My Son pray'd in the Old Chamber. Our time had been taken up by Son and Daughter Cooper's Visit; so that I only read the 130th and 143 Psalm. Twas on the Account of my Court-ship. I went to Mad. Winthrop; found her rocking her little Katee in the Cradle. I excus'd my Coming so late (near Eight). She set me an arm'd Chair and Cusheon; and so the Cradle was between her arm'd Chair and mine. Gave her the remnant of my Almonds; She did not eat of them as before; but laid them away; I said I came to enquire whether she had alter'd her mind since Friday, or remained of the same mind still. She said, Thereabouts. I told her I loved her, and was so fond as to think that she loved me: She said had a great respect for me. I told her, I had made her an offer, without asking any advice; she had so many to advise with, that twas a hindrance. The Fire was come to one short Brand besides the Block, which Brand was set up in end; at last it fell to pieces, and no Recruit was made: She gave me a Glass of Wine. I think I repeated again that I would go home and bewail my Rashness in making more haste than good Speed. I would endeavour to contain myself, and not go on to sollicit her to do that which she could not Consent to. Took leave of her. As came down the steps she bid me have a Care. Treated me Courteously. Told her she had enter'd the 4th year of her Widowhood. I had given her the News-Letter before; I did not bid her draw off her Glove as sometime I had done. Her Dress was not so clean as sometime it had been. Jehovah jireh![3]

Nov. 9, 1720. Dine at Bror Stoddard's: were so kind as to enquire of me if they should invite M'm Winthrop; I answer'd No. Thank'd my Sister Stoddard for her Courtesie; * * * She sent her servant home with me with a Lantern. Madam Winthrop's Shutters were open as I pass'd by.

1673–1729   1878

3. Again, "God will provide"; and although Sewall acknowledged defeat with Mrs. Winthrop, he achieved a third marriage sixteen months later, in his seventy-first year.

EDWARD TAYLOR
(1645?–1729)

During the lifetime of Edward Taylor only a few friends read his poems, which remained in manuscript. The quiet country pastor tended his flock at Westfield, then a frontier village, in the Connecticut valley, and regarded his poems as sacramental acts of private devotion and worship. Ezra Stiles, the poet's grandson, inherited the manuscript, along with Taylor's command "that his heirs should never publish" it; he therefore deposited it in the library at Yale College, of which he was the president. More than two centuries passed before it was discovered, and by that time little could be learned of the man besides what appears in the poetry.

The poetry alone is sufficient to establish him as a writer of a genuine power unequaled by any American poet until Bryant appeared, 150 years later. "A man of small stature but firm: of quick Passions—yet serious and grave," wrote his grandson Ezra Stiles; and Samuel Sewall remembered a sermon he had preached at the Old South Church in Boston, which "might have been preached at Paul's Cross." This poet was clearly a man of great spiritual passion, of large and liberal learning, enraptured by the Puritan dream to such a degree that he could express it in living song. His success was by no means invariable, but his best poems, a considerable number, justify the position that he at once attained in our literature when in 1939 Thomas H. Johnson published from manuscript a generous selection of the poems.

Taylor was born in Coventry, England, or nearby, probably in 1645, and most likely in a family of dissenters. Johnson points out that an ardent young Congregationalist was not then welcome at the British universities, and concludes that the persecutions of 1662 confirmed Taylor's resolution to emigrate. He taught school for a few years, but finally, in July, 1668, he arrived in Boston, seeking liberty and education. He carried letters to Increase Mather, already a prominent clergyman, and to John Hull, the Master of the Mint, the leading capitalist of the colony, and father of Sewall's first wife. The earnest young seeker captured the affections of his hosts—the Mathers became his intimates for life— and in a few days it was arranged for him to be off for Harvard, where he and Samuel Mather, the son of Increase, were classmates. He and Sewall were still closer—"Chamberfellows and Bed-fellows," as the latter records, adding that "he * * * drew me thither." Quite certainly young Taylor captivated everyone, although his college life was otherwise uneventful, save for some academic distinctions.

Upon graduation in 1671 he accepted a call from the congregation of Westfield, and spent the remaining fifty-eight years of his life in quiet usefulness as pastor to his Congregational flock. He married twice and became the father of thirteen children, most of whom he outlived. In 1720 Harvard conferred on him the degree of Master of Arts. Taylor died in 1729, "entirely enfeebled * * * longing and waiting for his Dismission."

Taylor's manuscript book is in several sections: "God's Determinations," which includes "The Preface" and "The Glory of and Grace in the Church Set Out"; "Five Poems," the source of "Huswifery" and "Upon a Spider * * * "; and the "Sacramental Meditations," in two series, from the first of which are drawn the remaining poems included in this volume. Never a servile imitator, Taylor was quite evidently acquainted with the serious British poetry of his times, especially the metaphysical poets—such as Donne, Crashaw, and Herbert—and the contemporaries of Milton, who published *Paradise Lost* the year before young Taylor set out for America. Dr. Samuel Johnson called Donne's poems "metaphysical" in disparagement, but poets of our century have restored them to honor. Readers of the seventeenth-century poets or of Hopkins or Yeats, Eliot or the earlier MacLeish, will recognize Taylor's metaphysical language, in which the extreme extension of an emotion has led to extravagant projection of the figure of speech, or to the association of ideas and images under almost unbearable tensions, as in the figure of the spinning wheel of "Huswifery" and in the metaphors of the bird of paradise and the bread of life in "Meditation Eight." Taylor's work was uneven; yet at his best he produced lines and passages of startling vitality, fusing lofty concept and homely detail in the memorable fashion of great poetry. He was a true mystic whose experience still convinces us, and one of the four or five American Puritans whose writings retain the liveliness of genuine literature.

There is as yet no definitive edition of Edward Taylor's poetry. A judicious selection of his poems, along with an authoritative biographical sketch, a critical introduction, and notes, may be found in Thomas H. Johnson's edition of *The Poetical Works of Edward Taylor*, 1939, supplemented by the poems which Johnson edits in "Some Edward Taylor Gleanings," *New England Quarterly*, XVI (June, 1943), 280–296, and in "The Topical Verses of Edward Taylor," *Publications of the Colonial Society of Massachusetts*, XXXIV (1937), 513–554. The Johnson text is followed here.

The Preface

Infinity, when all things it beheld,
In nothing, and of Nothing all did build,
Upon what Base was fixt the Lath,[1] wherein
He turn'd this Globe, and riggalld[2] it so trim?
Who blew the Bellows of his Furnace Vast?   5
Or held the Mould wherein the world was Cast?
Who laid its Corner Stone? Or whose Command?
Where stand the Pillars upon which it stands?
Who Lac'de and Fillitted[3] the earth so fine,
With Rivers like green Ribbons Smaragdine?[4]   10
Who made the Sea's its Selvedge,[5] and it locks
Like a Quilt Ball[6] within a Silver Box?
Who spread its Canopy? Or Curtains Spun?
Who in this Bowling Alley bowld the Sun?
Who made it always when it rises set: 15
To go at once both down, and up to get?
Who th' Curtain rods made for this Tapistry?
Who hung the twinckling Lanthorns in the Sky?
Who? who did this? or who is he? Why, know
It's Onely Might Almighty this did doe.   20
His hand hath made this noble worke which Stands
His Glorious Handywork not made by hands.
Who spake all things from nothing: and with ease

1. Lathe.
2. To make a groove for. *Cf.* archaic "regal" or "riggal," a groove or slot for a moving mechanical member.
3. A filet was a lace mesh often used in binding women's hair.
4. Emerald green, from the Latin *smaragdus*, "emerald."
5. The woven or finished edge of a fabric.
6. A ball with a cover quilted of small patches of contrasting colors, used as a toy or trinket.

Can speake all things to nothing, if he please.
Whose Little finger at his pleasure Can   25
Out mete[7] ten thousand worlds with halfe a span:
Whose Might Almighty can by half a looks[8]
Root up the rocks and rock the hills by th' roots.
Can take this mighty World up in his hande,
And shake it like a Squitchen[9] or a Wand.   30
Whose single Frown will make the Heavens shake
Like as an aspen leafe the Winde makes quake.
Oh! what a might is this! Whose single frown
Doth shake the world as it would shake it down?
Which All from Nothing fet,[1] from Nothing, All: 35
Hath All on Nothing set, lets Nothing fall.
Gave all to nothing Man indeed, whereby
Through nothing man all might him Glorify.
In Nothing is imbosst the brightest Gem
More pretious than all pretiousness in them.   40
But Nothing man did throw down all by sin:
And darkened[2] that lightsom Gem in him,
   That now his Brightest Diamond is grown
   Darker by far than any Coalpit Stone.

1682?   1939

Meditation One

What love is this of thine, that Cannot bee
   In thine Infinity, O Lord, Confinde,
Unless it in thy very Person see
   Infinity and Finity Conjoyn'd?
What! hath thy Godhead, as not satisfi'de,   5
   Marri'de our Manhood, making it its Bride?

Oh, Matchless Love! Filling Heaven to the brim!
   O'rerunning it: all running o're beside
This World! Nay, Overflowing Hell, wherein
   For thine Elect, there rose a mighty Tide!   10
That there our Veans might through thy Person bleed,
   To quench those flames, that else would on us feed.

Oh! that thy love might overflow my Heart!
   To fire the same with Love: for Love I would.

---

7. Measure out.
8. *half a looks:* So reads the original manuscript in the Yale University Library. This usage is not reported in the *New English Dictionary*, and its meaning is unknown.

9. "Possibly * * * the obsolete substantive *switching*, a switch or stick" [Johnson's note].
1. Fetched.
2. Read "darkenèd."

But oh! my streight'ned[3] Breast! my Lifeless Sparke!   15
My Fireless Flame! What Chilly Love, and Cold?
In measure small! In Manner Chilly! See!
Lord, blow the Coal: Thy Love Enflame in mee.

1682   1939

The Experience

Canticles I: 3. . . . . thy name is as ointment poured forth.[4]

Oh, that I always breath'd in such an aire
    As I suck't in, feeding on sweet Content!
Disht up unto my Soul ev'n in that pray're
    Pour'de out to God over last Sacrament.
        What Beam of Light wrapt up my sight to finde   5
        Me neerer God than ere Came in my minde?

Most strange it was! But yet more strange that shine
    Which fill'd my Soul then to the brim to spy
My nature with thy Nature all Divine
    Together joyn'd in Him that's Thou, and I.   10
        Flesh of my Flesh, Bone of my Bone: there's run
        Thy Godhead and my Manhood in thy Son.

Oh! that that Flame which thou didst on me Cast
    Might me enflame, and Lighten e[ve]ry where.
Then Heaven to me would be less at last,   15
    So much of heaven I should have while here.
        Oh! Sweet though Short! I'le not forget the same.
        My neerness, Lord, to thee did me Enflame.

I'le Claim my Right: Give place ye Angells Bright.
    Ye further from the Godhead stande than I.   20
My Nature is your Lord; and doth Unite
    Better than Yours unto the Deity.
        God's Throne is first and mine is next: to you
        Onely the place of Waiting-men is due.

Oh! that my Heart, thy Golden Harp might bee   25
    Well tun'd by Glorious Grace, that e'ry string
Screw'd to the highest pitch, might unto thee
    All Praises wrapt in sweetest Musick bring.

---

3. *I.e.*, straightened, here meaning "con-
stricted."
4. These words occur in the Song of
Solomon, a song of the union of lovers.
Taylor employs a similar language of
passion in describing the experience of
the Puritan "regeneration," a union of
"sanctified" man with God. See especially ll. 7–18.

I praise thee, Lord, and better praise thee would,
If what I had, my heart might ever hold.

1682–1683   30
                                                            1939

Huswifery

Make me, O Lord, thy Spin[n]ing Wheele compleat;
   Thy Holy Worde my Distaff make for mee.
Make mine Affections thy Swift Flyers neate,
   And make my Soule thy holy Spoole to bee.
My Conversation make to be thy Reele,[5]   5
And reele the yarn thereon spun of thy Wheele.

Make me thy Loome then, knit therein this Twine:
   And make thy Holy Spirit, Lord, winde quills:[6]
Then weave the Web thyselfe. The yarn is fine.
   Thine Ordinances make my Fulling Mills.[7]   10
Then dy the same in Heavenly Colours Choice,
All pinkt[8] with Varnish't[9] Flowers of Paradise.

Then cloath therewith mine Understanding, Will,
   Affections, Judgment, Conscience, Memory;
My Words and Actions, that their shine may fill   15
   My wayes with glory and thee glorify.
Then mine apparell shall display before yee
That I am Cloathd in Holy robes for glory.

1685?   1939

Meditation Eight

John VI: 51. I am the living bread.[1]

I ken[n]ing[2] through Astronomy Divine
   The Worlds bright Battlement, wherein I spy
A Golden Path my Pensill cannot line
   From that bright Throne unto my Threshold ly.
And while my puzzled thoughts about it pore,   5
I find the Bread of Life in't at my doore.

5. Among the parts of a spinning wheel, the *distaff* holds the raw wool or flax, the *flyers* regulate the spinning, the *spool* twists the yarn, and the *reel* receives the finished thread.
6. The spools of a loom.
7. Mills in which the cloth is cleansed with fuller's earth or soap.
8. *I.e.*, pinked, meaning "ornamented."
9. Here meaning "lustrous," "glossy."

1. In ll. 21–36 the poet elaborates the passage: "I am the living bread which came down out of heaven; if any man eat of this bread he shall live forever," in support of the doctrine of grace, the New Covenant between God and Adam's fallen children, confirmed by the gift of Christ, His son.
2. Recognizing, knowing.

When that this Bird of Paradise put in
    The Wicker Cage (my Corps) to tweedle[3] praise
Had peckt the Fruite forbid: and so did fling
    Away its Food, and lost its golden dayes,   10
    It fell into Celestiall Famine sore,
    And never could attain a morsell more.

Alas! alas! Poore Bird, what wilt thou doe?
    This Creatures field no food for Souls e're gave:
And if thou knock at Angells dores, they show   15
    An Empty Barrell: they no soul bread have.
    Alas! Poore Bird, the Worlds White Loafe is done,
    And cannot yield thee here the smallest Crumb.

In this sad state, Gods Tender Bowells[4] run
    Out streams of Grace: and he to end all strife,   20
The Purest Wheate in Heaven, his deare-dear Son
    Grinds, and kneads up into this Bread of Life:
    Which Bread of Life from Heaven down came and stands
    Disht on thy Table up by Angells Hands.

Did God mould up this Bread in Heaven, and bake,   25
    Which from his Table came, and to thine goeth?
Doth he bespeake thee thus: This Soule Bread take;
    Come, Eate thy fill of this, thy Gods White Loafe?
    Its Food too fine for Angells; yet come, take
    And Eate thy fill! Its Heavens Sugar Cake.   30

What Grace is this knead in this Loafe? This thing
    Souls are but petty things it to admire.
Yee Angells, help: This fill would to the brim
    Heav'ns whelm'd-down Chrystall meele Bowle, yea and higher.
    This Bread of Life dropt in thy mouth doth Cry: 35
    Eate, Eate me, Soul, and thou shalt never dy.

1684   1939

The Glory of and Grace in the Church Set Out

Come now behold
    Within this Knot[5] What Flowers do grow:
Spanglde like gold:
    Whence Wreaths of all Perfumes do flow.

3. *I.e.*, twiddle, here signifying "warble," in reference to the bird of paradise, his soul.

4. Here referring to a supposed inward center of compassion.

5. Clump.

Most Curious[6] Colours of all Sorts you shall   5
With all Sweet Spirits[7] s[c]ent. Yet that's not all.

    Oh! Look, and finde
  These Choicest Flowers most richly sweet
    Are Disciplinde
  With Artificiall Angells meet.[8]   10
An heap of Pearls is precious: but they Shall
When set by Art Excell. Yet that's not all.

    Christ's Spirit showers
  Down in his Word and Sacraments
    Upon these Flowers,   15
  The Clouds of Grace Divine Contents.
Such things of Wealthy Blessings on them fall
As make them sweetly thrive. Yet that's not all.

    Yet Still behold!
  All flourish not at once. We see   20
    While some Unfold
  Their blushing Leaves, some buds there bee:
Here's Faith, Hope, Charity in flower, which call
On yonders in the Bud. Yet that's not all.

    But as they stand   25
  Like Beauties reeching[9] in perfume
    A Divine Hand
  Doth hand them up to Glories room:
Where Each in sweet'ned Songs all Praises shall
Sing all ore Heaven for aye. And that's but all.   30

1682   1939

Upon a Spider Catching a Fly

    Thou sorrow, venom Elfe:
      Is this thy play,
  To spin a web out of thyselfe
    To Catch a Fly?
      For why?   5

  I saw a pettish[1] wasp
    Fall foule therein:

6. Amazing.
7. Essences, perfumes.
8. *Disciplinde * * * meet:* Taught
suitably by angel artificers.

9. *Cf.* "reeking"; an obsolete meaning
was "to emit sweet odors."
1. Peevish, ill-humored. *Cf.* "pet," l. 17.

Whom yet thy whorle[2] pins did no[t hasp]
  Lest he should fling
    His sting.   10

But as afraid, remote
  Didst stand hereat,
And with thy little fingers stroke
  And gently tap
    His back.   15

Thus gently him didst treate
  Lest he should pet,
And in a froppish,[3] aspish heate
  Should greatly fret
    Thy net.   20

Whereas the silly Fly,
  Caught by its leg,
Thou by the throate took'st hastily,
  And 'hinde the head
    Bite Dead.   25

This goes to pot, that not
  Nature doth call.[4]
Strive not above what strength hath got,
  Lest in the brawle
    Thou fall.   30

This Frey[5] seems thus to us:
  Hells Spider gets
His intrails spun to whip Cords[6] thus,
  And wove to nets,
    And sets.   35

To tangle Adams race
  In's stratagems
To their Destructions, Spoil'd, made base
  By venom things,
    Damn'd Sins.   40

But mighty, Gracious Lord,
  Communicate
Thy Grace to breake the Cord; afford

2. The whorl, or small flywheel of the spindle, whose "pins" secure, or "hasp," the spinning thread, as the whirling legs of the spider enmesh his victim.
3. Fretful.
4. *that not / Nature doth call: I.e.*, he "goes to pot" who does not call upon "Natural Reason," which, in the Puritan Covenant theology, was man's inherent endowment of capacity to know God's Truth.
5. *I.e.*, fray, or affray, here meaning "attack."
6. Tough cord, now of hemp, formerly of animal entrails, like catgut.

      Us Glorys Gate
        And State.   45

    We'l Nightingaile sing like,
      When pearcht on high
  In Glories Cage, thy glory, bright:
    [Yea,] thankfully,
      For joy.   50

1685?   1939

The Reflexion

Canticles II: 1. I am the rose of Sharon.[7]

Lord, art thou at the Table Head above
  Meat, Med'cine, Sweetness, sparkling Beautys, to
Enamour Souls with Flaming Flakes of Love,
    And not my Trencher,[8] nor my Cup o'reflow?
    Ben't I a bidden guest? Oh! sweat mine Eye: 5
  O'reflow with Teares: Oh! draw thy fountains dry.

Shall I not smell thy sweet, oh! Sharons Rose?
  Shall not mine Eye salute thy Beauty? Why?
Shall thy sweet leaves their Beautious sweets upclose?
    As halfe ashamde my sight should on them ly?   10
    Woe's me! For this my sighs shall be in grain,
  Offer'd on Sorrows Altar for the same.

Had not my Soule's, thy Conduit, Pipes stopt bin
  With mud, what Ravishment would'st thou Convay?
Let Graces Golden Spade dig till the Spring   15
    Of tears arise, and cleare this filth away.
    Lord, let thy Spirit raise my sighings till
  These Pipes my soule do with thy sweetness fill.

Earth once was Paradise of Heaven below,
  Till inkefac'd sin had it with poyson stockt;   20
And Chast this Paradise away into
  Heav'ns upmost Loft, and it in Glory Lockt.
    But thou, sweet Lord, hast with thy golden Key
  Unlock[t] the Doore, and made a golden day.

Once at thy Feast, I saw thee Pearle-like stand   25
  'Tween Heaven and Earth, where Heavens Bright glory all

7. In the Song of Solomon, the bride's
announcement of her readiness. Mystical
religious writers frequently substituted
Christ and the worshiper in "sanctification" instead of marriage. *Cf.* the note
to the epigraph of "The Experience."
8. Wooden platter.

In streams fell on thee, as a floodgate and,
    Like Sun Beams through thee on the World to Fall.
    Oh! Sugar sweet then! My Deare sweet Lord, I see
    Saints Heaven-lost Happiness restor'd by thee.   30

Shall Heaven and Earth's bright Glory all up lie,
    Like Sun Beams bundled in the sun in thee?
Dost thou sit Rose at Table Head, where I
    Do sit, and Carv'st no morsell sweet for mee?
    So much before, so little now! Sprindge,[9] Lord,   35
    Thy Rosie Leaves, and me their Glee afford.

Shall not thy Rose my Garden fresh perfume?
    Shall not thy Beauty my dull Heart assaile?
Shall not thy golden gleams run through this gloom?
    Shall my black Velvet Mask thy fair Face Vaile?   40
    Pass o're my Faults; shine forth, bright sun; arise!
    Enthrone thy Rosy-selfe within mine Eyes.

1683   1939

9. "Spread out, extend over" [Johnson's note].

COTTON MATHER
(1663–1728)

From his own day to the present, few of his critics have been able to express unalloyed enthusiasm for Cotton Mather, either as man or writer. Yet it is impossible to ignore the fantastic bulk of his writing, his contemporary influence, or the international reputation of his best works. In fact, in spite of the colossal mass, dullness, and personal bias of his work as a whole, it has been a valuable source for knowledge of the history and the men of colonial New England, while a number of his writings possess genuine and enduring power. Mather himself has been viewed as a pedantic egotist, a reactionary, and a bigoted witch-hunter; yet it seems only just to remember also that he was fighting a losing battle for the survival of an ideal and a theology that to him were life itself, while the tide of a new age, secular and materialistic, crumbled the defenses about his zealot's Zion.

The way of life that he belatedly defended was symbolized by the dynasty of which he was the last, in succession to his grandfather, Richard, and his father, Increase Mather. This priesthood had represented the dominant hierarchy of New England during more than a half century. Cotton Mather was enrolled in Harvard at eleven, already prodigious for his command of Latin, Greek, and Hebrew, and soon to become saturated with self-conscious piety and learning. Receiving his Master of Arts degree at eighteen, he entered the ministry at the Second Church in Boston as assistant to his father, whom he succeeded in due course. There he spent his life in a superhuman ferment of activity and publication which carried far beyond his parish duties into public issues, decorum, and morals, as well as theological dogma.

His personality, however, was not likely to sustain his chosen rôle even under favorable circumstances, and Boston was no longer the Puritan community of his father's youth. Encouraged by inherited authority and by his early reputation of unearthly genius, convinced that God had ordained him vicar by removing a speech defect, he became, as Moses Coit Tyler says in *A History of American Literature, 1607–1765*, a victim of circumstances, "stretched every instant of his life, on the rack of ostentatious exertion, intellectual and religious, * * * in deference to a dreadful system of ascetic and pharisaic formalism, in which his nature was hopelessly enmeshed." In his all-consuming study he amassed two thousand books, the largest colonial library of the time; his scientific speculations secured his election to the Royal Society; his ceaseless writing produced 444 printed books, fourteen of them in one year in which he also continued to perform his duties as pastor and observed twenty vigils and sixty fasts. It is reported that he kept 450 fasts during his life, and once

publicly humiliated himself for his sins. In modern terms this represents an advanced hysteria, a Puritan tragedy of genius. When he died in 1728, he had survived three wives—the last died insane—he had outlived all but two of fifteen children, and one of the survivors had gone far astray. His public leadership had failed, whether in support of the dark delusion of witchcraft or in the enlightened advocacy of smallpox vaccination; he had not even succeeded, as Jonathan Edwards later did, in reviving religious faith; yet his own faith had never wavered, however narrow it may seem to modern thought.

Mather's great literary defect was his style—pedantic, heavy with literary allusions and quotations in several languages, often arrogant, violent in its images, language, and bursts of passion. This "fantastic" style had flourished for a time in various European literatures from Italy to England, and Mather was among its last defenders. When he was deeply moved, however, he could make of it an impressive instrument, particularly in the biographical sketches (of which one is included in this volume) in *Magnalia Christi Americana* (1702), his best-known production. This ponderous work comprises seven books, including a history of the New England settlements, "lives" of governors, magistrates, and "sixty famous divines," records of "divine providences" and the "wars of the Lord" against Satan, witches, heretics, Quakers, and Indians— a pastiche of brilliance, beauty, and botchwork. The earlier

Wonders of the Invisible World (1693) is a vigorous analysis of the validity of evidence against witches, which still evokes the morbid fascination of reasoned error. Mather had not participated in the bloody trials of the previous year, but his influence then was on the side of the prosecution, although in 1700 he repudiated some of the convicting evidence as invalid. Bonifacius (1710), later called Essays to Do Good, quite remarkably establishes a practical system for the daily transaction of good deeds and benevolence—and delighted Franklin's rationalistic mind. Psalterium Americanum (1718), a translation of the psalms, advanced Mather's liberal leadership in the movement to restore psalm singing to worship. Parentator (1724), his life of his father, vies with his sketch of Eliot in Magnalia for gentleness and insight; and these qualities are again present in Manductio ad Ministerium (1726), a manual of guidance for young ministers. In these few of his many works he best revealed his occasional command of a literature of power.

There is no collected edition of the works of Cotton Mather. Editions are listed in J. T. Holmes, Cotton Mather: A Bibliography of His Works, 3 vols., with analyses and notes, 1940. Carefully chosen and edited is Kenneth B. Murdock's Selections from Cotton Mather, 1926. Magnalia Christi Americana; or The Ecclesiastical History of New England, was published in London, 1702, and in America, 2 vols., Hartford, 1820, and 2 vols., Hartford, 1853–1855. The passage reprinted below is from the latter text, Book III. The best full-length biography is Barrett Wendell's Cotton Mather: The Puritan Priest, 1891, 1926; see also Kenneth B. Murdock, "Cotton Mather," Dictionary of American Biography, 1933.

From Magnalia Christi Americana, Book III[1]
The Life of John Eliot

HIS FAMILY-GOVERNMENT[2]

The Apostle Paul, reciting and requiring Qualifications of a Gospel Minister, gives Order, that he be The Husband of one Wife, and one that ruleth well his own House, having his Children in subjection with all gravity. It seems, that a Man's Carriage in his own House is a part, or at least a sign, of his due Deportment in the House of God; and then, I am sure, our Eliot's was very Exemplary. That one Wife which was given to him truly from the Lord, he loved, prized, cherished, with a Kindness that notably represented the Compassion which he (thereby) taught his Church to expect from the Lord Jesus Christ; and after he had lived with

1. In 1691, Mather had published separately The Life and Death of the Renown'd Mr. John Eliot. Eliot came directly from Cambridge University to America (1631) and was called at once to the ministry at Roxbury, Massachusetts. As an Indian missionary, he established fourteen villages, inhabited by at least eleven hundred converted Indians, and he instigated the Society for the Propagation of the Gospel. His Indian translation was the first complete Bible printed in the colonies. The Puritan embodiment of gentle piety and sainthood, he died in 1690 at the age of eighty-six.
2. The two preceding sections of this biographical sketch have dealt with "The Birth, Age, and Family of Mr. Eliot," and "Mr. Eliot's Early Conversion, Sacred Employment, and Just Removal into America."

her for more than half an Hundred Years, he followed her to the Grave with *Lamentations* beyond those, which the Jews from the figure of a Letter in the Text, affirm, that *Abraham* deplored his aged *Sarah* with;[3] her Departure made a deeper Impression upon him than what any common Affliction could. His whole Conversation with her, had that *Sweetness*, and that *Gravity* and *Modesty* beautifying of it, that every one called them *Zachary* and *Elizabeth*.[4] His Family was a little *Bethel*,[5] for the Worship of God constantly and exactly maintained in it; and unto the daily Prayers of the Family, his manner was to prefix the *Reading* of the *Scripture*; which being done, 'twas also his manner to make his young People to chuse a certain Passage in the Chapter, and give him some *Observation* of their own upon it. By this Method he did mightily *sharpen* and *improve*, as well as *try*, their Understandings, and endeavour to make them *wise unto Salvation*. He was likewise very strict in the Education of his Children, and more careful to mend any *error* in their Hearts and Lives, than he could have been to cure a *Blemish* in their Bodies. No *Exorbitancies* or *Extravagancies* could find a Room under his Roof, nor was his House any other than a *School of Piety*; one might have there seen a perpetual mixture of a *Spartan* and a *Christian* Disciple. Whatever Decay there might be upon *Family-Religion* among us, as for our *Eliot*, we *knew him, that he would command his Children, and his Houshold after him, that they should keep the Way of the Lord.*

HIS WAY OF PREACHING

Such was he in his *lesser Family!* And in his *greater Family*, he manifested still more of his Regards to the Rule of a *Gospel-Ministry*. To his Congregation, he was a *Preacher* that made it his Care, to *give every one their Meat in due Season*. It was *Food* and not *Froth*; which in his publick Sermons, he entertained the Souls of his People with, he did not *starve* them with empty and windy Speculations, or with such things as *Animum non dant, quia non habent*;[6] much less did he *kill* them with such *Poyson* as is too commonly exposed by the *Arminian* and *Socinian*[7] Doctors that have too often sat in *Moses's* Chair. His way of *Preaching* was very *plain*; so that the very *Lambs* might wade, into his Discourses on those Texts and Themes, wherein *Elephants* might *swim*; and herewithal, it was very *powerful*, his Delivery was always very graceful and grateful; but when he was to use reproofs and warnings against

3. Genesis xxii: 2.
4. Zacharias the priest, and his wife Elizabeth, were permitted to be the parents of John the Baptist because "they were righteous before God, walking * * * blameless" (Luke I: 5–14).
5. Meaning "the house of God." Abraham and Jacob each gave this name to the place of his vision (Genesis xii: 8, and Genesis xxviii: 19).
6. Such things as "give no life, because they possess none."
7. Arminius and Socinus were sixteenth-century theologians regarded as heretics by orthodox Calvinists.

any *Sin*, his Voice would rise into a *Warmth* which had in it very much of *Energy* as well as *Decency*;[8] he would sound the *Trumpets* of God against all *Vice*, with a most penetrating Liveliness, and make his Pulpit another Mount *Sinai*,[9] for the Flashes of Lightning therein display'd against the Breaches of the *Law* given upon that *Burning Mountain*. And I observed, that there was usually a special Fervour in the Rebukes which he bestow'd upon *Carnality*, a carnal Frame and Life in Professors of Religion; when he was to brand the Earthly-mindedness of *Church-Members*, and the Allowance and the Indulgence which they often gave unto themselves in sensual Delights, here he was a right *Boanerges*;[1] he then spoke, as 'twas said one of the Ancients did, *Quot verba tot Fulmina*, as many *Thunderbolts* as *Words*.

It was another Property of his *Preaching*, that there was evermore much of CHRIST in it; and with *Paul*, he could say, *I determined to know nothing but Jesus Christ*; having that Blessed Name in his Discourses, with a Frequency like that, with which *Paul* mentions it in his *Epistles*. As 'twas noted of Dr. *Bodly*, that whatever Subject he were upon, in the Application still his Use of it would be, *to drive Men unto the Lord Jesus Christ*; in like manner, the Lord Jesus Christ was the Loadstone which gave a touch to all the Sermons of our *Eliot*; a Glorious, Precious, Lovely *Christ* was the Point of Heaven which they still verged unto. From this *Inclination* it was, that altho' he Printed several *English* Books before he dy'd, yet his Heart seemed not so much in any of them, as in that serious and savoury Book of his, Entituled, *The Harmony of the Gospels, in the Holy History of Jesus Christ*. From hence also 'twas, that he would give that Advice to young Preachers, *Pray let there be much of Christ in your Ministry*; and when he had heard a Sermon, which had any special Relish of a Blessed Jesus in it, he would say thereupon, *O blessed be God, that we have Christ so much and so well preached in poor* New-England!

Moreover, he lik'd no *Preaching*, but what had been *well studied* for; and he would very much commend a Sermon which he could perceive had required some good *Thinking* and *Reading* in the Author of it. I have been present, when he has unto a Preacher then just come home from the Assembly with him, thus expressed himself, *Brother, there was Oyl required for the Service of the Sanctuary; but it must be beaten Oyl; I praise God, that I saw your Oyl so well beaten to day; the Lord help us always by good Study to beat our Oyl, that there may be no knots in our Sermons left*

---

8. In its original sense, meaning "the fitting" or "the appropriate."

9. Where Moses received the Ten Commandments from God, who "descended upon it in fire;" hence the "Burning Mountain," later in the sentence. Its location is unidentified. See Exodus xix–xx.

1. Christ's appellation for James and John, translated as "sons of thunder" (Mark iii: 17).

undissolved, and that there may a clear light be thereby given in the House of God! And yet he likewise look'd for something in a Sermon beside and beyond the meer *Study* of *Man;* he was for having the *Spirit* of *God*, breathing in it and with it; and he was for speaking *those* things, from *those* Impressions and with *those* Affections, which might compel the Hearer to say, *The Spirit of God was here!* I have heard him complain, *It is a sad thing, when a Sermon shall have that one thing,* The Spirit of God *wanting in it.* * * *

ELIOT AS AN EVANGELIST.

The Titles of a *Christian* and of a *Minister,* have rendred our *Eliot* considerable; but there is one memorable Title more, by which he has been signalized unto us. An Honourable Person did once in Print put the Name of an *Evangelist* upon him; whereupon in a Letter of his to that Person afterwards Printed, his Expressions were, "There is a *Redundancy*, where you put the Title of *Evangelist* upon me; I beseech you to suppress all such things; let us do and speak and carry all things with Humility; it is the Lord who hath done what is done; and it is most becoming the Spirit of Jesus Christ to lift up him, and lay our selves low; I wish that Word could be obliterated."[2] My Reader sees what a Caution Mr. *Eliot* long since entred against our giving him the Title of an *Evangelist;* but his *Death* has now made it safe, and his *Life* had long made it just, for us to acknowledge him with such a Title. I know not whether that of an *Evangelist,* or one separated for the Employment of Preaching the Gospel in such Places whereunto Churches have hitherto been gathered, be not an *Office* that should be continued in our Days; but this I know, that our *Eliot* very notably did the *Service* and *Business* of such an Officer.

Cambden could not reach the Heighth of his Conceit, who bore in his *Shield* a Salvage of *America*, with his Hand pointing to the Sun, and this Motto, *Mihi Accessu, Tibi Recessu.*[3] Reader, Prepare to behold this *Device* Illustrated!

The Natives of the Country now Possessed by the *New-Englanders,* had been forlorn and wretched *Heathen* ever since their first herding here; and tho' we know not *When* or *How* those *Indians* first became Inhabitants of this mighty Continent, yet we may guess that probably the Devil decoy'd those miserable Salvages hither, in hopes that the Gospel of the Lord Jesus Christ would never come here to destroy or disturb his *Absolute Empire* over them.[4] But our *Eliot* was in such ill Terms with the Devil, as

2. In a letter to Edward Winslow, regarding his tribute to Eliot in a work dealing with the evangelists to the Indians.

3. "As I approach, you decline." That is, Eliot's luster would rival the sun's.
4. *I.e.*, the Indians, not having knowledge of God's covenant, must die "in sin," and belong to Satan.

to alarm him with sounding the *Silver Trumpets* of Heaven in his
Territories, and make some Noble and Zealous Attempts towards
outing him of his Ancient Possessions here. There were, I think,
Twenty several *Nations* (if I may call them so) of *Indians* upon
that spot of Ground, which fell under the Influence of our *Three
United Colonies;* and our *Eliot* was willing to rescue as many of
them as he could, from that old usurping *Landlord* of *America,* who
is *by the Wrath of God, the Prince of this World.*

I cannot find that any besides the Holy Spirit of God, first moved
him to the blessed Work of *Evangelizing* these perishing *Indians;*
'twas that Holy Spirit which laid before his Mind the Idea of that
which was on the *Seal* of the Massachuset Colony; A *poor Indian
having a Label going from his Mouth, with a,* COME OVER AND
HELP Us. It was the Spirit of our Lord Jesus Christ, which enkindled in him a *Pitty* for the dark Souls of these Natives, whom the
God of this World had blinded, through all the By-past Ages. He
was none of those that make, *The Salvation of the Heathen,* an
Article of their *Creed;* but (setting aside the unrevealed and extraordinary Steps which the *Holy one of Israel* may take out of his *usual
Paths*) he thought men to be *lost* if our *Gospel* be hidden from
them; and he was of the same Opinion with one of the Ancients,
who said, *Some have endeavoured to prove* Plato *a Christian, till
they prove themselves little better than Heathens.* It is indeed a
Principle in the Turkish *Alcoran,*[5] That *Let a Man's Religion be
what it will, he shall be saved, if he conscientiously live up to the
Rules of it:* But our *Eliot* was no *Mahometan.* He could most heartily
subscribe to that Passage in the Articles of the Church of *England.*
"They are to be held accursed, who presume to say, that every
Man shall be saved by the Law or Sect which he professeth, so
that he be diligent to frame his Life according to that Law, and
Light of Nature; for Holy Scripture doth set out unto us, only
the Name of Jesus Christ, whereby Men must be saved." And it
astonished him to see many dissembling Subscribers of those Articles, while they have grown up to such a *Phrensy,* as to deny peremptorily all *Church-state,* and all *Salvation* to all that are not under
Diocesan Bishops, yet at the same time to grant that the *Heathen* might be saved without the Knowledge of the Lord Jesus
Christ * * *

The exemplary *Charity* of this excellent Person in this important
Affair, will not be seen in its due Lustres, unless we make some
Reflections upon several Circumstances which he beheld these forlorn *Indians* in. Know then, that these doleful Creatures are the
veriest *Ruines of Mankind,* which are to be found any where upon
the Face of the Earth. No such *Estates* are to be expected among

5. The Koran.

them, as have been the *Baits* which the pretended *Converters* in other Countries have snapped at. One might see among them, what an *hard Master* the Devil is, to the most devoted of his *Vassals!* These abject Creatures, live in a Country full of *Mines*; we have already made entrance upon our *Iron*; and in the very Surface of the Ground among us, 'tis thought there lies *Copper* enough to supply all this World; besides other Mines hereafter to be exposed; but our shiftless *Indians* were never Owners of so much as a *Knife*, till we come among them; their Name for an *English-man* was a *Knife-man*; Stone was instead of Metal for their *Tools*; and for their *Coins*, they have only little *Beads* with Holes in them to string them upon a *Bracelet*, whereof some are *white*; and of these there go six for a Penny; some are *black* or *blew*; and of these, go *three* for a Penny; this *Wampam*, as they call it, is made of the *Shell-fish*, which lies upon the Sea Coast continually.

The[y] live in a Country, where *we* now have all the Conveniencies of human Life: But as for *them*, their *housing* is nothing but a few *Mats* ty'd about *Poles* fastened in the Earth, where a good *Fire* is their *Bed Clothes* in the coldest Seasons; their *Clothing* is but a Skin of a Beast, covering their *Hind-parts*, their *Fore-parts* having but a little Apron, where Nature calls for Secrecy; their *Diet* has not a greater Dainty than their *Nokehick*, that is a spoonful of their *parch'd meal*, with a spoonful of *Water*, which will strengthen them to travel a Day together; except we should mention the Flesh of *Deers*, *Bears*, *Mose*, *Rackoons*, and the like, which they have when they can *catch* them; as also a little *Fish*, which if they would preserve, 'twas by *drying*, not by *salting*; for they had not a grain of *Salt* in the World, I think, till we bestow'd it on them. Their *Physick* is, excepting a few odd *Specificks*, which some of them Encounter certain Cases with, nothing hardly, but an *Hot-House*, or a *Powaw*; their *Hot-House* is a little *Cave* about eight foot over, where after they have terribly heated it, a Crew of them go sit and sweat and smoke for an Hour together, and then immediately run into some very cold adjacent Brook, without the least Mischief to them; 'tis this way they recover themselves from some Diseases, particularly from the *French*;[6] but in most of their dangerous Distempers, 'tis a *Powaw* that must be sent for; that is, a *Priest*, who has more Familiarity with Satan than his Neighbours; this Conjurer comes and Roars, and Howls, and uses Magical Ceremonies over the Sick Man, and will be well paid for it, when he has done; if this don't effect the Cure, the *Man's Time is come, and there's an end*.

They live in a Country full of the best *Ship-Timber* under Heaven: But never saw a *Ship*, till some came from *Europe* hither; and then

6. Syphilis.

they were scar'd out of their Wits, to see the *Monster* come sailing in, and spitting Fire with a mighty noise, out of her floating side; they cross the Water in *Canoo's*, made sometimes of *Trees*, which they burn and hew, till they have hollow'd them; and sometimes of *Barks*, which they stitch into a light sort of a Vessel, to be easily carried over Land; if they over-set, it is but a little paddling like a Dog, and they are soon where they were.

Their way of living, is infinitely Barbarous: The Men are most abominably *slothful*; making their poor *Squaws*, or Wives, to plant and dress, and barn, and beat their Corn, and build their *Wigwams* for them; which perhaps may be the reason of their extraordinary Ease in Childbirth. In the mean time, their chief Employment, when they'll *condescend* unto any, is that of *Hunting*; wherein they'll go out some scores, if not Hundreds of them in a Company, driving all before them.

They continue in a Place, till they have burnt up all the *Wood* thereabouts, and then they pluck up Stakes; to follow the *Wood*, which they cannot fetch home unto themselves; hence when they enquire about the *English*, *Why come they hither!* They have themselves very Learnedly determined the Case, '*Twas because we wanted Firing*. No *Arts* are understood among them, unless just so far as to maintain their Brutish Conversation, which is little more than is to be found among the very *Bevers* upon our Streams. * * *

This was the miserable People, which our *Eliot* propounded unto himself, to teach and save! And he had a double Work incumbent on him; he was to make Men of them, e'er he could hope to see them *Saints*; they must be *civilized* e'er they could be *Christianized*; he could not, as *Gregory* once of our Nation, see any thing *Angelical*[7] to bespeak his Labours for their Eternal Welfare, all among them was *Diabolical*. To think on raising a Number of these hideous Creatures, unto the *Elevations* of our Holy Religion, must argue more than common or little Sentiments in the Undertaker; but the Faith of an *Eliot* could encounter it! * * *

The *First Step* which he judg'd necessary now to be taken by him, was to learn the *Indian* Language; for he saw them so stupid and senseless, that they would never do so much as enquire after the Religion of the Strangers now come into their Country, much less would they so far imitate us, as to leave off their beastly way of living, that they might be Partakers of any Spiritual Advantage by us: Unless we could first address them in a *Language* of their own. Behold, new Difficulties to be surmounted by our indefatigable *Eliot*! He hires a Native to teach him this exotick Language, and with a laborious Care and Skill, reduces it into a *Grammar*

7. Pope Gregory the Great (died 604), on first seeing specimens of the fair Britons, is reported to have exclaimed, "Not Angles, but angels!"

which afterwards he published. There is a Letter or two of our Alphabet, which the *Indians* never had in *theirs;* tho' there were enough of the *Dog* in their *Temper,* there can scarce be found an R in their *Language;* (any more than in the Language of the *Chinese,* or of the *Greenlanders*) save that the *Indians* to the Northward, who have a peculiar *Dialect,* pronounce an R where an N is pronounced by our *Indians;* but if their *Alphabat* be *short,* I am sure the *Words* composed of it are long enough to tire the Patience of any Scholar in the World; they are *Sesquipedalia Verba,*[8] of which their *Lingua* is composed; one would think, they had been growing ever since *Babel,* unto the Dimensions to which they are now extended. For instance, if my Reader will count how many Letters there are in this one Word, *Nummatchekodtantamooonganunnonash,* when he has done, for his Reward I'll tell him, it signifies no more in *English,* than *our Lusts,* and if I were to translate, *our Loves;* it must be nothing shorter than *Noowomantammooonkanunonnash.* Or, to give my Reader a longer Word than either of these, *Kummogkodonattoottummooetiteaongannunnonash,* is in English, *Our Question:* But I pray, Sir, count the Letters! Nor do we find in all this Language the least Affinity to, or Derivation from any *European* Speech that we are acquainted with. I know not what Thoughts it will produce in my Reader, when I inform him, that once finding that the *Dæmons* in a possessed young Woman, understood the *Latin* and *Greek* and *Hebrew* Languages,[9] my Curiosity led me to make Trial of this *Indian* Language, and the *Dæmons* did seem as if they did not understand it. This tedious Language our *Eliot* (the Anagram of whose Name was TOILE) quickly became a Master of; he employ'd a pregnant and witty *Indian,* who also spoke *English* well, for his Assistance in it; and compiling some Discourses by his Help, he would single out a *Word,* a *Noun,* a *Verb,* and pursue it through all its Variations: Having finished his Grammar, at the close he writes, *Prayers and Pains thro' Faith in Christ Jesus will do any thing!* And being by his *Prayers* and *Pains* thus furnished, he set himself in the Year 1646 to preach the Gospel of our Lord Jesus Christ, among these Desolate Outcasts. * * *

MR. ELIOT'S WAY OF OPENING THE MYSTERIES OF THE GOSPEL,
TO OUR INDIANS

'Twas in the Year 1646, that Mr. *Eliot,* accompany'd by three more, gave a Visit unto an Assembly of *Indians,* of whom he desired a Meeting at such a Time and Place, that he might lay before them the Things of their Eternal Peace. After a serious *Prayer,*

8. Literally, "foot-and-a-half words"; ridiculously long words.
9. Not uncommonly, witchcraft was detected when a "possessed" victim spoke in languages with which he was normally unfamiliar.

he gave them a *Sermon* which continued about a Quarter above an Hour, and contained the principal Articles of the Christian Religion, applying all to the Condition of the *Indians* present. Having done, he asked of them, Whether *they understood?* And with a General Reply they answered, *They understood all*. He then began what was his usual Method afterwards in treating with them; that is, he caused them to propound such *Questions* as they pleas'd unto himself; and he gave wise and good *Answers* to them all. Their *Questions* would often, tho' not always, refer to what he had newly preached; and he this way not only made a *Proof* of their profiting by his Ministry, but also gave an Edge to what he delivered unto them. Some of their *Questions* would be a little *Philosophical*, and required a good Measure of Learning in the Minister concerned with them; but for this our *Eliot* wanted not. He would also put proper *Questions* unto them, and at one of his first Exercises with them, he made the Young Ones capable of regarding those three Questions,

Q. 1. *Who made you and all the* World?

Q. 2. *Who do you look should save you from Sin and Hell?*

Q. 3. *How many Commandments has the Lord given you to keep?*

It was his Wisdom that he began with them upon such Principles as they themselves had already some Notions of; such as that of an *Heaven* for good, and *Hell* for bad People, when they dy'd. It broke his gracious Heart within him to see, what Floods of Tears fell from the eyes of several among those degenerate Salvages, at the first Addresses which he made unto them; yea, from the very worst of them all. He was very inquisitive to learn who were the *Powawes*, that is, the *Sorcerers*, and *Seducers*, that maintained the Worship of the Devil in any of their Societies; and having in one of his first Journeys to them, found out one of those Wretches, he made the *Indian* come unto him, and said, *Whether do you suppose* God, *or* Chepian (i.e. *the Devil*) *to be the Author of all Good?* The Conjurer answered, *God*. Upon this he added with a stern Countenance, *Why do you pray to* Chepian *then?* And the poor Man was not able to stand or speak before him; but at last made Promises of Reformation. * * *

THE CONCLUSION: OR, ELIOT EXPIRING.

By this time, I have doubtless made my Readers loth to have me tell what now remains of this little History; doubtless they are wishing that this *John* might have *Tarried unto the Second Coming of our Lord*.[1] But, alas, All-devouring *Death* at last snatch'd him from

1. See Jesus' rebuke to Peter, concerning John: "If I will that he tarry till I come * * * " (John xxi: 22).

us, and slighted all those Lamentations of ours, *My Father, My Father, the Chariots of Israel, and the Horsemen thereof!*[2]

When he was become a sort of *Miles Emeritus*,[3] and began to draw near his *End*, he grew still more Heavenly, more Savoury, more Divine, and scented more of the Spicy Country at which he was ready to put ashore. As the Historian observes of *Tiberius*, That when his *Life* and *Strength* were going from him, his *Vice* yet remained with him; on the contrary, the *Grace* of this Excellent Man rather increased than abated, when every thing else was dying with him. 'Tis too usual with *Old Men*, that when they are past *Work*, they are least sensible of their Inabilities and Incapacities, and can scarce endure to see another succeeding them in any part of their Office. But our *Eliot* was of a Temper quite contrary thereunto; for finding many Months before his Expiration, That he had not Strength enough to Edify his Congregation with Publick *Prayers*, and *Sermons*, he importun'd his People with some Impatience to call another Minister; professing himself unable to die with Comfort, until he could see a good Successor ordained, settled, fixed among them. For this Cause, he also cry'd mightily unto the Lord Jesus Christ our *Ascended Lord*, that he would give such a *Gift* unto *Roxbury*, and he sometimes call'd his whole Town together to join with him in a *Fast* for such a Blessing. As the Return of their Supplications, our Lord quickly bestow'd upon them, a Person young in Years, but old in Discretion, Gravity, and Experience; and one whom the Church of *Roxbury* hopes to find, *A Pastor after God's own Heart*.

It was Mr. *Nehemiah Walter*, who being by the Unanimous Vote and Choice of the Church there, become the *Pastor* of *Roxbury*, immediately found the Venerable *Eliot* Embracing and Cherishing of him, with the tender Affections of a Father. The good Old Man like Old *Aaron*,[4] as it were disrobed himself, with an unspeakable Satisfaction, when he beheld his Garments put upon a Son so dear unto him. After this, he for a Year or two before his *Translation*, could scarce be perswaded unto any *Publick Service*, but humbly pleaded, what none but he would ever have said, *It would be a Wrong to the Souls of the People, for him to do any thing among them, when they were supply'd so much to their Advantage otherwise.* If I mistake not, the last that ever he Preached was on a Publick *Fast*; when he fed his People with a very distinct and useful *Exposition* upon the Eighty Third Psalm; and he concluded with an Apology, begging his Hearers to pardon the *Poorness*, and *Meanness*, and *Brokenness*, (as he called it) of his Meditations; but added he,

2. The words of Elisha when Elijah the prophet was "taken up into heaven" in a chariot of fire (II Kings ii: 12).
3. Soldier emeritus; *i.e.*, honorably retired.

4. God commanded Moses to strip the aged High Priest, and bestow his office on his son, Eleazar; and Aaron died in the wilderness (Numbers xx: 22–27).

My dear Brother here, will by'nd by mend all.

But altho' he thus dismissed himself as one so near to the Age of *Ninety,* might well have done, from his *Publick Labours;* yet he would not give over his *Endeavours,* in a more private Sphere, to *Do good unto all.* He had always been an Enemy to *Idleness;* any one that should look into the little *Diary* that he kept in his *Almanacks,* would see that there was with him, *No Day without a Line;* and he was troubled particularly, when he saw how much *Time* was devoured by that Slavery to *Tobacco,* which too many debase themselves unto; and now he grew old, he was desirous that his *Works* should hold pace with his *Life;* the less *Time* he saw *left,* the less was he willing to have *lost.* He imagined that he could now do nothing to any purpose in any *Service* for God; and sometimes he would say with an Air peculiar to himself, *I wonder for what the Lord Jesus Christ lets me live; he knows that now I can do nothing for him!* And yet he could not forbear Essaying to *Do something* for his Lord; he conceived, that tho' the *English* could not be benefited by any *Gifts* which he now fancied himself to have only the *Ruines* of, yet who can tell but the *Negro's* might! He had long lamented it with a Bleeding and a Burning Passion, that the *English* used their *Negro's* but as their *Horses* or their *Oxen,* and that so little Care was taken about their immortal Souls; he look'd upon it as a Prodigy, that any wearing the *Name* of *Christians,* should so much have the *Heart* of *Devils* in them, as to prevent and hinder the Instruction of the poor *Blackamores,* and confine the Souls of their miserable Slaves to a *Destroying Ignorance,* meerly for fear of thereby losing the Benefit of their Vassalage; but now he made a Motion to the *English* within two or three Miles of him, that at such a time and Place they would send their *Negro's* once a Week unto him: For he would then *Catechise* them, and *Enlighten* them, to the utmost of his Power in the Things of their Everlasting Peace; however, he did not live to make much Progress in this Undertaking. * * *

It has been observed, That they who have spoke many considerable things in their *Lives,* usually speak few at their *Deaths.* But it was otherwise with our *Eliot,* who after much Speech of and for God in his *Life-time,* uttered some things little short of *Oracles* on his *Death-Bed,* which, 'tis a thousand Pities, they were not more exactly regarded and recorded. Those Authors that have taken the pains to Collect, *Apophthegmata Morientum,*[5] have not therein been unserviceable to the Living; but the *Apopthegms* of a Dying *Eliot* must have had in them a *Grace* and a *Strain* truly extraor[di]nary; and indeed the *vulgar Error* of the signal sweetness in the Song of a *Dying Swan,* was a very Truth in our Expiring *Eliot;* his last Breath smelt strong of Heaven, and was Articled into none but very gracious Notes; one

5. The wise words of the dying.

of the last whereof, was, *Welcome Joy!* and at last it went away calling upon the standers-by, to *Pray, pray, pray!* Which was the thing in which so vast a Portion of it, had been before Employ'd.

This was the Peace in the End of this *Perfect and upright Man;* thus was there another *Star* fetched away to be placed among the rest that the third Heaven is now enriched with. He had once, I think, a pleasant Fear, that the Old Saints of his Acquaintance, especially those two dearest Neighbours of his, *Cotton of Boston,* and *Mather of Dorchester,*[6] which were got safe to Heaven before him, would suspect him to be gone the wrong way, because he staid so long behind them. But they are now together with a Blessed Jesus, *beholding of his Glory,* and celebrating the High Praises of him that has *call'd them into his marvellous Light.* Whether *Heaven* was any more *Heaven* to him, because of his finding there, so many *Saints,* with whom he once had his Desirable Intimacies, yea, and so many *Saints* which had been the Seals of his own Ministry in this lower World, I cannot say; but it would be *Heaven* enough unto him, to go unto that *Jesus,* whom he had lov'd, preach'd, serv'd, and in whom he had been long assured, there does *All Fullness* dwell. In that Heaven I now leave him: Not without *Grynæus's* Pathetical Exclamations [*O, beatum illum diem!*[7]] "Blessed will be the Day, O Blessed the Day of our Arrival to the Glorious Assembly of Spirits, which this great Saint is now rejoicing with!" * * *

If the Dust of *dead Saints* could give us any Protection, we are not without it; here is a Spot of *American* Soyl that will afford a rich Crop of it, at the *Resurrection of the Just.* Poor *New-England* has been as Glastenbury of Old was called, *A Burying-place of Saints.*[8] But we cannot see a more terrible Prognostick, than Tombs filling apace with such *Bones,* as those of the Renowned *Eliot's;* the Whole Building of this Country trembles at the Fall of such a Pillar.

1695–1697   1702, 1853

6. In Puritan theology, "sanctification" (sainthood) is the last stage of grace in the process of "regeneration." Cotton Mather refers to his two grandfathers, John Cotton (died 1652) and Richard Mather (died 1669).

7. O! blessed that day!
8. Glastonbury Abbey in southeastern England, associated with St. Joseph of Arimathea, St. Dunstan, and others, an ancient place of pilgrimage.

JONATHAN EDWARDS
(1703–1758)

Jonathan Edwards, the last and most gifted defender of New England Calvinism, was in several respects the most remarkable American Puritan. Later even than Cotton Mather he attempted to revive the Puritan idealism in a new age of science, secularism, and mercantile activity. Where Mather militantly supported an institutional heirarchy, Edwards relied on spiritual insight; where Mather was aggressive and pedantic, Edwards possessed a profound learning supported by genuine mystical experience and the persuasive gifts of the logician. Unlike Mather, Edwards saw the fruits of his evangelism in the temporary revival of Puritan orthodoxy, but within sixteen years his own congregation had repudiated him. He was in all things too late born. If as a result he was at once identified with the past, he has at least held his position in history.

Edwards was born in 1703, in East Windsor, Connecticut. In childhood he wrote serious works, including a logical refutation of materialism and a pioneer study of the behavior of spiders. At thirteen he was enrolled at Yale. About 1717, before any other American thinker, he discovered, in Locke's *Essay Concerning Human Understanding*, a new empiricism, a theory of knowledge, and a psychology which he later used in support of such Calvinistic doctrines as predestination and the sovereignty of God, doctrines which, as *Personal Narrative* reveals, he had accepted for himself only after much soul-searching.

They became his foundation stone of faith during his ministry at Northampton, Massachusetts, where he was pastor from 1726 to 1750; they are equally fundamental to the fifteen books that he published, principally from Northampton. The "Great Awakening" of religious faith began there with his preaching, and spread in a wave of evangelism through the middle colonies, ironically producing, in a few years, organized schisms from Congregational and Presbyterian orthodoxy. This schismatic tendency was reflected in his own congregation after 1744. While his influence was being carried abroad by his writings, Edwards was confronted at home with a growing resistance to his severe orthodoxy, and finally, in 1750, with the decree of exclusion memorialized by his famous *Farewell Sermon* to his congregation.

At Stockbridge, Massachusetts, then a frontier village, he was appointed as pastor and Indian missionary, and there he completed his greatest writings, including *Freedom of the Will* (1754). Elected president of Nassau Hall (Princeton) in 1757, he assumed office in January, 1758, but died within three months as the result of an inoculation against smallpox.

He had gained a position as our country's first systematic philosopher, and earned a permanent place among those who have advanced the thought of the western world. For his use of the empiricism and psychology of Locke was truly an advance, although he employed it to defend a primitive Calvinistic orthodoxy that could not long sustain itself against the rationalistic "enlightenment" of the age of science which had already dawned. Yet no other writer has been so successful in suffusing this grim, Puritan determinism with "a divine and supernatural light" (as he said), in showing human predestination as the necessary corollary to the beauty of God's majestic sovereignty, in combining cold logic with the warmth of mystical insight. Too much has been made of an occasional sermon, such as "Sinners in the Hands of an Angry God," in which he held the "rebellious and disorderly" congregation of Enfield over the flaming pit of hell. This too was orthodoxy, but it was a phase of orthodoxy that his work as a whole has little to do with. More concerned with God's grace than His anger, Edwards is best understood in his masterpiece, *Freedom of the Will*, in *Personal Narrative*, and in such essays as "The Nature of True Virtue."

Except in the expression of mystical experience, and of the joy of nature and thought, Edwards' style tends to be reserved and somewhat tiresomely scrupulous; Perry Miller remarks (in *Jonathan Edwards*), even in controversy "he demol-

ishes at tedious length all possible positions of his opponents, including some that they do not hold * * * , and all the time hardly declares his own." But the beauty of this method is that there is nothing left but his own position, and whatever may be thought of his style, it enabled him, very often, to perform that miracle of metaphysics which he called "seeing the perfect idea of a thing."

All collected editions are entitled *The Works of President Edwards*. The first, an English publication, was edited by Edward Williams and Edward Parsons, 8 vols., Leeds, 1806–1811; it is authoritative, but rare. A trustworthy edition, with which the present text has been compared, is the first American edition, 8 vols., edited by Samuel Austin, Worcester, Mass., 1808–1809; reprinted, 4 vols., New York, 1843. An adequate and available selection is found in *Jonathan Edwards: Representative Selections*, edited by Clarence H. Faust and Thomas H. Johnson, American Writers Series, 1935. For biography, see Ola E. Winslow's *Jonathan Edwards*, 1940, which is readable and reliable; and Perry Miller's *Jonathan Edwards*, American Men of Letters Series, 1949, which is authoritative, and excellent for critical analysis.

Sarah Pierrepont

They say there is a young lady in——[1] who is beloved of that Great Being, who made and rules the world, and that there are certain seasons in which this Great Being, in some way or other invisible, comes to her and fills her mind with exceeding sweet delight, and that she hardly cares for anything, except to meditate on him—that she expects after a while to be received up where he is, to be raised up out of the world and caught up into heaven; being assured that he loves her too well to let her remain at a distance from him always. There she is to dwell with him, and to be ravished with his love and delight forever. Therefore, if you present all the world before her, with the richest of its treasures, she disregards it and cares not for it, and is unmindful of any pain or affliction. She has a strange sweetness

1. New Haven, Connecticut. Sarah was only thirteen when Edwards wrote this, about 1723. In 1727 he married Sarah, and she became a principal inspiration in his life and writing.

in her mind, and singular purity in her affections; is most just and conscientious in all her conduct; and you could not persuade her to do any thing wrong or sinful, if you would give her all the world, lest she should offend this Great Being. She is of a wonderful sweetness, calmness and universal benevolence of mind; especially after this Great God has manifested himself to her mind. She will sometimes go about from place to place, singing sweetly; and seems to be always full of joy and pleasure; and no one knows for what. She loves to be alone, walking in the fields and groves, and seems to have some one invisible always conversing with her.

1723?   1830

Personal Narrative[2]

I had a variety of concerns and exercises about my soul from my childhood; but had two more remarkable seasons of awakening, before I met with that change by which I was brought to those new dispositions, and that new sense of things, that I have since had. The first time was when I was a boy, some years before I went to college, at a time of remarkable awakening in my father's congregation. I was then very much affected for many months, and concerned about the things of religion, and my soul's salvation; and was abundant in duties. I used to pray five times a day in secret, and to spend much time in religious talk with other boys, and used to meet with them to pray together. I experienced I know not what kind of delight in religion. My mind was much engaged in it, and had much self-righteous pleasure; and it was my delight to abound in religious duties. I with some of my school-mates joined together, and built a booth in a swamp, in a very retired spot, for a place of prayer. And besides, I had particular secret places of my own in the woods, where I used to retire by myself; and was from time to time much affected. My affections seemed to be lively and easily moved, and I seemed to be in my element when engaged in religious duties. And I am ready to think, many are deceived with such affections, and such a kind of delight as I then had in religion, and mistake it for grace.

But in process of time, my convictions and affections wore off; and I entirely lost all those affections and delights and left off secret prayer, at least as to any constant performance of it; and returned like a dog to his vomit,[3] and went on in the ways of sin. Indeed I was

2. Celebrated for "mysticism" and "charm," this classic of religious experience was actually "the apparatus of psychological investigation * * * devoted, not to the defense of emotion against reason, but to a winnowing out of the one pure spiritual emotion from the horde of imitations" (Miller, *Jonathan Edwards*, p. 106). Written about 1740–1742, this essay was first published in a *Life* of Edwards by Samuel Hopkins (1765).
3. "—so a fool to his folly" (Proverbs xxvi: 11).

at times very uneasy, especially towards the latter part of my time at college; when it pleased God, to seize me with the pleurisy; in which he brought me nigh to the grave, and shook me over the pit of hell. And yet, it was not long after my recovery, before I fell again into my old ways of sin. But God would not suffer me to go on with my quietness; I had great and violent inward struggles, till, after many conflicts, with wicked inclinations, repeated resolutions, and bonds that I laid myself under by a kind of vows to God, I was brought wholly to break off all former wicked ways, and all ways of known outward sin; and to apply myself to seek salvation, and practice many religious duties; but without that kind of affection and delight which I had formerly experienced. My concern now wrought more by inward struggles and conflicts, and self-reflections. I made seeking my salvation the main business of my life. But yet, it seems to me, I sought after a miserable manner; which has made me sometimes since to question, whether ever it issued in that which was saving; being ready to doubt, whether such miserable seeking ever succeeded. I was indeed brought to seek salvation in a manner that I never was before; I felt a spirit to part with all things in the world, for an interest in Christ.—My concern continued and prevailed, with many exercising thoughts and inward struggles; but yet it never seemed to be proper to express that concern by the name of terror.

From my childhood up, my mind had been full of objections against the doctrine of God's sovereignty, in choosing whom he would to eternal life, and rejecting whom he pleased; leaving them eternally to perish, and be everlastingly tormented in hell. It used to appear like a horrible doctrine to me.[4] But I remember the time very well, when I seemed to be convinced, and fully satisfied, as to this sovereignty of God, and his justice in thus eternally disposing of men, according to his sovereign pleasure. But never could give an account, how, or by what means, I was thus convinced, not in the least imagining at the time, nor a long time after, that there was any extraordinary influence of God's Spirit in it; but only that now I saw further, and my reason apprehended the justice and reasonableness of it. However, my mind rested in it; and it put an end to all those cavils and objections. And there has been a wonderful alteration in my mind, with respect to the doctrine of God's sovereignty, from that day to this; so that I scarce ever have found so much as the rising of an objection against it, in the most absolute sense, in God's shewing mercy to whom he will shew mercy, and hardening whom he will.[5] God's absolute sovereignty and justice, with respect to salvation and

4. Referring to the Covenant theology of the Puritans. God's first covenant with Adam was eternal life in return for obedience—a covenant of justice. In Adam's fall, mankind forfeited this covenant. The New Covenant revealed through Jesus Christ was one of mercy; no one could earn or deserve God's grace. 5. Romans ix: 18. Paul's words were often quoted in support of the doctrine of grace.

damnation, is what my mind seems to rest assured of, as much as of any thing that I see with my eyes; at least it is so at times. But I have often, since that first conviction, had quite another kind of sense of God's sovereignty than I had then. I have often since had not only a conviction, but a delightful conviction. The doctrine has very often appeared exceeding pleasant, bright, and sweet.

Absolute sovereignty is what I love to ascribe to God. But my first conviction was not so.

The first instance that I remember of that sort of inward, sweet delight in God and divine things that I have lived much in since, was on reading those words, 1 Tim. i: 17. *Now unto the King eternal, immortal, invisible, the only wise God, be honor and glory forever and ever, Amen.* As I read the words, there came into my soul, and was as it were diffused through it, a sense of the glory of the Divine Being; a new sense, quite different from any thing I ever experienced before. Never any words of scripture seemed to me as these words did. I thought within myself, how excellent a being that was, and how happy I should be, if I might enjoy that God, and be wrapt up in heaven, and be as it were swallowed up in him forever! I kept saying, and as it were singing over these words of scripture to myself; and went to pray to God that I might enjoy him, and prayed in a manner quite different from what I used to do; with a new sort of affection. But it never came into my thought, that there was any thing spiritual, or of a saving nature in this.

From about that time, I began to have a new kind of apprehensions and ideas of Christ, and the work of redemption, and the glorious way of salvation by him. An inward, sweet sense of these things, at times, came into my heart; and my soul was led away in pleasant views and contemplations of them. And my mind was greatly engaged to spend my time in reading and meditating on Christ, on the beauty and excellency of his person, and the lovely way of salvation by free grace in him I found no books so delightful to me, as those that treated of these subjects. Those words, Cant.[6] ii: 1, used to be abundantly with me, *I am the Rose of Sharon, and the Lily of the valleys.* The words seemed to me, sweetly to represent the loveliness and beauty of Jesus Christ. The whole book of Canticles used to be pleasant to me, and I used to be much in reading it, about that time; and found, from time to time, an inward sweetness, that would carry me away, in my contemplations. This I know not how to express otherwise, than by a calm, sweet abstraction of soul from all the concerns of this world; and sometimes a kind of vision, or fixed ideas and imaginations, of being alone in the mountains, or some solitary wilderness, far from all mankind, sweetly conversing with

6. Canticles, or the Song of Solomon, a love poem interpreted by theologians as applying to Christ and mankind.

Christ, and wrapt and swallowed up in God. The sense I h
divine things, would often of a sudden kindle up, as it were, a :
burning in my heart; an ardor of soul, that I know not how to express.

Not long after I began to experience these things, I gave an
account to my father of some things that had passed in my mind.
I was pretty much affected by the discourse we had together; and
when the discourse was ended, I walked abroad alone, in a solitary
place in my father's pasture for contemplation. And as I was walking
there and looking up on the sky and clouds, there came into my mind
so sweet a sense of the glorious *majesty* and *grace* of God, that I
know not how to express. I seemed to see them both in a sweet conjunction; majesty and meekness joined together; it was a gentle, and
holy majesty; and also a majestic meekness; a high, great, and holy
gentleness.

After this my sense of divine things gradually increased, and became more and more lively, and had more of that inward sweetness.
The appearance of every thing was altered; there seemed to be, as it
were, a calm, sweet cast, or appearance of divine glory, in almost
every thing. God's excellency, his wisdom, his purity and love, seemed
to appear in every thing; in the sun, moon, and stars; in the clouds,
and blue sky; in the grass, flowers, trees; in the water, and all nature;
which used greatly to fix my mind. I often used to sit and view the
moon for continuance; and in the day, spent much time in viewing
the clouds and sky, to behold the sweet glory of God in these things;
in the mean time, singing forth, with a low voice, my contemplations
of the Creator and Redeemer. And scarce any thing, among all the
works of nature, was so delightful to me as thunder and lightning;
formerly, nothing had been so terrible to me. Before, I used to be
uncommonly terrified with thunder, and to be struck with terror
when I saw a thunder storm rising; but now, on the contrary, it
rejoiced me. I felt God, so to speak, at the first appearance of a
thunder storm; and used to take the opportunity, at such times, to
fix myself in order to view the clouds, and see the lightnings play,
and hear the majestic and awful voice of God's thunder, which
oftentimes was exceedingly entertaining, leading me to sweet contemplations of my great and glorious God. While thus engaged, it
always seemed natural to me to sing, or chant for my meditations;
or, to speak my thoughts in soliloquies with a singing voice.

I felt then great satisfaction, as to my good state; but that did not
content me. I had vehement longings of soul after God and Christ,
and after more holiness, wherewith my heart seemed to be full, and
ready to break; which often brought to my mind the words of the
Psalmist, Psal. cxix. 28: *My soul breaketh for the longing it hath.*
I often felt a mourning and lamenting in my heart, that I had not
turned to God sooner, that I might have had more time to grow in

grace. My mind was greatly fixed on divine things; almost perpetually in the contemplation of them. I spent most of my time in thinking of divine things, year after year; often walking alone in the woods, and solitary places, for meditation, soliloquy, and prayer, and converse with God; and it was always my manner, at such times, to sing forth my contemplations. I was almost constantly in ejaculatory prayer, wherever I was. Prayer seemed to be natural to me, as the breath by which the inward burnings of my heart had vent. The delights which I now felt in the things of religion, were of an exceedingly different kind from those before mentioned, that I had when a boy; and what I then had no more notion of, than one born blind has of pleasant and beautiful colors. They were of a more inward, pure, soul-animating and refreshing nature. Those former delights never reached the heart; and did not arise from any sight of the divine excellency of the things of God; or any taste of the soul-satisfying and life-giving good there is in them.

My sense of divine things seemed gradually to increase, until I went to preach at New York,[7] which was about a year and a half after they began; and while I was there, I felt them, very sensibly, in a higher degree than I had done before. My longings after God and holiness, were much increased. Pure and humble, holy and heavenly Christianity, appeared exceedingly amiable to me. I felt a burning desire to be in every thing a complete Christian; and conform to the blessed image of Christ; and that I might live, in all things, according to the pure and blessed rules of the gospel. I had an eager thirsting after progress in these things; which put me upon pursuing and pressing after them. It was my continual strife day and night, and constant inquiry, how I should *be* more holy, and *live* more holily, and more becoming a child of God, and a disciple of Christ. I now sought an increase of grace and holiness, and a holy life, with much more earnestness, than ever I sought grace before I had it. I used to be continually examining myself, and studying and contriving for likely ways and means, how I should live holily, with far greater diligence and earnestness, than ever I pursued any thing in my life; but yet with too great a dependance on my own strength; which afterwards proved a great damage to me. My experience had not then taught me, as it has done since my extreme feebleness and impotence, every manner of way; and the bottomless depths of secret corruption and deceit there was in my heart. However, I went on with my eager pursuit after more holiness, and conformity to Christ.

The heaven I desired was a heaven of holiness; to be with God, and to spend my eternity in divine love, and holy communion with Christ. My mind was very much taken up with contemplations on

7. August, 1722—May, 1723.

heaven, and the enjoyments there; and living there in perfect holiness, humility and love. And it used at that time to appear a great part of the happiness of heaven, that there the saints could express their love to Christ. It appeared to me a great clog and burden, that what I felt within, I could not express as I desired. The inward ardor of my soul, seemed to be hindered and pent up, and could not freely flame out as it would. I used often to think, how in heaven this principle should freely and fully vent and express itself. Heaven appeared exceedingly delightful, as a world of love; and that all happiness consisted in living in pure, humble, heavenly, divine love.

I remember the thoughts I used then to have of holiness; and said sometimes to myself, "I do certainly know that I love holiness, such as the gospel prescribes." It appeared to me, that there was nothing in it but what was ravishingly lovely; the highest beauty and amiableness—a *divine* beauty; far purer than any thing here upon earth; and that every thing else was like mire and defilement, in comparison of it.

Holiness, as I then wrote down some of my contemplations on it, appeared to me to be of a sweet, pleasant, charming, serene, calm nature; which brought an inexpressible purity, brightness, peacefulness and ravishment to the soul. In other words, that it made the soul like a field or garden of God, with all manner of pleasant flowers; all pleasant, delightful, and undisturbed; enjoying a sweet calm, and the gently vivifying beams of the sun. The soul of a true Christian, as I then wrote my meditations, appeared like such a little white flower as we see in the spring of the year; low and humble on the ground, opening its bosom to receive the pleasant beams of the sun's glory; rejoicing as it were in a calm rapture; diffusing around a sweet fragrancy; standing peacefully and lovingly, in the midst of other flowers round about; all in like manner opening their bosoms, to drink in the light of the sun. There was no part of creature holiness, that I had so great a sense of its loveliness, as humility, brokenness of heart and poverty of spirit; and there was nothing that I so earnestly longed for. My heart panted after this, to lie low before God, as in the dust; that I might be nothing, and that God might be ALL, that I might become as a little child.[8]

While at New York, I was sometimes much affected with reflections on my past life, considering how late it was before I began to be truly religious; and how wickedly I had lived till then; and once so as to weep abundantly, and for a considerable time together.

On *January* 12, 1723. I made a solemn dedication of myself to

8. This is the first climax of *Personal Narrative*, a theological case history of divine grace. In the Calvinistic theology, grace functioned through the stages of "regeneration"—after conviction of sin, repentance, and humiliation, man arrives at the stage of "justification"; he is relieved, not of original sin, but of its consequences. In the passages above, Edwards has been testing the psychological reality of his experience of "justification." *Cf.* Mark x: 15.

God, and wrote it down; giving up myself, and all that I had to God; to be for the future in no respect my own; to act as one that had no right to himself, in any respect. And solemnly vowed to take God for my whole portion and felicity; looking on nothing else as any part of my happiness, nor acting as if it were; and his law for the constant rule of my obedience; engaging to fight with all my might, against the world, the flesh and the devil, to the end of my life. But I have reason to be infinitely humbled, when I consider how much I have failed of answering my obligation.

I had then abundance of sweet religious conversation in the family where I lived, with Mr. John Smith and his pious mother. My heart was knit in affection to those in whom were appearances of true piety; and I could bear the thoughts of no other companions, but such as were holy, and the disciples of the blessed Jesus. I had great longings for the advancement of Christ's kingdom in the world; and my secret prayer used to be, in great part, taken up in praying for it. If I heard the least hint of any thing that happened, in any part of the world, that appeared, in some respect or other, to have a favorable aspect on the interest of Christ's kingdom, my soul eagerly catched at it; and it would much animate and refresh me. I used to be eager to read public news letters, mainly for that end; to see if I could not find some news favorable to the interest of religion in the world.

I very frequently used to retire into a solitary place, on the banks of Hudson's river, at some distance from the city, for contemplation on divine things, and secret converse with God; and had many sweet hours there. Sometimes Mr. Smith and I walked there together, to converse on the things of God; and our conversation used to turn much on the advancement of Christ's kingdom in the world, and the glorious things that God would accomplish for his church in the latter days. I had then, and at other times the greatest delight in the holy scriptures, of any book whatsoever. Oftentimes in reading it, every word seemed to touch my heart. I felt a harmony between something in my heart, and those sweet and powerful words. I seemed often to see so much light exhibited by every sentence, and such a refreshing food communicated, that I could not get along in reading; often dwelling long on one sentence, to see the wonders contained in it; and yet almost every sentence seemed to be full of wonders.

I came away from New York in the month of April, 1723, and had a most bitter parting with Madam Smith and her son. My heart seemed to sink within me at leaving the family and city, where I had enjoyed so many sweet and pleasant days. I went from New York to Weathersfield, by water, and as I sailed away, I kept sight of the city as long as I could. However, that night, after this sorrowful parting, I was greatly comforted in God at Westchester, where we went ashore to lodge; and had a pleasant time of it all the voyage to Saybrook. It was sweet to me to think of meeting dear Christians in heaven, where we should never part more. At Saybrook we went ashore to lodge, on Saturday, and there kept the Sabbath; where I had a sweet and refreshing season, walking alone in the fields.

After I came home to Windsor, I remained much in a like frame of mind, as when at New York; only sometimes I felt my heart ready to sink with the thoughts of my friends at New York. My support was in contemplations on the heavenly state; as I find in my Diary of May 1, 1723. It was a comfort to think of that state, where there is fulness of joy; where reigns heavenly, calm, and delightful love, without alloy; where there are continually the dearest expressions of this love; where is the enjoyment of the persons loved, without ever parting; where those persons who appear so lovely in this world, will really be inexpressibly more lovely and full of love to us. And how sweetly will the mutual lovers join together to sing the praises of God and the Lamb![9] How will it fill us with joy to think, that this enjoyment, these sweet exercises will never cease, but will last to all eternity! I continued much in the same frame, in the general, as when at New York, till I went to New Haven as tutor to the college; particularly once at Bolton, on a journey from Boston, while walking out alone in the fields. After I went to New Haven I sunk in religion; my mind being diverted from my eager pursuits after holiness, by some affairs that greatly perplexed and distracted my thoughts.

In September, 1725, I was taken ill at New Haven, and while endeavoring to go home to Windsor, was so ill at the North Village, that I could go no further; where I lay sick for about a quarter of a year. In this sickness God was pleased to visit me again with the sweet influences of his Spirit. My mind was greatly engaged there in divine, pleasant contemplations, and longings of soul. I observed that those who watched with me, would often be looking out wishfully for the morning; which brought to my mind those words of the Psalmist, and which my soul with delight made its own language, *My soul waiteth for the Lord, more than they that watch for the morning, I say, more than they that watch for the morning;*[1] and when the light of day came in at the windows, it refreshed my soul from one morning to another. It seemed to be some image of the light of God's glory.

I remember, about that time, I used greatly to long for the conversion of some that I was concerned with; I could gladly honor them, and with delight be a servant to them, and lie at their feet, if they

9. John repeatedly referred to Christ as the Lamb of God: he envisioned the heavenly host singing praises to God and the Lamb in Revelation xiv: 2–3 and xix: 5–7.

1. Psalm cxxx: 6.

were but truly holy. But some time after this, I was again greatly diverted in my mind with some temporal concerns that exceedingly took up my thoughts, greatly to the wounding of my soul; and went on through various exercises, that it would be tedious to relate, which gave me much more experience of my own heart, than ever I had before.

Since I came to this town,[2] I have often had sweet complacency in God, in views of his glorious perfections and the excellency of Jesus Christ. God has appeared to me a glorious and lovely being, chiefly on the account of his holiness. The holiness of God has always appeared to me the most lovely of all his attributes. The doctrines of God's absolute sovereignty, and free grace, in shewing mercy to whom he would shew mercy; and man's absolute dependance on the operations of God's Holy Spirit, have very often appeared to me as sweet and glorious doctrines. These doctrines have been much my delight. God's sovereignty has ever appeared to me, a great part of his glory. It has often been my delight to approach God, and adore him as a sovereign God, and ask sovereign mercy of him.

I have loved the doctrines of the gospel; they have been to my soul like green pastures. The gospel has seemed to me the richest treasure; the treasure that I have most desired, and longed that it might dwell richly in me. The way of salvation by Christ has appeared, in a general way, glorious and excellent, most pleasant and most beautiful. It has often seemed to me, that it would in a great measure spoil heaven, to receive it in any other way. That text has often been affecting and delightful to me. Isa. xxxii: 2. A *man shall be an hiding place from the wind, and a covert from the tempest*, &c.

It has often appeared to me delightful, to be united to Christ; to have him for my head, and to be a member of his body; also to have Christ for my teacher and prophet. I very often think with sweetness, and longings, and pantings of soul, of being a little child, taking hold of Christ, to be led by him through the wilderness of this world. That text, Matth. xviii: 3, has often been sweet to me, *except ye be converted and become as little children*, &c. I love to think of coming to Christ, to receive salvation of him, poor in spirit, and quite empty of self, humbly exalting him alone; cut off entirely from my own root, in order to grow into, and out of Christ; to have God in Christ to be all in all; and to live by faith on the Son of God, a life of humble unfeigned confidence in him. That scripture has often been sweet to me, Psal. cxv: 1. *Not unto us, O Lord, not unto us, but to thy name give glory, for thy mercy and for thy truth's sake.* And those words of Christ, Luke x: 21. *In that hour Jesus rejoiced in spirit, and said, I thank thee, O Father, Lord of heaven and earth, that thou hast hid these things from the wise and prudent, and hast*

2. Northampton, Massachusetts.

revealed them unto babes; even so, Father, for so it seemed good in thy sight. That sovereignty of God which Christ rejoiced in, seemed to me worthy of such joy; and that rejoicing seemed to show the excellency of Christ, and of what spirit he was.

Sometimes, only mentioning a single word caused my heart to burn within me; or only seeing the name of Christ, or the name of some attribute of God. And God has appeared glorious to me, on account of the Trinity. It has made me have exalting thoughts of God, that he subsists in three persons; Father, Son and Holy Ghost. The sweetest joys and delights I have experienced, have not been those that have arisen from a hope of my own good estate; but in a direct view of the glorious things of the gospel. When I enjoy this sweetness, it seems to carry me above the thoughts of my own estate; it seems at such times a loss that I cannot bear, to take off my eye from the glorious pleasant object I behold without me, to turn my eye in upon myself, and my own good estate.

My heart has been much on the advancement of Christ's kingdom in the world. The histories of the past advancement of Christ's kingdom have been sweet to me. When I have read histories of past ages, the pleasantest thing in all my reading has been, to read of the kingdom of Christ being promoted. And when I have expected, in my reading, to come to any such thing, I have rejoiced in the prospect, all the way as I read. And my mind has been much entertained and delighted with the scripture promises and prophecies, which relate to the future glorious advancement of Christ's kingdom upon earth.

I have sometimes had a sense of the excellent fulness of Christ, and his meetness and suitableness as a Saviour; whereby he has appeared to me, far above all, the chief of ten thousands. His blood and atonement have appeared sweet, and his righteousness sweet: which was always accompanied with ardency of spirit; and inward strugglings and breathings, and groanings that cannot be uttered, to be emptied of myself, and swallowed up in Christ.

Once as I rode out into the woods for my health, in 1737, having alighted from my horse in a retired place, as my manner commonly has been, to walk for divine contemplation and prayer, I had a view that for me was extraordinary, of the glory of the Son of God, as Mediator between God and man, and his wonderful, great, full, pure and sweet grace and love, and meek and gentle condescension. This grace that appeared so calm and sweet, appeared also great above the heavens. The person of Christ appeared ineffably excellent with an excellency great enough to swallow up all thought and conception—which continued as near as I can judge, about an hour; which kept me the greater part of the time in a flood of tears, and weeping aloud. I felt an ardency of soul to be, what I know not otherwise how to express, emptied and annihilated; to lie in the dust, and to be full of Christ alone; to love him with a holy and pure love; to trust in him; to live upon him; to serve and follow him; and to be perfectly sanctified and made pure, with a divine and heavenly purity. I have, several other times, had views very much of the same nature, and which have had the same effects.

I have many times had a sense of the glory of the third person in the Trinity, in his office of Sanctifier; in his holy operations, communicating divine light and life to the soul. God, in the communications of his Holy Spirit, has appeared as an infinite fountain of divine glory and sweetness; being full, and sufficient to fill and satisfy the soul; pouring forth itself in sweet communications; like the sun in its glory, sweetly and pleasantly diffusing light and life. And I have sometimes had an affecting sense of the excellency of the word of God, as a word of life; as the light of life; a sweet, excellent, life-giving word; accompanied with a thirsting after that word, that it might dwell richly in my heart.

Often, since I lived in this town, I have had very affecting views of my own sinfulness and vileness; very frequently to such a degree as to hold me in a kind of loud weeping, sometimes for a considerable time together; so that I have often been forced to shut myself up. I have had a vastly greater sense of my own wickedness, and the badness of my own heart, than ever I had before my conversion. It has often appeared to me, that if God should mark iniquity against me, I should appear the very worst of all mankind; of all that have been, since the beginning of the world to this time; and that I should have by far the lowest place in hell. When others, that have come to talk with me about their soul concerns, have expressed the sense they have had of their own wickedness, by saying that it seemed to them, that they were as bad as the devil himself; I thought their expression seemed exceedingly faint and feeble, to represent my wickedness.

My wickedness, as I am in myself, has long appeared to me perfectly ineffable, and swallowing up all thought and imagination; like an infinite deluge, or mountains over my head. I know not how to express better what my sins appear to me to be, than by heaping infinite upon infinite, and multiplying infinite by infinite. Very often, for these many years, these expressions are in my mind, and in my mouth, "Infinite upon infinite—Infinite upon infinite!" When I look into my heart, and take a view of my wickedness, it looks like an abyss infinitely deeper than hell. And it appears to me, that were it not for free grace, exalted and raised up to the infinite height of all the fulness and glory of the great Jehovah, and the arm of his power and grace stretched forth in all the majesty of his power, and in all the glory of his sovereignty, I should appear sunk down in my sins below hell itself; far beyond the sight of every thing, but the eye of sovereign grace, that can pierce even down to such a depth.

And yet, it seems to me, that my conviction of sin is exceedingly small, and faint; it is enough to amaze me, that I have no more sense of my sin. I know certainly, that I have very little sense of my sin-fulness. When I have had turns of weeping and crying for my sins, I thought I knew at the time, that my repentance was nothing to my sin.

I have greatly longed of late, for a broken heart, and to lie low before God; and, when I ask for humility, I cannot bear the thoughts of being no more humble than other Christians. It seems to me, that though their degrees of humility may be suitable for them, yet it would be a vile self-exaltation to me, not to be the lowest in humility of all mankind. Others speak of their longing to be "humbled to the dust"; that may be a proper expression for them, but I always think of myself, that I ought, and it is an expression that has long been natural for me to use in prayer, "to lie infinitely low before God." And it is affecting to think, how ignorant I was, when a young Chris-tian, of the bottomless, infinite depths of wickedness, pride, hypoc-risy and deceit, left in my heart.

I have a much greater sense of my universal, exceeding dependance on God's grace and strength, and mere good pleasure, of late, than I used formerly to have; and have experienced more of an abhorrence of my own righteousness. The very thought of any joy arising in me, on any consideration of my own amiableness, performances, or expe-riences, or any goodness of heart or life, is nauseous and detestable to me. And yet I am greatly afflicted with a proud and self-righteous spirit, much more sensibly than I used to be formerly. I see that serpent rising and putting forth its head continually, every where, all around me.

Though it seems to me, that, in some respects, I was a far better Christian, for two or three years after my first conversion, than I am now; and lived in a more constant delight and pleasure; yet, of late years, I have had a more full and constant sense of the absolute sovereignty of God, and a delight in that sovereignty; and have had more of a sense of the glory of Christ, as a Mediator revealed in the gospel. On one Saturday night, in particular, I had such a discovery of the excellency of the gospel above all other doctrines, that I could not but say to myself, "This is my chosen light, my chosen doctrine;" and of Christ, "This is my chosen Prophet." It appeared sweet, be-yond all expression, to follow Christ, and to be taught, and enlight-ened, and instructed by him; to learn of him, and live to him. An-other Saturday night, (*January*, 1739) I had such a sense, how sweet and blessed a thing it was to walk in the way of duty; to do that which was right and meet to be done, and agreeable to the holy mind of God; that it caused me to break forth into a kind of loud weeping, which held me some time, so that I was forced to shut myself up, and fasten the doors. I could not but, as it were, cry out, "How happy are they which do that which is right in the sight of God! They are blessed indeed, they are the happy ones!" I had, at the same time, a very affecting sense, how meet and suitable it was that God should govern the world, and order all things according to his own pleasure; and I rejoiced in it, that God reigned, and that his will was done.

1740?–1742   1765

The Nature of True Virtue[3]

Showing Wherein the Essence of True Virtue Consists

Whatever controversies and variety of opinions there are about the nature of virtue, yet all (excepting some skeptics, who deny any real difference between virtue and vice) mean by it, something *beautiful*, or rather some kind of *beauty*, or excellency.—It is not *all* beauty, that is called virtue; for instance, not the beauty of a building, of a flower, or of the rainbow: but some beauty belonging to Beings that have *perception* and *will*.—It is not all beauty of *mankind*, that is called virtue; for instance, not the external beauty of the countenance, or shape, gracefulness of motion, or harmony of voice: but it is a beauty that has its original seat in the mind.—But yet perhaps not *every* thing that may be called a beauty of mind, is properly called virtue. There is a beauty of understanding and speculation. There is something in the ideas and conceptions of great philosophers and statesmen, that may be called beautiful; which is a different thing from what is most commonly meant by virtue. But virtue is the beauty of those qualities and acts of the mind, that are of a *moral* nature, i. e., such as are attended with desert or worthiness of *praise*, or *blame*. Things of this sort, it is generally agreed, so far as I know, are not any thing belonging merely to speculation; but to the *disposition* and *will*, or (to use a general word, I suppose commonly well understood) the *heart*. Therefore I suppose, I shall not depart from the common opinion, when I say, that virtue is the beauty of the qualities and exercises of the heart, or those actions which proceed from them. So that when it is inquired, What is the nature of true *virtue?*—this is the same as to inquire, what that is which renders any habit, disposition, or exercise of the heart truly *beautiful*. I use the phrase *true* virtue, and speak of things *truly*

3. "The Nature of True Virtue" was Edwards' last work, composed after an illness and during the last three years of his life. It shows the man in the fullest maturity of his rational powers, perceptive insight, and unearthly holiness of spirit. He regarded it as unfinished; like many of his essays it was part of a large project never materialized, which he had tentatively entitled "A Rational Account of the Main Doctrines of the Christian Religion," intended to show "how all arts and sciences, the more they are perfected, the more they issue in divinity." The present essay was first published as part of Samuel Hopkins' *Life* (1765).

beautiful, because I suppose it will generally be allowed, that there is a distinction to be made between some things which are truly virtuous, and others which only seem to be virtuous, through a partial and imperfect view of things: that some actions and dispositions appear beautiful, if considered partially and superficially, or with regard to some things belonging to them, and in some of their circumstances and tendencies, which would appear otherwise in a more extensive and comprehensive view, wherein they are seen clearly in their whole nature and the extent of their connections in the universality of things.[4]—There is a general and a particular beauty. By a *particular* beauty, I mean that by which a thing appears beautiful when considered only with regard to its connection with, and tendency to some particular things within a limited, and, as it were, a private sphere. And a *general* beauty is that by which a thing appears beautiful when viewed most perfectly, comprehensively and universally, with regard to all its tendencies, and its connections with every thing it stands related to. The former may be without and against the latter. As, a few notes in a tune, taken only by themselves, and in their relation to one another, may be harmonious; which when considered with respect to all the notes in the tune, or the entire series of sounds they are connected with, may be very discordant and disagreeable.—(Of which more afterwards.)—*That only*, therefore, is what I mean by true virtue, which is *that*, belonging to the *heart* of an intelligent Being, that is beautiful by a *general* beauty, or beautiful in a comprehensive view as it is in itself, and as related to every thing that it stands in connection with. And therefore when we are inquiring concerning the nature of true virtue, viz., wherein this true and general beauty of the heart does most essentially consist—this is my answer to the inquiry:

True virtue most essentially consists in benevolence to Being in general. Or perhaps to speak more accurately, it is that consent, propensity and union of heart to Being in general, that is immediately exercised in a general good will.

The things which were before observed of the nature of true virtue, naturally lead us to such a notion of it. If it has its seat in the heart, and is the general goodness and beauty of the disposition and exercise of that, in the most comprehensive view, considered with regard to its universal tendency, and as related to every thing that it stands in connection with; what can it consist in, but a consent and good will to Being in general?—Beauty does not consist in discord and dissent, but in consent and agreement. And if every intelligent Being

4. This "is Edwards' supreme application of the method he learned at the beginning: 'Truth consists in having perfect and adequate ideas of things.' If we had perfect ideas, * * * we should have all things in one view. [Here] he looks hard upon a conception until it yields meaning beyond meaning. The book approaches * * * a naked idea" (Miller, *Jonathan Edwards*, p. 286).

is some way related to Being in general, and is a part of the universal system of existence; and so stands in connection with the whole; what can its general and true beauty be, but its union and consent with the great whole?

If any such thing can be supposed as a union of heart to some particular Being, or number of Beings, disposing it to benevolence to a private circle or system of Beings, which are but a small part of the whole; not implying a tendency to a union with the great system, and not at all inconsistent with enmity towards Being in general; this I suppose not to be of the nature of true virtue: although it may in some respects be good, and may appear beautiful in a confined and contracted view of things.—But of this more afterwards.

It is abundantly plain by the holy Scriptures, and generally allowed, not only by Christian divines, but by the more considerable deists, that virtue most essentially consists in love. And I suppose, it is owned by the most considerable writers, to consist in general love of benevolence, or kind affection: though it seems to me, the meaning of some in this affair is not sufficiently explained, which perhaps occasions some error or confusion in discourses on this subject.

When I say, true virtue consists in love to Being in general, I shall not be likely to be understood, that no one act of the mind or exercise of love is of the nature of true virtue, but what has Being in general, or the great system of universal existence, for its direct and immediate object: so that no exercise of love or kind affection to any one particular Being, that is but a small part of this whole, has any thing of the nature of true virtue. But, that the nature of true virtue consists in a disposition to benevolence towards Being in general. Though, from such a disposition may arise exercises of love to particular Beings, as objects are presented and occasions arise. No wonder, that he who is of a generally benevolent disposition, should be more disposed than another to have his heart moved with benevolent affection to particular persons, whom he is acquainted and conversant with, and from whom arise the greatest and most frequent occasions for exciting his benevolent temper. But my meaning is, that no affections towards particular persons or Beings are of the nature of true virtue, but such as arise from a generally benevolent temper, or from that habit or frame of mind, wherein consists a disposition to love Being in general.

And perhaps it is needless for me to give notice to my readers, that when I speak of an intelligent Being's having a heart united and benevolently disposed to Being in general, I thereby mean *intelligent* Being in general. Not inanimate things, or Beings that have no perception or will, which are not properly capable objects of benevolence.

Love is commonly distinguished into love of benevolence and love of complacence. Love of *benevolence* is that affection or propensity of the heart to any Being, which causes it to incline to its well being, or disposes it to desire and take pleasure in its happiness. And if I mistake not, it is agreeable to the common opinion, that beauty in the object is not always the ground of this propensity: but that there may be such a thing as benevolence, or a disposition to the welfare of those that are not considered as beautiful; unless mere existence be accounted a beauty. And benevolence or goodness in the Divine Being is generally supposed, not only to be prior to the beauty of many of its objects, but to their existence: so as to be the ground both of their existence and their beauty, rather than they the foundation of God's benevolence; as it is supposed that it is God's goodness which moved him to give them both Being and beauty. So that if all virtue primarily consists in that affection of heart to Being, which is exercised in benevolence, or an inclination to its good, then God's virtue is so extended as to include a propensity, not only to Being actually existing, and actually beautiful, but to possible Being, so as to incline him to give Being, beauty and happiness. But not now to insist particularly on this. What I would have observed at present, is, that it must be allowed, benevolence doth not necessarily presuppose beauty in its object.

What is commonly called love of *complacence*, presupposes beauty. For it is no other than delight in beauty; or complacence in the person or Being beloved for his beauty.

If virtue be the beauty of an intelligent Being, and virtue consists in love, then it is a plain inconsistence, to suppose that virtue primarily consists in any love to its object *for its beauty*; either in a love of complacence, which is delight in a Being for his beauty, or in a love of benevolence, that has the beauty of its object for its foundation. For that would be to suppose, that the beauty of intelligent beings primarily consists in love to beauty; or, that their virtue first of all consists in their love to virtue. Which is an inconsistence, and going in a circle. Because it makes virtue, or beauty of mind, the foundation or first motive of that love wherein virtue originally consists, or wherein the very first virtue consists; or, it supposes the first virtue to be the consequence and effect of virtue. So that virtue is originally the foundation and exciting cause of the very beginning or first Being of virtue. Which makes the first virtue, both the ground, and the consequence, both cause and effect of itself. Doubtless virtue primarily consists in something else besides any effect or consequence of virtue. If virtue consists primarily in love to virtue, then virtue, the thing loved, is the love of virtue: so that virtue must consist in the love of the love of virtue. And if it be inquired, what that virtue is, which virtue consists in the love of the love of, it must be answered, it is the love of virtue. So that there must be the love of the love of the love of virtue, and so on *in infinitum*. For there is no end of going back in a circle. We never come to any beginning, or foundation. For it is without beginning and hangs on nothing.

Therefore if the essence of virtue or beauty of mind lies in love, or a disposition to love, it must primarily consist in something *different* both from complacence, which is a delight in beauty, and also from any benevolence that has the beauty of its object for its foundation. Because it is absurd, to say that virtue is primarily and first of all the consequence of itself. For this makes virtue primarily prior to itself.

Nor can virtue primarily consist in *gratitude*; or one Being's benevolence to another for his benevolence to him. Because this implies the same inconsistence. For it supposes a benevolence prior to gratitude, that is the cause of gratitude. Therefore the first benevolence, or that benevolence which has none prior to it, cannot be gratitude.

Therefore there is room left for no other conclusion than that the primary object of virtuous love is Being, simply considered; or, that true virtue primarily consists, not in love to any particular Beings, because of their virtue or beauty, nor in gratitude, because they love us; but in a propensity and union of heart to Being simply considered; exciting absolute benevolence (if I may so call it) to Being in general.—I say, true virtue *primarily* consists in this. For I am far from asserting that there is no true virtue in any other love than this absolute benevolence. But I would express what appears to me to be the truth on this subject, in the following particulars.

The *first* object of a virtuous benevolence is *Being*, simply considered: and if Being, *simply* considered, be its object, then Being *in general* is its object; and the thing it has an ultimate propensity to, is the *highest good* of Being in general. And it will seek the good of every *individual* Being unless it be conceived as not consistent with the highest good of Being in general. In which case the good of a particular Being, or some Beings, may be given up for the sake of the highest good of Being in general. And particularly if there be any Being that is looked upon as statedly and irreclaimably opposite and an enemy to Being in general, then consent and adherence to Being in general will induce the truly virtuous heart to forsake that Being, and to oppose it.

And further, if Being, simply considered, be the first object of a truly virtuous benevolence, then that Being who has *most* of Being, or has the greatest share of existence, other things being equal, so far as such a Being is exhibited to our faculties or set in our view, will have the *greatest* share of the propensity and benevolent affection of the heart. I say, *other things being equal*, especially because there is a *secondary* object of virtuous benevolence, that I shall take notice of presently. Which is one thing that must be considered as the ground or motive to a purely virtuous benevolence. Pure benevolence in its first exercise is nothing else but Being's uniting consent, or propensity to Being; appearing true and pure by its extending to Being in general, and inclining to the general highest good, and to each Being, whose welfare is consistent with the highest general good, in proportion to the degree of *existence*[5] understood, other things being equal.

The *second* object of a virtuous propensity of heart is *benevolent* Being. A secondary ground of pure benevolence is virtuous benevolence itself in its object. When any one under the influence of general benevolence, sees another Being possessed of the like general benevolence, this attaches his heart to him, and draws forth greater love to him, than merely his having existence: because so far as the Being beloved has love to Being in general, so far his own Being is, as it were, enlarged, extends to, and in some sort comprehends, Being in general: and therefore he that is governed by love to Being in general must of necessity have complacence in him, and the greater degree of benevolence to him, as it were out of gratitude to him for his love to general existence, that his own heart is extended and united to, and so looks on its interest as its own. It is because his heart is thus united to Being in general, that he looks on a benevolent propensity to Being in general, wherever he sees it, as the beauty of the Being in whom it is; an excellency, that renders him worthy of esteem, complacence, and the greater good will.

But several things may be noted more particularly concerning this secondary ground of a truly virtuous love.

1. That loving a Being on *this ground* necessarily arises from pure benevolence to Being *in general*, and comes to the same thing. For he that has a simple and pure good will to general entity or existence, must love that temper in others, that agrees and conspires with itself. A spirit of consent to Being must agree with consent to Being. That which truly and sincerely seeks the good of others, must approve of, and love, that which joins with him in seeking the good of others.

2. This which has been now mentioned as a secondary ground of virtuous love, is the thing wherein true moral or spiritual *beauty* primarily consists. Yea, spiritual beauty consists wholly in this, and the various qualities and exercises of mind which proceed from it,

---

5. " * * * one Being may have more *existence* than another, as he may be *greater* than another. That which is *great*, has more existence, and is further from nothing, than that which is *little*. One Being may have every thing positive belonging to it, or every thing which goes to its positive existence (in opposition to defect) in a higher degree than another; or a greater capacity and power, greater understanding, every faculty and every positive quality in a higher degree. An *archangel* must be supposed to have more existence, and to be every way further removed from non-enity, than a *worm* or a *flea*" [Edwards' note].

and the external actions which proceed from these internal qualities and exercises. And in these things consists all true *virtue*, viz., in this love of Being, and the qualities and acts which arise from it.

3. As all spiritual beauty lies in these virtuous principles and acts, so it is primarily *on this account* they are beautiful, viz., that they imply *consent* and *union* with Being *in general*. This is the primary and most essential Beauty of every thing that can justly be called by the name of virtue, or is any moral excellency in the eye of one that has a perfect view of things. I say, the *primary* and *most essential* beauty—because there is a secondary and inferior sort of beauty; which I shall take notice of afterwards.

4. This spiritual beauty, that is but a *secondary* ground of a virtuous benevolence, is the ground, not only of benevolence, but *complacence*, and is the *primary* ground of the latter; that is, when the complacence is truly virtuous. Love to us in particular, and kindness received, may be a secondary ground. But this is the primary objective foundation of it.

5. It must be noted, that the *degree* of the *amiableness* or *valuableness* of true virtue, primarily consisting in consent and a benevolent propensity of heart to Being in general, in the eyes of one that is influenced by such a spirit, is not in the *simple* proportion of the degree of benevolent affection seen, but in a proportion *compounded* of the greatness of the benevolent Being or the degree of *Being* and the degree of *benevolence*. One that loves Being in general, will necessarily value good will to Being in general, wherever he sees it. But if he sees the same benevolence in *two* Beings, he will value it *more* in two, than in one only. Because it is a greater thing, more favorable to Being in general, to have two Beings to favor it, than only one of them. For there is more Being that favors Being: both together having more Being than one alone. So, if one Being be as great as two, has as much existence as both together, and has the same degree of general benevolence, it is more favorable to Being in general than if there were general benevolence in a Being that had but half that share of existence. As a large quantity of gold, with the same degree of preciousness, i. e. with the same excellent quality of matter, is more valuable than a small quantity of the same metal.

6. It is impossible that any one should truly *relish* this beauty, consisting in general benevolence, who has *not* that temper himself. I have observed, that if any Being is possessed of such a temper, he will unavoidably be pleased with the same temper in another. And it may in like manner be demonstrated, that it is such a spirit, and nothing else, which will relish such a spirit. For if a Being, destitute of benevolence, should love benevolence to Being in general, it would prize and seek that which it had no value for. Because to love an inclination to the good of Being in general, would imply a loving and

prizing the good of Being in general. For how should one love and value a *disposition* to a thing, or a *tendency to promote* a thing, and for that very reason, because it tends to promote it—when the *thing* itself is what he is regardless of, and has no value for, nor desires to have promoted.

1755–1758   1765

Diarists and Observers

SARAH KEMBLE KNIGHT
(1666–1727)

Sarah Kemble Knight was born in Boston, the daughter of Thomas Kemble, a merchant, reportedly an agent of Cromwell in selling prisoners of war. She married Captain Richard Knight, shipmaster, a widower considerably her senior. After her husband's death Mrs. Knight engaged in a variety of employments not usually associated with the women of her times. As court scrivener she learned something of the law, and seems occasionally to have employed such knowledge in the settlement of estates and in other semilegal activities. For a time, certainly in 1706, she conducted a school in Boston where, it is traditionally reported, Benjamin Franklin and Samuel Mather (both born in 1706) may have been pupils. At any rate, "Madam" Knight was an unusual woman, whose successful business activities included the management of a shop and a boardinghouse in Boston.

The death of a relative left her with an estate to settle, and on October 2, 1704, she set off on horseback from Boston to New York, not returning to Bos-

ton until March 3, 1705. Much of the country through which she traveled might have tested the hardihood of a horseman of less than her thirty-eight years. Her *Journal* of this courageous journey testifies to her keen sense of humor and to her unusual tolerance, and is important in its representation of American life at that time. Its lively portrayal of the New England backwoods and the cultivated prosperity of New York reminds us that the Puritan community was soon confronted with another America, in which, by 1704, worldly prosperity and secular sophistication are in strong contrast with large areas of ignorance, violence, and backwardness. It is valuable to compare Madam Knight's account with William Byrd's descriptions of characters he met with during his survey of the Virginia–North Carolina boundary dispute in 1728.

In 1712 Madam Knight moved to Connecticut, where she controlled property in both Norwich and New London. She engaged in Indian trading and farming, and she kept a shop and a "house of entertainment," probably an inn. At her death in 1727, she left an estate of £1,800, then a considerable sum, a testimony to her skill as a businesswoman.

The Journals of Madam Knight and Reverend Buckingham, with an introduction by Theodore Dwight, New York, 1825, was the first edition. *The Journal of Madam Knight*, a reprint of this, with a new introduction and fresh information, appeared in 1865. The standard edition is G. P. Winship's *Private Journal of a Journey from Boston to New York*, 1920, in which Dwight's introduction is reprinted. Useful biographical accounts are to be found in the introductions by Dwight and Winship, and in the article by Sidney Gunn in the *Dictionary of American Biography*, New York, 1933. The text below is that of the 1825 edition, with certain persistent abbreviations corrected.

From The Journal of Madam Knight

[*New England Frontier*]

[Oct. 2, 1704.]

About three o'clock afternoon, I begun my Journey from Boston to New-Haven; being about two Hundred Mile. My Kinsman, Capt. Robert Luist, waited on me as farr as Dedham, where I was to meet the Western post.

I vissitted the Reverd. Mr. Belcher, the Minister of the town, and tarried there till evening, in hopes the post would come along. But he not coming, I resolved to go to Billingses where he used to lodg, being 12 miles further. But being ignorant of the way, Madam Belcher seing no persuasions of her good spouses or hers could prevail with me to Lodg there that night, Very kindly went wyth me to the Tavern, where I hoped to get my guide, And desired the Hostess to inquire of her guests whether any of them would go with mee. But they, being tyed by the Lipps to a pewter engine,[1] scarcely allowed themselves time to say what clownish [A portion of the manuscript is missing.] Peices of eight, I told her no, I would not be accessary to such extortion.

Then John shan't go, sais shee. No, indeed, shan't hee; And held forth at that rate a long time, that I began to fear I was got among the Quaking tribe, beleeving not a Limbertong'd sister among them could out do Madm. Hostes.

Upon this, to my no small surprise, son John arrose, and gravely demanded what I would give him to go with me? Give you, sais I, are you John? Yes, says he, for want of a Better; And behold! this John look't as old as my Host, and perhaps had bin a man in the last Century. Well, Mr. John, sais I, make your demands. Why, half a piece of eight and a dram,[2] sais John. I agreed, and gave him a Dram (now) in hand to bind the bargain.

My hostess catechis'd John for going so cheap, saying his poor

1. *I.e.*, drinking from pewter mugs.
2. A Spanish dollar, then current, was a piece of eight, so called because it was worth eight Spanish reals. A dram was a small whisky or brandy glass; now called a jigger.

wife would break her heart [A portion of the manuscript is missing.] His shade on his Hors resembled a Globe on a Gate post. His habitt, Hors and furniture, its looks and goings Incomparably answered the rest.

Thus Jogging on with an easy pace, my Guide telling mee it was dangero's to Ride hard in the Night, (which his hors had the sence to avoid,) Hee entertained me with the Adventurs he had passed by late Rideing, and eminent Dangers he had escaped, so that, Remembring the Hero's in Parismus and the Knight of the Oracle, I didn't know but I had mett with a Prince disguis'd.

When we had Ridd about an how'r, wee come into a thick swamp, which by Reason of a great fogg, very much startled mee, it being now very Dark. But nothing dismay'd John: Hee had encountered a thousand and a thousand such Swamps, having a Universall Knowledge in the Woods; and readily Answered all my inquiries which were not a few.

In about an how'r, or something more, after we left the Swamp, we come to Billinges, where I was to Lodg. My Guide dismounted and very Complasantly help't me down and shewd the door, signing to me with his hand to Go in; which I Gladly did—But had not gone many steps into the Room, ere I was Interogated by a young Lady I understood afterwards was the Eldest daughter of the family, with these, or words to this purpose, (*viz.*) Law for mee—what in the world brings You here at this time a night?—I never see a woman on the Rode so Dreadfull late, in all the days of my versall life. Who are You? Where are You going? I'me scar'd out of my witts—with much now of the same Kind. I stood aghast, Prepareing to reply, when in comes my Guide—to him Madam turn'd, Roreing out: Lawfull heart, John, is it You?—how de do! Where in the world are you going with this woman? Who is she? John made no Answer but sat down in the corner, fumbled out his black Junk,[3] and saluted that instead of Debb; she then turned agen to mee and fell anew into her silly questions, without asking mee to sitt down.

I told her shee treated me very Rudely, and I did not think it my duty to answer her unmannerly Questions. But to get ridd of them, I told her I come there to have the post's[4] company with me tomorrow on my Journey, &c. Miss star'd awhile, drew a chair, bid me sitt, And then run upstairs and putts on two or three Rings, (or else I had not seen them before,) and returning, sett herself just before me, showing the way to Reding,[5] that I might see her Ornaments, perhaps to gain the more respect. But her Granam's new Rung sow, had it appeared, would affected me as much. I paid honest John

3. Oakum, or a piece of old rope; possibly jocose for a twist of tobacco leaves.
4. The post was the messenger who made scheduled trips with the mail, in this case on horseback.
5. Vernacular phrase for making a display of one's self.

with money and dram according to contract, and Dismist him, and pray'd Miss to shew me where I must Lodg. Shee conducted me to a parlour in a little back Lento,[6] which was almost fill'd with the bedsted, which was so high that I was forced to climb on a chair to gitt up to the wretched bed that lay on it; on which having Stretcht my tired Limbs, and lay'd my head on a Sad-colourd pillow, I began to think on the transactions of the past day.

[Oct. 3, 1704.]

About 8 in the morning, I with the Post proceeded forward without observing any thing remarkable; And about two, afternoon, Arrived at the Post's second stage, where the western Post mett him and exchanged Letters. Here, having called for something to eat, the woman bro't in a Twisted thing like a cable, but something whiter; and laying it on the bord, tugg'd for life to bring it into a capacity to spread; which having with great pains accomplished, she serv'd in a dish of Pork and Cabage, I suppose the remains of Dinner. The sause was of a deep Purple, which I tho't was boil'd in her dye Kettle; the bread was Indian, and every thing on the Table service Agreeable to these. I, being hungry, gott a little down; but my stomach was soon cloy'd, and what cabbage I swallowed serv'd me for a Cudd the whole day after.

Having here discharged the Ordnary[7] for self and Guide, (as I understood was the custom,) About Three, afternoon, went on with my Third Guide, who Rode very hard; and having crossed Providence Ferry, we come to a River which they Generally Ride thro'. But I dare not venture; so the Post got a Ladd and Cannoo to carry me to tother side, and hee rid thro' and Led my hors. The Canoo was very small and shallow, so that when we were in she seem'd redy to take in water, which greatly terrified mee, and caused me to be very circumspect, sitting with my hands fast on each side, my eyes stedy, not daring so much as to lodg my tongue a hair's breadth more on one side of my mouth than tother, nor so much as think on Lott's wife,[8] for a wry thought would have oversett our wherey: But was soon put out of this pain, by feeling the Cannoo on shore, which I as soon almost saluted with my feet; and Rewarding my sculler, again mounted and made the best of our way forwards. The Rode here was very even and the day pleasant, it being now near Sunsett. But the Post told mee we had neer 14 miles to Ride to the next Stage, (where we were to Lodg.) I askt him of the rest of the Rode, foreseeing we must travail in the night. Hee told mee there was a bad River we were to Ride thro', which was so very firce a hors could

---

6. Lean-to (a shed).
7. Paid for the meal, an "ordinary," the same for all comers.

8. Contrary to God's command, Lot's wife looked back upon His destruction of the wicked city of Sodom, and was turned to salt (Genesis xix: 26).

sometimes hardly stem it: But it was but narrow, and wee should soon be over. I cannot express the concern of mind this relation sett me in: no thoughts but those of the dang'ros River could entertain my Imagination, and they were as formidable as varios,[9] still Tormenting me with blackest Ideas of my Approaching fate—Sometimes seeing my self drowning, otherwhiles drowned, and at the best like a holy Sister Just come out of a Spiritual Bath in dripping Garments.

Now was the Glorious Luminary, with his swift Coursers arrived at his Stage, leaving poor me with the rest of this part of the lower world in darkness, with which wee were soon Surrounded. The only Glimering we now had was from the spangled Skies, Whose Imperfect Reflections rendered every Object formidable. Each lifeless Trunk, with its shatter'd Limbs, appear'd an Armed Enymie; and every little stump like a Ravenous devourer. Nor could I so much as discern my Guide, when at any distance, which added to the terror.

Thus, absolutely lost in Thought, and dying with the very thoughts of drowning, I come up with the Post, who I did not see till even with his Hors: he told mee he stopt for mee; and wee Rode on Very deliberatly a few paces, when we entred a Thickett of Trees and Shrubbs, and I perceived by the Hors's going, we were on the descent of a Hill, which, as wee come nearer the bottom, 'twas totaly dark, with the Trees that surrounded it. But I knew by the Going of the Hors wee had entred the water, which my Guide told mee was the hazzardos River he had told me off; and hee, Riding up close to my Side, Bid me not fear—we should be over Imediately. I now ralyed all the Courage I was mistrss of, Knowing that I must either Venture my fate of drowning, or be left like the Children in the wood. So, as the Post bid me, I gave Reins to my Nagg; and sitting as Stedy as Just before in the Cannoo, in a few minutes got safe to the other side, which hee told mee was the Narragansett country. * * *

Being come to mr. Havens', I was very civilly Received, and courteously entertained, in a clean comfortable House; and the Good woman was very active in helping off my Riding clothes, and then ask't what I would eat. I told her I had some Chocolett, if shee would prepare it; which with the help of some Milk, and a little clean brass Kettle, she soon affected to my satisfaction. I then betook me to my Apartment, which was a little Room parted from the Kitchen by a single bord partition; where, after I had noted the Occurances of the past day, I went to bed, which, tho' pretty hard, Yet neet and handsome. But I could get no sleep, because of the Clamor of some of the Town tope-ers in next Room, Who were entred into a strong debate concerning the Signifycation of the name

9. Various, conflicting.

of their Country, (*viz.*) Narraganset. One said it was named so by the Indians, because there grew a Brier there, of a Prodigious Highth and bigness, the like hardly ever known, called by the Indians Narragansett; and quotes an Indian of so Barberous a name for his Author, that I could not write it. His Antagonist Replyed no—It was from a Spring it had its name, which hee well knew where it was, which was extreem cold in summer, and as Hott as could be imagined in the winter, which was much resorted too by the natives, and by them called Narragansett, (Hott and Cold) and that was the originall of their places name—with a thousand Impertinances not worth notice, which He utter'd with such a Roreing voice and Thundering blows with the fist of wickedness on the Table, that it peirced my very head. I heartily fretted, and wish't 'um tongue tyed; but with as little succes as a friend of mine once, who was (as shee said) kept a whole night awake, on a Jorny, by a country Left.[1] and a Sergent, Insigne and a Deacon, contriving how to bring a triangle into a Square. They kept calling for tother Gill[2] which while they were swallowing, was some Intermission; But presently, like Oyle to fire, encreased the flame. I set my Candle on a Chest by the bed side, and setting up, fell to my old way of composing my Resentments, in the following manner:

> I ask thy Aid, O Potent Rum!
> To Charm these wrangling Topers Dum.
> Thou hast their Giddy Brains possest—
> The man confounded with the Beast—
> And I, poor I, can get no rest.
> Intoxicate them with thy fumes:
> O still their Tongues till morning comes!

And I know not but my wishes took effect; for the dispute soon ended with 'tother Dram; and so Good night!

[Oct. 4, 1704.]

About four in the morning, we set out for Kingston (for so was the Town called) with a french Docter in our company. Hee and the Post put on very furiously, so that I could not keep up with them, only as now and then they'd stop till they see mee. This Rode was poorly furnished with accommodations for Travellers, so that we were forced to ride 22 miles by the post's account, but neerer thirty by mine, before wee could bait[3] so much as our Horses, which I exceedingly complained of. But the post encourag'd mee, by sayng wee should be well accommodated anon at mr. Devills, a few miles further. But I questioned whether we ought to go to the Devil to

1. Lieutenant; *cf.* British pronunciation.
2. A rum glass, originally one holding a gill.
3. Obsolete meanings are, "to pasture" and "to stop for food."

be helpt out of affliction. However, like the rest of Deluded souls that post to the Infernal denn, Wee made all posible speed to this Devil's Habitation; where alliting, in full assurance of good accommodation, wee were going in. But meeting his two daughters, as I suposed twins, they so neerly resembled each other, both in features and habit, and look't as old as the Divel himselfe, and quite as Ugly, We desired entertainm't, but could hardly get a word out of 'um, till with our Importunity, telling them our necesity, &c. they call'd the old Sophister, who was as sparing of his words as his daughters had bin, and no, or none, was the reply's hee made us to our demands. Hee differed only in this from the old fellow in to'ther Country: hee let us depart. However, I thought it proper to warn poor Travailers to endeavor to Avoid falling into circumstances like ours, which at our next Stage I sat down and did as followeth:

> May all that dread the cruel feind of night
> Keep on, and not at this curs't Mansion light.
> 'Tis Hell; 'tis Hell! and Devills here do dwell:
> Here dwells the Devill—surely this's Hell.
> Nothing but Wants: a drop to cool yo'r Tongue
> Cant be procur'd these cruel Feinds among.
> Plenty of horrid Grins and looks sevear,
> Hunger and thirst, But pitty's bannish'd here—
> The Right hand keep, if Hell on Earth you fear!

Thus leaving this habitation of cruelty, we went forward; and arriving at an Ordinary[4] about two mile further, found tollerable accomodation. But our Hostes, being a pretty full mouth'd old creature, entertain'd our fellow travailer, the french Doctor, with Inumirable complaints of her bodily infirmities; and whispered to him so lou'd, that all the House had as full a hearing as hee; which was very divirting to the company, (of which there was a great many,) as one might see by their sneering. But poor weary I slipt out to enter my mind in my Jornal, and left my Great Landly with her Talkative Guests to themselves. * * *

[Connecticut]

[Oct. 7, 1704.]

* * * About two a clock afternoon we arrived at New Haven, where I was received with all Possible Respects and civility. Here I discharged Mr. Wheeler[5] with a reward to his satisfaction, and took some time to rest after so long and toilsome a Journey; and Inform'd myselfe of the manners and customs of the place, and at the same time employed myselfe in the afair I went there upon.

---

4. Here "Ordinary" refers to the inn that provides "ordinary" meals.

5. *I.e.*, she released Mr. Wheeler, her guide and companion, from his "charge."

They are Govern'd by the same Laws as wee in Boston, (or little differing,) thr'out this whole Colony of Connecticot, And much the same way of Church Government, and many of them good, Sociable people, and I hope Religious too: but a little too much Independent in their principalls, and, as I have been told, were formerly in their Zeal very Riggid in their Administrations towards such as their Lawes made Offenders, even to a harmless Kiss[6] or Innocent merriment among Young people. Whipping being a frequent and counted an easy Punishment, about which as other Crimes, the Judges were absolute in their Sentences. * * *

Their Diversions in this part of the Country are on Lecture days and Training days[7] mostly: on the former there is Riding from town to town.

And on training dayes The Youth divert themselves by Shooting at the Target, as they call it, (but it very much resembles a pillory,) where hee that hitts nearest the white has some yards of Red Ribbin presented him which being tied to his hattband, the two ends streeming down his back, he is Led away in Triumph, with great applause, as the winners of the Olympiack Games. They generally marry very young: the males oftener as I am told under twentie than above; they generally make public wedings, and have a way something singular (as they say) in some of them, *viz.* Just before Joyning hands the Bridegroom quitts the place, who is soon followed by the Bridesmen, and as it were, dragg'd back to duty—being the reverse to the former practice among us, to steal his Bride.

There are great plenty of Oysters all along by the sea side, as farr as I Rode in the Collony, and those very good. And they Generally lived very well and comfortably in their famelies. But too Indulgent (especially the farmers) to their slaves: suffering too great familiarity from them, permitting them to sit at Table and eat with them, (as they say to save time,) and into the dish goes the black hoof as freely as the white hand. They told me there was a farmer lived nere the Town where I lodgd who had some difference with his slave, concerning something the master had promised him and did not punctualy perform; which caused some hard words between them; But at length they put the matter to Arbitration and Bound themselves to stand at the award of such as they named—which done, the Arbitrators Having heard the Allegations of both parties, Order the master to pay 40s to black face, and acknowledge his fault. And so the matter ended: the poor master very honestly standing to the award.

There are every where in the Towns as I passed, a Number of Indians the Natives of the Country, and are the most salvage of all

6. In accordance with various community ordinances, even returning husbands might stand in the stocks for impetuously kissing their wives in public or on Sunday.

7. The delivery of a sermon was a "lecture"; training days were days set aside for compulsory military training.

the salvages of that kind that I had ever Seen: little or no care taken (as I heard upon enquiry) to make them otherwise. They have in some places Landes of their owne, and Govern'd by Law's of their own making;—they marry many wives and at pleasure put them away, and on the least dislike or fickle humour, on either side, saying *stand away* to one another is a sufficient Divorce. And indeed those uncomely *Stand aways* are too much in Vougue among the English in this (Indulgent Colony) as their Records plentifully prove, and that on very trivial matters, of which some have been told me, but are not proper to be Related by a Female pen, tho some of that foolish sex have had too large a share in the story.

If the natives committ any crime on their own precincts among themselves, The English takes no Cognezens of. But if on the English ground, they are punishable by our Laws. They mourn for their Dead by blackening their faces, and cutting their hair, after an Awkerd and frightfull manner; But can't bear You should mention the names of their dead Relations to them: they trade most for Rum, for which theyd hazzard their very lives; and the English fit them Generally as well, by seasoning it plentifully with water. * * *

They [the colonists] are generaly very plain in their dress, throuout all the Colony, as I saw, and follow one another in their modes; that You may know where they belong, especially the women, meet them where you will.

Their Cheif Red Letter day is St. Election, which is annualy Observed according to Charter, to choose their Govenr: a blessing they can never be thankfull enough for, as they will find, if ever it be their hard fortune to loose it. The present Govenor in Conecticott is the Honble John Winthrop Esq. A Gentleman of an Ancient and Honourable Family, whose Father was Govenor here sometime before, and his Grandfather had bin Govr of the Massachusetts. * * *

[New York City]

[Dec. 6, 1704.]

* * * The Cittie of New York is a pleasant, well compacted place, situated on a Commodius River which is a fine harbour for shipping. The Buildings Brick Generaly, very stately and high, though not altogether like ours in Boston. The Bricks in some of the Houses are of divers Coullers and laid in Checkers, being glazed look very agreeable. The inside of them are neat to admiration, the wooden work, for only the walls are plasterd, and the Sumers[8] and Gist[9] are plained and kept very white scowr'd as so is all the partitions if made of Bords. The fire places have no Jambs (as ours have) But the Backs run flush with the walls, and the Hearth is of Tyles and is as farr out into the Room at the Ends as before the fire, which is Generally Five foot in

8. A "summer" is a beam, lintel, or floor timber.   9. Joists.

the Low'r rooms, and the peice over where the mantle tree should be is made as ours with Joyners work, and as I suppose is fasten'd to iron rodds inside. The House where the Vendue[1] was, had Chimney Corners like ours, and they and the hearths were laid with the finest tile that I ever see, and the stair cases laid all with white tile which is ever clean, and so are the walls of the Kitchen which had a Brick floor. They were making Great preparations to Receive their Governor, Lord Cornbury from the Jerseys, and for that End raised the militia to Gard him on shore to the fort.

They are Generaly of the Church of England and have a New England Gentleman for their minister, and a very fine church set out with all Customary requisites. There are also a Dutch and Divers Conventicles as they call them, *viz.* Baptist, Quakers, &c. They are not strict in keeping the Sabbath as in Boston and other places where I had bin, but seem to deal with great exactness as farr as I see or Deall with. They are sociable to one another and Curteos and Civill to strangers and fare well in their houses. The English go very fasheonable in their dress. But the Dutch, especially the middling sort, differ from our women, in their habitt go loose, were French muches[2] which are like a Capp and a head band in one, leaving their ears bare, which are sett out with Jewells of a large size and many in number. And their fingers hoop't with Rings, some with large stones in them of many Coullers as were their pendants in their ears, which You should see very old women wear as well as Young.

They have Vendues very frequently and make thir Earnings very well by them, for they treat with good Liquor Liberally, and the Customers Drink as Liberally and Generally pay for't as well, by paying for that which they Bidd up Briskly for, after the sack[3] has gone plentifully about, tho' sometimes good penny worths are got there. Their Diversions in the Winter is Riding Sleys about three or four Miles out of Town, where they have Houses of entertainment at a place called the Bowery, and some go to friends Houses who handsomely treat them.

1704–1705   1825

1. Auction sale. *Cf.* the French *vendre,* "to sell."
2. Wear French headdress. *Cf.* the

French *mouchoir,* "handkerchief" or "kerchief."
3. A very dry wine. *Cf.* the French *sec,* "dry."

WILLIAM BYRD
(1674–1744)

William Byrd was born March 28, 1674, at the fall of the James River, in what is now Richmond, Virginia, a city he founded and named. At the age of seven he was sent to England for his education, under the direction of a grandfather. After a brief interval in Holland, where he learned something about the Dutch commercial system, he took up quarters in the Middle Temple, in London, for the study of law. He had already been elected a member of the Royal Society when, at the age of twenty-two, he returned to Virginia. In the tradition of his family, he was elected a member of the House of Burgesses, and he represented the colony on several occasions in England. In 1705, upon his father's death, he returned to Virginia, where he remained for the next ten years. Byrd inherited the family property—some 26,000 acres—and succeeded his father as Receiver-General of Revenues. He progressed from this office to membership in the Supreme Council, which functioned as a sort of Senate for the colony, retaining membership until his death, although exactly half of his seventy years were spent abroad.

His secret diaries—kept in an obsolete shorthand—form a unique and valuable account of life, day by day, on a colonial southern plantation. They defeat the myth that southern plantation life was characterized chiefly by silken ease, horse racing, and mint juleps. They further establish Byrd as a systematic student of literature: he read Greek, Hebrew, Latin, and French with facility. His library of 3,600 volumes was one of the largest private collections to be assembled in America before the Revolution. At the time of his death he had completed the building of Westover, one of the finest colonial Virginia mansions. His holdings in land amounted to approximately 186,000 acres in Virginia and North Carolina.

Prior to the publication of *The Secret Diary of William Byrd of Westover*, 1709–12 (1941), and *Another Secret Diary of William Byrd of Westover*, 1739–41 (1942), he was known for his *History of the Dividing Line Run in the Year 1728* and his *Secret History of the Line*—his accounts of the official survey, in which he participated, undertaken for the purpose of settling a boundary dispute between Virginia and North Carolina. Two other less extensive works are *A Progress to the Mines* (1732) and *A Journey to the Land of Eden* (1733), his journals of two visits in those years: to the iron mines of western Virginia, and to the interior of North Carolina.

Byrd's writings hold their place for the literary pleasure that they still provide, for the vitality and usefulness of their observation of American life, and for their foreshadowing, in the character of their author, of the liberal, patrician leadership which produced Washington and Jefferson in the next generation. If Byrd was the cavalier, he was an Americanized cavalier, who opposed the authoritarian pretensions of Governor Spotswood, and defended the American planter gentry in their efforts to preserve local determination of their own government and taxation. He was at home with the society, literature, and learning of London in that brilliant first quarter of the eighteenth century—with Wycherley and Congreve, or with the Earl of Orrery; but he also loved Williamsburg, by contrast a rustic capital. His literary style reflected the enlightened humanism and worldly security of his British literary contemporaries, but he employed it, without deterioration, in the description of a rugged frontier. Trained in science and the practical arts as well as in literature, he brought a practical observation to bear on the products of the land and the customs and characters of its inhabitants, both the Indians and the white frontiersmen. A Virginia gentleman, he was aware of the great social contrasts present in Virginia life, and he viewed the inhabitants of "Lubberland" with amusement; but he saw the potentialities both in the land and in its people. In his sketches of these people and his adventures among them, in his shrewd recapture of the good story, the droll character, and the memorable absurdity, he became, among other things, our first humorous writer of distinction.

The first publication of *The Westover Manuscripts* (containing the *History*, the *Progress*, and the *Journey*) was in 1841. A recent edition of these works is that edited by Mark Van Doren under the title *A Journey to the Land of Eden*, 1928. The Dietz Press, Richmond, published *The Secret Diary of William Byrd of Westover, 1709–1712*, edited by Louis B. Wright and Marion Tinling, 1941; *Another Secret Diary of William Byrd of Westover, 1739–1741*, edited by Maude H. Woodfin and Marion Tinling, 1942; and also *William Byrd's Natural History of Virginia*, edited by R. C. Beatty and William Mulloy, 1940.

The most reliable edition of the *History* and related materials is *William Byrd's Histories of the Dividing Line Betwixt Virginia and North Carolina*, edited by W. K. Boyd, 1929. This volume includes the previously unpublished *Secret History*. The present text is based on this edition, with the reduction of irregular capitals and the regularizing of abbreviated words.

R. C. Beatty's *William Byrd of Westover*, 1932, is a full-length biography; and Byrd is included in Louis B. Wright's *The First Gentlemen of Virginia*, 1940.

From The History of the Dividing Line[1]

[The Marooner]

[March 7, 1728.] While we continued here,[2] we were told that on the south shore, not far from the inlet, dwelt a marooner, that modestly called himself a hermit, though he forfeited that name by suffering a wanton female to cohabit with him. His habitation was a bower, covered with bark after the Indian fashion, which in that mild situation protected him pretty well from the weather. Like the ravens, he neither plowed nor sowed, but subsisted chiefly upon oysters, which his handmaid made a shift to gather from the adjacent rocks. Sometimes, too, for change of diet, he sent her to drive up the neighbor's cows, to moisten their mouths with a little milk. But as for raiment, he depended mostly upon his length of beard,

1. The official party, including commissioners and surveyors from both states, met on March 5, 1728, to begin the survey intended to establish the long-disputed boundary line between Virginia and North Carolina.

2. At Coratuck (or Currituck) Inlet, on the third day of the expedition.

and she upon her length of hair, part of which she brought decently forward, and the rest dangled behind quite down to her rump, like one of Herodotus'[3] East Indian pigmies. Thus did these wretches live in a dirty state of nature, and were mere Adamites, innocence only excepted. * * *

[*Lubberland*]

[March 10, 1728.] The sabbath happened very opportunely to give some ease to our jaded people, who rested religiously from every work, but that of cooking the kettle. We observed very few cornfields in our walks, and those very small, which seemed the stranger to us, because we could see no other tokens of husbandry or improvement. But, upon further inquiry, we were given to understand people only made corn for themselves and not for their stocks, which know very well how to get their own living. Both cattle and hogs ramble into the neighboring marshes and swamps, where they maintain themselves the whole winter long, and are not fetched home till the spring. Thus these indolent wretches, during one half of the year, lose the advantage of the milk of their cattle, as well as their dung, and many of the poor creatures perish in the mire, into the bargain, by this ill management. Some, who pique themselves more upon industry than their neighbors, will, now and then, in compliment to their cattle, cut down a tree whose limbs are loaded with the moss aforementioned. The trouble would be too great to climb the tree in order to gather this provender, but the shortest way (which in this country is always counted the best) is to fell it. * * * By this bad husbandry milk is so scarce, in the winter season, that were a big-bellied woman to long for it, she would lose her longing. And, in truth, I believe this is often the case, and at the same time a very good reason why so many people in this province are marked with a custard complexion.

The only business here is raising of hogs, which is managed with the least trouble, and affords the diet they are most fond of. The truth of it is, the inhabitants of North Carolina devour so much swine's flesh, that it fills them full of gross humors. For want too of a constant supply of salt, they are commonly obliged to eat it fresh, and that begets the highest taint of scurvy. Thus, whenever a severe cold happens to constitutions thus vitiated, it is apt to improve into the yaws, called there very justly the country distemper. This has all the symptoms of syphilis, with this aggravation, that no preparation of mercury will touch it. First it seizes the throat, next the palate, and lastly shows its spite to the poor nose, of which it is apt in a small time treacherously to undermine the foundation. This calamity

3. Herodotus, the Greek historian of the fifth century B.C., one of Byrd's favorite authors, described many strange peoples encountered on his extensive travels.

is so common and familiar here, that it ceases to be a scandal, and in the disputes that happen about beauty, the noses have in some companies much ado to carry it. Nay, it is said that once, after three good pork years, a motion had like to have been made in the house of burgesses, that a man with a nose should be incapable of holding any place of profit in the province; which extraordinary motion could never have been intended without some hopes of a majority.

[Indian Neighbors]

* * * I am sorry I cannot give a better account of the state of the poor Indians with respect to Christianity, although a great deal of pains has been and still continues to be taken with them. For my part, I must be of opinion, as I hinted before, that there is but one way of converting these poor infidels, and reclaiming them from barbarity, and that is, charitably to intermarry with them, according to the modern policy of the most Christian king in Canada and Louisiana.[4] Had the English done this at the first settlement of the colony, the infidelity of the Indians had been worn out at this day, with their dark complexions, and the country had swarmed with people more than it does with insects. It was certainly an unreasonable nicety, that prevented their entering into so good-natured an alliance. All nations of men have the same natural dignity, and we all know that very bright talents may be lodged under a very dark skin. The principal difference between one people and another proceeds only from the different opportunities of improvement. The Indians by no means want understanding, and are in their figure tall and well-proportioned. Even their copper-colored complexion would admit of blanching, if not in the first, at the farthest in the second generation. I may safely venture to say, the Indian women would have made altogether as honest wives for the first planters, as the damsels they used to purchase from aboard the ships. It is strange, therefore, that any good Christian should have refused a wholesome, straight bed-fellow, when he might have had so fair a portion with her, as the merit of saving her soul.

[March 13, 1728.] This being Sunday, we rested from our fatigue, and had leisure to reflect on the signal mercies of Providence.

The great plenty of meat wherewith Bearskin[5] furnished us in these lonely woods made us once more shorten the men's allowance of bread, from five to four pounds of biscuit a week. This was the more necessary, because we knew not yet how long our business might require us to be out.

In the afternoon our hunters went forth, and returned triumphantly with three brace of wild turkeys. They told us they could

---

4. Louis XV of France, reigned 1715–1774.   5. Their Indian guide and hunter.

see the mountains distinctly from every eminence, though the atmosphere was so thick with smoke that they appeared at a greater distance than they really were.

In the evening we examined our friend Bearskin, concerning the religion of his country, and he explained it to us, without any of that reserve to which his nation is subject. He told us he believed there was one supreme God, who had several subaltern deities under him. And that this master God made the world a long time ago. That he told the sun, the moon, and stars, their business in the beginning, which they, with good looking after, have faithfully performed ever since. That the same Power that made all things at first has taken care to keep them in the same method and motion ever since. He believed that God had formed many worlds before he formed this, but that those worlds either grew old and ruinous, or were destroyed for the dishonesty of the inhabitants. That God is very just and very good—ever well pleased with those men who possess those god-like qualities. That he takes good people into his safe protection, makes them very rich, fills their bellies plentifully, preserves them from sickness, and from being surprised or overcome by their enemies. But all such as tell lies, and cheat those they have dealings with, he never fails to punish with sickness, poverty and hunger, and, after all that, suffers them to be knocked on the head and scalped by those that fight against them. He believed that after death both good and bad people are conducted by a strong guard into a great road, in which departed souls travel together for some time, till at a certain distance this road forks into two paths, the one extremely level, and the other stony and mountainous. Here the good are parted from the bad by a flash of lightning, the first being hurried away to the right, the other to the left. The right hand road leads to a charming warm country, where the spring is everlasting, and every month is May; and as the year is always in its youth, so are the people, and particularly the women are bright as stars, and never scold. That in this happy climate there are deer, turkeys, elks, and buffaloes innumerable, perpetually fat and gentle, while the trees are loaded with delicious fruit quite throughout the four seasons. That the soil brings forth corn spontaneously, without the curse of labor, and so very wholesome, that none who have the happiness to eat of it are ever sick, grow old, or die. Near the entrance into this blessed land sits a venerable old man on a mat richly woven, who examines strictly all that are brought before him, and if they have behaved well, the guards are ordered to open the crystal gate, and let them enter into the land of delight. The left hand path is very rugged and uneven, leading to a dark and barren country, where it is always winter. The ground is the whole year round covered with snow, and nothing is to be seen upon the trees but icicles. All the people are hungry, yet have not a morsel of anything to eat, except a bitter kind of potato, that gives them the dry gripes, and fills their whole body with loathsome ulcers, that stink, and are insupportably painful. Here all the women are old and ugly, having claws like a panther, with which they fly upon the men that slight their passion. For it seems these haggard old furies are intolerably fond, and expect a vast deal of cherishing. They talk much, and exceedingly shrill, giving exquisite pain to the drum of the ear, which in that place of torment is so tender, that every sharp note wounds it to the quick. At the end of this path sits a dreadful old woman on a monstrous toad-stool, whose head is covered with rattle-snakes instead of tresses, with glaring white eyes, that strike a terror unspeakable into all that behold her. This hag pronounces sentence of woe upon all the miserable wretches that hold up their hands at her tribunal. After this they are delivered over to huge turkey-buzzards, like harpies, that fly away with them to the place above mentioned. Here, after they have been tormented a certain number of years, according to their several degrees of guilt, they are again driven back into this world, to try if they will mend their manners, and merit a place the next time in the regions of bliss. This was the substance of Bearskin's religion, and was as much to the purpose as could be expected from a mere state of nature, without one glimpse of revelation or philosophy. It contained, however, the three great articles of natural religion: the belief of a God; the moral distinction betwixt good and evil; and the expectation of rewards and punishments in another world. Indeed, the Indian notion of a future happiness is a little gross and sensual, like Mahomet's paradise. But how can it be otherwise, in a people that are contented with Nature as they find her, and have no other lights but what they receive from purblind tradition?

1728   1841

From A Progress to the Mines[6]

[Reading a Play in the Backwoods]

[Sept. 20, 1732.] I continued the bark,[7] and then tossed down my poached eggs, with as much ease as some good breeders slip children into the world. About nine I left the prudentest orders I could think of with my vizier, and then crossed the river to Shacco's. I made a running visit to three of my quarters,[8] where, besides finding all the people well, I had the pleasure to see better crops than usual

6. An account of a journey to the home and iron mines of former Governor Alexander Spotswood in the highlands of western Virginia. Byrd hoped to develop the iron on his own land. Goochland, named below as a stage, was about half

the distance.
7. Suffering from a fever, he has been taking doses of "bark" (quinine) and brandy.
8. *I.e.*, the living "quarters" for the slaves.

both of corn and tobacco. I parted there with my intendant, and pursued my journey to Mr. Randolph's, at Tuckahoe, without meeting with any adventure by the way. Here I found Mrs. Fleming, who was packing up her baggage with design to follow her husband the next day, who was gone to a new settlement in Goochland. Both he and she have been about seven years persuading themselves to remove to that retired part of the country, though they had the two strong arguments of health and interest for so doing. The widow smiled graciously upon me, and entertained me very handsomely. Here I learned all the tragical story of her daughter's humble marriage with her uncle's overseer. Besides the meanness of this mortal's aspect, the man has not one visible qualification, except impudence, to recommend him to a female's inclinations. But there is sometimes such a charm in that Hibernian endowment, that frail woman cannot withstand it, though it stand alone without any other recommendation. Had she run away with a gentleman or a pretty fellow, there might have been some excuse for her, though he were of inferior fortune: but to stoop to a dirty plebeian, without any kind of merit, is the lowest prostitution. I found the family justly enraged at it; and though I had more good nature than to join in her condemnation, yet I could devise no excuse for so senseless a prank as this young gentlewoman had played. Here good drink was more scarce than good victuals, the family being reduced to the last bottle of wine, which was therefore husbanded very carefully. But the water was excellent. The heir of the family did not come home till late in the evening. He is a pretty young man, but had the misfortune to become his own master too soon. This puts young fellows upon wrong pursuits, before they have sense to judge rightly for themselves. Though at the same time they have a strange conceit of their own sufficiency, when they grow near twenty years old, especially if they happen to have a small smattering of learning. It is then they fancy themselves wiser than all their tutors and governors, which makes them headstrong to all advice, and above all reproof and admonition.

[Sept. 21, 1732.] I was sorry in the morning to find myself stopped in my career by bad weather brought upon us by a northeast wind. This drives a world of raw unkindly vapors upon us from Newfoundland, laden with blight, coughs, and pleurisies. However, I complained not, lest I might be suspected to be tired of the good company. Though Mrs. Fleming was not so much upon her guard, but mutinied strongly at the rain, that hindered her from pursuing her dear husband. I said what I could to comfort a gentlewoman under so sad a disappointment. I told her a husband, that stayed so much at home as her's did, could be no such violent rarity, as for a woman to venture her precious health, to go daggling through the rain after him, or to be miserable if she happened to be prevented. That it was prudent for married people to fast sometimes from one another, that they might come together again with the better stomach. That the best things in this world, if constantly used, are apt to be cloying, which a little absence and abstinence would prevent. This was strange doctrine to a fond female, who fancies people should love with as little reason after marriage as before. In the afternoon monsieur Marij, the minister of the parish, came to make me a visit. He had been a Romish priest, but found reasons, either spiritual or temporal, to quit that gay religion. The fault of this new convert is, that he looks for as much respect from his protestant flock, as is paid to the popish clergy, which our ill-bred Hugonots do not understand. Madam Marij had so much curiosity as to want to come too; but another horse was wanting, and she believed it would have too vulgar an air to ride behind her husband. This woman was of the true exchange breed, full of discourse, but void of discretion, and married a parson, with the idle hopes he might some time or other come to be his grace of Canterbury. The gray mare is the better horse in that family, and the poor man submits to her wild vagaries for peace' sake. She has just enough of the fine lady to run in debt, and be of no signification in her household. And the only thing that can prevent her from undoing her loving husband will be, that nobody will trust them beyond the sixteen thousand,[9] which is soon run out in a Goochland store. The way of dealing there is for some small merchant or peddler to buy a Scots pennyworth of goods, and clap one hundred and fifty per cent. upon that. At this rate the parson cannot be paid much more for his preaching than it is worth. No sooner was our visitor retired, but the facetious widow was so kind as to let me into all this secret history, but was at the same time exceedingly sorry that the woman should be so indiscreet, and and the man so tame as to be governed by an unprofitable and fantastical wife.

[Sept. 22, 1732.] We had another wet day, to try both Mrs. Fleming's patience and my good breeding. The northeast wind commonly sticks by us three or four days, filling the atmosphere with damps, injurious both to man and beast. The worst of it was, we had no good liquor to warm our blood, and fortify our spirits against so strong a malignity. However, I was cheerful under all these misfortunes, and expressed no concern but a decent fear lest my long visit might be troublesome. Since I was like to have thus much leisure, I endeavored to find out what subject a dull married man could introduce that might best bring the widow to the use of her tongue. At length I discovered she was a notable quack, and therefore paid that regard to

9. *I.e.*, "sixteen thousand" pounds of tobacco, as this country clergyman's salary was reckoned.

her knowledge, as to put some questions to her about the bad distemper that raged then in the country. I mean the bloody flux, that was brought us in the negro-ship consigned to Col. Braxton. She told me she made use of very simple remedies in that case, with very good success. She did the business either with hartshorn drink, that had plantain leaves boiled in it, or else with a strong decoction of St. Andrew's cross, in new milk instead of water. I agreed with her that those remedies might be very good, but would be more effectual after a dose or two of Indian physic. But for fear this conversation might be too grave for a widow, I turned the discourse, and began to talk of plays, and finding her taste lay most towards comedy, I offered my service to read one to her, which she kindly accepted. She produced the second part of the Beggar's Opera,[1] which had diverted the town for forty nights successively, and gained four thousand pounds to the author. This was not owing altogether to the wit or humor that sparkled in it, but to some political reflections, that seemed to hit the ministry. But the great advantage of the author was, that his interest was solicited by the dutchess of Queensbury, which no man could refuse who had but half an eye in his head,[2] or half a guinea in his pocket. Her grace, like death, spared nobody, but even took my lord Selkirk[3] in for two guineas, to repair which extravagance he lived upon Scots herrings two months afterwards. But the best story was, she made a very smart officer in his majesty's guards give her a guinea, who swearing at the same time it was all he had in the world, she sent him fifty for it the next day, to reward his obedience. After having acquainted my company with the history of the play, I read three acts of it, and left Mrs. Fleming and Mr. Randolph to finish it, who read as well as most actors do at a rehearsal. Thus we killed the time, and triumphed over the bad weather.

1732   1841

1. *The Beggar's Opera*, by John Gay (1685–1732), on the London stage in 1728, had proved one of the most successful of British plays.
2. In the tradition of that age of literary patronage, the Duchess became his patroness, and Gay passed several years,

before his death at forty-seven, in the household of the Duke of Queensberry.
3. The first earl of Selkirk, William Douglas, of the ancient Scottish line; the jest concerning the frugality of the Scots is perennial.

JOHN WOOLMAN
(1720–1772)

John Woolman's *Journal* (1774) is a "Quaker classic of the inner Light," and countless non-

Quaker readers have been touched by its "exquisite purity and grace." Among the enduring autobiographies of the world, it shines apart, one of the few in which the record of the temporal life radiates a wholly spiritual and eternal light. The sentence with which, at thirty-six, Woolman began his *Journal*, contains the clue to its perfect candor and purity: "I have often felt a motion of love to leave some hints in writing of my experience of the goodness of God."

Such a vision of the interpenetration of the divine with the human had enkindled the evangelism of George Fox in England, about 1650. His followers called themselves Friends but found an unfriendly world, for they were double-dyed dissenters, differing both from the established church and from the Puritan sects. The American Puritans, themselves fugitives from persecution, had grievously persecuted the Quakers, whose "heresies" certainly threatened a hierarchy founded on belief in original depravity, predestination, and limited election for salvation by grace. Quakers believed that Christ was the atonement for all mankind's sins, that the "inward light" of God's immanence was available to all who sought "in the spirit and in truth."

Woolman's *Journal* is clearer to the reader who understands these principles of the Quakers, and their other fundamental testimony, that of quietness. The hysterical outbreaks of revivalism which marked the Puritan history are rare in the Quaker records; the Quaker trusted his "light" only in the controlled retrospect of his judg-

ment. This is nowhere better illustrated than in Woolman's strict discipline of impulsive "concerns" by means of "religious exercise" and the "draught" or "leading" of his mind. That this discipline of responsibility inevitably compelled Friends toward the service of the human community is illustrated by Woolman's unflagging interest in the whole life about him. For the Quaker mystic, salvation did not await a millennium; mortal and immortal life were wonderfully and strangely one. Woolman's *Journal* reveals those Quaker characteristics which have given the Friends an astonishing leadership, considering their numerical meagerness, in American thought and social action from the time of Penn to the present.

John Woolman was born in 1720, on a farm on the Rancocas in New Jersey, twenty miles from the Quaker city of the Penns. The young farmer experienced a growing companionship with nature, and a quietness favorable to the natural unfolding of a spirit essentially mystical. For his education there was the dame school, the Bible, the journals of Friends, some of them truly inspired, and always the close-knit community of the Quaker family and its meeting. At twenty he became a shopkeeper in nearby Mount Holly, and also learned the trade of the tailor. He prospered in his business and in his marriage, while his vocation soon led to his being "recorded" as a minister— the Friends' way of acknowledging by consensus the acceptability of the voluntary ministry that then provided their only leadership.

As his religious vocation grew, Woolman was led, at the age of thirty-six, to give up his shop altogether and live upon the income from intermittent tailoring, which provided sufficient means for his frugal life. Thus he was enabled to respond to his evangelical "concern"; he made extensive visitations among Friends throughout the colonies, sometimes for months at a time, preaching the way of "Divine Love." In his ministry and in the tracts which he published from time to time, he became a force in the growing movement for toleration; he attacked the economic exploitation which was already producing poverty and wretchedness among the masses; he preached unceasingly against slavery, and published one of the earliest works in the American literature of abolition. He led the movement which secured the freedom of slaves held by American Quakers—the first general emancipation of slaves in America. The abolition of slavery was one of the concerns which he carried abroad in 1772, on a visit to the Friends' Meetings in England. In protest against the poverty of the British workers and the cruel conditions imposed upon the coachmen, he traveled through England on foot, preaching at various Meetings. In York he was taken ill, and he died of smallpox on October 7, 1772, less than a month after the last entries made in his Journal.

Within two years The Works of John Woolman (Philadelphia, 1774) were published, including the Journal and his most important essays. That those responsible for this edition felt it desirable to "improve" Woolman's style is actually a mark of its individualistic distinction. In the presence of such straightforward language as Woolman wrote, rhetorical precisions often retire abashed. In the two revisions of his Journal manuscript he only sought, like George Fox, the Quaker founder, better to "use plainness of speech" to reveal the daily goodness of God. His writing is as plain as the best Friends' meetinghouse, and beautiful in the same way. In his style, his inward peace was the shaping element; if he was an artist, it was by nature. His passion for humanity and God was so great that only simplicity could contain it.

The standard collection is The Journal and Essays of John Woolman, edited by Amelia M. Gummere, 1922. This contains a biography. Other biographies are W. T. Shore, John Woolman, His Life and Our Times, 1913; and Janet Whitney, John Woolman, American Quaker, 1942. For material on the Society of Friends, see Rufus M. Jones, The Quakers in the American Colonies, 1921; and Elbert Russell, The History of Quakerism, 1942. Since Woolman left two revisions of the manuscript of the Journal, and since the first edition of the Works, 1774, was not accurate, it is natural that many variant readings appear in the more than forty editions that have been published in America and England. The edition published in Boston in 1871, with an introduction by John G. Whittier, provides a sound text based on the last manuscript, and we have followed it in our selections.

From The Journal of John Woolman

[*Quaker Faith and Practice*]

I was born in Northampton, in Burlington county, West-Jersey,[1] in the year 1720; and before I was seven years old I began to be acquainted with the operations of divine love. Through the care of my parents, I was taught to read nearly as soon as I was capable of it; and, as I went from school one seventh day,[2] I remember, while my companions went to play by the way, I went forward out of sight, and, sitting down, I read the 22d chapter of the Revelations. "He shewed me a pure river of water of life, clear as chrystal, proceeding out of the throne of God and of the lamb, &c." and, in reading it, my mind was drawn to seek after that pure habitation, which, I then believed, God had prepared for his servants. The place where I sat, and the sweetness that attended my mind, remain fresh in my memory.

This, and the like gracious visitations, had that effect upon me, that when boys used ill language it troubled me; and, through the continued mercies of God, I was preserved from it.

The pious instructions of my parents were often fresh in my mind when I happened to be among wicked children, and were of use to me. My parents, having a large family of children, used frequently, on first days after meeting,[3] to put us to read in the holy scriptures, or some religious books, one after another, the rest sitting by without much conversation; which, I have since often thought, was a good practice. From what I had read and heard, I believed there had been, in past ages, people who walked in uprightness before God, in a degree exceeding any that I knew, or heard of, now living; and the apprehension of there being less steadiness and firmness, amongst people in this age than in past ages, often troubled me while I was a child.

A thing remarkable in my childhood was, that once, going to a neighbour's house, I saw, on the way, a robin sitting on her nest, and as I came near she went off, but, having young ones, flew about, and with many cries expressed her concern for them; I stood and threw stones at her, till, one striking her, she fell down dead: at first I was pleased with the exploit, but after a few minutes was seized with horror, as having, in a sportive way, killed an innocent creature while she was careful for her young: I beheld her lying dead, and thought those young ones, for which she was so careful, must now

1. The colonial "Jerseys" included East Jersey and West Jersey. The Woolman plantation (farm) was near Mount Holly, site of an early Quaker community affiliated with the Philadelphia Friends, twenty miles distant.

2. *I.e.,* Saturday. Quakers substituted numbers for the usual names of the days of the week, both to gain simplicity and to avoid celebration of pagan gods.

3. Quakers, like the early Puritans, replaced the formal "church" by a simple "meetinghouse."

perish for want of their dam to nourish them; and, after some painful considerations on the subject, I climbed up the tree, took all the young birds, and killed them; supposing that better than to leave them to pine away and die miserably: and believed, in this case, that scripture-proverb was fulfilled, "The tender mercies of the wicked are cruel."[4] I then went on my errand, but, for some hours, could think of little else but the cruelties I had committed, and was much troubled. Thus He, whose tender mercies are over all his works, hath placed a principle in the human mind, which incites to exercise goodness towards every living creature; and this being singly attended to, people become tender-hearted and sympathising; but, being frequently and totally rejected, the mind becomes shut up in a contrary disposition.

About the twelfth year of my age, my father being abroad,[5] my mother reproved me for some misconduct, to which I made an undutiful reply; and, the next first day, as I was with my father returning from meeting, he told me he understood I had behaved amiss to my mother, and advised me to be more careful in future. I knew myself blameable, and in shame and confusion remained silent. Being thus awakened to a sense of my wickedness, I felt remorse in my mind, and, getting home, I retired and prayed to the Lord to forgive me; and do not remember that I ever, after that, spoke unhandsomely to either of my parents, however foolish in some other things. * * *

Advancing in age, the number of my acquaintances increased, and thereby my way grew more difficult; though I had found comfort in reading the holy scriptures, and thinking on heavenly things, I was now estranged therefrom: I knew I was going from the flock of Christ, and had no resolution to return; hence serious reflections were uneasy to me, and youthful vanities and diversions my greatest pleasure. Running in this road I found many like myself; and we associated in that which is the reverse to true friendship.[6]

But in this swift race it pleased God to visit me with sickness, so that I doubted of recovering; and then did darkness, horror, and amazement, with full force, seize me, even when my pain and distress of body was very great. I thought it would have been better for me never to have had a being, than to see the day which I now saw. I was filled with confusion; and in great affliction, both of mind and body, I lay and bewailed myself. I had not confidence to lift up my cries to God, whom I had thus offended; but, in a deep sense of my great folly, I was humbled before him; and, at length, that word which is as a fire and a hammer, broke and dissolved my rebellious

4. Proverbs xii: 10, "A righteous man regardeth the life of his beast: but the tender mercies of the wicked are cruel."
5. Then meaning "away from home."

6. The people known as Quakers called themselves Friends, or officially, the Religious Society of Friends.

heart,[7] and then my cries were put up in contrition; and in the multitude of his mercies I found inward relief, and felt a close engagement, that, if he was pleased to restore my health, I might walk humbly before him.

After my recovery, this exercise[8] remained with me a considerable time; but, by degrees, giving way to youthful vanities, they gained strength, and, getting with wanton[9] young people, I lost ground. The Lord had been very gracious, and spoke peace to me in the time of my distress; and I now most ungratefully turned again to folly; on which account, at times, I felt sharp reproof. I was not so hardy as to commit things scandalous; but to exceed in vanity, and promote mirth, was my chief study. Still I retained a love for pious people, and their company brought an awe upon me. My dear parents, several times, admonished me in the fear of the Lord, and their admonition entered into my heart, and had a good effect for a season; but, not getting deep enough to pray rightly, the tempter, when he came, found entrance. I remember once, having spent a part of the day in wantonness, as I went to bed at night, there lay in a window, near my bed, a Bible, which I opened, and first cast my eye on this text, "We lie down in our shame, and our confusion covers us":[1] this I knew to be my case: and, meeting with so unexpected a reproof, I was somewhat affected with it, and went to bed under remorse of conscience; which I soon cast off again.

Thus time passed on: my heart was replenished with mirth and wantonness, and pleasing scenes of vanity were presented to my imagination, till I attained the age of eighteen years; near which time I felt the judgements of God, in my soul, like a consuming fire; and, looking over my past life, the prospect was moving.—I was often sad, and longed to be delivered from those vanities; then again, my heart was strongly inclined to them, and there was in me a sore conflict: at times I turned to folly, and then again, sorrow and confusion took hold of me. In a while, I resolved totally to leave off some of my vanities; but there was a secret reserve, in my heart, of the more refined part of them, and I was not low enough to find true peace. Thus, for some months, I had great troubles; there remaining in me an unsubjected will, which rendered my labours fruitless, till at length, through the merciful continuance of heavenly visitations, I was made to bow down in spirit before the Lord. I remember one evening I had spent some time in reading a pious author; and, walking out alone, I humbly prayed to the Lord for his help, that I might be delivered from all those vanities which so ensnared me. Thus,

7. *Cf.* Jeremiah xxiii: 29: "Is not my word like as a fire? saith the Lord; and like a hammer that breaketh the rock in pieces?"

8. In the language of Friends, an experience or act conducive to religious faith.

9. Here meaning "worldly."

1. Jeremiah iii: 25.

being brought low, he helped me; and, as I learned to bear the cross, I felt refreshment to come from his presence; but, not keeping in that strength which gave victory, I lost ground again; the sense of which great affected me: and I sought desarts and lonely places, and there, with tears, did confess my sins to God, and humbly craved help of him. And I may say, with reverence, he was near to me in my troubles, and in those times of humiliation opened my ear to discipline. I was now led to look seriously at the means by which I was drawn from the pure truth, and learned this, that, if I would live in the life which the faithful servants of God lived in, I must not go into company as heretofore in my own will; but all the cravings of sense must be governed by a divine principle. In times of sorrow and abasement these instructions were sealed upon me, and I felt the power of Christ prevail over selfish desires, so that I was preserved in a good degree of steadiness; and, being young, and believing at that time that a single life was best for me, I was strengthened to keep from such company as had often been a snare to me.

I kept steadily to meetings; spent first day afternoons chiefly in reading the scriptures and other good books; and was early convinced, in my mind, that true religion consisted in an inward life, wherein the heart doth love and reverence God the Creator, and learns to exercise true justice and goodness, not only toward all men, but also toward the brute creatures.—That as the mind was moved, by an inward principle, to love God as an invisible incomprehensible Being, by the same principle it was moved to love him in all his manifestations in the visible world.—That, as by his breath the flame of life was kindled in all animal sensible creatures, to say we love God, and, at the same time exercise cruelty toward the least creature, is a contradiction in itself.

I found no narrowness respecting sects and opinions; but believed, that sincere upright-hearted people, in every society who truly love God, were accepted of him.

As I lived under the cross, and simply followed the openings[2] of truth, my mind, from day to day, was more enlightened; my former acquaintance were left to judge of me as they would, for I found it safest for me to live in private, and keep these things sealed up in my own breast. While I silently ponder on that change wrought in me, I find no language equal to it, nor any means to convey to another a clear idea of it. I looked upon the works of God in this visible creation, and an awfulness covered me; my heart was tender and often contrite, and universal love to my fellow-creatures increased in me: this will be understood by such as have trodden the same path. Some glances of real beauty may be seen in their faces, who dwell in true meakness.

There is a harmony in the sound of that voice to which divine

2. In the language of Friends, the intuitions or revelations of truth.

love gives utterance, and some appearance of right order in their temper and conduct, whose passions are regulated; yet all these do not fully shew forth that inward life to such as have not felt it: But this white stone[3] and new name is known rightly to such only as have it.

Though I have been thus strengthened to bear the cross, I still found myself in great danger, having many weaknesses attending me, and strong temptations to wrestle with; in the feeling whereof I frequently withdrew into private places, and often with tears besought the Lord to help me, whose gracious ear was open to my cry.

All this time I lived with my parents, and wrought on the plantation; and, having had schooling pretty well for a planter, I used to improve it in winter-evenings, and other leisure times; and, being now in the twenty-first year of my age, a man, in much business at shop-keeping and baking, asked me, if I would hire with him to tend shop and keep books. I acquainted my father with the proposal; and, after some deliberation, it was agreed for me to go.

At home I had lived retired; and now, having a prospect of being much in the way of company, I felt frequent and fervent cries in my heart to God, the father of mercies, that he would preserve me from all corruption; that in this more publick employment, I might serve him, my gracious Redeemer, in that humility and self-denial, with which I had been, in a small degree, exercised in a more private life. The man, who employed me, furnished a shop in Mount-Holly, about five miles from my father's house, and six from his own; and there I lived alone, and tended his shop. Shortly after my settlement here I was visited by several young people, my former acquaintance, who knew not but vanities would be as agreeable to me now as ever; and, at these times, I cried to the Lord, in secret, for wisdom and strength; for I felt myself encompassed with difficulties, and had fresh occasion to bewail the follies of time past, in contracting a familiarity with libertine people: and, as I had now left my father's house outwardly, I found my heavenly Father to be merciful to me beyond what I can express.

By day I was much amongst people, and had many trials to go through; but, in the evenings, I was mostly alone, and may with thankfulness acknowledge, that, in those times, the spirit of supplication was often poured upon me; under which I was frequently exercised, and felt my strength renewed.

In a few months after I came here, my master bought several Scotchmen, servants from on-board a vessel,[4] and brought them to Mount-Holly to sell; one of which was taken sick, and died.

---

3. Revelation ii: 17: "To him that overcometh will I give * * * a white stone, and in the stone a new name written * * * "

4. He bought the Scotsmen's indentures —the negotiable legal agreements by which servants were "bound" to work for a specified term of years to repay their passage to America.

In the latter part of his sickness, he, being delirious, used to curse and swear most sorrowfully; and, the next night after his burial, I was left to sleep alone in the same chamber where he died; I perceived in me a timorousness; I knew, however, I had not injured the man, but assisted in taking care of him according to my capacity; and was not free to ask any one, on that occasion, to sleep with me. Nature was feeble; but every trial was a fresh incitement to give myself up wholly to the service of God, for I found no helper like him in times of trouble. After a while, my former acquaintance gave over expecting me as one of their company; and I began to be known to some whose conversation was helpful to me: and now, as I had experienced the love of God, through Jesus Christ, to redeem me from many pollutions, and to be a succour to me through a sea of conflicts, with which no person was fully acquainted; and as my heart was often enlarged in this heavenly principle, I felt a tender compassion for the youth, who remained entangled in snares, like those which had entangled me from one time to another: this love and tenderness increased; and my mind was more strongly engaged for the good of my fellow-creatures. I went to meetings in an awful frame of mind, and endeavoured to be inwardly acquainted with the language of the true Shepherd; and, one day, being under a strong exercise of spirit, I stood up, and said some words in a meeting; but, not keeping close to the divine opening, I said more than was required of me; and being soon sensible of my error, I was afflicted in mind some weeks, without any light or comfort, even to that degree that I could not take satisfaction in any thing: I remembered God, and was troubled, and, in the depth of my distress, he had pity upon me, and sent the Comforter. I then felt forgiveness for my offence, and my mind became calm and quiet, being truly thankful to my gracious Redeemer for his mercies; and, after this, feeling the spring of divine love opened, and a concern[5] to speak, I said a few words in a meeting, in which I found peace; this, I believe, was about six weeks from the first time: and, as I was thus humbled and disciplined under the cross, my understanding became more strengthened to distinguish the pure spirit which inwardly moves upon the heart,[6] and taught me to wait in silence sometimes many weeks together, until I felt that rise which prepares the creature.

[Cases of Conscience]

About the twenty-third year of my age, I had many fresh and heavenly openings, in respect to the care and providence of the Almighty

5. In the Friends' terminology, a compelling inward motivation for an action or message approved by the judgment.
6. Friends hold themselves responsible to an "inward light" which, however, is genuine only when "disciplined understanding" distinguishes between selfish desire and the immanent radiance of God.

over his creatures in general, and over man as the most noble amongst those which are visible. And being clearly convinced in my judgement, that to place my whole trust in God was best for me, I felt renewed engagements, that in all things I might act on an inward principle of virtue, and pursue worldly business no farther, than as truth opened my way therein.

About the time called Christmas,[7] I observed many people from the country, and dwellers in town, who, resorting to public-houses, spent their time in drinking and vain sports, tending to corrupt one another; on which account I was much troubled. At one house, in particular, there was much disorder; and I believed it was a duty incumbent on me to go and speak to the master of that house. I considered I was young, and that several elderly friends in town had opportunity to see these things; but though I would gladly have been excused, yet I could not feel my mind clear.

The exercise was heavy: and as I was reading what the Almighty said to Ezekiel, respecting his duty as a watchman,[8] the matter was set home more clearly; and then, with prayers and tears, I besought the Lord for his assistance, who in loving-kindness, gave me a resigned heart: then, at a suitable opportunity, I went to the public-house; and, seeing the man amongst much company, I went to him, and told him, I wanted to speak with him; so we went aside, and there, in the fear of the Almighty, I expressed to him what rested on my mind; which he took kindly, and afterward shewed more regard to me than before. In a few years afterwards he died, middle-aged; and I often thought that, had I neglected my duty in that case, it would have given me great trouble; and I was humbly thankful to my gracious Father, who had supported me herein.

My employer having a negro woman, sold her, and desired me to write a bill of sale, the man being waiting who bought her: the thing was sudden; and, though the thoughts of writing an instrument of slavery for one of my fellow-creatures felt uneasy, yet I remembered I was hired by the year, that it was my master who directed me to do it, and that it was an elderly man, a member of our society,[9] who bought her; so, through weakness, I gave way, and wrote; but, at the executing it, I was so afflicted in my mind, that I said, before my master and the friend, that I believed slave-keeping to be a practice inconsistent with the Christian religion. This in some degree abated my uneasiness; yet, as often as I reflected seriously upon it, I thought I should have been clearer, if I had desired to have been excused from it, as a thing against my conscience; for such it was. And, some time

7. Early Friends ignored all special holidays, because they considered all days holy.
8. Ezekiel iii: 17, "Son of man, I have made thee a watchman unto the house of Israel: therefore hear the word at my mouth, and give them warning from me."
9. The Society of Friends. Woolman later led the successful movement to liberate the slaves held by Quakers—the first American emancipation.

after this, a young man, of our society, spoke to me to write a conveyance of a slave to him, he having lately taken a negro into his house: I told him I was not easy to write it; for, though many of our meeting and in other places kept slaves, I still believed the practice was not right, and desired to be excused from the writing. I spoke to him in good will; and he told me that keeping slaves was not altogether agreeable to his mind; but that the slave being a gift to his wife, he had accepted of her.

Until the year 1756, I continued to retail goods, besides following my trade as a tailor; about which time I grew uneasy on account of my business growing too cumbersome. I began with selling trimmings for garments, and from thence proceeded to sell cloths and linens; and at length, having got a considerable shop of goods, my trade increased every year, and the road to large business appeared open: but I felt a stop in my mind.

Through the mercies of the Almighty, I had, in a good degree, learned to be content with a plain way of living.[1] I had but a small family; and on serious reflection, I believed Truth did not require me to engage in many cumbering affairs. It had generally been my practice to buy and sell things really useful. Things that served chiefly to please the vain mind in people, I was not easy to trade in; seldom did it, and whenever I did, I found it to weaken me as a Christian.

The increase of business became my burthen; for though my natural inclination was toward merchandise, yet I believed Truth required me to live more free from outward cumbers. There was now a strife in my mind betwixt the two, and in this exercise my prayers were put up to the Lord, who graciously heard me, and gave me a heart resigned to his holy will; I then lessened my outward business; and as I had opportunity, told my customers of my intention, that they might consider what shop to turn to; and so in a while, wholly laid down merchandise, following my trade as a tailor, myself only, having no prentice. I also had a nursery of apple trees, in which I spent a good deal of time hoeing, grafting, trimming, and inoculating.

In merchandise it is the custom, where I lived, to sell chiefly on credit, and poor people often get in debt; and when payment is expected, having not wherewith to pay, and so their creditors often sue for it at law. Having often observed occurrences of this kind, I found it good for me to advise poor people to take such goods as were most useful and not costly.

In the time of trading, I had an opportunity of seeing that a too liberal use of spirituous liquors, and the custom of wearing too costly apparel, led some people into great inconveniences; and these two

1. Friends adopted "plainness," not to achieve asceticism, but to retain "the simplicity that is in Christ" described by Paul (II Corinthians xi: 3, and i: 12).

things appear to be often connected one with the other; for by not attending to that use of things which is consistent with universal righteousness, there is an increase of labor which extends beyond what our heavenly Father intends for us; and by great labor, and often by much sweating in the heat, there is, even among such who are not drunkards, a craving of some liquor to revive the spirits; that, partly by the luxurious drinking of some, and partly by the drinking of others, led to it through immoderate labor, very great quantities of rum are annually expended in our colonies; of which we should have no need, did we steadily attend to pure wisdom.

Where men take pleasure in feeling their minds elevated with strong drink, and so indulge this appetite as to disorder their understanding, neglect their duty as members in a family or civil society, and cast off all pretence to religion, their case is much to be pitied; and where such whose lives are for the most part regular, and whose examples have a strong influence on the minds of others, adhere to some customs which powerfully draw toward the use of more strong liquor than pure wisdom directeth the use of; this also, as it hinders the spreading of the spirit of meekness, and strengthens the hands of the more excessive drinkers, is a case to be lamented.

As every degree of luxury hath some connection with evil; for those who profess to be disciples of Christ, and are looked upon as leaders of the people, to have that mind in them, which was also in Christ, and so stand separate from every wrong way, is a means of help to the weaker. * * * I have felt an increasing care to attend to that holy Spirit which sets right bounds to our desires, and leads those who faithfully follow it, to apply all the gifts of Divine Providence to the purposes for which they were intended.

1756   1774

ST. JEAN DE CRÈVECŒUR
(1735–1813)

During the two decades before the Revolution, one of the most enthusiastic interpreters of the nascent American democracy was a visiting French aristocrat. Crèvecœur's discovery of the new world filled him with boundless excitement. As soldier of fortune, surveyor, and traveler, he went far and wide; and his observations provide some of the best surviving pictures of the diversity of tongues and types, the sharp contrasts of social behavior and local customs, that soon were to be welded into a new nation by common need and a common experience.

St. Jean de Crèvecœur (christened Michel-Guillaume Jean de Crèvecœur), born of a distinguished and ancient family near Caen, was educated strictly but well in a Jesuit school, and then visited England. At the age of nineteen he was in Canada, a lieutenant in the French army under Montcalm. In this service he surveyed and mapped large areas around the Great Lakes and in the Ohio country. He was in New York by 1759; he later roamed, an observant pilgrim, through the frontiers of New York, Pennsylvania, and the southern colonies. He became a citizen of New York in 1765, soon acquired a plantation in Orange County some sixty miles from the city, and married in 1769. There he remained, a successful planter, until the Revolution, writing down his impressions of rural America, "a land of happy farmers" and a haven of equality and freedom for the oppressed and dispossessed of Europe.

In spite of these liberal enthusiasms, his training was aristocratic, and he had sworn allegiance to Britain; his mildly Tory inclinations appear repeatedly in the *Letters*, particularly in those that he suppressed in his lifetime. In this equivocal mood he found himself suspected by both sides, and returned to France in 1780. *Letters from an American Farmer* appeared in London two years later; an enlarged but sentimentalized version in French was published in Paris in 1783. Volumes of letters and journals were then enormously popular,

and Crèvecœur's had the added advantage of topical interest. They were widely read on the continent and in England, and their author became, for a time, a celebrity in the flourishing literary world of Paris.

The influence of Franklin and French friends secured his appointment as French consul to New York, New Jersey, and Connecticut. He returned to America in 1783, to find his wife dead, his children adopted by a Boston family, and his plantation home wrecked by an Indian raid. Until 1790 he remained in New York, devoting himself to the cause of good relations between his mother country and his adopted land. The last twenty-three years of his life were spent in his ancestral Normandy. His only later publication was the *Voyage dans la Haute Pensylvanie et dans l'État de New-York* (1801). His suppressed letters from the earlier series remained unpublished and forgotten until their rediscovery by American scholars resulted in the *Sketches of Eighteenth Century America* (1925).

Crèvecœur exemplifies a number of ideals prevalent both in America and in Europe during the late eighteenth century. He subscribed in some degree to Rousseau's idealization of natural man as inherently good when free, and subject to corruption only by artificial urban society. He was an anticlerical like Thomas Paine, with a strong distrust for organized religion. Along with Jefferson and Franklin he held the physiocratic faith that agriculture was the basis of our economy; and he believed in humanitarian action to correct such abuses as slavery, civil disturbance, war, and the poverty of the masses.

Certain critics of his *Letters* have disparaged him as a sentimentalist. More sympathetic examination reveals the humanitarian whose pictures of America have by no means lost their interest through the long years.

A good and available edition of Crèvecœur is the *Letters from an American Farmer*, edited by W. P. Trent and Ludwig Lewisohn, 1904; see also *Sketches of Eighteenth Century America*, edited by H. L. Bourdin, R. H. Gabriel, and S. T. Williams, 1925. For biography and criticism, see Julia P. Mitchell, *St. Jean de Crèvecœur*, 1916; H. C. Rice, *Le Cultivateur Americain: Etude sur L'Œuvre de Saint John de Crèvecœur*, 1933; and the essay by Stanley T. Williams in the *Dictionary of American Biography*, 1930.

From Letters from an American Farmer

What Is an American?[1]

I wish I could be acquainted with the feelings and thoughts which must agitate the heart and present themselves to the mind of an enlightened Englishman, when he first lands on this continent. He must greatly rejoice that he lived at a time to see this fair country discovered[2] and settled; he must necessarily feel a share of national pride, when he views the chain of settlements which embellishes these extended shores. When he says to himself, this is the work of my countrymen, who, when convulsed by factions, afflicted by a variety of miseries and wants, restless and impatient, took refuge here. They brought along with them their national genius, to which they principally owe what liberty they enjoy, and what substance they possess. Here he sees the industry of his native country displayed in a new manner, and traces in their works the embryos of all the arts, sciences, and ingenuity which flourish in Europe. Here he beholds fair cities, substantial villages, extensive fields, an immense country filled with decent houses, good roads, orchards, meadows, and bridges, where an hundred years ago all was wild, woody, and uncultivated! What a train of pleasing ideas this fair spectacle must suggest; it is a prospect which must inspire a good citizen with the most heartfelt pleasure. The difficulty consists in the manner of viewing so extensive a scene. He is arrived on a new continent; a modern society offers itself to his contemplation, different from what he had hitherto seen. It is not composed, as in Europe, of great lords who possess everything, and of a herd of people who have nothing. Here are no aristocratical

1. Title of the third Letter (or essay), reproduced in part in this volume. The first three of the twelve Letters provide a discussion of American life and ideals in general. Four deal with the island of Nantucket—its topography, industry, social life, education, manners, and customs. One describes Martha's Vineyard and its whaling life; another, on Charleston, South Carolina, contains an attack on slavery. The book concludes with three essays including observations of nature, an account of a visit with John Bartram, the Philadelphia naturalist, and a final commentary on various subjects, showing a Tory bias.
2. Explored.

families, no courts, no kings, no bishops, no ecclesiastical dominion, no invisible power giving to a few a very visible one; no great manufacturers employing thousands, no great refinements of luxury. The rich and the poor are not so far removed from each other as they are in Europe. Some few towns excepted, we are all tillers of the earth, from Nova Scotia to West Florida. We are a people of cultivators, scattered over an immense territory, communicating with each other by means of good roads and navigable rivers, united by the silken bands of mild government, all respecting the laws, without dreading their power, because they are equitable. We are all animated with the spirit of an industry which is unfettered and unrestrained, because each person works for himself. If he travels through our rural districts he views not the hostile castle, and the haughty mansion, contrasted with the clay-built hut and miserable cabin, where cattle and men help to keep each other warm, and dwell in meanness, smoke, and indigence. A pleasing uniformity of recent competence appears throughout our habitations. The meanest of our log-houses is a dry and comfortable habitation. Lawyer or merchant are the fairest titles our towns afford; that of a farmer is the only appellation of the rural inhabitants of our country. It must take some time ere he can reconcile himself to our dictionary, which is but short in words of dignity, and names of honour. There, on a Sunday, he sees a congregation of respectable farmers and their wives, all clad in neat homespun, well mounted, or riding in their own humble waggons. There is not among them an esquire, saving the unlettered magistrate. There he sees a parson as simple as his flock, a farmer who does not riot on the labour of others. We have no princes, for whom we toil, starve, and bleed: we are the most perfect society now existing in the world. Here man is free as he ought to be; nor is this pleasing equality so transitory as many others are. Many ages will not see the shores of our great lakes replenished with inland nations, nor the unknown bounds of North America entirely peopled. Who can tell how far it extends? Who can tell the millions of men whom it will feed and contain? for no European foot has as yet travelled half the extent of this mighty continent!

The next wish of this traveller will be to know whence came all these people? they are a mixture of English, Scotch, Irish, French, Dutch, Germans, and Swedes. From this promiscuous breed, that race now called Americans have arisen. The eastern provinces [3] must indeed be excepted, as being the unmixed descendants of Englishmen. I have heard many wish that they had been more intermixed also: for my part, I am no wisher, and think it much better as it has happened. They exhibit a most conspicuous figure in this great and variegated picture; they too enter for a great share in the pleasing perspective displayed in these thirteen provinces. I know it is fashion-

3. New England.

able to reflect on them, but I respect them for what they have done; for the accuracy and wisdom with which they have settled their territory; for the decency of their manners; for their early love of letters; their ancient college,[4] the first in this hemisphere; for their industry; which to me who am but a farmer, is the criterion of everything. There never was a people, situated as they are, who with so ungrateful a soil have done more in so short a time. Do you think that the monarchical ingredients which are more prevalent in other governments, have purged them from all foul stains? Their histories assert the contrary.

In this great American asylum, the poor of Europe have by some means met together, and in consequence of various causes; to what purpose should they ask one another what countrymen they are? Alas, two thirds of them had no country. Can a wretch who wanders about, who works and starves, whose life is a continual scene of sore affliction or pinching penury; can that man call England or any other kingdom his country? A country that had no bread for him, whose fields procured him no harvest, who met with nothing but the frowns of the rich, the severity of the laws, with jails and punishments; who owned not a single foot of the extensive surface of this planet? No! urged by a variety of motives, here they came. Every thing has tended to regenerate them; new laws, a new mode of living, a new social system; here they are become men: in Europe they were as so many useless plants, wanting vegetative mould, and refreshing showers; they withered, and were mowed down by want, hunger, and war; but now by the power of transplantation, like all other plants they have taken root and flourished! Formerly they were not numbered in any civil lists of their country, except in those of the poor; here they rank as citizens. By what invisible power has this surprising metamorphosis been performed? By that of the laws and that of their industry. The laws, the indulgent laws, protect them as they arrive, stamping on them the symbol of adoption; they receive ample rewards for their labours; these accumulated rewards procure them lands; those lands confer on them the title of freemen, and to that title every benefit is affixed which men can possibly require. This is the great operation daily performed by our laws. From whence proceed these laws? From our government. Whence the government? It is derived from the original genius and strong desire of the people ratified and confirmed by the crown. This is the great chain which links us all, this is the picture which every province exhibits, Nova Scotia excepted. There the crown has done all;[5] either there were no people who had genius, or it was not much attended to: the consequence is, that the province is very

4. Harvard, founded in 1636, the first colonial college.
5. This satiric passage refers to the banishment, in 1755, of the French Acadians from Nova Scotia, which the British had conquered in 1710. (See Longfellow's *Evangeline*.)

thinly inhabited indeed; the power of the crown in conjunction with the musketos has prevented men from settling there. Yet some parts of it flourished once, and it contained a mild harmless set of people. But for the fault of a few leaders, the whole were banished. The greatest political error the crown ever committed in America, was to cut off men from a country which wanted nothing but men!

What attachment can a poor European emigrant have for a country where he had nothing? The knowledge of the language, the love of a few kindred as poor as himself, were the only cords that tied him: his country is now that which gives him land, bread, protection, and consequence. *Ubi panis ibi patria*,[6] is the motto of all emigrants. What then is the American, this new man? He is either an European, or the descendant of an European, hence that strange mixture of blood, which you will find in no other country. I could point out to you a family whose grandfather was an Englishman, whose wife was Dutch, whose son married a French woman, and whose present four sons have now four wives of different nations. *He* is an American, who, leaving behind him all his ancient prejudices and manners, receives new ones from the new mode of life he has embraced, the new government he obeys, and the new rank he holds. He becomes an American by being received in the broad lap of our great *Alma Mater*. Here individuals of all nations are melted into a new race of men, whose labours and posterity will one day cause great changes in the world. Americans are the western pilgrims, who are carrying along with them that great mass of arts, sciences, vigour, and industry which began long since in the east; they will finish the great circle. The Americans were once scattered all over Europe; here they are incorporated into one of the finest systems of population which has ever appeared, and which will hereafter become distinct by the power of the different climates they inhabit. The American ought therefore to love this country much better than that wherein either he or his forefathers were born. Here the rewards of his industry follow with equal steps the progress of his labour; his labour is founded on the basis of nature, *self-interest*; can it want a stronger allurement? Wives and children, who before in vain demanded of him a morsel of bread, now, fat and frolicsome, gladly help their father to clear those fields whence exuberant crops are to arise to feed and to clothe them all; without any part being claimed, either by a despotic prince, a rich abbot, or a mighty lord. Here religion demands but little of him; a small voluntary salary to the minister, and gratitude to God; can he refuse these? The American is a new man, who acts upon new principles; he must therefore entertain new ideas, and form new opinions. From involuntary idleness, servile dependence, penury, and useless labour, he has passed

6. Where there is bread, there is one's fatherland.

to toils of a very different nature, rewarded by ample subsistence.
—This is an American. * * *

Now we arrive near the great woods, near the last inhabited districts;[7] there men seem to be placed still farther beyond the reach of government, which in some measure leaves them to themselves. How can it pervade every corner; as they were driven there by misfortunes, necessity of beginnings, desire of acquiring large tracts of land, idleness, frequent want of economy, ancient debts; the reunion of such people does not afford a very pleasing spectacle. When discord, want of unity and friendship; when either drunkenness or idleness prevail in such remote districts; contention, inactivity, and wretchedness must ensue. There are not the same remedies to these evils as in a long established community. The few magistrates they have, are in general little better than the rest; they are often in a perfect state of war; that of man against man, sometimes decided by blows, sometimes by means of the law; that of man against every wild inhabitant of these venerable woods, of which they are come to dispossess them. There men appear to be no better than carnivorous animals of a superior rank, living on the flesh of wild animals when they can catch them, and when they are not able, they subsist on grain. He who would wish to see America in its proper light, and have a true idea of its feeble beginnings and barbarous rudiments, must visit our extended line of frontiers where the last settlers dwell, and where he may see the first labours of settlement, the mode of clearing the earth, in all their different appearances; where men are wholly left dependent on their native tempers, and on the spur of uncertain industry, which often fails when not sanctified by the efficacy of a few moral rules. There, remote from the power of example and check of shame, many families exhibit the most hideous parts of our society. They are a kind of forlorn hope, preceding by ten or twelve years the most respectable army of veterans which come after them. In that space, prosperity will polish some, vice and the law will drive off the rest, who uniting again with others like themselves will recede still farther; making room for more industrious people, who will finish their improvements, convert the loghouse into a convenient habitation, and rejoicing that the first heavy labours are finished, will change in a few years that hitherto barbarous country into a fine fertile, well regulated district. Such is our progress, such is the march of the Europeans toward the interior parts of this continent. In all societies there are off-casts; this impure part serves as our precursors or pioneers; my father himself was one of that class,[8] but he came upon honest principles, and was therefore one of the few

7. *I.e.*, what was then frontier. The observations of Madam Knight, William Byrd, and Crèvecœur, spanning a half century, all agree on the poverty and violence of these areas.

8. Actually, Crèvecœur's father never came to America.

who held fast; by good conduct and temperance, he transmitted to me his fair inheritance, when not above one in fourteen of his contemporaries had the same good fortune.

Forty years ago this smiling country was thus inhabited; it is now purged, a general decency of manners prevails throughout, and such has been the fate of our best countries. * * *

As I have endeavoured to show you how Europeans become Americans; it may not be disagreeable to show you likewise how the various Christian sects introduced, wear out, and how religious indifference becomes prevalent. When any considerable number of a particular sect happen to dwell contiguous to each other, they immediately erect a temple, and there worship the Divinity agreeably to their own peculiar ideas. Nobody disturbs them. If any new sect springs up in Europe it may happen that many of its professors will come and settle in America. As they bring their zeal with them, they are at liberty to make proselytes if they can, and to build a meeting and to follow the dictates of their consciences; for neither the government nor any other power interferes. If they are peaceable subjects, and are industrious, what is it to their neighbours how and in what manner they think fit to address their prayers to the Supreme Being? But if the sectaries are not settled close together, if they are mixed with other denominations, their zeal will cool for want of fuel, and will be extinguished in a little time. Then the Americans become as to religion, what they are as to country, allied to all. In them the name of Englishman, Frenchman, and European is lost, and in like manner, the strict modes of Christianity as practised in Europe are lost also. This effect will extend itself still farther hereafter, and though this may appear to you as a strange idea, yet it is a very true one. I shall be able perhaps hereafter to explain myself better; in the meanwhile, let the following example serve as my first justification.

Let us suppose you and I to be travelling; we observe that in this house, to the right, lives a Catholic, who prays to God as he has been taught, and believes in transubstantiation; he works and raises wheat, he has a large family of children, all hale and robust; his belief, his prayers offend nobody. About one mile farther on the same road, his next neighbour may be a good honest plodding German Lutheran, who addresses himself to the same God, the God of all, agreeably to the modes he has been educated in, and believes in consubstantiation; by so doing he scandalises nobody; he also works in his fields, embellishes the earth, clears swamps, etc. What has the world to do with his Lutheran principles? He persecutes nobody, and nobody persecutes him, he visits his neighbours, and his neighbours visit him. Next to him lives a seceder, the most enthusiastic of all sectaries; his zeal is hot and fiery, but separated as he is from others of the same complexion, he has no congregation of his own to resort to, where he might cabal and mingle religious pride with worldly obstinacy. He likewise raises good crops, his house is handsomely painted, his orchard is one of the fairest in the neighbourhood. How does it concern the welfare of the country, or of the province at large, what this man's religious sentiments are, or really whether he has any at all? He is a good farmer, he is a sober, peaceable, good citizen: William Penn himself would not wish for more. * * * Each of these people instruct their children as well as they can, but these instructions are feeble compared to those which are given to the youth of the poorest class in Europe. Their children will therefore grow up less zealous and more indifferent in matters of religion than their parents. The foolish vanity, or rather the fury of making Proselytes, is unknown here; they have no time, the seasons call for all their attention, and thus in a few years, this mixed neighbourhood will exhibit a strange religious medley, that will be neither pure Catholicism nor pure Calvinism. * * * The Quakers are the only people who retain a fondness for their own mode of worship; for be they ever so far separated from each other, they hold a sort of communion with the society, and seldom depart from its rules, at least in this country. Thus all sects are mixed as well as all nations; thus religious indifference is imperceptibly disseminated from one end of the continent to the other; which is at present one of the strongest characteristics of the Americans. Where this will reach no one can tell, perhaps it may leave a vacuum fit to receive other systems. Persecution, religious pride, the love of contradiction, are the food of what the world commonly calls religion. These motives have ceased here; zeal in Europe is confined; here it evaporates in the great distance it has to travel; there it is a grain of powder inclosed, here it burns away in the open air, and consumes without effect.

But to return to our back settlers. I must tell you, that there is something in the proximity of the woods, which is very singular. It is with men as it is with the plants and animals that grow and live in the forests; they are entirely different from those that live in the plains. I will candidly tell you all my thoughts but you are not to expect that I shall advance any reasons. By living in or near the woods, their actions are regulated by the wildness of the neighbourhood. The deer often come to eat their grain, the wolves to destroy their sheep, the bears to kill their hogs, the foxes to catch their poultry. This surrounding hostility immediately puts the gun into their hands; they watch these animals, they kill some; and thus by defending their property, they soon become professed hunters; this is the progress; once hunters, farewell to the plough. The chase renders them ferocious, gloomy, and unsociable; a hunter wants no neighbour, he rather hates them, because he dreads the competition. In a little time their success in the woods makes them neglect their tillage. They trust to the natural fecundity of the earth, and therefore do little; carelessness in fencing often exposes what little they sow to destruction; they are not at home to watch; in order therefore to make up the deficiency, they go oftener to the woods. That new mode of life brings along with it a new set of manners, which I cannot easily describe. These new manners being grafted on the old stock, produce a strange sort of lawless profligacy, the impressions of which are indelible. The manners of the Indian natives are respectable, compared with this European medley. Their wives and children live in sloth and inactivity; and having no proper pursuits, you may judge what education the latter receive. Their tender minds have nothing else to contemplate but the example of their parents; like them they grow up a mongrel breed, half civilised, half savage, except nature stamps on them some constitutional propensities. That rich, that voluptuous sentiment is gone that struck them so forcibly; the possession of their freeholds no longer conveys to their minds the same pleasure and pride. To all these reasons you must add, their lonely situation, and you cannot imagine what an effect on manners the great distances they live from each other has! Consider one of the last settlements in its first view: of what is it composed? Europeans who have not that sufficient share of knowledge they ought to have, in order to prosper; people who have suddenly passed from oppression, dread of government, and fear of laws, into the unlimited freedom of the woods. This sudden change must have a very great effect on most men, and on that class particularly. Eating of wild meat, whatever you may think, tends to alter their temper: though all the proof I can adduce, is, that I have seen it: and having no place of worship to resort to, what little society this might afford is denied them. The Sunday meetings, exclusive of religious benefits, were the only social bonds that might have inspired them with some degree of emulation in neatness. Is it then surprising to see men thus situated, immersed in great and heavy labours, degenerate a little? It is rather a wonder the effect is not more diffusive. The Moravians and the Quakers are the only instances in exception to what I have advanced. The first never settle singly, it is a colony of the society which emigrates; they carry with them their forms, worship, rules, and decency: the others never begin so hard, they are always able to buy improvements, in which there is a great advantage, for by that time the country is recovered from its first barbarity. * * *

Whatever has been said of the four New England provinces, no such degeneracy of manners has ever tarnished their annals; their back-settlers have been kept within the bounds of decency, and government, by means of wise laws, and by the influence of religion. What a detestable idea such people must have given to the natives of the Europeans! They trade with them, the worst of people are permitted to do that which none but persons of the best characters should be employed in. They get drunk with them, and often defraud the Indians. Their avarice, removed from the eyes of their superiors, knows no bounds; and aided by the little superiority of knowledge, these traders deceive them, and even sometimes shed blood. Hence those shocking violations, those sudden devastations which have so often stained our frontiers, when hundreds of innocent people have been sacrificed for the crimes of a few. It was in consequence of such behaviour, that the Indians took the hatchet against the Virginians in 1774. Thus are our first steps trod, thus are our first trees felled, in general, by the most vicious of our people; and thus the path is opened for the arrival of a second and better class, the true American freeholders; the most respectable set of people in this part of the world: respectable for their industry, their happy independence, the great share of freedom they possess, the good regulation of their families and for extending the trade and the dominion of our mother country. * * *

There is no wonder that this country has so many charms, and presents to Europeans so many temptations to remain in it. A traveller in Europe becomes a stranger as soon as he quits his own kingdom; but it is otherwise here. We know, properly speaking, no strangers; this is every person's country; the variety of our soils, situations, climates, governments, and produce, hath something which must please everybody. No sooner does an European arrive, no matter of what condition, than his eyes are opened upon the fair prospect; he hears his language spoke, he retraces many of his own country manners, he perpetually hears the names of families and towns with which he is acquainted; he sees happiness and prosperity in all places disseminated; he meets with hospitality, kindness, and plenty everywhere; he beholds hardly any poor, he seldom hears of punishments and executions; and he wonders at the elegance of our towns, those miracles of industry and freedom. He cannot admire enough our rural districts, our convenient roads, good taverns, and our many accommodations; he involuntarily loves a country where everything is so lovely. When in England, he was a mere Englishman; here he stands on a larger portion of the globe, not less than its fourth part, and may see the productions of the north, in iron and naval stores; the provisions of Ireland, the grain of Egypt, the indigo, the rice of China. He does not find, as in Europe, a crowded society, where every place is over-stocked; he does not feel that perpetual collision of parties, that difficulty of beginning, that contention which oversets so many. There is room for everybody in America; has he any particular talent, or industry? he exerts it in order to procure a livelihood, and it succeeds. Is he a merchant? the avenues of trade are infinite; is he eminent in any respect? he will be employed and respected. Does he love a country life? pleasant farms present themselves; he may purchase what he wants, and thereby become an American farmer. Is he a labourer, sober and industrious? he need not go many miles, nor receive many informations before he will be hired, well fed at the table of his employer, and paid four or five times more than he can get in Europe. Does he want uncultivated lands? thousands of acres present themselves, which he may purchase cheap. Whatever be his talents or inclinations, if they are moderate, he may satisfy them. I do not mean that every one who comes will grow rich in a little time; no, but he may procure an easy, decent maintenance, by his industry. * * *

An European, when he first arrives, seems limited in his intentions, as well as in his views; but he very suddenly alters his scale; two hundred miles formerly appeared a very great distance, it is now but a trifle; he no sooner breathes our air than he forms schemes, and embarks in designs he never would have thought of in his own country. There the plenitude of society confines many useful ideas, and often extinguishes the most laudable schemes which here ripen into maturity. Thus Europeans become Americans. * * *

Whenever I hear of any new settlement, I pay it a visit once or twice a year, on purpose to observe the different steps each settler takes, the gradual improvements, the different tempers of each family, on which their prosperity in a great nature depends; their different modifications of industry, their ingenuity, and contrivance; for being all poor, their life requires sagacity and prudence. In the evening I love to hear them tell their stories, they furnish me with new ideas; I sit still and listen to their ancient misfortunes, observing in many of them a strong degree of gratitude to God, and the government. Many a well meant sermon have I preached to some of them. When I found laziness and inattention to prevail, who could refrain from wishing well to these new countrymen, after having undergone so many fatigues. Who could withhold good advice? What a happy change it must be, to descend from the high, sterile, bleak lands of Scotland, where everything is barren and cold, to rest on some fertile farms in these middle provinces! Such a transition must have afforded the most pleasing satisfaction.

The following dialogue passed at an out-settlement, where I lately paid a visit:

Well, friend, how do you do now; I am come fifty odd miles on purpose to see you: how do you go on with your new cutting and slashing? Very well, good Sir, we learn the use of the axe bravely, we shall make it out; we have a belly full of victuals every day, our cows run about, and come home full of milk, our hogs get fat of themselves in the woods: Oh, this is a good country! God bless the king, and William Penn; we shall do very well by and by, if we keep our healths. Your log-house looks neat and light, where did you get these shingles? One of our neighbours is a New-England man, and he showed us how to split them out of chestnut-trees. Now for a barn, but all in good time, here are fine trees to build with. Who is to frame it, sure you don't understand that work yet? A countryman of ours who has been in America these ten years, offers to wait for his money until the second crop is lodged in it. What did you give for your land? Thirty-five shillings per acre, payable in seven years. How many acres have you got? An hundred and fifty. That is enough to begin with; is not your land pretty hard to clear? Yes, Sir, hard enough, but it would be harder still if it were ready cleared, for then we should have no timber, and I love the woods much; the land is nothing without them. Have not you found out any bees yet? No, Sir; and if we had we should not know what to do with them. I will tell you by and by. You are very kind. Farewell, honest man, God prosper you; whenever you travel toward ——, inquire for J. S. He will entertain you kindly, provided you bring him good tidings from your family and farm. In this manner I often visit them, and carefully examine their houses, their modes of ingenuity, their different ways; and make them all relate all they know, and describe all they feel. These are scenes which I believe you would willingly share with me. I well remember your philanthropic turn of mind. Is it not better to contemplate under these humble roofs, the rudiments of future wealth and population, than to behold the accumulated bundles of litigious papers in the office of a lawyer? To examine how the world is gradually settled, how the howling swamp is converted into a pleasing meadow, the rough ridge into a fine field; and to hear the cheerful whistling, the rural song, where there was no sound heard before, save the yell of the savage, the screech of the owl, or the hissing of the snake? Here an European, fatigued with luxury, riches, and pleasures, may find a sweet relaxation in a series of interesting scenes, as affecting as they are new. England, which now contains so many domes, so many castles, was once like this; a place woody and marshy; its inhabitants, now the favourite nation for arts and commerce, were once painted like our neighbours. The country will flourish in its turn, and the same observations will be made which I have just delineated. Posterity will look back with avidity and pleasure, to trace, if possible, the era of this or that particular settlement. * * *

After a foreigner from any part of Europe is arrived, and become a citizen; let him devoutly listen to the voice of our great parent, which says to him, "Welcome to my shores, distressed European; bless the hour in which thou didst see my verdant fields, my fair navigable rivers, and my green mountains!—If thou wilt work, I have bread for thee; if thou wilt be honest, sober, and industrious, I have

Reason and Revolution

BENJAMIN FRANKLIN

(1706–1790)

Franklin was the epitome of the Enlightenment, the versatile, practical embodiment of rational man in the eighteenth century. His mind approved and his behavior demonstrated the fundamental concepts of the Age of Reason—faith in the reality of the world as revealed to the senses, distrust of the mystical or mysterious, confidence in the attainment of progress by education and humanitarianism, and the assurance that an appeal to Reason would provide solutions for all human problems, including those of the society and the state. Many of his contemporaries ordered their personal lives by such beliefs, but it was Franklin's particular genius to make the rational life comprehensible and practicable to his countrymen.

In the years between his birth in Boston, in 1706, and his death in Philadelphia, in 1790, incredible political and economic changes occurred; after a successful struggle with France for domination of the North American continent, England recognized the independence of thirteen of her colonies in a

treaty signed in Paris; the philosophy of rational individualism undermined the position of established church and aristocracy; and the new empirical science, responding to Newton's discoveries, again awakened man's dream of mastering his physical world. Other men were pioneers in some of these events, but in all of them Benjamin Franklin actively participated—and left a written record unsurpassed for its penetration, objectivity, and wit.

His early years in Boston, spent reluctantly in his father's tallow shop and sporadically at school, were typical of the experience of a child in a colonial town; then, at the age of twelve, the boy was apprenticed to his brother James, a printer. There followed the long hours of work and the regimen of self-education so graphically recalled in Franklin's *Autobiography*, written many years later for his son, William. In 1722, when his brother was jailed for offending the authorities in his *New England Courant*, sixteen-year-old Benjamin took over the editorship of the paper, and under the pseudonym of Silence Dogood, continued his editorials on subjects ranging from the merits of higher education to freedom of the press. The next year, after disagreements with his brother, he took ship for Philadelphia, arriving in October, 1723, and created a favorite American anecdote by walking up from the Market Street wharf in the morning, munching on one of the "three great puffy rolls" he had purchased with his last pennies. He quickly found employment with Keimer, a printer, and after various activities, including a two-year stay in London, became sole owner of a printing firm which by his industry, frugality, and wise investments enabled him to retire from active business in 1748, when he was only forty-two years old. The years that lay ahead were to give him the varied experiences of a politician, statesman, and public citizen, but the discipline and adaptability which he urged upon his fellow citizens were characteristics of a proficient artisan devoted to his craft. Years later, although academic and international honors had been pressed upon him, he wrote as the opening words of his will, "I, Benjamin Franklin, of Philadelphia, printer * * *"

It was characteristic of Franklin that he not only printed legal forms, copies of Indian treaties, and acts of the Pennsylvania Assembly, but also made of a common aid to the farmer and merchant, the yearly almanac, a distinctive and indigenous creation. *Poor Richard's Almanack* gave the usual information on weather and currency, but the aphorisms, their sources ranging from Greek to English writers, became, by the turn of a phrase, American in vocabulary and implication.

His profession may have provided opportunity for acquaintance with the colonial leaders of Pennsylvania, but it was his unceasing energy and interest in humanity that directed his talents into a variety of civic projects. Franklin brought them about by perseverant ingenuity —such far-reaching institutions as the first circulating library, and more immediate measures, such as the lottery for the erection of steeple and chimes for Christ Church. Among the surviving monuments to his genius for the practical utilization of humane ideas are our first learned society—the American Philosophical Society; our first colonial hospital—the Pennsylvania Hospital; and the University of Pennsylvania, the first such institution to be founded upon the ideal of secular education which he formulated in a number of his writings.

His inquiring mind, energized by his confidence in the progress of rational man, turned as naturally to speculative thought as to ingenious inventions and to the improvement of the institutions of daily life. Nothing was more engrossing to Franklin than the manifestations of nature, so long in the realm of the theoretical or mystical, but now, with the stirring advance of eighteenth-century science, convincingly demonstrated to men's minds by scrupulous techniques of experimental observation. Franklin's curiosity ranged from the causes of earthquakes and the benefits of the Gulf Stream to navigation, to the possible association of lightning and electricity. As early as 1746 he became acquainted through correspondence with English scientists, and his enthusiastic assimilation of their information led to experiments with the Leyden jar and culminated in the famous kite-and-key experiment in 1752. His *Experiments and Observations on Electricity* (1751–1753) brought him international fame.

With the interest in science, the eighteenth century saw a corresponding growth of rationalism and skepticism in religion. Largely derivative from Shaftesbury and Locke, Deism, which stood a pole apart from the orthodoxy of the time, offered minds such as Franklin's an opportunity for reliance on a creative deity and freedom from the strictures of traditional theology. Franklin's earlier doubts became tempered in his later life to that benevolent eclecticism of moderation in action and a reasoned faith in God revealed in his letter to Thomas Paine.

Leadership in civic enterprises and business might in themselves have involved Franklin in the struggle for independence from England, but long before 1776 he had demonstrated qualities of statesmanship. He had learned the intricacies and intrigues of a proprietary colonial government in the fifteen years before 1751 during which he served as clerk of the Pennsylvania Assembly. And his consummate skill as diplomat in England, and in France in 1783,

was the result of long experience, which had begun with his mission, many years earlier, to obtain a treaty with the Ohio Indians.

In two lengthy trips to England between 1757 and 1775, he had served as colonial agent for Pennsylvania, Georgia, Massachusetts, and New Jersey, hoping for conciliation between England and the American colonies, but making a masterful defense against the Stamp Act. He returned to Philadelphia in time to serve in the Second Continental Congress and to be chosen, with Jefferson, as a member of the committee to draft the Declaration of Independence. After two years in France as the agent of Congress, Franklin successfully negotiated a treaty of alliance in 1778; and with John Jay and John Adams, he arranged the terms and signed the Treaty of Paris that ended the Revolution. The nine years he spent at Passy, near Paris, brought him the affectionate adulation of the French, and from his private press came beautifully printed and whimsical "Bagatelles," such as "The Whistle," "The Ephemera," and "To Madame Helvetius."

Franklin returned to Philadelphia in 1785, became president of the executive council of Pennsylvania for three years, and closed his brilliant career by serving as a member of the Constitutional Convention. His death in 1790 was the occasion for international mourning for a man who had become a symbol of democratic action in America and Europe. Six years earlier, when Jefferson was congratulated on replacing Franklin as minister at Paris, he responded, "No one can replace him, Sir; I am only his successor." There has been, in fact, no one since to replace him; he stands alone.

A new authoritative edition of Franklin's collected works is in process. The present most available edition is *The Writings of Benjamin Franklin*, 10 vols., edited by Albert H. Smyth, 1905–1907; but this omits certain texts to be found in John Bigelow's edition of *The Complete Works*, 10 vols., 1887–1889, which also contains Bigelow's edition of the *Autobiography*, 1868. A number of selections from Franklin's writings are available; especially well-balanced is *Franklin: Representative Selections*, edited by F. L. Mott and C. L. Jorgensen, American Writers Series, 1936. A modern biography, judicious and well documented, is *Benjamin Franklin*, by Carl

Van Doren, 1938. However, for special study, several other works are useful, especially James Parton, *Life and Times of Benjamin Franklin*, 2 vols., 1864; *The Life of Benjamin Franklin * * **, 3 vols., edited by John Bigelow, 1874 (1916); J. B. McMaster, *Benjamin Franklin as Man of Letters*, 1887; P. L. Ford, *The Many-Sided Franklin*, 1899; Bernard Fay, *Franklin, the Apostle of Modern Times*, 1929.

For special topics, and for the various recent collections of Franklin letters, see Bibliography, *Literary History of the United States*, edited by Robert E. Spiller, Willard Thorp, Thomas H. Johnson, and Henry Seidel Canby, Vol. III, 1948. For the textual problem of the *Autobiography*, see Max Farrand, *The Autobiography of Benjamin Franklin: A Restoration of a "Fair Copy,"* 1949; and *Benjamin Franklin's Memoirs, Parallel Text Edition*, edited by Max Farrand, 1949. The texts below are based on the Bigelow edition, unless otherwise noted. Except for the selections from *Poor Richard's Almanack*, all texts have been normalized in respect to spelling, punctuation, capitalization, and abbreviated forms.

From The Autobiography[1]

TWYFORD,[2] at the Bishop of St. Asaph's, 1771.

DEAR SON:

I have ever had a pleasure in obtaining any little anecdotes of my ancestors. You may remember the inquiries I made among the remains of my relations when you were with me in England,[3] and the journey I undertook for that purpose. Now imagining it may be equally agreeable to you to know the circumstances of *my* life, many of which you are yet unacquainted with, and expecting a week's uninterrupted leisure in my present country retirement, I sit down to write them for you. To which I have besides some other inducements. Having emerged from the poverty and obscurity in which I was born and bred to a state of affluence and some degree of reputation in the world, and having gone so far through life with a consid-

1. At sixty-five, Franklin wrote an account of his first twenty-four years, intended for his son, William, then colonial governor of New Jersey. Years later he was persuaded by friends to continue it. Additions in 1783, 1784, and 1788 more than doubled the size of the original manuscript, but brought the account only to the years 1757–1759, before the great period of Franklin's public service and international influence. He did not publish this work. The selections below are based on the collation of Bigelow with Farrand's edition of the original

manuscript in *Benjamin Franklin's Memoirs*. The language of our text is not "modernized," but mechanical handicaps to the present-day reader have been avoided.
2. In England, near Winchester. Franklin had become intimate with Jonathan Shipley, Bishop of St. Asaph's, who approved a more liberal policy for the colonies.
3. His son, William Franklin, went to England as his father's secretary in 1757, studied law there, and later served as royal governor of New Jersey.

erable share of felicity, the conducing means I made use of, which with the blessing of God so well succeeded, my posterity may like to know, as they may find some of them suitable to their own situations, and therefore fit to be imitated.

That felicity, when I reflected on it, has induced me sometimes to say that were it offered to my choice I should have no objection to a repetition of the same life from its beginning, only asking the advantages authors have in a second edition to correct some faults of the first. So would I, if I might, besides correcting the faults, change some sinister accidents and events of it for others more favorable. But though this was denied, I should still accept the offer. However, since such a repetition is not to be expected, the next thing most like living one's life over again seems to be a *recollection* of that life, and to make that recollection as durable as possible the putting it down in writing.

Hereby, too, I shall indulge the inclination so natural in old men to be talking of themselves and their own past actions; and I shall indulge it without being troublesome to others, who, through respect to age, might think themselves obliged to give me a hearing, since this may be read or not as any one pleases. And lastly (I may as well confess it, since my denial of it will be believed by nobody), perhaps I shall a good deal gratify my own *vanity*. Indeed, I scarce ever heard or saw the introductory words, "Without vanity I may say," etc., but some vain thing immediately followed. Most people dislike vanity in others, whatever share they have of it themselves; but I give it fair quarter wherever I meet with it, being persuaded that it is often productive of good to the possessor, and to others that are within his sphere of action; and therefore, in many cases, it would not be quite absurd if a man were to thank God for his vanity among the other comforts of life.

And now I speak of thanking God, I desire with all humility to acknowledge that I owe the mentioned happiness of my past life to His kind providence, which led me to the means I used and gave them success. My belief of this induces me to *hope*, though I must not *presume*, that the same goodness will still be exercised towards me, in continuing that happiness or in enabling me to bear a fatal reverse, which I may experience as others have done, the complexion of my future fortune being known to Him only in whose power it is to bless to us even our afflictions.

The notes one of my uncles (who had the same kind of curiosity in collecting family anecdotes) once put into my hands furnished me with several particulars relating to our ancestors. From these notes I learned that the family had lived in the same village, Ecton, in Northamptonshire, for three hundred years, and how much longer he knew not (perhaps from the time when the name Franklin, that before was the name of an order of people, was assumed by them for a surname when others took surnames all over the kingdom), on a freehold of about thirty acres, aided by the smith's business, which had continued in the family till his time, the eldest son being always bred to that business—a custom which he and my father both followed as to their eldest sons. When I searched the register at Ecton, I found an account of their births, marriages, and burials from the year 1555 only, there being no register kept in that parish at any time preceding. By that register I perceived that I was the youngest son of the youngest son for five generations back. My grandfather Thomas, who was born in 1598, lived at Ecton till he grew too old to follow business longer, when he went to live with his son John, a dyer at Banbury in Oxfordshire, with whom my father served an apprenticeship. There my grandfather died and lies buried. We saw his gravestone in 1758. His eldest son, Thomas, lived in the house of Ecton, and left it with the land to his only child, a daughter, who with her husband, one Fisher of Wellingborough, sold it to Mr. Isted, now lord of the manor there. My grandfather had four sons that grew up, viz.: Thomas, John, Benjamin, and Josiah. * * *

Josiah, my father, married young, and carried his wife with three children into New England about 1682. The conventicle[4] having been forbidden by law and frequently disturbed induced some considerable men of his acquaintance to remove to that country, and he was prevailed with to accompany them thither, where they expected to enjoy their mode of religion with freedom. By the same wife he had four children more born there, and by a second wife ten more, in all seventeen; of which I remember thirteen sitting at one time at his table, who all grew up to be men and women, and married; I was the youngest son, and the youngest child but two, and was born in Boston, New England. My mother, the second wife, was Abiah Folger, a daughter of Peter Folger,[5] one of the first settlers of New England, of whom honorable mention is made by Cotton Mather, in his church history of that country, entitled *Magnalia Christi Americana*, as "a godly, learned Englishman," if I remember the words rightly. I have heard that he wrote sundry small occasional pieces, but only one of them was printed, which I saw now many years since. * * *

My elder brothers were all put apprentices to different trades. I was put to the grammar school at eight years of age, my father intending to devote me, as the tithe of his sons, to the service of the church. My early readiness in learning to read (which must have been very

4. Religious assemblies of dissenters, made illegal by the Act of Uniformity, 1662.

5. Peter Folger (1617–1690), pioneer of Nantucket, a schoolmaster, published a volume of ballads condemning the Puritans for lack of religious toleration.

early, as I do not remember when I could not read) and the opinion of all his friends that I should certainly make a good scholar encouraged him in this purpose of his. My uncle Benjamin, too, approved of it, and proposed to give me all his shorthand volumes of sermons, I suppose as a stock to set up with, if I would learn his character.[6] I continued, however, at the grammar school not quite one year, though in that time I had risen gradually from the middle of the class of that year to be the head of it, and farther was removed into the next class above it, in order to go with that into the third at the end of the year. But my father, in the meantime, from a view of the expense of a college education, which having so large a family he could not well afford, and the mean living many so educated were afterwards able to obtain—reasons that he gave to his friends in my hearing—altered his first intention, took me from the grammar school, and sent me to a school for writing and arithmetic, kept by a then famous man, Mr. George Brownell, very successful in his profession generally, and that by mild, encouraging methods. Under him I acquired fair writing pretty soon, but I failed in the arithmetic, and made no progress in it. At ten years old I was taken home to assist my father in his business, which was that of a tallow-chandler and soap-boiler; a business he was not bred to, but had assumed on his arrival in New England, and on finding his dying trade would not maintain his family, being in little request. Accordingly, I was employed in cutting wick for the candles, filling the dipping mold and the molds for cast candles, attending the shop, going of errands, etc.

I disliked the trade, and had a strong inclination for the sea, but my father declared against it; however, living near the water, I was much in and about it, learned early to swim well and to manage boats; and when in a boat or canoe with other boys, I was commonly allowed to govern, especially in any case of difficulty; and upon other occasions I was generally a leader among the boys, and sometimes led them into scrapes, of which I will mention one instance, as it shows an early projecting public spirit, though not then justly conducted.

There was a salt-marsh that bounded part of the mill-pond, on the edge of which, at high water, we used to stand to fish for minnows. By much trampling, we had made it a mere quagmire. My proposal was to build a wharf there fit for us to stand upon, and I showed my comrades a large heap of stones which were intended for a new house near the marsh and which would very well suit our purpose. Accordingly, in the evening, when the workmen were gone, I assembled a number of my play-fellows, and, working with them diligently like so many emmets, sometimes two or three to a stone, we brought them all away and built our little wharf. The next morning the workmen were surprised at missing the stones, which were found

6. His shorthand.

in our wharf. Inquiry was made after the removers; we were discovered and complained of; several of us were corrected by our fathers; and, though I pleaded the usefulness of the work, mine convinced me that nothing was useful which was not honest. * * *

From a child I was fond of reading, and all the little money that came into my hands was ever laid out in books. Pleased with the *Pilgrim's Progress*, my first collection was of John Bunyan's works in separate little volumes. I afterwards sold them to enable me to buy R. Burton's *Historical Collections*; they were small chapman's books, and cheap, forty or fifty in all. My father's little library consisted chiefly of books in polemic divinity, most of which I read and have since often regretted that at a time when I had such a thirst for knowledge, more proper books had not fallen in my way, since it was now resolved I should not be a clergyman. *Plutarch's Lives* there was, in which I read abundantly, and I still think that time spent to great advantage. There was also a book of Defoe's,[7] called an *Essay on Projects*, and another of Dr. Mather's,[8] called *Essays to do Good*, which perhaps gave me a turn of thinking that had an influence on some of the principal future events of my life.

This bookish inclination at length determined my father to make me a printer, though he had already one son (James) of that profession. In 1717 my brother James returned from England with a press and letters to set up his business in Boston. I liked it much better than that of my father, but still had a hankering for the sea. To prevent the apprehended effect of such an inclination, my father was impatient to have me bound to my brother. I stood out some time, but at last was persuaded, and signed the indentures when I was yet but twelve years old. I was to serve as an apprentice till I was twenty-one years of age, only I was to be allowed journeyman's wages during the last year. In a little time I made great proficiency in the business and became a useful hand to my brother. I now had access to better books. An acquaintance with the apprentices of booksellers enabled me sometimes to borrow a small one, which I was careful to return soon and clean. Often I sat up in my room reading the greatest part of the night, when the book was borrowed in the evening and to be returned early in the morning, lest it should be missed or wanted.

And after some time an ingenious tradesman, Mr. Matthew Adams, who had a pretty collection of books, and who frequented our printing-house, took notice of me, invited me to his library, and very kindly lent me such books as I chose to read. I now took a fancy to poetry, and made some little pieces; my brother, thinking it

7. Daniel Defoe's *Essay upon Projects* (1697) advanced such liberal social proposals as insurance and popular education.

8. Cotton Mather's essays, originally entitled *Bonifacius* (1710), emphasized practical virtues, and influenced Franklin's early *Dogood Papers* (1722).

might turn to account, encouraged me, and put me on composing two occasional ballads. One was called *The Lighthouse Tragedy*, and contained an account of the drowning of Captain Worthilake with his two daughters; the other was a sailor's song, on the taking of Teach (or Blackbeard), the pirate.[9] They were wretched stuff, in the Grub-street-ballad style; and when they were printed he sent me about the town to sell them. The first sold wonderfully, the event being recent, having made a great noise. This flattered my vanity; but my father discouraged me by ridiculing my performances and telling me verse-makers were generally beggars. So I escaped being a poet, most probably a very bad one; but as prose writing has been of great use to me in the course of my life, and was a principal means of my advancement, I shall tell you how, in such a situation, I acquired what little ability I have in that way.

There was another bookish lad in the town, John Collins by name, with whom I was intimately acquainted. We sometimes disputed; and very fond we were of argument, and very desirous of confuting one another, which disputatious turn, by the way, is apt to become a very bad habit, making people often extremely disagreeable in company by the contradiction that is necessary to bring it into practice; and thence, besides souring and spoiling the conversation, is productive of disgusts and, perhaps, enmities where you may have occasion for friendship. I had caught it by reading my father's books of dispute about religion. Persons of good sense, I have since observed, seldom fall into it, except lawyers, university men, and men of all sorts that have been bred at Edinburgh. * * *

About this time I met with an odd volume of the *Spectator*.[1] It was the third. I had never before seen any of them. I bought it, read it over and over, and was much delighted with it. I thought the writing excellent, and wished, if possible, to imitate it. With that view I took some of the papers, and, making short hints of the sentiment in each sentence, laid them by a few days, and then, without looking at the book, tried to complete the papers again by expressing each hinted sentiment at length, and as fully as it had been expressed before, in any suitable words that should come to hand. Then I compared my *Spectator* with the original, discovered some of my faults, and corrected them. But I found I wanted a stock of words, or a readiness in recollecting and using them, which I thought I should have acquired before that time if I had gone on making verses; since the continual occasion for words of the same import, but of different length to suit the measure, or of different sound for the rhyme,

9. Narrative poems on the sensational news of the day were quickly printed as "broadsides" to be sold on the streets. During 1717–1718, George Worthilake, keeper of the Boston Light, was drowned with his family while rowing to Boston; and "Blackbeard," or Edward Teach, famed pirate of the southern coast, was killed by a British naval expedition.

1. Famous British periodical (1711–1712) largely the work of Joseph Addison and Sir Richard Steele.

would have laid me under a constant necessity of searching for variety and also have tended to fix that variety in my mind and make me master of it. Therefore, I took some of the tales and turned them into verse; and, after a time, when I had pretty well forgotten the prose, turned them back again. I also sometimes jumbled my collections of hints into confusion, and after some weeks endeavored to reduce them into the best order, before I began to form the full sentences and complete the paper. This was to teach me method in the arrangement of thoughts. By comparing my work afterwards with the original, I discovered many faults and amended them; but I sometimes had the pleasure of fancying that in certain particulars of small import I had been lucky enough to improve the method or the language, and this encouraged me to think I might possibly in time come to be a tolerable English writer, of which I was extremely ambitious. My time for these exercises and for reading was at night, after work, or before it began in the morning, or on Sundays, when I contrived to be in the printing-house alone, evading as much as I could the common attendance on public worship which my father used to exact of me when I was under his care, and which indeed I still thought a duty, though I could not, as it seemed to me, afford time to practice it.

When about sixteen years of age I happened to meet with a book, written by one Tryon,[2] recommending a vegetable diet. I determined to go into it. My brother, being yet unmarried, did not keep house, but boarded himself and his apprentices in another family. My refusing to eat flesh occasioned an inconveniency, and I was frequently chid for my singularity. I made myself acquainted with Tryon's manner of preparing some of his dishes, such as boiling potatoes or rice, making hasty pudding, and a few others, and then proposed to my brother, that if he would give me, weekly, half the money he paid for my board, I would board myself. He instantly agreed to it, and I presently found that I could save half what he paid me. This was an additional fund for buying books. But I had another advantage in it. My brother and the rest going from the printing-house to their meals, I remained there alone and dispatching presently my light repast, which often was no more than a biscuit or a slice of bread, a handful of raisins or a tart from the pastry-cook's, and a glass of water, had the rest of the time till their return for study, in which I made the greater progress, from that greater clearness of head and quicker apprehension which usually attend temperance in eating and drinking.

And now it was that, being on some occasion made ashamed of my ignorance in figures, which I had twice failed in learning when

2. Thomas Tryon (1634–1703) wrote several pamphlets on health and diet. Van Doren (*Benjamin Franklin*, p. 16) says Franklin read *The Way to Health* (1684, 1691).

at school, I took Cocker's book of arithmetic, and went through the whole by myself with great ease. I also read Seller's and Sturmy's books of navigation, and became acquainted with the little geometry they contain; but never proceeded far in that science. And I read about this time Locke[3] *On Human Understanding*, and the *Art of Thinking*, by Messrs. du Port Royal.

While I was intent on improving my language, I met with an English grammar (I think it was Greenwood's), at the end of which there were two little sketches of the arts of rhetoric and logic, the latter finishing with a specimen of a dispute in the Socratic method; and soon after I procured Xenophon's *Memorable Things of Socrates*,[4] wherein there are many instances of the same method. I was charmed with it, adopted it, dropped my abrupt contradiction and positive argumentation, and put on the humble inquirer and doubter. And being then, from reading Shaftesbury and Collins,[5] become a real doubter in many points of our religious doctrine, I found this method safest for myself and very embarrassing to those against whom I used it; therefore I took a delight in it, practiced it continually, and grew very artful and expert in drawing people, even of superior knowledge, into concessions, the consequences of which they did not foresee, entangling them in difficulties out of which they could not extricate themselves, and so obtaining victories that neither myself nor my cause always deserved. I continued this method some few years, but gradually left it, retaining only the habit of expressing myself in terms of modest diffidence; never using, when I advanced anything that may possibly be disputed, the words *certainly*, *undoubtedly*, or any others that give the air of positiveness to an opinion; but rather say, I conceive or apprehend a thing to be so or so; it appears to me, or I should think it so or so, for such and such reasons; or I imagine it to be so; or it is so, if I am not mistaken. This habit, I believe, has been of great advantage to me when I have had occasion to inculcate my opinions and persuade men into measures that I have been from time to time engaged in promoting; and, as the chief ends of conversation are to *inform* or to be *informed*, to *please* or to *persuade*, I wish well-meaning, sensible men would not lessen their power of doing good by a positive, assuming manner that seldom fails to disgust, tends to create opposi-

3. The empiricism of John Locke (1632–1704), especially his theory of the mind, strongly influenced Franklin's rationalism. The *Art of Thinking*, next mentioned, was a symposium (*L'art de penser*, 1662) by followers of Descartes, at the Abbey of Port Royal, which emphasized the Cartesian logic.
4. Title of Edward Bysshe's translation (1712) of Xenophon's *Memorabilia*. Note that Franklin was already familiar with the "Socratic method" of argument from reading James Greenwood's *Grammar* (1711), which emphasized, in the fashion of the day, the logical bases of grammar and rhetoric.
5. The Earl of Shaftesbury's collected essays, *Characteristics* * * * (1712, 1714), are here associated with Anthony Collins' *Discourse* * * * (1713), because both were "free thinking" in theology; Shaftesbury also influenced Franklin's rational view of morality.

tion and to defeat every one of those purposes for which speech was given to us, to wit, giving or receiving information or pleasure. For if you would *inform*, a positive dogmatical manner in advancing your sentiments may provoke contradiction and prevent a candid attention. If you wish information and improvement from the knowledge of others, and yet at the same time express yourself as firmly fixed in your present opinions, modest, sensible men, who do not love disputation, will probably leave you undisturbed in the possession of your error. And by such a manner, you can seldom hope to recommend yourself in *pleasing* your hearers, or to persuade those whose concurrence you desire. * * *

My brother had, in 1720 or 21, begun to print a newspaper. It was the second that appeared in America, and was called the *New England Courant*.[6] The only one before it was the *Boston News-Letter*. I remember his being dissuaded by some of his friends from the undertaking, as not likely to succeed, one newspaper being, in their judgment, enough for America. At this time (1771) there are not less than five-and-twenty. He went on, however, with the undertaking, and after having worked in composing the types and printing off the sheets, I was employed to carry the papers through the streets to the customers.

He had some ingenious men among his friends, who amused themselves by writing little pieces for this paper, which gained it credit and made it more in demand, and these gentlemen often visited us. Hearing their conversations, and their accounts of the approbation their papers were received with, I was excited to try my hand among them; but, being still a boy, and suspecting that my brother would object to printing anything of mine in his paper if he knew it to be mine, I contrived to disguise my hand and, writing an anonymous paper, I put it in at night under the door of the printing-house. It was found in the morning and communicated to his writing friends when they called in as usual. They read it, commented on it in my hearing, and I had the exquisite pleasure of finding it met with their approbation, and that, in their different guesses at the author, none were named but men of some character among us for learning and ingenuity. I suppose now that I was rather lucky in my judges, and that perhaps they were not really so very good ones as I then esteemed them.

Encouraged, however, by this, I wrote and conveyed in the same way to the press several more papers which were equally approved;[7] and I kept my secret till my small fund of sense for such perform-

6. Actually, James Franklin's *New England Courant* (1721–1726), was the fifth American newspaper. *Publick Occurrences* appeared in Boston, for one issue only, in 1690; it was followed by the Boston *News-Letter*, 1704, the Boston *Gazette*, 1719, and, in Philadelphia, the *American Weekly Mercury*, 1719.
7. *The Dogood Papers* (1722), his first published prose.

ances was pretty well exhausted, and then I discovered it, when I began to be considered a little more by my brother's acquaintance, and in a manner that did not quite please him, as he thought, probably with reason, that it tended to make me too vain. And perhaps this might be one occasion of the differences that we began to have about this time. Though a brother, he considered himself as my master, and me as his apprentice, and accordingly expected the same services from me as he would from another, while I thought he demeaned me too much in some he required of me, who from a brother expected more indulgence. Our disputes were often brought before our father, and I fancy I was either generally in the right, or else a better pleader, because the judgment was generally in my favor. But my brother was passionate, and had often beaten me, which I took extremely amiss; and, thinking my apprenticeship very tedious, I was continually wishing for some opportunity of shortening it, which at length offered in a manner unexpected.[8]

One of the pieces in our newspaper on some political point, which I have now forgotten, gave offense to the Assembly. He was taken up, censured, and imprisoned for a month, by the speaker's warrant, I suppose because he would not discover his author. I too was taken up and examined before the council; but, though I did not give them any satisfaction, they contented themselves with admonishing me, and dismissed me, considering me, perhaps, as an apprentice who was bound to keep his master's secrets.

During my brother's confinement, which I resented a good deal, notwithstanding our private differences, I had the management of the paper; and I made bold to give our rulers some rubs in it, which my brother took very kindly, while others began to consider me in an unfavorable light, as a young genius that had a turn for libeling and satire. My brother's discharge was accompanied with an order of the House (a very odd one), that "James Franklin should no longer print the paper called the *New England Courant.*"

There was a consultation held in our printing-house among his friends what he should do in this case. Some proposed to evade the order by changing the name of the paper; but my brother seeing inconveniences in that, it was finally concluded on as a better way to let it be printed for the future under the name of *Benjamin Franklin;*[9] and to avoid the censure of the Assembly, that might fall on him as still printing it by his apprentice, the contrivance was that my old indenture should be returned to me, with a full dis-

8. "I fancy his harsh and tyrranical treatment of me might be a means of impressing me with that aversion to arbitrary power that has stuck to me through my whole life" [Franklin's note].

9. In fact, James Franklin was arrested twice, on different charges; consequently, Benjamin edited the *Courant* for three weeks in June and July, 1722, and again for a week in February, 1723, before his name appeared as ostensible editor on February 11, 1723.

charge on the back of it, to be shown on occasion; but to secure to him the benefit of my service, I was to sign new indentures for the remainder of the term, which were to be kept private. A very flimsy scheme it was; however, it was immediately executed, and the paper went on accordingly under my name for several months.

At length, a fresh difference arising between my brother and me, I took upon me to assert my freedom, presuming that he would not venture to produce the new indentures. It was not fair in me to take this advantage, and this I therefore reckon one of the first errata of my life; but the unfairness of it weighed little with me when under the impression of resentment for the blows his passion too often urged him to bestow upon me, though he was otherwise not an ill-natured man; perhaps I was too saucy and provoking.

When he found I would leave him, he took care to prevent my getting employment in any other printing-house of the town, by going round and speaking to every master, who accordingly refused to give me work. I then thought of going to New York, as the nearest place where there was a printer; and I was the rather inclined to leave Boston when I reflected that I had already made myself a little obnoxious to the governing party, and, from the arbitrary proceedings of the Assembly in my brother's case, it was likely I might, if I stayed, soon bring myself into scrapes; and farther, that my indiscreet disputations about religion began to make me pointed at with horror by good people as an infidel or atheist. I determined on the point, but my father now siding with my brother, I was sensible that, if I attempted to go openly, means would be used to prevent me. My friend Collins, therefore, undertook to manage a little for me. He agreed with the captain of a New York sloop for my passage, under the notion of my being a young acquaintance of his, that had got a naughty girl with child, whose friends would compel me to marry her, and therefore I could not appear or come away publicly. So I sold some of my books to raise a little money, was taken on board privately, and as we had a fair wind, in three days I found myself in New York, near three hundred miles from home, a boy of but seventeen, without the least recommendation to, or knowledge of, any person in the place, and with very little money in my pocket.

My inclinations for the sea were by this time worn out, or I might now have gratified them. But, having a trade, and supposing myself a pretty good workman, I offered my service to the printer in the place, old Mr. William Bradford,[1] who had been the first printer in Pennsylvania, but removed from thence upon the quarrel of

---

1. William Bradford, the first Philadelphia printer (1685). In 1692 he supported George Keith in a schismatic attack on Penn's doctrines. In 1693 in New York he became the royal printer, and he founded that colony's first newspaper, the New York *Gazette* (1725).

George Keith. He could give me no employment, having little to do and help enough already; but, says he, "My son[2] at Philadelphia has lately lost his principal hand, Aquila Rose,[3] by death; if you go thither, I believe he may employ you." Philadelphia was one hundred miles further; I set out, however, in a boat for Amboy,[4] leaving my chest and things to follow me round by sea.

In crossing the bay, we met with a squall that tore our rotten sails to pieces, prevented our getting into the Kill,[5] and drove us upon Long Island. In our way, a drunken Dutchman, who was a passenger too, fell overboard; when he was sinking, I reached through the water to his shock pate, and drew him up, so that we got him in again. His ducking sobered him a little, and he went to sleep, taking first out of his pocket a book, which he desired I would dry for him. It proved to be my old favorite author, Bunyan's *Pilgrim's Progress*, in Dutch, finely printed on good paper, with copper cuts, a dress better than I had ever seen it wear in its own language. I have since found that it has been translated into most of the languages of Europe, and suppose it has been more generally read than any other book, except perhaps the Bible. Honest John was the first that I know of who mixed narration and dialogue, a method of writing very engaging to the reader, who in the most interesting parts finds himself, as it were, brought into the company and present at the discourse. Defoe in his *Crusoe*, his *Moll Flanders*, *Religious Courtship*, *Family Instructor*, and other pieces, has imitated it with success; and Richardson has done the same in his *Pamela*, etc.

When we drew near the island, we found it was at a place where there could be no landing, there being a great surf on the stony beach. So we dropped anchor, and swung round towards the shore. Some people came down to the water edge and hallowed to us, as we did to them; but the wind was so high, and the surf so loud, that we could not hear so as to understand each other. There were canoes on the shore, and we made signs, and hallowed that they should fetch us; but they either did not understand us, or thought it impracticable, so they went away, and night coming on, we had no remedy but to wait till the wind should abate; and in the mean time the boatman and I concluded to sleep if we could; and so crowded into the scuttle, with the Dutchman, who was still wet, and the spray, beating over the head of our boat, leaked through to us, so that we were soon almost as wet as he. In this manner we lay all night, with

---

2. Andrew Bradford (1686–1742), later Franklin's principal rival as a printer.
3. Aquila Rose (1695?–1723). His posthumous *Poems* * * * (1740) survives because Franklin assisted the poet's son in publishing them.
4. Perth Amboy, then the coastal capital of New Jersey. From there the shortest route across New Jersey was to Burlington, then capital of West Jersey, where the Delaware River would provide an easy passage of twenty miles to Philadelphia.
5. Dutch for "stream," here meaning "channel."

very little rest; but, the wind abating the next day, we made a shift to reach Amboy before night, having been thirty hours on the water, without victuals or any drink but a bottle of filthy rum, the water we sailed on being salt.

In the evening I found myself very feverish, and went into bed; but having read somewhere that cold water drank plentifully was good for a fever I followed the prescription, sweat plentifully most of the night; my fever left me, and in the morning, crossing the ferry, I proceeded on my journey on foot, having fifty miles to Burlington, where I was told I should find boats that would carry me the rest of the way to Philadelphia.

It rained very hard all the day; I was thoroughly soaked, and by noon a good deal tired; so I stopped at a poor inn, where I stayed all night, beginning now to wish I had never left home. I cut so miserable a figure, too, that I found, by the questions asked me, I was suspected to be some runaway servant, and in danger of being taken up on that suspicion. However, I proceeded the next day, and got in the evening to an inn, within eight or ten miles of Burlington, kept by one Dr. Brown. He entered into conversation with me while I took some refreshment, and, finding I had read a little, became very sociable and friendly. Our acquaintance continued as long as he lived. He had been, I imagine, an itinerant doctor, for there was no town in England or country in Europe of which he could not give a very particular account. He had some letters, and was ingenious, but much of an unbeliever, and wickedly undertook some years after to travesty the Bible in doggerel verse, as Cotton had done Virgil.[6] By this means he set many of the facts in a very ridiculous light, and might have hurt weak minds if his work had been published; but it never was.

At his house I lay that night, and the next morning reached Burlington, but had the mortification to find that the regular boats were gone a little before my coming, and no other expected to go till Tuesday, this being Saturday; wherefore I returned to an old woman in the town, of whom I had bought gingerbread to eat on the water, and asked her advice. She invited me to lodge at her house till a passage by water should offer; and, being tired with my foot traveling, I accepted the invitation. She, understanding I was a printer, would have had me stay at that town and follow my business, being ignorant of the stock necessary to begin with. She was very hospitable, gave me a dinner of ox-cheek with great good will, accepting only of a pot of ale in return; and I thought myself fixed till Tuesday should come. However, walking in the evening by the side of the river, a boat came by, which I found was going towards

6. Probably the English poet Charles Cotton (1630–1687), whose burlesque of Virgil (1664) was followed by par-odies of Lucian, a second part to Izaac Walton's *Compleat Angler*, and transla-tions of the essays of Montaigne.

Philadelphia, with several people in her. They took me in, and, as there was no wind, we rowed all the way; and about midnight, not having yet seen the city, some of the company were confident we must have passed it, and would row no farther; the others knew not where we were; so we put towards the shore, got into a creek, landed near an old fence, with the rails of which we made a fire, the night being cold (in October), and there we remained till daylight. Then one of the company knew the place to be Cooper's Creek, a little above Philadelphia,[7] which we saw as soon as we got out of the creek, and arrived there about eight or nine o'clock on the Sunday morning, and landed at the Market Street wharf.

I have been the more particular in this description of my journey, and shall be so of my first entry into that city, that you may in your mind compare such unlikely beginnings with the figure I have since made there. I was in my working dress, my best clothes being to come round by sea. I was dirty from my journey; my pockets were stuffed out with shirts and stockings; I knew no soul nor where to look for lodging. I was fatigued with traveling, rowing, and want of rest; I was very hungry; and my whole stock of cash consisted of a Dutch dollar and about a shilling in copper. The latter I gave the people of the boat for my passage, who at first refused it, on account of my rowing; but I insisted on their taking it, a man being sometimes more generous when he has but a little money than when he has plenty, perhaps through fear of being thought to have but little.

Then I walked up the street, gazing about, till near the market-house I met a boy with bread. I had made many a meal on bread, and, inquiring where he got it, I went immediately to the baker's he directed me to, in Second Street, and asked for biscuit, intending such as we had in Boston; but they, it seems, were not made in Philadelphia. Then I asked for a three-penny loaf, and was told they had none such. So, not considering or knowing the difference of money, and the greater cheapness nor the names of his bread, I bade him give me three-penny-worth of any sort. He gave me, accordingly, three great puffy rolls. I was surprised at the quantity, but took it, and, having no room in my pockets, walked off with a roll under each arm, and eating the other. Thus I went up Market Street as far as Fourth Street, passing by the door of Mr. Read, my future wife's father; when she, standing at the door, saw me, and thought I made, as I certainly did, a most awkward, ridiculous appearance. Then I turned and went down Chestnut Street and part of Walnut Street, eating my roll all the way, and, coming round, found myself again at Market Street wharf, near the boat I came in, to which I went for a draught of the river water; and, being filled with one of my rolls, gave the other two to a woman and her child that came down the

7. Actually on the New Jersey side, in present-day Camden.

river in the boat with us, and were waiting to go farther.

Thus refreshed, I walked again up the street, which by this time had many clean-dressed people in it, who were all walking the same way. I joined them, and thereby was led into the great meeting-house of the Quakers near the market. I sat down among them, and, after looking round awhile and hearing nothing said, being very drowsy through labor and want of rest the preceding night, I fell fast asleep, and continued so till the meeting broke up, when one was kind enough to rouse me. This was, therefore, the first house I was in, or slept in, in Philadelphia.

Walking down again toward the river and looking in the faces of people, I met a young Quaker man, whose countenance I liked, and accosting him, requested he would tell me where a stranger could get lodging. We were then near the sign of the Three Mariners. "Here," says he, "is one place that entertains strangers, but it is not a reputable house; if thee wilt walk with me, I'll show thee a better." He brought me to the Crooked Billet in Water Street. Here I got a dinner; and while I was eating it several sly questions were asked me, as it seemed to be suspected from my youth and appearance that I might be some runaway.

After dinner my sleepiness returned, and, being shown to a bed, I lay down without undressing, and slept till six in the evening, was called to supper, went to bed again very early, and slept soundly till next morning. Then I made myself as tidy as I could and went to Andrew Bradford the printer's. I found in the shop the old man his father, whom I had seen at New York, and who, traveling on horseback, had got to Philadelphia before me. He introduced me to his son, who received me civilly, gave me a breakfast, but told me he did not at present want a hand, being lately supplied with one; but there was another printer in town, lately set up, one Keimer, who perhaps might employ me; if not, I should be welcome to lodge at his house, and he would give me a little work to do now and then till fuller business should offer.

The old gentleman said he would go with me to the new printer; and when we found him, "Neighbor," says Bradford, "I have brought to see you a young man of your business; perhaps you may want such a one." He asked me a few questions, put a composing stick in my hand to see how I worked, and then said he would employ me soon, though he had just then nothing for me to do; and, taking old Bradford, whom he had never seen before, to be one of the town's people that had a good will for him, entered into a conversation on his present undertaking and prospects; while Bradford, not discovering [8] that he was the other printer's father, on Keimer's saying he expected soon to get the greatest part of the business into his own

8. Revealing.

hands, drew him on by artful questions, and starting little doubts, to explain all his views, what interest he relied on, and in what manner he intended to proceed. I, who stood by and heard all, saw immediately that one of them was a crafty old sophister, and the other a mere novice. Bradford left me with Keimer, who was greatly surprised when I told him who the old man was.

Keimer's printing-house, I found, consisted of an old shattered press, and one small, worn-out font of English,[9] which he was then using himself, composing an elegy on Aquila Rose, before mentioned, an ingenious young man, of excellent character, much respected in the town, clerk of the Assembly, and a pretty poet. Keimer made verses too, but very indifferently. He could not be said to write them, for his manner was to compose them in the types directly out of his head. So there being no copy, but one pair of cases,[1] and the elegy likely to require all the letter, no one could help him. I endeavored to put his press (which he had not yet used, and of which he understood nothing) into order fit to be worked with; and, promising to come and print off his elegy as soon as he should have got it ready, I returned to Bradford's, who gave me a little job to do for the present, and there I lodged and dieted. A few days after, Keimer sent for me to print off the elegy. And now he had got another pair of cases, and a pamphlet to reprint, on which he set me to work.

These two printers I found poorly qualified for their business. Bradford had not been bred to it, and was very illiterate; and Keimer, though something of a scholar, was a mere compositor, knowing nothing of presswork. He had been one of the French prophets, and could act their enthusiastic agitations. At this time he did not profess any particular religion, but something of all on occasion; was very ignorant of the world, and had, as I afterward found, a good deal of the knave in his composition. He did not like my lodging at Bradford's while I worked with him. He had a house, indeed, but without furniture, so he could not lodge me; but he got me a lodging at Mr. Read's, before mentioned, who was the owner of his house; and, my chest and clothes being come by this time, I made rather a more respectable appearance in the eyes of Miss Read than I had done when she first happened to see me eating my roll in the street.

I began now to have some acquaintance among the young people of the town that were lovers of reading, with whom I spent my evenings very pleasantly; and gaining money by my industry and frugality I lived very agreeably, forgetting Boston as much as I could,

9. The English, or 14-point, type would be oversized for most book and newspaper work.

1. The hand typesetter picked his capitals from boxes in the "upper case," his small letters from those in the "lower case."

and not desiring that any there should know where I resided, except my friend Collins, who was in my secret, and kept it when I wrote to him. At length, an incident happened that sent me back again much sooner than I had intended. I had a brother-in-law, Robert Holmes, master of a sloop that traded between Boston and Delaware. He being at Newcastle, forty miles below Philadelphia, heard there of me, and wrote me a letter mentioning the concern of my friends in Boston at my abrupt departure, assuring me of their good will to me, and that everything would be accommodated to my mind if I would return, to which he exhorted me very earnestly. I wrote an answer to his letter, thanked him for his advice, but stated my reasons for quitting Boston fully and in such a light as to convince him I was not so wrong as he had apprehended.

Sir William Keith,[2] governor of the province, was then at New castle, and Captain Holmes, happening to be in company with him when my letter came to hand, spoke to him of me, and showed him the letter. The Governor read it, and seemed surprised when he was told my age. He said I appeared a young man of promising parts, and therefore should be encouraged; the printers at Philadelphia were wretched ones; and if I would set up there he made no doubt I should succeed; for his part, he would procure me the public business, and do me every other service in his power. This my brother-in-law afterwards told me in Boston, but I knew as yet nothing of it; when, one day, Keimer and I being at work together near the window, we saw the Governor and another gentleman (which proved to be Colonel French of Newcastle), finely dressed, come directly across the street to our house, and heard them at the door.

Keimer ran down immediately, thinking it a visit to him; but the Governor inquired for me, came up, and with a condescension and politeness I had been quite unused to, made me many compliments, desired to be acquainted with me, blamed me kindly for not having made myself known to him when I first came to the place, and would have me away with him to the tavern, where he was going with Colonel French to taste, as he said, some excellent Madeira. I was not a little surprised, and Keimer stared like a pig poisoned. I went, however, with the Governor and Colonel French to a tavern at the corner of Third Street, and over the Madeira he proposed my setting up my business, laid before me the probabilities of success, and both he and Colonel French assured me I should have their interest and influence in procuring the public business of both governments. On my doubting whether my father would assist me in it, Sir William said he would give me a letter to him, in which he would state the advantages, and he did not doubt of prevailing with him. So it

2. Sir William Keith (1680–1749), governor of Pennsylvania (1717–1726), sided with the Assembly and the people; he opposed the Proprietors, who caused his dismissal.

was concluded I should return to Boston in the first vessel, with the Governor's letter recommending me to my father. In the mean time the intention was to be kept secret, and I went on working with Keimer as usual, the Governor sending for me now and then to dine with him—a very great honor I thought it—and conversing with me in the most affable, familiar, and friendly manner imaginable.[3] * * *

The sloop putting in at Newport, Rhode Island, I visited my brother John, who had been married and settled there some years. He received me very affectionately, for he always loved me. A friend of his, one Vernon, having some money due to him in Pennsylvania, about thirty-five pounds currency, desired I would receive it for him, and keep it till I had his directions what to remit it in. Accordingly, he gave me an order. This afterwards occasioned me a good deal of uneasiness.

At Newport we took in a number of passengers for New York, among which were two young women companions and a grave, sensible, matron-like Quaker woman, with her attendants. I had shown an obliging readiness to do her some little services, which impressed her, I suppose, with a degree of good will towards me; therefore, when she saw a daily growing familiarity between me and the two young women, which they appeared to encourage, she took me aside, and said, "Young man, I am concerned for thee, as thou has no friend with thee, and seems not to know much of the world, or of the snares youth is exposed to; depend upon it, those are very bad women; I can see it in all their actions; and if thee art not upon thy guard, they will draw thee into some danger; they are strangers to thee, and I advise thee, in a friendly concern for thy welfare, to have no acquaintance with them." As I seemed at first not to think so ill of them as she did, she mentioned some things she had observed and heard that had escaped my notice, but now convinced me she was right. I thanked her for her kind advice, and promised to follow it. When we arrived at New York, they told me where they lived, and invited me to come and see them; but I avoided it, and it was well I did; for the next day the captain missed a silver spoon and some other things, that had been taken out of his cabin, and, knowing that these were a couple of strumpets, he got a warrant to search their lodgings, found the stolen goods, and had the thieves punished. So, though we had escaped a sunken rock, which we scraped upon in the passage, I thought this escape of rather more importance to me.

At New York I found my friend Collins, who had arrived there

3. In April, 1724, Franklin returned to Boston, but could not win financial backing from his father, who thought him to be too young for the responsi-bility. His Boston friend John Collins, however, was impressed by his stories and decided to move to Philadelphia.

some time before me. We had been intimate from children, and had read the same books together; but he had the advantage of more time for reading and studying, and a wonderful genius for mathematical learning, in which he far outstripped me. While I lived in Boston, most of my hours of leisure for conversation were spent with him, and he continued a sober as well as an industrious lad; was much respected for his learning by several of the clergy and other gentlemen, and seemed to promise making a good figure in life. But, during my absence, he had acquired a habit of sotting with brandy; and I found by his own account, and what I heard from others, that he had been drunk every day since his arrival at New York, and behaved very oddly. He had gamed too, and lost his money, so that I was obliged to discharge his lodgings, and defray his expenses to and at Philadelphia, which proved extremely inconvenient to me.

The then governor of New York, Burnet[4] (son of Bishop Burnet), hearing from the captain that a young man, one of his passengers, had a great many books, desired he would bring me to see him. I waited upon him accordingly, and should have taken Collins with me but that he was not sober. The Governor treated me with great civility, showed me his library, which was a very large one, and we had a good deal of conversation about books and authors. This was the second governor who had done me the honor to take notice of me; which to a poor boy like me was very pleasing.

We proceeded to Philadelphia. I received on the way Vernon's money, without which we could hardly have finished our journey. Collins wished to be employed in some counting-house; but, whether they discovered his dramming by his breath, or by his behavior, though he had some recommendations, he met with no success in any application, and continued lodging and boarding at the same house with me, and at my expense. Knowing I had that money of Vernon's, he was continually borrowing of me, still promising repayment as soon as he should be in business. At length he had got so much of it that I was distressed to think what I should do in case of being called on to remit it.

His drinking continued, about which we sometimes quarrelled; for, when a little intoxicated, he was very fractious. Once, in a boat on the Delaware with some other young men, he refused to row in his turn. "I will be rowed home," says he. "We will not row you," says I. "You must, or stay all night on the water," says he, "just as you please." The others said, "Let us row; what signifies it?" But, my mind being soured with his other conduct, I continued to refuse. So he swore he would make me row, or throw me overboard; and coming along, stepping on the thwarts, toward me, when he came

4. William Burnet (1688–1729), governor of New York and New Jersey (1720–1728), then of Massachusetts (1728–1729), learned son of the brilliant historian Gilbert Burnet (1643–1716), Bishop of Salisbury.

up and struck at me, I clapped my hand under his crutch, and, rising, pitched him head-foremost into the river. I knew he was a good swimmer, and so was under little concern about him; but before he could get round to lay hold of the boat, we had with a few strokes pulled her out of his reach; and ever when he drew near the boat, we asked if he would row, striking a few strokes to slide her away from him. He was ready to die with vexation, and obstinately would not promise to row. However, seeing him at last beginning to tire, we lifted him in and brought him home dripping wet in the evening. We hardly exchanged a civil word afterwards, and a West India captain, who had a commission to procure a tutor for the sons of a gentleman at Barbados, happening to meet with him, agreed to carry him thither. He left me then, promising to remit me the first money he should receive in order to discharge the debt; but I never heard of him after.

The breaking into this money of Vernon's was one of the first great errata of my life; and this affair showed that my father was not much out in his judgment when he supposed me too young to manage business of importance. But Sir William, on reading his letter, said he was too prudent. There was great difference in persons; and discretion did not always accompany years, nor was youth always without it. "And since he will not set you up," says he, "I will do it myself. Give me an inventory of the things necessary to be had from England, and I will send for them. You shall repay me when you are able; I am resolved to have a good printer here, and I am sure you must succeed." This was spoken with such an appearance of cordiality, that I had not the least doubt of his meaning what he said. I had hitherto kept the proposition of my setting up a secret in Philadelphia, and I still kept it. Had it been known that I depended on the Governor, probably some friend that knew him better would have advised me not to rely on him, as I afterwards heard it as his known character to be liberal of promises which he never meant to keep. Yet, unsolicited as he was by me, how could I think his generous offers insincere? I believed him one of the best men in the world.

I presented him an inventory of a little printing-house, amounting by my computation to about one hundred pounds sterling. He liked it, but asked me if my being on the spot in England to choose the types and see that everything was good of the kind might not be of some advantage. "Then," says he, "when there, you may make acquaintances, and establish correspondences in the bookselling and stationery way." I agreed that this might be advantageous. "Then," says he, "get yourself ready to go with *Annis*," which was the annual ship, and the only one at that time usually passing between London and Philadelphia. But it would be some months before *Annis* sailed, so I continued working with Keimer, fretting about the money Collins had got from me, and in daily apprehensions of being called upon by Vernon, which, however, did not happen for some years after. * * *

My chief acquaintances at this time were Charles Osborne, Joseph Watson, and James Ralph,[5] all lovers of reading. The two first were clerks to an eminent scrivener or conveyancer in the town, Charles Brogden; the other was clerk to a merchant. Watson was a pious, sensible young man, of great integrity; the others rather more lax in their principles of religion, particularly Ralph, who, as well as Collins, had been unsettled by me, for which they both made me suffer. Osborne was sensible, candid, frank, sincere and affectionate to his friends, but in literary matters too fond of criticizing. Ralph was ingenious, genteel in his manners, and extremely eloquent; I think I never knew a prettier talker. Both of them great admirers of poetry, and began to try their hands in little pieces. Many pleasant walks we four had together on Sundays into the woods near Schuylkill, where we read to one another, and conferred on what we read.

Ralph was inclined to pursue the study of poetry, not doubting but he might become eminent in it and make his fortune by it, alleging that the best poets must when they first began to write make as many faults as he did. Osborne dissuaded him, assured him he had no genius for poetry, and advised him to think of nothing beyond the business he was bred to; that, in the mercantile way, though he had no stock, he might, by his diligence and punctuality, recommend himself to employment as a factor, and in time acquire wherewith to trade on his own account. I approved the amusing one's self with poetry now and then, so far as to improve one's language, but no farther. * * *

Ralph, though married, and having one child, had determined to accompany me in this voyage. It was thought he intended to establish a correspondence and obtain goods to sell on commission; but I found afterwards, that through some discontent with his wife's relations he purposed to leave her on their hands and never return again. Having taken leave of my friends, and interchanged some promises with Miss Read, I left Philadelphia in the ship, which anchored at Newcastle.[6] The Governor was there; but when I went to his lodging, the secretary came to me from him with the civillest message in the world, that he could not then see me, being engaged in business of the utmost importance, but should send the letters to me on board, wished me heartily a good voyage and a speedy re-

5. Ralph (died 1762) accompanied Franklin to England. He became known as a Neoclassical poet and as collaborator with Henry Fielding on the *Champion*, a periodical; and was author of an authoritative *History of England*.

6. Now New Castle, Delaware; originally a Swedish settlement, and an active port of entry. Delaware and Pennsylvania, both part of the grant to William Penn, remained long under the same governor.

turn, etc. I returned on board a little puzzled, but still not doubting.

Mr. Andrew Hamilton,[7] a famous lawyer of Philadelphia, had taken passage in the same ship for himself and son, and with Mr. Denham, a Quaker merchant, and Messrs. Onion and Russel, masters of an iron work in Maryland, had engaged the great cabin; so that Ralph and I were forced to take up with a berth in the steerage and, none on board knowing us, were considered as ordinary persons. But Mr. Hamilton and his son (it was James, since Governor) returned from Newcastle to Philadelphia, the father being recalled by a great fee to plead for a seized ship; and, just before we sailed, Colonel French coming on board and showing me great respect, I was more taken notice of, and with my friend Ralph invited by the other gentlemen to come into the cabin, there being now room. Accordingly, we removed thither. * * *

When we came into the Channel, the captain kept his word with me, and gave me an opportunity of examining the bag for the Governor's letters. I found none upon which my name was put as under my care * * * and after recollecting and comparing circumstances, I began to doubt his sincerity. I found my friend Denham, and opened the whole affair to him. He let me into Keith's character; told me there was not the least probability that he had written any letters for me; that no one who knew him had the smallest dependence on him; and he laughed at the notion of the Governor's giving me a letter of credit, having, as he said, no credit to give. On my expressing some concern about what I should do, he advised me to endeavor getting some employment in the way of my business. "Among the printers here," says he, "you will improve yourself, and when you return to America, you will set up to greater advantage." * * *

But what shall we think of a governor's playing such pitiful tricks, and imposing so grossly on a poor ignorant boy! It was a habit he had acquired. He wished to please everybody; and having little to give he gave expectations. He was otherwise an ingenious, sensible man, a pretty good writer, and a good governor for the people, though not for his constituents, the proprietaries, whose instructions he sometimes disregarded. Several of our best laws were of his planning and passed during his administration.

Ralph and I were inseparable companions. We took lodgings together in Little Britain[8] at three shillings and sixpence a week—as much as we could then afford. He found some relations, but they were poor and unable to assist him. He now let me know his inten-

---

7. Andrew Hamilton (died 1741), whose defense of John Peter Zenger, publisher of the New York *Weekly Journal*, established the principle of political freedom for the colonial press. His son James, four times governor of Pennsylvania before 1773, was a strongly conservative Tory.

8. In the heart of London, near St. Paul's.

tions of remaining in London, and that he never meant to return to Philadelphia. He had brought no money with him, the whole he could muster having been expended in paying his passage. I had fifteen pistoles;[9] so he borrowed occasionally of me to subsist while he was looking out for business. He first endeavored to get into the playhouse, believing himself qualified for an actor; but Wilkes,[1] to whom he applied, advised him candidly not to think of that employment, as it was impossible he should succeed in it. Then he proposed to Roberts, a publisher in Paternoster Row, to write for him a weekly paper like the *Spectator*, on certain conditions, which Roberts did not approve. Then he endeavored to get employment as a hackney writer, to copy for the stationers and lawyers about the Temple, but could find no vacancy.

I immediately got into work at Palmer's,[2] then a famous printing-house in Bartholomew Close, and here I continued near a year. I was pretty diligent, but spent with Ralph a good deal of my earnings in going to plays and other places of amusement. We had together consumed all my pistoles, and now just rubbed on from hand to mouth. He seemed quite to forget his wife and child, and I, by degrees, my engagements with Miss Read, to whom I never wrote more than one letter, and that was to let her know I was not likely soon to return. This was another of the great errata of my life, which I should wish to correct if I were to live it over again. In fact, by our expenses, I was constantly kept unable to pay my passage.

At Palmer's I was employed in composing for the second edition of Wollaston's *Religion of Nature*.[3] Some of his reasonings not appearing to me well founded, I wrote a little metaphysical piece in which I made remarks on them. It was entitled *A Dissertation on Liberty and Necessity, Pleasure and Pain*. I inscribed it to my friend Ralph; I printed a small number. It occasioned my being more considered by Mr. Palmer as a young man of some ingenuity, though he seriously expostulated with me upon the principles of my pamphlet, which to him appeared abominable. My printing this pamphlet was another erratum. While I lodged in Little Britain, I made

9. The pistole, or quarter doubloon, a Spanish coin, was then worth eighteen shillings in English currency.

1. Robert Wilks (1665?–1732), a prominent British comic actor, after 1709 associated in the management of the Haymarket and Drury Lane theaters.

2. Samuel Palmer (died 1732) was a prominent printer. Bartholomew Close was associated with the shops and lodgings of publishers, just as the Temple housed the legal profession. Both were in the center of London.

3. *The Religion of Nature Delineated* (1722), by William Wollaston (1660–

1724). According to Van Doren (*Benjamin Franklin*, pp. 51, 80), the book influenced his Deism. Wollaston argued that judgments of good and bad refer not only to religious revelation, but to a principle in Nature itself. Franklin's *Dissertation* * * * (1725), mentioned here, was a rebuttal, arguing that there are no natural vices or virtues—men simply respond to "necessity" on the basis of pain or pleasure. He soon abandoned this extreme materialism in favor of an eclectic Deism similar to Wollaston's, represented in his *Articles of Belief and Acts of Religion*, written in 1728 as his private creed.

an acquaintance with one Wilcox, a bookseller, whose shop was at the next door. He had an immense collection of second-hand books. Circulating libraries were not then in use; but we agreed that, on certain reasonable terms, which I have now forgotten, I might take, read, and return any of his books. This I esteemed a great advantage, and I made as much use of it as I could.

My pamphlet by some means falling into the hands of one Lyons,[4] a surgeon, author of a book entitled *The Infallibility of Human Judgment*, it occasioned an acquaintance between us. He took great notice of me, called on me often to converse on those subjects, carried me to the Horns, a pale alehouse in —— Lane, Cheapside, and introduced me to Dr. Mandeville,[5] author of the *Fable of the Bees*, who had a club there, of which he was the soul, being a most facetious, entertaining companion. Lyons, too, introduced me to Dr. Pemberton,[6] at Batson's Coffeehouse, who promised to give me an opportunity, some time or other, of seeing Sir Isaac Newton, of which I was extremely desirous; but this never happened.

I had brought over a few curiosities, among which the principal was a purse made of the asbestos, which purifies by fire. Sir Hans Sloane[7] heard of it, came to see me, and invited me to his house in Bloomsbury Square, where he showed me all his curiosities, and persuaded me to let him add that to the number, for which he paid me handsomely.

In our house there lodged a young woman, a milliner, who, I think, had a shop in the Cloisters. She had been genteelly bred, was sensible and lively, and of most pleasing conversation. Ralph read plays to her in the evenings; they grew intimate; she took another lodging, and he followed her. They lived together some time; but he being still out of business, and her income not sufficient to maintain them with her child, he took a resolution of going from London, to try for a country school, which he thought himself well qualified to undertake, as he wrote an excellent hand and was a master of arithmetic and accounts. This, however, he deemed a business below him, and confident of future better fortune, when he should be unwilling to have it known that he once was so meanly employed, he changed his name, and did me the honor to assume mine; for I soon after had a letter from him, acquainting me that he was settled in a small village (in Berkshire, I think it was), where he taught

---

4. According to Van Doren, William Lyons; his book is insignificant.
5. Bernard Mandeville (1670?–1733), Dutch-born physician. His political satire, *The Fable of the Bees: or, Private Vices, Public Benefits* (1714, revision of an earlier title, 1705) created sensational controversy by arguing that all acts of "virtue" spring from some selfishness.

6. Henry Pemberton was an editor and explicator of Newton; the latter, then eighty-four, was the scientific fountainhead of the Enlightenment.
7. Sir Hans Sloane (1660–1753), eminent botanist and physician, who left many thousands of bound volumes and manuscripts as the beginning of the British Museum collection.

reading and writing to ten or a dozen boys, at sixpence each per week, recommending Mrs. T. to my care, and desiring me to write to him, directing for Mr. Franklin, schoolmaster, at such a place.

He continued to write frequently, sending me large specimens of an epic poem which he was then composing, and desiring my remarks and corrections. These I gave him from time to time, but endeavored rather to discourage his proceeding. One of Young's *Satires* was then just published. I copied and sent him a great part of it, which set in a strong light the folly of pursuing the Muses with any hope of advancement by them. All was in vain; sheets of the poem continued to come by every post. In the meantime, Mrs. T., having on his account lost her friends and business, was often in distresses, and used to send for me and borrow what I could spare to help her out of them. I grew fond of her company, and being at this time under no religious restraints and presuming upon my importance to her, I attempted familiarities (another erratum), which she repulsed with a proper resentment, and acquainted him with my behavior. This made a breach between us; and when he returned again to London, he let me know he thought I had cancelled all the obligations he had been under to me. So I found I was never to expect his repaying me what I lent to him, or advanced for him. This was, however, not then of much consequence, as he was totally unable; and in the loss of his friendship I found myself relieved from a burden. I now began to think of getting a little money beforehand; and expecting better work I left Palmer's to work at Watts's,[8] near Lincoln's Inn Fields, a still greater printing-house. Here I continued all the rest of my stay in London. * * *

At Watts's printing-house I contracted an acquaintance with an ingenious young man, one Wygate, who, having wealthy relations, had been better educated than most printers; was a tolerable Latinist, spoke French, and loved reading. I taught him and a friend of his to swim at twice going into the river, and they soon became good swimmers. They introduced me to some gentlemen from the country who went to Chelsea[9] by water to see the College and Don Saltero's curiosities. In our return, at the request of the company, whose curiosity Wygate had excited, I stripped and leaped into the river, and swam from near Chelsea to Blackfriar's, performing on the way many feats of activity, both upon and under water, that surprised and pleased those to whom they were novelties.

I had from a child been ever delighted with this exercise, had

8. According to Van Doren (*Benjamin Franklin*, p. 53), James Watts (died 1763) employed fifty printers; his establishment was a good school for Franklin.
9. Now a borough of London, then a re-

sort for boats up the Thames. The old College there had become a veteran's hospital; Don Saltero, mentioned by Steele in the *Tatler*, maintained there a coffeehouse and museum patronized by scientific and literary London.

studied and practiced all Thevenot's[1] motions and positions, added some of my own, aiming at the graceful and easy as well as the useful. All these I took this occasion of exhibiting to the company, and was much flattered by their admiration; and Wygate, who was desirous of becoming a master, grew more and more attached to me on that account, as well as from the similarity of our studies. He at length proposed to me traveling all over Europe together, supporting ourselves everywhere by working at our business. I was once inclined to it; but, mentioning it to my good friend Mr. Denham, with whom I often spent an hour when I had leisure, he dissuaded me from it, advising me to think only of returning to Pennsylvania, which he was now about to do.

I must record one trait of this good man's character. He had formerly been in business at Bristol, but failed in debt to a number of people, compounded, and went to America. There, by a close application to business as a merchant, he acquired a plentiful fortune in a few years. Returning to England in the ship with me, he invited his old creditors to an entertainment, at which he thanked them for the easy composition they had favored him with, and, when they expected nothing but the treat, every man at the first remove found under his plate an order on a banker for the full amount of the unpaid remainder with interest.

He now told me he was about to return to Philadelphia, and should carry over a great quantity of goods in order to open a store there. He proposed to take me over as his clerk, to keep his books, in which he would instruct me, copy his letters, and attend the store. He added that as soon as I should be acquainted with mercantile business, he would promote me by sending me with a cargo of flour and bread, etc., to the West Indies, and procure me commissions from others which would be profitable; and if I managed well would establish me handsomely. The thing pleased me; for I was grown tired of London, remembered with pleasure the happy months I had spent in Pennsylvania, and wished again to see it; therefore I immediately agreed on the terms of fifty pounds a year, Pennsylvania money; less, indeed, than my present gettings as a compositor, but affording a better prospect. * * *

Thus I spent about eighteen months in London; most part of the time I worked hard at my business, and spent but little upon myself except in seeing plays and in books. My friend Ralph had kept me poor; he owed me about twenty-seven pounds, which I was now never likely to receive; a great sum out of my small earnings! I loved him, notwithstanding, for he had many amiable qualities, though

---

1. Melchissédech Thévenot's illustrated *Art of Swimming* (in French, 1695) was still the authority.

I had by no means improved my fortune; but I had picked up some very ingenious acquaintance, whose conversation was of great advantage to me; and I had read considerably.

We sailed from Gravesend on the 23rd of July, 1726. For the incidents of the voyage, I refer you to my Journal, where you will find them all minutely related. Perhaps the most important part of that journal is the *plan*[2] to be found in it, which I formed at sea, for regulating my future conduct in life. It is the more remarkable, as being formed when I was so young, and yet being pretty faithfully adhered to quite through to old age.

We landed in Philadelphia on the 11th of October, where I found sundry alterations. Keith was no longer governor, being superseded by Major Gordon.[3] I met him walking the streets as a common citizen. He seemed a little ashamed at seeing me, but passed without saying anything. I should have been as much ashamed at seeing Miss Read, had not her friends, despairing with reason of my return after the receipt of my letter, persuaded her to marry another, one Rogers, a potter, which was done in my absence. With him, however, she was never happy, and soon parted from him, refusing to cohabit with him or bear his name, it being now said that he had another wife. He was a worthless fellow, though an excellent workman, which was the temptation to her friends. He got into debt, ran away in 1727 or 28, and went to the West Indies, and died there. Keimer had got a better house, a shop well supplied with stationery, plenty of new types, a number of hands, though none good, and seemed to have a great deal of business.

Mr. Denham took a store in Water Street, where we opened our goods; I attended the business diligently, studied accounts, and grew, in a little time, expert at selling. We lodged and boarded together; he counseled me as a father, having a sincere regard for me. I respected and loved him, and we might have gone on together very happily; but, in the beginning of February, 1726/7,[4] when I had just passed my twenty-first year, we both were taken ill. My distemper was a pleurisy, which very nearly carried me off. I suffered a good deal, gave up the point in my own mind, and was rather disappointed when I found myself recovering, regretting, in some degree, that I must now, some time or other, have all that disagreeable work to do over again. I forget what his distemper was; it held him a long time, and at length carried him off. He left me a small legacy in a nuncupative will, as a token of his kindness for me, and he left me once more to the wide world; for the store was taken into the care of his execu-

2. The "Journal" (*Writings*, edited by Smyth, Vol. II, pp. 53–86) does not contain this "plan."
3. Major Patrick Gordon, colonial governor of Pennsylvania, 1726–1736.
4. In the Old Style (Julian) calendar, replaced in 1752 by the New Style (Gregorian) calendar, the year began on March 25. In the dual reckoning, Franklin was twenty-one on January 6/17, 1726/7.

tors, and my employment under him ended.

My brother-in-law, Holmes, being now at Philadelphia, advised my return to my business; and Keimer tempted me, with an offer of large wages by the year, to come and take the management of his printing-house, that he might better attend his stationer's shop. I had heard a bad character of him in London from his wife and her friends, and was not fond of having any more to do with him. I tried for farther employment as a merchant's clerk; but not readily meeting with any I closed again with Keimer. I found in his house these hands: Hugh Meredith, a Welsh Pennsylvanian, thirty years of age, bred to country work; honest, sensible, had a great deal of solid observation, was something of a reader, but given to drink. Stephen Potts, a young countryman of full age, bred to the same, of uncommon natural parts, and great wit and humor, but a little idle. These he had agreed with at extreme low wages per week, to be raised a shilling every three months, as they would deserve by improving in their business, and the expectation of these high wages, to come on hereafter, was what he had drawn them in with. Meredith was to work at press, Potts at book-binding, which he, by agreement, was to teach them, though he knew neither one nor the other. John ——, a wild Irishman, brought up to no business, whose service, for four years, Keimer had purchased from the captain of a ship; he, too, was to be made a pressman. George Webb, an Oxford scholar, whose time for four years he had likewise bought, intending him for a compositor, of whom more presently; and David Harry, a country boy, whom he had taken apprentice.

I soon perceived that the intention of engaging me at wages so much higher than he had been used to give was to have these raw, cheap hands formed through me; and, as soon as I had instructed them, then they being all articled to him, he should be able to do without me. I went on, however, very cheerfully, put his printing-house in order, which had been in great confusion, and brought his hands by degrees to mind their business and to do it better. * * *

Our printing-house often wanted sorts,[5] and there was no letter-founder in America; I had seen types cast at James's in London, but without much attention to the manner; however, I now contrived a mold, made use of the letters we had as puncheons, struck the matrices in lead, and thus supplied in a pretty tolerable way all deficiencies. I also engraved several things on occasion; I made the ink; I was warehouseman and everything, and, in short, quite a factotum.

But, however serviceable I might be, I found that my services became every day of less importance, as the other hands improved in the business; and when Keimer paid my second quarter's wages, he

5. Duplicate characters or letters in a type font.

let me know that he felt them too heavy, and thought I should make an abatement. He grew by degrees less civil, put on more of the master, frequently found fault, was captious, and seemed ready for an outbreaking. I went on, nevertheless, with a good deal of patience, thinking that his encumbered circumstances were partly the cause. At length a trifle snapped our connection; for a great noise happening near the courthouse, I put my head out of the window to see what was the matter. Keimer, being in the street, looked up and saw me, called out to me in a loud voice and angry tone to mind my business, adding some reproachful words, that nettled me the more for their publicity, all the neighbors who were looking out on the same occasion being witnesses how I was treated. He came up immediately into the printing-house, continued the quarrel, high words passed on both sides, he gave me the quarter's warning we had stipulated, expressing a wish that he had not been obliged to so long a warning. I told him his wish was unnecessary, for I would leave him that instant; and so, taking my hat, walked out of doors, desiring Meredith, whom I saw below, to take care of some things I left, and bring them to my lodging.

Meredith came accordingly in the evening, when we talked my affair over. He had conceived a great regard for me, and was very unwilling that I should leave the house while he remained in it. He dissuaded me from returning to my native country, which I began to think of; he reminded me that Keimer was in debt for all he possessed; that his creditors began to be uneasy; that he kept his shop miserably, sold often without profit for ready money, and often trusted without keeping accounts; that he must therefore fail, which would make a vacancy I might profit of. I objected my want of money. He then let me know that his father had a high opinion of me, and, from some discourse that had passed between them, he was sure would advance money to set us up, if I would enter into partnership with him. "My time," says he, "will be out with Keimer in the spring; by that time we may have our press and types in from London. I am sensible I am no workman; if you like it, your skill in the business shall be set against the stock I furnish, and we will share the profits equally."

The proposal was agreeable, and I consented; his father was in town and approved of it; the more as he saw I had great influence with his son, had prevailed on him to abstain long from dram-drinking, and he hoped might break him off that wretched habit entirely, when we came to be so closely connected. I gave an inventory to the father, who carried it to a merchant; the things were sent for. The secret was to be kept till they should arrive, and in the meantime I was to get work, if I could, at the other printing-house. But I found no vacancy there, and so remained idle a few days, when Keimer, on a prospect of being employed to print some paper money in New Jersey, which would require cuts and various types that I only could supply, and apprehending Bradford might engage me and get the job from him, sent me a very civil message, that old friends should not part for a few words, the effect of sudden passion, and wishing me to return. Meredith persuaded me to comply, as it would give more opportunity for his improvement under my daily instructions; so I returned, and we went on more smoothly than for some time before. The New Jersey job was obtained, I contrived a copperplate press for it, the first that had been seen in the country; I cut several ornaments and checks for the bills. We went together to Burlington, where I executed the whole to satisfaction; and he received so large a sum for the work as to be enabled thereby to keep his head much longer above water.

At Burlington[6] I made an acquaintance with many principal people of the province. Several of them had been appointed by the Assembly a committee to attend the press, and take care that no more bills were printed than the law directed. They were therefore, by turns, constantly with us, and generally he who attended brought with him a friend or two for company. My mind having been much more improved by reading than Keimer's, I suppose it was for that reason my conversation seemed to be more valued. They had me to their houses, introduced me to their friends, and showed me much civility; while he, though the master, was a little neglected. In truth, he was an odd fish; ignorant of common life, fond of rudely opposing received opinions, slovenly to extreme dirtiness, enthusiastic in some points of religion, and a little knavish withal. * * *

Before I enter upon my public appearance in business, it may be well to let you know the then state of my mind with regard to my principles and morals, that you may see how far those influenced the future events of my life. My parents had early given me religious impressions, and brought me through my childhood piously in the dissenting way. But I was scarce fifteen, when, after doubting by turns of several points, as I found them disputed in the different books I read, I began to doubt of Revelation itself. Some books against deism fell into my hands; they were said to be the substance of sermons preached at Boyle's lectures.[7] It happened that they wrought an effect on me quite contrary to what was intended by them; for the arguments of the deists, which were quoted to be refuted, appeared to me much stronger than the refutations; in short, I soon became a thorough deist. My arguments perverted some others, particularly Collins and Ralph; but each of them having afterwards wronged me greatly without the least compunction, and

6. Capital of West Jersey.
7. Robert Boyle (1627–1691), famous British pioneer physicist, discoverer of Boyle's law; endowed the Boyle Lectures for defense of Christianity.

recollecting Keith's conduct towards me (who was another free-thinker), and my own towards Vernon and Miss Read, which at times gave me great trouble, I began to suspect that this doctrine, though it might be true, was not very useful. My London pamphlet, which had for its motto these lines of Dryden—

> "Whatever is, is right. Tho' purblind Man
> Sees but a Part of the Chain, the nearest Link,
> His Eyes not carrying to the equal Beam,
> That poises all, above."[8]

—and from the attributes of God, his infinite wisdom, goodness, and power, concluded that nothing could possibly be wrong in the world, and that vice and virtue were empty distinctions, no such things existing, appeared now not so clever a performance as I once thought it; and I doubted whether some error had not insinuated itself unperceived into my argument, so as to infect all that followed, as is common in metaphysical reasonings.

I grew convinced that *truth, sincerity* and *integrity* in dealings between man and man were of the utmost importance to the felicity of life; and I formed written resolutions (which still remain in my journal book), to practice them ever while I lived. Revelation had indeed no weight with me as such; but I entertained an opinion that, though certain actions might not be bad *because* they were forbidden by it, or good *because* it commanded them, yet probably these actions might be forbidden *because* they were bad for us, or commanded *because* they were beneficial to us in their own natures, all the circumstances of things considered. And this persuasion, with the kind hand of Providence or some guardian angel, or accidental favorable circumstances and situations, or all together, preserved me through this dangerous time of youth, and the hazardous situations I was sometimes in among strangers, remote from the eye and advice of my father, without any *willful* gross immorality or injustice, that might have been expected from my want of religion. I say *willful*, because the instances I have mentioned had something of *necessity* in them, from my youth, inexperience, and the knavery of others. I had therefore a tolerable character to begin the world with; I valued it properly, and determined to preserve it.

We had not been long returned to Philadelphia before the new types arrived from London. We settled with Keimer, and left him by his consent before he heard of it. We found a house to hire near the market, and took it. To lessen the rent, which was then but twenty-four pounds a year, though I have since known it to let for seventy, we took in Thomas Godfrey,[9] a glazier, and his family, who

8. He apparently quotes from memory, with some slight variations. *Cf.* Dryden's *Oedipus* (London, 1679), Act III, Scene 2.

9. Thomas Godfrey, later a member of the Junto mentioned in the following

were to pay a considerable part of it to us, and we to board with them. We had scarce opened our letters and put our press in order, before George House, an acquaintance of mine, brought a countryman to us, whom he had met in the street inquiring for a printer. All our cash was now expended in the variety of particulars we had been obliged to procure, and this countryman's five shillings, being our first-fruits, and coming so seasonably, gave me more pleasure than any crown[1] I have since earned; and from the gratitude I felt towards House, has made me often more ready than perhaps I should otherwise have been to assist young beginners. * * *

I should have mentioned before that in the autumn of the preceding year, I had formed most of my ingenious acquaintance into a club of mutual improvement, which we called the Junto.[2] We met on Friday evenings. The rules that I drew up required that every member, in his turn, should produce one or more queries on any point of morals, politics, or natural philosophy, to be discussed by the company; and once in three months produce and read an essay of his own writing, on any subject he pleased. Our debates were to be under the direction of a president, and to be conducted in the sincere spirit of inquiry after truth, without fondness for dispute, or desire of victory; and, to prevent warmth, all expressions of positiveness in opinions, or direct contradiction, were after some time made contraband, and prohibited under small pecuniary penalties.

The first members were Joseph Breintnal, a copier of deeds for the scriveners, a good-natured, friendly, middle-aged man, a great lover of poetry, reading all he could meet with, and writing some that was tolerable; very ingenious in many little nicknackeries, and of sensible conversation. Thomas Godfrey, a self-taught mathematician, great in his way, and afterwards inventor of what is now called Hadley's quadrant. But he knew little out of his way, and was not a pleasing companion; as, like most great mathematicians I have met with, he expected universal precision in everything said, or was forever denying or distinguishing upon trifles, to the disturbance of all conversation. He soon left us. Nicholas Scull, a surveyor, afterwards surveyor-general, who loved books, and sometimes made a few verses. William Parsons, bred a shoemaker, but loving reading, had acquired a considerable share of mathematics, which he first studied with a view to astrology, that he afterwards laughed at. He also became surveyor-general. William Maugridge, a joiner,[3] a most exquisite mechanic, and a solid, sensible man. Hugh Meredith, Stephen

---

paragraph, a mathematician and the inventor of a quadrant long standard for navigation, was the father of Thomas Godfrey (1736–1763), who wrote the first American tragedy, *The Prince of Parthia* (1767).
1. Five shillings.

2. A faction or cabal, often secret (from the Spanish *junta*). This is the first American literary society of any duration; as Franklin shows, a number of its members achieved high distinction.
3. Cabinetmaker.

Potts, and George Webb I have characterized before. Robert Grace, a young gentleman of some fortune, generous, lively, and witty; a lover of punning and of his friends. And William Coleman, then a merchant's clerk, about my age, who had the coolest, clearest head, the best heart, and the exactest morals of almost any man I ever met with. He became afterwards a merchant of great note, and one of our provincial judges. Our friendship continued without interruption to his death, upwards of forty years. And the club continued almost as long, and was the best school of philosophy and politics that then existed in the province; for our queries, which were read the week preceding their discussion, put us on reading with attention upon the several subjects, that we might speak more to the purpose, and here, too, we acquired better habits of conversation, everything being studied in our rules which might prevent our disgusting each other. From hence the long continuance of the club, which I shall have frequent occasion to speak farther of hereafter.

But my giving this account of it here is to show something of the interest I had, every one of these exerting themselves in recommending business to us. Breintnal particularly procured us from the Quakers the printing forty sheets of their history,[4] the rest being to be done by Keimer; and upon this we worked exceeding hard, for the price was low. It was a folio, pro patria size, in pica, with long primer notes. I composed of it a sheet a day, and Meredith worked it off at press; it was often eleven at night, and sometimes later, before I had finished my distribution for the next day's work, for the little jobs sent in by our other friends now and then put us back. But so determined I was to continue doing a sheet a day of the folio that one night, when, having imposed my forms, I thought my day's work over, one of them by accident was broken, and two pages reduced to pi,[5] I immediately distributed and composed it over again before I went to bed. And this industry, visible to our neighbors, began to give us character and credit; particularly I was told that mention being made of the new printing-office at the merchants' every-night club, the general opinion was that it must fail, there being already two printers in the place, Keimer and Bradford; but Dr. Baird (whom you and I saw many years after at his native place, St. Andrew's in Scotland) gave a contrary opinion: "For the industry of that Franklin," says he, "is superior to anything I ever saw of the kind; I see him still at work when I go home from club, and he is at work again before his neighbors are out of bed." This struck the rest, and we soon after had offers from one of them to supply us

4. By William Sewel (or Sewell), a Dutch Quaker: *The History of the Rise, Increase, and Progress of the People Called Quakers* (Amsterdam, 1717; London, 1725; third edition, in English translation, Philadelphia. Samuel Keimer, 1728).

5. That is, he composed and locked up the type into the page forms (chases) for printing. The accident made a jumble (pi) of them (*cf.* "pied," meaning "disordered" printing).

with stationery; but as yet we did not choose to engage in shop business.

I mention this industry the more particularly and the more freely, though it seems to be talking in my own praise, that those of my posterity who shall read it may know the use of that virtue, when they see its effects in my favor throughout this relation.

George Webb, who had found a female friend that lent him wherewith to purchase his time of Keimer, now came to offer himself as a journeyman to us. We could not then employ him; but I foolishly let him know, as a secret, that I soon intended to begin a newspaper, and might then have work for him. My hopes of success, as I told him, were founded on this, that the then only newspaper,[6] printed by Bradford, was a paltry thing, wretchedly managed, no way entertaining, and yet was profitable to him; I therefore thought a good paper could scarcely fail of good encouragement. I requested Webb not to mention it; but he told it to Keimer, who immediately, to be beforehand with me, published proposals for printing one himself,[7] on which Webb was to be employed. I resented this; and to counteract them, as I could not yet begin our paper, I wrote several pieces of entertainment for Bradford's paper, under the title of the Busy Body, which Breintnal continued some months. By this means the attention of the public was fixed on that paper, and Keimer's proposals, which we burlesqued and ridiculed, were disregarded. He began his paper, however, and after carrying it on three quarters of a year, with at most only ninety subscribers, he offered it me for a trifle; and I, having been ready some time to go on with it, took it in hand directly; and it proved in a few years extremely profitable to me.

I perceive that I am apt to speak in the singular number, though our partnership still continued, the reason may be that in fact the whole management of the business lay upon me. Meredith was no compositor, a poor pressman, and seldom sober. My friends lamented my connection with him, but I was to make the best of it.

Our first papers made a quite different appearance from any before in the province; a better type, and better printed; but some spirited remarks of my writing on the dispute then going on between Governor Burnet and the Massachusetts Assembly struck the principal people, occasioned the paper and the manager of it to be much talked of, and in a few weeks brought them all to be our subscribers.

6. *American Weekly Mercury* (1719–1746). As Franklin explains, six of his "Busy Body Papers" in the *Mercury* (1729) "burlesqued and ridiculed" Keimer's new *Gazette* until Franklin was able to buy it himself.

7. Samuel Keimer published the first number of *The Universal Instructor in All Arts and Sciences and Pennslyvania Gazette* on December 24, 1728. Franklin bought him out "for a trifle," and assumed its publication as *The Pennsylvania Gazette*, dated September 25–October 2, 1729. It made him a fortune. In 1766 he relinquished it to David Hall, his partner; it continued publication until 1815.

Their example was followed by many, and our number went on growing continually. This was one of the first good effects of my having learned a little to scribble; another was that the leading men, seeing a newspaper now in the hands of one who could also handle a pen, thought it convenient to oblige and encourage me. Bradford still printed the votes, and laws, and other public business. He had printed an Address of the House to the Governor, in a coarse, blundering manner. We reprinted it elegantly and correctly, and sent one to every member. They were sensible of the difference: it strengthened the hands of our friends in the House, and they voted us their printers for the year ensuing. * * *

About this time[8] there was a cry among the people for more paper money, only fifteen thousand pounds being extant in the province, and that soon to be sunk. The wealthy inhabitants opposed any addition, being against all paper currency, from an apprehension that it would depreciate, as it had done in New England, to the prejudice of all creditors. We had discussed this point in our Junto, where I was on the side of an addition, being persuaded that the first small sum struck in 1723 had done much good by increasing the trade, employment, and number of inhabitants in the province, since I now saw all the old houses inhabited, and many new ones building: whereas I remembered well, that when I first walked about the streets of Philadelphia, eating my roll, I saw most of the houses in Walnut Street, between Second and Front streets, with bills on their doors to be let; and many likewise in Chestnut Street and other streets, which made me then think the inhabitants of the city were deserting it one after another.

Our debates possessed me so fully of the subject, that I wrote and printed an anonymous pamphlet[9] on it, entitled *The Nature and Necessity of a Paper Currency*. It was well received by the common people in general; but the rich men disliked it, for it increased and strengthened the clamor for more money; and they happening to have no writers among them that were able to answer it, their opposition slackened, and the point was carried by a majority in the House. My friends there, who conceived I had been of some service, thought fit to reward me by employing me in printing the money, a very profitable job and a great help to me.[1] This was another advantage gained by my being able to write.

The utility of this currency became by time and experience so evident as never afterwards to be much disputed; so that it grew soon to fifty-five thousand pounds, and in 1739 to eighty thousand pounds, since which it arose during war to upwards of three hundred and fifty thousand pounds—trade, building, and inhabitants all the

8. The winter of 1728–1729.
9. Dated April 3, 1729.

1. Franklin had bought out his partner, Hugh Meredith, in July, 1730, having borrowed money for the transaction.

while increasing—though I now think there are limits beyond which the quantity may be hurtful.

I soon after obtained through my friend Hamilton the printing of the Newcastle[2] paper money, another profitable job as I then thought it, small things appearing great to those in small circumstances; and these, to me, were really great advantages, as they were great encouragements. He procured for me, also, the printing of the laws and votes of that government, which continued in my hands as long as I followed the business.

I now opened a little stationer's shop. I had in it blanks of all sorts, the correctest that ever appeared among us, being assisted in that by my friend Breintnal. I had also paper, parchment, chapmen's books, etc. One Whitemash, a compositor I had known in London, an excellent workman, now came to me, and worked with me constantly and diligently; and I took an apprentice, the son of Aquila Rose.

I began now gradually to pay off the debt I was under for the printing-house. In order to secure my credit and character as a tradesman, I took care not only to be in *reality* industrious and frugal, but to avoid all *appearances* of the contrary. I dressed plainly; I was seen at no places of idle diversion. I never went out afishing or shooting; a book, indeed, sometimes debauched me from my work, but that was seldom, snug, and gave no scandal; and, to show that I was not above my business, I sometimes brought home the paper I purchased at the stores through the streets on a wheelbarrow. Thus being esteemed an industrious, thriving young man, and paying duly for what I bought, the merchants who imported stationery solicited my custom; others proposed supplying me with books; I went on swimmingly. In the meantime, Keimer's credit and business declining daily, he was at last forced to sell his printing-house to satisfy his creditors.[3] He went to Barbados, and there lived some years in very poor circumstances. * * *

There remained now no competitor with me at Philadelphia but the old one, Bradford, who was rich and easy, did a little printing now and then by straggling hands, but was not very anxious about it. However, as he kept the post-office, it was imagined he had better opportunities of obtaining news; his paper was thought a better distributer of advertisements than mine, and therefore had many more, which was a profitable thing to him, and a disadvantage to me; for, though I did indeed receive and send papers by the post, yet the public opinion was otherwise, for what I did send was by bribing the riders, who took them privately, Bradford being unkind enough to forbid it, which occasioned some resentment on my part;

2. *I.e.*, for Delaware.
3. In 1729, according to Van Doren, Keimer's apprentice, David Harry, took over his print shop, but he, too, failed in a few months.

and I thought so meanly of him for it, that when I afterward came into his situation[4] I took care never to imitate it.

I had hitherto continued to board with Godfrey, who lived in part of my house with his wife and children, and had one side of the shop for his glazier's business, though he worked little, being always absorbed in his mathematics. Mrs. Godfrey projected a match for me with a relation's daughter, took opportunities of bringing us often together, till a serious courtship on my part ensued, the girl being in herself very deserving. The old folks encouraged me by continual invitations to supper, and by leaving us together, till at length it was time to explain. Mrs. Godfrey managed our little treaty. I let her know that I expected as much money with their daughter as would pay off my remaining debt for the printing-house, which I believe was not then above a hundred pounds. She brought me word they had no such sum to spare; I said they might mortgage their house in the loan-office. The answer to this after some days was that they did not approve the match; that, on inquiry of Bradford, they had been informed the printing business was not a profitable one, the types would soon be worn out, and more wanted, that S. Keimer and D. Harry had failed one after the other, and I should probably soon follow them; and therefore I was forbidden the house, and the daughter shut up.

Whether this was a real change of sentiment or only artifice, on a supposition of our being too far engaged in affection to retract, and therefore that we should steal a marriage, which would leave them at liberty to give or withhold what they pleased, I know not; but I suspected the latter, resented it, and went no more. Mrs. Godfrey brought me afterwards some more favorable accounts of their disposition, and would have drawn me on again; but I declared absolutely my resolution to have nothing more to do with that family. This was resented by the Godfreys; we differed, and they removed, leaving me the whole house, and I resolved to take no more inmates.

But this affair having turned my thoughts to marriage, I looked around me and made overtures of acquaintance in other places; but soon found that, the business of a printer being generally thought a poor one, I was not to expect money with a wife, unless with such a one as I should not otherwise think agreeable. In the meantime that hard-to-be-governed passion of youth hurried me frequently into intrigues with low women that fell in my way, which were attended with some expense and great inconvenience, besides a continual risk of my health by a distemper, which of all things I dreaded, though by great good luck I escaped it.

4. Franklin became Deputy Postmaster-General for all the colonies in 1753. He required a fee for the carriage of news-papers, and made the service available to all publishers.

A friendly correspondence as neighbors and old acquaintances had continued between me and Mrs. Read's family, who all had a regard for me from the time of my first lodging in their house. I was often invited there and consulted in their affairs, wherein I sometimes was of service. I pitied poor Miss Read's unfortunate situation, who was generally dejected, seldom cheerful, and avoided company. I considered my giddiness and inconstancy when in London as in a great degree the cause of her unhappiness, though the mother was good enough to think the fault more her own than mine, as she had prevented our marrying before I went thither, and persuaded the other match in my absence. Our mutual affection was revived, but there were now great objections to our union. That match was indeed looked upon as invalid, a preceding wife being said to be living in England; but this could not easily be proved, because of the distance; and though there was a report of his death, it was not certain. Then, though it should be true, he had left many debts, which his successor might be called upon to pay. We ventured, however, over all these difficulties, and I took her to wife, September 1st, 1730. None of the inconveniences happened that we had apprehended; she proved a good and faithful helpmate, assisted me much by attending the shop; we throve together, and have ever mutually endeavored to make each other happy. Thus I corrected that great erratum as well as I could.

About this time, our club meeting not at a tavern but in a little room of Mr. Grace's, set apart for that purpose, a proposition was made by me, that, since our books were often referred to in our disquisitions upon the queries, it might be convenient to us to have them altogether where we met, that upon occasion they might be consulted; and by thus clubbing our books to a common library, we should, while we liked to keep them together, have each of us the advantage of using the books of all the other members, which would be nearly as beneficial as if each owned the whole. It was liked and agreed to, and we filled one end of the room with such books as we could best spare. The number was not so great as we expected; and though they had been of great use, yet some inconveniences occurring for want of due care of them, the collection, after about a year, was separated, and each took his books home again.

And now I set on foot my first project of a public nature, that for a subscription library. I drew up the proposals, got them put into form by our great scrivener, Brockden, and, by the help of my friends in the Junto, procured fifty subscribers of forty shillings each to begin with, and ten shillings a year for fifty years, the term our company was to continue.[5] We afterwards obtained a charter, the company

5. Founded in 1731, this Library Company of Philadelphia is still in existence, housing an important collection of early Americana.

being increased to one hundred. This was the mother of all the North American subscription libraries, now so numerous. It is become a great thing itself, and continually increasing. These libraries have improved the general conversation of the Americans, made the common tradesmen and farmers as intelligent as most gentlemen from other countries, and perhaps have contributed in some degree to the stand so generally made throughout the colonies in defence of their privileges.[6] * * *

This library afforded me the means of improvement by constant study, for which I set apart an hour or two each day, and thus repaired in some degree the loss of the learned education my father once intended for me. Reading was the only amusement I allowed myself. I spent no time in taverns, games, or frolics of any kind; and my industry in my business continued as indefatigable as it was necessary. I was indebted for my printing-house; I had a young family coming on to be educated, and I had to contend with, for business, two printers who were established in the place before me. My circumstances, however, grew daily easier. My original habits of frugality continuing, and my father having, among his instructions to me when a boy, frequently repeated a proverb of Solomon,[7] "Seest thou a man diligent in his calling; he shall stand before kings, he shall not stand before mean men," I from thence considered industry as a means of obtaining wealth and distinction, which encouraged me, though I did not think that I should ever literally *stand before kings*, which, however, has since happened; for I have stood before *five*, and even had the honor of sitting down with one—the King of Denmark—to dinner. * * *

I had been religiously educated as a Presbyterian; and though some of the dogmas of that persuasion, such as *the eternal decrees of God, election, reprobation, etc.*, appeared to me unintelligible, others doubtful, and I early absented myself from the public assemblies of the sect, Sunday being my studying day, I never was without some religious principles. I never doubted, for instance, the existence of the Deity; that he made the world, and governed it by his Providence; that the most acceptable service of God was the doing good to man; that our souls are immortal; and that all crime will be punished, and virtue rewarded, either here or hereafter. These I esteemed the essentials of every religion; and, being to be found in all the religions we had in our country, I respected them all, though with different degrees of respect, as I found them more or less mixed

6. The first manuscript, dated 1771, ends here. It is followed by a brief correspondence, dated 1783, in which friends urge him to complete his autobiography. The third section, which is given in part below, is headed "Continuation of the Account of my Life, begun at Passy, near Paris, 1784."
7. Proverbs xxii: 29.

with other articles, which, without any tendency to inspire, promote, or confirm morality, served principally to divide us, and make us unfriendly to one another. This respect to all, with an opinion that the worst had some good effects, induced me to avoid all discourse that might tend to lessen the good opinion another might have of his own religion; and as our province increased in people, and new places of worship were continually wanted, and generally erected by voluntary contribution, my mite for such purpose, whatever might be the sect, was never refused.

Though I seldom attended any public worship, I had still an opinion of its propriety, and of its utility when rightly conducted, and I regularly paid my annual subscription for the support of the only Presbyterian minister or meeting we had in Philadelphia. He used to visit me sometimes as a friend, and admonish me to attend his administrations, and I was now and then prevailed on to do so, once for five Sundays successively. Had he been in my opinion a good preacher, perhaps I might have continued, notwithstanding the occasion I had for the Sunday's leisure in my course of study; but his discourses were chiefly either polemic arguments, or explications of the peculiar doctrines of our sect, and were all to me very dry, uninteresting, and unedifying, since not a single moral principle was inculcated or enforced, their aim seeming to be rather to make us Presbyterians than good citizens. * * *

It was about this time I conceived the bold and arduous project of arriving at moral perfection. I wished to live without committing any fault at any time; I would conquer all that either natural inclination, custom, or company might lead me into. As I knew, or thought I knew, what was right and wrong, I did not see why I might not always do the one and avoid the other. But I soon found I had undertaken a task of more difficulty than I had imagined. While my care was employed in guarding against one fault, I was often surprised by another; habit took the advantage of inattention; inclination was sometimes too strong for reason. I concluded, at length, that the mere speculative conviction that it was our interest to be completely virtuous was not sufficient to prevent our slipping; and that the contrary habits must be broken, and good ones acquired and established, before we can have any dependence on a steady, uniform rectitude of conduct. For this purpose I therefore contrived the following method.

In the various enumerations of the moral virtues I had met with in my reading, I found the catalogue more or less numerous, as different writers included more or fewer ideas under the same name. Temperance, for example, was by some confined to eating and drinking, while by others it was extended to mean the moderating every other pleasure, appetite, inclination, or passion, bodily or mental, even to our avarice and ambition. I proposed to myself, for the sake of clearness, to use rather more names, with fewer ideas annexed to each, than a few names with more ideas; and I included under thirteen names of virtues all that at that time occurred to me as necessary or desirable, and annexed to each a short precept, which fully expressed the extent I gave to its meaning.

These names of virtues, with their precepts, were:

1. TEMPERANCE. Eat not to dullness; drink not to elevation.

2. SILENCE. Speak not but what may benefit others or yourself; avoid trifling conversation.

3. ORDER. Let all your things have their places; let each part of your business have its time.

4. RESOLUTION. Resolve to perform what you ought; perform without fail what you resolve.

5. FRUGALITY. Make no expense but to do good to others or yourself; *i.e.*, waste nothing.

6. INDUSTRY. Lose no time; be always employed in something useful; cut off all unnecessary actions.

7. SINCERITY. Use no hurtful deceit; think innocently and justly, and, if you speak, speak accordingly.

8. JUSTICE. Wrong none by doing injuries, or omitting the benefits that are your duty.

9. MODERATION. Avoid extremes; forbear resenting injuries so much as you think they deserve.

10. CLEANLINESS. Tolerate no uncleanliness in body, clothes, or habitation.

11. TRANQUILLITY. Be not disturbed at trifles, or at accidents common or unavoidable.

12. CHASTITY. Rarely use venery but for health or offspring, never to dullness, weakness, or the injury of your own or another's peace or reputation.

13. HUMILITY. Imitate Jesus and Socrates.

My intention being to acquire the *habitude* of all these virtues, I judged it would be well not to distract my attention by attempting the whole at once, but to fix it on one of them at a time; and, when I should be master of that, then to proceed to another, and so on, till I should have gone through the thirteen; and, as the previous acquisition of some might facilitate the acquisition of certain others, I arranged them with that view, as they stand above. *Temperance* first, as it tends to procure that coolness and clearness of head, which is so necessary where constant vigilance was to be kept up, and guard maintained against the unremitting attraction of ancient habits, and the force of perpetual temptations. This being acquired and established, *Silence* would be more easy; and my desire being to gain knowledge at the same time that I improved in virtue, and considering that in conversation it was obtained rather by the use of the ears than of the tongue, and therefore wishing to break a habit I was getting into of prattling, punning, and joking, which only made me acceptable to trifling company, I gave *Silence* the second place. This and the next, *Order*, I expected would allow me more time for attending to my project and my studies. *Resolution*, once become habitual, would keep me firm in my endeavors to obtain all the subsequent virtues; *Frugality* and *Industry* freeing me from my remaining debt, and producing affluence and independence, would make more easy the practice of *Sincerity* and *Justice*, etc., etc. Conceiving then, that, agreeably to the advice of Pythagoras[8] in his Golden Verses, daily examination would be necessary, I contrived the following method for conducting that examination.

I made a little book, in which I allotted a page for each of the virtues. I ruled each page with red ink, so as to have seven columns, one for each day of the week, marking each column with a letter for the day. I crossed these columns with thirteen red lines, marking the beginning of each line with the first letter of one of the virtues, on which line, and in its proper column, I might mark, by a little black spot, every fault I found upon examination to have been committed respecting that virtue upon that day.

I determined to give a week's strict attention to each of the virtues successively. Thus, in the first week, my great guard was to avoid even the least offence against *Temperance*, leaving the other virtues to their ordinary chance, only marking every evening the faults of the day. Thus, if in the first week I could keep my first line, marked T, clear of spots, I supposed the habit of that virtue so much strengthened, and its opposite weakened, that I might venture extending my attention to include the next, and for the following week keep both lines clear of spots. Proceeding thus to the last, I could go through a course complete in thirteen weeks, and four courses in a year. And like him who, having a garden to weed, does not attempt to eradicate all the bad herbs at once, which would exceed his reach and his strength, but works on one of the beds at a time, and, having accomplished the first, proceeds to a second, so I should have, I hoped, the encouraging pleasure of seeing on my pages the progress I made in virtue, by clearing successively my lines of their spots, till in the end, by a number of courses, I should be happy in viewing a clean book, after a thirteen weeks' daily examination.

8. Influential Greek philosopher-mathematician (*fl.* 530 B.C.), whose teachings survive only in the traditions of his disciples. Franklin refers to the Pythagorean discipline of "passionate intellectual contemplation."

Form of the pages.

TEMPERANCE.							
EAT NOT TO DULLNESS; DRINK NOT TO ELEVATION.							
	S.	M.	T.	W.	T.	F.	S.
T.							
S.	*	*		*		*	
O.	* *	*	*	*		*	*
R.			*			*	
F.		*			*		
I.			*				
S.							
J.							
M.							
C.							
T.							
C.							
H.							

* * *

The precept of *Order* requiring that *every part of my business should have its allotted time*, one page in my little book contained the following scheme of employment for the twenty-four hours of a natural day.

THE MORNING.
Question. What good shall I do this day?

$$
\left.\begin{array}{r} 5 \\ 6 \\ \\ \\ \\ 7 \end{array}\right\}
$$
Rise, wash and address *Powerful Goodness!* [9] Contrive day's business, and take the resolution of the day; prosecute the present study, and breakfast.

$$
\left.\begin{array}{r} 8 \\ 9 \\ 10 \\ 11 \end{array}\right\}
$$
Work.

9. Franklin's daily prayer, prefixed to his "tables of examinations," was as follows: "O powerful Goodness! bounti- ful Father! merciful Guide! Increase in me that wisdom which discovers my truest interest. Strengthen my resolu-

made it a rule to forbear all direct contradiction to the sentiments of others, and all positive assertion of my own. I even forbid myself, agreeably to the old laws of our Junto, the use of every word or expression in the language that imported a fixed opinion, such as *certainly, undoubtedly*, etc., and I adopted, instead of them, *I conceive, I apprehend*, or *I imagine* a thing to be so or so; or it *so appears to me at present*. When another asserted something that I thought an error, I denied myself the pleasure of contradicting him abruptly, and of showing immediately some absurdity in his proposition; and in answering I began by observing that in certain cases or circumstances his opinion would be right, but in the present case there *appeared* or *seemed* to me some difference, etc. I soon found the advantage of this change in my manner; the conversations I engaged in went on more pleasantly. The modest way in which I proposed my opinions procured them a readier reception and less contradiction; I had less mortification when I was found to be in the wrong, and I more easily prevailed with others to give up their mistakes and join with me when I happened to be in the right.

And this mode, which I at first put on with some violence to natural inclination, became at length so easy, and so habitual to me, that perhaps for these fifty years past no one has ever heard a dogmatical expression escape me. And to this habit (after my character of integrity) I think it principally owing that I had early so much weight with my fellow-citizens when I proposed new institutions, or alterations in the old, and so much influence in public councils when I became a member; for I was but a bad speaker, never eloquent, subject to much hesitation in my choice of words, hardly correct in language, and yet I generally carried my points.

In reality, there is, perhaps, no one of our natural passions so hard to subdue as *pride*. Disguise it, struggle with it, beat it down, stifle it, mortify it as much as one pleases, it is still alive, and will every now and then peep out and show itself; you will see it, perhaps, often in this history; for, even if I could conceive that I had completely overcome it, I should probably be proud of my humility.[1] * * *

In 1732 I first published my almanac,[2] under the name of *Richard Saunders*; it was continued by me about twenty-five years, commonly called *Poor Richard's Almanack*. I endeavored to make it both entertaining and useful, and it accordingly came to be in such demand that I reaped considerable profit from it, vending annually near ten

1. "Thus far written at Passy, 1784" [Franklin's note]. Then, beginning a new manuscript, Franklin wrote: "I am now about to write at home [Philadelphia], August, 1788, but cannot have the help expected from my papers, many of them being lost in the war. * * *" The selections following describe some of the practical projects, from 1731 to 1753, which increased his reputation prior to his call to highest national service in the period of the Revolution.
2. *Poor Richard's Almanack*. He published it from 1733 to 1758, then sold it. See the selections in this volume, immediately following the *Autobiography*.

thousand. And observing that it was generally read, scarce any neighborhood in the province being without it, I considered it as a proper vehicle for conveying instruction among the common people, who bought scarcely any other books; I therefore filled all the little spaces that occurred between the remarkable days in the calendar with proverbial sentences, chiefly such as inculcated industry and frugality, as the means of procuring wealth, and thereby securing virtue; it being more difficult for a man in want, to act always honestly, as, to use here one of those proverbs, *it is hard for an empty sack to stand upright.*

These proverbs, which contained the wisdom of many ages and nations, I assembled and formed into a connected discourse prefixed to the Almanac of 1757, as the harangue of a wise old man to the people attending an auction.[3] The bringing all these scattered counsels thus into a focus enabled them to make greater impression. The piece, being universally approved, was copied in all the newspapers of the continent; reprinted in Britain on a broadside, to be stuck up in houses; two translations were made of it in French, and great numbers bought by the clergy and gentry, to distribute gratis among their poor parishioners and tenants. In Pennsylvania, as it discouraged useless expense in foreign superfluities, some thought it had its share of influence in producing that growing plenty of money which was observable for several years after its publication.

I considered my newspaper, also, as another means of communicating instruction, and in that view frequently reprinted in it extracts from the *Spectator*, and other moral writers; and sometimes published little pieces of my own, which had been first composed for reading in our Junto. Of these are a Socratic dialogue, tending to prove that, whatever might be his parts and abilities, a vicious man could not properly be called a man of sense; and a discourse on self-denial, showing that virtue was not secure till its practice became a habitude, and was free from the opposition of contrary inclinations. These may be found in the papers about the beginning of 1735.

In the conduct of my newspaper, I carefully excluded all libeling and personal abuse, which is of late years become so disgraceful to our country. Whenever I was solicited to insert anything of that kind, and the writers pleaded, as they generally did, the liberty of the press, and that a newspaper was like a stage-coach, in which any one who would pay had a right to a place, my answer was, that I would print the piece separately if desired, and the author might have as many copies as he pleased to distribute himself, but that I would not take upon me to spread his detraction; and that, having contracted with my subscribers to furnish them with what might

3. "The Way to Wealth"; included in this volume.

be either useful or entertaining, I could not fill their papers with private altercation, in which they had no concern, without doing them manifest injustice. Now, many of our printers make no scruple of gratifying the malice of individuals by false accusations of the fairest characters among ourselves, augmenting animosity even to the producing of duels; and are, moreover, so indiscreet as to print scurrilous reflections on the government of neighboring states, and even on the conduct of our best national allies, which may be attended with the most pernicious consequences. These things I mention as a caution to young printers, and that they may be encouraged not to pollute their presses and disgrace their profession by such infamous practices, but refuse steadily, as they may see by my example that such a course of conduct will not, on the whole, be injurious to their interests. * * *

In 1739 arrived among us from Ireland the Reverend Mr. Whitefield,[4] who had made himself remarkable there as an itinerant preacher. He was at first permitted to preach in some of our churches; but the clergy taking a dislike to him soon refused him their pulpits, and he was obliged to preach in the fields. The multitudes of all sects and denominations that attended his sermons were enormous, and it was matter of speculation to me, who was one of the number, to observe the extraordinary influence of his oratory on his hearers, and how much they admired and respected him, notwithstanding his common abuse of them, by assuring them they were naturally *half beasts and half devils*. It was wonderful to see the change soon made in the manners of our inhabitants. From being thoughtless or indifferent about religion, it seemed as if all the world were growing religious, so that one could not walk through the town in an evening without hearing psalms sung in different families of every street.

And it being found inconvenient to assemble in the open air, subject to its inclemencies, the building of a house to meet in was no sooner proposed, and persons appointed to receive contributions, but sufficient sums were soon received to procure the ground and erect the building, which was one hundred feet long and seventy broad, about the size of Westminster Hall; and the work was carried on with such spirit as to be finished in a much shorter time than could have been expected.[5] Both house and ground were vested in trustees, expressly for the use of any preacher of any religious persuasion who might desire to say something to the people at Phila-

4. George Whitefield (1714–1770), a British evangelist, was associated with the founding of the Methodist denomination, but split from the Wesleys on theological grounds, to become the leader of the Calvinistic Methodists. In his early American pilgrimages (1738–41) he became an evangelist of the "Great Awakening" (*cf.* the headnote to Jonathan Edwards).

5. Then called the New Building, it was used before completion (1739) for Whitefield's audiences, and later housed the Charity School, Academy, and College of Philadelphia (the University of Pennsylvania).

delphia; the design in building not being to accommodate any particular sect, but the inhabitants in general; so that even if the Mufti of Constantinople were to send a missionary to preach Mohammedanism to us, he would find a pulpit at his service.

Mr. Whitefield, in leaving us, went preaching all the way through the colonies to Georgia. * * * He used, indeed, sometimes to pray for my conversion, but never had the satisfaction of believing that his prayers were heard. Ours was a mere civil friendship, sincere on both sides, and lasted to his death. The following instance will show something of the terms on which we stood. Upon one of his arrivals from England at Boston, he wrote to me that he should come soon to Philadelphia, but knew not where he could lodge when there, as he understood his old friend and host, Mr. Benezet,[6] was removed to Germantown. My answer was, "You know my house; if you can make shift with its scanty accommodations, you will be most heartily welcome." He replied, that if I made that kind offer for Christ's sake, I should not miss of a reward. And I returned, "Don't let me be mistaken; it was not for Christ's sake, but for your sake." One of our common acquaintance jocosely remarked that, knowing it to be the custom of the saints, when they received any favor, to shift the burden of the obligation from off their own shoulders, and place it in heaven, I had contrived to fix it on earth.

The last time I saw Mr. Whitefield was in London, when he consulted me about his Orphan House concern, and his purpose of appropriating it to the establishment of a college. * * *

I had, on the whole, abundant reason to be satisfied with my being established in Pennsylvania. There were, however, two things that I regretted, there being no provision for defense, nor for a complete education of youth; no militia, nor any college. I therefore, in 1743, drew up a proposal for establishing an academy; and at that time, thinking the Reverend Mr. Peters,[7] who was out of employ, a fit person to superintend such an institution, I communicated the project to him; but he, having more profitable views in the service of the proprietaries, which succeeded, declined the undertaking; and, not knowing another at that time suitable for such a trust, I let the scheme lie a while dormant. I succeeded better the next year, 1744, in proposing and establishing a Philosophical Society.[8] The paper I wrote for that purpose will be found among my writings, when collected. * * *

6. Anthony Benezet (1713–1784), a French-born Quaker, settled in Philadelphia in 1731, and became a pioneer in the work for such humanitarian reforms as abolition, temperance, and the rights of Indians and Negroes.
7. Richard Peters had been Rector of Christ's Church, Philadelphia, and was expecting appointment as Secretary of the colony.
8. The American Philosophical Society (1743–), first learned scientific society in North America. Its first three presidents were Franklin, David Rittenhouse, and Thomas Jefferson.

Peace being concluded, and the association business therefore at an end, I turned my thoughts again to the affair of establishing an academy. The first step I took was to associate in the design a number of active friends, of whom the Junto furnished a good part; the next was to write and publish a pamphlet, entitled *Proposals Relating to the Education of Youth in Pennsylvania*.[9] This I distributed among the principal inhabitants gratis; and as soon as I could suppose their minds a little prepared by the perusal of it, I set on foot a subscription for opening and supporting an academy; it was to be paid in quotas yearly for five years; by so dividing it, I judged the subscription might be larger, and I believe it was so, amounting to no less, if I remember right, than five thousand pounds.

In the introduction to these proposals, I stated their publication, not as an act of mine, but of some *public-spirited gentlemen*, avoiding as much as I could, according to my usual rule, the presenting myself to the public as the author of any scheme for their benefit.

The subscribers, to carry the project into immediate execution, chose out of their number twenty-four trustees, and appointed Mr. Francis, then attorney-general, and myself to draw up constitutions for the government of the academy; which being done and signed, a house was hired, masters engaged, and the schools opened, I think, in the same year, 1749.

The scholars increasing fast, the house was soon found too small, and we were looking out for a piece of ground, properly situated, with intention to build, when Providence threw into our way a large house ready built, which, with a few alterations, might well serve our purpose. This was the building before mentioned, erected by the hearers of Mr. Whitefield, and was obtained for us in the following manner.

It is to be noted that the contributions to this building being made by people of different sects, care was taken in the nomination of trustees, in whom the building and ground was to be vested, that a predominancy should not be given to any sect, lest in time that predominancy might be a means of appropriating the whole to the use of such sect, contrary to the original intention. It was therefore that one of each sect was appointed, viz., one Church-of-England man, one Presbyterian, one Baptist, one Moravian, etc.; those, in case of vacancy by death, were to fill it by election from among the contributors. The Moravian happened not to please his colleagues, and on his death they resolved to have no other of that sect. The difficulty then was, how to avoid having two of some other sect, by means of the new choice.

9. This pamphlet, which appeared in 1749, made the proposal, then radical, for college education on a secular basis, free from ecclesiastical concerns and de- nominational bias. It carried over the spirit of the "Proposal for Promoting Useful Knowledge" (1743) which he mentions in the preceding paragraph.

Several persons were named, and for that reason not agreed to. At length one mentioned me, with the observation that I was merely an honest man, and of no sect at all, which prevailed with them to choose me. The enthusiasm which existed when the house was built had long since abated, and its trustees had not been able to procure fresh contributions for paying the ground-rent and discharging some other debts the building had occasioned, which embarrassed them greatly. Being now a member of both sets of trustees, that for the building and that for the academy, I had a good opportunity of negotiating with both, and brought them finally to an agreement, by which the trustees for the building were to cede it to those of the academy, the latter undertaking to discharge the debt, to keep forever open in the building a large hall for occasional preachers, according to the original intention, and maintain a free school for the instruction of poor children. Writings were accordingly drawn, and on paying the debts the trustees of the academy were put in possession of the premises; and by dividing the great and lofty hall into stories, and different rooms above and below for the several schools, and purchasing some additional ground, the whole was soon made fit for our purpose, and the scholars removed into the building. The care and trouble of agreeing with the workmen, purchasing materials, and superintending the work, fell upon me; and I went through it the more cheerfully, as it did not then interfere with my private business, having the year before taken a very able, industrious, and honest partner, Mr. David Hall, with whose character I was well acquainted, as he had worked for me four years. He took off my hands all care of the printing-office, paying me punctually my share of the profits. This partnership continued eighteen years, successfully for us both.

The trustees of the academy, after a while, were incorporated by a charter from the governor; their funds were increased by contributions in Britain and grants of land from the proprietaries, to which the Assembly has since made considerable addition; and thus was established the present University of Philadelphia.[1] I have been continued one of its trustees from the beginning, now near forty years, and have had the very great pleasure of seeing a number of the youth who have received their education in it distinguished by their improved abilities, serviceable in public stations, and ornaments to their country. * * *

Before I proceed in relating the part I had in public affairs * * * , it may not be amiss here to give some account of the rise and progress

1. Now the University of Pennsylvania. The University dates from 1765, when the medical school was added to the College of Philadelphia. The latter, chartered 1755, absorbed the Academy, chartered 1749, and the Charity School, whose charter, granted to the trustees of the New Building, is dated 1740. Instruction was continued in the Charity School and the Academy for more than a century under these trusts, which sprang chiefly from Franklin's efforts.

of my philosophical reputation.

In 1746, being at Boston, I met there with a Dr. Spence, who was lately arrived from Scotland and showed me some electric experiments. They were imperfectly performed, as he was not very expert; but, being on a subject quite new to me, they equally surprised and pleased me. Soon after my return to Philadelphia, our library company received from Mr. P. Collinson,[2] Fellow of the Royal Society of London, a present of a glass tube, with some account of the use of it in making such experiments. I eagerly seized the opportunity of repeating what I had seen at Boston; and by much practice, acquired great readiness in performing those, also, which we had an account of from England, adding a number of new ones. I say much practice, for my house was continually full for some time with people who came to see these new wonders.

To divide a little this incumbrance among my friends, I caused a number of similar tubes to be blown at our glass-house, with which they furnished themselves, so that we had at length several performers. Among these, the principal was Mr. Kinnersley,[3] an ingenious neighbor, who, being out of business, I encouraged to undertake showing the experiments for money, and drew up for him two lectures, in which the experiments were ranged in such order, and accompanied with such explanations in such method, as that the foregoing should assist in comprehending the following. He procured an elegant apparatus for the purpose, in which all the little machines that I had roughly made for myself were nicely formed by instrument-makers. His lectures were well attended, and gave great satisfaction; and after some time he went through the colonies, exhibiting them in every capital town, and picked up some money. In the West India islands, indeed, it was with difficulty the experiments could be made, from the general moisture of the air.

Obliged as as we were to Mr. Collinson for his present of the tube, etc., I thought it right he should be informed of our success in using it, and wrote him several letters containing accounts of our experiments. He got them read in the Royal Society, where they were not at first thought worth so much notice as to be printed in their *Transactions*. One paper, which I wrote for Mr. Kinnersley on the sameness of lightning with electricity, I sent to Dr. Mitchel,[4]

2. Peter Collinson (1694–1768), Quaker merchant, transmitted in London the reports of Franklin's electrical experiments. One of Franklin's letters to Collinson is reprinted in this volume.
3. Ebenezer Kinnersley, a Baptist clergyman, then without a pastorate. The lectures that Franklin mentions occurred in 1751–1752. He served as English master at the Academy of Philadelphia, 1753–1773, and died in 1778. Kinnersley's experimental contributions to the knowledge of electricity were considerable; detractors charged Franklin with appropriating his friend's ideas, but Kinnersley himself rose to Franklin's defense.
4. Dr. John Mitchell, of Virginia and London, one of Franklin's earliest scientific correspondents. Years later, in negotiating the peace treaty with England (1783), Franklin used a map of the southern colonies made by Mitchell.

an acquaintance of mine, and one of the members also of that society, who wrote me word that it had been read, but was laughed at by the connoisseurs. The papers, however, being shown to Dr. Fothergill,[5] he thought them of too much value to be stifled, and advised the printing of them. Mr. Collinson then gave them to Cave for publication in his *Gentleman's Magazine;*[6] but he chose to print them separately in a pamphlet, and Dr. Fothergill wrote the preface. Cave, it seems, judged rightly for his profit, for by the additions that arrived afterward they swelled to a quarto volume, which has had five editions, and cost him nothing for copy-money.

It was, however, some time before those papers were much taken notice of in England. A copy of them happening to fall into the hands of the Count de Buffon,[7] a philosopher deservedly of great reputation in France, and, indeed, all over Europe, he prevailed with M. Dalibard[8] to translate them into French, and they were printed at Paris. The publication offended the Abbé Nollet, preceptor in natural philosophy to the royal family, and an able experimenter, who had formed and published a theory of electricity, which then had the general vogue. He could not at first believe that such a work came from America, and said it must have been fabricated by his enemies at Paris to decry his system. Afterwards, having been assured that there really existed such a person as Franklin at Philadelphia, which he had doubted, he wrote and published a volume of letters, chiefly addressed to me, defending his theory, and denying the verity of my experiments, and of the positions deduced from them.

I once purposed answering the Abbé, and actually began the answer; but, on consideration that my writings contained a description of experiments which any one might repeat and verify, and if not to be verified, could not be defended; or of observations offered as conjectures, and not delivered dogmatically, therefore not laying me under any obligation to defend them; and reflecting that a dispute between two persons, writing in different languages, might be lengthened greatly by mistranslations, and thence misconceptions of one another's meaning, much of one of the Abbé's letters being founded on an error in the translation, I concluded to let my papers shift for themselves, believing it was better to spend

5. John Fothergill (1712–1780), London Quaker and physician, developed internationally famous botanical gardens. A longtime friend and correspondent, he aided Franklin in drafting the scheme of reconciliation rejected by Parliament (1774).
6. A famous periodical (1731–1754) published in London by Edward Cave, prominent printer and journalist.
7. Comte Georges Louis Leclerc de Buffon (1707–1788), famous naturalist, directed the Paris Jardin des Plantes and the Royal Museum.
8. Thomas-François D'Alibard, Parisian scientist. In the *Experiments and Observations on Electricity* * * * (1751), the pamphlet in question, Franklin had described a possible lightning rod. D'Alibard set up such a rod at Marly, near Paris, and on May 10, 1752, successfully drew "lightning from the clouds" before Franklin had tested his device. See Franklin's reference to this below.

what time I could spare from public business in making new experiments than in disputing about those already made. I therefore never answered M. Nollet, and the event gave me no cause to repent my silence; for my friend M. le Roy,[9] of the Royal Academy of Sciences, took up my cause and refuted him; my book was translated into the Italian, German, and Latin languages; and the doctrine it contained was by degrees universally adopted by the philosophers of Europe, in preference to that of the Abbé; so that he lived to see himself the last of his sect, except Monsieur B——, of Paris, his *élève* and immediate disciple.

What gave my book the more sudden and general celebrity was the success of one of its proposed experiments, made by Messrs. Dalibard and De Lor at Marly, for drawing lightning from the clouds. This engaged the public attention everywhere. M. de Lor, who had an apparatus for experimental philosophy, and lectured in that branch of science, undertook to repeat what he called the Philadelphia Experiments, and after they were performed before the king and court, all the curious of Paris flocked to see them. I will not swell this narrative with an account of that capital experiment, nor of the infinite pleasure I received in the success of a similar one I made soon after with a kite at Philadelphia, as both are to be found in the histories of electricity.[1]

Dr. Wright, an English physician, when at Paris wrote to a friend who was of the Royal Society an account of the high esteem my experiments were in among the learned abroad, and of their wonder that my writings had been so little noticed in England. The society, on this, resumed the consideration of the letters that had been read to them; and the celebrated Dr. Watson[2] drew up a summary account of them, and of all I had afterwards sent to England on the subject, which he accompanied with some praise of the writer. This summary was then printed in their *Transactions*; and some members of the society in London, particularly the very ingenious Mr. Canton,[3] having verified the experiment of procuring lightning from the clouds by a pointed rod, and acquainting them with the success, they soon made me more than amends for the slight with which they had before treated me. Without my having made any application for that honor, they chose me a member, and voted that I should be excused the customary payments, which would have

9. Jean-Baptiste Le Roy, distinguished French physicist, later intimate with Franklin at Passy (1776–1785) where Le Roy was in charge of the king's laboratory.

1. For example, in Joseph Priestley's *History * * * of Electricity* (1767), which contains an account of the "kite and key" experiment, approved in manuscript by Franklin, as having been performed in June, 1752. Franklin's only

account of it is contained in the letter to Collinson (October, 1752).

2. Later Sir William Watson (1715–1787), English physician and early pioneer in electrical experiments, whose theories resembled Franklin's.

3. John Canton (1718–1772), English physicist, the first in England to verify Franklin's hypothesis identifying lightning with electricity.

amounted to twenty-five guineas; and ever since have given me their *Transactions* gratis. They also presented me with the gold medal of Sir Godfrey Copley for the year 1753,[4] the delivery of which was accompanied by a very handsome speech of the president, Lord Macclesfield, wherein I was highly honored.

From Poor Richard's Almanack[5]

Preface to Poor Richard, 1733

COURTEOUS READER,

I might in this place attempt to gain thy Favour, by declaring that I write Almanacks with no other View than that of the publick Good; but in this I should not be sincere; and Men are now adays too wise to be deceiv'd by Pretences how specious soever. The plain Truth of the Matter is, I am excessive poor, and my Wife, good Woman, is, I tell her, excessive proud; she cannot bear, she says, to sit spinning in her Shift of Tow, while I do nothing but gaze at the Stars; and has threatned more than once to burn all my Books and Rattling-Traps (as she calls my Instruments) if I do not make some profitable Use of them for the Good of my Family. The Printer has offer'd me some considerable share of the Profits, and I have thus begun to comply with my Dame's Desire.

Indeed this Motive would have had Force enough to have made me publish an Almanack many Years since, had it not been over-powered by my Regard for my good Friend and Fellow Student Mr. *Titan Leeds*,[6] whose Interest I was extreamly unwilling to hurt: But this Obstacle (I am far from speaking it with Pleasure) is soon to be removed, since inexorable Death, who was never known to respect Merit, has already prepared the mortal Dart, the fatal Sister has already extended her destroying Shears, and that ingenious Man must soon be taken from us. He dies, by my Calculation made at his

---

4. Sir Godfrey Copley (died 1709) founded the Copley Medal, given annually by the British Royal Society, an award of high distinction.
5. Franklin published his almanac annually from 1733 to 1758, then sold it, but it continued publication until 1796. Besides the usual astronomical and agricultural data of an almanac, Franklin inserted useful information, literary selections, and especially the editorial wisdom of the fictional Richard Saunders, who, with his wife, Bridget, became favorite literary characters. Poor Richard's proverbs, often old, but always newly minted for Americans, are still current homely wisdom. *The Way to Wealth* was a collection of the most utilitarian, hence the best remembered, of

these maxims, prepared for Poor Richard's preface of 1758. This is preceded in the present selections by Poor Richard's first two prefaces, those of 1733 and 1734. See also Franklin's account in the *Autobiography*. The selections from the *Almanack* follow Franklin's original text without typographical alterations.
6. Titan Leeds (1699–1738), Franklin's rival in Philadelphia, publisher of *The American Almanack*. Inspired by Swift's famous Bickerstaff hoax, Franklin immortalized Leeds by the mock prediction, from astronomical "evidence," of his imminent death. Leed's denial only served to publicize the controversy, in which Poor Richard was still persisting when his victim died, five years later.

Request, on Oct. 17. 1733. 3 h. 29 m. P. M. at the very instant of the ☌ of ☉ and ☿ : By his own Calculation he will survive till the 26th of the same Month. This small Difference between us we have disputed whenever we have met these 9 Years past; but at length he is inclinable to agree with my Judgment: Which of us is most exact, a little Time will now determine. As therefore these Provinces may not longer expect to see any of his Performances after this Year, I think my self free to take up the Task, and request a share of the publick Encouragement; which I am the more apt to hope for on this Account, that the Buyer of my Almanack may consider himself, not only as purchasing an useful Utensil, but as performing an Act of Charity, to his poor *Friend and Servant*

R. Saunders.

Preface to Poor Richard, 1734

Courteous Readers,

Your kind and charitable Assistance last Year, in purchasing so large an Impression of my Almanacks, has made my Circumstances much more easy in the World, and requires my grateful Acknowledgment. My Wife has been enabled to get a Pot of her own, and is no longer oblig'd to borrow one from a Neighbour; nor have we ever since been without something of our own to put in it. She has also got a pair of Shoes, two new Shifts, and a new warm Petticoat; and for my part, I have bought a second-hand Coat, so good, that I am now not asham'd to go to Town or be seen there. These Things have render'd her Temper so much more pacifick than it us'd to be, that I may say, I have slept more, and more quietly within this last Year, than in the three foregoing Years put together. Accept my hearty Thanks therefor, and my sincere Wishes for your Health and Prosperity.

In the Preface to my last Almanack, I foretold the Death of my dear old Friend and Fellow-Student, the learned and ingenious Mr. *Titan Leeds*, which was to be on the 17th of *October*, 1733, 3 h. 29 m. P. M. at the very Instant of the ☌ of ☉ and ☿. By his own Calculation he was to survive till the 26th of the same Month, and expire in the Time of the Eclipse, near 11 o'clock A. M. At which of these Times he died, or whether he be really yet dead, I cannot at this present Writing positively assure my Readers; forasmuch as a Disorder in my own Family demanded my Presence, and would not permit me as I had intended, to be with him in his last Moments, to receive his last Embrace, to close his Eyes, and do the Duty of a Friend in performing the last Offices to the Departed. Therefore it is that I cannot positively affirm whether he be dead or not; for the Stars only show to the Skilful, what will happen in the natural and universal Chain of Causes and Effects; but 'tis well known, that the

Events which would otherwise certainly happen at certain Times in the Course of Nature are sometimes set aside or postpon'd for wise and good Reasons by the immediate particular Dispositions of Providence; which particular Dispositions the Stars can by no Means discover or foreshow. There is however (and I cannot speak it without Sorrow) there is the strongest Probability that my dear Friend is *no more;* for there appears in his Name, as I am assured, an Almanack for the Year 1734, in which I am treated in a very gross and unhandsome Manner; in which I am called *a false Predicter, an Ignorant, a conceited Scribler, a Fool, and a Lyar.* Mr. *Leeds* was too well bred to use any Man so indecently and so scurrilously, and moreover his Esteem and Affection for me was extraordinary: So that it is to be feared that Pamphlet may be only a Contrivance of somebody or other, who hopes perhaps to sell two or three Year's Almanacks still, by the sole Force and Virtue of Mr. *Leeds's* Name; but certainly, to put Words into the Mouth of a Gentleman and a Man of Letters, against his Friend, which the meanest and most scandalous of the People might be asham'd to utter even in a drunken Quarrel, is an unpardonable Injury to his Memory, and an Imposition upon the Publick.

Mr. *Leeds* was not only profoundly skilful in the useful Science he profess'd, but he was a Man of *exemplary Sobriety*, a most *sincere Friend*, and an *exact Performer of his Word*. These valuable Qualifications, with many others so much endear'd him to me, that although it should be so, that, contrary to all Probability, contrary to my Prediction and his own, he might possibly be yet alive, yet my Loss of Honour as a Prognosticator, cannot afford me so much Mortification, as his Life, Health and Safety would give me Joy and Satisfaction.

I am, *Courteous and Kind Reader*
Your poor Friend and Servant,

Octob. 30. 1733.   R. Saunders

The Way to Wealth: Preface to Poor Richard, 1758 [7]

Courteous Reader,

I have heard that nothing gives an Author so great Pleasure, as to find his Works respectfully quoted by other learned Authors. This Pleasure I have seldom enjoyed; for tho' I have been, if I may say it

7. In 1757, on a voyage to England to represent the grievances of Pennsylvania against the Crown and the Proprietors, Franklin wrote the preface for his almanac of 1758. He imagined an old man, Father Abraham, addressing an auction, in a speech drawn almost entirely from Poor Richard's maxims on virtue and economy over the past twenty-five years. The result was an American classic of prudential virtue. In 1759 it was separately published as *Father Abraham's Speech*. It has been republished many times. It omits Poor Richard's many worldly and even sophisticated epigrams, but it remains a compendium of the homely practicality of the common American folk. It has been here printed in its original spelling and punctuation.

without Vanity, an *eminent Author* of Almanacks annually now a full Quarter of a Century, my Brother Authors in the same Way, for what Reason I know not, have ever been very sparing in their Applauses; and no other Author has taken the least Notice of me, so that did not my Writings produce me some *solid Pudding*, the great Deficiency of *Praise* would have quite discouraged me.

I concluded at length, that the People were the best Judges of my Merit; for they buy my Works; and besides, in my Rambles, where I am not personally known, I have frequently heard one or other of my Adages repeated, with, *as Poor Richard says,* at the End on't; this gave me some Satisfaction, as it showed not only that my Instructions were regarded, but discovered likewise some Respect for my Authority; and I own, that to encourage the Practice of remembering and repeating those wise Sentences, I have sometimes *quoted* myself with great Gravity.

Judge then how much I must have been gratified by an Incident I am going to relate to you. I stopt my Horse lately where a great Number of People were collected at a Vendue of Merchant Goods. The Hour of Sale not being come, they were conversing on the Badness of the Times, and one of the Company call'd to a plain clean old Man, with white Locks, *Pray, Father Abraham, what think you of the Times? Won't these heavy Taxes quite ruin the Country? How shall we ever be able to pay them? What would you advise us to?*——Father *Abraham* stood up, and reply'd, If you'd have my Advice, I'll give it you in short, for a *Word to the Wise is enough,* and *many Words won't fill a Bushel,* as *Poor Richard* says. They join'd in desiring him to speak his Mind, and gathering round him, he proceeded as follows;

"Friends, says he, and Neighbours, the Taxes are indeed very heavy, and if those laid on by the Government were the only Ones we had to pay, we might more easily discharge them; but we have many others, and much more grievous to some of us. We are taxed twice as much by our *Idleness,* three times as much by our *Pride,* and four times as much by our *Folly,* and from these Taxes the Commissioners cannot ease or deliver us by allowing an Abatement. However let us hearken to good Advice, and something may be done for us; *God helps them that help themselves,* as *Poor Richard* says, in his Almanack of 1733.

It would be thought a hard Government that should tax its People one tenth Part of their *Time,* to be employed in its Service. But *Idleness* taxes many of us much more, if we reckon all that is spent in absolute *Sloth,* or doing of nothing, with that which is spent in idle Employments or Amusements, that amount to nothing. *Sloth,* by bringing on Diseases, absolutely shortens Life. *Sloth, like Rust, consumes faster than Labour wears, while the used Key is always bright,* as Poor Richard says. But *dost thou love Life, then do not squander Time, for that's the Stuff Life is made of,* as Poor Richard says.—How much more than is necessary do we spend in Sleep! forgetting that *The sleeping Fox catches no Poultry,* and that *there will be sleeping enough in the Grave,* as Poor Richard says. If Time be of all Things the most precious, *wasting Time* must be, as *Poor Richard* says, *the greatest Prodigality,* since, as he elsewhere tells us, *Lost Time is never found again;* and what we call *Time-enough, always proves little enough:* Let us then up and be doing, and doing to the Purpose; so by Diligence shall we do more with less Perplexity. *Sloth makes all Things difficult, but Industry all easy,* as *Poor Richard* says; and *He that riseth late, must trot all Day, and shall scarce overtake his Business at Night.* While *Laziness travels so slowly, that Poverty soon overtakes him,* as we read in *Poor Richard,* who adds, *Drive thy Business, let not that drive thee;* and *Early to Bed, and early to rise, makes a Man healthy, wealthy and wise.*

So what signifies *wishing* and *hoping* for better Times. We may make these Times better if we bestir ourselves. *Industry need not wish,* as *Poor Richard* says, and *He that lives upon Hope will die fasting. There are no Gains, without Pains;* then *Help Hands, for I have no Lands,* or if I have, they are smartly taxed. And, as *Poor Richard* likewise observes, *He that hath a Trade hath an Estate,* and *He that hath a Calling, hath an Office of Profit and Honour;* but then the *Trade* must be worked at, and the *Calling* well followed, or neither the *Estate,* nor the *Office,* will enable us to pay our Taxes.— If we are industrious we shall never starve; for, as *Poor Richard* says, *At the working Man's House* Hunger *looks in, but dares not enter.* Nor will the Bailiff or the Constable enter, for *Industry pays Debts, while Despair encreaseth them,* says *Poor Richard.*—What though you have found no Treasure, nor has any rich Relation left you a Legacy, *Diligence is the Mother of Good luck,* as Poor Richard says, *and God gives all Things to Industry.* Then *plough deep, while Sluggards sleep, and you shall have Corn to sell and to keep,* says Poor Dick. Work while it is called To-day, for you know not how much you may be hindered To-morrow, which makes *Poor Richard* say, *One To-day is worth two To-morrows;* and farther, *Have you somewhat to do To-morrow, do it To-day.* If you were a Servant, would you not be ashamed that a good Master should catch you idle? Are you then your own Master, *be ashamed to catch yourself idle,* as *Poor Dick* says. When there is so much to be done for yourself, your Family, your Country, and your gracious King, be up by Peep of Day; *Let not the Sun look down and say, Inglorious here he lies.* Handle your Tools without Mittens; remember that *the Cat in Gloves catches no Mice,* as *Poor Richard* says. 'Tis true there is much to be done, and perhaps you are weak handed, but stick to it steadily, and you will see great Effects, for *constant Dropping wears away Stones*, and by *Diligence and Patience the Mouse ate in two the Cable*; and *little Strokes fell great Oaks*, as *Poor Richard* says in his Almanack, the Year I cannot just now remember.

Methinks I hear some of you say, *Must a Man afford himself no Leisure?*—I will tell thee, my Friend, what *Poor Richard* says, *Employ thy Time well if thou meanest to gain Leisure*; and *since thou art not sure of a Minute, throw not away an Hour*. Leisure, is Time for doing something useful; this Leisure the diligent Man will obtain, but the lazy Man never; so that, as *Poor Richard* says, a *Life of Leisure and a Life of Laziness are two Things*. Do you imagine that Sloth will afford you more Comfort than Labour? No, for as *Poor Richard* says, *Trouble springs from Idleness, and grievous Toil from needless Ease*. *Many without Labour, would live by their* WITS *only, but they break for want of Stock*. Whereas Industry gives Comfort, and Plenty, and Respect: *Fly Pleasures, and they'll follow you. The diligent Spinner has a large Shift*; and *now I have a Sheep and a Cow, every Body bids me Good morrow*; all which is well said by *Poor Richard*.

But with our Industry, we must likewise be *steady, settled* and *careful*, and oversee our own Affairs *with our own Eyes*, and not trust too much to others; for, as *Poor Richard* says,

> *I never saw an oft removed Tree,*
> *Nor yet an oft removed Family,*
> *That throve so well as those that settled be.*

And again, *Three Removes is as bad as a Fire*; and again, *Keep thy Shop, and thy Shop will keep thee*; and again, *If you would have your Business done, go; If not, send*. And again,

> *He that by the Plough would thrive,*
> *Himself must either hold or drive.*

And again, *The Eye of a Master will do more Work than both His Hands*; and again, *Want of Care does us more Damage than Want of Knowledge*; and again, *Not to oversee Workmen, is to leave them your Purse open*. Trusting too much to others Care is the Ruin of many; for, as the *Almanack* says, *In the Affairs of this World, Men are saved, not by Faith, but by the Want of it*; but a Man's own Care is profitable; for, saith *Poor Dick*, *Learning is to the Studious, and Riches to the Careful*, as well as *Power to the Bold*, and *Heaven to the Virtuous*. And farther, *If you would have a faithful Servant, and one that you like, serve yourself*. And again, he adviseth to Circumspection and Care, even in the smallest Matters, because sometimes *a little Neglect may breed great Mischief*; adding, *For want of a Nail the Shoe was lost; for want of a Shoe the Horse was lost; and for want of a Horse the Rider was lost,* being overtaken and slain by the Enemy, all for want of Care about a Horse shoe Nail.

So much for Industry, my Friends, and Attention to one's own Business; but to these we must add *Frugality,* if we would make our *Industry* more certainly successful. A Man may, if he knows not how to save as he gets, *keep his Nose all his Life to the Grindstone,* and die not worth a *Groat* at last. *A fat Kitchen makes a lean Will,* as *Poor Richard* says; and,

> *Many Estates are spent in the Getting,*
> *Since Women for Tea forsook Spinning and Knitting,*
> *And Men for Punch forsook Hewing and Splitting.*

If you would be wealthy, says he, in another Almanack, *think of Saving as well as of Getting: The* Indies *have not made* Spain *rich, because her* Outgoes *are greater than her* Incomes. Away then with your expensive Follies, and you will not have so much Cause to complain of hard Times, heavy Taxes, and chargeable Families; for, as *Poor Dick* says,

> *Women and Wine, Game and Deceit,*
> *Make the Wealth small, and the Wants great.*

And farther, *What maintains one Vice, would bring up two Children.* You may think perhaps, That a *little* Tea, or a *little* Punch now and then, Diet a *little* more costly, Clothes a *little* finer, and a *little* Entertainment now and then, can be no *great* Matter; but remember what *Poor Richard* says, *Many* a Little *makes a Mickle;* and farther, *Beware of little Expences; a small Leak will sink a great Ship;* and again, *Who Dainties love, shall Beggars prove;* and moreover, *Fools make Feasts, and wise Men eat them.*

Here you are all got together at this Vendue of *Fineries* and *Knicknacks.* You call them *Goods,* but if you do not take Care, they will prove *Evils* to some of you. You expect they will be sold *cheap,* and perhaps they may for less than they cost; but if you have no Occasion for them, they must be *dear* to you. Remember what *Poor Richard* says, *Buy what thou hast no Need of, and ere long thou shalt sell thy Necessaries.* And again, *At a great Pennyworth pause a while:* He means, that perhaps the Cheapness is *apparent* only, and not *real;* or the Bargain, by straitning thee in thy Business, may do thee more Harm than Good. For in another place he says, *Many have been ruined by buying good Pennyworths.* Again, *Poor Richard* says, *'Tis foolish to lay out Money in a Purchase of Repentance;* and yet this Folly is practised every Day at Vendues, for want of minding the Almanack. *Wise Men,* as *Poor Dick* says, *learn by others Harms, Fools scarcely by their own;* but *Felix quem faciunt aliena Pericula cautum.*[8] Many a one, for the Sake of Finery on the Back, have gone

8. He is fortunate who is made cautious by the misfortunes of another.

with a hungry Belly, and half starved their Families; *Silks and Sattins, Scarlet and Velvets*, as *Poor Richard* says, *put out the Kitchen Fire*. These are not the *Necessaries* of Life; they can scarcely be called the *Conveniences*, and yet only because they look pretty, how many *want* to *have* them. The *artificial* Wants of Mankind thus become more numerous than the *natural*; and, as *Poor Dick* says, *For one poor Person, there are an hundred* indigent. By these, and other Extravagancies, the Genteel are reduced to Poverty, and forced to borrow of those whom they formerly despised, but who through *Industry* and *Frugality* have maintained their Standing; in which Case it appears plainly, that a *Ploughman on his Legs is higher than a Gentleman on his Knees*, as *Poor Richard* says. Perhaps they have had a small Estate left them which they knew not the Getting of; they think *'tis Day, and will never be Night*; that a little to be spent out of so much, is not worth minding; (*a Child and a Fool*, as *Poor Richard* says, *imagine* Twenty Shillings *and Twenty Years can never be spent*) but, *always taking out of, the Mealtub, and never putting in, soon comes to the Bottom*; then, as *Poor Dick* says, *When the Well's dry, they know the Worth of Water*. But this they might have known before, if they had taken his Advice; *If you would know the Value of Money, go and try to borrow some*; for, *he that goes a borrowing goes a sorrowing*; and indeed so does he that lends to such People, when he goes *to get it in again*.—*Poor Dick* farther advises, and says,

> *Fond* Pride of Dress *is sure a very Curse;*
> *E'er* Fancy *you consult, consult your Purse.*

And again, *Pride is as loud a Beggar as Want, and a great deal more saucy*. When you have bought one fine Thing you must buy ten more, that your Appearance may be all of a Piece; but *Poor Dick* says, *'Tis easier to suppress the first Desire, than to satisfy all that follow it*. And 'tis as truly Folly for the Poor to ape the Rich, as for the Frog to swell, in order to equal the Ox.

> *Great Estates may venture more,*
> *But little Boats should keep near Shore.*

'Tis however a Folly soon punished; for *Pride that dines on Vanity sups on Contempt*, as *Poor Richard* says. And in another Place, *Pride breakfasted with Plenty, dined with Poverty, and supped with Infamy*. And after all, of what Use is this *Pride of Appearance*, for which so much is risked, so much is suffered? It cannot promote Health, or ease Pain; it makes no Increase of Merit in the Person, it creates Envy, it hastens Misfortune.

> *What is a Butterfly? At best*
> *He's but a Caterpillar drest.*
> *The gaudy Fop's his Picture just,*

as *Poor Richard* says.

But what Madness must it be to *run in Debt* for these Super-fluities! We are offered, by the Terms of this Vendue, *Six Months Credit*; and that perhaps has induced some of us to attend it, because we cannot spare the ready Money, and hope now to be fine without it. But, ah, think what you do when you run in Debt; *You give to another, Power over your Liberty*. If you cannot pay at the Time, you will be ashamed to see your Creditor; you will be in Fear when you speak to him; you will make poor pitiful sneaking Excuses, and by Degrees come to lose your Veracity, and sink into base downright lying; for, as *Poor Richard* says, *The second Vice is Lying, the first is running in Debt*. And again, to the same Purpose, *Lying rides upon Debt's Back*. Whereas a freeborn *Englishman* ought not to be ashamed or afraid to see or speak to any Man living. But Poverty often deprives a Man of all Spirit and Virtue: *'Tis hard for an empty Bag to stand upright*, as *Poor Richard* truly says. What would you think of that Prince, or that Government, who should issue an Edict forbidding you to dress like a Gentleman or a Gentlewoman, on Pain of Imprisonment or Servitude? Would you not say, that you are free, have a Right to dress as you please, and that such an Edict would be a Breach of your Privileges, and such a Government tyrannical? And yet you are about to put yourself under that Tyranny when you run in Debt for such Dress! Your Creditor has Authority at his Pleasure to deprive you of your Liberty, by confining you in Goal [*sic*] for Life, or to sell you for a Servant, if you should not be able to pay him! When you have got your Bargain, you may, perhaps, think little of Payment; but *Creditors*, *Poor Richard* tells us, *have better Memories than Debtors*; and in another Place says, *Creditors are a superstitious Sect, great Observers of set Days and Times*. The Day comes round before you are aware, and the Demand is made before you are prepared to satisfy it. Or if you bear your Debt in Mind, the Term which at first seemed so long, will, as it lessens, appear extreamly short. *Time* will seem to have added Wings to Heels as well as Shoulders. *Those have a short Lent*, saith *Poor Richard*, *who owe Money to be paid at Easter*. Then since, as he says, *The Borrower is a Slave to the Lender, and the Debtor to the Creditor*, disdain the Chain, preserve your Freedom; and maintain your Independency: Be *industrious* and *free*; be *frugal* and *free*. At present, perhaps, you may think yourself in thriving Circumstances, and that you can bear a little Extravangance [*sic*] without Injury;

> *For Age and Want, save while you may;*
> *No Morning Sun lasts a whole Day,*

as *Poor Richard* says—Gain may be temporary and uncertain, but ever while you live, Expence is constant and certain; and *'tis easier*

to build two Chimnies than to keep one in Fuel, as Poor Richard
says. So *rather go to Bed supperless than rise in Debt*.

> Get what you can, and what you get hold;
> 'Tis the Stone that will turn all your Lead into Gold,

as *Poor Richard* says. And when you have got the Philosopher's Stone,
sure you will no longer complain of bad Times, or the Difficulty of
paying Taxes.

This Doctrine, my Friends, is *Reason* and *Wisdom*; but after all,
do not depend too much upon your own *Industry*, and *Frugality*,
and *Prudence*, though excellent Things, for they may all be blasted
without the Blessing of Heaven; and therefore ask that Blessing
humbly, and be not uncharitable to those that at present seem to
want it, but comfort and help them. Remember *Job* suffered, and
was afterwards prosperous.

And now to conclude, *Experience keeps a dear School, but Fools
will learn in no other, and scarce in that*; for it is true, *we may give
Advice, but we cannot give Conduct*, as *Poor Richard* says: However, remember this, *They that won't be counselled, can't be helped*,
as *Poor Richard* says: And farther, That *if you will not hear Reason,
she'll surely rap your Knuckles*.

Thus the old Gentleman ended his Harangue. The People heard
it, and approved the Doctrine and immediately practised the contrary, just as if it had been a common Sermon; for the Vendue
opened, and they began to buy extravagantly, notwithstanding all his
Cautions, and their own Fear of Taxes.—I found the good Man had
thoroughly studied my Almanacks, and digested all I had dropt on
those Topics during the Course of Five-and-twenty Years. The frequent Mention he made of me must have tired any one else, but my
Vanity was wonderfully delighted with it, though I was conscious
that not a tenth Part of the Wisdom was my own which he ascribed
to me, but rather the *Gleanings* I had made of the Sense of all Ages
and Nations. However, I resolved to be the better for the Echo of it;
and though I had at first determined to buy Stuff for a new Coat, I
went away resolved to wear my old One a little longer. *Reader*, if
thou wilt do the same, thy Profit will be as great as mine.

I am, as ever,
Thine to serve thee,

July 7, 1757. RICHARD SAUNDERS.

An Edict by the King of Prussia[9]

DANTZIC, Sept. 5, [1773].

We have long wondered here at the supineness of the English na-

---

9. First published in the *Gentleman's
Magazine*, October, 1773, this ironic
hoax, often favorably compared with
those of Swift, made a "fair hit," as

tion, under the Prussian impositions upon its trade entering our port. We did not, till lately, know the claims, ancient and modern, that hang over that nation; and therefore could not suspect that it might submit to those impositions from a sense of duty or from principles of equity. The following Edict, just made publick, may, if serious, throw some light upon this matter.

"FREDERIC, by the grace of God, King of Prussia,[1] &c. &c. &c., to all present and to come, (*à tous présens et à venir,*) Health. The peace now enjoyed throughout our dominions, having afforded us leisure to apply ourselves to the regulation of commerce, the improvement of our finances, and at the same time the easing our domestic subjects in their taxes: For these causes, and other good considerations us thereunto moving, we hereby make known, that, after having deliberated these affairs in our council, present our dear brothers, and other great officers of the state, members of the same, we, of our certain knowledge, full power, and authority royal, have made and issued this present Edict, viz.

"Whereas it is well known to all the world, that the first German settlements made in the Island of Britain, were by colonies of people, subject to our renowned ducal ancestors, and drawn from their dominions, under the conduct of Hengist, Horsa, Hella, Uff, Cerdicus, Ida, and others; and that the said colonies have flourished under the protection of our august house for ages past; have never been emancipated therefrom; and yet have hitherto yielded little profit to the same: And whereas we ourself have in the last war fought for and defended the said colonies, against the power of France, and thereby enabled them to make conquests from the said power in America, for which we have not yet received adequate compensation: And whereas it is just and expedient that a revenue should be raised from the said colonies in Britain, towards our indemnification; and that those who are descendants of our ancient subjects, and thence still owe us due obedience, should contribute to the replenishing of our royal coffers as they must have done, had their ancestors remained in the territories now to us appertaining: We do therefore hereby ordain and command, that, from and after the date of these presents, there shall be levied and paid to our officers of the *customs*, on all goods, wares, and merchandizes, and on all grain and other produce of the earth, exported from the said Island of Britain, and on all goods of whatever kind imported into the same, a duty of four and a half per cent *ad valorem*, for the use of us and our successors. And

---

Franklin said, in the minds of British readers (letter to William Franklin, October 6, 1773). With "deadpan" seriousness, Franklin supposes that the fifth-century immigration of German tribes into Britain (the foundation of the Anglo-Saxon stock) gives modern Germany rights of taxation in modern England—a mock analogy with the British claims on the American colonies.

1. Frederick II (the Great), King of Prussia (1740–1786), ruled the lands from which sprang the ancient invaders of Britain named in the following paragraph.

that the said duty may more effectually be collected, we do hereby ordain, that all ships or vessels bound from Great Britain to any other part of the world, or from any other part of the world to Great Britain, shall in their respective voyages touch at our port of Koningsberg, there to be unladen, searched, and charged with the said duties.[2]

"And whereas there hath been from time to time discovered in the said island of Great Britain, by our colonists there, many mines or beds of iron-stone; and sundry subjects, of our ancient dominion, skilful in converting the said stone into metal, have in time past transported themselves thither, carrying with them and communicating that art; and the inhabitants of the said island, presuming that they had a natural right to make the best use they could of the natural productions of their country for their own benefit, have not only built furnaces for smelting the said stone into iron, but have erected plating-forges, slitting-mills, and steel-furnaces, for the more convenient manufacturing of the same; thereby endangering a diminution of the said manufacture in our ancient dominion;—we do therefore hereby farther ordain, that, from and after the date hereof, no mill or other engine for slitting or rolling of iron, or any plating-forge to work with a tilt-hammer, or any furnace for making steel, shall be erected or continued in the said island of Great Britain: And the Lord Lieutenant of every county in the said island is hereby commanded, on information of any such erection within his county, to order and by force to cause the same to be abated and destroyed; as he shall answer the neglect thereof to us at his peril. But we are nevertheless graciously pleased to permit the inhabitants of the said island to transport their iron into Prussia, there to be manufactured, and to them returned; they paying our Prussian subjects for the workmanship, with all the costs of commission, freight, and risk, coming and returning; any thing herein contained to the contrary notwithstanding.

"We do not, however, think fit to extend this our indulgence to the article of wool; but, meaning to encourage, not only the manufacturing of woollen cloth, but also the raising of wool, in our ancient dominions, and to prevent both, as much as may be, in our said island, we do hereby absolutely forbid the transportation of wool from thence, even to the mother country, Prussia; and that those islanders may be farther and more effectually restrained in making any advantage of their own wool in the way of manufacture, we command that none shall be carried out of one county into another; nor shall any worsted, bay, or woollen yarn, cloth, says, bays, kerseys,

---

2. Provisions strongly resembling the British Navigation Acts, taxing American commerce, a principal cause of the Revolution. In the following paragraphs, Franklin substitutes such British staples as iron and wool for American products, such as tobacco and molasses, exploited by the British.

serges, frizes, druggets, cloth-serges, shalloons, or any other drapery stuffs, or woollen manufactures whatsoever, made up or mixed with wool in any of the said counties, be carried into any other county, or be water-borne even across the smallest river or creek, on penalty of forfeiture of the same, together with the boats, carriages, horses, &c., that shall be employed in removing them. Nevertheless, our loving subjects there are hereby permitted (if they think proper) to use all their wool as manure for the improvement of their lands.

"And whereas the art and mystery of making hats hath arrived at great perfection in Prussia, and the making of hats by our remoter subjects ought to be as much as possible restrained: And forasmuch as the islanders before mentioned, being in possession of wool, beaver and other furs, have presumptuously conceived they had a right to make some advantage thereof, by manufacturing the same into hats, to the prejudice of our domestic manufacture: We do therefore hereby strictly command and ordain, that no hats or felts whatsoever, dyed or undyed, finished or unfinished, shall be loaded or put into or upon any vessel, cart, carriage, or horse, to be transported or conveyed out of one county in the said island into another county, or to any other place whatsoever, by any person or persons whatsoever; on pain of forfeiting the same, with a penalty of five hundred pounds sterling for every offence. Nor shall any hatmaker, in any of the said counties, employ more than two apprentices, on penalty of five pounds sterling per month; we intending hereby, that such hatmakers, being so restrained, both in the production and sale of their commodity, may find no advantage in continuing their business. But, lest the said islanders should suffer inconveniency by the want of hats, we are farther graciously pleased to permit them to send their beaver furs to Prussia; and we also permit hats made thereof to be exported from Prussia to Britain; the people thus favoured to pay all costs and charges of manufacturing, interest, commission to our merchants, insurance and freight going and returning, as in the case of iron.

"And, lastly, being willing farther to favour our said colonies in Britain, we do hereby also ordain and command, that all the *thieves*, highway and street robbers, house-breakers, forgerers, murderers, s–d—tes,[3] and villains of every denomination, who have forfeited their lives to the law in Prussia; but whom we, in our great clemency, do not think fit here to hang, shall be emptied out of our gaols into the said island of Great Britain, for the better peopling of that country.

"We flatter ourselves, that these our royal regulations and commands will be thought just and reasonable by our much-favoured

---

3. Sodomites. The exporting of British criminals as American colonists was a long-established abuse.

colonists in England; the said regulations being copied from their statutes of 10 and 11 William III. c. 10, 5 Geo. II. c. 22, 23, Geo. II. c. 29, 4 Geo. I. c. 11, and from other equitable laws made by their parliaments; or from instructions given by their Princes; or from resolutions of both House, entered into for the good government of their *own colonies in Ireland and America.*

"And all persons in the said island are hereby cautioned not to oppose in any wise the execution of this our Edict, or any part thereof, such opposition being high treason; of which all who are suspected shall be transported in fetters from Britain to Prussia, there to be tried and executed according to the Prussian law.

"Such is our pleasure.

"Given at Potsdam, this twenty-fifth day of the month of August, one thousand seven hundred and seventy-three, and in the thirty-third year of our reign.

"By the King, in his Council.

"Rechtmaessig,[4] *Sec.*"

Some take this Edict to be merely one of the King's *Jeux d'Esprit:* others suppose it serious, and that he means a quarrel with England; but all here think the assertion it concludes with, "that these regulations are copied from acts of the English parliament respecting their colonies," a very injurious one; it being impossible to believe, that a people distinguished for their love of liberty, a nation so wise, so liberal in its sentiments, so just and equitable towards its neighbours, should, from mean and injudicious views of petty immediate profit, treat its own children in a manner so arbitrary and tyrannical!

The Sale of the Hessians[5]

*From the Count de Schaumbergh to the Baron
Hohendorf, Commanding the Hessian
Troops in America*

ROME, February 18, 1777.

MONSIEUR LE BARON:—

On my return from Naples, I received at Rome your letter of the 27th December of last year. I have learned with unspeakable pleasure the courage our troops exhibited at Trenton,[6] and you can-

4. The German word for "legally authorized," placed beside the seal.
5. The exact date and place of the first publication of this satire are unknown. It is reported first in French; the English version was in circulation in 1778, and it has reappeared many times. The English purchase of thousands of mercenaries from Hesse evoked profound anger in America, and Franklin distorted the facts for satiric effect. It has

not been proved (but was generally suspected) that Frederick II, Landgrave of Hesse-Cassel, pocketed a profit on the death indemnities. He was reportedly paid £30 per head for at least 15,700 Hessians killed on American soil. (J. F. Watson, *Annals of Philadelphia,* Vol. II, p. 66).
6. At the Battle of Trenton (Christmas night, 1776) Washington routed the Hessian defenders and took 950 prisoners,

not imagine my joy on being told that of the 1,950 Hessians engaged in the fight, but 345 escaped. There were just 1,605 men killed, and I cannot sufficiently commend your prudence in sending an exact list of the dead to my minister in London. This precaution was the more necessary, as the report sent to the English ministry does not give but 1,455 dead. This would make 483,450 florins instead of 643,500 which I am entitled to demand under our convention. You will comprehend the prejudice which such an error would work in my finances, and I do not doubt you will take the necessary pains to prove that Lord North's[7] list is false and yours correct.

The court of London objects that there were a hundred wounded who ought not to be included in the list, nor paid for as dead; but I trust you will not overlook my instructions to you on quitting Cassel, and that you will not have tried by human succor to recall the life of the unfortunates whose days could not be lengthened but by the loss of a leg or an arm. That would be making them a pernicious present, and I am sure they would rather die than live in a condition no longer fit for my service. I do not mean by this that you should assassinate them; we should be humane, my dear Baron, but you may insinuate to the surgeons with entire propriety that a crippled man is a reproach to their profession, and that there is no wiser course than to let every one of them die when he ceases to be fit to fight.

I am about to send to you some new recruits. Don't economize them. Remember glory before all things. Glory is true wealth. There is nothing degrades the soldier like the love of money. He must care only for honour and reputation, but this reputation must be acquired in the midst of dangers. A battle gained without costing the conqueror any blood is an inglorious success, while the conquered cover themselves with glory by perishing with their arms in their hands. Do you remember that of the 300 Lacedæmonians who defended the defile of Thermopylæ, not one returned? How happy should I be could I say the same of my brave Hessians!

It is true that their king, Leonidas, perished with them: but things have changed, and it is no longer the custom for princes of the empire to go and fight in America for a cause with which they have no concern. And besides, to whom should they pay the thirty guineas[8] per man if I did not stay in Europe to receive them? Then, it is necessary also that I be ready to send recruits to replace the men you lose. For this purpose I must return to Hesse. It is true, grown men are becoming scarce there, but I will send you boys. Besides, the

leaving twenty or thirty dead, including their commander. Franklin's exaggeration is a satiric license.
7. Frederick North, Earl of Guilford, British prime minister (1770–1782).

8. The exact death bounty is not known, but Franklin's figure here verifies that quoted by Watson from an independent source.

scarcer the commodity the higher the price. I am assured that the women and little girls have begun to till our lands, and they get on not badly. You did right to send back to Europe that Dr. Crumeras who was so successful in curing dysentery. Don't bother with a man who is subject to looseness of the bowels. That disease makes bad soldiers. One coward will do more mischief in an engagement than ten brave men will do good. Better that they burst in their barracks than fly in a battle, and tarnish the glory of our arms. Besides, you know that they pay me as killed for all who die from disease, and I don't get a farthing for runaways. My trip to Italy, which has cost me enormously, makes it desirable that there should be a great mortality among them. You will therefore promise promotion to all who expose themselves; you will exhort them to seek glory in the midst of dangers; you will say to Major Maundorff that I am not at all content with his saving the 345 men who escaped the massacre of Trenton. Through the whole campaign he has not had ten men killed in consequence of his orders. Finally, let it be your principal object to prolong the war and avoid a decisive engagement on either side, for I have made arrangements for a grand Italian opera, and I do not wish to be obliged to give it up. Meantime I pray God, my dear Baron de Hohendorf, to have you in his holy and gracious keeping.

Letter to Peter Collinson[1]

[*Kite and Key*]

[PHILADELPHIA] Oct. 19, 1752.

SIR,

As frequent mention is made in public papers from *Europe* of the success of the *Philadelphia* experiment for drawing the electric fire from clouds by means of pointed rods of iron erected on high buildings, &c., it may be agreeable to the curious to be informed, that the same experiment has succeeded in *Philadelphia*, though made in a different and more easy manner, which is as follows:

Make a small cross of two light strips of cedar, the arms so long as to reach to the four corners of a large thin silk handkerchief when extended; tie the corners of the handkerchief to the extremities of the cross, so you have the body of a kite; which being properly accommodated with a tail, loop, and string, will rise in the air, like those made of paper; but this being of silk, is fitter to bear the wet

1. Franklin gives an account of these experiments in the *Autobiography*, above. This letter was among the documents read to the Royal Society in London on December 21, 1752, concerning Franklin's identification of lightning with electricity, for which he received the Copley Medal in 1753 and was elected a Fellow of the Society in 1756. The letter was printed in the *Gentleman's Magazine*, December, 1752.

and wind of a thunder-gust without tearing. To the top of the up-right stick of the cross is to be fixed a very sharp-pointed wire, rising a foot or more above the wood. To the end of the twine, next the hand, is to be tied a silk ribbon, and where the silk and twine join, a key may be fastened. This kite is to be raised when a thunder-gust appears to be coming on, and the person who holds the string must stand within a door or window, or under some cover, so that the silk ribbon may not be wet; and care must be taken that the twine does not touch the frame of the door or window. As soon as any of the thunder-clouds come over the kite, the pointed wire will draw the electric fire from them, and the kite, with all the twine, will be electrified, and the loose filaments of the twine will stand out every way, and be attracted by an approaching finger. And when the rain has wet the kite and twine, so that it can conduct the electric fire freely, you will find it stream out plentifully from the key on the approach of your knuckle. At this key the phial[2] may be charged; and from electric fire thus obtained, spirits may be kindled, and all the other electric experiments be performed, which are usually done by the help of a rubbed glass globe or tube, and thereby the same-ness of the electric matter with that of lightning completely demon-strated.

B. FRANKLIN.

The Ephemera[3]

You may remember, my dear friend, that when we lately spent that happy day in the delightful garden and sweet society of the Moulin Joly,[4] I stopt a little in one of our walks, and staid some time behind the company. We had been shown numberless skeletons of a kind of little fly, called an ephemera, whose successive genera-tions, we were told, were bred and expired within the day. I hap-pened to see a living company of them on a leaf, who appeared to be engaged in conversation. You know I understand all the inferior animal tongues; my too great application of the study of them is the best excuse I can give for the little progress I have made in your charming language.[5] I listened through curiosity to the discourse

2. The Leyden jar, an early experi-mental electrical condenser.

3. In France as American representative (1776–85) Franklin had a small press for propaganda releases, on which he also printed his "Bagatelles," charming trifles to amuse his friends. "The Ephem-era," unlike most of these essays, shows his characteristic speculative curiosity as well as the wit that captivated the French. Madame Brillon, for whom he wrote this, was a young Passy matron

at least thirty-five years his junior, with whom he played simultaneously the father and gallant. Franklin wrote this, the first Bagatelle, in 1778; it was printed both in French and English, but the dates are not established.

4. Name of an island in the Seine, loca-tion of the home of a friend, where they had spent a day together.

5. He had asked her to correct his French; she thought correction impaired his style and distracted him with the

of these little creatures; but as they, in their national vivacity, spoke three or four together, I could make but little of their conversation. I found, however, by some broken expressions that I heard now and then, they were disputing warmly on the merits of two foreign musicians, one a *cousin*, the other a *moscheto*;[6] in which dispute they spent their time, seemingly as regardless of the shortness of life as if they had been sure of living a month. Happy people! thought I, you live certainly under a wise, just, and mild government, since you have no public grievances to complain of, nor any subject of contention but the perfections and imperfections of foreign music. I turned my head from them to an old grey-headed one, who was single on another leaf, and talking to himself. Being amused with his soliloquy, I put it down in writing, in hopes it will likewise amuse her to whom I am so much indebted for the most pleasing of all amusements, her delicious company and heavenly harmony.[7]

"It was," said he, "the opinion of learned philosophers of our race, who lived and flourished long before my time, that this vast world, the Moulin Joly, could not itself subsist more than eighteen hours; and I think there was some foundation for that opinion, since, by the apparent motion of the great luminary that gives life to all nature, and which in my time has evidently declined considerably towards the ocean at the end of our earth, it must then finish its course, be extinguished in the waters that surround us, and leave the world in cold and darkness, necessarily producing universal death and destruction. I have lived seven of those hours, a great age, being no less than four hundred and twenty minutes of time. How very few of us continue so long! I have seen generations born, flourish, and expire. My present friends are the children and grandchildren of the friends of my youth, who are now, alas, no more! And I must soon follow them; for, by the course of nature, though still in health, I cannot expect to live above seven or eight minutes longer. What now avails all my toil and labor, in amassing honey-dew on this leaf, which I cannot live to enjoy! What the political struggles I have been engaged in, for the good of my compatriot inhabitants of this bush, or my philosophical studies for the benefit of our race in general! for, in politics, what can laws do without morals? Our present race of ephemeræ will in a course of minutes become corrupt, like those of other and older bushes, and consequently as wretched. And in philosophy how small our progress! Alas! art is long, and life is short! My friends would comfort me with the idea of a name, they say, I shall leave behind me, and they tell me I have lived long

statement that it was "always good French to say: '*Je vous aime*'" (Van Doren).

6. The *cousin* is a gnat, the *moscheto* a mosquito; Franklin here makes a playful reference to the continuous rivalries, in Paris, between opposing musical schools.

7. Madame Brillon, an accomplished musician, played and sang, and set verses to music for Franklin.

enough to nature and to glory. But what will fame be to an ephemera who no longer exists? And what will become of all history in the eighteenth hour, when the world itself, even the whole Moulin Joly, shall come to its end, and be buried in universal ruin?"

To me, after all my eager pursuits, no solid pleasures now remain, but the reflection of a long life spent in meaning well, the sensible conversation of a few good lady ephemerae, and now and then a kind smile and a tune from the ever amiable *Brillante*.[8]

B. FRANKLIN.

1778

To Madame Helvetius[9]

Mortified at the barbarous resolution pronounced by you so positively yesterday evening, that you would remain single the rest of your life as a compliment due to the memory of your husband, I retired to my chamber. Throwing myself upon my bed, I dreamt that I was dead, and was transported to the Elysian Fields.

I was asked whether I wished to see any persons in particular; to which I replied that I wished to see the philosophers. "There are two who live here at hand in this garden; they are good neighbors, and very friendly towards one another."—"Who are they?"—"Socrates and Helvetius."—"I esteem them both highly; but let me see Helvetius first, because I understand a little French, but not a word of Greek." I was conducted to him, he received me with much courtesy, having known me, he said, by character, some time past. He asked me a thousand questions relative to the war, the present state of religion, of liberty, of the government in France. "You do not inquire, then," said I, "after your dear friend, Madame Helvetius; yet she loves you exceedingly. I was in her company not more than an hour ago." "Ah," said he, "you make me recur to my past happiness, which ought to be forgotten in order to be happy here. For many years I could think of nothing but her, though at length I am consoled. I have taken another wife, the most like her that I could find; she is not indeed altogether so handsome, but she has a great fund of wit and good-sense, and her whole study is to please me. She is at this moment gone to fetch the best nectar and ambrosia to regale me; stay here awhile and you will see her." "I

8. This pun on her name, Brillon, appears also in Franklin's letters.
9. Another *Bagatelle*. Madame Helvetius, widow of the philosopher Claude Adrien Helvetius, who had died in 1771, was Franklin's neighbor at Auteuil; a famous beauty in her youth, she was now the gay and sympathetic hostess of two generations of intellectuals. Frank-

lin became her intimate companion and proposed marriage, which she wisely declined; he perpetuated the offer in such pleasantries as this famous essay, which he gave her, in French, in December, 1779. The first printings, in French and English, are not dated; however, it has been many times reprinted.

ve," said I, "that your former friend is more faithful to you
ou are to her; she has had several good offers, but has refused
them all. I will confess to you that I loved her extremely; but she
was cruel to me, and rejected me peremptorily for your sake." "I
pity you sincerely," said he, "for she is an excellent woman, handsome and amiable. But do not the Abbé de la R * * * * and
the Abbé M * * * * visit her?"[1]—"Certainly they do; not one
of your friends has dropped her acquaintance."—"If you had
gained the Abbé M * * * * with a bribe of good coffee and
cream, perhaps you would have succeeded; for he is as deep a
reasoner as Duns Scotus or St. Thomas;[2] he arranges and methodizes
his arguments in such a manner that they are almost irresistible. Or
if by a fine edition of some old classic you had gained the Abbé
de la R * * * * to speak *against* you, that would have been still better,
as I always observed that when he recommended any thing to her,
she had a great inclination to do directly the contrary." As he finished
these words the new Madame Helvetius entered with the nectar,
and I recognized her immediately as my former American friend, Mrs.
Franklin![3] I reclaimed her, but she answered me coldly: "I was a
good wife to you for forty-nine years and four months, nearly half
a century; let that content you. I have formed a new connection here,
which will last to eternity."

Indignant at this refusal of my Eurydice,[4] I immediately resolved
to quit those ungrateful shades, and return to this good world again,
to behold the sun and you! Here I am; let us *avenge ourselves!*

[1]779

Letter to Joseph Priestley[5]
[*Science and Humanity*]

PASSY, Feb. 8, 1780.

DEAR SIR,

Your kind letter of September 27 came to hand but very lately,
the bearer having stayed long in Holland. I always rejoice to hear

---

1. Van Doren writes (*Benjamin Franklin*, p. 648): "The witty Abbé Morellet,
who had met Franklin in England, lived
near Madame Helvetius if not in her
house. The book-loving Abbé de la
Roche was comfortably domesticated
with her. * * *"
2. Duns Scotus (1265?–1308), Scottish
scholastic theologian, and St. Thomas
Aquinas (1225?–1274), Italian scholastic and founder of Thomist philosophy—both proverbial for skill in dialectics.

3. Franklin's wife, Deborah, had died
in 1774.
4. In the Greek myth, Eurydice, having
died, was sought by her husband, Orpheus, in Pluto's realm of death.
5. Joseph Priestley (1733–1804), British chemist and liberal, supported the
American and French revolutions. Subjected to hostility and violence, he emigrated to Philadelphia (1791). His research and writing advanced science and
religious liberalism, especially Unitarianism. His correspondence with
Franklin was considerable.

of your being still employed in experimental researches into nature, and of the Success you meet with. The rapid Progress *true* Science now makes, occasions my regretting sometimes that I was born so soon. It is impossible to imagine the height to which may be carried, in a thousand years, the power of man over matter. We may perhaps learn to deprive large masses of their gravity, and give them absolute levity, for the sake of easy transport. Agriculture may diminish its labour and double its produce; all diseases may by sure means be prevented or cured, not excepting even that of old age, and our lives lengthened at pleasure even beyond the antediluvian standard. O that moral science were in as fair a way of improvement, that men would cease to be wolves to one another, and that human beings would at length learn what they now improperly call humanity![6]

I am glad my little paper on the *Aurora Borealis* pleased. If it should occasion further enquiry, and so produce a better hypothesis, it will not be wholly useless. I am ever, with the greatest and most sincere esteem, dear sir, yours very affectionately

B. FRANKLIN.

Letter to Sir Joseph Banks[7]
[*War and Peace*]

PASSY, 27 July, 1783.

DEAR SIR,

I received your very kind letter by Dr. Blagden,[8] and esteem myself much honoured by your friendly remembrance. I have been too much and too closely engaged in public affairs, since his being here, to enjoy all the benefit of his conversation you were so good as to intend me. I hope soon to have more leisure, and to spend a part of it in those studies, that are much more agreeable to me than political operations.

I join with you most cordially in rejoicing at the return of peace. I hope it will be lasting, and that mankind will at length, as they call themselves reasonable creatures, have reason and sense enough to settle their differences without cutting throats; for, in my opinion, *there never was a good war, or a bad peace.* What vast additions to the conveniences and comforts of living might mankind have acquired, if the money spent in wars had been employed in works of

6. The belief in moral progress, common to the thought of the Enlightenment, persists in Franklin's writing and correspondence. Often he expressed its goal as the abolition of war. See the letter next following, to Sir Joseph Banks.

7. Sir Joseph Banks (1743–1820), President of the Royal Society of London, of which Franklin had been elected a Fellow in 1756.
8. Sir Charles Blagden (1748–1820), fellow member with Franklin and Banks of the Royal Society, was a distinguished physicist and physician.

public utility! What an extension of agriculture, even to the tops of our mountains; what rivers rendered navigable, or joined by canals: what bridges, aqueducts, new roads, and other public works, edifices, and improvements, rendering England a complete paradise, might have been obtained by spending those millions in doing good, which in the last war have been spent in doing mischief; in bringing misery into thousands of families, and destroying the lives of so many thousands of working people, who might have performed the useful labour!

I am pleased with the late astronomical discoveries made by our society. Furnished as all Europe now is with academies of science, with nice instruments and the spirit of experiment, the progress of human knowledge will be rapid, and discoveries made, of which we have at present no conception. I begin to be almost sorry I was born so soon, since I cannot have the happiness of knowing what will be known 100 years hence.

I wish continued success to the labours of the royal society, and that you may long adorn their chair; being, with the highest esteem, dear Sir, &c.,

B. FRANKLIN.

P.S. Dr. Blagden will acquaint you with the experiment of a vast globe sent up into the air, much talked of here, and which, if prosecuted, may furnish means of new knowledge.[9]

Letter to [Thomas Paine?][1]
[*Reason and Religion*]

PHILA. July 3, 1786[?].

DEAR SIR,

I have read your manuscript with some attention. By the argument it contains against the doctrines of a particular providence, though you allow a general providence, you strike at the foundation of all religion. For without the belief of a providence, that takes cognizance of, guards, and guides, and may favour particular persons, there is no motive to worship a deity, to fear its displeasure, or to pray for its protection. I will not enter into any discussion of your principles, though you seem to desire it. At present I shall only give you my opinion, that, though your reasonings are subtile, and may

9. The first balloon to rise successfully was sent up by the brothers Mongolfier at Annonay, near Lyons, France, in June, 1783. Franklin was very much interested in the scientific and practical possibilities. See letter (above) to Priestley.

1. This letter, without salutation in the original rough draft, was assumed by early editors of Franklin's works to have been addressed to Thomas Paine, with reference to his deistic writings. Smyth, noting that the *Age of Reason* did not appear for almost ten years, leaves it unassigned. The cordial and generous tone of Franklin's other letters to Paine in this period would suggest that this letter was written to a less familiar acquaintance. Its importance, however, lies in its expression of Franklin's religious ideas at this late date.

prevail with some readers, you will not succeed so as to change the general sentiments of mankind on that subject, and the consequence of printing this piece will be a great deal of odium drawn upon yourself, mischief to you, and no benefit to others. He that spits against the wind, spits in his own face.

But, were you to succeed, do you imagine any good would be done by it? You yourself may find it easy to live a virtuous life, without the assistance afforded by religion; you having a clear perception of the advantages of virtue, and the disadvantages of vice, and possessing a strength of resolution sufficient to enable you to resist common temptations. But think how great a proportion of mankind consists of weak and ignorant men and women, and of inexperienced and inconsiderate youth of both sexes, who have need of the motives of religion to restrain them from vice, to support their virtue, and retain them in the practice of it till it becomes *habitual*, which is the great point for its security. And perhaps you are indebted to her originally, that is, to your religious education, for the habits of virtue upon which you now justly value yourself. You might easily display your excellent talents of reasoning upon a less hazardous subject, and thereby obtain a rank with our most distinguished authors. For among us it is not necessary, as among the hottentots, that a youth, to be received into the company of men, should prove his manhood by beating his mother.

I would advise you, therefore, not to attempt unchaining the tiger, but to burn this piece before it is seen by any other person; whereby you will save yourself a great deal of mortification from the enemies it may raise against you, and perhaps a good deal of regret and repentance. If men are so wicked as we now see them *with religion*, what would they be *if without it*. I intend this letter itself as a *proof* of my friendship, and therefore add no *professions* to it; but subscribe simply yours,

B. F.

THOMAS PAINE
(1737–1809)

Thomas Paine, with his natural gift for pamphleteering and rebellion, was appropriately born into an age of revolution. "My country is the world, and my religion is to do good," he once declared; and he served the rebels of three countries.

This "Great Commoner of Mankind," son of a nominal Quaker of Thetford, England, was early apprenticed to his father, a staymaker. At nineteen, he went to sea for perhaps two years, then followed his father's trade again as master staymaker in several English communities. For nearly twelve years, beginning in 1762, he was employed as an excise officer. His leisure was devoted to the eager pursuit of books and ideas, particularly the study of social philosophy and the new science. After three years in the excise service, he was dismissed for a neglect of duty, but he was reinstated following a year spent as a teacher near London.

The young excise collector learned social science at first hand, seeing the hardships of the tax-burdened masses and the hopelessness of humble workers of his own class. His first wife having died, he acquired, in his second marriage, a small tobacconist's shop in Lewes, where he was stationed; but he still lived constantly on the edge of privation. In 1772 he wrote his first pamphlet, *The Case of the Officers of the Excise,* and he spent the next winter in London, representing his fellow workers in a petition to Parliament for a living wage. Suddenly he was dismissed, possibly for his agency in this civil revolt, although the official charge was that he had neglected his duties at Lewes. Within two months of losing his position, he lost his shop through bankruptcy and his wife by separation. This was his unhappy situation at thirty-seven, when Franklin met him in London and recognized his peculiar talents in their American perspective. In 1774 Paine made his way to Philadelphia, bearing a cautious letter from Franklin recommending him as "an ingenious worthy young man."

In Philadelphia, Paine edited the *Pennsylvania Magazine,* and contributed to the *Pennsylvania Journal.* As the relations of the colonies with England approached a crisis, readers of the two Philadelphia papers recognized a political satirist of genius. On January 10, 1776, his famous pamphlet *Common Sense* appeared. It boldly advocated a "Declaration for Independence," and brought the separatist agitation to a crisis. This was a courageous act of high treason against England; Paine knew quite well that publication of the pamphlet could cost him his life, even though it was signed simply "By an Englishman." In three months it sold probably a hundred thousand copies; they circulated from hand to hand. It was also reprinted abroad. Paine became forthwith the most articulate spokesman of the American Revolution. He enlisted, was appointed aide-de-camp to General Greene, and served through the engagements of 1776 in New York, New Jersey, and Pennsylvania; but his chief contribution was a series of sixteen pamphlets (1776–1783) entitled *The American Crisis* and signed "Common Sense." The first of these, with its blast at the "summer soldier and the sunshine patriot," appeared in the black month of December, 1776, just after Washington's retreat across New Jersey. It was read at once to all regiments, and like the twelve later *Crisis* pamphlets that dealt directly with the military engagements, it restored the morale and inspired the success of that citizens' army. The last of the *Crisis* papers, the sixteenth, appeared on December 9, 1783, at the end of the war. Meanwhile Paine had served on various committees of the Continental Congress; he had been clerk of the Pennsylvania Assembly, received an honorary degree from the College of Philadelphia (the University of Pennsylvania), gone to France to help negotiate a loan for the colonies, and published much concerning the war and the eventual federal union of the colonies.

The war over, he turned to invention, perfecting the model of an iron bridge without piers. In 1787 he went to Paris and London, and secured foreign patents for his bridge. In both countries he was received as an important international figure; Burke and Fox became his friends, and Lafayette presented him with a key to the Bastille to be transmitted to General Washington. In England, the patronage of the great terminated suddenly. Paine's *Rights of Man* (Part I, 1791; Part II, 1792), answering Burke's recent *Reflections on the French Revolution*, not only championed Rousseau's doctrines of freedom, but also suggested the overthrow of the British monarchy. On May 21, 1792, Paine was indicted for treason, and he was forced to seek refuge in France, where he had taken part in the early events of the Revolution during his visits in 1789 and 1791.

The French revolutionaries received him enthusiastically; he was elected a member of the National Convention, representing four districts. But when he opposed the execution of Louis

XVI and the Reign of Terror, he was imprisoned in the Luxembourg. He had already sent to press in Paris the first part of *The Age of Reason*, a deistic treatise advocating a rationalistic view of religion. Set free as a result of the death of Robespierre and the friendly intercession of James Monroe, then American ambassador to France, he recuperated for many months in Monroe's home, where he completed *The Age of Reason* (1794–1795), and wrote his last important treatise, *Agrarian Justice* (1797). In 1802 he returned to America, only to find that his patriotic services had been forgotten in the wave of resentment against his "atheistical" beliefs and the reaction of conservatives against the French Revolution. During his remaining years, neglected by all but his vilifiers, he remained in obscurity, for the most part on his farm in New Rochelle. There he was buried in 1809, after a year of illness in New York; his funeral was attended by six people, two of them Negroes. In 1819, William Cobbett, returning to England, transported Paine's remains to their native soil, in token of repentance for his earlier condemnation. At Cobbett's death no one knew where Paine was buried; his final resting place is still unknown.

Paine's writings, his doctrines of the social contract, political liberalism, and the equality of all men, resulted less from his own originality than from his journalistic ability to make vigorous restatements of the popular liberal thought of the eighteenth century. Even the much debated *Age of Reason* was an extensive formulation of Deism, a familiar theological concept of contemporary rationalism, the advanced thought of that era. But his prose still possesses many of the qualities that made it stimulating and inspiring to his contemporaries. His excellence lies in the fiery ardor and determination of his words, the conviction of his courageous and indomitable spirit, and the sincerity and passion of his belief in the rights of the humblest man.

The comprehensive edition of Paine's works is that of Moncure D. Conway, *The Writings of Thomas Paine*, 4 vols., 1894–1896; and the most nearly definitive biography is Conway's *The Life of Thomas Paine*, 2 vols., 1892. Shorter lives have been written by F. J. Gould, 1925; by Crane Brinton in the *Dictionary of American Biography*, 1934; and by Hesketh Pearson, 1937. Longer, and authoritative, is W. E. Woodward, *Tom Paine: America's Godfather*, 1945. A careful text is the one-volume edition of A. W. Peach, *Selections from the Works of Thomas Paine*, 1928; an excellent one-volume scholarly edition with introduction is *Thomas Paine: Representative Selections*, edited by H. H. Clark, American Writers Series, 1944. In this volume the Conway edition is followed, except as noted.

From Common Sense

Thoughts on the Present State of American Affairs[1]

In the following pages I offer nothing more than simple facts, plain arguments, and common sense; and have no other preliminaries to settle with the reader, than that he will divest himself of prejudice and prepossession, and suffer his reason and his feelings to determine for themselves; that he will put on, or rather that he will not put off, the true character of a man, and generously enlarge his views beyond the present day.

Volumes have been written on the subject of the struggle between England and America. Men of all ranks have embarked in the controversy, from different motives, and with various designs; but all have been ineffectual, and the period of debate is closed. Arms as the last resource decide the contest; the appeal was the choice of the king, and the continent has accepted the challenge.

It hath been reported of the late Mr. Pelham[2] (who though an able minister was not without his faults) that on his being attacked in the House of Commons on the score that his measures were only of a temporary kind, replied, "*They will last my time.*" Should a thought so fatal and unmanly possess the colonies in the present contest, the name of Ancestors will be remembered by future generations with detestation.

The sun never shined on a cause of greater worth. 'Tis not the affair of a city, a county, a province, or a kingdom; but of a continent

1. "Thoughts on the Present State of American Affairs" was Part III of *Common Sense*. Part I discussed the British constitution in relation to "the origin and design of government"; Part II analyzed the weaknesses of "monarchy and hereditary succession." The American Declaration of Independence was promulgated six months later, on July 4.
2. Henry Pelham, British prime minister (1744–1754).

—of at least one-eighth part of the habitable globe. 'Tis not the concern of a day, a year, or an age; posterity are virtually involved in the contest, and will be more or less affected even to the end of time by the proceedings now. Now is the seedtime of continental union, faith, and honor. The least fracture now will be like a name engraved with the point of a pin on the tender rind of a young oak; the wound would enlarge with the tree, and posterity read it in full grown characters.

By referring the matter from argument to arms, a new era for politics is struck—a new method of thinking has arisen. All plans, proposals, &c. prior to the nineteenth of April,[3] i.e. to the commencement of hostilities, are like the almanacks of the last year; which though proper then, are superseded and useless now. Whatever was advanced by the advocates on either side of the question then, terminated in one and the same point, viz. a union with Great Britain; the only difference between the parties was the method of effecting it; the one proposing force, the other friendship; but it has so far happened that the first has failed, and the second has withdrawn her influence.

As much has been said of the advantages of reconciliation, which, like an agreeable dream, has passed away and left us as we were, it is but right that we should examine the contrary side of the argument, and inquire into some of the many material injuries which these colonies sustain, and always will sustain, by being connected with and dependent on Great Britain. To examine that connection and dependence on the principles of nature and common sense; to see what we have to trust to, if separated, and what we are to expect, if dependent.

I have heard it asserted by some, that as America has flourished under her former connection with Great Britain, the same connection is necessary towards her future happiness, and will always have the same effect. Nothing can be more fallacious than this kind of argument. We may as well assert that because a child has thrived upon milk, that it is never to have meat, or that the first twenty years of our lives is to become a precedent for the next twenty. But even this is admitting more than is true; for I answer roundly that America would have flourished as much, and probably much more, had no European power taken any notice of her. The commerce by which she hath enriched herself are the necessaries of life, and will always have a market while eating is the custom of Europe.

But she has protected us, say some. That she hath engrossed us is true, and defended the continent at our expense as well as her own is admitted; and she would have defended Turkey from the same

3. April 19, 1775, the date of the battles of Lexington and Concord, where American minutemen defended their ammunition stores against British troops—the first armed engagements of the Revolution.

motive, viz. for the sake of trade and dominion.

Alas! we have been long led away by ancient prejudices and made large sacrifices to superstition. We have boasted the protection of Great Britain without considering that her motive was *interest*, not *attachment*; and that she did not protect us from *our enemies* on *our account*, but from her enemies on her own account, from those who had no quarrel with us on any *other account*, and who will always be our enemies on the *same account*. Let Britain waive her pretensions to the continent, or the continent throw off the dependence, and we should be at peace with France and Spain were they at war with Britain. The miseries of Hanover's[4] last war ought to warn us against connections.

It hath lately been asserted in parliament, that the colonies have no relation to each other but through the parent country, i.e. that Pennsylvania and the Jerseys, and so on for the rest, are sister colonies by the way of England; this is certainly a very roundabout way of proving relationship, but it is the nearest and only true way of proving enmity (or enemyship, if I may so call it). France and Spain never were, nor perhaps ever will be, our enemies as *Americans*, but as our being the *subjects of Great Britain*.

But Britain is the parent country, say some. Then the more shame upon her conduct. Even brutes do not devour their young, nor savages make war upon their families; wherefore, the assertion, if true, turns to her reproach; but it happens not to be true, or only partly so, and the phrase *parent* or *mother country* hath been jesuitically adopted by the King and his parasites, with a low papistical design of gaining an unfair bias on the credulous weakness of our minds. Europe, and not England, is the parent country of America. This new world hath been the asylum for the persecuted lovers of civil and religious liberty from *every part* of Europe. Hither have they fled, not from the tender embraces of the mother, but from the cruelty of the monster; and it is so far true of England, that the same tyranny which drove the first emigrants from home pursues their descendants still.

In this extensive quarter of the globe, we forget the narrow limits of three hundred and sixty miles (the extent of England) and carry our friendship on a larger scale; we claim brotherhood with every European Christian, and triumph in the generosity of the sentiment.

It is pleasant to observe by what regular gradations we surmount the force of local prejudices as we enlarge our acquaintance with the world. A man born in any town in England divided into parishes, will naturally associate most with his fellow parishioners (because their interests in many cases will be common) and distinguish him

4. The Prussian house of Hanover occupied the British throne from 1714 to 1901. Paine thus connects the repeated French invasions of Hanover, during the Seven Years' War (1756–1763), with the Franco-British rivalries.

by the name of *neighbor*; if he meet him but a few miles from home, he drops the narrow idea of a street, and salutes him by the name of *townsman*; if he travel out of the county and meet him in any other, he forgets the minor divisions of street and town, and calls him *country-man, i.e. county-man*; but if in their foreign excursions they should associate in France, or any other part of *Europe*, their local remembrance would be enlarged into that of *Englishman*. And by a just parity of reasoning, all Europeans meeting in America, or any other quarter of the globe, are *countrymen*; for England, Holland, Germany, or Sweden, when compared with the whole, stand in the same places on the larger scale, which the divisions of street, town, and county do on the smaller ones; distinctions too limited for continental minds. Not one third of the inhabitants, even of this province,[5] are of English descent. Wherefore, I reprobate the phrase of parent or mother country applied to England only, as being false, selfish, narrow, and ungenerous.

But, admitting that we were all of English descent, what does it amount to? Nothing. Britain, being now an open enemy, extinguishes every other name and title; and to say that reconciliation is our duty, is truly farcical. The first king of England, of the present line (William the Conqueror) was a Frenchman, and half the peers of England are descendants from the same country; wherefore, by the same method of reasoning, England ought to be governed by France.

Much hath been said of the united strength of Britain and the colonies, that in conjunction they might bid defiance to the world. But this is mere presumption, the fate of war is uncertain; neither do the expressions mean anything, for this continent would never suffer itself to be drained of inhabitants to support the British arms in either Asia, Africa, or Europe.

Besides, what have we to do with setting the world at defiance? Our plan is commerce, and that, well attended to, will secure us the peace and friendship of all Europe; because it is the interest of all Europe to have America a *free port*. Her trade will always be a protection, and her barrenness of gold and silver secure her from invaders.

I challenge the warmest advocate for reconciliation to show a single advantage that this continent can reap, by being connected with Great Britain. I repeat the challenge, not a single advantage is derived. Our corn will fetch its price in any market in Europe, and our imported goods must be paid for, buy them where we will.

But the injuries and disadvantages which we sustain by that connection are without number; and our duty to mankind at large, as well as to ourselves, instruct us to renounce the alliance: because any submission to, or dependence on, Great Britain, tends directly

5. *I.e.*, Pennsylvania.

to involve this continent in European wars and quarrels, and set us at variance with nations who would otherwise seek our friendship, and against whom we have neither anger nor complaint. As Europe is our market for trade, we ought to form no partial connection with any part of it. 'Tis the true interest of America to steer clear of European contentions, which she never can do while by her dependence on Britain she is made the makeweight in the scale of British politics.

Europe is too thickly planted with kingdoms to be long at peace, and whenever a war breaks out between England and any foreign power, the trade of America goes to ruin, *because of her connection with Britain*. The next war may not turn out like the last,[6] and should it not, the advocates for reconciliation now will be wishing for separation then, because neutrality in that case would be a safer convoy than a man of war. Everything that is right or reasonable pleads for separation. The blood of the slain, the weeping voice of nature cries, 'TIS TIME TO PART. Even the distance at which the Almighty hath placed England and America is a strong and natural proof that the authority of the one over the other, was never the design of heaven. The time likewise at which the continent was discovered, adds weight to the argument, and the manner in which it was peopled, increases the force of it. The Reformation was preceded by the discovery of America, as if the Almighty graciously meant to open a sanctuary to the persecuted in future years, when home should afford neither friendship nor safety.

The authority of Great Britain over this continent is a form of government which sooner or later must have an end. And a serious mind can draw no true pleasure by looking forward, under the painful and positive conviction that what he calls "the present constitution" is merely temporary. As parents, we can have no joy, knowing that *this government* is not sufficiently lasting to insure anything which we may bequeath to posterity; and by a plain method of argument, as we are running the next generation into debt, we ought to do the work of it, otherwise we use them meanly and pitifully. In order to discover the line of our duty rightly, we should take our children in our hand, and fix our station a few years farther into life; that eminence will present a prospect which a few present fears and prejudices conceal from our sight.

Though I would carefully avoid giving unnecessary offense, yet I am inclined to believe that all those who espouse the doctrine of reconciliation may be included within the following descriptions: Interested men, who are not to be trusted, weak men who *cannot* see, prejudiced men who *will not* see, and a certain set of moderate men who think better of the European world than it deserves; and

6. The British were victorious in the French and Indian War, the American phase of the Seven Years' War.

this last class, by an ill-judged deliberation, will be the cause of more calamities to this continent than all the other three.

It is the good fortune of many to live distant from the scene of present sorrow; the evil is not sufficiently brought to *their* doors to make *them* feel the precariousness with which all American property is possessed. But let our imaginations transport us a few moments to Boston;[7] that seat of wretchedness will teach us wisdom, and instruct us forever to renounce a power in whom we can have no trust. The inhabitants of that unfortunate city, who but a few months ago were in ease and affluence, have now no other alternative than to stay and starve, or turn out to beg. Endangered by the fire of their friends if they continue within the city, and plundered by the soldiery if they leave it, in their present situation they are prisoners without the hope of redemption, and in a general attack for their relief they would be exposed to the fury of both armies.

Men of passive tempers look somewhat lightly over the offenses of Great Britain, and, still hoping for the best, are apt to call out, *Come, come, we shall be friends again for all this.* But examine the passions and feelings of mankind; bring the doctrine of reconciliation to the touchstone of nature, and then tell me whether you can hereafter love, honor, and faithfully serve the power that hath carried fire and sword into your land? If you cannot do all these, then are you only deceiving yourselves, and by your delay bringing ruin upon posterity. Your future connection with Britain, whom you can neither love nor honor, will be forced and unnatural, and being formed only on the plan of present convenience, will in a little time fall into a relapse more wretched than the first. But if you say you can still pass the violations over, then I ask, Hath your house been burnt? Hath your property been destroyed before your face? Are your wife and children destitute of a bed to lie on, or bread to live on? Have you lost a parent or child by their hands, and yourself the ruined and wretched survivor? If you have not, then are you not a judge of those who have. But if you have, and can still shake hands with the murderers, then are you unworthy the name of husband, father, friend, or lover; and whatever may be your rank or title in life, you have the heart of a coward, and the spirit of a sycophant.

This is not inflaming or exaggerating matters, but trying them by those feelings and affections which nature justifies, and without which we should be incapable of discharging the social duties of life, or enjoying the felicities of it. I mean not to exhibit horror for the purpose of provoking revenge, but to awaken us from fatal and unmanly slumbers, that we may pursue determinately some fixed object. 'Tis not in the power of Britain or of Europe to conquer America,

7. Boston was then under British military occupation, and subject, then and later, to American siege.

if she doth not conquer herself by *delay* and *timidity*. The present winter is worth an age if rightly employed, but if lost or neglected the whole continent will partake of the misfortune; and there is no punishment which that man doth not deserve, be he who, or what, or where he will, that may be the means of sacrificing a season so precious and useful.

It is repugnant to reason, to the universal order of things, to all examples from former ages, to suppose that this continent can long remain subject to any external power. The most sanguine in Britain doth not think so. The utmost stretch of human wisdom cannot, at this time, compass a plan, short of separation, which can promise the continent even a year's security. Reconciliation is *now* a fallacious dream. Nature has deserted the connection, and art cannot supply her place. For, as Milton wisely expresses, "Never can true reconcilement grow where wounds of deadly hate have pierced so deep."[8]

Every quiet method for peace hath been ineffectual. Our prayers have been rejected with disdain; and have tended to convince us that nothing flatters vanity or confirms obstinacy in kings more than repeated petitioning—and nothing hath contributed more than that very measure to make the kings of Europe absolute. Witness Denmark and Sweden.[9] Wherefore, since nothing but blows will do, for God's sake let us come to a final separation, and not leave the next generation to be cutting throats under the violated unmeaning names of parent and child.

To say they will never attempt it again is idle and visionary; we thought so at the repeal of the stamp act, yet a year or two undeceived us; as well may we suppose that nations which have been once defeated will never renew the quarrel.

As to government matters, it is not in the power of Britain to do this continent justice: the business of it will soon be too weighty and intricate to be managed with any tolerable degree of convenience, by a power so distant from us, and so very ignorant of us; for if they cannot conquer us they cannot govern us. To be always running three or four thousand miles with a tale or a petition, waiting four or five months for an answer, which, when obtained, requires five or six more to explain it in, will in a few years be looked upon as folly and childishness. There was a time when it was proper, and there is a proper time for it to cease.

Small islands not capable of protecting themselves are the proper objects for government to take under their care; but there is something absurd in supposing a continent to be perpetually governed by an island. In no instance hath nature made the satellite larger than its primary planet; and as England and America, with respect

8. *Paradise Lost*, Book IV, ll. 98–99.
9. Both Denmark and Sweden had recently been threatened by monarchical absolutism; Gustavus III of Sweden had imprisoned the entire Council in 1772.

to each other, reverse the common order of nature, it is evident that they belong to different systems. England to Europe: America to itself.

I am not induced by motives of pride, party, or resentment to espouse the doctrine of separation and independence; I am clearly, positively, and conscientiously persuaded that 'tis the true interest of this continent to be so; that everything short of *that* is mere patch-work, that it can afford no lasting felicity—that it is leaving the sword to our children, and shrinking back at a time when a little more, a little further, would have rendered this continent the glory of the earth.

As Britain hath not manifested the least inclination towards a compromise, we may be assured that no terms can be obtained worthy the acceptance of the continent, or any ways equal to the expense of blood and treasure we have been already put to.

The object contended for ought always to bear some just proportion to the expense. The removal of North[1] or the whole detestable junto, is a matter unworthy the millions we have expended. A temporary stoppage of trade was an inconvenience which would have sufficiently balanced the repeal of all the acts complained of, had such repeals been obtained; but if the whole continent must take up arms, if every man must be a soldier, 'tis scarcely worth our while to fight against a contemptible ministry only. Dearly, dearly do we pay for the repeal of the acts, if that is all we fight for; for, in a just estimation, 'tis as great a folly to pay a Bunker-hill price[2] for law as for land. As I have always considered the independency of this continent an event which sooner or later must arrive, so from the late rapid progress of the continent to maturity, the event cannot be far off. Wherefore, on the breaking out of hostilities, it was not worth the while to have disputed a matter which time would have finally redressed, unless we meant to be in earnest; otherwise it is like wasting an estate on a suit at law, to regulate the trespasses of a tenant whose lease is just expiring. No man was a warmer wisher for a reconciliation than myself, before the fatal nineteenth of April, 1775,[3] but the moment the event of that day was made known, I rejected the hardened, sullen-tempered Pharaoh of England[4] forever; and disdain the wretch, that with the pretended title of FATHER OF HIS PEOPLE can unfeelingly hear of their slaughter, and composedly sleep with their blood upon his soul.

But admitting that matters were now made up, what would be the event? I answer, the ruin of the continent. And that for several

1. Frederick North, Earl of Guilford, prime minister (1770–1782), was held responsible for the British policy of colonial exploitation by taxation.
2. American casualties at Bunker Hill (June 17, 1775) were reported to be one third of those engaged.
3. Date of the battles of Concord and Lexington.
4. King George III; here likened to the "hardened Pharoah," despotic captor of the Israelites (Exodus vii: 13–14).

reasons.

First. The powers of governing still remaining in the hands of the king, he will have a negative over the whole legislation of this continent. And as he hath shown himself such an inveterate enemy to liberty, and discovered such a thirst for arbitrary power, is he, or is he not, a proper person to say to these colonies, *You shall make no laws but what I please!* And is there any inhabitant of America so ignorant as not to know, that according to what is called the *present constitution*, this continent can make no laws but what the king gives leave to; and is there any man so unwise as not to see, that (considering what has happened) he will suffer no law to be made here but such as suits *his* purpose? We may be as effectually enslaved by the want of laws in America, as by submitting to laws made for us in England. After matters are made up (as it is called), can there be any doubt but the whole power of the crown will be exerted to keep this continent as low and humble as possible? Instead of going forward we shall go backward, or be perpetually quarrelling, or ridiculously petitioning. We are already greater than the king wishes us to be, and will he not hereafter endeavor to make us less? To bring the matter to one point, Is the power who is jealous of our prosperity, a proper power to govern us? Whoever says No to this question is an independent, for independency means no more than this, whether we shall make our own laws, or whether the king, the greatest enemy this continent hath, or can have, shall tell us, *There shall be no laws but such as I like.*

But the king, you'll say, has a negative in England; the people there can make no laws without his consent. In point of right and good order, it is something very ridiculous that a youth of twenty-one (which hath often happened) shall say to several millions of people older and wiser than himself, "I forbid this or that act of yours to be law." But in this place I decline this sort of reply, though I will never cease to expose the absurdity of it, and only answer that England being the king's residence, and America not so, makes quite another case. The king's negative here is ten times more dangerous and fatal than it can be in England; for *there* he will scarcely refuse his consent to a bill for putting England into as strong a state of defense as possible, and in America he would never suffer such a bill to be passed.

America is only a secondary object in the system of British politics, England consults the good of *this* country no further than it answers her *own* purpose. Wherefore, her own interest leads her to suppress the growth of *ours* in every case which doth not promote *her* advantage, or in the least interfere with it. A pretty state we should soon be in under such a secondhand government, considering what has happened! Men do not change from enemies to friends by the alteration of a name: and in order to show that reconciliation *now* is a dangerous doctrine, I affirm *that it would be policy in the king at this time to repeal the acts for the sake of reinstating himself in the government of the provinces;* in order that HE MAY ACCOMPLISH BY CRAFT AND SUBTLETY, IN THE LONG RUN, WHAT HE CANNOT DO BY FORCE AND VIOLENCE IN THE SHORT ONE. Reconciliation and ruin are nearly related.

Secondly. That as even the best terms which we can expect to obtain can amount to no more than a temporary expedient, or a kind of government by guardianship, which can last no longer than till the colonies come of age, so the general face and state of things in the interim will be unsettled and unpromising. Emigrants of property will not choose to come to a country whose form of government hangs but by a thread, and who is every day tottering on the brink of commotion and disturbance; and numbers of the present inhabitants would lay hold of the interval to dispose of their effects, and quit the continent.

But the most powerful of all arguments is, that nothing but independence, i.e. a continental form of government, can keep the peace of the continent and preserve it inviolate from civil wars. I dread the event of a reconciliation with Britain *now*, as it is more than probable that it will be followed by a revolt somewhere or other, the consequences of which may be far more fatal than all the malice of Britain.

Thousands are already ruined by British barbarity; (thousands more will probably suffer the same fate). Those men have other feelings than us who have nothing suffered. All they *now* possess is liberty; what they before enjoyed is sacrificed to its service, and having nothing more to lose they disdain submission. Besides, the general temper of the colonies towards a British government will be like that of a youth who is nearly out of his time; they will care very little about her. And a government which cannot preserve the peace is no government at all, and in that case we pay our money for nothing; and pray what is it that Britain can do, whose power will be wholly on paper, should a civil tumult break out the very day after reconciliation? I have heard some men say, many of whom I believe spoke without thinking, that they dreaded an independence, fearing that it would produce civil wars. It is but seldom that our first thoughts are truly correct, and that is the case here; for there is ten times more to dread from a patched up connection than from independence. I make the sufferer's case my own, and I protest, that were I driven from house and home, my property destroyed, and my circumstances ruined, that as a man, sensible of injuries, I could never relish the doctrine of reconciliation, or consider myself bound thereby.

The colonies have manifested such a spirit of good order and obedience to continental government as is sufficient to make every reasonable person easy and happy on that head. No man can assign the least pretense for his fears on any other grounds than such as are truly childish and ridiculous, viz., that one colony will be striving for superiority over another.

Where there are no distinctions there can be no superiority; perfect equality affords no temptation. The republics of Europe are all (and we may say always) in peace. Holland and Switzerland are without wars, foreign or domestic. Monarchical governments, it is true, are never long at rest: the crown itself is a temptation to enterprising ruffians at *home*; and that degree of pride and insolence ever attendant on regal authority, swells into a rupture with foreign powers in instances where a republican government, by being formed on more natural principles, would negotiate the mistake.

If there is any true cause of fear respecting independence, it is because no plan is yet laid down. Men do not see their way out. Wherefore, as an opening into that business I offer the following hints; at the same time modestly affirming that I have no other opinion of them myself than that they may be the means of giving rise to something better. Could the straggling thoughts of individuals be collected, they would frequently form materials for wise and able men to improve into useful matter.

Let the assemblies be annual, with a president only. The representation more equal, their business wholly domestic, and subject to the authority of a continental congress.

Let each colony be divided into six, eight, or ten, convenient districts, each district to send a proper number of delegates to congress, so that each colony send at least thirty. The whole number in congress will be at least 390. Each congress to sit and to choose a president by the following method. When the delegates are met, let a colony be taken from the whole thirteen colonies by lot, after which let the congress choose (by ballot) a president from out of the delegates of that province. In the next congress, let a colony be taken by lot from twelve only, omitting that colony from which the president was taken in the former congress, and so proceeding on till the whole thirteen shall have had their proper rotation. And in order that nothing may pass into a law but what is satisfactorily just, not less than three fifths of the congress to be called a majority. He that will promote discord, under a government so equally formed as this, would have joined Lucifer[5] in his revolt.

But as there is a peculiar delicacy from whom, or in what manner, this business must first arise, and as it seems most agreeable and consistent that it should come from some intermediate body be-

5. This was the name of Satan before he revolted against God; *cf*. Isaiah xiv: 12–20.

tween the governed and the governors, that is, between the congress and the people, let a CONTINENTAL CONFERENCE be held in the following manner, and for the following purpose:

A committee of twenty-six members of congress, viz., two for each colony. Two members from each house of assembly, or provincial convention; and five representatives of the people at large, to be chosen in the capital city or town of each province, for, and in behalf of the whole province, by as many qualified voters as shall think proper to attend from all parts of the province for that purpose; or, if more convenient, the representatives may be chosen in two or three of the most populous parts thereof. In this CONFERENCE, thus assembled, will be united the two grand principles of business, *knowledge* and *power*. The members of congress, assemblies, or conventions, by having had experience in national concerns, will be able and useful counsellors, and the whole, being empowered by the people, will have a truly legal authority.

The conferring members being met, let their business be to frame a CONTINENTAL CHARTER, or Charter of the United Colonies (answering to what is called the Magna Charta of England); fixing the number and manner of choosing members of congress, members of assembly, with their date of sitting, and drawing the line of business and jurisdiction between them (always remembering, that our strength is continental, not provincial); securing freedom and property to all men, and above all things the free exercise of religion, according to the dictates of conscience; with such other matter as it is necessary for a charter to contain. Immediately after which, the said conference to dissolve, and the bodies which shall be chosen conformable to the said charter, to be the legislators and governors of this continent for the time being: Whose peace and happiness, may God preserve. AMEN.

Should any body of men be hereafter delegated for this or some similar purpose, I offer them the following extracts from that wise observer on governments, Dragonetti. "The science," says he, "of the politician consists in fixing the true point of happiness and freedom. Those men would deserve the gratitude of ages, who should discover a mode of government that contained the greatest sum of individual happiness, with the least national expense." [6]

But where, say some, is the king of America? I'll tell you, friend, he reigns above, and doth not make havoc of mankind like the Royal Brute of Great Britain. Yet that we may not appear to be defective even in earthly honors, let a day be solemnly set apart for proclaiming the charter; let it be brought forth placed on the divine law, the Word of God; let a crown be placed thereon, by which the world

---

6. "Dragonetti on 'Virtues and Rewards'" [Paine's note]. He referred to   Giacinto Dragonetti, author of *Le Virtù ed i Premi* (1767).

may know, that so far as we approve of monarchy, that in America THE LAW IS KING. For as in absolute governments the king is law, so in free countries the law *ought* to BE king, and there ought to be no other. But lest any ill use should afterwards arise, let the crown at the conclusion of the ceremony be demolished, and scattered among the people whose right it is.[7] * * *

O ye that love mankind! Ye that dare oppose not only the tyranny but the tyrant, stand forth! Every spot of the old world is overrun with oppression. Freedom hath been hunted round the globe. Asia and Africa have long expelled her. Europe regards her like a stranger, and England hath given her warning to depart. O receive the fugitive, and prepare in time an asylum for mankind.

1776

The American Crisis[8]

These are the times that try men's souls: The summer soldier and the sunshine patriot will in this crisis, shrink from the service of his country; but he that stands it Now, deserves the love and thanks of man and woman. Tyranny, like hell, is not easily conquered; yet we have this consolation with us, that the harder the conflict, the more glorious the triumph. What we obtain too cheap, we esteem to[o] lightly:——'Tis dearness only that gives everything its value. Heaven knows how to put a proper price upon its goods; and it would be strange indeed, if so celestial an article as FREEDOM should not be highly rated. Britain, with an army to enforce her tyranny, has declared that she has a right (not only to) TAX but "to BIND *us in* ALL CASES WHATSOEVER", and if being *bound in that manner*, is not slavery, then is there not such a thing as slavery upon earth. Even the expression is impious for so unlimited a power can belong only to God.

Whether the Independence of the Continent was declared too soon, or delayed too long, I will not now enter into as an argument; my own simple opinion is, that had it been eight months earlier, it would have been much better. We did not make a proper use of last winter, neither could we, while we were in a dependent state. However, the fault, if it were one, was all our own; we have none to blame but ourselves. But no great deal is lost yet; all that Howe[9] has been

---

7. Popular sovereignty and a government by social contract are recurrent themes in Paine's later writings; *cf.* the Declaration of Independence.
8. The first of the sixteen pamphlets now known as *The Crisis*, this originally appeared undated in the *Pennsylvania Journal*, December 19, 1776. There were three pamphlet editions within the week,

one undated, one dated December 19, and one dated December 23. Since Paine later referred to the last as authoritative, it is reproduced here. The last number of *The Crisis*, the sixteenth, appeared on December 9, 1783.
9. Lord William Howe had taken command of the British troops in America in 1775.

doing for this month past, is rather a ravage than a conquest, which the spirit of the Jersies[1] a year ago would have quickly repulsed, and which time and a little resolution will soon recover.

I have as little superstition in me as any man living, but my secret opinion has ever been, and still is, that God Almighty will not give up a people to military destruction, or leave them unsupportedly to perish, who have so earnestly and so repeatedly sought to avoid the calamities of war, by every decent method which wisdom could invent. Neither have I so much of the infidel in me, as to suppose that he has relinquished the government of the world, and given us up to the care of devils; and as I do not, I cannot see on what grounds the king of Britain can look up to heaven for help against us: a common murderer, a highwayman, or a house-breaker, has as good a pretence as he.

'Tis surprising to see how rapidly a panic will sometimes run through a country. All nations and ages have been subject to them: Britain has trembled like an ague at the report of a French fleet of flat-bottomed boats; and in the fourteenth century the whole English army, after ravaging the kingdom of France, was driven back like men petrified with fear; and this brave exploit was performed by a few broken forces collected and headed by a woman, Joan of Arc. Would that heaven might inspire some Jersey maid to spirit up her countrymen, and save her fair fellow sufferers from ravage and ravishment! Yet panics, in some cases, have their uses; they produce as much good as hurt. Their duration is always short; the mind soon grows through them, and acquires a firmer habit than before. But their peculiar advantage is, that they are the touchstones of sincerity and hypocrisy, and bring things and men to light, which might otherwise have lain forever undiscovered. In fact, they have the same effect on secret traitors which an imaginary apparition would have upon a private murderer. They sift out the hidden thoughts of man, and hold them up in public to the world. Many a disguised tory has lately shown his head, that shall penitentially solemnize with curses the day on which Howe arrived upon the Delaware.

As I was with the troops at Fort-Lee, and marched with them to the edge of Pennsylvania, I am well acquainted with many circumstances, which those who live at a distance, know but little or nothing of.[2] Our situation there was exceedingly cramped, the place being a narrow neck of land between the North-River[3] and the

1. The colony was divided into East and West Jersey.
2. On November 20, General Greene made the hasty retreat southward from the Hudson forts to Newark, New Jersey. There, according to tradition, Paine wrote this *Crisis* paper on a drumhead. In less than a month it was printed, and Washington had it read to each regiment of the army, now encamped in Pennsylvania. A few days later, on Christmas night, they struck successfully across the Delaware at Trenton, and nine days later they attacked at Princeton. Paine participated in both battles.
3. The Hudson.

Hackensack. Our force was inconsiderable, being not one-fourth so great as Howe could bring against us. We had no army at hand to have relieved the garrison, had we shut ourselves up and stood on our defence. Our ammunition, light artillery, and the best part of our stores, had been removed, on the apprehension that Howe would endeavor to penetrate the Jerseys,[4] in which case Fort-Lee could be of no use to us; for it must occur to every thinking man, whether in the army or not, that these kind of field forts are only for temporary purposes, and last in use no longer than the enemy directs his force against the particular object, which such forts are raised to defend.[5] Such was our situation and condition at Fort-Lee on the morning of the 20th of November, when an officer arrived with information that the enemy with 200 boats had landed about seven miles above: Major General Green,[6] who commanded the garrison, immediately ordered them under arms, and sent express to General Washington at the town of Hackensack, distant by the way of the ferry, six miles. Our first object was to secure the bridge over the Hackensack, which laid up the river between the enemy and us, about six miles from us, and three from them. General Washington arrived in about three-quarters of an hour, and marched at the head of the troops towards the bridge, which place I expected we should have a brush for; however, they did not choose to dispute it with us, and the greatest part of our troops went over the bridge, the rest over the ferry, except some which passed at a mill on a small creek, between the bridge and the ferry, and made their way through some marshy grounds up to the town of Hackensack, and there passed the river. We brought off as much baggage as the wagons could contain, the rest was lost. The simple object was to bring off the garrison, and march them on till they could be strengthened by the Jersey or Pennsylvania militia, so as to be enabled to make a stand. We staid four days at Newark, collected our out-posts with some of the Jersey militia, and marched out twice to meet the enemy, on being informed that they were advancing, though our numbers were greatly inferior to theirs. Howe, in my little opinion, committed a great error in generalship in not throwing a body of forces off from Staten-Island through Amboy, by which means he might have seized all our stores at Brunswick,[7] and intercepted our march into Pennsylvania; but if we believe the power of hell to be limited, we must likewise believe that their agents are under some providential control.

4. Cf. "Jersies" above. The *Crisis* papers, printed, sometimes reprinted, under pressure, were never definitively edited by Paine.
5. Propagandist Paine naturally belittles the British success—actually the capture of Fort Lee and Fort Washington, the strategic defenses of the Hudson, together with enough men and materiel to make a field regiment.
6. *I. e.*, Greene. Nathaniel Greene commanded one of the divisions against Trenton, a month later.
7. Now Perth Amboy and New Brunswick. By holding this line Howe could have blocked Greene's only strategic retreat to Pennsylvania.

I shall not now attempt to give all the particulars of our retreat to the Delaware; suffice it for the present to say, that both officers and men, though greatly harassed and fatigued, frequently without rest, covering, or provision, the inevitable consequences of a long retreat, bore it with a manly and martial spirit. All their wishes centered in one, which was, that the country would turn out and help them to drive the enemy back. Voltaire[8] has remarked that King William never appeared to full advantage but in difficulties and in action; the same remark may be made on General Washington, for the character fits him. There is a natural firmness in some minds which cannot be unlocked by trifles, but which, when unlocked, discovers a cabinet of fortitude; and I reckon it among those kind of public blessings, which we do not immediately see, that God hath blessed him with uninterrupted health, and given him a mind that can even flourish upon care.

I shall conclude this paper with some miscellaneous remarks on the state of our affairs; and shall begin with asking the following question, Why is it that the enemy have left the New-England provinces, and made these middle ones the seat of war? The answer is easy: New England is not infested with tories, and we are. I have been tender in raising the cry against these men, and used numberless arguments to show them their danger, but it will not do to sacrifice a world either to their folly or their baseness. The period is now arrived, in which either they or we must change our sentiments, or one or both must fall. And what is a tory? Good God! what is he? I should not be afraid to go with a hundred Whigs against a thousand tories, were they to attempt to get into arms. Every tory is a coward; for servile, slavish, self-interested fear is the foundation of toryism; and a man under such influence, though he may be cruel, never can be brave.

But, before the line of irrecoverable separation be drawn between us, let us reason the matter together: Your conduct is an invitation to the enemy, yet not one in a thousand of you has heart enough to join him. Howe is as much deceived by you as the American cause is injured by you. He expects you will all take up arms, and flock to his standard, with muskets on your shoulders. Your opinions are of no use to him, unless you support him personally, for 'tis soldiers, and not tories, that he wants.

I once felt all that kind of anger, which a man ought to feel, against the mean principles that are held by the tories: A noted one, who kept a tavern at Amboy, was standing at his door, with as pretty a child in his hand, about eight or nine years old, as I ever saw, and after speaking his mind as freely as he thought was prudent, finished

8. The French man of letters Voltaire (1694–1778), then very popular in America, made this remark concerning William III of England (died 1702) in his principal historical treatise, *Le Siècle de Louis XIV* (1751), Chapter 17.

with this unfatherly expression, "Well! give me peace in my day." Not a man lives on the continent but fully believes that a separation must some time or other finally take place, and a generous parent should have said, "If there must be trouble, let it be in my day, that my child may have peace;" and this single reflection, well applied, is sufficient to awaken every man to duty. Not a place upon earth might be so happy as America. Her situation is remote from all the wrangling world, and she has nothing to do but to trade with them. A man can distinguish himself between temper and principle, and I am as confident, as I am that God governs the world, that America will never be happy till she gets clear of foreign dominion. Wars, without ceasing, will break out till that period arrives, and the continent must in the end be conqueror; for though the flame of liberty may sometimes cease to shine, the coal can never expire.

America did not, nor does not want force; but she wanted a proper application of that force. Wisdom is not the purchase of a day, and it is no wonder that we should err at the first setting off. From an excess of tenderness, we were unwilling to raise an army, and trusted our cause to the temporary defence of a well-meaning militia. A summer's experience has now taught us better; yet with those troops, while they were collected, we were able to set bounds to the progress of the enemy, and, thank God! they are again assembling. I always considered militia as the best troops in the world for a sudden exertion, but they will not do for a long campaign. Howe, it is probable, will make an attempt on this city;[9] should he fail on this side the Delaware, he is ruined. If he succeeds, our cause is not ruined. He stakes all on his side against a part on ours; admitting he succeeds, the consequence will be, that armies from both ends of the continent will march to assist their suffering friends in the middle states; for he cannot go everywhere, it is impossible. I consider Howe as the greatest enemy the tories have; he is bringing a war into their country, which, had it not been for him and partly for themselves, they had been clear of. Should he now be expelled, I wish with all the devotion of a Christian, that the names of whig and tory may never more be mentioned; but should the tories give him encouragement to come, or assistance if he come, I as sincerely wish that our next year's arms may expel them from the continent, and the Congress appropriate their possessions to the relief of those who have suffered in well-doing. A single successful battle next year will settle the whole. America could carry on a two years' war by the confiscation of the property of disaffected persons, and be made happy by their expulsion. Say not that this is revenge, call it rather the soft resentment of a suffering people, who, having no object in view but the

9. Philadelphia. As Paine predicts, it was occupied by the British (September 26, 1777).

GOOD of ALL, have staked their OWN ALL upon a seemingly doubtful event. Yet it is folly to argue against determined hardness; eloquence may strike the ear, and the language of sorrow draw forth the tear of compassion, but nothing can reach the heart that is steeled with prejudice.

Quitting this class of men, I turn with the warm ardor of a friend to those who have nobly stood, and are yet determined to stand the matter out: I call not upon a few, but upon all: not on THIS state or THAT state, but on EVERY state: up and help us; lay your shoulders to the wheel; better have too much force than too little, when so great an object is at stake. Let it be told to the future world, that in the depth of winter, when nothing but hope and virtue could survive, that the city and the country, alarmed at one common danger, came forth to meet and to repulse it. Say not that thousands are gone, turn out your tens of thousands;[1] throw not the burden of the day upon Providence, but *"show your faith by your works,"*[2] that God may bless you. It matters not where you live, or what rank of life you hold, the evil or the blessing will reach you all. The far and the near, the home counties and the back,[3] the rich and the poor, will suffer or rejoice alike. The heart that feels not now is dead; the blood of his children will curse his cowardice, who shrinks back at a time when a little might have saved the whole, and made *them* happy. I love the man that can smile in trouble, that can gather strength from distress, and grow brave by reflection. 'Tis the business of little minds to shrink; but he whose heart is firm, and whose conscience approves his conduct, will pursue his principles unto death. My own line of reasoning is to myself as straight and clear as a ray of light. Not all the treasures of the world, so far as I believe, could have induced me to support an offensive war, for I think it murder; but if a thief breaks into my house, burns and destroys my property, and kills or threatens to kill me, or those that are in it, and to *"bind me in all cases whatsoever"* to his absolute will, am I to suffer it? What signifies it to me, whether he who does it is a king or a common man; my countryman or not my countryman; whether it be done by an individual villain, or an army of them? If we reason to the root of things we shall find no difference; neither can any just cause be assigned why we should punish in the one case and pardon in the other. Let them call me rebel, and welcome, I feel no concern from it; but I should suffer the misery of devils, were I to make a whore of my soul by swearing allegiance to one whose character is that of a sottish, stupid, stubborn, worthless, brutish man. I conceive likewise a horrid idea in receiving mercy from a being, who at the last day shall be shrieking to the rocks and mountains to cover him, and fleeing with terror from the orphan,

1. *Cf.* I Samuel xviii: 7: "Saul hath slain his thousands, and David his ten thousands."
2. *Cf.* James ii: 18.
3. *I.e.*, both well-settled "counties," and backwoods.

250 · *Thomas Paine*

the widow, and the slain of America.

There are cases which cannot be overdone by language, and this is one. There are persons, too, who see not the full extent of the evil which threatens them; they solace themselves with hopes that the enemy, if he succeed, will be merciful. It is the madness of folly, to expect mercy from those who have refused to do justice; and even mercy, where conquest is the object, is only a trick of war; The cunning of the fox is as murderous as the violence of the wolf, and we ought to guard equally against both. Howe's first object is, partly by threats and partly by promises, to terrify or seduce the people to deliver up their arms and receive mercy. The ministry recommended the same plan to Gage,[4] and this is what the tories call making their peace, *"a peace which passeth all understanding"*[5] indeed! A peace which would be the immediate forerunner of a worse ruin than any we have yet thought of. Ye men of Pennsylvania, do reason upon these things! Were the back counties to give up their arms, they would fall an easy prey to the Indians, who are all armed: this perhaps is what some tories would not be sorry for. Were the home counties to deliver up their arms, they would be exposed to the resentment of the back counties, who would then have it in their power to chastise their defection at pleasure. And were any one state to give up its arms, THAT state must be garrisoned by all Howe's army of Britons and Hessians[6] to preserve it from the anger of the rest. Mutual fear is the principal link in the chain of mutual love, and woe be to that state that breaks the compact. Howe is mercifully inviting you to barbarous destruction, and men must be either rogues or fools that will not see it. I dwell not upon the vapors of imagination; I bring reason to your ears, and, in language as plain as A, B, C, hold up truth to your eyes.

I thank God that I fear not. I see no real cause for fear. I know our situation well, and can see the way out of it. While our army was collected, Howe dared not risk a battle; and it is no credit to him that he decamped from the White Plains,[7] and waited a mean opportunity to ravage the defenceless Jerseys; but it is great credit to us, that, with a handful of men, we sustained an orderly retreat for near an hundred miles, brought off our ammunition, all our fieldpieces, the greatest part of our stores, and had four rivers to pass. None can say that our retreat was precipitate, for we were near three weeks in performing it, that the country[8] might have time to come in. Twice we marched back to meet the enemy, and remained out till dark.

4. General Thomas Gage, Howe's predecessor, commanded the British armies in America from 1763 to 1775.
5. Ironic word play on Philippians iv: 7, where Paul refers to "the peace of God."
6. Already a term of disdain for the German mercenaries from Hesse and

elsewhere, many thousands of whom were employed in the British army.
7. At White Plains, New York, Howe had successfully attacked Washington's positions in October, but failed to follow up his advantage.
8. The militia, or local volunteers.

The sign of fear was not seen in our camp, and had not some of the cowardly and disaffected inhabitants spread false alarms through the country, the Jersies had never been ravaged. Once more we are again collected and collecting, our new army at both ends of the continent is recruiting fast, and we shall be able to open the next campaign with sixty thousand men, well-armed and clothed. This is our situation, and who will may know it. By perseverance and fortitude we have the prospect of a glorious issue; by cowardice and submission, the sad choice of a variety of evils—a ravaged country—a depopulated city—habitations without safety, and slavery without hope—our homes turned into barracks and bawdy-houses for Hessians, and a future race to provide for, whose fathers we shall doubt of. Look on this picture and weep over it! and if there yet remains one thoughtless wretch who believes it not, let him suffer it unlamented.

COMMON SENSE

December 23, 1776

From The Age of Reason[9]
BEING AN INVESTIGATION OF TRUE AND OF FABULOUS THEOLOGY

To My Fellow-Citizens of the
UNITED STATES OF AMERICA

I put the following work under your protection. It contains my opinion upon religion. You will do me the justice to remember that I have always strenuously supported the right of every man to his own opinion, however different that opinion might be to mine. He who denies to another this right makes a slave of himself to his present opinion, because he precludes himself the right of changing it.

The most formidable weapon against errors of every kind is reason. I have never used any other, and I trust I never shall.

Your affectionate friend and fellow-citizen.

THOMAS PAINE

Paris, 8th Pluviose,
Second Year of the French Republic, one and indivisible.
January 27, O. S. 1794.

9. *The Age of Reason* presents a paradox in literary history. The author declared that he wrote it in an effort to offset the collapse of religion and the growth of atheism during the French Revolution; yet his book caused him to be regarded as the archatheist himself. Paine's object was to define a rational Deism based on natural morals, and the rational universe suggested by the Newtonian physics. His God was the First Cause, the Designer of this rational universe. The selections below attempt to preserve this argument, while excluding, for lack of space, his detailed refutation, in Part II, of nonrational elements and episodes in the Old and New Testaments. The text is selected from Part I of the first English edition (Paris, 1794), with divisions suggested by the French translation which appeared almost simultaneously. Part II was published in 1795 in both Paris and London, and a London edition of both Parts appeared that year.

[Profession of Faith]

It has been my intention for several years past to publish my thoughts upon Religion. I am well aware of the difficulties that attend the subject; and from that consideration had reserved it to a more advanced period of life. I intended it to be the last offering I should make to my fellow-citizens of all nations, and that at a time when the purity of the motive that induced me to it could not admit of a question, even by those who might disapprove the work.

The circumstance that has now taken place in France,[1] of the total abolition of the whole national order of priesthood and of everything appertaining to compulsive systems or religion and compulsive articles of faith, has not only precipitated my intention, but rendered a work of this kind exceedingly necessary; lest, in the general wreck of superstition, of false systems of government, and false theology, we lose sight of morality, of humanity, and of the theology that is true.

As several of my colleagues, and others of my fellow-citizens of France, have given me the example of making their voluntary and individual profession of faith, I also will make mine; and I do this with all that sincerity and frankness with which the mind of man communicates with itself.

I believe in one God, and no more; and I hope for happiness beyond this life.

I believe in the equality of man, and I believe that religious duties consist in doing justice, loving mercy, and endeavoring to make our fellow-creatures happy.

But lest it should be supposed that I believe many other things in addition to these, I shall, in the progress of this work, declare the things I do not believe and my reasons for not believing them.

I do not believe in the creed professed by the Jewish church, by the Roman church, by the Greek church, by the Turkish church, by the Protestant church, nor by any church that I know of. My own mind is my own church.

All national institutions of churches—whether Jewish, Christian, or Turkish—appear to me no other than human inventions set up to terrify and enslave mankind and monopolize power and profit.

I do not mean by this declaration to condemn those who believe otherwise. They have the same right to their belief as I have to mine. But it is necessary to the happiness of man that he be mentally faithful to himself. Infidelity does not consist in believing or in disbelieving; it consists in professing to believe what he does not believe.

It is impossible to calculate the moral mischief, if I may so express

1. Since 1792 the more radical leaders of the French Revolution had discredited the clergy by forced confessions, closed the churches, abolished the Christian calendar and Sabbath, enshrined the Goddess of Reason in Notre Dame, and begun to promote a pagan cult.

it, that mental lying has produced in society. When a man has so far corrupted and prostituted the chastity of his mind as to subscribe his professional belief to things he does not believe, he has prepared himself for the commission of every other crime. He takes up the trade of a priest for the sake of gain, and, in order to *qualify* himself for that trade, he begins with a perjury. Can we conceive anything more destructive to morality than this?

Soon after I had published the pamphlet, COMMON SENSE, in America, I saw the exceeding probability that a revolution in the system of government would be followed by a revolution in the system of religion. The adulterous connection of church and state, wherever it had taken place, whether Jewish, Christian, or Turkish, had so effectually prohibited, by pains and penalties, every discussion upon established creeds and upon first principles of religion, that until the system of government should be changed those subjects could not be brought fairly and openly before the world; but that whenever this should be done, a revolution in the system of religion would follow. Human inventions and priestcraft would be detected, and man would return to the pure, unmixed, and unadulterated belief of one God, and no more.

[Of Myth and Miracle]

Every national church or religion has established itself by pretending some special mission from God, communicated to certain individuals. The Jews have their Moses; the Christians their Jesus Christ, their apostles and saints; and the Turks their Mahomet—as if the way to God was not open to every man alike.

Each of those churches show certain books which they call *revelation*, or the word of God. The Jews say that their word of God was given by God to Moses face to face; the Christians say that their word of God came by divine inspiration; and the Turks say that their word of God (the Koran) was brought by an angel from heaven. Each of those churches accuse the other of unbelief; and, for my own part, I disbelieve them all.

As it is necessary to affix right ideas to words, I will, before I proceed further into the subject, offer some observations on the word *revelation*. Revelation, when applied to religion, means something communicated *immediately* from God to man.

No one will deny or dispute the power of the Almighty to make such a communication, if he pleases. But admitting, for the sake of a case, that something has been revealed to a certain person, and not revealed to any other person, it is revelation to that person only. When he tells it to a second person, a second to a third, a third to a fourth, and so on, it ceases to be a revelation to all those persons. It is a revelation to the first person only, and *hearsay* to every other; and, consequently, they are not obliged to believe it.

It is a contradiction in terms and ideas to call anything a revelation that comes to us at second-hand, either verbally or in writing. Revelation is necessarily limited to the first communication. After this, it is only an account of something which that person says was a revelation made to him; and though he may find himself obliged to believe it, it cannot be incumbent upon me to believe it in the same manner, for it was not a revelation to *me*, and I have only his word for it that it was made to *him*.

When Moses told the children of Israel that he received the two tables of commandments from the hand of God, they were not obliged to believe him, because they had no other authority for it than his telling them so; and I have no other authority for it than some historian telling me so. The commandments carry no internal evidence of divinity with them. They contain some good moral precepts, such as any man qualified to be a lawgiver, or a legislator, could produce himself, without having recourse to supernatural intervention.[2]

When I am told that the Koran was written in heaven, and brought to Mahomet by an angel, the account comes too near the same kind of hearsay evidence and secondhand authority as the former. I did not see the angel myself, and therefore I have a right not to believe it.

When also I am told that a woman, called the Virgin Mary, said, or gave out, that she was with child without any cohabitation with a man, and that her betrothed husband, Joseph, said that an angel told him so, I have a right to believe them or not; such a circumstance required a much stronger evidence than their bare word for it; but we have not even this; for neither Joseph nor Mary wrote any such matter themselves. It is only reported by others that *they said so*. It is hearsay upon hearsay, and I do not choose to rest my belief upon such evidence.

It is, however, not difficult to account for the credit that was given to the story of Jesus Christ being the Son of God. He was born at a time when the heathen mythology had still some fashion and repute in the world, and that mythology had prepared the people for the belief of such a story. Almost all the extraordinary men that lived under the heathen mythology were reputed to be the sons of some of their gods. It was not a new thing, at that time, to believe a man to have been celestially begotten; the intercourse of gods with women was then a matter of familiar opinion. Their Jupiter, according to their accounts, had cohabited with hundreds; the story therefore had nothing in either new, wonderful, or obscene; it was conforma-

2. "It is, however, necessary to except the declaration * * * that God visits the sins of the fathers upon the children. This is contrary to every principle of moral justice" [Paine's note].

ble to the opinions that then prevailed among the people called Gentiles, or mythologists, and it was those people only that believed it. The Jews, who had kept strictly to the belief of one God and no more, and who had always rejected the heathen mythology, never credited the story.

It is curious to observe how the theory of what is called the Christian church sprung out of the tail of the heathen mythology. A direct incorporation took place, in the first instance, by making the reputed founder to be celestially begotten. The trinity of gods that then followed was no other than a reduction of the former plurality, which was about twenty or thirty thousand. The statue of Mary succeeded the statue of Diana of Ephesus.[3] The deification of heroes changed into the canonization of saints. The mythologists had gods for everything; the Christian mythologists had saints for everything. The church became as crowded with the one as the pantheon had been with the other; and Rome was the place of both. The Christian theory is little else than the idolatry of the ancient mythologists, accommodated to the purposes of power and revenue; and it yet remains to reason and philosophy to abolish the amphibious fraud.

[Christian Revelation and Nature]

Nothing that is here said can apply, even with the most distant disrespect, to the real character of Jesus Christ. He was a virtuous and an amiable man. The morality that he preached and practiced was of the most benevolent kind; and though similar systems of morality had been preached by Confucius, and by some of the Greek philosophers, many years before, by the Quakers since, and by many good men in all ages, it has not been exceeded by any.

Jesus Christ wrote no account of himself, of his birth, parentage, or anything else. Not a line of what is called the New Testament is of his writing. The history of him is altogether the work of other people; and as to the account given of his resurrection and ascension, it was the necessary counterpart to the story of his birth. His historians, having brought him into the world in supernatural manner, were obliged to take him out again in the same manner, or the first part of the story must have fallen to the ground.

The wretched contrivance with which this latter part is told exceeds everything that went before it. * * * A small number of persons, not more than eight or nine, are introduced as proxies for the whole world, to say they *saw it*, and all the rest of the world are called upon to believe it. But it appears that Thomas did not believe the resurrection;[4] and, as they say, would not believe without having ocular and manual demonstration himself. So *neither will I*; and the reason is equally as good for me, and for every other person, as for

3. See Acts xix: 23–41.   4. See John xx: 19–25.

Thomas. * * *

But some perhaps will say: Are we to have no word of God—no revelation? I answer: Yes; there is a word of God; there is a revelation.

THE WORD OF GOD IS THE CREATION WE BEHOLD; and it is in *this* word, which no human invention can counterfeit or alter, that God speaketh universally to man.

Human language is local and changeable, and is therefore incapable of being used as the means of unchangeable and universal information. The idea that God sent Jesus Christ to publish, as they say, the glad tidings to all nations from one end of the earth unto the other, is consistent only with the ignorance of those who knew nothing of the extent of the world, and who believed, as those world-saviors believed and continued to believe for several centuries (and that in contradiction to the discoveries of philosophers and the experience of navigators), that the earth was flat like a trencher; and that a man might walk to the end of it. * * *

It is always necessary that the means that are to accomplish any end be equal to the accomplishment of that end, or the end cannot be accomplished. It is in this that the difference between finite and infinite power and wisdom discovers itself. Man frequently fails in accomplishing his ends from a natural inability of the power to the purpose; and frequently from the want of wisdom to apply power properly. But it is impossible for infinite power and wisdom to fail as man faileth. The means it useth are always equal to the end; but human language, more especially as there is not a universal language, is incapable of being used as a universal means of unchangeable and uniform information; and therefore it is not the means that God useth in manifesting himself universally to man.

It is only in the CREATION that all our ideas and conceptions of a *word of God* can unite. The creation speaketh a universal language, independently of human speech or human languages, multiplied and various as they be. It is an ever existing original which every man can read. It cannot be forged; it cannot be counterfeited; it cannot be lost; it cannot be altered; it cannot be suppressed. It does not depend upon the will of man whether it shall be published or not; it publishes itself from one end of the earth to the other. It preaches to all nations and to all worlds; and this *word of God* reveals to man all that is necessary for man to know of God.

Do we want to contemplate his power? We see it in the immensity of the creation. Do we want to contemplate his wisdom? We see it in the unchangeable order by which the incomprehensible whole is governed. Do we want to contemplate his munificence? We see it in the abundance with which he fills the earth. Do we want to contemplate his mercy? We see it in his not withholding that abundance even from the unthankful. In fine, do we want to know what

God is? Search not the book called the Scripture, which any human hand might make, but the scripture called the Creation.

[First Cause: God of Reason]

The only idea man can affix to the name of God is that of a *first cause*, the cause of all things. And incomprehensibly difficult as it is for man to conceive what a first cause is, he arrives at the belief of it from the tenfold greater difficulty of disbelieving it. It is difficult beyond description to conceive that space can have no end; but it is more difficult to conceive an end. It is difficult beyond the power of man to conceive an eternal duration of what we call time; but it is more impossible to conceive a time when there shall be no time. In like manner of reasoning, everything we behold carries in itself the internal evidence that it did not make itself. Every man is an evidence to himself that he did not make himself; neither could his father make himself, nor his grandfather, nor any of his race; neither could any tree, plant, or animal make itself; and it is the conviction arising from this evidence that carries us on, as it were, by necessity, to the belief of a first cause eternally existing, of a nature totally different to any material existence we know of, and by the power of which all things exist; and this first cause, man calls God.

It is only by the exercise of reason that man can discover God. Take away that reason and he would be incapable of understanding anything; and, in this case, it would be just as consistent to read even the book called the Bible to a horse as to a man. How then is it that those people pretend to reject reason?

Almost the only parts of the book called the Bible that convey to us any idea of God are some chapters in Job, and the 19th Psalm; I recollect no other. Those parts are true *deistical* compositions; for they treat of the *Deity* through his works. They take the book of Creation as the word of God; they refer to no other book; and all the inferences they make are drawn from that volume.

I insert, in this place, the 19th Psalm, as paraphrased into English verse by Addison.[5] I recollect not the prose, and where I write this I have not the opportunity of seeing it.

> The spacious firmament on high,
> With all the blue ethereal sky,
> And spangled heavens, a shining frame,
> Their great original proclaim.[6]

> The unwearied sun, from day to day,
> Does his Creator's power display,

---

5. Joseph Addison (1672–1719), British poet and essayist.

6. In the first edition, the stanzas were not indicated by spacing.

And publishes to every land
The work of an Almighty hand.

Soon as the evening shades prevail
The moon takes up the wondrous tale,
And nightly to the listening earth
Repeats the story of her birth;

Whilst all the stars that round her burn
And all the planets, in their turn,
Confirm the tidings as they roll
And spread the truth from pole to pole.

What though in solemn silence all
Move round the dark terrestrial ball;
What though nor real voice, nor sound,
Amidst their radiant orbs be found.

In reason's ear they all rejoice,
And utter forth a glorious voice;
Forever singing as they shine,
THE HAND THAT MADE US IS DIVINE.

What more does man want to know than that the hand or power
that made these things is divine, is omnipotent? Let him believe this
with the force it is impossible to repel, if he permits his reason to
act, and his rule of moral life will follow of course.

The allusions in Job have, all of them, the same tendency with
this Psalm; that of deducing or proving a truth, that would otherwise be unknown, from truths already known.

I recollect not enough of the passages in Job to insert them correctly; but there is one that occurs to me that is applicable to the
subject I am speaking upon: "Canst thou by searching find out God?
Canst thou find out the Almighty to perfection?"[7]

I know not how the printers have pointed this passage, for I keep
no Bible; but it contains two distinct questions that admit of distinct
answers.

First, Canst thou by *searching* find out God? Yes, because, in
the first place, I know I did not make myself, and yet I have existence;
and by *searching* into the nature of other things, I find that no other
thing could make itself; and yet millions of other things exist; therefore it is that I know, by positive conclusion resulting from this
search, that there is a power superior to all those things, and that
power is God.

Secondly, Canst thou find out the Almighty to *perfection*? No,

7. This is Job xi: 7. See the following
chapter, verses 7–16, for Job's acknowledgment of the God of Nature as First
Cause, and see also chapters xxxviii–xli.

not only because the power and wisdom he had manifested in the structure of the Creation that I behold is to me incomprehensible; but because even this manifestation, great as it is, is probably but a small display of that immensity of power and wisdom by which millions of other worlds, to me invisible by their distance, were created and continue to exist.

It is evident that both these questions were put to the reason of the person to whom they are supposed to have been addressed; and it is only by admitting the first question to be answered affirmatively that the second could follow. It would have been unnecessary, and even absurd, to have put a second question more difficult than the first, if the first question had been answered negatively. The two questions have different objects; the first refers to the existence of God, the second to his attributes. Reason can discover the one, but it falls infinitely short in discovering the whole of the other.

[Recapitulation]

Having now extended the subject to a greater length than I first intended, I shall bring it to a close by abstracting a summary from the whole.

First—That the idea or belief of a word of God existing in print, or in writing, or in speech, is inconsistent in itself for the reasons already assigned. These reasons, among others, are the want of a universal language; the mutability of language; the errors to which translations are subject; the possibility of totally suppressing such a word; the probability of altering it, or fabricating the whole, and imposing it upon the world.

Secondly—That the creation we behold is the real and ever-existing word of God in which we cannot be deceived. It proclaimeth his power, it demonstrates his wisdom, it manifests his goodness and beneficence.

Thirdly—That the moral duty of man consists in imitating the moral goodness and beneficence of God manifested in the creation towards all his creatures. That seeing, as we daily do, the goodness of God to all men, it is an example calling upon all men to practice the same towards each other; and consequently that everything of persecution and revenge between man and man, and everything of cruelty to animals is a violation of moral duty.

I trouble not myself about the manner of future existence. I content myself with believing, even to positive conviction, that the power that gave me existence is able to continue it in any form and manner he pleases, either with or without this body; and it appears more probable to me that I shall continue to exist hereafter than that I should have had existence, as I now have, before that existence began.

It is certain that in one point all nations of the earth and all religious agree. All believe in a God. The things in which they disagree are the redundancies annexed to that belief; and, therefore, if ever a universal religion should prevail, it will not be believing anything new, but in getting rid of redundancies and believing as man believed at first. Adam, if ever there was such a man, was created a Deist; but in the meantime let every man follow, as he has a right to do, the religion and the worship he prefers.

1794

THOMAS JEFFERSON
(1743–1826)

It may be that Thomas Jefferson's thought and personality have influenced his countrymen more deeply, and remained more effectively alive, than those of any other American. Yet, of the eight titles published by him, only one represents what can be called a book in the usual sense. It is estimated that fifty volumes will be required for the definitive edition of his writings, composed chiefly of state papers, a few treatises, and the incredible twenty-five thousand letters, many of great length, by which he was always "sowing useful truths," as he called it. His words could not be contained by a letter or confined at their first destination; they were reborn in the public ideals and acts of the American people, and indeed in their daily speech. This is partly because he embodied their best meanings in such public utterances as the Virginia Statute for Religious Freedom, in the Declaration of Independence, of which he was the principal author, in the *Notes on the State of Virginia*, a veritable storehouse of humane ideas and liberal democracy, which he pub-

lished in 1784–1785, in his addresses as president, and in his autobiography, published three years after his death.

This Virginian planter-aristocrat had as vigorous humanitarian sympathies as Franklin, and though thirty-seven years his junior, he was just as much a product of the Enlightenment. His mind, like Franklin's, ranged curiously over many fields of knowledge—law, philosophy, government, architecture, education, religion, science, agriculture, mechanics—and whatever he touched, he enriched in some measure. He knew that he was not profound, but he read widely, impelled by the same practical reason as Franklin—to gain understanding. The development of rational science from Bacon to Newton; the history of English law from King Alfred to Blackstone; the tradition of English liberty in Harrington, Milton, Hobbes, Locke, and Algernon Sydney; the challenging ideas of contemporary French liberalism in Montesquieu, Helvetius, Voltaire, and the physiocrats—from acquaintance with these, indeed, he did gain understanding. This understanding he applied, with simple American directness, to a conception of democracy for a new land of plenty, where the people might have a fresh start toward liberty, selfhood, and that excellence which he sought in all things. This patrician humanist looked to merit and ability alone, not to privilege; the natural rights of man must be secured by law inalienably for all, irrespective of station. For him, government, a necessary evil, found sanction only in the common consent of a social contract; its purpose was the benefit of the individual, not his exploitation; it must provide freedom of speech, thought, association, press, worship, education, and enterprise. In a letter to Benjamin Rush in 1800, he stated his conviction, unaltered throughout his life: "I have sworn upon the altar of God, eternal hostility against every form of tyranny over the mind of man."

These ideas found practical expression in Jefferson's forty years of a public life so active that only its highest moments can be mentioned here. He was born in Albemarle County, Virginia, April 13, 1743. Years of private study were supplemented by two years at William and Mary College. He then prepared for the practice of law, but his election to the Virginia House of Burgesses in 1769 drew him into public life. He represented Virginia in the Second Continental Congress in 1775; the following year—with John Adams, Benjamin Franklin, Roger Sherman, and Robert R. Livingston—he drafted the Declaration of Independence. Again

in the Virginia legislature, he devoted himself to codifying and liberalizing the laws and to the cause of toleration represented in his bill for the establishment of religious freedom, finally adopted later, in 1786. He was governor of Virginia (1779–1781), and delegate to the Congress of the Confederation, before going to Paris to assist Franklin and Adams in treaty negotiations (1784). He remained in Paris to succeed Franklin as American minister (1785–1789). As the first American secretary of state (1790–1793) in Washington's cabinet, his opposition to the extreme Federalism and the aristocratic tendencies of Alexander Hamilton, secretary of the treasury, drew the support of those who favored equalitarian measures and greater local independence, thus defining the constitutional questions that have since continued to provide the issues for the two American parties. On these issues he was narrowly defeated by John Adams in 1796, and accepted the vice-presidency, then awarded the unsuccessful candidate. On the same issues he won the election of 1800, and served for two terms as president. Among the many acts of his administration may be noted his measures to prevent unwarranted encroachment of the federal powers upon the domain of the states, and his concern for the expansion of the country, reflected in the Louisiana Purchase (1803) and in his sponsorship of the expedition of Lewis and Clark (1803–1806).

In 1809 he "retired" to a very active life at Monticello, a monument to his architectural genius, whose gradual perfection had been his hobby since 1767. The sale of his library of ten thousand volumes to the national government partially relieved his financial obligations and provided the foundation of the national library of his dreams (now the Library of Congress). His democratic theories of education, formulated through the years, soon took concrete form in the University of Virginia (1819), whose notable buildings he designed, and whose first Rector he became. His correspondence, in which he now expressed the seasoned experience and the accumulated wisdom of a lifetime, grew to enormous proportions, which, as he said, often denied him "the leisure of reading a single page in a week." The only American of his time to be elected to the Institute of France, Jefferson experimented in agriculture, paleontology, geography, and botany, and was president of the American Philosophical Society for eighteen years. It was fitting that his death in 1826 should occur on the fiftieth anniversary of the signing of the Declaration of Independence.

The earliest reliable edition of Jefferson's works is *The Writings of Thomas Jefferson*, 10 vols., edited by P. L. Ford, 1892–1899. The Memorial Edition, edited by A. A. Lipscomb and A. E. Bergh, 20 vols., 1903–1907, contains additional texts not in the Ford edition. A definitive edition, in preparation under the direction of Julian P. Boyd, is expected to comprise at least fifty volumes, of which nine have appeared at this date (1955), entitled *Papers of Thomas Jefferson* (Princeton University Press). Many important letters have been published, but there is no definitive edition of them. See especially *Thomas Jefferson Correspondence * * ***, edited by W. C. Ford, 1916; *Correspondence Between John Adams and Thomas Jefferson*, edited by Paul Wilstach, 1925; *The Best Letters of Thomas Jefferson*, edited by J. G. de Roulhac Hamilton, 1926. Available single-volume collections are *The Complete Jefferson * * ** except his Letters*, edited by Saul K. Padover, 1943; and *Life and Selected Writings of Thomas Jefferson*, edited by A. Koch and W. Peden, 1944. *Alexander Hamilton and Thomas Jefferson: Representative Selections*, edited by F. C. Prescott, American Writers Series, 1934, is a good critical selection contrasting the two political philosophies.

Biographies and special studies are numerous. Among the available general treatments, see A. J. Nock, *Jefferson*, 1926; and Gilbert Chinard, *Thomas Jefferson: The Apostle of Americanism*, 1929. Dumas Malone has in progress a four-volume biography, of which two volumes have appeared: *Jefferson, The Virginian*, 1948, and *Jefferson and the Rights of Man*, 1951. Also authoritative is Malone's "Jefferson" in the *Dictionary of American Biography*, 1933. Important special studies are Adrienne Koch, *The Philosophy of Thomas Jefferson*, 1943; K. Lehmann, *Thomas Jefferson, American Humanist*, 1947; C. G. Bowers, *Jefferson and Hamilton*, 1925, and *Jefferson in Power*, 1936.

The Declaration of Independence

In CONGRESS, July 4, 1776.

THE UNANIMOUS DECLARATION of the thirteen united STATES OF AMERICA.[1]

When in the Course of human events, it becomes necessary for one people to dissolve the political bands which have connected them with another, and to assume among the powers of the earth, the

---

1. Richard Henry Lee of Virginia, on June 7, 1776, proposed a resolution in Congress that "these united Colonies are, and of right ought to be, free and inde-

separate and equal station to which the Laws of Nature and of Nature's God entitle them, a decent respect to the opinions of mankind requires that they should declare the causes which impel them to the separation.————We hold these truths to be self-evident, that all men are created equal, that they are endowed by their Creator with certain unalienable Rights, that among these are Life, Liberty and the pursuit of Happiness.[2]—That to secure these rights, Governments are instituted among Men, deriving their just powers from the consent of the governed,—That whenever any Form of Government becomes destructive of these ends, it is the Right of the People to alter or to abolish it, and to institute new Government, laying its foundation on such principles and organizing its powers in such form, as to them shall seem most likely to effect their Safety and Happiness. Prudence, indeed, will dictate that Governments long established should not be changed for light and transient causes; and accordingly all experience hath shewn, that mankind are more disposed to suffer, while evils are sufferable, than to right themselves by abolishing the forms to which they are accustomed. But when a long train of abuses and usurpations, pursuing invariably the same Object evinces a design to reduce them under absolute Despotism, it is their right, it is their duty, to throw off such Government, and to provide new Guards for their future security.—Such has been the patient sufferance of these Colonies; and such is now the necessity which constrains them to alter their former Systems of Government. The history of the present King of Great Britain[3] is a history of repeated injuries and usurpations, all having in direct object the establishment of an absolute Tyranny over these States. To prove this, let Facts be submitted to a candid world.————He has refused his Assent to Laws, the most wholesome and necessary for the public good.————He has forbidden his Governors to pass Laws of immediate and pressing importance, unless suspended in their operation till his Assent should be obtained; and when so suspended, he has utterly

pendent States." Final action was postponed, but on June 11 a committee of five was appointed, which on June 28 presented the draft of a Declaration of Independence. It was substantially the work of Jefferson, although Franklin made fundamental contributions, and the influence of John Adams is evident. On July 2, Lee's original resolution was passed. On July 4, the Declaration was passed after some changes during debate; the Liberty Bell rang from the State House steeple in Philadelphia, and that night printed broadside copies were hastily run off for public distribution. On August 2, an engrossed parchment copy was signed by all the delegates but three, who also signed shortly thereafter. Printed copies, with all the signatures, appeared in January, 1777. The

philosophical and political ideals expressed in the Declaration can be traced far back in history, and their immediate roots are found in eighteenth-century thought, while the final draft represented a consensus among the delegates; however, the document still reflects the authorship of Jefferson, his precise clarity and powerful grace of thought. The text printed here is that authorized by the State Department: *The Declaration of Independence, 1776* (1911).

2. *Cf.* John Locke, *Second Treatise of Government*, where he identified natural rights as those to "life, liberty, and estate [property]."

3. George III, king from 1760 to 1820, was the responsible engineer of those policies of his government which evoked rebellion.

neglected to attend to them.———He has refused to pass other Laws for the accommodation of large districts of people, unless those people would relinquish the right of Representation in the Legislature, a right inestimable to them and formidable to tyrants only. ———He has called together legislative bodies at places unusual, uncomfortable, and distant from the depository of their public Records, for the sole purpose of fatiguing them into compliance with his measures.———He has dissolved Representative Houses repeatedly, for opposing with manly firmness his invasions on the rights of the people.———He has refused for a long time, after such dissolutions, to cause others to be elected; whereby the Legislative powers, incapable of Annihilation, have returned to the People at large for their exercise; the State remaining in the mean time exposed to all the dangers of invasion from without, and convulsions within.———He has endeavoured to prevent the population of these States; for that purpose obstructing the Laws for Naturalization of Foreigners; refusing to pass others to encourage their migrations hither, and raising the conditions of new Appropriations of Lands.———He has obstructed the Administration of Justice, by refusing his Assent to Laws for establishing Judiciary powers.———He has made Judges dependent on his Will alone, for the tenure of their officers, and the amount and payment of their salaries.———He has erected a multitude of New Offices, and sent hither swarms of Officers to harass our people, and eat out their substance.———He has kept among us, in times of peace, Standing Armies without the Consent of our legislatures.———He has affected to render the Military independent of and superior to the Civil power.———He has combined with others[4] to subject us to a jurisdiction foreign to our constitution, and unacknowledged by our laws; giving his Assent to their Acts of pretended Legislation:—For Quartering large bodies of armed troops among us:—For protecting them, by a mock Trial, from punishment for any Murders which they should commit on the Inhabitants of these States:—For cutting off our Trade with all parts of the world:—For imposing Taxes on us without our Consent:—For depriving us in many cases, of the benefits of Trial by Jury:—For transporting us beyond Seas to be tried for pretended offences:—For abolishing the free System of English Laws in a neighbouring Province,[5] establishing therein an Arbitrary government, and enlarging its Boundaries so as to render it at once an example and fit instrument for introducing the same absolute rule into these Colonies:—For taking away our Charters, abolishing our most valuable Laws, and altering fundamentally the Forms of our Governments:—For suspending our own

4. The British Parliament.
5. The Quebec Act (1774) promised concessions to the French Catholics, and restored the French civil law, thus alien-ating the Province of Quebec from the seaboard colonies in the growing controversy.

Legislatures, and declaring themselves invested with power to legislate for us in all cases whatsoever.—He has abdicated Government here, by declaring us out of his Protection and waging War against us:—He has plundered our seas, ravaged our Coasts, burnt our towns, and destroyed the lives of our people.—He is at this time transporting large Armies of foreign Mercenaries[6] to compleat the works of death, desolation and tyranny, already begun with circumstances of Cruelty & perfidy scarcely paralleled in the most barbarous ages, and totally unworthy the Head of a civilized nation.—He has constrained our fellow Citizens taken Captive on the high Seas to bear Arms against their Country, to become the executioners of their friends and Brethren, or to fall themselves by their Hands.—He has excited domestic insurrections amongst us, and has endeavoured to bring on the inhabitants of our frontiers, the merciless Indian Savages, whose known rule of warfare, is an undistinguished destruction of all ages, sexes and conditions. In every stage of these Oppressions We have Petitioned for Redress in the most humble terms: Our repeated Petitions have been answered only by repeated injury. A Prince, whose character is thus marked by every act which may define a Tyrant, is unfit to be the ruler of a free people. Nor have We been wanting in attentions to our British brethren. We have warned them from time to time of attempts by their legislature to extend an unwarrantable jurisdiction over us. We have reminded them of the circumstances of our emigration and settlement here. We have appealed to their native justice and magnanimity, and we have conjured them by the ties of our common kindred to disavow these usurpations, which, would inevitably interrupt our connections and correspondence. They too have been deaf to the voice of justice and of consanguinity. We must, therefore, acquiesce in the necessity, which denounces[7] our Separation, and hold them, as we hold the rest of mankind, Enemies in War, in Peace Friends.

WE, THEREFORE, the Representatives of the UNITED STATES OF AMERICA, in General Congress Assembled, appealing to the Supreme Judge of the world for the rectitude of our intentions, do, in the Name and by Authority of the good People of these Colonies, solemnly publish and declare, That these United Colonies are, and of Right ought to be FREE AND INDEPENDENT STATES; that they are Absolved from all Allegiance to the British Crown, and that all political connection between them and the State of Great Britain, is and ought to be totally dissolved; and that as Free and Independent States, they have full Power to levy War, conclude Peace, contract Alliances, establish Commerce, and to do all other Acts and Things which Independent States may of right do.——And for the support

6. German soldiers, principally Hessians, hired by the British for colonial service.
7. Proclaims.

of this Declaration, with a firm reliance on the protection of divine Providence, we mutually pledge to each other our Lives, our Fortunes and our sacred Honor.

1776

First Inaugural Address[8]

Friends and Fellow-Citizens:

Called upon to undertake the duties of the first executive office of our country, I avail myself of the presence of that portion of my fellow-citizens which is here assembled, to express my grateful thanks for the favor with which they have been pleased to look towards me, to declare a sincere consciousness that the task is above my talents, and that I approach it with those anxious and awful presentiments which the greatness of the charge and the weakness of my powers so justly inspire. A rising nation spread over a wide and fruitful land, traversing all the seas with the rich productions of their industry, engaged in commerce with nations who feel power and forget right, advancing rapidly to destinies beyond the reach of mortal eye; when I contemplate these transcendent objects, and see the honor, the happiness, and the hopes of this beloved country committed to the issue and the auspices of this day, I shrink from the contemplation, and humble myself before the magnitude of the undertaking.

Utterly, indeed, should I despair, did not the presence of many whom I here see remind me that in the other high authorities provided by our constitution I shall find resources of wisdom, of virtue, and of zeal on which to rely under all difficulties. To you then, gentlemen, who are charged with the sovereign functions of legislation, and to those associated with you, I look with encouragement for that guidance and support which may enable us to steer with safety the vessel in which we are all embarked, amidst the conflicting elements of a troubled sea.

During the contest of opinion[9] through which we have passed, the animation of discussions and of exertions has sometimes worn an aspect which might impose on strangers unused to think freely and to speak and to write what they think. But this being now decided by the voice of the nation, announced according to the rules

8. In accordance with Article II of the Constitution, subsequently changed by the Twelfth Amendment, Jefferson had become vice-president in 1796, as the candidate defeated by the Federalist, John Adams. In 1800 he ran against Aaron Burr, both of them Democratic Republicans (Democrats). The electoral vote was a tie, a result that prompted the adoption of the Twelfth Amendment.

The election was settled by a vote in the House of Representatives, where Jefferson, supported by Hamilton, defeated Burr, whose resentment ultimately led to the Burr–Hamilton duel and Hamilton's death. The inauguration occurred on March 4, 1801, before the Congress, in the Senate Chamber of the still-unfinished Capitol.

9. *I.e.*, the bitterly contested election.

of the Constitution, all will, of course, arrange themselves under the will of the law, and unite in common efforts for the common good. All too will bear in mind this sacred principle, that though the will of the majority is in all cases to prevail, that will, to be rightful, must be reasonable; that the minority possess their equal rights, which equal laws must protect, and to violate would be oppression. Let us then, fellow-citizens, unite with one heart and one mind; let us restore to social intercourse that harmony and affection without which liberty, and even life itself, are but dreary things. And let us reflect that having banished from our land that religious intolerance under which mankind so long bled and suffered, we have yet gained little if we countenance a political intolerance as despotic, as wicked, and capable of as bitter and bloody persecutions. During the throes and convulsions of the ancient world, during the agonizing spasms of infuriated man, seeking through blood and slaughter his long-lost liberty, it was not wonderful that the agitation of the billows should reach even this distant and peaceful shore;[1] that this should be more felt and feared by some and less by others; and should divide opinions as to measures of safety. But every difference of opinion is not a difference of principle. We have called by different names brethren of the same principle. We are all republicans; we are all federalists.[2] If there be any among us who would wish to dissolve this Union, or to change its republican form, let them stand undisturbed as monuments of the safety with which error of opinion may be tolerated, where reason is left free to combat it.[3] I know, indeed, that some honest men have feared that a republican government cannot be strong; that this Government is not strong enough. But would the honest patriot, in the full tide of successful experiment, abandon a government which has so far kept us free and firm, on the theoretic and visionary fear that this Government, the world's best hope, may by possibility want energy to preserve itself? I trust not. I believe this, on the contrary, the strongest government on earth. I believe it the only one where every man, at the call of the law would fly to the standard of the law; would meet invasions of the public order as his own personal concern. Sometimes it is said that man cannot be trusted with the government of himself. Can he then, be trusted with the government of others? Or have we found angels in the form of kings to govern him? Let history answer this question.

Let us then, pursue with courage and confidence our own federal and republican principles, our attachment to union and representative government. Kindly separated by nature and a wide ocean from

1. The Reign of Terror (1794) in the French Revolution alarmed American conservatives and intensified the strife between the parties.
2. The two contesting political parties. The "Democratic Republicans" (the official name) were the ancestors of the Democratic party; Jefferson is referring not to politics but to common principles.
3. This is probably the first important official recognition of the guarantee of freedom of thought and opinion.

the exterminating havoc of one quarter of the globe; too high-minded
to endure the degradations of the others; possessing a chosen country, with room enough for our descendants to the hundredth and
thousandth generation;[4] entertaining a due sense of our equal right
to the use of our own faculties, to the acquisitions of our own industry, to honor and confidence from our fellow-citizens, resulting
not from birth, but from our actions and their sense of them; enlightened by a benign religion, professed indeed and practiced in
various forms yet all of them inculcating honesty, truth, temperance,
gratitude, and the love of man, acknowledging and adoring an over-
ruling Providence, which by all its dispensations proves that it delights in the happiness of man here and his greater happiness hereafter: with all these blessings, what more is necessary to make us
a happy and a prosperous people? Still one thing more, fellow-citizens
—a wise and frugal government, which shall restrain men from injuring one another, shall leave them otherwise free to regulate their
own pursuits of industry and improvement, and shall not take from
the mouth of labor the bread it has earned. This is the sum of good
government; and this is necessary to close the circle of our felicities.

About to enter, fellow-citizens, on the exercise of duties which
comprehend everything dear and valuable to you, it is proper you
should understand what I deem the essential principle of this government, and consequently those which ought to shape its administration. I will compress them in the narrowest compass they will bear,
stating the general principle but not all its limitations. Equal and
exact justice to all men of whatever state or persuasion, religious or
political; peace, commerce and honest friendship with all nations, entangling alliances with none;[5] the support of the state governments
in all their rights, as the most competent administrations for our
domestic concerns, and the surest bulwarks against anti-republican
tendencies; the preservation of the general government in its whole
constitutional vigor, as the sheet-anchor of our peace at home and
safety abroad; a jealous care of the right of election by the people;
a mild and safe corrective of abuses which are lopped by the sword
of revolution, where peaceable remedies are unprovided; absolute
acquiescence in the decisions of the majority, the vital principle of
republics, from which is no appeal but to force, the vital principle
and immediate parent of despotism; a well-disciplined militia, our
best reliance in peace and for the first moments of war, till regulars
may relieve them; the supremacy of the civil over the military authority—economy in the public expense, that labor may be lightly

4. The pessimistic "law" of Malthus on
the imbalance of population and subsistence had just been propounded in
An Essay on the Principle of Population
(1798).

5. Reaffirming Washington's injunction,
in the "Farewell Address," that we must
not "entangle our peace and prosperity"
in foreign alliances.

burdened; the honest payment of our debts, and sacred preservation of the public faith; encouragement of agriculture, and of commerce as its handmaid; the diffusion of information and arraignment of all abuses at the bar of the public reason; freedom of religion, freedom of the press, and freedom of person, under the protection of the habeas corpus;[6] and trial by juries impartially selected. These principles form the bright constellation which has gone before us, and guided our steps through an age of revolution and reformation. The wisdom of our sages and blood of our heroes have been devoted to their attainment; they should be the creed of our political faith; the text of civic instruction; the touchstone by which to try the services of those we trust; and should we wander from them in moments of error or alarm, let us hasten to retrace our steps and to regain the road which alone leads to peace, liberty, and safety.

I repair then, fellow-citizens, to the post which you have assigned me. With experience enough in subordinate stations to know the difficulties of this, the greatest of all, I have learned to expect that it will rarely fall to the lot of imperfect man to retire from this station with the reputation and the favor which bring him into it. Without pretentions to that high confidence you reposed in our first and greatest revolutionary character,[7] whose preëminent services had entitled him to the first place in his country's love, and had destined for him the fairest page in the volume of faithful history, I ask so much confidence only as may give firmness and effect to the legal administration of your affairs. I shall often go wrong through defect of judgment. When right, I shall often be thought wrong by those whose positions will not command a view of the whole ground. I ask your indulgence for my own errors, which will never be intentional; and your support against the errors of others who may condemn what they would not, if seen in all its parts. The approbation implied by your suffrage is a great consolation to me for the past; and my future solicitude will be to retain the good opinion of those who have bestowed it in advance, to conciliate that of others by doing them all the good in my power, and to be instrumental to the happiness and freedom of all.

Relying then on the patronage of your good-will, I advance with obedience to the work, ready to retire from it whenever you become sensible how much better choice it is in your power to make. And may that Infinite Power which rules the destinies of the universe lead our councils to what is best, and give them a favorable issue for your peace and prosperity.

1801

6. The guarantee that the individual will not be held under unlawful arrest.

7. George Washington.

From Notes on the State of Virginia[8]

[*A Southerner on Slavery*][9]

There must doubtless be an unhappy influence on the manners of our people produced by the existence of slavery among us. The whole commerce between master and slave is a perpetual exercise of the most boisterous passions, the most unremitting despotism on the one part, and degrading submissions on the other. Our children see this and learn to imitate it, for man is an imitative animal. This quality is the germ of all education in him. From his cradle to his grave he is learning to do what he sees others do. If a parent could find no motive either in his philanthropy or his self-love for restraining the intemperance of passion toward his slave, it should always be a sufficient one that his child is present. But generally it is not sufficient. The parent storms, the child looks on, catches the lineaments of wrath, puts on the same airs in the circle of smaller slaves, gives a loose to the worst of passions, and thus nursed, educated, and daily exercised in tyranny, cannot but be stamped by it with odious peculiarities. The man must be a prodigy who can retain his manners and morals undepraved by such circumstances. And with what execration should the statesman be loaded who, permitting one-half of the citizens thus to trample on the rights of the other, transforms those into despots, and these into enemies, destroys the morals of the one part, and the *amor patriae*[1] of the other. For if a slave can have a country in this world, it must be any other in preference to that in which he is born to live and labor for another; in which he must lock up the faculties of his nature, contribute as far as depends on his individual endeavors to the evanishment of the human race, or entail[2] his own miserable condition on the endless generations proceeding from him. With the morals of the people, their industry also is destroyed. For in a warm climate, no man will labor for himself who can make another labor for him. This is so true that, of the proprietors of slaves, a very small proportion indeed are ever seen to labor. And can the liberties of a nation be thought secure when we have removed their only firm basis, a conviction in the minds of the

8. *Notes on the State of Virginia* resulted from an official inquiry received by Jefferson in 1781, the year of his retirement as governor of his state. The Marquis de Barbé-Marbois, secretary of the French legation at Philadelphia, formulated a series of questions of interest to him in official negotiations. Jefferson's extended reply, in twenty-three sections, dealt with natural resources, geography, landscape, inhabitants (including the Indians), slavery, government, laws and civil rights, education, religious freedom, social customs, and a number of other topics. Two hundred copies, dated 1782, were printed for private distribution in 1784–1785. The appearance of a French translation caused Jefferson to issue an authorized London edition in 1787, reprinted in Philadelphia in 1788. Additional material and notes appeared in the editions of 1800 and 1853.

9. From Query 18.

1. Love of country.

2. A legal term meaning "to settle on an heir" (as by bequest or inheritance).

people that these liberties are of the gift of God? That they are not to be violated but with His wrath? Indeed, I tremble for my country when I reflect that God is just; that His justice cannot sleep forever; that considering numbers, nature, and natural means only, a revolution of the wheel of fortune, an exchange of situation, is among possible events; that it may become probable by supernatural interference! The Almighty has no attribute which can take side with us in such a contest. But it is impossible to be temperate and to pursue this subject through the various considerations of policy, of morals, of history natural and civil. We must be contented to hope they will force their way into everyone's mind. I think a change already perceptible, since the origin of the present revolution.[3] The spirit of the master is abating, that of the slave rising from the dust, his condition mollifying, the way, I hope, preparing, under the auspices of heaven, for a total emancipation, and that this is disposed, in the order of events, to be with the consent of the masters, rather than by their extirpation.

* * * It is a problem[4] which I give to the master to solve, whether the religious precepts against the violation of property were not framed for him as well as his slave? And whether the slave may not as justifiably take a little from one who has taken all from him, as he may slay one who would slay him? That a change in the relations in which a man is placed should change his ideas of moral right and wrong, is neither new, nor peculiar to the color of the blacks. Homer tells us it was so two thousand six hundred years ago:

> Jove fix'd it certain, that whatever day
> Makes a man a slave, takes his worth away.

But the slaves of which Homer speaks were whites. Notwithstanding these considerations which must weaken their respect for the laws of property, we find among them numerous instances of the most rigid integrity, and as many as among their better instructed masters, of benevolence, gratitude, and unshaken fidelity. The opinion that they are inferior in the faculties of reason and imagination must be hazarded with great diffidence.

[An American on Dictators[5]]

In December 1776, our circumstances being much distressed, it was proposed in the house of delegates to create a dictator, invested

---

3. *I.e.*, the American Revolution.
4. The following related paragraphs are from Query 14.
5. From Query 13. Jefferson's abhorrence of dictatorship is emphasized by the fact that he wrote this in the crisis of 1781, when British troops occupied the strategic eastern part of Virginia, and the legislature had fled for temporary security to Staunton. The entire Query, from which the following is the concluding passage, deals with defects in the constitution of Virginia.

with every power legislative, executive, and judiciary, civil and military, of life and of death, over our persons and over our properties; and in June 1781, again under calamity, the same proposition was repeated, and wanted a few votes only of being passed.—One who entered into this contest from a pure love of liberty, and a sense of injured rights, who determined to make every sacrifice, and to meet every danger, for the re-establishment of those rights on a firm basis, who did not mean to expend his blood and substance for the wretched purpose of changing this master for that, but to place the powers of governing him in a plurality of hands of his own choice, so that the corrupt will of no one man might in future oppress him, must stand confounded and dismayed when he is told, that a considerable portion of that plurality had meditated the surrender of them into a single hand, and, in lieu of a limited monarch, to deliver him over to a despotic one![6] How must he find his efforts and sacrifices abused and baffled, if he may still, by a single vote, be laid prostrate at the feet of one man! In God's name, from whence have they derived this power? Is it from our ancient laws? None such can be produced. Is it from any principle in our new constitution expressed or implied? Every lineament of that expressed or implied, is in full opposition to it. Its fundamental principle is, that the state shall be governed as a commonwealth. It provides a republican organization, proscribes under the name of prerogative the exercise of all powers undefined by the laws; places on this basis the whole system of our laws; and by consolidating them together, chooses that they shall be left to stand or fall together, never providing for any circumstances, nor admitting that such could arise, wherein either should be suspended; no, not for a moment. Our ancient laws expressly declare, that those who are but delegates themselves shall not delegate to others powers which require judgment and integrity in their exercise. Or was this proposition moved on a supposed right in the movers, of abandoning their posts in a moment of distress? The same laws forbid the abandonment of that post, even on ordinary occasions; and much more a transfer of their powers into other hands and other forms, without consulting the people. They never admit the idea that these, like sheep or cattle, may be given from hand to hand without an appeal to their own will.—Was it from the necessity of the case? Necessities which dissolve a government, do not convey its authority to an oligarchy or a monarchy. They throw back, into the hands of the people, the powers they had delegated, and leave them as individuals to shift for themselves. A leader may offer, but not impose himself, nor be imposed on them. Much less can their necks be submitted to his sword, their breath be held at his

6. Chinard notes (*Thomas Jefferson*, p. 129), that Jefferson's later resistance to the extreme Federalists, in the contro- versies concerning the Constitution, "already exists in germ, in this declaration."

will or caprice. The necessity which should operate these tremendous effects should at least be palpable and irresistible. Yet in both instances, where it was feared, or pretended with us, it was belied by the event. It was belied, too, by the preceding experience of our sister states, several of whom had grappled through greater difficulties without abandoning their forms of government. When the proposition was first made, Massachusetts had found even the government of committees sufficient to carry them through an invasion. But we at the time of that proposition,[7] were under no invasion. When the second was made, there had been added to this example those of Rhode Island, New York, New Jersey, and Pennsylvania, in all of which the republican form had been found equal to the task of carrying them through the severest trials. In this state alone did there exist so little virtue, that fear was to be fixed in the hearts of the people, and to become the motive of their exertions, and the principle of their government? The very thought alone was treason against the people; was treason against mankind in general; as rivetting forever the chains which bow down their necks by giving to their oppressors a proof, which they would have trumpeted through the universe, of the imbecility of republican government, in times of pressing danger, to shield them from harm. Those who assume the right of giving away the reins of government in any case, must be sure that the herd, whom they hand on to the rods and hatchet of the dictator, will lay their necks on the block when he shall nod to them. But if our assemblies supposed such a resignation in the people, I hope they mistook their character. I am of opinion, that the government, instead of being braced and invigorated for greater exertions under their difficulties, would have been thrown back upon the bungling machinery of county committees for administration, till a convention could have been called, and its wheels again set into regular motion. What a cruel moment was this for creating such an embarrassment, for putting to the proof the attachment of our countrymen to republican government! Those who meant well, of the advocates for this measure, (and most of them meant well, for I know them personally, had been their fellow-laborers in the common cause, and had often proved the purity of their principles), had been seduced in their judgment by the example of an ancient republic, whose constitution and circumstances were fundamentally different. They had sought this precedent in the history of Rome, where alone it was to be found, and where at length, too, it had proved fatal. They had taken it from a republic rent by the most bitter factions and tumults, where the government was of a heavy-handed unfeeling aristocracy, over a people ferocious, and rendered desperate by poverty and wretchedness; tumults which could not be allayed under the

7. In 1776 Virginia had not been invaded, as it was in 1781.

most trying circumstances, but by the omnipotent hand of a single despot. Their constitution, therefore, allowed a temporary tyrant to be erected, under the name of a Dictator; and that temporary tyrant, after a few examples, became perpetual. They misapplied this precedent to a people mild in their dispositions, patient under their trial, united for the public liberty, and affectionate to their leaders. But if from the constitution of the Roman government there resulted to their Senate a power of submitting all their rights to the will of one man, does it follow that the assembly of Virginia have the same authority? What clause in our constitution has substituted that of Rome, by way of residuary provision, for all cases not otherwise provided for? Or if they may step ad libitum[8] into any other form of government for precedents to rule us by, for what oppression may not a precedent be found in this world of the *bellum omnium in omnia?*[9] Searching for the foundations of this proposition, I can find none which may pretend a color of right or reason, but the defect before developed, that there being no barrier between the legislative, executive, and judiciary departments, the legislature may seize the whole: that having seized it, and possessing a right to fix their own quorum, they may reduce that quorum to one, whom they may call a chairman, speaker, dictator, or by any other name they please.—Our situation is indeed perilous, and I hope my countrymen will be sensible of it, and will apply, at a proper season, the proper remedy; which is a convention to fix the constitution, to amend its defects, to bind up the several branches of government by certain laws, which, when they transgress, their acts shall become nullities; to render unnecessary an appeal to the people, or in other words a rebellion, on every infraction of their rights, on the peril that their acquiescence shall be construed into an intention to surrender those rights.

1781   1784-1785

Letter to Dr. Benjamin Rush[1]
[*The Christian Deist*]

WASHINGTON, April 21, 1803.

DEAR SIR,—

In some of the delightful conversations with you, in the evenings of 1798–99, and which serve as an anodyne to the afflictions of the

---

8. At pleasure; *i.e.*, whenever they wish.
9. This world of the general turmoil in all things.
1. Because of his deistic faith, Jefferson was often accused by his contemporaries of being irreligious. To the reader of today, the large number and the tenor of his religious references may

suggest precisely the opposite judgment. "On religious tenets," he declared, "our reason must ultimately decide, as it is the only oracle which God has given us" (Memorial Edition, Vol. XIV, p. 197). And see his emphasis on "freedom of religion" in the First Inaugural Address. Benjamin Rush (1745?–1813), whose

crisis through which our country was then laboring, the Christian religion was sometimes our topic; and I then promised you, that one day or other, I would give you my views of it. They are the result of a life of inquiry and reflection, and very different from that anti-Christian system imputed to me by those who know nothing of my opinions. To the corruptions of Christianity I am, indeed, opposed; but not to the genuine precepts of Jesus himself. I am a Christian, in the only sense he wished any one to be; sincerely attached to his doctrines, in preference to all others; ascribing to himself every *human* excellence; and believing he never claimed any other. At the short interval since these conversations, when I could justifiably abstract my mind from public affairs, the subject has been under my contemplation. But the more I considered it, the more it expanded beyond the measure of either my time or information. In the moment of my late departure from Monticello, I received from Dr. Priestley,[2] his little treatise of "Socrates and Jesus Compared." This being a section of the general view I had taken of the field, it became a subject of reflection while on the road, and unoccupied otherwise. The result was, to arrange in my mind a syllabus, or outline of such an estimate of the comparative merits of Christianity, as I wished to see executed by some one of more leisure and information for the task, than myself. This I now send you, as the only discharge of my promise I can probably ever execute. And in confiding it to you, I know it will not be exposed to the malignant perversions of those who make every word from me a text for new misrepresentations and calumnies.[3] I am moreover averse to the communication of my religious tenets to the public; because it would countenance the presumption of those who have endeavored to draw them before that tribunal, and to seduce public opinion to erect itself into that inquisition over the rights of conscience, which the laws have so justly proscribed. It behooves every man who values liberty of conscience for himself, to resist invasions of it in the case of others; or their case may, by change of circumstances, become his own.[4] It behooves him, too, in his own case, to give no example of concession, betraying the common right of independent opinion, by answering questions of faith, which the laws have left between God and himself. Accept my affectionate salutations.

correspondence with Jefferson was considerable, was a Philadelphia scientist, physician, and political leader, congressional signer of the Declaration of Independence, surgeon in the Continental army, and first professor of chemistry at the University of Pennsylvania.

2. Joseph Priestley (1733–1804), British-born scientist and clergyman, emigrated to Pennsylvania (1794) because of persecution for his republican sympathies. His writings anticipated the Unitarian theology and Bentham's theories of the state.

3. Then in his first term as president, Jefferson was subjected to much abuse by political enemies.

4. *Cf.* The amendments to the Constitution of the United States forming the Bill of Rights, especially Amendments I and V.

SYLLABUS OF AN ESTIMATE OF THE MERIT OF THE DOCTRINES OF
JESUS, COMPARED WITH THOSE OF OTHERS.

In a comparative view of the Ethics of the enlightened nations
of antiquity, of the Jews and of Jesus, no notice should be taken of
the corruptions of reason among the ancients, to wit, the idolatry
and superstition of the vulgar, nor of the corruptions of Christianity
by the learned among its professors.

Let a just view be taken of the moral principles inculcated by the
most esteemed of the sects of ancient philosophy, or of their individuals; particularly Pythagoras, Socrates, Epicurus, Cicero, Epictetus, Seneca, Antoninus.

I. Philosophers. 1. Their precepts related chiefly to ourselves, and
the government of those passions which, unrestrained, would disturb
our tranquillity of mind.[5] In this branch of philosophy they were
really great.

2. In developing our duties to others, they were short and defective. They embraced, indeed, the circles of kindred and friends, and
inculcated partiotism, or the love of our country in the aggregate,
as a primary obligation; toward our neighbors and countrymen they
taught justice, but scarcely viewed them as within the circle of benevolence. Still less have they inculcated peace, charity, and love to our
fellow men, or embraced with benevolence the whole family of
mankind.

II. Jews. 1. Their system was Deism; that is, the belief of one
only God. But their ideas of him and of his attributes were degrading
and injurious.

2. Their Ethics were not only imperfect, but often irreconcilable
with the sound dictates of reason and morality, as they respect intercourse with those around us; and repulsive and anti-social, as respecting other nations. They needed reformation, therefore, in an eminent
degree.

III. Jesus. In this state of things among the Jews, Jesus appeared.
His parentage was obscure; his condition poor; his education null;
his natural endowments great; his life correct and innocent; he was
meek, benevolent, patient, firm, disinterested, and of the sublimest
eloquence.

The disadvantages under which his doctrines appear are remarkable.

1. Like Socrates and Epictetus, he wrote nothing himself.

2. But he had not, like them, a Xenophon or an Arrian to write
for him. I name not Plato, who only used the name of Socrates to
cover the whimsies of his own brain. On the contrary,[6] all the learned

5. Jefferson's footnote here points out
that, of Seneca's fundmental tenets,
seven out of ten relate "to ourselves";
and that, of Cicero's precepts, the ratio
is six out of eleven, wholly or in principal
part.

6. *I.e.,* in the case of Jesus.

of his country, entrenched in its power and riches, were opposed to him, lest his labors should undermine their advantages; and the commiting to writing his life and doctrines fell on unlettered and ignorant men;[7] who wrote, too, from memory, and not till long after the transactions had passed.

3. According to the ordinary fate of those who attempt to enlighten and reform mankind, he fell an early victim to the jealousy and combination of the altar and the throne, at about thirty-three years of age, his reason having not yet attained the *maximum* of its energy, nor the course of his preaching, which was but of three years at most, presented occasions for developing a complete system of morals.

4. Hence the doctrines which he really delivered were defective as a whole, and fragments only of what he did deliver have come to us mutilated, misstated, and often unintelligible.

5. They have been still more disfigured by the corruptions of schismatizing followers, who have found an interest in sophisticating and perverting the simple doctrines he taught, by engrafting on them the mysticisms of a Grecian sophist, frittering them into subtleties, and obscuring them with jargon, until they have caused good men to reject the whole in disgust, and to view Jesus himself as an impostor.

Notwithstanding these disadvantages, a system of morals is presented to us, which, if filled up in the true style and spirit of the rich fragments he left us, would be the most perfect and sublime that has ever been taught by man.

The question of his being a member of the Godhead, or in direct communication with it, claimed for him by some of his followers, and denied by others, is foreign to the present view, which is merely an estimate of the intrinsic merit of his doctrines.

1. He corrected the Deism of the Jews, confirming them in their belief of one only God, and giving them juster notions of his attributes and government.

2. His moral doctrines, relating to kindred and friends, were more pure and perfect than those of the most correct of the philosophers, and greatly more so than those of the Jews; and they went far beyond both in inculcating universal philanthropy, not only to kindred and friends, to neighbors and countrymen, but to all mankind, gathering all into one family, under the bonds of love, charity, peace, common wants and common aids. A development of this head will evince the peculiar superiority of the system of Jesus over all others.

3. The precepts of philosophy, and of the Hebrew code, laid hold of actions only. He pushed his scrutinies into the heart of man;

7. Modern scholarship would moderate this view, especially in connection with Luke and Paul.

erected his tribunal in the region of his thoughts, and purified the waters at the fountain head.

4. He taught, emphatically, the doctrines of a future state, which was either doubted, or disbelieved by the Jews; and wielded it with efficacy, as an important incentive, supplementary to the other motives to moral conduct.

Letter to John Adams[8]
[*The True Aristocracy*]

MONTICELLO, October 28, 1813.

* * * I agree with you that there is a natural aristocracy among men. The grounds of this are virtue and talents. Formerly, bodily powers gave place among the aristoi.[9] But since the invention of gunpowder has armed the weak as well as the strong with missile death, bodily strength, like beauty, good humor, politeness and other accomplishments, has become but an auxiliary ground for distinction. There is also an artificial aristocracy, founded on wealth and birth, without either virtue or talents; for with these it would belong to the first class. The natural aristocracy I consider as the most precious gift of nature, for the instruction, the trusts, and government of society. And indeed, it would have been inconsistent in creation to have formed man for the social state, and not to have provided virtue and wisdom enough to manage the concerns of the society. May we not even say, that that form of government is the best, which provides the most effectually for a pure selection of these natural aristoi into the offices of government? The artificial aristocracy is a mischievous ingredient in government, and provision should be made to prevent its ascendency. On the question, what is the best provision, you and I differ; but we differ as rational friends, using the free exercise of our own reason, and mutually indulging its errors. You think it best to put the pseudo-aristoi[1] into a separate chamber of legislation, where they may be hindered from doing mischief by their coordinate branches, and where, also, they may be a protection to wealth against the Agrarian and plundering enterprises of the ma-

---

8. The Jefferson–Adams correspondence, comprising more than 150 letters, is one of the greatest in the annals of history. The two patriots had become estranged in politics; the Federalist Adams won the presidency in 1796, despite the opposition of Jefferson, who then succeeded him in 1801, when his Democratic Republican party bitterly attacked the conservatism of the Massachusetts incumbent. Reconciled in 1812, they exchanged their experienced wisdom on the issues of their world until they died, both on the anniversary of national independence, in 1826.

9. In Greek, literally, "the best." In two letters Adams has learnedly argued from ancient and recent examples that, without attention to aristocracy, "no society can pretend to establish a free government. * * * The five pillars of aristocracy are beauty, wealth, birth, genius, and virtue"; but "any one of the first three" outweighs either or both of the others. Jefferson emphasizes genius and virtue.

1. See above, "artificial aristocracy, founded on wealth and birth."

jority of the people. I think that to give them power in order to prevent them from doing mischief, is arming them for it, and increasing instead of remedying the evil. For if the co-ordinate branches can arrest their action, so may they that of the co-ordinates. Mischief may be done negatively as well as positively. Of this, a cabal in the Senate of the United States has furnished many proofs. Nor do I believe them necessary to protect the wealthy; because enough of these will find their way into every branch of the legislation, to protect themselves. From fifteen to twenty legislatures of our own, in action for thirty years past, have proved that no fears of an equalization of property are to be apprehended from them. I think the best remedy is exactly that provided by all our constitutions, to leave to the citizens the free election and separation of the aristoi from the pseudo-aristoi, of the wheat from the chaff. In general they will elect the really good and wise. In some instances, wealth may corrupt, and birth blind them; but not in sufficient degree to endanger the society.

It is probable that our difference of opinion may, in some measure, be produced by a difference of character in those among whom we lived. From what I have seen of Massachusetts and Connecticut myself, and still more from what I have heard, and the character given of the former by yourself (volume I, page 111),[2] who know them so much better, there seems to be in those two States a traditionary reverence for certain families, which has rendered the offices of the government nearly hereditary in those families. I presume that from an early period of your history, members of those families happening to possess virtue and talents, have honestly exercised them for the good of the people, and by their services have endeared their names to them. In coupling Connecticut with you, I mean it politically only, not morally. For having made the Bible the common law of their land, they seemed to have modeled their morality on the story of Jacob and Laban.[3] But although this hereditary succession to office with you, may, in some degree, be founded in real family merit, yet in a much higher degree, it has proceeded from your strict alliance of Church and State. These families are canonised in the eyes of the people on common principles, "you tickle me, and I will tickle you." In Virginia we have nothing of this. Our clergy, before the revolution, having been secured against rivalship by fixed salaries, did not give themselves the trouble of acquiring influence over the people. Of wealth, there were great accumulations in particular families, handed down from generation to generation, under the English law of entails.[4] But the only object of ambition for the wealthy was a

2. Referring to Adams' *Defense of the Constitutions of Government of the United States of America* (3 vols., Philadelphia, 1797; earlier editions, London, 1787 and 1794).

3. Genesis xxvii–xxxi. A dynastic family was founded on the relations in marriage between Jacob and Laban's daughters.
4. An entailed estate could not be sold or given away and was passed on as a whole from generation to generation.

seat in the King's Council. All their court then was paid to the crown and its creatures; and they Philipised[5] in all collisions between the King and the people. Hence they were unpopular; and that unpopularity continues attached to their names. A Randolph, a Carter, or a Burwell must have great personal superiority over a common competitor to be elected by the people even at this day. At the first session of our legislature after the Declaration of Independence, we passed a law abolishing entails. And this was followed by one abolishing the privilege of primogeniture, and dividing the lands of intestates equally among all their children, or other representatives.[6] These laws, drawn by myself, laid the ax to the foot of pseudo-aristocracy. And had another which I prepared been adopted by the legislature, our work would have been complete. It was a bill for the more general diffusion of learning. This proposed to divide every county into wards of five or six miles square, like your townships; to establish in each ward a free school for reading, writing and common arithmetic; to provide for the annual selection of the best subjects from these schools, who might receive, at the public expense, a higher degree of education at a district school; and from these district schools to select a certain number of the most promising subjects, to be completed at an University, where all the useful sciences should be taught. Worth and genius would thus have been sought out from every condition of life, and completely prepared by education for defeating the competition of wealth and birth for public trusts. My proposition had, for a further object, to impart to these wards those portions of self-government for which they are best qualified, by confiding to them the care of their poor, their roads, police, elections, the nomination of jurors, administration of justice in small cases, elementary exercises of militia; in short, to have made them little republics, with a warden at the head of each, for all those concerns which, being under their eye, they would better manage than the larger republics of the county or State. A general call of ward meetings by their wardens on the same day through the State, would at any time produce the genuine sense of the people on any required point, and would enable the State to act in mass, as your people have so often done, and with so much effect by their town meetings. The law for religious freedom, which made a part of this system, having put down the aristocracy of the clergy, and restored to the citizen the freedom of the mind, and those of entails and descents nurturing an equality of condition among them, this on education would have raised the mass of the people to the high ground of moral respecta-

5. In reference to the leaders whom Philip II of Macedon bribed to support his policies intended to destroy the independence of the Greek cities.

6. Jefferson had fostered this legislation against hereditary wealth in Virginia. Primogeniture secured the estate to the oldest son. Intestates are those who leave no will and testament at death.

bility necessary to their own safety, and to orderly government; and would have completed the great object of qualifying them to select the veritable aristoi, for the trusts of government, to the exclusion of the pseudalists; and the same Theognis who has furnished the epigraphs of your two letters, assures us that Οὐδεμίαν πω Κύρν᾽, ἀγαθοὶ πόλιν ὤλεσαν ἄνδρες.[7]

Although this law has not yet been acted on but in a small and inefficient degree, it is still considered as before the legislature, with other bills of the revised code, not yet taken up, and I have great hope that some patriotic spirit will, at a favorable moment, call it up, and make it the keystone of the arch of our government.

With respect to aristocracy, we should further consider, that before the establishment of the American States, nothing was known to history but the man of the old world, crowded within limits either small or overcharged, and steeped in the vices which that situation generates. A government adapted to such men would be one thing; but a very different one, that for the man of these States. Here every one may have land to labor for himself, if he chooses; or, preferring the exercise of any other industry, may exact for it such compensation as not only to afford a comfortable subsistence, but wherewith to provide for a cessation from labor in old age. Every one, by his property, or by his satisfactory situation, is interested in the support of law and order. And such men may safely and advantageously reserve to themselves a wholesome control over their public affairs, and a degree of freedom, which, in the hands of the *canaille*[8] of the cities of Europe, would be instantly perverted to the demolition and destruction of everything public and private. The history of the last twenty-five years of France,[9] and of the last forty years in America, nay of its last two hundred years, proves the truth of both parts of this observation.

But even in Europe a change has sensibly taken place in the mind of man. Science had liberated the ideas of those who read and reflect, and the American example had kindled feelings of right in the people. An insurrection has consequently begun, of science, talents, and courage, against rank and birth, which have fallen into contempt. It has failed in its first effort, because the mobs of the cities, the instrument used for its accomplishment, debased by ignorance, poverty and vice, could not be restrained to rational action. But the world will recover from the panic of this first catastrophe. Science is progressive, and talents and enterprise on the alert. Resort may be had to the people of the country, a more governable power from their principles and subordination; and rank, and birth, and tinsel-aristocracy will finally shrink into insignificance, even there. This, however, we have

7. Good men, Curnus, have not yet destroyed any state (Theognis, I, 43).
8. Rabble.

9. *I.e.*, since the beginning of the French Revolution.

no right to meddle with. It suffices for us, if the moral and physical condition of our own citizens qualifies them to select the able and good for the direction of their government, with a recurrence of elections at such short periods as will enable them to displace an unfaithful servant, before the mischief he meditates may be irremediable.

I have thus stated my opinion on a point on which we differ, not with a view to controversy, for we are both too old to change opinions which are the result of a long life of inquiry and reflection; but on the suggestions of a former letter of yours, that we ought not to die before we have explained ourselves to each other. We acted in perfect harmony, through a long and perilous contest for our liberty and independence. A constitution has been acquired, which, though neither of us thinks perfect, yet both consider as competent to render our fellow citizens the happiest and the securest on whom the sun has ever shone. If we do not think exactly alike as to its imperfections, it matters little to our country, which, after devoting to it long lives of disinterested labor, we have delivered over to our successors in life, who will be able to take care of it and of themselves.

Of the pamphlet on aristocracy which has been sent to you, or who may be its author, I have heard nothing but through your letter. If the person you suspect, it may be known from the quaint, mystical, and hyperbolical ideas, involved in affected, new-fangled and pedantic terms which stamp his writings. Whatever it be, I hope your quiet is not to be affected at this day by the rudeness or intemperance of scribblers; but that you may continue in tranquillity to live and to rejoice in the prosperity of our country, until it shall be your own wish to take your seat among the aristoi who have gone before you. Ever and affectionately yours.

Letter to Dr. Walter Jones[1]
[*The Character of Washington*]

MONTICELLO, January 2, 1814.

DEAR SIR,—

Your favor of November the 25th reached this place December the 21st, having been near a month on the way. * * *

You say that in taking General Washington on your shoulders, to bear him harmless through the federal coalition, you encounter a perilous topic. I do not think so. You have given the genuine history of the course of his mind through the trying scenes in which it was engaged, and of the seductions by which it was deceived, but not

1. Dr. Walter Jones, graduate in medicine from Edinburgh (1770), served as medical officer in the Continental army and was twice elected congressman from Virginia.

depraved. I think I knew General Washington intimately and thoroughly; and were I called on to delineate his character, it should be in terms like these.

His mind was great and powerful, without being of the very first order; his penetration strong, though not so acute as that of a Newton, Bacon, or Locke;[2] and as far as he saw, no judgment was ever sounder. It was slow in operation, being little aided by invention or imagination, but sure in conclusion. Hence the common remark of his officers, of the advantage he derived from councils of war, where hearing all suggestions, he selected whatever was best; and certainly no general ever planned his battles more judiciously. But if deranged during the course of the action, if any member of his plan was dislocated by sudden circumstances, he was slow in re-adjustment. The consequence was, that he often failed in the field, and rarely against an enemy in station, as at Boston and York.[3] He was incapable of fear, meeting personal dangers with the calmest unconcern. Perhaps the strongest feature in his character was prudence, never acting until every circumstance, every consideration, was maturely weighed; refraining if he saw a doubt, but, when once decided, going through with his purpose, whatever obstacles opposed. His integrity was most pure, his justice the most inflexible I have ever known, no motives of interest or consanguinity, of friendship or hatred, being able to bias his decision. He was, indeed, in every sense of the words, a wise, a good, and a great man. His temper was naturally irritable and high toned; but reflection and resolution had obtained a firm and habitual ascendency over it. If ever, however, it broke its bonds, he was most tremendous in his wrath. In his expenses he was honorable, but exact; liberal in contributions to whatever promised utility; but frowning and unyielding on all visionary projects, and all unworthy calls on his charity. His heart was not warm in its affections; but he exactly calculated every man's value, and gave him a solid esteem proportioned to it. His person, you know, was fine, his stature exactly what one would wish, his deportment easy, erect, and noble; the best horseman of his age, and the most graceful figure that could be seen on horseback. Although in the circle of his friends, where he might be unreserved with safety, he took a free share in conversation, his colloquial talents were not above mediocrity, possessing neither copiousness of ideas, nor fluency of words. In public, when called on for a sudden opinion, he was unready, short, and embarrassed. Yet he wrote readily, rather diffusely, in an easy and correct style. This he had acquired by conversation with the world, for his education was

2. These powerfully influenced the thought of American intellectuals in Jefferson's age: Sir Isaac Newton (1642–1727) formulated the new physical science; Francis Bacon (1561–1626), especially in *Novum Organum*, founded this new empirical science; and John Locke (1632–1704) provided psychological sanctions for rationalism.
3. Yorktown.

merely reading, writing, and common arithmetic, to which he added surveying at a later day. His time was employed in action chiefly, reading little, and that only in agriculture and English history. His correspondence became necessarily extensive, and, with journalizing[4] his agricultural proceedings, occupied most of his leisure hours within doors. On the whole, his character was, in its mass, perfect, in nothing bad, in few points indifferent; and it may truly be said, that never did nature and fortune combine more perfectly to make a man great, and to place him in the same constellation with whatever worthies have merited from man an everlasting remembrance. For his was the singular destiny and merit, of leading the armies of his country successfully through an arduous war, for the establishment of its independence; of conducting its councils through the birth of a government, new in its forms and principles, until it had settled down into a quiet and orderly train; and of scrupulously obeying the laws through the whole of his career, civil and military, of which the history of the world furnishes no other example.

How, then, can it be perilous for you to take such a man on your shoulders? I am satisfied the great body of republicans[5] think of him as I do. We were, indeed, dissatisfied with him on his ratification of the British treaty.[6] But this was short lived. We knew his honesty, the wiles with which he was encompassed, and that age had already begun to relax the firmness of his purposes; and I am convinced he is more deeply seated in the love and gratitude of the republicans, than in the Pharisaical homage of the federal monarchists. For he was no monarchist from preference of his judgment. The soundness of that gave him correct views of the rights of man, and his severe justice devoted him to them. He has often declared to me that he considered our new Constitution as an experiment on the practicability of republican government, and with what dose of liberty man could be trusted for his own good; that he was determined the experiment should have a fair trial, and would lose the last drop of his blood in support of it. And these declarations he repeated to me the oftener and more pointedly, because he knew my suspicions of Colonel Hamilton's[7] views, and probably had heard from him the same declarations which I had, to wit, "that the British constitution, with its unequal representation, corruption, and other existing abuses, was the most perfect government which had ever been established on earth, and that a reformation of those abuses would make it an impracticable government." I do not believe that General Washington had not a firm confidence in the durability of our government. He was natu-

---

4. Washington kept a daily "journal" or diary.
5. Now Democrats.
6. The United States had made unpopular economic concessions to Great Britain in return for the evacuation of British outposts in the northwestern areas (Jay's Treaty, 1794).
7. Alexander Hamilton.

rally distrustful of men, and inclined to gloomy apprehensions; and I was ever persuaded that a belief that we must at length end in something like a British constitution, had some weight in his adoption of the ceremonies of levees, birthdays, pompous meetings with Congress, and other forms of the same character, calculated to prepare us gradually for a change which he believed possible, and to let it come on with as little shock as might be to the public mind.

These are my opinions of General Washington, which I would vouch at the judgment seat of God, having been formed on an acquaintance of thirty years. I served with him in the Virginia legislature from 1769 to the Revolutionary war, and again a short time in Congress, until he left us to take command of the army. During the war and after it we corresponded occasionally, and in the four years of my continuance in the office of Secretary of State, our intercourse was daily, confidential, and cordial. After I retired from that office, great and malignant pains were taken by our federal monarchists, and not entirely without effect, to make him view me as a theorist, holding French principles[8] of government, which would lead infallibly to licentiousness and anarchy. And to this he listened the more easily, from my known disapprobation of the British treaty. I never saw him afterwards, or these malignant insinuations should have been dissipated before his just judgment, as mists before the sun. I felt on his death, with my countrymen, that "verily a great man hath fallen this day in Israel."[9]

More time and recollection would enable me to add many other traits of his character; but why add them to you who knew him well? And I cannot justify to myself a longer detention of your paper.

Vale, proprieque tuum, me esse tibi persuadeas.[1]

Letter to President Monroe
[*The Monroe Doctrine*][2]

MONTICELLO, October 24, 1823.

DEAR SIR:

The question presented by the letters you have sent me, is the most momentous which has ever been offered to my contemplation since that of Independence. That made us a nation, this sets our

8. Federalist conservatives pictured Jeffersonians as atheists likely to introduce a Reign of Terror as in the French Revolution.
9. David's words when Abner, his former enemy, was slain (II Samuel iii: 38).
1. Farewell, you persuade me to be especially yours.
2. James Monroe, president 1817–1825, sent to Congress on December 2, 1823, his foreign-policy message since famous as the Monroe Doctrine. The Holy Alliance—Russia, Austria, Prussia, and France—had made threatening overtures against the sovereignty of the United States and South American governments. Before promulgating his policy of America for Americans, the President sought Jefferson's advice and received the following reply.

compass and points the course which we are to steer through the ocean of time opening on us. And never could we embark on it under circumstances more auspicious. Our first and fundamental maxim should be, never to entangle ourselves in the broils of Europe. Our second, never to suffer Europe to intermeddle with the cis-Atlantic affairs. America, North and South, has a set of interests distinct from those of Europe, and peculiarly her own. She should therefore have a system of her own, separate and apart from that of Europe. While the last is laboring to become the domicile of despotism, our endeavor should surely be, to make our hemisphere that of freedom. One nation,[3] most of all, could disturb us in this pursuit; she now offers to lead, aid, and accompany us in it. By acceding to her proposition, we detach her from the bands, bring her mighty weight into the scale of free government, and emancipate a continent at one stroke, which might otherwise linger long in doubt and difficulty. Great Britain is the nation which can do us the most harm of any one, or all on earth; and with her on our side we need not fear of the whole world. With her then, we should most sedulously cherish a cordial friendship; and nothing would tend more to knit our affections than to be fighting once more, side by side, in the same cause. Not that I would purchase even her amity at the price of taking part in her wars. But the war in which the present proposition might engage us, should that be its consequence, is not her war, but ours. Its object is to introduce and establish the American system, of keeping out of our land all foreign powers, of never permitting those of Europe to intermeddle with the affairs of our nations. It is to maintain our own principle, not to depart from it. And if, to facilitate this, we can effect a division in the body of the European powers, and draw over to our side its most powerful member, surely we should do it. But I am clearly of Mr. Canning's[4] opinion, that it will prevent instead of provoking war. With Great Britain withdrawn from their scale and shifted into that of our two continents, all Europe combined would not undertake such a war. For how would they propose to get at either enemy without superior fleets? Nor is the occasion to be slighted which this proposition offers, of declaring our protest against the atrocious violations of the rights of nations, by the interference of any one in the internal affairs of another, so flagitiously begun by Bonaparte, and now continued by the equally lawless Alliance, calling itself Holy.

But we have first to ask ourselves a question. Do we wish to acquire to our own confederacy any one or more of the Spanish provinces? I candidly confess, that I have ever looked on Cuba as the

3. England.
4. George Canning (1770–1827) had just become British foreign secretary, and within the year led the movement to recognize the independence of the revolted Spanish colonies in South America.

most interesting addition which could ever be made to our system of States. The control which, with Florida Point, this island would give us over the Gulf of Mexico, and the countries and isthmus bordering on it, as well as all those whose waters flow into it, would fill up the measure of our political well-being. Yet, as I am sensible that this can never be obtained, even with her own consent, but by war; and its independence, which is our second interest, (and especially its independence of England,) can be secured without it, I have no hesitation in abandoning my first wish to future chances, and accepting its independence, with peace and the friendship of England, rather than its association, at the expense of war and her enmity.

I could honestly, therefore, join in the declaration proposed, that we aim not at the acquisition of any of those possessions, that we will not stand in the way of any amicable arrangement between them and the Mother country; but that we will oppose, with all our means, the forcible interposition of any other power, as auxiliary, stipendiary, or under any other form or pretext, and most especially, their transfer to any power by conquest, cession, or acquisition in any other way. I should think it, therefore, advisable, that the Executive should encourage the British government to a continuance in the dispositions expressed in these letters, by an assurance of his concurrence with them as far as his authority goes; and that as it may lead to war, the declaration of which requires an act of Congress, the case shall be laid before them for consideration at their first meeting, and under the reasonable aspect in which it is seen by himself.

I have been so long weaned from political subjects, and have so long ceased to take any interest in them, that I am sensible I am not qualified to offer opinions on them worthy of any attention. But the question now proposed involves consequences so lasting, and effects so decisive of our future destinies, as to rekindle all the interest I have heretofore felt on such occasions, and to induce me to the hazard of opinions, which will prove only my wish to contribute still my mite towards anything which may be useful to our country. And praying you to accept it at only what it is worth, I add the assurance of my constant and affectionate friendship and respect.

THE FEDERALIST
(1787–1788)

The essays of *The Federalist* were the product of an American crisis, written under pressure, as Hamilton said, "in the cabin of a Hudson River sloop; by the dim candle of country inn." The immediate urgency, in 1787, was for ratification of the Constitution of the United States, a document which had resulted from extended debate and vast compromises of opposed opinion in the Constitutional Convention. The eighty-five *Federalist* essays, all but eight of them published in New York periodicals between October, 1787, and May, 1788, accomplished much more than the influencing of ratification in New York or other doubtful states. Recognized as the fundamental commentary on the Constitution, they have influenced American constitutional law from the time of the first chief justice of the Supreme Court, John Jay, who wrote at least five of them. They have served political science the world over as a principal statement of the theory of a republic; and finally, they have won lasting approval in the world literature of political philosophy.

The signature of "Publius" temporarily masked the collaboration of three powerful American statesmen. The authorship of a number of the essays is still in doubt, and a few may have resulted from collaboration. Hamilton certainly instigated the project and is credited with thirty-five or more of the papers; Madison probably wrote thirty; and Jay, as before mentioned, certainly five.

These three men represented, in temperament and experience, the gaping diversities of opinion that had been resolved in the Constitutional Convention. The weakness of the Confederation (1778), which vested the principal sovereignty in the individual states, had convinced nearly all leaders of the need to en-

large the federal sovereignty; to secure, as Hamilton said (*Federalist*, No. XXXVII), "stability and energy in government, with the inviolable attention due to liberty and to the republican form." But the liberal Madison had differed widely from such conservatives as Hamilton respecting the degree of individual and local sovereignty that must be relinquished. Like Jefferson a planter-aristocrat deeply read in the liberal philosophy of the time, he was an individualist who cherished the idea that government was at best but a necessary evil, continually subject to the free social consent of the individual. He had a physiocrat's confidence in the land as the source of wealth; he had fostered, in the Virginia constitution, those principles of civil liberty which he later helped to enlarge into the Bill of Rights, the first ten amendments to the federal Constitution. Thomas Jefferson, whose ideals have been the foundation stone of American freedom, was all this time absent as American minister to France, but he could have had no better spokesman than James Madison.

Alexander Hamilton and John Jay, on the contrary, represented the conservatism of the mercantile and banking interests centered in New York, and both were allied by marriage with powerful and conservative New York families. Both were fundamentally devoted to republican principles, but neither one was temperamentally able to have confidence in the people as a whole. Each had hoped for what Hamilton, in the Constitutional

Convention, had demanded: "One General Government [of] complete sovereignty, [because] two sovereignties cannot exist within the same limits." As for the people, Hamilton declared that the powers of government should rest with "the wealthy, the good, and the wise," while Jay later summed up his economic philosophy with the dictum that "those who own the country ought to govern it."

Yet in order to secure a republic with adequate federal sovereignty, men of this opinion had been willing to make compromises with the views of many who felt as Jefferson or Madison did. *The Federalist* was the final proof that both parties were convinced of the effectiveness of these adjustments, and the resulting system of checks and balances provided in the Constitution to express the correspondence of the two American ideals —individualism, and effective action, by consensus, for the general good of the whole federal society.

In its entirety *The Federalist* discusses the theory and the proposed function of almost every aspect of the Constitution. No selection can be adequate, but we have included three papers, each of fundamental significance and high literary merit, representing the three authors. The leaders of the American Revolution—such men as Franklin and Paine, Washington, John Adams, and Jefferson—under the urgency of a stirring necessity, created a literature which still possesses a living power and beauty. They developed an American style of simple candor and clear precision for the expression of ideas, whether at the level of utility or nobility. Among these writers the authors of *The Federalist* have an enduring place.

The Federalist papers were first collected in *The Federalist: A Collection of Essays written in Favour of the New Constitution * * * *, New York, 1788. Standard editions are those of Henry Cabot Lodge, 1891, and P. L. Ford, 1898. E. M. Earle, 1938, included also the texts of the Articles of Confederation, the Convocation for the Constitutional Convention, the Constitution, and its Amendments. Selections, with a useful introduction and bibliography, are found in *Alexander Hamilton and Thomas Jefferson: Representative Selections*, edited by F. C. Prescott, American Writers Series, 1934.

No. II
[One Union Indivisible]

To the People of the State of New York:[1]

When the people of America reflect that they are now called upon to decide a question, which, in its consequences, must prove one of the most important that ever engaged their attention, the propriety of their taking a very comprehensive, as well as a very serious, view of it, will be evident.

Nothing is more certain than the indispensable necessity of gov-

1. *The Federalist*, No. II (written by John Jay) appeared in the *Independent Journal*, New York, October 31, 1787.

ernment, and it is equally undeniable that, whenever and however it is instituted, the people must cede to it some of their natural rights, in order to vest it with requisite powers. It is well worthy of consideration therefore, whether it would conduce more to the interest of the people of America that they should, to all general purposes, be one nation, under one federal government, or that they should divide themselves into separate confederacies, and give to the head of each the same kind of powers which they are advised to place in one national government.

It has until lately been a received and uncontradicted opinion that the prosperity of the people of America depended on their continuing firmly united, and the wishes, prayers, and efforts of our best and wisest citizens have been constantly directed to that object. But politicians now appear, who insist that this opinion is erroneous, and that instead of looking for safety and happiness in union, we ought to seek it in a division of the States into distinct confederacies or sovereignties. However extraordinary this new doctrine may appear, it nevertheless has its advocates; and certain characters who were much opposed to it formerly are at present of the number. Whatever may be the arguments or inducements which have wrought this change in the sentiments and declarations of these gentlemen, it certainly would not be wise in the people at large to adopt these new political tenets without being fully convinced that they are founded in truth and sound policy.

It has often given me pleasure to observe that independent America was not composed of detached and distant territories, but that one connected, fertile, wide-spreading country was the portion of our western sons of liberty. Providence has in a particular manner blessed it with a variety of soils and productions, and watered it with innumerable streams, for the delight and accommodation of its inhabitants. A succession of navigable waters forms a kind of chain round its borders, as if to bind it together; while the most noble rivers in the world, running at convenient distances, present them with highways for the easy communication of friendly aids, and the mutual transportation and exchange of their various commodities.

With equal pleasure I have so often taken notice that Providence has been pleased to give this one connected country to one united people—a people descended from the same ancestors, speaking the same language, professing the same religion, attached to the same principles of government, very similar in their manners and customs, and who, by their joint counsels, arms, and efforts, fighting side by side throughout a long and bloody war, have nobly established general liberty and independence.

This country and this people seem to have been made for each other, and it appears as if it was the design of Providence that an inheritance so proper and convenient for a band of brethren united to each other by the strongest ties, should never be split into a number of unsocial, jealous, and alien sovereignties.

Similar sentiments have hitherto prevailed among all orders and denominations of men among us. To all general purposes we have uniformly been one people; each individual citizen everywhere enjoying the same national rights, privileges, and protection. As a nation we have made peace and war; as a nation we have formed alliances, and made treaties, and entered into various compacts and conventions with foreign states.

A strong sense of the value and blessings of union induced the people, at a very early period, to institute a federal government to preserve and perpetuate it. They formed it almost as soon as they had a political existence; nay, at a time when their habitations were in flames, when many of their citizens were bleeding, and when the progress of hostility and desolation left little room for those calm and mature inquiries and reflections which must ever precede the formation of a wise and well-balanced government for a free people. It is not to be wondered at that a government, instituted in times so inauspicious, should on experiment be found greatly deficient and inadequate to the purpose it was intended to answer.

This intelligent people perceived and regretted these defects. Still continuing no less attached to union than enamored of liberty, they observed the danger which immediately threatened the former and more remotely the latter; and being persuaded that ample security for both could only be found in a national government more wisely framed, they, as with one voice, convened the late convention at Philadelphia, to take that important subject under consideration.

This convention, composed of men who possessed the confidence of the people, and many of whom had become highly distinguished by their patriotism, virtue, and wisdom, in times which tried the minds and hearts of men, undertook the arduous task. In the mild season of peace, with minds unoccupied by other subjects, they passed many months in cool, uninterrupted, and daily consultation; and finally, without having been awed by power, or influenced by any passions except love for their country, they presented and recommended to the people the plan produced by their joint and very unanimous councils.

Admit, for so is the fact, that this plan is only *recommended*, not imposed, yet let it be remembered that it is neither recommended to *blind* approbation, nor to *blind* reprobation; but to that sedate and candid consideration which the magnitude and importance of the subject demand, and which it certainly ought to receive. But this (as was remarked in the foregoing number of this paper) is more to be wished than expected, that it may be so considered and examined.

Experience on a former occasion teaches us not to be too sanguine in such hopes. It is not yet forgotten that well-grounded apprehensions of imminent danger induced the people of America to form the memorable Congress of 1774. That body recommended certain measures to their constituents, and the event proved their wisdom; yet it is fresh in our memories how soon the press began to teem with pamphlets and weekly papers against those very measures. Not only many of the officers of government, who obeyed the dictates of personal interest, but others, from a mistaken estimate of consequences, or the undue influence of former attachments, or whose ambition aimed at objects which did not correspond with the public good, were indefatigable in their efforts to persuade the people to reject the advice of that patriotic Congress. Many, indeed, were deceived and deluded, but the great majority of the people reasoned and decided judiciously; and happy they are in reflecting that they did so.

They considered that the Congress was composed of many wise and experienced men. That, being convened from different parts of the country, they brought with them and communicated to each other a variety of useful information. That, in the course of the time they passed together in inquiring into and discussing the true interests of their country, they must have acquired very accurate knowledge on that head. That they were individually interested in the public liberty and prosperity, and therefore that it was not less their inclination than their duty to recommend only such measures as, after the most mature deliberation, they really thought prudent and advisable.

These and similar considerations then induced the people to rely greatly on the judgment and integrity of the Congress; and they took their advice, notwithstanding the various arts and endeavors used to deter them from it. But if the people at large had reason to confide in the men of that Congress, few of whom had been fully tried or generally known, still greater reason have they now to respect the judgment and advice of the convention, for it is well known that some of the most distinguished members of that Congress, who have been since tried and justly approved for patriotism and abilities, and who have grown old in acquiring political information, were also members of this convention, and carried into it their accumulated knowledge and experience.

It is worthy of remark that not only the first, but every succeeding Congress, as well as the late convention, have invariably joined with the people in thinking that the prosperity of America depended on its Union. To preserve and perpetuate it was the great object of the people in forming that convention, and it is also the great object of the plan which the convention has advised them to adopt. With what propriety, therefore, or for what good purposes, are attempts at this particular period made by some men to depreciate the importance of the Union? Or why is it suggested that three or four confederacies would be better than one? I am persuaded in my own mind that the people have always thought right on this subject, and that their universal and uniform attachment to the cause of the Union rests on great and weighty reasons, which I shall endeavor to develop and explain in some ensuing papers. They who promote the idea of substituting a number of distinct confederacies in the room of the plan of the convention, seem clearly to foresee that the rejection of it would put the continuance of the Union in the utmost jeopardy. That certainly would be the case, and I sincerely wish that it may be as clearly foreseen by every good citizen, that whenever the dissolution of the Union arrives, America will have reason to exclaim, in the words of the poet: "FAREWELL! A LONG FAREWELL TO ALL MY GREATNESS."[2]   PUBLIUS [John Jay]

No. IX
[State Sovereignty and Federal Sovereignty]

TO THE PEOPLE OF THE STATE OF NEW YORK:[3]

A firm Union will be of the utmost moment to the peace and liberty of the States, as a barrier against domestic faction and insurrection. It is impossible to read the history of the petty republics of Greece and Italy without feeling sensations of horror and disgust at the distractions with which they were continually agitated, and at the rapid succession of revolutions by which they were kept in a state of perpetual vibration between the extremes of tyranny and anarchy. If they exhibit occasional calms, these only serve as short-lived contrasts to the furious storms that are to succeed. If now and then intervals of felicity open to view, we behold them with a mixture of regret arising from the reflection that the pleasing scenes before us are soon to be overwhelmed by the tempestuous waves of sedition and party rage. If momentary rays of glory break forth from the gloom, while they dazzle us with a transient and fleeting brilliancy, they at the same time admonish us to lament that the vices of government should pervert the direction and tarnish the luster of those bright talents and exalted endowments for which the favored soils that produced them have been so justly celebrated.

From the disorders that disfigure the annals of those republics the advocates of despotism have drawn arguments, not only against the forms of republican government, but against the very principles of civil liberty. They have decried all free government as inconsistent

2. Shakespeare, *King Henry VIII*, Act III, Scene 2.
3. *The Federalist*, No. IX (written by Alexander Hamilton) appeared in the *Independent Journal*, New York, November 21, 1787.

with the order of society, and have indulged themselves in malicious exultation over its friends and partisans. Happily for mankind, stupendous fabrics reared on the basis of liberty, which have flourished for ages, have, in a few glorious instances, refuted their gloomy sophisms. And, I trust, America will be the broad and solid foundation of other edifices, not less magnificent, which will be equally permanent monuments of their errors.

But it is not to be denied that the portraits they have sketched of republican government were too just copies of the originals from which they were taken. If it had been found impracticable to have devised models of a more perfect structure, the enlightened friends to liberty would have been obliged to abandon the cause of that species of government as indefensible. The science of politics, however, like most other sciences, has received great improvement. The efficacy of various principles is now well understood, which were either not known at all, or imperfectly known to the ancients. The regular distribution of power into distinct departments; the introduction of legislative balances and checks; the institution of courts composed of judges holding their offices during good behavior; the representation of the people in the legislature by deputies of their own election: these are wholly new discoveries, or have made their principal progress towards perfection in modern times. They are means, and powerful means by which the excellences of republican government may be retained and its imperfections lessened or avoided. To this catalogue of circumstances that tend to the amelioration of popular systems of civil government, I shall venture, however novel it may appear to some, to add one more, on a principle which has been made the foundation of an objection to the new Constitution; I mean the ENLARGEMENT of the ORBIT within which such systems are to revolve, either in respect to the dimensions of a single State, or to the consolidation of several smaller States into one great Confederacy. The latter is that which immediately concerns the object under consideration. It will, however, be of use to examine the principle in its application to a single State, which shall be attended to in another place.

The utility of a Confederacy, as well to suppress faction and to guard the internal tranquillity of States, as to increase their external force and security, is in reality not a new idea. It has been practiced upon in different countries and ages, and has received the sanction of the most approved writers on the subject of politics. The opponents of the plan proposed have, with great assiduity, cited and circulated the observations of Montesquieu[4] on the necessity of a contracted territory for a republican government. But they seem not

4. Charles de Secondat, Baron de la Brède et de Montesquieu (1689–1755), French political philosopher; his *Spirit of Laws* is cited in Note 5.

to have been apprised of the sentiments of that great man expressed in another part of his work, nor to have adverted to the consequences of the principle to which they subscribe with such ready acquiescence.

When Montesquieu recommends a small extent for republics, the standards he had in view were of dimensions far short of the limits of almost every one of these States. Neither Virginia, Massachusetts, Pennsylvania, New York, North Carolina, nor Georgia can by any means be compared with the models from which he reasoned and to which the terms of his description apply. If we therefore take his ideas on this point as the criterion of truth, we shall be driven to the alternative either of taking refuge at once in the arms of monarchy, or of splitting ourselves into an infinity of little jealous, clashing, tumultuous commonwealths, the wretched nurseries of unceasing discord, and the miserable objects of universal pity or contempt. Some of the writers who have come forward on the other side of the question seem to have been aware of the dilemma; and have even been bold enough to hint at the division of the larger States as a desirable thing. Such an infatuated policy, such a desperate expedient, might, by the multiplication of petty offices, answer the views of men who possess not qualifications to extend their influence beyond the narrow circles of personal intrigue, but it could never promote the greatness or happiness of the people of America.

Referring the examination of the principle itself to another place, as has been already mentioned, it will be sufficient to remark here that, in the sense of the author who has been most emphatically quoted upon the occasion, it would only dictate a reduction of the SIZE of the more considerable MEMBERS of the Union, but would not militate against their being all comprehended in one confederate government. And this is the true question, in the discussion of which we are at present interested.

So far are the suggestions of Montesquieu from standing in opposition to a general Union of the States, that he explicitly treats of a CONFEDERATE REPUBLIC as the expedient for extending the sphere of popular government, and reconciling the advantages of monarchy with those of republicanism.

"It is very probable" (says he[5]), "that mankind would have been obliged at length to live constantly under the government of a single person, had they not contrived a kind of constitution that has all the internal advantages of a republican, together with the external force of a monarchial government. I mean a CONFEDERATE REPUBLIC.

"This form of government is a convention by which several smaller *states* agree to become members of a larger *one*, which they intend to form. It is a kind of assemblage of societies that constitute a new

5. "*Spirit of Laws*, vol. i. book ix. chap. i." [Publius' note].

one, capable of increasing, by means of new associations, till they arrive to such a degree of power as to be able to provide for the security of the united body.

"A republic of this kind, able to withstand an external force, may support itself without any internal corruptions. The form of this society prevents all manner of inconveniences.

"If a single member should attempt to usurp the supreme authority, he could not be supposed to have an equal authority and credit in all the confederate states. Were he to have too great influence over one, this would alarm the rest. Were he to subdue a part, that which would still remain free might oppose him with forces independent of those which he had usurped, and overpower him before he could be settled in his usurpation.

"Should a popular insurrection happen in one of the confederate states, the others are able to quell it. Should abuses creep into one part, they are reformed by those that remain sound. The state may be destroyed on one side, and not on the other; the confederacy may be dissolved, and the confederate preserve their sovereignty.

"As this government is composed of small republics, it enjoys the internal happiness of each; and with respect to its external situation, it is possessed, by means of the association, of all the advantages of large monarchies."

I have thought it proper to quote at length these interesting passages, because they contain a luminous abridgment of the principal arguments in favor of the Union, and must effectually remove the false impressions which a misapplication of other parts of the work was calculated to make. They have, at the same time, an intimate connection with the more immediate design of this paper; which is, to illustrate the tendency of the Union to repress domestic faction and insurrection.

A distinction, more subtle than accurate, has been raised between a *Confederacy* and a *consolidation* of the States. The essential characteristic of the first is said to be the restriction of its authority to the members in their collective capacities, without reaching to the individuals of whom they are composed. It is contended that the national council ought to have no concern with any object of internal administration. An exact equality of suffrage between the members has also been insisted upon as a leading feature of a confederate government. These positions are, in the main, arbitrary; they are supported neither by principle nor precedent. It has indeed happened that governments of this kind have generally operated in the manner which the distinction, taken notice of, supposes to be inherent in their nature; but there have been in most of them extensive exceptions to the practice, which serve to prove, as far as example will go, that there is no absolute rule on the subject. And it will be clearly shown, in the course of this investigation, that, as far as the principle contended for has prevailed, it has been the cause of incurable disorder and imbecility in the government.

The definition of a *Confederate Republic* seems simply to be "an assemblage of societies," or an association of two or more states into one state. The extent, modifications, and objects of the federal authority are mere matters of discretion. So long as the separate organization of the members be not abolished; so long as it exists, by a constitutional necessity, for local purposes; though it should be in perfect subordination to the general authority of the union, it would still be, in fact and in theory, an association of states, or a confederacy. The proposed Constitution, so far from implying an abolition of the State governments, makes them constituent parts of the national sovereignty, by allowing them a direct representation in the Senate, and leaves in their possession certain exclusive and very important portions of sovereign power. This fully corresponds, in every rational import of the terms, with the idea of a federal government.

In the Lycian confederacy, which consisted of twenty-three CITIES or republics, the largest were entitled to *three* votes in the COMMON COUNCIL, those of the middle class to *two*, and the smallest to *one*. The COMMON COUNCIL had the appointment of all the judges and magistrates of the respective CITIES. This was certainly the most delicate species of interference in their internal administration; for if there be anything that seems exclusively appropriated to the local jurisdictions, it is the appointment of their own officers. Yet Montesquieu, speaking of this association says: "Were I to give a model of an excellent Confederate Republic, it would be that of Lycia." Thus we perceive that the distinctions insisted upon were not within the contemplation of this enlightened civilian; and we shall be led to conclude, that they are the novel refinements of an erroneous theory.

PUBLIUS [Alexander Hamilton]

No. X
[Majority Rule, Freedom for Minorities]

TO THE PEOPLE OF THE STATE OF NEW YORK:[6]

Among the numerous advantages promised by a well-constructed union, none deserves to be more accurately developed than its tendency to break and control the violence of faction. The friend of popular governments never finds himself so much alarmed for their character and fate as when he contemplates their propensity to this

6. *The Federalist*, No. X (written by James Madison) appeared in the New York *Daily Advertiser*, November 23, 1787.

dangerous vice. He will not fail, therefore, to set a due value on any plan which, without violating the principles to which he is attached, provides a proper cure for it. The instability, injustice, and confusion introduced into the public councils have, in truth, been the mortal diseases under which popular governments have everywhere perished; as they continue to be the favorite and fruitful topics from which the adversaries to liberty derive their most specious declamations. The valuable improvements made by the American constitutions on the popular models, both ancient and modern, cannot certainly be too much admired; but it would be an unwarrantable partiality, to contend that they have as effectually obviated the danger on this side as was wished and expected. Complaints are everywhere heard from our most considerate and virtuous citizens, equally the friends of public and private faith and of public and personal liberty, that our governments are too unstable; that the public good is disregarded in the conflicts of rival parties; and that measures are too often decided, not according to the rules of justice, and the rights of the minor party, but by the superior force of an interested and overbearing majority. However anxiously we may wish that these complaints had no foundation, the evidence of known facts will not permit us to deny that they are in some degree true. It will be found, indeed, on a candid review of our situation, that some of the distresses under which we labor have been erroneously charged on the operation of our governments; but it will be found, at the same time, that other causes will not alone account for many of our heaviest misfortunes; and, particularly, for that prevailing and increasing distrust of public engagements, and alarm for private rights, which are echoed from one end of the continent to the other. These must be chiefly, if not wholly, effects of the unsteadiness and injustice with which a factious spirit has tainted our public administrations.

By a faction, I understand a number of citizens, whether amounting to a majority or minority of the whole, who are united and actuated by some common impulse of passion, or of interest, adverse to the rights of other citizens or to the permanent and aggregate interests of the community.

There are two methods of curing the mischiefs of faction: the one, by removing its causes; the other, by controlling its effects.

There are again two methods of removing the causes of faction: the one, by destroying the liberty which is essential to its existence; the other, by giving to every citizen the same opinions, the same passions, and the same interests.

It could never be more truly said than of the first remedy, that it was worse than the disease. Liberty is to faction what air is to fire, an ailment without which it instantly expires. But it could not be less folly to abolish liberty, which is essential to political life, because it nourishes faction, than it would be to wish the annihilation of air, which is essential to animal life, because it imparts to fire its destructive agency.

The second expedient is as impracticable as the first would be unwise. As long as the reason of man continues fallible, and he is at liberty to exercise it, different opinions will be formed. As long as the connection subsists between his reason and his self-love, his opinions and his passions will have a reciprocal influence on each other; and the former will be objects to which the latter will attach themselves. The diversity in the faculties of men, from which the rights of property originate, is not less an insuperable obstacle to a uniformity of interests. The protection of these faculties is the first object of government. From the protection of different and unequal faculties of acquiring property, the possession of different degrees and kinds of property immediately results; and from the influence of these on the sentiments and views of the respective proprietors ensues a division of the society into different interests and parties.

The latent causes of faction are thus sown in the nature of man; and we see them everywhere brought into different degrees of activity, according to the different circumstances of civil society. A zeal for different opinions concerning religion, concerning government and many other points, as well of speculation as of practice; an attachment to different leaders ambitiously contending for pre-eminence and power, or to persons of other descriptions whose fortunes have been interesting to the human passions, have, in turn, divided mankind into parties, inflamed them with mutual animosity, and rendered them much more disposed to vex and oppress each other, than to co-operate for their common good. So strong is this propensity of mankind to fall into mutual animosities, that where no substantial occasion presents itself, the most frivolous and fanciful distinctions have been sufficient to kindle their unfriendly passions and excite their most violent conflicts. But the most common and durable source of factions has been the various and unequal distribution of property. Those who hold and those who are without property have ever formed distinct interests in society. Those who are creditors and those who are debtors fall under a like discrimination. A landed interest, a manufacturing interest, a mercantile interest, a moneyed interest, with many lesser interests, grow up of necessity in civilized nations, and divide them into different classes, actuated by different sentiments and views. The regulation of these various and interfering interests forms the principal task of modern legislation, and involves the spirit of party and faction in the necessary and ordinary operations of the government.

No man is allowed to be a judge in his own cause; because his interest would certainly bias his judgment and, not improbably, corrupt his integrity. With equal, nay, with greater reason, a body of men are unfit to be both judges and parties at the same time; yet what are many of the most important acts of legislation, but so many judicial determinations, not indeed concerning the rights of single persons, but concerning the rights of large bodies of citizens? and what are the different classes of legislators, but advocates and parties to the causes which they determine? Is a law proposed concerning private debts?—it is a question to which the creditors are parties on one side, and the debtors on the other. Justice ought to hold the balance between them. Yet the parties are, and must be, themselves the judges; and the most numerous party, or, in other words, the most powerful faction, must be expected to prevail. Shall domestic manufactures be encouraged, and in what degree by restrictions on foreign manufactures? are questions which would be differently decided by the landed and the manufacturing classes, and probably by neither with a sole regard to justice and the public good. The apportionment of taxes on the various descriptions of property is an act which seems to require the most exact impartiality; yet there is, perhaps, no legislative act in which greater opportunity and temptation are given to a predominant party, to trample on the rules of justice. Every shilling with which they overburden the inferior number is a shilling saved to their own pockets.

It is in vain to say that enlightened statesmen will be able to adjust these clashing interests and render them all subservient to the public good. Enlightened statesmen will not always be at the helm; nor, in many cases, can such an adjustment be made at all, without taking into view indirect and remote considerations, which will rarely prevail over the immediate interest which one party may find in disregarding the rights of another or the good of the whole.

The inference to which we are brought is that the causes of faction cannot be removed and that relief is only to be sought in the means of controlling its effects.

If a faction consists of less than a majority, relief is supplied by the republican principle, which enables the majority to defeat its sinister views by regular vote. It may clog the administration, it may convulse the society; but it will be unable to execute and mask its violence under the forms of the Constitution. When a majority is included in a faction, the form of popular government, on the other hand, enables it to sacrifice to its ruling passion or interest both the public good and the rights of other citizens. To secure the public good, and private rights, against the danger of such a faction, and at the same time to preserve the spirit and the form of popular government, is then the great object to which our inquiries are directed. Let me add that it is the great *desideratum*, by which alone this form of government can be rescued from the opprobrium under which it has so long labored, and be recommended to the esteem and adoption of mankind.

By what means is this object attainable? Evidently by one of two only. Either the existence of the same passion or interest in a majority, at the same time, must be prevented; or the majority, having such co-existent passion or interest, must be rendered, by their number and local situation, unable to concert and carry into effect schemes of oppression. If the impulse and the opportunity be suffered to coincide, we well know that neither moral nor religious motives can be relied on as an adequate control. They are not found to be such on the injustice and violence of individuals, and lose their efficacy in proportion to the number combined together; that is, in proportion as their efficacy becomes needful.

From this view of the subject it may be concluded that a pure democracy, by which I mean a society consisting of a small number of citizens, who assemble and administer the government in person, can admit of no cure for the mischiefs of faction. A common passion or interest will, in almost every case, be felt by a majority of the whole; a communication and concert results from the form of government itself; and there is nothing to check the inducements to sacrifice the weaker party or an obnoxious individual. Hence it is that such democracies have ever been spectacles of turbulence and contention; have ever been found incompatible with personal security, or the rights of property, and have in general been as short in their lives as they have been violent in their deaths. Theoretic politicians, who have patronized this species of government, have erroneously supposed that by reducing mankind to a perfect equality in their political rights, they would at the same time be perfectly equalized and assimilated in their possessions, their opinions, and their passions.

A republic, by which I mean a government in which the scheme of representation takes place, opens a different prospect, and promises the cure for which we are seeking. Let us examine the points in which it varies from pure democracy, and we shall comprehend both the nature of the cure and the efficacy which it must derive from the union.

The two great points of difference between a democracy and a republic are: First, the delegation of the government, in the latter, to a small number of citizens elected by the rest; secondly, the greater number of citizens, and greater sphere of country, over which the latter may be extended.

The effect of the first difference is, on the one hand, to refine and enlarge the public views, by passing them through the medium of a chosen body of citizens, whose wisdom may best discern the true interest of their country, and whose patriotism and love of justice will be least likely to sacrifice it to temporary or partial considerations. Under such a regulation, it may well happen that the public voice, pronounced by the representatives of the people, will be more consonant to the public good than if pronounced by the people themselves, convened for the purpose. On the other hand, the effect may be inverted. Men of factious tempers, of local prejudices, or of sinister designs, may by intrigue, by corruption, or by other means, first obtain the suffrages, and then betray the interests of the people. The question resulting is, whether small or extensive republics are most favorable to the election of proper guardians of the public weal; and it is clearly decided in favor of the latter by two obvious considerations.

In the first place, it is to be remarked that, however small the republic may be, the representatives must be raised to a certain number, in order to guard against the cabals of a few; and that, however large it may be, they must be limited to a certain number, in order to guard against the confusion of a multitude. Hence, the number of representatives in the two cases not being in proportion to that of the constituents, and being proportionally greatest in the small republic, it follows that if the proportion of fit characters be not less in the large than in the small republic, the former will present a greater option, and consequently a greater probability of a fit choice.

In the next place, as each representative will be chosen by a greater number of citizens in the large than in the small republic, it will be more difficult for unworthy candidates to practise with success the vicious arts, by which elections are too often carried; and the suffrages of the people, being more free, will be more likely to centre in men who possess the most attractive merit and the most diffusive and established characters.

It must be confessed that in this as in most other cases, there is a mean, on both sides of which inconveniences will be found to lie. By enlarging too much the number of electors, you render the representative too little acquainted with all their local circumstances and lesser interests; as by reducing it too much, you render him unduly attached to these, and too little fit to comprehend and pursue great and national objects. The federal Constitution forms a happy combination in this respect; the great and aggregate interests being referred to the national, the local and particular to the State, legislatures.

The other point of difference is, the greater number of citizens and extent of territory which may be brought within the compass of republican than of democratic government; and it is this circumstance principally which renders factious combinations less to be dreaded in the former, than in the latter. The smaller the society,

the fewer probably will be the distinct parties and interests composing it; the fewer the distinct parties and interests, the more frequently will a majority be found of the same party; and the smaller
the number of individuals composing a majority, and the smaller the
compass within which they are placed, the more easily will they concert and execute their plans of oppression. Extend the sphere, and
you take in a greater variety of parties and interests; you make it less
probable that a majority of the whole will have a common motive
to invade the rights of other citizens; or if such a common motive
exists, it will be more difficult for all who feel it to discover their own
strength, and to act in unison with each other. Besides other impediments, it may be remarked that where there is a consciousness of
unjust or dishonorable purposes, communication is always checked
by distrust, in proportion to the number whose concurrence is necessary.

Hence it clearly appears that the same advantage which a republic
has over a democracy, in controlling the effects of faction, is enjoyed
by a large over a small republic—is enjoyed by the Union over the
States composing it. Does the advantage consist in the substitution
of representatives, whose enlightened views and virtuous sentiments
render them superior to local prejudices, and to schemes of injustice? It will not be denied that the representation of the Union will
be most likely to possess these requisite endowments. Does it consist in the greater security afforded by a greater variety of parties,
against the event of any one party being able to outnumber and
oppress the rest? In an equal degree does the increased variety of
parties, comprised within the Union, increase this security. Does it,
in fine, consist in the greater obstacles opposed to the concert and
accomplishment of the secret wishes of an unjust and interested
majority? Here, again, the extent of the Union gives it the most palpable advantage.

The influence of factious leaders may kindle a flame within their
particular States, but will be unable to spread a general conflagration
through the other States. A religious sect may degenerate into a
political faction in a part of the confederacy; but the variety of sects
dispersed over the entire face of it must secure the national councils
against any danger from that source. A rage for paper money, for
an abolition of debts, for an equal division of property, or for any
other improper and wicked project will be less apt to pervade the
whole body of the Union than a particular member of it; in the same
proportion as such a malady is more likely to taint a particular county
or district than an entire State.

In the extent and proper structure of the Union, therefore, we
behold a republican remedy for the diseases most incident to republican government. And according to the degree of pleasure and pride

we feel in being republicans, ought to be our zeal in cherishing the spirit and supporting the character of federalists.

PUBLIUS [James Madison]

PHILIP FRENEAU
(1752–1832)

Judged in his own time by his political opponents as "a writer of wretched and insolent doggerel, an incendiary journalist," Philip Freneau was nevertheless our second important poet. His double rôle as poet and political journalist in the transitional age of the Revolution is consistent with the contradictions of his poetry. [Freneau was neoclassical by training and taste yet romantic in essential spirit.] He was also at once a satirist and a sentimentalist, a humanitarian but also a bitter polemicist, a poet of Reason yet the celebrant of "lovely Fancy," and a deistic optimist most inspired by themes of death and transcience.

Freneau was born on January 2, 1752, in New York, of French Huguenot and Scottish stock. He was tutored for Princeton ("that hotbed of Whiggery") where he established close friendships with a future president, James Madison, and a future novelist, Hugh Henry Brackenridge. In collaboration with the latter he produced his earliest work; slightly later, in "The Power of Fancy" (1770), a genuine independence appears. After graduation and an unsatisfactory teaching experience, he gained his first popular success in New York in 1775 as a satirist of the British. That year Freneau made his first voyage to the West Indies, where he wrote "The House of Night," foreshadowing the Gothic mood of Poe and Coleridge—F. L. Pattee calls it "the first distinctly romantic note heard in America" —and "The Beauties of Santa Cruz," blending the praise of nature with social protest in his characteristic later manner. This poetry foretold achievement of a distinguished order, but he was soon diverted from literature into the tide of revolution. As passenger on an American ship, which he helped to defend in an attack by the British in 1780, he was taken prisoner. "The British Prison Ship" (1781), a good piece of invective, reveals the rigors and brutality of his captivity. In truth he now could say: "An age employed in edging steel / Can no poetic rapture feel." In the closing year of the war he became the prolific propagandist, celebrating American victories and leaders, while continuing to hurl his vitriol at the British in many poems. "The poet of the Revolution" they called him, a compliment not wholly to his advantage, since its persistence long obscured the fact that his later poems were his best, and these were quite different. The earlier poems were collected (1786) in *The Poems* of *Philip Freneau Written Chiefly During the Late War.*

For a few years, writing with sporadic fluency, Freneau earned his living variously as farmer, journalist, and sea captain. His *Miscellaneous Works,* essays and new poems, appeared in 1788. In 1789 he married, and almost literally flung himself, as political journalist, into the raging controversies between the Jeffersonian Democrats, whom he supported, and Hamilton's Federalists. In New York he edited the *Daily Advertiser.* In 1791, probably with Jefferson's support, he established in Philadelphia the *National Gazette,* and campaigned against the opinions of the powerful *Gazette of the United States,* edited by John Fenno, and supported by Hamilton. Simultaneously he served as translating clerk in Jefferson's Department of State. He was soon a power in journalism and politics. Jefferson asserted that his paper "saved our Constitution, which was fast galloping into monarchy"; but Washington muttered against "that rascal Freneau," while Irving's urbanity was disturbed by "a barking cur." When Jefferson withdrew from politics temporarily in 1793, Freneau resigned and his paper failed, in the midst of a Federalist tide which ended only with Jefferson's election to the presidency in 1801. Freneau's social and religious liberalism, in which he resembled Paine, gave the Federalists a deadly weapon against him; indeed his political enemies so besmirched his reputation that he has only recently been recognized as a courageous champion of American popular government.

Reduced in fortune and political ambition, he settled in 1794 at his plantation homestead, Mount Pleasant, near Freehold, New Jersey, where he edited, each for a year, a New Jersey paper and a New York magazine. On his own hand press he published new essays and poems, and revisions of earlier pieces. Collections appeared in 1795 and 1799. His poverty drove him at fifty to resume plowing the sea instead of his "sandy patrimony"; he was captain of coastwise trading vessels from 1803 to 1807. Again he turned to his farm for subsistence, but in 1815 his home burned down, and he gathered together the remnants of his family and possessions in a little farmhouse nearer town. In 1815 he collected the important poems of his later period, including the interesting work inspired by the War of 1812, in *A Collection of Poems * * * Written Between the Year 1797 and the Present Time.* After he was seventy, he worked on the public roads; "he went," says Leary, "from house to house as tinker, mending clocks, and doing other small jobs of repairing." He continued almost until his death to send poems to the newspapers. Poor and nearly forgotten, he died of exposure in 1832 at the age of eighty, after losing his way in a blizzard, as he returned, it is said, from a tavern.

As a poet, Freneau heralded American literary independence; his close observation of nature (before Bryant) distinguished his treatment of indigenous wild life and other native American subjects. In contrast with the ornate style of his early couplets, he later developed a natural, simple, and concrete diction, best illustrated in such nature lyrics as "The Wild Honey Suckle" and "The Indian Burying Ground." Freneau did not establish trends, but he represented qualities that were to be characteristic of the next half century. He has been called the "Father of American Poetry," and it is ultimately that Freneau is important. In the main, as Harry H. Clark remarks, "he is worthy of study as a cross-section of an intensely significant period in our political and literary history rather than as an intrinsically wise political theorist or a profound creator of poetic beauty."

The standard edition of the poetry is *The Poems of Philip Freneau*, 3 vols., edited by F. L. Pattee, 1902–1907. An excellent volume of selections is *Poems of Freneau*, edited by H. H. Clark, 1929. Additional poems are found in *The Last Poems of Philip Freneau*, edited by Lewis Leary, 1946. Freneau's prose has not been collected, although H. H. Clark has projected an edition and has published a facsimile of the 1799 edition of *Letters on Various Interesting and Important Subjects*, 1943. An authoritative critical biography is *That Rascal Freneau: A Study in Literary Failure*, by Lewis Leary, 1941. Another biography is that of Pattee, in Volume I of his edition of the *Poems;* while H. H. Clark's edition contains a penetrating critical introduction.

To Sir Toby[1]

A SUGAR PLANTER IN THE INTERIOR PARTS OF JAMAICA

If there exists a hell—the case is clear—
Sir Toby's slaves enjoy that portion here:
Here are no blazing brimstone lakes, 'tis true;
But kindled Rum too often burns as blue,
In which some fiend, whom nature must detest,   5
Steeps Toby's brand and marks poor Cudjoe's[2] breast.
Here whips on whips excite perpetual fears,
And mingled howlings vibrate on my ears;
Here nature's plagues abound, to fret and tease,
Snakes, scorpions, despots, lizards, centipedes.   10
No art, no care escapes the busy lash;
All have their dues—and all are paid in cash.
The eternal driver keeps a steady eye
On a black herd, who would his vengeance fly,
But chained, imprisoned, on a burning soil,   15
For the mean avarice of a tyrant, toil!
The lengthy cart-whip guards this monster's reign—
And cracks, like pistols, from the fields of cane.

1. In the West Indies Freneau encountered Negro slavery in its fullest excesses, and he became an early voice in protest. (See Leary, *That Rascal Freneau*, pp. 68–69.) However, the present satire was written and published later, in 1784, when he commanded a trading vessel to and from the Caribbean.
2. *I.e.,* "cudge," then a vernacular term for a Negro slave. The line refers to the branding of slaves.

Ye powers who formed these wretched tribes, relate,
What had they done, to merit such a fate!   20
Why were they brought from Eboe's[2a] sultry waste,
To see that plenty which they must not taste—
Food, which they cannot buy, and dare not steal,
Yams and potatoes—many a scanty meal!—

One, with a gibbet wakes his negro's fears,   25
One to the windmill nails him by the ears;
One keeps his slave in darkened dens, unfed,
One puts the wretch in pickle ere he's dead:
This, from a tree suspends him by the thumbs,
That, from his table grudges even the crumbs!   30

O'er yond' rough hills a tribe of females go,
Each with her gourd, her infant, and her hoe;
Scorched by a sun that has no mercy here,
Driven by a devil, whom men call overseer—
In chains, twelve wretches to their labors haste;   35
Twice twelve I saw, with iron collars graced!—

Are such the fruits that spring from vast domains?
Is wealth, thus got, Sir Toby, worth your pains!—
Who would your wealth on terms like these possess,
Where all we see is pregnant with distress—   40
Angola's[3] natives scourged by ruffian hands,
And toil's hard product shipp'd to foreign lands.

Talk not of blossoms and your endless spring;
What joy, what smile, can scenes of misery bring?—
Though Nature here has every blessing spread,   45
Poor is the labourer—and how meanly fed!—

Here Stygian[4] paintings light and shade renew,
Pictures of hell, that Virgil's pencil drew:[5]
Here, surly Charons[6] make their annual trip,
And ghosts arrive in every Guinea ship,   50
To find what beasts these western isles afford,
Plutonian[7] scourges, and despotic lords:—

Here, they, of stuff determined to be free,
Must climb the rude cliffs of the Liguanee;[1]
Beyond the clouds, in skulking haste repair,   55
And hardly safe from brother traitors there.

1784   1784, 1795

2a. "A small Negro kingdom near the
river Senegal" [Freneau's note].
3. Portuguese province in West Africa.
4. Pertaining to the river Styx; hence,
"hellish."
5. Virgil, in the *Aeneid* (Book VI), describes the descent of Aeneas into the
infernal regions to seek his father's advice.

6. In Greek myth, Charon ferried the
dead across the River Styx to Hades—
here he is associated with the captains of
slave ships.
7. Pluto ruled Hades.
1. *I.e.*, Liguanea, the highland plateau
of Kingston, Jamaica, rimmed at the
north by mountains.

To the Memory of the Brave Americans[2]

UNDER GENERAL GREENE, IN SOUTH CAROLINA, WHO FELL
IN THE ACTION OF SEPTEMBER 8, 1781.

At Eutaw Springs the valiant died;
　　Their limbs with dust are covered o'er—
Weep on, ye springs, your tearful tide;
　　How many heroes are no more!

If in this wreck of ruin, they　　　　　　　　　　5
　　Can yet be thought to claim a tear,
O smite your gentle breast, and say
　　The friends of freedom slumber here!

Thou, who shalt trace this bloody plain,
　　If goodness rules thy generous breast,　　　10
Sigh for the wasted rural reign;
　　Sigh for the shepherds, sunk to rest!

Stranger, their humble graves adorn;
　　You too may fall, and ask a tear;
'Tis not the beauty of the morn　　　　　　　　15
　　That proves the evening shall be clear.—

They saw their injured country's woe;
　　The flaming town, the wasted field;
Then rushed to meet the insulting foe;
　　They took the spear—but left the shield.　　20

Led by thy conquering genius, Greene,
　　The Britons they compelled to fly;
None distant viewed the fatal plain,
　　None grieved, in such a cause to die—

But, like the Parthian,[3] famed of old,　　　　25
　　Who, flying, still their arrows threw,
These routed Britons, full as bold,
　　Retreated, and retreating slew.

Now rest in peace, our patriot band;
　　Though far from nature's limits thrown,　　30
We trust they find a happier land,
　　A brighter sunshine of their own.

1781　　　　　　　　　　　　　　　　　　　　　　　1781, 1786

2. General Nathaniel Greene's fine generalship in the South in 1781 was crucial. Although he lost several hundred men at Eutaw Springs, he prevented the relief of Cornwallis, who surrendered at Yorktown on October 19. The poem appeared in the *Freeman's Journal*, November 21, 1781.

3. The Parthians, famous cavalrymen of ancient Persia, destroyed their enemies by feigning flight, then suddenly wheeling to discharge their arrows.

On Mr. Paine's Rights of Man[4]

Thus briefly sketched the sacred RIGHTS OF MAN,
How inconsistent with the ROYAL PLAN!
Which for itself exclusive honour craves,
Where some are masters born, and millions slaves.
With what contempt must every eye look down   5
On that base, childish bauble called a *crown*,
The gilded bait, that lures the crowd, to come,
Bow down their necks, and meet a slavish doom;
The source of half the miseries men endure,
The quack that kills them, while it seems to cure.   10

    Roused by the REASON of his manly page,
Once more shall PAINE a listening world engage:
From Reason's source, a bold reform he brings,
In raising *mankind*, he pulls down *kings*,
Who, source of discord, patrons of all wrong,   15
On blood and murder have been fed too long:
Hid from the world, and tutored to be base,
The curse, the scourge, the ruin of our race,
Their's was the task, a dull designing few,
To shackle beings that they scarcely knew,   20
Who made this globe the residence of slaves,
And built their thrones on systems formed by knaves
—Advance, bright years, to work their final fall,
And haste the period that shall crush them all.

    Who, that has read and scanned the historic page   25
But glows, at every line, with kindling rage,
To see by them the rights of men aspersed
Freedom restrained, and Nature's law reversed,
Men, ranked with beasts, by monarchs willed away,
And bound young fools, or madmen to obey: 30
Now driven to wars, and now oppressed at home,
Compelled in crowds o'er distant seas to roam,
From India's climes the plundered prize to bring
To glad the strumpet, or to glut the king.

    COLUMBIA, hail! immortal be thy reign: 35
Without a king, we till the smiling plain;
Without a king, we trace the unbounded sea,
And traffic round the globe, through each degree;

---

4. See headnote on Thomas Paine, above. *The Rights of Man*, Part I, ran serially in the New York *Daily Advertiser*, May 6–27, 1791, and Freneau's poem appeared at the end of the concluding installment. The poem was popular; it reappeared in three other papers within a month. Freneau had been attracted, during the Revolution, by Paine's emphasis on "natural rights"; and like Jefferson, he believed that the new work might offset the current conservative reaction in America.

Each foreign clime our honoured flag reveres,
Which asks no monarch, to support the STARS: 40
Without a *king*, the laws maintain their sway,
While honour bids each generous heart obey.
Be ours the task the ambitious to restrain,
And this great lesson teach—that kings are vain;
That warring realms to certain ruin haste,   45
That kings subsist by war, and wars are waste:
So shall our nation, formed on Virtue's plan,
Remain the guardian of the Rights of Man,
A vast Republic, famed through every clime,
Without a king, to see the end of time.   50

1791   1795

The Wild Honey Suckle[5]

Fair flower, that dost so comely grow,
Hid in this silent, dull retreat,
Untouched thy honied blossoms blow,
Unseen thy little branches greet:
   No roving foot shall crush thee here,   5
   No busy hand provoke a tear.

By Nature's self in white arrayed,
She bade thee shun the vulgar eye,
And planted here the guardian shade,
And sent soft waters murmuring by;   10
   Thus quietly thy summer goes,
   Thy days declining to repose.

Smit with those charms, that must decay,
I grieve to see your future doom;
They died—nor were those flowers more gay,   15
The flowers that did in Eden bloom;
   Unpitying frosts, and Autumn's power
   Shall leave no vestige of this flower.

From morning suns and evening dews
At first thy little being came:
If nothing once, you nothing lose,   20
For when you die you are the same;
   The space between, is but an hour,
   The frail duration of a flower.

1786   1786, 1788

5. Then the popular name for a familiar shrub, *azalea viscosa*, sometimes "swamp honeysuckle." *Cf.* Emerson, "The Rhodora."

The Indian Burying Ground

In spite of all the learned have said,
  I still my old opinion keep;
The posture, that we give the dead,
  Points out the soul's eternal sleep.

Not so the ancients of these lands—
  The Indian, when from life released,
Again is seated with his friends,
  And shares again the joyous feast.[6]

His imaged birds, and painted bowl,
  And venison, for a journey dressed,
Bespeak the nature of the soul,
  Activity, that knows no rest.

His bow, for action ready bent,
  And arrows, with a head of stone,
Can only mean that life is spent,
  And not the old ideas gone.

Thou, stranger, that shalt come this way,
  No fraud upon the dead commit—
Observe the swelling turf, and say
  They do not lie, but here they sit.

Here still a lofty rock remains,
  On which the curious eye may trace
(Now wasted, half, by wearing rains)
  The fancies of a ruder race.

Here still an aged elm aspires,
  Beneath whose far-projecting shade
(And which the shepherd still admires)
  The children of the forest played!

There oft a restless Indian queen
  (Pale Shebah,[7] with her braided hair)
And many a barbarous form is seen
  To chide the man that lingers there.

By midnight moons, o'er moistening dews;
  In habit for the chase arrayed,

5

10

15

20

25

30

6. "The North American Indians bury their dead in a sitting posture; decorating the corpse with wampum, the images of birds, quadrupeds, &c: And (if that of a warrior) with bows, arrows, tomhawks [*sic*], and other military weapons" [Freneau's note].
7. The Queen of Sheba, a powerful Arabian country, paid a visit in homage to Solomon (I Kings x; II Chronicles ix) and became legendary in literature for her beauty and wisdom.

The hunter still the deer pursues,   35
    The hunter and the deer, a shade!

And long shall timorous fancy see
    The painted chief, and pointed spear,
And Reason's self shall bow the knee
    To shadows and delusions here.   40

1787   1788

On a Honey Bee

DRINKING FROM A GLASS OF WINE AND DROWNED THEREIN[8]

Thou, born to sip the lake or spring,
    Or quaff the waters of the stream,
Why hither come, on vagrant wing?—
    Does Bacchus tempting seem—
        Did he for you this glass prepare?—   5
        Will I admit you to a share?

Did storms harass or foes perplex,
    Did wasps or king-birds bring dismay—
Did wars distress, or labors vex,
    Or did you miss your way?—   10
        A better seat you could not take
        Than on the margin of this lake.

Welcome!—I hail you to my glass:
    All welcome, here, you find;
Here, let the cloud of trouble pass,   15
    Here, be all care resigned.—
        This fluid never fails to please,
        And drown the griefs of men or bees.

What forced you here we cannot know,
    And you will scarcely tell—   20
But cheery we would have you go
    And bid a glad farewell:
        On lighter wings we bid you fly,
        Your dart will now all foes defy.

Yet take not, oh! too deep a drink,   25
    And in this ocean die;
Here bigger bees than you might sink,
    Even bees full six feet high.

8. Originally, "On a Bee Drinking from a Glass of Water" (*Time-Piece*, Sept. 6, 1797), this was twice revised, and reprinted with the present title in *Poems* (1809).

Like Pharaoh, then, you would be said
To perish in a sea of red.[1]   30

Do as you please, your will is mine;
   Enjoy it without fear—
And your grave will be this glass of wine,
   Your epitaph—a tear;
      Go, take your seat on Charon's[2] boat,   35
      We'll tell the hive, you died afloat.

1797, 1809

To a Caty-Did[3]

In a branch of willow hid
Sings the evening Caty-did:
From the lofty locust bough
Feeding on a drop of dew,
In her suit of green array'd   5
Hear her singing in the shade
   Caty-did, Caty-did, Caty-did!

While upon a leaf you tread,
Or repose your little head,
On your sheet of shadows laid,   10
All the day you nothing said:
Half the night your cheery tongue
Revell'd out its little song,
   Nothing else but Caty-did.

From your lodgings on the leaf   15
Did you utter joy or grief?—
Did you only mean to say,
I have had my summer's day,
And am passing, soon, away
To the grave of Caty-did:—   20
   Poor, unhappy Caty-did!

But you would have utter'd more
Had you known of nature's power—
From the world when you retreat,
And a leaf's your winding sheet,   25

1. Pharaoh, king of Egypt, attempting to pursue the Israelites across the Red Sea, lost his army by drowning (Exodus xiv: 1–27).
2. The ferryman of the dead.
3. "A well-known insect, when full grown, about two inches in length, and of the exact color of a green leaf. It is of the genus cicada, or grasshopper kind, inhabiting the green foliage of trees and singing such a song as Caty-did in the evening, towards autumn" [Freneau's note].

Long before your spirit fled,
Who can tell but nature said,
Live again, my Caty-did!
    Live and chatter, Caty-did.

Tell me, what did Caty do?   30
Did she mean to trouble you?—
Why was Caty not forbid
To trouble little Caty-did?—
Wrong, indeed at you to fling,
Hurting no one while you sing   35
    Caty-did! Caty-did! Caty-did!

Why continue to complain?
Caty tells me, she again
Will not give you plague or pain:—
Caty says you may be hid,   40
Caty will not go to bed
While you sing us Caty-did.
    Caty-did! Caty-did! Caty-did!

But, while singing, you forgot
To tell us what did Caty not: 45
Caty-did not think of cold,
Flocks retiring to the fold,
Winter, with his wrinkles old,
Winter, that yourself foretold
    When you gave us Caty-did.   50

Stay securely in your nest;
Caty now, will do her best,
All she can, to make you blest;
But, you want no human aid—
Nature, when she form'd you, said,   55
"Independent you are made,
My dear little Caty-did:
Soon yourself must disappear
With the verdure of the year,"—
And to go, we know not where,   60
    With your song of Caty-did.

1815

On the Universality and Other Attributes
of the God of Nature[4]

All that we see, about, abroad,
What is it all, but nature's God?
In meaner works discovered here
No less than in the starry sphere.

In seas, on earth, this God is seen;   5
All that exist, upon him lean;
He lives in all, and never strayed
A moment from the works he made:

His system fixed on general laws
Bespeaks a wise creating cause;   10
Impartially he rules mankind
And all that on this globe we find.

Unchanged in all that seems to change,
Unbounded space is his great range;
To one vast purpose always true,   15
No time, with him, is old or new.

In all the attributes divine
Unlimited perfectings shine;
In these enwrapt, in these complete,
All virtues in that centre meet.   20

This power doth all powers transcend,
To all intelligence a friend,
Exists, the greatest and the best[5]
Throughout all the worlds, to make them blest.

All that he did he first approved,   25
He all things into being loved;
O'er all he made he still presides,
For them in life, or death provides.

1815

4. Characteristic phrase of Deism, the rationalistic creed of Freneau now at sixty-three as in his youth. For Deism, see Franklin, Paine, and Jefferson, above.

5. *"Jupiter, optimus, maximus.*—Cicero" [Freneau's note]. The comparison of pagan and Christian concepts of God was characteristic of Deism; *Cf.* Paine, *The Age of Reason.*

The New Nation and the House Divided *

* This introduction should be read in conjunction with the Chronological Table beginning on page 1332.

The history of the United States from the beginning of the nineteenth century to the Civil War had almost an epical character. During the early years the new nation successfully defended itself against the sniping of three foreign enemies, while such American statesmen as Washington and Jefferson, Madison, and Monroe slowly won for their country the respect if not the affection of European powers. Within a half century, American pioneers had pushed across the forest and mountain barriers, the great rivers and deserts, to the shores of the Pacific, and northwest into Alaska. The power, imagination, and opportunity quickened by political freedom and nationalism were expressed in the development, more rapid than ever before seen, of government, trade, shipping, manufactures, agricultural wealth and an expanding system of roads and waterways. While the material genius of the country expressed itself luxuriantly, cultural institutions, already strong in the colonies, expanded rapidly; and such authors as Irving, Cooper, Hawthorne, Poe, Emerson, Longfellow, Melville, and Whitman forged a new literature, rich in native character and tradition, and recognized as American by the world at large. If American literature, like the European literature of the time, was romantic in character, it was not so by imitation, but by virtue of the abounding strangeness of this new continent, and the experience of a way of life in which, for a time, it seemed that the theoretical possibility of uninterrupted human progress might be concretely realized. And then, slowly revealed, the tragic flaw in the American state came into view, the widening, unhealing breach between the sections—and the appalling catastrophe of the Civil War rang down the curtain on an epoch.

REGIONAL INFLUENCES

The city of New York, which by 1800, with a population of sixty thousand, had become the largest city in the United States, was destined to be for several decades the literary capital, the city of the so-called Knickerbocker authors, who derived this label from Washington Irving's *Knickerbocker's History of New York* (1809). Prominent among the Knickerbockers were many writers now of only minor interest: such poets as Drake and Halleck, and such men of letters as Charles Fenno Hoffman, Paulding, Verplanck, and Willis. Irving was the only author of this immediate group to achieve high literary distinction, but two other great New York writers, Bryant and Cooper, shared to some degree the Knickerbocker spirit. This spirit was a large-minded, romantic acceptance of life, ranging from Bryant's serious religion of nature to Irving's fantasy and burlesque, and encouraging, especially among its essayists, a worldly sophistication and witty gaiety. The New York theater flourished, and in the development of newspaper journalism the city soon led the nation.

Philadelphia, which had been called "the Athens of America" during the late colonial period, continued to produce literary works, but few of its writers rose to prominence, and many of the more talented found their way to New York, as they have been doing ever since. Philadelphia continued as the center of a new popular periodical literature, represented by *Godey's* and *Graham's*; it long remained an incubating ground for liberal ideas and humanitarian reform; and it maintained leadership in the development of science and technology. Meanwhile, the South built a flourishing agrarian civilization and a distinguished planter-aristocracy on the shaky foundations of slavery, while expending a great deal of its energy, and much of its traditional genius for statesmanship, in defending that doomed institution. At Richmond, and more importantly at Charleston, there developed small coteries of writers, but none were of national prominence except Poe and the Charlestonian William Gilmore Simms. The latter was greatly praised and widely popular, but today few beside the literary specialist are acquainted with his faintly Byronic poetry, or with his many novels of frontier adventure. Cooper has outlived this later rival because of his true sense of history and his creation of a few living characters.

In this first period of our national literature, however, the most spectacular development was the movement generally known as the "renaissance" of New England. It began in a new intellectualism, Unitarian and transcendental, which was crowned by the appearance of the works of Emerson in the late thirties, and by the later masterpieces of Thoreau. New England contributed vitally to the reform movements, especially abolition; it produced, in such figures as Hawthorne, Longfellow, Holmes, and Lowell, creators of a literature which combined a high democratic idealism with a patrician intellectual leadership.

ROMANTICISM

The remarkable and opulent literature which developed in various regions is best explained by reference to certain stirring events of our national history, infused by the surging romanticism which had its sources both at home and abroad. Romanticism is not an organized system, but rather a particular attitude toward the realities of man, nature, and society. From the middle of the eighteenth century, the romantic spirit gradually strengthened, especially in Germany, France, and England; in English literature it flourished earlier than in America, particularly among such writers as Burns, Wordsworth, Coleridge, Shelley, Keats, and Byron. In reaction against the neoclassical spirit, the romantic preferred freedom to formalism and emphasized individualism instead of authority. He exalted the imagination above either rationalism or strict fidelity to factual delineation. He rejected the validity of material reality in favor of innate or intuitive perception by the heart of man: *"intimations* of immortality" were taken to *prove* immortality. In consequence, the romantic gave faith and credence to ideality and elevation—to a reality that was considered more lofty, and truer, than the evidence of substantial things. Romantic reliance upon the importance of the subconscious, inner life was illustrated in Emerson's intuitionalism, and also produced a profound interest in abnormal psychology, shown, for instance, by Poe and Hawthorne.

Yet in its view of nature, the romantic movement was essentially simple, as compared with that of rationalism: its universe was beautiful, and man was the chosen and favored creature in it, as in the nature poems of Wordsworth, Bryant, or Longfellow. In another manifestation, romanticism reveled in strangeness and mystery, producing in one direction the medievalism of Keats and Lowell, and in another the fantastic visions of Coleridge or Poe.

One impulse of romanticism was humanitarian; it romanticized the "common man"; it produced an age of reform movements; it developed a lavish enthusiasm for the primitive—for ancient ballads, epics, and folk literature, and for the "noble savage," usually in the idealization of the American Indian. In some manifestations, especially in America, it reveled in broad forms of humor and burlesque. In every country, romanticism produced a luxuriant new literature, with wide variations among authors, but everywhere certain characteristics persisted: opulence and freedom, devotion to individualism, a reliance upon the good of nature and "natural" man, and an abiding faith in the boundless resources of the human spirit and imagination.

Basically, the romantic spirit is rebellious; it thrives in turbulent times, in revolution and conflict; it encourages an optimistic expectation of improvement. These conditions of romanticism had been present in the American and French revolutions. The later period, which produced such American romantics as Bryant, Irving, and Cooper, was also a time of hopeful challenge. During the youth of this generation, the young republic asserted its independence over and over again: in two diplomatic victories over the French, in leading the world against the Barbary pirates, in resisting British pretensions by war in 1812; and finally, in announcing its western hegemony by the Monroe Doctrine of 1823. Internally an even more astonishing accomplishment extended the American dominion from the Northwest Territory to Oregon, from Louisiana to the Rockies and (by means of the Mexican War in 1848), through the southwest from Texas to California. For such romantics as Bryant, Irving, Cooper, and their lesser emulators this expansion was a contagious influence, and these frontiers were an invitation to adventure, strongly reflected in their writings.

However, a number of our most powerful romantic authors had been brooding upon problems for which optimism and expansion provided no answers. In Poe and Hawthorne the spiritual questioning of romanticism found its first great American representatives. In their chief works they sought the reality of man in the hidden recesses of the mind and the spirit, and probed these obscure sources of behavior and moral judgment. Poe, like Keats and Coleridge, embodied his revelations in aesthetic symbolism, except in his tales of detection and science—a form of narrative that he invented. By contrast, Hawthorne, equipped with a penetrating sense of history, found his symbolism in man's conflict with the vestiges of the past, indelibly fixed in his moral nature and his social environment. Before Poe and Hawthorne, symbolic litera-

ture had appeared in America only in the expression of the rapt visions of early religious mystics, such as Edwards and Woolman; now Poe especially carried symbolic idealism to a level so advanced that he became the inspiration for certain of the French symbolists, and hence a strong influence on the literary expression of the twentieth century. Melville, another great original, stands closer to the tradition of Hawthorne than to any other. Like Hawthorne, he was obsessed by the enigma of evil, but while the New Englander prevailingly took the Puritan morality as a point of departure, Melville drew symbols from land and sea for his explorations into the shadowed heart of the universe.

THE SPIRIT OF REFORM
Early in the nineteenth century the new republic began to experience the social disorders inevitably attendant upon its unprecedented expansion in territory, population, and industrial activity. American writers responded with a swelling tide of literature devoted to humanitarian reform movements. During the thirty years before the Civil War the population of the United States increased from thirteen to thirty million white Americans. Although nearly half of the nation's population had pushed beyond the Alleghenies by 1830, there were already at that time increasing concentrations in eastern urban and industrial centers, where recent immigrants accounted for about 12 per cent of the nation. The remarkable development of industry and financial institutions

was accompanied by economic crises and a kind of poverty that the younger agrarian nation had not known. Even the frontier, for all its glamor, adventure, and homestead land, was the scene of back-breaking labor, and of stringently limited educational and cultural opportunity. The election in 1800 of Jefferson, a patrician who trusted the people, has been regarded as breaking the ruling authority of "the rich, the well-born, and the able," and in 1828 the frontier elected its own popular hero, Andrew Jackson, with a direct mandate from the common people. The increasing determination of these masses to be heard in the national government remained a powerful influence against the entrenchment of monopoly and privilege. For these masses Negro slavery was an intolerable threat against the enterprise of free men; and the spirit of the frontier, no less than the moral abhorrence which impelled the North, was influential in precipitating the Civil War.

Respect for the common man and a belief in his capacities was a romantic assumption honored by writers on every hand. Bryant, as a great metropolitan editor, espoused human and civil rights, supported the nascent labor movement and many other reforms, and steadily opposed the extension of slavery. Hawthorne and Melville continued to regard the improvement of society as indispensable for the spirit of mankind. The transcendentalists in general resembled Thoreau rather than Emerson in their active and often rebellious participation in support of various reforms, and especially abolition. Fundamentally, if in varying measure, the reform spirit infused the writing of such New England Brahmins as Longfellow, Lowell, and even Holmes, while Whittier, a man of the people, spent himself, and perhaps mortgaged his artistic potential, in humanitarian causes. New reform movements and organizations flourished, and reform became a profession attracting talented and powerful leadership. Well-directed groups joined forces with British reformers to improve the standards of criminology, to abolish inhuman punishments and imprisonment for debt, to clean up the loathsome jails and provide rehabilitation instead of punishment. Societies for aid to the physically handicapped bore fruit in schools for the deaf and the blind, and asylums for the insane—Dorothea Dix added this interest to her earlier crusade for prison reform.

The American Temperance Society was founded in 1826, and many lecturers, some as prominent as Channing, Beecher, and Garrison, drew large audiences, while local church communities organized auxiliaries of pledge-signers. The women's rights movement drew such strong leaders as Margaret Fuller, journalist of transcendentalism, Elizabeth Cady Stanton, and Lucretia Mott. In 1848, the movement rose to the national scale with the meeting of the first women's congress at Seneca Falls, New York. Women crusaded for equality with men in educational opportunities and employment, in marriage and property ownership; and they were a vigorous auxiliary to the temperance movement and to the campaigns for factory reforms affecting women and child workers, especially in the New England cotton mills.

TRANSCENDENTALISM

The many important modifications in religious doctrine and in sectarian organizations, especially among Protestant denominations, were of importance for literature principally in New England, where a strong intellectualist mysticism among Unitarian thinkers stimulated the transcendental movement. Even so, Unitarianism and transcendentalism became a concern of our major literature only because of the great stature of Emerson and Thoreau. All other transcendental writers, for example, Bronson Alcott, Margaret Fuller, the Channings, and Orestes Brownson, were at most of secondary importance.

Yet for the history of ideas in the United States, transcendentalism wrote an important chapter. It was the expression for one age of an intuitional idealism which has taken various forms in American thought as a countercurrent to rationalistic and authoritarian orthodoxies from early times; whether among dissenters from Puritanism, or Puritan and Quaker mystics, or, as late as 1897, in William James's hypothesis of a "Will to Believe."

Transcendentalism was a philosophical dissent from Unitarianism, which represented the compromise of rational Deism with Calvinism, retaining the rationalists' acceptance of liberal scientific thought, and rejecting extreme concepts concerning the original depravity and the inherited guilt of man. In Unitarianism the Godhead was conceived as Unity, not Trinity; it was the human potential in the acts and words of Jesus that gave them sublime importance; and the Holy Ghost was the divine spark in every man. The rising young transcendentalists asserted that the Unitarian creed had become conventional and complacent in its orthodox fidelity to Christian dogmas of supernaturalism. Transcendentalists rejected Locke's materialistic psychology in favor of the idealism of the German thinker Immanuel Kant (*The Critique of Pure Reason*, 1781), who declared that the "transcendental" knowledge in the mind of man was innate, or *a priori*; the transcendentalists interpreted this view as supporting the belief that intuition surpassed reason as a guide to the truth. Thus they evolved a theological monism, in which the divine immanence of God coexisted with the universe and the individual; they asserted the doctrine of correspondence between the microcosm of the individual mind and the macrocosmic Oversoul of the universe; and hence they derived an enlarged conception of the sanctity of the individual and his freedom to follow his intuitional knowledge.

American transcendentalists were influenced by such British writers as Wordsworth, Coleridge, and Carlyle; they drew on such German idealistic philosophers as Kant, Hegel, Fichte, and Schelling, and on the writings of Goethe, Richter, Herder, and others; they sought confirmation among the ancients: the Greek philosophers, especially Plato, the Neoplatonists, and the Hindu wisdom of the age-old Vedas. They read the Christian mystics from the Middle Ages to Swedenborg.

The Transcendental Club, an informal group, met oftenest at Emerson's Concord home, and its members were chiefly responsible for *The Dial* (1840–1844), the famous little magazine that Emerson edited for two of its four years. One group of transcendentalists concerned themselves with reform movements and social revolt; Thoreau is the most noteworthy of these in respect to literary values. Brook Farm (1841) and Fruitlands (1842) were agrarian experiments in communal living supported briefly by transcendentalists concerned with the social order.

INEVITABLE CONFLICT

From colonial days, antislavery leaders had preached gradual emancipation; but in 1831, a group led by William Lloyd Garrison, editor of the newly founded abolition magazine, *The Liberator*, had formed the militant New England Anti-Slavery Society. Two years later, all such organizations met together in Philadelphia to found the American Anti-Slavery Society. Among the many who attended was Whittier, who thereafter gave the bulk of his limited strength to the cause. The crusade for abolition was carried on in press and pulpit, and on the lecture platform. The succeeding events are too well-known to require formal discussion.

When the Mexican War threatened, Lowell abandoned the dream world of *Sir Launfal* and lighted the caustic flame of the *Biglow Papers*. Longfellow's "Building of the Ship," like Whittier's "Ichabod," reveals the varied emotional reactions of the period. Thoreau's resistance to the Mexican War involved an act of civil disobedience, and he then published the famous essay of that title, initiating a philosophy of pacific resistance. Upon the enactment of the strengthened Fugitive Slave Law of 1850, even the pacifistic Emerson wrote firmly in his *Journal*, "I will not obey it, by God." Act by act, as the following texts reveal, our literature reflects the later events of the drama: the Kansas-Nebraska Bill, the Kansas insurrections, John Brown's life and death, the Lincoln-Douglas debates, the disruption of the Democrats, the new Republican party, the election of Lincoln, and the war itself.

Romantic Rediscovery: Nature, Man, Society

WASHINGTON IRVING
(1783–1859)

As a writer, Washington Irving was so naturally endowed that he seemed to drift into his career at the whim of circumstances and his own inclinations. Humorists are always likely to be taken for granted, and there has been no searching revaluation of Irving such as should have been provoked by the perceptive biography by Stanley T. Williams (1935). Actually, with Poe and Hawthorne, Irving has survived all other American writers of fiction before Melville, and he still finds new readers with every passing generation. He was the first great prose stylist of American romanticism, and his familiar style was destined to outlive the formal prose of such contemporaries as Scott and Cooper, and to provide a model for the prevailing prose narrative of the future.

The apparent ease of his writing is not simply that of the gifted amateur; it results from his purposeful identification of his whole personality with what he wrote. He was urbane and worldly, yet humorous and gentle; a robust connoisseur, yet innately reserved; a patrician, yet sympathetic toward the people. His vast reading, following only the impulse of his own enthusiasms, resulted in a rich if random literary inheritance, revealed in all that he wrote. His response to the period of Addison, Swift, and Johnson, with its great and graceful style, and his enthusiasm for the current European romanticism, enabled him to combine these with his independent literary personality and American roots.

It is instructive to consider the number of his literary innovations. He was our first great belletrist, writing always for pleasure, and to produce pleasure; yet readers of all classes responded to him in a country in which the didactic and utilitarian had formerly prevailed. He gave an impetus both to the extravagant American humor of which Mark Twain became the classic, and to the urbane wit that has survived in writers rang-

323

ing from Holmes and Lowell to the *New Yorker* wits of the present century. In his *Sketch Book* appeared the first modern short stories and the first great American juvenile literature. He was among the first of the moderns to write good history and biography as literary entertainment. He introduced the familiar essay to America. On his own whimsical terms, Irving restored the waning Gothic romances which Poe soon infused with psychological subtleties. The scope of his life and his writing was international, and produced a certain breadth of view in his readers; yet his best-known stories awakened an interest in the life of American regions from the Hudson valley to the prairies of the West. His influence abroad, as writer, as visitor, and as diplomat, was that of a gifted cultural ambassador, at home on both continents, at a time when his young country badly needed such representation. He was the only American writer of his generation who could chide the British in an atmosphere of good humor.

The events of Irving's life are characterized by the same casual approach and distinguished results. Gently born and well educated, the youngest of eleven children of a prosperous New York merchant, he began a genteel reading for the law at sixteen, but preferred a literary Bohemianism. At nineteen he published, in his brother's newspaper, his "Jonathan Oldstyle" satires of New York life. By the age of twenty-three, when he was admitted to the New York bar,

he had roamed the Hudson valley and been a literary vagabond in England, Holland, France, and Italy, reading and studying what pleased him, which was a great deal, and reveling in the gay world of the theater. Back in New York, he joined with his brother, William, and James Kirke Paulding, in 1807, in producing the *Salmagundi* papers, Addisonian commentaries on New York society and frivolities. A *History of New York, by Diedrich Knickerbocker* (1809), a rollicking burlesque of a current serious history of the early Dutch settlers, has become a classic of humor, and might have launched an immediate career for its author.

A personal tragedy, however, changed his course for a time; the death of his fiancée, Matilda Hoffman, coincided with the demands of the family cutlery firm, and in 1810 he went to Washington as representative of the business. In 1815 he again turned restlessly to his European roving, with headquarters in England during the next seventeen years, but his literary career was soon to catch up with him again. In 1818 the failure of the Irving firm, which had bountifully supported his leisure, threw family responsibilities upon him, and he loyally plunged into the authorship for which he had almost unconsciously prepared himself. The *Sketch Book* appeared serially in 1819–1820, and in volume form shortly thereafter it at once had an international success. *Bracebridge Hall* followed in 1822; then he first went to Germany in pursuit of an interest in German romanticism, which flavored the *Tales of a Traveller* (1824) and other later writings. Meanwhile in Paris he had met John Howard Payne, the American dramatist and actor; his collaboration with him resulted brilliantly in *Charles the Second; or The Merry Monarch*, one of the most successful social comedies of its time.

From 1826 to 1829 he was in Spain on diplomatic business, residing for a time in the Alhambra. His reading at that period, including the study of Spanish historical sources, resulted in a number of important works: *A History of the Life and Voyages of Christopher Columbus* (1828), *A Chronicle of the Conquest of Granada* (1829), *Voyages and Discoveries of the Companions of Columbus* (1831), a famous volume of stories and sketches—*The Alhambra* (1832), and "Legends of the Conquest of Spain" (in *The Crayon Miscellany*, 1835).

Before *The Alhambra* appeared, he was on his way back to the United States after two years as secretary of the American legation in London (1829–1831). American reviewers had commented, often with irritation, on his seeming preference for Europe, but the charges were exaggerated. After seventeen years abroad he returned with the desire to portray his own country again, and although such western adventures as *A Tour of the Prairies* (1835), *Astoria* (a novel on Astor's fur trade, 1836), and

The Adventures of Captain Bonneville (explorations in the Rocky Mountains, 1837), are not among his best work, they broke new trails in our literature. In 1836 he made his home at Sunnyside, near Tarrytown, so lovingly described years before as "Sleepy Hollow." He had already declined a nomination to Congress; now he declined to run for mayor of New York, or to become Van Buren's secretary of the navy. Instead he wrote a good *Life of Oliver Goldsmith* (1840), and began the *Life of George Washington* (published 1855–1859), long a standard work. From 1842 to 1845 he served as minister to Spain, then settled at Sunnyside, which he remodeled and enlarged, while preparing the revised edition of his works, and completing his *Washington*. The fifth and last volume of the latter appeared just before his death in 1859.

The standard edition of Irving's work is *The Works of Washington Irving*, Author's Uniform Revised Edition, 21 vols., 1860–1861, reissued in 12 vols., 1881, the source of the texts here reprinted. *The Journals of Washington Irving*, 3 vols., 1919, were edited by W. P. Trent and G. S. Hellman, and a number of volumes of the letters have been published. Several later editions of Irving's works, and editions of individual volumes, are easily available; note especially *Knickerbocker's History of New York*, edited by Stanley T. Williams and Tremaine McDowell, 1927. *Washington Irving: Representative Selections*, edited by Henry A. Pochmann, American Writers Series, 1934, has a useful introduction and bibliography.

Pierre M. Irving published the first standard *Life and Letters * * * *, 4 vols., 1862–1864; other good lives are those by Charles Dudley Warner, 1890, and G. S. Hellman, 1925. However, the definitive biographical and critical study is that by Stanley T. Williams: *The Life of Washington Irving*, 2 vols., 1935.

From A History of New York, by Diedrich Knickerbocker[1]

Book III: In Which Is Recorded the Golden Reign of Wouter Van Twiller

CHAPTER I: OF THE RENOWNED WOUTER VAN TWILLER,[2] HIS UNPARALLELED VIRTUES—AS LIKEWISE HIS UNUTTERABLE WISDOM IN THE LAW CASE OF WANDLE SCHOONHOVEN AND BARENT BLEECKER—AND THE GREAT ADMIRATION OF THE PUBLIC THEREAT

Grievous and very much to be commiserated is the task of the feeling historian, who writes the history of his native land. If it fall to his lot to be the recorder of calamity or crime, the mournful page is watered with his tears—nor can he recall the most prosperous and blissful era, without a melancholy sigh at the reflection, that it has passed away for ever! I know not whether it be owing to an immoderate love for the simplicity of former times, or to that certain tenderness of heart incident to all sentimental historians; but I candidly confess that I cannot look back on the happier days of our city, which I now describe, without great dejection of spirit. With faltering hand do I withdraw the curtain of oblivion, that veils the modest merit of our venerable ancestors, and as their figures rise to my mental vision, humble myself before their mighty shades.

Such are my feelings when I revisit the family mansion of the Knickerbockers, and spend a lonely hour in the chamber where hang the portraits of my forefathers, shrouded in dust, like the forms they represent. With pious reverence do I gaze on the countenances of those renowned burghers, who have preceded me in the steady march of existence—whose sober and temperate blood now meanders through my veins, flowing slower and slower in its feeble conduits, until its current shall soon be stopped for ever!

These, I say to myself, are but frail memorials of the mighty men who flourished in the days of the patriarchs; but who, alas, have long since mouldered in that tomb, towards which my steps are insensibly

1. Published on December 6, 1809, simultaneously in Philadelphia, New York, Boston, Baltimore, and Charleston, this work was conceived as a parody of a serious history—Samuel Mitchell's *Picture of New York* (1807). But the element of parody was almost lost in the gusty independence of Irving's burlesque, a classic of humorous literature. In the comic treatment of the early Dutch governors there are satirical resemblances to the persons and policies of American leaders—especially John Adams, Jefferson, and Madison. (See the verbatim reprint of 1809 text, with notes by Stanley T. Williams and Tremaine McDowell, 1927; and the Notes, pp. 379–383, in

Pochmann's *Washington Irving: Representative Selections*, 1934.) In several revisions Irving refined the broadest extravagances of the first text. His last edition (1848) is followed here. The work is in eight books. The first two, ridiculing pedantry and solemnity in historical writing, are a burlesque history of the world from the Creation to the establishment of New Amsterdam. The subsequent books deal with governors Wouter Van Twiller (in the section here given in part), William the Testy, and Peter Stuyvesant "the Headstrong."
2. Wouter Van Twiller (1580?–1656), Dutch governor of New Netherland, 1633–1637.

and irresistibly hastening! As I pace the darkened chamber and lose myself in melancholy musings, the shadowy images around me almost seem to steal once more into existence—their countenances to assume the animation of life—their eyes to pursue me in every movement! Carried away by the delusions of fancy, I almost imagine myself surrounded by the shades of the departed, and holding sweet converse with the worthies of antiquity! Ah, hapless Diedrich! born in a degenerate age, abandoned to the buffetings of fortune—a stranger and a weary pilgrim in thy native land—blest with no weeping wife, nor family of helpless children; but doomed to wander neglected through those crowded streets, and elbowed by foreign upstarts from those fair abodes where once thine ancestors held sovereign empire!

Let me not, however, lose the historian in the man, nor suffer the doting recollections of age to overcome me, while dwelling with fond garrulity on the virtuous days of the patriarchs—on those sweet days of simplicity and ease, which never more will dawn on the lovely island of Manna-hata.[3]

These melancholy reflections have been forced from me by the growing wealth and importance of New Amsterdam, which, I plainly perceive, are to involve it in all kinds of perils and disasters. Already, as I observed at the close of my last book, they had awakened the attentions of the mother country. The usual mark of protection shown by mother countries to wealthy colonies was forthwith manifested; a governor being sent out to rule over the province and squeeze out of it as much revenue as possible. The arrival of a governor of course put an end to the protectorate of Oloffe the Dreamer.[4] He appears, however, to have dreamt to some purpose during his sway, as we find him afterwards living as a patroon on a great landed estate on the banks of the Hudson; having virtually forfeited all right to his ancient appellation of Kortlandt or Lackland.[5]

It was in the year of our Lord 1629[6] that Mynheer Wouter Van Twiller was appointed governor of the province of Nieuw Nederlandts, under the commission and control of their High Mightinesses the Lords States General of the United Netherlands, and the privileged West India Company.

This renowned old gentleman arrived at New Amsterdam in the merry month of June, the sweetest month in all the year; when Dan Apollo seems to dance up the transparent firmament—when the robin, the thrush, and a thousand other wanton songsters make the

3. Whitman also substituted for "Manhattan" this Indian form, meaning "the place of God," but in Irving's burlesque etymology, the meaning, previously given, is "the place of the jolly toper."
4. Oloff Stevenszen Van Cortlandt (1600–1684), whom Irving ridiculed in an earlier passage, actually was a prominent merchant and mayor (*cf.* Van Cortlandt Park and Street).
5. Irving had already translated the name as "short-of-land."
6. Actually 1633. Van Twiller was not, as Irving suggests, the first governor.

woods to resound with amorous ditties, and the luxurious little boblincon revels among the clover blossoms of the meadows—all which happy coincidence persuaded the old dames of New Amsterdam, who were skilled in the art of foretelling events, that this was to be a happy and prosperous administration.

The renowned Wouter (or Walter) Van Twiller, was descended from a long line of Dutch burgomasters, who had successively dozed away their lives, and grown fat upon the bench of magistracy in Rotterdam; and who had comported themselves with such singular wisdom and propriety, that they were never either heard or talked of— which, next to being universally applauded, should be the object of ambition of all magistrates and rulers. There are two opposite ways by which some men make a figure in the world; one by talking faster than they think; and the other by holding their tongues and not thinking at all. By the first, many a smatterer acquires the reputation of a man of quick parts; by the other, many a dunderpate, like the owl, the stupidest of birds, comes to be considered the very type of wisdom. This, by the way, is a casual remark, which I would not, for the universe, have it thought I apply to Governor Van Twiller. It is true he was a man shut up within himself, like an oyster, and rarely spoke except in monosyllables; but then it was allowed he seldom said a foolish thing. So invincible was his gravity that he was never known to laugh or even to smile through the whole course of a long and prosperous life. Nay if a joke were uttered in his presence, that set light minded hearers in a roar, it was observed to throw him into a state of perplexity. Sometimes he would deign to inquire into the matter, and when, after much explanation, the joke was made as plain as a pike-staff, he would continue to smoke his pipe in silence, and at length, knocking out the ashes would exclaim, "Well! I see nothing in all that to laugh about."

With all his reflective habits, he never made up his mind on a subject. His adherents accounted for this by the astonishing magnitude of his ideas. He conceived every subject on so grand a scale that he had not room in his head to turn it over and examine both sides of it. Certain it is that if any matter were propounded to him on which ordinary mortals would rashly determine at first glance, he would put on a vague, mysterious look; shake his capacious head; smoke some time in profound silence, and at length observe that "he had his doubts about the matter"; which gained him the reputation of a man slow of belief and not easily imposed upon. What is more, it gained him a lasting name: for to this habit of the mind has been attributed his surname of Twiller; which is said to be a corruption of the original Twijfler, or, in plain English, *Doubter*.

The person of this illustrious old gentleman was formed and proportioned, as though it had been moulded by the hands of some cunning Dutch statuary,[7] as a model of majesty and lordly grandeur. He was exactly five feet six inches in height, and six feet five inches in circumference. His head was a perfect sphere, and of such stupendous dimensions, that dame Nature, with all her sex's ingenuity, would have been puzzled to construct a neck capable of supporting it; wherefore she wisely declined the attempt, and settled it firmly on the top of his back bone, just between the shoulders. His body was oblong and particularly capacious at bottom; which was wisely ordered by Providence, seeing that he was a man of sedentary habits, and very averse to the idle labor of walking. His legs were short, but sturdy in proportion to the weight they had to sustain; so that when erect he had not a little the appearance of a beer barrel on skids. His face, that infallible index of the mind, presented a vast expanse, unfurrowed by any of those lines and angles which disfigure the human countenance with what is termed expression. Two small grey eyes twinkled feebly in the midst, like two stars of lesser magnitude in a hazy firmament; and his full-fed cheeks, which seemed to have taken toll of every thing that went into his mouth, were curiously mottled and streaked with dusky red, like a spitzenberg apple.

His habits were as regular as his person. He daily took his four stated meals, appropriating exactly an hour to each; he smoked and doubted eight hours, and he slept the remaining twelve of the four and twenty. Such was the renowned Wouter Van Twiller—a true philosopher, for his mind was either elevated above, or tranquilly settled below, the cares and perplexities of this world. He had lived in it for years, without feeling the least curiosity to know whether the sun revolved round it, or it round the sun; and he had watched, for at least half a century, the smoke curling from his pipe to the ceiling, without once troubling his head with any of those numerous theories, by which a philosopher would have perplexed his brain, in accounting for its rising above the surrounding atmosphere.

In his council he presided with great state and solemnity. He sat in a huge chair of solid oak, hewn in the celebrated forest of the Hague, fabricated by an experienced timmerman[8] of Amsterdam, and curiously carved about the arms and feet, into exact imitations of gigantic eagle's claws. Instead of a sceptre he swayed a long Turkish pipe, wrought with jasmin and amber, which had been presented to a stadtholder[9] of Holland, at the conclusion of a treaty with one of the petty Barbary powers.[1] In this stately chair would he sit, and this magnificent pipe would he smoke, shaking his right knee with a constant motion, and fixing his eye for hours together upon a little print of Amsterdam, which hung in a black frame against the oppo-

---

7. Then meaning "sculptor."
8. Dutch, "cabinetmaker."
9. Dutch, "governor."

1. The Barbary States of North Africa, whose centuries of piracy on Christian shipping Jefferson had just quelled in expeditions, 1801–1805.

site wall of the council chamber. Nay, it has even been said, that when any deliberation of extraordinary length and intricacy was on the carpet, the renowned Wouter would shut his eyes for full two hours at a time, that he might not be disturbed by external objects —and at such times the internal commotion of his mind was evinced by certain regular guttural sounds, which his admirers declared were merely the noise of conflict, made by his contending doubts and opinions.

It is with infinite difficulty I have been enabled to collect these biographical anecdotes of the great man under consideration. The facts respecting him were so scattered and vague, and divers of them so questionable in point of authenticity, that I have had to give up the search after many, and decline the admission of still more, which would have tended to heighten the coloring of his portrait.

I have been the more anxious to delineate fully the person and habits of Wouter Van Twiller, from the consideration that he was not only the first, but also the best governor that ever presided over this ancient and respectable province; and so tranquil and benevolent was his reign, that I do not find throughout the whole of it, a single instance of any offender being brought to punishment—a most indubitable sign of a merciful governor, and a case unparalleled, excepting in the reign of the illustrious King Log,[2] from whom, it is hinted, the renowned Van Twiller was a lineal descendant.

The very outset of the career of this excellent magistrate was distinguished by an example of legal acumen, that gave flattering presage of a wise and equitable administration. The morning after he had been installed in office, and at the moment that he was making his breakfast from a prodigious earthen dish, filled with milk and Indian pudding, he was interrupted by the appearance of Wandle Schoonhoven, a very important old burgher of New Amsterdam, who complained bitterly of one Barent Bleecker,[3] inasmuch as he refused to come to a settlement of accounts, seeing that there was a heavy balance in favor of the said Wandle. Governor Van Twiller, as I have already observed, was a man of few words; he was likewise a mortal enemy to multiplying writings—or being disturbed at his breakfast. Having listened attentively to the statement of Wandle Schoonhoven, giving an occasional grunt, as he shovelled a spoonful of Indian pudding[4] into his mouth—either as a sign that he relished the dish, or comprehended the story—he called unto him his constable, and pulling out of his breeches pocket a huge jack-knife, dispatched it after the defendant as a summons, accompanied by his tobacco-box

2. See "The Frogs Desiring a King," in *Aesop's Fables*. The gods appointed a log, which served them silently; they grew dissatisfied, and were sent a stork, which ate them.

3. Two familiar family names in New Amsterdam, the latter surviving in Bleecker Street, New York.
4. Usually a corn-meal mush, or hasty pudding.

as a warrant.

This summary process was as effectual in those simple days as was the seal ring of the great Haroun Alraschid[5] among the true believers. The two parties being confronted before him, each produced a book of accounts, written in a language and character that would have puzzled any but a High Dutch commentator, or a learned decipherer of Egyptian obelisks. The sage Wouter took them one after the other, and having poised them in his hands, and attentively counted over the number of leaves, fell straightway into a very great doubt, and smoked for half an hour without saying a word; at length, laying his finger beside his nose, and shutting his eyes for a moment, with the air of a man who has just caught a subtle idea by the tail, he slowly took his pipe from his mouth, puffed forth a column of tobacco smoke, and with marvellous gravity and solemnity pronounced—that having carefully counted over the leaves and weighed the books, it was found, that one was just as thick and as heavy as the other—therefore it was the final opinion of the court that the accounts were equally balanced—therefore Wandle should give Barent a receipt, and Barent should give Wandle a receipt—and the constable should pay the costs.

This decision being straightway made known, diffused general joy throughout New Amsterdam, for the people immediately perceived, that they had a very wise and equitable magistrate to rule over them. But its happiest effect was, that not another lawsuit took place throughout the whole of his administration—and the office of constable fell into such decay, that there was not one of those losel[6] scouts known in the province for many years. I am the more particular in dwelling on this transaction, not only because I deem it one of the most sage and righteous judgments on record, and well worthy the attention of modern magistrates; but because it was a miraculous event in the history of the renowned Wouter—being the only time he was ever known to come to a decision in the whole course of his life.

CHAPTER IV: CONTAINING FURTHER PARTICULARS OF THE GOLDEN AGE, AND WHAT CONSTITUTED A FINE LADY AND GENTLEMAN IN THE DAYS OF WALTER THE DOUBTER

In this dulcet period of my history, when the beauteous island of Manna-hata presented a scene, the very counterpart of those glowing pictures drawn of the golden reign of Saturn,[7] there was, as I have before observed, a happy ignorance, an honest simplicity preva-

5. Harun al-Rashid (764?–809), most famous Caliph of Baghdad, immortalized in the legendary *Arabian Nights*.
6. Worthless.

7. Roman mythology deified Saturn, fabled as king of an aboriginal "golden age," and as god of the seed-sowing; hence there is a double analogy with the epoch of Van Twiller.

lent among its inhabitants, which, were I even able to depict, would be but little understood by the degenerate age for which I am doomed to write. Even the female sex, those arch innovators upon the tranquillity, the honesty, and gray-beard customs of society, seemed for a while to conduct themselves with incredible sobriety and comeliness.

Their hair, untortured by the abominations of art, was scrupulously pomatumed back from their foreheads with a candle, and covered with a little cap of quilted calico, which fitted exactly to their heads. Their petticoats of linsey-woolsey were striped with a variety of gorgeous dyes—though I must confess these gallant garments were rather short, scarce reaching below the knee; but then they made up in the number, which generally equalled that of the gentleman's small clothes; and what is still more praiseworthy, they were all of their own manufacture—of which circumstance, as may well be supposed, they were not a little vain.

These were the honest days in which every woman staid at home, read the Bible, and wore pockets—ay, and that too of a goodly size, fashioned with patchwork into many curious devices, and ostentatiously worn on the outside. These, in fact, were convenient receptacles, where all good housewives carefully stored away such things as they wished to have at hand; by which means they often came to be incredibly crammed—and I remember there was a story current when I was a boy that the Lady of Wouter Van Twiller once had occasion to empty her right pocket in search of a wooden ladle, when the contents filled a couple of corn baskets, and the utensil was discovered lying among some rubbish in one corner—but we must not give too much faith to all these stories; the anecdotes of those remote periods being very subject to exaggeration.

Besides these notable pockets, they likewise wore scissors and pincushions suspended from their girdles by red ribands, or among the more opulent and showy classes, by brass, and even silver chains—indubitable tokens of thrifty housewives and industrious spinsters. I cannot say much in vindication of the shortness of the petticoats; it doubtless was introduced for the purpose of giving the stockings a chance to be seen, which were generally of blue worsted with magnificent red clocks—or perhaps to display a well-turned ankle, and a neat, though serviceable foot, set off by a high-heeled leathern shoe, with a large and splendid silver buckle. Thus we find that the gentle sex in all ages have shown the same disposition to infringe a little upon the laws of decorum, in order to betray a lurking beauty, or gratify an innocent love of finery.

From the sketch here given, it will be seen that our good grandmothers differed considerably in their ideas of a fine figure from their scantily dressed descendants of the present day. A fine lady, in those times, waddled under more clothes, even on a fair summer's day, than would have clad the whole bevy of a modern ball-room. Nor were they the less admired by the gentlemen in consequence thereof. On the contrary, the greatness of a lover's passion seemed to increase in proportion to the magnitude of its object—and a voluminous damsel arrayed in a dozen of petticoats, was declared by a Low Dutch[8] sonneteer of the province to be radiant as a sunflower, and luxuriant as a full-blown cabbage. Certain it is, that in those days the heart of a lover could not contain more than one lady at a time; whereas the heart of a modern gallant has often room enough to accommodate half a dozen. The reason of which I conclude to be, that either the hearts of the gentlemen have grown larger, or the persons of the ladies smaller—this, however, is a question for physiologists to determine.

But there was a secret charm in these petticoats, which, no doubt, entered into the consideration of the prudent gallants. The wardrobe of a lady was in those days her only fortune; and she who had a good stock of petticoats and stockings, was as absolutely an heiress as is a Kamschatka[9] damsel with a store of bearskins, or a Lapland belle with a plenty of reindeer. The ladies, therefore, were very anxious to display these powerful attractions to the greatest advantage; and the best rooms in the house, instead of being adorned with caricatures of dame Nature, in water colors and needle work, were always hung round with abundance of homespun garments, the manufacture and the property of the females—a piece of laudable ostentation that still prevails among the heiresses of our Dutch villages.

The gentlemen, in fact, who figured in the circles of the gay world in these ancient times, corresponded, in most particulars, with the beauteous damsels whose smiles they were ambitious to deserve. True it is, their merits would make but a very inconsiderable impression upon the heart of a modern fair; they neither drove their curricles, nor sported their tandems,[1] for as yet those gaudy vehicles were not even dreamt of—neither did they distinguish themselves by their brilliancy at the table, and their consequent rencontres with watchmen, for our forefathers were of too pacific a disposition to need those guardians of the night, every soul throughout the town being sound asleep before nine o'clock. Neither did they establish their claims to gentility at the expense of their tailors—for as yet those offenders against the pockets of society, and the tranquillity of all aspiring young gentlemen, were unknown in New Amsterdam; every good housewife made the clothes of her husband and family, and even the goede vrouw[2] of Van Twiller himself thought it no

8. That is, of Holland; cf. the "Low Countries" (Holland, Belgium, and Luxemburg).
9. A Russian peninsula on the Bering Sea.

1. A curricle was a light, two-wheeled racing carriage popular with the young bloods of Irving's period; in the tandem the two horses were harnessed in file instead of abreast.
2. Dutch, "good wife."

disparagement to cut out her husband's linsey-woolsey galligaskins.[3]

Not but what there were some two or three youngsters who manifested the first dawning of what is called fire and spirit; who held all labor in contempt; skulked about docks and market-places; loitered in the sunshine, squandered what little money they could procure at hustle-cap and chuck-farthing;[4] swore, boxed, fought cocks, and raced their neighbor's horses—in short, who promised to be the wonder, the talk, and abomination of the town, had not their stylish career been unfortunately cut short by an affair of honor with a whipping-post.

Far other, however, was the truly fashionable gentleman of those days—his dress, which served for both morning and evening, street and drawing-room, was a linsey-woolsey coat, made, perhaps, by the fair hands of the mistress of his affections, and gallantly bedecked with abundance of large brass buttons—half a score of breeches heightened the proportions of his figure—his shoes were decorated by enormous copper buckles—a low-crowned broad-rimmed hat overshadowed his burly visage, and his hair dangled down his back in a prodigious queue of eelskin.

Thus equipped, he would manfully sally forth with pipe in mouth to besiege some fair damsel's obdurate heart—not such a pipe, good reader, as that which Acis did sweetly tune in praise of his Galatea,[5] but one of true Delft manufacture, and furnished with a charge of fragrant tobacco. With this would he resolutely set himself down before the fortress, and rarely failed, in the process of time, to smoke the fair enemy into a surrender, upon honorable terms.

Such was the happy reign of Wouter Van Twiller, celebrated in many a long forgotten song as the real golden age, the rest being nothing but counterfeit copper-washed coin. In that delightful period, a sweet and holy calm reigned over the whole province. The burgomaster smoked his pipe in peace—the substantial solace of his domestic cares, after her daily toils were done, sat soberly at the door, with her arms crossed over her apron of snowy white, without being insulted with ribald street walkers or vagabond boys—those unlucky urchins who do so infest our streets, displaying, under the roses of youth, the thorns and briers of iniquity. Then it was that the lover with ten breeches, and the damsel with petticoats of half a score, indulged in all the innocent endearments of virtuous love without fear and without reproach; for what had that virtue to fear, which was defended by a shield of good linsey-woolseys, equal at least to the seven bull hides of the invincible Ajax.[6]

3. The voluminous knee breeches then worn by the Dutch, the commoner kind being made of linsey-woolsey, a coarse mixture of linen and wool.
4. Two coin games. The latter survives as pitch-penny. In the former, the coins to be matched were shaken out of a hat or cap.

5. The myth of Acis, loved by Galatea, a river nymph, and murdered by a rival, provided a familiar theme for eighteenth-century poets. *Cf.* Ovid, *Metamorphoses*, Book XIII, 750–897.
6. Referring to the legendary shield of Ajax, one of the greatest warriors of the Greeks in the siege of Troy; *cf.*

Ah blissful, and never to be forgotten age! when every thing was better than it has ever been since, or ever will be again—when Buttermilk Channel[7] was quite dry at low water—when the shad in the Hudson were all salmon, and when the moon shone with a pure and resplendent whiteness, instead of that melancholy yellow light which is the consequence of her sickening at the abominations she every night witnesses in this degenerate city!

Happy would it have been for New Amsterdam could it always have existed in this state of blissful ignorance and lowly simplicity, but alas! the days of childhood are too sweet to last! Cities, like men, grow out of them in time, and are doomed alike to grow into the bustle, the cares, and miseries of the world. Let no man congratulate himself, when he beholds the child of his bosom or the city of his birth increasing in magnitude and importance—let the history of his own life teach him the dangers of the one, and this excellent little history of Manna-hata convince him of the calamities of the other.

1809, 1860–1861

The Author's Account of Himself[8]

(I am of this mind with Homer, that as the snaile that crept out of her shel was turned eftsoons into a toad, and thereby was forced to make a stoole to sit on; so the traveller that stragleth from his owne country is in a short time transformed into so monstrous a shape, that he is faine to alter his mansion with his manners, and to live where he cannot where he would.—LYLY'S EUPHUES*)* [9]

I was always fond of visiting new scenes, and observing strange characters and manners. Even when a mere child I began my travels, and made many tours of discovery into foreign parts and unknown regions of my native city, to the frequent alarm of my parents, and the emolument of the town-crier. As I grew into boyhood, I extended the range of my observations. My holiday afternoons were spent in rambles about the surrounding country. I made myself familiar with all its places famous in history or fable. I knew every spot where a

Homer's *Iliad*.

7. In New York harbor, between Governor's Island and Long Island (Brooklyn).

8. *The Sketch Book of Geoffrey Crayon, Gent.* appeared in seven installments in New York, 1819–1820, including a maximum of thirty-six pieces—the count varies slightly in later collections. All but two, says Irving, "were written in England," but, "circumstances compelled me to send them piece-meal to the United States"—a reference, no doubt, to the failure of the Irving business in 1818, which caused him again to turn to his pen for support. The bulk of these pieces, appreciative if whimsical essays on English life, manners, and tradition, confirmed his position as unofficial ambassador of good will to the mother coun-

try, while he did not sacrifice his strong American preferences, which appear, for instance, in "The Author's Account of Himself" and in "English Writers on America," below. The American survival of this work was assured by "Rip Van Winkle" and "The Legend of Sleepy Hollow," in which Irving's genius blended German legends with the social life and character of colonial Dutch Americans of the lower Hudson valley.

9. John Lyly (1554–1606), an Elizabethan whose florid romances temporarily provided a high-flown fashionable speech for the court and society. The hero of his *Euphues* (1578) is a foppish young Athenian traveler; the quotation is from Lyly's second volume, *Euphues and His England* (1580).

murder or robbery had been committed, or a ghost seen. I visited the neighboring villages, and added greatly to my stock of knowledge, by noting their habits and customs, and conversing with their sages and great men. I even journeyed one long summer's day to the summit of the most distant hill, whence I stretched my eye over many a mile of terra incognita,[1] and was astonished to find how vast a globe I inhabited.

This rambling propensity strengthened with my years. Books of voyages and travels became my passion, and in devouring their contents, I neglected the regular exercises of the school. How wistfully would I wander about the pier-heads in fine weather, and watch the parting ships, bound to distant climes—with what longing eyes would I gaze after their lessening sails, and waft myself in imagination to the ends of the earth!

Further reading and thinking, though they brought this vague inclination into more reasonable bounds, only served to make it more decided. I visited various parts of my own country; and had I been merely a lover of fine scenery, I should have felt little desire to see elsewhere its gratification, for on no country have the charms of nature been more prodigally lavished. Her mighty lakes, like oceans of liquid silver; her mountains, with their bright aerial tints; her valleys, teeming with wild fertility; her tremendous cataracts, thundering in their solitudes; her boundless plains, waving with spontaneous verdure; her broad deep rivers, rolling in solemn silence to the ocean; her trackless forests, where vegetation puts forth all its magnificence; her skies, kindling with the magic of summer clouds and glorious sunshine;—no, never need an American look beyond his own country for the sublime and beautiful of natural scenery.

But Europe held forth the charms of storied and poetical association. There were to be seen the masterpieces of art, the refinements of highly-cultivated society, the quaint peculiarities of ancient and local custom. My native country was full of youthful promise: Europe was rich in the accumulated treasures of age. Her very ruins told the history of times gone by, and every mouldering stone was a chronicle. I longed to wander over the scenes of renowned achievement—to tread, as it were, in the footsteps of antiquity—to loiter about the ruined castle—to meditate on the falling tower—to escape, in short, from the commonplace realities of the present, and lose myself among the shadowy grandeurs of the past.

I had, beside all this, an earnest desire to see the great men of the earth. We have, it is true, our great men in America: not a city but has an ample share of them. I have mingled among them in my time, and been almost withered by the shade into which they cast me; for there is nothing so baleful to a small man as the shade of a great one, particularly the great man of a city. But I was anxious to see the

1. The unknown (unexplored) earth, as designated on ancient maps.

great men of Europe; for I had read in the works of various philosophers, that all animals degenerated in America, and man among
the number.[2] A great man of Europe, thought I, must therefore be as
superior to a great man of America, as a peak of the Alps to a highland
of the Hudson; and in this idea I was confirmed, by observing the
comparative importance and swelling magnitude of many English
travellers among us, who, I was assured, were very little people in
their own country. I will visit this land of wonders, thought I, and see
the gigantic race from which I am degenerated.

It has been either my good or evil lot to have my roving passion gratified. I have wandered through different countries, and witnessed many of the shifting scenes of life. I cannot say that I have
studied them with the eye of a philosopher; but rather with the
sauntering gaze with which humble lovers of the picturesque stroll
from the window of one print-shop to another; caught sometimes
by the delineations of beauty, sometimes by the distortions of caricature, and sometimes by the loveliness of landscape. As it is the fashion for modern tourists to travel pencil in hand, and bring home their
portfolios filled with sketches, I am disposed to get up a few for the
entertainment of my friends. When, however, I look over the hints
and memorandums I have taken down for the purpose, my heart
almost fails me at finding how my idle humor has led me aside from
the great objects studied by every regular traveller who would make
a book. I fear I shall give equal disappointment with an unlucky landscape painter, who had travelled on the continent, but, following the
bent of his vagrant inclination, had sketched in nooks, and corners,
and by-places. His sketch-book was accordingly crowded with cottages, and landscapes, and obscure ruins; but he had neglected to
paint St. Peter's, or the Coliseum; the cascade of Terni,[3] or the bay
of Naples; and had not a single glacier or volcano in his whole
collection.

1819, 1860–1861

Rip Van Winkle[4]

A POSTHUMOUS WRITING OF DIEDRICH KNICKERBOCKER

> *By Woden,[5] God of Saxons,*
> *From whence comes Wensday, that is Wodensday.*
> *Truth is a thing that ever I will keep*

2. Then a prevalent slander in European, especially British, literature.

3. North of Rome, in the Apennines,
where the series of successive falls in
the river were then an inevitable goal of
the sight-seer.

4. This famous tale (ending the first
installment of the *Sketch Book*) has
been regarded as the first American
short story. Within ten years (1829) it
began in Philadelphia its long stage
career. This involved adaptations and inheritance by many authors and actors,
until it was stabilized in the version
acted by the third Joseph Jefferson
(1829–1905).

5. Sometimes Wodan or Odin; in Norse
and Teutonic mythology, the god of war
and wisdom—also "the Thunderer."

Unto thylke day in which I creep into
My sepulchre—

CARTWRIGHT [6]

[The following Tale was found among the papers of the late Diedrich Knickerbocker, an old gentleman of New York, who was very
curious in the Dutch history of the province, and the manners of
the descendants from its primitive settlers. His historical researches,
however, did not lie so much among books as among men; for the
former are lamentably scanty on his favorite topics; whereas he found
the old burghers, and still more their wives, rich in that legendary
lore, so invaluable to true history. Whenever, therefore, he happened upon a genuine Dutch family, snugly shut up in its low-roofed
farmhouse, under a spreading sycamore, he looked upon it as a little
clasped volume of black-letter, and studied it with the zeal of a bookworm.[7]

The result of all these researches was a history of the province
during the reign of the Dutch governors, which he published some
years since. There have been various opinions as to the literary character of his work, and, to tell the truth, it is not a whit better than
it should be. Its chief merit is its scrupulous accuracy, which indeed
was a little questioned on its first appearance, but has since been
completely established; and it is now admitted into all historical
collections, as a book of unquestionable authority.

The old gentleman died shortly after the publication of his work,
and now that he is dead and gone, it cannot do much harm to his
memory to say that his time might have been much better employed
in weightier labors. He, however, was apt to ride his hobby his own
way; and though it did now and then kick up the dust a little in the
eyes of his neighbors, and grieve the spirit of some friends, for whom
he felt the truest deference and affection; yet his errors and follies
are remembered "more in sorrow than in anger,"[8] and it begins to
be suspected, that he never intended to injure or offend. But however his memory may be appreciated by critics, it is still held dear by
many folk, whose good opinion is well worth having; particularly by
certain biscuit-bakers, who have gone so far as to imprint his likeness
on their new-year cakes; and have thus given him a chance for immortality, almost equal to the being stamped on a Waterloo Medal,[9]

6. William Cartwright (1611–1643),
short-lived prodigy of the "Tribe of
Ben," of whom Jonson said, "My son
Cartwright writes all like a man."
7. Thus, in the *Sketch Book*, Irving perpetuated the fictitious Dutch historian,
Knickerbocker, from his earlier *History
of New York*. But in a footnote at the
end of "Rip Van Winkle" he gave a clue
to the German source of the folk tale
by denying that Knickerbocker had
based it on a "superstition about the

Emperor Frederick *der Rothbart.*" This
led to the identification of a probable
source, "Peter Klaus the Goatherd," in a
collection of German legends that Irving
had read (see H. A. Pochmann, "Irving's
German Sources in *The Sketch Book*,"
Studies in Philology, XXVII, July, 1930,
489–94).
8. Shakespeare's *Hamlet*, Act I, Scene
2, ll. 231–232.
9. A silver medal presented by the
British crown to all participants in the

or a Queen Anne's Farthing.[1]]

Whoever has made a voyage up the Hudson must remember the Kaatskill mountains. They are a dismembered branch of the great Appalachian family, and are seen away to the west of the river, swelling up to a noble height, and lording it over the surrounding country. Every change of season, every change of weather, indeed, every hour of the day, produces some change in the magical hues and shapes of these mountains, and they are regarded by all the good wives, far and near, as perfect barometers. When the weather is fair and settled, they are clothed in blue and purple, and print their bold outlines on the clear evening sky; but, sometimes, when the rest of the landscape is cloudless, they will gather a hood of gray vapors about their summits, which, in the last rays of the setting sun, will glow and light up like a crown of glory.

At the foot of these fairy mountains, the voyager may have descried the light smoke curling up from a village, whose shingle-roofs gleam among the trees, just where the blue tints of the upland melt away into the fresh green of the nearer landscape. It is a little village, of great antiquity, having been founded by some of the Dutch colonists, in the early times of the province, just about the beginning of the government of the good Peter Stuyvesant, (may he rest in peace!) and there were some of the houses of the original settlers standing within a few years, built of small yellow bricks brought from Holland, having latticed windows and gable fronts, surmounted with weathercocks.

In that same village, and in one of these very houses (which, to tell the precise truth, was sadly time-worn and weather-beaten), there lived many years since, while the country was yet a province of Great Britain, a simple good-natured fellow, of the name of Rip Van Winkle. He was a descendant of the Van Winkles who figured so gallantly in the chivalrous days of Peter Stuyvesant, and accompanied him to the siege of Fort Christina.[2] He inherited, however, but little of the martial character of his ancestors. I have observed that he was a simple good-natured man; he was, moreover, a kind neighbor, and an obedient hen-pecked husband. Indeed, to the latter circumstance might be owing that meekness of spirit which gained him such universal popularity; for those men are most apt to be obsequious and conciliating abroad, who are under the discipline of shrews at home. Their tempers, doubtless, are rendered pliant and malleable in the fiery furnace of domestic tribulation; and a curtain

Battle of Waterloo (June 18, 1815) or in the engagements of the two previous days.
1. In the reign of Queen Anne (1702–1714) farthings (bronze coins worth a quarter of a penny) bearing her image were minted.

2. Referring to events treated in his *History of New York*. Stuyvesant was the autocratic governor of New Amsterdam (1647–1664); he seized Fort Christina from the Swedes on the Delaware in 1655.

lecture is worth all the sermons in the world for teaching the virtues of patience and long-suffering. A termagant wife may, therefore, in some respects, be considered a tolerable blessing; and if so, Rip Van Winkle was thrice blessed.

Certain it is, that he was a great favorite among all the good wives of the village, who, as usual, with the amiable sex, took his part in all family squabbles; and never failed, whenever they talked those matters over in their evening gossipings, to lay all the blame on Dame Van Winkle. The children of the village, too, would shout with joy whenever he approached. He assisted at their sports, made their playthings, taught them to fly kites and shoot marbles, and told them long stories of ghosts, witches, and Indians. Whenever he went dodging about the village, he was surrounded by a troop of them, hanging on his skirts, clambering on his back, and playing a thousand tricks on him with impunity; and not a dog would bark at him throughout the neighborhood.

The great error in Rip's composition was an insuperable aversion to all kinds of profitable labor. It could not be from the want of assiduity or perseverance; for he would sit on a wet rock, with a rod as long and heavy as a Tartar's lance, and fish all day without a murmur, even though he should not be encouraged by a single nibble. He would carry a fowling-piece on his shoulder for hours together, trudging through woods and swamps, and up hill and down dale, to shoot a few squirrels or wild pigeons. He would never refuse to assist a neighbor even in the roughest toil, and was a foremost man at all country frolics for husking Indian corn, or building stone-fences; the women of the village, too, used to employ him to run their errands, and to do such little old jobs as their less obliging husbands would not do for them. In a word Rip was ready to attend to anybody's business but his own; but as to doing family duty, and keeping his farm in order, he found it impossible.

In fact, he declared it was of no use to work on his farm; it was the most pestilent little piece of ground in the whole country; every thing about it went wrong, and would go wrong, in spite of him. His fences were continually falling to pieces; his cow would either go astray, or get among the cabbages; weeds were sure to grow quicker in his fields than anywhere else; the rain always made a point of setting in just as he had some outdoor work to do; so that though his patrimonial estate had dwindled away under his management, acre by acre, until there was little more left than a mere patch of Indian corn and potatoes, yet it was the worst conditioned farm in the neighborhood.

His children, too, were as ragged and wild as if they belonged to nobody. His son Rip, an urchin begotten in his own likeness, promised to inherit the habits, with the old clothes of his father. He was generally seen trooping like a colt at his mother's heels, equipped in a pair of his father's cast-off galligaskins,[3] which he had much ado to hold up with one hand, as a fine lady does her train in bad weather.

Rip Van Winkle, however, was one of those happy mortals, of foolish, well-oiled dispositions, who take the world easy, eat white bread or brown, whichever can be got with least thought or trouble, and would rather starve on a penny than work for a pound. If left to himself, he would have whistled life away in perfect contentment; but his wife kept continually dinning in his ears about his idleness, his carelessness, and the ruin he was bringing on his family. Morning, noon, and night, her tongue was incessantly going, and every thing he said or did was sure to produce a torrent of household eloquence. Rip had but one way of replying to all lectures of the kind, and that, by frequent use, had grown into a habit. He shrugged his shoulders, shook his head, cast up his eyes, but said nothing. This, however, always provoked a fresh volley from his wife; so that he was fain to draw off his forces, and take to the outside of the house—the only side which, in truth, belongs to a hen-pecked husband.

Rip's sole domestic adherent was his dog Wolf, who was as much hen-pecked as his master; for Dame Van Winkle regarded them as companions in idleness, and even looked upon Wolf with an evil eye, as the cause of his master's going so often astray. True it is, in all points of spirit befitting an honorable dog, he was as courageous an animal as ever scoured the woods—but what courage can withstand the ever-during and all-besetting terrors of a woman's tongue? The moment Wolf entered the house his crest fell, his tail drooped to the ground, or curled between his legs, he sneaked about with a gallows air, casting many a sidelong glance at Dame Van Winkle, and at the least flourish of a broomstick or ladle, he would fly to the door with yelping precipitation.

Times grew worse and worse with Rip Van Winkle as years of matrimony rolled on; a tart temper never mellows with age, and a sharp tongue is the only edged tool that grows keener with constant use. For a long while he used to console himself, when driven from home, by frequenting a kind of perpetual club of the sages, philosophers, and other idle personages of the village; which held its sessions on a bench before a small inn, designated by a rubicund portrait of His Majesty George the Third. Here they used to sit in the shade through a long lazy summer's day, talking listlessly over village gossip, or telling endless sleepy stories about nothing. But it would have been worth any statesman's money to have heard the profound discussions that sometimes took place, when by chance an old newspaper fell into their hands from some passing traveller. How solemnly they would listen to the contents, as drawled out by Derrick Van

3. Knee breeches.

Bummel, the schoolmaster, a dapper learned little man, who was not to be daunted by the most gigantic word in the dictionary; and how sagely they would deliberate upon public events some months after they had taken place.

The opinions of this junto were completely controlled by Nicholas Vedder, a patriarch of the village, and landlord of the inn, at the door of which he took his seat from morning till night, just moving sufficiently to avoid the sun and keep in the shade of a large tree; so that the neighbors could tell the hour by his movements as accurately as by a sun-dial. It is true he was rarely heard to speak, but smoked his pipe incessantly. His adherents, however (for every great man has his adherents), perfectly understood him, and knew how to gather his opinions. When any thing that was read or related displeased him, he **was** observed to smoke his pipe vehemently, and to send forth short, frequent and angry puffs; but when pleased, he would inhale the smoke slowly and tranquilly, and emit it in light and placid clouds; and sometimes, taking the pipe from his mouth, and letting the fragrant vapor curl about his nose, would gravely nod his head in token of perfect approbation.

From even this stronghold the unlucky Rip was at length routed by his termagant wife, who would suddenly break in upon the tranquillity of the assemblage and call the members all to naught; nor was that august personage, Nicholas Vedder himself, sacred from the daring tongue of this terrible virago, who charged him outright with encouraging her husband in habits of idleness.

Poor Rip was at last reduced almost to despair; and his only alternative, to escape from the labor of the farm and clamor of his wife, was to take gun in hand and stroll away into the woods. Here he would sometimes seat himself at the foot of a tree, and share the contents of his wallet with Wolf, with whom he sympathized as a fellow-sufferer in persecution. "Poor Wolf," he would say, "thy mistress leads thee a dog's life of it; but never mind, my lad, whilst I live thou shalt never want a friend to stand by thee!" Wolf would wag his tail, look wistfully in his master's face, and if dogs can feel pity I verily believe he reciprocated the sentiment with all his heart.

In a long ramble of the kind on a fine autumnal day, Rip had unconsciously scrambled to one of the highest parts of the Kaatskill mountains. He was after his favorite sport of squirrel shooting, and the still solitudes had echoed and re-echoed with the reports of his gun. Panting and fatigued, he threw himself, late in the afternoon, on a green knoll, covered with mountain herbage, that crowned the brow of a precipice. From an opening between the trees he could overlook all the lower country for many a mile of rich woodland. He saw at a distance the lordly Hudson, far, far below him, moving on its silent but majestic course, with the reflection of a purple cloud, or the sail of a lagging bark, here and there sleeping on its glassy bosom, and at last losing itself in the blue highlands.

On the other side he looked down into a deep mountain glen, wild, lonely, and shagged, the bottom filled with fragments from the impending cliffs, and scarcely lighted by the reflected rays of the setting sun. For some time Rip lay musing on this scene; evening was gradually advancing; the mountains began to throw their long blue shadows over the valleys; he saw that it would be dark long before he could reach the village, and he heaved a heavy sigh when he thought of encountering the terrors of Dame Van Winkle.

As he was about to descend, he heard a voice from a distance, hallooing, "Rip Van Winkle! Rip Van Winkle!" He looked round, but could see nothing but a crow winging its solitary flight across the mountain. He thought his fancy must have deceived him, and turned again to descend, when he heard the same cry through the still evening air; "Rip Van Winkle! Rip Van Winkle!"—at the same time Wolf bristled up his back, and giving a low growl, skulked to his master's side, looking fearfully down into the glen. Rip now felt a vague apprehension stealing over him; he looked anxiously in the same direction, and perceived a strange figure slowly toiling up the rocks, and bending under the weight of something he carried on his back. He was surprised to see any human being in this lonely and unfrequented place, but supposing it to be some one of the neighborhood in need of his assistance, he hastened down to yield it.

On nearer approach he was still more surprised at the singularity of the stranger's appearance. He was a short square-built old fellow, with thick bushy hair, and a grizzled beard. His dress was of the antique Dutch fashion—a cloth jerkin strapped round the waist— several pair of breeches, the outer one of ample volume, decorated with rows of buttons down the sides, and bunches at the knees. He bore on his shoulder a stout keg, that seemed full of liquor, and made signs for Rip to approach and assist him with the load. Though rather shy and distrustful of this new acquaintance, Rip complied with his usual alacrity; and mutually relieving one another, they clambered up a narrow gully, apparently the dry bed of a mountain torrent. As they ascended, Rip every now and then heard long rolling peals, like distant thunder, that seemed to issue out of a deep ravine, or rather cleft, between lofty rocks, toward which their rugged path conducted. He paused for an instant, but supposing it to be the muttering of one of those transient thunder-showers which often take place in mountain heights, he proceeded. Passing through the ravine, they came to a hollow, like a small amphitheatre, surrounded by perpendicular precipices, over the brinks of which impending trees shot their branches, so that you only caught glimpses of the azure sky and the bright evening cloud. During the whole time Rip and his companion had labored on in silence; for though the former marvelled greatly what could be the object of carrying a keg of liquor up this wild mountain, yet there was something strange and incomprehensible about the unknown, that inspired awe and checked familiarity.

On entering the amphitheatre, new objects of wonder presented themselves. On a level spot in the centre was a company of oddlooking personages playing at nine-pins. They were dressed in a quaint outlandish fashion; some wore short doublets, others jerkins, with long knives in their belts, and most of them had enormous breeches, of similar style with that of the guide's. Their visages, too, were peculiar: one had a large head, broad face, and small piggish eyes: the face of another seemed to consist entirely of nose, and was surmounted by a white sugar-loaf hat, set off with a little red cock's tail. They all had beards, of various shapes and colors. There was one who seemed to be the commander. He was a stout old gentleman, with a weather-beaten countenance; he wore a laced doublet, broad belt and hanger,[4] high crowned hat and feather, red stockings, and high-heeled shoes, with roses[5] in them. The whole group reminded Rip of the figures in an old Flemish painting, in the parlor of Dominie Van Shaick, the village parson, and which had been brought over from Holland at the time of the settlement.

What seemed particularly odd to Rip was, that though these folks were evidently amusing themselves, yet they maintained the gravest faces, the most mysterious silence, and were, withal, the most melancholy party of pleasure he had ever witnessed. Nothing interrupted the stillness of the scene but the noise of the balls, which, whenever they were rolled, echoed along the mountains like rumbling peals of thunder.

As Rip and his companion approached them, they suddenly desisted from their play, and stared at him with such fixed statue-like gaze, and such strange, uncouth, lack-lustre countenances, that his heart turned within him, and his knees smote together. His companion now emptied the contents of the keg into large flagons, and made signs to him to wait upon the company. He obeyed with fear and trembling; they quaffed the liquor in profound silence, and then returned to their game.

By degrees Rip's awe and apprehension subsided. He even ventured, when no eye was fixed upon him, to taste the beverage, which he found had much of the flavor of excellent Hollands.[6] He was naturally a thirsty soul, and was soon tempted to repeat the draught. One taste provoked another; and he reiterated his visits to the flagon so often that at length his senses were overpowered, his eyes swam

4. A short, curved sword worn at the side.
5. Rosettes.

6. A Dutch gin long famous for excellence.

in his head, his head gradually declined, and he fell into a deep sleep.

On waking, he found himself on the green knoll whence he had first seen the old man of the glen. He rubbed his eyes—it was a bright sunny morning. The birds were hopping and twittering among the bushes, and the eagle was wheeling aloft, and breasting the pure mountain breeze. "Surely," thought Rip, "I have not slept here all night." He recalled the occurrences before he fell asleep. The strange man with a keg of liquor—the mountain ravine—the wild retreat among the rocks—the wobegone party at nine-pins—the flagon—"Oh! that flagon! that wicked flagon!" thought Rip—"what excuse shall I make to Dame Van Winkle!"

He looked round for his gun, but in place of the clean well-oiled fowling-piece, he found an old firelock lying by him, the barrel incrusted with rust, the lock falling off, and the stock worm-eaten. He now suspected that the grave roysters of the mountain had put a trick upon him, and, having dosed him with liquor, had robbed him of his gun. Wolf, too, had disappeared, but he might have strayed away after a squirrel or partridge. He whistled after him and shouted his name, but all in vain; the echoes repeated his whistle and shout, but no dog was to be seen.

He determined to revisit the scene of the last evening's gambol, and if he met with any of the party, to demand his dog and gun. As he rose to walk, he found himself stiff in the joints, and wanting in his usual activity. "These mountain beds do not agree with me," thought Rip, "and if this frolic should lay me up with a fit of the rheumatism, I shall have a blessed time with Dame Van Winkle." With some difficulty he got down into the glen: he found the gully up which he and his companion had ascended the preceding evening; but to his astonishment a mountain stream was now foaming down it, leaping from rock to rock, and filling the glen with babbling murmurs. He, however, made shift to scramble up its sides, working his toilsome way through thickets of birch, sassafras, and witch-hazel, and sometimes tripped up or entangled by the wild grapevines that twisted their coils or tendrils from tree to tree, and spread a kind of network in his path.

At length he reached to where the ravine had opened through the cliffs to the amphitheatre; but no traces of such opening remained. The rocks presented a high impenetrable wall over which the torrent came tumbling in a sheet of feathery foam, and fell into a broad deep basin, black from the shadows of the surrounding forest. Here, then, poor Rip was brought to a stand. He again called and whistled after his dog; he was only answered by the cawing of a flock of idle crows, sporting high in air about a dry tree that overhung a sunny precipice; and who, secure in their elevation, seemed to look down and scoff at the poor man's perplexities. What was to be done? the morning was passing away, and Rip felt famished for want of his breakfast. He grieved to give up his dog and gun; he dreaded to meet his wife; but it would not do to starve among the mountains. He shook his head, shouldered the rusty firelock, and, with a heart full of trouble and anxiety, turned his steps homeward.

As he approached the village he met a number of people, but none whom he knew, which somewhat surprised him, for he had thought himself acquainted with every one in the country round. Their dress, too, was of a different fashion from that to which he was accustomed. They all stared at him with equal marks of surprise, and whenever they cast their eyes upon him, invariably stroked their chins. The constant recurrence of this gesture induced Rip, involuntarily, to do the same, when, to his astonishment, he found his beard had grown a foot long!

He had now entered the skirts of the village. A troop of strange children ran at his heels, hooting after him, and pointing at his gray beard. The dogs, too, not one of which he recognized for an old acquaintance, barked at him as he passed. The very village was altered; it was larger and more populous. There were rows of houses which he had never seen before, and those which had been his familiar haunts had disappeared. Strange names were over the doors—strange faces at the windows—every thing was strange. His mind now misgave him; he began to doubt whether both he and the world around him were not bewitched. Surely this was his native village, which he had left but the day before. There stood the Kaatskill mountains —there ran the silver Hudson at a distance—there was every hill and dale precisely as it had always been—Rip was sorely perplexed —"That flagon last night," thought he, "has addled my poor head sadly!"

It was with some difficulty that he found the way to his own house, which he approached with silent awe, expecting every moment to hear the shrill voice of Dame Van Winkle. He found the house gone to decay—the roof fallen in, the windows shattered, and the doors off the hinges. A half-starved dog that looked like Wolf was skulking about it. Rip called him by name, but the cur snarled, showed his teeth, and passed on. This was an unkind cut indeed—"My very dog," sighed poor Rip, "has forgotten me!"

He entered the house, which, to tell the truth, Dame Van Winkle had always kept in neat order. It was empty, forlorn, and apparently abandoned. This desolateness overcame all his connubial fears—he called loudly for his wife and children—the lonely chambers rang for a moment with his voice, and then all again was silence.

He now hurried forth, and hastened to his old resort, the village inn—but it too was gone. A large rickety wooden building stood in its place, with great gaping windows, some of them broken and mended with old hats and petticoats, and over the door was painted, "the Union Hotel, by Jonathan Doolittle." Instead of the great tree that used to shelter the quiet little Dutch inn of yore, there now was reared a tall naked pole, with something on the top that looked like a red night-cap,[7] and from it was fluttering a flag, on which was a singular assemblage of stars and stripes—all this was strange and incomprehensible. He recognized on the sign, however, the ruby face of King George, under which he had smoked so many a peaceful pipe; but even this was singularly metamorphosed. The red coat was changed for one of blue and buff, a sword was held in the hand instead of a sceptre, the head was decorated with a cocked hat, and underneath was painted in large characters, GENERAL WASHINGTON.

There was, as usual, a crowd of folk about the door, but none that Rip recollected. The very character of the people seemed changed. There was a busy, bustling, disputatious tone about it, instead of the accustomed phlegm and drowsy tranquillity. He looked in vain for the sage Nicholas Vedder, with his broad face, double chin, and fair long pipe, uttering clouds of tobacco-smoke instead of idle speeches; or Van Bummel, the schoolmaster, doling forth the contents of an ancient newspaper. In place of these, a lean, bilious-looking fellow, with his pockets full of handbills, was haranguing vehemently about rights of citizens—elections—members of congress—liberty—Bunker's Hill—heroes of seventy-six—and other words, which were a perfect Babylonish jargon[8] to the bewildered Van Winkle.

The appearance of Rip, with his long grizzled beard, his rusty fowling-piece, his uncouth dress, and an army of women and children at his heels, soon attracted the attention of the tavern politicians. They crowded round him, eyeing him from head to foot with great curiosity. The orator bustled up to him, and, drawing him partly aside, inquired "on which side he voted?" Rip stared in vacant stupidity. Another short but busy little fellow pulled him by the arm, and, rising on tiptoe, inquired in his ear, "Whether he was Federal or Democrat?"[9] Rip was equally at a loss to comprehend the question; when a knowing, self-important old gentleman, in a sharp cocked hat, made his way through the crowd, putting them to the right and left with his elbows as he passed, and planting himself before Van Winkle, with one arm akimbo, the other resting on his cane, his keen eyes and sharp hat penetrating, as it were, into his very soul, demanded in an austere tone, "what brought him to the election with a gun on his shoulder, and a mob at his heels, and whether he meant to breed a riot in the village?"—"Alas! gentlemen," cried Rip,

7. The "liberty cap," familiar symbol of the French Revolution, was often displayed in the United States.
8. *Cf.* Genesis xi: 1–9. The "confusion of tongues" occurred at Babel.
9. The earliest American political parties—Federalist (Hamiltonian) and Democratic Republican (Jeffersonian).

somewhat dismayed, "I am a poor quiet man, a native of the place, and a loyal subject of the king, God bless him!"

Here a general shout burst from the by-standers—"A tory! a tory! a spy! a refugee! hustle him! away with him!" It was with great difficulty that the self-important man in the cocked hat restored order; and, having assumed a tenfold austerity of brow, demanded again of the unknown culprit, what he came there for, and whom he was seeking? The poor man humbly assured him that he meant no harm, but merely came there in search of some of his neighbors, who used to keep about the tavern.

"Well—who are they?—name them."

Rip bethought himself a moment, and inquired, "Where's Nicholas Vedder?"

There was a silence for a little while, when an old man replied, in a thin piping voice, "Nicholas Vedder! why, he is dead and gone these eighteen years! There was a wooden tombstone in the churchyard that used to tell all about him, but that's rotten and gone too."

"Where's Brom Dutcher?"

"Oh, he went off to the army in the beginning of the war; some say he was killed at the storming of Stony Point[1]—others say he was drowned in a squall at the foot of Antony's Nose.[2] I don't know—he never came back again."

"Where's Van Bummel, the schoolmaster?"

"He went off to the wars too, was a great militia general, and is now in congress."

Rip's heart died away at hearing of these sad changes in his home and friends, and finding himself thus alone in the world. Every answer puzzled him too, by treating of such enormous lapses of time, and of matters which he could not understand: war—congress—Stony Point;—he had no courage to ask after any more friends, but cried out in despair, "Does nobody here know Rip Van Winkle?"

"Oh, Rip Van Winkle!" exclaimed two or three, "Oh, to be sure! that's Rip Van Winkle yonder, leaning against the tree."

Rip looked, and beheld a precise counterpart of himself, as he went up the mountain: apparently as lazy, and certainly as ragged. The poor fellow was now completely confounded. He doubted his own identity, and whether he was himself or another man. In the midst of his bewilderment, the man in the cocked hat demanded who he was, and what was his name?

"God knows," exclaimed he, at his wit's end; "I'm not myself—I'm somebody else—that's me yonder—no—that's somebody else got into my shoes—I was myself last night, but I fell asleep on the

1. A strategic headland on the Hudson below West Point, captured by Mad Anthony Wayne, July 18, 1779, in one of the most daring and brilliant exploits of the Revolution.
2. Another fortified promontory on the Hudson, scene of a bloody contest in 1777.

mountain, and they've changed my gun, and every thing's changed, and I'm changed, and I can't tell what's my name, or who I am!"

The by-standers began now to look at each other, nod, wink significantly, and tap their fingers against their foreheads. There was a whisper, also, about securing the gun, and keeping the old fellow from doing mischief, at the very suggestion of which the self-important man in the cocked hat retired with some precipitation. At this critical moment a fresh comely woman pressed through the throng to get a peep at the gray-bearded man. She had a chubby child in her arms, which, frightened at his looks, began to cry. "Hush, Rip," cried she, "hush, you little fool; the old man won't hurt you." The name of the child, the air of the mother, the tone of her voice, all awakened a train of recollections in his mind. "What is your name, my good woman?" asked he.

"Judith Gardenier."

"And your father's name?"

"Ah, poor man, Rip Van Winkle was his name, but it's twenty years since he went away from home with his gun, and never has been heard of since—his dog came home without him; but whether he shot himself, or was carried away by the Indians, nobody can tell. I was then but a little girl."

Rip had but one question more to ask; but he put it with a faltering voice:

"Where's your mother?"

"Oh, she too had died but a short time since; she broke a blood-vessel in a fit of passion at a New-England peddler."

There was a drop of comfort, at least, in this intelligence. The honest man could contain himself no longer. He caught his daughter and her child in his arms. "I am your father!" cried he—"Young Rip Van Winkle once—old Rip Van Winkle now!—Does nobody know poor Rip Van Winkle?"

All stood amazed, until an old woman, tottering out from among the crowd, put her hand to her brow, and peering under it in his face for a moment, exclaimed, "Sure enough! it is Rip Van Winkle—it is himself! Welcome home again, old neighbor—Why, where have you been these twenty long years?"

Rip's story was soon told, for the whole twenty years had been to him but as one night. The neighbors stared when they heard it; some were seen to wink at each other, and put their tongues in their cheeks: and the self-important man in the cocked hat, who, when the alarm was over, had returned to the field, screwed down the corners of his mouth, and shook his head—upon which there was a general shaking of the head throughout the assemblage.

It was determined, however, to take the opinion of old Peter Vanderdonk, who was seen slowly advancing up the road. He was a descendant of the historian[3] of that name, who wrote one of the earliest accounts of the province. Peter was the most ancient inhabitant of the village, and well versed in all the wonderful events and traditions of the neighborhood. He recollected Rip at once, and corroborated his story in the most satisfactory manner. He assured the company that it was a fact, handed down from his ancestor the historian, that the Kaatskill mountains had always been haunted by strange beings. That it was affirmed that the great Hendrick Hudson, the first discoverer of the river and country, kept a kind of vigil there every twenty years, with his crew of the Half-moon; being permitted in this way to revisit the scenes of his enterprise, and keep a guardian eye upon the river, and the great city called by his name.[4] That his father had once seen them in their old Dutch dresses playing at nine-pins in a hollow of the mountain; and that he himself had heard, one summer afternoon, the sound of their balls, like distant peals of thunder.

To make a long story short, the company broke up, and returned to the more important concerns of the election. Rip's daughter took him home to live with her; she had a snug, well-furnished house, and a stout cheery farmer for a husband, whom Rip recollected for one of the urchins that used to climb upon his back. As to Rip's son and heir, who was the ditto of himself, seen leaning against the tree, he was employed to work on the farm; but evinced an hereditary disposition to attend to any thing else but his business.

Rip now resumed his old walks and habits; he soon found many of his former cronies, though all rather the worse for the wear and tear of time; and preferred making friends among the rising generation, with whom he soon grew into great favor.

Having nothing to do at home, and being arrived at that happy age when a man can be idle with impunity, he took his place once more on the bench at the inn door, and was reverenced as one of the patriarchs of the village, and a chronicle of the old times "before the war." It was some time before he could get into the regular track of gossip, or could be made to comprehend the strange events that had taken place during his torpor. How that there had been a revolutionary war—that the country had thrown off the yoke of old England—and that, instead of being a subject of His Majesty George the Third, he was now a free citizen of the United States. Rip, in fact, was no politician; the changes of states and empires made but little impression on him; but there was one species of despotism

3. Adriaen Van der Donck (*ca.* 1620–1655), Dutch lawyer and founder of Yonkers, wrote a description of New Netherland, published in Dutch (Amsterdam, 1655).
4. The town of Hudson handled a considerable shipping in Irving's youth.

Henry (not Hendrick) Hudson, an English adventurer, discovered and explored the river for the East Indian Company in 1609; abandoned on Hudson Bay by mutineers in 1611, he passed from history into legend.

under which he had long groaned, and that was—petticoat govern-ment. Happily that was at an end; he had got his neck out of the yoke of matrimony, and could go in and out whenever he pleased, without dreading the tyranny of Dame Van Winkle. Whenever her name was mentioned, however, he shook his head, shrugged his shoulders, and cast up his eyes; which might pass either for an expres-sion of resignation to his fate, or joy at his deliverance.

He used to tell his story to every stranger that arrived at Mr. Doo-little's hotel. He was observed, at first, to vary on some points every time he told it, which was, doubtless, owing to his having so recently awaked. It at last settled down precisely to the tale I have related, and not a man, woman, or child in the neighborhood, but knew it by heart. Some always pretended to doubt the reality of it, and in-sisted that Rip had been out of his head, and that this was one point on which he always remained flighty. The old Dutch inhabitants, however, almost universally gave it full credit. Even to this day they never hear a thunderstorm of a summer afternoon about the Kaatskill, but they say Hendrick Hudson and his crew are at their game of nine-pins; and it is a common wish of all hen-pecked husbands in the neighborhood, when life hangs heavy on their hands, that they might have a quieting draught out of Rip Van Winkle's flagon.

1819, 1860–1861

English Writers on America[5]

Methinks I see in my mind a noble and puissant nation, rousing herself like a strong man after sleep, and shaking her invisible locks: methings I see her as an eagle, mew-ing her mighty youth, and kindling her endazzled eyes at the full mid-day beam.
—MILTON ON THE LIBERTY OF THE PRESS [6]

It is with feelings of deep regret that I observe the literary animos-ity daily growing up between England and America. Great curiosity has been awakened of late with respect to the United States, and the London press has teemed with volumes of travels through the Republic; but they seem intended to diffuse error rather than knowl-edge; and so successful have they been, that, notwithstanding the constant intercourse between the nations, there is no people con-cerning whom the great mass of the British public have less pure information, or entertain more numerous prejudices.

English travellers are the best and the worst in the world. Where no motives of pride or interest intervene, none can equal them for profound and philosophical views of society, or faithful and graphical

5. This piece represents a strong note in the *Sketch Book*. Persistent disparage-ment of America, by British and some-times by continental writers, after 1750, though not surprising, was a steady source of irritation. In a tradition that

included Franklin, Lowell, and Charles Francis Adams, Irving was one of the best emissaries of our culture, and apparently his candid rebuttals, as in this essay, did not lessen his influence.
6. *I.e.*, in the *Areopagitica* (1644).

descriptions of external objects; but when either the interest or reputation of their own country comes in collision with that of another, they go to the opposite extreme, and forget their usual probity and candor in the indulgence of splenetic remark and an illiberal spirit of ridicule.

Hence, their travels are more honest and accurate, the more remote the country described. I would place implicit confidence in an Englishman's descriptions of the regions beyond the cataracts of the Nile; of unknown islands in the Yellow Sea; of the interior of India; or of any other tract which other travellers might be apt to picture out with the illusions of their fancies; but I would cautiously receive his account of his immediate neighbors and of those nations with which he is in habits of most frequent intercourse. However I might be disposed to trust his probity, I dare not trust his prejudices.

It has also been the peculiar lot of our country to be visited by the worst kind of English travellers. While men of philosophical spirit and cultivated minds have been sent from England to ransack the poles, to penetrate the deserts, and to study the manners and customs of barbarous nations, with which she can have no permanent intercourse of profit or pleasure; it has been left to the broken-down tradesman, the scheming adventurer, the wandering mechanic, the Manchester and Birmingham agent,[7] to be her oracles respecting America. From such sources she is content to receive her information respecting a country in a singular state of moral and physical development; a country in which one of the greatest political experiments in the history of the world is now performing, and which presents the most profound and momentous studies to the statesman and philosopher.

That such men should give prejudiced accounts of America is not a matter of surprise. The themes it offers for contemplation are too vast and elevated for their capacities. The national character is yet in a state of fermentation: it may have its frothiness and sediment, but its ingredients are sound and wholesome: it has already given proofs of powerful and generous qualities; and the whole promises to settle down into something substantially excellent. But the causes which are operating to strengthen and ennoble it, and its daily indications of admirable properties, are all lost upon these purblind observers, who are only affected by the little asperities incident to its present situation. They are capable of judging only of the surface of things, of those matters which come in contact with their private interests and personal gratifications. They miss some of the snug conveniences and petty comforts which belong to an old, highly finished, and over-populous state of society, where the ranks of useful labor are crowded, and many earn a painful and servile subsistence by studying the very caprices of appetite and self-indulgence. These minor comforts, how-

7. Business representatives of the aggressive British industry of those cities.

ever, are all-important in the estimation of narrow minds; which either do not perceive, or will not acknowledge, that they are more than counterbalanced among us by great and generally diffused blessings.

They may, perhaps, have been disappointed in some unreasonable expectation of sudden gain. They may have pictured America to themselves an El Dorado, where gold and silver abounded, and the natives were lacking in sagacity; and where they were to become strangely and suddenly rich, in some unforeseen but easy manner. The same weakness of mind that indulges absurd expectations produces petulance in disappointment. Such persons become embittered against the country on finding that there, as everywhere else, a man must sow before he can reap; must win wealth by industry and talent; and must contend with the common difficulties of nature and the shrewdness of an intelligent and enterprising people.

Perhaps, through mistaken, or ill-directed hospitality, or from the prompt disposition to cheer and countenance the stranger, prevalent among my countrymen, they may have been treated with unwonted respect in America; and having been accustomed all their lives to consider themselves below the surface of good society, and brought up in a servile feeling of inferiority, they become arrogant on the common boon of civility: they attribute to the lowliness of others their own elevation; and underrate a society where there are no artificial distinctions, and where, by any chance, such individuals as themselves can rise to consequence.

One would suppose, however, that information coming from such sources, on a subject where the truth is so desirable, would be received with caution by the censors of the press; that the motives of these men, their veracity, their opportunities of inquiry and observation, and their capacities for judging correctly, would be rigorously scrutinized before their evidence was admitted, in such sweeping extent, against a kindred nation. The very reverse, however, is the case, and it furnishes a striking instance of human inconsistency. Nothing can surpass the vigilance with which English critics will examine the credibility of the traveller who publishes an account of some distant, and comparatively unimportant country. How warily will they compare the measurements of a pyramid or the descriptions of a ruin; and how sternly will they censure any inaccuracy in these contributions of merely curious knowledge: while they will receive, with eagerness and unhesitating faith, the gross misrepresentations of coarse and obscure writers concerning a country with which their own is placed in the most important and delicate relations. Nay, they will even make these apocryphal volumes textbooks, on which to enlarge with a zeal and an ability worthy of a more generous cause.

I shall not, however, dwell on this irksome and hackneyed topic; nor should I have adverted to it, but for the undue interest apparently taken in it by my countrymen, and certain injurious effects which I apprehend it might produce upon the national feeling. We attach too much consequence to these attacks. They cannot do us any essential injury. The tissue of misrepresentations attempted to be woven round us are like cobwebs woven round the limbs of an infant giant. Our country continually outgrows them. One falsehood after another falls off of itself. We have but to live on, and every day we live a whole volume of refutation. All the writers of England united, if we could for a moment suppose their great minds stooping to so unworthy a combination, could not conceal our rapidly growing importance and matchless prosperity. They could not conceal that these are owing, not merely to physical and local, but also to moral causes —to the political liberty, the general diffusion of knowledge, the prevalence of sound, moral, and religious principles which give force and sustained energy to the character of a people; and which, in fact, have been the acknowledged and wonderful supporters of their own national power, and glory.

But why are we so exquisitely alive to the aspersions of England? Why do we suffer ourselves to be so affected by the contumely she has endeavored to cast upon us? It is not in the opinion of England alone that honor lives, and reputation has its being. The world at large is the arbiter of a nation's fame; with its thousand eyes it witnesses a nation's deeds, and from their collective testimony is national glory or national disgrace established.

For ourselves, therefore, it is comparatively of but little importance whether England does us justice or not; it is, perhaps, of far more importance to herself. She is instilling anger and resentment into the bosom of a youthful nation, to grow with its growth, and strengthen with its strength. If in America, as some of her writers are laboring to convince her, she is hereafter to find an invidious rival and a gigantic foe, she may thank those very writers for having provoked rivalship and irritated hostility. Everyone knows the all-pervading influence of literature at the present day, and how much the opinions and passions of mankind are under its control. The mere contests of the sword are temporary, their wounds are but in the flesh, and it is the pride of the generous to forgive and forget them; but the slanders of the pen pierce to the heart; they rankle longest in the noblest spirits; they dwell ever present in the mind, and render it morbidly sensitive to the most trifling collision. It is but seldom that any one overt act produces hostilities between two nations; there exists, most commonly, a previous jealousy and ill-wind, a predisposition to take offense. Trace these to their cause, and how often will they be found to originate in the mischievous effusions of mercenary writers, who, secure in their closets, and for ignominious bread, concoct and circulate the venom that is to inflame the generous and the brave.

I am not laying too much stress upon this point, for it applies most emphatically to our particular case. Over no nation does the press hold a more absolute control than over the people of America, for the universal education of the poorest classes makes every individual a reader. There is nothing published in England on the subject of our country, that does not circulate through every part of it. There is not a calumny dropped from an English pen, nor an unworthy sarcasm uttered by an English statesman, that does not go to blight good will and add to the mass of latent resentment. Possessing, then, as England does, the fountain-head from whence the literature of the language flows, how completely is it in her power, and how truly is it her duty, to make it the medium of amiable and magnanimous feeling—a stream where two nations meet together and drink in peace and kindness. Should she, however, persist in turning it to waters of bitterness, the time may come when she may repent her folly. The present friendship of America may be of but little moment to her, but the future destinies of that country do not admit of a doubt; over those of England, there lower some shadows of uncertainty. Should, then, a day of gloom arrive—should these reverses overtake her from which the proudest empires have not been exempt—she may look back with regret at her infatuation in repulsing from her side a nation she might have grappled to her bosom, and thus destroying her only chance for real friendship beyond the boundaries of her own dominions.[8]

There is a general impression in England that the people of the United States are inimical to the parent country. It is one of the errors which have been diligently propagated by designing writers. There is, doubtless, considerable political hostility, and a general soreness at the illiberality of the English press; but, collectively speaking, the prepossessions of the people are strongly in favor of England. Indeed, at one time they amounted, in many parts of the Union, to an absurd degree of bigotry. The bare name of Englishman was a passport to the confidence and hospitality of every family, and too often gave a transient currency to the worthless and the ungrateful. Throughout the country there was something of enthusiasm connected with the idea of England. We looked to it with a hallowed feeling of tenderness and veneration, as the land of our forefathers —the august repository of the monuments and antiquities of our race—the birthplace and mausoleum of the sages and heroes of our paternal history. After our own country, there was none in whose

8. One of the earliest expressions of the possible common destiny, in the future, of the English-speaking world.

glory we more delighted—none whose good opinion we were more anxious to possess—none towards which our hearts yearned with such throbbings of warm consanguinity. Even during the late war,[9] whenever there was the least opportunity for kind feelings to spring forth, it was the delight of the generous spirits of our country to show that, in the midst of hostilities, they still kept alive the sparks of future friendship.

Is all this to be at an end? Is this golden band of kindred sympathies, so rare betweeen nations, to be broken for ever?—Perhaps it is for the best—it may dispel an illusion which might have kept us in mental vassalage; which might have interfered occasionally with our true interests, and prevented the growth of proper national pride. But it is hard to give up the kindred tie! and there are feelings dearer than interest—closer to the heart than pride—that will still make us cast back a look of regret, as we wander farther and farther from the paternal roof, and lament the waywardness of the parent that would repel the affections of the child.

Shortsighted and injudicious, however, as the conduct of England may be in this system of aspersion, recrimination on our part would be equally ill-judged. I speak not of a prompt and spirited vindication of our country nor the keenest castigation of her slanderers—but I allude to a disposition to retaliate in kind; to retort sarcasm and inspire prejudice, which seems to be growing widely among our writers. Let us guard particularly against such a temper, for it will redouble the evil instead of redressing the wrong. Nothing is so easy and inviting as the retort of abuse and sarcasm; but it is a paltry and unprofitable contest. It is the alternative of a morbid mind, fretted into petulance rather than warmed into indignation. If England is willing to permit the mean jealousies of trade or the rancorous animosities of politics to deprave the integrity of her press and poison the fountain of public opinion, let us beware of her example. She may deem it her interest to diffuse error and engender antipathy, for the purpose of checking emigration; we have no purpose of the kind to serve. Neither have we any spirit of national jealousy to gratify; for as yet, in all our rivalships with England, we are the rising and the gaining party. There can be no end to answer, therefore, but the gratification of resentment—a mere spirit of retaliation; and even that is impotent. Our retorts are never republished in England; they fall short, therefore, of their aim; but they foster a querulous and peevish temper among our writers; they sour the sweet flow of our early literature and sow thorns and brambles among its blossoms. What is still worse, they circulate through our own country, and, as far as they have effect, excite virulent national prejudices. This last is the evil most especially to be deprecated. Governed, as we

9. The War of 1812.

are, entirely by public opinion, the utmost care should be taken to preserve the purity of the public mind. Knowledge is power,[1] and truth is knowledge; whoever, therefore, knowingly propagates a prejudice willfully saps the foundation of his country's strength.

The members of a republic, above all other men, should be candid and dispassionate. They are, individually, portions of the sovereign mind and sovereign will, and should be enabled to come to all questions of national concern with calm and unbiased judgments. From the peculiar nature of our relations with England, we must have more frequent questions of a difficult and delicate character with her than with any other nation—questions that affect the most acute and excitable feelings; and as, in the adjusting of these, our national measures must ultimately be determined by popular sentiment, we cannot be too anxiously attentive to purify it from all latent passion or prepossession.

Opening, too, as we do, an asylum for strangers from every portion of the earth, we should receive all with impartiality. It should be our pride to exhibit an example of one nation, at least, destitute of national antipathies and exercising not merely the overt acts of hospitality, but those more rare and noble courtesies which spring from liberality of opinion.[2]

What have we to do with national prejudices? They are the inveterate diseases of old countries, contracted in rude and ignorant ages, when nations knew but little of each other, and looked beyond their own boundaries with distrust and hostility. We, on the contrary, have sprung into national existence in an enlightened and philosophic age, when the different parts of the habitable world and the various branches of the human family have been indefatigably studied and made known to each other; and we forego the advantages of our birth if we do not shake off the national prejudices, as we would the local superstitions, of the old world.

But above all let us not be influenced by any angry feelings so far as to shut our eyes to the perception of what is really excellent and amiable in the English character. We are a young people, necessarily an imitative one, and must take our examples and models, in a great degree, from the existing nations of Europe. There is no country more worthy of our study than England. The spirit of her constitution is most analogous to ours. The manners of her people—their intellectual activity—their freedom of opinion—their habits of thinking on those subjects which concern the dearest interests and most sacred charities of private life, are all congenial to the American

---

1. A familiar translation of Francis Bacon's "Nam et ipsa scientia potestas est," in *Meditationes Sacrae, De Haeresibus*.

2. The rising tide of emigration was then a cause of concern in Britain. By the end of the century immigrants were arriving in the United States at the rate of a million a year.

character, and, in fact, are all intrinsically excellent; for it is in the moral feeling of the people that the deep foundations of British prosperity are laid, and however the superstructure may be timeworn or overrun by abuses, there must be something solid in the basis, admirable in the materials, and stable in the structure of an edifice that so long has towered unshaken amidst the tempests of the world.

Let it be the pride of our writers, therefore, discarding all feelings of irritation, and disdaining to retaliate the illiberality of British authors, to speak of the English nation without prejudice and with determined candor. While they rebuke the indiscriminating bigotry with which some of our countrymen admire and imitate everything English, merely because it is English, let them frankly point out what is really worthy of approbation. We may thus place England before us as a perpetual volume of reference, wherein are recorded sound deductions from ages of experience; and while we avoid the errors and absurdities which may have crept into the page, we may draw thence golden maxims of practical wisdom, wherewith to strengthen and to embellish our national character.

1820, 1860–1861

The Legend of Sleepy Hollow[3]

FOUND AMONG THE PAPERS OF THE LATE DIEDRICH KNICKERBOCKER

A pleasing land of drowsy head it was,
Of dreams that wave before the half-shut eye,
And of gay castles in the clouds that pass,
For ever flushing round a summer sky.
—CASTLE OF INDOLENCE [4]

In the bosom of one of those spacious coves which indent the eastern shore of the Hudson, at that broad expansion of the river denominated by the ancient Dutch navigators the Tappan Zee, and where they always prudently shortened sail, and implored the protection of St. Nicholas when they crossed, there lies a small market-town or rural port, which by some is called Greensburgh, but which is more generally and properly known by the name of Tarry Town.[5] This name was given, we are told, in former days, by the good housewives of the adjacent country, from the inveterate propensity of their husbands to linger about the village tavern on market days. Be that as it may, I do not vouch for the fact, but merely advert to it, for the sake of being precise and authentic. Not far from this village,

3. First appeared in the fourth installment of the New York serial edition of the *Sketch Book*. Again Irving naturalized in the Hudson valley certain elements found in German folk tales, and others common to folk literature.
4. By James Thomson (1700–1748),

Scottish poet.
5. Now Tarrytown, about fifteen miles above New York City limits; the expansion of the Hudson there is still called the Tappan Sea. After 1835 Irving made his home at Sunnyside, in the quiet valley described below.

perhaps about two miles, there is a little valley, or rather lap of land, among high hills, which is one of the quietest places in the whole world. A small brook glides through it, with just murmur enough to lull one to repose; and the occasional whistle of a quail, or tapping of a woodpecker, is almost the only sound that ever breaks in upon the uniform tranquillity.

I recollect that, when a stripling, my first exploit in squirrel-shooting was in a grove of tall walnut-trees that shades one side of the valley. I had wandered into it at noon time, when all nature is peculiarly quiet, and was startled by the roar of my own gun, as it broke the Sabbath stillness around, and was prolonged and rever-berated by the angry echoes. If ever I should wish for a retreat, whither I might steal from the world and its distractions, and dream quietly away the remnant of a troubled life, I know of none more promising than this little valley.

From the listless repose of the place, and the peculiar character of its inhabitants, who are descendants from the original Dutch set-tlers, this sequestered glen has long been known by the name of SLEEPY HOLLOW, and its rustic lads are called the Sleepy Hollow Boys throughout all the neighboring country. A drowsy, dreamy in-fluence seems to hang over the land, and to pervade the very atmos-phere. Some say that the place was bewitched by a high German doctor, during the early days of the settlement; others, that an old Indian chief, the prophet or wizard of his tribe, held his powwows there before the country was discovered by Master Hendrick Hudson. Certain it is, the place still continues under the sway of some witch-ing power, that holds a spell over the minds of the good people, causing them to walk in a continual reverie. They are given to all kinds of marvellous beliefs; are subject to trances and visions; and frequently see strange sights, and hear music and voices in the air. The whole neighborhood abounds with local tales, haunted spots, and twilight superstitions; stars shoot and meteors glare oftener across the valley than in any other part of the country, and the night-mare, with her whole nine fold,[6] seems to make it the favorite scene of her gambols.

The dominant spirit, however, that haunts this enchanted region, and seems to be commander-in-chief of all the powers of the air, is the apparition of a figure on horseback without a head. It is said by some to be the ghost of a Hessian[7] trooper, whose head had been carried away by a cannon-ball, in some nameless battle during the revolutionary war; and who is ever and anon seen by the country

6. Reads "the nightmare and her nine fold" in Shakespeare's *King Lear*, Act III, Scene 4, l. 128. The nightmare, in folk superstition, was a demon; her nine foals (offspring of a mare) were imps.
7. The soldiers hired by the British from Hesse, Germany; see Franklin, "The Sale of the Hessians," in this volume.

folk, hurrying along in the gloom of night, as if on the wings of the wind. His haunts are not confined to the valley, but extend at times to the adjacent roads, and especially to the vicinity of a church at no great distance. Indeed, certain of the most authentic historians of those parts, who have been careful in collecting and collating the floating facts concerning this spectre, allege that the body of the trooper, having been buried in the church-yard, the ghost rides forth to the scene of battle in nightly quest of his head; and that the rushing speed with which he sometimes passes along the Hollow, like a midnight blast, is owing to his being belated, and in a hurry to get back to the church-yard before daybreak.[8]

Such is the general purport of this legendary superstition, which has furnished materials for many a wild story in that region of shadows; and the spectre is known, at all the country firesides, by the name of the Headless Horseman of Sleepy Hollow.

It is remarkable that the visionary propensity I have mentioned is not confined to the native inhabitants of the valley, but is unconsciously imbibed by every one who resides there for a time. However wide awake they may have been before they entered that sleepy region, they are sure, in a little time, to inhale the witching influence of the air, and begin to grow imaginative—to dream dreams, and see apparitions.

I mention this peaceful spot with all possible laud; for it is in such little retired Dutch valleys, found here and there embosomed in the great State of New-York, that population, manners, and customs, remain fixed; while the great torrent of migration and improvement, which is making such incessant changes in other parts of this restless country, sweeps by them unobserved. They are like those little nooks of still water which border a rapid stream; where we may see the straw and bubble riding quietly at anchor, or slowly revolving in their mimic harbor, undisturbed by the rush of the passing current. Though many years have elapsed since I trod the drowsy shades of Sleepy Hollow, yet I question whether I should not still find the same trees and the same families vegetating in its sheltered bosom.

In this by-place of nature, there abode, in a remote period of American history, that is to say, some thirty years since, a worthy wight of the name of Ichabod Crane; who sojourned, or, as he expressed it, "tarried," in Sleepy Hollow, for the purpose of instructing the children of the vicinity. He was a native of Connecticut; a State which supplies the Union with pioneers for the mind as well as for the forest, and sends forth yearly its legions of frontier woodsmen and country schoolmasters. The cognomen of Crane was not inapplicable to his person. He was tall, but exceedingly lank, with nar-

8. *Hamlet*, Act I, Scene 1, ll. 157–164, perpetuated the superstition that the spirits must be in their graves before the "bird of dawning" crows. Irving quotes the lines in the sketch entitled "Christmas."

row shoulders, long arms and legs, hands that dangled a mile out of his sleeves, feet that might have served for shovels, and his whole frame most loosely hung together. His head was small, and flat at top, with huge ears, large green glassy eyes, and a long snipe nose, so that it looked like a weather-cock, perched upon his spindle neck, to tell which way the wind blew. To see him striding along the profile of a hill on a windy day, with his clothes bagging and fluttering about him, one might have mistaken him for the genius of famine descending upon the earth, or some scarecrow eloped from a cornfield.

His school-house was a low building of one large room, rudely constructed of logs; the windows partly glazed, and partly patched with leaves of old copy-books. It was most ingeniously secured at vacant hours, by a withe twisted in the handle of the door, and stakes set against the window shutters; so that, though a thief might get in with perfect ease, he would find some embarrassment in getting out; an idea most probably borrowed by the architect, Yost Van Houten, from the mystery of an eel-pot. The school-house stood in a rather lonely but pleasant situation, just at the foot of a woody hill, with a brook running close by, and a formidable birch tree growing at one end of it. From hence the low murmur of his pupils' voices, conning over their lessons, might be heard in a drowsy summer's day, like the hum of a bee-hive; interrupted now and then by the authoritative voice of the master, in the tone of menace or command; or, peradventure, by the appalling sound of the birch, as he urged some tardy loiterer along the flowery path of knowledge. Truth to say, he was a conscientious man, and ever bore in mind the golden maxim, "Spare the rod and spoil the child."[9]—Ichabod Crane's scholars certainly were not spoiled.

I would not have it imagined, however, that he was one of those cruel potentates of the school, who joy in the smart of their subjects; on the contrary, he administered justice with discrimination rather than severity; taking the burthen off the backs of the weak, and laying it on those of the strong. Your mere puny stripling, that winced at the least flourish of the rod, was passed by with indulgence; but the claims of justice were satisfied by inflicting a double portion on some little, tough, wrong-headed, broad-skirted Dutch urchin, who sulked and swelled and grew dogged and sullen beneath the birch. All this he called "doing his duty by their parents"; and he never inflicted a chastisement without following it by the assurance, so consolatory to the smarting urchin, that "he would remember it, and thank him for it the longest day he had to live."

When school hours were over, he was even the companion and playmate of the larger boys; and on holiday afternoons would convoy

9. This phrasing is from *Hudibras*, II, 843 (1664), by Samuel Butler (1612–1680), British satirist; but the maxim originates in Proverbs xiii: 24.

some of the smaller ones home, who happened to have pretty sisters, or good housewives for mothers, noted for the comforts of the cupboard. Indeed it behooved him to keep on good terms with his pupils. The revenue arising from his school was small, and would have been scarcely sufficient to furnish him with daily bread, for he was a huge feeder, and though lank, had the dilating powers of an anaconda; but to help out his maintenance, he was, according to country custom in those parts, boarded and lodged at the houses of the farmers, whose children he instructed. With these he lived successively a week at a time; thus going the rounds of the neighborhood, with all his worldly effects tied up in a cotton handkerchief.

That all this might not be too onerous on the purses of his rustic patrons, who are apt to consider the costs of schooling a grievous burden, and schoolmasters as mere drones, he had various ways of rendering himself both useful and agreeable. He assisted the farmers occasionally in the lighter labors of their farms; helped to make hay; mended the fences; took the horses to water; drove the cows from pasture; and cut wood for the winter fire. He laid aside, too, all the dominant dignity and absolute sway with which he lorded it in his little empire, the school, and became wonderfully gentle and ingratiating. He found favor in the eyes of the mothers, by petting the children, particularly the youngest; and like the lion bold, which whilom so magnanimously the lamb did hold,[1] he would sit with a child on one knee, and rock a cradle with his foot for whole hours together.

In addition to his other vocations, he was the singing-master of the neighborhood, and picked up many bright shillings by instructing the young folks in psalmody. It was a matter of no little vanity to him, on Sundays, to take his station in front of the church gallery, with a band of chosen singers; where, in his own mind, he completely carried away the palm from the parson. Certain it is, his voice resounded far above all the rest of the congregation; and there are peculiar quavers still to be heard in that church, and which may even be heard half a mile off, quite to the opposite side of the mill-pond, on a still Sunday morning, which are said to be legitimately descended from the nose of Ichabod Crane. Thus, by divers little make-shifts in that ingenious way which is commonly denominated "by hook and by crook," the worthy pedagogue got on tolerably enough, and was thought, by all who understood nothing of the labor of headwork, to have a wonderfully easy life of it.

The schoolmaster is generally a man of some importance in the female circle of a rural neighborhood; being considered a kind of idle gentlemanlike personage, of vastly superior taste and accomplish-

1. *The New England Primer*, for "L," read, "The lion bold the lamb doth hold"—a conception probably derived from Milton, *Paradise Lost*, Book IV, l. 343; but see also Isaiah xi: 6–9.

ments to the rough country swains, and, indeed, inferior in learning only to the parson. His appearance, therefore, is apt to occasion some little stir at the tea-table of a farmhouse, and the addition of a supernumerary dish of cakes or sweetmeats, or peradventure, the parade of a silver tea-pot. Our man of letters, therefore, was peculiarly happy in the smiles of all the country damsels. How he would figure among them in the churchyard, between services on Sundays! gathering grapes for them from the wild vines that overrun the surrounding trees; reciting for their amusement all the epitaphs on the tombstones; or sauntering, with a whole bevy of them, along the banks of the adjacent mill-pond; while the more bashful country bumpkins hung sheepishly back, envying his superior elegance and address.

From his half itinerant life, also, he was a kind of travelling gazette, carrying the whole budget of local gossip from house to house; so that his appearance was always greeted with satisfaction. He was, moreover, esteemed by the women as a man of great erudition, for he had read several books quite through, and was a perfect master of Cotton Mather's history of New England Witchcraft,[2] in which, by the way, he most firmly and potently believed.

He was, in fact, an odd mixture of small shrewdness and simple credulity. His appetite for the marvellous, and his powers of digesting it, were equally extraordinary; and both had been increased by his residence in this spellbound region. No tale was too gross or monstrous for his capacious swallow. It was often his delight, after his school was dismissed in the afternoon, to stretch himself on the rich bed of clover, bordering the little brook that whimpered by his school-house, and there con over old Mather's direful tales, until the gathering dusk of the evening made the printed page a mere mist before his eyes. Then, as he wended his way, by swamp and stream and awful woodland, to the farmhouse where he happened to be quartered, every sound of nature, at that witching hour, fluttered his excited imagination: the moan of the whip-poor-will[3] from the hill-side; the boding cry of the tree-toad, that harbinger of storm; the dreary hooting of the screech-owl, or the sudden rustling in the thicket of birds frightened from their roost. The fire-flies, too, which sparkled most vividly in the darkest places, now and then startled him, as one of uncommon brightness would stream across his path; and if, by chance, a huge blockhead of a beetle came winging his blundering flight against him, the poor varlet was ready to give up the ghost, with the idea that he was struck with a witch's token. His only resource on such occasions, either to drown thought, or drive

2. See selections from Mather in this volume. He wrote of witchcraft in *Memorable Providences Relating to Witchcrafts* * * * (1689) and *The Wonders of the Invisible World* (1693).

3. "The whip-poor-will is a bird which is only heard at night. It receives its name from its note, which is thought to resemble those words" [Irving's note, in editions after 1820].

away evil spirits, was to sing psalm tunes;—and the good people of Sleepy Hollow, as they sat by their doors of an evening, were often filled with awe, at hearing his nasal melody, "in linked sweetness long drawn out,"[4] floating from the distant hill, or along the dusky road.

Another of his sources of fearful pleasure was, to pass long winter evenings with the old Dutch wives, as they sat spinning by the fire, with a row of apples roasting and spluttering along the hearth, and listen to their marvellous tales of ghosts and goblins, and haunted fields, and haunted brooks, and haunted bridges, and haunted houses, and particularly of the headless horseman, or galloping Hessian of the Hollow, as they sometimes called him. He would delight them equally by his anecdotes of witchcraft, and of the direful omens and portentous sights and sounds in the air, which prevailed in the earlier times of Connecticut; and would frighten them wofully with speculations upon comets and shooting stars; and with the alarming fact that the world did absolutely turn round, and that they were half the time topsy-turvy!

But if there was a pleasure in all this, while snugly cuddling in the chimney corner of a chamber that was all of a ruddy glow from the crackling wood fire, and where, of course, no spectre dared to show his face, it was dearly purchased by the terrors of his subsequent walk homewards. What fearful shapes and shadows beset his path amidst the dim and ghastly glare of a snowy night!—With what wistful look did he eye every trembling ray of light streaming across the waste fields from some distant window!—How often was he appalled by some shrub covered with snow, which, like a sheeted spectre, beset his very path!—How often did he shrink with curdling awe at the sound of his own steps on the frosty crust beneath his feet; and dread to look over his shoulder, lest he should behold some uncouth being tramping close behind him!—and how often was he thrown into complete dismay by some rushing blast, howling among the trees, in the idea that it was the Galloping Hessian on one of his nightly scourings!

All these, however, were mere terrors of the night, phantoms of the mind that walk in darkness; and though he had seen many spectres in his time, and been more than once beset by Satan in divers shapes, in his lonely perambulations, yet daylight put an end to all these evils; and he would have passed a pleasant life of it, in despite of the devil and all his works, if his path had not been crossed by a being that causes more perplexity to mortal man than ghosts, goblins, and the whole race of witches put together, and that was—a woman.

Among the musical disciples who assembled, one evening in each week, to receive his instructions in psalmody, was Katrina Van Tassel, the daughter and only child of a substantial Dutch farmer.

4. Milton, "L'Allegro," l. 140; but for "in," read "of."

She was a blooming lass of fresh eighteen; plump as a partridge; ripe and melting and rosy cheeked as one of her father's peaches, and universally famed, not merely for her beauty, but her vast expectations. She was withal a little of a coquette, as might be perceived even in her dress, which was a mixture of ancient and modern fashions, as most suited to set off her charms. She wore the ornaments of pure yellow gold, which her great-great-grandmother had brought over from Saardam;[5] the tempting stomacher of the older time; and withal a provokingly short petticoat, to display the prettiest foot and ankle in the country round.

Ichabod Crane had a soft and foolish heart towards the sex; and it is not to be wondered at, that so tempting a morsel soon found favor in his eyes; more especially after he had visited her in her paternal mansion. Old Baltus Van Tassel was a perfect picture of a thriving, contented, liberal-hearted farmer. He seldom, it is true, sent either his eyes or his thoughts beyond the boundaries of his own farm; but within those every thing was snug, happy, and well-conditioned. He was satisfied with his wealth, but not proud of it; and piqued himself upon the hearty abundance, rather than the style in which he lived. His stronghold was situated on the banks of the Hudson, in one of those green, sheltered, fertile nooks, in which the Dutch farmers are so fond of nestling. A great elm-tree spread its broad branches over it; at the foot of which bubbled up a spring of the softest and sweetest water, in a little well, formed of a barrel; and then stole sparkling away through the grass, to a neighboring brook, that bubbled along among alders and dwarf willows. Hard by the farmhouse was a vast barn, that might have served for a church; every window and crevice of which seemed bursting forth with the treasures of the farm; the flail was busily resounding within it from morning to night; swallows and martins skimmed twittering about the eaves; and rows of pigeons, some with one eye turned up, as if watching the weather, some with their heads under their wings, or buried in their bosoms, and others swelling, and cooing, and bowing about their dames, were enjoying the sunshine on the roof. Sleek unwieldy porkers were grunting in the repose and abundance of their pens; whence sallied forth, now and then, troops of sucking pigs, as if to snuff the air. A stately squadron of snowy geese were riding in an adjoining pond, convoying whole fleets of ducks; regiments of turkeys were gobbling through the farmyard, and guinea fowls fretting about it, like ill-tempered housewives, with their peevish discontented cry. Before the barn door strutted the gallant cock, that pattern of a husband, a warrior, and a fine gentleman, clapping his burnished wings, and crowing in the pride and gladness of his heart—sometimes tearing up the earth with his feet, and then

5. Modern Zaandam, four miles from Amsterdam, Holland.

generously calling his ever-hungry family of wives and children to enjoy the rich morsel which he had discovered.

The pedagogue's mouth watered, as he looked upon this sumptuous promise of luxurious winter fare. In his devouring mind's eye, he pictured to himself every roasting-pig running about with a pudding in his belly, and an apple in his mouth; the pigeons were snugly put to bed in a comfortable pie, and tucked in with a coverlet of crust; the geese were swimming in their own gravy; and the ducks pairing cosily in dishes, like snug married couples, with a decent competency of onion sauce. In the porkers he saw carved out the future sleek side of bacon, and juicy relishing ham; not a turkey but he beheld daintily trussed up, with its gizzard under its wing, and, peradventure, a necklace of savory sausages; and even bright chanticleer himself lay sprawling on his back, in a side-dish, with uplifted claws, as if craving that quarter which his chivalrous spirit disdained to ask while living.

As the enraptured Ichabod fancied all this, and as he rolled his great green eyes over the fat meadowlands, the rich fields of wheat, of rye, of buckwheat, and Indian corn, and the orchards burthened with ruddy fruit, which surrounded the warm tenement of Van Tassel, his heart yearned after the damsel who was to inherit these domains, and his imagination expanded with the idea, how they might be readily turned into cash, and the money invested in immense tracts of wild land, and shingle palaces in the wilderness. Nay, his busy fancy already realized his hopes, and presented to him the blooming Katrina, with a whole family of children, mounted on the top of a wagon loaded with household trumpery, with pots and kettles dangling beneath; and he beheld himself bestriding a pacing mare, with a colt at her heels, setting out for Kentucky, Tennessee, or the Lord knows where.

When he entered the house the conquest of his heart was complete. It was one of those spacious farmhouses, with high-ridged, but lowly-sloping roofs, built in the style handed down from the first Dutch settlers; the low projecting eaves forming a piazza along the front, capable of being closed up in bad weather. Under this were hung flails, harness, various utensils of husbandry, and nets for fishing in the neighboring river. Benches were built along the sides for summer use; and a great spinning-wheel at one end, and a churn at the other, showed the various uses to which this important porch might be devoted. From this piazza the wondering Ichabod entered the hall, which formed the centre of the mansion and the place of usual residence. Here, rows of resplendent pewter, ranged on a long dresser, dazzled his eyes. In one corner stood a huge bag of wool ready to be spun; in another a quantity of linsey-woolsey just from the loom; ears of Indian corn, and strings of dried apples and peaches, hung in gay festoons along the walls, mingled with the gaud of red peppers; and a door left ajar gave him a peep into the best parlor, where the claw-footed chairs, and dark mahogany tables, shone like mirrors; andirons, with their accompanying shovel and tongs, glistened from their covert of asparagus tops; mock-oranges and conch-shells decorated the mantel-piece; strings of various colored birds' eggs were suspended above it: a great ostrich egg was hung from the centre of the room, and a corner cupboard, knowingly left open, displayed immense treasures of old silver and well-mended china.

From the moment Ichabod laid his eyes upon these regions of delight, the peace of his mind was at an end, and his only study was how to gain the affections of the peerless daughter of Van Tassel. In this enterprise, however, he had more real difficulties than generally fell to the lot of a knight-errant of yore, who seldom had any thing but giants, enchanters, fiery dragons, and such like easily-conquered adversaries, to contend with; and had to make his way merely through gates of iron and brass, and walls of adamant, to the castle keep, where the lady of his heart was confined; all which he achieved as easily as a man would carve his way to the centre of a Christmas pie; and then the lady gave him her hand as a matter of course. Ichabod, on the contrary, had to win his way to the heart of a country coquette, beset with a labyrinth of whims and caprices, which were for ever presenting new difficulties and impediments; and he had to encounter a host of fearful adversaries of real flesh and blood, and numerous rustic admirers, who beset every portal to her heart; keeping a watchful and angry eye upon each other, but ready to fly out in the common cause against any new competitor.

Among these the most formidable was a burly, roaring, roystering blade, of the name of Abraham, or, according to the Dutch abbreviation, Brom Van Brunt, the hero of the country round, which rang with his feats of strength and hardihood. He was broad-shouldered and double-jointed, with short curly black hair, and a bluff, but not unpleasant countenance, having a mingled air of fun and arrogance. From his Herculean frame and great powers of limb, he had received the nickname of BROM BONES, by which he was universally known. He was famed for great knowledge and skill in horsemanship, being as dexterous on horseback as a Tartar. He was foremost at all races and cock-fights; and, with the ascendency which bodily strength acquires in rustic life, was the umpire in all disputes, setting his hat on one side, and giving his decisions with an air and tone admitting of no gainsay or appeal. He was always ready for either a fight or a frolic; but had more mischief than ill-will in his composition; and, with all his over-bearing roughness, there was a strong dash of waggish good humor at bottom. He had three or four boon companions, who regarded him as their model, and at the head of whom he scoured the country, attending every scene of feud or merriment for miles round. In cold weather he was distinguished by a fur cap, surmounted with a flaunting fox's tail; and when the folks at a country gathering descried this well-known crest at a distance, whisking about among a squad of hard riders, they always stood by for a squall. Sometimes his crew would be heard dashing along past the farmhouses at midnight, with whoop and halloo, like a troop of Don Cossacks;[6] and the old dames, startled out of their sleep, would listen for a moment till the hurry-scurry had clattered by, and then exclaim, "Ay, there goes Brom Bones and his gang!" The neighbors looked upon him with a mixture of awe, admiration, and good will; and when any madcap prank, or rustic brawl, occurred in the vicinity, always shook their heads, and warranted Brom Bones was at the bottom of it.

This rantipole[7] hero had for some time singled out the blooming Katrina for the object of his uncouth gallantries, and though his amorous toyings were something like the gentle caresses and endearments of a bear, yet it was whispered that she did not altogether discourage his hopes. Certain it is, his advances were signals for rival candidates to retire, who felt no inclination to cross a lion in his amours; insomuch, that when his horse was seen tied to Van Tassel's paling, on a Sunday night, a sure sign that his master was courting, or, as it is termed, "sparking," within, all other suitors passed by in despair, and carried the war into other quarters.

Such was the formidable rival with whom Ichabod Crane had to contend, and, considering all things, a stouter man than he would have shrunk from the competition, and a wiser man would have despaired. He had, however, a happy mixture of pliability and perseverance in his nature; he was in form and spirit like a supple-jack[8]— yielding, but tough; though he bent, he never broke; and though he bowed beneath the slightest pressure, yet, the moment it was away— jerk! he was as erect, and carried his head as high as ever.

To have taken the field openly against his rival would have been madness; for he was not a man to be thwarted in his armours, any more than that stormy lover, Achilles.[9] Ichabod, therefore, made his advances in a quiet and gently-insinuating manner. Under cover of his character of singing-master, he made frequent visits at the farmhouse; not that he had any thing to apprehend from the meddlesome interference of parents, which is so often a stumbling-block in the path of lovers. Balt Van Tassel was an easy indulgent soul; he loved his daughter better even than his pipe, and like a reasonable man and an excellent father, let her have her way in every thing. His

6. The Cossacks of the Don valley in Russia were adventuresome horsemen, famous as Czarist cavalry.
7. Reckless; *cf.* "rant."
8. Various pliant, woody vines, then used for walking sticks.
9. The Greek hero of the *Iliad* returned after death to claim his promised bride, Polyxena, daughter of the Trojan king, Priam.

notable little wife, too, had enough to do to attend to her house-keeping and manage her poultry; for, as she sagely observed, ducks and geese are foolish things, and must be looked after, but girls can take care of themselves. Thus while the busy dame bustled about the house, or plied her spinning-wheel at one end of the piazza, honest Balt would sit smoking his evening pipe at the other, watching the achievements of a little wooden warrior, who, armed with a sword in each hand, was most valiantly fighting the wind on the pinnacle of the barn. In the mean time, Ichabod would carry on his suit with the daughter by the side of the spring under the great elm, or saun-tering along in the twilight, that hour so favorable to the lover's eloquence.

I profess not to know how women's hearts are wooed and won. To me they have always been matters of riddle and admiration. Some seem to have but one vulnerable point, or door of access; while others have a thousand avenues, and may be captured in a thousand differ-ent ways. It is a great triumph of skill to gain the former, but a still greater proof of generalship to maintain possession of the latter, for the man must battle for his fortress at every door and window. He who wins a thousand common hearts is therefore entitled to some renown; but he who keeps undisputed sway over the heart of a coquette, is indeed a hero. Certain it is, this was not the case with the redoubtable Brom Bones; and from the moment Ichabod Crane made his advances, the interests of the former evidently declined; his horse was no longer seen tied at the palings on Sunday nights, and a deadly feud gradually arose between him and the preceptor of Sleepy Hollow.

Brom, who had a degree of rough chivalry in his nature, would fain have carried matters to open warfare, and have settled their pretensions to the lady, according to the mode of those most concise and simple reasoners, the knights-errant of yore—by single combat; but Ichabod was too conscious of the superior might of his adversary to enter the lists against him: he had overheard a boast of Bones, that he would "double the schoolmaster up, and lay him on a shelf of his own school-house"; and he was too wary to give him an op-portunity. There was something extremely provoking in this ob-stinately pacific system; it left Brom no alternative but to draw upon the funds of rustic waggery in his disposition, and to play off boorish practical jokes upon his rival: Ichabod became the object of whimsical persecution to Bones, and his gang of rough riders. They harried his hitherto peaceful domains; smoked out his singing school, by stop-ping up the chimney; broke into the school-house at night, in spite of its formidable fastenings of withe and window stakes, and turned every thing topsy-turvy: so that the poor schoolmaster began to think all the witches in the country held their meetings there. But what was still more annoying, Brom took all opportunities of turning him into ridicule in presence of his mistress, and had a scoundrel dog whom he taught to whine in the most ludicrous manner, and introduced as a rival of Ichabod's to instruct her in psalmody.

In this way matters went on for some time, without producing any material effect on the relative situation of the contending powers. On a fine autumnal afternoon, Ichabod, in pensive mood, sat enthroned on the lofty stool whence he usually watched all the concerns of his little literary realm. In his hand he swayed a ferule, that sceptre of despotic power; the birch of justice reposed on three nails, behind the throne, a constant terror to evil doers; while on the desk before him might be seen sundry contraband articles and prohibited weapons, detected upon the persons of idle urchins; such as half-munched apples, popguns, whirligigs, fly-cages, and whole legions of rampant little paper game-cocks. Apparently there had been some appalling act of justice recently inflicted, for his scholars were all busily intent upon their books, or slyly whispering behind them with one eye kept upon the master; and a kind of buzzing stillness reigned throughout the schoolroom. It was suddenly interrupted by the appearance of a negro, in tow-cloth jacket and trowsers, a round-crowned fragment of a hat, like the cap of Mercury,[1] and mounted on the back of a ragged, wild, half-broken colt, which he managed with a rope by way of halter. He came clattering up to the school door with an invitation to Ichabod to attend a merry-making or "quilting frolic," to be held that evening at Mynheer Van Tassel's; and having delivered his message with that air of importance, and effort at fine language, which a negro is apt to display on petty embassies of the kind, he dashed over the brook, and was seen scampering away up the hollow, full of the importance and hurry of his mission.

All was now bustle and hubbub in the late quiet schoolroom. The scholars were hurried through their lessons, without stopping at trifles; those who were nimble skipped over half with impunity, and those who were tardy, had a smart application now and then in the rear, to quicken their speed, or help them over a tall word. Books were flung aside without being put away on the shelves, inkstands were overturned, benches thrown down, and the whole school was turned loose an hour before the usual time, bursting forth like a legion of young imps, yelping and racketing about the green, in joy at their early emancipation.

The gallant Ichabod now spent at least an extra half hour at his toilet, brushing and furbishing up his best, and indeed only suit of rusty black, and arranging his looks [sic] by a bit of broken looking-glass, that hung up in the school-house. That he might make his appearance before his mistress in the true style of a cavalier, he borrowed

1. The winged cap, symbol of the speed of this messenger of the gods.

a horse from the farmer with whom he was domiciliated, a choleric old Dutchman, of the name of Hans Van Ripper, and, thus gallantly mounted, issued forth, like a knight-errant in quest of adventures. But it is meet I should, in the true spirit of romantic story, give some account of the looks and equipments of my hero and his steed. The animal he bestrode was a broken-down plough-horse, that had out-lived almost every thing but his viciousness. He was gaunt and shagged, with a ewe neck and a head like a hammer; his rusty mane and tail were tangled and knotted with burrs; one eye had lost its pupil, and was glaring and spectral; but the other had the gleam of a genuine devil in it. Still he must have had fire and mettle in his day, if we may judge from the name he bore of Gunpowder. He had, in fact, been a favorite steed of his master's, the choleric Van Ripper, who was a furious rider, and had infused, very probably, some of his own spirit into the animal; for, old and broken-down as he looked, there was more of the lurking devil in him than in any young filly in the country.

Ichabod was a suitable figure for such a steed. He rode with short stirrups, which brought his knees nearly up to the pommel of the saddle; his sharp elbows stuck out like grasshoppers'; he carried his whip perpendicularly in his hand, like a sceptre, and, as his horse jogged on, the motion of his arms was not unlike the flapping of a pair of wings. A small wool hat rested on the top of his nose, for so his scanty strip of forehead might be called; and the skirts of his black coat fluttered out almost to the horse's tail. Such was the appearance of Ichabod and his steed, as they shambled out of the gate of Hans Van Ripper, and it was altogether such an apparition as is seldom to be met with in broad daylight.

It was, as I have said, a fine autumnal day, the sky was clear and serene, and nature wore that rich and golden livery which we always associate with the idea of abundance. The forests had put on their sober brown and yellow, while some trees of the tenderer kind had been nipped by the frosts into brilliant dyes of orange, purple, and scarlet. Streaming files of wild ducks began to make their appearance high in the air; the bark of the squirrel might be heard from the groves of beech and hickory nuts, and the pensive whistle of the quail at intervals from the neighboring stubble-field.

The small birds were taking their farewell banquets. In the fulness of their revelry, they fluttered, chirping and frolicking, from bush to bush, and tree to tree, capricious from the very profusion and variety around them. There was the honest cock-robin, the favorite game of stripling sportsmen, with its loud querulous note; and the twittering blackbirds flying in sable clouds; and the golden-winged woodpecker, with his crimson crest, his broad black gorget, and splendid plumage; and the cedar bird, with its red-tipt wings and yellow-tipt tail, and its little monteiro cap[2] of feathers; and the blue jay, that noisy coxcomb, in his gay light-blue coat and white underclothes; screaming and chattering, nodding and bobbing and bowing, and pretending to be on good terms with every songster of the grove.

As Ichabod jogged slowly on his way, his eye, ever open to every symptom of culinary abundance, ranged with delight over the treasures of jolly autumn. On all sides he beheld vast store of apples; some hanging in oppressive opulence on the trees; some gathered into baskets and barrels for the market; others heaped up in rich piles for the cider-press. Farther on he beheld great fields of Indian corn, with its golden ears peeping from their leafy coverts, and holding out the promise of cakes and hasty pudding; and the yellow pumpkins lying beneath them, turning up their fair round bellies to the sun, and giving ample prospects of the most luxurious of pies; and anon he passed the fragrant buckwheat fields, breathing the odor of the bee-hive, and as he beheld them, soft anticipations stole over his mind of dainty slapjacks, well buttered, and garnished with honey or treacle, by the delicate little dimpled hand of Katrina Van Tassel.

Thus feeding his mind with many sweet thoughts and "sugared suppositions," he journeyed along the sides of a range of hills which look out upon some of the goodliest scenes of the mighty Hudson. The sun gradually wheeled his broad disk down into the west. The wide bosom of the Tappan Zee lay motionless and glassy, excepting that here and there a gentle undulation waved and prolonged the blue shadow of the distant mountain. A few amber clouds floated in the sky, without a breath of air to move them. The horizon was of a fine golden tint, changing gradually into a pure apple green, and from that into the deep blue of the mid-heaven. A slanting ray lingered on the woody crests of the precipices that overhung some parts of the river, giving greater depth to the dark-gray and purple of their rocky sides. A sloop was loitering in the distance, dropping slowly down with the tide, her sail hanging uselessly against the mast; and as the reflection of the sky gleamed along the still water, it seemed as if the vessel was suspended in the air.

It was toward evening that Ichabod arrived at the castle of the Heer Van Tassel, which he found thronged with the pride and flower of the adjacent country. Old farmers, a spare leathern-faced race, in homespun coats and breeches, blue stockings, huge shoes, and magnificent pewter buckles. Their brisk withered little dames, in close crimped caps, longwaisted shortgowns, homespun petticoats, with scissors and pin-cushions, and gay calico pockets hanging on the outside. Buxom lasses, almost as antiquated as their mothers, except-

---

2. Usually "montera" (Spanish), a hunting cap with flaps; here referring to the crest of the cedar waxwing.

ing where a straw hat, a fine ribbon, or perhaps a white frock, gave symptoms of city innovation. The sons, in short square-skirted coats with rows of stupendous brass buttons, and their hair generally queued in the fashion of the times, especially if they could procure an eel-skin for the purpose, it being esteemed, throughout the country, as a potent nourisher and strengthener of the hair.

Brom Bones, however, was the hero of the scene, having come to the gathering on his favorite steed Daredevil, a creature, like himself, full of mettle and mischief, and which no one but himself could manage. He was, in fact, noted for preferring vicious animals, given to all kinds of tricks, which kept the rider in constant risk of his neck, for he held a tractable well-broken horse as unworthy of a lad of spirit.

Fain would I pause to dwell upon the world of charms that burst upon the enraptured gaze of my hero, as he entered the state parlor of Van Tassel's mansion. Not those of the bevy of buxom lasses, with their luxurious display of red and white; but the ample charms of a genuine Dutch country tea-table, in the sumptuous time of autumn. Such heaped-up platters of cakes of various and almost indescribable kinds, known only to experienced Dutch housewives! There was the doughty dough-nut, the tenderer oly koek,[3] and the crisp and crumbling cruller; sweet cakes and short cakes, ginger cakes and honey cakes, and the whole family of cakes. And then there were apple pies and peach pies and pumpkin pies; besides slices of ham and smoked beef; and moreover delectable dishes of preserved plums, and peaches, and pears, and quinces; not to mention broiled shad and roasted chickens; together with bowls of milk and cream, all mingled higgledy-piggledy, pretty much as I have enumerated them, with the motherly tea-pot sending up its clouds of vapor from the midst—Heaven bless the mark! I want breath and time to discuss this banquet as it deserves, and am too eager to get on with my story. Happily, Ichabod Crane was not in so great a hurry as his historian, but did ample justice to every dainty.

He was a kind and thankful creature, whose heart dilated in proportion as his skin was filled with good cheer; and whose spirits rose with eating as some men's do with drink. He could not help, too, rolling his large eyes round him as he ate, and chuckling with the possibility that he might one day be lord of all this scene of almost unimaginable luxury and splendor. Then, he thought, how soon he'd turn his back upon the old school-house; snap his fingers in the face of Hans Van Ripper, and every other niggardly patron, and kick any itinerant pedagogue out of doors that should dare to call him comrade!

3. Literally translated "oil cake," a deep-fried dainty similar to the cruller but more delicate.

Old Baltus Van Tassel moved about among his guests with a face dilated with content and good humor, round and jolly as the harvest moon. His hospitable attentions were brief, but expressive, being confined to a shake of the hand, a slap on the shoulder, a loud laugh, and a pressing invitation to "fall to, and help themselves."

And now the sound of the music from the common room, or hall, summoned to the dance. The musician was an old grayheaded negro, who had been the itinerant orchestra of the neighborhood for more than half a century. His instrument was as old and battered as himself. The greater part of the time he scraped on two or three strings, accompanying every movement of the bow with a motion of the head; bowing almost to the ground, and stamping with his foot whenever a fresh couple were to start.

Ichabod prided himself upon his dancing as much as upon his vocal powers. Not a limb, not a fibre about him was idle; and to have seen his loosely hung frame in full motion, and clattering about the room, you would have thought Saint Vitus[4] himself, that blessed patron of the dance, was figuring before you in person. He was the admiration of all the negroes; who, having gathered, of all ages and sizes, from the farm and the neighborhood, stood forming a pyramid of shining black faces at every door and window, gazing with delight at the scene, rolling their white eye-balls, and showing grinning rows of ivory from ear to ear. How could the flogger of urchins be otherwise than animated and joyous? the lady of his heart was his partner in the dance, and smiling graciously in reply to all his amorous oglings; while Brom Bones, sorely smitten with love and jealousy, sat brooding by himself in one corner.

When the dance was at an end, Ichabod was attracted to a knot of the sager folks, who, with old Van Tassel, sat smoking at one end of the piazza, gossiping over former times, and drawing out long stories about the war.

This neighborhood, at the time of which I am speaking, was one of those highly-favored places which abound with chronicle and great men. The British and American line had run near it during the war; it had, therefore, been the scene of marauding, and infested with refugees, cow-boys,[5] and all kinds of border chivalry. Just sufficient time had elapsed to enable each story-teller to dress up his tale with a little becoming fiction, and, in the indistinctness of his recollection, to make himself the hero of every exploit.

There was the story of Doffue Martling, a large blue-bearded Dutchman, who had nearly taken a British frigate with an old iron nine-pounder from a mud breastwork, only that his gun burst at the

4. St. Vitus, martyred under Diocletian, legendary in Germany as the patron of health, was supplicated on his festival by dancing before his image.

5. A term applied during the Revolution to bands of Tory guerrillas operating near New York.

sixth discharge. And there was an old gentleman who shall be nameless, being too rich a mynheer to be lightly mentioned, who, in the battle of Whiteplains,[6] being an excellent master of defence, parried a musket ball with a small sword, insomuch that he absolutely felt it whiz round the blade, and glance off at the hilt: in proof of which, he was ready at any time to show the sword, with the hilt a little bent. There were several more that had been equally great in the field, not one of whom but was persuaded that he had a considerable hand in bringing the war to a happy termination.

But all these were nothing to the tales of ghosts and apparitions that succeeded. The neighborhood is rich in legendary treasures of the kind. Local tales and superstitions thrive best in these sheltered long-settled retreats; but are trampled under foot by the shifting throng that forms the population of most of our country places. Besides, there is no encouragement for ghosts in most of our villages, for they have scarcely had time to finish their first nap, and turn themselves in their graves, before their surviving friends have travelled away from the neighborhood; so that when they turn out at night to walk their rounds, they have no acquaintance left to call upon. This is perhaps the reason why we so seldom hear of ghosts except in our long-established Dutch communities.

The immediate cause, however, the prevalence of supernatural stories in these parts, was doubtless owing to the vicinity of Sleepy Hollow. There was a contagion in the very air that blew from that haunted region; it breathed forth an atmosphere of dreams and fancies infecting all the land. Several of the Sleepy Hollow people were present at Van Tassel's, and, as usual, were doling out their wild and wonderful legends. Many dismal tales were told about funeral trains, and mourning cries and wailings heard and seen about the great tree where the unfortunate Major André[7] was taken, and which stood in the neighborhood. Some mention was made also of the woman in white, that haunted the dark glen at Raven Rock, and was often heard to shriek on winter nights before a storm, having perished there in the snow. The chief part of the stories, however, turned upon the favorite spectre of Sleepy Hollow, the headless horseman, who had been heard several times of late, patrolling the country; and, it was said, tethered his horse nightly among the graves in the churchyard.

The sequestered situation of this church seems always to have made it a favorite haunt of troubled spirits. It stands on a knoll, surrounded by locust-trees and lofty elms, from among which its decent whitewashed walls shine modestly forth, like Christian purity beaming through the shades of retirement. A gentle slope descends from

6. White Plains, scene of Washington's defeat by Howe, October 28, 1776.
7. Major John André (1751–1780), gallant British spy, apprehended as agent of Arnold's disloyalty, and executed.

it to a silver sheet of water, bordered by high trees, between which, peeps may be caught at the blue hills of the Hudson. To look upon its grass-grown yard, where the sunbeams seem to sleep so quietly, one would think that there at least the dead might rest in peace. On one side of the church extends a wide woody dell, along which raves a large brook among broken rocks and trunks of fallen trees. Over a deep black part of the stream, not far from the church, was formerly thrown a wooden bridge; the road that led to it, and the bridge itself, were thickly shaded by overhanging trees, which cast a gloom about it, even in the daytime; but occasioned a fearful darkness at night. This was one of the favorite haunts of the headless horseman; and the place where he was most frequently encountered. The tale was told of old Brouwer, a most heretical disbeliever in ghosts, how he met the horseman returning from his foray into Sleepy Hollow, and was obliged to get up behind him; how they galloped over bush and brake, over hill and swamp, until they reached the bridge; when the horseman suddenly turned into a skeleton, threw old Brouwer into the brook, and sprang away over the tree-tops with a clap of thunder.

This story was immediately matched by a thrice marvellous adventure of Brom Bones, who made light of the galloping Hessian as an arrant jockey.[8] He affirmed that, on returning one night from the neighboring village of Sing Sing, he had been overtaken by this midnight trooper; that he had offered to race with him for a bowl of punch, and should have won it too, for Daredevil beat the goblin-horse all hollow, but, just as they came to the church-bridge, the Hessian bolted, and vanished in a flash of fire.

All these tales, told in that drowsy undertone with which men talk in the dark, the countenances of the listeners only now and then receiving a casual gleam from the glare of a pipe, sank deep in the mind of Ichabod. He repaid them in kind with large extracts from his invaluable author, Cotton Mather, and added many marvellous events that had taken place in his native State of Connecticut, and fearful sights which he had seen in his nightly walks about Sleepy Hollow.

The revel now gradually broke up. The old farmers gathered together their families in their wagons, and were heard for some time rattling along the hollow roads, and over the distant hills. Some of the damsels mounted on pillions behind their favorite swains, and their light-hearted laughter, mingling with the clatter of hoofs, echoed along the silent woodlands, sounding fainter and fainter until they gradually died away—and the late scene of noise and frolic was all silent and deserted. Ichabod only lingered behind, according to the custom of country lovers, to have a tête-à-tête with the heiress, fully convinced that he was now on the high road to success. What

8. Cheat or trickster.

passed at this interview I will not pretend to say, for in fact I do not know. Something, however, I fear me, must have gone wrong, for he certainly sallied forth, after no very great interval, with an air quite desolate and chop-fallen.—Oh these women! these women! Could that girl have been playing off any of her coquettish tricks? —Was her encouragement of the poor pedagogue all a mere sham to secure her conquest of his rival?—Heaven only knows, not I!— Let it suffice to say, Ichabod stole forth with the air of one who had been sacking a hen-roost, rather than a fair lady's heart. Without looking to the right or left to notice the scene of rural wealth, on which he had so often gloated, he went straight to the stable, and with several hearty cuffs and kicks, roused his steed most uncourteously from the comfortable quarters in which he was soundly sleeping, dreaming of mountains of corn and oats, and whole valleys of timothy and clover.

It was the very witching time of night[9] that Ichabod, heavy-hearted and crest-fallen, pursued his travel homewards, along the sides of the lofty hills which rise above Tarry Town, and which he had traversed so cheerily in the afternoon. The hour was as dismal as himself. Far below him, the Tappan Zee spread its dusky and indistinct waste of waters, with here and there the tall mast of a sloop, riding quietly at anchor under the land. In the dead hush of midnight, he could even hear the barking of the watch dog from the opposite shore of the Hudson; but it was so vague and faint as only to give an idea of his distance from this faithful companion of man. Now and then, too, the long-drawn crowing of a cock, accidentally awakened, would sound far, far off, from some farmhouse away among the hills—but it was like a dreaming sound in his ear. No signs of life occurred near him, but occasionally the melancholy chirp of a cricket, or perhaps the guttural twang of a bull-frog, from a neighboring marsh, as if sleeping uncomfortably, and turning suddenly in his bed.

All the stories of ghosts and goblins that he had heard in the afternoon, now came crowding upon his recollection. The night grew darker and darker; the stars seemed to sink deeper in the sky, and driving clouds occasionally hid them from his sight. He had never felt so lonely and dismal. He was, moreover, approaching the very place where many of the scenes of the ghost stories had been laid. In the centre of the road stood an enormous tulip-tree, which towered like a giant above all the other trees of the neighborhood, and formed a kind of landmark. Its limbs were gnarled, and fantastic, large enough to form trunks for ordinary trees, twisting down almost to the earth, and rising again into the air. It was connected with the tragical story of the unfortunate André, who had been taken

9. *Cf. Hamlet,* Act III, Scene 2, l. 406.

prisoner hard by; and was universally known by the name of Major André's tree. The common people regarded it with a mixture of respect and superstition, partly out of sympathy for the fate of its ill-starred namesake, and partly from the tales of strange sights and doleful lamentations told concerning it.

As Ichabod approached this fearful tree, he began to whistle: he thought his whistle was answered—it was but a blast sweeping sharply through the dry branches. As he approached a little nearer, he thought he saw something white, hanging in the midst of the tree —he paused and ceased whistling; but on looking more narrowly, perceived that it was a place where the tree had been scathed by lightning, and the white wood laid bare. Suddenly he heard a groan —his teeth chattered and his knees smote against the saddle: it was but the rubbing of one huge bough upon another, as they were swayed about by the breeze. He passed the tree in safety, but new perils lay before him.

About two hundred yards from the tree a small brook crossed the road, and ran into a marshy and thickly-wooded glen, known by the name of Wiley's swamp. A few rough logs, laid side by side, served for a bridge over this stream. On that side of the road where the brook entered the wood, a group of oaks and chestnuts, matted thick with wild grapevines, threw a cavernous gloom over it. To pass this bridge was the severest trial. It was at this identical spot that the unfortunate André was captured, and under the covert of those chestnuts and vines were the sturdy yeomen concealed who surprised him. This has ever since been considered a haunted stream, and fearful are the feelings of the schoolboy who has to pass it alone after dark.

As he approached the stream his heart began to thump; he summoned up, however, all his resolution, gave his horse half a score of kicks in the ribs, and attempted to dash briskly across the bridge; but instead of starting forward, the perverse old animal made a lateral movement, and ran broadside against the fence. Ichabod, whose fears increased with the delay, jerked the reins on the other side, and kicked lustily with the contrary foot: it was all in vain; his steed started, it is true, but it was only to plunge to the opposite side of the road into a thicket of brambles and alder bushes. The schoolmaster now bestowed both whip and heel upon the starveling ribs of old Gunpowder, who dashed forward, snuffling and snorting, but came to a stand just by the bridge, with a suddenness that had nearly sent his rider sprawling over his head. Just at this moment a plashy tramp by the side of the bridge caught the sensitive ear of Ichabod. In the dark shadow of the grove, on the margin of the brook, he beheld something huge, misshapen, black and towering. It stirred not, but seemed gathered up in the gloom, like some gigantic monster ready to spring upon the traveller.

The hair of the affrighted pedagogue rose upon his head with terror. What was to be done? To turn and fly was now too late; and besides, what chance was there of escaping ghost or goblin, if such it was, which could ride upon the wings of the wind? Summoning up, therefore, a show of courage, he demanded in stammering accents—"Who are you?" He received no reply. He repeated his demand in a still more agitated voice. Still there was no answer. Once more he cudgelled the sides of the inflexible Gunpowder, and, shutting his eyes, broke forth with involuntary fervor into a psalm tune. Just then the shadowy object of alarm put itself in motion, and, with a scramble and a bound, stood at once in the middle of the road. Though the night was dark and dismal, yet the form of the unknown might now in some degree be ascertained. He appeared to be a horseman of large dimensions, and mounted on a black horse of powerful frame. He made no offer of molestation or sociability, but kept aloof on one side of the road, jogging along on the blind side of old Gunpowder, who had now got over his fright and waywardness.

Ichabod, who had no relish for this strange midnight companion, and bethought himself of the adventure of Brom Bones with the Galloping Hessian, now quickened his steed, in hopes of leaving him behind. The stranger, however, quickened his horse to an equal pace. Ichabod pulled up, and fell into a walk, thinking to lag behind—the other did the same. His heart began to sink within him; he endeavored to resume his psalm tune, but his parched tongue clove to the roof of his mouth, and he could not utter a stave. There was something in the moody and dogged silence of this pertinacious companion, that was mysterious and appalling. It was soon fearfully accounted for. On mounting a rising ground, which brought the figure of his fellow-traveller in relief against the sky, gigantic in height, and muffled in a cloak, Ichabod was horror-struck, on perceiving that he was headless!—but his horror was still more increased, on observing that the head, which should have rested on his shoulders, was carried before him on the pommel of the saddle: his terror rose to desperation; he rained a shower of kicks and blows upon Gunpowder, hoping, by a sudden movement, to give his companion the slip—but the spectre started full jump with him. Away then they dashed, through thick and thin; stones flying, and sparks flashing at every bound. Ichabod's flimsy garments fluttered in the air, as he stretched his long lank body away over his horse's head, in the eagerness of his flight.

They had now reached the road which turns off to Sleepy Hollow; but Gunpowder, who seemed possessed with a demon, instead of keeping up it, made an opposite turn, and plunged headlong down hill to the left. This road leads through a sandy hollow, shaded by trees for about a quarter of a mile, where it crosses the bridge famous in goblin story, and just beyond swells the green knoll on which stands the whitewashed church.

As yet the panic of the steed had given his unskilful rider an apparent advantage in the chase; but just as he had got half way through the hollow, the girths of the saddle gave way, and he felt it slipping from under him. He seized it by the pommel, and endeavored to hold it firm, but in vain; and had just time to save himself by clasping old Gunpowder round the neck, when the saddle fell to the earth, and he heard it trampled under foot by his pursuer. For a moment the terror of Hans Van Ripper's wrath passed across his mind—for it was his Sunday saddle; but this was no time for petty fears; the goblin was hard on his haunches; and (unskilful rider that he was!) he had much ado to maintain his seat; sometimes slipping on one side, sometimes on another, and sometimes jolted on the high ridge of his horse's back-bone, with a violence that he verily feared would cleave him asunder.

An opening in the trees now cheered him with the hopes that the church bridge was at hand. The wavering reflection of a silver star in the bosom of the brook told him that he was not mistaken. He saw the walls of the church dimly glaring under the trees beyond. He recollected the place where Brom Bones's ghostly competitor had disappeared. "If I can but reach that bridge,"[1] thought Ichabod, "I am safe." Just then he heard the black steed panting and blowing close behind him; he even fancied that he felt his hot breath. Another convulsive kick in the ribs and old Gunpowder sprang upon the bridge; he thundered over the resounding planks; he gained the opposite side; and now Ichabod cast a look behind to see if his pursuer should vanish, according to rule, in a flash of fire and brimstone. Just then he saw the goblin rising in his stirrups, and in the very act of hurling his head at him. Ichabod endeavored to dodge the horrible missile, but too late. It encountered his cranium with a tremendous crash—he was tumbled headlong into the dust, and Gunpowder, the black steed, and the goblin rider, passed by like a whirlwind.

The next morning the old horse was found without his saddle, and with the bridle under his feet, soberly cropping the grass at his master's gate. Ichabod did not make his appearance at breakfast—dinner-hour came, but no Ichabod. The boys assembled at the school-house, and strolled idly about the banks of the brook; but no schoolmaster. Hans Van Ripper now began to feel some uneasiness about the fate of poor Ichabod, and his saddle. An inquiry was set on foot, and after diligent investigation they came upon his traces. In one part of the road leading to the church was found the saddle trampled in the dirt; the tracks of horses' hoofs deeply dented in the road, and evi-

---

1. It was commonly held that witches cannot cross water. *Cf.* Burns's "Tam O'Shanter."

dently at furious speed, were traced to the bridge, beyond which, on the bank of a broad part of the brook, where the water ran deep and black, was found the hat of the unfortunate Ichabod, and close beside it a shattered pumpkin.

The brook was searched, but the body of the schoolmaster was not to be discovered. Hans Van Ripper, as executor of his estate, examined the bundle which contained all his worldly effects. They consisted of two shirts and a half; two stocks for the neck; a pair or two of worsted stockings; an old pair of corduroy small-clothes; a rusty razor; a book of psalm tunes, full of dogs' ears; and a broken pitch-pipe. As to the books and furniture of the schoolhouse, they belonged to the community, excepting Cotton Mather's History of Witchcraft, a New England Almanac, and a book of dreams and fortune-telling; in which last was a sheet of foolscap much scribbled and blotted in several fruitless attempts to make a copy of verses in honor of the heiress of Van Tassel. These magic books and the poetic scrawl were forthwith consigned to the flames by Hans Van Ripper; who from that time forward determined to send his children no more to school; observing, that he never knew any good come of this same reading and writing. Whatever money the schoolmaster possessed, and he had received his quarter's pay but a day or two before, he must have had about his person at the time of his disappearance.

The mysterious event caused much speculation at the church on the following Sunday. Knots of gazers and gossips were collected in the churchyard, at the bridge, and at the spot where the hat and pumpkin had been found. The stories of Brouwer, of Bones, and a whole budget of others, were called to mind; and when they had diligently considered them all, and compared them with the symptoms of the present case, they shook their heads, and came to the conclusion that Ichabod had been carried off by the galloping Hessian. As he was a bachelor, and in nobody's debt, nobody troubled his head any more about him. The school was removed to a different quarter of the hollow, and another pedagogue reigned in his stead.

It is true, an old farmer, who had been down to New York on a visit several years after, and from whom this account of the ghostly adventure was received, brought home the intelligence that Ichabod Crane was still alive; that he had left the neighborhood, partly through fear of the goblin and Hans Van Ripper, and partly in mortification at having been suddenly dismissed by the heiress; that he had changed his quarters to a distant part of the country; had kept school and studied law at the same time, had been admitted to the bar, turned politician, electioneered, written for the newspapers, and finally had been made a justice of the Ten Pound Court.[2] Brom Bones too, who,

2. A petty magistrate's court, limited to cases involving no more than £10.

shortly after his rival's disappearance, conducted the blooming Katrina in triumph to the altar, was observed to look exceedingly knowing whenever the story of Ichabod was related, and always burst into a hearty laugh at the mention of the pumpkin; which led some to suspect that he knew more about the matter than he chose to tell.

The old country wives, however, who are the best judges of these matters, maintain to this day that Ichabod was spirited away by supernatural means; and it is a favorite story often told about the neighborhood round the winter evening fire. The bridge became more than ever an object of superstitious awe, and that may be the reason why the road has been altered of late years, so as to approach the church by the border of the mill-pond. The school-house being deserted, soon fell to decay, and was reported to be haunted by the ghost of the unfortunate pedagogue; and the plough boy, loitering homeward of a still summer evening, has often fancied his voice at a distance, chanting a melancholy psalm tune among the tranquil solitudes of Sleepy Hollow.

POSTSCRIPT, FOUND IN THE HANDWRITING OF MR. KNICKERBOCKER

The preceding Tale is given, almost in the precise words in which I heard it related at a Corporation meeting of the ancient city of Manhattoes, at which were present many of its sagest and most illustrious burghers. The narrator was a pleasant, shabby, gentlemanly old fellow, in pepper-and-salt clothes, with a sadly humorous face; and one whom I strongly suspected of being poor,—he made such efforts to be entertaining. When his story was concluded, there was much laughter and approbation, particularly from two or three deputy aldermen, who had been asleep the greater part of the time. There was, however, one tall, dry-looking old gentleman, with beetling eyebrows, who maintained a grave and rather severe face throughout: now and then folding his arms, inclining his head, and looking down upon the floor, as if turning a doubt over in his mind. He was one of your wary men, who never laugh, but upon good grounds—when they have reason and the law on their side. When the mirth of the rest of the company had subsided, and silence was restored, he leaned one arm on the elbow of his chair, and sticking the other akimbo, demanded, with a slight, but exceedingly sage motion of the head, and contraction of the brow, what was the moral of the story, and what it went to prove?

The story-teller, who was just putting a glass of wine to his lips, as a refreshment after his toils, paused for a moment, looked at his inquirer with an air of infinite deference, and, lowering the glass slowly to the table, observed, that the story was intended most logically to prove:—

"That there is no situation in life but has its advantages and pleasures—providing we will but take a joke as we find it:

"That, therefore, he that runs races with goblin troopers is likely to have rough riding of it.

"Ergo, for a country schoolmaster to be refused the hand of a Dutch heiress, is a certain step to high preferment, in the state."

The cautious old gentleman knit his brows tenfold closer after this explanation, being sorely puzzled by the ratiocination of the syllogism; while, methought, the one in pepper-and-salt eyed him with something of a triumphant leer. At length he observed, that all this was very well, but still he thought the story a little on the extravagant—there were one or two points on which he had his doubts.

"Faith, sir," replied the story-teller, "as to that matter, I don't believe one-half of it myself."

D. K.

1820, 1860–1861

To the Reader[3]

Worthy and Dear Reader!—Hast thou ever been waylaid in the midst of a pleasant tour by some treacherous malady: thy heels tripped up, and thou left to count the tedious minutes as they passed, in the solitude of an inn chamber? If thou hast, thou wilt be able to pity me. Behold me, interrupted in the course of my journeying up the fair banks of the Rhine, and laid up by indisposition in this old frontier town of Mentz. I have worn out every source of amusement. I know the sound of every clock that strikes, and bell that rings, in the place. I know to a second when to listen for the first tap of the Prussian drum, as it summons the garrison to parade, or at what hour to expect the distant sound of the Austrian military band. All these have grown wearisome to me; and even the well-known step of my doctor, as he slowly paces the corridor, with healing in the creak of his shoes, no longer affords an agreeable interruption to the monotony of my apartment.

For a time I attempted to beguile the weary hours, by studying German under the tuition of mine host's pretty little daughter, Katrine; but I soon found even German had not power to charm a languid ear, and that the conjugating of *ich liebe*[4] might be powerless, however rosy the lips which uttered it.

I tried to read, but my mind would not fix itself. I turned over

3. *Tales of a Traveller* was published in London, in two volumes, August 25, 1824. In New York it appeared in four installments, August 24 to October 9, 1824. The first installment bore the subtitle "Strange Stories by a Nervous Gentleman." This contained the two pieces reprinted below: "To the

Reader," which became the introduction for the collected volume, and the "Adventure of the German Student." In this publication Irving still used the name Geoffrey Crayon, his whimsical pseudonym in the *Sketch Book.*
4. "I love."

volume after volume, but threw them by with distaste: "Well, then," said I at length, in despair, "if I cannot read a book, I will write one." Never was there a more lucky idea; it at once gave me occupation and amusement. The writing of a book was considered in old times as an enterprise of toil and difficulty, insomuch that the most trifling lucubration was denominated a "work," and the world talked with awe and reverence of "the labors of the learned."—These matters are better understood nowadays.

Thanks to the improvements in all kind of manufactures, the art of book-making has been made familiar to the meanest capacity. Everybody is an author. The scribbling of a quarto is the mere pastime of the idle; the young gentleman throws off his brace of duodecimos in the intervals of the sporting season, and the young lady produces her set of volumes with the same facility that her great-grandmother worked a set of chair-bottoms.

The idea having struck me, therefore, to write a book, the reader will easily perceive that the execution of it was no difficult matter. I rummaged my portfolio, and cast about, in my recollection, for those floating materials which a man naturally collects in travelling; and here I have arranged them in this little work.

As I know this to be a story-telling and a story-reading age, and that the world is fond of being taught by apologue, I have digested the instruction I would convey into a number of tales. They may not possess the power of amusement, which the tales told by many of my contemporaries possess; but then I value myself on the sound moral which each of them contains. This may not be apparent at first, but the reader will be sure to find it out in the end. I am for curing the world by gentle alteratives, not by violent doses; indeed, the patient should never be conscious that he is taking a dose. I have learnt this much from experience under the hands of the worthy Hippocrates of Mentz.[5]

I am not, therefore, for those barefaced tales which carry their moral on the surface, staring one in the face; they are enough to deter the squeamish reader. On the contrary, I have often hid my moral from sight, and disguised it as much as possible by sweets and spices, so that while the simple reader is listening with open mouth to a ghost or a love story, he may have a bolus of sound morality popped down his throat, and be never the wiser for the fraud.[6]

As the public is apt to be curious about the sources whence an

---

5. A whimsical pronunciation for the city named Mainz in German and Mayence in French. See the date line concluding the letter.

6. "Many years later * * * a flattering review * * * asserted: 'His most comical pieces have always a serious end in view.' 'You laugh,' said Irving to his nephew, with [an] air of whimsical significance * * * , 'but it is true. I have kept that to myself hitherto, but that man has found me out. He has detected the moral.'" [Quoted by Pochmann, *Washington Irving: Representative Selections*, p. 386].

author draws his stories, doubtless that it may know how far to put faith in them, I would observe, that the Adventure of the German Student, or rather the latter part of it, is founded on an anecdote related to me as existing somewhere in French; and, indeed, I have been told, since writing it, that an ingenious tale has been founded on it by an English writer; but I have never met with either the former or the latter in print. Some of the circumstances in the Adventure of the Mysterious Picture, and in the Story of the Young Italian, are vague recollections of anecdotes related to me some years since; but from what source derived, I do not know. The Adventure of the Young Painter among the banditti is taken almost entirely from an authentic narrative in manuscript.

As to the other tales contained in this work, and indeed to my tales generally, I can make but one observation; I am an old traveller; I have read somewhat, heard and seen more, and dreamt more than all. My brain is filled, therefore, with all kinds of odds and ends. In travelling, these heterogeneous matters have become shaken up in my mind, as the articles are apt to be in an ill-packed travelling trunk; so that when I attempt to draw forth a fact, I cannot determine whether I have read, heard, or dreamt it; and I am always at a loss to know how much to believe of my own stories.

These matters being premised, fall to, worthy reader, with good appetite; and, above all, with good humor, to what is here set before thee. If the tales I have furnished should prove to be bad, they will at least be found short; so that no one will be wearied long on the same theme. "Variety is charming," as some poet observes.

There is a certain relief in change, even though it be from bad to worse! As I have often found in travelling in a stage-coach, that it is often a comfort to shift one's position, and be bruised in a new place.

Ever thine,

Geoffrey Crayon.

Dated from the HOTEL DE DARMSTADT,
    ci-devant HOTEL DE PARIS,
        MENTZ, *otherwise called* MAYENCE.

Adventure of the German Student[7]

On a stormy night, in the tempestuous times of the French revolution, a young German was returning to his lodgings, at a late hour,

7. The Gothic story, employing physical and psychological terror in a weird or mysterious setting, had enjoyed a vogue toward the end of the previous century, especially in German literature and among British writers from Walpole to Ann Radcliffe and "Monk" Lewis. An earlier American author, Charles Brockden Brown, had succeeded notably in this vein. Irving gave a humorously perverse twist to the Gothic tale; the present story, which appeared

across the old part of Paris. The lightning gleamed, and the loud claps of thunder rattled through the lofty narrow streets—but I should first tell you something about this young German.

Gottfried Wolfgang was a young man of good family. He had studied for some time at Gottingen, but being of a visionary and enthusiastic character, he had wandered into those wild and speculative doctrines which have so often bewildered German students. His secluded life, his intense application, and the singular nature of his studies, had an effect on both mind and body. His health was impaired; his imagination diseased. He had been indulging in fanciful speculations on spiritual essences, until, like Swedenborg, he had an ideal world of his own around him. He took up a notion, I do not know from what cause, that there was an evil influence hanging over him; an evil genius or spirit seeking to ensnare him and ensure his perdition. Such an idea working on his melancholy temperament, produced the most gloomy effects. He became haggard and desponding. His friends discovered the mental malady preying upon him, and determined that the best cure was a change of scene; he was sent, therefore, to finish his studies amidst the splendors and gayeties of Paris.

Wolfgang arrived at Paris at the breaking out of the revolution.[8] The popular delirium at first caught his enthusiastic mind, and he was captivated by the political and philosophical theories of the day: but the scenes of blood which followed shocked his sensitive nature, disgusted him with society and the world, and made him more than ever a recluse. He shut himself up in a solitary apartment in the *Pays Latin*,[9] the quarter of students. There, in a gloomy street not far from the monastic walls of the Sorbonne, he pursued his favorite speculations. Sometimes he spent hours together in the great libraries of Paris, those catacombs of departed authors, rummaging among their hoards of dusty and obsolete works in quest of food for his unhealthy appetite. He was, in a manner, a literary ghoul, feeding in the charnel-house of decayed literature.

Wolfgang, though solitary and recluse, was of an ardent temperament, but for a time it operated merely upon his imagination. He was too shy and ignorant of the world to make any advances to the fair, but he was a passionate admirer of female beauty, and in his lonely chamber would often lose himself in reveries on forms and faces which he had seen, and his fancy would deck out images of loveliness far surpassing the reality.

While his mind was in this excited and sublimated state, a dream

in *Tales of a Traveller*, is an excellent example of his success. This literary impulse later reached its American perfection in the psychological subtleties of Poe.

8. The French Revolution is generally dated from 1789; the Republic was declared in 1792.

9. The Latin Quarter, adjacent to the University (*cf.* Sorbonne, below), occupied by students, artists, and Bohemians.

produced an extraordinary effect upon him. It was of a female face of transcendent beauty. So strong was the impression made, that he dreamt of it again and again. It haunted his thoughts by day, his slumbers by night; in fine, he became passionately enamoured of this shadow of a dream. This lasted so long that it became one of those fixed ideas which haunt the minds of melancholy men, and are at times mistaken for madness.

Such was Gottfried Wolfgang, and such his situation at the time I mentioned. He was returning home late one stormy night, through some of the old and gloomy streets of the *Marais*, the ancient part of Paris. The loud claps of thunder rattled among the high houses of the narrow streets. He came to the *Place de Grève*, the square where public executions are performed. The lightning quivered about the pinnacles of the ancient *Hôtel de Ville*,[1] and shed flickering gleams over the open space in front. As Wolfgang was crossing the square, he shrank back with horror at finding himself close by the guillotine. It was the height of the reign of terror, when this dreadful instrument of death stood ever ready, and its scaffold was continually running with the blood of the virtuous and the brave. It had that very day been actively employed in the work of carnage, and there it stood in grim array, amidst a silent and sleeping city, waiting for fresh victims.

Wolfgang's heart sickened within him, and he was turning shuddering from the horrible engine, when he beheld a shadowy form, cowering as it were at the foot of the steps which led up to the scaffold. A succession of vivid flashes of lightning revealed it more distinctly. It was a female figure, dressed in black. She was seated on one of the lower steps of the scaffold, leaning forward, her face hid in her lap; and her long dishevelled tresses hanging to the ground, streaming with the rain which fell in torrents. Wolfgang paused. There was something awful in this solitary monument of woe. The female had the appearance of being above the common order. He knew the times to be full of vicissitude, and that many a fair head, which had once been pillowed on down, now wandered houseless. Perhaps this was some poor mourner whom the dreadful axe had rendered desolate, and who sat here heart-broken on the strand of existence, from which all that was dear to her had been launched into eternity.

He approached, and addressed her in the accents of sympathy. She raised her head and gazed wildly at him. What was his astonishment at beholding, by the bright glare of the lightning, the very face which had haunted him in his dreams. It was pale and disconsolate, but ravishingly beautiful.

Trembling with violent and conflicting emotions, Wolfgang again

1. City hall.

accosted her. He spoke something of her being exposed at such an hour of the night, and to the fury of such a storm, and offered to conduct her to her friends. She pointed to the guillotine with a gesture of dreadful signification.

"I have no friend on earth!" said she.

"But you have a home," said Wolfgang.

"Yes—in the grave!"

The heart of the student melted at the words.

"If a stranger dare make an offer," said he, "without danger of being misunderstood, I would offer my humble dwelling as a shelter; myself as a devoted friend. I am friendless myself in Paris, and a stranger in the land; but if my life could be of service, it is at your disposal, and should be sacrificed before harm or indignity should come to you."

There was an honest earnestness in the young man's manner that had its effect. His foreign accent, too, was in his favor; it showed him not to be a hackneyed inhabitant of Paris. Indeed, there is an eloquence in true enthusiasm that is not to be doubted. The homeless stranger confided herself implicitly to the protection of the student.

He supported her faltering steps across the *Pont Neuf,* and by the place where the statue of Henry the Fourth had been overthrown by the populace. The storm had abated, and the thunder rumbled at a distance. All Paris was quiet; that great volcano of human passion slumbered for a while, to gather fresh strength for the next day's eruption. The student conducted his charge through the ancient streets of the *Pays Latin,* and by the dusky walls of the Sorbonne, to the great dingy hotel which he inhabited. The old portress who admitted them stared with surprise at the unusual sight of the melancholy Wolfgang with a female companion.

On entering his apartment, the student, for the first time, blushed at the scantiness and indifference of his dwelling. He had but one chamber—an old-fashioned saloon—heavily carved, and fantastically furnished with the remains of former magnificence, for it was one of those hotels in the quarter of the Luxembourg palace, which had once belonged to nobility. It was lumbered with books and papers, and all the usual apparatus of a student, and his bed stood in a recess at one end.

When lights were brought, and Wolfgang had a better opportunity of contemplating the stranger, he was more than ever intoxicated by her beauty. Her face was pale, but of a dazzling fairness, set off by a profusion of raven hair that hung clustering about it. Her eyes were large and brilliant, with a singular expression approaching almost to wildness. As far as her black dress permitted her shape to be seen, it was of perfect symmetry. Her whole appearance was highly striking, though she was dressed in the simplest style. The only thing approaching to an ornament which she wore, was a broad black band round her neck, clasped by diamonds.

The perplexity now commenced with the student how to dispose of the helpless being thus thrown upon his protection. He thought of abandoning his chamber to her, and seeking shelter for himself elsewhere. Still he was so fascinated by her charms, there seemed to be such a spell upon his thoughts and senses, that he could not tear himself from her presence. Her manner, too, was singular and unaccountable. She spoke no more of the guillotine. Her grief had abated. The attentions of the student had first won her confidence, and then, apparently, her heart. She was evidently an enthusiast like himself, and enthusiasts soon understood each other.

In the infatuation of the moment, Wolfgang avowed his passion for her. He told her the story of his mysterious dream, and how she had possessed his heart before he had even seen her. She was strangely affected by his recital, and acknowledged to have felt an impulse towards him equally unaccountable. It was the time for wild theory and wild actions. Old prejudices and superstitions were done away; every thing was under the sway of the "Goddess of Reason."[2] Among other rubbish of the old times, the forms and ceremonies of marriage began to be considered superfluous bonds for honorable minds. Social compacts were the vogue. Wolfgang was too much of a theorist not to be tainted by the liberal doctrines of the day.

"Why should we separate?" said he: "our hearts are united; in the eye of reason and honor we are as one. What need is there of sordid forms to bind high souls together?"

The stranger listened with emotion: she had evidently received illumination at the same school.

"You have no home nor family," continued he; "let me be every thing to you, or rather let us be every thing to one another. If form is necessary, form shall be observed—there is my hand. I pledge myself to you for ever."

"For ever?" said the stranger, solemnly.

"For ever!" repeated Wolfgang.

The stranger clasped the hand extended to her: "then I am yours," murmured she, and sank upon his bosom.

The next morning the student left his bride sleeping, and sallied forth at an early hour to seek more spacious apartments suitable to the change in his situation. When he returned, he found the stranger lying with her head hanging over the bed, and one arm thrown over it. He spoke to her, but received no reply. He advanced to awaken her from her uneasy posture. On taking her hand, it was cold—there was no pulsation—her face was pallid and ghastly.—In a word she

2. The "Goddess of Reason" had been literally enthroned, in recognition of the rationalistic program of the Revolution concerning government and social institutions, including marriage.

was a corpse.

Horrified and frantic, he alarmed the house. A scene of confusion ensued. The police was summoned. As the officer of police entered the room, he started back on beholding the corpse.

"Good heaven!" cried he, "how did this woman come here?"

"Do you know anything about her?" said Wolfgang, eagerly.

"Do I?" exclaimed the officer: "she was guillotined yesterday."

He stepped forward; undid the black collar round the neck of the corpse, and the head rolled on the floor!

The student burst into a frenzy. "The fiend! the fiend has gained possession of me!" shrieked he: "I am lost for ever."

They tried to soothe him, but in vain. He was possessed with the frightful belief that an evil spirit had reanimated the dead body to ensnare him. He went distracted, and died in a mad-house.

Here the old gentleman with the haunted head finished his narrative.

"And is this really a fact?" said the inquisitive gentleman.

"A fact not to be doubted," replied the other. "I had it from the best authority. The student told it me himself. I saw him in a mad-house in Paris."

1824, 1860–61

JAMES FENIMORE COOPER
(1789–1851)

The novels of Cooper, appearing immediately after the heyday of the works of Sir Walter Scott, at first attained phenomenal popularity, then survived primarily because of their appeal for younger readers. In Europe, Cooper has been perhaps the most popular American author of his century. Unfortunately he inherited a formal rhetoric which soon went out of fashion, and many of his idealized situations and characters, especially his women, forbid close analysis. Yet he is respectfully remembered as a master of adventurous narrative, and even more, as the creator of an American hero-myth. For the serious reader of today, Cooper has gained stature as a critic of American society, not only in his novels of American history, but also in the comparative judgments of Europe and the United States to be found in his excellent volumes of travels, and in the critical commentaries which, as a patrician democrat, he addressed to his countrymen during the Jacksonian age of equalitarian excess.

The son of Judge William Cooper and Susan Fenimore, Cooper was born at Burlington, New Jersey, September 15, 1789. The next year his father settled on the family estate, now Cooperstown, at the foot of Otsego Lake, in New York. There the family was dominant; Judge Cooper was by nature the landed proprietor. Young Cooper was privately tutored; then he attended Yale for three years, without achieving a degree. After a year at sea before the mast, he was commissioned a midshipman in the United States Navy in 1808. Three years later he married Susan Augusta De-Lancey, daughter of a wealthy family in Mamaroneck, Westchester County, New York; he then resigned his commission and became the country gentleman, devoting himself to his family, and to agricultural, political, financial, and social interests in Cooperstown and in Westchester County.

According to a charming legend, Cooper's first novel (*Precaution*, 1820) was a response to his wife's challenge to improve on the current British society fiction, and the failure of this work turned him to historical novels. *The Spy* (1821), a novel of the Revolution, foreshadowed his typical hero in Harvey Birch, and launched his career as the American rival of Sir Walter Scott in the popular field of historical romance. In the remaining thirty years of his life, he poured out a staggering total of thirty-three novels, numerous volumes of social comment, a *History of the Navy*, and five volumes of travels.

In the *Leather-Stocking Tales* the American frontier hero first materialized, to run his limitless course to the present day, through the romance, dime novel, drama, movies, and television. Fearless and miraculously resourceful, he survives the rigors of nature and the villainy of man by superior strength and skill, and by the help of heaven, for he is always quaintly moral. In short, he is the knight of the Christian romances transplanted to the soil of democracy and the American forest and frontier. Cooper's Natty Bumppo appears in the five novels under various names which, like a knight of old, he has gained by his exploits. Deerslayer merges into Hawk-eye, Pathfinder, and Leather-Stocking.

Cooper did not plan these novels as a series, nor did he publish them in the chronological order of the events in their hero's life. In *The Pioneers* (1823), the author's third novel, Natty Bumppo first appeared, as a seasoned scout in advancing years, accompanied by the dying Chingachgook, the old Indian chief who has been his faithful comrade in adventure. The *Leather-Stocking Tales* are named below in the order of events in the life of Natty Bumppo: *The Deerslayer* (1841), early adventures with the hostile Hurons, on Lake Otsego, New York, in 1740–1745; *The Last of the Mohicans* (1826), an adventure of the French and Indian Wars, in the Lake George country in 1757; *The Pathfinder* (1840), continuing the same border warfare in 1760, in the St. Lawrence and Lake Ontario country; *The Pioneers* (1823), described above, taking place in 1793, as the eastern forest frontier begins to disappear, and old Chingachgook dies; and *The Prairie* (1827), set in the new frontier of the western plains in 1804, where the aged Leather-Stocking, having assisted some white pioneers and the Pawnees against the Sioux, takes leave of life amid people who can still value his devotion to a dying chivalry.

Almost as popular in their own day as the *Leather-Stocking Tales* were Cooper's romances of seafaring and naval combat; of these *The Pilot* (1823) set the pattern and provided the typical heroes in Long Tom Coffin and the mysterious "Pilot," generally taken to represent the gallant John Paul Jones. Later novels of the sea included, notably, *The Red Rover* (1828), *The Water-Witch* (1830), *The Two Admirals* (1842), and *The Wing-and-Wing* (1842).

Cooper's earnestness as a social critic was strongly evident in his novels based on European history. *The Bravo* (1831), *The Heidenmauer* (1832), and *The Headsman* (1833), are satires of European feudalism, but follow the conventional pattern which Scott had established for historical romance. From 1826 to 1833 Cooper lived observantly abroad, ostensibly as American consul at Lyon, but actually as a persistent traveler. His novels of foreign locale, as well as his travel books and volumes of social comment, reflect his continuous awareness of contrasts in society, behavior, and government between the United States and Europe, particularly Great Britain. Abroad he was regarded as a champion of American life; but at home, his comments ironically gained him a reputation as a defender of the aristocracy. His *Sketches of Switzerland* and *Gleanings in Europe*, published in five volumes between 1836 and 1838, are now regarded as genuine contributions to our literature of travel, but at the time they antagonized equalitarian democrats, and the breach was widened by such commentaries and novels as *A Letter to His Countrymen* (1834), and *Homeward Bound*, *Home as Found*, and *The American Democrat*, all published in 1838.

He had returned to Cooperstown in 1834. Soon the unbalanced reviews of such works led him to institute a number of lawsuits for slander; and the fact that he generally won his cases at law did not pacify his enemies or reduce public bitterness. In addition he was involved in litigation over the trespass of the community on his lands, and the controversy of the "Three Mile Point," beginning in 1837, confirmed his reputation as an aristocratic reactionary. Curiously enough, however, his popularity as a novelist, then or later, was affected but little.

Among the best contributions of his prolific later years is a trilogy of novels, *Satanstoe* (1845), *The Chainbearer* (1845), and *The Redskins* (1846), in which the author employs the fiction of certain "Littlepage Manuscripts," purported to contain records of three generations of a great family of upstate New York landholders. The novels form a consecutive social history of three generations of Dutch patroon society in the Hudson valley, ending with the Anti-

Rent Wars of the 1840's, when the tenants successfully opposed the feudal leases and perpetual sovereignty of the lords of the manor. Thus was founded the family novel of several volumes. Uneven in quality, the *Littlepage Manuscripts* succeed by their fine sense of history and their narrative intensity, and they are the last of Cooper's works to do so. Cooper died in 1851 on the day before his sixty-second birthday.

Cooper's novels, especially the *Leather-Stocking Tales*, have been reprinted many times but never critically edited, thus the authoritative *Descriptive Bibliography of the Writings of James Fenimore Cooper*, by Robert E. Spiller and P. C. Blackburn, 1934, is indispensable for serious study. The Author's Revised Edition appeared in 12 vols. in 1851, followed by an edition illustrated by F. O. C. Darley, 32 vols., 1859–1861. The Household Edition, 32 vols., 1876–1884, contains valuable introductory essays by Susan Fenimore Cooper, the novelist's daughter. The *Works*, 33 vols., 1895–1900, is still procurable. See also *Gleanings in Europe*, 2 vols., edited by Robert E. Spiller, 1928–1930, and *The American Democrat*, edited by H. L. Mencken, 1931. An excellent collection of the nonfiction is *Cooper: Representative Selections*, edited by Robert E. Spiller, American Writers Series, 1936.

There is no definitive biography; but *Fenimore Cooper, Critic of His Times*, by Robert E. Spiller, 1931, is an authoritative and penetrating study, and may be supplemented by the same author's Introduction to the *Representative Selections* (listed above). The comments by Susan Fenimore Cooper in *The Cooper Gallery*, 1865, are informative; and T. R. Lounsbury's pioneer biography, 1882, is still useful. The most recent biographical study is by James Grossman, 1949. *The Correspondence*, in part, has been compiled by J. F. Cooper, 2 vols., 1922.

From Gleanings in Europe: England[1]

[*English and American Traits*]

It would be an occupation of interest, to note the changes, moral and physical, that time, climate, and different institutions, have produced between the people of England, and those of America.

Physically, I do not think the change as great as is usually imagined. Dress makes a sensible difference in appearance, and I find that the Americans, who have been under the hands of the English tailors, are not easily distinguished from the English themselves. The principal points of distinction strike me to be these. We are taller, and less fleshy; more disposed to stoop; have more prominent features, and faces less full; are less ruddy, and more tanned; have much smaller hands and feet, anti-democratical as it may be; and are more slouching in gait. The exceptions, of course, are numerous; but I think these distinctions may be deemed national. The American, who has become Europeanized by dress, however, is so very different a looking animal from what he is at home, that too much stress is not to be laid on them. Then the great extent of the United States is creating certain physical differences in our own population, that render all such comparisons liable to many qualifications.

1. Cooper traveled extensively in Europe from 1826 to 1833, and published several volumes on his travels. The following is from *England* (London, 1837), which appeared the same year in the United States with the full title given here.

As to stature and physical force, I see no reason to think that the animal has deteriorated in America. As between England and the Old Atlantic states, the difference is not striking, after one allows for the disparity in numbers, and the density of the population here, the eye always seeking exceptions; but I incline to believe that the south-west will turn the scale to our side. I believe it to be a fact, that the aborigines of that portion of the Union were larger than those of our section of the country.

There are obvious physical differences among the English themselves. One county is said to have an undue proportion of red heads, another to have men taller than the common, this again men that are shorter, and all to show traces of their remote origins. It is probable that some of these peculiarities have descended to ourselves, though they have become blended by the unusual admixture of the population.

Morally, we live under the influence of systems so completely the converse of each other, that it is matter of surprise so many points of resemblance still remain. The immediate tendency of the English system is, to create an extreme deference in all the subordinate classes for their superiors; while that of the American is to run into the opposite feeling. The effects of both these tendencies are certainly observable; though relatively, that of our own much less, I think, than that of England. It gives good models a rather better chance here, than they have with us.

In England, the disaffected to the government are among precisely those who most sustain government in America; and the disaffected in America, (if so strong a word can properly be used, as applied to natives,) are of a class whose interests it is to sustain government in England. These facts give very different aspects to the general features of society. Walking in Regent-street lately, I witnessed an attempt of the police to compel some hackney coachmen to quit their boxes, and go with them before the magistrate. A crowd of a thousand people collected immediately, and its feeling was decidedly against the ministers of the law; so much so, indeed, as to render it doubtful whether the coachmen, whose conduct had been flagrantly criminal, would not be rescued. Now, in America, I think the feeling of such a crowd, would have been just the other way. It would have taken an interest in supporting the authorities of the country, instead of an interest in opposing them. This was not the case of a mob, you will remember, in which passion puts down reason; but an ordinary occurrence of the exercise of the power of the police. Instances of this nature might be multiplied, to show that the mass of the two people act under the influence of feelings diametrically opposed to each other.

On the other hand, Englishmen of the higher classes are, with very few exceptions, and these exceptions are usually instances of mere party opposition, attached to their system, sensitive of the subject of its merits or defects, and ever ready to defend it when assailed. The American of the same class is accustomed to sneer at democracy, to cavil at its fruits, and to colour and exaggerate its faults. Though this latter disposition may be, to a degree, accounted for by the facts, that all merit is comparative, and most of our people have not had the opportunities to compare; and that it is natural to resist most that which most annoys, although the substitution of any other for the actual system would produce even greater discontent; still, I think, the general tendency of aristocratical institutions on the one hand, and of democratical on the other, is to produce this broad difference in feeling, as between classes.

Both the Americans and the English are charged with being offensively boastful and arrogant as nations, and too much disposed to compare themselves advantageously with their neighbours. I have visited no country in which a similar disposition does not exist, and as communities are merely aggregations of men, I fancy that the disposition of a people to take this view of their own merits, is no more than carrying out the well known principle of individual vanity. The English and ourselves, however, well may, and probably do, differ from other nations in one circumstance connected with such a failing. The mass in both nations are better instructed, and are of more account than the mass in other countries, and their sentiments form more of a public opinion than elsewhere. When the bulk of a people are in a condition to make themselves heard, one is not to expect much refinement or delicacy, in the sentiments they utter. The English do not strike me as being a vainer nation than the French, although, in the way of ordinary intercourse, I believe that both they and we are more boastful.

The English are to be particularly distinguished from the Americans in the circumstance of their being a proud people. This is a useful and even an ennobling quality, when it is sustained by facts, though apt to render a people both uncomfortable and unpleasant, when the glory on which they pique themselves is passed away. We are almost entirely wanting in national pride, though abundantly supplied with an irritable vanity that might rise to pride, had we greater confidence in our facts. Most intelligent Englishmen are ready enough to admit the obvious faults of their climate, and even of their social condition; but it is an uncommon American that will concede anything material on such points, unless it can be made to bear on democracy. We have the sensitiveness of provincials, increased by the consciousness of having our spurs to earn, on all matters of glory and renown, and our jealousy extends even to the reputations of the cats and dogs. It is but an indifferent compliment to human nature to add, that the man who will join complacently, and I may say ignorantly, in the abuse of foreigners against the institutions of the country, and even against its people, always reserving a saving clause in favour of his own particular class, will take fire if an innuendo is hazarded against its beef, or a suggestion made that the four thousand feet of the Round Peak are not equal to the thirteen thousand feet of the Jung Frau. The English are tolerably free from this weakness, and travelling is daily increasing this species of liberality, at least. I presume that the insular situation of England, and our own distance from Europe, are equally the causes of these traits; though there may be said to be a "property qualification" in the very nature of man, that disposes him to view his own things with complacency, and those of his neighbours with digust. Bishop Heber, in one of his letters to Lord Grenville, in speaking of the highest peaks of the Himalayas, throws into a parenthesis, "which I feel some exultation in saying, is completely within the limits of the British empire;" a sort of sentiment, of which I dare say, neither St. Chrysostom[2] nor Polycarp[3] was entirely free.

On the subject of sensibility to comments on their national habits and national characters, neither France nor England is by any means as philosophical or indifferent as one might suppose. As a rule, I believe all men are more easily enraged when their real faults are censured, than when their virtues are called in question; and if the defect happen to be unavoidable, or one for which they are not fairly responsible, the resentment is two-fold that which would attend a comment on a vice. The only difference I can discover between the English and ourselves in this particular, is easily to be traced to our greater provincialism, youth, and the consciousness that we are obliged to anticipate some of our renown. I should say that the English are *thin-skinned*, and the Americans *raw*. Both resent fair, frank, and manly comments with the same bad taste, resorting to calumny, blackguardism, and abuse, when wit and pleasantry would prove both more effective and wiser, and, perhaps, reformation wisest of all. I can only account for this peculiarity, by supposing that the institutions and political facts of the two countries have rendered vulgar-minded men of more account than is usually the case; and that their influence has created a species of public opinion which is less under the correction of taste, principles, and manners, than is the case in nations where the mass is more depressed. Of the fact itself, there can be no question.

In order to appreciate the effect of refinement on this nation, it will be necessary to recur to some of its statistical facts. England, including Wales, contains rather less than fifty-eight thousand square

2. John of Antioch (347?–407) Greek Church Father and saint, later called Chrysostom. 3. St. Polycarp, Bishop of Smyrna, born about 69 A.D., was martyred in 155.

miles of territory; the state of New York, about forty-three thousand. On the former surface, there is a population of something like fifteen millions; on the latter, a population of less than two. One gives a proportion of about two hundred and sixty to the square mile, and the other a proportion of less than fifty. These premises, alone would show us the immense advantage that any given portion of surface in England must possess over the same extent of surface in America, in all those arts and improvements that depend on physical force. If there were ten men of education, and refinement, and fortune, in a county of New York, of one thousand square miles in extent, there ought to be more than fifty men of the same character and means, in an English county of equal territory. This is supposing that the real premises offer nothing more against us than the dispro-portion between numbers and surface; whereas, in fact, time, wealth, and an older civilization more than quadruple the odds. Even these do not make up the sum of the adverse elements. Though England has but fifteen millions of souls, the empire she controls has nearly ten times that population, and a very undue proportion of the re-sults of so great a physical force centre in this small spot.

The consideration of these truths suggest several useful heads of reflection. In the first place, they show us, if not the absolute im-possibility, the great improbability, that the civilization, refinement, knowledge, wealth, and tastes of even the best portions of America can equal those of this country, and suggest the expediency of look-ing to other points for our sources of pride. I have said, that the two countries act under the influence of moral agencies that are almost the converse of each other. The condensation of improvement and cultivation is so great here, that even the base of society is affected by it, even to deportment; whereas, with us, these properties are so dispersed, as to render it difficult for those who are lucky enough to possess them, to keep what they have got, in face of the overshadow-ing influence of a lower school, instead of being able to impart them to society. Our standard, in nearly all things, as it is popular, is neces-sarily one of mediocrity; a highly respectable, and, circumstances considered, a singularly creditable one, but still a mediocrity; whereas, the condition of these people has enabled them to raise a standard which, however much it may be and is wanting in the better elements of a pure taste, has immensely the advantage of our own in most of the obvious blandishments of life. More than half of the peculiari-ties of America—peculiarities for which it is usual to seek a cause in the institutions, simply because they are so peculiar themselves —are to be traced to facts like these; or, in other words, to the dis-proportion between surface and numbers, the want of any other commercial towns, and our distance from the rest of the world.

Every condition of society has its own advantages, and its own disadvantages. To claim perfection for any one in particular, would be to deny the nature of man. Their comparative merits are to be decided, only, by the comparative gross results, and it is in this sense, that I contend for the superiority of our own. The utilitarian school, as it has been popularly construed, is not to my taste, either; for I believe there is great utility in the grace and elegance of life, and no one would feel more disposed to resist a system in which these essential properties are proscribed. That we are wanting in both, I am ready to allow; but I think the reason is to be found in facts entirely independent of the institutions, and that the time will come when the civilization of America will look down that of any other section of the world, if the country can pass that state of probation during which it is and will be exposed to the assaults of secret combinations to destroy it; and during which, moreover, it is, in an especial degree, liable to be affected by inherited opinions, and opinions that have been obtained under a system that has so many of the forms, while it has so few of the principles of our own, as easily to be confounded with it, by the ignorant and the unreflecting.

We over-estimate the effects of intelligence as between ourselves and the English. The mass of information, here, probably exceeds that of America, though it is less equally distributed. In *general* knowledge of a practical nature, too, I think no people can compete with our own. But there is a species of information, that is both useful and refining, in which there are few European nations that do not surpass us. I allude, in particular, to most things that serve to embellish life. In addition to this superiority, the Europeans of the better classes very obviously possess over us an important advantage, in their intimate associations with each other, by which means they insensibly imbibe a great deal of current knowledge, of which the similar classes in America are nearly ignorant; or, which, if known at all, is only known through the medium of books. In the exhibition of this knowledge, which embraces all that belongs to what is commonly termed a knowledge of the world, the difference between the European and the American is the difference that is seen between the man who has passed all his days in good society, and the man who has got his knowledge of it from novels and plays.

In a correct estimate of their government, and in an acquaintance with its general action, the English are much our superiors, though we know most of details. This arises from the circumstances that the rights of an Englishman are little more than franchises, which require no very profound examination to be understood; while those of the American depend on principles that demand study, and which are constantly exposed to the antagonist influence of opinions that have been formed under another system. It is true the English monarchy, as a monarchy and as it now exists, is a pure mystification; but the supremacy of parliament being admitted, there can arise no great difficulty on the score of interpretation. The American system, moreover, is complicated and double, and the only true Whig and Tory parties that can exist must have their origin in the circumstance. To these reasons may be added the general fact, that the educated Englishman reasons on his institutions like an Englishman only; while his American counterpart oftener reasons on the institutions of the republic like an Englishman, too, than like an American. A single fact will show you what I mean, although a hundred might be quoted. In England the government is composed, in theory, of three bases and one summit; in America, it is composed of one base and three summits. In one, there is supposed to be a balance in the powers of the state; and, as this is impossible in practice, it has resulted in a consolidated authority in its action; in the other, there is but one power, that of the entire people, and the balance is in the action of their agents. A very little reflection will show that the maxims of two such systems ought to be as different as the systems themselves.

The English are to be distinguished from the Americans by greater independence of personal habits. Not only the institutions, but the physical condition of our own country has a tendency to reduce us all to the same level of usages. The steam-boats, the overgrown taverns, the speculative character of the enterprises, and the consequent disposition to do all things in common, aid the tendency of the system in bringing about such a result. In England a man dines by himself, in a room filled with other hermits; he eats at his leisure, drinks his wine in silence, reads the paper by the hour; and, in all things, encourages his individuality and insists on his particular humours. The American is compelled to submit to a common rule; he eats when others eat, sleeps when others sleep, and he is lucky, indeed, if he can read a paper in a tavern without having a stranger looking over each shoulder. The Englishman would stare at a proposal that should invade his habits under the pretence of a common wish, while the American would be very apt to yield tacitly, though this common wish should be no more than an impudent assertion of some one who had contrived to effect his own purposes, under the popular plea. The Englishman is so much attached to his independence that he instinctively resists every effort to invade it, and nothing would be more likely to arouse him than to say the mass thinks differently from himself; whereas the American ever seems ready to resign his own opinion to that which is made to seem to be the opinion of the public. I say *seems* to be, for so manifest is the power of public opinion, that one of the commonest expedients of all American managers, is to create an impression that the public thinks in a particular way, in order to bring the common mind in subjection. One often renders himself ridiculous by a foolish obstinacy, and the other is as often contemptible by a weak compliance. A portion of what may be called the *community* of character and habits in America is doubtless owing to the rustic nature of its society, for one more easily maintains his independence in a capital than in a village, but I think the chief reasons are to be found in the practice of referring every thing to the common mind.

It is usual to ascribe the solitary and unsocial habits of English life to the natural dispositions of the people, but, I think, unjustly. The climate is made to bear the blame of no small portion of this peculiarity. Climate, probably, has an influence on us all, for we know that we are more elastic and more ready to be pleased in a clear bracing air, than in one that is close and *siroccoish*,[4] but, on the whole I am led to think, the English owe their habits to their institutions, more than to any natural causes.

I know no subject, no feeling, nothing, on which an Englishman, as a rule, so completely loses sight of all the better points of his character, on which he is so uniformly bigoted and unjust, so ready to listen to misrepresentation and caricature, and so unwilling to receive truth—on which, in short, he is so little himself in general, as on those connected with America.

As the result of this hasty and imperfect comparison, I am led to believe, that a national character somewhere between the two, would be preferable to either, as it is actually found. This may be saying no more than that man does not exist in a condition of perfection; but were the inequalities named, pared off from both people, an ingenious critic might still find faults of sufficient magnitude to preserve the identity with the human race, and qualities of sufficient elevation, to entitle both to be considered among the greatest and best nations of modern, if not of any other, times.

In most things that pertain to taste, the English have greatly the advantage of us, though *taste* is certainly not the strong side of English character. On this point, alone, one might write a book, but a very few remarks must now satisfy you. In nothing, however, is this superiority more apparent, than in their simplicity, and, particularly, in their simplicity of language. They call a spade, a spade. I very well know, that neither men nor women, in America, who are properly educated, and who are accustomed to its really better tone, differ much, if any, from the English in this particular; but, in this case, as in most others, in which *national* peculiarities are sought, the better tone of America is over-shadowed by its mediocrity. Although I deem the government of this country the very quintessence of hocus pocus, having scarcely a single practice that does not violate its theory, I believe that there is more honesty of public sentiment in England,

4. *Cf.* sirocco.

than in America. The defect at home, I ascribe, in common with the majority of our national failings, to the greater activity, and greater *unresisted* force of ignorance and cupidity, there, than here. High qualities are nowhere collected in a sufficient phalanx to present a front to the enemy, in America.

The besetting, the degrading vice of America, is the moral coward-ice by which men are led to truckle to what is called public opinion; though this opinion is as inconstant as the winds—though, in all cases that enlist the feelings of factions, there are *two* and sometimes twenty, each differing from all the others, and though, nine times in ten, these opinions are mere engines set in motion by the most corrupt and the least respectable portion of the community, for un-worthy purposes. The English are a more respectable and constant nation than the Americans, as relates to this peculiarity; probably, because the condensed masses of intelligence and character enable the superior portion of the community to produce a greater impres-sion on the inferior, by their collective force. In standing prejudices, they strike me as being worse than ourselves; but in passing impres-sions, greatly our superiors.

For the last I have endeavoured to account, and I think the first may be ascribed to a system that is sustained by errors that it is not the interest of the more enlightened to remove, but which, instead of weakening in the ignorant, they rather encourage in themselves.

1828   1837

From The American Democrat

An Aristocrat and a Democrat

We live in an age when the words aristocrat and democrat are much used, without regard to the real significations. An aristocrat is one of a few who possess the political power of a country; a democrat, one of the many. The words are also properly applied to those who entertain notions favorable to aristocratical or democratical forms of government. Such persons are not necessarily either aristocrats or democrats in fact, but merely so in opinion. Thus a member of a democratical government may have an aristocratical bias, and vice versa.

To call a man who has the habits and opinions of a gentleman, an aristocrat from that fact alone, is an abuse of terms and betrays ignorance of the true principles of government, as well as of the world. It must be an equivocal freedom under which every one is not the master of his own innocent acts and associations; and he is a sneak-ing democrat indeed who will submit to be dictated to, in those habits over which neither law nor morality assumes a right of control.

Some men fancy that a democrat can only be one who seeks the level, social, mental and moral, of the majority, a rule that would at once exclude all men of refinement, education, and taste from the class. These persons are enemies of democracy, as they at once render it impracticable. They are usually great sticklers for their own associations and habits, too, though unable to comprehend any of a nature that are superior. They are, in truth, aristocrats in principle, though assuming a contrary pretension, the groundwork of all their feelings and arguments being self. Such is not the intention of liberty, whose aim is to leave every man to be the master of his own acts; denying hereditary honors, it is true, as unjust and unnecessary, but not denying the inevitable consequences of civilization.

The law of God is the only rule of conduct in this, as in other matters. Each man should do as he would be done by. Were the question put to the greatest advocate of indiscriminate association, whether he would submit to have his company and habits dictated to him, he would be one of the first to resist the tyranny; for they who are the most rigid in maintaining their own claims in such matters, are usually the loudest in decrying those whom they fancy to be better off than themselves. Indeed, it may be taken as a rule in social intercourse, that he who is the most apt to question the pretensions of others is the most conscious of the doubtful position he himself occupies; thus establishing the very claims he affects to deny, by letting his jealousy of it be seen. Manners, education, and refinement, are positive things, and they bring with them innocent tastes which are productive of high enjoyments; and it is as unjust to deny their possessors their indulgence as it would be to insist on the less fortunate's passing the time they would rather devote to athletic amusements, in listening to operas for which they have no relish, sung in a language they do not understand.

All that democracy means, is as equal a participation in rights as is practicable; and to pretend that social equality is a condition of popular institutions is to assume that the latter are destructive of civilization, for, as nothing is more self-evident than the impossibility of raising all men to the highest standard of tastes and refinement, the alternative would be to reduce the entire community to the lowest. The whole embarrassment on this point exists in the difficulty of making men comprehend qualities they do not themselves possess. We can all perceive the difference between ourselves and our inferiors, but when it comes to a question of the difference between us and our superiors, we fail to appreciate merits of which we have no proper conceptions. In face of this obvious difficulty, there is the safe and just governing rule, already mentioned, or that of permitting every one to be the undisturbed judge of his own habits and associations, so long as they are innocent and do not impair the rights of others to be equally judges for themselves. It follows, that social intercourse must regulate itself, independently of institutions, with the exception that the latter, while they withhold no natural, bestow no factitious advantages beyond those which are inseparable from the rights of property, and general civilization.

In a democracy, men are just as free to aim at the highest attainable places in society, as to attain the largest fortunes; and it would be clearly unworthy of all noble sentiment to say that the grovelling competition for money shall alone be free, while that which enlists all the liberal acquirements and elevated sentiments of the race, is denied the democrat. Such an avowal would be at once a declaration of the inferiority of the system, since nothing but ignorance and vulgarity could be its fruits.

The democratic gentleman must differ in many essential particulars from the aristocratical gentleman, though in their ordinary habits and tastes they are virtually identical. Their principles vary; and, to a slight degree, their deportment accordingly. The democrat, recognizing the right of all to participate in power, will be more liberal in his general sentiments, a quality of superiority in itself; but in conceding this much to his fellow man, he will proudly maintain his own independence of vulgar domination as indispensable to his personal habits. The same principles and manliness that would induce him to depose a royal despot would induce him to resist a vulgar tyrant.

There is no more capital, though more common error, than to suppose him an aristocrat who maintains his independence of habits; for democracy asserts the control of the majority, only in matters of law, and not in matters of custom. The very object of the institution is the utmost practicable personal liberty, and to affirm the contrary would be sacrificing the end to the means.

An aristocrat, therefore, is merely one who fortifies his exclusive privileges by positive institutions, and a democrat, one who is willing to admit of a free competition in all things. To say, however, that the last supposes this competition will lead to nothing is an assumption that means are employed without any reference to an end. He is the purest democrat who best maintains his rights, and no rights can be dearer to a man of cultivation than exemptions from unseasonable invasions on his time by the coarse minded and ignorant.

1838

WILLIAM CULLEN BRYANT
(1794–1878)

It is not surprising that the early life of Bryant should have provided a myth, but it is unfortunate that the myth should continue to obscure his impressive reality. In the fresh morning of the national literature came the boy poet, uttering full-grown songs, especially a "Thanatopsis" of beautiful death; the image swiftly merged with that of the venerable and bearded patriarch, spiritual psalmist of the new nation—"as quiet, as cool, and as dignified," wrote Lowell, "as a smooth, silent iceberg" whose only "flame" reflected the "chill Northern Lights." Bryant was then fifty-four, and only the younger Longfellow approached him in reputation; but Lowell's lines, if jocose, were addressed less to a poet than to a revered national monument.

In reality the man was one of the great personalities of his age, an individual whose force, courage, and dynamic liberalism as an editor provided effective leadership in American cultural and political life from the Age of Jackson through the Civil War and Reconstruction period. As poet and critic he gave an American formulation to the romantic movement; he provided an example of disciplined imagination and precise expression; he opposed to the usual insipid generalization about nature his close observation of the natural object; and finally, he encouraged American poets to seek cultural independence from

Europe by writing of their own American experience. To be sure, Bryant inherited, with his American generation, a measure of neoclassical restraint and didacticism that troubles the reader of a later generation. Yet in spite of the vast changes in the sensibility of readers and the nature of modern experience, a few of his poems are timeless, while the reader who can recapture the sense of that older time will find in many others a moving inspiration and a genuine insight.

Born in Cummington, in the Berkshire foothills of western Massachusetts, a fine natural setting for the boyhood of a poet of nature, Bryant benefited also from the companionship of his father, Dr. Peter Bryant, an enthusiastic naturalist and a persistent walker in the woods. No wonder that he later remembered his reading, at the age of sixteen, the *Lyrical Ballads* of Wordsworth and Coleridge, when "a thousand springs seemed to gush up at once into my heart, and the face of nature, of a sudden, to change into a strange freshness." He was then at Williams College, where he remained only a year, but his reading had already included much beyond the elementary schooling provided at Cummington—he had access to his father's ample library and to those of two clergymen, one his uncle, who tutored him in classical languages and literature. He had written verses from the age of nine; when he was only fourteen his father sent to a Boston publisher his satire, *The Embargo* (1808), which reflected the Federalist resentment against Jefferson's trade restrictions, intended to avert war with England. The next year a second volume of his juvenile poems appeared in Boston, and in 1811, after one year at college, he wrote the first draft of "Thanatopsis." These early poems reflected influences that he soon learned to absorb in his own independent style: the neoclassical forms of Addison, Pope, and Johnson; the attitudes of the "graveyard school," especially as represented by Blair, Thomson, Young, Gray, and Henry Kirke White; and finally, the mature romanticism of Scott, Cowper, Burns, Coleridge, and Wordsworth.

For a time, literature became secondary to the law. After four years of preparation, he was admitted to the bar, and practiced at Great Barrington from 1816 to 1825. In this interval he married, and held a political office, but the man of letters would not be suppressed. In 1817 his publication of "Thanatopsis" drew general attention to his genius; it was widely copied and became at once a familiar poem. He began to write sporadically for the magazines, and his essay on "Early American Verse" (1818) established him as a discerning critic. In 1821 he was called to read "The Ages" as the Phi Beta Kappa poem at Harvard. His first collected *Poems* appeared in Boston in 1821. In 1825 he accepted a minor editorial position in New York, and within a year

he became assistant editor of the New York *Evening Post*.

In New York, to the end of his days, he was a dominant leader in literature and in public causes. He became the intimate of Cooper and of such Knickerbockers as Irving, Halleck, and Verplanck, and the friend, often the adviser, of later arrivals. During his first year in New York he delivered before the Athenaeum his influential lectures on poetry, and thereafter he was increasingly active as a public speaker and as a poet on special occasions. Although public responsibility drained his time and energy, he continued to publish poems in the periodicals. Further collections and new volumes appeared in 1832, 1842, 1844, 1846, 1854, and 1864. In spite of the sometimes long intervals between volumes, he remained a familiar poet of the people; an illustrated edition of 1846 became a popular favorite, and his last approved collection, the Household Edition of 1876, remained in print into the present century. He made six extensive tours abroad and published two widely read volumes of *Letters of a Traveller*. In his declining years he furnished his countrymen with good poetic translations of the *Iliad* (1870) and the *Odyssey* (1871–1872). His *Library of Poetry and Song* (1871–1872) was the first great critical anthology in America. Meanwhile he had become editor in chief of the *Evening Post* (1829), which soon became his property, and, under his management, one of our first great national newspapers.

Bryant's persistent themes, besides religion and nature, dealt with humanitarian reform and national morality. Although his boyhood satire was leveled at Jefferson's embargo, he became a great leader of the northern Democrats; just as in religion, having rejected, in "Thanatopsis'" the strict Calvinism of Cummington, he passed through a stage of Deism to become, in mature life, a prominent leader of the Unitarian movement. As a liberal Democrat he waged continual newspaper warfare for various freedoms—freedom of speech, of religion, and of labor association and collective bargaining, free trade, and the freedom of the masses from oppressive debtor laws and the exploitation of banking and currency regulations. In defense of one freedom he helped destroy the Democratic party, for he waged continuous warfare for free soil and, finally, the freedom of the slaves. Having supported the antislavery Democratic "Barnburners" during the Mexican War, he became an active organizer of the Republican party (1855–1856). In his eighty-fourth year, on a warm May day, he delivered the address at the unveiling of Mazzini's statue in New York. On returning home, he was stricken on his doorstep, and he died a few days later. As a poet his range was not large and his thoughts were not profound, but he was able to express the common idealism of his countrymen at a level of propriety and dignity so high as to make him, for the time, their most revered spokesman. As a magnanimous editor and public leader, certainly, he must rank with the great men of his age.

The Poetical Works of William Cullen Bryant, Household Edition, 1876, is his final text and provides the basis for the text of poems reprinted below. *The Life and Works of William Cullen Bryant*, 6 vols., edited by Parke Godwin, 1883–1884, is the standard collection; there is no comprehensive collection of Bryant's prose, and most of his editorial writing has not been garnered from the *Post*. The Roslyn Edition of the *Poetical Works*, edited by H. C. Sturges, 1903, is the best available one-volume edition, containing also a good bibliography. Tremaine McDowell's *Bryant: Representative Selections*, American Writers Series, 1935, is excellent in text, introduction, and notes.

Parke Godwin's *Life* (1883), the first two volumes of his *Life and Works*, is sound for its time. Reliable one-volume studies are John Bigelow, *William Cullen Bryant*, American Men of Letters Series, 1890; W. A. Bradley, *William Cullen Bryant*, 1905; and H. H. Peckham, *Gotham Yankee*, 1950. Allan Nevins, *The Evening Post: A Century of Journalism*, 1922, gives much new light on Bryant.

Thanatopsis[1]

To him who in the love of Nature holds
Communion with her visible forms, she speaks

1. "Thanatopsis" (meaning "a meditation on death"), written in Bryant's seventeenth year (1811), was frequently revised, before and after its first publication (*North American Review*, September, 1817). It is still one of the most familiar of American poems. Recalling the British "graveyard school" in general, and specifically the poems of Henry Kirke White, Blair, Southey, and Cowper, it asserts its independence by its American largeness of landscape. It also expresses Bryant's early rejection of orthodox Calvinism—the young Deist stoically compares death with the crumbling of the insensible clod. In a few years he had swung to the Unitarian position (see "To a Waterfowl") and become a leader of Unitarian liberalism.

A various language; for his gayer hours
She has a voice of gladness, and a smile
And eloquence of beauty, and she glides   5
Into his darker musings, with a mild
And healing sympathy, that steals away
Their sharpness, ere he is aware. When thoughts
Of the last bitter hour come like a blight
Over thy spirit, and sad images   10
Of the stern agony, and shroud, and pall,
And breathless darkness, and the narrow house,
Make thee to shudder, and grow sick at heart,—
Go forth, under the open sky, and list
To Nature's teachings, while from all around—   15
Earth and her waters, and the depths of air,—
Comes a still voice—
                    Yet a few days, and thee
The all-beholding sun shall see no more
In all his course; nor yet in the cold ground,
Where thy pale form was laid, with many tears,   20
Nor in the embrace of ocean, shall exist
Thy image. Earth, that nourished thee, shall claim
Thy growth, to be resolved to earth again,
And, lost each human trace, surrendering up
Thine individual being, shalt thou go   25
To mix forever with the elements,
To be a brother to the insensible rock
And to the sluggish clod, which the rude swain
Turns with his share,[2] and treads upon. The oak
Shall send his roots abroad, and pierce thy mould. 30

    Yet not to thine eternal resting-place
Shalt thou retire alone, nor couldst thou wish
Couch more magnificent. Thou shalt lie down
With patriarchs of the infant world, with kings,
The powerful of the earth, the wise, the good,   35
Fair forms, and hoary seers of ages past,
All in one mighty sepulchre. The hills
Rock-ribbed and ancient as the sun, the vales
Stretching in pensive quietness between;
The venerable woods—rivers that move   40
In majesty, and the complaining brooks
That make the meadows green; and, poured round all,
Old Ocean's gray and melancholy waste,—
Are but the solemn decorations all

2. Plowshare.

Of the great tomb of man. The golden sun,   45
The planets, all the infinite host of heaven,
Are shining on the sad abodes of death,
Through the still lapse of ages. All that tread
The globe are but a handful to the tribes
That slumber in its bosom.—Take the wings   50
Of morning, pierce the Barcan[3] wilderness,
Or lose thyself in the continuous woods
Where rolls the Oregon,[4] and hears no sound,
Save his own dashings—yet the dead are there:
And millions in those solitudes, since first   55
The flight of years began, have laid them down
In their last sleep—the dead reign there alone.
So shalt thou rest, and what if thou withdraw
In silence from the living, and no friend
Take note of thy departure? All that breathe   60
Will share thy destiny. The gay will laugh
When thou are gone, the solemn brood of care
Plod on, and each one as before will chase
His favorite phantom; yet all these shall leave
Their mirth and their employments, and shall come   65
And make their bed with thee. As the long train
Of ages glide away, the sons of men,
The youth in life's green spring, and he who goes
In the full strength of years, matron and maid,
The speechless babe, and the gray-headed man—   70
Shall one by one be gathered to thy side,
By those, who in their turn shall follow them.

So live, that when thy summons comes to join
The innumerable caravan, which moves
To that mysterious realm, where each shall take   75
His chamber in the silent halls of death,
Thou go not, like the quarry-slave at night,
Scourged to his dungeon, but, sustained and soothed
By an unfaltering trust, approach thy grave,
Like one who wraps the drapery of his couch   80
About him, and lies down to pleasant dreams.

1811   1817, 1821

3. The desert of Barca (in Libya, North
Africa) is compared with the "Great
American Desert" then shown on maps.

4. The Indian name; now the Columbia
River.

The Yellow Violet

When beechen buds begin to swell,
And woods the blue-bird's warble know,
The yellow violet's modest bell
Peeps from the last year's leaves below.

Ere russet fields their green resume,   5
Sweet flower, I love, in forest bare,
To meet thee, when thy faint perfume
Alone is in the virgin air.

Of all her train, the hands of Spring
First plant thee in the watery mould,   10
And I have seen thee blossoming
Beside the snow-bank's edges cold.

Thy parent sun, who bade thee view
Pale skies, and chilling moisture sip,
Has bathed thee in his own bright hue,   15
And streaked with jet thy glowing lip.

Yet slight thy form, and low thy seat,
And earthward bent thy gentle eye,
Unapt the passing view to meet
When loftier flowers are flaunting nigh.   20

Oft, in the sunless April day,
Thy early smile has stayed my walk;
But midst the gorgeous blooms of May,
I passed thee on thy humble stalk.

So they, who climb to wealth, forget   25
The friends in darker fortunes tried.
I copied them—but I regret
That I should ape the ways of pride.

And when again the genial hour
Awakes the painted tribes of light,   30
I'll not o'erlook the modest flower
That made the woods of April bright.

1814   1821

To a Waterfowl

Whither, 'midst falling dew,
While glow the heavens with the last steps of day,

Far, through their rosy depths, dost thou pursue
    Thy solitary way?

Vainly the fowler's eye   5
Might mark thy distant flight, to do thee wrong,
As, darkly seen against the crimson sky,
    Thy figure floats along.

Seek'st thou the plashy brink
Of weedy lake, or marge of river wide,   10
Or where the rocking billows rise and sink
    On the chafed ocean side?

There is a Power, whose care
Teaches thy way along that pathless coast, —
The desert and illimitable air,   15
    Lone wandering, but not lost.

All day thy wings have fann'd,
At that far height, the cold thin atmosphere;
Yet stoop not, weary, to the welcome land,
    Though the dark night is near.   20

And soon that toil shall end,
Soon shalt thou find a summer home, and rest,
And scream among thy fellows; reeds shall bend,
    Soon, o'er thy sheltered nest.

Thou'rt gone, the abyss of heaven   25
Hath swallowed up thy form, yet, on my heart
Deeply hath sunk the lesson thou hast given,
    And shall not soon depart.

He, who, from zone to zone,
Guides through the boundless sky thy certain flight,   30
In the long way that I must trace alone,
    Will lead my steps aright.

1815   1818, 1821

A Forest Hymn

The groves were God's first temples. Ere man learned
To hew the shaft, and lay the architrave,
And spread the roof above them—ere he framed
The lofty vault, to gather and roll back
The sound of anthems; in the darkling wood,   5
Amid the cool and silence, he knelt down,

And offered to the Mightiest solemn thanks
And supplication. For his simple heart
Might not resist the sacred influences
Which, from the stilly twilight of the place,   10
And from the gray old trunks that high in heaven
Mingled their mossy boughs, and from the sound
Of the invisible breath that swayed at once
All their green tops, stole over him, and bowed
His spirit with the thought of boundless power   15
And inaccessible majesty. Ah, why
Should we, in the world's riper years, neglect
God's ancient sanctuaries, and adore
Only among the crowd, and under roofs
That our frail hands have raised? Let me, at least,   20
Here, in the shadow of this aged wood,
Offer one hymn—thrice happy, if it find
Acceptance in His ear.

                    Father, thy hand
Hath reared these venerable columns, thou
Didst weave this verdant roof. Thou didst look down   25
Upon the naked earth, and, forthwith, rose
All these fair ranks of trees. They, in thy sun,
Budded, and shook their green leaves in thy breeze,
And shot toward heaven. The century-living crow
Whose birth was in their tops, grew old and died   30
Among their branches, till, at last, they stood,
As now they stand, massy, and tall, and dark,
Fit shrine for humble worshipper to hold
Communion with his Maker. These dim vaults,
These winding aisles, of human pomp or pride   35
Report not. No fantastic carvings show
The boast of our vain race to change the form
Of thy fair works. But thou art here—thou fill'st
The solitude. Thou art in the soft winds
That run along the summit of these trees   40
In music; thou art in the cooler breath
That from the inmost darkness of the place
Comes, scarcely felt; the barky trunks, the ground,
The fresh moist ground, are all instinct with thee.
Here is continual worship;—Nature, here,   45
In the tranquillity that thou dost love,
Enjoys thy presence. Noiselessly, around,
From perch to perch, the solitary bird
Passes; and yon clear spring, that, midst its herbs,

Wells softly forth and wandering steeps the roots   50
Of half the mighty forest, tells no tale
Of all the good it does. Thou hast not left
Thyself without a witness, in the shades,
Of thy perfections. Grandeur, strength, and grace
Are here to speak of thee. This mighty oak—   55
By whose immovable stem I stand and seem
Almost annihilated—not a prince,
In all that proud old world beyond the deep,
E'er wore his crown as loftily as he
Wears the green coronal of leaves with which   60
Thy hand had graced him. Nestled at his root
Is beauty, such as blooms not in the glare
Of the broad sun. That delicate forest flower,
With scented breath and look so like a smile,
Seems, as it issues from the shapeless mould,   65
An emanation of the indwelling Life,
A visible token of the upholding Love,
That are the soul of this great universe.

My heart is awed within me when I think
Of the great miracle that still goes on,   70
In silence, round me—the perpetual work
Of thy creation, finished, yet renewed
Forever. Written on thy works I read
The lesson of thy own eternity.
Lo! all grow old and die—but see again,   75
How on the faltering footsteps of decay
Youth presses—ever gay and beautiful youth
In all its beautiful forms. These lofty trees
Wave not less proudly that their ancestors
Moulder beneath them. Oh, there is not lost   80
One of earth's charms: upon her bosom yet,
After the flight of untold centuries,
The freshness of her far beginning lies
And yet shall lie. Life mocks the idle hate
Of his arch-enemy Death—yea, seats himself   85
Upon the tyrant's throne—the sepulchre,
And of the triumphs of his ghastly foe
Makes his own nourishment. For he came forth
From thine own bosom, and shall have no end.

There have been holy men who hid themselves   90
Deep in the woody wilderness, and gave
Their lives to thought and prayer, till they outlived
The generation born with them, nor seemed

Less aged than the hoary trees and rocks
Around them;—and there have been holy men
Who deemed it were not well to pass life thus.
But let me often to these solitudes
Retire, and in thy presence reassure
My feeble virtue. Here its enemies,
The passions, at thy plainer footsteps shrink
And tremble and are still. O God! when thou
Dost scare the world with tempests, set on fire
The heavens with falling thunderbolts, or fill,
With all the waters of the firmament,
The swift dark whirlwind that uproots the woods
And drowns the villages; when, at thy call,
Uprises the great deep and throws himself
Upon the continent, and overwhelms
Its cities—who forgets not, at the sight
Of these tremendous tokens of thy power,
His pride, and lays his strifes and follies by?
Oh, from these sterner aspects of thy face
Spare me and mine, nor let us need the wrath
Of the mad unchained elements to teach
Who rules them. Be it ours to meditate,
In these calm shades, thy milder majesty,
And to the beautiful order of thy works
Learn to conform the order of our lives.

1825, 1832

The Past

Thou unrelenting Past!
Strong are the barriers round thy dark domain,
   And fetters, sure and fast,
Hold all that enter thy unbreathing reign.

   Far in thy realm withdrawn,
Old empires sit in sullenness and gloom,
   And glorious ages gone
Lie deep within the shadow of thy womb.

   Childhood, with all its mirth,
Youth, Manhood, Age that draws us to the ground,
   And last, Man's Life on earth,
Glide to thy dim dominions, and are bound.

   Thou hast my better years;
Thou hast my earlier friends, the good, the kind,

Yielded to thee with tears—   15
The venerable form,[5] the exalted mind.

My spirit yearns to bring
The lost ones back—yearns with desire intense,
    And struggles hard to wring
Thy bolts apart, and pluck thy captives thence.   20

In vain; thy gates deny
All passage save to those who hence depart;
    Nor to the streaming eye
Thou giv'st them back—nor to the broken heart.

In thy abysses hide   25
Beauty and excellence unknown; to thee
    Earth's wonder and her pride
Are gathered, as the waters to the sea;

Labors of good to man,
Unpublished charity, unbroken faith,   30
    Love, that midst grief began,
And grew with years, and faltered not in death.

Full many a mighty name
Lurks in thy depths, unuttered, unrevered;
    With thee are silent fame,   35
Forgotten arts, and wisdom disappeared.

Thine for a space are they—
Yet shalt thou yield thy treasures up at last:
    Thy gates shall yet give way,
Thy bolts shall fall, inexorable Past!   40

All that of good and fair
Has gone into thy womb from earliest time,
    Shall then come forth to wear
The glory and the beauty of its prime.

They have not perished—no!   45
Kind words, remembered voices once so sweet,
    Smiles, radiant long ago,
And features, the great soul's apparent seat.

All shall come back; each tie
Of pure affection shall be knit again;   50
    Alone shall Evil die,
And Sorrow dwell a prisoner in thy reign.

5. Identified as his father, Dr. Peter Bryant, who died in 1820. *Cf.* the last stanza.

And then shall I behold
Him, by whose kind paternal side I sprung,
   And her, who, still and cold,
Fills the next grave—the beautiful and young.[6]

1828, 1832

To the Fringed Gentian[7]

Thou blossom bright with autumn dew,
And colored with the heaven's own blue,
That openest when the quiet light
Succeeds the keen and frosty night—

Thou comest not when violets lean
O'er wandering brooks and springs unseen,
Or columbines, in purple dressed,
Nod o'er the ground-bird's hidden nest.

Thou waitest late and com'st alone,
When woods are bare and birds are flown,
And frosts and shortening days portend
The aged year is near his end.

Then doth thy sweet and quiet eye
Look through its fringes to the sky,
Blue—blue—as if that sky let fall
A flower from its cerulean wall.

I would that thus, when I shall see
The hour of death draw near to me,
Hope, blossoming within my heart,
May look to heaven as I depart.

1829

1832

The Prairies[8]

These are the gardens of the Desert, these
The unshorn fields, boundless and beautiful,
For which the speech of England has no name[9]—

6. His favorite sister, Mrs. Sarah Bryant Shaw, who died in 1824.
7. "Draw your own images, in describing nature, from what you observe around you," Bryant wrote his brother (Godwin, *Life*, Vol. I, p. 281). A botanist from youth, he took the lead in opposition to stereotyped references to nature. For a discussion of his success-

ful realism in this direction see Norman Foerster, "Bryant," in his *Nature in American Literature* (1923). And *cf.* "Robert of Lincoln," below.
8. Written on the poet's first sight of the prairies, on a visit to his brothers in Illinois in 1832.
9. "Prairie," in the tongue of the French settlers, signified "meadow."

The Prairies. I behold them for the first,
And my heart swells, while the dilated sight   5
Takes in the encircling vastness. Lo! they stretch
In airy undulations, far away,
As if the Ocean, in his gentlest swell,
Stood still, with all his rounded billows fixed,
And motionless forever. Motionless?—   10
No—they are all unchained again. The clouds
Sweep over with their shadows, and, beneath,
The surface rolls and fluctuates to the eye;[1]
Dark hollows seem to glide along and chase
The sunny ridges. Breezes of the South!   15
Who toss the golden and the flame-like flowers,
And pass the prairie-hawk that, poised on high,
Flaps his broad wings, yet moves not[2]—ye have played
Among the palms of Mexico and vines
Of Texas, and have crisped the limpid brooks   20
That from the fountains of Sonora[3] glide
Into the calm Pacific—have ye fanned
A nobler or a lovelier scene than this?
Man hath no part in all this glorious work:
The hand that built the firmament hath heaved   25
And smoothed these verdant swells, and sown their slopes
With herbage, planted them with island-groves,
And hedged them round with forests. Fitting floor
For this magnificent temple of the sky—
With flowers whose glory and whose multitude   30
Rival the constellations! The great heavens
Seem to stoop down upon the scene in love,—
A nearer vault, and of a tenderer blue,
Than that which bends above our Eastern hills.

As o'er the verdant waste I guide my steed,   35
Among the high rank grass that sweeps his sides
The hollow beating of his footstep seems
A sacrilegious sound. I think of those
Upon whose rest he tramples. Are they here—
The dead of other days?—and did the dust   40
Of these fair solitudes once stir with life
And burn with passion? Let the mighty mounds[4]

1. "* * * when the shadows of the clouds are passing rapidly over them, the face of the ground seems to fluctuate and toss like billows of the sea" [Bryant's note].
2. "I have seen the prairie-hawk balancing himself in the air for hours together, apparently over the same spot, probably watching his prey" [Bryant's note].
3. State in northwest Mexico.
4. Ascribed to the supposed ancient "Mound Builders"; now associated with Indian burials. See Bryant's earlier reference to former civilizations on this continent in "Thanatopsis," ll. 50–57.

That overlook the rivers, or that rise
In the dim forest crowded with old oaks,
Answer. A race, that long has passed away,   45
Built them; a disciplined and populous race
Heaped, with long toil, the earth, while yet the Greek
Was hewing the Pentelicus[5] to forms
Of symmetry, and rearing on its rock
The glittering Parthenon. These ample fields   50
Nourished their harvests, here their herds were fed,
When haply by their stalls the bison lowed,
And bowed his manèd shoulder to the yoke.
All day this desert murmured with their toils,
Till twilight blushed, and lovers walked, and wooed 55
In a forgotten language, and old tunes,
From instruments of unremembered form,
Gave the soft winds a voice. The red-man came—
The roaming hunter-tribes, warlike and fierce,
And the mound-builders vanished from the earth.   60
The solitude of centuries untold
Has settled where they dwelt. The prairie-wolf
Hunts in their meadows, and his fresh-dug den
Yawns by my path. The gopher mines the ground
Where stood their swarming cities. All is gone;   65
All—save the piles of earth that hold their bones,
The platforms where they worshipped unknown gods,
The barriers which they builded from the soil
To keep the foe at bay—till o'er the walls
The wild beleaguerers broke, and, one by one,   70
The strongholds of the plain were forced, and heaped
With corpses. The brown vultures of the wood
Flocked to those vast uncovered sepulchres,
And sat, unscared and silent, at their feast.
Haply some solitary fugitive,   75
Lurking in marsh and forest, till the sense
Of desolation and of fear became
Bitterer than death, yielded himself to die.
Man's better nature triumphed then. Kind words
Welcomed and soothed him; the rude conquerors   80
Seated the captive with their chiefs; he chose
A bride among their maidens, and at length
Seemed to forget—yet ne'er forgot—the wife
Of his first love, and her sweet little ones,
Butchered, amid their shrieks, with all his race.   85

5. Or Pentelikon, a Greek mountain; source of the fine marble of such ancient buildings in nearby Athens as the Parthenon (l. 50), celebrated temple of Athena.

Thus change the forms of being. Thus arise
Races of living things, glorious in strength,
And perish, as the quickening breath of God
Fills them, or is withdrawn. The red-man, too,
Has left the blooming wilds he ranged so long,   90
And, nearer to the Rocky Mountains, sought
A wilder hunting-ground. The beaver builds
No longer by these streams, but far away,
On waters whose blue surface ne'er gave back
The white man's face—among Missouri's springs,   95
And pools whose issues swell the Oregon[6]—
He rears his little Venice. In these plains
The bison feeds no more. Twice twenty leagues
Beyond remotest smoke of hunter's camp,
Roams the majestic brute, in herds that shake   100
The earth with thundering steps—yet here I meet
His ancient footprints stamped beside the pool.

Still this great solitude is quick with life.
Myriads of insects, gaudy as the flowers
They flutter over, gentle quadrupeds,   105
And birds, that scarce have learned the fear of man,
Are here, and sliding reptiles of the ground,
Startlingly beautiful. The graceful deer
Bounds to the wood at my approach. The bee,
A more adventurous colonist than man,   110
With whom he came across the eastern deep,
Fills the savannas with his murmurings,
And hides his sweets, as in the golden age,
Within the hollow oak. I listen long
To his domestic hum, and think I hear   115
The sound of that advancing multitude
Which soon shall fill these deserts. From the ground
Comes up the laugh of children, the soft voice
Of maidens, and the sweet and solemn hymn
Of Sabbath worshippers. The low of herds   120
Blends with the rustling of the heavy grain
Over the dark brown furrows. All at once
A fresher wind sweeps by, and breaks my dream,
And I am in the wilderness alone.

1832   1833, 1834

6. *Cf.* "Thanatopsis." Now the Columbia River.

The Battle-Field[7]

Once this soft turf, this rivulet's sands,
   Were trampled by a hurrying crowd,
And fiery hearts and armed hands
   Encountered in the battle-cloud.

Ah! never shall the land forget 5
   How gushed the life-blood of her brave—
Gushed, warm with hope and courage yet,
   Upon the soil they fought to save.

Now all is calm, and fresh, and still;
   Alone the chirp of flitting bird,
And talk of children on the hill, 10
   And bell of wandering kine, are heard.

No solemn host goes trailing by
   The black-mouthed gun and staggering wain;
Men start not at the battle-cry,
   Oh, be it never heard again! 15

Soon rested those who fought; but thou
   Who minglest in the harder strife
For truths which men receive not now,
   Thy warfare only ends with life. 20

A friendless warfare! lingering long
   Through weary day and weary year;
A wild and many-weaponed throng
   Hang on thy front, and flank, and rear.

Yet nerve thy spirit to the proof, 25
   And blench not at thy chosen lot,
The timid good may stand aloof,
   The sage may frown—yet faint thou not.

Nor heed the shaft too surely cast,
   The foul and hissing bolt of scorn;
For with thy side shall dwell, at last, 30
   The victory of endurance born.

7. The battlefield is that of political justice; as a great liberal editor, Bryant was constantly and savagely attacked. An abolition Democrat, he was vilified by the slavery Democrats for his free-soil and antislavery editorials, while conservatives of both parties attacked him for his humanitarian, liberal attitude toward banking, currency, and debtor laws, criminal and penal procedures, freedom of speech and of contract and labor association. His editorials, reprinted below, on free speech and labor were written within a year of this poem, whose ninth stanza provides one of the familiar quotations of literature.

Truth, crushed to earth, shall rise again;
 Th' eternal years of God are hers;
But Error, wounded, writhes in pain,   35
 And dies among his worshippers.

Yea, though thou lie upon the dust,
 When they who helped thee flee in fear,
Die full of hope and manly trust,
 Like those who fell in battle here.   40

Another hand thy sword shall wield,
 Another hand the standard wave,
Till from the trumpet's mouth is pealed
 The blast of triumph o'er thy grave.

1837   1837, 1839

Robert of Lincoln[8]

Merrily swinging on brier and weed,
 Near to the nest of his little dame,
Over the mountain-side or mead,
 Robert of Lincoln is telling his name:
  Bob-o'-link, bob-o'-link,   5
  Spink, spank, spink;
Snug and safe is that nest of ours,
Hidden among the summer flowers.
   Chee, chee, chee.

Robert of Lincoln is gayly drest,   10
 Wearing a bright black wedding-coat;
White are his shoulders and white his crest.
 Hear him call in his merry note:
  Bob-o'-link, bob-o'-link,
  Spink, spank, spink;   15
Look, what a nice new coat is mine,
Sure there was never a bird so fine.
   Chee, chee, chee.

Robert of Lincoln's Quaker wife,
 Pretty and quiet, with plain brown wings, 20
Passing at home a patient life,

8. The bobolink is a familiar bird in the Berkshires of western Massachusetts, where Bryant in youth began his intimate study of nature with his father, a naturalist and physician. The descriptions of the bird's remarkable mating garb (ll. 10–14), of his unusual song uttered in flight, and of his domestic character, distinguish this among all bird poems for accuracy and charm. (See R. T. Peterson's *Field Guide to the Birds*, pp. 199 and 209; he records the sound of the flight note as "pink"—compare Bryant's "spink.")

Broods in the grass while her husband sings:
    Bob-o'-link, bob-o'-link,
    Spink, spank, spink;
Brood, kind creature; you need not fear
Thieves and robbers while I am here.
        Chee, chee, chee.

Modest and shy as a nun is she;
    One weak chirp is her only note.
Braggart and prince of braggarts is he,
    Pouring boasts from his little throat:
    Bob-o'-link, bob-o'-link,
    Spink, spank, spink;
Never was I afraid of man;
Catch me, cowardly knaves, if you can!
        Chee, chee, chee.

Six white eggs on a bed of hay,
    Flecked with purple, a pretty sight!
There as the mother sits all day,
    Robert is singing with all his might:
    Bob-o'-link, bob-o'-link,
    Spink, spank, spink;
Nice good wife, that never goes out,
Keeping house while I frolic about.
        Chee, chee, chee.

Soon as the little ones chip the shell,
    Six wide mouths are open for food;
Robert of Lincoln bestirs him well,
    Gathering seeds for the hungry brood.
    Bob-o'-link, bob-o'-link,
    Spink, spank, spink;
This new life is likely to be
Hard for a gay young fellow like me.
        Chee, chee, chee.

Robert of Lincoln at length is made
    Sober with work, and silent with care;
Off is his holiday garment laid,
    Half forgotten that merry air:
    Bob-o'-link, bob-o'-link,
    Spink, spank, spink;
Nobody knows but my mate and I
Where our nest and our nestlings lie.
        Chee, chee, chee.

Summer wanes; the children are grown;
   Fun and frolic no more he knows;   65
Robert of Lincoln's a humdrum crone;
   Off he flies, and we sing as he goes:
      Bob-o'-link, bob-o'-link,
      Spink, spank, spink;
When you can pipe that merry old strain,   70
Robert of Lincoln, come back again.
      Chee, chee, chee.

1855   1855, 1864

The Death of Lincoln[1]

Oh, slow to smite and swift to spare,
   Gentle and merciful and just!
Who, in the fear of God, didst bear
   The sword of power, a nation's trust!

In sorrow by thy bier we stand,   5
   Amid the awe that hushes all,
And speak the anguish of a land
   That shook with horror at thy fall.

Thy task is done; the bond are free:
   We bear thee to an honored grave,   10
Whose proudest monument shall be
   The broken fetters of the slave

Pure was thy life; its bloody close
   Hath placed thee with the sons of light,
Among the noble host of those   15
   Who perished in the cause of Right.

1865   1866, 1871

The Flood of Years[2]

A mighty Hand, from an exhaustless Urn,
Pours forth the never-ending Flood of Years,

1. Lincoln died by the assassin's bullet on April 15, 1865, and his funeral train at once started its long pilgrimage to Springfield, Illinois. According to Godwin, Bryant wrote his poem at the request of the Committee of Arrangements for the ceremony in the city of New York. As "Abraham Lincoln: Poetical Tribute to the Memory of Abraham Lincoln" the poem appeared in the *Atlantic Monthly* for January, 1866.

2. For the stages of Bryant's religious thought see the poems "Thanatopsis" and "To a Waterfowl." According to Godwin, when Bryant was questioned concerning the faith expressed in "The Flood of Years," he replied, "I believe in the everlasting life of the soul; and it seems to me that immortality would be but an imperfect gift without the recognition in the life to come of those who are dear to us."

Among the nations. How the rushing waves
Bear all before them! On their foremost edge,
And there alone, is Life. The Present there
Tosses and foams, and fills the air with roar
Of mingled noises. There are they who toil,
And they who strive, and they who feast, and they
Who hurry to and fro. The sturdy swain—
Woodman and delver with the spade—is there,
And busy artisan beside his bench,
And pallid student with his written roll.
A moment on the mounting billow seen,
The flood sweeps over them and they are gone.
There groups of revellers whose brows are twined
With roses, ride the topmost swell awhile,
And as they raise their flowing cups and touch
The clinking brim to brim, are whirled beneath
The waves and disappear. I hear the jar
Of beaten drums, and thunders that break forth
From cannon, where the advancing billow sends
Up to the sight long files of armèd men,
That hurry to the charge through flame and smoke.
The torrent bears them under, whelmed and hid
Slayer and slain, in heaps of bloody foam.
Down go the steed and rider, the plumed chief
Sinks with his followers; the head that wears
The imperial diadem goes down beside
The felon's with cropped ear and branded cheek.
A funeral-train—the torrent sweeps away
Bearers and bier and mourners. By the bed
Of one who dies men gather sorrowing,
And women weep aloud; the flood rolls on;
The wail is stifled and the sobbing group
Borne under. Hark to that shrill, sudden shout,
The cry of an applauding multitude,
Swayed by some loud-voiced orator who wields
The living mass as if he were its soul!
The waters choke the shout and all is still.
Lo! next a kneeling crowd, and one who spreads
The hands in prayer, the engulfing wave o'ertakes
And swallows them and him. A sculptor wields
The chisel, and the stricken marble grows
To beauty; at his easel, eager-eyed,
A painter stands, and sunshine at his touch
Gathers upon his canvas, and life glows;
A poet, as he paces to and fro,

Murmurs his sounding lines. Awhile they ride
The advancing billow, till its tossing crest
Strikes them and flings them under, while their tasks   50
Are yet unfinished. See a mother smile
On her young babe that smiles to her again;
The torrent wrests it from her arms; she shrieks
And weeps, and amidst her tears is carried down.
A beam like that of moonlight turns the spray   55
To glistening pearls; two lovers, hand in hand,
Rise on the billowy swell and fondly look
Into each other's eyes. The rushing flood
Flings them apart: the youth goes down; the maid
With hands outstretched in vain, and streaming eyes,   60
Waits for the next high wave to follow him.
An aged man succeeds; his bending form
Sinks slowly. Mingling with the sullen stream
Gleam the white locks, and then are seen no more.

  Lo! wider grows the stream—a sea-like flood   65
Saps earth's walled cities; massive palaces
Crumble before it; fortresses and towers
Dissolve in the swift waters; populous realms
Swept by the torrent see their ancient tribes
Engulfed and lost; their very languages   70
Stifled, and never to be uttered more.

  I pause and turn my eyes, and looking back
Where that tumultuous flood has been, I see
The silent ocean of the Past, a waste
Of waters weltering over graves, its shores   75
Strewn with the wreck of fleets where mast and hull
Drop away piecemeal; battlemented walls
Frown idly, green with moss, and temples stand
Unroofed, forsaken by the worshipper.
There lie memorial stones, whence time has gnawed   80
The graven legends, thrones of kings o'erturned,
The broken altars of forgotten gods,
Foundations of old cities and long streets
Where never fall of human foot is heard,
On all the desolate pavement. I behold   85
Dim glimmerings of lost jewels, far within
The sleeping waters, diamond, sardonyx,
Ruby and topaz, pearl and chrysolite,
Once glittering at the banquet on fair brows
That long ago were dust, and all around   90
Strewn on the surface of that silent sea
Are withering bridal wreaths, and glossy locks

Shorn from dear brows, by loving hands, and scrolls
O'er written, haply with fond words of love
And vows of friendship, and fair pages flung   95
Fresh from the printer's engine. There they lie
A moment, and then sink away from sight.

    I looked, and the quick tears are in my eyes,
For I behold in every one of these
A blighted hope, a separate history   100
Of human sorrows, telling of dear ties
Suddenly broken, dreams of happiness
Dissolved in air, and happy days too brief
That sorrowfully ended, and I think
How painfully must the poor heart have beat   105
In bosoms without number, as the blow
Was struck that slew their hope and broke their peace.

    Sadly I turn and look before, where yet
The Flood must pass, and I behold a mist
Where swarm dissolving forms, the brood of Hope,   110
Divinely fair, that rest on banks of flowers,
Or wander among rainbows, fading soon
And reappearing, haply giving place
To forms of grisly aspect such as Fear
Shapes from the idle air—where serpents lift   115
The head to strike, and skeletons stretch forth
The bony arm in menace. Further on
A belt of darkness seems to bar the way
Long, low, and distant, where the Life to come
Touches the Life that is. The Flood of Years   120
Rolls toward it near and nearer. It must pass
That dismal barrier. What is there beyond?
Hear what the wise and good have said. Beyond
That belt of darkness, still the Years roll on
More gently, but with not less mighty sweep.   125
They gather up again and softly bear
All the sweet lives that late were overwhelmed
And lost to sight, all that in them was good,
Noble, and truly great, and worthy of love—
The lives of infants and ingenuous youths,   130
Sages and saintly women who have made
Their households happy; all are raised and borne
By that great current in its onward sweep,
Wandering and rippling with caressing waves
Around green islands fragrant with the breath   135
Of flowers that never wither. So they pass
From stage to stage along the shining course

Of that bright river, broadening like a sea.
As its smooth eddies curl along their way
They bring old friends together; hands are clasped   140
In joy unspeakable; the mother's arms
Again are folded round the child she loved
And lost. Old sorrows are forgotten now,
Or but remembered to make sweet the hour
That overpays them; wounded hearts that bled   145
Or broke are healed forever. In the room
Of this grief-shadowed present, there shall be
A Present in whose reign no grief shall gnaw
The heart, and never shall a tender tie
Be broken; in whose reign the eternal Change   150
That waits on growth and action shall proceed
With everlasting Concord hand in hand.

1876   1876

From Lectures on Poetry[3]

Lecture Fourth: On Originality and Imitation

I propose in this lecture to say a few words on the true use and
value of imitation in poetry. I mean not what is technically called the
imitation of nature, but the studying and copying of models of poetic
composition. There is hardly any praise of which writers in the
present age, particularly writers in verse, are more ambitious than
that of originality. This ambition is a laudable one, for a captivating
originality is everything in the art. Whether it consists in presenting
familiar things in a new and striking yet natural light, or in revealing
secrets of emotion and thought which have lain undetected from the
birth of literature, it is one of the most abundant and sure sources
of poetic delight. It strikes us with the same sort of feeling as the finding of some beautiful spot in our familiar walks which we had never
observed before, or the exhibition of some virtue in the character of a
friend which we were ignorant that he possessed. It is of itself a
material addition to the literary riches of the country in which it is
produced; and it impresses something of its character upon that
literature, which lasts as long as the productions in which it is contained are read and remembered.

3. Newly arrived in New York, Bryant
gave four lectures before the Athenaeum
Society in April, 1826: "On the Nature
of Poetry," "On the Value and Uses of
Poetry," "On Poetry in its Relation to
Our Age and Country," and the one here
reprinted—"On Originality and Imitation." He affirmed his romantic faith in
originality, while asserting the poet's responsibility to the rich tradition of the
past. Independent originality will function principally in the fusion of imagination and emotion; for the American poet,
he insisted that this fusion was most
likely to occur in the use of native
themes and materials.

Nor does it lose its peculiar charm with the lapse of time, for there is an enduring freshness and vividness in its pictures of nature, of action and emotion, that fade not with years. The poetry of Shakespear, for instance, maintains its original power over the mind, and no more loses its living beauty by the lapse of ages than the universe grows dim and deformed in the sight of men.

It is not at all strange that a quality of so much importance to the poet should be sought after with great ardor, and that, in the zeal of pursuit, mistakes should sometimes be made as to that characteristic of it which alone is really valuable. Poets have often been willing to purchase the praise of it at the sacrifice of what is better. They have been led, by their overeagerness to attain it, into puerile conceits, into extravagant vagaries of imagination, into overstrained exaggerations of passion, into mawkish and childish simplicity. It has given birth to outrages upon moral principle, upon decency, upon common sense; it has produced, in short, irregularities and affectations of every kind. The grandiloquous nonsense of euphuism, which threatened to overlay and smother English literature in its very cradle, the laborious wit of the metaphysical poets who were contemporaries of Milton, the puling effeminacy of the cockney school, which has found no small favor at the present day—are all children of this fruitful parent.

It seems to me that all these errors arise from not paying sufficient attention to the consideration that poetry is an art; that, like all other arts, it is founded upon a series of experiments—experiments, in this instance, made upon the imagination and the feelings of mankind; that a great deal of its effect depends upon the degree of success with which a sagacious and strong mind seizes and applies the skill of others, and that to slight the experiences of our predecessors on this subject is a pretty certain way to go wrong. For, if we consider the matter a little more narrowly, we shall find that the most original of poets is not without very great obligations to his predecessors and his contemporaries. The art of poetry is not perfected in a day. It is brought to excellence, by slow degrees, from the first rude and imperfect attempts at versification to the finished productions of its greatest masters. The gorgeousness of poetic imagery, the curious felicities of poetic language, the music of poetic numbers, the spells of words that act like magic on the heart, are not created by one poet in any language, in any country. An innumerable multitude of sentiments, of illustrations, of impassioned forms of expression, of harmonious combinations of words, both fixed in books and floating in conversation, must previously exist either in the vernacular language of the poet or in some other which he has studied, and whose beauties and riches he seeks to transplant into his own, before he can produce any work which is destined to live.

Genius, therefore, with all its pride in its own strength, is but a dependent quality, and cannot put forth its whole powers nor claim all its honors without an amount of aid from the talents and labors of others which it is difficult to calculate. In those fortunate circumstances which permit its most perfect exercises, it takes, it is true, a pre-eminent station; but, after all, it is elevated upon the shoulders of its fellows. It may create something in literature, but it does not create all, great as its merit may be. What it does is infinitely less than what is done for it; the new treasures it finds are far less in value than the old of which it makes use. There is no warrant for the notion maintained by some, that the first poets in any language were great poets, or that, whatever their rank, they did not learn their art from the great poets in other languages. It might as well be expected that a self-taught architect would arise in a country whose inhabitants live in caves, and, without models or instruction, raise the majestic Parthenon and pile up St. Peter's into the clouds.

That there were poets in the English language before Chaucer, some of whom were not unworthy to be his predecessors, is attested by extant monuments of their verse; and, if there had not been, he might have learned his art from the polished poets of Italy, whom he studied and loved. Italy had versifiers before Dante, and, if they were not his masters, he at least found masters in the harmonious poets of a kindred dialect, the Provençal. In the Provençal language, the earliest of the cultivated tongues of modern Europe, there arose no great poet. The reason was that their literature had scarcely been brought to that degree of perfection which produces the finest specimens of poetry when the hour of its decline had come. It possessed, it is true, authors innumerable, revivers of the same art, enrichers of the same idiom, and polishers of the same system of versification, yet they never looked for models out of their own literature; they did not study the remains of ancient poetry to avail themselves of its riches; they confined themselves to such improvements and enlargements of the art as were made among themselves; and therefore their progress, though wonderful for the circumstances in which they were placed, was yet limited in comparison with that of those nations who have had access to the treasures they neglected.

In Roman literature there were poets before Lucretius, who is thought to have carried the poetry of the Latins to its highest measure of perfection; before even Ennius, who boasted of having introduced the melody of the hexameter into Latin verse. But Ennius and Lucretius and Horace and Virgil, and all the Roman poets, were, moreover, disciples of the Greeks, and sought to transfuse the spirit of the Grecian literature into their domestic tongue. Of the Greek poets we discover no instructors. The oldest of their poems which we possess, the writings of Homer, are also among the most perfect. Yet we should forget all reverence for probability were we to suppose that the art of poetry was born with him. The inferior and more mechanical parts of it must have been the fruit of long and zealous cultivation; centuries must have elapsed, and thousands of trials must have been made, before the musical and various hexameter could have been brought to the perfection in which we find it in his works. His poems themselves are full of allusions to a long antiquity of poetry. All the early traditions of Greece are sprinkled with the names of its minstrels, and the heroic fables of that country are probably, in a great measure, the work of these primitive bards. Orpheus, whose verse recalled the dead, Sinus and Musæus, whom Virgil, the disciple of Homer, seats in that elysium where he forgets to place his master, are examples of a sort of immortality conferred on mere names in literature, the dim but venerable shadows of the fathers of poetry, whose works have been lost for thousands of years. These were undoubtedly the ancient bards from whose compositions Homer kindled his imagination, and, catching a double portion of their spirit, emulated and surpassed them.

At the present day, however, a writer of poems writes in a language which preceding poets have polished, refined, and filled with forcible, graceful, and musical expressions. He is not only taught by them to overcome the difficulties of rhythmical construction, but he is shown, as it were, the secrets of the mechanism by which he moves the mind of his reader; he is shown ways of kindling the imagination and of interesting the passions which his own sagacity might never have discovered; his mind is filled with the beauty of their sentiments, and their enthusiasm is breathed into his soul. He owes much, also, to his contemporaries as well as to those who have gone before him. He reads their works, and whatever excellence he beholds in them, inspires him with a strong desire to rival it—stronger, perhaps, than that excited by the writings of his predecessors; for such is our reverence for the dead that we are willing to concede to them that superiority which we are anxious to snatch from the living. Even if he should refuse to read the writings of his brethren, he cannot escape the action of their minds on his own. He necessarily comes to partake somewhat of the character of their genius, which is impressed not only on all contemporary literature, but even on the daily thoughts of those with whom he associates. In short, his mind is in a great degree formed by the labors of others; he walks in a path which they have made smooth and plain, and is supported by their strength. Whoever would entirely disclaim imitation, and aspire to the praises of complete originality, should be altogether ignorant of any poetry written by others, and of all those aids which the cultivation of poetry has lent to prose. Deprive an author of these advantages, and what sort of poetry does any one imagine that he would produce? I dare say it would be sufficiently original, but who will affirm that it could be read?

The poet must do precisely what is done by the mathematician, who takes up his science where his predecessors have left it, and pushes its limits as much farther, and makes as many new applications of principles, as he can. He must found himself on the excellence already attained in his art, and if, in addition to this, he delights us with new modes of sublimity, of beauty, and of human emotion, he deserves the praise of originality and of genius. If he has nothing of all this, he is entitled to no other honor than belongs to him who keeps alive the practice of a delightful and beautiful art.

This very necessity, however, of a certain degree of dependence upon models in poetry has at some periods led into an opposite fault to the inordinate desire of originality. The student, instead of copying nature with the aid of knowledge derived from these models, has been induced to make them the original, from which the copy was to be drawn. He has been led to take an imperfect work—and all human works are imperfect—as the standard of perfection, and to dwell upon it with such reverence that he comes to see beauties where no beauties are, and excellence in place of positive defects. Thus the study of poetry, which should encourage the free and unlimited aspirations of the mind after all that is noble and beautiful, has been perverted into a contrivance to chill and repress them. It has seduced its admirers from an admiration of the works of God to an idolatry for the works of men; it has carried them from living and inexhaustible sources of poetic inspiration to drink at comparatively scanty and impure channels; it has made them to linger by the side of these instead of using them as guides to ascend to their original fountain.

It is of high importance, then, to inquire what are the proper limits of poetic imitation, or, in other words, by what means the examples and labors of others may be made use of in strengthening, and prevented from enfeebling, the native vigor of genius. No better rule has been given for this purpose than to take no particular poem nor poet, nor class of poets, as the pattern of poetic composition, but to study the beauties of all. All good poems have their peculiar merits and faults, all great poets their points of strength and weakness, all schools of poetry their agreements with good taste and their offences against it. To confine the attention and limit the admiration to one particular sort of excellence, not only tends to narrow the range of the intellectual powers, but most surely brings along with it the peculiar defects to which that sort of excellence is allied, and into which it is most apt to deviate. Thus, a poet of the Lake school, by endeavoring too earnestly after simplicity, may run into childishness; a follower of Byron, in his pursuit of energy of thought, and the intense expression of passion, may degenerate into abruptness, extravagance, or obscurity; a disciple of Scott, in his zeal for easy writing, may find himself inditing something little better than doggerel, or, at least, very dull and feeble verse; an imitator of Leigh Hunt, too intent on keeping up the vivacity and joyousness of the poetic temperament, may forget his common sense; and a poet of the school of Pope may write very polished, well-balanced verses with a great deal of antithesis and very little true feeling.

Still, these several schools have all their excellences; they have all some qualities to be admired and loved and dwelt upon. Let the student of poetry dwell upon them as long as he pleases, let him study them until they are incorporated into his mind, but let him give his admiration to no one of them exclusively. It is remarkable to what degree the great founders of the several styles of English poetry, even of the least lofty, varied, and original, have pursued this universal search after excellence. When Pope—brilliant, witty, harmonious, and, within a certain compass, a great master of language—had fixed the poetical taste of his age, we all know what a crowd of imitators arose in his train, and how rapidly poetry declined. But the imitators of Pope failed to do what Pope did. Great as was his partiality for the French school, and closely as he formed himself on the model of Boileau, he yet disdained not to learn much from other instructors. He went back for gems of thought and graces of style to the earlier writers of English verse—to the poets of the Elizabethan age, and, farther still, to the venerable Chaucer. He was a passionate admirer and a restorer of Shakespeare, and, by recommending him to the English people, prepared the way for the downfall of his own school, but not, I hope, for the oblivion of his own writings.

This relish of poetic excellence in all its forms, and in whatever school or style of poetry it is found, does not, I apprehend, lead to a less lively apprehension of the several merits of these styles, while at the same time it opens the eyes of the student to their several defects and errors. In this way the mind forms to itself a higher standard of excellence than exists in any of them—a standard compounded of the characteristic merits of all, and free from any of their imperfections. To this standard it will refer all their compositions; to this it will naturally aspire; and, by the contemplation of this, it will divest itself of that blind and idolatrous reverence for certain models of composition and certain dogmas of ancient criticism which are the death of the hopes and inspirations of the poet.

It is long since the authority of great names was disregarded in matters of science. Ages ago the schools shook themselves loose from the fetters of Aristotle. He no more now delivers the oracles of philosophy than the priests of Apollo deliver the oracles of religion. Why should the chains of authority be worn any longer by the heart and the imagination than by the reason? This is a question which the age has already answered. The genius of modern times has gone out in every direction in search of originality. Its ardor has not always been compensated by the discovery of its object, but under its auspices a fresh, vigorous, and highly original poetry has grown up. The fertile soil of modern literature has thrown up, it is true, weeds among the flowers, but the flowers are of immortal bloom and fragrance, and the weeds are soon outworn. It is no longer necessary that a narrative poem should be written on the model of the ancient epic; a lyric composition is not relished the more, perhaps not so much, for being Pindaric or Horatian; and it is not required that a satire should remind the reader of Juvenal. It is enough for the age if beautiful diction, glowing imagery, strong emotion, and fine thought are so combined as to give them their fullest effect upon the mind. The end of poetry is then attained, no matter by what system of rules.

If it were to be asked which is the more likely to produce specimens of poetry worthy of going down to posterity, which is the more favorable to the enlargement of the human mind and the vigorous action of all its faculties on the variety of objects and their relations by which it is surrounded—an age distinguished for too great carefulness of imitation, or an age remarkable for an excessive ambition of originality—I think that a wise decision must be in favor of the latter. Whatever errors in taste may spring from the zeal for new developments of genius and the disdain of imitation, their influence is of short duration. The fantastic brood of extravagances and absurdities to which they give birth soon die and are forgotten, for nothing is immortal in literature but what is truly excellent. On the other hand, such an age may and does produce poems worthy to live. The works of the early Italian poets were composed in such an age; the proudest monuments of English verse are the growth of such a spirit; the old poetry of Spain, the modern poetry of Germany, grew into beauty and strength under such auspices. Men walked, as they should ever do, with a confident step by the side of these ancient masters, of whom they learned this art; they studied their works, not that they might resemble, but that they might surpass them.

But one of the best fruits of such an age is the remarkable activity into which it calls the human intellect. Those things which are ours rather by memory than by the natural growth of the mind lie on its surface, already wrought into distinct shape, and are brought into use with little effort. But for the native conceptions of the mind, the offspring of strong mental excitement, it is necessary to go deeper and to toil more intensely. It is not without a vigorous exercise that the intellect searches for these among its stores, extricates them from the obscurity in which they are first beheld, ascertains their parts and detains them until they are moulded into distinctness and symmetry, and embodied in language.

But when once a tame and frigid taste has possessed the tribe of poets, when all their powers are employed in servilely copying the works of their predecessors, it is not only impossible that any great work should be produced among them, but the period of a literary reformation, of the awakening of genius, is postponed to a distant futurity. It is the quality of such a state of literature, by the imposing precision of its rules and the ridicule it throws on everything out of its own beaten track, to perpetuate itself indefinitely. The happy appearance of some extraordinary genius, educated under different influences than those operating on the age, and compelling admiration by the force of his talents; or, perhaps, some great moral or political revolution, by unsettling old opinions and familiarizing men to daring speculations—can alone have any effect to remove it. The mind grows indolent, or, at least, enfeebled, by the want of those higher exercises to which it was destined. At the same time, the spirit of poetry, as seen in its power of elevating the mind, of humanizing the affections, and expelling sordid appetites, is no longer felt, or only felt by a few, who conceal in their own bosoms the secret of its power over them.

1825   1884

From The Right of Workmen to Strike[4]

Sentence was passed on Saturday on the twenty "men who had determined not to work." The punishment selected, on due consideration, by the judge, was that officers appointed for the purpose should immediately demand from each of the delinquents a sum of money which was named in the sentence of the court. The amount demanded would not have fallen short of the savings of many years. Either the offenders had not parted with these savings, or their brother workmen raised the ransom money for them on the spot. The fine was paid over as required. All is now well; justice has been satisfied. But if the expenses of their families had anticipated the law, and left nothing in their hands, or if friends had not been ready to buy the freedom of their comrades, they would have been sent to prison, and there they would have staid, until their wives and children, besides earning their own bread, had saved enough to re-

4. *Cf.* "The Battle-Field," above. This editorial appeared in his *Evening Post* at the height of the battle for the recognition of the workers' right to collective bargaining. Under the common law, labor unions were still prosecuted as "conspiracies." The first successful association—the Mechanics Union of Trade Associations—had just been formed in Philadelphia (1827). In New York City, in 1829, the first successful workers' party polled nearly one third of the votes cast. Throughout the thirties, indictments for conspiracy were persistently employed against the insurgent union movement.

deem the captives from their cells. Such had been their punishment. What was their offence? They had committed the crime of unanimously declining to go to work at the wages offered to them by their masters. They had said to one another, "Let us come out from the meanness and misery of our caste. Let us begin to do what every order more privileged and more honoured is doing every day. By the means which we believe to be the best let us raise ourselves and our families above the humbleness of our condition. We may be wrong, but we cannot help believing that we might do much if we were true brothers to each other, and would resolve not to sell the only thing which is our own, the cunning of our hands, for less than it is worth." What other things they may have done is nothing to the purpose: it was for this they were condemned; it is for this they are to endure the penalty of the law.

We call upon a candid and generous community to mark that the punishment inflicted upon these twenty "men who had determined not to work" is not directed against the offence of conspiring to prevent others by force from working at low wages, but expressly against the offence of settling by pre-concert the compensation which they thought they were entitled to obtain. It is certainly superfluous to repeat, that this journal would be the very last to oppose a law levelled at any attempt to molest the labourer who chooses to work for less than the prices settled by the union. We have said, and to cut off cavil, we say it now again, that a conspiracy to deter, by threats of violence, a fellow workman from arranging his own terms with his employers, is a conspiracy to commit a felony—a conspiracy which, being a crime against liberty, we should be the first to condemn—a conspiracy which no strike should, for its own sake, countenance for a moment—a conspiracy already punishable by the statute, and far easier to reach than the one of which "the twenty" stood accused; but a conspiracy, we must add, that has not a single feature in common with the base and barbarous prohibition under which the offenders were indicted and condemned.

They were condemned because they had determined not to work for the wages that were offered them! Can any thing be imagined more abhorrent to every sentiment of generosity or justice, than the law which arms the rich with the legal right to fix, by assize, the wages of the poor? If this is not SLAVERY, we have forgotten its definition. Strike the right of associating for the sale of labour from the privileges of a freeman, and you may as well at once bind him to a master, or ascribe him to the soil. If it be not in the colour of his skin, and in the poor franchise of naming his own terms in a contract for his work, what advantage has the labourer of the North over the bondman of the South? Punish by human laws a "determination not to work," make it penal by any other penalty than idleness inflicts, and it matters little whether the task-masters be one or many, an individual or an order, the hateful scheme of slavery will have gained a foothold in the land. And then the meanness of this law, which visits with its malice those who cling to it for protection, and shelters with all its fences those who are raised above its threats. A late solicitation for its aid against employers, is treated with derision and contempt, but the moment the "masters" invoked its intervention, it came down from its high place with most indecent haste, and has now discharged its fury upon the naked heads of wretches so forlorn, that their worst faults multiply their titles to a liberty which they must learn to win from livelier sensibilities than the barren benevolence of Wealth, or the tardy magnanimity of Power. * * *

"Self-created societies," says Judge Edwards, "are unknown to the constitution and laws, and will not be permitted to rear their crest and extend their baneful influence over any portion of the community." If there is any sense in this passage it means that self-created societies are unlawful, and must be put down by the courts. Down then with every literary, every religious, and every charitable association not incorporated! What nonsense is this! Self-created societies *are* known to the constitution and laws, for they are not prohibited, and the laws which allow them will, if justly administered, protect them. But suppose in charity that the reporter has put this absurdity into the mouth of Judge Edwards, and that he meant only those self-created societies which have an effect upon trade and commerce. Gather up then and sweep to the penitentiary all those who are confederated to carry on any business or trade in concert, by fixed rules, and see how many men you would leave at large in this city. The members of every partnership in the place will come under the penalties of the law, and not only these, but every person pursuing any occupation whatever, who governs himself by a mutual understanding with others that follow the same occupation. * * *

1836   June 13, 1836; 1884

Freedom of Speech[5]

A meeting of the people of Cincinnati have proclaimed the right of silencing the expression of unpopular opinions by violence. We

5. Another of Bryant's *Evening Post* editorials, this appeared at the height of a concerted effort in 1835–1836, to abridge freedom of speech and the press in respect to abolitionist pronouncements. The American Anti-Slavery Society was newly established (1833) at Philadelphia, and with Garrison's new *Liberator* was fomenting an abolitionist literature. Abolitionist groups petitioned Congress in 1834–1835, and flooded the country with propaganda. In the spring of 1836, Charles Pinckney of South Carolina offered his famous "Gag-rule" resolution to Congress, proposing that all abolitionist petitions and resolutions be tabled and ignored—a direct violation of the Constitution.

refer our readers to the proceedings of an anti-abolition meeting lately held in that city. They will be found in another part of this paper.

If the meeting had contented itself with declaring its disapprobation of the tenets of the abolitionists, we should have had nothing to say. They might have exhausted the resources of rhetoric and of language—they might have indulged in the very extravagance and wantonness of vehement condemnation, for aught we cared; they would still have been in the exercise of a right which the constitution and the laws secure to them. But when they go further, and declare that they have not only a right to condemn certain opinions in others, but the right to coerce those who hold them to silence, it is time to make an immediate and decided stand, and to meet the threat of coercion with defiance.

The Cincinnati meeting, in the concluding resolution offered by Wilson N. Brown, and adopted with the rest, declare in so many words that if they cannot put down the abolitionist press by fair means they will do it by foul; if they cannot silence it by remonstrance, they will silence it by violence; if they cannot persuade it to desist, they will stir up mobs against it, inflame them to madness, and turn their brutal rage against the dwellings, the property, the persons, the lives of the wretched abolitionists and their families. In announcing that they will put them down by force all this is included. Fire, robbery, bloodshed, are the common excesses of an enraged mob. There is no extreme of cruelty and destruction to which in the drunkenness and delirium of its fury it may not proceed. The commotions of the elements can as easily be appeased by appeals to the quality of mercy as these commotions of the human mind; the whirlwind and the lightning might as well be expected to pause and turn aside to spare the helpless and innocent, as an infuriated multitude.

If the abolitionists *must* be put down, and if the community are of that opinion, there is no necessity of violence to effect the object. The community have the power in their own hands; the majority may make a law declaring the discussion of slavery in a certain manner to be a crime, and imposing penalties. The law may then be put in force against the offenders, and their mouths may be gagged in due form, and with all the solemnities of justice.

What is the reason this is not done? The answer is ready. The community are for leaving the liberty of the press untrammelled—there is not a committee that can be raised in any of the State legislatures north of the Potomac who will report in favor of imposing penalties on those who declaim against slavery—there is not a legislature who would sanction such a report—and there is not a single free state the people of which would sustain a legislature in so doing. These are facts, and the advocates of mob law know them to be so.

Who then are the men that issue this invitation to silence the press by violence? Who but an insolent brawling minority, a few noisy fanatics who claim that their own opinions shall be the measure of freedom for the rest of the community, and who undertake to overawe a vast pacific majority by threats of wanton outrage and plunder? These men are for erecting an oligarchy of their own and riding rough shod over the people and the people's rights. They claim a right to repeal the laws established by the majority in favor of the freedom of the press. They make new laws of their own to which they require that the rest of the community shall submit, and in case of a refusal, they threaten to execute them by the ministry of a mob. There is no tyranny or oppression exercised in any part of the world more absolute or more frightful than that which they would establish.

So far as we are concerned we are determined that this despotism shall neither be submitted to nor encouraged. In whatever form it makes its appearance we shall raise our voice against it. We are resolved that the subject of slavery shall be as it ever has been, as free a subject of discussion and argument and declamation, as the difference between whiggism and democracy, or as the difference between the Arminians and the Calvinists. If the press chooses to be silent on the subject it shall be the silence of perfect free will, and not the silence of fear. We hold that this combination of the few to govern the many by the terror of illegal violence, is as wicked and indefensible as a conspiracy to rob on the highway. We hold it to be the duty of good citizens to protest against it whenever and wherever it shows itself, and to resist it if necessary to the death.

One piece of justice must be done to the South. Thousands there are of persons in that quarter of the country who disapprove, as heartily as any citizen of the North can do, the employment of violence against the presses or the preachers of the anti-slavery party. There are great numbers also, as we are well informed, who think that only harm could result from directing the penalties of the law against those who discuss the question of slavery. They are for leaving the mode of discussing this question solely to the calm and considerate good sense of the North, satisfied that the least show of a determination to abridge the liberty of speech in this matter is but throwing oil on the flames.

1836   August 8, 1836; 1884

Symbolic and Ethical Idealism

NATHANIEL HAWTHORNE
(1804–1864)

To understand Hawthorne the reader must set aside an attractive legend. Only accidental circumstances support the tradition of the shy recluse, brooding in solitude upon the gloomier aspects of Puritan New England, whose writings are a kind of spiritual autobiography. Instead, during most of his life, Hawthorne was decidedly a public figure, capable, when necessary, of a certain urbanity. As a writer, he set out quite consciously to exploit his antiquarian enthusiasms and his understanding of the colonial history of New England. He was absorbed by the enigmas of evil and of moral responsibility, interwoven with man's destiny in nature and in eternity; but in this interest he was not unusual, for he shared it with such contemporaries as Poe, Emerson, and Melville, and with others more remote, such as Milton and Shakespeare.

It is true that for some years after his graduation from college he lived quietly in quiet Salem, but a young man engrossed in historical study and in learning the writer's craft is not notably queer if he does not seek society or marriage, especially if he is poor. In later years Hawthorne successfully managed his official duties, made a large circle of friends, and performed the extrovert functions of a foreign consul with competence, if without joy. The true Hawthorne is revealed just as much by "The Old Manse," an essay light-spirited and affectionate, as by "Rappaccini's Daughter," "Ethan Brand," or *The Scarlet Letter*. We understand better his full manliness and humanity now that Professor Randall Stewart has restored their pristine vigor to the gently henpecked texts that Mrs. Hawthorne published of his *Note-Books*.

Born in Salem, Massachusetts, July 8, 1804, Hawthorne was five generations removed from his Puritan American forebears.

When the boy was twelve, his widowed mother took him to live with her brother in Maine, but old Salem had already enkindled his antiquarian inclination. To Salem he returned to prepare for College. At Bowdoin College (1821–1825), where he was, he said, "An idle student," but "always reading," he made a friend of Longfellow, his classmate, and lifelong intimates of Horatio Bridge and of Franklin Pierce, later president of the United States.

The next twelve years, of so-called "seclusion," in his mother's Salem home, were years of literary apprenticeship. He read widely, preparing himself to be the chronicler of the antiquities and the spiritual temper of colonial New England. His first novel, *Fanshawe* (1828), an abortive chronicle of Bowdoin life, was recalled and almost completely destroyed. He made observant walking trips about Massachusetts; remote portions of New England he frequently visited as the guest of his uncle, whose extensive stage-coach business provided the means. In 1832 there appeared in a gift book, *The Token*, his first published tales, including "The Gentle Boy." Other stories followed, in *The Token* and various magazines, to be collected in 1837 as *Twice-Told Tales* (enlarged in 1842), a volume of masterpieces, but only a few discerning critics, such as Poe, then understood what he was doing.

He had become secretly engaged to Sophia Peabody in 1838, and since his stories were not gaining popular support, he secured remunerative employment in the Boston Custom House. Seven months at Brook Farm, a socialistic co-operative, led him to abandon the idea of taking his bride there; on their marriage in 1842 they settled in Concord, at the Old Manse, Emerson's ancestral home. There he spent four idyllic years, during which the stories of *Mosses from an Old Manse* (1846) were published serially and as a volume.

His sales were still meager, and he returned to Salem as surveyor in the Custom House (1846–1849). He lost this position, with other Democrats, at the next election, but in 1850 he published *The Scarlet Letter*, which made his fame, changed his fortune, and gave to our literature its first symbolic novel, a year before the appearance of Melville's *Moby-Dick*. In this novel were concentrated the entire resources of Hawthorne's creative personality and experience.

After a short time in the Berkshires, Hawthorne settled in 1852 at the Wayside, Concord, which became his permanent home. He was at the height of his creative activity. *The House of the Seven Gables* (1851), a great novel of family decadence, was followed by *The Blithedale Romance* (1852), a minor novel on the Brook Farm experiment. Among the tales of *The Snow-Image* (1851), were "Ethan Brand" and "The Great Stone Face." *A Wonder Book* (1852) and *Tanglewood Tales* (1853) entered the literature of juvenile classics.

The *Life of Franklin Pierce*

(1852) was recognized handsomely by the new president, who appointed his college friend as consul at Liverpool (1853–1857). Hawthorne faithfully performed the duties, which he found uncongenial, while seeing much of England and recording his impressions in the *English Note-Books* (published after his death) and *Our Old Home* (1863), a sheaf of essays. A long holiday on the Continent resulted in the *French and Italian Note-Books* (not published in his lifetime), and *The Marble Faun* (1860), a novel with an Italian setting, whose moral allegory, while not satisfactorily clarified, continues to interest the student of Hawthorne's thought. In 1860 Hawthorne brought his family back to the Wayside, where he died four years later, in 1864.

Although in many of his stories, and in the two great novels, Hawthorne created genuine characters and situations, he holds his permanent audience primarily by the interest and the consistent vitality of his criticism of life. Beyond his remarkable sense of the past, which gives a genuine ring to the historical reconstructions, beyond his precise and simple style, which is in the great tradition of familiar narrative, the principal appeal of his work is in the quality of its allegory, always richly ambivalent, providing enigmas which each reader solves in his own terms. Reference is made, in the stories below, to his discovery of the Puritan past of his family, the persecutors of Quakers and "witches"; but wherever his interest started, it led him to a long investigation of the problems of moral and social responsibility. His enemies are intolerance, the hypocrisy that hides the common sin, and the greed that refuses to share joy; he fears beyond everything withdrawal from mankind, the cynical suspicion, the arrogant perfectionism that cannot bide its mortal time—whatever divorces the pride-ridden intellect from the common heart of humanity. It is not enough to call him the critic of the Puritan; the Quaker or the transcendental extremist might be equally guilty; and Wakefield, Aylmer, and Ethan Brand are not Puritans. His remedy is in nature and in the sweetness of a world freed not from sin, but from the corrosive sense of guilt.

A new complete edition of Hawthorne's works is needed. At present the standard edition is *The Complete Works of Nathaniel Hawthorne*, 12 vols., edited by George P. Lathrop, 1883. *The Heart of Hawthorne's Journals* was edited by Newton Arvin, 1929. Randall Stewart edited *The American Notebooks of Nathaniel Hawthorne*, 1932, and *The English Notebooks*, 1941. One-volume collections are the *Complete Novels and Selected Tales*, edited by Norman Holmes Pearson, 1939; *Hawthorne's Short Stories*, edited by Newton Arvin, 1946; and *Hawthorne: Representative Selections*, edited by Austin Warren, American Writers Series, 1934.

The best interpretative biography is *Nathaniel Hawthorne*, by Randall Stewart, 1948. George E. Woodberry's *Nathaniel Hawthorne*, 1902, long the standard biography, is still not superseded for its scope and data. For special points of view see also Julian Hawthorne, *Nathaniel Hawthorne and His Wife*, 2 vols., 1884; Robert Cantwell, *Nathaniel Hawthorne: The American Years*, 1948; Mark Van Doren, *Nathaniel Hawthorne*, 1949.

The Gentle Boy[1]

In the course of the year 1656, several of the people called Quakers, led, as they professed, by the inward movement of the spirit, made their appearance in New England. Their reputation, as holders of mystic and pernicious principles, having spread before them, the Puritans early endeavored to banish, and to prevent the further intrusion of the rising sect. But the measures by which it was intended to purge the land of heresy, though more than sufficiently vigorous, were entirely unsuccessful. The Quakers, esteeming persecution as a divine call to the post of danger, laid claim to a holy courage, unknown to the Puritans themselves, who had shunned the cross, by providing for the peaceable exercise of their religion in a distant wilderness. Though it was the singular fact, that every nation of the earth rejected the wandering enthusiasts who practised peace towards all men, the place of greatest uneasiness and peril, and therefore, in their eyes the most eligible, was the province of Massachusetts Bay.

The fines, imprisonments, and stripes, liberally distributed by our pious forefathers;[2] the popular antipathy, so strong that it endured nearly a hundred years after actual persecution had ceased, were attractions as powerful for the Quakers, as peace, honor, and reward, would have been for the worldly minded. Every European vessel brought new cargoes of the sect, eager to testify against the oppression which they hoped to share; and when shipmasters were restrained by heavy fines from affording them passage, they made long and circuitous journeys through the Indian country, and appeared in the province as if conveyed by a supernatural power. Their enthusiasm, heightened almost to madness by the treatment which they received, produced actions contrary to the rules of decency, as well as of rational religion, and presented a singular contrast to the calm and staid deportment of their sectarian successors of the present

1. "The Gentle Boy" and three lesser pieces, the first published tales of Hawthorne, appeared in *The Token* (an annual gift book) for 1832. It was collected in the *Twice-Told Tales* of 1837. This story foreshadows Hawthorne's great novels, *The Scarlet Letter* and *The House of the Seven Gables*. Like the former, it concerns intolerance in a colonial Puritan community. Hawthorne remembered that his great-great-grandfather, Judge William Hathorne, during the 1650's sentenced Quakers to be whipped through the streets, as recorded in William Sewel's *History of the Rise, Increase, and Progress of the People Called Quakers* (Amsterdam, 1717; English translation, London, 1725). William's son, John Hathorne, was a member of the court that condemned the witches of Salem in 1692, and unlike his collaborator Samuel Sewall, never declared repentance. The dying curse of a victim, "Wizard" Maule, descended, in *The House of the Seven Gables*, upon the Pyncheon family. Such facts provide background for Hawthorne's work in general. However, "The Gentle Boy" stands on its own merits as one of Hawthorne's best historical reconstructions, and a sensitive story of action and character.

2. In "The Custom House," his prefatory essay to *The Scarlet Letter*, Hawthorne wrote of ancestor William Hathorne: "He was likewise a bitter persecutor, as witness the Quakers, [a memory] which will last longer, it is to be feared, than any record of his better deeds. * * * "

day. The command of the spirit, inaudible except to the soul, and not to be controverted on grounds of human wisdom, was made a plea for most indecorous exhibitions, which, abstractedly considered, well deserved the moderate chastisement of the rod. These extravagances, and the persecution which was at once their cause and consequence, continued to increase, till, in the year 1659, the government of Massachusetts Bay indulged two members of the Quaker sect with the crown of martyrdom.

An indelible stain of blood is upon the hands of all who consented to this act, but a large share of the awful responsibility must rest upon the person then at the head of the government. He was a man of narrow mind and imperfect education, and his uncompromising bigotry was made hot and mischievous by violent and hasty passions; he exerted his influence indecorously and unjustifiably to compass the death of the enthusiasts; and his whole conduct, in respect to them, was marked by brutal cruelty. The Quakers, whose revengeful feelings were not less deep because they were inactive, remembered this man and his associates in after times. The historian[3] of the sect affirms that, by the wrath of Heaven, a blight fell upon the land in the vicinity of the "bloody town" of Boston, so that no wheat would grow there; and he takes his stand, as it were, among the graves of the ancient persecutors, and triumphantly recounts the judgments that overtook them, in old age or at the parting hour. He tells us that they died suddenly and violently and in madness; but nothing can exceed the bitter mockery with which he records the loathsome disease, and "death by rottenness," of the fierce and cruel governor.[4]

On the evening of the autumn day that had witnessed the martyrdom of two men of the Quaker persuasion, a Puritan settler was returning from the metropolis to the neighboring country town in which he resided. The air was cool, the sky clear, and the lingering twilight was made brighter by the rays of a young moon, which had now nearly reached the verge of the horizon. The traveller, a man of middle age, wrapped in a gray frieze cloak, quickened his pace when he had reached the outskirts of the town, for a gloomy extent of nearly four miles lay between him and his home. The low, straw-thatched houses were scattered at considerable intervals along the road, and the country having been settled but about thirty years, the tracts of original forest still bore no small proportion to the cultivated ground. The autumn wind wandered among the branches, whirling away the leaves from all except the pine-trees, and moaning as if it lamented the desolation of which it was the instrument. The road had penetrated the mass of woods that lay nearest to the town, and

3. William Sewel; *cf.* Note 1, above.
4. John Endecott (or Endicott), several times governor, as at the period of this story (1655–1664). Longfellow used his persecution of the Quakers as background for *The New England Tragedies*, in which Judge Hathorne also appears.

was just emerging into an open space, when the traveller's ears were saluted by a sound more mournful than even that of the wind. It was like the wailing of some one in distress, and it seemed to proceed from beneath a tall and lonely fir-tree, in the centre of a cleared but uninclosed and uncultivated field. The Puritan could not but remember that this was the very spot which had been made accursed a few hours before by the execution of the Quakers, whose bodies had been thrown together into one hasty grave, beneath the tree on which they suffered. He struggled, however, against the superstitious fears which belonged to the age, and compelled himself to pause and listen.

"The voice is most likely mortal, nor have I cause to tremble if it be otherwise," thought he, straining his eyes through the dim moonlight. "Methinks it is like the wailing of a child; some infant, it may be, which has strayed from its mother, and chanced upon this place of death. For the ease of mine own conscience I must search this matter out."

He therefore left the path, and walked somewhat fearfully across the field. Though now so desolate, its soil was pressed down and trampled by the thousand footsteps of those who had witnessed the spectacle of that day, all of whom had now retired, leaving the dead to their loneliness. The traveller at length reached the fir-tree, which from the middle upward was covered with living branches, although a scaffold had been erected beneath, and other preparations made for the work of death. Under this unhappy tree, which in after times was believed to drop poison with its dew, sat the one solitary mourner for innocent blood. It was a slender and light clad little boy, who leaned his face upon a hillock of fresh-turned and half-frozen earth, and wailed bitterly, yet in a suppressed tone, as if his grief might receive the punishment of crime. The Puritan, whose approach had been unperceived, laid his hand upon the child's shoulder, and addressed him compassionately.

"You have chosen a dreary lodging, my poor boy, and no wonder that you weep," said he. "But dry your eyes, and tell me where your mother dwells. I promise you, if the journey be not too far, I will leave you in her arms to-night."

The boy had hushed his wailing at once, and turned his face upward to the stranger. It was a pale, bright-eyed countenance, certainly not more than six years old, but sorrow, fear, and want had destroyed much of its infantile expression. The Puritan seeing the boy's frightened gaze, and feeling that he trembled under his hand, endeavored to reassure him.

"Nay, if I intended to do you harm, little lad, the readiest way were to leave you here. What! you do not fear to sit beneath the gallows on a new-made grave, and yet you tremble at a friend's touch.

Take heart, child, and tell me what is your name and where is your home?"

"Friend," replied the little boy, in a sweet though faltering voice, "they call me Ilbrahim, and my home is here."

The pale, spiritual face, the eyes that seemed to mingle with the moonlight, the sweet, airy voice, and the outlandish name, almost made the Puritan believe that the boy was in truth a being which had sprung up out of the grave on which he sat. But perceiving that the apparition stood the test of a short mental prayer, and remembering that the arm which he had touched was lifelike, he adopted a more rational supposition. "The poor child is stricken in his intellect," thought he, "but verily his words are fearful in a place like this." He then spoke soothingly, intending to humor the boy's fantasy.

"Your home will scarce be comfortable, Ilbrahim, this cold autumn night, and I fear you are ill-provided with food. I am hastening to a warm supper and bed, and if you will go with me you shall share them!"

"I thank thee, friend, but though I be hungry, and shivering with cold, thou wilt not give me food nor lodging," replied the boy, in the quiet tone which despair had taught him, even so young. "My father was of the people whom all men hate. They have laid him under this heap of earth, and here is my home."

The Puritan, who had laid hold of little Ilbrahim's hand, relinquished it as if he were touching a loathsome reptile. But he possessed a compassionate heart, which not even religious prejudice could harden into stone.

"God forbid that I should leave this child to perish, though he comes of the accursed sect," said he to himself. "Do we not all spring from an evil root? Are we not all in darkness till the light doth shine upon us? He shall not perish, neither in body, nor, if prayer and instruction may avail for him, in soul." He then spoke aloud and kindly to Ilbrahim, who had again hid his face in the cold earth of the grave. "Was every door in the land shut against you, my child, that you have wandered to this unhallowed spot?"

"They drove me forth from the prison when they took my father thence," said the boy, "and I stood afar off watching the crowd of people, and when they were gone I came hither, and found only his grave. I knew that my father was sleeping here, and I said this shall be my home."

"No, child, no; not while I have a roof over my head, or a morsel to share with you!" exclaimed the Puritan, whose sympathies were now fully excited. "Rise up and come with me, and fear not any harm."

The boy wept afresh, and clung to the heap of earth as if the cold heart beneath it were warmer to him than any in a living breast. The traveller, however, continued to entreat him tenderly, and seeming to acquire some degree of confidence, he at length arose. But his slender limbs tottered with weakness, his little head grew dizzy, and he leaned against the tree of death for support.

"My poor boy, are you so feeble?" said the Puritan. "When did you taste food last?"

"I ate of bread and water with my father in the prison," replied Ilbrahim, "but they brought him none neither yesterday nor to-day, saying that he had eaten enough to bear him to his journey's end. Trouble not thyself for my hunger, kind friend, for I have lacked food many times ere now."

The traveller took the child in his arms and wrapped his cloak about him, while his heart stirred with shame and anger against the gratuitous cruelty of the instruments in this persecution. In the awakened warmth of his feelings he resolved that, at whatever risk, he would not forsake the poor little defenceless being whom Heaven had confided to his care. With this determination he left the accursed field, and resumed the homeward path from which the wailing of the boy had called him. The light and motionless burden scarcely impeded his progress, and he soon beheld the fire rays from the windows of the cottage which he, a native of a distant clime, had built in the western wilderness. It was surrounded by a considerable extent of cultivated ground, and the dwelling was situated in the nook of a wood-covered hill, whither it seemed to have crept for protection.

"Look up, child," said the Puritan to Ilbrahim, whose faint head had sunk upon his shoulder, "there is our home."

At the word "home," a thrill passed through the child's frame, but he continued silent. A few moments brought them to a cottage door, at which the owner knocked; for at that early period, when savages were wandering everywhere among the settlers, bolt and bar were indispensable to the security of a dwelling. The summons was answered by a bond-servant, a coarse-clad and dull-featured piece of humanity, who, after ascertaining that his master was the applicant, undid the door, and held a flaring pine-knot torch to light him in. Farther back in the passage-way, the red blaze discovered a matronly woman, but no little crowd of children came bounding forth to greet their father's return. As the Puritan entered, he thrust aside his cloak, and displayed Ilbrahim's face to the female.

"Dorothy, here is a little outcast, whom Providence hath put into our hands," observed he. "Be kind to him, even as if he were of those dear ones who have departed from us."

"What pale and bright-eyed little boy is this, Tobias?" she inquired. "Is he one whom the wilderness folk have ravished from some Christian mother?"

"No, Dorothy, this poor child is no captive from the wilderness," he replied. "The heathen savage would have given him to eat of his scanty morsel, and to drink of his birchen cup; but Christian men, alas! had cast him out to die."

Then he told her how he had found him beneath the gallows, upon his father's grave; and how his heart had prompted him, like the speaking of an inward voice, to take the little outcast home, and be kind unto him. He acknowledged his resolution to feed and clothe him, as if he were his own child, and to afford him the instruction which should counteract the pernicious errors hitherto instilled into his infant mind. Dorothy was gifted with even a quicker tenderness than her husband, and she approved of all his doings and intentions.

"Have you a mother, dear child?" she inquired.

The tears burst forth from his full heart, as he attempted to reply; but Dorothy at length understood that he had a mother, who, like the rest of her sect, was a persecuted wanderer. She had been taken from the prison a short time before, carried into the uninhabited wilderness, and left to perish there by hunger or wild beasts. This was no uncommon method of disposing of the Quakers, and they were accustomed to boast that the inhabitants of the desert were more hospitable to them than civilized man.

"Fear not, little boy, you shall not need a mother, and a kind one," said Dorothy, when she had gathered this information. "Dry your tears, Ilbrahim, and be my child, as I will be your mother."

The good woman prepared the little bed, from which her own children had successively been borne to another resting-place. Before Ilbrahim would consent to occupy it, he knelt down, and as Dorothy listened to his simple and affecting prayer, she marvelled how the parents that had taught it to him could have been judged worthy of death. When the boy had fallen asleep, she bent over his pale and spiritual countenance, pressed a kiss upon his white brow, drew the bedclothes up about his neck, and went away with a pensive gladness in her heart.

Tobias Pearson was not among the earliest emigrants from the old country. He had remained in England during the first years of the civil war, in which he had borne some share as a cornet of dragoons, under Cromwell. But when the ambitious designs of his leader began to develop themselves, he quitted the army of the Parliament, and sought a refuge from the strife, which was no longer holy, among the people of his persuasion in the colony of Massachusetts. A more worldly consideration had perhaps an influence in drawing him thither; for New England offered advantages to men of unprosperous fortunes, as well as to dissatisfied religionists, and Pearson had hitherto found it difficult to provide for a wife and increasing family. To this supposed impurity of motive the more bigoted Puritans were inclined to impute the removal by death of all the children, for whose earthly good the father had been over-thoughtful. They had left their native country blooming like roses, and like roses they had perished in a foreign soil. Those expounders of the ways of Providence, who had thus judged their brother, and attributed his domestic sorrows to his sin, were not more charitable when they saw him and Dorothy endeavoring to fill up the void in their hearts by the adoption of an infant of the accursed sect. Nor did they fail to communicate their disapprobation to Tobias; but the latter, in reply, merely pointed at the little, quiet, lovely boy, whose appearance and deportment were indeed as powerful arguments as could possibly have been adduced in his own favor. Even his beauty, however, and his willing manners, sometimes produced an effect ultimately unfavorable; for the bigots, when the outer surfaces of their iron hearts had been softened and again grew hard, affirmed that no merely natural cause could have so worked upon them.

Their antipathy to the poor infant was also increased by the ill success of divers theological discussions, in which it was attempted to convince him of the errors of his sect. Ilbrahim, it is true, was not a skilful controversialist; but the feeling of his religion was strong as instinct in him, and he could neither be enticed nor driven from the faith which his father had died for. The odium of this stubbornness was shared in a great measure by the child's protectors, insomuch that Tobias and Dorothy very shortly began to experience a most bitter species of persecution, in the cold regards of many a friend whom they had valued. The common people manifested their opinions more openly. Pearson was a man of some consideration, being a representative to the General Court, and an approved lieutenant in the trainbands, yet within a week after his adoption of Ilbrahim he had been both hissed and hooted. Once, also, when walking through a solitary piece of woods, he heard a loud voice from some invisible speaker; and it cried, "What shall be done to the backslider? Lo! the scourge is knotted for him, even the whip of nine cords, and every cord three knots!" These insults irritated Pearson's temper for the moment; they entered also into his heart, and became imperceptible but powerful workers towards an end which his most secret thought had not yet whispered.

On the second Sabbath after Ilbrahim became a member of their family, Pearson and his wife deemed it proper that he should appear with them at public worship. They had anticipated some opposition to this measure from the boy, but he prepared himself in silence, and at the appointed hour was clad in the new mourning suit which Dorothy had wrought for him. As the parish was then, and during many subsequent years, unprovided with a bell, the signal for the commencement of religious exercises was the beat of a drum. At the first sound of that martial call to the place of holy and quiet thoughts, Tobias and Dorothy set forth, each holding a hand of little Ilbrahim, like two parents linked together by the infant of their love. On their path through the leafless woods they were overtaken by many persons of their acquaintance, all of whom avoided them, and passed by on the other side; but a severer trial awaited their constancy when they had descended the hill, and drew near the pine-built and undecorated house of prayer. Around the door, from which the drummer still sent forth his thundering summons, was drawn up a formidable phalanx, including several of the oldest members of the congregation, many of the middle aged, and nearly all the younger males. Pearson found it difficult to sustain their united and disapproving gaze, but Dorothy, whose mind was differently circumstanced, merely drew the boy closer to her, and faltered not in her approach. As they entered the door, they overheard the muttered sentiments of the assemblage, and when the reviling voices of the little children smote Ilbrahim's ear, he wept.

The interior aspect of the meeting-house was rude. The low ceiling, the unplastered walls, the naked wood work, and the undraperied pulpit, offered nothing to excite the devotion, which, without such external aids, often remains latent in the heart. The floor of the building was occupied by rows of long, cushionless benches, supplying the place of pews, and the broad aisle formed a sexual division, impassable except by children beneath a certain age.

Pearson and Dorothy separated at the door of the meeting-house, and Ilbrahim, being within the years of infancy, was retained under the care of the latter. The wrinkled beldams involved themselves in their rusty cloaks as he passed by; even the mild-featured maidens seemed to dread contamination; and many a stern old man arose, and turned his repulsive and unheavenly countenance upon the gentle boy, as if the sanctuary were polluted by his presence. He was a sweet infant of the skies that had strayed away from his home, and all the inhabitants of this miserable world closed up their impure hearts against him, drew back their earth-soiled garments from his touch, and said, "We are holier than thou."

Ilbrahim, seated by the side of his adopted mother, and retaining fast hold of her hand, assumed a grave and decorous demeanor, such as might befit a person of matured taste and understanding, who should find himself in a temple dedicated to some worship which he did not recognize, but felt himself bound to respect. The exercises had not yet commenced, however, when the boy's attention was arrested by an event, apparently of trifling interest. A woman, having her face muffled in a hood, and a cloak drawn completely about her form, advanced slowly up the broad aisle and took a place upon the foremost bench. Ilbrahim's faint color varied, his nerves fluttered, he was unable to turn his eyes from the muffled female.

When the preliminary prayer and hymn were over, the minister arose, and having turned the hour-glass which stood by the great Bible, commenced his discourse. He was now well stricken in years, a man of pale, thin countenance, and his gray hairs were closely covered by a black velvet skullcap. In his younger days he had practically learned the meaning of persecution from Archbishop Laud,[5] and he was not now disposed to forget the lesson against which he had murmured then. Introducing the often discussed subject of the Quakers, he gave a history of that sect, and a description of their tenets, in which error predominated, and prejudice distorted the aspect of what was true. He adverted to the recent measures in the province, and cautioned his hearers of weaker parts against calling in question the just severity which God-fearing magistrates had at length been compelled to exercise. He spoke of the danger of pity, in some cases a commendable and Christian virtue, but inapplicable to this pernicious sect. He observed that such was their devilish obstinacy in error, that even the little children, the sucking babes, were hardened and desperate heretics. He affirmed that no man, without Heaven's especial warrant, should attempt their conversion, lest while he lent his hand to draw them from the slough, he should himself be precipitated into its lowest depths.

The sands of the second hour were principally in the lower half of the glass when the sermon concluded. An approving murmur followed, and the clergyman, having given out a hymn, took his seat with much self-congratulation, and endeavored to read the effect of his eloquence in the visages of the people. But while voices from all parts of the house were tuning themselves to sing, a scene occurred, which, though not very unusual at that period in the province, happened to be without precedent in this parish.

The muffled female, who had hitherto sat motionless in the front rank of the audience, now arose, and with slow, stately, and unwavering step, ascended the pulpit stairs. The quiverings of incipient harmony were hushed, and the divine sat in speechless and almost terrified astonishment, while she undid the door, and stood up in the sacred desk from which his maledictions had just been thundered. She then divested herself of the cloak and hood, and appeared in a most singular array. A shapeless robe of sackcloth was girded about her waist with a knotted cord; her raven hair fell down upon her shoulders, and its blackness was defiled by pale streaks of ashes, which she had strown upon her head. Her eyebrows, dark and strongly de-

5. William Laud (1573–1645), created Archbishop of Canterbury in 1633, whose persecution of Calvinists and Presbyterians caused many to seek religious freedom in America.

fined, added to the deathly whiteness of a countenance, which, emaciated with want, and wild with enthusiasm and strange sorrows, retained no trace of earlier beauty. This figure stood gazing earnestly on the audience, and there was no sound, nor any movement, except a faint shuddering which every man observed in his neighbor, but was scarcely conscious of in himself. At length, when her fit of inspiration came, she spoke, for the first few moments, in a low voice, and not invariably distinct utterance. Her discourse gave evidence of an imagination hopelessly entangled with her reason; it was a vague and incomprehensible rhapsody, which, however, seemed to spread its own atmosphere round the hearer's soul, and to move his feelings by some influence unconnected with the words. As she proceeded, beautiful but shadowy images would sometimes be seen, like bright things moving in a turbid river; or a strong and singularly-shaped idea leaped forth, and seized at once on the understanding or the heart. But the course of her unearthly eloquence soon led her to the persecutions of her sect, and from thence the step was short to her own peculiar sorrows. She was naturally a woman of mighty passions, and hatred and revenge now wrapped themselves in the garb of piety; the character of her speech was changed, her images became distinct though wild, and her denunciations had an almost hellish bitterness.

"The Governor and his mighty men," she said, "have gathered together, taking counsel among themselves and saying, 'What shall we do unto this people—even unto the people that have come into this land to put our iniquity to the blush?' And lo! the devil entereth into the council chamber, like a lame man of low stature and gravely apparelled, with a dark and twisted countenance, and a bright, downcast eye. And he standeth up among the rulers; yea, he goeth to and fro, whispering to each; and every man lends his ear, for his word is 'Slay, slay!' But I say unto ye, Woe to them that slay! Woe to them that shed the blood of saints! Woe to them that have slain the husband, and cast forth the child, the tender infant, to wander homeless and hungry and cold, till he die; and have saved the mother alive, in the cruelty of their tender mercies! Woe to them in their lifetime! cursed are they in the delight and pleasure of their hearts! Woe to them in their death hour, whether it come swiftly with blood and violence, or after long and lingering pain! Woe, in the dark house, in the rottenness of the grave, when the children's children shall revile the ashes of the fathers! Woe, woe, woe, at the judgment, when all the persecuted and all the slain in this bloody land, and the father, the mother, and the child, shall await them in a day that they cannot escape! Seed of the faith, seed of the faith, ye whose hearts are moving with a power that ye know not, arise, wash your hands of this innocent blood! Lift your voices, chosen ones; cry aloud, and call down a woe and a judgment with me!"

Having thus given vent to the flood of malignity which she mistook for inspiration, the speaker was silent. Her voice was succeeded by the hysteric shrieks of several women, but the feelings of the audience generally had not been drawn onward in the current with her own. They remained stupefied, stranded as it were, in the midst of a torrent, which deafened them by its roaring, but might not move them by its violence. The clergyman, who could not hitherto have ejected the usurper of his pulpit otherwise than by bodily force, now addressed her in the tone of just indignation and legitimate authority.

"Get you down, woman, from the holy place which you profane," he said. "Is it to the Lord's house that you come to pour forth the foulness of your heart and the inspiration of the devil? Get you down, and remember that the sentence of death is on you; yea, and shall be executed, were it but for this day's work!"

"I go, friend, I go, for the voice hath had its utterance," replied she, in a depressed and even mild tone. "I have done my mission unto thee and to thy people. Reward me with stripes, imprisonment, or death, as ye shall be permitted."

The weakness of exhausted passion caused her steps to totter as she descended the pulpit stairs. The people, in the meanwhile, were stirring to and fro on the floor of the house, whispering among themselves, and glancing towards the intruder. Many of them now recognized her as the woman who had assaulted the Governor with frightful language as he passed by the window of her prison; they knew, also, that she was adjudged to suffer death, and had been preserved only by an involuntary banishment into the wilderness. The new outrage, by which she had provoked her fate, seemed to render further lenity impossible; and a gentleman in military dress, with a stout man of inferior rank, drew towards the door of the meeting-house, and awaited her approach.

Scarcely did her feet press the floor, however, when an unexpected scene occurred. In that moment of her peril, when every eye frowned with death, a little timid boy pressed forth, and threw his arms round his mother.

"I am here, mother; it is I, and I will go with thee to prison," he exclaimed.

She gazed at him with a doubtful and almost frightened expression, for she knew that the boy had been cast out to perish, and she had not hoped to see his face again. She feared, perhaps, that it was but one of the happy visions with which her excited fancy had often deceived her, in the solitude of the desert or in prison. But when she felt his hand warm within her own, and heard his little eloquence of childish love, she began to know that she was yet a mother.

"Blessed art thou, my son," she sobbed. "My heart was withered; yea, dead with thee and with thy father; and now it leaps as in the first moment when I pressed thee to my bosom."

She knelt down and embraced him again and again while the joy that could find no words expressed itself in broken accents, like the bubbles gushing up to vanish at the surface of a deep fountain. The sorrows of past years, and the darker peril that was nigh, cast not a shadow on the brightness of that fleeting moment. Soon, however, the spectators saw a change upon her face, as the consciousness of her sad estate returned, and grief supplied the fount of tears which joy had opened. By the words she uttered, it would seem that the indulgence of natural love had given her mind a momentary sense of its errors, and made her know how far she had strayed from duty in following the dictates of a wild fanaticism.

"In a doleful hour art thou returned to me, poor boy," she said, "for thy mother's path has gone darkening onward, till now the end is death. Son, son, I have borne thee in my arms when my limbs were tottering, and I have fed thee with the food that I was fainting for; yet I have ill performed a mother's part by thee in life, and now I leave thee no inheritance but woe and shame. Thou wilt go seeking through the world, and find all hearts closed against thee and their sweet affections turned to bitterness for my sake. My child, my child, how many a pang awaits thy gentle spirit, and I the cause of all!"

She hid her face on Ilbrahim's head, and her long, raven hair, discolored with the ashes of her mourning, fell down about him like a veil. A low and interrupted moan was the voice of her heart's anguish, and it did not fail to move the sympathies of many who mistook their involuntary virtue for a sin. Sobs were audible in the female section of the house, and every man who was a father drew his hand across his eyes. Tobias Pearson was agitated and uneasy, but a certain feeling like the consciousness of guilt oppressed him, so that he could not go forth and offer himself as the protector of the child. Dorothy, however, had watched her husband's eye. Her mind was free from the influence that had begun to work on his, and she drew near the Quaker woman, and addressed her in the hearing of all the congregation.

"Stranger, trust this boy to me, and I will be his mother," she said, taking Ilbrahim's hand. "Providence has signally marked out my husband to protect him, and he has fed at our table and lodged under our roof now many days, till our hearts have grown very strongly unto him. Leave the tender child with us, and be at ease concerning his welfare."

The Quaker rose from the ground, but drew the boy closer to her, while she gazed earnestly in Dorothy's face. Her mild but saddened features, and neat matronly attire, harmonized together, and were like a verse of fireside poetry. Her very aspect proved that she was blameless, so far as mortal could be so, in respect to God and man; while the enthusiast,[6] in her robe of sackcloth and girdle of knotted cord, had as evidently violated the duties of the present life and the future, by fixing her attention wholly on the latter. The two females, as they held each a hand of Ilbrahim, formed a practical allegory; it was rational piety and unbridled fanaticism contending for the empire of a young heart.

"Thou art not of our people," said the Quaker, mournfully.

"No, we are not of your people," replied Dorothy, with mildness, "but we are Christians, looking upward to the same heaven with you. Doubt not that your boy shall meet you there, if there be a blessing on our tender and prayerful guidance of him. Thither, I trust, my own children have gone before me, for I also have been a mother; I am no longer so," she added, in a faltering tone, "and your son will have all my care."

"But will ye lead him in the path which his parents have trodden?" demanded the Quaker. "Can ye teach him the enlightened faith which his father has died for, and for which I, even I, am soon to become an unworthy martyr? The boy has been baptized in blood; will ye keep the mark fresh and ruddy upon his forehead?"

"I will not deceive you," answered Dorothy. "If your child become our child, we must breed him up in the instruction which Heaven has imparted to us; we must pray for him the prayers of our own faith; we must do towards him according to the dictates of our own consciences, and not of yours. Were we to act otherwise, we should abuse your trust, even in complying with your wishes."

The mother looked down upon her boy with a troubled countenance, and then turned her eyes upward to heaven. She seemed to pray internally, and the contention of her soul was evident.

"Friend," she said at length to Dorothy, "I doubt not that my son shall receive all earthly tenderness at thy hands. Nay, I will believe that even thy imperfect lights may guide him to a better world, for surely thou art on the path thither. But thou hast spoken of a husband. Doth he stand here among this multitude of people? Let him come forth, for I must know to whom I commit this most precious trust."

She turned her face upon the male auditors, and after a momentary delay, Tobias Pearson came forth from among them. The Quaker saw the dress which marked his military rank, and shook her head; but then she noted the hesitating air, the eyes that struggled with her own, and were vanquished; the color that went and came, and could find no resting-place. As she gazed, an unmirthful smile

6. In its archaic meaning, "one possessed." The "unbridled fanaticism" of Ilbrahim's mother is as reprehensible to Hawthorne as Puritan intolerance.

spread over her features, like sunshine that grows melancholy in some desolate spot. Her lips moved inaudibly, but at length she spake.

"I hear it, I hear it. The voice speaketh within me and saith, 'Leave thy child, Catharine, for his place is here, and go hence, for I have other work for thee. Break the bonds of natural affection, martyr thy love, and know that in all these things eternal wisdom hath its ends.' I go, friends; I go. Take ye my boy, my precious jewel. I go hence, trusting that all shall be well, and that even for his infant hands there is a labor in the vineyard."

She knelt down and whispered to Ilbrahim, who at first struggled and clung to his mother, with sobs and tears, but remained passive when she had kissed his cheek and arisen from the ground. Having held her hands over his head in mental prayer, she was ready to depart.

"Farewell, friends in mine extremity," she said to Pearson and his wife; "the good deed ye have done me is a treasure laid up in heaven, to be returned a thousand-fold hereafter. And farewell ye, mine enemies, to whom it is not permitted to harm so much as a hair of my head, nor to stay my footsteps even for a moment. The day is coming when ye shall call upon me to witness for ye to this one sin uncommitted, and I will rise up and answer."

She turned her steps towards the door, and the men, who had stationed themselves to guard it, withdrew, and suffered her to pass. A general sentiment of pity overcame the virulence of religious hatred. Sanctified by her love and her affliction, she went forth, and all the people gazed after her till she had journeyed up the hill, and was lost behind its brow. She went, the apostle of her own unquiet heart, to renew the wanderings of past years. For her voice had been already heard in many lands of Christendom; and she had pined in the cells of a Catholic Inquisition before she felt the lash and lay in the dungeons of the Puritans. Her mission had extended also to the followers of the Prophet,[7] and from them she had received the courtesy and kindness which all the contending sects of our purer religion united to deny her. Her husband and herself had resided many months in Turkey, where even the Sultan's countenance was gracious to them; in that pagan land, too, was Ilbrahim's birthplace, and his oriental name was a mark of gratitude for the good deeds of an unbeliever.

When Pearson and his wife had thus acquired all the rights over Ilbrahim that could be delegated, their affection for him became like the memory of their native land, or their mild sorrow for the dead, a piece of the immovable furniture of their hearts. The boy, also, after a week or two of mental disquiet, began to gratify his protectors by many inadvertent proofs that he considered them as

7. Mohammed.

parents, and their house as home. Before the winter snows were melted, the persecuted infant, the little wanderer from a remote and heathen country, seemed native in the New England cottage, and inseparable from the warmth and security of its hearth. Under the influence of kind treatment, and in the consciousness that he was loved, Ilbrahim's demeanor lost a premature manliness, which had resulted from his earlier situation; he became more childlike, and his natural character displayed itself with freedom. It was in many respects a beautiful one, yet the disordered imaginations of both his father and mother had perhaps propagated a certain unhealthiness in the mind of the boy. In his general state, Ilbrahim would derive enjoyment from the most trifling events, and from every object about him; he seemed to discover rich treasures of happiness, by a faculty analogous to that of the witch hazel, which points to hidden gold where all is barren to the eye. His airy gayety, coming to him from a thousand sources, communicated itself to the family, and Ilbrahim was like a domesticated sunbeam, brightening moody countenances, and chasing away the gloom from the dark corners of the cottage.

On the other hand, as the susceptibility of pleasure is also that of pain, the exuberant cheerfulness of the boy's prevailing temper sometimes yielded to moments of deep depression. His sorrows could not always be followed up to their original source, but most frequently they appeared to flow, though Ilbrahim was young to be sad for such a cause, from wounded love. The flightiness of his mirth rendered him often guilty of offences against the decorum of a Puritan household, and on these occasions he did not invariably escape rebuke. But the slightest word of real bitterness, which he was infallible in distinguishing from pretended anger, seemed to sink into his heart and poison all his enjoyments, till he became sensible that he was entirely forgiven. Of the malice, which generally accompanies a superfluity of sensitiveness, Ilbrahim was altogether destitute: when trodden upon, he would not turn; when wounded, he could but die. His mind was wanting in the stamina for self-support; it was a plant that would twine beautifully round something stronger than itself, but if repulsed, or torn away, it had no choice but to wither on the ground. Dorothy's acuteness taught her that severity would crush the spirit of the child, and she nurtured him with the gentle care of one who handles a butterfly. Her husband manifested an equal affection, although it grew daily less productive of familiar caresses.

The feelings of the neighboring people, in regard to the Quaker infant and his protectors, had not undergone a favorable change, in spite of the momentary triumph which the desolate mother had obtained over their sympathies. The scorn and bitterness, of which he was the object, were very grievous to Ilbrahim, especially when any circumstance made him sensible that the children, his equals in age, partook of the enmity of their parents. His tender and social nature had already overflowed in attachments to everything about him, and still there was a residue of unappropriated love, which he yearned to bestow upon the little ones who were taught to hate him. As the warm days of spring came on, Ilbrahim was accustomed to remain for hours, silent and inactive, within hearing of the children's voices at their play; yet, with his usual delicacy of feeling, he avoided their notice, and would flee and hide himself from the smallest individual among them. Chance, however, at length seemed to open a medium of communication between his heart and theirs; it was by means of a boy about two years older than Ilbrahim, who was injured by a fall from a tree in the vicinity of Pearson's habitation. As the sufferer's own home was at some distance, Dorothy willingly received him under her roof, and became his tender and careful nurse.

Ilbrahim was the unconscious possessor of much skill in physiognomy, and it would have deterred him, in other circumstances, from attempting to make a friend of this boy. The countenance of the latter immediately impressed a beholder disagreeably, but it required some examination to discover that the cause was a very slight distortion of the mouth, and the irregular, broken line, and near approach of the eyebrows. Analogous, perhaps, to these trifling deformities, was an almost imperceptible twist of every joint, and the uneven prominence of the breast; forming a body, regular in its general outline, but faulty in almost all its details. The disposition of the boy was sullen and reserved, and the village schoolmaster stigmatized him as obtuse in intellect; although, at a later period of life, he evinced ambition and very peculiar talents. But whatever might be his personal or moral irregularities, Ilbrahim's heart seized upon, and clung to him, from the moment that he was brought wounded into the cottage; the child of persecution seemed to compare his own fate with that of the sufferer, and to feel that even different modes of misfortune had created a sort of relationship between them. Food, rest, and the fresh air, for which he languished, were neglected; he nestled continually by the bedside of the little stranger, and, with a fond jealousy, endeavored to be the medium of all the cares that were bestowed upon him. As the boy became convalescent, Ilbrahim contrived games suitable to his situation, or amused him by a faculty which he had perhaps breathed in with the air of his barbaric birthplace. It was that of reciting imaginary adventures, on the spur of the moment, and apparently in inexhaustible succession. His tales were of course monstrous, disjointed, and without aim; but they were curious on account of a vein of human tenderness which ran through them all, and was like a sweet, familiar face, encountered in the midst of wild and unearthly scenery. The auditor paid much attention to these romances, and sometimes interrupted them by brief remarks upon the incidents, displaying shrewdness above his years, mingled with a moral obliquity which grated very harshly against Ilbrahim's instinctive rectitude. Nothing, however, could arrest the progress of the latter's affection, and there were many proofs that it met with a response from the dark and stubborn nature on which it was lavished. The boy's parents at length removed him, to complete his cure under their own roof.

Ilbrahim did not visit his new friend after his departure; but he made anxious and continual inquiries respecting him, and informed himself of the day when he was to reappear among his playmates. On a pleasant summer afternoon, the children of the neighborhood had assembled in the little forest-crowned amphitheatre behind the meeting-house, and the recovering invalid was there, leaning on a staff. The glee of a score of untainted bosoms was heard in light and airy voices, which danced among the trees like sunshine become audible; the grown men of this weary world, as they journeyed by the spot, marvelled why life, beginning in such brightness, should proceed in gloom; and their hearts, or their imaginations, answered them and said, that the bliss of childhood gushes from its innocence. But it happened that an unexpected addition was made to the heavenly little band. It was Ilbrahim, who came towards the children with a look of sweet confidence on his fair and spiritual face, as if, having manifested his love to one of them, he had no longer to fear a repulse from their society. A hush came over their mirth the moment they beheld him, and they stood whispering to each other while he drew nigh; but, all at once, the devil of their fathers entered into the unbreeched fanatics, and sending up a fierce, shrill cry, they rushed upon the poor Quaker child. In an instant, he was the centre of a brood of baby-fiends, who lifted sticks against him, pelted him with stones, and displayed an instinct of destruction far more loathsome than the bloodthirstiness of manhood.

The invalid, in the meanwhile, stood apart from the tumult, crying out with a loud voice, "Fear not, Ilbrahim, come hither and take my hand;" and his unhappy friend endeavored to obey him. After watching the victim's struggling approach with a calm smile and unabashed eye, the foul-hearted little villain lifted his staff and struck Ilbrahim on the mouth, so forcibly that the blood issued in a stream. The poor child's arms had been raised to guard his head from the storm of blows; but now he dropped them at once. His persecutors beat him down, trampled upon him, dragged him by his long, fair locks, and Ilbrahim was on the point of becoming as veritable a martyr as ever entered bleeding into heaven. The uproar, however, attracted the notice of a few neighbors, who put themselves to the trouble of rescuing the little heretic, and of conveying him to Pearson's door.

Ilbrahim's bodily harm was severe, but long and careful nursing accomplished his recovery; the injury done to his sensitive spirit was more serious, though not so visible. Its signs were principally of a negative character, and to be discovered only by those who had previously known him. His gait was thenceforth slow, even, and unvaried by the sudden bursts of sprightlier motion, which had once corresponded to his overflowing gladness; his countenance was heavier, and its former play of expression, the dance of sunshine reflected from moving water, was destroyed by the cloud over his existence; his notice was attracted in a far less degree by passing events, and he appeared to find greater difficulty in comprehending what was new to him than at a happier period. A stranger, founding his judgment upon these circumstances, would have said that the dulness of the child's intellect widely contradicted the promise of his features; but the secret was in the direction of Ilbrahim's thoughts, which were brooding within him when they should naturally have been wandering abroad. An attempt of Dorothy to revive his former sportiveness was the single occasion on which his quiet demeanor yielded to a violent display of grief; he burst into passionate weeping, and ran and hid himself, for his heart had become so miserably sore that even the hand of kindness tortured it like fire. Sometimes, at night and probably in his dreams, he was heard to cry "Mother! Mother!" as if her place, which a stranger had supplied while Ilbrahim was happy, admitted of no substitute in his extreme affliction. Perhaps, among the many life-weary wretches then upon the earth, there was not one who combined innocence and misery like this poor, broken-hearted infant, so soon the victim of his own heavenly nature.

While this melancholy change had taken place in Ilbrahim, one of an earlier origin and of different character had come to its perfection in his adopted father. The incident with which this tale commences found Pearson in a state of religious dulness, yet mentally disquieted, and longing for a more fervid faith than he possessed. The first effect of his kindness to Ilbrahim was to produce softened feeling, and incipent love for the child's whole sect; but joined to this, and resulting perhaps from self-suspicion, was a proud and ostentatious contempt of all their tenets and practical extravagances. In the course of much thought, however, for the subject struggled irresistibly into his mind, the foolishness of the doctrine began to be less evident, and the points which had particularly offended his reason assumed another aspect, or vanished entirely away. The work within him appeared to go on even while he slept, and that which had been a doubt, when he lay down to rest, would often hold the place of a truth, confirmed by some forgotten demonstration, when he recalled his thoughts in the morning. But while he was thus becoming assimilated to the enthusiasts, his contempt, in nowise decreasing towards them, grew very fierce against himself; he imagined, also, that every face of his acquaintance wore a sneer, and that every word addressed to him was a gibe. Such was his state of mind at the period of Ilbrahim's misfortune; and the emotions consequent upon that event completed the change, of which the child had been the original instrument.

In the mean time, neither the fierceness of the persecutors, nor the infatuation of their victims, had decreased. The dungeons were never empty; the streets of almost every village echoed daily with the lash; the life of a woman, whose mild and Christian spirit no cruelty could embitter, had been sacrificed; and more innocent blood was yet to pollute the hands that were so often raised in prayer. Early after the Restoration, the English Quakers represented to Charles II that a "vein of blood was open in his dominions;" but though the displeasure of the voluptuous king was roused, his interference was not prompt. And now the tale must stride forward over many months, leaving Pearson to encounter ignominy and misfortune; his wife to a firm endurance of a thousand sorrows; poor Ilbrahim to pine and droop like a cankered rosebud; his mother to wander on a mistaken errand, neglectful of the holiest trust which can be committed to a woman.

A winter evening, a night of storm, had darkened over Pearson's habitation, and there were no cheerful faces to drive the gloom from his broad hearth. The fire, it is true, sent forth a glowing heat and a ruddy light, and large logs, dripping with half-melted snow, lay ready to be cast upon the embers. But the apartment was saddened in its aspect by the absence of much of the homely wealth which had once adorned it; for the exaction of repeated fines, and his own neglect of temporal affairs, had greatly impoverished the owner. And with the furniture of peace, the implements of war had likewise disappeared; the sword was broken, the helm and cuirass were cast away forever; the soldier had done with battles, and might not lift so much as his naked hand to guard his head. But the Holy Book remained, and the table on which it rested was drawn before the fire, while two of the persecuted sect sought comfort from its pages.

He who listened, while the other read, was the master of the house, now emaciated in form, and altered as to the expression and healthiness of his countenance; for his mind had dwelt too long among visionary thoughts, and his body had been worn by imprisonment and stripes. The hale and weather-beaten old man who sat beside him had sustained less injury from a far longer course of the same mode of life. In person he was tall and dignified, and, which alone would have made him hateful to the Puritans, his gray locks fell from beneath the broad-brimmed hat, and rested on his shoulders.[8] As the old man

8. The Puritan wore his hair cut short, hence the derisive term "roundhead."

read the sacred page the snow drifted against the windows, or eddied in at the crevices of the door, while a blast kept laughing in the chimney, and the blaze leaped fiercely up to seek it. And sometimes, when the wind struck the hill at a certain angle, and swept down by the cottage across the wintry plain, its voice was the most doleful that can be conceived; it came as if the Past were speaking, as if the Dead had contributed each a whisper, as if the Desolation of Ages were breathed in that one lamenting sound.

The Quaker at length closed the book, retaining however his hand between the pages which he had been reading, while he looked steadfastly at Pearson. The attitude and features of the latter might have indicated the endurance of bodily pain; he leaned his forehead on his hands, his teeth were firmly closed, and his frame was tremulous at intervals with a nervous agitation.

"Friend Tobias," inquired the old man, compassionately, "hast thou found no comfort in these many blessed passages of Scripture?"

"Thy voice has fallen on my ear like a sound afar off and indistinct," replied Pearson without lifting his eyes. "Yea, and when I have hearkened carefully the words seemed cold and lifeless, and intended for another and a lesser grief than mine. Remove the book," he added, in a tone of sullen bitterness. "I have no part in its consolations, and they do but fret my sorrow the more."

"Nay, feeble brother, be not as one who hath never known the light," said the elder Quaker earnestly, but with mildness. "Art thou he that wouldst be content to give all, and endure all, for conscience' sake; desiring even peculiar trials, that thy faith might be purified and thy heart weaned from worldly desires? And wilt thou sink beneath an affliction which happens alike to them that have their portion here below, and to them that lay up treasure in heaven? Faint not, for thy burden is yet light."

"It is heavy! It is heavier than I can bear!" exclaimed Pearson, with the impatience of a variable spirit. "From my youth upward I have been a man marked out for wrath; and year by year, yea, day after day, I have endured sorrows such as others know not in their lifetime. And now I speak not of the love that has been turned to hatred, the honor to ignominy, the ease and plentifulness of all things to danger, want, and nakedness. All this I could have borne, and counted myself blessed. But when my heart was desolate with many losses I fixed it upon the child of a stranger, and he became dearer to me than all my buried ones; and now he too must die as if my love were poison. Verily, I am an accursed man, and I will lay me down in the dust and lift up my head no more."

"Thou sinnest, brother, but it is not for me to rebuke thee; for I also have had my hours of darkness, wherein I have murmured against the cross," said the old Quaker. He continued, perhaps in the hope of distracting his companion's thoughts from his own sorrows. "Even of late was the light obscured within me, when the men of blood had banished me on pain of death, and the constables led me onward from village to village towards the wilderness. A strong and cruel hand was wielding the knotted cords; they sunk deep into the flesh, and thou mightst have tracked every reel and totter of my footsteps by the blood that followed. As we went on"—

"Have I not borne all this; and have I murmured?" interrupted Pearson impatiently.

"Nay, friend, but hear me," continued the other. "As we journeyed on, night darkened on our path, so that no man could see the rage of the persecutors or the constancy of my endurance, though Heaven forbid that I should glory therein. The lights began to glimmer in the cottage windows, and I could discern the inmates as they gathered in comfort and security, every man with his wife and children by their own evening hearth. At length we came to a tract of fertile land; in the dim light, the forest was not visible around it; and behold! there was a straw-thatched dwelling, which bore the very aspect of my home, far over the wild ocean, far in our own England. Then came bitter thoughts upon me; yea, remembrances that were like death to my soul. The happiness of my early days was painted to me; the disquiet of my manhood, the altered faith of my declining years. I remembered how I had been moved to go forth a wanderer when my daughter, the youngest, the dearest of my flock, lay on her dying bed, and"—

"Couldst thou obey the command at such a moment?" exclaimed Pearson, shuddering.

"Yea, yea," replied the old man hurriedly. "I was kneeling by her bedside when the voice spoke loud within me; but immediately I rose, and took my staff, and gat me gone. Oh! that it were permitted me to forget her woful look when I thus withdrew my arm, and left her journeying through the dark valley alone! for her soul was faint, and she had leaned upon my prayers. Now in that night of horror I was assailed by the thought that I had been an erring Christian and a cruel parent; yea, even my daughter, with her pale, dying features, seemed to stand by me and whisper, 'Father, you are deceived; go home and shelter your gray head.' O Thou, to whom I have looked in my farthest wanderings," continued the Quaker, raising his agitated eyes to heaven, "inflict not upon the bloodiest of our persecutors the unmitigated agony of my soul, when I believed that all I had done and suffered for Thee was at the instigation of a mocking fiend! But I yielded not; I knelt down and wrestled with the tempter, while the scourge bit more fiercely into the flesh. My prayer was heard, and I went on in peace and joy towards the wilderness."

The old man, though his fanaticism had generally all the calmness of reason, was deeply moved while reciting this tale; and his unwonted emotion seemed to rebuke and keep down that of his companion. They sat in silence, with their faces to the fire, imagining, perhaps, in its red embers new scenes of persecution yet to be encountered. The snow still drifted hard against the windows, and sometimes, as the blaze of the logs had gradually sunk, came down the spacious chimney and hissed upon the hearth. A cautious footstep might now and then be heard in a neighboring apartment, and the sound invariably drew the eyes of both Quakers to the door which led thither. When a fierce and riotous gust of wind had led his thoughts, by a natural association, to homeless travellers on such a night, Pearson resumed the conversation.

"I have well-nigh sunk under my own share of this trial," observed he, sighing heavily; "yet I would that it might be doubled to me, if so the child's mother could be spared. Her wounds have been deep and many, but this will be the sorest of all."

"Fear not for Catharine," replied the old Quaker, "for I know that valiant woman, and have seen how she can bear the cross. A mother's heart, indeed, is strong in her, and may seem to contend mightily with her faith; but soon she will stand up and give thanks that her son has been thus early an accepted sacrifice. The boy hath done his work, and she will feel that he is taken hence in kindness both to him and her. Blessed, blessed are they that with so little suffering can enter into peace!"

The fitful rush of the wind was now disturbed by a portentous sound; it was a quick and heavy knocking at the outer door. Pearson's wan countenance grew paler, for many a visit of persecution had taught him what to dread; the old man, on the other hand, stood up erect, and his glance was firm as that of the tried soldier who awaits his enemy.

"The men of blood have come to seek me," he observed with calmness. "They have heard how I was moved to return from banishment; and now am I to be led to prison, and thence to death. It is an end I have long looked for. I will open unto them, lest they say, 'Lo, he feareth!' "

"Nay, I will present myself before them," said Pearson, with recovered fortitude. "It may be that they seek me alone, and know not that thou abidest with me."

"Let us go boldly, both one and the other," rejoined his companion. "It is not fitting that thou or I should shrink."

They therefore proceeded through the entry to the door, which they opened, bidding the applicant "Come in, in God's name!" A furious blast of wind drove the storm into their faces, and extinguished the lamp; they had barely time to discern a figure, so white from head to foot with the drifted snow that it seemed like Winter's self, come in human shape, to seek refuge from its own desolation.

"Enter, friend, and do thy errand, be it what it may," said Pearson. "It must needs be pressing, since thou comest on such a bitter night."

"Peace be with this household," said the stranger, when they stood on the floor of the inner apartment.

Pearson started, the elder Quaker stirred the slumbering embers of the fire till they sent up a clear and lofty blaze; it was a female voice that had spoken; it was a female form that shone out, cold and wintry, in that comfortable light.

"Catharine, blessed woman!" exclaimed the old man, "art thou come to this darkened land again? art thou come to bear a valiant testimony as in former years? The scourge hath not prevailed against thee, and from the dungeon hast thou come forth triumphant; but strengthen, strengthen now thy heart, Catharine, for Heaven will prove thee yet this once, ere thou go to thy reward."

"Rejoice, friends!" she replied. "Thou who hast long been of our people, and thou whom a little child hath led to us, rejoice! Lo! I come, the messenger of glad tidings, for the day of persecution is overpast. The heart of the king, even Charles, hath been moved in gentleness towards us, and he hath sent forth his letters to stay the hands of the men of blood. A ship's company of our friends hath arrived at yonder town, and I also sailed joyfully among them."

As Catharine spoke, her eyes were roaming about the room, in search of him for whose sake security was dear to her. Pearson made a silent appeal to the old man, nor did the latter shrink from the painful task assigned him.

"Sister," he began, in a softened yet perfectly calm tone, "thou tellest us of His love, manifested in temporal good; and now must we speak to thee of that selfsame love, displayed in chastenings.[9] Hitherto, Catharine, thou hast been as one journeying in a darksome and difficult path, and leading an infant by the hand; fain wouldst thou have looked heavenward continually, but still the cares of that little child have drawn thine eyes and thy affections to the earth. Sister! go on rejoicing, for his tottering footsteps shall impede thine own no more."

But the unhappy mother was not thus to be consoled; she shook like a leaf, she turned white as the very snow that hung drifted into her hair. The firm old man extended his hand and held her up, keeping his eye upon hers, as if to repress any outbreak of passion.

"I am a woman, I am but a woman; will He try me above my strength?" said Catharine very quickly, and almost in a whisper. "I have been wounded sore: I have suffered much; many things in the body; many in the mind; crucified in myself, and in them that were dearest to me. Surely," added she, with a long shudder, "He hath

9. Hebrews xii: 6: "For whom the Lord loveth he chasteneth * * * "

spared me in this one thing." She broke forth with sudden and irre-pressible violence. "Tell me, man of cold heart, what has God done to me? Hath He cast me down, never to rise again? Hath He crushed my very heart in his hand? And thou, to whom I committed my child, how hast thou fulfilled thy trust? Give me back the boy, well, sound, alive, alive; or earth and Heaven shall avenge me!"

The agonized shriek of Catharine was answered by the faint, the very faint, voice of a child.

On this day it had become evident to Pearson, to his aged guest, and to Dorothy, that Ilbrahim's brief and troubled pilgrimage drew near its close. The two former would willingly have remained by him to make use of the prayers and pious discourses which they deemed appropriate to the time, and which, if they be impotent as to the departing traveller's reception in the world whither he goes, may at least sustain him in bidding adieu to earth. But though Ilbrahim ut-tered no complaint, he was disturbed by the faces that looked upon him; so that Dorothy's entreaties, and their own conviction that the child's feet might tread heaven's pavement and not soil it, had induced the two Quakers to remove. Ilbrahim then closed his eyes and grew calm, and, except for now and then a kind and low word to his nurse, might have been thought to slumber. As nightfall came on, however, and the storm began to rise, something seemed to trouble the repose of the boy's mind, and to render his sense of hear-ing active and acute. If a passing wind lingered to shake the case-ment, he strove to turn his head towards it; if the door jarred to and fro upon its hinges, he looked long and anxiously thitherward; if the heavy voice of the old man, as he read the Scriptures, rose but a little higher, the child almost held his dying breath to listen; if a snow-drift swept by the cottage, with a sound like the trailing of a garment, Ilbrahim seemed to watch that some visitant should enter.

But, after a little time, he relinquished whatever secret hope had agitated him, and with one low, complaining whisper, turned his cheek upon the pillow. He then addressed Dorothy with his usual sweetness, and besought her to draw near him; she did so, and Ilbra-him took her hand in both of his, grasping it with a gentle pressure, as if to assure himself that he retained it. At intervals, and without disturbing the repose of his countenance, a very faint trembling passed over him from head to foot, as if a mild but somewhat cool wind had breathed upon him, and made him shiver. As the boy thus led her by the hand, in his quiet progress over the borders of eternity, Dorothy almost imagined that she could discern the near, though dim, delightfulness of the home he was about to reach; she would not have enticed the little wanderer back, though she bemoaned her-self that she must leave him and return. But just when Ilbrahim's feet were pressing on the soil of Paradise he heard a voice behind him, and it recalled him a few, few paces of the weary path which he had travelled. As Dorothy looked upon his features, she perceived that their placid expression was again disturbed; her own thoughts had been so wrapped in him, that all sounds of the storm, and of human speech, were lost to her; but when Catharine's shriek pierced through the room, the boy strove to raise himself.

"Friend, she is come! Open unto her!" cried he.

In a moment his mother was kneeling by the bedside; she drew Ilbrahim to her bosom, and he nestled there, with no violence of joy, but contentedly, as if he were hushing himself to sleep. He looked into her face, and reading its agony, said, with feeble earnestness, "Mourn not, dearest mother. I am happy now." And with these words the gentle boy was dead.

The king's mandate to stay the New England persecutors was effectual in preventing further martyrdoms; but the colonial authorities, trusting in the remoteness of their situation, and perhaps in the supposed instability of the royal government, shortly renewed their severities in all other respects. Catharine's fanaticism had become wilder by the sundering of all human ties; and wherever a scourge was lifted there was she to receive the blow; and whenever a dungeon was unbarred thither she came, to cast herself upon the floor. But in process of time a more Christian spirit—a spirit of forbearance, though not of cordiality or approbation—began to pervade the land in regard to the persecuted sect. And then, when the rigid old Pilgrims eyed her rather in pity than in wrath; when the matrons fed her with the fragments of their children's food, and offered her a lodging on a hard and lowly bed; when no little crowd of schoolboys left their sports to cast stones after the roving enthusiast; then did Catharine return to Pearson's dwelling and made that her home.

As if Ilbrahim's sweetness yet lingered round his ashes; as if his gentle spirit came down from heaven to teach his parent a true religion, her fierce and vindictive nature was softened by the same griefs which had once irritated it. When the course of years had made the features of the unobtrusive mourner familiar in the settlement, she became a subject of not deep, but general, interest; a being on whom the otherwise superfluous sympathies of all might be bestowed. Every one spoke of her with that degree of pity which it is pleasant to experience; every one was ready to do her the little kindnesses which are not costly, yet manifest good will; and when at last she died, a long train of her once bitter persecutors followed her, with decent sadness and tears that were not painful, to her place by Ilbrahim's green and sunken grave.

1832, 1837

Young Goodman Brown[1]

Young Goodman Brown came forth at sunset into the street at Salem village; but put his head back, after crossing the threshold, to exchange a parting kiss with his young wife. And Faith, as the wife was aptly named, thrust her own pretty head into the street, letting the wind play with the pink ribbons of her cap while she called to Goodman Brown.

"Dearest heart," whispered she, softly and rather sadly, when her lips were close to his ear, "prithee put off your journey until sunrise and sleep in your own bed to-night. A lone woman is troubled with such dreams and such thoughts that she's afeared of herself sometimes. Pray tarry with me this night, dear husband, of all nights in the year."

"My love and my Faith," replied young Goodman Brown, "of all nights in the year, this one night must I tarry away from thee. My journey, as thou callest it, forth and back again, must needs be done 'twixt now and sunrise. What, my sweet, pretty wife, dost thou doubt me already, and we but three months married?"

"Then God bless you!" said Faith, with the pink ribbons; "and may you find all well when you come back."

"Amen!" cried Goodman Brown. "Say thy prayers, dear Faith, and go to bed at dusk, and no harm will come to thee."

So they parted; and the young man pursued his way until, being about to turn the corner by the meeting-house, he looked back and saw the head of Faith still peeping after him with a melancholy air, in spite of her pink ribbons.

"Poor little Faith!" thought he, for his heart smote him. "What a wretch am I to leave her on such an errand! She talks of dreams, too. Methought as she spoke there was trouble in her face, as if a dream had warned her what work is to be done to-night. But no, no; 't would kill her to think it. Well, she's a blessed angel on earth; and after this one night I'll cling to her skirts and follow her to heaven."

With this excellent resolve for the future, Goodman Brown felt himself justified in making more haste on his present evil purpose. He had taken a dreary road, darkened by all the gloomiest trees of the forest, which barely stood aside to let the narrow path creep through, and closed immediately behind. It was all as lonely as

1. Medieval literature abounds in descriptions of the "Witches' Sabbath," a midnight orgy of evil rites at which Satan himself sometimes presided. Hawthorne was certainly familiar with Cotton Mather's description, in *The Wonders of the Invisible World* (1693), of such "Diabolical Sacraments" as taking place in Massachusetts. Hawthorne's story is a memorable portrayal of a Puritan community, but its theme is universal. The concept of mankind's natural depravity was a principal determinant in Puritan thought, but Goodman Brown's corruption through his loss of simple faith in the goodness of mankind represents a timeless tragedy. This story appeared in the *New England Magazine* for April, 1835, and was collected in *Mosses from an Old Manse* (1846).

could be; and there is this peculiarity in such a solitude, that the traveller knows not who may be concealed by the innumerable trunks and the thick boughs overhead; so that with lonely footsteps he may yet be passing through an unseen multitude.

"There may be a devilish Indian behind every tree," said Goodman Brown to himself; and he glanced fearfully behind him as he added, "What if the devil himself should be at my very elbow!"

His head being turned back, he passed a crook of the road, and, looking forward again, beheld the figure of a man, in grave and decent attire, seated at the foot of an old tree. He arose at Goodman Brown's approach and walked onward side by side with him.

"You are late, Goodman Brown," said he. "The clock of the Old South[2] was striking as I came through Boston, and that is full fifteen minutes agone."

"Faith kept me back a while," replied the young man, with a tremor in his voice, caused by the sudden appearance of his companion, though not wholly unexpected.

It was now deep dusk in the forest, and deepest in that part of it where these two were journeying. As nearly as could be discerned, the second traveller was about fifty years old, apparently in the same rank of life as Goodman Brown, and bearing a considerable resemblance to him, though perhaps more in expression than features. Still they might have been taken for father and son. And yet, though the elder person was as simply clad as the younger, and as simple in manner too, he had an indescribable air of one who knew the world, and who would not have felt abashed at the governor's dinner table or in King William's court,[3] were it possible that his affairs should call him thither. But the only thing about him that could be fixed upon as remarkable was his staff, which bore the likeness of a great black snake, so curiously wrought that it might almost be seen to twist and wriggle itself like a living serpent. This, of course, must have been an ocular deception, assisted by the uncertain light.

"Come, Goodman Brown," cried his fellow-traveller, "this is a dull pace for the beginning of a journey. Take my staff, if you are so soon weary."

"Friend," said the other, exchanging his slow pace for a full stop, "having kept covenant by meeting thee here, it is my purpose now to return whence I came. I have scruples touching the matter thou wot'st of."

"Sayest thou so?" replied he of the serpent, smiling apart. "Let us walk on, nevertheless, reasoning as we go; and if I convince thee not

---

2. *I.e.,* Old South Church, Boston, famous as the secret rendezvous of American patriots before the Revolution. However, the Church was erected in 1729, while the story seems to be set somewhat earlier, before 1702. See the reference to "King William's court," just below.
3. William III was King of England from 1689 to 1702.

thou shalt turn back. We are but a little way in the forest yet."

"Too far! too far!" exclaimed the goodman, unconsciously resuming his walk. "My father never went into the woods on such an errand, nor his father before him. We have been a race of honest men and good Christians since the days of the martyrs; and shall I be the first of the name of Brown that ever took this path and kept"—

"Such company, thou wouldst say," observed the elder person, interpreting his pause. "Well said, Goodman Brown! I have been as well acquainted with your family as with ever a one among the Puritans; and that's no trifle to say. I helped your grandfather, the constable, when he lashed the Quaker woman so smartly through the streets of Salem; and it was I that brought your father a pitch-pine knot, kindled at my own heart, to set fire to an Indian village, in King Philip's war.[4] They were my good friends, both; and many a pleasant walk have we had along this path, and returned merrily after midnight. I would fain be friends with you for their sake."

"If it be as thou sayest," replied Goodman Brown, "I marvel they never spoke of these matters; or, verily, I marvel not, seeing that the least rumor of the sort would have driven them from New England. We are a people of prayer, and good works to boot, and abide no such wickedness."

"Wickedness or not," said the traveller with the twisted staff, "I have a very general acquaintance here in New England. The deacons of many a church have drunk the communion wine with me; the selectmen of divers towns make me their chairman; and a majority of the Great and General Court are firm supporters of my interest. The governor and I, too— But these are state secrets."

"Can this be so?" cried Goodman Brown, with a stare of amazement at his undisturbed companion. "Howbeit, I have nothing to do with the governor and council; they have their own ways, and are no rule for a simple husbandman[5] like me. But, were I to go on with thee, how should I meet the eye of that good old man, our minister, at Salem village? Oh, his voice would make me tremble both Sabbath day and lecture day."[6]

Thus far the elder traveller had listened with due gravity; but now burst into a fit of irrepressible mirth, shaking himself so violently that his snake-like staff actually seemed to wriggle in sympathy.

"Ha! ha! ha!" shouted he again and again; then composing himself, "Well, go on, Goodman Brown, go on; but, prithee, don't kill me with laughing."

"Well, then, to end the matter at once," said Goodman Brown,

---

4. King Philip, or Metacomet, was the last leader of Indian resistance in southern New England, which ended with his death in 1676.
5. Generally, "farmer," but then sometimes denoting any man of humble station, conventionally addressed as "Goodman."
6. The day of the midweek sermon, generally Thursday.

considerably nettled, "there is my wife, Faith. It would break her dear little heart; and I'd rather break my own."

"Nay, if that be the case," answered the other, "e'en go thy ways, Goodman Brown. I would not for twenty old women like the one hobbling before us that Faith should come to any harm."

As he spoke he pointed his staff at a female figure on the path, in whom Goodman Brown recognized a very pious and exemplary dame, who had taught him his catechism in youth, and was still his moral and spiritual adviser, jointly with the minister and Deacon Gookin.

"A marvel, truly, that Goody⁷ Cloyse should be so far in the wilderness at nightfall," said he. "But with your leave, friend, I shall take a cut through the woods until we have left this Christian woman behind. Being a stranger to you, she might ask whom I was consorting with and whither I was going."

"Be it so," said his fellow-traveller. "Betake you to the woods, and let me keep the path."

Accordingly the young man turned aside, but took care to watch his companion, who advanced softly along the road until he had come within a staff's length of the old dame. She, meanwhile, was making the best of her way, with singular speed for so aged a woman, and mumbling some indistinct words—a prayer, doubtless—as she went. The traveller put forth his staff and touched her withered neck with what seemed the serpent's tail.

"The devil!" screamed the pious old lady.

"Then Goody Cloyse knows her old friend?" observed the traveller, confronting her and leaning on his writhing stick.

"Ah, forsooth, and is it your worship indeed?" cried the good dame. "Yea, truly is it, and in the very image of my old gossip, Goodman Brown, the grandfather of the silly fellow that now is. But—would your worship believe it?—my broomstick hath strangely disappeared, stolen, as I suspect, by that unhanged witch, Goody Cory, and that, too, when I was all anointed with the juice of smallage,⁸ and cinquefoil, and wolf's bane"—

"Mingled with fine wheat and the fat of a new-born babe," said the shape of old Goodman Brown.

"Ah, your worship knows the recipe," cried the old lady, cackling aloud. "So, as I was saying, being all ready for the meeting, and no horse to ride on, I made up my mind to foot it; for they tell me there is a nice young man to be taken into communion to-night. But now your good worship will lend me your arm, and we shall be there in

---

7. A contraction of "Goodwife," then a term of civility in addressing a wife of humble station (*cf.* "Goodman"). Goody Cloyse, like Goody Cory and Martha Carrier, who appear later, were among the "witches" of Salem sentenced in 1692 by the court of magistrates of which Hawthorne's forebear was a member.

8. Wild celery. In the literature of witchcraft a plant credited with magic powers.

a twinkling."

"That can hardly be," answered her friend. "I may not spare you my arm, Goody Cloyse; but here is my staff, if you will."

So saying, he threw it down at her feet, where, perhaps, it assumed life, being one of the rods which its owner had formerly lent to the Egyptian magi. Of this fact, however, Goodman Brown could not take cognizance. He had cast up his eyes in astonishment, and, looking down again, beheld neither Goody Cloyse nor the serpentine staff, but his fellow-traveller alone, who waited for him as calmly as if nothing had happened.

"That old woman taught me my catechism," said the young man; and there was a world of meaning in this simple comment.

They continued to walk onward, while the elder traveller exhorted his companion to make good speed and persevere in the path, discoursing so aptly that his arguments seemed rather to spring up in the bosom of his auditor than to be suggested by himself. As they went, he plucked a branch of maple to serve for a walking stick, and began to strip it of the twigs and little boughs, which were wet with evening dew. The moment his fingers touched them they became strangely withered and dried up as with a week's sunshine. Thus the pair proceeded, at a good free pace, until suddenly, in a gloomy hollow of the road, Goodman Brown sat himself down on the stump of a tree and refused to go any farther.

"Friend," said he, stubbornly, "my mind is made up. Not another step will I budge on this errand. What if a wretched old woman do choose to go to the devil when I thought she was going to heaven: is that any reason why I should quit my dear Faith and go after her?"

"You will think better of this by and by," said his acquaintance, composedly. "Sit here and rest yourself a while; and when you feel like moving again, there is my staff to help you along."

Without more words, he threw his companion the maple stick, and was as speedily out of sight as if he had vanished into the deepening gloom. The young man sat a few moments by the roadside, applauding himself greatly, and thinking with how clear a conscience he should meet the minister in his morning walk, nor shrink from the eye of good old Deacon Gookin. And what calm sleep would be his that very night, which was to have been spent so wickedly, but so purely and sweetly now, in the arms of Faith! Amidst these pleasant and praiseworthy meditations, Goodman Brown heard the tramp of horses along the road, and deemed it advisable to conceal himself within the verge of the forest, conscious of the guilty purpose that had brought him thither, though now so happily turned from it.

On came the hoof tramps and the voices of the riders, two grave old voices, conversing soberly as they drew near. These mingled sounds appeared to pass along the road, within a few yards of the young man's hiding-place; but, owing doubtless to the depth of the gloom at that particular spot, neither the travellers nor their steeds were visible. Though their figures brushed the small boughs by the way-side, it could not be seen that they intercepted, even for a moment, the faint gleam from the strip of bright sky athwart which they must have passed. Goodman Brown alternately crouched and stood on tiptoe, pulling aside the branches and thrusting forth his head as far as he durst without discerning so much as a shadow. It vexed him the more, because he could have sworn, were such a thing possible, that he recognized the voices of the minister and Deacon Gookin, jogging along quietly, as they were wont to do, when bound to some ordination or ecclesiastical council. While yet within hearing, one of the riders stopped to pluck a switch.

"Of the two, reverend sir," said the voice like the deacon's, "I had rather miss an ordination dinner than to-night's meeting. They tell me that some of our community are to be here from Falmouth and beyond, and others from Connecticut and Rhode Island, besides several of the Indian powwows, who, after their fashion, know almost as much deviltry as the best of us. Moreover, there is a goodly young woman to be taken into communion."

"Mighty well, Deacon Gookin!" replied the solemn old tones of the minister. "Spur up, or we shall be late. Nothing can be done, you know, until I get on the ground."

The hoofs clattered again; and the voices, talking so strangely in the empty air, passed on through the forest, where no church had ever been gathered or solitary Christian prayed. Whither, then, could these holy men be journeying so deep into the heathen wilderness? Young Goodman Brown caught hold of a tree for support, being ready to sink down on the ground, faint and overburdened with the heavy sickness of his heart. He looked up to the sky, doubting whether there really was a heaven above him. Yet there was the blue arch, and the stars brightening in it.

"With heaven above and Faith below, I will yet stand firm against the devil!" cried Goodman Brown.

While he still gazed upward into the deep arch of the firmament and had lifted his hands to pray, a cloud, though no wind was stirring, hurried across the zenith and hid the brightening stars. The blue sky was still visible, except directly overhead, where this black mass of cloud was sweeping swiftly northward. Aloft in the air, as if from the depths of the cloud, came a confused and doubtful sound of voices. Once the listener fancied that he could distinguish the accents of towns-people of his own, men and women, both pious and ungodly, many of whom he had met at the communion table, and had seen others rioting at the tavern. The next moment, so indistinct were the sounds, he doubted whether he had heard aught but the murmur of the old forest, whispering without a wind. Then came a stronger swell of those familiar tones, heard daily in the sunshine at Salem village, but never until now from a cloud of night. There was one voice, of a young woman, uttering lamentations, yet with an uncertain sorrow, and entreating for some favor, which, perhaps, it would grieve her to obtain; and all the unseen multitude, both saints and sinners, seemed to encourage her onward.

"Faith!" shouted Goodman Brown, in a voice of agony and desperation; and the echoes of the forest mocked him, crying, "Faith! Faith!" as if bewildered wretches were seeking her all through the wilderness.

The cry of grief, rage, and terror was yet piercing the night, when the unhappy husband held his breath for a response. There was a scream, drowned immediately in a louder murmur of voices, fading into far-off laughter, as the dark cloud swept away, leaving the clear and silent sky above Goodman Brown. But something fluttered lightly down through the air and caught on the branch of a tree. The young man seized it, and beheld a pink ribbon.

"My Faith is gone!" cried he, after one stupefied moment. "There is no good on earth; and sin is but a name. Come, devil; for to thee is this world given."

And, maddened with despair, so that he laughed loud and long, did Goodman Brown grasp his staff and set forth again, at such a rate that he seemed to fly along the forest path rather than to walk or run. The road grew wilder and drearier and more faintly traced, and vanished at length, leaving him in the heart of the dark wilderness, still rushing onward with the instinct that guides mortal man to evil. The whole forest was peopled with frightful sounds—the creaking of the trees, the howling of wild beasts, and the yell of Indians; while sometimes the wind tolled like a distant church bell, and sometimes gave a broad roar around the traveller, as if all Nature were laughing him to scorn. But he was himself the chief horror of the scene, and shrank not from its other horrors.

"Ha! ha! ha!" roared Goodman Brown when the wind laughed at him. "Let us hear which will laugh loudest. Think not to frighten me with your deviltry. Come witch, come wizard, come Indian powwow, come devil himself, and here comes Goodman Brown. You may as well fear him as he fear you."

In truth, all through the haunted forest there could be nothing more frightful than the figure of Goodman Brown. On he flew among the black pines, brandishing his staff with frenzied gestures, now giving vent to an inspiration of horrid blasphemy, and now shouting forth such laughter as set all the echoes of the forest laughing like demons around him. The fiend in his own shape is less hideous than when he rages in the breast of man. Thus sped the demoniac on his course, until, quivering among the trees, he saw a red light before him, as when the felled trunks and branches of a clearing have been set on fire, and throw up their lurid blaze against the sky, at the hour of midnight. He paused, in a lull of the tempest that had driven him onward, and heard the swell of what seemed a hymn, rolling solemnly from a distance with the weight of many voices. He knew the tune; it was a familiar one in the choir of the village meeting-house. The verse died heavily away, and was lengthened by a chorus, not of human voices, but of all the sounds of the benighted wilderness pealing in awful harmony together. Goodman Brown cried out, and his cry was lost to his own ear by its unison with the cry of the desert.

In the interval of silence he stole forward until the light glared full upon his eyes. At one extremity of an open space, hemmed in by the dark wall of the forest, arose a rock, bearing some rude, natural resemblance either to an altar or a pulpit, and surrounded by four blazing pines, their tops aflame, their stems untouched, like candles at an evening meeting. The mass of foliage that had overgrown the summit of the rock was all on fire, blazing high into the night and fitfully illuminating the whole field. Each pendent twig and leafy festoon was in a blaze. As the red light arose and fell, a numerous congregation alternately shone forth, then disappeared in shadow, and again grew, as it were, out of the darkness, peopling the heart of the solitary woods at once.

"A grave and dark-clad company," quoth Goodman Brown.

In truth they were such. Among them, quivering to and fro between gloom and splendor, appeared faces that would be seen next day at the council board of the province, and others which, Sabbath after Sabbath, looked devoutly heavenward, and benignantly over the crowded pews, from the holiest pulpits in the land. Some affirm that the lady of the governor was there. At least there were high dames well known to her, and wives of honored husbands, and widows, a great multitude, and ancient maidens, all of excellent repute, and fair young girls, who trembled lest their mothers should espy them. Either the sudden gleams of light flashing over the obscure field bedazzled Goodman Brown, or he recognized a score of the church members of Salem village famous for their especial sanctity. Good old Deacon Gookin had arrived, and waited at the skirts of that venerable saint, his revered pastor. But, irreverently consorting with these grave, reputable, and pious people, these elders of the church, these chaste dames and dewy virgins, there were men of dissolute lives and women of spotted fame, wretches given over to all mean and filthy vice, and suspected even of horrid crimes. It was strange to see that the good shrank not from the wicked, nor were the sinners abashed by the saints. Scattered also among their pale-faced enemies were the Indian priests, or powwows, who had often scared their native forest with more hideous incantations than any known to English witchcraft.

"But where is Faith?" thought Goodman Brown; and, as hope came into his heart, he trembled.

Another verse of the hymn arose, a slow and mournful strain, such as the pious love, but joined to words which expressed all that our nature can conceive of sin, and darkly hinted at far more. Unfathomable to mere mortals is the lore of fiends. Verse after verse was sung; and still the chorus of the desert swelled between like the deepest tone of a mighty organ; and with the final peal of that dreadful anthem there came a sound, as if the roaring wind, the rushing streams, the howling beasts, and every other voice of the unconcerted wilderness were mingling and according with the voice of guilty man in homage to the prince of all. The four blazing pines threw up a loftier flame, and obscurely discovered shapes and visages of horror on the smoke wreaths above the impious assembly. At the same moment the fire on the rock shot redly forth and formed a glowing arch above its base, where now appeared a figure. With reverence be it spoken, the figure bore no slight similitude, both in garb and manner, to some grave divine of the New England churches.

"Bring forth the converts!" cried a voice that echoed through the field and rolled into the forest.

At the word, Goodman Brown stepped forth from the shadow of the trees and approached the congregation, with whom he felt a loathful brotherhood by the sympathy of all that was wicked in his heart. He could have well-nigh sworn that the shape of his own dead father beckoned him to advance, looking downward from a smoke wreath, while a woman, with dim features of despair, threw out her hand to warn him back. Was it his mother? But he had no power to retreat one step, nor to resist, even in thought, when the minister and good old Deacon Gookin seized his arms and led him to the blazing rock. Thither came also the slender form of a veiled female, led between Goody Cloyse, that pious teacher of the catechism, and Martha Carrier, who had received the devil's promise to be queen of hell. A rampant hag was she. And there stood the proselytes beneath the canopy of fire.

"Welcome, my children," said the dark figure, "to the communion of your race. Ye have found thus young your nature and your destiny. My children, look behind you!"

They turned; and flashing forth, as it were, in a sheet of flame, the fiend worshippers were seen; the smile of welcome gleamed darkly on every visage.

"There," resumed the sable form, "are all whom ye have reverenced from youth. Ye deemed them holier than yourselves and

shrank from your own sin, contrasting it with their lives of righteousness and prayerful aspirations heavenward. Yet here are they all in
my worshipping assembly. This night it shall be granted you to
know their secret deeds: how hoary-bearded elders of the church have
whispered wanton words to the young maids of their households;
how many a woman, eager for widows' weeds, has given her husband
a drink at bedtime and let him sleep his last sleep in her bosom; how
beardless youths have made haste to inherit their fathers' wealth;
and how fair damsels—blush not, sweet ones—have dug little graves
in the garden, and bidden me, the sole guest, to an infant's funeral.
By the sympathy of your human hearts for sin ye shall scent out all
the places—whether in church, bedchamber, street, field, or forest
—where crime has been committed, and shall exult to behold the
whole earth one stain of guilt, one mighty blood spot. Far more than
this. It shall be yours to penetrate, in every bosom, the deep mystery
of sin, the fountain of all wicked arts, and which inexhaustibly supplies more evil impulses than human power—than my power at its
utmost—can make manifest in deeds. And now, my children, look
upon each other."

They did so; and, by the blaze of the hell-kindled torches, the
wretched man beheld his Faith, and the wife her husband, trembling
before that unhallowed altar.

"Lo, there ye stand, my children," said the figure, in a deep and
solemn tone, almost sad with its despairing awfulness, as if his once
angelic nature could yet mourn for our miserable race. "Depending
upon one another's hearts, ye had still hoped that virtue were not
all a dream. Now are ye undeceived. Evil is the nature of mankind.
Evil must be your only happiness. Welcome again, my children, to
the communion of your race."

"Welcome," repeated the fiend worshippers, in one cry of despair
and triumph.

And there they stood, the only pair, as it seemed, who were yet
hesitating on the verge of wickedness in this dark world. A basin was
hollowed, naturally, in the rock. Did it contain water, reddened by
the lurid light? or was it blood? or, perchance, a liquid flame? Herein
did the shape of evil dip his hand and prepare to lay the mark of
baptism upon their foreheads, that they might be partakers of the
mystery of sin, more conscious of the secret guilt of others, both in
deed and thought, than they could now be of their own. The husband
cast one look at his pale wife, and Faith at him. What polluted
wretches would the next glance show them to each other, shuddering alike at what they disclosed and what they saw!

"Faith! Faith!" cried the husband, "look up to heaven, and resist
the wicked one."

Whether Faith obeyed he knew not. Hardly had he spoken when

he found himself amid calm night and solitude, listening to a roar of the wind which died heavily away through the forest. He staggered against the rock, and felt it chill and damp; while a hanging twig, that had been all on fire, besprinkled his cheek with the coldest dew.

The next morning young Goodman Brown came slowly into the street of Salem village, staring around him like a bewildered man. The good old minister was taking a walk along the graveyard to get an appetite for breakfast and meditate his sermon, and bestowed a blessing, as he passed, on Goodman Brown. He shrank from the venerable saint as if to avoid an anathema. Old Deacon Gookin was at domestic worship, and the holy words of his prayer were heard through the open window. "What God doth the wizard pray to?" quoth Goodman Brown. Goody Cloyse, that excellent old Christian, stood in the early sunshine at her own lattice, catechizing a little girl who had brought her a pint of morning's milk. Goodman Brown snatched away the child as from the grasp of the fiend himself. Turning the corner by the meeting-house, he spied the head of Faith, with the pink ribbons, gazing anxiously forth, and bursting into such joy at sight of him that she skipped along the street and almost kissed her husband before the whole village. But Goodman Brown looked sternly and sadly into her face, and passed on without a greeting.

Had Goodman Brown fallen asleep in the forest and only dreamed a wild dream of a witch-meeting?

Be it so if you will; but, alas! it was a dream of evil omen for young Goodman Brown. A stern, a sad, a darkly meditative, a distrustful, if not a desperate man did he become from the night of that fearful dream. On the Sabbath day, when the congregation were singing a holy psalm, he could not listen because an anthem of sin rushed loudly upon his ear and drowned all the blessed strain. When the minister spoke from the pulpit with power and fervid eloquence, and, with his hand on the open Bible, of the sacred truths of our religion, and of saint-like lives and triumphant deaths, and of future bliss or misery unutterable, then did Goodman Brown turn pale, dreading lest the roof should thunder down upon the gray blasphemer and his hearers. Often, awaking suddenly at midnight, he shrank from the bosom of Faith; and at morning or eventide, when the family knelt down at prayer, he scowled and muttered to himself, and gazed sternly at his wife, and turned away. And when he had lived long, and was borne to his grave a hoary corpse, followed by Faith, an aged woman, and children and grandchildren, a goodly procession, besides neighbors not a few, they carved no hopeful verse upon his tombstone, for his dying hour was gloom.

1835, 1846.

The Minister's Black Veil

A Parable[9]

The sexton stood in the porch of Milford meeting-house, pulling busily at the bell-rope. The old people of the village came stooping along the street. Children, with bright faces, tripped merrily beside their parents, or mimicked a graver gait, in the conscious dignity of their Sunday clothes. Spruce bachelors looked sidelong at the pretty maidens, and fancied that the Sabbath sunshine made them prettier than on week days. When the throng had mostly streamed into the porch, the sexton began to toll the bell, keeping his eye on the Reverend Mr. Hooper's door. The first glimpse of the clergyman's figure was the signal for the bell to cease its summons.

"But what has good Parson Hooper got upon his face?" cried the sexton in astonishment.

All within hearing immediately turned about, and beheld the semblance of Mr. Hooper, pacing slowly his meditative way towards the meeting-house. With one accord they started, expressing more wonder than if some strange minister were coming to dust the cushions of Mr. Hooper's pulpit.

"Are you sure it is our parson?" inquired Goodman Gray of the sexton.

"Of a certainty it is good Mr. Hooper," replied the sexton. "He was to have exchanged pulpits with Parson Shute, of Westbury; but Parson Shute sent to excuse himself yesterday, being to preach a funeral sermon."

The cause of so much amazement may appear sufficiently slight. Mr. Hooper, a gentlemanly person, of about thirty, though still a bachelor, was dressed with due clerical neatness, as if a careful wife had starched his band, and brushed the weekly dust from his Sunday's garb. There was but one thing remarkable in his appearance. Swathed about his forehead, and hanging down over his face, so low as to be shaken by his breath, Mr. Hooper had on a black veil. On a nearer view it seemed to consist of two folds of crape, which entirely con-

9. The interpretation of this parable has intrigued generations of readers. The dying speech of Parson Hooper connects the symbol of his black veil with the hypocritical secret sins of mankind. But see also Poe's interpretation in his review of Hawthorne's *Twice-Told Tales*. In this interpretation, the story is associated with *The Scarlet Letter* as much as with *Young Goodman Brown*. A clue has also been sought in Hawthorne's footnote to the title of the story, which reads as follows: "Another clergyman in New England, Mr. Joseph Moody, of York, Maine, who died about eighty years since, made himself remarkable by the same eccentricity that is here related of the Reverend Mr. Hooper. In his case, however, the symbol had a different import. In early life he had accidentally killed a beloved friend; and from that day till the hour of his own death, he hid his face from men." Stewart suggests (*Nathaniel Hawthorne*, p. 257) that Hawthorne purposely refrained from emphasizing a single cause for the destructive estrangement of Hooper from mankind. The story first appeared in *The Token* for 1836, and was collected in *Twice-Told Tales* (1837).

cealed his features, except the mouth and chin, but probably did not intercept his sight, further than to give a darkened aspect to all living and inanimate things. With this gloomy shade before him, good Mr. Hooper walked onward, at a slow and quiet pace, stooping somewhat, and looking on the ground, as is customary with abstracted men, yet nodding kindly to those of his parishioners who still waited on the meeting-house steps. But so wonder-struck were they that his greeting hardly met with a return.

"I can't really feel as if good Mr. Hooper's face was behind that piece of crape," said the sexton.

"I don't like it," muttered an old woman, as she hobbled into the meeting-house. "He has changed himself into something awful, only by hiding his face."

"Our parson has gone mad!" cried Goodman Gray, following him across the threshold.

A rumor of some unaccountable phenomenon had preceded Mr. Hooper into the meeting-house, and set all the congregation astir. Few could refrain from twisting their heads towards the door; many stood upright, and turned directly about; while several little boys clambered upon the seats, and came down again with a terrible racket. There was a general bustle, a rustling of the women's gowns and shuffling of the men's feet, greatly at variance with that hushed repose which should attend the entrance of the minister. But Mr. Hooper appeared not to notice the perturbation of his people. He entered with an almost noiseless step, bent his head mildly to the pews on each side, and bowed as he passed his oldest parishioner, a white-haired great-grandsire, who occupied an arm-chair in the centre of the aisle. It was strange to observe how slowly this venerable man became conscious of something singular in the appearance of his pastor. He seemed not fully to partake of the prevailing wonder, till Mr. Hooper had ascended the stairs, and showed himself in the pulpit, face to face with his congregation, except for the black veil. That mysterious emblem was never once withdrawn. It shook with his measured breath, as he gave out the psalm; it threw its obscurity between him and the holy page, as he read the Scriptures; and while he prayed, the veil lay heavily on his uplifted countenance. Did he seek to hide it from the dread Being whom he was addressing?

Such was the effect of this simple piece of crape, that more than one woman of delicate nerves was forced to leave the meeting-house. Yet perhaps the pale-faced congregation was almost as fearful a sight to the minister, as his black veil to them.

Mr. Hooper had the reputation of a good preacher, but not an energetic one: he strove to win his people heavenward by mild, persuasive influences, rather than to drive them thither by the thunders of the Word. The sermon which he now delivered was marked by the same characteristics of style and manner as the general series of his pulpit oratory. But there was something, either in the sentiment of the discourse itself, or in the imagination of the auditors, which made it greatly the most powerful effort that they had ever heard from their pastor's lips. It was tinged, rather more darkly than usual, with the gentle gloom of Mr. Hooper's temperament. The subject had reference to secret sin, and those sad mysteries which we hide from our nearest and dearest, and would fain conceal from our own consciousness, even forgetting that the Omniscient can detect them. A subtle power was breathed into his words. Each member of the congregation, the most innocent girl, and the man of hardened breast, felt as if the preacher had crept upon them, behind his awful veil, and discovered their hoarded iniquity of deed or thought. Many spread their clasped hands on their bosoms. There was nothing terrible in what Mr. Hooper said, at least, no violence; and yet, with every tremor of his melancholy voice, the hearers quaked. An unsought pathos came hand in hand with awe. So sensible were the audience of some unwonted attribute in their minister, that they longed for a breath of wind to blow aside the veil, almost believing that a stranger's visage would be discovered, though the form, gesture, and voice were those of Mr. Hooper.

At the close of the services, the people hurried out with indecorous confusion, eager to communicate their pent-up amazement, and conscious of lighter spirits the moment they lost sight of the black veil. Some gathered in little circles, huddled closely together, with their mouths all whispering in the centre; some went homeward alone, wrapt in silent meditation; some talked loudly, and profaned the Sabbath day with ostentatious laughter. A few shook their sagacious heads, intimating that they could penetrate the mystery; while one or two affirmed that there was no mystery at all, but only that Mr. Hooper's eyes were so weakened by the midnight lamp, as to require a shade. After a brief interval, forth came good Mr. Hooper also, in the rear of his flock. Turning his veiled face from one group to another, he paid due reverence to the hoary heads, saluted the middle aged with kind dignity as their friend and spiritual guide, greeted the young with mingled authority and love, and laid his hands on the little children's heads to bless them. Such was always his custom on the Sabbath day. Strange and bewildered looks repaid him for his courtesy. None, as on former occasions, aspired to the honor of walking by their pastor's side. Old Squire Saunders, doubtless by an accidental lapse of memory, neglected to invite Mr. Hooper to his table, where the good clergyman had been wont to bless the food, almost every Sunday since his settlement. He returned, therefore, to the parsonage, and, at the moment of closing the door, was observed to look back upon the people, all of whom had their eyes fixed upon the minister. A sad smile gleamed faintly from beneath the black veil, and flickered about his mouth, glimmering as he disappeared.

"How strange," said a lady, "that a simple black veil, such as any woman might wear on her bonnet, should become such a terrible thing on Mr. Hooper's face!"

"Something must surely be amiss with Mr. Hooper's intellects," observed her husband, the physician of the village. "But the strangest part of the affair is the effect of this vagary, even on a sober-minded man like myself. The black veil, though it covers only our pastor's face, throws its influence over his whole person, and makes him ghostlike from head to foot. Do you not feel it so?"

"Truly do I," replied the lady; "and I would not be alone with him for the world. I wonder he is not afraid to be alone with himself!"

"Men sometimes are so," said her husband.

The afternoon service was attended with similar circumstances. At its conclusion, the bell tolled for the funeral of a young lady. The relatives and friends were assembled in the house, and the more distant acquaintances stood about the door, speaking of the good qualities of the deceased, when their talk was interrupted by the appearance of Mr. Hooper, still covered with his black veil. It was now an appropriate emblem. The clergyman stepped into the room where the corpse was laid, and bent over the coffin, to take a last farewell of his deceased parishioner. As he stooped, the veil hung straight down from his forehead, so that, if her eyelids had not been closed forever, the dead maiden might have seen his face. Could Mr. Hooper be fearful of her glance, that he so hastily caught back the black veil? A person who watched the interview between the dead and living, scrupled not to affirm, that, at the instant when the clergyman's features were disclosed, the corpse had slightly shuddered, rustling the shroud and muslin cap, though the countenance retained the composure of death. A superstitious old woman was the only witness of this prodigy. From the coffin Mr. Hooper passed into the chamber of the mourners, and thence to the head of the staircase, to make the funeral prayer. It was a tender and heart-dissolving prayer, full of sorrow, yet so imbued with celestial hopes, that the music of a heavenly harp, swept by the fingers of the dead, seemed faintly to be heard among the saddest accents of the minister. The people trembled, though they but darkly understood him when he prayed that they, and himself, and all of mortal race, might be ready, as he trusted this young maiden had been, for the dreadful hour that should snatch the veil from their faces. The bearers went heavily forth, and the mourners followed, saddening all the street, with the dead before them, and Mr. Hooper in his black veil behind.

"Why do you look back?" said one in the procession to his partner. "I had a fancy," replied she, "that the minister and the maiden's spirit were walking hand in hand."

"And so had I, at the same moment," said the other.

That night, the handsomest couple in Milford village were to be joined in wedlock. Though reckoned a melancholy man, Mr. Hooper had a placid cheerfulness for such occasions, which often excited a sympathetic smile where livelier merriment would have been thrown away. There was no quality of his disposition which made him more beloved than this. The company at the wedding awaited his arrival with impatience, trusting that the strange awe, which had gathered over him throughout the day, would now be dispelled. But such was not the result. When Mr. Hooper came, the first thing that their eyes rested on was the same horrible black veil, which had added deeper gloom to the funeral, and could portend nothing but evil to the wedding. Such was its immediate effect on the guests that a cloud seemed to have rolled duskily from beneath the black crape, and dimmed the light of the candles. The bridal pair stood up before the minister. But the bride's cold fingers quivered in the tremulous hand of the bridegroom, and her deathlike paleness caused a whisper that the maiden who had been buried a few hours before was come from her grave to be married. If ever another wedding were so dismal, it was that famous one where they tolled the wedding knell. After performing the ceremony, Mr. Hooper raised a glass of wine to his lips, wishing happiness to the new-married couple in a strain of mild pleasantry that ought to have brightened the features of the guests, like a cheerful gleam from the hearth. At that instant, catching a glimpse of his figure in the looking-glass, the black veil involved his own spirit in the horror with which it overwhelmed all others. His frame shuddered, his lips grew white, he spilt the untasted wine upon the carpet, and rushed forth into the darkness. For the Earth, too, had on her Black Veil.

The next day, the whole village of Milford talked of little else than Parson Hooper's black veil. That, and the mystery concealed behind it, supplied a topic for discussion between acquaintances meeting in the street, and good women gossiping at their open windows. It was the first item of news that the tavern-keeper told to his guests. The children babbled of it on their way to school. One imitative little imp covered his face with an old black handkerchief, thereby so affrighting his playmates that the panic seized himself, and he well-nigh lost his wits by his own waggery.

It was remarkable that of all the busybodies and impertinent people in the parish, not one ventured to put the plain question to Mr. Hooper, wherefore he did this thing. Hitherto, whenever there appeared the slightest call for such interference, he had never lacked advisers, nor shown himself averse to be guided by their judgment. It he erred at all, it was by so painful a degree of self-distrust, that even the mildest censure would lead him to consider an indifferent action as a crime. Yet, though so well acquainted with this amiable weakness, no individual among his parishioners chose to make the black veil a subject of friendly remonstrance. There was a feeling of dread, neither plainly confessed nor carefully concealed, which caused each to shift the responsibility upon another, till at length it was found expedient to send a deputation of the church, in order to deal with Mr. Hooper about the mystery, before it should grow into a scandal. Never did an embassy so ill discharge its duties. The minister received them with friendly courtesy, but became silent, after they were seated, leaving to his visitors the whole burden of introducing their important business. The topic, it might be supposed, was obvious enough. There was the black veil swathed round Mr. Hooper's forehead, and concealing every feature above his placid mouth, on which, at times, they could perceive the glimmering of a melancholy smile. But that piece of crape, to their imagination, seemed to hang down before his heart, the symbol of a fearful secret between him and them. Were the veil but cast aside, they might speak freely of it, but not till then. Thus they sat a considerable time, speechless, confused, and shrinking uneasily from Mr. Hooper's eye, which they felt to be fixed upon them with an invisible glance. Finally, the deputies returned abashed to their constituents, pronouncing the matter too weighty to be handled, except by a council of the churches, if, indeed, it might not require a general synod.

But there was one person in the village unappalled by the awe with which the black veil had impressed all beside herself. When the deputies returned without an explanation, or even venturing to demand one, she, with the calm energy of her character, determined to chase away the strange cloud that appeared to be settling round Mr. Hooper, every moment more darkly than before. As his plighted wife, it should be her privilege to know what the black veil concealed. At the minister's first visit, therefore, she entered upon the subject with a direct simplicity, which made the task easier both for him and her. After he had seated himself, she fixed her eyes steadfastly upon the veil, but could discern nothing of the dreadful gloom that had so overawed the multitude: it was but a double fold of crape, hanging down from his forehead to his mouth, and slightly stirring with his breath.

"No," said she aloud, and smiling, "there is nothing terrible in this piece of crape, except that it hides a face which I am always glad to look upon. Come, good sir, let the sun shine from behind the cloud. First lay aside your black veil: then tell me why you put it on."

Mr. Hooper's smile glimmered faintly.

"There is an hour to come," said he, "when all of us shall cast aside our veils. Take it not amiss, beloved friend, if I wear this piece of crape till then."

"Your words are a mystery, too," returned the young lady. "Take away the veil from them, at least."

"Elizabeth, I will," said he, "so far as my vow may suffer me. Know, then, this veil is a type and a symbol, and I am bound to wear it ever, both in light and darkness, in solitude and before the gaze of multitudes, and as with strangers, so with my familiar friends. No mortal eye will see it withdrawn. This dismal shade must separate me from the world: even you, Elizabeth, can never come behind it!"

"What grievous affliction hath befallen you," she earnestly inquired, "that you should thus darken your eyes forever?"

"If it be a sign of mourning," replied Mr. Hooper, "I, perhaps, like most other mortals, have sorrows dark enough to be typified by a black veil."

"But what if the world will not believe that it is the type of an innocent sorrow?" urged Elizabeth. "Beloved and respected as you are, there may be whispers that you hide your face under the consciousness of secret sin. For the sake of your holy office, do away this scandal!"

The color rose into her cheeks as she intimated the nature of the rumors that were already abroad in the village. But Mr. Hooper's mildness did not forsake him. He even smiled again—that same sad smile, which always appeared like a faint glimmering of light, proceeding from the obscurity beneath the veil.

"If I hide my face for sorrow, there is cause enough," he merely replied; "and if I cover it for secret sin, what mortal might not do the same?"

And with this gentle, but unconquerable obstinacy did he resist all her entreaties. At length Elizabeth sat silent. For a few moments she appeared lost in thought, considering, probably, what new methods might be tried to withdraw her lover from so dark a fantasy, which, if it had no other meaning, was perhaps a symptom of mental disease. Though of a firmer character than his own, the tears rolled down her cheeks. But, in an instant, as it were, a new feeling took the place of sorrow: her eyes were fixed insensibly on the black veil, when, like a sudden twilight in the air, its terrors fell around her. She arose, and stood trembling before him.

"And do you feel it then, at last?" said he mournfully.

She made no reply, but covered her eyes with her hand, and turned to leave the room. He rushed forward and caught her arm.

"Have patience with me, Elizabeth!" cried he, passionately. "Do not desert me, though this veil must be between us here on earth. Be mine, and hereafter there shall be no veil over my face, no dark-

ness between our souls! It is but a mortal veil—it is not for eternity!
O! you know not how lonely I am, and how frightened, to be alone
behind my black veil. Do not leave me in this miserable obscurity
forever!"

"Lift the veil but once, and look me in the face," said she.

"Never! It cannot be!" replied Mr. Hooper.

"Then farewell!" said Elizabeth.

She withdrew her arm from his grasp, and slowly departed, pausing
at the door, to give one long shuddering gaze, that seemed almost
to penetrate the mystery of the black veil. But, even amid his grief,
Mr. Hooper smiled to think that only a material emblem had separated him from happiness, though the horrors, which it shadowed
forth, must be drawn darkly between the fondest of lovers.

From that time no attempts were made to remove Mr. Hooper's
black veil, or, by a direct appeal, to discover the secret which it was
supposed to hide. By persons who claimed a superiority to popular
prejudice, it was reckoned merely an eccentric whim, such as often
mingles with the sober actions of men otherwise rational, and tinges
them all with its own semblance of insanity. But with the multitude,
good Mr. Hooper was irreparably a bugbear. He could not walk the
street with any peace of mind, so conscious was he that the gentle
and timid would turn aside to avoid him, and that others would
make it a point of hardihood to throw themselves in his way. The
impertinence of the latter class compelled him to give up his customary walk at sunset to the burial ground; for when he leaned pen-
sively over the gate, there would always be faces behind the gravestones, peeping at his black veil. A fable went the rounds that the
stare of the dead people drove him thence. It grieved him, to the
very depth of his kind heart, to observe how the children fled from
his approach, breaking up their merriest sports, while his melancholy
figure was yet afar off. Their instinctive dread caused him to feel
more strongly than aught else, that a preternatural horror was interwoven with the threads of the black crape. In truth, his own antipathy
to the veil was known to be so great, that he never willingly passed
before a mirror, nor stooped to drink at a still fountain, lest, in its
peaceful bosom, he should be affrighted by himself. This was what
gave plausibility to the whispers, that Mr. Hooper's conscience tortured him for some great crime too horrible to be entirely concealed,
or otherwise than so obscurely intimated. Thus, from beneath the
black veil, there rolled a cloud into the sunshine, an ambiguity of
sin or sorrow, which enveloped the poor minister, so that love or
sympathy could never reach him. It was said that ghost and fiend
consorted with him there. With self-shudderings and outward terrors,
he walked continually in its shadow, groping darkly within his own
soul, or gazing through a medium that saddened the whole world.

Even the lawless wind, it was believed, respected his dreadful secret, and never blew aside the veil. But still good Mr. Hooper sadly smiled at the pale visages of the worldly throng as he passed by.

Among all its bad influences, the black veil had the one desirable effect, of making its wearer a very efficient clergyman. By the aid of his mysterious emblem—for there was no other apparent cause— he became a man of awful power over souls that were in agony for sin. His converts always regarded him with a dread peculiar to themselves, affirming, though but figuratively, that, before he brought them to celestial light, they had been with him behind the black veil. Its gloom, indeed, enabled him to sympathize with all dark affections. Dying sinners cried aloud for Mr. Hooper, and would not yield their breath till he appeared; though ever, as he stooped to whisper consolation, they shuddered at the veiled face so near their own. Such were the terrors of the black veil, even when Death had bared his visage! Strangers came long distances to attend service at his church, with the mere idle purpose of gazing at his figure, because it was forbidden them to behold his face. But many were made to quake ere they departed! Once, during Governor Belcher's[1] administration, Mr. Hooper was appointed to preach the election sermon. Covered with his black veil, he stood before the chief magistrate, the council, and the representatives, and wrought so deep an impression, that the legislative measures of that year were characterized by all the gloom and piety of our earliest ancestral sway.

In this manner Mr. Hooper spent a long life, irreproachable in outward act, yet shrouded in dismal suspicions; kind and loving, though unloved, and dimly feared; a man apart from men, shunned in their health and joy, but ever summoned to their aid in mortal anguish. As years wore on, shedding their snows above his sable veil, he acquired a name throughout the New England churches, and they called him Father Hooper. Nearly all his parishioners, who were of mature age when he was settled, had been borne away by many a funeral: he had one congregation in the church, and a more crowded one in the churchyard; and having wrought so late into the evening, and done his work so well, it was now good Father Hooper's turn to rest.

Several persons were visible by the shaded candle-light, in the death chamber of the old clergyman. Natural connections he had none. But there was the decorously grave, though unmoved physician, seeking only to mitigate the last pangs of the patient whom he could not save. There were the deacons, and other eminently pious members of his church. There, also, was the Reverend Mr. Clark, of Westbury, a young and zealous divine, who had ridden in haste to pray by the

1. Jonathan Belcher was governor of Massachusetts and New Hampshire from 1730 to 1741.

bedside of the expiring minister. There was the nurse, no hired hand-maiden of death, but one whose calm affection had endured thus long in secrecy, in solitude, amid the chill of age, and would not perish, even at the dying hour. Who, but Elizabeth! And there lay the hoary head of good Father Hooper upon the death pillow, with the black veil still swathed about his brow, and reaching down over his face, so that each more difficult gasp of his faint breath caused it to stir. All through life that piece of crape had hung between him and the world: it had separated him from cheerful brotherhood and woman's love, and kept him in that saddest of all prisons, his own heart; and still it lay upon his face, as if to deepen the gloom of his darksome chamber, and shade him from the sunshine of eternity.

For some time previous, his mind had been confused, wavering doubtfully between the past and the present, and hovering forward, as it were, at intervals, into the indistinctness of the world to come. There had been feverish turns, which tossed him from side to side, and wore away what little strength he had. But in his most convulsive struggles, and in the wildest vagaries of his intellect, when no other thought retained its sober influence, he still showed an awful solicitude lest the black veil should slip aside. Even if his bewildered soul could have forgotten, there was a faithful woman at his pillow, who, with averted eyes, would have covered that aged face, which she had last beheld in the comeliness of manhood. At length the death-stricken old man lay quietly in the torpor of mental and bodily exhaustion, with an imperceptible pulse, and breath that grew fainter and fainter, except when a long, deep, and irregular inspiration seemed to prelude the flight of his spirit.

The minister of Westbury approached the bedside.

"Venerable Father Hooper," said he, "the moment of your release is at hand. Are you ready for the lifting of the veil that shuts in time from eternity?"

Father Hooper at first replied merely by a feeble motion of his head; then, apprehensive, perhaps, that his meaning might be doubtful, he exerted himself to speak.

"Yea," said he, in faint accents, "my soul hath a patient weariness until that veil be lifted."

"And is it fitting," resumed the Reverend Mr. Clark, "that a man so given to prayer, of such a blameless example, holy in deed and thought, so far as mortal judgment may pronounce; is it fitting that a father in the church should leave a shadow on his memory, that may seem to blacken a life so pure? I pray you, my venerable brother, let not this thing be! Suffer us to be gladdened by your triumphant aspect as you go to your reward. Before the veil of eternity be lifted, let me cast aside this black veil from your face!"

And thus speaking, the Reverend Mr. Clark bent forward to reveal the mystery of so many years. But, exerting a sudden energy, that made all the beholders stand aghast, Father Hooper snatched both his hands from beneath the bedclothes, and pressed them strongly on the black veil, resolute to struggle, if the minister of Westbury would contend with a dying man.

"Never!" cried the veiled clergyman. "On earth, never!"

"Dark old man!" exclaimed the affrighted minister, "with what horrible crime upon your soul are you now passing to the judgment?"

Father Hooper's breath heaved; it rattled in his throat; but, with a mighty effort, grasping forward with his hands, he caught hold of life, and held it back till he should speak. He even raised himself in bed; and there he sat, shivering with the arms of death around him, while the black veil hung down, awful, at that last moment, in the gathered terrors of a lifetime. And yet the faint, sad smile, so often there, now seemed to glimmer from its obscurity, and linger on Father Hooper's lips.

"Why do you tremble at me alone?" cried he, turning his veiled face round the circle of pale spectators. "Tremble also at each other! Have men avoided me, and women shown no pity, and children screamed and fled, only for my black veil? What, but the mystery which it obscurely typifies, has made this piece of crape so awful? When the friend shows his inmost heart to his friend; the lover to his best beloved; when man does not vainly shrink from the eye of his Creator, loathsomely treasuring up the secret of his sin; then deem me a monster, for the symbol beneath which I have lived, and die! I look around me, and lo! on every visage a Black Veil!"

While his auditors shrank from one another, in mutual affright, Father Hooper fell back upon his pillow, a veiled corpse, with a faint smile lingering on the lips. Still veiled, they laid him in his coffin, and a veiled corpse they bore him to the grave. The grass of many years has sprung up and withered on that grave, the burial stone is moss-grown, and good Mr. Hooper's face is dust; but awful is still the thought that it mouldered beneath the Black Veil!

1836, 1837

Wakefield[2]

In some old magazine or newspaper, I recollect a story, told as truth, of a man—let us call him Wakefield—who absented himself for a long time from his wife. The fact thus abstractedly stated is not very uncommon, nor—without a proper distinction of circumstances—to be condemned either as naughty or nonsensical. How-

2. "Wakefield" was first published in the *New England Magazine* for May, 1835; it was collected in *Twice-Told Tales* (1837).

beit, this, though far from the most aggravated, is perhaps the strangest instance on record of marital delinquency; and, moreover, as remarkable a freak as may be found in the whole list of human oddities. The wedded couple lived in London. The man, under pretence of going a journey, took lodgings in the next street to his own house, and there, unheard of by his wife or friends, and without the shadow of a reason for such self-banishment, dwelt upwards of twenty years. During that period, he beheld his home every day, and frequently the forlorn Mrs. Wakefield. And after so great a gap in his matrimonial felicity—when his death was reckoned certain, his estate settled, his name dismissed from memory, and his wife, long, long ago, resigned to her autumnal widowhood—he entered the door one evening, quietly, as from a day's absence, and became a loving spouse till death.

This outline is all that I remember. But the incident, though of the purest originality, unexampled, and probably never to be repeated, is one, I think, which appeals to the generous sympathies of mankind. We know, each for himself, that none of us would perpetrate such a folly, yet feel as if some other might. To my own contemplations, at least, it has often recurred, always exciting wonder, but with a sense that the story must be true and a conception of its hero's character. Whenever any subject so forcibly affects the mind, time is well spent in thinking of it. If the reader choose, let him do his own meditation; or if he prefer to ramble with me through the twenty years of Wakefield's vagary, I bid him welcome; trusting that there will be a pervading spirit and a moral, even should we fail to find them, done up neatly, and condensed into the final sentence. Thought has always its efficacy, and every striking incident its moral.

What sort of a man was Wakefield? We are free to shape out our own idea, and call it by his name. He was now in the meridian of life; his matrimonial affections, never violent, were sobered into a calm, habitual sentiment; of all husbands, he was likely to be the most constant, because a certain sluggishness would keep his heart at rest, wherever it might be placed. He was intellectual, but not actively so; his mind occupied itself in long and lazy musings, that tended to no purpose, or had not vigour to attain it; his thoughts were seldom so energetic as to seize hold of words. Imagination, in the proper meaning of the term, made no part of Wakefield's gifts. With a cold but not depraved nor wandering heart, and a mind never feverish with riotous thoughts, nor perplexed with originality, who could have anticipated that our friend would entitle himself to a foremost place among the doers of eccentric deeds? Had his acquaintances been asked, who was the man in London, the surest to perform nothing to-day which should be remembered on the morrow, they would have thought of Wakefield. Only the wife of his bosom might have hesitated. She, without having analysed his character, was partly aware of a quiet selfishness, that had rusted into his inactive mind, —of a peculiar sort of vanity, the most uneasy attribute about him, —of a disposition to craft, which had seldom produced more positive effects than the keeping of petty secrets, hardly worth revealing,— and, lastly, of what she called a little strangeness, sometimes, in the good man. This latter quality is indefinable, and perhaps nonexistent.

Let us now imagine Wakefield bidding adieu to his wife. It is the dusk of an October evening. His equipment is a drab great-coat, a hat covered with an oil-cloth, top-boots, an umbrella in one hand and a small portmanteau in the other. He has informed Mrs. Wakefield that he is to take the night coach into the country. She would fain inquire the length of his journey, its object, and the probable time of his return; but, indulgent to his harmless love of mystery, interrogates him only by a look. He tells her not to expect him positively by the return coach, not to be alarmed should he tarry three or four days; but, at all events, to look for him at supper on Friday evening. Wakefield himself, be it considered, has no suspicion of what is before him. He holds out his hand; she gives her own, and meets his parting kiss, in the matter-of-course way of a ten years' matrimony; and forth goes the middle-aged Mr. Wakefield, almost resolved to perplex his good lady by a whole week's absence. After the door has closed behind him, she perceives it thrust partly open, and a vision of her husband's face, through the aperture, smiling on her, and gone in a moment. For the time, this little incident is dismissed without a thought. But, long afterwards, when she has been more years a widow than a wife, that smile recurs, and flickers across all her reminiscences of Wakefield's visage. In her many musings, she surrounds the original smile with a multitude of fantasies, which make it strange and awful; as, for instance, if she imagines him in a coffin, that parting look is frozen on his pale features; or, if she dreams of him in heaven, still his blessed spirit wears a quiet and crafty smile. Yet, for its sake, when all others have given him up for dead, she sometimes doubts whether she is a widow.

But our business is with the husband. We must hurry after him, along the street, ere he lose his individuality, and melt into the great mass of London life. It would be vain searching for him there. Let us follow close at his heels, therefore, until, after several superfluous turns and doublings, we find him comfortably established by the fireside of a small apartment, previously bespoken. He is in the next street to his own, and at his journey's end. He can scarcely trust his good fortune in having got thither unperceived,—recollecting that, at one time, he was delayed by the throng, in the very focus of a lighted lantern; and, again, there were footsteps, that seemed to tread behind his own, distinct from the multitudinous tramp around him;

and, anon, he heard a voice shouting afar, and fancied that it called his name. Doubtless, a dozen busybodies had been watching him, and told his wife the whole affair. Poor Wakefield! Little knowest thou thine own insignificance in this great world! No mortal eye but mine has traced thee. Go quietly to thy bed, foolish man; and, on the morrow, if thou wilt be wise, get thee home to good Mrs. Wakefield, and tell her the truth. Remove not thyself, even for a little week, from thy place in her chaste bosom. Were she, for a single moment, to deem thee dead, or lost, or lastingly divided from her, thou wouldst be woefully conscious of a change in thy true wife, forever after. It is perilous to make a chasm in human affections; not that they gape so long and wide, but so quickly close again!

Almost repenting of his frolic, or whatever it may be termed, Wakefield lies down betimes, and starting from his first nap, spreads forth his arms into the wide and solitary waste of the unaccustomed bed. "No,"—thinks he, gathering the bedclothes about him,—"I will not sleep alone another night."

In the morning, he rises earlier than usual, and sets himself to consider what he really means to do. Such are his loose and rambling modes of thought that he has taken this very singular step, with the consciousness of a purpose, indeed, but without being able to define it sufficiently for his own contemplation. The vagueness of the project, and the convulsive effort with which he plunges into the execution of it, are equally characteristic of a feeble-minded man. Wakefield sifts his ideas, however, as minutely as he may, and finds himself curious to know the progress of matters at home,—how his exemplary wife will endure her widowhood of a week; and, briefly, how the little sphere of creatures and circumstances, in which he was a central object, will be affected by his removal. A morbid vanity, therefore, lies nearest the bottom of the affair. But, how is he to attain his ends? Not, certainly, by keeping close in this comfortable lodging, where, though he slept and awoke in the next street to his home, he is as effectually abroad, as if the stage-coach had been whirling him away all night. Yet, should he reappear, the whole project is knocked on the head. His poor brains being hopelessly puzzled with this dilemma, he at length ventures out, partly resolving to cross the head of the street, and send one hasty glance towards his forsaken domicile. Habit—for he is a man of habits—takes him by the hand, and guides him, wholly unaware to his own door, where, just at the critical moment, he is aroused by the scraping of his foot upon the step. Wakefield! whither are you going?

At that instant, his fate was turning on the pivot. Little dreaming of the doom to which his first backward step devotes him, he hurries away, breathless with agitation hitherto unfelt, and hardly dares turn his head, at the distant corner. Can it be that nobody caught sight of him? Will not the whole household—the decent Mrs. Wakefield, the smart maid-servant, and the dirty little footboy—raise a hue and cry, through London streets, in pursuit of their fugitive lord and master? Wonderful escape! He gathers courage to pause and look homeward, but is perplexed with a sense of change about the familiar edifice, such as affects us all, when, after a separation of months or years, we again see some hill or lake, or work of art, with which we were friends of old. In ordinary cases, this indescribable impression is caused by the comparison and contrast between our imperfect reminiscences and the reality. In Wakefield, the magic of a single night has wrought a similar transformation, because, in that brief period, a great moral change has been effected. But this is a secret from himself. Before leaving the spot, he catches a far and momentary glimpse of his wife, passing athwart the front window, with her face turned towards the head of the street. The crafty nincompoop takes to his heels, scared with the idea, that, among a thousand such atoms of mortality, her eye must have detected him. Right glad is his heart, though his brain be somewhat dizzy, when he finds himself by the coalfire of his lodgings.

So much for the commencement of this long whim-wham.[3] After the initial conception, and the stirring up of the man's sluggish temperament to put it in practice, the whole matter evolves itself in a natural train. We may suppose him, as the result of deep deliberation, buying a new wig, of reddish hair, and selecting sundry garments, in a fashion unlike his customary suit of brown, from a Jew's old-clothes bag. It is accomplished. Wakefield is another man. The new system being now established, a retrograde movement to the old would be almost as difficult as the step that placed him in his unparalleled position. Furthermore, he is rendered obstinate by a sulkiness, occasionally incident to his temper, and brought on, at present, by the inadequate sensation which he conceives to have been produced in the bosom of Mrs. Wakefield. He will not go back until she be frightened half to death. Well, twice or thrice has she passed before his sight, each time with a heavier step, a paler cheek, and more anxious brow; and in the third week of his non-appearance, he detects a portent of evil entering the house, in the guise of an apothecary. Next day, the knocker is muffled. Towards nightfall comes the chariot of a physician, and deposits its big-wigged and solemn burden at Wakefield's door, whence, after a quarter of an hour's visit, he emerges, perchance the herald of a funeral. Dear woman! Will she die? By this time, Wakefield is excited to something like energy of feeling, but still lingers away from his wife's bedside, pleading with his conscience, that she must not be disturbed at such a juncture. If aught else restrains him, he does not know it.

3. Archaic colloquialism for a whimsical eccentricity of behavior.

In the course of a few weeks, she gradually recovers; the crisis is over; her heart is sad, perhaps, but quiet; and, let him return soon or late, it will never be feverish for him again. Such ideas glimmer through the mist of Wakefield's mind, and render him indistinctly conscious that an almost impassable gulf divides his hired apartment from his former home. "It is but in the next street!" he sometimes says. Fool! it is in another world. Hitherto, he has put off his return from one particular day to another; henceforward, he leaves the precise time undetermined. Not to-morrow,—probably next week,—pretty soon. Poor man! The dead have nearly as much chance of revisiting their earthly homes, as the self-banished Wakefield.

Would that I had a folio to write, instead of an article of a dozen pages! Then might I exemplify how an influence, beyond our control, lays its strong hand on every deed which we do, and weaves its consequences into an iron tissue of necessity. Wakefield is spell-bound. We must leave him, for ten years or so, to haunt around his house, without once crossing the threshold, and to be faithful to his wife, with all the affection of which his heart is capable, while he is slowly fading out of hers. Long since, it must be remarked, he has lost the perception of singularity in his conduct.

Now for a scene! Amid the throng of a London street, we distinguish a man, now waxing elderly, with few characteristics to attract careless observers, yet bearing, in his whole aspect, the handwriting of no common fate, for such as have the skill to read it. He is meagre; his low and narrow forehead is deeply wrinkled; his eyes, small and lustreless, sometimes wander apprehensively about him, but oftener seem to look inward. He bends his head, and moves with an indescribable obliquity of gait, as if unwilling to display his full front to the world. Watch him, long enough to see what we have described, and you will allow, that circumstances—which often produce remarkable men from nature's ordinary handiwork—have produced one such here. Next, leaving him to sidle along the footwalk, cast your eyes in the opposite direction, where a portly female, considerably in the wane of life, with a prayer-book in her hand, is proceeding to yonder church. She has the placid mien of settled widowhood. Her regrets have either died away, or have become so essential to her heart, that they would be poorly exchanged for joy. Just as the lean man and well-conditioned woman are passing, a slight obstruction occurs, and brings these two figures directly in contact. Their hands touch; the pressure of the crowd forces her bosom against his shoulder; they stand, face to face, staring into each other's eyes. After a ten years' separation, thus Wakefield meets his wife!

The throng eddies away, and carries them asunder. The sober widow, resuming her former pace, proceeds to church, but pauses in the portal, and throws a perplexed glance along the street. She passes in, however, opening her prayer-book as she goes. And the man! with so wild a face, that busy and selfish London stands to gaze after him, he hurries to his lodgings, bolts the door, and throws himself upon the bed. The latent feelings of years break out; his feeble mind acquires a brief energy from their strength; all the miserable strangeness of his life is revealed to him at a glance: and he cries out, passionately, "Wakefield! Wakefield! You are mad!"

Perhaps he was so. The singularity of his situation must have so moulded him to himself, that, considered in regard to his fellow-creatures and the business of life, he could not be said to possess his right mind. He had contrived, or rather he had happened, to dissever himself from the world,—to vanish,—to give up his place and privileges with living men, without being admitted among the dead. The life of a hermit is nowise parallel to his. He was in the bustle of the city, as of old; but the crowd swept by, and saw him not; he was, we may figuratively say, always beside his wife, and at his hearth, yet must never feel the warmth of the one, nor the affection of the other. It was Wakefield's unprecedented fate, to retain his original share of human sympathies, and to be still involved in human interests, while he had lost his reciprocal influence on them. It would be a most curious speculation, to trace out the effect of such circumstances on his heart and intellect, separately, and in unison. Yet, changed as he was, he would seldom be conscious of it, but deem himself the same man as ever; glimpses of the truth, indeed, would come, but only for the moment; and still he would keep saying, "I shall soon go back!" nor reflect that he had been saying so for twenty years.

I conceive, also, that these twenty years would appear, in the retrospect, scarcely longer than the week to which Wakefield had at first limited his absence. He would look on the affair as no more than an interlude in the main business of his life. When, after a little while more, he should deem it time to re-enter his parlour, his wife would clap her hands for joy, on beholding the middle-aged Mr. Wakefield. Alas, what a mistake! Would Time but await the close of our favourite follies, we should be young men, all of us, and till Doomsday.

One evening, in the twentieth year since he vanished, Wakefield is taking his customary walk towards the dwelling which he still calls his own. It is a gusty night of autumn, with frequent showers, that patter down upon the pavement, and are gone, before a man can put up his umbrella. Pausing near the house, Wakefield discerns, through the parlour windows of the second floor, the red glow, and the glimmer and fitful flash of a comfortable fire. On the ceiling appears a grotesque shadow of good Mrs. Wakefield. The cap, the nose and chin, and the broad waist form an admirable caricature, which dances, moreover, with the up-flickering and down-sinking blaze, almost too merrily for the shade of an elderly widow. At this instant, a shower chances to fall, and is driven, by the unmannerly gust, full into Wakefield's face and bosom. He is quite penetrated with its autumnal chill. Shall he stand, wet and shivering here, when his own hearth has a good fire to warm him, and his own wife will run to fetch the gray coat and small clothes, which doubtless she has kept carefully in the closet of their bedchamber? No! Wakefield is no such fool. He ascends the steps,—heavily!—for twenty years have stiffened his legs, since he came down,—but he knows it not. Stay, Wakefield! Would you go to the sole home that is left you? Then step into your grave! The door opens. As he passes in, we have a parting glimpse of his visage, and recognize the crafty smile, which was the precursor of the little joke that he has ever since been playing off at his wife's expense. How unmercifully has he quizzed the poor woman! Well, a good night's rest to Wakefield!

This happy event—supposing it to be such—could only have occurred at an unpremeditated moment. We will not follow our friend across the threshold. He has left us much food for thought, a portion of which shall lend its wisdom to a moral, and be shaped into a figure. Amid the seeming confusion of our mysterious world, individuals are so nicely adjusted to a system, and systems to one another, and to a whole, that, by stepping aside for a moment, a man exposes himself to a fearful risk of losing his place for ever. Like Wakefield, he may become, as it were, the Outcast of the Universe.

1835, 1837

The Birthmark[4]

In the latter part of the last century there lived a man of science, an eminent proficient in every branch of natural philosophy, who not long before our story opens had made experience of a spiritual affinity more attractive than any chemical one. He had left his laboratory to the care of an assistant, cleared his fine countenance from the furnace smoke, washed the stain of acids from his fingers, and persuaded a beautiful woman to become his wife. In those days when the comparatively recent discovery of electricity and other kindred

4. Hawthorne often made the point that a strictly scientific view of life destroyed human values (cf. "Rappaccini's Daughter" and "Ethan Brand," below). In "The Birthmark" he associates intellectual arrogance with the demand for moral perfection, often reflected in a puritanical abasement of mortal life in the pursuit of an immediate heaven. Hawthorne recognized this persistent human dilemma in an early memorandum of the idea for this story (*The American Notebooks*, entries for 1837): "A person to be the death of his beloved in trying to raise her to more than mortal perfection; yet this should be a comfort to him for having aimed so highly and holily." *Cf.* the tragic and bewildered speech of Aylmer's dying wife. The story appeared in *The Pioneer* for March, 1843, and was collected in *Mosses from an Old Manse* (1846).

mysteries of Nature seemed to open paths into the region of miracle, it was not unusual for the love of science to rival the love of woman in its depth and absorbing energy. The higher intellect, the imagination, the spirit, and even the heart might all find their congenial aliment in pursuits which, as some of their ardent votaries believed, would ascend from one step of powerful intelligence to another, until the philosopher should lay his hand on the secret of creative force and perhaps make new worlds for himself. We know not whether Aylmer possessed this degree of faith in man's ultimate control over Nature. He had devoted himself, however, too unreservedly to scientific studies ever to be weaned from them by any second passion. His love for his young wife might prove the stronger of the two; but it could only be by intertwining itself with his love of science, and uniting the strength of the latter to his own.

Such a union accordingly took place, and was attended with truly remarkable consequences and a deeply impressive moral. One day, very soon after their marriage, Aylmer sat gazing at his wife with a trouble in his countenance that grew stronger until he spoke.

"Georgiana," said he, "has it never occurred to you that the mark upon your cheek might be removed?"

"No, indeed," said she, smiling; but perceiving the seriousness of his manner, she blushed deeply. "To tell you the truth it has been so often called a charm that I was simple enough to imagine it might be so."

"Ah, upon another face perhaps it might," replied her husband; "but never on yours. No, dearest Georgiana, you came so nearly perfect from the hand of Nature that this slightest possible defect, which we hesitate whether to term a defect or a beauty, shocks me, as being the visible mark of earthly imperfection."

"Shocks you, my husband!" cried Georgiana, deeply hurt; at first reddening with momentary anger, but then bursting into tears. "Then why did you take me from my mother's side? You cannot love what shocks you!"

To explain this conversation it must be mentioned that in the centre of Georgiana's left cheek there was a singular mark, deeply interwoven, as it were, with the texture and substance of her face. In the usual state of her complexion—a healthy though delicate bloom—the mark wore a tint of deeper crimson, which imperfectly defined its shape amid the surrounding rosiness. When she blushed it gradually became more indistinct, and finally vanished amid the triumphant rush of blood that bathed the whole cheek with its brilliant glow. But if any shifting motion caused her to turn pale there was the mark again, a crimson stain upon the snow, in what Aylmer sometimes deemed an almost fearful distinctness. Its shape bore not a little similarity to the human hand, though of the smallest pygmy size. Georgiana's lovers were wont to say that some fairy at her birth hour had laid her tiny hand upon the infant's cheek, and left this impress there in token of the magic endowments that were to give her such sway over all hearts. Many a desperate swain would have risked life for the privilege of pressing his lips to the mysterious hand. It must not be concealed, however, that the impression wrought by this fairy sign manual varied exceedingly, according to the difference of temperament in the beholders. Some fastidious persons—but they were exclusively of her own sex—affirmed that the bloody hand, as they chose to call it, quite destroyed the effect of Georgiana's beauty, and rendered her countenance even hideous. But it would be as reasonable to say that one of those small blue stains which sometimes occur in the purest statuary marble would convert the Eve of Powers[5] to a monster. Masculine observers, if the birthmark did not heighten their admiration, contented themselves with wishing it away, that the world might possess one living specimen of ideal loveliness without the semblance of a flaw. After his marriage,—for he thought little or nothing about the matter before,—Aylmer discovered that this was the case with himself.

Had she been less beautiful,—if Envy's self could have found aught else to sneer at,—he might have felt his affection heightened by the prettiness of this mimic hand, now vaguely portrayed, now lost, now stealing forth again and glimmering to and fro with every pulse of emotion that throbbed within her heart; but seeing her otherwise so perfect, he found this one defect grow more and more intolerable with every moment of their united lives. It was the fatal flaw of humanity which Nature, in one shape or another, stamps ineffaceably on all her productions, either to imply that they are temporary and finite, or that their perfection must be wrought by toil and pain. The crimson hand expressed the ineludible gripe in which mortality clutches the highest and purest of earthly mold, degrading them into kindred with the lowest, and even with the very brutes, like whom their visible frames return to dust. In this manner, selecting it as the symbol of his wife's liability to sin, sorrow, decay, and death, Aylmer's sombre imagination was not long in rendering the birthmark a frightful object, causing him more trouble and horror than ever Georgiana's beauty, whether of soul or sense, had given him delight.

At all the seasons which should have been their happiest, he invariably and without intending it, nay, in spite of a purpose to the contrary, reverted to this one disastrous topic. Trifling as it at first appeared, it so connected itself with innumerable trains of thought and modes of feeling that it became the central point of all. With the morning twilight Aylmer opened his eyes upon his wife's face

5. Hiram Powers (1805–1873), American sculptor, whose studio in Florence became a center for the expatriate American art colony. Hawthorne refers to his masterpiece, "Eve Before the Fall."

and recognized the symbol of imperfection; and when they sat together at the evening hearth his eyes wandered stealthily to her cheek, and beheld, flickering with the blaze of the wood fire, the spectral hand that wrote mortality where he would fain have worshipped. Georgiana soon learned to shudder at his gaze. It needed but a glance with the peculiar expression that his face often wore to change the roses of her cheek into a deathlike paleness, amid which the crimson hand was brought strongly out, like a bas-relief of ruby on the whitest marble.

Late one night when the lights were growing dim, so as hardly to betray the stain on the poor wife's cheek, she herself, for the first time, voluntarily took up the subject.

"Do you remember, my dear Aylmer," said she, with a feeble attempt at a smile, "have you any recollection of a dream last night about this odious hand?"

"None! none whatever!" replied Aylmer, starting; but then he added, in a dry, cold tone, affected for the sake of concealing the real depth of his emotion, "I might well dream of it; for before I fell asleep it had taken a pretty firm hold of my fancy."

"And you did dream of it?" continued Georgiana, hastily; for she dreaded lest a gush of tears should interrupt what she had to say. "A terrible dream! I wonder that you can forget it. Is it possible to forget this one expression?—'It is in her heart now; we must have it out!' Reflect, my husband; for by all means I would have you recall that dream."

The mind is in a sad state when Sleep, the all-involving, cannot confine her spectres within the dim region of her sway, but suffers them to break forth, affrighting this actual life with secrets that perchance belong to a deeper one. Aylmer now remembered his dream. He had fancied himself with his servant Aminadab, attempting an operation for the removal of the birthmark; but the deeper went the knife, the deeper sank the hand, until at length its tiny grasp appeared to have caught hold of Georgiana's heart; whence, however, her husband was inexorably resolved to cut or wrench it away.

When the dream had shaped itself perfectly in his memory, Aylmer sat in his wife's presence with a guilty feeling. Truth often finds its way to the mind close muffled in robes of sleep, and then speaks with uncompromising directness of matters in regard to which we practise an unconscious self-deception during our waking moments. Until now he had not been aware of the tyrannizing influence acquired by one idea over his mind, and of the lengths which he might find in his heart to go for the sake of giving himself peace.

"Aylmer," resumed Georgiana, solemnly, "I know not what may be the cost to both of us to rid me of this fatal birthmark. Perhaps its removal may cause cureless deformity; or it may be the stain goes as deep as life itself. Again: do we know that there is a possibility, on any terms, of unclasping the firm gripe of this little hand which was laid upon me before I came into the world?"

"Dearest Georgiana, I have spent much thought upon the subject," hastily interrupted Aylmer. "I am convinced of the perfect practicability of its removal."

"If there be the remotest possibility of it," continued Georgiana, "let the attempt be made at whatever risk. Danger is nothing to me; for life, while this hateful mark makes me the object of your horror and disgust,—life is a burden which I would fling down with joy. Either remove this dreadful hand, or take my wretched life! You have deep science. All the world bears witness of it. You have achieved great wonders. Cannot you remove this little, little mark, which I cover with the tips of two small fingers? Is this beyond your power, for the sake of your own peace, and to save your poor wife from madness?"

"Noblest, dearest, tenderest wife," cried Aylmer, rapturously, "doubt not my power. I have already given this matter the deepest thought—thought which might almost have enlightened me to create a being less perfect than yourself. Georgiana, you have led me deeper than ever into the heart of science. I feel myself fully competent to render this dear cheek as faultless as its fellow; and then, most beloved, what will be my triumph when I shall have corrected what Nature left imperfect in her fairest work! Even Pygmalion,[6] when his sculptured woman assumed life, felt not greater ecstasy than mine will be."

"It is resolved, then," said Georgiana, faintly smiling. "And, Aylmer, spare me not, though you should find the birthmark take refuge in my heart at last."

Her husband tenderly kissed her cheek—her right cheek—not that which bore the impress of the crimson hand.

The next day Aylmer apprised his wife of a plan that he had formed whereby he might have opportunity for the intense thought and constant watchfulness which the proposed operation would require; while Georgiana, likewise, would enjoy the perfect repose essential to its success. They were to seclude themselves in the extensive apartments occupied by Aylmer as a laboratory, and where, during his toilsome youth, he had made discoveries in the elemental powers of Nature that had roused the admiration of all the learned societies in Europe. Seated calmly in this laboratory, the pale philosopher had investigated the secrets of the highest cloud region and of the profoundest mines; he had satisfied himself of the causes that kindled and kept alive the fires of the volcano; and had explained the

6. *Cf.* the Greek legend of Pygmalion and Galatea, in which this transformation was permitted by Aphrodite, the goddess of love.

mystery of fountains, and how it is that they gush forth, some so bright and pure, and others with such rich medicinal virtues, from the dark bosom of the earth. Here, too, at an earlier period, he had studied the wonders of the human frame, and attempted to fathom the very process by which Nature assimilates all her precious influences from earth and air, and from the spiritual world, to create and foster man, her masterpiece. The latter pursuit, however, Aylmer had long laid aside in unwilling recognition of the truth—against which all seekers sooner or later stumble—that our great creative Mother, while she amuses us with apparently working in the broadest sunshine, is yet severely careful to keep her own secrets, and, in spite of her pretended openness, shows us nothing but results. She permits us, indeed, to mar, but seldom to mend, and, like a jealous patentee, on no account to make. Now, however, Aylmer resumed these half-forgotten investigations; not, of course, with such hopes or wishes as first suggested them; but because they involved much physiological truth and lay in the path of his proposed scheme for the treatment of Georgiana.

As he led her over the threshold of the laboratory, Georgiana was cold and tremulous. Aylmer looked cheerfully into her face, with intent to reassure her, but was so startled with the intense glow of the birthmark upon the whiteness of her cheek that he could not restrain a strong convulsive shudder. His wife fainted.

"Aminadab! Aminadab!" shouted Aylmer, stamping violently on the floor.

Forthwith there issued from an inner apartment a man of low stature, but bulky frame, with shaggy hair hanging about his visage, which was grimed with the vapors of the furnace. This personage had been Aylmer's underworker during his whole scientific career, and was admirably fitted for that office by his great mechanical readiness, and the skill with which, while incapable of comprehending a single principle, he executed all the details of his master's experiments. With his vast strength, his shaggy hair, his smoky aspect, and the indescribable earthiness that incrusted him, he seemed to represent man's physical nature; while Aylmer's slender figure, and pale, intellectual face, were no less apt a type of the spiritual element.

"Throw open the door of the boudoir, Aminadab," said Aylmer, "and burn a pastil."

"Yes, master," answered Aminadab, looking intently at the lifeless form of Georgiana; and then he muttered to himself, "If she were my wife, I'd never part with that birthmark."

When Georgiana recovered consciousness she found herself breathing an atmosphere of penetrating fragrance, the gentle potency of which had recalled her from her deathlike faintness. The scene around her looked like enchantment. Aylmer had converted those smoky, dingy, sombre rooms, where he had spent his brightest years in recondite pursuits, into a series of beautiful apartments not unfit to be the secluded abode of a lovely woman. The walls were hung with gorgeous curtains, which imparted the combination of grandeur and grace that no other species of adornment can achieve; and as they fell from the ceiling to the floor, their rich and ponderous folds, concealing all angles and straight lines, appeared to shut in the scene from infinite space. For aught Georgiana knew, it might be a pavilion among the clouds. And Aylmer, excluding the sunshine, which would have interfered with his chemical processes, had supplied its place with perfumed lamps, emitting flames of various hue, but all uniting in a soft, impurpled radiance. He now knelt by his wife's side, watching her earnestly, but without alarm; for he was confident in his science, and felt that he could draw a magic circle round her within which no evil might intrude.

"Where am I? Ah, I remember," said Georgiana, faintly; and she placed her hand over her cheek to hide the terrible mark from her husband's eyes.

"Fear not, dearest!" exclaimed he. "Do not shrink from me! Believe me, Georgiana, I even rejoice in this single imperfection, since it will be such a rapture to remove it."

"Oh, spare me!" sadly replied his wife. "Pray do not look at it again. I never can forget that convulsive shudder."

In order to soothe Georgiana, and, as it were, to release her mind from the burden of actual things, Aylmer now put in practice some of the light and playful secrets which science had taught him among its profounder lore. Airy figures, absolutely bodiless ideas, and forms of unsubstantial beauty came and danced before her, imprinting their momentary footsteps on beams of light. Though she had some indistinct idea of the method of these optical phenomena, still the illusion was almost perfect enough to warrant the belief that her husband possessed sway over the spiritual world. Then again, when she felt a wish to look forth from her seclusion, immediately, as if her thoughts were answered, the procession of external existence flitted across a screen. The scenery and the figures of actual life were perfectly represented, but with that bewitching, yet indescribable difference which always makes a picture, an image, or a shadow so much more attractive than the original. When wearied of this, Aylmer bade her cast her eyes upon a vessel containing a quantity of earth. She did so, with little interest at first; but was soon startled to perceive the germ of a plant shooting upward from the soil. Then came the slender stalk; the leaves gradually unfolded themselves; and amid them was a perfect and lovely flower.

"It is magical!" cried Georgiana. "I dare not touch it."

"Nay, pluck it," answered Aylmer,—"pluck it, and inhale its brief perfume while you may. The flower will wither in a few moments and leave nothing save its brown seed vessels; but thence may be perpetuated a race as ephemeral as itself."

But Georgiana had no sooner touched the flower than the whole plant suffered a blight, its leaves turning coal-black as if by the agency of fire.

"There was too powerful a stimulus," said Aylmer, thoughtfully.

To make up for this abortive experiment, he proposed to take her portrait by a scientific process of his own invention. It was to be effected by rays of light striking upon a polished plate of metal. Georgiana assented; but, on looking at the result, was affrighted to find the features of the portrait blurred and indefinable; while the minute figure of a hand appeared where the cheek should have been. Aylmer snatched the metallic plate and threw it into a jar of corrosive acid.

Soon, however, he forgot these mortifying failures. In the intervals of study and chemical experiment he came to her flushed and exhausted, but seemed invigorated by her presence, and spoke in glowing language of the resources of his art. He gave a history of the long dynasty of the alchemists, who spent so many ages in quest of the universal solvent by which the golden principle might be elicited from all things vile and base. Aylmer appeared to believe that, by the plainest scientific logic, it was altogether within the limits of possibility to discover this long-sought medium; "but," he added, "a philosopher who should go deep enough to acquire the power would attain too lofty a wisdom to stoop to the exercise of it." Not less singular were his opinions in regard to the elixir vitæ.[7] He more than intimated that it was at his option to concoct a liquid that should prolong life for years, perhaps interminably; but that it would produce a discord in Nature which all the world, and chiefly the quaffer of the immortal nostrum, would find cause to curse.

"Aylmer, are you in earnest?" asked Georgiana, looking at him with amazement and fear. "It is terrible to possess such power, or even to dream of possessing it."

"Oh, do not tremble, my love," said her husband. "I would not wrong either you or myself by working such inharmonious effects upon our lives; but I would have you consider how trifling, in comparison, is the skill requisite to remove this little hand."

At the mention of the birthmark, Georgiana, as usual, shrank as if a redhot iron had touched her cheek.

Again Aylmer applied himself to his labors. She could hear his voice in the distant furnace room giving directions to Aminadab, whose harsh, uncouth, misshapen tones were audible in response, more like the grunt or growl of a brute than human speech. After

7. The elixir of life, whose function Hawthorne describes. The other "solvent" sought by the alchemists, for transmuting base substances into gold, is more usually referred to as "the philosopher's stone."

hours of absence, Aylmer reappeared and proposed that she should now examine his cabinet of chemical products and natural treasures of the earth. Among the former he showed her a small vial, in which, he remarked, was contained a gentle yet most powerful fragrance, capable of impregnating all the breezes that blow across the kingdom. They were of inestimable value, the contents of that little vial; and, as he said so, he threw some of the perfume into the air and filled the room with piercing and invigorating delight.

"And what is this?" asked Georgiana, pointing to a small crystal globe containing a gold-colored liquid. "It is so beautiful to the eye that I could imagine it the elixir of life."

"In one sense it is," replied Aylmer; "or, rather, the elixir of immortality. It is the most precious poison that ever was concocted in this world. By its aid I could apportion the lifetime of any mortal at whom you might point your finger. The strength of the dose would determine whether he were to linger out years, or drop dead in the midst of a breath. No king on his guarded throne could keep his life if I, in my private station, should deem that the welfare of millions justified me in depriving him of it."

"Why do you keep such a terrific drug?" inquired Georgiana in horror.

"Do not mistrust me, dearest," said her husband, smiling; "its virtuous potency is yet greater than its harmful one. But see! here is a powerful cosmetic. With a few drops of this in a vase of water, freckles may be washed away as easily as the hands are cleansed. A stronger infusion would take the blood out of the cheek, and leave the rosiest beauty a pale ghost."

"Is it with this lotion that you intend to bathe my cheek?" asked Georgiana, anxiously.

"Oh, no," hastily replied her husband; "this is merely superficial. Your case demands a remedy that shall go deeper."

In his interviews with Georgiana, Aylmer generally made minute inquiries as to her sensations and whether the confinement of the rooms and the temperature of the atmosphere agreed with her. These questions had such a particular drift that Georgiana began to conjecture that she was already subjected to certain physical influences, either breathed in with the fragrant air or taken with her food. She fancied likewise, but it might be altogether fancy, that there was a stirring up of her system—a strange, indefinite sensation creeping through her veins, and tingling, half painfully, half pleasurably, at her heart. Still, whenever she dared to look into the mirror, there she beheld herself pale as a white rose and with the crimson birthmark stamped upon her cheek. Not even Aylmer now hated it so much as she.

To dispel the tedium of the hours which her husband found it necessary to devote to the processes of combination and analysis, Georgiana turned over the volumes of his scientific library. In many dark old tomes she met with chapters full of romance and poetry. They were the works of the philosophers of the middle ages, such as Albertus Magnus, Cornelius Agrippa, Paracelsus, and the famous friar who created the prophetic Brazen Head.[8] All these antique naturalists stood in advance of their centuries, yet were imbued with some of their credulity, and therefore were believed, and perhaps imagined themselves to have acquired from the investigation of Nature a power above Nature, and from physics a sway over the spiritual world. Hardly less curious and imaginative were the early volumes of the Transactions of the Royal Society, in which the members, knowing little of the limits of natural possibility, were continually recording wonders or proposing methods whereby wonders might be wrought.

But to Georgiana the most engrossing volume was a large folio from her husband's own hand, in which he had recorded every experiment of his scientific career, its original aim, the methods adopted for its development, and its final success or failure, with the circumstances to which either event was attributable. The book, in truth, was both the history and emblem of his ardent, ambitious, imaginative, yet practical and laborious life. He handled physical details as if there were nothing beyond them; yet spiritualized them all, and redeemed himself from materialism by his strong and eager aspiration towards the infinite. In his grasp the veriest clod of earth assumed a soul. Georgiana, as she read, reverenced Aylmer and loved him more profoundly than ever, but with a less entire dependence on his judgment than heretofore. Much as he had accomplished, she could not but observe that his most splendid successes were almost invariably failures, if compared with the ideal at which he aimed. His brightest diamonds were the merest pebbles, and felt to be so by himself, in comparison with the inestimable gems which lay hidden beyond his reach. The volume, rich with achievements that had won renown for its author, was yet as melancholy a record as ever mortal hand had penned. It was the sad confession and continual exemplification of the shortcomings of the composite man, the spirit burdened with clay and working in matter, and of the despair that assails the higher nature at finding itself so miserably thwarted by the earthly part. Perhaps every man of genius in whatever sphere might recognize the

---

8. These important pioneers of science were all popularly regarded as "magicians": St. Albertus Magnus (died 1280), German theologian; Cornelius Agrippa (died 1535), German theologian, whose scientific contributions verged on the occult, as did those of Paracelsus (died 1541), a Swiss scientist whose theory of disease advanced modern medicine. The "famous friar" was Roger Bacon (died 1294), English Franciscan scholar, early pioneer of modern inductive science, to whom were popularly attributed occult writings and magical devices such as the apocryphal "Brazen Head" here mentioned.

image of his own experience in Aylmer's journal.

So deeply did these reflections affect Georgiana that she laid her face upon the open volume and burst into tears. In this situation she was found by her husband.

"It is dangerous to read in a sorcerer's books," said he with a smile, though his countenance was uneasy and displeased. "Georgiana, there are pages in that volume which I can scarcely glance over and keep my senses. Take heed lest it prove as detrimental to you."

"It has made me worship you more than ever," said she.

"Ah, wait for this one success," rejoined he, "then worship me if you will. I shall deem myself hardly unworthy of it. But come, I have sought you for the luxury of your voice. Sing to me, dearest."

So she poured out the liquid music of her voice to quench the thirst of his spirit. He then took his leave with a boyish exuberance of gaiety, assuring her that her seclusion would endure but a little longer, and that the result was already certain. Scarcely had he departed when Georgiana felt irresistibly impelled to follow him. She had forgotten to inform Aylmer of a symptom which for two or three hours past had begun to excite her attention. It was a sensation in the fatal birthmark, not painful, but which induced a restlessness throughout her system. Hastening after her husband, she intruded for the first time into the laboratory.

The first thing that struck her eye was the furnace, that hot and feverish worker, with the intense glow of its fire, which by the quantities of soot clustered above it seemed to have been burning for ages. There was a distilling apparatus in full operation. Around the room were retorts, tubes, cylinders, crucibles, and other apparatus of chemical research. An electrical machine stood ready for immediate use. The atmosphere felt oppressively close; and was tainted with gaseous odors which had been tormented forth by the processes of science. The severe and homely simplicity of the apartment with its naked walls and brick pavement, looked strange, accustomed as Georgiana had become to the fantastic elegance of her boudoir. But what chiefly, indeed almost solely, drew her attention, was the aspect of Aylmer himself.

He was pale as death, anxious and absorbed, and hung over the furnace as if it depended upon his utmost watchfulness whether the liquid which it was distilling should be the draught of immortal happiness or misery. How different from the sanguine and joyous mien that he had assumed for Georgiana's encouragement!

"Carefully now, Aminadab; carefully, thou human machine; carefully, thou man of clay!" muttered Aylmer, more to himself than his assistant. "Now, if there be a thought too much or too little, it is all over."

"Ho! ho!" mumbled Aminadab. "Look, master! look!"

Aylmer raised his eyes hastily, and at first reddened, then grew paler than ever, on beholding Georgiana. He rushed towards her and seized her arm with a gripe that left the print of his fingers upon it.

"Why do you come hither? Have you no trust in your husband?" cried he, impetuously. "Would you throw the blight of that fatal birthmark over my labors? It is not well done. Go, prying woman, go!"

"Nay, Aylmer," said Georgiana with the firmness of which she possessed no stinted endowment, "it is not you that have a right to complain. You mistrust your wife; you have concealed the anxiety with which you watch the development of this experiment. Think not so unworthily of me, my husband. Tell me all the risk we run, and fear not that I shall shrink; for my share in it is far less than your own."

"No, no, Georgiana!" said Aylmer, impatiently; "it must not be."

"I submit," replied she calmly. "And, Aylmer, I shall quaff whatever draught you bring me; but it will be on the same principle that would induce me to take a dose of poison if offered by your hand."

"My noble wife," said Aylmer, deeply moved; "I knew not the height and depth of your nature until now. Nothing shall be concealed. Know, then, that this crimson hand, superficial as it seems, has clutched its grasp into your being with a strength of which I had no previous conception.[9] I have already administered agents powerful enough to do aught except to change your entire physical system. Only one thing remains to be tried. If that fail us we are ruined."

"Why did you hesitate to tell me this?" asked she.

"Because, Georgiana," said Aylmer, in a low voice, "there is danger."

"Danger? There is but one danger—that this horrible stigma shall be left upon my cheek!" cried Georgiana. "Remove it, remove it, whatever be the cost, or we shall both go mad!"

"Heaven knows your words are too true," said Aylmer, sadly. "And now, dearest, return to your boudoir. In a little while all will be tested."

He conducted her back and took leave of her with a solemn tenderness which spoke far more than his words how much was now at stake. After his departure Georgiana became rapt in musings. She considered the character of Aylmer, and did it completer justice than at any previous moment. Her heart exulted, while it trembled, at his honorable love—so pure and lofty that it would accept nothing less than perfection nor miserably make itself contented with an earthlier nature than he had dreamed of. She felt how much more precious was such a sentiment than that meaner kind which would have

9. In ancient superstition, the shape of the stigma often suggested hidden po-   tentialities or experience, good or bad, in the person so marked.

borne with the imperfection for her sake, and have been guilty of treason to holy love by degrading its perfect idea to the level of the actual; and with her whole spirit she prayed that, for a single moment, she might satisfy his highest and deepest conception. Longer than one moment she well knew it could not be; for his spirit was ever on the march, ever ascending, and each instant required something that was beyond the scope of the instant before.

The sound of her husband's footsteps aroused her. He bore a crystal goblet containing a liquor colorless as water, but bright enough to be the draught of immortality. Aylmer was pale; but it seemed rather the consequence of a highly-wrought state of mind and tension of spirit than of fear or doubt.

"The concoction of the draught has been perfect," said he, in answer to Georgiana's look. "Unless all my science have deceived me, it cannot fail."

"Save on your account, my dearest Aylmer," observed his wife, "I might wish to put off this birthmark of mortality by relinquishing mortality itself in preference to any other mode. Life is but a sad possession to those who have attained precisely the degree of moral advancement at which I stand. Were I weaker and blinder it might be happiness. Were I stronger, it might be endured hopefully. But, being what I find myself, me thinks I am of all mortals the most fit to die."

"You are fit for heaven without tasting death!" replied her husband. "But why do we speak of dying? The draught cannot fail. Behold its effect upon this plant."

On the window seat there stood a geranium diseased with yellow blotches, which had overspread all its leaves. Aylmer poured a small quantity of the liquid upon the soil in which it grew. In a little time, when the roots of the plant had taken up the moisture, the unsightly blotches began to be extinguished in a living verdure.

"There needed no proof," said Georgiana, quietly. "Give me the goblet. I joyfully stake all upon your word."

"Drink, then, thou lofty creature!" exclaimed Aylmer, with fervid admiration. "There is no taint of imperfection on thy spirit. Thy sensible frame, too, shall soon be all perfect."

She quaffed the liquid and returned the goblet to his hand.

"It is grateful," said she with a placid smile. "Methinks it is like water from a heavenly fountain; for it contains I know not what of unobtrusive fragrance and deliciousness. It allays a feverish thirst that had parched me for many days. Now, dearest, let me sleep. My earthly senses are closing over my spirit like the leaves around the heart of a rose at sunset."

She spoke the last words with a gentle reluctance, as if it required almost more energy than she could command to pronounce the faint and lingering syllables. Scarcely had they loitered through her lips ere she was lost in slumber. Aylmer sat by her side, watching her aspect with the emotions proper to a man the whole value of whose existence was involved in the process now to be tested. Mingled with this mood, however, was the philosophic investigation characteristic of the man of science. Not the minutest symptom escaped him. A heightened flush of the cheek, a slight irregularity of breath, a quiver of the eyelid, a hardly perceptible tremor through the frame, —such were the details which, as the moments passed, he wrote down in his folio volume. Intense thought had set its stamp upon every previous page of that volume, but the thoughts of years were all concentrated upon the last.

While thus employed, he failed not to gaze often at the fatal hand, and not without a shudder. Yet once, by a strange and unaccountable impulse, he pressed it with his lips. His spirit recoiled, however, in the very act; and Georgiana, out of the midst of her deep sleep, moved uneasily and murmured as if in remonstrance. Again Aylmer resumed his watch. Nor was it without avail. The crimson hand, which at first had been strongly visible upon the marble paleness of Georgiana's cheek, now grew more faintly outlined. She remained not less pale than ever; but the birthmark, with every breath that came and went, lost somewhat of its former distinctness. Its presence had been awful; its departure was more awful still. Watch the stain of the rainbow fading out of the sky, and you will know how that mysterious symbol passed away.

"By Heaven! it is well-nigh gone!" said Aylmer to himself, in almost irrepressible ecstasy. "I can scarcely trace it now. Success! success! And now it is like the faintest rose color. The lightest flush of blood across her cheek would overcome it. But she is so pale!"

He drew aside the window curtain and suffered the light of natural day to fall into the room and rest upon her cheek. At the same time he heard a gross, hoarse chuckle, which he had long known as his servant Aminadab's expression of delight.

"Ah, clod! ah, earthly mass!" cried Aylmer, laughing a sort of frenzy, "you have served me well! Matter and spirit—earth and heaven—have both done their part in this! Laugh, thing of the senses! You have earned the right to laugh."

These exclamations broke Georgiana's sleep. She slowly unclosed her eyes and gazed into the mirror which her husband had arranged for that purpose. A faint smile flitted over her lips when she recognized how barely perceptible was now that crimson hand which had once blazed forth with such disastrous brilliancy as to scare away all their happiness. But then her eyes sought Aylmer's face with a trouble and anxiety that he could by no means account for.

"My poor Aylmer!" murmured she.

"Poor? Nay, richest, happiest, most favored!" exclaimed he. "My peerless bride, it is successful! You are perfect!"

"My poor Aylmer," she repeated, with a more than human tenderness, "you have aimed loftily; you have done nobly. Do not repent that with so high and pure a feeling, you have rejected the best the earth could offer. Aylmer, dearest Aylmer, I am dying!"

Alas! it was too true! The fatal hand had grappled with the mystery of life, and was the bond by which an angelic spirit kept itself in union with a mortal frame. As the last crimson tint of the birthmark—that sole token of human imperfection—faded from her cheek, the parting breath of the now perfect woman passed into the atmosphere, and her soul, lingering a moment near her husband, took its heavenward flight. Then a hoarse, chuckling laugh was heard again! Thus ever does the gross fatality of earth exult in its invariable triumph over the immortal essence which, in this dim sphere of half development, demands the completeness of a higher state. Yet, had Aylmer reached a profounder wisdom, he need not thus have flung away the happiness which would have woven his mortal life of the selfsame texture with the celestial. The momentary circumstance was too strong for him; he failed to look beyond the shadowy scope of time, and living once for all in eternity, to find the perfect future in the present.

1843, 1846

Rappaccini's Daughter[1]

A young man, named Giovanni Guasconti, came, very long ago, from the more southern region of Italy, to pursue his studies at the University of Padua. Giovanni, who had but a scanty supply of gold ducats in his pocket, took lodgings in a high and gloomy chamber of an old edifice which looked not unworthy to have been the palace of a Paduan noble, and which, in fact, exhibited over its entrance the armorial bearings of a family long since extinct. The young stranger, who was not unstudied in the great poem of his country,

1. It may be part of the perennial charm of this allegorical tale that there has been no general agreement as to its interpretation. In "Rappaccini's Daughter," the symbols and elements are complex, and seem at first to be contradictory. One notes the theme of intellectual arrogance again, in the figures of Rappaccini and Baglioni, reminiscent of such stories as "The Birthmark" and "Ethan Brand." As the consequence of Rappaccini's arrogance, there is the "awful doom" of Beatrice—she is isolated from her kind, as were Young Goodman Brown, Parson Hooper, and Wakefield, for their various mistakes. At the same time, one notes in the love story of Giovanni and Beatrice that Giovanni first saw the garden as an "Eden of poisonous flowers," replete with its "Adam," its particular "tree" (Beatrice's), and its reptile. Thus it forms an association with Hawthorne's attack on the puritanical concept of original depravity in *The Scarlet Letter*. "Rappaccini's Daughter" was first published in the *Democratic Review* for December, 1844, and was collected in *Mosses from an Old Manse* (1846).

recollected that one of the ancestors of this family, and perhaps an occupant of this very mansion, had been pictured by Dante as a partaker of the immortal agonies of his Inferno. These reminiscences and associations, together with the tendency to heartbreak natural to a young man for the first time out of his native sphere, caused Giovanni to sigh heavily as he looked around the desolate and ill-furnished apartment.

"Holy Virgin, signor!" cried old Dame Lisabetta, who, won by the youth's remarkable beauty of person, was kindly endeavoring to give the chamber a habitable air, "what a sigh was that to come out of a young man's heart! Do you find this old mansion gloomy? For the love of Heaven, then, put your head out of the window, and you will see as bright sunshine as you have left in Naples."

Guasconti mechanically did as the old woman advised, but could not quite agree with her that the Paduan sunshine was as cheerful as that of southern Italy. Such as it was, however, it fell upon a garden beneath the window and expended its fostering influences on a variety of plants, which seemed to have been cultivated with exceeding care.

"Does this garden belong to the house?" asked Giovanni.

"Heaven forbid, signor, unless it were fruitful of better pot herbs than any that grow there now," answered old Lisabetta. "No; that garden is cultivated by the own hands of Signor Giacomo Rappaccini, the famous doctor, who, I warrant him, has been heard of as far as Naples. It is said that he distils these plants into medicines that are as potent as a charm. Oftentimes you may see the signor doctor at work, and perchance the signora, his daughter, too, gathering the strange flowers that grow in the garden."

The old woman had now done what she could for the aspect of the chamber; and, commending the young man to the protection of the saints, took her departure.

Giovanni still found no better occupation than to look down into the garden beneath his window. From its appearance, he judged it to be one of those botanic gardens which were of earlier date in Padua than elsewhere in Italy or in the world. Or, not improbably, it might once have been the pleasure-place of an opulent family; for there was the ruin of a marble fountain, in the centre, sculptured with rare art, but so wofully shattered that it was impossible to trace the original design from the chaos of remaining fragments. The water, however, continued to gush and sparkle into the sunbeams as cheerfully as ever. A little gurgling sound ascended to the young man's window, and made him feel as if the fountain were an immortal spirit that sung its song unceasingly and without heeding the vicissitudes around it, while one century imbodied it in marble and another scattered the perishable garniture on the soil. All about the pool into which the water subsided grew various plants, that seemed to require a plentiful supply of moisture for the nourishment of gigantic leaves, and, in some instances, flowers gorgeously magnificent. There was one shrub in particular, set in a marble vase in the midst of the pool, that bore a profusion of purple blossoms, each of which had the lustre and richness of a gem; and the whole together made a show so resplendent that it seemed enough to illuminate the garden, even had there been no sunshine. Every portion of the soil was peopled with plants and herbs, which, if less beautiful, still bore tokens of assiduous care, as if all had their individual virtues, known to the scientific mind that fostered them. Some were placed in urns, rich with old carving, and others in common garden pots; some crept serpent-like along the ground or climbed on high, using whatever means of ascent was offered them. One plant had wreathed itself round a statue of Vertumnus,[2] which was thus quite veiled and shrouded in a drapery of hanging foliage, so happily arranged that it might have served a sculptor for a study.

While Giovanni stood at the window he heard a rustling behind a screen of leaves, and became aware that a person was at work in the garden. His figure soon emerged into view, and showed itself to be that of no common laborer, but a tall, emaciated, sallow, and sickly-looking man, dressed in a scholar's garb of black. He was beyond the middle term of life, with gray hair, a thin, gray beard, and a face singularly marked with intellect and cultivation, but which could never, even in his more youthful days, have expressed much warmth of heart.

Nothing could exceed the intentness with which this scientific gardener examined every shrub which grew in his path: it seemed as if he was looking into their inmost nature, making observations in regard to their creative essence, and discovering why one leaf grew in this shape and another in that, and wherefore such and such flowers differed among themselves in hue and perfume. Nevertheless, in spite of this deep intelligence on his part, there was no approach to intimacy between himself and these vegetable existences. On the contrary, he avoided their actual touch or the direct inhaling of their odors with a caution that impressed Giovanni most disagreeably; for the man's demeanor was that of one walking among malignant influences, such as savage beasts, or deadly snakes, or evil spirits, which, should he allow them one moment of license, would wreak upon him some terrible fatality. It was strangely frightful to the young man's imagination to see this air of insecurity in a person cultivating a garden, that most simple and innocent of human toils, and which had been alike the joy and labor of the unfallen parents of the race. Was this garden, then, the Eden of the present world?

2. Roman deity of the gardens and orchards, who presided over the change of seasons.

And this man, with such a perception of harm in what his own hands caused to grow,—was he the Adam?

The distrustful gardener, while plucking away the dead leaves or pruning the too luxuriant growth of the shrubs, defended his hands with a pair of thick gloves. Nor were these his only armor. When, in his walk through the garden, he came to the magnificent plant that hung its purple gems beside the marble fountain, he placed a kind of mask over his mouth and nostrils, as if all this beauty did but conceal a deadlier malice; but, finding his task still too dangerous, he drew back, removed the mask, and called loudly, but in the infirm voice of a person affected with inward disease,—

"Beatrice! Beatrice!"

"Here am I, my father. What would you?" cried a rich and youthful voice from the window of the opposite house—a voice as rich as a tropical sunset, and which made Giovanni, though he knew not why, think of deep hues of purple or crimson and of perfumes heavily delectable. "Are you in the garden?"

"Yes, Beatrice," answered the gardener, "and I need your help."

Soon there emerged from under a sculptured portal the figure of a young girl, arrayed with as much richness of taste as the most splendid of the flowers, beautiful as the day, and with a bloom so deep and vivid that one shade more would have been too much. She looked redundant with life, health, and energy; all of which attributes were bound down and compressed, as it were, and girdled tensely, in their luxuriance, by her virgin zone.[3] Yet Giovanni's fancy must have grown morbid while he looked down into the garden; for the impression which the fair stranger made upon him was as if here were another flower, the human sister of those vegetable ones, as beautiful as they, more beautiful than the richest of them, but still to be touched only with a glove, nor to be approached without a mask. As Beatrice came down the garden path, it was observable that she handled and inhaled the odor of several of the plants which her father had most sedulously avoided.

"Here, Beatrice," said the latter, "see how many needful offices require to be done to our chief treasure. Yet, shattered as I am, my life might pay the penalty of approaching it so closely as circumstances demand. Henceforth, I fear, this plant must be consigned to your sole charge."

"And gladly will I undertake it," cried again the rich tones of the young lady, as she bent towards the magnificent plant and opened her arms as if to embrace it. "Yes, my sister, my splendor, it shall be Beatrice's task to nurse and serve thee; and thou shalt reward her with thy kisses and perfumed breath, which to her is as the breath of

3. Originally, a belt or girdle. In Mediterranean countries, unmarried women wore a distinctive variety of belt, hence a "virgin zone."

life."

Then, with all the tenderness in her manner that was so strikingly expressed in her words, she busied herself with such attentions as the plant seemed to require; and Giovanni, at his lofty window, rubbed his eyes and almost doubted whether it were a girl tending her favorite flower, or one sister performing the duties of affection to another. The scene soon terminated. Whether Dr. Rappaccini had finished his labors in the garden, or that his watchful eye had caught the stranger's face, he now took his daughter's arm and retired. Night was already closing in; oppressive exhalations seemed to proceed from the plants and steal upward past the open window; and Giovanni, closing the lattice, went to his couch and dreamed of a rich flower and beautiful girl. Flower and maiden were different, and yet the same, and fraught with some strange peril in either shape.

But there is an influence in the light of morning that tends to rectify whatever errors of fancy, or even of judgment, we may have incurred during the sun's decline, or among the shadows of the night, or in the less wholesome glow of moonshine. Giovanni's first movement, on starting from sleep, was to throw open the window and gaze down into the garden which his dreams had made so fertile of mysteries. He was surprised and a little ashamed to find how real and matter-of-fact an affair it proved to be, in the first rays of the sun which gilded the dew-drops that hung upon leaf and blossom, and, while giving a brighter beauty to each rare flower, brought everything within the limits of ordinary experience. The young man rejoiced that, in the heart of the barren city, he had the privilege of overlooking this spot of lovely and luxuriant vegetation. It would serve, he said to himself, as a symbolic language to keep him in communion with Nature. Neither the sickly and thoughtworn Dr. Giacomo Rappaccini, it is true, nor his brilliant daughter, were now visible; so that Giovanni could not determine how much of the singularity which he attributed to both was due to their own qualities and how much to his wonder-working fancy; but he was inclined to take a most rational view of the whole matter.

In the course of the day he paid his respects to Signor Pietro Baglioni, professor of medicine in the university, a physician of eminent repute, to whom Giovanni had brought a letter of introduction. The professor was an elderly personage, apparently of genial nature, and habits that might almost be called jovial. He kept the young man to dinner, and made himself very agreeable by the freedom and liveliness of his conversation, especially when warmed by a flask or two of Tuscan wine. Giovanni, conceiving that men of science, inhabitants of the same city, must needs be on familiar terms with one another, took an opportunity to mention the name of Dr. Rappaccini. But the professor did not respond with so much cordiality as he had anticipated.

"Ill would it become a teacher of the divine art of medicine," said Professor Pietro Baglioni, in answer to a question of Giovanni, "to withhold due and well-considered praise of a physician so eminently skilled as Rappaccini; but, on the other hand, I should answer it but scantily to my conscience were I to permit a worthy youth like yourself, Signor Giovanni, the son of an ancient friend, to imbibe erroneous ideas respecting a man who might hereafter chance to hold your life and death in his hands. The truth is, our worshipful Dr. Rappaccini has as much science as any member of the faculty—with perhaps one single exception—in Padua, or all Italy; but there are certain grave objections to his professional character."

"And what are they?" asked the young man.

"Has my friend Giovanni any disease of body or heart, that he is so inquisitive about physicians?" said the professor, with a smile. "But as for Rappaccini, it is said of him—and I, who know the man well, can answer for its truth—that he cares infinitely more for science than for mankind. His patients are interesting to him only as subjects for some new experiment. He would sacrifice human life, his own among the rest, or whatever else was dearest to him, for the sake of adding so much as a grain of mustard seed to the great heap of his accumulated knowledge."

"Methinks he is an awful man indeed," remarked Guasconti, mentally recalling the cold and purely intellectual aspect of Rappaccini. "And yet, worshipful professor, is it not a noble spirit? Are there many men capable of so spiritual a love of science?"

"God forbid," answered the professor, somewhat testily; "at least, unless they take sounder views of the healing art than those adopted by Rappaccini. It is his theory that all medicinal virtues are comprised within those substances which we term vegetable poisons. These he cultivates with his own hands, and is said even to have produced new varieties of poison, more horribly deleterious than Nature, without the assistance of this learned person, would ever have plagued the world withal. That the signor doctor does less mischief than might be expected with such dangerous substances is undeniable. Now and then, it must be owned, he has effected, or seemed to effect, a marvellous cure; but, to tell you my private mind, Signor Giovanni, he should receive little credit for such instances of success, —they being probably the work of chance,—but should be held strictly accountable for his failures, which may justly be considered his own work."

The youth might have taken Baglioni's opinions with many grains of allowance had he known that there was a professional warfare of long continuance between him and Dr. Rappaccini, in which the latter was generally thought to have gained the advantage. If the reader be inclined to judge for himself, we refer him to certain black-letter tracts on both sides, preserved in the medical department of the University of Padua.

"I know not, most learned professor," returned Giovanni, after musing on what had been said of Rappaccini's exclusive zeal for science,—"I know not how dearly this physician may love his art; but surely there is one object more dear to him. He has a daughter."

"Aha!" cried the professor, with a laugh. "So now our friend Giovanni's secret is out. You have heard of this daughter, whom all the young men in Padua are wild about, though not half a dozen have ever had the good hap to see her face. I know little of the Signora Beatrice save that Rappaccini is said to have instructed her deeply in his science, and that, young and beautiful as fame reports her, she is already qualified to fill a professor's chair. Perchance her father destines her for mine! Other absurd rumors there be, not worth talking about or listening to. So now, Signor Giovanni, drink off your glass of lachryma."[4]

Guasconti returned to his lodgings somewhat heated with the wine he had quaffed, and which caused his brain to swim with strange fantasies in reference to Dr. Rappaccini and the beautiful Beatrice. On his way, happening to pass by a florist's, he bought a fresh bouquet of flowers.

Ascending to his chamber, he seated himself near the window, but within the shadow thrown by the depth of the wall, so that he could look down into the garden with little risk of being discovered. All beneath his eye was a solitude. The strange plants were basking in the sunshine, and now and then nodding gently to one another, as if in acknowledgment of sympathy and kindred. In the midst, by the shattered fountain, grew the magnificent shrub, with its purple gems clustering all over it; they glowed in the air, and gleamed back again out of the depths of the pool, which thus seemed to overflow with colored radiance from the rich reflection that was steeped in it. At first, as we have said, the garden was a solitude. Soon, however,— as Giovanni had half hoped, half feared, would be the case,—a figure appeared beneath the antique sculptured portal, and came down between the rows of plants, inhaling their various perfumes as if she were one of those beings of old classic fable that lived upon sweet odors. On again beholding Beatrice, the young man was even startled to perceive how much her beauty exceeded his recollection of it; so brilliant, so vivid, was its character, that she glowed amid the sunlight, and, as Giovanni whispered to himself, positively illuminated the more shadowy intervals of the garden path. Her face being now more revealed than on the former occasion, he was struck by its expression of simplicity and sweetness,—qualities that had not entered

4. In full, Lachryma Christi (tears of Christ), an esteemed Italian wine from the Neapolitan area.

into his idea of her character, and which made him ask anew what manner of mortal she might be. Nor did he fail again to observe, or imagine, an analogy between the beautiful girl and the gorgeous shrub that hung its gemlike flowers over the fountain,—a resemblance which Beatrice seemed to have indulged a fantastic humor in heightening, both by the arrangement of her dress and the selection of its hues.

Approaching the shrub, she threw open her arms, as with a passionate ardor, and drew its branches into an intimate embrace—so intimate that her features were hidden in its leafy bosom and her glistening ringlets all intermingled with the flowers.

"Give me thy breath, my sister," exclaimed Beatrice; "for I am faint with common air. And give me this flower of thine, which I separate with gentlest fingers from the stem and place it close beside my heart."

With these words the beautiful daughter of Rappaccini plucked one of the richest blossoms of the shrub, and was about to fasten it in her bosom. But now, unless Giovanni's draughts of wine had bewildered his senses, a singular incident occurred. A small orange-colored reptile, of the lizard or chameleon species, chanced to be creeping along the path, just at the feet of Beatrice. It appeared to Giovanni,—but, at the distance from which he gazed, he could scarcely have seen anything so minute,—it appeared to him, however, that a drop or two of moisture from the broken stem of the flower descended upon the lizard's head. For an instant the reptile contorted itself violently, and then lay motionless in the sunshine.[5] Beatrice observed this remarkable phenomenon, and crossed herself, sadly, but without surprise; nor did she therefore hesitate to arrange the fatal flower in her bosom. There it blushed, and almost glimmered with the dazzling effect of a precious stone, adding to her dress and aspect the one appropriate charm which nothing else in the world could have supplied. But Giovanni, out of the shadow of his window, bent forward and shrank back, and murmured and trembled.

"Am I awake? Have I my senses?" said he to himself. "What is this being? Beautiful shall I call her, or inexpressibly terrible?"

Beatrice now strayed carelessly through the garden, approaching closer beneath Giovanni's window, so that he was compelled to thrust his head quite out of its concealment in order to gratify the intense and painful curiosity which she excited. At this moment there came a beautiful insect over the garden wall; it had, perhaps, wandered through the city, and found no flowers or verdure among

5. The presence of the reptile in the garden reminds the reader that Giovanni's first sight of the place had suggested a Garden of Eden of which the Adam was Rappaccini. But here the reptile is a harmless lizard, and the fruit of Beatrice's particular "tree" has killed it.

those antique haunts of men until the heavy perfumes of Dr. Rappaccini's shrubs had lured it from afar. Without alighting on the flowers, this winged brightness seemed to be attracted by Beatrice, and lingered in the air and fluttered about her head. Now, here it could not be but that Giovanni Guasconti's eyes deceived him. Be that as it might, he fancied that, while Beatrice was gazing at the insect with childish delight, it grew faint and fell at her feet; its bright wings shivered; it was dead—from no cause that he could discern, unless it were the atmosphere of her breath. Again Beatrice crossed herself and sighed heavily as she bent over the dead insect.

An impulsive movement of Giovanni drew her eyes to the window. There she beheld the beautiful head of the young man—rather a Grecian than an Italian head, with fair, regular features, and a glistening of gold among his ringlets—gazing down upon her like a being that hovered in mid air. Scarcely knowing what he did, Giovanni threw down the bouquet which he had hitherto held in his hand.

"Signora," said he, "there are pure and healthful flowers. Wear them for the sake of Giovanni Guasconti."

"Thanks, signor," replied Beatrice, with her rich voice, that came forth as it were like a gush of music, and with a mirthful expression half childish and half woman-like. "I accept your gift, and would fain recompense it with this precious purple flower; but if I toss it into the air it will not reach you. So Signor Guasconti must even content himself with my thanks."

She lifted the bouquet from the ground, and then, as if inwardly ashamed at having stepped aside from her maidenly reserve to respond to a stranger's greeting, passed swiftly homeward through the garden. But few as the moments were, it seemed to Giovanni, when she was on the point of vanishing beneath the sculptured portal, that his beautiful bouquet was already beginning to wither in her grasp. It was an idle thought; there could be no possibility of distinguishing a faded flower from a fresh one at so great a distance.

For many days after this incident the young man avoided the window that looked into Dr. Rappaccini's garden, as if something ugly and monstrous would have blasted his eyesight had he been betrayed into a glance. He felt conscious of having put himself, to a certain extent, within the influence of an unintelligible power by the communication which he had opened with Beatrice. The wisest course would have been, if his heart were in any real danger, to quit his lodgings and Padua itself at once; the next wiser, to have accustomed himself, as far as possible, to the familiar and daylight view of Beatrice—thus bringing her rigidly and systematically within the limits of ordinary experience. Least of all, while avoiding her sight, ought Giovanni to have remained so near this extraordinary being that the proximity and possibility even of intercourse should give a kind of substance and reality to the wild vagaries which his imagination ran riot continually in producing. Guasconti had not a deep heart—or, at all events, its depths were not sounded now; but he had a quick fancy, and an ardent southern temperament, which rose every instant to a higher fever pitch. Whether or no Beatrice possessed those terrible attributes, that fatal breath, the affinity with those so beautiful and deadly flowers which were indicated by what Giovanni had witnessed, she had at least instilled a fierce and subtle poison into his system. It was not love, although her rich beauty was a madness to him; nor horror, even while he fancied her spirit to be imbued with the same baneful essence that seemed to pervade her physical frame; but a wild offspring of both love and horror that had each parent in it, and burned like one and shivered like the other. Giovanni knew not what to dread; still less did he know what to hope; yet hope and dread kept a continual warfare in his breast, alternately vanquishing one another and starting up afresh to renew the contest. Blessed are all simple emotions, be they dark or bright! It is the lurid intermixture of the two that produces the illuminating blaze of the infernal regions.

Sometimes he endeavored to assuage the fever of his spirit by a rapid walk through the streets of Padua or beyond its gates: his footsteps kept time with the throbbings of his brain, so that the walk was apt to accelerate itself to a race. One day he found himself arrested; his arm was seized by a portly personage, who had turned back on recognizing the young man and expended much breath in overtaking him.

"Signor Giovanni! Stay, my young friend!" cried he. "Have you forgotten me? That might well be the case if I were as much altered as yourself."

It was Baglioni, whom Giovanni had avoided ever since their first meeting, from a doubt that the professor's sagacity would look too deeply into his secrets. Endeavoring to recover himself, he stared forth wildly from his inner world into the outer one and spoke like a man in a dream.

"Yes; I am Giovanni Guasconti. You are Professor Pietro Baglioni. Now let me pass!"

"Not yet, not yet, Signor Giovanni Guasconti," said the professor, smiling, but at the same time scrutinizing the youth with an earnest glance. "What! did I grow up side by side with your father? and shall his son pass me like a stranger in these old streets of Padua? Stand still, Signor Giovanni; for we must have a word or two before we part."

"Speedily, then, most worshipful professor, speedily," said Giovanni, with feverish impatience. "Does not your worship see that I am in haste?"

Now, while he was speaking there came a man in black along the street, stooping and moving feebly like a person in inferior health. His face was all overspread with a most sickly and sallow hue, but yet so pervaded with an expression of piercing and active intellect that an observer might easily have overlooked the merely physical attributes and have seen only this wonderful energy. As he passed, this person exchanged a cold and distant salutation with Baglioni, but fixed his eyes upon Giovanni with an intentness that seemed to bring out whatever was within him worthy of notice. Neverthe-less, there was a peculiar quietness in the look, as if taking merely a speculative, not a human, interest in the young man.

"It is Dr. Rappaccini!" whispered the professor when the stranger had passed. "Has he ever seen your face before?"

"Not that I know," answered Giovanni, starting at the name.

"He *has* seen you! he must have seen you!" said Baglioni, hastily. "For some purpose or other, this man of science is making a study of you. I know that look of his! It is the same that coldly illuminates his face as he bends over a bird, a mouse, or a butterfly, which, in pursuance of some experiment, he has killed by the perfume of a flower; a look as deep as Nature itself, but without Nature's warmth of love. Signor Giovanni, I will stake my life upon it, you are the subject of one of Rappaccini's experiments!"

"Will you make a fool of me?" cried Giovanni, passionately. "*That*, signor professor, were an untoward experiment."

"Patience! patience!" replied the imperturbable professor. "I tell thee, my poor Giovanni, that Rappaccini has a scientific interest in thee. Thou hast fallen into fearful hands! And the Signora Bea-trice,—what part does she act in this mystery?"

But Guasconti, finding Baglioni's pertinacity intolerable, here broke away, and was gone before the professor could again seize his arm. He looked after the young man intently and shook his head.

"This must not be," said Baglioni to himself. "The youth is the son of my old friend, and shall not come to any harm from which the arcana of medical science can preserve him. Besides, it is too insufferable an impertinence in Rappaccini, thus to snatch the lad out of my own hands, as I may say, and make use of him for his infernal experiments. This daughter of his! It shall be looked to. Perchance, most learned Rappaccini, I may foil you where you little dream of it!"

Meanwhile Giovanni had pursued a circuitous route, and at length found himself at the door of his lodgings. As he crossed the threshold he was met by old Lisabetta, who smirked and smiled, and was evidently desirous to attract his attention; vainly, however, as the ebullition of his feelings had momentarily subsided into a cold and dull vacuity. He turned his eyes full upon the withered face that was puckering itself into a smile, but seemed to behold it not. The old dame, therefore, laid her grasp upon his cloak.

"Signor! signor!" whispered she, still with a smile over the whole breadth of her visage, so that it looked not unlike a grotesque carving in wood, darkened by centuries. "Listen, signor! There is a private entrance into the garden!"

"What do you say?" exclaimed Giovanni, turning quickly about, as if an inanimate thing should start into feverish life. "A private entrance into Dr. Rappaccini's garden?"

"Hush! hush! not so loud!" whispered Lisabetta, putting her hand over his mouth. "Yes; into the worshipful doctor's garden, where you may see all his fine shrubbery. Many a young man in Padua would give gold to be admitted among those flowers."

Giovanni put a piece of gold into her hand.

"Show me the way," said he.

A surmise, probably excited by his conversation with Baglioni, crossed his mind, that this interposition of old Lisabetta might perchance be connected with the intrigue, whatever were its nature, in which the professor seemed to suppose that Dr. Rappaccini was involving him. But such a suspicion, though it disturbed Giovanni, was inadequate to restrain him. The instant that he was aware of the possibility of approaching Beatrice, it seemed an absolute necessity of his existence to do so. It mattered not whether she were angel or demon; he was irrevocably within her sphere, and must obey the law that whirled him onward, in ever-lessening circles, towards a result which he did not attempt to foreshadow; and yet, strange to say, there came across him a sudden doubt whether this intense interest on his part were not delusory; whether it were really of so deep and positive a nature as to justify him in now thrusting himself into an incalculable position; whether it were not merely the fantasy of a young man's brain, only slightly or not at all connected with his heart.

He paused, hesitated, turned half about, but again went on. His withered guide led him along several obscure passages, and finally undid a door, through which, as it was opened, there came the sight and sound of rustling leaves, with the broken sunshine glimmering among them. Giovanni stepped forth, and, forcing himself through the entanglement of a shrub that wreathed its tendrils over the hidden entrance, stood beneath his own window in the open area of Dr. Rappaccini's garden.

How often is it the case that, when impossibilities have come to pass and dreams have condensed their misty substance into tangible realities, we find ourselves calm, and even coldly self-possessed, amid circumstances which it would have been a delirium of joy or agony to anticipate! Fate delights to thwart us thus. Passion will choose his own time to rush upon the scene, and lingers sluggishly behind when an appropriate adjustment of events would seem to summon his appearance. So was it now with Giovanni. Day after day his pulses had throbbed with feverish blood at the improbable idea of an interview with Beatrice, and of standing with her, face to face, in this very garden, basking in the Oriental sunshine of her beauty, and snatching from her full gaze the mystery which he deemed the riddle of his own existence. But now there was a singular and untimely equanimity within his breast. He threw a glance around the garden to discover if Beatrice or her father were present, and, perceiving that he was alone, began a critical observation of the plants.

The aspect of one and all of them dissatisfied him; their gorgeousness seemed fierce, passionate, and even unnatural. There was hardly an individual shrub which a wanderer, straying by himself through a forest, would not have been startled to find growing wild, as if an unearthly face had glared at him out of the thicket. Several also would have shocked a delicate instinct by an appearance of artificialness indicating that there had been such commixture, and, as it were, adultery, of various vegetable species, that the production was no longer of God's making, but the monstrous offspring of man's depraved fancy, glowing with only an evil mockery of beauty. They were probably the result of experiment, which in one or two cases had succeeded in mingling plants individually lovely into a compound possessing the questionable and ominous character that distinguished the whole growth of the garden. In fine, Giovanni recognized but two or three plants in the collection, and those of a kind that he well knew to be poisonous. While busy with these contemplations he heard the rustling of a silken garment, and, turning, beheld Beatrice emerging from beneath the sculptured portal.

Giovanni had not considered with himself what should be his deportment; whether he should apologize for his intrusion into the garden, or assume that he was there with the privity at least, if not by the desire, of Dr. Rappaccini or his daughter; but Beatrice's manner placed him at his ease, though leaving him still in doubt by what agency he had gained admittance. She came lightly along the path and met him near the broken fountain. There was surprise in her face, but brightened by a simple and kind expression of pleasure.

"You are a connoisseur in flowers, signor," said Beatrice, with a smile, alluding to the bouquet which he had flung her from the window. "It is no marvel, therefore, if the sight of my father's rare collection has tempted you to take a nearer view. If he were here, he could tell you many strange and interesting facts as to the nature and habits of these shrubs; for he has spent a lifetime in such studies, and this garden is his world."

"And yourself, lady," observed Giovanni, "if fame says true,—you likewise are deeply skilled in the virtues indicated by these rich blossoms and these spicy perfumes. Would you deign to be my instructress, I should prove an apter scholar than if taught by Signor Rappaccini himself."

"Are there such idle rumors?" asked Beatrice, with the music of a pleasant laugh. "Do people say that I am skilled in my father's science of plants? What a jest is there! No; though I have grown up among these flowers, I know no more of them than their hues and perfume; and sometimes methinks I would fain rid myself of even that small knowledge. There are many flowers here, and those not the least brilliant, that shock and offend me when they meet my eye. But pray, signor, do not believe these stories about my science. Believe nothing of me save what you see with your own eyes."

"And must I believe all that I have seen with my own eyes?" asked Giovanni, pointedly, while the recollection of former scenes made him shrink. "No, signora; you demand too little of me. Bid me believe nothing save what comes from your own lips."

It would appear that Beatrice understood him. There came a deep flush to her cheek; but she looked full into Giovanni's eyes, and responded to his gaze of uneasy suspicion with a queenlike haughtiness.

"I do so bid you, signor," she replied. "Forget whatever you may have fancied in regard to me. If true to the outward senses, still it may be false in its essence; but the words of Beatrice Rappaccini's lips are true from the depths of the heart outward. Those you may believe."

A fervor glowed in her whole aspect and beamed upon Giovanni's consciousness like the light of truth itself; but while she spoke there was a fragrance in the atmosphere around her, rich and delightful, though evanescent, yet which the young man, from an indefinable reluctance, scarcely dared to draw into his lungs. It might be the odor of the flowers. Could it be Beatrice's breath which thus embalmed her words with a strange richness, as if by steeping them in her heart? A faintness passed like a shadow over Giovanni and flitted away; he seemed to gaze through the beautiful girl's eyes into her transparent soul, and felt no more doubt or fear.

The tinge of passion that had colored Beatrice's manner vanished; she became gay, and appeared to derive a pure delight from her communion with the youth not unlike what the maiden of a lonely island might have felt conversing with a voyager from the civilized world. Evidently her experience of life had been confined within the limits of that garden. She talked now about matters as simple as the daylight or summer clouds, and now asked questions in reference to the city, or Giovanni's distant home, his friends, his mother, and his sisters—questions indicating such seclusion, and such lack of familiarity with modes and forms, that Giovanni responded as if to an infant. Her spirit gushed out before him like a fresh rill that was just catching its first glimpse of the sunlight and wondering at the reflections of earth and sky which were flung into its bosom. There came thoughts, too, from a deep source, and fantasies of a gemlike brilliancy, as if diamonds and rubies sparkled upward among the bubbles of the fountain. Ever and anon there gleamed across the young man's mind a sense of wonder that he should be walking side by side with the being who had so wrought upon his imagination, whom he had idealized in such hues of terror, in whom he had positively witnessed such manifestations of dreadful attributes,—that he should be conversing with Beatrice like a brother, and should find her so human and so maidenlike. But such reflections were only momentary; the effect of her character was too real not to make itself familiar at once.

In this free intercourse they had strayed through the garden, and now, after many turns among its avenues, were come to the shattered fountain, beside which grew the magnificent shrub, with its treasury of glowing blossoms. A fragrance was diffused from it which Giovanni recognized as identical with that which he had attributed to Beatrice's breath, but incomparably more powerful. As her eyes fell upon it, Giovanni beheld her press her hand to her bosom as if her heart were throbbing suddenly and painfully.

"For the first time in my life," murmured she, addressing the shrub, "I had forgotten thee."

"I remember, signora," said Giovanni, "that you once promised to reward me with one of these living gems for the bouquet which I had the happy boldness to fling to your feet. Permit me now to pluck it as a memorial of this interview."

He made a step towards the shrub with extended hand; but Beatrice darted forward, uttering a shriek that went through his heart like a dagger. She caught his hand and drew it back with the whole force of her slender figure. Giovanni felt her touch thrilling through his fibres.

"Touch it not!" exclaimed she, in a voice of agony. "Not for thy life! It is fatal!"

Then, hiding her face, she fled from him and vanished beneath the sculptured portal. As Giovanni followed her with his eyes, he beheld the emanciated figure and pale intelligence of Dr. Rappaccini, who had been watching the scene, he knew not how long, within the shadow of the entrance.

No sooner was Guasconti alone in his chamber than the image of Beatrice came back to his passionate musings, invested with all the witchery that had been gathering around it ever since his first glimpse of her, and now likewise imbued with a tender warmth of girlish womanhood. She was human; her nature was endowed with all gentle and feminine qualities; she was worthiest to be worshipped; she was capable, surely, on her part, of the height and heroism of love. Those tokens which he had hitherto considered as proofs of a frightful peculiarity in her physical and moral system were now either forgotten, or, by the subtle sophistry of passion transmitted into a golden crown of enchantment, rendering Beatrice the more admirable by so much as she was the more unique. Whatever had looked ugly was now beautiful; or, if incapable of such a change, it stole away and hid itself among those shapeless half ideas which throng the dim region beyond the daylight of our perfect consciousness. Thus did he spend the night, nor fell asleep until the dawn had begun to awake the slumbering flowers in Dr. Rappaccini's garden, whither Giovanni's dreams doubtless led him. Up rose the sun in his due season, and, flinging his beams upon the young man's eyelids, awoke him to a sense of pain. When thoroughly aroused, he became sensible of a burning and tingling agony in his hand—in his right hand—the very hand which Beatrice had grasped in her own when he was on the point of plucking one of the gemlike flowers. On the back of that hand there was now a purple print like that of four small fingers, and the likeness of a slender thumb upon his wrist.

Oh, how stubbornly does love,—or even that cunning semblance of love which flourishes in the imagination, but strikes no depth of root into the heart,—how stubbornly does it hold its faith until the moment comes when it is doomed to vanish into thin mist! Giovanni wrapped a handkerchief about his hand and wondered what evil thing had stung him, and soon forgot his pain in a reverie of Beatrice.

After the first interview, a second was in the inevitable course of what we call fate. A third; a fourth; and a meeting with Beatrice in the garden was no longer an incident in Giovanni's daily life, but the whole space in which he might be said to live; for the anticipation and memory of that ecstatic hour made up the remainder. Nor was it otherwise with the daughter of Rappaccini. She watched for the youth's appearance, and flew to his side with confidence as unreserved as if they had been playmates from early infancy—as if they were such playmates still. If, by any unwonted chance, he failed to come at the appointed moment, she stood beneath the window and sent up the rich sweetness of her tones to float around him in his chamber and echo and reverberate throughout his heart: "Giovanni! Giovanni! Why tarriest thou? Come down!" And down he hastened into that Eden of poisonous flowers.

But, with all this intimate familiarity, there was still a reserve in Beatrice's demeanor, so rigidly and invariably sustained that the idea of infringing it scarcely occurred to his imagination. By all appreciable signs, they loved; they had looked love with eyes that conveyed the holy secret from the depths of one soul into the depths of the other, as if it were too sacred to be whispered by the way; they had even spoken love in those gushes of passion when their spirits darted forth in articulated breath like tongues of long-hidden flame; and yet there had been no seal of lips, no clasp of hands, nor any slightest caress such as love claims and hallows. He had never touched one of the gleaming ringlets of her hair; her garment—so marked was the physical barrier between them—had never been waved against him by a breeze. On the few occasions when Giovanni had seemed tempted to overstep the limit, Beatrice grew so sad, so stern, and withal wore such a look of desolate separation, shuddering at itself, that not a spoken word was requisite to repel him. At such times he was startled at the horrible suspicions that rose, monster-like, out of the caverns of his heart and stared him in the face; his love grew thin and faint as the morning mist, his doubts alone had substance. But, when Beatrice's face brightened again after the momentary shadow, she was transformed at once from the mysterious, questionable being whom he had watched with so much awe and horror; she was now the beautiful and unsophisticated girl whom he felt his spirit knew with a certainty beyond all other knowledge.

A considerable time had now passed since Giovanni's last meeting with Baglioni. One morning, however, he was disagreeably surprised by a visit from the professor, whom he had scarcely thought of for whole weeks, and would willingly have forgotten still longer. Given up as he had long been to a pervading excitement, he could tolerate no companions except upon condition of their perfect sympathy with his present state of feeling. Such sympathy was not to be expected from Professor Baglioni.

The visitor chatted carelessly for a few moments about the gossip of the city and the university, and then took up another topic.

"I have been reading an old classic author lately," said he, "and met with a story that strangely interested me. Possibly you may remember it.[6] It is of an Indian prince, who sent a beautiful woman as a present to Alexander the Great. She was as lovely as the dawn and gorgeous as the sunset; but what especially distinguished her was a certain rich perfume in her breath—richer than a garden of Persian roses. Alexander, as was natural to a youthful conqueror, fell in love at first sight with this magnificent stranger; but a certain sage physician, happening to be present, discovered a terrible secret in regard to her."

"And what was that?" asked Giovanni, turning his eyes downward to avoid those of the professor.

6. Baglioni's story finds its source in a passage copied by Hawthorne, in his *American Notebooks*, from Sir Thomas Browne's *Vulgar Errors* (1646), Book VII, Caption 17.

"That this lovely woman," continued Baglioni, with emphasis, "had been nourished with poisons from her birth upward, until her whole nature was so imbued with them that she herself had become the deadliest poison in existence. Poison was her element of life. With that rich perfume of her breath she blasted the very air. Her love would have been poison—her embrace death. Is not this a marvellous tale?"

"A childish fable," answered Giovanni, nervously starting from his chair. "I marvel how your worship finds time to read such nonsense among your graver studies."

"By the by," said the professor, looking uneasily about him, "what singular fragrance is this in your apartment? Is it the perfume of your gloves? It is faint, but delicious; and yet, after all, by no means agreeable. Were I to breathe it long, methinks it would make me ill. It is like the breath of a flower; but I see no flowers in the chamber."

"Nor are there any," replied Giovanni, who had turned pale as the professor spoke; "nor, I think, is there any fragrance except in your worship's imagination. Odors, being a sort of element combined of the sensual and the spiritual, are apt to deceive us in this manner. The recollection of a perfume, the bare idea of it, may easily be mistaken for a present reality."

"Ay; but my sober imagination does not often play such tricks," said Baglioni; "and, were I to fancy any kind of odor, it would be that of some vile apothecary drug, wherewith my fingers are likely enough to be imbued. Our worshipful friend Rappaccini, as I have heard, tinctures his medicaments with odors richer than those of Araby. Doubtless, likewise, the fair and learned Signora Beatrice would minister to her patients with draughts as sweet as a maiden's breath; but woe to him that sips them!"

Giovanni's face evinced many contending emotions. The tone in which the professor alluded to the pure and lovely daughter of Rappaccini was a torture to his soul; and yet the intimation of a view of her character, opposite to his own, gave instantaneous distinctness to a thousand dim suspicions, which now grinned at him like so many demons. But he strove hard to quell them and to respond to Baglioni with a true lover's perfect faith.

"Signor professor," said he, "you were my father's friend; perchance, too, it is your purpose to act a friendly part towards his son. I would fain feel nothing towards you save respect and deference; but I pray you to observe, signor, that there is one subject on which we must not speak. You know not the Signora Beatrice. You cannot, therefore, estimate the wrong—the blasphemy, I may even say— that is offered to her character by a light or injurious word."

"Giovanni! my poor Giovanni!" answered the professor, with a calm expression of pity, "I know this wretched girl far better than yourself. You shall hear the truth in respect to the poisoner Rappaccini and his poisonous daughter; yes, poisonous as she is beautiful. Listen; for, even should you do violence to my gray hairs, it shall not silence me. That old fable of the Indian woman has become a truth by the deep and deadly science of Rappaccini and in the person of the lovely Beatrice."

Giovanni groaned and hid his face.

"Her father," continued Baglioni, "was not restrained by natural affection from offering up his child in this horrible manner as the victim of his insane zeal for science; for, let us do him justice, he is as true a man of science as ever distilled his own heart in an alembic. What, then, will be your fate? Beyond a doubt you are selected as the material of some new experiment. Perhaps the result is to be death; perhaps a fate more awful still. Rappaccini, with what he calls the interest of science before his eyes, will hesitate at nothing."

"It is a dream," muttered Giovanni to himself; "surely it is a dream."

"But," resumed the professor, "be of good cheer, son of my friend. It is not yet too late for the rescue. Possibly we may even succeed in bringing back this miserable child within the limits of ordinary nature, from which her father's madness has estranged her. Behold this little silver vase! It was wrought by the hands of the renowned Benvenuto Cellini,[7] and is well worthy to be a love gift to the fairest dame in Italy. But its contents are invaluable. One little sip of this antidote would have rendered the most virulent poisons of the Borgias[8] innocuous. Doubt not that it will be as efficacious against those of Rappaccini. Bestow the vase, and the precious liquid within it, on your Beatrice, and hopefully await the result."

Baglioni laid a small, exquisitely wrought silver vial on the table and withdrew, leaving what he had said to produce its effect upon the young man's mind.

"We will thwart Rappaccini yet," thought he, chuckling to himself, as he descended the stairs; "but, let us confess the truth of him, he is a wonderful man—a wonderful man indeed; a vile empiric, however, in his practice, and therefore not to be tolerated by those who respect the good old rules of the medical profession."

Throughout Giovanni's whole acquaintance with Beatrice, he had occasionally, as we have said, been haunted by dark surmises as to her character; yet so thoroughly had she made herself felt by him as a simple, natural, most affectionate, and guileless creature, that the image now held up by Professor Baglioni looked as strange and incredible as if it were not in accordance with his own original con-

7. Benvenuto Cellini (1500–1571), famous Italian sculptor, and perhaps the greatest goldsmith of the Renaissance.

8. Italian family influential in the papacy and politics (1455–1519), charged with the poisoning of numerous enemies.

ception. True, there were ugly recollections connected with his first glimpses of the beautiful girl; he could not quite forget the bouquet that withered in her grasp, and the insect that perished amid the sunny air, by no ostensible agency save the fragrance of her breath. These incidents, however, dissolving in the pure light of her character, had no longer the efficacy of facts, but were acknowledged as mistaken fantasies, by whatever testimony of the senses they might appear to be substantiated. There is something truer and more real than what we can see with the eyes and touch with the finger. On such better evidence had Giovanni founded his confidence in Beatrice, though rather by the necessary force of her high attributes than by any deep and generous faith on his part. But now his spirit was incapable of sustaining itself at the height to which the early enthusiasm of passion had exalted it; he fell down, grovelling among earthly doubts, and defiled therewith the pure whiteness of Beatrice's image. Not that he gave her up; he did but distrust. He resolved to institute some decisive test that should satisfy him, once for all, whether there were those dreadful peculiarities in her physical nature which could not be supposed to exist without some corresponding monstrosity of soul. His eyes, gazing down afar, might have deceived him as to the lizard, the insect, and the flowers; but if he could witness, at the distance of a few paces, the sudden blight of one fresh and healthful flower in Beatrice's hand, there would be room for no further question. With this idea he hastened to the florist's and purchased a bouquet that was still gemmed with the morning dew-drops.

It was now the customary hour of his daily interview with Beatrice. Before descending into the garden, Giovanni failed not to look at his figure in the mirror,—a vanity to be expected in a beautiful young man, yet, as displaying itself at that troubled and feverish moment, the token of a certain shallowness of feeling and insincerity of character. He did gaze, however, and said to himself that his features had never before possessed so rich a grace, nor his eyes such vivacity, nor his cheeks so warm a hue of superabundant life.

"At least," thought he, "her poison has not yet insinuated itself into my system. I am no flower to perish in her grasp."

With that thought he turned his eyes on the bouquet, which he had never once laid aside from his hand. A thrill of indefinable horror shot through his frame on perceiving that those dewy flowers were already beginning to droop; they wore the aspect of things that had been fresh and lovely yesterday. Giovanni grew white as marble, and stood motionless before the mirror, staring at his own reflection there as at the likeness of something frightful. He remembered Baglioni's remark about the fragrance that seemed to pervade the chamber. It must have been the poison in his breath! Then he shuddered— shuddered at himself. Recovering from his stupor, he began to watch with curious eye a spider that was busily at work hanging its web from the antique cornice of the apartment, crossing and recrossing the artful system of interwoven lines—as vigorous and active a spider as ever dangled from an old ceiling. Giovanni bent towards the insect, and emitted a deep, long breath. The spider suddenly ceased its toil; the web vibrated with a tremor originating in the body of the small artisan. Again Giovanni sent forth a breath, deeper, longer, and imbued with a venomous feeling out of his heart: he knew not whether he were wicked, or only desperate. The spider made a convulsive gripe with his limbs and hung dead across the window.

"Accursed! accursed!" muttered Giovanni, addressing himself. "Hast thou grown so poisonous that this deadly insect perishes by thy breath?"

At that moment a rich, sweet voice came floating up from the garden.

"Giovanni! Giovanni! It is past the hour! Why tarriest thou? Come down!"

"Yes," muttered Giovanni again. "She is the only being whom my breath may not slay! Would that it might!"

He rushed down, and in an instant was standing before the bright and loving eyes of Beatrice. A moment ago his wrath and despair had been so fierce that he could have desired nothing so much as to wither her by a glance; but with her actual presence there came influences which had too real an existence to be at once shaken off: recollections of the delicate and benign power of her feminine nature, which had so often enveloped him in a religious calm; recollections of many a holy and passionate outgush of her heart, when the pure fountain had been unsealed from its depths and made visible in its transparency to his mental eye; recollections which, had Giovanni known how to estimate them, would have assured him that all this ugly mystery was but an earthly illusion, and that, whatever mist of evil might seem to have gathered over her, the real Beatrice was a heavenly angel. Incapable as he was of such high faith, still her presence had not utterly lost its magic. Giovanni's rage was quelled into an aspect of sullen insensibility. Beatrice, with a quick spiritual sense, immediately felt that there was a gulf of blackness between them which neither he nor she could pass. They walked on together, sad and silent, and came thus to the marble fountain and to its pool of water on the ground, in the midst of which grew the shrub that bore gem-like blossoms. Giovanni was affrighted at the eager enjoyment—the appetite, as it were—with which he found himself inhaling the fragrance of the flowers.

"Beatrice," asked he, abruptly, "whence came this shrub?"

"My father created it," answered she, with simplicity.

"Created it! created it!" repeated Giovanni. "What mean you,

Beatrice?"

"He is a man fearfully acquainted with the secrets of Nature," replied Beatrice; "and, at the hour when I first drew breath, this plant sprang from the soil, the offspring of his science, of his intellect, while I was but his earthly child. Approach it not!" continued she, observing with terror that Giovanni was drawing nearer to the shrub. "It has qualities that you little dream of. But I, dearest Giovanni,—I grew up and blossomed with the plant and was nourished with its breath. It was my sister, and I loved it with a human affection; for, alas!—hast thou not suspected it?—there was an awful doom."

Here Giovanni frowned so darkly upon her that Beatrice paused and trembled. But her faith in his tenderness reassured her, and made her blush that she had doubted for an instant.

"There was an awful doom," she continued, "the effect of my father's fatal love of science, which estranged me from all society of my kind. Until Heaven sent thee, dearest Giovanni, oh, how lonely was thy poor Beatrice!"

"Was it a hard doom?" asked Giovanni, fixing his eyes upon her.

"Only of late have I known how hard it was," answered she, tenderly. "Oh, yes; but my heart was torpid, and therefore quiet."

Giovanni's rage broke forth from his sullen gloom like a lightning flash out of a dark cloud.

"Accursed one!" cried he, with venomous scorn and anger. "And, finding thy solitude wearisome, thou hast severed me likewise from all the warmth of life and enticed me into thy region of unspeakable horror!"

"Giovanni!" exclaimed Beatrice, turning her large bright eyes upon his face. The force of his words had not found its way into her mind; she was merely thunderstruck.

"Yes, poisonous thing!" repeated Giovanni, beside himself with passion. "Thou hast done it! Thou hast blasted me! Thou hast filled my veins with poison! Thou hast made me as hateful, as ugly, as loathsome and deadly a creature as thyself—a world's wonder of hideous monstrosity! Now, if our breath be happily as fatal to ourselves as to all others, let us join our lips in one kiss of unutterable hatred, and so die!"

"What has befallen me?" murmured Beatrice, with a low moan out of her heart. "Holy Virgin, pity me, a poor heartbroken child!"

"Thou,—dost thou pray?" cried Giovanni, still with the same fiendish scorn. "Thy very prayers, as they come from thy lips, taint the atmosphere with death. Yes, yes; let us pray! Let us to church and dip our fingers in the holy water at the portal! They that come after us will perish as by a pestilence! Let us sign crosses in the air! It will be scattering curses abroad in the likeness of holy symbols!"

"Giovanni," said Beatrice, calmly, for her grief was beyond passion, "why dost thou join thyself with me thus in those terrible words? I, it is true, am the horrible thing thou namest me. But thou, —what hast thou to do, save with one other shudder at my hideous misery to go forth out of the garden and mingle with thy race, and forget that there ever crawled on earth such a monster as poor Beatrice?"

"Dost thou pretend ignorance?" asked Giovanni, scowling upon her. "Behold! this power have I gained from the pure daughter of Rappaccini."

There was a swarm of summer insects flitting through the air in search of the food promised by the flower odors of the fatal garden. They circled round Giovanni's head, and were evidently attracted towards him by the same influence which had drawn them for an instant within the sphere of several of the shrubs. He sent forth a breath among them, and smiled bitterly at Beatrice as at least a score of the insects fell dead upon the ground.

"I see it! I see it!" shrieked Beatrice. "It is my father's fatal science! No, no, Giovanni; it was not I! Never! never! I dreamed only to love thee and be with thee a little time, and so to let thee pass away, leaving but thine image in mine heart; for, Giovanni, believe it, though my body be nourished with poison, my spirit is God's creature, and craves love as its daily food. But my father,—he has united us in this fearful sympathy. Yes; spurn me, tread upon me, kill me! Oh, what is death after such words as thine? But it was not I. Not for a world of bliss would I have done it."

Giovanni's passion had exhausted itself in its outburst from his lips. There now came across him a sense, mournful, and not without tenderness, of the intimate and peculiar relationship between Beatrice and himself. They stood, as it were, in an utter solitude, which would be made none the less solitary by the densest throng of human life. Ought not, then, the desert of humanity around them to press this insulated pair closer together? If they should be cruel to one another, who was there to be kind to them? Besides, thought Giovanni, might there not still be a hope of his returning within the limits of ordinary nature, and leading Beatrice, the redeemed Beatrice, by the hand? O, weak, and selfish, and unworthy spirit, that could dream of an earthly union and earthly happiness as possible, after such deep love had been so bitterly wronged as was Beatrice's love by Giovanni's blighting words! No, no; there could be no such hope. She must pass heavily, with that broken heart, across the borders of Time—she must bathe her hurts in some fount of paradise, and forget her grief in the light of immortality, and *there* be well.

But Giovanni did not know it.

"Dear Beatrice," said he, approaching her, while she shrank away as always at his approach, but now with a different impulse, "dearest Beatrice, our fate is not yet so desperate. Behold! there is a medicine, potent, as a wise physician has assured me, and almost divine in its efficacy. It is composed of ingredients the most opposite to those by which thy awful father has brought this calamity upon thee and me. It is distilled of blessed herbs. Shall we not quaff it together, and thus be purified from evil?"

"Give it me!" said Beatrice, extending her hand to receive the little silver vial which Giovanni took from his bosom. She added, with a peculiar emphasis, "I will drink; but do thou await the result."

She put Baglioni's antidote to her lips; and, at the same moment, the figure of Rappaccini emerged from the portal and came slowly towards the marble fountain. As he drew near, the pale man of science seemed to gaze with a triumphant expression at the beautiful youth and maiden, as might an artist who should spend his life in achieving a picture or a group of statuary and finally be satisfied with his success. He paused; his bent form grew erect with conscious power; he spread out his hands over them in the attitude of a father imploring a blessing upon his children; but those were the same hands that had thrown poison into the stream of their lives. Giovanni trembled. Beatrice shuddered nervously, and pressed her hand upon her heart.

"My daughter," said Rappaccini, "thou art no longer lonely in the world. Pluck one of those precious gems from thy sister shrub and bid thy bridegroom wear it in his bosom. It will not harm him now. My science and the sympathy between thee and him have so wrought within his system that he now stands from common men, as thou dost, daughter of my pride and triumph, from ordinary women. Pass on, then, through the world, most dear to one another and dreadful to all besides!"

"My father," said Beatrice, feebly,—and still as she spoke she kept her hand upon her heart,—"wherefore didst thou inflict this miserable doom upon thy child?"

"Miserable!" exclaimed Rappaccini. "What mean you, foolish girl? Dost thou deem it misery to be endowed with marvellous gifts against which no power nor strength could avail an enemy—misery, to be able to quell the mightiest with a breath—misery, to be as terrible as thou art beautiful? Wouldst thou, then, have preferred the condition of a weak woman, exposed to all evil and capable of none?"

"I would fain have been loved, not feared," murmured Beatrice, sinking down upon the ground. "But now it matters not. I am going, father, where the evil which thou hast striven to mingle with my being will pass away like a dream—like the fragrance of these poison-ous flowers, which will no longer taint my breath among the flowers of Eden. Farewell, Giovanni! Thy words of hatred are like lead within my heart; but they, too, will fall away as I ascend. Oh, was there not, from the first, more poison in thy nature than in mine?"

To Beatrice,—so radically had her earthly part been wrought upon by Rappaccini's skill,—as poison had been life, so the powerful antidote was death; and thus the poor victim of man's ingenuity and of thwarted nature, and of the fatality that attends all such efforts of perverted wisdom, perished there, at the feet of her father and Giovanni. Just at that moment Professor Pietro Baglioni looked forth from the window, and called loudly, in a tone of triumph mixed with horror, to the thunderstricken man of science,—

"Rappaccini! Rappaccini! and is *this* the upshot of your experiment!"

1844, 1846

Ethan Brand[9]

A *Chapter from an Abortive Romance*

Bartram the lime-burner, a rough, heavy-looking man, begrimed with charcoal, sat watching his kiln, at nightfall, while his little son played at building houses with the scattered fragments of marble, when, on the hillside below them, they heard a roar of laughter, not mirthful, but slow, and even solemn, like a wind shaking the boughs of the forest.

"Father, what is that?" asked the little boy, leaving his play, and pressing betwixt his father's knees.

"Oh, some drunken man, I suppose," answered the lime-burner; "some merry fellow from the bar-room in the village, who dared not laugh loud enough within doors lest he should blow the roof of the house off. So here he is, shaking his jolly sides at the foot of Graylock."[1]

"But, father," said the child, more sensitive than the obtuse,

9. "Ethan Brand" represents the savage culmination of Hawthorne's recurrent theme, the awful consequences of intellectual withdrawal from humanity—the repudiation of involvement with the general heart of man. The germ of the story is found in a memorandum, dated 1844, in *The American Notebooks* (edited by Randall Stewart, p. 106): "The Unpardonable Sin might consist in a want of love and reverence for the Human Soul; in consequence of which, the investigator pried into its dark depths * * * from a cold philosophical curiosity,—content that it should be wicked in whatever kind or degree, and only desiring to study it out. Would not this, in other words, be the separation of the intellect from the heart?" In the same source (pp. 36–67 *passim*) are detailed descriptions of the principal characters and scenes of this tale, including the lime-kiln; these were written during a holiday that Hawthorne spent near North Adams, Massachusetts, in the summer of 1838. "Ethan Brand", was first published in the *Boston Museum* for January 5, 1850, and was reprinted in the *Dollar Magazine* for May, 1850; it was collected in *The Snow-Image and Other Tales* (London, 1851, Boston, 1852).

1. The highest elevation in Massachusetts—Mount Greylock, in the Berkshires.

middle-aged clown, "he does not laugh like a man that is glad. So the noise frightens me!"

"Don't be a fool, child!" cried his father, gruffly. "You will never make a man, I do believe; there is too much of your mother in you. I have known the rustling of a leaf startle you. Hark! Here comes the merry fellow now. You shall see that there is no harm in him."

Bartram and his little son, while they were talking thus, sat watching the same lime-kiln that had been the scene of Ethan Brand's solitary and meditative life, before he began his search for the Unpardonable Sin. Many years, as we have seen, had now elapsed, since that portentous night when the IDEA was first developed.[2] The kiln, however, on the mountain-side, stood unimpaired, and was in nothing changed since he had thrown his dark thoughts into the intense glow of its furnace, and melted them, as it were, into the one thought that took possession of his life. It was a rude, round, tower-like structure about twenty feet high, heavily built of rough stones, and with a hillock of earth heaped about the larger part of its circumference; so that the blocks and fragments of marble might be drawn by cart-loads, and thrown in at the top. There was an opening at the bottom of the tower, like an oven-mouth, but large enough to admit a man in a stooping posture, and provided with a massive iron door. With the smoke and jets of flame issuing from the chinks and crevices of this door, which seemed to give admittance into the hillside, it resembled nothing so much as the private entrance to the infernal regions, which the shepherds of the Delectable Mountains[3] were accustomed to show to pilgrims.

There are many such lime-kilns in that tract of country, for the purpose of burning the white marble which composes a large part of the substance of the hills. Some of them, built years ago, and long deserted, with weeds growing in the vacant round of the interior, which is open to the sky, and grass and wild-flowers rooting themselves into the chinks of the stones, look already like relics of antiquity, and may yet be overspread with the lichens of centuries to come. Others, where the lime-burner still feeds his daily and night-long fire, afford points of interest to the wanderer among the hills, who seats himself on a log of wood or a fragment of marble, to hold a chat with the solitary man. It is a lonesome, and, when the character is inclined to thought, may be an intensely thoughtful occupation; as it proved in the case of Ethan Brand, who had mused to such strange purpose, in days gone by, while the fire in this very kiln was burning.

2. *Cf.* the subtitle of this story, declaring it to be "A Chapter from an Abortive Romance." Another vestige of the longer work survives in the reference to "the Esther of our tale," below.

3. A place of temptation for Christian in Bunyan's *Pilgrim's Progress* (Part II, 1684), which also permitted him to see, in the distance, the Celestial City.

The man who now watched the fire was of a different order, and troubled himself with no thoughts save the very few that were requisite to his business. At frequent intervals, he flung back the clashing weight of the iron door, and, turning his face from the insufferable glare, thrust in huge logs of oak, or stirred the immense brands with a long pole. Within the furnace were seen the curling and riotous flames, and the burning marble, almost molten with the intensity of heat; while without, the reflection of the fire quivered on the dark intricacy of the surrounding forest, and showed in the foreground a bright and ruddy little picture of the hut, the spring beside its door, the athletic and coal-begrimed figure of the lime-burner, and the half-frightened child, shrinking into the protection of his father's shadow. And when again the iron door was closed, then reappeared the tender light of the half-full moon, which vainly strove to trace out the indistinct shapes of the neighboring mountains; and, in the upper sky, there was a flitting congregation of clouds, still faintly tinged with the rosy sunset, though thus far down into the valley the sunshine had vanished long and long ago.

The little boy now crept still closer to his father, as footsteps were heard ascending the hillside, and a human form thrust aside the bushes that clustered beneath the trees.

"Halloo! who is it?" cried the lime-burner, vexed at his son's timidity, yet half infected by it. "Come forward, and show yourself, like a man, or I'll fling this chunk of marble at your head!"

"You offer me a rough welcome," said a gloomy voice, as the unknown man drew nigh. "Yet I neither claim nor desire a kinder one, even at my own fireside."

To obtain a distincter view, Bartram threw open the iron door of the kiln, whence immediately issued a gush of fierce light, that smote full upon the stranger's face and figure. To a careless eye there appeared nothing very remarkable in his aspect, which was that of a man in a coarse, brown, country-made suit of clothes, tall and thin, with the staff and heavy shoes of a wayfarer. As he advanced, he fixed his eyes—which were very bright—intently upon the brightness of the furnace, as if he beheld, or expected to behold, some object worthy of note within it.

"Good evening, stranger," said the lime-burner; "whence come you, so late in the day?"

"I come from my search," answered the wayfarer; "for, at last, it is finished."

"Drunk!—or crazy!" muttered Bartram to himself. "I shall have trouble with the fellow. The sooner I drive him away, the better."

The little boy, all in a tremble, whispered to his father, and begged him to shut the door of the kiln, so that there might not be so much light; for that there was something in the man's face which he was afraid to look at, yet could not look away from. And, indeed, even the lime-burner's dull and torpid sense began to be impressed by an indescribable something in that thin, rugged, thoughtful visage, with the grizzled hair hanging wildly about it, and those deeply sunken eyes, which gleamed like fires within the entrance of a mysterious cavern. But, as he closed the door, the stranger turned towards him, and spoke in a quiet, familiar way, that made Bartram feel as if he were a sane and sensible man, after all.

"Your task draws to an end, I see," said he. "This marble has already been burning three days. A few hours more will convert the stone to lime."

"Why, who are you?" exclaimed the lime-burner. "You seem as well acquainted with my business as I am myself."

"And well I may be," said the stranger; "for I followed the same craft many a long year, and here, too, on this very spot. But you are a new-comer in these parts. Did you never hear of Ethan Brand?"

"The man that went in search of the Unpardonable Sin?" asked Bartram, with a laugh.

"The same," answered the stranger. "He has found what he sought, and therefore he comes back again."

"What! then you are Ethan Brand himself?" cried the lime-burner, in amazement. "I am a new-comer here, as you say, and they call it eighteen years since you left the foot of Graylock. But, I can tell you, the good folks still talk about Ethan Brand, in the village yonder, and what a strange errand took him away from his lime-kiln. Well, and so you have found the Unpardonable Sin?"

"Even so!" said the stranger, calmly.

"If the question is a fair one," proceeded Bartram, "where might it be?"

Ethan Brand laid his finger on his own heart.

"Here!" replied he.

And then, without mirth in his countenance, but as if moved by an involuntary recognition of the infinite absurdity of seeking throughout the world for what was the closest of all things to himself, and looking into every heart, save his own, for what was hidden in no other breast, he broke into a laugh of scorn. It was the same slow, heavy laugh, that had almost appalled the lime-burner when it heralded the wayfarer's approach.

The solitary mountain-side was made dismal by it. Laughter, when out of place, mistimed, or bursting forth from a disordered state of feeling, may be the most terrible modulation of the human voice. The laughter of one asleep, even if it be a little child,—the mad-man's laugh,—the wild, screaming laugh of a born idiot,—are sounds that we sometimes tremble to hear, and would always willingly forget. Poets have imagined no utterance of fiends or hobgoblins so fearfully appropriate as a laugh. And even the obtuse lime-burner felt his nerves shaken, as this strange man looked inward at his own heart, and burst into laughter that rolled away into the night, and was indistinctly reverberated among the hills.

"Joe," said he to his little son, "scamper down to the tavern in the village, and tell the jolly fellows there that Ethan Brand has come back, and that he has found the Unpardonable Sin!"

The boy darted away on his errand, to which Ethan Brand made no objection, nor seemed hardly to notice it. He sat on a log of wood, looking steadfastly at the iron door of the kiln. When the child was out of sight, and his swift and light footsteps ceased to be heard treading first on the fallen leaves and then on the rocky mountain-path, the lime-burner began to regret his departure. He felt that the little fellow's presence had been a barrier between his guest and himself, and that he must now deal, heart to heart, with a man who, on his own confession, had committed the one only crime for which Heaven could afford no mercy. That crime, in its indistinct black-ness, seemed to overshadow him. The lime-burner's own sins rose up within him, and made his memory riotous with a throng of evil shapes that asserted their kindred with the Master Sin, whatever it might be, which it was within the scope of man's corrupted nature to conceive and cherish. They were all of one family; they went to and fro between his breast and Ethan Brand's, and carried dark greetings from one to the other.

Then Bartram remembered the stories which had grown tradi-tionary in reference to this strange man, who had come upon him like a shadow of the night, and was making himself at home in his old place, after so long absence that the dead people, dead and buried for years, would have had more right to be at home, in any familiar spot, than he. Ethan Brand, it was said, had conversed with Satan himself in the lurid blaze of this very kiln. The legend had been matter of mirth heretofore, but looked grisly now. According to this tale, before Ethan Brand departed on his search, he had been accus-tomed to evoke a fiend from the hot furnace of the lime-kiln, night after night, in order to confer with him about the Unpardonable Sin; the man and the fiend each laboring to frame the image of some mode of guilt which could neither be atoned for nor forgiven. And, with the first gleam of light upon the mountaintop, the fiend crept in at the iron door, there to abide the intensest element of fire, until again summoned forth to share in the dreadful task of extending man's possible guilt beyond the scope of Heaven's else infinite mercy.

While the lime-burner was struggling with the horror of these thoughts, Ethan Brand rose from the log, and flung open the door of the kiln. The action was in such accordance with the idea in Bar-tram's mind, that he almost expected to see the Evil One issue forth, red-hot, from the raging furnace.

"Hold! hold!" cried he, with a tremulous attempt to laugh; for he was ashamed of his fears, although they overmastered him. "Don't, for mercy's sake, bring out your Devil now!"

"Man!" sternly replied Ethan Brand, "what need have I of the Devil? I have left him behind me, on my track. It is with such half-way sinners as you that he busies himself. Fear not, because I open the door. I do but act by old custom, and am going to trim your fire, like a lime-burner, as I was once."

He stirred the vast coals, thrust in more wood, and bent forward to gaze into the hollow prison-house of the fire, regardless of the fierce glow that reddened upon his face. The lime-burner sat watching him, and half suspected this strange guest of a purpose, if not to evoke a fiend, at least to plunge bodily into the flames, and thus vanish from the sight of man. Ethan Brand, however, drew quietly back, and closed the door of the kiln.

"I have looked," said he, "into many a human heart that was seven times hotter with sinful passions than yonder furnace is with fire. But I found not there what I sought. No, not the Unpardonable Sin!"

"What is the Unpardonable Sin?" asked the lime-burner; and then he shrank farther from his companion, trembling lest his question should be answered.

"It is a sin that grew within my own breast," replied Ethan Brand, standing erect, with a pride that distinguishes all enthusiasts of his stamp. "A sin that grew nowhere else! The sin of an intellect that triumphed over the sense of brotherhood with man and reverence for God, and sacrificed everything to its own mighty claims! The only sin that deserves a recompense of immortal agony! Freely, were it to do again, would I incur the guilt. Unshrinkingly I accept the retribution!"

"The man's head is turned," muttered the lime-burner to himself. "He may be a sinner like the rest of us,—nothing more likely, —but, I'll be sworn, he is a madman too."

Nevertheless, he felt uncomfortable at his situation, alone with Ethan Brand on the wild mountain-side, and was right glad to hear the rough murmur of tongues, and the footsteps of what seemed a pretty numerous party, stumbling over the stones and rustling through the underbrush. Soon appeared the whole lazy regiment that was wont to infest the village tavern, comprehending three or four individuals who had drunk flip beside the bar-room fire through all the winters, and smoked their pipes beneath the stoop through all the summers, since Ethan Brand's departure. Laughing boisterously, and mingling all their voices together in unceremonious talk, they now burst into the moonshine and narrow streaks of firelight that illuminated the open space before the lime-kiln. Bartram set the door ajar again, flooding the spot with light, that the whole company might get a fair view of Ethan Brand, and he of them.

There, among other old acquaintances, was a once ubiquitous man, now almost extinct, but whom we were formerly sure to encounter at the hotel of every thriving village throughout the country. It was the stage-agent. The present specimen of the genus was a wilted and smoke-dried man, wrinkled and red-nosed, in a smartly cut, brown, bob-tailed coat, with brass buttons, who, for a length of time unknown, had kept his desk and corner in the bar-room, and was still puffing what seemed to be the same cigar that he had lighted twenty years before. He had great fame as a dry joker, though, perhaps, less on account of any intrinsic humor than from a certain flavor of brandy-toddy and tobacco-smoke, which impregnated all his ideas and expressions, as well as his person. Another well-remembered, though strangely altered, face was that of Lawyer Giles, as people still called him in courtesy; an elderly ragamuffin, in his soiled shirt-sleeves and tow-cloth trousers. This poor fellow had been an attorney, in what he called his better days, a sharp practitioner, and in great vogue among the village litigants; but flip, and sling, and toddy, and cocktails, imbibed at all hours, morning, noon, and night, had caused him to slide from intellectual to various kinds and degrees of bodily labor, till at last, to adopt his own phrase, he slid into a soap-vat. In other words, Giles was now a soap-boiler, in a small way. He had come to be but the fragment of a human being, a part of one foot having been chopped off by an axe, and an entire hand torn away by the devilish grip of a steam-engine. Yet, though the corporeal hand was gone, a spiritual member remained; for, stretching forth the stump, Giles steadfastly averred that he felt an invisible thumb and fingers with as vivid a sensation as before the real ones were amputated. A maimed and miserable wretch he was; but one, nevertheless, whom the world could not trample on, and had no right to scorn, either in this or any previous stage of his misfortunes, since he had still kept up the courage and spirit of a man, asked nothing in charity, and with his one hand—and that the left one—fought a stern battle against want and hostile circumstances.

Among the throng, too, came another personage, who, with certain points of similarity to Lawyer Giles, had many more of difference. It was the village doctor; a man of some fifty years, whom, at an earlier period of his life, we introduced as paying a professional visit to Ethan Brand during the latter's supposed insanity. He was now a purple-visaged, rude, and brutal, yet half-gentlemanly figure, with something wild, ruined, and desperate in his talk, and in all the details of his gesture and manners. Brandy possessed this man like an evil spirit, and made him as surly and savage as a wild beast, and as miserable as a lost soul; but there was supposed to be in him such wonderful skill, such native gifts of healing, beyond any which medical science could impart, that society caught hold of him, and would not let him sink out of its reach. So, swaying to and fro upon his horse, and grumbling thick accents at the bedside, he visited all the sick-chambers for miles about among the mountain towns, and sometimes raised a dying man, as it were, by miracle, or quite as often, no doubt, sent his patient to a grave that was dug many a year too soon. The doctor had an everlasting pipe in his mouth, and, as somebody said, in allusion to his habit of swearing, it was always alight with hell-fire.

These three worthies pressed forward, and greeted Ethan Brand each after his own fashion, earnestly inviting him to partake of the contents of a certain black bottle, in which, as they averred, he would find something far better worth seeking for than the Unpardonable Sin. No mind, which has wrought itself by intense and solitary meditation into a high state of enthusiasm, can endure the kind of contact with low and vulgar modes of thought and feeling to which Ethan Brand was now subjected. It made him doubt—and, strange to say, it was a painful doubt—whether he had indeed found the Unpardonable Sin, and found it within himself. The whole question on which he had exhausted life, and more than life, looked like a delusion.

"Leave me," he said bitterly, "ye brute beasts, that have made yourselves so, shrivelling up your souls with fiery liquors! I have done with you. Years and years ago, I groped into your hearts, and found nothing there for my purpose. Get ye gone!"

"Why, you uncivil scoundrel," cried the fierce doctor, "is that the way you respond to the kindness of your best friends? Then let me tell you the truth. You have no more found the Unpardonable Sin than yonder boy Joe has. You are but a crazy fellow,—I told you so twenty years ago,—neither better nor worse than a crazy fellow, and the fit companion of old Humphrey, here!"

He pointed to an old man, shabbily dressed, with long white hair, thin visage, and unsteady eyes. For some years past this aged person had been wandering about among the hills, inquiring of all travellers whom he met for his daughter. The girl, it seemed, had gone off with a company of circus-performers; and occasionally tidings of her came to the village, and fine stories were told of her glittering appearance as she rode on horseback in the ring, or performed marvellous feats on the tight-rope.

The white-haired father now approached Ethan Brand, and gazed unsteadily into his face.

"They tell me you have been all over the earth," said he, wringing his hands with earnestness. "You must have seen my daughter, for she makes a grand figure in the world, and everybody goes to see her. Did she send any word to her old father, or say when she was coming back?"

Ethan Brand's eye quailed beneath the old man's. That daughter, from whom he so earnestly desired a word of greeting, was the Esther of our tale, the very girl whom, with such cold and remorseless purpose, Ethan Brand had made the subject of a psychological experiment, and wasted, absorbed, and perhaps annihilated her soul, in the process.

"Yes," murmured he, turning away from the hoary wanderer; "it is no delusion. There is an Unpardonable Sin!"

While these things were passing, a merry scene was going forward in the area of cheerful light, beside the spring and before the door of the hut. A number of the youth of the village, young men and girls, had hurried up the hillside, impelled by curiosity to see Ethan Brand, the hero of so many a legend familiar to their childhood. Finding nothing, however, very remarkable in his aspect,— nothing but a sunburnt wayfarer, in plain garb and dusty shoes, who sat looking into the fire as if he fancied pictures among the coals,— these young people speedily grew tired of observing him. As it happened, there was other amusement at hand. An old German Jew, travelling with a diorama[4] on his back, was passing down the mountain-road towards the village just as the party turned aside from it, and, in hopes of eking out the profits of the day, the showman had kept them company to the lime-kiln.

"Come, old Dutchman," cried one of the young men, "let us see your pictures, if you can swear they are worth looking at!"

"Oh, yes, Captain," answered the Jew,—whether as a matter of courtesy or craft, he styled everybody Captain,—"I shall show you, indeed, some very superb pictures!"

So, placing his box in a proper position, he invited the young men and girls to look through the glass orifices of the machine, and proceeded to exhibit a series of the most outrageous scratchings and daubings, as specimens of the fine arts, that ever an itinerant showman had the face to impose upon his circle of spectators. The pictures were worn out, moreover, tattered, full of cracks and wrinkles, dingy with tobacco-smoke, and otherwise in a most pitiable condition. Some purported to be cities, public edifices, and ruined castles in Europe; others represented Napoleon's battles and Nelson's seafights; and in the midst of these would be seen a gigantic, brown, hairy hand,—which might have been mistaken for the Hand of Destiny, though, in truth, it was only the showman's,—pointing its forefinger to various scenes of the conflict, while its owner gave his-

4. A box or chamber with a lens for viewing enlarged pictures, either trans- parencies or stereoscopic (three-dimensional) views.

torical illustrations. When, with much merriment at its abominable deficiency of merit, the exhibition was concluded, the German bade little Joe put his head into the box. Viewed through the magnifying-glasses, the boy's round, rosy visage assumed the strangest imaginable aspect of an immense Titanic child, the mouth grinning broadly, and the eyes and every other feature overflowing with fun at the joke. Suddenly, however, that merry face turned pale, and its expression changed to horror, for this easily impressed and excitable child had become sensible that the eye of Ethan Brand was fixed upon him through the glass.

"You make the little man to be afraid, Captain," said the German Jew, turning up the dark and strong outline of his visage, from his stooping posture. "But look again, and, by chance, I shall cause you to see somewhat that is very fine, upon my word!"

Ethan Brand gazed into the box for an instant, and then starting back, looked fixedly at the German. What had he seen? Nothing, apparently; for a curious youth, who had peeped in almost at the same moment, beheld only a vacant space of canvas.

"I remember you now," muttered Ethan Brand to the showman.

"Ah, Captain," whispered the Jew of Nuremberg, with a dark smile, "I find it to be a heavy matter in my show-box,—this Unpardonable Sin! By my faith, Captain, it has wearied my shoulders, this long day, to carry it over the mountain."

"Peace," answered Ethan Brand, sternly, "or get thee into the furnace yonder!"

The Jew's exhibition had scarcely concluded, when a great, elderly dog—who seemed to be his own master, as no person in the company laid claim to him—saw fit to render himself the object of public notice. Hitherto, he had shown himself a very quiet, well-disposed old dog, going round from one to another, and, by way of being sociable, offering his rough head to be patted by any kindly hand that would take so much trouble. But now, all of a sudden, this grave and venerable quadruped, of his own mere motion, and without the slightest suggestion from anybody else, began to run round after his tail, which, to heighten the absurdity of the proceeding, was a great deal shorter than it should have been. Never was seen such headlong eagerness in pursuit of an object that could not possibly be attained; never was heard such a tremendous outbreak of growling, snarling, barking, and snapping,—as if one end of the ridiculous brute's body were at deadly and most unforgivable enmity with the other. Faster and faster, round about went the cur; and faster and still faster fled the unapproachable brevity of his tail; and louder and fiercer grew his yells of rage and animosity; until, utterly exhausted, and as far from the goal as ever, the foolish old dog ceased his performance as suddenly as he had begun it. The next moment he was as mild, quiet, sensible, and respectable in his deportment, as when he first scraped acquaintance with the company.

As may be supposed, the exhibition was greeted with universal laughter, clapping of hands, and shouts of encore, to which the canine performer responded by wagging all that there was to wag of his tail, but appeared totally unable to repeat his very successful effort to amuse the spectators.

Meanwhile, Ethan Brand had resumed his seat upon the log, and moved, it might be, by a perception of some remote analogy between his own case and that of this self-pursuing cur, he broke into the awful laugh, which, more than any other token, expressed the condition of his inward being. From that moment, the merriment of the party was at an end; they stood aghast, dreading lest the inauspicious sound should be reverberated around the horizon, and that mountain would thunder it to mountain, and so the horror be prolonged upon their ears. Then, whispering one to another that it was late,—that the moon was almost down,—that the August night was growing chill,—they hurried homewards, leaving the lime-burner and little Joe to deal as they might with their unwelcome guest. Save for these three human beings, the open space on the hillside was a solitude, set in a vast gloom of forest. Beyond that darksome verge, the firelight glimmered on the stately trunks and almost black foliage of pines, intermixed with the lighter verdure of sapling oaks, maples, and poplars, while here and there lay the gigantic corpses of dead trees, decaying on the leaf-strewn soil. And it seemed to little Joe—a timorous and imaginative child—that the silent forest was holding its breath until some fearful thing should happen.

Ethan Brand thrust more wood into the fire, and closed the door of the kiln; then looking over his shoulder at the lime-burner and his son, he bade, rather than advised, them to retire to rest.

"For myself, I cannot sleep," said he. "I have matters that it concerns me to meditate upon. I will watch the fire, as I used to do in the old time."

"And call the Devil out of the furnace to keep you company, I suppose," muttered Bartram, who had been making intimate acquaintance with the black bottle above mentioned. "But watch, if you like, and call as many devils as you like! For my part, I shall be all the better for a snooze. Come, Joe!"

As the boy followed his father into the hut, he looked back at the wayfarer, and the tears came into his eyes, for his tender spirit had an intuition of the bleak and terrible loneliness in which this man had enveloped himself.

When they had gone, Ethan Brand sat listening to the crackling of the kindled wood, and looking at the little spirts of fire that issued through the chinks of the door. These trifles, however, once so familiar, had but the slightest hold of his attention, while deep within his mind he was reviewing the gradual but marvellous change that had been wrought upon him by the search to which he had devoted himself. He remembered how the night dew had fallen upon him,—how the dark forest had whispered to him,—how the stars had gleamed upon him,—a simple and loving man, watching his fire in the years gone by, and ever musing as it burned. He remembered with what tenderness, with what love and sympathy for mankind, and what pity for human guilt and woe, he had first begun to contemplate those ideas which afterwards became the inspiration of his life; with what reverence he had then looked into the heart of man, viewing it as a temple originally divine, and, however desecrated, still to be held sacred by a brother; with what awful fear he had deprecated the success of his pursuit, and prayed that the Unpardonable Sin might never be revealed to him. Then ensued that vast intellectual development, which, in its progress, disturbed the counterpoise between his mind and heart. The Idea that possessed his life had operated as a means of education; it had gone on cultivating his powers to the highest point of which they were susceptible; it had raised him from the level of an unlettered laborer to stand on a starlit eminence, whither the philosophers of the earth, laden with the lore of universities, might vainly strive to clamber after him. So much for the intellect! But where was the heart? That, indeed, had withered,—had contracted,—had hardened,—had perished! It had ceased to partake of the universal throb. He had lost his hold of the magnetic chain of humanity. He was no longer a brother-man, opening the chambers or the dungeons of our common nature by the key of holy sympathy, which gave him a right to share in all its secrets; he was now a cold observer, looking on mankind as the subject of his experiment, and, at length, converting man and woman to be his puppets, and pulling the wires that moved them to such degrees of crime as were demanded for his study.

Thus Ethan Brand became a fiend. He began to be so from the moment that his moral nature had ceased to keep the pace of improvement with his intellect. And now, as his highest effort and inevitable development,—as the bright and gorgeous flower, and rich, delicious fruit of his life's labor,—he had produced the Unpardonable Sin!

"What more have I to seek? what more to achieve?" said Ethan Brand to himself. "My task is done, and well done!"

Starting from the log with a certain alacrity in his gait and ascending the hillock of earth that was raised against the stone circumference of the lime-kiln, he thus reached the top of the structure. It was a space of perhaps ten feet across, from edge to edge, presenting a view of the upper surface of the immense mass of broken marble with which the kiln was heaped. All these innumerable blocks and fragments of marble were red-hot and vividly on fire, sending up great spouts of blue flame, which quivered aloft and danced madly, as within a magic circle, and sank and rose again, with continual and multitudinous activity. As the lonely man bent forward over this terrible body of fire, the blasting heat smote up against his person with a breath that, it might be supposed, would have scorched and shrivelled him up in a moment.

Ethan Brand stood erect, and raised his arms on high. The blue flames played upon his face, and imparted the wild and ghastly light which alone could have suited its expression; it was that of a fiend on the verge of plunging into his gulf of intensest torment.

"O Mother Earth," cried he, "who art no more my Mother, and into whose bosom this frame shall never be resolved! O mankind, whose brotherhood I have cast off, and trampled thy great heart beneath my feet! O stars of heaven, that shone on me of old, as if to light me onward and upward!—farewell all, and forever. Come, deadly element of Fire,—henceforth my familiar frame! Embrace me, as I do thee!"

That night the sound of a fearful peal of laughter rolled heavily through the sleep of the lime-burner and his little son; dim shapes of horror and anguish haunted their dreams, and seemed still present in the rude hovel, when they opened their eyes to the daylight.

"Up, boy, up!" cried the lime-burner, staring about him. "Thank Heaven, the night is gone, at last; and rather than pass such another, I would watch my lime-kiln, wide awake, for a twelvemonth. This Ethan Brand, with his humbug of an Unpardonable Sin, has done me no such mighty favor, in taking my place!"

He issued from the hut, followed by little Joe, who kept fast hold of his father's hand. The early sunshine was already pouring its gold upon the mountain-tops, and though the valleys were still in shadow, they smiled cheerfully in the promise of the bright day that was hastening onward. The village, completely shut in by hills, which swelled away gently about it, looked as if it had rested peacefully in the hollow of the great hand of Providence. Every dwelling was distinctly visible; the little spires of the two churches pointed upwards, and caught a foreglimmering of brightness from the sun-gilt skies upon their gilded weathercocks. The tavern was astir, and the figure of the old, smoke-dried stage-agent, cigar in mouth, was seen beneath the stoop. Old Graylock was glorified with a golden cloud upon his head. Scattered likewise over the breasts of the surrounding mountains, there were heaps of hoary mist, in fantastic shapes, some of them far down into the valley, others high up towards the summits, and still others, of the same family of mist or cloud, hovering in the gold radiance of the upper atmosphere. Stepping from one to another of the clouds that rested on the hills, and thence to the loftier brotherhood that sailed in air, it seemed almost as if a mortal man might thus ascend into the heavenly regions. Earth was so mingled with sky that it was a day-dream to look at it.

To supply that charm of the familiar and homely, which Nature so readily adopts into a scene like this, the stage coach was rattling down the mountain-road, and the driver sounded his horn, while Echo caught up the notes, and intertwined them into a rich and varied and elaborate harmony, of which the original performer could lay claim to little share. The great hills played a concert among themselves, each contributing a strain of airy sweetness.

Little Joe's face brightened at once.

"Dear father," cried he, skipping cheerily to and fro, "that strange man is gone, and the sky and the mountains all seem glad of it!"

"Yes," growled the lime-burner, with an oath, "but he has let the fire go down, and no thanks to him if five hundred bushels of lime are not spoiled. If I catch the fellow hereabouts again, I shall feel like tossing him into the furnace!"

With his long pole in his hand, he ascended to the top of the kiln. After a moment's pause, he called to his son.

"Come up here, Joe!" said he.

So little Joe ran up the hillock, and stood by his father's side. The marble was all burnt into perfect, snow-white lime. But on its surface, in the midst of the circle,—snow-white too, and thoroughly converted into lime,—lay a human skeleton, in the attitude of a person who, after long toil, lies down to long repose. Within the ribs—strange to say—was the shape of a human heart.

"Was the fellow's heart made of marble?" cried Bartram, in some perplexity at this phenomenon. "At any rate, it is burnt into what looks like special good lime; and, taking all the bones together, my kiln is half a bushel the richer for him."

So saying, the rude lime-burner lifted his pole, and, letting it fall upon the skeleton, the relics of Ethan Brand were crumbled into fragments.

1850, 1851–1852

The Old Manse[5]

The Author Makes the Reader Acquainted with his Abode

Between two tall gateposts of rough-hewn stone (the gate itself having fallen from its hinges at some unknown epoch) we beheld the

5. The historic Emerson house in Concord, Massachusetts. Emerson's grandfather, the Reverend William Emerson, built it in 1765. When Ralph Waldo Emerson, six years a widower, married again and moved to Concord, he tem-

gray front of the old parsonage terminating the vista of an avenue of black ash-trees. It was now a twelvemonth since the funeral procession of the venerable clergyman,[6] its last inhabitant, had turned from that gateway towards the village burying-ground. The wheel-track leading to the door, as well as the whole breadth of the avenue, was almost overgrown with grass, affording dainty mouthfuls to two or three vagrant cows and an old white horse who had his own living to pick up along the roadside. The glimmering shadows that lay half asleep between the door of the house and the public highway were a kind of spiritual medium, seen through which the edifice had not quite the aspect of belonging to the material world. Certainly it had little in common with those ordinary abodes which stand so imminent upon the road that every passer-by can thrust his head, as it were, into the domestic circle. From these quiet windows the figures of passing travellers looked too remote and dim to disturb the sense of privacy. In its near retirement and accessible seclusion it was the very spot for the residence of a clergyman,—a man not estranged from human life, yet enveloped in the midst of it with a veil woven of intermingled gloom and brightness. It was worthy to have been one of the time-honored parsonages of England in which, through many generations, a succession of holy occupants pass from youth to age, and bequeath each an inheritance of sanctity to pervade the house and hover over it as with an atmosphere.

Nor, in truth, had the Old Manse ever been profaned by a lay occupant until that memorable summer afternoon when I entered it as my home. A priest[7] had built it; a priest had succeeded to it; other priestly men from time to time had dwelt in it; and children born in its chambers had grown up to assume the priestly character. It was awful to reflect how many sermons must have been written there. The latest inhabitant alone—he by whose translation to paradise the dwelling was left vacant—had penned nearly three thousand discourses, besides the better, if not the greater, number that gushed living from his lips. How often, no doubt, had he paced to and fro along the avenue, attuning his meditations to the sighs and gentle murmurs, and deep and solemn peals of the wind among the lofty tops of the trees! In that variety of natural utterances he could find something accordant with every passage of his sermon, were it of tenderness or reverential fear. The boughs over my head seemed shadowy with solemn thoughts as well as with rustling leaves. I took

porarily occupied this house, and began there the composition of his first important prose work, *Nature*. When Hawthorne was married, in 1842, he rented the Old Manse, and remained there until 1846, completing there most of the tales in *Mosses from an Old Manse* (1846). The present essay, written as an introduction for that volume, represents

Hawthorne's familiar style at its best. Its intimate revelation of the man himself, and of the life of his New England, contributes much to the understanding of his fictional creations.
6. The Reverend Ezra Ripley, the former occupant, died in 1841.
7. Clergyman.

shame to myself for having been so long a writer of idle stories, and ventured to hope that wisdom would descend upon me with the falling leaves of the avenue, and that I should light upon an intellectual treasure in the Old Manse well worth those hoards of long-hidden gold which people seek for in moss-grown houses. Profound treatises of morality; a layman's unprofessional and therefore unprejudiced views of religion; histories (such as Bancroft[8] might have written had he taken up his abode here as he once purposed) bright with picture, gleaming over a depth of philosophic thought,—these were the works that might fitly have flowed from such a retirement. In the humblest event I resolved at least to achieve a novel that should evolve some deep lesson and should possess physical substance enough to stand alone.

In furtherance of my design, and as if to leave me no pretext for not fulfilling it, there was in the rear of the house the most delightful little nook of a study that ever afforded its snug seclusion to a scholar. It was here that Emerson wrote Nature; for he was then an inhabitant of the Manse, and used to watch the Assyrian dawn and Paphian sunset and moonrise[9] from the summit of our eastern hill. When I first saw the room its walls were blackened with the smoke of unnumbered years, and made still blacker by the grim prints of Puritan ministers that hung around. These worthies looked strangely like bad angels, or at least like men who had wrestled so continually and so sternly with the devil that somewhat of his sooty fierceness had been imparted to their own visages. They had all vanished now; a cheerful coat of paint and golden-tinted paper-hangings lighted up the small apartment; while the shadow of a willow-tree that swept against the overhanging eaves attempered the cheery western sunshine. In place of the grim prints there was the sweet and lovely head of one of Raphael's Madonnas and two pleasant little pictures of the Lake of Como. The only other decorations were a purple vase of flowers, always fresh, and a bronze one containing graceful ferns. My books (few, and by no means choice; for they were chiefly such waifs as chance had thrown in my way) stood in order about the room, seldom to be disturbed.

The study had three windows, set with little, old-fashioned panes of glass, each with a crack across it. The two on the western side looked, or rather peeped, between the willow branches down into the orchard, with glimpses of the river through the trees. The third, facing northward, commanded a broader view of the river at a spot where its hitherto obscure waters gleam forth into the light of history. It was at this window that the clergyman who then dwelt in

---

8. George Bancroft (1800–1891) had already published three volumes of his monumental *History of the United States*. As customs collector of Boston he had been influential in securing Hawthorne's appointment to his staff (1839).
9. An apt paraphrase of a sentence to be found in Emerson's *Nature*.

the Manse stood watching the outbreak of a long and deadly struggle between two nations; he saw the irregular array of his parishioners on the farther side of the river and the glittering line of the British on the hither bank. He awaited in an agony of suspense the rattle of the musketry. It came, and there needed but a gentle wind to sweep the battle smoke around this quiet house.[1]

Perhaps the reader, whom I cannot help considering as my guest in the Old Manse and entitled to all courtesy in the way of sight-showing,—perhaps he will choose to take a nearer view of the memorable spot. We stand now on the river's brink. It may well be called the Concord, the river of peace and quietness; for it is certainly the most unexcitable and sluggish stream that ever loitered imperceptibly towards its eternity—the sea. Positively, I had lived three weeks beside it before it grew quite clear to my perception which way the current flowed. It never has a vivacious aspect except when a northwestern breeze is vexing its surface on a sunshiny day. From the incurable indolence of its nature, the stream is happily incapable of becoming the slave of human ingenuity, as is the fate of so many a wild, free mountain torrent. While all things else are compelled to subserve some useful purpose, it idles its sluggish life away in lazy liberty, without turning a solitary spindle or affording even water-power enough to grind the corn that grows upon its banks. The torpor of its movement allows it nowhere a bright, pebbly shore, nor so much as a narrow strip of glistening sand, in any part of its course. It slumbers between broad prairies, kissing the long meadow grass, and bathes the overhanging boughs of elder bushes and willows or the roots of elms and ash-trees and clumps of maples. Flags and rushes grow along its plashy shore; the yellow water-lily spreads its broad, flat leaves on the margin; and the fragrant white pond-lily abounds, generally selecting a position just so far from the river's brink that it cannot be grasped save at the hazard of plunging in.

It is a marvel whence this perfect flower derives its loveliness and perfume, springing as it does from the black mud over which the river sleeps, and where lurk the slimy eel and speckled frog and the mud turtle, whom continual washing cannot cleanse. It is the very same black mud out of which the yellow lily sucks its obscene life and noisome odor. Thus we see, too, in the world that some persons assimilate only what is ugly and evil from the same moral circumstances which supply good and beautiful results—the fragrance of celestial flowers—to the daily life of others.

The reader must not, from any testimony of mine, contract a dislike towards our slumberous stream. In the light of a calm and

---

1. Referring to the tradition that the Reverend William Emerson had watched from this house the Battle of Concord Bridge (April 19, 1775), which his grandson, Ralph Waldo Emerson, had commemorated in the "Concord Hymn" (1837).

golden sunset it becomes lovely beyond expression; the more lovely for the quietude that so well accords with the hour, when even the wind, after blustering all day long, usually hushes itself to rest. Each tree and rock, and every blade of grass, is distinctly imaged, and, however unsightly in reality, assumes ideal beauty in the reflection. The minutest things of earth and the broad aspect of the firmament are pictured equally without effort and with the same felicity of success. All the sky glows downward at our feet; the rich clouds float through the unruffled bosom of the stream like heavenly thoughts through a peaceful heart. We will not, then, malign our river as gross and impure while it can glorify itself with so adequate a picture of the heaven that broods above it; or, if we remember its tawny hue and the muddiness of its bed, let it be a symbol that the earthliest human soul has an infinite spiritual capacity and may contain the better world within its depths. But, indeed, the same lesson might be drawn out of any mud puddle in the streets of a city; and, being taught us everywhere, it must be true.

Come, we have pursued a somewhat devious track in our walk to the battleground. Here we are, at the point where the river was crossed by the old bridge, the possession of which was the immediate object of the contest. On the hither side grow two or three elms, throwing a wide circumference of shade, but which must have been planted at some period within the threescore years and ten that have passed since the battle day. On the farther shore, overhung by a clump of elder bushes, we discern the stone abutment of the bridge. Looking down into the river, I once discovered some heavy fragments of the timbers, all green with half a century's growth of water moss; for during that length of time the tramp of horses and human footsteps has ceased along this ancient highway. The stream has here about the breadth of twenty strokes of a swimmer's arm,—a space not too wide when the bullets were whistling across. Old people who dwell hereabouts will point out the very spots on the western bank where our countrymen fell down and died; and on this side of the river an obelisk of granite has grown up from the soil that was fertilized with British blood. The monument, not more than twenty feet in height, is such as it befitted the inhabitants of a village to erect in illustration of a matter of local interest rather than what was suitable to commemorate an epoch of national history. Still, by the fathers of the village this famous deed was done; and their descendants might rightfully claim the privilege of building a memorial.

A humbler token of the fight, yet a more interesting one than the granite obelisk, may be seen close under the stone-wall which separates the battleground from the precincts of the parsonage. It is the grave—marked by a small, mossgrown fragment of stone at the head and another at the foot—the grave of two British soldiers who were slain in the skirmish, and have ever since slept peacefully where Zechariah Brown and Thomas Davis buried them. Soon was their warfare ended; a weary night march from Boston, a rattling volley of musketry across the river, and then these many years of rest. In the long procession of slain invaders who passed into eternity from the battlefields of the revolution, these two nameless soldiers led the way.

Lowell, the poet, as we were once standing over this grave, told me a tradition in reference to one of the inhabitants below. The story has something deeply impressive, though its circumstances cannot altogether be reconciled with probability. A youth in the service of the clergyman happened to be chopping wood, that April morning, at the back door of the Manse, and when the noise of battle rang from side to side of the bridge he hastened across the intervening field to see what might be going forward. It is rather strange, by the way, that this lad should have been so diligently at work when the whole population of town and country were startled out of their customary business by the advance of the British troops. Be that as it might, the tradition says that the lad now left his task and hurried to the battle-field with the axe still in his hand. The British had by this time retreated, the Americans were in pursuit; and the late scene of strife was thus deserted by both parties. Two soldiers lay on the ground—one was a corpse; but, as the young New Englander drew nigh, the other Briton raised himself painfully upon his hands and knees and gave a ghastly stare into his face. The boy,—it must have been a nervous impulse, without purpose, without thought, and betokening a sensitive and impressible nature rather than a hardened one,—the boy uplifted his axe and dealt the wounded soldier a fierce and fatal blow upon the head.

I could wish that the grave might be opened; for I would fain know whether either of the skeleton soldiers has the mark of an axe in his skull. The story comes home to me like truth. Oftentimes, as an intellectual and moral exercise, I have sought to follow that poor youth through his subsequent career, and observe how his soul was tortured by the blood stain, contracted as it had been before the long custom of war had robbed human life of its sanctity, and while it still seemed murderous to slay a brother man. This one circumstance has borne more fruit for me than all that history tells us of the fight.

Many strangers come in the summer time to view the battleground. For my own part, I have never found my imagination much excited by this or any other scene of historic celebrity; nor would the placid margin of the river have lost any of its charm for me had men never fought and died there. There is a wilder interest in the tract of land—perhaps a hundred yards in breadth—which extends between the battle-field and the northern face of our Old Manse, with its contiguous avenue and orchard. Here, in some unknown age, before the white man came, stood an Indian village, convenient to the river, whence its inhabitants must have drawn so large a part of their subsistence. The site is identified by the spear and arrow heads, the chisels, and other implements of war, labor, and the chase, which the plough turns up from the soil. You see a splinter of stone, half hidden beneath a sod; it looks like nothing worthy of note; but, if you have faith enough to pick it up, behold a relic! Thoreau, who has a strange faculty of finding what the Indians have left behind them, first set me on the search; and I afterwards enriched myself with some very perfect specimens, so rudely wrought that it seemed almost as if chance had fashioned them. Their great charm consists in this rudeness and in the individuality of each article, so different from the productions of civilized machinery, which shapes everything on one pattern. There is exquisite delight, too, in picking up for one's self an arrowhead that was dropped centuries ago and has never been handled since, and which we thus receive directly from the hand of the red hunter, who purposed to shoot it at his game or at an enemy. Such an incident builds up again the Indian village and its encircling forest, and recalls to life the painted chiefs and warriors, the squaws at their household toil, and the children sporting among the wigwams, while the little wind-rocked papoose swings from the branch of the tree. It can hardly be told whether it is a joy or a pain, after such a momentary vision, to gaze around in the broad daylight of reality and see stone fences, white houses, potato fields, and men doggedly hoeing in their shirt-sleeves and homespun pantaloons. But this is nonsense. The Old Manse is better than a thousand wigwams.

The Old Manse! We had almost forgotten it, but will return thither through the orchard. This was set out by the last clergyman, in the decline of his life, when the neighbors laughed at the hoary-headed man for planting trees from which he could have no prospect of gathering fruit. Even had that been the case, there was only so much the better motive for planting them, in the pure and unselfish hope of benefiting his successors,—an end so seldom achieved by more ambitious efforts. But the old minister, before reaching his patriarchal age of ninety, ate the apples from this orchard during many years, and added silver and gold to his annual stipend by disposing of the superfluity. It is pleasant to think of him walking among the trees in the quiet afternoons of early autumn and picking up here and there a windfall, while he observes how heavily the branches are weighed down, and computes the number of empty flour barrels that will be filled by their burden. He loved each tree, doubtless, as if it had been his own child. An orchard has a relation to mankind, and readily connects itself with matters of the heart. The trees possess a domestic character; they have lost the wild nature of their forest kindred, and have grown humanized by receiving the care of man as well as by contributing to his wants. There is so much individuality of character, too, among apple-trees that it gives them an additional claim to be the objects of human interest. One is harsh and crabbed in its manifestations; another gives us fruit as mild as charity. One is churlish and illiberal, evidently grudging the few apples that it bears; another exhausts itself in free-hearted benevolence. The variety of grotesque shapes into which apple-trees contort themselves has its effect on those who get acquainted with them: they stretch out their crooked branches, and take such hold of the imagination that we remember them as humorists and odd-fellows. And what is more melancholy than the old apple-trees that linger about the spot where once stood a homestead, but where there is now only a ruined chimney rising out of a grassy and weed-grown cellar? They offer their fruit to every wayfarer,—apples that are bitter sweet with the moral of Time's vicissitude.

I have met with no other such pleasant trouble in the world as that of finding myself, with only the two or three mouths which it was my privilege to feed, the sole inheritor of the old clergyman's wealth of fruits. Throughout the summer there were cherries and currants; and then came autumn, with his immense burden of apples, dropping them continually from his overladen shoulders as he trudged along. In the stillest afternoon, if I listened, the thump of a great apple was audible, falling without a breath of wind, from the mere necessity of perfect ripeness. And, besides, there were pear-trees, that flung down bushels upon bushels of heavy pears; and peach-trees, which, in a good year, tormented me with peaches, neither to be eaten nor kept, nor, without labor and perplexity, to be given away. The idea of an infinite generosity and exhaustless bounty on the part of our Mother Nature was well worth obtaining through such cares as these. That feeling can be enjoyed in perfection only by the natives of summer islands, where the bread-fruit, the cocoa, the palm, and the orange grow spontaneously and hold forth the ever-ready meal; but likewise almost as well by a man long habituated to city life, who plunges into such a solitude as that of the Old Manse, where he plucks the fruit of trees that he did not plant, and which therefore, to my heterodox taste, bear the closest resemblance to those that grew in Eden. It has been an apothegm these five thousand years, that toil sweetens the bread it earns. For my part (speaking from hard experience, acquired while belaboring the rugged furrows of Brook Farm[2]), I relish best the free gifts of Providence.

Not that it can be disputed that the light toil requisite to cultivate a moderately-sized garden imparts such zest to kitchen vegetables as

2. A socialistic community of transcendentalists and Fourierists, in which Hawthorne spent some time in 1841, and lost some money.

is never found in those of the market gardener. Childless men, if they would know something of the bliss of paternity, should plant a seed, —be it squash, bean, Indian corn, or perhaps a mere flower or worthless weed,—should plant it with their own hands, and nurse it from infancy to maturity altogether by their own care. If there be not too many of them, each individual plant becomes an object of separate interest. My garden, that skirted the avenue of the Manse, was of precisely the right extent. An hour or two of morning labor was all that it required. But I used to visit and revisit it a dozen times a day, and stand in deep contemplation over my vegetable progeny with a love that nobody could share or conceive of who had never taken part in the process of creation. It was one of the most bewitching sights in the world to observe a hill of beans thrusting aside the soil, or a row of early peas just peeping forth sufficiently to trace a line of delicate green. Later in the season the humming-birds were attracted by the blossoms of a peculiar variety of bean; and they were a joy to me, those little spiritual visitants, for deigning to sip airy food out of my nectar cups. Multitudes of bees used to bury themselves in the yellow blossoms of the summer squashes. This, too, was a deep satisfaction; although when they had laden themselves with sweets they flew away to some unknown hive, which would give back nothing in requital of what my garden had contributed. But I was glad thus to fling a benefaction upon the passing breeze with the certainty that somebody must profit by it, and that there would be a little more honey in the world to allay the sourness and bitterness which mankind is always complaining of. Yes, indeed; my life was the sweeter for that honey.

Speaking of summer squashes, I must say a word of their beautiful and varied forms. They presented an endless diversity of urns and vases, shallow or deep, scalloped or plain, moulded in patterns which a sculptor would do well to copy, since Art has never invented anything more graceful. A hundred squashes in the garden were worthy, in my eyes at least, of being rendered indestructible in marble. If ever Providence (but I know it never will) should assign me a superfluity of gold, part of it shall be expended for a service of plate, or most delicate porcelain, to be wrought into the shapes of summer squashes gathered from vines which I will plant with my own hands. As dishes for containing vegetables they would be peculiarly appropriate.

But not merely the squeamish love of the beautiful was gratified by my toil in the kitchen garden. There was a hearty enjoyment, likewise, in observing the growth of the crook-necked winter squashes, from the first little bulb, with the withered blossom adhering to it, until they lay strewn upon the soil, big, round fellows, hiding their heads beneath the leaves, but turning up their great yellow rotundities to the noontide sun. Gazing at them, I felt that by my agency something worth living for had been done. A new substance was born into the world. They were real and tangible existences, which the mind could seize hold of and rejoice in. A cabbage, too,—especially the early Dutch cabbage, which swells to a monstrous circumference, until its ambitious heart often bursts asunder,—is a matter to be proud of when we can claim a share with the earth and sky in producing it. But, after all, the hugest pleasure is reserved until these vegetable children of ours are smoking on the table, and we, like Saturn, make a meal of them.

What with the river, the battle-field, the orchard and the garden, the reader begins to despair of finding his way back into the Old Manse. But in agreeable weather it is the truest hospitality to keep him out-of-doors. I never grew quite acquainted with my habitation till a long spell of sulky rain had confined me beneath its roof. There could not be a more sombre aspect of external Nature than as then seen from the windows of my study. The great willow-tree had caught and retained among its leaves a whole cataract of water, to be shaken down at intervals by the frequent gusts of wind. All day long, and for a week together, the rain was drip-drip-dripping and splash-splash-splashing from the eaves, and bubbling and foaming into the tubs beneath the spouts. The old, unpainted shingles of the house and out-buildings were black with moisture; and the mosses of ancient growth upon the walls looked green and fresh, as if they were the newest things and afterthought of Time. The usually mirrored surface of the river was blurred by an infinity of raindrops; the whole landscape had a completely water-soaked appearance, conveying the impression that the earth was wet through like a sponge; while the summit of a wooded hill, about a mile distant, was enveloped in a dense mist, where the demon of the tempest seemed to have his abiding-place and to be plotting still direr inclemencies.

Nature has no kindness, no hospitality, during a rain. In the fiercest heat of sunny days she retains a secret mercy, and welcomes the wayfarer to shady nooks of the woods whither the sun cannot penetrate; but she provides no shelter against her storms. It makes us shiver to think of those deep, umbrageous recesses, those overshadowing banks, where we found such enjoyment during the sultry afternoons. Not a twig of foliage there but would dash a little shower into our faces. Looking reproachfully towards the impenetrable sky,—if sky there be above that dismal uniformity of cloud,—we are apt to murmur against the whole system of the universe, since it involves the extinction of so many summer days in so short a life by the hissing and spluttering rain. In such spells of weather—and it is to be supposed such weather came—Eve's bower in paradise must have been but a cheerless and aguish kind of shelter, nowise comparable to the old parsonage, which had resources of its own to beguile the week's imprisonment. The idea of sleeping on a couch of wet roses!

Happy the man who in a rainy day can betake himself to a huge garret, stored, like that of the Manse, with lumber[3] that each generation has left behind it from a period before the revolution. Our garret was an arched hall, dimly illuminated through small and dusty windows, it was but a twilight at the best; and there were nooks, or rather caverns, of deep obscurity, the secrets of which I never learned, being too reverent of their dust and cobwebs. The beams and rafters, roughly hewn and with strips of bark still on them, and the rude masonry of the chimneys, made the garret look wild and uncivilized,—an aspect unlike what was seen elsewhere in the quiet and decorous old house. But on one side there was a little whitewashed apartment which bore the traditional title of the Saint's Chamber, because holy men in their youth had slept and studied and prayed there. With its elevated retirement, its one window, its small fireplace, and its closet, convenient for an oratory,[4] it was the very spot where a young man might inspire himself with solemn enthusiasm and cherish saintly dreams. The occupants, at various epochs, had left brief records and ejaculations inscribed upon the walls. There, too, hung a tattered and shrivelled roll of canvas, which on inspection proved to be the forcibly wrought picture of a clergyman, in wig, band, and gown, holding a Bible in his hand. As I turned his face towards the light he eyed me with an air of authority such as men of his profession seldom assume in our days. The original had been pastor of the parish more than a century ago, a friend of Whitefield,[5] and almost his equal in fervid eloquence. I bowed before the effigy of the dignified divine, and felt as if I had now met face to face with the ghost by whom, as there was reason to apprehend, the Manse was haunted.

Houses of any antiquity in New England are so invariably possessed with spirits that the matter seems hardly worth alluding to. Our ghost used to heave deep sighs in a particular corner of the parlor, and sometimes rustled paper, as if he were turning over a sermon in the long upper entry,—where nevertheless he was invisible in spite of the bright moonshine that fell through the eastern window. Not improbably he wished me to edit and publish a selection from a chest full of manuscript discourses that stood in the garret. Once, while Hillard[6] and other friends sat talking with us in the twilight, there

3. Household odds and ends.
4. Private chapel for prayer.
5. George Whitefield, British evangelist in America of the "Great Awakening" (1738–40), and of Methodism (1744 and later), preached twice at Concord on the invitation of the Reverend

Daniel Bliss, a maternal ancestor of Emerson.
6. George Stillman Hillard (1808–1879), Boston lawyer, with whom Hawthorne had made his residence in Boston, was a frequent visitor at the Old Manse.

came a rustling noise as of a minister's silk gown, sweeping through the very midst of the company so closely as almost to brush against the chairs. Still there was nothing visible. A yet stranger business was that of a ghostly servant maid, who used to be heard in the kitchen at deepest midnight, grinding coffee, cooking, ironing,—performing, in short, all kinds of domestic labor,—although no traces of anything accomplished could be detected the next morning. Some neglected duty of her servitude—some ill-starched ministerial band—disturbed the poor damsel in her grave and kept her at work without any wages.

But to return from this digression. A part of my predecessor's library was stored in the garret,—no unfit receptacle indeed for such dreary trash as comprised the greater number of volumes. The old books would have been worth nothing at an auction. In this venerable garret, however, they possessed an interest, quite apart from their literary value, as heirlooms, many of which had been transmitted down through a series of consecrated hands from the days of the mighty Puritan divines. Autographs of famous names were to be seen in faded ink on some of their flyleaves; and there were marginal observations or interpolated pages closely covered with manuscript in illegible shorthand, perhaps concealing matter of profound truth and wisdom. The world will never be the better for it. A few of the books were Latin folios, written by Catholic authors; others demolished Papistry, as with a sledge-hammer, in plain English. A dissertation on the book of Job—which only Job himself could have had patience to read—filled at least a score of small, thickset quartos, at the rate of two or three volumes to a chapter. Then there was a vast folio body of divinity—too corpulent a body, it might be feared, to comprehend the spiritual element of religion. Volumes of this form dated back two hundred years or more, and were generally bound in black leather, exhibiting precisely such an appearance as we should attribute to books of enchantment. Others equally antique were of a size proper to be carried in the large waistcoat pockets of old times,—diminutive, but as black as their bulkier brethren, and abundantly interfused with Greek and Latin quotations. These little old volumes impressed me as if they had been intended for very large ones, but had been unfortunately blighted at an early stage of their growth.

The rain pattered upon the roof and the sky gloomed through the dusty garret windows, while I burrowed among these venerable books in search of any living thought which should burn like a coal of fire, or glow like an inextinguishable gem, beneath the dead trumpery that had long hidden it. But I found no such treasure; all was dead alike; and I could not but muse deeply and wonderingly upon the humiliating fact that the works of man's intellect decay like those of his hands. Thought grows mouldy. What was good and nourishing food for the spirits of one generation affords no sustenance for the next. Books of religion, however, cannot be considered a fair test of the enduring and vivacious properties of human thought, because such books so seldom really touch upon their ostensible subject, and have, therefore, so little business to be written at all. So long as an unlettered soul can attain to saving grace, there would seem to be no deadly error in holding theological libraries to be accumulations of, for the most part, stupendous impertinence.

Many of the books had accrued in the latter years of the last clergyman's lifetime. These threatened to be of even less interest than the elder works, a century hence, to any curious inquirer who should then rummage them as I was doing now. Volumes of the "Liberal Preacher" and "Christian Examiner,"[7] occasional sermons, controversial pamphlets, tracts, and other productions of a like fugitive nature took the place of the thick and heavy volumes of past time. In a physical point of view there was much the same difference as between a feather and a lump of lead; but, intellectually regarded, the specific gravity of old and new was about upon a par. Both also were alike frigid. The elder books, nevertheless, seemed to have been earnestly written, and might be conceived to have possessed warmth at some former period; although, with the lapse of time, the heated masses had cooled down even to the freezing point. The frigidity of the modern productions, on the other hand, was characteristic and inherent, and evidently had little to do with the writer's qualities of mind and heart. In fine, of this whole dusty heap of literature I tossed aside all the sacred part, and felt myself none the less a Christian for eschewing it. There appeared no hope of either mounting to the better world on a Gothic staircase of ancient folios or of flying thither on the wings of a modern tract.

Nothing, strange to say, retained any sap except what had been written for the passing day and year without the remotest pretension or idea or permanence. There were a few old newspapers, and still older almanacs, which reproduced to my mental eye the epochs when they had issued from the press with a distinctness that was altogether unaccountable. It was as if I had found bits of magic looking-glass among the books, with the images of a vanished century in them. I turned my eyes towards the tattered picture above mentioned, and asked of the austere divine wherefore it was that he and his brethren, after the most painful rummaging and groping into their minds, had been able to produce nothing half so real as these newspaper scribblers and almanac makers had thrown off in the effervescence of a moment. The portrait responded not; so I sought an answer for myself. It is the age itself that writes newspapers and

7. Theological magazines.

almanacs, which, therefore, have a distinct purpose and meaning at the time, and a kind of intelligible truth for all times; whereas most other works—being written by men who, in the very act, set themselves apart from their age—are likely to possess little significance when new, and none at all when old. Genius, indeed, melts many ages into one, and thus effects something permanent, yet still with a similarity of office to that of the more ephemeral writer. A work of genius is but the newspaper of a century, or perchance of a hundred centuries.

Lightly as I have spoken of these old books, there yet lingers with me a superstitious reverence for literature of all kinds. A bound volume has a charm in my eyes similar to what scraps of manuscript possess for the good Mussulman. He imagines that those wind-wafted records are perhaps hallowed by some sacred verse; and I, that every new book or antique one may contain the "open sesame,"—the spell to disclose treasures hidden in some unsuspected cave of Truth. Thus it was not without sadness that I turned away from the library of the Old Manse.

Blessed was the sunshine when it came again at the close of another stormy day, beaming from the edge of the western horizon; while the massive firmament of clouds threw down all the gloom it could, but served only to kindle the golden light into a more brilliant glow by the strongly contrasted shadows. Heaven smiled at the earth, so long unseen, from beneath its heavy eyelid. Tomorrow for the hill-tops and the wood paths.

Or it might be that Ellery Channing[8] came up the avenue to join me in a fishing excursion on the river. Strange and happy times were those when we cast aside all irksome forms and strait-laced habitudes, and delivered ourselves up to the free air, to live like the Indians or any less conventional race during one bright semicircle of the sun. Rowing our boat against the current, between wide meadows, we turned aside into the Assabeth.[9] A more lovely stream than this, for a mile above its junction with the Concord, has never flowed on earth,—nowhere, indeed, except to lave the interior regions of a poet's imagination. It is sheltered from the breeze by woods and a hill-side; so that elsewhere there might be a hurricane, and here scarcely a ripple across the shaded water. The current lingers along so gently that the mere force of the boatman's will seems sufficient to propel his craft against it. It comes flowing softly through the midmost privacy and deepest heart of a wood which whispers it to be quiet; while the stream whispers back again from its sedgy borders, as if river and wood were hushing one another to sleep. Yes; the river sleeps along its course and dreams of the sky and of the clustering

8. William Ellery Channing (1818–1901), nephew of the Unitarian leader of the same name, was a minor transcendentalist author.
9. A branch of the Concord River.

foliage, amid which fall showers of broken sunlight, imparting specks of vivid cheerfulness, in contrast with the quiet depth of the prevailing tint. Of all this scene, the slumbering river has a dream picture in its bosom. Which, after all, was the most real—the picture, or the original?—the objects palpable to our grosser senses, or their apotheosis in the stream beneath? Surely the disembodied images stand in closer relation to the soul. But both the original and the reflection had here an ideal charm; and, had it been a thought more wild, I could have fancied that this river had strayed forth out of the rich scenery of my companion's inner world; only the vegetation along its banks should then have had an Oriental[1] character.

Gentle and unobtrusive as the river is, yet the tranquil woods seem hardly satisfied to allow it passage. The trees are rooted on the very verge of the water, and dip their pendent branches into it. At one spot there is a lofty bank, on the slope of which grow some hemlocks, declining across the stream with outstretched arms, as if resolute to take the plunge. In other places the banks are almost on a level with the water; so that the quiet congregation of trees set their feet in the flood, and are fringed with foliage down to the surface. Cardinal flowers kindle their spiral flames and illuminate the dark nooks among the shrubbery. The pond-lily grows abundantly along the margin—that delicious flower, which, as Thoreau tells me, opens its virigin bosom to the first sunlight and perfects its being through the magic of that genial kiss. He has beheld beds of them unfolding in due succession as the sunrise stole gradually from flower to flower—a sight not to be hoped for unless when a poet adjusts his inward eye to a proper focus with the outward organ. Grape-vines here and there twine themselves around shrub and tree and hang their clusters over the water within reach of the boatman's hand. Oftentimes they unite two trees of alien race in an inextricable twine, marrying the hemlock and the maple against their will, and enriching them with a purple offspring of which neither is the parent. One of these ambitious parasites has climbed into the upper branches of a tall, white pine, and is still ascending from bough to bough, unsatisfied till it shall crown the tree's airy summit with a wreath of its broad foliage and a cluster of its grapes.

The winding course of the stream continually shut out the scene behind us, and revealed as calm and lovely a one before. We glided from depth to depth, and breathed new seclusion at every turn. The shy kingfisher flew from the withered branch close at hand to another at a distance, uttering a shrill cry of anger or alarm. Ducks that had been floating there since the preceding eve were startled at our approach, and skimmed along the glassy river, breaking its dark sur-

1. The previous passage has suggested to Hawthorne the transcendentalist's absorption in oriental idealistic thought.

face with a bright streak. The pickerel leaped from among the lily-pads. The turtle, sunning itself upon a rock or at the root of a tree, slid suddenly into the water with a plunge. The painted Indian who paddled his canoe along the Assabeth three hundred years ago could hardly have seen a wilder gentleness displayed upon its banks and reflected in its bosom than we did. Nor could the same Indian have prepared his noontide meal with more simplicity. We drew up our skiff at some point where the overarching shade formed a natural bower, and there kindled a fire with the pine cones and decayed branches that lay strewn plentifully around. Soon the smoke ascended among the trees, impregnated with a savory incense, not heavy, dull, and surfeiting, like the steam of cookery within doors, but sprightly and piquant. The smell of our feast was akin to the woodland odors with which it mingled: there was no sacrilege committed by our intrusion there: the sacred solitude was hospitable, and granted us free leave to cook and eat in the recess that was at once our kitchen and banqueting hall. It is strange what humble offices may be performed in a beautiful scene without destroying its poetry. Our fire, red gleaming among the trees, and we beside it, busied with culinary rites and spreading out our meal on a mossgrown log, all seemed in unison with the river gliding by and the foliage rustling over us. And, what was strangest, neither did our mirth seem to disturb the propriety of the solemn woods; although the hobgoblins of the old wilderness and the will-of-the-wisps that glimmered in the marshy places might have come trooping to share our table talk, and have added their shrill laughter to our merriment. It was the very spot in which to utter the extremest nonsense or the profoundest wisdom, or that ethereal product of the mind which partakes of both, and may become one or the other, in correspondence with the faith and insight of the auditor.

So amid sunshine and shadow, rustling leaves and sighing waters, up gushed our talk like the babble of a fountain. The evanescent spray was Ellery's; and his, too, the lumps of golden thought that lay glimmering in the fountain's bed and brightened both our faces by the reflection. Could he have drawn out that virgin gold and stamped it with the mint mark that alone gives currency, the world might have had the profit, and he the fame. My mind was the richer merely by the knowledge that it was there. But the chief profit of those wild days to him and me lay, not in any definite idea, not in any angular or rounded truth, which we dug out of the shapeless mass of problematical stuff, but in the freedom which we thereby won from all custom and conventionalism and fettering influences of man on man. We were so free to-day that it was impossible to be slaves again to-morrow. When we crossed the threshold of the house or trod the thronged pavements of a city, still the leaves of the trees that overhang the Assabeth were whispering to us, "Be free! be free!" Therefore along that shady river-bank there are spots, marked with a heap of ashes and half-consumed brands, only less sacred in my remembrance than the hearth of a household fire.

And yet how sweet, as we floated homeward adown the golden river at sunset,—how sweet was it to return within the system of human society, not as to a dungeon and a chain, but as to a stately edifice, whence we could go forth at will into statelier simplicity! How gently, too, did the sight of the Old Manse, best seen from the river, overshadowed with its willow and all environed about with the foliage of its orchard and avenue,—how gently did its gray, homely aspect rebuke the speculative extravagances of the day! It had grown sacred in connection with the artificial life against which we inveighed; it had been a home for many years in spite of all; it was my home too; and, with these thoughts, it seemed to me that all the artifice and conventionalism of life was but an impalpable thinness upon its surface, and that the depth below was none the worse for it. Once, as we turned our boat to the bank, there was a cloud, in the shape of an immensely gigantic figure of a hound, couched above the house, as if keeping guard over it. Gazing at this symbol, I prayed that the upper influences might long protect the institutions that had grown out of the heart of mankind.

If ever my readers should decide to give up civilized life, cities, houses, and whatever moral or material enormities in addition to these the perverted ingenuity of our race has contrived, let it be in the early autumn. Then Nature will love him better than at any other season, and will take him to her bosom with a more motherly tenderness. I could scarcely endure the roof of the old house above me in those first autumnal days. How early in the summer, too, the prophecy of autumn comes! Earlier in some years than in others; sometimes even in the first weeks of July. There is no other feeling like what is caused by this faint, doubtful, yet real perception—if it be not rather a foreboding—of the year's decay, so blessedly sweet and sad in the same breath.

Did I say that there was no feeling like it? Ah, but there is a half-acknowledged melancholy like to this when we stand in the perfected vigor of our life and feel that Time has now given us all his flowers, and that the next work of his never idle fingers must be to steal them one by one away.

I have forgotten whether the song of the cricket be not as early a token of autumn's approach as any other,—that song which may be called an audible stillness; for though very loud and heard afar, yet the mind does not take note of it as a sound, so completely is its individual existence merged among the accompanying characteristics of the season. Alas for the pleasant summer time! In August the grass is still verdant on the hills and in the valleys; the foliage of the trees is as dense as ever, and as green; the flowers gleam forth in richer abundance along the margin of the river, and by the stone walls, and deep among the woods; the days, too, are as fervid now as they were a month ago; and yet in every breath of wind and in every beam of sunshine we hear the whispered farewell and behold the parting smile of a dear friend. There is a coolness amid all the heat, a mildness in the blazing noon. Not a breeze can stir but it thrills us with the breath of autumn. A pensive glory is seen in the far golden gleams, among the shadows of the trees. The flowers—even the brightest of them, and they are the most gorgeous of the year—have this gentle sadness wedded to their pomp, and typify the character of the delicious time each within itself. The brilliant cardinal flower has never seemed gay to me.

Still later in the season Nature's tenderness waxes stronger. It is impossible not to be fond of our mother now; for she is so fond of us! At other periods she does not make this impression on me, or only at rare intervals; but in those genial days of autumn, when she has perfected her harvests and accomplished every needful thing that was given her to do, then she overflows with a blessed superfluity of love. She has leisure to caress her children now. It is good to be alive at such times. Thank Heaven for breath—yes, for mere breath—when it is made up of a heavenly breeze like this! It comes with a real kiss upon our cheeks; it would linger fondly around us if it might; but, since it must be gone, it embraces us with its whole kindly heart and passes onward to embrace likewise the next thing that it meets. A blessing is flung abroad and scattered far and wide over the earth, to be gathered up by all who choose. I recline upon the still unwithered grass and whisper to myself, "O perfect day! O beautiful world! O beneficent God!" And it is the promise of a blessed eternity; for our Creator would never have made such lovely days and have given us the deep hearts to enjoy them, above and beyond all thought, unless we were meant to be immortal. This sunshine is the golden pledge thereof. It beams through the gates of paradise and shows us glimpses far inward.

By and by, in a little time, the outward world puts on a drear austerity. On some October morning there is a heavy hoar-frost on the grass and along the tops of the fences; and at sunrise the leaves fall from the trees of our avenue without a breath of wind, quietly descending by their own weight. All summer long they have murmured like the noise of waters; they have roared loudly while the branches were wrestling with the thunder gust; they have made music both glad and solemn; they have attuned my thoughts by their quiet sound as I paced to and fro beneath the arch of intermingling boughs. Now they can only rustle under my feet. Henceforth the gray parsonage begins to assume a larger importance, and draws to its fireside,—for the abomination of the air-tight stove is reserved till wintry weather,—draws closer and closer to its fireside the vagrant impulses that had gone wandering about through the summer.

When summer was dead and buried the Old Manse became as lonely as a hermitage. Not that ever—in my time at least—it had been thronged with company; but, at no rare intervals, we welcomed some friend out of the dusty glare and tumult of the world, and rejoiced to share with him the transparent obscurity that was floating over us. In one respect our precincts were like the Enchanted Ground through which the pilgrim travelled on his way to the Celestial City![2] The guests, each and all, felt a slumberous influence upon them; they fell asleep in chairs, or took a more deliberate siesta on the sofa, or were seen stretched among the shadows of the orchard, looking up dreamily through the boughs. They could not have paid a more acceptable compliment to my abode, nor to my own qualities as a host. I held it as a proof that they left their cares behind them as they passed between the stone gate-posts at the entrance of our avenue, and that the so powerful opiate was the abundance of peace and quiet within and all around us. Others could give them pleasure and amusement or instruction—these could be picked up anywhere; but it was for me to give them rest—rest in a life of trouble. What better could be done for those weary and world-worn spirits?—for him whose career of perpetual action was impeded and harassed by the rarest of his powers[3] and the richest of his acquirements?—for another who had thrown his ardent heart from earliest youth into the strife of politics,[4] and now, perchance, began to suspect that one lifetime is too brief for the accomplishment of any lofty aim?—for her on whose feminine nature had been imposed the heavy gift of intellectual power, such as a strong man might have staggered under, and with it the necessity to act upon the world?[5]—in a word, not to multiply instances, what better could be done for anybody who came within our magic circle than to throw the spell of a tranquil spirit over him? And when it had wrought its full effect, then we dismissed him, with but misty reminiscences, as if he had been dreaming of us.

Were I to adopt a pet idea, as so many people do, and fondle it in my embraces to the exclusion of all others, it would be, that the

2. In *Pilgrim's Progress* Christian is warned of the Enchanted Ground as affording temptation to linger on the journey to the Celestial City.
3. This is considered to be a reference to Horatio Bridge, Hawthorne's intimate from college days, who had sacrificed literary ambitions in his career as naval officer. In 1845 Hawthorne had edited, from Bridge's diary, *The Journal of an African Cruiser*.
4. Franklin Pierce, another college friend, later president of the United States (1853–1857).
5. Possibly Margaret Fuller, who was a visitor there. Editor of *The Dial* (1840–1842), she was the only prominent woman transcendentalist, and an early feminist.

great want which mankind labors under at this present period is sleep. The world should recline its vast head on the first convenient pillow and take an age-long nap. It has gone distracted through a morbid activity, and, while preternaturally wide awake, is nevertheless tormented by visions that seem real to it now, but would assume their true aspect and character were all things once set right by an interval of sound repose. This is the only method of getting rid of old delusions and avoiding new ones; of regenerating our race, so that it might in due time awake as an infant out of dewy slumber; of restoring to us the simple perception of what is right, and the single-hearted desire to achieve it, both of which have long been lost in consequence of this weary activity of brain and torpor or passion of the heart that now afflict the universe. Stimulants, the only mode of treatment hitherto attempted, cannot quell the disease; they do but heighten the delirium.

Let not the above paragraph ever be quoted against the author; for, though tinctured with its modicum of truth, it is the result and expression of what he knew, while he was writing, to be but a distorted survey of the state and prospects of mankind. There were circumstances around me which made it difficult to view the world precisely as it exists; for, severe and sober as was the Old Manse, it was necessary to go but a little way beyond its threshold before meeting with stranger moral shapes of men than might have been encountered elsewhere in a circuit of a thousand miles.

These hobgoblins of flesh and blood were attracted thither by the widespreading influence of a great original thinker, who had his earthly abode at the opposite extremity of our village. His mind acted upon other minds of a certain constitution with wonderful magnetism, and drew many men upon long pilgrimages to speak with him face to face. Young visionaries—to whom just so much of insight had been imparted as to make life all a labyrinth around them—came to seek the clew that should guide them out of their self-involved bewilderment. Grayheaded theorists—whose systems, at first air, had finally imprisoned them in an iron frame-work—travelled painfully to his door, not to ask deliverance, but to invite the free spirit into their own thraldom. People that had lighted on a new thought, or a thought that they fancied new, came to Emerson, as the finder of a glittering gem hastens to a lapidary, to ascertain its quality and value. Uncertain, troubled, earnest wanderers through the midnight of the moral world beheld his intellectual fire as a beacon burning on a hill-top, and, climbing the difficult ascent, looked forth into the surrounding obscurity more hopefully than hitherto. The light revealed objects unseen before,—mountains, gleaming lakes, glimpses of a creation among the chaos; but, also as was unavoidable, it attracted bats and owls and the whole host of night birds, which flapped their dusky wings against the gazer's eyes, and sometimes were mistaken for fowls of angelic feather. Such delusions always hover nigh whenever a beacon fire of truth is kindled.

For myself, there had been epochs of my life when I, too, might have asked of this prophet the master word that should solve me the riddle of the universe; but now, being happy, I felt as if there were no question to be put, and therefore admired Emerson as a poet of deep beauty and austere tenderness, but sought nothing from him as a philosopher. It was good, nevertheless, to meet him in the woodpaths, or sometimes in our avenue, with that pure intellectual gleam diffused about his presence like the garment of a shining one; and he so quiet, so simple, so without pretension, encountering each man alive as if expecting to receive more than he could impart. And, in truth, the heart of many an ordinary man had, perchance, inscriptions which he could not read. But it was impossible to dwell in his vicinity without inhaling more or less the mountain atmosphere of his lofty thought, which, in the brains of some people, wrought a singular giddiness,—new truth being as heady as new wine. Never was a poor little country village infested with such a variety of queer, strangely-dressed, oddly-behaved mortals, most of whom took upon themselves to be important agents of the world's destiny, yet were simply bores of a very intense water. Such, I imagine, is the invariable character of persons who crowd so closely about an original thinker as to draw in his unuttered breath and thus become imbued with a false originality. This triteness of novelty is enough to make any man of common sense blaspheme at all ideas of less than a century's standing, and pray that the world may be petrified and rendered immovable in precisely the worst moral and physical state that it ever yet arrived at, rather than be benefited by such schemes of such philosophers.

And now I begin to feel—and perhaps should have sooner felt—that we have talked enough of the Old Manse. Mine honored reader, it may be, will vilify the poor author as an egotist for babbling through so many pages about a moss-grown country parsonage, and his life within its walls and on the river and in the woods, and the influences that wrought upon him from all these sources. My conscience, however, does not reproach me with betraying anything too sacredly individual to be revealed by a human spirit to its brother or sister spirit. How narrow—how shallow and scanty too—is the stream of thought that has been flowing from my pen, compared with the broad tide of dim emotions, ideas, and associations which swell around me from that portion of my existence! How little have I told! and of that little, how almost nothing is even tinctured with any quality that makes it exclusively my own! Has the reader gone wandering, hand in hand with me, through the inner passages of my being? and have we groped together into all its chambers and examined their treasures or their rubbish? Not so. We have been standing on the greensward but just within the cavern's mouth, where the common sunshine is free to penetrate, and where every footstep is therefore free to come. I have appealed to no sentiment or sensibilities save such as are diffused among us all. So far as I am a man of really individual attributes I veil my face; nor am I, nor have I ever been, one of those supremely hospitable people who serve up their own hearts, delicately fried, with brain sauce, as a tidbit for their beloved public.

Glancing back over what I have written, it seems but the scattered reminiscences of a single summer. In fairyland there is no measurement of time; and, in a spot so sheltered from the turmoil of life's ocean, three years hastened away with a noiseless flight, as the breezy sunshine chases the cloud shadows across the depths of a still valley. Now came hints, growing more and more distinct, that the owner of the old house was pining for his native air. Carpenters next appeared, making a tremendous racket among the out-buildings, strewing the green grass with pine shavings and chips of chestnut joists, and vexing the whole antiquity of the place with their discordant renovations. Soon, moreover, they divested our abode of the veil of woodbine which had crept over a large portion of its southern face. All the aged mosses were cleared unsparingly away; and there were horrible whispers about brushing up the external walls with a coat of paint—a purpose as little to my taste as might be that of rouging the venerable cheeks of one's grandmother. But the hand that renovates is always more sacrilegious than that which destroys. In fine, we gathered up our household goods, drank a farewell cup of tea in our pleasant little breakfast room,—delicately fragrant tea, an unpurchasable luxury, one of the many angel gifts that had fallen like dew upon us,—and passed forth between the tall stone gateposts as uncertain as the wandering Arabs where our tent might next be pitched. Providence took me by the hand, and—an oddity of dispensation which, I trust, there is no irreverence in smiling at —has led me, as the newspapers announce while I am writing, from the Old Manse into a custom house.[6] As a story teller, I have often contrived strange vicissitudes for my imaginary personages, but none like this.

The treasure of intellectual good which I hoped to find in our secluded dwelling had never come to light. No profound treatise of ethics, no philosophic history, no novel even, that could stand unsupported on its edges. All that I had to show, as a man of letters,

6. Hawthorne had just been appointed surveyor in the Salem Custom House (1846–1849).

were these few tales and essays, which had blossomed out like flowers in the calm summer of my heart and mind. Save editing (an easy task) the journal of my friend of many years, the African Cruiser, I had done nothing else. With these idle weeds and withering blossoms I have intermixed some that were produced long ago,—old, faded things, reminding me of flowers pressed between the leaves of a book,—and now offer the bouquet, such as it is, to any whom it may please. These fitful sketches, with so little of external life about them, yet claiming no profundity of purpose,—so reserved, even while they sometimes seem so frank,—often but half in earnest, and never, even when most so, expressing satisfactorily the thoughts which they profess to image,—such trifles, I truly feel, afford no solid basis for a literary reputation. Nevertheless, the public—if my limited number of readers, whom I venture to regard rather as a circle of friends, may be termed a public—will receive them the more kindly, as the last offering, the last collection, of this nature which it is my purpose ever to put forth. Unless I could do better, I have done enough in this kind. For myself the book will always retain one charm—as reminding me of the river, with its delightful solitudes, and of the avenue, the garden, and the orchard, and especially the dear old Manse, with the little study on its western side, and the sunshine glimmering through the willow branches while I wrote.

Let the reader, if he will do me so much honor, imagine himself my guest, and that, having seen whatever may be worthy of notice within and about the Old Manse, he has finally been ushered into my study. There, after seating him in an antique elbow chair, an heirloom of the house, I take forth a roll of manuscript and entreat his attention to the following tales—an act of personal inhospitality, however, which I never was guilty of, nor ever will be, even to my worst enemy.

1846

EDGAR ALLAN POE
(1809–1849)

A century and more after his death, Poe is still among the most popular of American authors. Cheap reprints of his stories and poems circulate even from newsstands, but unlike most authors of extreme popularity, Poe has also exerted a continuous influence on the most advanced writers and critics.

His works are directed toward universal human responses, which change very little, if at all, with the passing of time and events. He influenced the course of creative writing and criticism by emphasizing the art that appeals simultaneously to reason and to emotion, and by insisting that the work of art is not a fragment of the author's life, nor an adjunct to some didactic purpose, but an object created in the cause of beauty—which he defined in its largest spiritual implications. This creative act, according to Poe, involves the utmost concentration and unity, together with the most scrupulous use of words.

This definition of sensibility was directly opposed to the view implicit in the prevailing American literature of Poe's generation, as represented in general by the works of Emerson, Hawthorne, Longfellow, Whittier, and Holmes, all born in the years from 1803 to 1809. These others turned toward Wordsworth, while Poe took Coleridge as his lodestar in his search for a consistent theory of art. Hawthorne's symbolism links him with Poe, but Hawthorne's impulses were primarily didactic, while Poe taught no moral lessons except the discipline of beauty. Only in Melville, among the authors before the Civil War, does one find a similar sensibility expressed in symbolism. The literary tradition of Poe, preserved by European symbolism, especially in France, played a considerable part in shaping the spirit of our twentieth-century literature, particularly in its demand for the intellectual analysis and controlled perception of emotional consciousness.

The familiar legend of Poe is at variance with his actual personality. Finding himself in conflict with the prevailing spirit of his age, he took refuge in the Byronic myth of the lonely and misunderstood artist. Indeed, his neurotic personality sometimes resembled that of his own fictional characters; it is much easier to see now, than it was then, how vastly sublimated are the actual events which first suggested "To Helen" or "Ligeia."

The son of itinerant actors, he was born in Boston, January 19, 1809. His father, David Poe, apparently deserted his wife and disappeared about eighteen months later. Elizabeth Arnold Poe, an English-born actress, died during a tour, in Richmond in 1811, and her infant son became the ward of the Allan family, although he was never legally adopted. John Allan was a substantial Scottish tobacco exporter; Mrs. Allan lavished on the young poet the erratic affections of the childless wife of a somewhat unfaithful husband. In time this situation led to tensions and jealousies which permanently estranged Poe from his foster father; but in youth he enjoyed the genteel and thorough education, with none of the worldly expectations, of a young Virginia gentleman.

Allan's business interests took him abroad, and Poe lived with the family in England and Scotland from 1815 to 1820, attending a fine classical preparatory school at Stoke Newington for three years. When he was eleven, the family returned to Richmond, where he continued his studies at a local academy. His precocious adoration of Jane Stith Stanard, the young mother of a schoolfellow, later inspired the lyric "To Helen," according to his own report. At this period he considered himself engaged to Sarah Elmira Royster. Her father's objections to a stripling with no prospects resulted in her engagement to another while Poe was at the University of Virginia in 1826. His gambling debts prompted Allan to remove him from the University within a year, in spite of his obvious academic competence.

Unable to come to terms with Allan, who wanted to employ him in the business, Poe ran away to Boston, where he published *Tamerlane and Other Poems* (1827), significantly signed "By a Bostonian"; then he disappeared into the army under the name of "Edgar A. Perry." The death of Mrs. Allan produced a temporary reconciliation with Allan, who offered to seek an appointment to West Point for the young sergeant major. Poe secured a discharge from the army, and published *Al Aaraaf, Tamerlane, and Minor Poems* (1829). Before entering West Point (July 1, 1830) he again had a violent disagreement with Allan, who still declined to assure his prospects. Finding himself unsuited to the life at the Academy, he provoked a dismissal by an infraction of duty, and left three weeks before March 6, 1831, when he was officially excluded. Allan, who had married again, refused to befriend him; two years later his death ended all expectations. Meanwhile, in New York, Poe had published *Poems* (1831), again without results that would suggest his ability to survive by writing.

From 1831 to 1835 Poe lived as a hack writer in Baltimore, with his aunt, the motherly Mrs. Maria Poe Clemm, whose daughter, Virginia, later became his wife. This period of poverty and struggle is almost a merciful blank on the record.

In 1832 the *Philadelphia Saturday Courier* published Poe's first five short stories, a part of the *Tales of the Folio Club*. In 1833 his first characteristic short story, combining pseudoscience and terror, won a prize of fifty dollars and publication in the *Baltimore Saturday Visitor*. "MS Found in a Bottle" appeared on October 12, heralding the success of the formula for popular fiction which Poe was slowly developing by a close study of periodical literature. The prize story won him friends, and ultimately an assistant editorship on the Richmond *Southern Literary Messenger* (1835–1837). In September, 1835, Poe secretly married his cousin, Virginia Clemm; the ceremony was repeated publicly in Richmond eight months later, when Virginia was not quite fourteen.

Poe's experience with the *Messenger* set a pattern which was to continue, with minor variations, in later editorial associations. He was a brilliant editor; he secured important contributors; he attracted attention by his own critical articles. He failed through personal instability. His devotion to Virginia was beset by some insecurity never satisfactorily explained; he had periods of quarrelsomeness which estranged him from his editorial associates. Apparently he left the *Messenger* of his own accord, but during a time of strained relations, with a project for a magazine of his own which he long cherished without result.

After a few months in New York, Poe settled down to his period of greatest accomplishment (1838–1844) in Philadelphia. There he was editor of, or associated with, *Burton's Gentleman's Magazine* (1839), *Graham's Magazine* (1841–1842), and *The Saturday Museum* (1843). He became well-known in literary circles as a result of the vitality of his critical articles, which were a by-product of his editorial functions, the publication of new poems and revised versions of others, and the appearance of some of his greatest stories in *Graham's*. He collected from earlier periodicals his *Tales of the Grotesque and Arabesque* (2 vols., 1840). His fame was assured by "The Gold Bug," which won the prize of one hundred dollars offered in 1843 by the Philadelphia *Dollar Newspaper*.

Unable to hold a permanent editorial connection in Philadelphia, Poe moved in 1844 to New York, where he found sporadic employment on the *Evening Mirror* and the *Broadway Journal*. For some time it had been evident that Virginia must soon die of tuberculosis, and this apprehension, added to grueling poverty, had increased Poe's eccentricities. Even an occasional escape by alcohol could not go unnoticed in anyone for whom only a moderate indulgence was ruinous, and Poe's reputation, in these years, suffered in consequence. His can-

did reviews and critical articles increased the number of his enemies, who besmirched his reputation by gossip concerning a number of literary ladies with whom his relations were actually indiscreet but innocent. Yet in 1845 he climaxed his literary life. "The Raven" appeared in the *Mirror*, and in *The Raven and Other Poems*, his major volume of poems. His *Tales* also appeared in New York and London. The Poes found a little cottage at Fordham (now part of New York City) in 1846, and Virginia died there the following January. Poe was feverishly at work on *Eureka* (1848), then deemed the work of a demented mind, but now critically important as a "prose poem" in which he attempted to unify the laws of physical science with those of aesthetic reality.

His life ended, as it had been lived, in events so strange that he might have invented them. In 1849, learning that Sarah Elmira Royster, his childhood sweetheart, was a widow, he visited Richmond and secured her consent to marry him. About two months later he left for Philadelphia on a business engagement. Six days thereafter he was found unconscious on the streets of Baltimore, and he died in delirium after four days, on October 7, 1849.

During a short life of poverty, anxiety, and fantastic tragedy Poe achieved the establishment of a new symbolic poetry within the small compass of forty-eight poems; the formalization of the new short story; the invention of the story of detection and the broadening of science fiction;

the foundation of a new fiction of psychological analysis and symbolism; and the slow development, in various stages, of an important critical theory and a discipline of analytical criticism.

Of the seven multivolume editions of the works of Poe, beginning with Griswold's four-volume collection in 1850, all but one is out of print. This is *Works of Edgar Allan Poe*, 10 vols., edited by E. C. Stedman and G. E. Woodberry, 1894–1895, a reliable edition, reprinted in 1914. Unless otherwise noted, this is the source of the present texts. A more complete edition, most reliable, is the so-called Virginia Edition, 17 vols., edited by J. A. Harrison, 1902. *The Poems of Edgar Allan Poe*, edited by Killis Campbell, 1917, shows the evolution of the texts, and contains valuable notes; the same editor published a scholarly edition of *Poe's Short Stories*, 1927. *The Complete Poems and Stories of Edgar Allan Poe*, edited by A. H. Quinn and E. H. O'Neill, 1946, is excellent. *Edgar Allan Poe: Representative Selections*, edited by M. Alterton and H. Craig, American Writers Series, 1935, contains an excellent critical introduction and notes, with a good bibliography.

The standard scholarly biography is *Edgar Allan Poe*, by A. H. Quinn, 1941. The following are valuable for their critical quality: G. E. Woodberry, *The Life of Edgar Allan Poe, Personal and Literary*, 2 vols., 1885; rev. 1909; Hervey Allen, *Israfel—The Life and Times of Edgar Allan Poe*, 2 vols., 1926; and N. B. Fagin, *The Histrionic Mr. Poe*, 1949. A special study of unique merit is Killis Campbell, *The Mind of Poe and Other Studies*, 1933. The latest and most complete source for Poe's letters is *The Letters of Edgar Allan Poe*, 2 vols., edited by J. W. Ostrom, 1948.

Romance

Romance, who loves to nod and sing,
With drowsy head and folded wing,
Among the green leaves as they shake
Far down within some shadowy lake,
To me a painted paroquet 5
Hath been—a most familiar bird—
Taught me my alphabet to say,
To lisp my very earliest word,
While in the wild wood I did lie,
A child—with a most knowing eye. 10

Of late, eternal Condor[1] years
So shake the very Heaven on high
With tumult as they thunder by,
I have no time for idle cares
Through gazing on the unquiet sky. 15
And when an hour with calmer wings
Its down upon my spirit flings—
That little time with lyre and rhyme
To while away—forbidden things!
My heart would feel to be a crime 20
Unless it trembled with the strings.

1829

1. The Andean vulture, noted for courage and ruthlessness; a familiar figure in South American literature.

Song from Al Aaraaf[2]

" 'Neath blue-bell or streamer—
    Or tufted wild spray
That keeps from the dreamer
    The moonbeam[3] away—
Bright beings![4] that ponder,   5
    With half closing eyes,
On the stars which your wonder
    Hath drawn from the skies,
Till they glance thro' the shade, and
    Come down to your brow   10
Like—eyes of the maiden
    Who calls on you now—
Arise! from your dreaming
    In violet bowers,
To duty beseeming   15
    These star-litten hours—
And shake from your tresses,
    Encumber'd with dew,
The breath of those kisses
    That cumber them too   20
(O, how, without you, Love!
    Could angels be blest?)—
Those kisses of true love
    That lull'd ye to rest!
Up!—shake from your wing   25
    Each hindering thing:
The dew of the night—
    It would weigh down your flight;
And true love caresses—
    O! leave them apart: 30
They are light on the tresses,
    But lead on the heart.

2. "Al Aaraaf" was an ambitious allegory of 422 lines, not well organized as a whole. In Nesace's song, here reprinted, the singer is represented as the spirit of ideal or intellectual beauty, and Ligeia, to whom she sings, is the personification of the harmony of nature. Ligeia, whose name Poe borrowed from one of the Sirens, is herself also a heavenly singer. The dwellers in Al Aaraaf have defeated Nesace by faults of knowledge or faults of love, and the two have met in some remote but divine sphere, where Nesace has come in her exile from Al Aaraaf. In the Koran, Al Aaraaf is a limbo of souls who made no final choice of good or bad. However, Poe identifies it, in a note, as the star discovered by the Swedish astronomer Tycho Brahe, which, after a few nights of splendor, suddenly disappeared. The song occurs in Part II, ll. 68–155, of "Al Aaraaf."

3. Poe notes "that the moon, in Egypt, has the effect of producing blindness to those who sleep with the face exposed to its rays."

4. Addressing the spirits accompanying her, whose "duty" (l. 15) was to warn the inhabitants of other spheres against falling into the errors of Al Aaraaf.

"Ligeia! Ligeia!
  My beautiful one!
Whose harshest idea   35
  Will to melody run,
O! is it thy will
  On the breezes to toss?
Or, capriciously still,
  Like the lone Albatross,[5]   40
Incumbent on night
  (As she on the air)
To keep watch with delight
  On the harmony there?

"Ligeia! wherever   45
  Thy image may be,
No magic shall sever
  Thy music from thee.
Thou hast bound many eyes
  In a dreamy sleep—   50
But the strains still arise
  Which *thy* vigilance keep:
The sound of the rain
  Which leaps down to the flower,
And dances again   55
  In the rhythm of the shower—
The murmur[6] that springs
  From the growing of grass
Are the music of things—
  But are modell'd,[7] alas!—   60
Away, then, my dearest,
  O! hie thee away
To springs that lie clearest
  Beneath the moon-ray—
To lone lake that smiles,   65
  In its dream of deep rest,
At the many star-isles
  That enjewel its breast—
Where wild flowers, creeping,
  Have mingled their shade,   70
On its margin is sleeping
  Full many a maid—

5. "The Albatross is said to sleep on the wing" [Poe's note].

6. "I met with this idea in an old English tale, which I am unable to obtain and quote from memory: The verie essence and, as it were, springe-heade and origine of all musicke is the very pleasaunte sounde which the trees of the forest do make when they growe" [Poe's note].

7. *I.e.*, they are imitations of the divine ideal.

Some have left the cool glade, and
    Have slept with the bee[8]—
Arouse them, my maiden,   75
    On moorland and lea—
Go! breathe on their slumber,
    All softly in ear,
The musical number
    They slumber'd to hear—   80
For what can awaken
    An angel so soon,
Whose sleep hath been taken
    Beneath the cold moon,
As the spell which no slumber   85
    Of witchery may test,
The rhythmical number
    Which lull'd him to rest?"

1829, 1845

Sonnet—To Science[9]

Science! true daughter of Old Time thou art!
    Who alterest all things with thy peering eyes.
Why preyest thou thus upon the poet's heart,
    Vulture, whose wings are dull realities?
How should he love thee? or how deem thee wise?   5
    Who wouldst not leave him in his wandering
To seek for treasure in the jewelled skies,
    Albeit he soared with an undaunted wing?
Hast thou not dragged Diana[1] from her car?
    And driven the Hamadryad from the wood   10
To seek a shelter in some happier star?
    Hast thou not torn the Naiad from her flood,
The Elfin from the green grass, and from me
The summer dream beneath the tamarind[2] tree?

1829   1829, 1845

8. "The wild bee will not sleep in the shade if there be moonlight. The rhyme in this verse, as in one about sixty lines before, has an appearance of affectation. It is, however, imitated from Sir W. Scott, or rather from Claud Halcro—in whose mouth I admired its effect: 'O! were there an island, / Tho' ever so wild / Where woman might smile, and / No man be beguiled, &c.'" [Poe's note]. The passage is in Scott's *The Pirate*, Chapter 12. *Cf.* Poe's rhymes: "glade, and" (l. 73) with "maiden" (l. 75).

9. In three volumes, Poe printed this sonnet just before "Al Aaraaf," with which it is connected in meaning. At that time he saw the artist's imagination as being in conflict with the scientific, especially the metaphysical. *Cf.* his strong disapproval of Wordsworth in "Letter to B——," reprinted with Poe's criticism below. Lines 10 and 11 refer directly to the exile of Nesace ("The Hamadryad") in "Al Aaraaf."

1. Roman goddess, whose "car" was the moon. She was revered for her chastity; *cf.* "Dian" in Ulalume."

2. An oriental tree probably unknown in actuality to Poe, but idealized in Eastern poetry.

Lenore[3]

Ah, broken is the golden bowl![4]—the spirit flown forever!
Let the bell toll!—a saintly soul floats on the Stygian[5] river:—
And, Guy De Vere, hast *thou* no tear?—weep now or never more!
See! on yon drear and rigid bier low lies thy love, Lenore!
Come, let the burial rite be read—the funeral song be sung!—   5
An anthem for the queenliest dead that ever died so young—
A dirge for her the doubly dead in that she died so young.

"Wretches![6] ye loved her for her wealth, and ye hated her for her
     pride;
And, when she fell in feeble health, ye blessed her—that she died:—
How *shall* the ritual, then, be read—the requiem how be sung   10
By you—by yours, the evil eye,—by yours, the slanderous tongue
That did to death the innocence that died, and died so young?"

Peccavimus;[7] yet rave not thus! but let a Sabbath song
Go up to God so solemnly the dead may feel no wrong!
The sweet Lenore hath gone before, with Hope that flew beside,   15
Leaving thee wild for the dear child that should have been thy
     bride—
For her, the fair and debonair, that now so lowly lies,
The life upon her yellow hair, but not within her eyes—
The life still there upon her hair, the death upon her eyes.

"Avaunt!—avaunt! to friends from fiends the indignant ghost is
     riven—
        20
From Hell unto a high estate within the utmost Heaven—
From moan and groan to a golden throne beside the King of
     Heaven:—
Let *no* bell toll, then, lest her soul, amid its hallowed mirth,
Should catch the note as it doth float up from the damnèd Earth!
And I—to-night my heart is light:—no dirge will I upraise,   25
But waft the angel on her flight with a Pæan of old days!"

1831, 1849

---

3. "Lenore" first appeared as "A
Pæan" in the 1831 volume, and was revised three times. The final form, given
here, appeared in the *Richmond Whig*,
September 18, 1849. Originally it was
in short lines, indicated in general by the
internal rimes in the present text. The
dirge for the delicate girl killed by the
cruelty or falseness of her family or
lover was conventional in romantic
poetry; but this poem recalls the poet's
resentment at the marriage, which he

ascribed to a cruel intrigue, of his sweetheart, Miss Royster, to an older man
of wealth; and his grief at the death of
his foster mother, Mrs. Allan.
4. *Cf.* Ecclesiastes xii: 6.
5. The river Styx, in Greek mythology,
separates the world of the living from
the Hades of death.
6. Stanzas 2 and 4, between quotation
marks, are the lover's address to the
"wretches," Lenore's false friends.
7. We have sinned.

The Sleeper[8]

At midnight, in the month of June,
I stand beneath the mystic moon.
An opiate vapor, dewy, dim,[9]
Exhales from out her golden rim,
And, softly dripping, drop by drop,   5
Upon the quiet mountain top,
Steals drowsily and musically
Into the universal valley.
The rosemary[1] nods upon the grave;
The lily lolls upon the wave;   10
Wrapping the fog about its breast,
The ruin moulders into rest;
Looking like Lethe,[2] see! the lake
A conscious slumber seems to take,
And would not, for the world, awake.   15
All Beauty sleeps!—and lo! where lies
(Her casement open to the skies)
Irene, with her Destinies!

Oh, lady bright! can it be right—
This window open to the night?   20
The wanton airs, from the tree-top,
Laughingly through the lattice drop—
The bodiless airs, a wizard rout,
Flit through thy chamber in and out,
And wave the curtain canopy   25
So fitfully—so carefully—
Above the closed and fringed lid
'Neath which thy slumb'ring soul lies hid,
That, o'er the floor and down the wall,
Like ghosts the shadows rise and fall!   30
Oh, lady dear, hast thou no fear?
Why and what art thou dreaming here?
Sure thou art come o'er far-off seas,
A wonder to these garden trees!
Strange is thy pallor! strange thy dress!   35
Strange, above all, thy length of tress,[3]
And this all solemn silentness!

8. As "Irene" in the 1831 volume, the poem contained only the substance of "The Sleeper," which emerged in the 1845 volume as given here, after several revisions.
9. The superstition that night air and moonlight had deadly effects, especially on delicate girls, outlived the century.

1. The flower of rosemary is a symbol of fidelity or remembrance; cf. Ophelia in *Hamlet*, Act IV, Scene v, l. 174.
2. In Greek mythology, a river of Hades whose water provided forgetfulness.
3. A familiar superstition held that the hair grew very rapidly just after death.

The lady sleeps! Oh, may her sleep,
Which is enduring, so be deep!
Heaven have her in its sacred keep!
This chamber changed for one more holy,   40
This bed for one more melancholy,
I pray to God that she may lie
Forever with unopened eye,
While the dim sheeted ghosts go by!   45

My love, she sleeps! Oh, may her sleep,
As it is lasting, so be deep!
Soft may the worms about her creep![4]
Far in the forest, dim and old,
For her may some tall vault unfold—   50
Some vault that oft hath flung its black
And winged panels fluttering back,
Triumphant, o'er the crested palls,
Of her grand family funerals—

Some sepulchre, remote, alone,   55
Against whose portal she hath thrown,
In childhood, many an idle stone—
Some tomb from out whose sounding door
She ne'er shall force an echo more,
Thrilling to think, poor child of sin!   60
It was the dead who groaned within.

1831, 1845

Israfel[5]

In Heaven a spirit doth dwell
"Whose heart-strings are a lute";
None sing so wildly well

4. The good taste of this line has been called in question, but the figure was common to the romance of melancholy. Campbell (*The Poems of Edgar Allan Poe*, p. 213) cites Shelley (*Rosalind and Helen*, l. 345): "And the crawling worms were cradling her"; and Byron (*Giaour*, ll. 945–946): "It is as if the dead could feel / The icy worm around them steal * * * "

5. As in "Al Aaraaf," with which this may be compared, Poe here attempts to express a poetic creed, emphasized by the motto which he had printed, either above or below the text, in a number of editions: "And the angel Israfel, [whose heart-strings are a lute,] and who has the sweetest voice of all God's creatures.

—KORAN." Except for the phrase within brackets, this quotation was adapted from George Sale's translation of the Koran, Section IV (1734), in which Israfel is represented as one of the four angels beside the throne of God. In 1845 and subsequent editions, Poe interpolated the bracketed words, also the second line of his poem. Campbell (*The Poems of Edgar Allan Poe*, p. 203) finds the source of this line in De Béranger's "Le Refus" (ll. 41–42), which Poe used in 1839 as the motto for "The Fall of the House of Usher," as follows: "Son cœur est un luth suspendu; / Sitôt qu'on le touche il résonne" ("His heart is a suspended lute; Whenever one touches it, it resounds").

As the angel Israfel,
And the giddy stars (so legends tell)   5
Ceasing their hymns, attend the spell
    Of his voice, all mute.

Tottering above
    In her highest noon,
    The enamored moon   10
Blushes with love,
    While, to listen, the red levin[6]
    (With the rapid Pleiads,[7] even,
    Which were seven)
    Pauses in Heaven.   15

And they say (the starry choir
    And the other listening things)
That Israfeli's fire
Is owing to that lyre
    By which he sits and sings—   20
The trembling living wire
    Of those unusual strings.

But the skies that angel trod,
    Where deep thoughts are a duty—
Where Love's a grown-up God—   25
    Where the Houri[8] glances are
Imbued with all the beauty
    Which we worship in a star.

Therefore, thou art not wrong,
    Israfeli, who despisest   30
An unimpassioned song;
To thee the laurels belong,
    Best bard, because the wisest!
Merrily live, and long!

The ecstasies above   35
    With thy burning measures suit—
Thy grief, thy joy, thy hate, thy love,
    With the fervor of thy lute—
    Well may the stars be mute!

Yes, Heaven is thine; but this   40
    Is a world of sweets and sours;
    Our flowers are merely—flowers,
And the shadow of thy perfect bliss
    Is the sunshine of ours.

---

6. Lightning.
7. The constellation, represented in classic myth as seven sisters.

8. A nymph of the Mohammedan paradise.

If I could dwell
Where Israfel
 Hath dwelt, and he where I,
He might not sing so wildly well
 A mortal melody,
While a bolder note than this might swell
 From my lyre within the sky.   50

       1831, 1845

To Helen[9]

Helen, thy beauty is to me
 Like those Nicean[1] barks of yore,
That gently, o'er a perfumed sea,
 The weary, way-worn wanderer bore
 To his own native shore.   5

On desperate seas long wont to roam,
 Thy hyacinth hair,[2] thy classic face,
Thy Naiad[3] airs have brought me home
 To the glory that was Greece
And the grandeur that was Rome.[4]   10

Lo! in yon brilliant window-niche
 How statue-like I see thee stand!
 The agate lamp within thy hand,[5]
Ah! Psyche, from the regions which
 Are Holy Land!   15

1823   1831, 1845

9. Poe traced the inspiration of this lyric to "the first purely ideal love of my soul," Mrs. Jane Stith Stanard, a young Richmond neighbor, who died in 1824. Poe approved Lowell's statement that he wrote the first draft a year earlier, at fourteen. It was rigorously revised; the personal element is almost wholly sublimated in the idealization of the tradition of pure beauty in art.
1. No wholly convincing identification has been made. Perhaps Poe used this word merely because it is musical and suggestive. All guesses have suggested Mediterranean and classical associations, referring to cultural pilgrimages of Catullus, Bacchus, or Ulysses, thus conforming to the sense of the following three lines. The conjectures, with supporting references, are summarized in Campbell (*Poems*, p. 201); the Catullus theory is added by J. J. Jones in "Poe's 'Nicéan Barks' " (*American Literature*, II, 1931, 433–438).

2. In "Ligeia" (below), Poe associates "the Homeric epithet, 'hyacinthine' " with "raven-black * * * and naturally-curling tresses"; in another story, "The Assignation," a girl's hair resembles the "clustered curls" of "the young hyacinth"; and in classic myth, the flower preserved the memory of Apollo's love for the dead young Hyacinthus. *Cf.* the following phrase, "thy classic face."
3. The naiads of classical myth were nymphs associated with fresh water (lakes, rivers, fountains). *Cf.* "desperate seas," above.
4. Compare these perfect lines with those of the first version (*Poems*, 1831): "To the beauty of fair Greece, / And the grandeur of old Rome."
5. Byron's early influence has been perceived in these three lines (Campbell, *Poems*, p. 203); but it has not been recalled that Byron once emulated Leander, the legendary Greek lover, who nightly swam the Hellespont, guided to

The City in the Sea[6]

Lo! Death has reared himself a throne
In a strange city lying alone
Far down within the dim West,
Where the good and the bad and the worst and the best
Have gone to their eternal rest.   5
There shrines and palaces and towers
(Time-eaten towers that tremble not!)
Resemble nothing that is ours.
Around, by lifting winds forgot,
Resignedly beneath the sky   10
The melancholy waters lie.

No rays from the holy heaven come down
On the long night-time of that town;
But light from out the lurid sea
Streams up the turrets silently—   15
Gleams up the pinnacles far and free—
Up domes—up spires—up kingly halls—
Up fanes—up Babylon-like[7] walls—
Up shadowy long-forgotten bowers
Of sculptured ivy and stone flowers—   20
Up many and many a marvellous shrine
Whose wreathèd friezes intertwine
The viol, the violet, and the vine.

Resignedly beneath the sky
The melancholy waters lie.   25
So blend the turrets and shadows there
That all seem pendulous in air,
While from a proud tower in the town
Death looks gigantically down.

There open fanes and gaping graves   30
Yawn level with the luminous waves;
But not the riches there that lie
In each idol's diamond eye—
Not the gaily-jewelled dead
Tempt the waters from their bed;   35

Hero's arms by her lamp, aloft on a tower. Byron wrote passionately of these lovers in *The Bride of Abydos*, II, stanza 1. Lamps and vessels were sometimes made of agate in antiquity, and the stone was a talismanic symbol of immortality.
6. The meanings of this poem are emphasized by its earlier titles: "The Doomed City" (1831); "The City of Sin"

(1836). Parallels with Byron and Shelley are noted by Campbell (*Poems*, p. 208), but observe the prevalence, in Poe's poems and tales, of the theme of the dominion of evil.
7. Babylon, in Biblical literature, is the symbol of the wicked city doomed. See, for example, Revelation xvi: 18–19; and Isaiah xiv.

For no ripples curl, alas!
Along that wilderness of glass—
No swellings tell that winds may be
Upon some far-off happier sea—
No heavings hint that winds have been   40
On seas less hideously serene.

But lo, a stir is in the air!
The wave—there is a movement there!
As if the towers had thrust aside,
In slightly sinking, the dull tide—   45
As if their tops had feebly given
A void within the filmy Heaven.
The waves have now a redder glow—
The hours are breathing faint and low—
And when, amid no earthly moans,   50
Down, down that town shall settle hence,
Hell, rising from a thousand thrones,
Shall do it reverence.

                                          1831, 1845

The Coliseum[8]

Type of the antique Rome! Rich reliquary
Of lofty contemplation left to Time
By buried centuries of pomp and power!
At length—at length—after so many days
Of weary pilgrimage and burning thirst   5
(Thirst for the springs of lore that in thee lie),
I kneel, an altered and an humble man,
Amid thy shadows, and so drink within
My very soul thy grandeur, gloom, and glory!

Vastness! and Age! and Memories of Eld!
Silence! and Desolation! and dim Night!   10
I feel ye now—I feel ye in your strength—
O spells more sure than e'er Judæan king[9]
Taught in the gardens of Gethsemane!
O charms more potent than the rapt Chaldee[1]   15
Ever drew down from out the quiet stars!

8. This appeared, with many minor alterations, in five magazines before being
collected in the volume of 1845. While
Byron's feeling for antiquity is recalled
in several lines, the poem bears the genuine stamp of Poe, and represents his
best blank verse.

9. Jesus Christ. Gethsemane (l. 14) was
the scene of his agony and arrest. *Cf.*
Matthew xxvi: 36.
1. A Semitic people of Babylonia, the
fabled astrologers of antiquity.

Ah, dream too bright to last!
　　Ah, starry Hope! that didst arise
But to be overcast!
　　A voice from out the Future cries,　　　　10
"On! on!"—but o'er the Past
　　(Dim gulf!) my spirit hovering lies
Mute, motionless, aghast!

For, alas! alas! with me
　　The light of Life is o'er!　　　　　　　　15
　　No more—no more—no more—
(Such language holds the solemn sea
　　To the sands upon the shore)
Shall bloom the thunder-blasted tree,
　　Or the stricken eagle soar!　　　　　　　20

And all my days are trances,
　　And all my nightly dreams
Are where thy dark eye glances,
　　And where thy footstep gleams—
In what ethereal dances,　　　　　　　　　25
　　By what eternal streams.

1834, 1845

Sonnet—Silence

There are some qualities—some incorporate things,
　　That have a double life, which thus is made
A type of that twin entity which springs
　　From matter and light, evinced in solid and shade.
There is a two-fold *Silence*—sea and shore—　　　5
　　Body and soul. One dwells in lonely places,
　　Newly with grass o'ergrown; some solemn graces,
Some human memories and tearful lore,
Render him terrorless: his name's "No More."
He is the corporate Silence: dread him not!　　　　10
　　No power hath he of evil in himself;
But should some urgent fate (untimely lot!)
　　Bring thee to meet his shadow (nameless elf,
That haunteth the lone regions where hath trod
No foot of man), commend thyself to God!　　　　15

1840, 1845

he published in six versions before the 1845 collection, supports the theory that it refers to Miss Royster, lost sweetheart of his youth, whom he regarded as symbolically dead.

Dream-Land

By a route obscure and lonely,
Haunted by ill angels only,
Where an Eidolon,[5] named NIGHT,
On a black throne reigns upright,
I have reached these lands but newly   5
From an ultimate dim Thule[6]—
From a wild weird clime that lieth, sublime,
    Out of SPACE—out of TIME.

Bottomless vales and boundless floods,
And chasms, and caves, and Titan woods,   10
With forms that no man can discover
For the tears that drip all over;
Mountains toppling evermore
Into seas without a shore;
Seas that restlessly aspire,   15
Surging, unto skies of fire;
Lakes that endlessly outspread
Their lone waters, lone and dead,—
Their still waters, still and chilly
With the snows of the lolling lily.   20

By the lakes that thus outspread
Their lone waters, lone and dead,—
Their sad waters, sad and chilly
With the snows of the lolling lily,—
By the mountains—near the river   25
Murmuring lowly, murmuring ever,
By the grey woods,—by the swamp
Where the toad and the newt encamp,—
By the dismal tarns and pools
    Where dwell the Ghouls,—   30
By each spot the most unholy—
In each nook most melancholy,—
There the traveller meets, aghast,
Sheeted Memories of the Past—
Shrouded forms that start and sigh   35
As they pass the wanderer by—
White-robed forms of friends long given,
In agony, to the Earth—and Heaven.

---

5. Literally, an image. *Cf.* "The Raven"
(ll. 46–47), in which Night is also personified as a symbol of Death.

6. In antiquity, the farthest northern
limits of the habitable world.

For the heart whose woes are legion
'T is a peaceful, soothing region—   40
For the spirit that walks in shadow
'T is—oh, 't is an Eldorado![7]
But the traveller, travelling through it,
May not—dare not openly view it;
Never its mysteries are exposed   45
To the weak human eye unclosed;
So wills its King, who hath forbid
The uplifting of the fringéd lid;
And thus the sad Soul that here passes
Beholds it but through darkened glasses.   50

By a route obscure and lonely,
Haunted by ill angels only,
Where an Eidolon, named NIGHT,
On a black throne reigns upright,
I have wandered home but newly   55
From this ultimate dim Thule.

1844, 1845

The Raven[8]

Once upon a midnight dreary, while I pondered, weak and weary,
Over many a quaint and curious volume of forgotten lore,
While I nodded, nearly napping, suddenly there came a tapping,
As of some one gently rapping, rapping at my chamber door.
" 'Tis some visitor," I muttered, "tapping at my chamber door—   5
    Only this and nothing more."

Ah, distinctly I remember it was in the bleak December,
And each separate dying ember wrought its ghost upon the floor.
Eagerly I wished the morrow;—vainly I had sought to borrow
From my books surcease of sorrow—sorrow for the lost Lenore—   10
For the rare and radiant maiden whom the angels name Lenore—
    Nameless here for evermore.

7. Literally, "The golden"; a legendary city of treasure in Spanish America, sought by explorers—hence, any unattainable, rich goal.
8. Poe left some sixteen manuscript versions of this poem, which was published in eleven magazines before his death. The standard version, followed here, is that of the 1845 edition of the *Poems*. His recapitulation of its creation (see "The Philosophy of Composition") is an excellent example of analytical criticism, substantiating his assertion that he had carefully calculated this poem for popular appeal. Yet the "lost Lenore" is a central experience in Poe's life; the power of the poem depends in considerable degree upon the tension between calculated effect and genuine emotional experience. Lenore is variously identified as Miss Royster, a youthful sweetheart, and as Virginia, his wife, whose long and hopeless illness was ended by death in 1847.

And the silken sad uncertain rustling of each purple curtain
Thrilled me—filled me with fantastic terrors never felt before;
So that now, to still the beating of my heart, I stood repeating,   15
" 'Tis some visitor entreating entrance at my chamber door—
Some late visitor entreating entrance at my chamber door;—
      This it is and nothing more."

Presently my soul grew stronger; hesitating then no longer,
"Sir," said I, "or Madam, truly your forgiveness I implore;   20
But the fact is I was napping, and so gently you came rapping,
And so faintly you came tapping, tapping at my chamber door,
That I scarce was sure I heard you"—here I opened wide the door;—
      Darkness there, and nothing more.

Deep into that darkness peering, long I stood there wondering, fear-
    ing,   25
Doubting, dreaming dreams no mortals ever dared to dream before;
But the silence was unbroken, and the stillness gave no token,
And the only word there spoken was the whispered word, "Lenore!"
This I whispered, and an echo murmured back the word, "Lenore!"—
      Merely this and nothing more.   30

Back into the chamber turning, all my soul within me burning,
Soon again I heard a tapping somewhat louder than before.
"Surely," said I, "surely that is something at my window lattice;
Let me see, then, what thereat is, and this mystery explore—
Let my heart be still a moment and this mystery explore;—   35
      'Tis the wind and nothing more."

Open here I flung the shutter, when, with many a flirt and flutter,
In there stepped a stately raven of the saintly days of yore;
Not the least obeisance made he; not a minute stopped or stayed he;
But, with mien of lord or lady, perched above my chamber door—   40
Perched upon a bust of Pallas[9] just above my chamber door—
      Perched, and sat, and nothing more.

Then this ebony bird beguiling my sad fancy into smiling,
By the grave and stern decorum of the countenance it wore,
"Though thy crest be shorn and shaven, thou," I said, "art sure no
    craven,   45
Ghastly grim and ancient raven wandering from the Nightly shore—
Tell me what thy lordly name is on the Night's Plutonian shore!"[1]
      Quoth the raven, "Nevermore."

9. Poe's conscious selection of Pallas
Athena, goddess of wisdom, for the
raven's perch, recalls his reported attempt, in an early draft, to have the
bitter truth revealed by an owl, Athena's
traditional bird of wisdom.
1. The infernal regions were ruled by
Pluto.

Much I marvelled this ungainly fowl to hear discourse so plainly,
Though its answer little meaning—little relevancy bore; 50
For we cannot help agreeing that no living human being
Ever yet was blessed with seeing bird above his chamber door—
Bird or beast upon the sculptured bust above his chamber door,
   With such name as "Nevermore."

But the raven, sitting lonely on the placid bust, spoke only 55
That one word, as if his soul in that one word he did outpour.
Nothing farther then he uttered—not a feather then he fluttered—
Till I scarcely more than muttered, "Other friends have flown be-
  fore—
On the morrow *he* will leave me as my hopes have flown before."
   Then the bird said, "Nevermore." 60

Startled at the stillness broken by reply so aptly spoken,
"Doubtless," said I, "what it utters is its only stock and store,
Caught from some unhappy master whom unmerciful Disaster
Followed fast and followed faster till his songs one burden bore—
Till the dirges of his Hope that melancholy burden bore 65
   Of 'Never—nevermore.' "

But the raven still beguiling all my sad soul into smiling,
Straight I wheeled a cushioned seat in front of bird and bust and
  door;
Then, upon the velvet sinking, I betook myself to linking
Fancy unto fancy, thinking what this ominous bird of yore— 70
What this grim, ungainly, ghastly, gaunt, and ominous bird of yore
   Meant in croaking "Nevermore."

This I sat engaged in guessing, but no syllable expressing
To the fowl whose fiery eyes now burned into my bosom's core;
This and more I sat divining, with my head at ease reclining 75
On the cushion's velvet lining that the lamplight gloated[2] o'er,
But whose velvet violet lining with the lamplight gloating o'er,
   She shall press, ah, nevermore!

Then, methought, the air grew denser, perfumed from an unseen
  censer
Swung by angels whose faint foot-falls tinkled on the tufted floor. 80
"Wretch," I cried, "thy God hath lent thee—by these angels he hath
  sent thee
Respite—respite and nepenthe[3] from thy memories of Lenore!
Quaff, oh quaff this kind nepenthe and forget this lost Lenore!"
   Quoth the raven, "Nevermore."

2. A double meaning is inherent in the rare usage of the word "gloated" in the sense of "to refract light from."

3. In classical mythology, a potion banishing sorrow, as in the *Odyssey*, IV, 419–430.

"Prophet!" said I, "thing of evil!—prophet still, if bird or devil!—
Whether Tempter sent, or whether tempest tossed thee here
    ashore,
Desolate, yet all undaunted, on this desert land enchanted—   87
On this home by Horror haunted,—tell me truly, I implore—
Is there—*is* there balm in Gilead?[4]—tell me—tell me, I implore!"
          Quoth the raven, "Nevermore."   90

"Prophet!" said I, "thing of evil!—prophet still, if bird or devil!
By that heaven that bends above us—by that God we both
    adore—
Tell this soul with sorrow laden if, within the distant Aidenn,[5]
It shall clasp a sainted maiden whom the angels name Lenore—
Clasp a rare and radiant maiden whom the angels name Lenore." 95
          Quoth the raven, "Nevermore."

"Be that word our sign of parting, bird or fiend!" I shrieked, up-
    starting—
"Get thee back into the tempest and the Night's Plutonian shore!
Leave no black plume as a token of that lie thy soul hath spoken!
Leave my loneliness unbroken!—quit the bust above my door!   100
Take thy beak from out my heart, and take thy form from off
    my door!"
          Quoth the raven, "Nevermore."

And the raven, never flitting, still is sitting, *still* is sitting
On the pallid bust of Pallas just above my chamber door;
And his eyes have all the seeming of a demon's that is dreaming, 105
And the lamp-light o'er him streaming throws his shadow on the
    floor;
And my soul from out that shadow that lies floating on the floor
          Shall be lifted—nevermore!

1842–1844   1845

Ulalume[6]

    The skies they were ashen and sober;
      The leaves they were crispèd and sere—
      The leaves they were withering and sere:

4. *Cf.* Jeremiah viii: 22: "Is there no
balm in Gilead?"—a reference to an
esteemed medicinal herb from that region.
5. Variant spelling and pronunciation
for "Eden."
6. "Ulalume" appears variously with
and without the tenth stanza, given here.
The poem appeared in four magazines

during Poe's last years of life, 1847–
1849. In one of these, the tenth stanza
was dropped, as it was in Griswold's
edition of Poe's *Works* the next year
(1850). But, in the same year Griswold
included the poem, *with* the tenth stanza,
in the tenth edition of his *Poets and
Poetry of America*. This text also agrees
with the Ingram manuscript (J. P.

It was night, in the lonesome October
  Of my most immemorial[7] year:
It was hard by the dim lake of Auber,
  In the misty mid region of Weir[8]—
It was down by the dank tarn of Auber,
  In the ghoul-haunted woodland of Weir.

Here once, through an alley Titanic,[9]
  Of cypress, I roamed with my Soul—
Of cypress, with Psyche,[1] my Soul.
These were days when my heart was volcanic
  As the scoriac[2] rivers that roll—
  As the lavas that restlessly roll
Their sulphurous currents down Yaanek[3]
  In the ultimate climes of the pole—
That groan as they roll down Mount Yaanek
  In the realms of the boreal pole.

Our talk had been serious and sober,
  But our thoughts they were palsied and sere—
  Our memories were treacherous and sere;
For we knew not the month was October,
  And we marked not the night of the year
  (Ah, night of all nights in the year!)—
We noted not the dim lake of Auber
  (Though once we had journeyed down here)—
We remembered not the dank tarn of Auber,
  Nor the ghoul-haunted woodland of Weir.

And now, as the night was senescent
  And star-dials pointed to morn—
  As the star-dials hinted of morn—
At the end of our path a liquescent
  And nebulous lustre was born,
Out of which a miraculous crescent
  Arose with a duplicate horn—

5

10

15

20

25

30

35

Morgan Library, New York) that Poe wrote only a month before his death, except for a slight variant in line 28. We have here followed the Ingram reading, since that seems to have been Poe's last preference. Campbell (*The Poems of Edgar Allan Poe,* p. 273) suggests that Poe may have derived the name "Ulalume" from Latin *ululare,* "to wail."

7. Poe's invention of an intensive, meaning "most memorable." In the years 1846–1847, Poe's troubles reached their crisis in his illness, poverty, literary quarrels, and the increasing illness and death of Virginia.

8. Auber and Weir are invented poetic place names.

9. Implying both "enormous" and "primeval," since the Titans were the earliest race of Greek gods.

1. The Greek word meant "the soul," the spiritual personality. Cf. Psyche's speech, ll. 51–55.

2. A coinage. Cf. "scoria," meaning "slaggy lava."

3. An imaginary volcano.

Astarte's[4] bediamonded crescent
  Distinct with its duplicate horn.

And I said: "She is warmer than Dian;
  She rolls through an ether of sighs—
  She revels in a region of sighs.
She has seen that the tears are not dry on
  These cheeks, where the worm never dies,[5]
And has come past the stars of the Lion,[6]
  To point us the path to the skies—
  To the Lethean peace of the skies[7]—
Come up, in despite of the Lion,
  To shine on us with her bright eyes—
Come up through the lair of the Lion,
  With love in her luminous eyes."

But Psyche, uplifting her finger,
  Said: "Sadly this star I mistrust—
  Her pallor I strangely mistrust:
Ah, hasten!—ah, let us not linger!
  Ah, fly!—let us fly!—for we must."
In terror she spoke, letting sink her
  Wings till they trailed in the dust—
In agony sobbed, letting sink her
  Plumes till they trailed in the dust—
  Till they sorrowfully trailed in the dust.

I replied: "This is nothing but dreaming:
  Let us on by this tremulous light!
  Let us bathe in this crystalline light!
Its Sibyllic[8] splendor is beaming
  With Hope and in Beauty to-night:—
  See!—it flickers up the sky through the night!
Ah, we safely may trust to its gleaming,
  And be sure it will lead us aright—
We surely may trust to a gleaming,
  That cannot but guide us aright,
  Since it flickers up to Heaven through the night."

Thus I pacified Psyche and kissed her,
  And tempted her out of her gloom—
  And conquered her scruples and gloom;

4. The Phoenician goddess of fertility, and the Ashtoreth of the Old Testament, there condemned for her carnality. A moon goddess, she is here compared with Diana (Dian, l. 39), the Roman huntress of the moon, renowned for chastity.
5. *Cf.* Isaiah lxvi: 24.
6. The constellation Leo, here suggesting a danger in the Zodiac, through which Astarte has passed.
7. In classical mythology, the Lethe was the river of forgetfulness.
8. Usually, "Sibylline"; from "Sibyl," any one of several prophetesses of classic myth.

And we passed to the end of the vista,   75
    But were stopped by the door of a tomb—
    By the door of a legended tomb;
And I said: "What is written, sweet sister,
    On the door of this legended tomb?"
She replied: "Ulalume—Ulalume—   80
    'Tis the vault of thy lost Ulalume!"

Then my heart it grew ashen and sober
    As the leaves that were crispèd and sere—
    As the leaves that were withering and sere;
And I cried: "It was surely October   85
    On *this* very night of last year
    That I journeyed—I journeyed down here!—
    That I brought a dread burden down here—
    On this night of all nights in the year,
    Ah, what demon has tempted me here?   90
Well I know, now, this dim lake of Auber—
    This misty mid region of Weir—
Well I know, now, this dank tarn of Auber,
    This ghoul-haunted woodland of Weir."

Said we, then—the two, then: "Ah, can it   95
    Have been that the woodlandish ghouls—
    The pitiful, the merciful ghouls—
To bar up our way and to ban it
    From the secret that lies in these wolds—
    From the thing that lies hidden in these wolds—   100
Have drawn up the spectre of a planet
    From the limbo of lunary souls—
This sinfully scintillant planet
    From the Hell of the planetary souls?"

1847, 1850

The Bells[9]

I

Hear the sledges with the bells—
    Silver bells!
What a world of merriment their melody foretells!
    How they tinkle, tinkle, tinkle,
    In the icy air of night!   5

9. "The Bells" survives in four manuscripts, the earliest, only seventeen lines
long, written during the summer of 1848.
The last, completed a year later, appeared after the poet's death in *Sartain's
Union Magazine* for November, 1849,
and is reproduced here.

While the stars that oversprinkle
All the heavens, seem to twinkle
  With a crystalline delight;
    Keeping time, time, time,
    In a sort of Runic[1] rhyme,
To the tintinnabulation[2] that so musically wells
    From the bells, bells, bells, bells,
      Bells, bells, bells—
From the jingling and the tinkling of the bells.

II

    Hear the mellow wedding bells—
        Golden bells!
What a world of happiness their harmony foretells!
    Through the balmy air of night
    How they ring out their delight!—
      From the molten-golden notes,
        And all in tune,
      What a liquid ditty floats
To the turtle-dove that listens, while she gloats
        On the moon!
      Oh, from out the sounding cells,
What a gush of euphony voluminously wells!
        How it swells!
        How it dwells
      On the Future!—how it tells
      Of the rapture that impels
    To the swinging and the ringing
      Of the bells, bells, bells—
Of the bells, bells, bells, bells,
      Bells, bells, bells—
To the rhyming and the chiming of the bells!

III

  Hear the loud alarum bells—
      Brazen bells!
What a tale of terror, now, their turbulency tells!
    In the startled ear of night
    How they scream out their affright!
      Too much horrified to speak,
      They can only shriek, shriek,
        Out of tune,
In a clamorous appealing to the mercy of the fire,
In a mad expostulation with the deaf and frantic fire,
      Leaping higher, higher, higher,

10

15

20

25

30

35

40

45

1. Runes were the characters in an ancient Teutonic alphabet. Poe here recalls
the use of these characters in magic and
prophecy.
2. Poe's coinage. Cf. Latin, tintinnabulum, "a small bell."

With a desperate desire,
And a resolute endeavor
Now—now to sit, or never,
By the side of the pale-faced moon.   50
    Oh, the bells, bells, bells!
    What a tale their terror tells
        Of Despair!
How they clang, and clash, and roar!
What a horror they outpour   55
On the bosom of the palpitating air!
    Yet the ear, it fully knows,
        By the twanging
        And the clanging,
    How the danger ebbs and flows;   60
    Yet the ear distinctly tells,
        In the jangling
        And the wrangling,
How the danger sinks and swells,
By the sinking or the swelling in the anger of the bells—   65
        Of the bells,—
Of the bells, bells, bells, bells,
    Bells, bells, bells—
In the clamor and the clangor of the bells!

IV

Hear the tolling of the bells—   70
        Iron bells!
What a world of solemn thought their monody compels!
    In the silence of the night,
    How we shiver with affright
At the melancholy menace of their tone!   75
    For every sound that floats
    From the rust within their throats
        Is a groan.
    And the people—ah, the people—
    They that dwell up in the steeple,   80
        All alone,
And who tolling, tolling, tolling,
    In that muffled monotone,
Feel a glory in so rolling
    On the human heart a stone—   85
They are neither man nor woman—
They are neither brute nor human—
        They are Ghouls:—
And their king it is who tolls:—
    And he rolls, rolls, rolls,   90
        Rolls

A pæan from the bells!
And his merry bosom swells
        With the pæan of the bells!
And he dances, and he yells;   95
    Keeping time, time, time,
    In a sort of Runic rhyme,
        To the pæan of the bells—
            Of the bells:
    Keeping time, time, time,   100
    In a sort of Runic rhyme,
        To the throbbing of the bells—
    Of the bells, bells, bells—
        To the sobbing of the bells;
    Keeping time, time, time,   105
        As he knells, knells, knells,
    In a happy Runic rhyme,
        To the rolling of the bells—
    Of the bells, bells, bells:—
        To the tolling of the bells—   110
    Of the bells, bells, bells, bells,
        Bells, bells, bells—
To the moaning and the groaning of the bells.

1848–1849   1849

Annabel Lee[3]

It was many and many a year ago,
        In a kingdom by the sea,
That a maiden there lived whom you may know
        By the name of Annabel Lee;—
And this maiden she lived with no other thought   5
        Than to love and be loved by me.

She was a child and *I* was a child,
        In this kingdom by the sea,
But we loved with a love that was more than love—
        I and my Annabel Lee—   10
With a love that the wingéd seraphs of Heaven
        Coveted her and me.

And this was the reason that, long ago,
        In this kingdom by the sea,

3. The text is that of first publication, in the New York *Tribune* for October 9, 1849, two days after the poet's death. The poem appeared in two other maga-zines within three months, and was col-lected in Griswold's edition of Poe's *Works* (1850).

A wind blew out of a cloud by night 15
 Chilling my Annabel Lee;
So that her highborn kinsmen came
 And bore her away from me,
To shut her up in a sepulchre
 In this kingdom by the sea. 20

The angels, not half so happy in Heaven,
 Went envying her and me:—
Yes! that was the reason (as all men know,
 In this kingdom by the sea)
That the wind came out of the cloud, chilling 25
 And killing my Annabel Lee.

But our love it was stronger by far than the love
 Of those who were older than we—
 Of many far wiser than we—
And neither the angels in Heaven above 30
 Nor the demons down under the sea,
Can ever dissever my soul from the soul
 Of the beautiful Annabel Lee:—

For the moon never beams without bringing me dreams
 Of the beautiful Annabel Lee; 35
And the stars never rise but I see the bright eyes
 Of the beautiful Annabel Lee;
And so, all the night-tide, I lie down by the side
Of my darling, my darling, my life and my bride,
 In her sepulchre there by the sea— 40
 In her tomb by the side of the sea.

1849, 1850

Ligeia[4]

And the will therein lieth, which dieth not. Who knoweth the mysteries of the will, with its vigor? For God is but a great will pervading all things by nature of its intentness. Man doth not yield himself to the angels, nor unto death utterly, save only through the weakness of his feeble will.

—JOSEPH GLANVILL [5]

I cannot, for my soul, remember how, when, or even precisely where, I first became acquainted with the lady Ligeia. Long years

4. Poe once declared that "Ligeia" was his best tale. It is his most complex story of reincarnation and the survival of personality. This is also the theme of the stories, "Morella," and "Berenice." Either burial alive or reincarnation occurs in "The Fall of the House of Usher." In the poems, psychic survival is a persistent overtone, appearing variously in "Al Aaraaf," "Israfel," "Ulalume," "The Raven," "Annabel Lee,"

and—with the serenity of complete sublimation—in "To Helen." "Ligeia" first appeared in the *American Museum* for September, 1838, and was collected in Poe's *Tales of the Grotesque and Arabesque* (1840).
5. The source of this epigraph has never been discovered. If Poe invented it, he ascribed it to a likely author. Joseph Glanvill (1636–1680), an English ecclesiastical theorist, was associated with

have since elapsed, and my memory is feeble through much suffering. Or, perhaps, I cannot *now* bring these points to mind, because, in truth, the character of my beloved, her rare learning, her singular yet placid cast of beauty, and the thrilling and enthralling eloquence of her low musical language, made their way into my heart by paces so steadily and stealthily progressive that they have been unnoticed and unknown. Yet I believe that I met her first and most frequently in some large, old, decaying city near the Rhine. Of her family—I have surely heard her speak. That it is of a remotely ancient date cannot be doubted. Ligeia! Ligeia! Buried in studies of a nature more than all else adapted to deaden impressions of the outward world, it is by that sweet word alone—by Ligeia—that I bring before mine eyes in fancy the image of her who is no more. And now, while I write, a recollection flashes upon me that I have *never known* the paternal name of her who was my friend and my betrothed, and who became the partner of my studies, and finally the wife of my bosom. Was it a playful charge on the part of my Ligeia? or was it a test of my strength of affection, that I should institute no inquiries upon this point? or was it rather a caprice of my own—a wildly romantic offering on the shrine of the most passionate devotion? I but indistinctly recall the fact itself—what wonder that I have utterly forgotten the circumstances which originated or attended it. And, indeed, if ever that spirit which is entitled *Romance*—if ever she, the wan and the misty-winged *Ashtophet*[6] of idolatrous Egypt, presided, as they tell, over marriages ill-omened, then most surely she presided over mine.

There is one dear topic, however, on which my memory fails me not. It is the *person* of Ligeia. In stature she was tall, somewhat slender, and, in her latter days, even emaciated. I would in vain attempt to portray the majesty, the quiet ease, of her demeanor, or the incomprehensible lightness and elasticity of her footfall. She came and departed as a shadow. I was never made aware of her entrance into my closed study save by the dear music of her low sweet voice, as she placed her marble hand upon my shoulder. In beauty of face no maiden ever equalled her. It was the radiance of an opium dream—an airy and spirit-lifting vision more wildly divine than the phantasies which hovered about the slumbering souls of the daughters of Delos.[7] Yet her features were not of that regular mould which we have been falsely taught to worship in the classical labors of the

the Cambridge Platonists. Their intuitional idealism partly embraced cabbalism, an ancient Hebrew occultism emphasizing spiritualistic manifestations and the eternity of the soul.

6. Apparently Poe's invention of a deity, suggesting the Phoenician and Egyptian goddess of fertility, Ashtoreth, combined with Tophet, hell, or an imaginary place of chaos associated in the Old Testament with Egyptian worship of Moloch. *Cf.* Isaiah xxx: 33; II Kings xxiii: 10.

7. Delos, a Greek island of the Cyclades, the mythological birthplace of the twins

heathen. "There is no exquisite beauty," says Bacon, Lord Verulam,[8] speaking truly of all the forms and *genera* of beauty, "without some *strangeness* in the proportion." Yet, although I saw that the features of Ligeia were not of a classic regularity—although I perceived that her loveliness was indeed "exquisite," and felt that there was much of "strangeness" pervading it, yet I have tried in vain to detect the irregularity and to trace home my own perception of "the strange." I examined the contour of the lofty and pale forehead—it was faultless—how cold indeed that word when applied to a majesty so divine!—the skin rivalling the purest ivory, the commanding extent and repose, the gentle prominence of the regions above the temples; and then the raven-black, the glossy, the luxuriant and naturally-curling tresses, setting forth the full force of the Homeric epithet, "hyacinthine!"[9] I looked at the delicate outlines of the nose—and nowhere but in the graceful medallions of the Hebrews had I beheld a similar perfection. There were the same luxurious smoothness of surface, the same scarcely perceptible tendency to the aquiline, the same harmoniously curved nostrils speaking the free spirit. I regarded the sweet mouth. Here was indeed the triumph of all things heavenly—the magnificent turn of the short upper lip—the soft, voluptuous slumber of the under—the dimples which sported, and the color which spoke—the teeth glancing back, with a brilliancy almost startling, every ray of the holy light which fell upon them in her serene and placid, yet most exultingly radiant of all smiles. I scrutinized the formation of the chin—and here, too, I found the gentleness of breadth, the softness and the majesty, the fullness and the spirituality, of the Greek—the contour which the god Apollo revealed but in a dream, to Cleomenes,[1] the son of the Athenian. And then I peered into the large eyes of Ligeia.

For eyes we have no models in the remotely antique. It might have been, too, that in these eyes of my beloved lay the secret to which Lord Verulam alludes. They were, I must believe, far larger than the ordinary eyes of our own race. They were even fuller than the fullest of the gazelle eyes of the tribe of the valley of Nourjahad.[2] Yet it was only at intervals—in moments of intense excitement—that peculiarity became more than slightly noticeable in Ligeia. And at such moments was her beauty—in my heated fancy thus it ap-

Apollo and Artemis, became a shrine. Artemis was attended by maidens sworn to chastity, perhaps Poe's "daughters of Delos," although this obscure reference may have been introduced merely for its alliterative quality. However, in some cults Artemis became a moon goddess identified with Astarte (Ashtoreth), whom Poe has just recalled above.

8. Francis Bacon, *Essayes* (1625), "Of Beauty." Bacon wrote "excellent beauty," not "exquisite."

9. *Cf.* "To Helen."

1. The Venus de' Medici bears the signature of Cleomenes, possibly a late forgery; and Apollo, patron of the arts, is suggested by Poe as the source of the sculptor's inspiration.

2. *The History of Nourjahad* (1767), an oriental romance by Frances Sheridan (1724–1766), was still familiar.

peared perhaps—the beauty of beings either above or apart from the earth—the beauty of the fabulous Houri[3] of the Turk. The hue of the orbs was the most brilliant of black, and, far over them, hung jetty lashes of great length. The brows, slightly irregular in outline, had the same tint. The "strangeness," however, which I found in the eyes, was of a nature distinct from the formation, or the color, or the brilliancy of the features, and must, after all, be referred to the *expression*. Ah, word of no meaning! behind whose vast latitude of mere sound we intrench our ignorance of so much of the spiritual. The expression of the eyes of Ligeia! How for long hours have I pondered upon it! How have I, through the whole of a midsummer night, struggled to fathom it! What was it—that something more profound than the well of Democritus[4]—which lay far within the pupils of my beloved? What *was* it? I was possessed with a passion to discover. Those eyes! those large, those shining, those divine orbs! they became to me twin stars of Leda,[5] and I to them devoutest of astrologers.

There is no point, among the many incomprehensible anomalies of the science of mind, more thrillingly exciting than the fact—never, I believe, noticed in the schools—that, in our endeavors to recall to memory something long forgotten, we often find ourselves *upon the very verge* of remembrance, without being able, in the end, to remember. And thus how frequently, in my intense scrutiny of Ligeia's eyes, have I felt approaching the full knowledge of their expression—felt it approaching—yet not quite be mine—and so at length entirely depart! And (strange, oh strangest mystery of all!) I found, in the commonest objects of the universe, a circle of analogies to that expression. I mean to say that, subsequently to the period when Ligeia's beauty passed into my spirit, there dwelling as in a shrine, I derived, from many existences in the material world, a sentiment such as I felt always aroused within me by her large and luminous orbs. Yet not the more could I define that sentiment, or analyze, or even steadily view it. I recognized it, let me repeat, sometimes in the survey of a rapidly-growing vine—in the contemplation of a moth, a butterfly, a chrysalis, a stream of running water. I have felt it in the ocean; in the falling of a meteor. I have felt it in the glances of unusually aged people. And there are one or two stars in heaven (one especially, a star of the sixth magnitude, double and changeable, to be found near the large star in Lyra[6]) in a telescopic

3. A nymph of the Mohammedan paradise.
4. Democritus, the Greek "laughing philosopher" of the fifth century B.C., one of whose surviving fragments is the source of the proverb, "Truth lies at the bottom of a well."
5. In the constellation Gemini, according to Greek myth, the two bright stars are Castor and Pollux, twin sons of the mortal Leda and the god Zeus, who visited her as a swan.
6. The constellation contains two double stars. Poe's "large star" is Vega, or Alpha Lyrae, of the first magnitude. The other, lower and to the left, is Epsilon Lyrae, requiring a telescope, as he says, for observation.

scrutiny of which I have been made aware of the feeling. I have been filled with it by certain sounds from stringed instruments, and not unfrequently by passages from books. Among innumerable other instances, I well remember something in a volume of Joseph Glanvill, which (perhaps merely from its quaintness—who shall say?) never failed to inspire me with the sentiment;—"And the will therein lieth, which dieth not. Who knoweth the mysteries of the will, with its vigor? For God is but a great will pervading all things by nature of its intentness. Man doth not yield him to the angels, nor unto death utterly, save only through the weakness of his feeble will."

Length of years, and subsequent reflection, have enabled me to trace, indeed, some remote connection between this passage in the English moralist and a portion of the character of Ligeia. An *intensity* in thought, action, or speech, was possibly, in her, a result, or at least an index, of that gigantic volition which, during our long intercourse, failed to give other and more immediate evidence of its existence. Of all the women whom I have ever known, she, the outwardly calm, the ever-placid Ligeia, was the most violently a prey to the tumultuous vultures of stern passion. And of such passion I could form no estimate, save by the miraculous expansion of those eyes which at once so delighted and appalled me—by the almost magical melody, modulation, distinctness and placidity of her very low voice—and by the fierce energy (rendered doubly effective by contrast with her manner of utterance) of the wild words which she habitually uttered.

I have spoken of the learning of Ligeia: it was immense—such as I have never known in woman. In the classical tongues was she deeply proficient, and as far as my own acquaintance extended in regard to the modern dialects of Europe, I have never known her at fault. Indeed upon any theme of the most admired, because simply the most abstruse of the boasted erudition of the academy, have I *ever* found Ligeia at fault? How singularly—how thrillingly, this one point in the nature of my wife has forced itself, at this late period only, upon my attention! I said her knowledge was such as I have never known in woman—but where breathes the man who has traversed, and successfully, *all* the wide areas of moral, physical, and mathematical science? I saw not then what I now clearly perceive, that the acquisitions of Ligeia were gigantic, were astounding; yet I was sufficiently aware of her infinite supremacy to resign myself, with a child-like confidence, to her guidance through the chaotic world of metaphysical investigation at which I was most busily occupied during the earlier years of our marriage. With how vast a triumph—with how vivid a delight—with how much of all that is ethereal in hope —did I *feel*, as she bent over me in studies but little sought—but less known—that delicious vista by slow degrees expanding before me, down whose long, gorgeous, and all untrodden path, I might at length pass onward to the goal of a wisdom too divinely precious not to be forbidden!

How poignant, then, must have been the grief with which, after some years, I beheld my well-grounded expectations take wings to themselves and fly away! Without Ligeia I was but as a child groping benighted. Her presence, her readings alone, rendered vividly luminous the many mysteries of the transcendentalism in which we were immersed. Wanting the radiant lustre of her eyes, letters, lambent and golden, grew duller than Saturnian lead.[7] And now those eyes shone less and less frequently upon the pages over which I pored. Ligeia grew ill. The wild eyes blazed with a too—too glorious effulgence; the pale fingers became of the transparent waxen hue of the grave, and the blue veins upon the lofty forehead swelled and sank impetuously with the tides of the most gentle emotion. I saw that she must die—and I struggled desperately in spirit with the grim Azrael.[8] And the struggles of the passionate wife were, to my astonishment, even more energetic than my own. There had been much in her stern nature to impress me with the belief that, to her, death would have come without its terrors;—but not so. Words are impotent to convey any just idea of the fierceness of resistance with which she wrestled with the Shadow. I groaned in anguish at the pitiable spectacle. I would have soothed—I would have reasoned; but, in the intensity of her wild desire for life,—for life—*but* for life —solace and reason were alike the uttermost of folly. Yet not until the last instance, amid the most convulsive writhings of her fierce spirit, was shaken the external placidity of her demeanor. Her voice grew more gentle—grew more low—yet I would not wish to dwell upon the wild meaning of the quietly uttered words. My brain reeled as I hearkened entranced, to a melody more than mortal—to assumptions and aspirations which mortality had never before known.

That she loved me I should not have doubted; and I might have been easily aware that, in a bosom such as hers, love would have reigned no ordinary passion. But in death only, was I fully impressed with the strength of her affection. For long hours, detaining my hand, would she pour out before me the overflowing of a heart whose more than passionate devotion amounted to idolatry. How had I deserved to be so blessed by such confessions?—how had I deserved to be so cursed with the removal of my beloved in the hour of her making them? But upon this subject I cannot bear to dilate. Let me say only, that in Ligeia's more than womanly abandonment to a love, alas! all unmerited, all unworthily bestowed, I at length recognized the principle of her longing with so wildly earnest a desire for the life

7. In ancient alchemy and chemistry, lead bore the name of Saturn. *Cf.* "saturnine."

8. In Mohammedan and Hebrew mythology, the Angel of Death.

which was now fleeing so rapidly away. It is this wild longing—it is this eager vehemence of desire for life—*but* for life—that I have no power to portray—no utterance capable of expressing.

At high noon of the night in which she departed, beckoning me, peremptorily, to her side, she bade me repeat certain verses composed by herself not many days before. I obeyed her.——They were these:[9]

> Lo! 'tis a gala night
> Within the lonesome latter years!
> An angel throng, bewinged, bedight
> In veils, and drowned in tears,
> Sit in a theatre, to see
> A play of hopes and fears,
> While the orchestra breathes fitfully
> The music of the spheres.
>
> Mimes, in the form of God on high,
> Mutter and mumble low,
> And hither and thither fly—
> Mere puppets they, who come and go
> At bidding of vast formless things
> That shift the scenery to and fro,
> Flapping from out their Condor wings
> Invisible Wo!
>
> That motley drama!—oh, be sure
> It shall not be forgot!
> With its Phantom chased forever more,
> By a crowd that seize it not,
> Through a circle that ever returneth in
> To the self-same spot,
> And much of Madness and more of Sin
> And Horror the soul of the plot.
>
> But see, amid the mimic rout,
> A crawling shape intrude!
> A blood-red thing that writhes from out
> The scenic solitude!
> It writhes!—it writhes! with mortal pangs
> The mimes become its food,
> And the seraphs sob at vermin fangs
> In human gore imbued.
>
> Out—out are the lights—out all!
> And over each quivering form,

9. This poem was not a part of the story as first published in 1838. Entitled "The Conqueror Worm," it appeared separately in *Graham's Magazine* for January, 1843; it was first incorporated in the version of the tale printed in the *Broadway Journal* for September 27, 1845.

> The curtain, a funeral pall,
>   Comes down with the rush of a storm,
> And the angels, all pallid and wan,
>   Uprising, unveiling, affirm
> That the play is the tragedy, "Man,"
>   And its hero the Conqueror Worm.

"O God!" half shrieked Ligeia, leaping to her feet and extending her arms aloft with a spasmodic movement, as I made an end of these lines—"O God! O Divine Father!—shall these things be undeviatingly so?—shall this Conqueror be not once conquered? Are we not part and parcel in Thee? Who—who knoweth the mysteries of the will with its vigor? Man doth not yield him to the angels, *nor unto death utterly,* save only through the weakness of his feeble will."

And now, as if exhausted with emotion, she suffered her white arms to fall, and returned solemnly to her bed of Death. And as she breathed her last sighs, there came mingled with them a low murmur from her lips. I bent to them my ear and distinguished, again, the concluding words of the passage in Glanvill—"*Man doth not yield him to the angels, nor unto death utterly, save only through the weakness of his feeble will.*"

She died;—and I, crushed into the very dust with sorrow, could no longer endure the lonely desolation of my dwelling in the dim and decaying city by the Rhine. I had no lack of what the world calls wealth. Ligeia had brought me far more, very far more than ordinarily falls to the lot of mortals. After a few months, therefore, of weary and aimless wandering, I purchased, and put in some repair, an abbey, which I shall not name, in one of the wildest and least frequented portions of fair England. The gloomy and dreary grandeur of the building, the almost savage aspect of the domain, the many melancholy and time-honored memories connected with both, had much in unison with the feelings of utter abandonment which had driven me into that remote and unsocial region of the country. Yet although the external abbey, with its verdant decay hanging about it, suffered but little alteration, I gave way, with a child-like perversity, and perchance with a faint hope of alleviating my sorrows, to a display of more than regal magnificence within.— For such follies, even in childhood, I had imbibed a taste and now they came back to me as if in the dotage of grief. Alas, I feel how much even of incipient madness might have been discovered in the gorgeous and fantastic draperies, in the solemn carvings of Egypt, in the wild cornices and furniture, in the Bedlam patterns of the carpets of tufted gold! I had become a bounden slave in the trammels of opium, and my labors and my orders had taken a coloring from my dreams. But these absurdities I must not pause to detail. Let me speak only of that one chamber, ever accursed, whither in a moment of mental alienation, I led from the altar as my bride—as the successor of the unforgotten Ligeia—the fair-haired and blue-eyed Lady Rowena Trevanion, of Tremaine.

There is no individual portion of the architecture and decoration of that bridal chamber which is not now visibly before me. Where were the souls of the haughty family of the bride, when, through thirst of gold, they permitted to pass the threshold of an apartment so bedecked, a maiden and a daughter so beloved? I have said that I minutely remember the details of the chamber—yet I am sadly forgetful on topics of deep moment—and here there was no system, no keeping, in the fantastic display, to take hold upon the memory. The room lay in a high turret of the castellated abbey, was pentagonal in shape, and of capacious size. Occupying the whole southern face of the pentagon was the sole window—an immense sheet of unbroken glass from Venice—a single pane, and tinted of a leaden hue, so that the rays of either the sun or moon, passing through it, fell with a ghastly lustre on the objects within. Over the upper portion of this huge window, extended the trellice-work of an aged vine, which clambered up the massy walls of the turret. The ceiling, of gloomy-looking oak, was excessively lofty, vaulted, and elaborately fretted with the wildest and most grotesque specimens of a semi-Gothic, semi-Druidical device. From out the most central recess of this melancholy vaulting, depended, by a single chain of gold with long links, a huge censer of the same metal, Saracenic in pattern, and with many perforations so contrived that there writhed in and out of them, as if endued with a serpent vitality, a continual succession of parti-colored fires.

Some few ottomans and golden candelabra, of Eastern figure, were in various stations about—and there was the couch, too—the bridal couch—of an Indian model, and low, and sculptured of solid ebony, with a pall-like canopy above. In each of the angles of the chamber stood on end a gigantic sarcophagus of black granite, from the tombs of the kings over against Luxor,[1] with their aged lids full of immemorial sculpture. But in the draping of the apartment lay, alas! the chief phantasy of all. The lofty walls, gigantic in height—even unproportionably so—were hung from summit to foot, in vast folds, with a heavy and massive-looking tapestry—tapestry of a material which was found alike as a carpet on the floor, as a covering for the ottomans and the ebony bed, as a canopy for the bed, and as the gorgeous volutes of the curtains which partially shaded the window. The material was the richest cloth of gold. It was spotted all over,

1. The ancient site of Thebes, in middle Egypt, on the Nile. The fascination of Egypt for romantic writers reflected the remarkable development of Egyptology since Jean François Champollion began deciphering hieroglyphics early in the century.

at irregular intervals, with arabesque figures, about a foot in diameter, and wrought upon the cloth in patterns of the most jetty black. But these figures partook of the true character of the arabesque only when regarded from a single point of view. By a contrivance now common, and indeed traceable to a very remote period of antiquity, they were made changeable in aspect. To one entering the room, they bore the appearance of simple monstrosities; but upon a farther advance, this appearance gradually departed; and step by step, as the visitor moved his station in the chamber, he saw himself surrounded by an endless succession of the ghastly forms which belong to the superstition of the Norman, or arise in the guilty slumbers of the monk. The phantasmagoric effect was vastly heightened by the artificial introduction of a strong continual current of wind behind the draperies—giving a hideous and uneasy animation to the whole.

In halls such as these—in a bridal chamber such as this—I passed, with the Lady of Tremaine, the unhallowed hours of the first month of our marriage—passed them with but little disquietude. That my wife dreaded the fierce moodiness of my temper—that she shunned me and loved me but little—I could not help perceiving; but it gave me rather pleasure than otherwise. I loathed her with a hatred belonging more to demon than to man. My memory flew back (oh, with what intensity of regret!) to Ligeia, the beloved, the august, the beautiful, the entombed. I revelled in recollections of her purity, of her wisdom, of her lofty, her ethereal nature, of her passionate, her idolatrous love. Now, then, did my spirit fully and freely burn with more than all the fires of her own. In the excitement of my opium dreams (for I was habitually fettered in the shackles of the drug) I would call aloud upon her name, during the silence of the night, or among the sheltered recesses of the glens by day, as if, through the wild eagerness, the solemn passion, the consuming ardor of my longing for the departed, I could restore her to the pathway she had abandoned—ah, *could* it be forever?—upon the earth.

About the commencement of the second month of the marriage, the Lady Rowena was attacked with sudden illness, from which her recovery was slow. The fever which consumed her rendered her nights uneasy; and in her perturbed state of half-slumber, she spoke of sounds, and of motions, in and about the chamber of the turret, which I concluded had no origin save in the distemper of her fancy, or perhaps in the phantasmagoric influence of the chamber itself. She became at length convalescent—finally well. Yet but a brief period elapsed, ere a second more violent disorder again threw her upon a bed of suffering; and from this attack her frame, at all times feeble, never altogether recovered. Her illnesses were, after this epoch, of alarming character, and of more alarming recurrence, defying alike the knowledge and the great exertions of her physicians. With the increase of the chronic disease which had thus, apparently, taken too sure hold upon her constitution to be eradicated by human means, I could not fail to observe a similar increase in the nervous irritation of her temperament, and in her excitability by trivial causes of fear. She spoke again, and now more frequently and pertinaciously, of the sounds—of the slight sounds—and of the unusual motions among the tapestries, to which she had formerly alluded.

One night, near the closing in of September, she pressed this distressing subject with more than usual emphasis upon my attention. She had just awakened from an unquiet slumber, and I had been watching, with feelings half of anxiety, half of a vague terror, the workings of her emaciated countenance. I sat by the side of her ebony bed, upon one of the ottomans of India. She partly arose, and spoke, in an earnest low whisper, of sounds which she *then* heard, but which I could not hear—of motions which she *then* saw, but which I could not perceive. The wind was rushing hurriedly behind the tapestries, and I wished to show her (what, let me confess it, I could not *all* believe) that those almost inarticulate breathings, of those very gentle variations of the figures upon the wall, were but the natural effects of that customary rushing of the wind. But a deadly pallor, overspreading her face, had proved to me that my exertions to reassure her would be fruitless. She appeared to be fainting, and no attendants were within call. I remembered where was deposited a decanter of light wine which had been ordered by her physicians, and hastened across the chamber to procure it. But, as I stepped beneath the light of the censer, two circumstances of a startling nature attracted my attention. I had felt that some palpable although invisible object had passed lightly by my person; and I saw that there lay upon the golden carpet, in the very middle of the rich lustre thrown from the censer, a shadow—a faint, indefinite shadow of angelic aspect—such as might be fancied for the shadow of a shade. But I was wild with the excitement of an immoderate dose of opium, and heeded these things but little, nor spoke of them to Rowena. Having found the wine, I recrossed the chamber, and poured out a goblet-ful, which I held to the lips of the fainting lady. She had now partially recovered, however, and took the vessel herself, while I sank upon an ottoman near me, with my eyes fastened upon her person. It was then that I became distinctly aware of a gentle foot-fall upon the carpet, and near the couch; and in a second thereafter, as Rowena was in the act of raising the wine to her lips, I saw, or may have dreamed that I saw, fall within the goblet, as if from some invisible spring in the atmosphere of the room, three or four large drops of a brilliant and ruby colored fluid. If this I saw—not so Rowena. She swallowed the wine unhesitatingly, and I forbore to speak to her of a circumstance which must, after all, I considered, have been but the suggestion of a vivid imagination, rendered morbidly active by the terror of the lady, by the opium, and by the hour.

Yet I cannot conceal it from my own perception that, immediately subsequent to the fall of the ruby-drops, a rapid change for the worse took place in the disorder of my wife; so that, on the third subsequent night, the hands of her menials prepared her for the tomb, and on the fourth, I sat alone, with her shrouded body, in that fantastic chamber which had received her as my bride.—Wild visions, opium-engendered, flitted, shadow-like, before me. I gazed with unquiet eye upon the sarcophagi in the angles of the room, upon the varying figures of the drapery, and upon the writhing of the parti-colored fires in the censer overhead. My eyes then fell, as I called to mind the circumstances of a former night, to the spot beneath the glare of the censer where I had seen the faint traces of the shadow. It was there, however, no longer; and breathing with greater freedom, I turned my glances to the pallid and rigid figure upon the bed. Then rushed upon me a thousand memories of Ligeia—and then came back upon my heart, with the turbulent violence of a flood, the whole of that unutterable wo with which I had regarded *her* thus enshrouded. The night waned; and still, with a bosom full of bitter thoughts of the one only and supremely beloved, I remained gazing upon the body of Rowena.

It might have been midnight, or perhaps earlier, or later, for I had taken no note of time, when a sob, low, gentle, but very distinct, startled me from my revery.—I *felt* that it came from the bed of ebony—the bed of death. I listened in an agony of superstitious terror —but there was no repetition of the sound. I strained my vision to detect any motion in the corpse—but there was not the slightest perceptible. Yet I could not have been deceived. I *had* heard the noise, however faint, and my soul was awakened within me. I resolutely and perseveringly kept my attention riveted upon the body. Many minutes elapsed before any circumstance occurred tending to throw light upon the mystery. At length it became evident that a slight, a very feeble, and barely noticeable tinge of color had flushed up within the cheeks, and along the sunken small veins of the eyelids. Through a species of unutterable horror and awe, for which the language of mortality has no sufficiently energetic expression, I felt my heart cease to beat, my limbs grow rigid where I sat. Yet a sense of duty finally operated to restore my self-possession. I could no longer doubt that we had been precipitate in our preparations—that Rowena still lived. It was necessary that some immediate exertion be made; yet the turret was altogether apart from the portion of the abbey tenanted by the servants—there were none within call—I had no means of summoning them to my aid without leaving the room for many minutes—and this I could not venture to do. I therefore struggled alone in my endeavors to call back the spirit still hovering.

In a short period it was certain, however, that a relapse had taken place; the color disappeared from both eyelid and cheek, leaving a wanness even more than that of marble; the lips became doubly shrivelled and pinched up in the ghastly expression of death; a repulsive clamminess and coldness overspread rapidly the surface of the body; and all the usual rigorous stiffness immediately supervened. I fell back with a shudder upon the couch from which I had been so startlingly aroused, and again gave myself up to passionate waking visions of Ligeia.

An hour thus elapsed when (could it be possible?) I was a second time aware of some vague sound issuing from the region of the bed. I listened—in extremity of horror. The sound came again—it was a sigh. Rushing to the corpse, I saw—distinctly saw—a tremor upon the lips. In a minute afterward they relaxed, disclosing a bright line of the pearly teeth. Amazement now struggled in my bosom with the profound awe which had hitherto reigned there alone. I felt that my vision grew dim, that my reason wandered; and it was only by a violent effort that I at length succeeded in nerving myself to the task which duty thus once more had pointed out. There was now a partial glow upon the forehead and upon the cheek and throat; a perceptible warmth pervaded the whole frame; there was even a slight pulsation at the heart. The lady *lived*; and with redoubled ardor I betook myself to the task of restoration. I chafed and bathed the temples and the hands, and used every exertion which experience, and no little medical reading, could suggest. But in vain. Suddenly, the color fled, the pulsation ceased, the lips resumed the expression of the dead, and, in an instant afterward, the whole body took upon itself the icy chilliness, the livid hue, the intense rigidity, the sunken outline, and all the loathsome peculiarities of that which has been, for many days, a tenant of the tomb.

And again I sunk into visions of Ligeia—and again (what marvel that I shudder while I write?) *again* there reached my ears a low sob from the region of the ebony bed. But why shall I minutely detail the unspeakable horrors of that night? Why shall I pause to relate how, time after time, until near the period of the gray dawn, this hideous drama of revivification was repeated; how each terrific relapse was only into a sterner and apparently more irredeemable death; how each agony wore the aspect of a struggle with some invisible foe; and how each struggle was succeeded by I know not what of wild change in the personal appearance of the corpse? Let me hurry to a conclusion.

The greater part of the fearful night had worn away, and she who had been dead, once again stirred—and now more vigorously than hitherto, although arousing from a dissolution more appalling in its utter hopelessness than any. I had long ceased to struggle or to move, and remained sitting rigidly upon the ottoman, a helpless prey to a whirl of violent emotions, of which extreme awe was perhaps the least terrible, the least consuming. The corpse, I repeat, stirred, and now more vigorously than before. The hues of life flushed up with unwonted energy into the countenance—the limbs relaxed—and, save that the eyelids were yet pressed heavily together, and that the bandages and draperies of the grave still imparted their charnel character to the figure, I might have dreamed that Rowena had indeed shaken off, utterly, the fetters of Death. But if this idea was not, even then, altogether adopted, I could at least doubt no longer, when, arising from the bed, tottering, with feeble steps, with closed eyes, and with the manner of one bewildered in a dream, the thing that was enshrouded advanced boldly and palpably into the middle of the apartment.

I trembled not—I stirred not—for a crowd of unutterable fancies connected with the air, the stature, the demeanor of the figure, rushing hurriedly through my brain, had paralyzed—had chilled me into stone. I stirred not—but gazed upon the apparition. There was a mad disorder in my thoughts—a tumult unappeasable. Could it, indeed, be the *living* Rowena who confronted me? Could it indeed be Rowena *at all*—the fair-haired, the blue-eyed Lady Rowena Trevanion of Tremaine? Why, *why* should I doubt it? The bandage lay heavily about the mouth—but then might it not be the mouth of the breathing Lady of Tremaine? And the cheeks—there were the roses as in her noon of life—yes, these might indeed be the fair cheeks of the living Lady of Tremaine. And the chin, with its dimples, as in health, might it not be hers?—but *had she then grown taller since her malady?* What inexpressible madness seized me with that thought? One bound, and I had reached her feet! Shrinking from my touch, she let fall from her head, unloosened, the ghastly cerements which had confined it, and there streamed forth, into the rushing asmosphere of the chamber, huge masses of long and dishevelled hair; *it was blacker than the raven wings of the midnight!* And now slowly opened *the eyes* of the figure which stood before me. "Here then, at least," I shrieked aloud, "can I never—can I never be mistaken—these are the full, and the black, and the wild eyes—of my lost love—of the lady—of the LADY LIGEIA!"

1838, 1840

The Fall of the House of Usher

Son cœur est un luth suspendu;
Sitôt qu'on le touche il résonne.
—DE BÉRANGER.[2]

During the whole of a dull, dark, and soundless day in the autumn of the year, when the clouds hung oppressively low in the heavens,

2. Pierre Jean de Béranger, from "Le Refus" (ll. 41–42); translated, "His heart is a suspended lute; Whenever one touches it, it resounds." *Cf.* "Israfel."

I had been passing alone, on horseback, through a singularly dreary tract of country, and at length found myself, as the shades of the evening drew on, within view of the melancholy House of Usher. I know not how it was—but, with the first glimpse of the building, a sense of insufferable gloom pervaded my spirit. I say insufferable; for the feeling was unrelieved by any of that half-pleasurable, because poetic, sentiment with which the mind usually receives even the sternest natural images of the desolate or terrible. I looked upon the scene before me—upon the mere house, and the simple land-scape features of the domain—upon the bleak walls—upon the vacant eye-like windows—upon a few rank sedges—and upon a few white trunks of decayed trees—with an utter depression of soul which I can compare to no earthly sensation more properly than to the after-dream of the reveller upon opium—the bitter lapse into every-day life—the hideous dropping off of the veil. There was an iciness, a sinking, a sickening of the heart—an unredeemed dreariness of thought which no goading of the imagination could torture into aught of the sublime. What was it—I paused to think—what was it that so unnerved me in the contemplation of the House of Usher? It was a mystery all insoluble; nor could I grapple with the shadowy fancies that crowded upon me as I pondered. I was forced to fall back upon the unsatisfactory conclusion, that while, beyond doubt, there *are* combinations of very simple natural objects which have the power of thus affecting us, still the analysis of this power lies among considerations beyond our depth. It was possible, I reflected, that a mere different arrangement of the particulars of the scene, of the details of the picture, would be sufficient to modify, or perhaps to annihilate its capacity for sorrowful impression; and, acting upon this idea, I reined my horse to the precipitous brink of a black and lurid tarn that lay in unruffled lustre by the dwelling, and gazed down—but with a shudder even more thrilling than before—upon the remodelled and inverted images of the gray sedge, and the ghastly tree-stems, and the vacant and eye-like windows.

Nevertheless, in this mansion of gloom I now proposed to myself a sojourn of some weeks. Its proprietor, Roderick Usher, had been one of my boon companions in boyhood; but many years had elapsed since our last meeting. A letter, however, had lately reached me in a distant part of the country—a letter from him—which, in its wildly importunate nature, had admitted of no other than a personal reply. The MS. gave evidence of nervous agitation. The writer spoke of acute bodily illness—of a mental disorder which oppressed him—and of an earnest desire to see me, as his best and indeed his only personal friend, with a view of attempting, by the cheerfulness of my society, some alleviation of his malady. It was the manner in which all this, and much more, was said—it was the apparent *heart* that went with his request—which allowed me no room for hesitation; and I accordingly obeyed forthwith what I still considered a very singular summons.

Although, as boys, we had been even intimate associates, yet I really knew little of my friend. His reserve had been always excessive and habitual. I was aware, however, that his very ancient family had been noted, time out of mind, for a peculiar sensibility of temperament, displaying itself, through long ages, in many works of exalted art, and manifested, of late, in repeated deeds of munificent yet unobtrusive charity, as well as in a passionate devotion to the intricacies, perhaps even more than to the orthodox and easily recognizable beauties, of musical science. I had learned, too, the very remarkable fact, that the stem of the Usher race, all time-honored as it was, had put forth, at no period, any enduring branch; in other words, that the entire family lay in the direct line of descent, and had always, with very trifling and very temporary variation, so lain. It was this deficiency, I considered, while running over in thought the perfect keeping of the character of the premises with the accredited character of the people, and while speculating upon the possible influence which the one, in the long lapse of centuries, might have exercised upon the other—it was this deficiency, perhaps, of collateral issue, and the consequent undeviating transmission, from sire to son, of the patrimony with the name, which had, at length, so identified the two as to merge the original title of the estate in the quaint and equivocal appellation of the "House of Usher"—an appellation which seemed to include, in the minds of the peasantry who used it, both the family and the family mansion.

I have said that the sole effect of my somewhat childish experiment—that of looking down within the tarn—had been to deepen the first singular impression. There can be no doubt that the consciousness of the rapid increase of my superstition—for why should I not so term it?—served mainly to accelerate the increase itself. Such, I have long known, is the paradoxical law of all sentiments having terror as a basis. And it might have been for this reason only, that, when I again uplifted my eyes to the house itself, from its image in the pool, there grew in my mind a strange fancy—a fancy so ridiculous, indeed, that I but mention it to show the vivid force of the sensations which oppressed me. I had so worked upon my imagination as really to believe that about the whole mansion and domain there hung an atmosphere peculiar to themselves and their immediate vicinity—an atmosphere which had no affinity with the air of heaven, but which had reeked up from the decayed trees, and the gray wall, and the silent tarn—a pestilent and mystic vapor, dull, sluggish, faintly discernible, and leaden-hued.

Shaking off from my spirit what *must* have been a dream, I scanned more narrowly the real aspect of the building. Its principal feature seemed to be that of an excessive antiquity. The discoloration of ages had been great. Minute fungi overspread the whole exterior, hanging in a fine tangled web-work from the eaves. Yet all this was apart from any extraordinary dilapidation. No portion of the masonry had fallen; and there appeared to be a wild inconsistency between its still perfect adaptation of parts, and the crumbling condition of the individual stones. In this there was much that reminded me of the specious totality of old wood-work which has rotted for long years in some neglected vault, with no disturbance from the breath of the external air. Beyond this indication of extensive decay, however, the fabric gave little token of instability. Perhaps the eye of a scrutinizing observer might have discovered a barely perceptible fissure, which, extending from the roof of the building in front, made its way down the wall in a zigzag direction, until it became lost in the sullen waters of the tarn.

Noticing these things, I rode over a short causeway to the house. A servant in waiting took my horse, and I entered the Gothic archway of the hall. A valet, of stealthy step, thence conducted me, in silence, through many dark and intricate passages in my progress to the *studio* of his master. Much that I encountered on the way contributed, I know not how, to heighten the vague sentiments of which I have already spoken. While the objects around me—while the carvings of the ceilings, the sombre tapestries of the walls, the ebon blackness of the floors, and the phantasmagoric armorial trophies which rattled as I strode, were but matters to which, or to such as which, I had been accustomed from my infancy—while I hesitated not to acknowledge how familiar was all this—I still wondered to find how unfamiliar were the fancies which ordinary images were stirring up. On one of the staircases, I met the physician of the family. His countenance, I thought, wore a mingled expression of low cunning and perplexity. He accosted me with trepidation and passed on. The valet now threw open a door and ushered me into the presence of his master.

The room in which I found myself was very large and lofty. The windows were long, narrow, and pointed, and at so vast a distance from the black oaken floor as to be altogether inaccessible from within. Feeble gleams of encrimsoned light made their way through the trellissed panes, and served to render sufficiently distinct the more prominent objects around; the eye, however, struggled in vain to reach the remoter angles of the chamber, or the recesses of the vaulted and fretted ceiling. Dark draperies hung upon the walls. The general furniture was profuse, comfortless, antique, and tattered.

Many books and musical instruments lay scattered about, but failed to give any vitality to the scene. I felt that I breathed an atmosphere of sorrow. An air of stern, deep, and irredeemable gloom hung over and pervaded all.

Upon my entrance, Usher arose from a sofa on which he had been lying at full length, and greeted me with a vivacious warmth which had much in it, I at first thought, of an overdone cordiality—of the constrained effort of the *ennuyé*[3] man of the world. A glance, however, at his countenance convinced me of his perfect sincerity. We sat down; and for some moments, while he spoke not, I gazed upon him with a feeling half of pity, half of awe. Surely, man had never before so terribly altered, in so brief a period, as had Roderick Usher! It was with difficulty that I could bring myself to admit the identity of the wan being before me with the companion of my early boyhood. Yet the character of his face had been at all times remarkable.[4] A cadaverousness of complexion; an eye large, liquid, and luminous beyond comparison; lips somewhat thin and very pallid, but of a surpassingly beautiful curve; a nose of a delicate Hebrew model, but with a breadth of nostril unusual in similar formations; a finely moulded chin, speaking, in its want of prominence, of a want of moral energy; hair of a more than web-like softness and tenuity;—these features, with an inordinate expansion above the regions of the temple, made up altogether a countenance not easily to be forgotten. And now in the mere exaggeration of the prevailing character of these features, and of the expression they were wont to convey, lay so much of change that I doubted to whom I spoke. The now ghastly pallor of the skin, and the now miraculous lustre of the eye, above all things startled and even awed me. The silken hair, too, had been suffered to grow all unheeded, and as, in its wild gossamer texture, it floated rather than fell about the face, I could not, even with effort, connect its Arabesque expression with any idea of simple humanity.

In the manner of my friend I was at once struck with an incoherence—an inconsistency; and I soon found this to arise from a series of feeble and futile struggles to overcome an habitual trepidancy—an excessive nervous agitation. For something of this nature I had indeed been prepared, no less by his letter, than by reminiscences of certain boyish traits, and by conclusions deduced[5] from his peculiar physical conformation and temperament. His action was alternately vivacious and sullen. His voice varied rapidly from a tremulous indecision (when the animal spirits seemed utterly in abeyance) to that species of energetic concision—that abrupt, weighty, unhurried, and hollow-sounding enunciation—that leaden, self-balanced, and per-

---

3. Bored.
4. Hervey Allen wrote: "The description of Roderick Usher is the most perfect pen-portrait of Poe himself."

5. Poe, like many intelligent contemporaries, trusted the phrenological deduction of character from external characteristics.

fectly modulated guttural utterance, which may be observed in the lost drunkard, or the irreclaimable eater of opium, during the periods of his most intense excitement.

It was thus that he spoke of the object of my visit, of his earnest desire to see me, and of the solace he expected me to afford him. He entered, at some length, into what he conceived to be the nature of his malady. It was, he said, a constitutional and a family evil, and one for which he despaired to find a remedy—a mere nervous affection, he immediately added, which would undoubtedly soon pass off. It displayed itself in a host of unnatural sensations. Some of these, as he detailed them, interested and bewildered me; although, perhaps, the terms and the general manner of their narration had their weight. He suffered much from a morbid acuteness of the senses; the most insipid food was alone endurable; he could wear only garments of certain texture; the odors of all flowers were oppressive; his eyes were tortured by even a faint light; and there were but peculiar sounds, and these from stringed instruments, which did not inspire him with horror.

To an anomalous species of terror I found him a bounden slave. "I shall perish," said he, "I *must* perish in this deplorable folly. Thus, thus, and not otherwise, shall I be lost. I dread the events of the future, not in themselves, but in their results. I shudder at the thought of any, even the most trivial, incident, which may operate upon this intolerable agitation of soul. I have, indeed, no abhorrence of danger, except in its absolute effect—in terror. In this unnerved, in this pitiable, condition I feel that the period will sooner or later arrive when I must abandon life and reason together, in some struggle with the grim phantasm, FEAR."

I learned, moreover, at intervals, and through broken and equivocal hints, another singular feature of his mental condition. He was enchained by certain superstitious impressions in regard to the dwelling which he tenanted, and whence, for many years, he had never ventured forth—in regard to an influence whose supposititious force was conveyed in terms too shadowy here to be re-stated—an influence which some peculiarities in the mere form and substance of his family mansion had, by dint of long sufferance, he said, obtained over his spirit—an effect which the *physique* of the gray walls and turrets, and of the dim tarn into which they all looked down, had, at length, brought about upon the *morale* of his existence.

He admitted, however, although with hesitation, that much of the peculiar gloom which thus afflicted him could be traced to a more natural and far more palpable origin—to the severe and long-continued illness—indeed to the evidently approaching dissolution—of a tenderly beloved sister, his sole companion for long years, his last and only relative on earth. "Her decease," he said, with a bitterness which I can never forget, "would leave him (him, the hopeless and the frail) the last of the ancient race of the Ushers." While he spoke, the lady Madeline (for so was she called) passed through a remote portion of the apartment, and, without having noticed my presence, disappeared. I regarded her with an utter astonishment not unmingled with dread; and yet I found it impossible to account for such feelings. A sensation of stupor oppressed me as my eyes followed her retreating steps. When a door, at length, closed upon her, my glance sought instinctively and eagerly the countenance of the brother; but he had buried his face in his hands, and I could only perceive that a far more than ordinary wanness had overspread the emaciated fingers through which trickled many passionate tears.

The disease of the lady Madeline had long baffled the skill of her physicians. A settled apathy, a gradual wasting away of the person, and frequent although transient affections of a partially cataleptical character were the unusual diagnosis. Hitherto she had steadily borne up against the pressure of her malady, and had not betaken herself finally to bed; but on the closing in of the evening of my arrival at the house, she succumbed (as her brother told me at night with inexpressible agitation) to the prostrating power of the destroyer; and I learned that the glimpse I had obtained of her person would thus probably be the last I should obtain—that the lady, at least while living, would be seen by me no more.

For several days ensuing, her name was unmentioned by either Usher or myself; and during this period I was busied in earnest endeavors to alleviate the melancholy of my friend. We painted and read together, or I listened, as if in a dream, to the wild improvisations of his speaking guitar. And thus, as a closer and still closer intimacy admitted me more unreservedly into the recesses of his spirit, the more bitterly did I perceive the futility of all attempt at cheering a mind from which darkness, as if an inherent positive quality, poured forth upon all objects of the moral and physical universe in one unceasing radiation of gloom.

I shall ever bear about me a memory of the many solemn hours I thus spent alone with the master of the House of Usher. Yet I should fail in any attempt to convey an idea of the exact character of the studies, or of the occupations, in which he involved me, or led me the way. An excited and highly distempered ideality threw a sulphureous lustre over all. His long improvised dirges will ring forever in my ears. Among other things, I hold painfully in mind a certain singular perversion and amplification of the wild air of the last waltz of Von Weber.[6] From the paintings over which his elaborate fancy brooded, and which grew, touch by touch, into

6. Karl Maria Von Weber (1786–1826), pioneer of German romantic opera, did not compose "The Last Waltz of Von Weber." It was one of the *Danses Brilliantes* (1822) by Karl Gottlieb Reissiger (1798–1859).

vaguenesses at which I shuddered the more thrillingly, because I shuddered knowing not why—from these paintings (vivid as their images now are before me) I would in vain endeavor to educe more than a small portion which should lie within the compass of merely written words. By the utter simplicity, by the nakedness of his designs, he arrested and overawed attention. If ever mortal painted an idea, that mortal was Roderick Usher. For me at least, in the circumstances then surrounding me, there arose out of the pure abstractions which the hypochondriac contrived to throw upon his canvas, an intensity of intolerable awe, no shadow of which felt I ever yet in the contemplation of the certainly glowing yet too concrete reveries of Fuseli.[7]

One of the phantasmagoric conceptions of my friend, partaking not so rigidly of the spirit of abstraction, may be shadowed forth, although feebly, in words. A small picture presented the interior of an immensely long and rectangular vault or tunnel, with low walls, smooth, white, and without interruption or device. Certain accessory points of the design served well to convey the idea that this excavation lay at an exceeding depth below the surface of the earth. No outlet was observed in any portion of its vast extent, and no torch or other artificial source of light was discernible; yet a flood of intense rays rolled throughout, and bathed the whole in a ghastly and inappropriate splendor.

I have just spoken of that morbid condition of the auditory nerve which rendered all music intolerable to the sufferer, with the exception of certain effects of stringed instruments. It was, perhaps, the narrow limits to which he thus confined himself upon the guitar which gave birth, in great measure, to the fantastic character of his performances. But the fervid *facility* of his *impromptus* could not be so accounted for. They must have been, and were, in the notes, as well as in the words of his wild fantasias (for he not unfrequently accompanied himself with rhymed verbal improvisations), the result of that intense mental collectedness and concentration to which I have previously alluded as observable only in particular moments of the highest artificial excitement. The words of one of these rhapsodies I have easily remembered. I was, perhaps, the more forcibly impressed with it as he gave it, because, in the under or mystic current of its meaning, I fancied that I perceived, and for the first time, a full consciousness on the part of Usher of the tottering of his lofty reason upon her throne. The verses, which were entitled "The Haunted Palace,"[8] ran very nearly, if not accurately, thus:—

7. Swiss-born Johann Heinrich Füssli (1742–1825). As Henry Fuseli he became, in London, a romantic impressionist and illustrator of Shakespeare and Milton.

8. This poem was published in the *Baltimore Museum* for April, 1839, five months before it appeared as part of the present story.

I.

In the greenest of our valleys,
    By good angels tenanted,
Once a fair and stately palace—
    Radiant palace—reared its head.
In the monarch Thought's dominion—
    It stood there!
Never seraph spread a pinion
    Over fabric half so fair.

II.

Banners yellow, glorious, golden,
    On its roof did float and flow
(This—all this—was in the olden
    Time long ago);
And every gentle air that dallied,
    In that sweet day,
Along the ramparts plumed and pallid,
    A winged odor went away.

III.

Wanderers in that happy valley
    Through two luminous windows saw
Spirits moving musically
    To a lute's well-tunèd law;
Round about a throne, where sitting
    (Porphyrogene!)[9]
In state his glory well befitting,
    The ruler of the realm was seen.

IV.

And all with pearl and ruby glowing
    Was the fair palace door,
Through which came flowing, flowing, flowing
    And sparkling evermore,
A troop of Echoes whose sweet duty
    Was but to sing,
In voices of surpassing beauty,
    The wit and wisdom of their king.

V.

But evil things, in robes of sorrow,
    Assailed the monarch's high estate;
(Ah, let us mourn, for never morrow
    Shall dawn upon him, desolate!)
And, round about his home, the glory
    That blushed and bloomed

---

9. A Greek derivative; "born to the purple"—a mark of royalty.

Is but a dim-remembered story
Of the old time entombed.

VI.

And travellers now within that valley,
Through the red-litten windows see
Vast forms that move fantastically
To a discordant melody;
While, like a rapid ghastly river,
Through the pale door;
A hideous throng rush out forever,
And laugh—but smile no more.

I well remember that suggestions arising from this ballad led us into a train of thought wherein there became manifest an opinion of Usher's which I mention not so much on account of its novelty (for other men[1] have thought thus), as on account of the pertinacity with which he maintained it. This opinion, in its general form, was that of the sentience of all vegetable things. But, in his disordered fancy, the idea had assumed a more daring character, and trespassed, under certain conditions, upon the kingdom of inorganization. I lack words to express the full extent, or the earnest *abandon* of his persuasion. The belief, however, was connected (as I have previously hinted) with the gray stones of the home of his forefathers. The conditions of the sentience had been here, he imagined, fulfilled in the method of collocation of these stones—in the order of their arrangement, as well as in that of the many *fungi* which overspread them, and of the decayed trees which stood around—above all, in the long undisturbed endurance of this arrangement, and in its reduplication in the still waters of the tarn. Its evidence—the evidence of the sentience—was to be seen, he said (and I here started as he spoke), in the gradual yet certain condensation of an atmosphere of their own about the waters and the walls. The result was discoverable, he added, in that silent yet importunate and terrible influence which for centuries had moulded the destinies of his family, and which made *him* what I now saw him—what he was. Such opinions need no comment, and I will make none.

Our books[2]—the books which, for years, had formed no small por-

---

1. "Watson, Dr. Percival, Spallanzani, and especially the Bishop of Llandaff.— See 'Chemical Essays,' vol. v" [Poe's note].

2. Usher's library is occult and fantastically learned, suggesting his own state of mind and foreshadowing the later burial and resurrection of his sister, Madeline. *Vert-Vert* and *Chartreuse*, by Jean Baptiste Gresset (1709–1777), are lusty, anticlerical satires; in the novel of Machiavelli (1469–1527), an infernal demon visits the earth to prove that women are the damnation of men; in *Heaven and Hell* (1758), the mystical scientist Swedenborg argues the continuity of spiritual identity; while the following title, by Ludwig Holberg (1684–1754) again suggests a round trip into the world of death. The next three writers are exponents of chiromancy, or occult divination by palm-

tion of the mental existence of the invalid—were, as might be supposed, in strict keeping with this character of phantasm. We pored together over such works as the *Ververt et Chartreuse* of Gresset; the *Belphegor* of Machiavelli; the *Heaven and Hell* of Swedenborg; the *Subterranean Voyage of Nicholas Klimm* of Holberg; the *Chiromancy* of Robert Flud, of Jean D'Indaginé, and of De la Chambre; the *Journey into the Blue Distance* of Tieck; and the *City of the Sun* of Campanella. One favorite volume was a small octavo edition of the *Directorium Inquisitorium*, by the Dominican Eymeric de Gironne; and there were passages in Pomponius Mela, about the old African Satyrs and Ægipans, over which Usher would sit dreaming for hours. His chief delight, however, was found in the perusal of an exceedingly rare and curious book in quarto Gothic—the manual of a forgotten church—the *Vigiliæ Mortuorum secundum Chorum Ecclesiæ Maguntinæ*.

I could not help thinking of the wild ritual of this work, and of its probable influence upon the hypochondriac, when, one evening, having informed me abruptly that the lady Madeline was no more, he stated his intention of preserving her corpse for a fortnight (previously to its final interment), in one of the numerous vaults within the main walls of the building. The worldly reason, however, assigned for this singular proceeding, was one which I did not feel at liberty to dispute. The brother had been led to his resolution (so he told me) by consideration of the unusual character of the malady of the deceased, of certain obtrusive and eager inquiries on the part of her medical men,[3] and of the remote and exposed situation of the burial-ground of the family. I will not deny that when I called to mind the sinister countenance of the person whom I met upon the staircase, on the day of my arrival at the house, I had no desire to oppose what I regarded as at best but a harmless, and by no means an unnatural, precaution.

At the request of Usher, I personally aided him in the arrangements for the temporary entombment. The body having been encoffined, we two alone bore it to its rest. The vault in which we placed it (and which had been so long unopened that our torches, half smothered in its oppressive atmosphere, gave us little opportunity for investiga-

istry: Robert Flud (1574–1637), British Rosicrucian and pseudoscientist; and two Frenchmen—Jean D'Indaginé (*Chiromantia*, 1522), and Marin Cureau de la Chambre, (*Principes de la Chiromancie*, 1653). The next two titles again suggest the journey to another world. Ludwig Tieck (1773–1853), a German poet, did not, however, publish a work of the title here attributed to him; the book by Tomaso Campanella (1568–1639), Italian philosopher, describes an ideal otherworld. *Inquisitorum Directorium* was an account of procedures and tortures, by Nicolas Eymeric de Girone (*ca.* 1320–1399), once inquisitor-general for Castile. Pomponius Mela was a Roman of the first century A.D., but his *Geography*, when printed at Milan in 1471, was still given credence for such wonders as the "Ægipans," reputed goatmen of Africa. The last title, translated as *The Vigils of the Dead * * ** , has not been identified; but there were many such titles in the Middle Ages.

3. The stealing of the bodies of the dead for medical students and scientists was then a common practice.

tion) was small, damp, and entirely without means of admission for light; lying, at great depth, immediately beneath that portion of the building in which was my own sleeping apartment. It had been used, apparently, in remote feudal times, for the worst purposes of a donjon-keep, and, in later days, as a place of deposit for powder, or some other highly combustible substance, as a portion of its floor, and the whole interior of a long archway through which we reached it, were carefully sheathed with copper. The door, of massive iron, had been, also, similarly protected. Its immense weight caused an unusually sharp, grating sound, as it moved upon its hinges.

Having deposited our mournful burden upon tressels within this region of horror, we partially turned aside the yet unscrewed lid of the coffin, and looked upon the face of the tenant. A striking similitude between the brother and sister now first arrested my attention; and Usher, divining, perhaps, my thoughts, murmured out some few words from which I learned that the deceased and himself had been twins, and that sympathies of a scarcely intelligible nature had always existed between them. Our glances, however, rested not long upon the dead—for we could not regard her unawed. The disease which had thus entombed the lady in the maturity of youth, had left, as usual in all maladies of a strictly cataleptical character, the mockery of a faint blush upon the bosom and the face, and that suspiciously lingering smile upon the lip which is so terrible in death. We replaced and screwed down the lid, and, having secured the door of iron, made our way, with toil, into the scarcely less gloomy apartments of the upper portion of the house.

And now, some days of bitter grief having elapsed, an observable change came over the features of the mental disorder of my friend. His ordinary manner had vanished. His ordinary occupations were neglected or forgotten. He roamed from chamber to chamber with hurried, unequal, and objectless step. The pallor of his countenance had assumed, if possible, a more ghastly hue—but the luminousness of his eye had utterly gone out. The once occasional huskiness of his tone was heard no more; and a tremulous quaver, as if of extreme terror, habitually characterized his utterance. There were times, indeed, when I thought his unceasingly agitated mind was laboring with some oppressive secret, to divulge which he struggled for the necessary courage. At times, again, I was obliged to resolve all into the mere inexplicable vagaries of madness, for I beheld him gazing upon vacancy for long hours, in an attitude of the profoundest attention, as if listening to some imaginary sound. It was no wonder that his condition terrified—that it infected me. I felt creeping upon me, by slow yet certain degrees, the wild influences of his own fantastic yet impressive superstitions.

It was, especially, upon retiring to bed late in the night of the seventh or eighth day after the placing of the lady Madeline within the donjon, that I experienced the full power of such feelings. Sleep came not near my couch—while the hours waned and waned away. I struggled to reason off the nervousness which had dominion over me. I endeavored to believe that much, if not all of what I felt, was due to the bewildering influence of the gloomy furniture of the room—of the dark and tattered draperies, which, tortured into motion by the breath of a rising tempest, swayed fitfully to and fro upon the walls, and rustled uneasily about the decorations of the bed. But my efforts were fruitless. An irrepressible tremor gradually pervaded my frame; and, at length, there sat upon my very heart an incubus of utterly causeless alarm. Shaking this off with a gasp and a struggle, I uplifted myself upon the pillows, and, peering earnestly within the intense darkness of the chamber, hearkened—I know not why, except that an instinctive spirit prompted me—to certain low and indefinite sounds which came, through the pauses of the storm, at long intervals, I knew not whence. Overpowered by an intense sentiment of horror, unaccountable yet unendurable, I threw on my clothes with haste (for I felt that I should sleep no more during the night), and endeavored to arouse myself from the pitiable condition into which I had fallen, by pacing rapidly to and fro through the apartment.

I had taken but few turns in this manner, when a light step on an adjoining staircase arrested my attention. I presently recognized it as that of Usher. In an instant afterward he rapped, with a gentle touch, at my door, and entered, bearing a lamp. His countenance was, as usual, cadaverously wan—but, moreover, there was a species of mad hilarity in his eyes—an evidently restrained *hysteria* in his whole demeanor. His air appalled me—but any thing was preferable to the solitude which I had so long endured, and I even welcomed his presence as a relief.

"And you have not seen it?" he said abruptly, after having stared about him for some moments in silence—"you have not then seen it?—but, stay! you shall." Thus speaking, and having carefully shaded his lamp, he hurried to one of the casements, and threw it freely open to the storm.

The impetuous fury of the entering gust nearly lifted us from our feet. It was, indeed, a tempestuous yet sternly beautiful night, and one wildly singular in its terror and its beauty. A whirlwind had apparently collected its force in our vicinity; for there were frequent and violent alterations in the direction of the wind; and the exceeding density of the clouds (which hung so low as to press upon the turrets of the house) did not prevent our perceiving the life-like velocity with which they flew careering from all points against each other, without passing away into the distance. I say that even their exceeding density did not prevent our perceiving this—yet we had no glimpse of the moon or stars, nor was there any flashing forth of the lightning. But the under surfaces of the huge masses of agitated vapor, as well as all terrestrial objects immediately around us, were glowing in the unnatural light of a faintly luminous and distinctly visible gaseous exhalation which hung about and enshrouded the mansion.

"You must not—you shall not behold this!" said I, shuddering, to Usher, as I led him, with a gentle violence, from the window to a seat. "These appearances, which bewilder you, are merely electrical phenomena not uncommon—or it may be that they have their ghastly origin in the rank miasma of the tarn. Let us close this casement;—the air is chilling and dangerous to your frame. Here is one of your favorite romances. I will read, and you shall listen:—and so we will pass away this terrible night together."

The antique volume which I had taken up was the "Mad Trist" of Sir Launcelot Canning;[4] but I had called it a favorite of Usher's more in sad jest than in earnest; for, in truth, there is little in its uncouth and unimaginative prolixity which could have had interest for the lofty and spiritual ideality of my friend. It was, however, the only book immediately at hand; and I indulged a vague hope that the excitement which now agitated the hypochondriac, might find relief (for the history of mental disorder is full of similar anomalies) even in the extremeness of the folly which I should read. Could I have judged, indeed, by the wild overstrained air of vivacity with which he hearkened, or apparently hearkened, to the words of the tale, I might well have congratulated myself upon the success of my design.

I had arrived at that well-known portion of the story where Ethelred, the hero of the Trist, having sought in vain for peaceable admission into the dwelling of the hermit, proceeds to make good an entrance by force. Here, it will be remembered, the words of the narrative run thus:

"And Ethelred, who was by nature of a doughty heart, and who was now mighty withal, on account of the powerfulness of the wine which he had drunken, waited no longer to hold parley with the hermit, who, in sooth, was of an obstinate and maliceful turn, but, feeling the rain upon his shoulders, and fearing the rising of the tempest, uplifted his mace outright, and, with blows, made quickly room in the plankings of the door for his gauntleted hand; and now pulling therewith sturdily, he so cracked, and ripped, and tore all asunder, that the noise of the dry and hollow-sounding wood alarumed and reverberated throughout the forest."

At the termination of this sentence I started and, for a moment, paused; for it appeared to me (although I at once concluded that my

4. Not identified; possibly Poe invented the book and the author for his purpose.

excited fancy had deceived me)—it appeared to me that, from some very remote portion of the mansion, there came, indistinctly to my ears, what might have been, in its exact similarity of character, the echo (but a stifled and dull one certainly) of the very cracking and ripping sound which Sir Launcelot had so particularly described. It was, beyond doubt, the coincidence alone which had arrested my attention; for, amid the rattling of the sashes of the casements, and the ordinary commingled noises of the still increasing storm, the sound, in itself, had nothing, surely, which should have interested or disturbed me. I continued the story:

"But the good champion Ethelred, now entering within the door, was sore enraged and amazed to perceive no signal of the maliceful hermit; but, in the stead thereof, a dragon of a scaly and prodigious demeanor, and of a fiery tongue, which sate in guard before a palace of gold, with a floor of silver; and upon the wall there hung a shield of shining brass with this legend enwritten—

> Who entereth herein, a conqueror hath bin;
> Who slayeth the dragon, the shield he shall win.

And Ethelred uplifted his mace, and struck upon the head of the dragon, which fell before him, and gave up his pesty breath, with a shriek so horrid and harsh, and withal so piercing, that Ethelred had fain to close his ears with his hands against the dreadful noise of it, the like whereof was never before heard."

Here again I paused abruptly, and now with a feeling of wild amazement—for there could be no doubt whatever that, in this instance, I did actually hear (although from what direction it proceeded I found it impossible to say) a low and apparently distant, but harsh, protracted, and most unusual screaming or grating sound—the exact counterpart of what my fancy had already conjured up for the dragon's unnatural shriek as described by the romancer.

Oppressed, as I certainly was, upon the occurrence of this second and most extraordinary coincidence, by a thousand conflicting sensations, in which wonder and extreme terror were predominant, I still retained sufficient presence of mind to avoid exciting, by any observation, the sensitive nervousness of my companion. I was by no means certain that he had noticed the sounds in question; although, assuredly, a strange alteration had, during the last few minutes, taken place in his demeanor. From a position fronting my own, he had gradually brought round his chair, so as to sit with his face to the door of the chamber; and thus I could but partially perceive his features, although I saw that his lips trembled as if he were murmuring inaudibly. His head had dropped upon his breast—yet I knew that he was not asleep, from the wide and rigid opening of the eye as I caught a glance of it in profile. The motion of his body, too, was at variance with this idea—for he rocked from side to side with a gentle yet constant and uniform sway. Having rapidly taken notice of all this, I resumed the narrative of Sir Launcelot, which thus proceeded:

"And now, the champion, having escaped from the terrible fury of the dragon, bethinking himself of the brazen shield, and of the breaking up of the enchantment which was upon it, removed the carcass from out of the way before him, and approached valorously over the silver pavement of the castle to where the shield was upon the wall; which in sooth tarried not for his full coming, but fell down at his feet upon the silver floor, with a mighty great and terrible ringing sound."

No sooner had these syllables passed my lips, than—as if a shield of brass had indeed, at the moment, fallen heavily upon a floor of silver —I became aware of a distinct, hollow, metallic, and clangorous, yet apparently muffled, reverberation. Completely unnerved, I leaped to my feet; but the measured rocking movement of Usher was undisturbed. I rushed to the chair in which he sat. His eyes were bent fixedly before him, and throughout his whole countenance there reigned a stony rigidity. But, as I placed my hand upon his shoulder, there came a strong shudder over his whole person; a sickly smile quivered about his lips; and I saw that he spoke in a low, hurried, and gibbering murmur, as if unconscious of my presence. Bending closely over him, I at length drank in the hideous import of his words.

"Now hear it?—yes, I hear it, and *have* heard it. Long—long—long —many minutes, many hours, many days, have I heard it—yet I dared not—oh, pity me, miserable wretch that I am!—I dared not— I *dared* not speak! *We have put her living in the tomb!* Said I not that my senses were acute? I *now* tell you that I heard her feeble first movements in the hollow coffin. I heard them—many, many days ago —yet I dared not—*I dared not speak!* And now—to-night—Ethelred—ha! ha!—the breaking of the hermit's door, and the death-cry of the dragon, and the clangor of the shield—say, rather, the rending of her coffin, and the grating of the iron hinges of her prison, and her struggles within the coppered archway of the vault! Oh! whither shall I fly? Will she not be here anon? Is she not hurrying to upbraid me for my haste? Have I not heard her footstep on the stair? Do I not distinguish that heavy and horrible beating of her heart? Madman!"—here he sprang furiously to his feet, and shrieked out his syllables, as if in the effort he were giving up his soul—"MADMAN! I TELL YOU THAT SHE NOW STANDS WITHOUT THE DOOR!"

As if in the superhuman energy of his utterance there had been found the potency of a spell, the huge antique panels to which the speaker pointed threw slowly back, upon the instant, their ponderous and ebony jaws. It was the work of the rushing gust—but then without those doors there *did* stand the lofty and enshrouded figure of the lady Madeline of Usher. There was blood upon her white robes, and the evidence of some bitter struggle upon every portion of her emaciated frame. For a moment she remained trembling and reeling to and fro upon the threshold—then, with a low moaning cry, fell heavily inward upon the person of her brother, and in her violent and now final death-agonies, bore him to the floor a corpse, and a victim to the terrors he had anticipated.

From that chamber, and from that mansion, I fled aghast. The storm was still abroad in all its wrath as I found myself crossing the old causeway. Suddenly there shot along the path a wild light, and I turned to see whence a gleam so unusual could have issued; for the vast house and its shadows were alone behind me. The radiance was that of the full, setting, and blood-red moon, which now shone vividly through that once barely discernible fissure, of which I have before spoken as extending from the roof of the building, in a zigzag direction, to the base. While I gazed, this fissure rapidly widened—there came a fierce breath of the whirlwind—the entire orb of the satellite burst at once upon my sight—my brain reeled as I saw the mighty walls rushing asunder—there was a long tumultuous shouting sound like the voice of a thousand waters[5]—and the deep and dank tarn at my feet closed sullenly and silently over the fragments of the HOUSE OF USHER.

1839, 1840

The Murders in the Rue Morgue[6]

What song the Syrens sang, or what name Achilles assumed when he hid himself among women, although puzzling questions, are not beyond *all* conjecture.
—SIR THOMAS BROWNE [7]

The mental features discoursed of as the analytical, are, in themselves, but little susceptible of analysis. We appreciate them only in their effects. We know of them, among other things, that they are always to their possessor, when inordinately possessed, a source of the

5. *Cf.* Ezekiel xliii: 2: "[God's] voice was like a noise of many waters."
6. The centennial of the detective story was spontaneously recognized in 1941, when a number of American and British periodicals published articles and special numbers acknowledging Poe's invention of the form. The first such story, "The Murders in the Rue Morgue," appeared in *Graham's Magazine* in April, 1841. It contained all the ingredients, now classic, of this fiction: the crime unusually violent or malicious; the blundering police official reluctantly cooperating with the unofficial detective: the impossible conditions, such as the room here completely locked from the inside; the cool courage and flawless deduction of the detective; the surpris-

ing application of well-known facts or scientific data; the clue "hidden" in the obvious place or the "insignificant" detail; and the innocent suspect dramatically saved from unjust punishment. These ingredients Poe employed variously in a number of detective stories. In science fiction, of which he was also the pioneer, he employed similar deductive processes, as well as his characteristic elements of shock or horror (*cf.* "A Descent into the Maelström"). The story was somewhat revised before being collected with the author's *Tales* (1845), the text given here.
7. Sir Thomas Browne (1605–1682), British physician and antiquary. The quotation is from Chapter 5 of *Hydriotaphia, or Urn-Burial* (1658).

liveliest enjoyment. As the strong man exults in his physical ability, delighting in such exercises as call his muscles into action, so glories the analyst in that moral activity which *disentangles*. He derives pleasure from even the most trivial occupations bringing his talent into play. He is fond of enigmas, of conundrums, hieroglyphics; exhibiting in his solutions of each a degree of *acumen* which appears to the ordinary apprehension præternatural. His results, brought about by the very soul and essence of method, have, in truth, the whole air of intuition.

The faculty of re-solution is possibly much invigorated by mathematical study, and especially by that highest branch of it which, unjustly, and merely on account of its retrograde operations, has been called, as if *par excellence*, analysis. Yet to calculate is not in itself to analyze. A chess-player, for example, does the one, without effort at the other. It follows that the game of chess, in its effects upon mental character, is greatly misunderstood. I am not now writing a treatise, but simply prefacing a somewhat peculiar narrative by observations very much at random; I will, therefore, take occasion to assert that the higher powers of the reflective intellect are more decidedly and more usefully tasked by the unostentatious game of draughts than by all the elaborate frivolity of chess.[8] In this latter, where the pieces have different and *bizarre* motions, with various and variable values, what is only complex, is mistaken (a not unusual error) for what is profound. The *attention* is here called powerfully into play. If it flag for an instant, an oversight is committed, resulting in injury or defeat. The possible moves being not only manifold, but involute, the chances of such oversights are multiplied; and in nine cases out of ten, it is the more concentrative rather than the more acute player who conquers. In draughts, on the contrary, where the moves are *unique* and have but little variation, the probabilities of inadvertence are diminished, and the mere attention being left comparatively unemployed, what advantages are obtained by either party are obtained by superior *acumen*. To be less abstract, let us suppose a game of draughts where the pieces are reduced to four kings, and where, of course, no oversight is to be expected. It is obvious that here the victory can be decided (the players being at all equal) only by some *recherché*[9] movement, the result of some strong exertion of the intellect. Deprived of ordinary resources, the analyst throws himself into the spirit of his opponent, identifies himself therewith, and not unfrequently sees thus, at a glance, the sole methods (sometimes indeed absurdly simple ones) by which he may seduce into error or hurry into miscalculation.

Whist[1] has long been known for its influence upon what is termed

8. "Draughts" is the British term for "checkers." This theory of chess, as a game of logical calculation, Poe had already expounded in "Maelzel's Chess-Player" (1836), exposing an automaton as being actuated by the exhibitor.
9. Studied or refined.
1. The ancestor of the modern game of bridge.

the calculating power; and men of the highest order of intellect have been known to take an apparently unaccountable delight in it, while eschewing chess as frivolous. Beyond doubt there is nothing of a similar nature so greatly tasking the faculty of analysis. The best chess-player in Christendom *may* be little more than the best player of chess; but proficiency in whist implies capacity for success in all these more important undertakings where mind struggles with mind. When I say proficiency, I mean that perfection in the game which includes a comprehension of *all* the sources whence legitimate advantage may be derived. These are not only manifold, but multiform, and lie frequently among recesses of thought altogether inaccessible to the ordinary understanding. To observe attentively is to remember distinctly; and, so far, the concentrative chess-player will do very well at whist; while the rules of Hoyle (themselves based upon the mere mechanism of the game) are sufficiently and generally comprehensible. Thus to have a retentive memory, and proceed by "the book" are points commonly regarded as the sum total of good playing. But it is in matters beyond the limits of mere rule that the skill of the analyst is evinced. He makes, in silence, a host of observations and inferences. So, perhaps, do his companions; and the difference in the extent of the information obtained, lies not so much in the validity of the inference as in the quality of the observation. The necessary knowledge is that of *what* to observe. Our player confines himself not at all; nor, because the game is the object, does he reject deductions from things external to the game. He examines the countenance of his partner, comparing it carefully with that of each of his opponents. He considers the mode of assorting the cards in each hand; often counting trump by trump, and honor by honor, through the glances bestowed by their holders upon each. He notes every variation of face as the play progresses, gathering a fund of thought from the differences in the expression of certainty, of surprise, of triumph, or chagrin. From the manner of gathering up a trick he judges whether the person taking it, can make another in the suit. He recognizes what is played through feint, by the manner with which it is thrown upon the table. A casual or inadvertent word; the accidental dropping or turning of a card, with the accompanying anxiety or carelessness in regard to its concealment; the counting of the tricks, with the order of their arrangement; embarrassment, hesitation, eagerness, or trepidation—all afford, to his apparently intuitive perception, indications of the true state of affairs. The first two or three rounds having been played, he is in full possession of the contents of each hand, and thenceforward puts down his cards with as absolute a precision of purpose as if the rest of the party had turned outward the faces of their own.

The analytical power should not be confounded with simple ingenuity; for while the analyst is necessarily ingenious, the ingenious man is often remarkably incapable of analysis. The constructive or combining power, by which ingenuity is usually manifested, and to which the phrenologists[2] (I believe erroneously) have assigned a separate organ, supposing it a primitive faculty, has been so frequently seen in those whose intellect bordered otherwise upon idiocy, as to have attracted general observation among writers on morals. Between ingenuity and the analytic ability there exists a difference far greater, indeed, than that between the fancy and the imagination, but of a character very strictly analogous. It will be found, in fact, that the ingenious are always fanciful, and the *truly* imaginative never otherwise than analytic.

The narrative which follows will appear to the reader somewhat in the light of a commentary upon the propositions just advanced.

Residing in Paris during the spring and part of the summer of 18—, I there became acquainted with a Monsieur C. Auguste Dupin.[3] This young gentleman was of an excellent, indeed of an illustrious family, but, by a variety of untoward events, had been reduced to such poverty that the energy of his character succumbed beneath it, and he ceased to bestir himself in the world, or to care for the retrieval of his fortunes. By courtesy of his creditors, there still remained in his possession a small remnant of his patrimony; and, upon the income arising from this, he managed, by means of a rigorous economy, to procure the necessities of life, without troubling himself about its superfluities. Books, indeed, were his sole luxuries, and in Paris these are easily obtained.

Our first meeting was at an obscure library in the Rue Montmartre, where the accident of our both being in search of the same very rare and very remarkable volume, brought us into closer communion. We saw each other again and again. I was deeply interested in the little family history which he detailed to me with all that candor which a Frenchman indulges whenever mere self is the theme. I was astonished, too, at the vast extent of his reading; and, above all, I felt my soul enkindled within me by the wild fervor, and the vivid freshness of his imagination. Seeking in Paris the objects I then sought, I felt that the society of such a man would be to me a treasure beyond price; and this feeling I frankly confided to him. It was at length arranged that we should live together during my stay in the city; and as my worldly circumstances were somewhat less em-

2. According to phrenology, which was then taken seriously, the conformation of the skull indicated mental faculties and traits of character.

3. Quinn notes, in *Edgar Allan Poe*, " * * * a name which he borrowed from the heroine, Marie Dupin, of a story, 'Marie Laurent,' the first of a series of 'Unpublished Passages in the Life of Vidocq * * * ' " (*Burton's Gentleman's Magazine*, 1838). François Eugène Vidocq (1775–1857), a former criminal, became a Parisian police official and organized the detective bureau. His sensational *Memoires* (1828), probably spurious, are reflected in some minor details of Poe's stories.

barrassed than his own, I was permitted to be at the expense of renting, and furnishing in a style which suited the rather fantastic gloom of our common temper, a time-eaten and grotesque mansion, long deserted through superstitions into which we did not inquire, and tottering to its fall in a retired and desolate portion of the Faubourg St. Germain.[4]

Had the routine of our life at this place been known to the world, we should have been regarded as madmen—although, perhaps, as madmen of a harmless nature. Our seclusion was perfect. We admitted no visitors. Indeed the locality of our retirement had been carefully kept a secret from my own former associates; and it had been many years since Dupin had ceased to know or be known in Paris. We existed within ourselves alone.

It was a freak of fancy in my friend (for what else shall I call it?) to be enamored of the night for her own sake; and into this *bizarrerie*, as into all his others, I quietly fell; giving myself up to his wild whims with a perfect *abandon*. The sable divinity would not herself dwell with us always; but we could counterfeit her presence. At the first dawn of the morning we closed all the massy shutters of our old building; lighted a couple of tapers which, strongly perfumed, threw out only the ghastliest and feeblest of rays. By the aid of these we then busied our souls in dreams—reading, writing, or conversing, until warned by the clock of the advent of the true Darkness. Then we sallied forth into the streets, arm in arm, continuing the topics of the day, or roaming far and wide until a late hour, seeking, amid the wild lights and shadows of the populous city, that infinity of mental excitement which quiet observation can afford.

At such times I could not help remarking and admiring (although from his rich ideality I had been prepared to expect it) a peculiar analytic ability in Dupin. He seemed, too, to take an eager delight in its exercise—if not exactly in its display—and did not hesitate to confess the pleasure thus derived. He boasted to me, with a low chuckling laugh, that most men, in respect to himself, wore windows in their bosoms, and was wont to follow up such assertions by direct and very startling proofs of his intimate knowledge of my own. His manner at these moments was frigid and abstract; his eyes were vacant in expression; while his voice, usually a rich tenor, rose into a treble which would have sounded petulant but for the deliberateness and entire distinctness of the enunciation. Observing him in these moods, I often dwelt meditatively upon the old philosophy of the Bi-Part Soul, and amused myself with the fancy of a double Dupin—the creative and the resolvent.

Let it not be supposed, from what I have just said, that I am

4. Dilapidated mansions of the former nobility still stood in this run-down quarter of Paris.

detailing any mystery, or penning any romance. What I have described in the Frenchman was merely the result of an excited, or perhaps of a diseased, intelligence. But of the character of his remarks at the periods in question an example will best convey the idea.

We were strolling one night down a long dirty street, in the vicinity of the Palais Royal. Being both, apparently, occupied with thought, neither of us had spoken a syllable for fifteen minutes at least. All at once Dupin broke forth with these words:

"He is a very little fellow, that's true, and would do better for the *Théâtre des Variétés*."[5]

"There can be no doubt of that," I replied, unwittingly, and not at first observing (so much had I been absorbed in reflection) the extraordinary manner in which the speaker had chimed in with my meditations. In an instant afterward I recollected myself, and my astonishment was profound.

"Dupin," said I, gravely, "this is beyond my comprehension. I do not hesitate to say that I am amazed, and can scarcely credit my senses. How was it possible you should know I was thinking of ——?" Here I paused, to ascertain beyond a doubt whether he really knew of whom I thought.

"—— of Chantilly," said he, "why do you pause? You were remarking to yourself that his diminutive figure unfitted him for tragedy."

This was precisely what had formed the subject of my reflections. Chantilly was a *quondam* cobbler of the Rue St. Denis, who, becoming stage-mad, had attempted the *rôle* of Xerxes, in Crébillon's[6] tragedy so called, and been notoriously Pasquinaded[7] for his pains.

"Tell me, for Heaven's sake," I exclaimed, "the method—if method there is—by which you have been enabled to fathom my soul in this matter." In fact, I was even more startled than I would have been willing to express.

"It was the fruiterer," replied my friend, "who brought you to the conclusion that the mender of soles was not of sufficient height for Xerxes *et id genus omne*."[8]

"The fruiterer!—you astonish me—I know no fruiterer whomsoever."

"The man who ran up against you as we entered the street—it may have been fifteen minutes ago."

I now remembered that, in fact, a fruiterer, carrying upon his head a large basket of apples, had nearly thrown me down, by accident, as we passed from the Rue C—— into the thoroughfare where we stood;

5. French vaudeville.
6. Prosper Jolyot de Crébillon (1674–1762), author of *Xerxes* (1714), a tragedy of the Persian conqueror.
7. Ridiculed. "Anthony Pasquin" was

the pen name of John Williams (1761–1818), whose bitter and satiric dramatic criticism made his name traditional in Paris and London.
8. And all that sort.

but what this had to do with Chantilly I could not possibly understand.

There was not a particle of *charlatânerie* about Dupin. "I will explain," he said, "and that you may comprehend all clearly, we will first retrace the course of your meditations, from the moment in which I spoke to you until that of the *rencontre* with the fruiterer in question. The larger links of the chain run thus—Chantilly, Orion, Dr. Nichols, Epicurus, Stereotomy, the street stones, the fruiterer."

There are few persons who have not, at some period of their lives, amused themselves in retracing the steps by which particular conclusions of their own minds have been attained. The occupation is often full of interest; and he who attempts it for the first time is astonished by the apparently illimitable distance and incoherence between the starting-point and the goal. What, then, must have been my amazement, when I heard the Frenchman speak what he had just spoken, and when I could not help acknowledging that he had spoken the truth. He continued:

"We had been talking of horses, if I remember aright, just before leaving the Rue C——. This was the last subject we discussed. As we crossed into this street, a fruiterer, with a large basket upon his head, brushing quickly past us, thrust you upon a pile of paving stones collected at a spot where the causeway is undergoing repair. You stepped upon one of the loose fragments, slipped, slightly strained your ankle, appeared vexed or sulky, muttered a few words, turned to look at the pile, and then proceeded in silence. I was not particularly attentive to what you did; but observation has become with me, of late, a species of necessity.

"You kept your eyes upon the ground—glancing, with a petulant expression, at the holes and ruts in the pavement (so that I saw you were still thinking of the stones), until we reached the little alley called Lamartine, which has been paved, by way of experiment, with the overlapping and riveted blocks. Here your countenance brightened up, and, perceiving your lips move, I could not doubt that you murmured the word 'stereotomy,'[9] a term very affectedly applied to this species of pavement. I knew that you could not say to yourself 'stereotomy' without being brought to think of atomies, and thus of the theories of Epicurus; and since, when we discussed this subject not very long ago, I mentioned to you how singularly, yet with how little notice, the vague guesses of that noble Greek had met with confirmation in the late nebular cosmogony, I felt that you could not avoid casting your eyes upward to the great *nebula* in Orion, and I certainly expected that you would do so. You did look up; and I was now assured that I had correctly followed your steps. But in that bitter

9. Greek compound denoting the cutting of a solid object, here meaning "stone-cutting."

tirade upon Chantilly, which appeared in yesterday's '*Musée*,' the satirist, making so disgraceful allusions to the cobbler's change of name upon assuming the buskin, quoted a Latin line about which we have often conversed. I mean the line

Perdidit antiquum litera prima sonum.[1]

I had told you that this was in reference to Orion, formerly written Urion; and, from certain pungencies connected with this explanation, I was aware that you could not have forgotten it. It was clear, therefore, that you would not fail to combine the two ideas of Orion and Chantilly. That you did combine them I saw by the character of the smile which passed over your lips. You thought of the poor cobbler's immolation. So far, you had been stooping in your gait; but now I saw you draw yourself up to your full height. I was then sure that you reflected upon the diminutive figure of Chantilly. At this point I interrupted your meditations to remark that as, in fact, he *was* a very little fellow—that Chantilly—he would do better at the *Théâtre des Variétés.*"

Not long after this, we were looking over an evening edition of the *Gazette des Tribunaux*, when the following paragraphs arrested our attention.

"EXTRAORDINARY MURDERS.—This morning, about three o'clock, the inhabitants of the Quartier St. Roch were aroused from sleep by a succession of terrific shrieks, issuing, apparently, from the fourth story of a house in the Rue Morgue, known to be in the sole occupancy of one Madame L'Espanaye, and her daughter, Mademoiselle Camille L'Espanaye. After some delay, occasioned by a fruitless attempt to procure admission in the usual manner, the gateway was broken in with a crowbar, and eight or ten of the neighbors entered, accompanied by two *gendarmes*. By this time the cries had ceased; but, as the party rushed up the first flight of stairs, two or more rough voices, in angry contention, were distinguished, and seemed to proceed from the upper part of the house. As the second landing was reached, these sounds, also, had ceased, and every thing remained perfectly quiet. The party spread themselves, and hurried from room to room. Upon arriving at a large back chamber in the fourth story (the door of which, being found locked, with the key inside, was forced open), a spectacle presented itself which struck every one present not less with horror than with astonishment.

"The apartment was in the wildest disorder—the furniture broken and thrown about in all directions. There was only one bedstead; and from this the bed had been removed, and thrown into the middle of the floor. On a chair lay a razor, besmeared with blood. On the hearth were two or three long and thick tresses of gray human hair,

1. The first letter destroys the antique sound (impression).

also dabbled with blood, and seeming to have been pulled out by the roots. Upon the floor were found four Napoleons,[2] an ear-ring of topaz, three large silver spoons, three smaller of *métal d'Alger*,[3] and two bags, containing nearly four thousand francs in gold. The drawers of a *bureau*, which stood in one corner, were open, and had been, apparently, rifled, although many articles still remained in them. A small iron safe was discovered under the *bed* (not under the bedstead). It was open, with the key still in the door. It had no contents beyond a few old letters, and other papers of little consequence.

"Of Madame L'Espanaye no traces were here seen; but an unusual quantity of soot being observed in the fire-place, a search was made in the chimney, and (horrible to relate!) the corpse of the daughter, head downward, was dragged therefrom; it having been thus forced up the narrow aperture for a considerable distance. The body was quite warm. Upon examining it, many excoriations were perceived, no doubt occasioned by the violence with which it had been thrust up and disengaged. Upon the face were many severe scratches, and, upon the throat, dark bruises, and deep indentations of finger nails, as if the deceased had been throttled to death.

"After a thorough investigation of every portion of the house without farther discovery, the party made its way into a small paved yard in the rear of the building, where lay the corpse of the old lady, with her throat so entirely cut that, upon an attempt to raise her, the head fell off. The body, as well as the head, was fearfully mutilated—the former so much so as scarcely to retain any semblance of humanity.

"To this horrible mystery there is not as yet, we believe, the slightest clew."

The next day's paper had these additional particulars:

"*The Tragedy in the Rue Morgue.*—Many individuals have been examined in relation to this most extraordinary and frightful affair," [the word '*affaire*' has not yet, in France, that levity of import which it conveys with us] "but nothing whatever has transpired to throw light upon it. We give below all the material testimony elicited.

"*Pauline Dubourg*, laundress, deposes that she has known both the deceased for three years, having washed for them during that period. The old lady and her daughter seemed on good terms—very affectionate toward each other. They were excellent pay. Could not speak in regard to their mode or means of living. Believe that Madame L. told fortunes for a living. Was reputed to have money put by. Never met any person in the house when she called for the clothes or took them home. Was sure that they had no servant in employ. There appeared to be no furniture in any part of the building except in the

---

2. A former French coin, worth twenty francs.　　3. An alloy then used to imitate silver.

fourth story.

"*Pierre Moreau,* tobacconist, deposes that he has been in the habit of selling small quantities of tobacco and snuff to Madame L'Espanaye for nearly four years. Was born in the neighborhood, and has always resided there. The deceased and her daughter had occupied the house in which the corpses were found, for more than six years. It was formerly occupied by a jeweller, who under-let the upper rooms to various persons. The house was the property of Madame L. She became dissatisfied with the abuse of the premises by her tenant, and moved into them herself, refusing to let any portion. The old lady was childish. Witness had seen the daughter some five or six times during the six years. The two lived an exceedingly retired life— were reputed to have money. Had heard it said among the neighbors that Madame L. told fortunes—did not believe it. Had never seen any person enter the door except the old lady and her daughter, a porter once or twice, and a physician some eight or ten times.

"Many other persons, neighbors, gave evidence to the same effect. No one was spoken of as frequenting the house. It was not known whether there were any living connections of Madame L. and her daughter. The shutters of the front windows were seldom opened. Those in the rear were always closed, with the exception of the large back room, fourth story. The house was a good house—not very old.

"*Isidore Musèt, gendarme,*[4] deposes that he was called to the house about three o'clock in the morning, and found some twenty or thirty persons at the gateway, endeavoring to gain admittance. Forced it open, at length, with a bayonet—not with a crowbar. Had but little difficulty in getting it open, on account of its being a double or folding gate, and bolted neither at bottom nor top. The shrieks were continued until the gate was forced—and then suddenly ceased. They seemed to be screams of some person (or persons) in great agony— were loud and drawn out, not short and quick. Witness led the way up stairs. Upon reaching the first landing, heard two voices in loud and angry contention—the one a gruff voice, the other much shriller —a very strange voice. Could distinguish some words of the former, which was that of a Frenchman. Was positive that it was not a woman's voice. Could distinguish the words '*sacré*' and '*diable.*'[5] The shrill voice was that of a foreigner. Could not be sure whether it was the voice of a man or of a woman. Could not make out what was said, but believed the language to be Spanish. The state of the room and of the bodies was described by this witness as we described them yesterday.

"*Henri Duval,* a neighbor, and by trade a silver-smith, deposes that he was one of the party who first entered the house. Corroborates the

---

4. French policeman.
5. All-purpose semiprofanity in France; literally "sacred" and "devil." *Cf.* be-

low, *mon Dieu,* literally "my God!" but translated "Heavens!"

testimony of Musèt in general. As soon as they forced an entrance, they reclosed the door, to keep out the crowd, which collected very fast, notwithstanding the lateness of the hour. The shrill voice, this witness thinks, was that of an Italian. Was certain it was not French. Could not be sure that it was a man's voice. It might have been a woman's. Was not acquainted with the Italian language. Could not distinguish the words, but was convinced by the intonation that the speaker was an Italian. Knew Madame L. and her daughter. Had conversed with both frequently. Was sure that the shrill voice was not that of either of the deceased.

"—— *Odenheimer, restaurateur.*—This witness volunteered his testimony. Not speaking French, was examined through an interpreter. Is a native of Amsterdam. Was passing the house at the time of the shrieks. They lasted for several minutes—probably ten. They were long and loud—very awful and distressing. Was one of those who entered the building. Corroborated the previous evidence in every respect but one. Was sure that the shrill voice was that of a man—of a Frenchman. Could not distinguish the words uttered. They were loud and quick—unequal—spoken apparently in fear as well as in anger. The voice was harsh—not so much shrill as harsh. Could not call it a shrill voice. The gruff voice said repeatedly, '*sacré*,' '*diable*,' and once '*mon Dieu*.'

"*Jules Mignaud*, banker, of the firm of Mignaud et Fils, Rue Deloraine. Is the elder Mignaud. Madame L'Espanaye had some property. Had opened an account with his banking house in the spring of the year —— (eight years previously). Made frequent deposits in small sums. Had checked for nothing until the third day before her death, when she took out in person the sum of 4000 francs. This sum was paid in gold, and a clerk sent home with the money.

"*Adolphe Le Bon*, clerk to Mignaud et Fils, deposes that on the day in question, about noon, he accompaned Madame L'Espanaye to her residence with the 4000 francs, put up in two bags. Upon the door being opened, Mademoiselle L. appeared and took from his hands one of the bags, while the old lady relieved him of the other. He then bowed and departed. Did not see any person in the street at the time. It is a by-street—very lonely.

"*William Bird*, tailor, deposes that he was one of the party who entered the house. Is an Englishman. Has lived in Paris two years. Was one of the first to ascend the stairs. Heard the voices in contention. The gruff voice was that of a Frenchman. Could make out several words, but cannot now remember all. Heard distinctly '*sacré* and '*mon Dieu*.' There was a sound at the moment as if of several persons struggling—a scraping and scuffling sound. The shrill voice was very loud—louder than the gruff one. Is sure that it was not the voice of an Englishman. Appeared to be that of a German. Might have been a woman's voice. Does not understand German.

"Four of the above-named witnesses, being recalled, deposed that the door of the chamber in which was found the body of Mademoiselle L. was locked on the inside when the party reached it. Every thing was perfectly silent—no groans or noises of any kind. Upon forcing the door no person was seen. The windows, both of the back and front room, were down and firmly fastened from within. A door between the two rooms was closed but not locked. The door leading from the front room into the passage was locked, with the key on the inside. A small room in the front of the house, on the fourth story, at the head of the passage, was open, the door being ajar. This room was crowded with old beds, boxes, and so forth. These were carefully removed and searched. There was not an inch of any portion of the house which was not carefully searched. Sweeps were sent up and down the chimneys. The house was a four-story one, with garrets (*mansardes*). A trap-door on the roof was nailed down very securely —did not appear to have been opened for years. The time elapsing between the hearing of the voices in contention and the breaking open of the room door was variously stated by the witnesses. Some made it as short as three minutes—some as long as five. The door was opened with difficulty.

"*Alfonzo Garcio*, undertaker, deposes that he resides in the Rue Morgue. Is a native of Spain. Was one of the party who entered the house. Did not proceed up stairs. Is nervous, and was apprehensive of the consequences of agitation. Heard the voices in contention. The gruff voice was that of a Frenchman. Could not distinguish what was said. The shrill voice was that of an Englishman—is sure of this. Does not understand the English language, but judges by the intonation.

"*Alberto Montani*, confectioner, deposes that he was among the first to ascend the stairs. Heard the voices in question. The gruff voice was that of a Frenchman. Distinguished several words. The speaker appeared to be expostulating. Could not make out the words of the shrill voice. Spoke quick and unevenly. Thinks it the voice of a Russian. Corroborates the general testimony. Is an Italian. Never conversed with a native of Russia.

"Several witnesses, recalled, here testified that the chimneys of all the rooms on the fourth story were too narrow to admit the passage of a human being. By 'sweeps' were meant cylindrical sweeping-brushes, such as are employed by those who clean chimneys. These brushes were passed up and down every flue in the house. There is no back passage by which any one could have descended while the party proceeded up stairs. The body of Mademoiselle L'Espanaye was so firmly wedged in the chimney that it could not be got down until four or five of the party united their strength.

"*Paul Dumas*, physician, deposes that he was called to view the bodies about daybreak. They were both then lying on the sacking of the bedstead in the chamber where Mademoiselle L. was found. The corpse of the young lady was much bruised and excoriated. The fact that it had been thrust up the chimney would sufficiently account for these appearances. The throat was greatly chafed. There were several deep scratches just below the chin, together with a series of livid spots which were evidently the impression of fingers. The face was fearfully discolored, and the eyeballs protruded. The tongue had been partially bitten through. A large bruise was discovered upon the pit of the stomach, produced, apparently, by the pressure of a knee. In the opinion of M. Dumas, Mademoiselle L'Espanaye had been throttled to death by some person or persons unknown. The corpse of the mother was horribly mutilated. All the bones of the right leg and arm were more or less shattered. The left *tibia* much splintered, as well as all the ribs of the left side. Whole body dreadfully bruised and discolored. It was not possible to say how the injuries had been inflicted. A heavy club of wood, or a broad bar of iron—a chair—any large, heavy, and obtuse weapon would have produced such results, if wielded by the hands of a very powerful man. No woman could have inflicted the blows with any weapon. The head of the deceased, when seen by witness, was entirely separated from the body, and was also greatly shattered. The throat had evidently been cut with some very sharp instrument—probably with a razor.

"*Alexandre Etienne*, surgeon, was called with M. Dumas to view the bodies. Corroborated the testimony, and the opinions of M. Dumas.

"Nothing further of importance was elicited, although several other persons were examined. A murder so mysterious, and so perplexing in all its particulars, was never before committed in Paris—if indeed a murder has been committed at all. The police are entirely at fault[6]—an unusual occurrence in affairs of this nature. There is not, however, the shadow of a clew apparent."

The evening edition of the paper stated that the greatest excitement still continued in the Quartier St. Roch—that the premises in question had been carefully re-searched, and fresh examinations of witnesses instituted, but all to no purpose. A postscript, however, mentioned that Adolphe Le Bon had been arrested and imprisoned—although nothing appeared to criminate him beyond the facts already detailed.

Dupin seemed singularly interested in the progress of this affair—at least so I judged from his manner, for he made no comments. It was only after the announcement that Le Bon had been imprisoned, that he asked me my opinion respecting the murders.

6. A French idiom rendered literally; it means "at a loss."

I could merely agree with all Paris in considering them an insoluble mystery. I saw no means by which it would be possible to trace the murderer.

"We must not judge of the means," said Dupin, "by this shell of an examination. The Parisian police, so much extolled for *acumen*, are cunning, but no more. There is no method in their proceedings, beyond the method of the moment. They make a vast parade of measures; but, not unfrequently, these are so ill-adapted to the objects proposed, as to put us in mind of Monsieur Jourdain's calling for his *robe-de-chambre—pour mieux entendre la musique.*[7] The results attained by them are not unfrequently surprising, but, for the most part, are brought about by simple diligence and activity. When these qualities are unavailing, their schemes fail. Vidocq, for example, was a good guesser, and a persevering man. But, without educated thought, he erred continually by the very intensity of his investigations. He impaired his vision by holding the object too close. He might see, perhaps, one or two points with unusual clearness, but in so doing he, necessarily, lost sight of the matter as a whole. Thus there is such a thing as being too profound. Truth is not always in a well. In fact, as regards the more important knowledge, I do believe that she is invariably superficial. The depth lies in the valleys where we seek her, and not upon the mountain-tops where she is found. The modes and sources of this kind of error are well typified in the contemplation of the heavenly bodies. To look at a star by glances— to view it in a side-long way, by turning toward it the exterior portions of the *retina* (more susceptible of feeble impressions of light than the interior), is to behold the star distinctly—is to have the best appreciation of its lustre—a lustre which grows dim just in proportion as we turn our vision *fully* upon it. A greater number of rays actually fall upon the eye in the latter case, but, in the former, there is the more refined capacity for comprehension. By undue profundity we perplex and enfeeble thought; and it is possible to make even Venus herself vanish from the firmament by a scrutiny too sustained, too concentrated, or too direct.

"As for these murders, let us enter into some examinations for ourselves, before we make up an opinion respecting them. An inquiry will afford us amusement," [I thought this an odd term, so applied, but said nothing] "and besides, Le Bon once rendered me a service for which I am not ungrateful. We will go and see the premises with our own eyes. I know G——, the Prefect of Police, and shall have no difficulty in obtaining the necessary permission."

The permission was obtained, and we proceeded at once to the Rue Morgue. This is one of those miserable thoroughfares which inter-

7. In Molière's famous comedy, *Le Bourgeois Gentilhomme* (1670), M. Jourdain attests his cultural frustrations by "calling for his dressing gown in order to hear the music better."

vene between the Rue Richelieu and the Rue St. Roch. It was late in the afternoon when we reached it, as this quarter is at a great distance from that in which we resided. The house was readily found; for there were still many persons gazing up at the closed shutters, with an objectless curiosity, from the opposite side of the way. It was an ordinary Parisian house, with a gateway, on one side of which was a glazed watch-box, with a sliding panel in the window, indicating a *loge de concierge.*[8] Before going in we walked up the street, turned down an alley, and then, again turning, passed in the rear of the building—Dupin, meanwhile, examining the whole neighborhood, as well as the house, with a minuteness of attention for which I could see no possible object.

Retracing our steps we came again to the front of the dwelling, rang, and, having shown our credentials, were admitted by the agents in charge. We went up stairs—into the chamber where the body of Mademoiselle L'Espanaye had been found, and where both the deceased still lay. The disorders of the room had, as usual, been suffered to exist. I saw nothing beyond what had been stated in the *Gazette des Tribunaux.* Dupin scrutinized every thing—not excepting the bodies of the victims. We then went into the other rooms, and into the yard; a *gendarme* accompanying us throughout. The examination occupied us until dark, when we took our departure. On our way home my companion stepped in for a moment at the office of one of the daily papers.

I have said that the whims of my friend were manifold, and that *Je les ménageais:*[9]—for this phrase there is no English equivalent. It was his humor, now, to decline all conversation on the subject of the murder, until about noon the next day. He then asked me, suddenly, if I had observed any thing *peculiar* at the scene of the atrocity.

There was something in his manner of emphasizing the word *"peculiar,"* which caused me to shudder, without knowing why.

"No, nothing *peculiar,*" I said; "nothing more, at least, than we both saw stated in the paper."

"The *Gazette,*" he replied, "has not entered, I fear, into the unusual horror of the thing. But dismiss the idle opinions of this print. It appears to me that this mystery is considered insoluble, for the very reason which should cause it to be regarded as easy of solution— I mean for the *outré*[1] character of its features. The police are confounded by the seeming absence of motive—not for the murder itself—but for the atrocity of the murder. They are puzzled, too, by the seeming impossibility of reconciling the voices heard in contention, with the facts that no one was discovered upstairs but the assassinated Mademoiselle L'Espanaye, and that there were no

8. Janitor's lodge or quarters.
9. Poe suggests the idiomatic subtlety; here read, approximately, "I humored them with tactful respect."
1. Excessive or outrageous.

means of egress without the notice of the party ascending. The wild disorder of the room; the corpse thrust, with the head downward, up the chimney; the frightful mutilation of the body of the old lady; these considerations, with those just mentioned, and others which I need not mention, have sufficed to paralyze the powers, by putting completely at fault the boasted *acumen*, of the government agents. They have fallen into the gross but common error of confounding the unusual with the abstruse. But it is by these deviations from the plane of the ordinary, that reason feels its way, if at all, in its search for the true. In investigations such as we are now pursuing, it should not be so much asked 'what has occurred,' as 'what has occurred that has never occurred before.' In fact, the facility with which I shall arrive, or have arrived, at the solution of this mystery, is in the direct ratio of its apparent insolubility in the eyes of the police."

I stared at the speaker in mute astonishment.

"I am now awaiting," continued he, looking toward the door of our apartment—"I am now awaiting a person who, although perhaps not the perpetrator of these butcheries, must have been in some measure implicated in their perpetration. Of the worst portion of the crimes committed, it is probable that he is innocent. I hope that I am right in this supposition; for upon it I build my expectation of reading the entire riddle. I look for the man here—in this room—every moment. It is true that he may not arrive; but the probability is that he will. Should he come, it will be necessary to detain him. Here are pistols; and we both know how to use them when occasion demands their use."

I took the pistols, scarcely knowing what I did, or believing what I heard, while Dupin went on, very much as if in a soliloquy. I have already spoken of his abstract manner at such times. His discourse was addressed to myself; but his voice, although by no means loud, had that intonation which is commonly employed in speaking to some one at a great distance. His eyes, vacant in expression, regarded only the wall.

"That the voices heard in contention," he said, "by the party upon the stairs, were not the voices of the women themselves, was fully proved by the evidence. This relieves us of all doubt upon the question whether the old lady could have first destroyed the daughter, and afterward have committed suicide. I speak of this point chiefly for the sake of method; for the strength of Madame L'Espanaye would have been utterly unequal to the task of thrusting her daughter's corpse up the chimney as it was found; and the nature of the wounds upon her own person entirely precludes the idea of self-destruction. Murder, then, has been committed by some third party; and the voices of this third party were those heard in contention. Let me now advert—not to the whole testimony respecting these voices—but to what was *peculiar* in that testimony. Did you observe any thing peculiar about it?"

I remarked that, while all the witnesses agreed in supposing the gruff voice to be that of a Frenchman, there was much disagreement in regard to the shrill, or, as one individual termed it, the harsh voice.

"That was the evidence itself," said Dupin, "but it was not the peculiarity of the evidence. You have observed nothing distinctive. Yet there *was* something to be observed. The witnesses, as you re-mark, agreed about the gruff voice; they were here unanimous. But in regard to the shrill voice, the peculiarity is—not that they dis-agreed—but that, while an Italian, an Englishman, a Spaniard, a Hollander, and a Frenchman attempted to describe it, each one spoke of it as that *of a foreigner*. Each is sure that it was not the voice of one of his own countrymen. Each likens it—not to the voice of an individual of any nation with whose language he is conversant —but the converse. The Frenchman supposes it the voice of a Spaniard, and 'might have distinguished some words *had he been acquainted with the Spanish*.' The Dutchman maintains it to have been that of a Frenchman; but we find it stated that '*not understand-ing French this witness was examined through an interpreter*.' The Englishman thinks it the voice of a German, and '*does not under-stand German*.' The Spaniard 'is sure' that it was that of an English-man, but 'judges by the intonation' altogether, '*as he has no knowl-edge of the English*.' The Italian believes it the voice of a Russian, but '*has never conversed with a native of Russia*.' A second French-man differs, moreover, with the first, and is positive that the voice was that of an Italian; but, *not being cognizant of that tongue*, is, like the Spaniard, 'convinced by the intonation.' Now, how strangely unusual must that voice have really been, about which such testi-mony as this *could* have been elicited!—in whose *tones*, even, deni-zens of the five great divisions of Europe could recognize nothing familiar! You will say that it might have been the voice of an Asiatic —of an African. Neither Asiatics nor Africans abound in Paris; but, without denying the inference, I will now merely call your attention to three points. The voice is termed by one witness 'harsh rather than shrill.' It is represented by two others to have been 'quick and un-equal.' No words—no sounds resembling words—were by any witness mentioned as distinguishable.

"I know not," continued Dupin, "what impression I may have made, so far, upon your own understanding; but I do not hesitate to say that legitimate deductions even from this portion of the testi-mony—the portion respecting the gruff and shrill voices—are in themselves sufficient to engender a suspicion which should give direc-tion to all farther progress in the investigation of the mystery. I said 'legitimate deductions'; but my meaning is not thus fully expressed.

I designed to imply that the deductions are the *sole* proper ones, and that the suspicion arises *inevitably* from them as the single result. What the suspicion is, however, I will not say just yet. I merely wish you to bear in mind that, with myself, it was sufficiently forcible to give a definite form—a certain tendency—to my inquiries in the chamber.

"Let us now transport ourselves, in fancy, to this chamber. What shall we first seek here? The means of egress employed by the murderers. It is not too much to say that neither of us believe in præternatural events. Madame and Mademoiselle L'Espanaye were not destroyed by spirits. The doers of the deed were material and escaped materially. Then how? Fortunately there is but one mode of reasoning upon the point, and that mode *must* lead us to a definite decision. Let us examine, each by each, the possible means of egress. It is clear that the assassins were in the room where Mademoiselle L'Espanaye was found, or at least in the room adjoining, when the party ascended the stairs. It is, then, only from these two apartments that we have to seek issues. The police have laid bare the floors, the ceiling, and the masonry of the walls, in every direction. No *secret* issues could have escaped their vigilance. But, not trusting to *their* eyes, I examined with my own. There were, then, *no* secret issues. Both doors leading from the rooms into the passage were securely locked, with the keys inside. Let us turn to the chimneys. These, although of ordinary width for some eight or ten feet above the hearths, will not admit, throughout their extent, the body of a large cat. The impossibility of egress, by means already stated, being thus absolute, we are reduced to the windows. Through those of the front room no one could have escaped without notice from the crowd in the street. The murderers *must* have passed, then, through those of the back room. Now, brought to this conclusion in so unequivocal a manner as we are, it is not our part, as reasoners, to reject it on account of apparent impossibilities. It is only left for us to prove that these apparent 'impossibilities' are, in reality, not such.

"There are two windows in the chamber. One of them is unobstructed by furniture, and is wholly visible. The lower portion of the other is hidden from view by the head of the unwieldy bedstead which is thrust close up against it. The former was found securely fastened from within. It resisted the utmost force of those who endeavored to raise it. A large gimlet-hole had been pierced in its frame to the left, and a very stout nail was found fitted therein, nearly to the head. Upon examining the other window, a similar nail was seen similarly fitted in it; and a vigorous attempt to raise this sash failed also. The police were now entirely satisfied that egress had not been in these directions. And, *therefore*, it was thought a matter of supererogation to withdraw the nails and open the windows.

"My own examination was somewhat more particular, and was so for the reason I have just given—because here it was, I knew, that all apparent impossibilities *must* be proved to be not such in reality.

"I proceeded to think thus—*a posteriori*.[2] The murderers *did* escape from one of these windows. This being so, they could not have re-fastened the sashes from the inside, as they were found fastened; —the consideration which put a stop, through its obviousness, to the scrutiny of the police in this quarter. Yet the sashes *were* fastened. They *must*, then, have the power of fastening themselves. There was no escape from this conclusion. I stepping to the unobstructed casement, withdrew the nail with some difficulty, and attempted to raise the sash. It resisted all my efforts, as I had anticipated. A concealed spring must, I now knew, exist; and this corroboration of my idea convinced me that my premises, at least, were correct, however mysterious still appeared the circumstances attending the nails. A careful search soon brought to light the hidden spring. I pressed it, and, satisfied with the discovery, forbore to upraise the sash.

"I now replaced the nail and regarded it attentively. A person passing out through this window might have reclosed it, and the spring would have caught—but the nail could not have been replaced. The conclusion was plain, and again narrowed in the field of my investigations. The assassins *must* have escaped through the other window. Supposing, then, the springs upon each sash to be the same, as was probable, there *must* be found a difference between the nails, or at least between the modes of their fixture. Getting upon the sacking of the bedstead, I looked over the head-board minutely at the second casement. Passing my hand down behind the board, I readily discovered and pressed the spring, which was, as I had supposed, identical in character with its neighbor. I now looked at the nail. It was as stout as the other, and apparently fitted in the same manner— driven in nearly up to the head.

"You will say that I was puzzled; but, if you think so, you must have misunderstood the nature of the inductions. To use a sporting phrase, I had not been once 'at fault.' The scent had never for an instant been lost. There was no flaw in any link of the chain. I had traced the secret to its ultimate result,—and that result was *the nail*. It had, I say, in every respect, the appearance of its fellow in the other window; but this fact was an absolute nullity (conclusive as it might seem to be) when compared with the consideration that here, at this point, terminated the clew. 'There *must* be something wrong,' I said, 'about the nail.' I touched it; and the head, with about a quarter of an inch of the shank, came off in my fingers. The rest of the shank was in the gimlet-hole, where it had been broken off.

2. In logic, inductive reasoning, based on observation.

The fracture was an old one (for its edges were incrusted with rust), and had apparently been accomplished by the blow of a hammer, which had partially imbedded, in the top of the bottom sash, the head portion of the nail. I now carefully replaced this head portion in the indentation whence I had taken it, and the resemblance to a perfect nail was complete—the fissure was invisible. Pressing the spring, I gently raised the sash for a few inches; the head went up with it, remaining firm in its bed. I closed the window, and the semblance of the whole nail was again perfect.

"This riddle, so far, was now unriddled. The assassin had escaped through the window which looked upon the bed. Dropping of its own accord upon his exit (or perhaps purposely closed), it had become fastened by the spring; and it was the retention of this spring which had been mistaken by the police for that of the nail,—farther inquiry being thus considered unnecessary.

"The next question is that of the mode of descent. Upon this point I had been satisfied in my walk with you around the building. About five feet and a half from the casement in question there runs a lightning-rod. From this rod it would have been impossible for any one to reach the window itself, to say nothing of entering it. I observed, however, that the shutters of the fourth story were of the peculiar kind called by Parisian carpenters *ferrades*—a kind rarely employed at the present day, but frequently seen upon very old mansions at Lyons and Bordeaux. They are in the form of an ordinary door (a single, not a folding door), except that the lower half is latticed or worked in open trellis—thus affording an excellent hold for the hands. In the present instance these shutters are fully three feet and a half broad. When we saw them from the rear of the house, they were both about half open—that is to say they stood off at right angles from the wall. It is probable that the police, as well as myself, examined the back of the tenement; but, if so, in looking at these *ferrades* in the line of their breadth (as they must have done), they did not perceive this great breadth itself, or, at all events, failed to take it into due consideration. In fact, having once satisfied themselves that no egress could have been made in this quarter, they would naturally bestow here a very cursory examination. It was clear to me, however, that the shutter belonging to the window at the head of the bed, would, if swung fully back to the wall, reach to within two feet of the lightning-rod. It was also evident that, by exertion of a very unusual degree of activity and courage, an entrance into the window, from the rod, might have been thus effected. By reaching to the distance of two feet and a half (we now suppose the shutter open to its whole extent) a robber might have taken a firm grasp upon the trellis-work. Letting go, then, his hold upon the rod, placing his feet securely against the wall, and springing boldly from it, he might have swung the shutter so as to close it, and, if we imagine the window open at the time, might even have swung himself into the room.

"I wish you to bear especially in mind that I have spoken of a *very* unusual degree of activity as requisite to success in so hazardous and so difficult a feat. It is my design to show you first, that the thing might possibly have been accomplished:—but, secondly and *chiefly*, I wish to impress upon your understanding the *very extraordinary* —the almost præternatural character of that agility which could have accomplished it.

"You will say, no doubt, using the language of the law, that 'to make out my case,' I should rather undervalue than insist upon a full estimation of the activity required in this matter. This may be the practice in law, but it is not the usage of reason. My ultimate object is only the truth. My immediate purpose is to lead you to place in juxtaposition, that *very unusual* activity of which I have just spoken, with that *very peculiar* shrill (or harsh) and *unequal* voice, about whose nationality no two persons could be found to agree, and in whose utterance no syllabification could be detected."

At these words a vague and half-formed conception of the meaning of Dupin flitted over my mind. I seemed to be upon the verge of comprehension, without power to comprehend—as men, at times, find themselves upon the brink of remembrance, without being able, in the end, to remember. My friend went on with his discourse.

"You will see," he said, "that I have shifted the question from the mode of egress to that of ingress. It was my design to convey the idea that both were effected in the same manner, at the same point. Let us now revert to the interior of the room. Let us survey the appearances here. The drawers of the bureau, it is said, had been rifled, although many articles of apparel still remained within them. The conclusion here is absurd. It is a mere guess—a very silly one— and no more. How are we to know that the articles found in the drawers were not all these drawers had originally contained? Madame L'Espanaye and her daughter lived an exceedingly retired life—saw no company—seldom went out—had little use for numerous changes of habiliment. Those found were at least of as good quality as any likely to be possessed by these ladies. If a thief had taken any, why did he not take the best—why did he not take all? In a word, why did he abandon four thousand francs in gold to encumber himself with a bundle of linen? The gold *was* abandoned. Nearly the whole sum mentioned by Monsieur Mignaud, the banker, was discovered, in bags, upon the floor. I wish you, therefore, to discard from your thoughts the blundering idea of *motive*, engendered in the brains of the police by that portion of the evidence which speaks of money delivered at the door of the house. Coincidences ten times as remarkable as this (the delivery of the money, and murder committed within three days upon the party receiving it), happen to all of us every hour of our lives, without attracting even momentary notice. Coincidences, in general, are great stumbling-blocks in the way of that class of thinkers who have been educated to know nothing of the theory of probabilities—that theory to which the most glorious objects of human research are indebted for the most glorious of illustration. In the present instance, had the gold been gone, the fact of its delivery three days before would have formed something more than a coincidence. It would have been corroborative of this idea of motive. But, under the real circumstances of the case, if we are to suppose gold the motive of this outrage, we must also imagine the perpetrator so vacillating an idiot as to have abandoned his gold and his motive together.

"Keeping now steadily in mind the points to which I have drawn your attention—that peculiar voice, that unusual agility, and that startling absence of motive in a murder so singularly atrocious as this—let us glance at the butchery itself. Here is a woman strangled to death by manual strength, and thrust up a chimney head downward. Ordinary assassins employ no such mode of murder as this. Least of all, do they thus dispose of the murdered. In the manner of thrusting the corpse up the chimney, you will admit that there was something *excessively outré*—something altogether irreconcilable with our common notions of human action, even when we suppose the actors the most depraved of men. Think, too, how great must have been that strength which could have thrust the body *up* such an aperture so forcibly that the united vigor of several persons was found barely sufficient to drag it *down!*

"Turn, now, to other indications of the employment of a vigor most marvellous. On the hearth were thick tresses—very thick tresses —of gray human hair. These had been torn out by the roots. You are aware of the great force necessary in tearing thus from the head even twenty or thirty hairs together. You saw the locks in question as well as myself. Their roots (a hideous sight!) were clotted with fragments of the flesh of the scalp—sure token of the prodigious power which had been exerted in uprooting perhaps half a million of hairs at a time. The throat of the old lady was not merely cut, but the head absolutely severed from the body: the instrument was a mere razor. I wish you also to look at the *brutal* ferocity of these deeds. Of the bruises upon the body of Madame L'Espanaye I do not speak. Monsieur Dumas, and his worthy coadjutor Monsieur Etienne, have pronounced that they were inflicted by some obtuse instrument; and so far these gentlemen are very correct. The obtuse instrument was clearly the stone pavement in the yard, upon which the victim had fallen from the window which looked in upon the bed. This idea, however simple it may now seem, escaped the police for the same reason that the breadth of the shutters escaped them —because, by the affair of the nails, their perceptions had been hermetically sealed against the possibility of the windows having ever been opened at all.

"If now, in addition to all these things, you have properly reflected upon the odd disorder of the chamber, we have gone so far as to combine the ideas of an agility astounding, a strength superhuman, a ferocity brutal, a butchery without motive, a *grotesquerie* in horror absolutely alien from humanity, and a voice foreign in tone to the ears of men of many nations, and devoid of all distinct or intelligible syllabification. What result, then, has ensued? What impression have I made upon your fancy?"

I felt a creeping of the flesh as Dupin asked me the question. "A madman," I said, "has done this deed—some raving maniac, escaped from a neighboring *Maison de Santé*."[3]

"In some respects," he replied, "your idea is not irrelevant. But the voices of madmen, even in their wildest paroxysms, are never found to tally with that peculiar voice heard upon the stairs. Madmen are of some nation, and their language, however incoherent in its words, has always the coherence of syllabification. Besides, the hair of a madman is not such as I now hold in my hand. I disentangled this little tuft from the rigidly clutched fingers of Madame L'Espanaye. Tell me what you can make of it."

"Dupin!" I said, completely unnerved; "this hair is most unusual —this is no *human* hair."

"I have not asserted that it is," said he; "but, before we decide this point, I wish you to glance at the little sketch I have here traced upon this paper. It is a *facsimile* drawing of what has been described in one portion of the testimony as 'dark bruises and deep indentations of finger nails' upon the throat of Mademoiselle L'Espanaye, and in another (by Messrs. Dumas and Etienne) as a 'series of livid spots, evidently the impression of fingers.'

"You will perceive," continued my friend, spreading out the paper upon the table before us, "that this drawing gives the idea of a firm and fixed hold. There is no *slipping* apparent. Each finger has retained—possibly until the death of the victim—the fearful grasp by which it originally imbedded itself. Attempt, now, to place all your fingers, at the same time, in the respective impressions as you see them."

I made the attempt in vain.

"We are possibly not giving this matter a fair trial," he said. "The paper is spread out upon a plane surface; but the human throat is cylindrical. Here is a billet of wood, the circumference of which

3. Private hospital or nursing home.

is about that of the throat. Wrap the drawing around it, and try the experiment again."

I did so; but the difficulty was even more obvious than before. "This," I said, "is the mark of no human hand."

"Read now," replied Dupin, "this passage from Cuvier."[4]

It was a minute anatomical and generally descriptive account of the large fulvous Ourang-Outang of the East Indian Islands. The gigantic stature, the prodigious strength and activity, the wild ferocity, and the imitative propensities of these mammalia are sufficiently well known to all. I understood the full horrors of the murder at once.

"The description of the digits," said I, as I made an end of the reading, "is in exact accordance with this drawing. I see that no animal but an Ourang-Outang, of the species here mentioned, could have impressed the indentations as you have traced them. This tuft of tawny hair, too, is identical in character with that of the beast of Cuvier. But I cannot possibly comprehend the particulars of this frightful mystery. Besides, there were *two* voices heard in contention, and one of them was unquestionably the voice of a Frenchman."

"True; and you will remember an expression attributed almost unanimously, by the evidence, to this voice,—the expression, '*mon Dieu!*' This, under the circumstances, has been justly characterized by one of the witnesses (Montani, the confectioner) as an expression of remonstrance or expostulation. Upon these two words, therefore, I have mainly built my hopes of a full solution of the riddle. A Frenchman was cognizant of the murder. It is possible—indeed it is far more than probable—that he was innocent of all participation in the bloody transactions which took place. The Ourang-Outang may have escaped from him. He may have traced it to the chamber; but, under the agitating circumstances which ensued, he could never have recaptured it. It is still at large. I will not pursue these guesses —for I have no right to call them more—since the shades of reflection upon which they are based are scarcely of sufficient depth to be appreciable by my own intellect, and since I could not pretend to make them intelligible to the understanding of another. We will call them guesses, then, and speak of them as such. If the Frenchman in question is indeed, as I suppose, innocent of this atrocity, this advertisement, which I left last night, upon our return home, at the office of *Le Monde* (a paper devoted to the shipping interest, and much sought by sailors), will bring him to our residence."

He handed me a paper, and I read thus:

"CAUGHT—*In the Bois de Boulogne, early in the morning of the —— inst.* (the morning of the murder), *a very large, tawny Ourang-*

4. Baron Georges Léopold Chrétien Frédéric Dagobert Cuvier (1769– 1832), pioneer of comparative anatomy, originator of the present system of animal classification, and voluminous writer on biology.

Outang of the Bornese species. The owner (who is ascertained to be a sailor, belonging to a Maltese vessel) may have the animal again, upon identifying it satisfactorily, and paying a few charges arising from its capture and keeping. Call at No. —— Rue ——, Faubourg St. Germain—au troisième."[5]

"How was it possible," I asked, "that you should know the man to be a sailor, and belonging to a Maltese vessel?"

"I do *not* know it," said Dupin. "I am not *sure* of it. Here, however, is a small piece of ribbon, which from its form, and from its greasy appearance, has evidently been used in tying the hair in one of those long *queues* of which sailors are so fond. Moreover, this knot is one which few besides sailors can tie, and is peculiar to the Maltese. I picked the ribbon up at the foot of the lightning-rod. It could not have belonged to either of the deceased. Now if, after all, I am wrong in my induction from this ribbon, that the Frenchman was a sailor belonging to a Maltese vessel, still I can have done no harm in saying what I did in the advertisement. If I am in error, he will merely suppose that I have been misled by some circumstance into which he will not take the trouble to inquire. But if I am right, a great point is gained. Cognizant although innocent of the murder, the Frenchman will naturally hesitate about replying to the advertisement—about demanding the Ourang-Outang. He will reason thus:—'I am innocent; I am poor; my Ourang-Outang is of great value—to one in my circumstances a fortune of itself—why should I lose it through idle apprehensions of danger? Here it is, within my grasp. It was found in the Bois de Boulogne—at a vast distance from the scene of that butchery. How can it ever be suspected that a brute beast should have done the deed? The police are at fault—they have failed to procure the slightest clew. Should they even trace the animal, it would be impossible to prove me cognizant of the murder, or to implicate me in guilt on account of that cognizance. Above all, *I am known*. The advertiser designates me as the possessor of the beast. I am not sure to what limit his knowledge may extend. Should I avoid claiming a property of so great value, which it is known that I possess, I will render the animal at least, liable to suspicion. It is not my policy to attract attention either to myself or to the beast. I will answer the advertisement, get the Ourang-Outang, and keep it close until this matter has blown over.'"

At this moment we heard a step upon the stairs.

"Be ready," said Dupin, "with your pistols, but neither use them nor show them until at a signal from myself."

The front door of the house had been left open, and the visitor

5. On the fourth floor (the French start numbering with our second floor).

had entered, without ringing, and advanced several steps upon the staircase. Now, however, he seemed to hesitate. Presently we heard him descending. Dupin was moving quickly to the door, when we again heard him coming up. He did not turn back a second time, but stepped up with decision, and rapped at the door of our chamber.

"Come in," said Dupin, in a cheerful and hearty tone.

A man entered. He was a sailor, evidently,—a tall, stout, and muscular-looking person, with a certain dare-devil expression of countenance, not altogether unprepossessing. His face, greatly sunburnt, was more than half hidden by whisker and *mustachio*. He had with him a huge oaken cudgel, but appeared to be otherwise unarmed. He bowed awkwardly, and bade us "good evening," in French accents, which, although somewhat Neufchatelish,[6] were still sufficiently indicative of a Parisian origin.

"Sit down, my friend," said Dupin. "I suppose you have called about the Ourang-Outang. Upon my word, I almost envy you the possession of him; a remarkably fine, and no doubt a very valuable animal. How old do you suppose him to be?"

The sailor drew a long breath, with the air of a man relieved of some intolerable burden, and then replied, in an assured tone:

"I have no way of telling—but he can't be more than four or five years old. Have you got him here?"

"Oh, no; we had no conveniences for keeping him here. He is at a livery stable in the Rue Dubourg, just by. You can get him in the morning. Of course you are prepared to identify the property?"

"To be sure I am, sir."

"I shall be sorry to part with him," said Dupin.

"I don't mean that you should be at all this trouble for nothing, sir," said the man. "Couldn't expect it. Am very willing to pay a reward for the finding of the animal—that is to say, any thing in reason."

"Well," replied my friend, "that is all very fair, to be sure. Let me think!—what should I have? Oh! I will tell you. My reward shall be this. You shall give me all the information in your power about these murders in the Rue Morgue."

Dupin said the last words in a very low tone, and very quietly. Just as quietly, too, he walked toward the door, locked it, and put the key in his pocket. He then drew a pistol from his bosom and placed it, without the least flurry, upon the table.

The sailor's face flushed up as if he were struggling with suffocation. He started to his feet and grasped his cudgel; but the next moment he fell back into his seat, trembling violently, and with the countenance of death itself. He spoke not a word. I pitied him from the bottom of my heart.

6. Neufchâtel is a city in northern France.

"My friend," said Dupin, in a kind tone, "you are alarming your-self unnecessarily—you are indeed. We mean you no harm what-ever. I pledge you the honor of a gentleman, and of a Frenchman, that we intend you no injury. I perfectly well know that you are innocent of the atrocities in the Rue Morgue. It will not do, how-ever, to deny that you are in some measure implicated in them. From what I have already said, you must know that I have had means of information about this matter—means of which you could never have dreamed. Now the thing stands thus. You have done nothing which you could have avoided—nothing, certainly, which renders you culpable. You were not even guilty of robbery, when you might have robbed with impunity. You have nothing to conceal. You have no reason for concealment. On the other hand, you are bound by every principle of honor to confess all you know. An innocent man is now imprisoned, charged with that crime of which you can point out the perpetrator."

The sailor had recovered his presence of mind, in a great measure, while Dupin uttered these words; but his original boldness of bearing was all gone.

"So help me God!" said he, after a brief pause, "I *will* tell you all I know about this affair;—but I do not expect you to believe one half I say—I would be a fool indeed if I did. Still, I *am* innocent, and I will make a clean breast if I die for it."

What he stated was, in substance, this. He had lately made a voy-age to the Indian Archipelago. A party, of which he formed one, landed at Borneo, and passed into the interior on an excursion of pleasure. Himself and a companion had captured the Ourang-Outang. This companion dying, the animal fell into his own exclusive posses-sion. After great trouble, occasioned by the intractable ferocity of his captive during the home voyage, he at length succeeded in lodg-ing it safely at his own residence in Paris, where, not to attract to-ward himself the unpleasant curiosity of his neighbors, he kept it carefully secluded, until such time as it should recover from a wound in the foot, received from a splinter on board ship. His ultimate design was to sell it.

Returning home from some sailors' frolic on the night, or rather in the morning, of the murder, he found the beast occupying his own bedroom, into which it had broken from a closet adjoining, where it had been, as was thought, securely confined. Razor in hand, and fully lathered, it was sitting before a looking-glass, attempting the operation of shaving, in which it had no doubt previously watched its master through the keyhole of the closet. Terrified at the sight of so dangerous a weapon in the possession of an animal so ferocious, and so well able to use it, the man, for some moments, was at a loss what to do. He had been accustomed, however, to quiet the creature, even in its fiercest moods, by the use of a whip, and to this he now resorted. Upon sight of it, the Ourang-Outang sprang at once through the door of the chamber, down the stairs, and thence, through a window, unfortunately open, into the street.

The Frenchman followed in despair; the ape, razor still in hand, occasionally stopping to look back and gesticulate at his pursuer, until the latter had nearly come up with it. It then again made off. In this manner the chase continued for a long time. The streets were profoundly quiet, as it was nearly three o'clock in the morning. In passing down an alley in the rear of the Rue Morgue, the fugitive's attention was arrested by a light gleaming from the open window of Madame L'Espanaye's chamber, in the fourth story of her house. Rushing to the building, it perceived the lightning-rod, clambered up with inconceivable agility, grasped the shutter, which was thrown fully back against the wall, and, by its means, swung itself directly upon the headboard of the bed. The whole feat did not occupy a minute. The shutter was kicked open again by the Ourang-Outang as it entered the room.

The sailor, in the meantime, was both rejoiced and perplexed. He had strong hopes of now recapturing the brute, as it could scarcely escape from the trap into which it had ventured, except by the rod, where it might be intercepted as it came down. On the other hand, there was much cause for anxiety as to what it might do in the house. This latter reflection urged the man still to follow the fugitive. A lightning-rod is ascended without difficulty, especially by a sailor; but, when he had arrived as high as the window, which lay far to his left, his career was stopped; the most that he could accomplish was to reach over so as to obtain a glimpse of the interior of the room. At this glimpse he nearly fell from his hold through excess of horror. Now it was that those hideous shrieks arose upon the night, which had startled from slumber the inmates of the Rue Morgue. Madame L'Espanaye and her daughter, habited in their night clothes, had apparently been occupied in arranging some papers in the iron chest already mentioned, which had been wheeled into the middle of the room. It was open, and its contents lay beside it on the floor. The victims must have been sitting with their backs toward the window; and, from the time elapsing between the ingress of the beast and the screams, it seems probable that it was not immediately perceived. The flapping-to of the shutter would naturally have been attributed to the wind.

As the sailor looked in, the gigantic animal had seized Madame L'Espanaye by the hair (which was loose, as she had been combing it), and was flourishing the razor about her face, in imitation of the motions of a barber. The daughter lay prostrate and motionless; she had swooned. The screams and struggles of the old lady (during which the hair was torn from her head) had the effect of changing the probably pacific purposes of the Ourang-Outang into those of wrath. With one determined sweep of its muscular arm it nearly severed her head from her body. The sight of blood inflamed its anger into phrensy. Gnashing its teeth, and flashing fire from its eyes, it flew upon the body of the girl, and imbedded its fearful talons in her throat, retaining its grasp until she expired. Its wandering and wild glances fell at this moment upon the head of the bed, over which the face of its master, rigid with horror, was just discernible. The fury of the beast, who no doubt bore still in mind the dreaded whip, was instantly converted into fear. Conscious of having deserved punishment, it seemed desirous of concealing its bloody deeds, and skipped about the chamber in an agony of nervous agitation; throwing down and breaking the furniture as it moved, and dragging the bed from the bedstead. In conclusion, it seized first the corpse of the daughter, and thrust it up the chimney, as it was found; then that of the old lady, which it immediately hurled through the window headlong.

As the ape approached the casement with its mutilated burden, the sailor shrank aghast to the rod, and, rather gliding than clambering down it, hurried at once home—dreading the consequences of the butchery, and gladly abandoning, in his terror, all solicitude about the fate of the Ourang-Outang. The words heard by the party upon the staircase were the Frenchman's exclamations of horror and affright, commingled with the fiendish jabberings of the brute.

I have scarcely any thing to add. The Ourang-Outang must have escaped from the chamber, by the rod, just before the breaking of the door. It must have closed the window as it passed through it. It was subsequently caught by the owner himself, who obtained for it a very large sum at the *Jardin des Plantes*.[7] Le Bon was instantly released, upon our narration of the circumstances (with some comments from Dupin) at the *bureau* of the Prefect of Police. This functionary, however well disposed to my friend, could not altogether conceal his chagrin at the turn which affairs had taken, and was fain to indulge in a sarcasm or two about the propriety of every person minding his own business.

"Let him talk," said Dupin, who had not thought it necessary to reply. "Let him discourse; it will ease his conscience. I am satisfied with having defeated him in his own castle. Nevertheless, that he failed in the solution of this mystery, is by no means that matter for wonder which he supposes it; for, in truth, our friend the Prefect is somewhat too cunning to be profound. In his wisdom is no *stamen*.[8] It is all head and no body, like the pictures of the Goddess Laverna[9]

7. A botanical garden, as the name suggests, but also the zoological garden of Paris.

8. Staying power: the plural, "stamina," is now used as the singular.

9. A Roman deity of the underworld;

—or, at best, all head and shoulders, like a codfish. But he is a good creature after all. I like him especially for one master stroke of cant, by which he has attained his reputation for ingenuity. I mean the way he has *'de nier ce qui est, et d'expliquer ce qui n'est pas.'*"[1]

1841, 1845

A Descent into the Maelström[2]

> The ways of God in Nature, as in Providence, are not as *our* ways; nor are the models that we frame any way commensurate to the vastness, profundity, and unsearchableness of His works, *which have a depth in them greater than the well of Democritus.*
>
> —JOSEPH GLANVILL [3]

We had now reached the summit of the loftiest crag. For some minutes the old man seemed too much exhausted to speak.

"Not long ago," said he at length, "and I could have guided you on this route as well as the youngest of my sons; but, about three years past, there happened to me an event such as never happened before to mortal man—or at least such as no man ever survived to tell of—and the six hours of deadly terror which I then endured have broken me up body and soul. You suppose me a *very* old man —but I am not. It took less than a single day to change these hairs from a jetty black to white, to weaken my limbs, and to unstring my nerves, so that I tremble at the least exertion, and am frightened at a shadow. Do you know I can scarcely look over this little cliff without getting giddy?"

The "little cliff," upon whose edge he had so carelessly thrown himself down to rest that the weightier portion of his body hung over it, while he was only kept from falling by the tenure of his elbow on its extreme and slippery edge—this "little cliff" arose, a

Poe probably refers to her function as protectress of thieves.

1. "Of denying [ignoring] whatever is, and of explaining what does not exist." Poe's note refers the passage to *La Nouvelle Héloïse* (1761), a romance by Jean Jacques Rousseau (1712–1778).

2. An example of Poe's direct use of his knowledge of science in the plot and action of an exciting story. Scientific and pseudoscientific lore had been employed since the beginning of modern fiction with Defoe. Use of it was intensified by the Gothic novelists of the eighteenth century, whose emphasis on the occult influenced Poe in such tales as "Ligeia." But in the present story, as in his early "MS Found in a Bottle," Poe intensifies the effect by making the scientific facts intrinsic to the action. In this sense he is the forerunner of the science fiction of today. Actually, his interest in science appears in all varieties of his fiction—accessory to the solution of a mystery in such stories as "The Gold Bug" or "The Murders in the Rue Morgue," implemented with psychological analysis in stories such as "The Pit and the Pendulum." The rational methods of science underlie his own fictional techniques as well as the methods of detection employed in his detective stories. *Eureka*, the last work of his life, was an effort to reconcile the laws of physics with metaphysical reality. "A Descent into the Maelström" first appeared in *Graham's Magazine* for May, 1841, and was collected in the *Tales* (1845).

3. For Joseph Glanvill (1636–1680) see epigraph to "Ligeia." The motto is quoted, with slight changes, from Glanvill's *Essays on Several Important Subjects in Philosophy and Religion* (London, 1676). Democritus is credited with the idea that Truth is to be found at the bottom of a deep well.

sheer unobstructed precipice of black shining rock, some fifteen or sixteen hundred feet from the world of crags beneath us. Nothing would have tempted me to within half-a-dozen yards of its brink. In truth, so deeply was I excited by the perilous position of my companion, that I fell at full length upon the ground, clung to the shrubs around me, and dared not even glance upward at the sky—while I struggled in vain to divest myself of the idea that the very foundations of the mountain were in danger from the fury of the winds. It was long before I could reason myself into sufficient courage to sit up and look out into the distance.

"You must get over these fancies," said the guide, "for I have brought you here that you might have the best possible view of the scene of that event I mentioned—and to tell you the whole story with the spot just under your eye.

"We are now," he continued in that particularising manner which distinguished him—"we are now close upon the Norwegian coast—in the sixty-eighth degree of latitude—in the great province of Nordland—and in the dreary district of Lofoden.[4] The mountain upon whose top we sit is Helseggen, the Cloudy. Now raise yourself up a little higher—hold on to the grass if you feel giddy—so—and look out, beyond the belt of vapour beneath us, into the sea."

I looked dizzily, and beheld a wide expanse of ocean, whose waters wore so inky a hue as to bring at once to my mind the Nubian geographer's account of the *Mare Tenebrarum*.[5] A panorama more deplorably desolate no human imagination can conceive. To the right and left, as far as the eye could reach, there lay outstretched, like ramparts of the world, lines of horridly black and beetling cliff, whose character of gloom was but the more forcibly illustrated by the surf which reared high up against it its white and ghastly crest, howling and shrieking for ever. Just opposite the promontory upon whose apex we were placed, and at a distance of some five or six miles out at sea, there was visible a small, bleak-looking island; or, more properly, its position was discernible through the wilderness of surge in which it was enveloped. About two miles nearer the land arose another of smaller size, hideously craggy and barren, and encompassed at various intervals by a cluster of dark rocks.

The appearance of the ocean, in the space between the more distant island and the shore, had something very unusual about it.

4. The Lofoten Islands are, as Poe suggests, a cluster off the coast of northwest Norway, at latitude 68 degrees N. The maelström also is actual. In the narrow strait between Moskenesöy and Vaeröy (Poe's "Moskoe" and "Vurrgh") the rapid fall of an unusually large tide causes currents and whirlpools which became proverbial for destruction in the days of small vessels. Poe of course exaggerates the whirlpool for the effects of his story; but the report of conical vortices in the ocean was still regarded as likely, and was supported by the folklore of the sea.
5. Sea of darkness; the unexplored outer Atlantic as sometimes designated on ancient maps. The "Nubian geographer" was probably Claudius Ptolemaeus (Ptolemy) of Alexandria, in the second century A.D., founder of the Ptolemaic system of geography and astronomy.

Although at the time so strong a gale was blowing landward that a brig in the remote offing lay to under a double-reefed trysail, and constantly plunged her whole hull out of sight, still there was here nothing like a regular swell, but only a short, quick, angry cross dashing of water in every direction—as well in the teeth of the wind as otherwise. Of foam there was little except in the immediate vicinity of the rocks.

"The island in the distance," resumed the old man, "is called by the Norwegians Vurrgh. The one midway is Moskoe. That a mile to the northward is Ambaaren. Yonder are Iflesen, Hoeyholm, Kieldholm, Suarven, and Buckholm. Farther off—between Moskoe and Vurrgh—are Otterholm, Flimen, Sandflesen, and Skarholm. These are the true names of the places—but why it has been thought necessary to name them at all, is more than either you or I can understand. Do you hear anything? Do you see any change in the water?"

We had now been about ten minutes upon the top of Helseggen, to which we had ascended from the interior of Lofoden, so that we had caught no glimpse of the sea until it had burst upon us from the summit. As the old man spoke, I became aware of a loud and gradually increasing sound, like the moaning of a vast herd of buffaloes upon an American prairie; and at the same moment I perceived that what seamen term the *chopping* character of the ocean beneath us, was rapidly changing into a current which set to the eastward. Even while I gazed this current acquired a monstrous velocity. Each moment added to its speed—to its headlong impetuosity. In five minutes the whole sea as far as Vurrgh was lashed into ungovernable fury; but it was between Moskoe and the coast that the main uproar held its sway. Here the vast bed of the waters, seamed and scarred into a thousand conflicting channels, burst suddenly into frenzied convulsion—heaving, boiling, hissing,—gyrating in gigantic and innumerable vortices, and all whirling and plunging on to the eastward with a rapidity which water never elsewhere assumes except in precipitous descents.

In a few minutes more, there came over the scene another radical alteration. The general surface grew somewhat more smooth, and the whirlpools one by one disappeared, while prodigious streaks of foam became apparent where none had been seen before. These streaks at length, spreading out to a great distance, and entering into combination, took unto themselves the gyratory motion of the subsided vortices, and seemed to form the germ of another more vast. Suddenly—very suddenly—this assumed a distinct and definite existence in a circle of more than a mile in diameter. The edge of the whirl was represented by a broad belt of gleaming spray; but no particle of this slipped into the mouth of the terrific funnel, whose interior, as far as the eye could fathom it, was a smooth, shining, and jet-black wall of water, inclined to the horizon at an angle of some forty-five degrees, speeding dizzily round and round with a swaying and sweltering motion, and sending forth to the wind an appalling voice, half-shriek, half-roar, such as not even the mighty cataract of Niagara ever lifts up in its agony to Heaven.

The mountain trembled to its very base, and the rock rocked. I threw myself upon my face, and clung to the scant herbage in an excess of nervous agitation.

"This," said I at length, to the old man—"this *can* be nothing else than the great whirlpool of the Maelström."

"So it is sometimes termed," said he. "We Norwegians call it the Moskoe-ström, from the island of Moskoe in the midway."

The ordinary accounts of this vortex had by no means prepared me for what I saw. That of Jonas Ramus,[6] which is perhaps the most circumstantial of any, cannot impart the faintest conception either of the magnificence, or of the horror of the scene—or of the wild bewildering sense of *the novel* which confounds the beholder. I am not sure from what point of view the writer in question surveyed it, nor at what time; but it could neither have been from the summit of Helseggen, nor during a storm. There are some passages of his description, nevertheless, which may be quoted for their details, although their effect is exceedingly feeble in conveying an impression of the spectacle.

"Between Lofoden and Moskoe,' he says, "the depth of the water is between thirty-five and forty fathoms; but on the other side, toward Ver (Vurrgh) this depth decreases so as not to afford a convenient passage for a vessel, without the risk of splitting on the rocks, which happens even in the calmest weather. When it is flood, the stream runs up the country between Lofoden and Moskoe with a boisterous rapidity, but the roar of its impetuous ebb to the sea is scarce equalled by the loudest and most dreadful cataracts—the noise being heard several leagues off, and the vortices or pits are of such an extent and depth, that if a ship comes within its attraction it is inevitably absorbed and carried down to the bottom and there beat to pieces against the rocks, and when the water relaxes the fragments thereof are thrown up again. But these intervals of tranquillity are only at the turn of the ebb and flood, and in calm weather, and last but a quarter of an hour, its violence gradually returning. When the stream is most boisterous, and its fury heightened by a storm, it is dangerous to come within a Norway mile[7] of it. Boats, yachts, and ships have been carried away by not guarding against it before they were within its reach. It likewise happens frequently that whales come too near the stream, and are overpowered by its violence, and then

6. Identified as the writer on this subject whom he quoted below, with variations, from the current *Encyclopædia* *Britannica* (Quinn, Edgar Allan Poe, pp. 312–313).
7. About four and a half English miles.

it is impossible to describe their howlings and bellowings in their fruitless struggles to disengage themselves. A bear once, attempting to swim from Lofoden to Moskoe, was caught by the stream and borne down, while he roared terribly, so as to be heard on shore. Large stocks of firs and pine trees, after being absorbed by the current, rise again broken and torn to such a degree as if bristles grew upon them. This plainly shows the bottom to consist of craggy rocks, among which they are whirled to and fro. This stream is regulated by the flux and reflux of the sea—it being constantly high and low water every six hours. In the year 1645, early in the morning of Sexagesima Sunday,[8] it raged with such noise and impetuosity that the very stones of the houses on the coast fell to the ground."

In regard to the depth of the water, I could not see how this could have been ascertained at all in the immediate vicinity of the vortex. The "forty fathoms" must have reference only to portions of the channel close upon the shore either of Moskoe or Lofoden. The depth in the centre of the Moskoe-ström must be immeasurably greater; and no better proof of this fact is necessary than can be obtained from even the sidelong glance into the abyss of the whirl which may be had from the highest crag of Helseggen. Looking down from this pinnacle upon the howling Phlegethon[9] below, I could not help smiling at the simplicity with which the honest Jonas Ramus records, as a matter difficult of belief, the anecdotes of the whales and the bears; for it appeared to me, in fact, a self-evident thing that the largest ship of the line in existence coming within the influence of that deadly attraction could resist it as little as a feather the hurricane, and must disappear bodily and at once.

The attempts to account for the phenomenon—some of which I remember seemed to me sufficiently plausible in perusal—now wore a very different and unsatisfactory aspect. The idea generally received is that this, as well as three smaller vortices among the Ferroe Islands, "have no other cause than the collision of waves rising and falling at flux and reflux against a ridge of rocks and shelves, which confines the water so that it precipitates itself like a cataract; and thus the higher the flood rises the deeper must the fall be, and the natural result of all is a whirlpool or vortex, the prodigious suction of which is sufficiently known by lesser experiments."—These are the words of the Encyclopædia Britannica. Kircher[1] and others imagine that in the centre of the channel of the Maelström is an abyss penetrating the globe, and issuing in some very remote part—the Gulf of Bothnia being somewhat decidedly named in one instance. This opinion, idle in itself, was the one to which, as I gazed, my imagination most readily assented; and, mentioning it to the guide, I was rather sur-

8. The second Sunday before Lent.
9. In Greek myth, a river in Hades, flowing with fire instead of water.

1. Athanasius Kircher (1601–1680), German Jesuit scholar and early archae-ologist.

prised to hear him say that, although it was the view almost universally entertained of the subject by the Norwegians, it nevertheless was not his own. As to the former notion he confessed his inability to comprehend it; and here I agreed with him—for, however conclusive on paper, it becomes altogether unintelligible, and even absurd, amid the thunder of the abyss.

"You have had a good look at the whirl now," said the old man, "and if you will creep round this crag so as to get in its lee, and deaden the roar of the water, I will tell you a story that will convince you I ought to know something of the Moskoe-ström."

I placed myself as desired, and he proceeded.

"Myself and my two brothers once owned a schooner-rigged smack of about seventy tons burthen, with which we were in the habit of fishing among the islands beyond Moskoe, nearly to Vurrgh. In all violent eddies at sea there is good fishing at proper opportunities if one has only the courage to attempt it, but among the whole of the Lofoden coastmen, we three were the only ones who made a regular business of going out to the islands, as I tell you. The usual grounds are a great way lower down to the southward. There fish can be got at all hours, without much risk, and therefore these places are preferred. The choice spots over here among the rocks, however, not only yield the finest variety, but in far greater abundance, so that we often got in a single day what the more timid of the craft could not scrape together in a week. In fact, we made it a matter of desperate speculation—the risk of life standing instead of labour, and courage answering for capital.

"We kept the smack in a cove about five miles higher up the coast than this; and it was our practice, in fine weather, to take advantage of the fifteen minutes' slack to push across the main channel of the Moskoe-ström, far above the pool, and then drop down upon anchorage somewhere near Otterholm, or Sandflesen, where the eddies are not so violent as elsewhere. Here we used to remain until nearly time for slack-water again, when we weighed and made for home. We never set out upon this expedition without a steady side wind for going and coming—one that we felt sure would not fail us before our return—and we seldom made a miscalculation upon this point. Twice during six years we were forced to stay all night at anchor on account of a dead calm, which is a rare thing indeed just about here; and once we had to remain on the grounds nearly a week, starving to death, owing to a gale which blew up shortly after our arrival, and made the channel too boisterous to be thought of. Upon this occasion we should have been driven out to sea in spite of everything (for the whirlpools threw us round and round so violently that at length we fouled our anchor and dragged it) if it had not been that we drifted into one of the innumerable cross currents—here to-day and gone to-morrow—which drove us under the lee of Flimen, where, by good luck, we brought up.

"I could not tell you the twentieth part of the difficulties we encountered 'on the grounds'—it is a bad spot to be in, even in good weather—but we made shift always to run the gauntlet of the Moskoe-ström itself without accident; although at times my heart has been in my mouth when we happened to be a minute or so behind or before the slack. The wind sometimes was not as strong as we thought it at starting, and then we made rather less way than we could wish, while the current rendered the smack unmanageable. My eldest brother had a son eighteen years old, and I had two stout boys of my own. These would have been of great assistance at such times in using the sweeps, as well as afterward in fishing, but somehow, although we ran the risk ourselves we had not the heart to let the young ones get into the danger—for, after all is said and done, it *was* a horrible danger, and that is the truth.

"It is now within a few days of three years since what I am going to tell you occurred. It was on the tenth day of July 18—, a day which the people of this part of the world will never forget—for it was one in which blew the most terrible hurricane that ever came out of the heavens; and yet all the morning, and indeed until late in the afternoon, there was a gentle and steady breeze from the southwest, while the sun shone brightly, so that the oldest seaman among us could not have foreseen what was to follow.

"The three of us—my two brothers and myself—had crossed over to the islands about 2 o'clock P.M., and had soon nearly loaded the smack with fine fish, which, we all remarked, were more plentiful that day than we had ever known them. It was just seven *by my watch* when we weighed and started for home, so as to make the worst of the Ström at slack water, which we knew would be at eight.

"We set out with a fresh wind on our starboard quarter, and for some time spanked along at a great rate, never dreaming of danger, for indeed we saw not the slightest reason to apprehend it. All at once we were taken aback by a breeze from over Helseggen. This was most unusual—something that had never happened to us before—and I began to feel a little uneasy without exactly knowing why. We put the boat on the wind, but could make no headway at all for the eddies, and I was just upon the point of proposing to return to the anchorage, when, looking astern, we saw the whole horizon covered with a singular copper-coloured cloud that rose with the most amazing velocity.

"In the meantime the breeze that had headed us off fell away, and we were dead becalmed, drifting about in every direction. This state of things, however, did not last long enough to give us time to think about it. In less than a minute the storm was upon us—in less than two the sky was entirely overcast—and what with this and the driving spray it became suddenly so dark that we could not see each other in the smack.

"Such a hurricane as then blew it is folly to attempt describing. The oldest seaman in Norway never experienced anything like it. We had let our sails go by the run before it cleverly took us; but, at the first puff, both our masts went by the board as if they had been sawed off—the mainmast taking with it my youngest brother, who had lashed himself to it for safety.

"Our boat was the lightest feather of a thing that ever sat upon water. It had a complete flush deck, with only a small hatch near the bow, and this hatch it had always been our custom to batten down when about to cross the Ström by way of precaution against the chopping seas. But for this circumstance we should have foundered at once—for we lay entirely buried for some moments. How my elder brother escaped destruction I cannot say, for I never had an opportunity of ascertaining. For my part, as soon as I had let the foresail run, I threw myself flat on deck, with my feet against the narrow gunwale of the bow, and with my hands grasping a ring-bolt near the foot of the fore-mast. It was mere instinct that prompted me to do this—which was undoubtedly the very best thing I could have done—for I was too much flurried to think.

"For some moments we were completely deluged, as I say, and all this time I held my breath, and clung to the bolt. When I could stand it no longer I raised myself upon my knees, still keeping hold with my hands, and thus got my head clear. Presently our little boat gave herself a shake, just as a dog does in coming out of the water, and thus rid herself in some measure of the seas. I was now trying to get the better of the stupor that had come over me, and to collect my senses so as to see what was to be done, when I felt somebody grasp my arm. It was my elder brother, and my heart leaped for joy, for I had made sure that he was overboard—but the next moment all this joy was turned into horror—for he put his mouth close to my ear, and screamed out the word '*Moskoe-ström!*'

"No one ever will know what my feelings were at that moment. I shook from head to foot, as if I had had the most violent fit of the ague. I knew what he meant by that one word well enough—I knew what he wished to make me understand. With the wind that now drove us on we were bound for the whirl of the Ström, and nothing could save us!

"You perceive that in crossing the Ström *channel*, we always went a long way up above the whirl, even in the calmest weather, and then had to wait and watch carefully for the slack—but now we were driving right upon the pool itself, and in such a hurricane as this! 'To be sure,' I thought, 'we shall get there just about the slack—

there is some little hope in that'—but in the next moment I cursed myself for being so great a fool as to dream of hope at all. I knew very well that we were doomed had we been ten times a ninety-gun ship.

"By this time the first fury of the tempest had spent itself, or perhaps we did not feel it so much as we scudded before it, but at all events the seas, which at first had been kept down by the wind and lay flat and frothing, now got up into absolute mountains. A singular change, too, had come over the heavens. Around in every direction it was still as black as pitch, but nearly overhead there burst out, all at once, a circular rift of clear sky—as clear as I ever saw, and of a deep bright blue—and through it there blazed forth the full moon with a lustre that I never before knew her to wear. She lit up everything about us with the greatest distinctness—but, O God, what a scene it was to light up!

"I now made one or two attempts to speak to my brother—but, in some manner which I could not understand, the din had so increased that I could not make him hear a single word, although I screamed at the top of my voice in his ear. Presently he shook his head, looking as pale as death, and held up one of his fingers as if to say '*listen!*'

"At first I could not make out what he meant—but soon a hideous thought flashed upon me. I dragged my watch from its fob. It was not going. I glanced at its face by the moonlight, and then burst into tears as I flung it far away into the ocean. *It had run down at seven o'clock! We were behind the time of the slack, and the whirl of the Ström was in full fury!*

"When a boat is well built, properly trimmed, and not deep laden, the waves in a strong gale, when she is going large, seem always to slip from beneath her—which appears very strange to a landsman—and this is what is called *riding*, in sea-phrase.

"Well, so far we had ridden the swells very cleverly, but presently a gigantic sea happened to take us right under the counter, and bore us with it as it rose—up—up—as if into the sky. I would not have believed that any wave could rise so high. And then down we came with a sweep, a slide, and a plunge, that made me feel sick and dizzy, as if I was falling from some lofty mountain-top in a dream. But while we were up I had thrown a quick glance around—and that one glance was all sufficient. I saw our exact position in an instant. The Moskoeström whirlpool was about a quarter of a mile dead ahead—but no more like the every-day Moskoe-ström, than the whirl as you now see it is like a mill-race. If I had not known where we were, and what we had to expect, I should not have recognised the place at all. As it was, I involuntarily closed my eyes in horror. The lids clenched themselves together as if in a spasm.

"It could not have been more than two minutes afterward until we suddenly felt the waves subside, and were enveloped in foam. The boat made a sharp half turn to larboard, and then shot off in its new direction like a thunderbolt. At the same moment the roaring noise of the water was completely drowned in a kind of shrill shriek—such a sound as you might imagine given out by the waste-pipes of many thousand steam-vessels letting off their steam all together. We were now in the belt of surf that always surrounds the whirl; and I thought of course that another moment would plunge us into the abyss—down which we could only see indistinctly on account of the amazing velocity with which we were borne along. The boat did not seem to sink into the water at all, but to skim like an air-bubble upon the surface of the surge. Her starboard side was next the whirl, and on the larboard arose the world of ocean we had left. It stood like a huge writhing wall between us and the horizon.

"It may appear strange, but now, when we were in the very jaws of the gulf, I felt more composed than when we were only approaching it. Having made up my mind to hope no more, I got rid of a good deal of that terror which unmanned me at first. I suppose it was despair that strung my nerves.

"It may look like boasting—but what I tell you is truth—I began to reflect how magnificent a thing it was to die in such a manner, and how foolish it was in me to think of so paltry a consideration as my own individual life in view of so wonderful a manifestation of God's power. I do believe that I blushed with shame when this idea crossed my mind. After a little while I became possessed with the keenest curiosity about the whirl itself. I positively felt a *wish* to explore its depths, even at the sacrifice I was going to make; and my principal grief was that I should never be able to tell my old companions on shore about the mysteries I should see. These, no doubt, were singular fancies to occupy a man's mind in such extremity, and I have often thought since that the revolutions of the boat around the pool might have rendered me a little light-headed.

"There was another circumstance which tended to restore my self-possession, and this was the cessation of the wind, which could not reach us in our present situation—for, as you saw yourself, the belt of such is considerably lower than the general bed of the ocean, and this latter now towered above us, a high, black, mountainous ridge. If you have never been at sea in a heavy gale you can form no idea of the confusion of mind occasioned by the wind and spray together. They blind, deafen, and strangle you, and take away all power of action or reflection. But we were now, in a great measure, rid of these annoyances—just as death-condemned felons in prison are allowed petty indulgences, forbidden them while their doom is yet uncertain.

"How often we made the circuit of the belt it is impossible to say.

We careered round and round for perhaps an hour, flying rather than floating, getting gradually more and more into the middle of the surge, and then nearer and nearer to its horrible inner edge. All this time I had never let go of the ring-bolt. My brother was at the stern, holding on to a small empty water-cask which had been securely lashed under the coop of the counter, and was the only thing on deck that had not been swept overboard when the gale first took us. As we approached the brink of the pit he let go his hold upon this, and made for the ring, from which, in the agony of his terror, he endeavoured to force my hands, as it was not large enough to afford us both a secure grasp. I never felt deeper grief than when I saw him attempt this act—although I knew he was a madman when he did it—a raving maniac through sheer fright. I did not care, however, to contest the point with him. I knew it could make no difference whether either of us held on at all, so I let him have the bolt, and went astern to the cask. This there was no great difficulty in doing, for the smack flew round steadily enough, and upon an even keel, only swaying to and fro with the immense sweeps and swelters of the whirl. Scarcely had I secured myself in my new position when we gave a wild lurch to starboard, and rushed headlong into the abyss. I muttered a hurried prayer to God, and thought all was over.

"As I felt the sickening sweep of the descent I had instinctively tightened my hold upon the barrel, and closed my eyes. For some seconds I dared not open them, while I expected instant destruction, and wondered that I was not already in my death-struggles with the water. But moment after moment elapsed. I still lived. The sense of falling had ceased; and the motion of the vessel seemed much as it had been before while in the belt of foam, with the exception that she now lay more along. I took courage, and looked once again upon the scene.

"Never shall I forget the sensations of awe, horror, and admiration with which I gazed about me. The boat appeared to be hanging, as if by magic, midway down, upon the interior surface of a funnel vast in circumference, prodigious in depth, and whose perfectly smooth sides might have been mistaken for ebony but for the bewildering rapidity with which they spun around, and for the gleaming and ghastly radiance they shot forth, as the rays of the full moon, from that circular rift amid the clouds which I have already described, streamed in a flood of golden glory along the black walls, and far away down into the inmost recesses of the abyss.

"At first I was too much confused to observe anything accurately. The general burst of terrific grandeur was all that I beheld. When I recovered myself a little, however, my gaze fell instinctively downward. In this direction I was able to obtain an unobstructed view from the manner in which the smack hung on the inclined surface of the pool. She was quite upon an even keel—that is to say, her deck lay in a plane parallel with that of the water—but this latter sloped at an angle of more than forty-five degrees, so that we seemed to be lying upon our beam-ends. I could not help observing, nevertheless, that I had scarcely more difficulty in maintaining my hold and footing in this situation than if we had been upon a dead level, and this, I suppose, was owing to the speed at which we revolved.

"The rays of the moon seemed to search the very bottom of the profound gulf; but still I could make out nothing distinctly, on account of a thick mist in which everything there was enveloped, and over which there hung a magnificent rainbow, like that narrow and tottering bridge which Mussulmen say is the only pathway between Time and Eternity. This mist or spray was no doubt occasioned by the clashing of the great walls of the funnel as they all met together at the bottom, but the yell that went up to the Heavens from out of that mist I dare not attempt to describe.

"Our first slide into the abyss itself, from the belt of foam above, had carried us a great distance down the slope, but our farther descent was by no means proportionate. Round and round we swept—not with any uniform movement—but in dizzying swings and jerks, that sent us some times only a few hundred yards—sometimes nearly the complete circuit of the whirl. Our progress downward at each revolution was slow but very perceptible.

"Looking about me upon the wide waste of liquid ebony on which we were thus borne, I perceived that our boat was not the only object in the embrace of the whirl. Both above and below us were visible fragments of vessels, large masses of building timber and trunks of trees, with many smaller articles, such as pieces of house furniture, broken boxes, barrels, and staves. I have already described the unnatural curiosity which had taken the place of my original terrors. It appeared to grow upon me as I drew nearer and nearer to my dreadful doom. I now began to watch, with a strange interest, the numerous things that floated in our company. I *must* have been delirious, for I even sought *amusement* in speculating upon the relative velocities of their several descents toward the foam below. 'This fir-tree,' I found myself at one time saying, 'will certainly be the next thing that takes the awful plunge and disappears,'—and then I was disappointed to find that the wreck of a Dutch merchant ship overtook it and went down before. At length, after making several guesses of this nature, and being deceived in all, this fact—the fact of my invariable miscalculation—set me upon a train of reflection that made my limbs again tremble, and my heart beat heavily once more.

"It was not a new terror that thus affected me, but the dawn of a more exciting *hope*. This hope arose partly from memory, and partly from present observation. I called to mind the great variety of buoyant matter that strewed the coast of Lofoden, having been absorbed and then thrown forth by the Moskoe-ström. By far the greater number of the articles were shattered in the most extraordinary way—so chafed and roughened as to have the appearance of being stuck full of splinters—but then I distinctly recollected that there were *some* of them which were not disfigured at all. Now I could not account for this difference except by supposing that the roughened fragments were the only ones which had been *completely absorbed*— that the others had entered the whirl at so late a period of the tide, or, for some reason, had descended so slowly after entering, that they did not reach the bottom before the turn of the flood came, or of the ebb, as the case might be. I conceived it possible, in either instance, that they might thus be whirled up again to the level of the ocean, without undergoing the fate of those which had been drawn in more early, or absorbed more rapidly. I made also three important observations. The first was that, as a general rule, the larger the bodies were the more rapid their descent; the second, that, between two masses of equal extent, the one spherical and the other of *any other shape*, the superiority in speed of descent was with the sphere; the third, that, between two masses of equal size, the one cylindrical and the other of any other shape, the cylinder was absorbed the more slowly. Since my escape I have had several conversations on this subject with an old schoolmaster of the district, and it was from him that I learned the use of the words 'cylinder' and 'sphere.' He explained to me—although I have forgotten the explanation—how what I observed was in fact the natural consequence of the forms of the floating fragments, and showed me how it happened that a cylinder swimming in a vortex offered more resistance to its suction, and was drawn in with greater difficulty than an equally bulky body of any form whatever.[2]

"There was one startling circumstance which went a great way in enforcing these observations and rendering me anxious to turn them to account, and this was that at every revolution we passed something like a barrel, or else the yard or the mast of a vessel, while many of these things which had been on our level when I first opened my eyes upon the wonders of the whirlpool were now high up above us, and seemed to have moved but little from their original station.

"I no longer hesitated what to do. I resolved to lash myself securely to the water-cask upon which I now held, to cut it loose from the counter, and to throw myself with it into the water. I attracted my brother's attention by signs, pointed to the floating barrels that came near us, and did everything in my power to make him understand

2. "See Archimedes, *De Incidentibus in Fluido*, lib. 2" [Poe's note]. The title is translated, "Concerning the falling into [*i.e.*, floating in] liquids." Archimedes (287?–212 b.c.) was the Greek physicist who first discovered the relations between the displacement of fluid and levitation or buoyancy.

what I was about to do. I thought at length that he comprehended my design, but whether this was the case or not, he shook his head despairingly, and refused to move from his station by the ring-bolt. It was impossible to reach him, the emergency admitted of no delay, and so, with a bitter struggle, I resigned him to his fate, fastened myself to the cask by means of the lashings which secured it to the counter, and precipitated myself with it into the sea without another moment's hesitation.

"The result was precisely what I had hoped it might be. As it is myself who now tell you this tale—as you see that I *did* escape—and as you are already in possession of the mode in which this escape was effected, and must therefore anticipate all that I have further to say, I will bring my story quickly to conclusion. It might have been an hour or thereabout after my quitting the smack, when, having descended to a vast distance beneath me, it made three or four wild gyrations in rapid succession, and, bearing my loved brother with it, plunged headlong at once and for ever into the chaos of foam below. The barrel to which I was attached sunk very little farther than half the distance between the bottom of the gulf and the spot at which I leaped overboard, before a great change took place in the character of the whirlpool. The slope of the sides of the vast funnel became momently less and less sharp. The gyrations of the whirl grew gradually less and less violent. By degrees the froth and the rainbow disappeared, and the bottom of the gulf seemed slowly to uprise. The sky was clear, the winds had gone down, and the full moon was setting radiantly in the west, when I found myself on the surface of the ocean, in full view of the shores of Lofoden, and above the spot where the pool of the Moskoe-ström *had been*. It was the hour of the slack—but the sea still heaved in mountainous waves from the effects of the hurricane. I was borne violently into the channel of the Ström, and in a few minutes was hurried down the coast into the 'grounds' of the fishermen. A boat picked me up, exhausted from fatigue and (now that the danger was removed) speechless from the memory of its horror. Those who drew me on board were my old mates and daily companions, but they knew me no more than they would have known a traveller from the spirit-land. My hair, which had been raven-black the day before, was as white as you see it now. They say, too, that the whole expression of my countenance had changed. I told them my story—they did not believe it. I now tell it to *you*, and I can scarcely expect you to put more faith in it than did the merry fishermen of Lofoden."

1841, 1845

The Cask of Amontillado[3]

The thousand injuries of Fortunato I had borne as I best could; but when he ventured upon insult, I vowed revenge. You, who so well know the nature of my soul, will not suppose, however, that I gave utterance to a threat. *At length* I would be avenged; this was a point definitely settled—but the very definitiveness with which it was resolved precluded the idea of risk. I must not only punish, but punish with impunity. A wrong is unredressed when retribution overtakes its redresser. It is equally unredressed when the avenger fails to make himself felt as such to him who has done the wrong.

It must be understood, that neither by word nor deed had I given Fortunato cause to doubt my good-will. I continued, as was my wont, to smile in his face, and he did not perceive that my smile *now* was at the thought of his immolation.

He had a weak point—this Fortunato—although in other regards he was a man to be respected and even feared. He prided himself on his connoisseurship in wine. Few Italians have the true virtuoso spirit. For the most part their enthusiasm is adopted to suit the time and opportunity—to practise imposture upon the British and Austrian *millionnaires*. In painting and gemmary Fortunato, like his countrymen, was a quack—but in the matter of old wines he was sincere. In this respect I did not differ from him materially: I was skilful in the Italian vintages myself, and bought largely whenever I could.

It was about dusk, one evening during the supreme madness of the carnival season, that I encountered my friend. He accosted me with excessive warmth, for he had been drinking much. The man wore motley. He had on a tight-fitting parti-striped dress, and his head was surmounted by the conical cap and bells. I was so pleased to see him, that I thought I should never have done wringing his hand.

I said to him: "My dear Fortunato, you are luckily met. How remarkably well you are looking to-day! But I have received a pipe[4] of what passes for Amontillado,[5] and I have my doubts."

"How?" said he. "Amontillado? A pipe? Impossible! And in the middle of the carnival!"

"I have my doubts," I replied; "and I was silly enough to pay the full Amontillado price without consulting you in the matter. You were not to be found, and I was fearful of losing a bargain."

"Amontillado!"

---

3. Originally published in *Godey's Lady's Book* for November, 1846, this story was first collected by Griswold in his edition of Poe's *Works* (1850). It is one of those later stories, written from 1841 on, in which Poe best exemplifies the principles of concentration and thematic totality which he enounced in 1842, in his review (reprinted in this volume) of Hawthorne's *Twice-told Tales*. It also illustrates his best command of dialogue, social situation, and the swift dramatic climax.

4. A French derivative; in England and the United States a large cask with the volume of two hogsheads.

5. A pale, dry sherry, much esteemed, originating in Montilla, Spain.

"I have my doubts."

"Amontillado!"

"And I must satisfy them."

"Amontillado!"

"As you are engaged, I am on my way to Luchesi. If any one has a critical turn, it is he. He will tell me——"

"Luchesi cannot tell Amontillado from Sherry."

"And yet some fools will have it that his taste is a match for your own."

"Come, let us go."

"Whither?"

"To your vaults."

"My friend, no; I will not impose upon your good nature. I perceive you have an engagement. Luchesi——"

"I have no engagement;—come."

"My friend, no. It is not the engagement, but the severe cold with which I perceive you are afflicted. The vaults are insufferably damp. They are encrusted with nitre."

"Let us go, nevertheless. The cold is merely nothing. Amontillado! You have been imposed upon. And as for Luchesi, he cannot distinguish Sherry from Amontillado."

Thus speaking, Fortunato possessed himself of my arm. Putting on a mask of black silk, and drawing a *roquelaire*[6] closely about my person, I suffered him to hurry me to my palazzo.

There were no attendants at home; they had absconded to make merry in honor of the time. I had told them that I should not return until the morning, and had given them explicit orders not to stir from the house. These orders were sufficient, I well knew, to insure their immediate disappearance, one and all, as soon as my back was turned.

I took from their sconces two flambeaux, and giving one to Fortunato, bowed him through several suites of rooms to the archway that led into the vaults. I passed down a long and winding staircase, requesting him to be cautious as he followed. We came at length to the foot of the descent, and stood together on the damp ground of the catacombs of the Montresors.

The gait of my friend was unsteady, and the bells upon his cap jingled as he strode.

"The pipe?" said he.

"It is farther on," said I; "but observe the white web-work which gleams from these cavern walls."

He turned toward me, and looked into my eyes with two filmy orbs that distilled the rheum of intoxication.

6. A short cloak.

"Nitre?" he asked, at length.

"Nitre," I replied. "How long have you had that cough?"

"Ugh! ugh! ugh!—ugh! ugh! ugh!—ugh! ugh! ugh!—ugh! ugh!
ugh!—ugh! ugh! ugh!"

My poor friend found it impossible to reply for many minutes.

"It is nothing," he said, at last.

"Come," I said, with decision, "we will go back; your health is
precious. You are rich, respected, admired, beloved; you are happy, as
once I was. You are a man to be missed. For me it is no matter. We
will go back; you will be ill, and I cannot be responsible. Besides, there
is Luchesi——"

"Enough," he said; "the cough is a mere nothing; it will not kill
me. I shall not die of a cough."

"True—true," I replied; "and, indeed, I had no intention of alarming you unnecessarily; but you should use all proper caution. A
draught of this Medoc[7] will defend us from the damps."

Here I knocked off the neck of a bottle which I drew from a long
row of its fellows that lay upon the mould.

"Drink," I said, presenting him the wine.

He raised it to his lips with a leer. He paused and nodded to me
familiarly, while his bells jingled.

"I drink," he said, "to the buried that repose around us."

"And I to your long life."

He again took my arm, and we proceeded.

"These vaults," he said, "are extensive."

"The Montresors," I replied, "were a great and numerous family."

"I forget your arms."

"A huge human foot d'or, in a field azure;[8] the foot crushes a serpent rampant whose fangs are imbedded in the heel."

"And the motto?"

"*Nemo me impune lacessit.*"[9]

"Good!" he said.

The wine sparkled in his eyes and the bells jingled. My own fancy
grew warm with the Medoc. We had passed through walls of piled
bones, with casks and puncheons intermingling, into the inmost
recesses of the catacombs. I paused again, and this time I made bold
to seize Fortunato by an arm above the elbow.

"The nitre!" I said; "see, it increases. It hangs like moss upon the
vaults. We are below the river's bed. The drops of moisture trickle
among the bones. Come, we will go back ere it is too late. Your

7. Correctly, "Médoc," a claret from the
Médoc, near Bordeaux, France. Except
for the varieties branded by certain vineyards, however, it is not a connoisseur's
wine.
8. The coat of arms bore a golden foot
on an azure field. "Rampant," in the
following sentence, means "rearing up."
Fortunato intended an insult in pretending to forget the coat of arms.
9. "No one attacks me with impunity."
This is the legend of the royal arms of
Scotland.

cough——"

"It is nothing," he said; "let us go on. But first, another draught of the Medoc."

I broke and reached him a flagon of De Grâve.[1] He emptied it at a breath. His eyes flashed with a fierce light. He laughed and threw the bottle upward with a gesticulation I did not understand.

I looked at him in surprise. He repeated the movement—a grotesque one.

"You do not comprehend?" he said.

"Not I," I replied.

"Then you are not of the brotherhood."

"How?"

"You are not of the masons."[2]

"Yes, yes," I said; "yes, yes."

"You? Impossible! A mason?"

"A mason," I replied.

"A sign," he said.

"It is this," I answered, producing a trowel from beneath the folds of my *roquelaire.*

"You jest," he exclaimed, recoiling a few paces. "But let us proceed to the Amontillado."

"Be it so," I said, replacing the tool beneath the cloak, and again offering him my arm. He leaned upon it heavily. We continued our route in search of the Amontillado. We passed through a range of low arches, descended, passed on, and descending again, arrived at a deep crypt, in which the foulness of the air caused our flambeaux rather to glow than flame.

At the most remote end of the crypt there appeared another less spacious. Its walls had been lined with human remains, piled to the vault overhead, in the fashion of the great catacombs of Paris.[3] Three sides of this interior crypt were still ornamented in this manner. From the fourth the bones had been thrown down, and lay promiscuously upon the earth, forming at one point a mound of some size. Within the wall thus exposed by the displacing of the bones, we perceived a still interior recess, in depth about four feet, in width three, in height six or seven. It seemed to have been constructed for no especial use within itself, but formed merely the interval between two of the colossal supports of the roof of the catacombs, and was backed by one of their circumscribing walls of solid granite.

It was in vain that Fortunato, uplifting his dull torch, endeavored to pry into the depth of the recess. Its termination the feeble light

1. Correctly, "Grâves," a light wine from the Bordeaux area.
2. Properly, "Masons"; an allusion to the secret society of Freemasons. The trowel, ironically shown by Montresor, is a symbol of their supposed origin as a guild of stoneworkers.
3. Like the earlier catacombs of Italy, those of Paris were subterranean galleries with recessed niches for burial vaults.

did not enable us to see.

"Proceed," I said; "herein is the Amontillado. As for Luchesi——"

"He is an ignoramus," interrupted my friend, as he stepped unsteadily forward, while I followed immediately at his heels. In an instant he had reached the extremity of the niche, and finding his progress arrested by the rock, stood stupidly bewildered. A moment more and I had fettered him to the granite. In its surface were two iron staples, distant from each other about two feet, horizontally. From one of these depended a short chain, from the other a padlock. Throwing the links about his waist, it was but the work of a few seconds to secure it. He was too much astounded to resist. Withdrawing the key I stepped back from the recess.

"Pass your hand," I said, "over the wall; you cannot help feeling the nitre. Indeed it is *very* damp. Once more let me *implore* you to return. No? Then I must positively leave you. But I must first render you all the little attentions in my power."

"The Amontillado!" ejaculated my friend, not yet recovered from his astonishment.

"True," I replied; "the Amontillado."

As I said these words I busied myself among the pile of bones of which I have before spoken. Throwing them aside, I soon uncovered a quantity of building stone and mortar. With these materials and with the aid of my trowel, I began vigorously to wall up the entrance of the niche.

I had scarcely laid the first tier of the masonry when I discovered that the intoxication of Fortunato had in a great measure worn off. The earliest indication I had of this was a low moaning cry from the depth of the recess. It was *not* the cry of a drunken man. There was then a long and obstinate silence. I laid the second tier, and the third, and the fourth; and then I heard the furious vibrations of the chain. The noise lasted for several minutes, during which, that I might hearken to it with the more satisfaction, I ceased my labors and sat down upon the bones. When at last the clanking subsided, I resumed the trowel, and finished without interruption the fifth, the sixth, and the seventh tier. The wall was now nearly upon a level with my breast. I again paused, and holding the flambeaux over the masonwork, threw a few feeble rays upon the figure within.

A succession of loud and shrill screams, bursting suddenly from the throat of the chained form, seemed to thrust me violently back. For a brief moment I hesitated—I trembled. Unsheathing my rapier, I began to grope with it about the recess; but the thought of an instant reassured me. I placed my hand upon the solid fabric of the catacombs, and felt satisfied. I reapproached the wall. I replied to the yells of him who clamored. I re-echoed—I aided—I surpassed them in volume and in strength. I did this, and the clamorer grew still.

It was now midnight, and my task was drawing to a close. I had completed the eighth, the ninth, and the tenth tier. I had finished a portion of the last and the eleventh; there remained but a single stone to be fitted and plastered in. I struggled with its weight; I placed it partially in its destined position. But now there came from out the niche a low laugh that erected the hairs upon my head. It was succeeded by a sad voice, which I had difficulty in recognizing as that of the noble Fortunato. The voice said—

"Ha! ha! ha!—he! he!—a very good joke indeed—an excellent jest. We will have many a rich laugh about it at the palazzo—he! he! he!—over our wine—he! he! he!"

"The Amontillado!" I said.

"He! he! he!—he! he! he!—yes, the Amontillado. But is it not getting late? Will not they be awaiting us at the palazzo, the Lady Fortunato and the rest? Let us be gone."

"Yes," I said, "let us be gone."

"*For the love of God, Montresor!*"

"Yes," I said, "for the love of God!"

But to these words I hearkened in vain for a reply. I grew impatient. I called aloud:

"Fortunato!"

No answer. I called again:

"Fortunato!"

No answer still. I thrust a torch through the remaining aperture and let it fall within. There came forth in return only a jingling of the bells. My heart grew sick—on account of the dampness of the catacombs. I hastened to make an end of my labor. I forced the last stone into its position; I plastered it up. Against the new masonry I re-erected the old rampart of bones. For the half of a century no mortal has disturbed them. *In pace requiescat!*[4]

1846, 1850

Letter to B——[5]

It has been said, that a good critique on a poem may be written by one who is no poet himself. This, according to *your* idea and *mine* of poetry, I feel to be false—the less poetical the critic, the less just

4. May he rest in peace!
5. This article appeared first as the preface to Poe's *Poems*, 1831, where it was entitled "Letter to Mr. ——." It was reprinted, as "Letter to B——," in the *Southern Literary Messenger* for July, 1836. The following text is that of 1831, but we have retained the more familiar title of 1836. In 1831, the article opened, as a letter, with a salutation to

"Dear B——," and a short introductory paragraph which served no purpose save to suggest that Poe was addressing his publisher. This paragraph and the salutation were wisely dropped in the 1836 text, and we have omitted them here. It seems likely that "B" was a real person, Elam Bliss of New York, the publisher of the *Poems* (1831). The letter is Poe's first considerable statement of

the critique, and the converse. On this account, and because there are but few B——s in the world, I would be as much ashamed of the world's good opinion as proud of your own. Another than yourself might here observe "Shakspeare is in possession of the world's good opinion, and yet Shakspeare is the greatest of poets. It appears then that the world judge correctly, why should you be ashamed of their favorable judgment?" The difficulty lies in the interpretation of the word "judgment" or "opinion." The opinion is the world's, truly, but it may be called theirs as a man would call a book his, having bought it; he did not write the book, but it is his; they did not originate the opinion, but it is theirs. A fool, for example, thinks Shakspeare a great poet—yet the fool has never read Shakspeare. But the fool's neighbor, who is a step higher on the Andes of the mind, whose head (that is to say his more exalted thought) is too far above the fool to be seen or understood, but whose feet (by which I mean his every day actions) are sufficiently near to be discerned, and by means of which that superiority is ascertained, which *but* for them would never have been discovered—this neighbor asserts that Shakspeare is a great poet —the fool believes him, and it is henceforward his *opinion*. This neighbor's own opinion has, in like manner, been adopted from one above *him*, and so, ascendingly, to a few gifted individuals, who kneel around the summit, beholding, face to face, the master spirit who stands upon the pinnacle.   *   *   *   *

You are aware of the great barrier in the path of an American writer. He is read, if at all, in preference to the combined and established wit of the world. I say established; for it is with literature as with law or empire—an established name is an estate in tenure, or a throne in possession. Besides, one might suppose that books, like their authors, improve by travel—their having crossed the sea is, with us, so great a distinction. Our antiquaries abandon time for distance; our very fops glance from the binding to the bottom of the title-page, where the mystic characters which spell London, Paris, or Genoa, are precisely so many letters of recommendation.

      *   *   *   *

I mentioned just now a vulgar error as regards criticism. I think the notion that no poet can form a correct estimate of his own writings is another. I remarked before, that in proportion to the poetical talent, would be the justice of a critique upon poetry. Therefore, a bad poet would, I grant, make a false critique, and his self-love would infallibly bias his little judgment in his favor; but a poet, who is indeed a poet, could not, I think, fail of making a just critique. Whatever should be deducted on the score of self-love, might be replaced

poetic theory, later to be modified (*cf.* "The Poetic Principle"). The asterisks in the present text appeared in both versions, and do not represent omitted passages.

on account of his intimate acquaintance with the subject; in short, we have more instances of false criticism than of just, where one's own writings are the test, simply because we have more bad poets than good. There are of course many objections to what I say: Milton is a great example of the contrary; but his opinion with respect to the Paradise Regained, is by no means fairly ascertained. By what trivial circumstances men are often led to assert what they do not really believe! Perhaps an inadvertent word has descended to posterity. But, in fact, the Paradise Regained is little, if at all, inferior to the Paradise Lost, and is only supposed so to be because men do not like epics, whatever they may say to the contrary, and reading those of Milton in their natural order, are too much wearied with the first to derive any pleasure from the second.

I dare say Milton preferred Comus to either—if so—justly.

*   *   *   *   *

As I am speaking of poetry, it will not be amiss to touch slightly upon the most singular heresy in its modern history—the heresy of what is called very foolishly, the Lake School. Some years ago I might have been induced, by an occasion like the present, to attempt a formal refutation of their doctrine; at present it would be a work of supererogation. The wise must bow to the wisdom of such men as Coleridge and Southey, but being wise, have laughed at poetical theories so prosaically exemplified.

Aristotle, with singular assurance, has declared poetry the most philosophical of all writing[6]—but it required a Wordsworth to pronounce it the most metaphysical. He seems to think that the end of poetry is, or should be, instruction—yet it is a truism that the end of our existence is happiness; if so, the end of every separate part of our existence—every thing connected with our existence should be still happiness. Therefore the end of instruction should be happiness; and happiness is another name for pleasure;—therefore the end of instruction should be pleasure: yet we see the above mentioned opinion implies precisely the reverse.

To proceed: *ceteris paribus*,[7] he who pleases, is of more importance to his fellow men than he who instructs, since utility is happiness, and pleasure is the end already obtained which instruction is merely the means of obtaining.

I see no reason, then, why our metaphysical poets should plume themselves so much on the utility of their works, unless indeed they refer to instruction with eternity in view; in which case, sincere respect for their piety would not allow me to express my contempt for their judgment; contempt which it would be difficult to conceal, since their writings are professedly to be understood by the few, and it is

6. Poe's footnote here quotes the Greek phrase translated in his text, from Aristotle, *Poetics*, ix, 3.
7. Other things being equal.

the many who stand in need of salvation. In such case I should no doubt be tempted to think of the devil in Melmoth,[8] who labors indefatigably through three octavo volumes, to accomplish the destruction of one or two souls, while any common devil would have demolished one or two thousand.

*   *   *   *   *

Against the subtleties which would make poetry a study—not a passion—it becomes the metaphysician to reason—but the poet to protest. Yet Wordsworth and Coleridge are men in years; the one imbued in contemplation from his childhood, the other a giant in intellect and learning. The diffidence, then, with which I venture to dispute their authority would be overwhelming, did I not feel, from the bottom of my heart, that learning has little to do with the imagination—intellect with the passions—or age with poetry.   *   *   *   *

"Trifles, like straws, upon the surface flow,
    He who would search for pearls must dive below,"[9]

are lines which have done much mischief. As regards the greater truths, men oftener err by seeking them at the bottom than at the top; the depth lies in the huge abysses where wisdom is sought—not in the palpable palaces where she is found. The ancients were not always right in hiding the goddess in a well:[1] witness the light which Bacon has thrown upon philosophy; witness the principles of our divine faith—that moral mechanism by which the simplicity of a child may overbalance the wisdom of a man.

Poetry, above all things, is a beautiful painting whose tints, to minute inspection, are confusion worse confounded, but start boldly out to the cursory glance of the connoisseur.

We see an instance of Coleridge's liability to err in his Biographia Literaria[2]—professedly his literary life and opinions, but, in fact, a treatise *de omni scibili et quibusdam aliis*.[3] He goes wrong by reason of his very profundity, and of his error we have a natural type in the contemplation of a star. He who regards it directly and intensely sees, it is true, the star, but it is the star without a ray—while he who surveys it less inquisitively is conscious of all for which the star is useful to us below—its brilliancy and its beauty.

*   *   *   *   *

As to Wordsworth, I have no faith in him. That he had, in youth, the feelings of a poet, I believe—for there are glimpses of extreme

8. *Melmoth the Wanderer* (1820); Gothic prose romance by Charles Robert Maturin, Irish clergyman.
9. From Dryden, *All For Love*, Prologue, ll. 25–26. For "Trifles" read "Errors."

1. *Cf.* Democritus: "Truth lies at the bottom of a well."
2. Coleridge's major critical work, published in 1817.
3. Concerning everything that can be known, and certain other things as well.

delicacy in his writings—(and delicacy is the poet's own kingdom—his *El Dorado*)—but they have the appearance of a better day recollected; and glimpses, at best, are little evidence of present poetic fire—we know that a few straggling flowers spring up daily in the crevices of the Avalanche.

He was to blame in wearing away his youth in contemplation with the end of poetizing in his manhood. With the increase of his judgment the light which should make it apparent has faded away. His judgment consequently is too correct. This may not be understood, but the old Goths of Germany would have understood it, who used to debate matters of importance to their State twice, once when drunk, and once when sober—sober that they might not be deficient in formality—drunk lest they should be destitute of vigor.

The long wordy discussions by which he tries to reason us into admiration of his poetry, speak very little in his favor: they are full of such assertions as this—(I have opened one of his volumes at random) "Of genius the only proof is the act of doing well what is worthy to be done, and what was never done before"[4]—indeed! then it follows that in doing what is *un*worthy to be done, or what *has* been done before, no genius can be evinced: yet the picking of pockets is an unworthy act, pockets have been picked time immemorial, and Barrington,[5] the pick-pocket, in point of genius, would have thought hard of a comparison with William Wordsworth, the poet.

Again—in estimating the merit of certain poems, whether they be Ossian's or M'Pherson's,[6] can surely be of little consequence, yet, in order to prove their worthlessness, Mr. W. has expended many pages in the controversy. *Tantœne animis?*[7] Can great minds descend to such absurdity? But worse still: that he may bear down every argument in favor of these poems, he triumphantly drags forward a passage in his abomination of which he expects the reader to sympathize. It is the beginning of the epic poem Temora. "The blue waves of Ullin roll in light; the green hills are covered with day; trees shake their dusky heads in the breeze." And this—this gorgeous, yet simple imagery—where all is alive and panting with immortality—than which earth has nothing more grand, nor paradise more beautiful—this—William Wordsworth, the author of Peter Bell, has *selected* to dignify with his imperial contempt. We shall see what better he, in his own person, has to offer.[8] Imprimis:

4. Wordsworth, in "Essay, Supplementary to the Preface" (1815).
5. George Barrington, pseudonym for George Waldron (1755–1840?), Irish writer; an incorrigible and gifted pickpocket, deported 1790.
6. James Macpherson (1736–1796) published *Fingal* (1762) and *Temora* (1763), alleged translations from manuscripts of Ossian, legendary Irish bard and warrior of the third century Finn Saga. Their authenticity was never

proved, but their enormous popularity stimulated the extravagant elements of romanticism that Wordsworth opposed.
7. In idiomatic English, "Why all the resentment?"
8. Poe quotes below two extreme illustrations of Wordsworth's poetry of the commonplace: first, from an early version of "The Idiot Boy"; second, from "The Pet Lamb," with Poe's dashes introduced to emphasize banality of phrase.

> "And now she's at the poney's [*sic*] head,
> And now she's at the poney's tail,
> On that side now, and now on this,
> And almost stifled her with bliss—
> A few sad tears does Betty shed,
> She pats the poney where or when
> She knows not: happy Betty Foy!
> O Johnny! never mind the Doctor!"

Secondly:

> "The dew was falling fast, the—stars began to blink,
> I heard a voice, it said—drink, pretty creature, drink;
> And looking o'er the hedge, be—fore me I espied
> A snow-white mountain lamb with a—maiden at its side.
> No other sheep were near, the lamb was all alone,
> And by a slender cord was—tether'd to a stone."

Now we have no doubt this is all true; we *will* believe it, indeed we will, Mr. W. Is it sympathy for the sheep you wish to excite? I love a sheep from the bottom of my heart.

*　　　*　　　*　　　*

But there *are* occasions, dear B——, there are occasions when even Wordsworth is reasonable. Even Stamboul, it is said, shall have an end, and the most unlucky blunders must come to a conclusion. Here is an extract from his preface.

"Those who have been accustomed to the phraseology of modern writers, if they persist in reading this book to a conclusion (*impossible!*) will, no doubt, have to struggle with feelings of awkwardness; (ha! ha! ha!) they will look round for poetry (ha! ha! ha! ha!) and will be induced to inquire by what species of courtesy these attempts have been permitted to assume that title." Ha! ha! ha! ha! ha!

Yet let not Mr. W. despair; he has given immortality to a wagon, and the bee Sophocles has eternalized a sore toe [*sic*], and dignified a tragedy with a chorus of turkeys.

*　　　*　　　*

Of Coleridge I cannot speak but with reverence. His towering intellect! his gigantic power! To use an author quoted by himself, "J'ai trouvé souvent que la plupart des sectes ont raison dans une bonne partie de ce quelles avancent, mais non pas en ce quelles nient,"[9] and, to employ his own language, he has imprisoned his own conceptions by the barrier he has erected against those of others. It is lamentable to think that such a mind should be buried in meta-

9. In *Biographia Literaria*, Chapter 11; Coleridge quotes from Leibnitz, *Trois Lettres à M. Redmond de Mont-Mort*. The French passage is translated: "I have frequently observed that most sects are right, for the most part, in what they advocate, but not in what they deny."

physics, and, like the Nyctanthes, waste its perfume upon the night alone. In reading that man's poetry I tremble, like one who stands upon a volcano, conscious, from the very darkness bursting from the crater, of the fire and the light that are weltering below.

*　　*　　*　　*　　*

What is Poetry? Poetry! that Proteus-like idea, with as many appellations as the nine-titled Corcyra![1] Give me, I demanded of a scholar some time ago, give me a definition of poetry? "Tres volontiers,"[2]—and he proceeded to his library, brought me a Dr. Johnson, and overwhelmed me with a definition. Shade of the immortal Shakspeare! I imagined to myself the scowl of your spiritual eye upon the profanity of that scurrilous Ursa Major.[3] Think of poetry, dear B——, think of poetry, and then think of—Dr. Samuel Johnson! Think of all that is airy and fairy-like, and then of all that is hideous and unwieldy; think of his huge bulk, the Elephant! and then—and then think of the Tempest—the Midsummer Night's Dream—Prospero—Oberon—and Titania!

*　　*　　*　　*　　*

A poem,[4] in my opinion, is opposed to a work of science by having, for its *immediate* object, pleasure, not truth; to romance, by having for its object an *indefinite* instead of a *definite* pleasure, being a poem only so far as this object is attained: romance presenting perceptible images with definite, poetry with *in*definite sensations, to which end music is an *essential*, since the comprehension of sweet sound is our most indefinite conception. Music, when combined with a pleasurable idea, is poetry; music without the idea is simply music; the idea without the music is prose from its very definitiveness.

What was meant by the invective against "him who had no music in his soul?"

*　　*　　*　　*　　*

To sum up this long rigmarole, I have, dear B——, what you no doubt perceive, for the metaphysical poets, *as* poets, the most sovereign contempt. That they have followers proves nothing—

> No Indian prince has to his palace
> More followers than a thief to the gallows.[5]

1831

1. In Greek myth, Proteus, god of the sea, was able quickly to change his appearance; Corcyra (modern Corfu), Greek island and ancient port, has had a variety of names.
2. Very willingly.
3. The constellation of the Great Bear; here used in humorous allusion to the burly truculence of Dr. Samuel Johnson.
4. This famous pronouncement, regarded by some critics as the first formulation of Poe's poetics, may be interestingly compared with "The Poetic Principle," his last word on the subject (see below). A comparison of the present passage with Coleridge's definition of poetry, in *Biographia Literaria*, Chapter 14, will suggest the similarities and differences between the two poet-critics.
5. From Samuel Butler (1612–1680), *Hudibras*, Part II (1664), Canto I, ll. 272–273.

Twice-Told Tales, By Nathaniel Hawthorne[6]

A Review

We said a few hurried words about Mr. Hawthorne in our last number, with the design of speaking more fully in the present. We are still, however, pressed for room, and must necessarily discuss his volumes more briefly and more at random than their high merits deserve.

The book professes to be a collection of *tales*, yet is, in two respects, misnamed. These pieces are now in their third republication, and, of course, are thrice-told.[7] Moreover, they are by no means *all* tales, either in the ordinary or in the legitimate understanding of the term. Many of them are pure essays; for example, "Sights from a Steeple," "Sunday at Home," "Little Annie's Ramble," "A Rill from the Town Pump," "The Toll-Gatherer's Day," "The Haunted Mind," "The Sister Years," "Snow-Flakes," "Night Sketches," and "Foot-Prints on the Sea-Shore." We mention these matters chiefly on account of their discrepancy with that marked precision and finish by which the body of the work is distinguished.

Of the essays just named, we must be content to speak in brief. They are each and all beautiful, without being characterized by the polish and adaptation so visible in the tales proper. A painter would at once note their leading or predominant feature, and style it *repose*. There is no attempt at effect. All is quiet, thoughtful, subdued. Yet this repose may exist simultaneously with high originality of thought; and Mr. Hawthorne has demonstrated the fact. At every turn we meet with novel combinations; yet these combinations never surpass the limits of the quiet. We are soothed as we read; and withal is a calm astonishment that ideas so apparently obvious have never occurred or been presented to us before. Herein our author differs materially from Lamb or Hunt or Hazlitt—who, with vivid originality of manner and expression, have less of the true novelty of thought than is generally supposed, and whose originality, at best, has an uneasy and meretricious quaintness, replete with startling effects unfounded in nature, and inducing trains of reflection which lead to no satisfactory result. The Essays of Hawthorne have much of the character of Irving, with more of originality, and less of finish; while, compared with the Spectator, they have a vast superiority at

---

6. This is one of Poe's most important critical articles. In the fourth paragraph begins the famous formulation of the short story as a literary *genre*, which Poe was the first to define, and was already illustrating in his own stories, at the height of his maturity. Apart from this, of course, the essay is one of Poe's most characteristic critiques. It first ap-

peared in *Graham's Magazine* for May, 1842, although Poe had printed a brief notice of five paragraphs in the April issue (see his opening sentence).
7. These stories had in most cases been published in magazines, then in a collected edition in 1837; the present edition was a republication of the 1837 volume.

all points. The Spectator, Mr. Irving, and Mr. Hawthorne have in common that tranquil and subdued manner which we have chosen to denominate *repose*; but, in the case of the two former, this repose is attained rather by the absence of novel combination, or of originality, than otherwise, and consists chiefly in the calm, quiet, unostentatious expression of commonplace thoughts, in an unambitious, unadulterated Saxon. In them, by strong effort, we are made to conceive the absence of all. In the essays before us the absence of effort is too obvious to be mistaken, and a strong undercurrent of *suggestion* runs continuously beneath the upper stream of the tranquil thesis. In short, these effusions of Mr. Hawthorne are the product of a truly imaginative intellect, restrained, and in some measure repressed, by fastidiousness of taste, by constitutional melancholy, and by indolence.

But it is of his tales that we desire principally to speak. The tale proper, in our opinion, affords unquestionably the fairest field for the exercise of the loftiest talent, which can be afforded by the wide domains of mere prose. Were we bidden to say how the highest genius could be most advantageously employed for the best display of its own powers, we should answer, without hesitation—in the composition of a rhymed poem, not to exceed in length what might be perused in an hour. Within this limit alone can the highest order of true poetry exist. We need only here say, upon this topic, that, in almost all classes of composition, the unity of effect or impression is a point of the greatest importance. It is clear, moreover, that this unity cannot be thoroughly preserved in productions whose perusal cannot be completed at one sitting. We may continue the reading of a prose composition, from the very nature of prose itself, much longer than we can persevere, to any good purpose, in the perusal of a poem. This latter, if truly fulfilling the demands of the poetic sentiment, induces an exaltation of the soul which cannot be long sustained. All high excitements are necessarily transient. Thus a long poem is a paradox. And, without unity of impression, the deepest effects cannot be brought about. Epics were the offspring of an imperfect sense of Art, and their reign is no more. A poem *too* brief may produce a vivid, but never an intense or enduring impression. Without a certain continuity of effort—without a certain duration or repetition of purpose—the soul is never deeply moved. There must be the dropping of the water upon the rock. De Béranger[8] has wrought brilliant things —pungent and spirit-stirring—but, like all immassive bodies, they lack *momentum*, and thus fail to satisfy the Poetic Sentiment. They sparkle and excite, but, from want of continuity, fail deeply to impress. Extreme brevity will degenerate into epigrammatism; but the

8. *Cf.* "Israfel," epigraph to "The Fall of the House of Usher," and "The Poetic Principle" for other references to Pierre Jean de Béranger (1780–1857), French lyric poet.

sin of extreme length is even more unpardonable. *In medio tutissimus ibis.*[9]

Were we called upon, however, to designate that class of composition which, next to such a poem as we have suggested, should best fulfil the demands of high genius—should offer it the most advantageous field of exertion—we should unhesitatingly speak of the prose tale, as Mr. Hawthorne has here exemplified it. We allude to the short prose narrative, requiring from a half-hour to one or two hours in its perusal. The ordinary novel is objectionable, from its length, for reasons already stated in substance. As it cannot be read at one sitting, it deprives itself, of course, of the immense force derivable from *totality*. Worldly interests intervening during the pauses of perusal, modify, annul, or counteract, in a greater or less degree, the impressions of the book. But simple cessation in reading would, of itself, be sufficient to destroy the true unity. In the brief tale, however, the author is enabled to carry out the fulness of his intention, be it what it may. During the hour of perusal the soul of the reader is at the writer's control. There are no external or extrinsic influences—resulting from weariness or interruption.

A skilful literary artist has constructed a tale. If wise, he has not fashioned his thoughts to accommodate his incidents; but having conceived, with deliberate care, a certain unique or single *effect* to be wrought out, he then invents such incidents—he then combines such events as may best aid him in establishing this preconceived effect. If his very initial sentence tend not to the outbringing of this effect, then he has failed in his first step. In the whole composition there should be no word written, of which the tendency, direct or indirect, is not to the one pre-established design. And by such means, with such care and skill, a picture is at length painted which leaves in the mind of him who contemplates it with a kindred art, a sense of the fullest satisfaction. The idea of the tale has been presented unblemished, because undisturbed; and this is an end unattainable by the novel. Undue brevity is just as exceptionable here as in the poem; but undue length is yet more to be avoided.

We have said that the tale has a point of superiority even over the poem. In fact, while the *rhythm* of this latter is an essential aid in the development of the poem's highest idea—the idea of the Beautiful—the artificialities of this rhythm are an inseparable bar to the development of all points of thought or expression which have their basis in *Truth*. But Truth is often, and in very great degree, the aim of the tale. Some of the finest tales are tales of ratiocination. Thus the field of this species of composition, if not in so elevated a region

9. "You travel most safely in the middle [moderate] course": Ovid, in the *Metamorphoses;* the advice of Helios to his son Phaëthon, who insists on driving the chariot of the sun for a day, and nearly burns up the earth by neglecting his father's injunction.

on the mountain of Mind, is a table-land of far vaster extent than the domain of the mere poem. Its products are never so rich, but infinitely more numerous, and more appreciable by the mass of mankind. The writer of the prose tale, in short, may bring to his theme a vast variety of modes or inflections of thought and expression—(the ratiocinative, for example, the sarcastic, or the humorous) which are not only antagonistical to the nature of the poem, but absolutely forbidden by one of its most peculiar and indispensable adjuncts; we allude, of course, to rhythm. It may be added here, *par parenthèse*,[1] that the author who aims at the purely beautiful in a prose tale is laboring at a great disadvantage. For Beauty can be better treated in the poem. Not so with terror, or passion, or horror, or a multitude of such other points. And here it will be seen how full of prejudice are the usual animadversions against those *tales of effect*, many fine examples of which were found in the earlier numbers of *Blackwood*.[2] The impressions produced were wrought in a legitimate sphere of action, and constituted a legitimate although sometimes an exaggerated interest. They were relished by every man of genius: although there were found many men of genius who condemned them without just ground. The true critic will but demand that the design intended be accomplished, to the fullest extent, by the means most advantageously applicable.

We have very few American tales of real merit—we may say, indeed, none, with the exception of *The Tales of a Traveller* of Washington Irving, and these *Twice-Told Tales* of Mr. Hawthorne. Some of the pieces of Mr. John Neal[3] abound in vigor and originality; but, in general, his compositions of this class are excessively diffuse, extravagant, and indicative of an imperfect sentiment of Art. Articles at random are, now and then, met with in our periodicals which might be advantageously compared with the best effusions of the British Magazines; but, upon the whole, we are far behind our progenitors in this department of literature.

Of Mr. Hawthorne's tales we should say, emphatically, that they belong to the highest region of Art—an Art subservient to genius of a very lofty order. We had supposed, with good reason for so supposing, that he had been thrust into his present position by one of the impudent *cliques* which beset our literature, and whose pretensions it is our full purpose to expose at the earliest opportunity; but we have been most agreeably mistaken. We know of few compositions which the critic can more honestly commend than these *Twice-Told Tales*. As Americans, we feel proud of the book.

---

1. Parenthetically.
2. The *Edinburgh Monthly Magazine* (1817) soon simply called *Blackwood's Magazine*, was noted from the beginning for fiction creating the mood of "terror, or passion, or horror" that Poe here associates with "effect."
3. John Neal (1793–1876), voluminous American writer and journalist, had been a *Blackwood's* author.

Mr. Hawthorne's distinctive trait is invention, creation, imagination, originality—a trait which, in the literature of fiction, is positively worth all the rest. But the nature of the originality, so far as regards its manifestation in letters, is but imperfectly understood. The inventive or original mind as frequently displays itself in novelty of *tone* as in novelty of matter. Mr. Hawthorne is original at *all* points.

It would be a matter of some difficulty to designate the best of these tales; we repeat that, without exception, they are beautiful. "Wakefield" is remarkable for the skill with which an old idea—a well-known incident—is worked up or discussed. A man of whims conceives the purpose of quitting his wife and residing *incognito*, for twenty years, in her immediate neighborhood. Something of this kind actually happened in London. The force of Mr. Hawthorne's tale lies in the analysis of the motives which must or might have impelled the husband to such folly, in the first instance, with the possible causes of his perseverance. Upon this thesis a sketch of singular power has been constructed.

"The Wedding Knell" is full of the boldest imagination—an imagination fully controlled by taste. The most captious critic could find no flaw in this production.

"The Minister's Black Veil" is a masterly composition, of which the sole defect is that to the rabble its exquisite skill will be *caviare*.[4] The *obvious* meaning of this article will be found to smother its insinuated one. The *moral* put into the mouth of the dying minister will be supposed to convey the *true* import of the narrative; and that a crime of dark dye (having reference to the "young lady") has been committed, is a point which only minds congenial with that of the author will perceive.

"Mr. Higginbotham's Catastrophe" is vividly original, and managed most dexterously.

"Dr. Heidegger's Experiment" is exceedingly well imagined, and executed with surpassing ability. The artist breathes in every line of it.

"The White Old Maid" is objectionable even more than the "Minister's Black Veil," on the score of its mysticism. Even with the thoughtful and analytic, there will be much trouble in penetrating its entire import.

"The Hollow of the Three Hills" we would quote in full had we space;—not as evincing higher talent than any of the other pieces, but as affording an excellent example of the author's peculiar ability. The subject is commonplace. A witch subjects the Distant and the Past to the view of a mourner. It has been the fashion to describe, in such cases, a mirror in which the images of the absent appear;

4. *Cf. Hamlet*, Act II, Scene 2, 1. 465: "The play, I remember, pleased not the million; 'twas caviare to the general."

or a cloud of smoke is made to arise, and thence the figures are gradually unfolded. Mr. Hawthorne has wonderfully heightened his effect by making the ear, in place of the eye, the medium by which the fantasy is conveyed. The head of the mourner is enveloped in the cloak of the witch, and within its magic folds there arise sounds which have an all-sufficient intelligence. Throughout this article also, the artist is conspicuous—not more in positive than in negative merits. Not only is all done that should be done, but (what perhaps is an end with more difficulty attained) there is nothing done which should not be. Every word *tells*, and there is not a word which does *not* tell.

In "Howe's Masquerade" we observe something which resembles plagiarism[5]—but which *may be* a very flattering coincidence of thought. We quote the passage in question.

[Quotation.]

The idea here is, that the figure in the cloak is the phantom or reduplication of Sir William Howe; but in an article called "William Wilson," one of the *Tales of the Grotesque and Arabesque*, we have not only the same idea, but the same idea similarly presented in several respects. We quote two paragraphs, which our readers may compare with what has been already given. We have italicized, above, the immediate particulars of resemblance.

[Quotation.]

Here it will be observed that, not only are the two general conceptions identical, but there are various *points* of similarity. In each case the figure seen is the wraith or duplication of the beholder. In each case the scene is a masquerade. In each case the figure is cloaked. In each, there is a quarrel—that is to say, angry words pass between the parties. In each the beholder is enraged. In each the cloak and sword fall upon the floor. The "villain, unmuffle yourself," of Mr. H. is precisely paralleled by a passage at page 56 of "William Wilson."

In the way of objection we have scarcely a word to say of these tales. There is, perhaps, a somewhat too general or prevalent *tone* —a tone of melancholy and mysticism. The subjects are insufficiently varied. There is not so much of *versatility* evinced as we might well be warranted in expecting from the high powers of Mr. Hawthorne. But beyond these trivial exceptions we have really none to make. The style is purity itself. Force abounds. High imagination gleams

5. Charges of plagiarism abounded in this period. What Poe did not know was that "Howe's Masquerade" had been first published by Hawthorne in the *Democratic Review* more than a year before his own "William Wilson" ap-peared. *Cf.* Quinn, *Edgar Allan Poe*, p. 336. As in most other editions, the quoted passages, in which Poe finds "flattering" resemblances, have been omitted as irrelevant here.

from every page. Mr. Hawthorne is a man of the truest genius. We only regret that the limits of our Magazine will not permit us to pay him that full tribute of commendation, which, under other circumstances, we should be so eager to pay.

1842, 1894

The Philosophy of Composition[6]

Charles Dickens, in a note now lying before me, alluding to an examination I once made of the mechanism of *Barnaby Rudge*,[7] says—"By the way, are you aware that Godwin wrote his *Caleb Williams* backward?[8] He first involved his hero in a web of difficulties, forming the second volume, and then, for the first, cast about him for some mode of accounting for what had been done."

I cannot think this the *precise* mode of procedure on the part of Godwin—and indeed what he himself acknowledges, is not altogether in accordance with Mr. Dickens's idea—but the author of *Caleb Williams* was too good an artist not to perceive the advantage derivable from at least a somewhat similar process. Nothing is more clear than that every plot, worth the name, must be elaborated to its *dénouement*[9] before anything be attempted with the pen. It is only with the *dénouement* constantly in view that we can give a plot its indispensable air of consequence, or causation, by making the incidents, and especially the tone at all points, tend to the development of the intention.

There is a radical error, I think, in the usual mode of constructing a story. Either history affords a thesis—or one is suggested by an incident of the day—or, at best, the author sets himself to work in the combination of striking events to form merely the basis of his

6. This essay has survived endless discussions as to whether Poe actually composed "The Raven" in the manner described. It retains its fascination and its usefulness because it convincingly shows what elements, somehow or other, went into "The Raven," and what processes, at one time or another, occurred in the creative mind of the author during the four years in which he repeatedly returned to this work. If, in the limited scope of a lecture (for which the paper was probably intended), Poe distorted the time sequence or foreshortened the perspective of ideas concerned in the process, the critical truth of his "best specimen of analysis," as he called it, is not diminished. He was concerned to demonstrate that a poem, like any other work of art, is fabricated of materials selected for consciously determined purposes; that these plastic potentials are shaped by the creative intelligence to make them most useful in communicating the intended effect or idea. This concept, in accord with his theory of creation, which he believed valid for fiction as well as for poetry, was directly opposed to the romantic assumption that the artist is himself an instrument responding intuitively to pressures of inspiration. Thus the essay is a source of information concerning Poe's theories and practice, while providing, at the same time, a model of analytical criticism. It was first published in *Graham's Magazine* for April, 1846.

7. In 1841, while Dickens' *Barnaby Rudge* was appearing serially, Poe wrote a review in which he succeeded in naming the murderer, still supposedly shrouded in mystery.

8. See Godwin's Preface to *Caleb Williams* (1794) for confirmation.

9. Literally, the "untying"; hence, the "solution" of a fictional plot.

narrative—designing, generally, to fill in with description, dialogue, or autorial [sic] comment, whatever crevices of fact, or action, may, from page to page, render themselves apparent.

I prefer commencing with the consideration of an *effect*. Keeping originality *always* in view—for he is false to himself who ventures to dispense with so obvious and so easily attainable a source of interest—I say to myself, in the first place, "Of the innumerable effects, or impressions, of which the heart, the intellect, or (more generally) the soul is susceptible, what one shall I, on the present occasion, select?" Having chosen a novel, first, and secondly a vivid effect, I consider whether it can be best wrought by incident or tone— whether by ordinary incidents and peculiar tone, or the converse, or by peculiarity both of incident and tone—afterward looking about me (or rather within) for such combinations of event, or tone, as shall best aid me in the construction of the effect.

I have often thought how interesting a magazine paper might be written by any author who would—that is to say who could—detail, step by step, the processes by which any one of his compositions attained its ultimate point of completion. Why such a paper has never been given to the world, I am much at a loss to say—but, perhaps, the autorial vanity has had more to do with the omission than any one other cause. Most writers—poets in especial—prefer having it understood that they compose by a species of fine frenzy—an ecstatic intuition—and would positively shudder at letting the public take a peep behind the scenes, at the elaborate and vacillating crudities of thought—at the true purposes seized only at the last moment—at the innumerable glimpses of idea that arrived not at the maturity of full view—at the fully matured fancies discarded in despair as unmanageable—at the cautious selections and rejections—at the painful erasures and interpolations—in a word, at the wheels and pinions—the tackle for scene-shifting—the step-ladders and demon-traps—the cock's feathers, the red paint, and the black patches, which, in ninety-nine cases out of the hundred, constitute the properties of the literary *histrio*.[1]

I am aware, on the other hand, that the case is by no means common, in which an author is at all in condition to retrace the steps by which his conclusions have been attained. In general, suggestions, having arisen pell-mell, are pursued and forgotten in a similar manner.

For my own part, I have neither sympathy with the repugnance alluded to, nor at any time the least difficulty in recalling to mind the progressive steps of any of my compositions; and, since the interest of an analysis, or reconstruction, such as I have considered a *desideratum*, is quite independent of any real or fancied interest in

1. Actor.

the thing analyzed, it will not be regarded as a breach of decorum on my part to show the *modus operandi*[2] by which some one of my own works was put together. I select *The Raven*, as most generally known. It is my design to render it manifest that no one point in its composition is referrible either to accident or intuition—that the work proceeded, step by step, to its completion with the precision and rigid consequence of a mathematical problem.

Let us dismiss, as irrelevant to the poem, *per se*, the circumstance —or say the necessity—which, in the first place, gave rise to the intention of composing *a* poem that should suit at once the popular and the critical taste.

We commence, then, with this intention.

The initial consideration was that of extent. If any literary work is too long to be read at one sitting, we must be content to dispense with the immensely important effect derivable from unity of impression—for, if two sittings be required, the affairs of the world interfere, and every thing like totality is at once destroyed. But since, *ceteris paribus*,[3] no poet can afford to dispense with *any thing* that may advance his design, it but remains to be seen whether there is, in extent, any advantage to counterbalance the loss of unity which attends it. Here I say no, at once. What we term a long poem is, in fact, merely a succession of brief ones—that is to say, of brief poetical effects. It is needless to demonstrate that a poem is such, only inasmuch as it intensely excites, by elevating, the soul; and all intense excitements are, through a psychal[4] necessity, brief. For this reason, at least one half of the *Paradise Lost* is essentially prose—a succession of poetical excitements interspersed, *inevitably*, with corresponding depressions —the whole being deprived, through the extremeness of its length, of the vastly important artistic element, totality, or unity, of effect.

It appears evident, then, that there is a distinct limit, as regards length, to all works of literary art—the limit of a single sitting— and that, although in certain classes of prose composition, such as *Robinson Crusoe* (demanding no unity) this limit may be advantageously overpassed, it can never properly be overpassed in a poem. Within this limit, the extent of a poem may be made to bear mathematical relation to its merit—in other words, to the excitement or elevation—again in other words, to the degree of the true poetical effect which it is capable of inducing; for it is clear that the brevity must be in direct ratio of the intensity of the intended effect:—this, with one proviso—that a certain degree of duration is absolutely requisite for the production of any effect at all.

Holding in view these considerations, as well as that degree of excitement which I deemed not above the popular, while not below

2. Method of performance.
3. Other things being equal.

4. Psychological.

the critical, taste, I reached at once what I conceived the proper *length* for my intended poem—a length of about one hundred lines. It is, in fact, a hundred and eight.

My next thought concerned the choice of an impression, or effect, to be conveyed; and here I may as well observe that, throughout the construction, I kept steadily in view the design of rendering the work *universally* appreciable. I should be carried too far out of my immediate topic were I to demonstrate a point upon which I have repeatedly insisted, and which, with the poetical, stands not in the slightest need of demonstration—the point, I mean, that Beauty is the sole legitimate province of the poem. A few words, however, in elucidation of my real meaning, which some of my friends have evinced a disposition to misrepresent. That pleasure which is at once the most intense, the most elevating, and the most pure, is, I believe, found in the contemplation of the beautiful. When, indeed, men speak of Beauty, they mean, precisely, not a quality, as is supposed, but an effect—they refer, in short, just to that intense and pure elevation of *soul*—*not* of intellect, or of heart—upon which I have commented, and which is experienced in consequence of contemplating "the beautiful." Now I designate Beauty as the province of the poem, merely because it is an obvious rule of Art that effects should be made to spring from direct causes—that objects should be attained through means best adapted for their attainment—no one as yet having been weak enough to deny that the peculiar elevation alluded to is *most readily* attained in the poem. Now the object, Truth, or the satisfaction of the intellect, and the object Passion, or the excitement of the heart, are, although attainable, to a certain extent, in poetry, far more readily attainable in prose. Truth, in fact, demands a precision, and Passion a *homeliness* (the truly passionate will comprehend me) which are absolutely antagonistic to that Beauty which, I maintain, is the excitement, or pleasurable elevation, of the soul. It by no means follows from any thing here said, that passion, or even truth, may not be introduced, and even profitably introduced, into a poem—for they may serve in elucidation, or aid the general effect, as do discords in music, by contrast—but the true artist will always contrive, first, to tone them into proper subservience to the predominant aim, and, secondly, to enveil them, as far as possible, in that Beauty which is the atmosphere and the essence of the poem.

Regarding, then, Beauty as my province, my next question referred to the *tone* of its highest manifestation—and all experience has shown that this tone is one of *sadness*. Beauty of whatever kind, in its supreme development, invariably excites the sensitive soul to tears. Melancholy is thus the most legitimate of all the poetical tones.

The length, the province, and the tone, being thus determined, I betook myself to ordinary induction, with the view of obtaining some artistic piquancy which might serve me as a key-note in the construction of the poem—some pivot upon which the whole structure might turn. In carefully thinking over all the usual artistic effects —or more properly *points*, in the theatrical sense—I did not fail to perceive immediately that no one had been so universally employed as that of the *refrain*. The universality of its employment sufficed to assure me of its intrinsic value, and spared me the necessity of submitting it to analysis. I considered it, however, with regard to its susceptibility of improvement, and soon saw it to be in a primitive condition. As commonly used, the *refrain*, or burden, not only is limited to lyric verse, but depends for its impression upon the force of monotone—both in sound and thought. The pleasure is deduced solely from the sense of identity—of repetition. I resolved to diversify, and so heighten, the effect, by adhering, in general, to the monotone of sound, while I continually varied that of thought: that is to say, I determined to produce continuously novel effects, by the variation of the *application* of the refrain—the refrain itself remaining, for the most part, unvaried.

These points being settled, I next bethought me of the *nature* of my refrain. Since its application was to be repeatedly varied, it was clear that the refrain itself must be brief, for there would have been an insurmountable difficulty in frequent variations of application in any sentence of length. In proportion to the brevity of the sentence, would, of course, be the facility of the variation. This led me at once to a single word as the best refrain.

The question now arose as to the *character* of the word. Having made up my mind to a refrain, the division of the poem into stanzas was, of course, a corollary: the refrain forming the close of each stanza. That such a close, to have force, must be sonorous and susceptible of protracted emphasis, admitted no doubt; and these considerations inevitably led me to the long *o* as the most sonorous vowel, in connection with *r* as the most producible consonant.

The sound of the refrain being thus determined, it became necessary to select a word embodying this sound, and at the same time in the fullest possible keeping with that melancholy which I had predetermined as the tone of the poem. In such a search it would have been absolutely impossible to overlook the word "Nevermore." In fact, it was the very first which presented itself.

The next *desideratum* was a pretext for the continuous use of the one word "Nevermore." In observing the difficulty which I at once found in inventing a sufficiently plausible reason for its continuous repetition, I did not fail to perceive that this difficulty arose solely from the pre-assumption that the word was to be so continuously or monotonously spoken by a *human* being—I did not fail to perceive, in short, that the difficulty lay in the reconciliation of this monotony with the exercise of reason on the part of the creature repeating the word. Here, then, immediately arose the idea of a *non-reasoning* creature capable of speech; and, very naturally, a parrot, in the first instance, suggested itself, but was superseded forthwith by a Raven, as equally capable of speech, and infinitely more in keeping with the intended *tone*.

I had now gone so far as the conception of a Raven—the bird of ill omen—monotonously repeating the one word, "Nevermore" at the conclusion of each stanza, in a poem of melancholy tone, and in length about one hundred lines. Now, never losing sight of the object *supremeness*, or perfection, at all points, I asked myself—"Of all melancholy topics, what, according to the *universal* understanding of mankind, is the *most* melancholy?" "Death"—was the obvious reply. "And when," I said, "is this most melancholy of topics most poetical?" From what I have already explained at some length, the answer, here also, is obvious—"When it most closely allies itself to *Beauty*." The death, then, of a beautiful woman is, unquestionably, the most poetical topic in the world—and equally is it beyond doubt that the lips best suited for such topic are those of a bereaved lover.

I had now to combine the two ideas, of a lover lamenting his deceased mistress, and a Raven continuously repeating the word "Nevermore." I had to combine these, bearing in mind my design of varying, at every turn, the *application* of the word repeated; but the only intelligible mode of such combination is that of imagining the Raven employing the word in answer to the queries of the lover. And here it was that I saw at once the opportunity afforded for the effect on which I had been depending—that is to say, the effect of the *variation of application*. I saw that I could make the first query propounded by the lover—the first query to which the Raven should reply "Nevermore"—that I could make this first query a commonplace one—the second less so—the third still less, and so on—until at length the lover, startled from his original *nonchalance* by the melancholy character of the word itself—by its frequent repetition—and by a consideration of the ominous reputation of the fowl that uttered it—is at length excited to superstition, and wildly propounds queries of a far different character—queries whose solution he has passionately at heart—propounds them half in superstition and half in that species of despair which delights in self-torture—propounds them not altogether because he believes in the prophetic or demoniac character of the bird (which, reason assures him, is merely repeating a lesson learned by rote) but because he experiences a phrenzied pleasure in so modeling his questions as to receive from the *expected* "Nevermore" the most delicious because the most intolerable of sorrow. Perceiving the opportunity thus afforded me—or, more strictly, thus forced upon me in the progress of the construction—

I first established in mind the climax, or concluding query—that query to which "Nevermore" should be in the last place an answer—that in reply to which this word "Nevermore" should involve the utmost conceivable amount of sorrow and despair.

Here then the poem may be said to have its beginning—at the end, where all works of art should begin—for it was here, at this point of my preconsiderations, that I first put pen to paper in the composition of the stanza:

"Prophet," said I, "thing of evil! prophet still if bird or devil!
By that heaven that bends above us—by that God we both adore,
Tell this soul with sorrow laden, if within the distant Aidenn,
It shall clasp a sainted maiden whom the angels name Lenore—
Clasp a rare and radiant maiden whom the angels name Lenore."
           Quoth the Raven, "Nevermore."

I composed this stanza, at this point, first, that by establishing the climax, I might the better vary and graduate, as regards seriousness and importance, the preceding queries of the lover; and secondly, that I might definitely settle the rhythm, the meter, and the length and general arrangement of the stanza,—as well as graduate the stanzas which were to precede, so that none of them might surpass this in rhythmical effect. Had I been able, in the subsequent composition, to construct more vigorous stanzas, I should, without scruple, have purposely enfeebled them, so as not to interfere with the climacteric effect.

And here I may as well say a few words of the versification. My first object (as usual) was originality. The extent to which this has been neglected, in versification, is one of the most unaccountable things in the world. Admitting that there is little possibility of variety in mere *rhythm*, it is still clear that the possible varieties of meter and stanza are absolutely infinite—and yet, *for centuries, no man, in verse, has ever done, or ever seemed to think of doing, an original thing.* The fact is, that originality (unless in minds of very unusual force) is by no means a matter, as some suppose, of impulse or intuition. In general, to be found, it must be elaborately sought, and although a positive merit of the highest class, demands in its attainment less of invention than negation.

Of course, I pretend to no originality in either the rhythm or meter of *The Raven.* The former is trochaic—the latter is octameter acatalectic, alternating with heptameter catalectic repeated in the refrain of the fifth verse, and terminating with tetrameter catalectic. Less pedantically—the feet employed throughout (trochees) consist of a long syllable followed by a short: the first line of the stanza consists of eight of these feet—the second of seven and a half (in effect two-thirds)—the third of eight—the fourth of seven and a half—the fifth the same—the sixth three and a half. Now, each of these lines, taken individually, has been employed before; and what originality *The Raven* has, is in their *combination into stanza*; nothing even remotely approaching this combination has ever been attempted. The effect of this originality of combination is aided by other unusual, and some altogether novel effects, arising from an extension of the application of the principles of rhyme and alliteration.

The next point to be considered was the mode of bringing together the lover and the Raven—and the first branch of this consideration was the *locale*. For this the most natural suggestion might seem to be a forest, or the fields—but it has always appeared to me that a close *circumscription of space* is absolutely necessary to the effect of in-sulated incident:—it has the force of a frame to a picture. It has an indisputable moral power in keeping concentrated the attention, and, of course, must not be confounded with mere unity of place.

I determined, then, to place the lover in his chamber—in a chamber rendered sacred to him by memories of her who had frequented it. The room is represented as richly furnished—this in mere pursuance of the ideas I have already explained on the subject of Beauty, as the sole true poetical thesis.

The *locale* being thus determined, I had now to introduce the bird—and the thought of introducing him through the window, was inevitable. The idea of making the lover suppose, in the first instance, that the flapping of the wings of the bird against the shutter, is a "tapping" at the door, originated in a wish to increase, by prolonging, the reader's curiosity, and in a desire to admit the incidental effect arising from the lover's throwing open the door, finding all dark, and thence adopting the half-fancy that it was the spirit of his mistress that knocked.

I made the night tempestuous, first, to account for the Raven's seeking admission, and secondly, for the effect of contrast with the (physical) serenity within the chamber.

I made the bird alight on the bust of Pallas, also for the effect of contrast between the marble and the plumage—it being understood that the bust was absolutely *suggested* by the bird—the bust of *Pallas* being chosen, first, as most in keeping with the scholarship of the lover, and secondly, for the sonorousness of the word, *Pallas*, itself.

About the middle of the poem, also, I have availed myself of the force of contrast, with a view of deepening the ultimate impression. For example, an air of the fantastic—approaching as nearly to the ludicrous as was admissible—is given to the Raven's entrance. He comes in "with many a flirt and flutter."

Not the *least obeisance made he*—not a moment stopped or stayed he,
But with *mien of lord or lady*, perched above my chamber door.

In the two stanzas which follow, the design is more obviously carried out:—

Then this ebony bird beguiling my sad fancy into smiling
By the *grave and stern decorum of the countenance it wore*,
"Though thy *crest be shorn and shaven* thou," I said, "art sure no craven,
Ghastly grim and ancient Raven wandering from the nightly shore—
Tell me what thy lordly name is on the Night's Plutonian shore?"
      Quoth the Raven, "Nevermore."

Much I marvelled *this ungainly fowl* to hear discourse so plainly
Though its answer little meaning—little relevancy bore;
For we cannot help agreeing that no living human being
Ever yet was blessed with seeing bird above his chamber door—
Bird or beast upon the sculptured bust above his chamber door,
      With such name as "Nevermore."

The effect of the *dénouement* being thus provided for, I immediately drop the fantastic for a tone of the most profound seriousness—this tone commencing in the stanza directly following the one last quoted, with the line,

But the Raven, sitting lonely on that placid bust, spoke only, etc.

From this epoch the lover no longer jests—no longer sees any thing even of the fantastic in the Raven's demeanor. He speaks of him as a "grim, ungainly, ghastly, gaunt, and ominous bird of yore," and feels the "fiery eyes" burning into his "bosom's core." This revolution of thought, or fancy, on the lover's part, is intended to induce a similar one on the part of the reader—to bring the mind into a proper frame for the *dénouement*—which is now brought about as rapidly and as *directly* as possible.

With the *dénouement* proper—with the Raven's reply, "Nevermore," to the lover's final demand if he shall meet his mistress in another world—the poem, in its obvious phase, that of a simple narrative, may be said to have its completion. So far, every thing is within the limits of the accountable—of the real. A raven, having learned by rote the single word "Nevermore," and having escaped from the custody of its owner, is driven at midnight, through the violence of a storm, to seek admission at a window from which a light still gleams—the chamber-window of a student, occupied half in poring over a volume, half in dreaming of a beloved mistress deceased. The casement being thrown open at the fluttering of the bird's wings, the bird itself perches on the most convenient seat out of the immediate reach of the student, who, amused by the incident and the oddity of the visitor's demeanor, demands of it, in jest and without looking for a reply, its name. The raven addressed, answers with its customary word, "Nevermore"—a word which finds immediate echo in the melancholy heart of the student, who, giving utterance aloud to certain thoughts suggested by the occasion, is again startled by the fowl's repetition of "Nevermore." The student now guesses the state of the case, but is impelled, as I have before explained, by the human thirst for self-torture, and in part by superstition, to propound such queries to the bird as will bring him, the lover, the most of the luxury of sorrow, through the anticipated answer "Nevermore." With the indulgence, to the extreme, of this self-torture, the narration, in what I have termed its first or obvious phase, has a natural termination, and so far there has been no overstepping of the limits of the real.

But in subjects so handled, however skilfully, or with however vivid an array of incident, there is always a certain hardness or nakedness, which repels the artistical eye. Two things are invariably required—first, some amount of complexity, or more properly, adaptation; and, secondly, some amount of suggestiveness—some under-current, however indefinite, of meaning. It is this latter, in especial, which imparts to a work of art so much of that *richness* (to borrow from colloquy a forcible term) which we are too fond of confounding with *the ideal*. It is the *excess* of the suggested meaning—it is the rendering this the upper instead of the under current of the theme—which turns into prose (and that of the very flattest kind) the so-called poetry of the so-called transcendentalists.

Holding these opinions, I added the two concluding stanzas of the poem—their suggestiveness being thus made to pervade all the narrative which has preceded them. The undercurrent of meaning is rendered first apparent in the lines—

"Take thy beak from out *my heart*, and take thy form from off my
    door!"
       Quoth the Raven, "Nevermore!"

It will be observed that the words, "from out my heart," involve the first metaphorical expression in the poem. They, with the answer, "Nevermore," dispose the mind to seek a moral in all that has been previously narrated. The reader begins now to regard the Raven as emblematical—but it is not until the very last line of the very last stanza, that the intention of making him emblematical of *Mournful and Never-ending Remembrance* is permitted distinctly to be seen:

And the Raven, never flitting, still is sitting, still is sitting,
On the pallid bust of Pallas, just above my chamber door;
And his eyes have all the seeming of a demon's that is dreaming,
And the lamplight o'er him streaming throws his shadow on the floor;
And my soul *from out that shadow* that lies floating on the floor
      Shall be lifted—nevermore.

1846

From The Poetic Principle[5]

In speaking of the Poetic Principle, I have no design to be either thorough or profound. While discussing, very much at random, the essentiality of what we call Poetry, my principal purpose will be to cite for consideration some few of those minor English or American poems which best suit my own taste, or which, upon my own fancy, have left the most definite impression. By "minor poems" I mean, of course, poems of little length. And here, in the beginning, permit me to say a few words in regard to a somewhat peculiar principle, which, whether rightfully or wrongfully, has always had its influence in my own critical estimate of the poem. I hold that a long poem does not exist. I maintain that the phrase, "a long poem," is simply a flat contradiction in terms.

I need scarcely observe that a poem deserves its title only inasmuch as it excites, by elevating the soul. The value of the poem is in the ratio of this elevating excitement. But all excitements are, through a psychal[6] necessity, transient. That degree of excitement which would entitle a poem to be so called at all, cannot be sustained throughout a composition of any great length. After the lapse of half an hour, at the very utmost, it flags—fails—a revulsion ensues— and then the poem is, in effect, and in fact, no longer such.

There are, no doubt, many who have found difficulty in reconciling the critical dictum that the "Paradise Lost" is to be devoutly admired throughout, with the absolute impossibility of maintaining for it, during perusal, the amount of enthusiasm which that critical dictum would demand. This great work, in fact, is to be regarded as poetical only when, losing sight of that vital requisite in all works of Art, Unity, we view it merely as a series of minor poems. If, to preserve its Unity—its totality of effect or impression—we read it (as would be necessary) at a single sitting, the result is but a constant alternation of excitement and depression. After a passage of what we feel to be true poetry, there follows, inevitably, a passage of platitude which no critical pre-judgment can force us to admire; but if, upon completing the work, we read it again, omitting the first book—that is to say, commencing with the second—we shall be surprised at now finding that admirable which we before condemned—

5. Poe's final statement of his poetic credo refines and clarifies much that he said in earlier essays. His analytical reconsideration of these principles through the years now results in an assured consistency where previously contradictions appeared. This is especially noticeable in his recognition of moral truth as a principal objective. He still insists on the primary rôle of beauty; he still rejects didacticism; but he now clearly understands that intel-

lectual and spiritual truth are often principal factors in the functioning of aesthetic response. This composition was prepared as a lecture, and delivered several times in the last year of Poe's life. The next year it was printed three times: in the *Home Journal* for August 31, 1850; in *Sartain's Union Magazine* for October, 1850, and in Griswold's edition of the *Works* (1850).
6. Psychological.

that damnable which we had previously so much admired. It follows from all this that the ultimate, aggregate, or absolute effect of even the best epic under the sun, is a nullity; and this is precisely the fact.

In regard to the Iliad, we have, if not positive proof, at least very good reason, for believing it intended as a series of lyrics; but, granting the epic intention, I can say only that the work is based in an imperfect sense of Art. The modern epic is, of the supposititious ancient model, but an inconsiderate and blindfold imitation. But the day of these artistic anomalies is over. If, at any time, any very long poem were popular in reality, which I doubt, it is at least clear that no very long poem will ever be popular again.

That the extent of a poetical work is, *ceteris paribus*,[7] the measure of its merit, seems undoubtedly, when we thus state it, a proposition sufficiently absurd—yet we are indebted for it to the Quarterly Reviews. Surely there can be nothing in mere size, abstractly considered—there can be nothing in mere bulk, so far as a volume is concerned, which has so continuously elicited admiration from these saturnine pamphlets! A mountain, to be sure, by the mere sentiment of physical magnitude which it conveys, does impress us with a sense of the sublime—but no man is impressed after *this* fashion by the material grandeur of even "The Columbiad."[8] Even the Quarterlies have not instructed us to be so impressed by it. As yet, they have not insisted on our estimating Lamartine[9] by the cubic foot, or Pollok[1] by the pound—but what else are we to infer from their continued prating about "sustained effort"? If, by "sustained effort," any little gentleman has accomplished an epic, let us frankly commend him for the effort—if this indeed be a thing commendable—but let us forbear praising the epic on the effort's account. It is to be hoped that common sense, in the time to come, will prefer deciding upon a work of Art, rather by the impression it makes—by the effect it produces—than by the time it took to impress the effect, or by the amount of "sustained effort" which had been found necessary in effecting the impression. The fact is, that perseverance is one thing and genius quite another—nor can all the Quarterlies in Christendom confound them. By-and-by, this proposition, with many which I have just been urging, will be received as self-evident. In the meantime, by being generally condemned as falsities, they will not be essentially damaged as truths.

On the other hand, it is clear that a poem may be improperly brief. Undue brevity degenerates into mere epigrammatism. A very short poem, while now and then producing a brilliant or vivid, never

---

7. Other things being equal.
8. An enormous American "national epic," published in 1807 by Joel Barlow (1754–1812).
9. Alphonse de Lamartine (1790–

1869), popular and influential French romantic poet, who wrote voluminously.
1. Robert Pollok (1798–1827), Scottish poet; author (1827) of a verse essay of overwhelming length and dullness.

produces a profound or enduring effect. There must be the steady pressing down of the stamp upon the wax. De Béranger[2] has wrought innumerable things, pungent and spirit-stirring; but in general they have been too imponderous to stamp themselves deeply into the public attention, and thus, as so many feathers of fancy, have been blown aloft only to be whistled down the wind.

A remarkable instance of the effect of undue brevity in depressing a poem—in keeping it out of the popular view—is afforded by the following exquisite little Serenade:

> I arise from dreams of thee
>   In the first sweet sleep of night,
> When the winds are breathing low,
>   And the stars are shining bright;
> I arise from dreams of thee,
>   And a spirit in my feet
> Has led me—who knows how?—
>   To thy chamber-window, sweet!
>
> The wandering airs, they faint
>   On the dark, the silent stream—
> The champak odors fail
>   Like sweet thoughts in a dream;
> The nightingale's complaint,
>   It dies upon her heart,
> As I must die on thine,
>   O, beloved as thou art!
>
> O, lift me from the grass!
>   I die, I faint, I fail!
> Let thy love in kisses rain
>   On my lips and eyelids pale.
> My cheek is cold and white, alas!
>   My heart beats loud and fast:
> Oh! press it close to thine again,
>   Where it will break at last!

Very few perhaps are familiar with these lines—yet no less a poet than Shelley is their author. Their warm, yet delicate and ethereal imagination will be appreciated by all—but by none so thoroughly as by him who has himself arisen from sweet dreams of one beloved, to bathe in the aromatic air of a southern midsummer night.

One of the finest poems by Willis[3]—the very best in my opinion which he has ever written—has, no doubt, through this same defect

2. Pierre Jean de Béranger (1780–1857), French lyric poet of the masses; *Cf.* review of *Twice-Told Tales.*

3. Nathaniel Parker Willis (1806–1867), then a popular poet and editor in New York.

of undue brevity, been kept back from its proper position, not less in the critical than in the popular view.

> The shadows lay along Broadway,
>   'Twas near the twilight-tide—
> And slowly there a lady fair
>   Was walking in her pride.
> Alone walk'd she; but, viewlessly,
>   Walk'd spirits at her side.
>
> Peace charm'd the street beneath her feet,
>   And Honour charm'd the air;
> And all astir looked kind on her,
>   And call'd her good and fair—
> For all God ever gave to her
>   She kept with chary care.
>
> She kept with care her beauties rare
>   From lovers warm and true—
> For her heart was cold to all but gold,
>   And the rich came not to woo—
> But honour'd well are charms to sell,
>   If priests the selling do.
>
> Now walking there was one more fair—
>   A slight girl, lily-pale;
> And she had unseen company
>   To make the spirit quail—
> 'Twixt Want and Scorn she walk'd forlorn,
>   And nothing could avail.
>
> No mercy now can clear her brow
>   For this world's peace to pray;
> For, as love's wild prayer dissolved in air,
>   Her woman's heart gave way!—
> But the sin forgiven by Christ in Heaven
>   By man is cursed alway!

In this composition we find it difficult to recognize the Willis who has written so many mere "verses of society." The lines are not only richly ideal, but full of energy; while they breathe an earnestness—an evident sincerity of sentiment—for which we look in vain throughout all the other works of this author.

While the epic mania—while the idea that, to merit in poetry, prolixity is indispensable—has for some years past been gradually dying out of the public mind by mere dint of its own absurdity—we find it succeeded by a heresy too palpably false to be long tolerated, but one which, in the brief period it has already endured, may be said to have accomplished more in the corruption of our Poetical Literature than all its other enemies combined. I allude to the heresy of The Didactic. It has been assumed, tacitly and avowedly, directly and indirectly, that the ultimate object of all Poetry is Truth. Every poem, it is said, should inculcate a moral; and by this moral is the poetical merit of the work to be adjudged. We Americans especially have patronized this happy idea; and we Bostonians, very especially, have developed it in full. We have taken it into our heads that to write a poem simply for the poem's sake, and to acknowledge such to have been our design, would be to confess ourselves radically wanting in the true Poetic dignity and force:—but the simple fact is, that would we but permit ourselves to look into our own souls, we should immediately there discover that under the sun there neither exists nor can exist any work more thoroughly dignified—more supremely noble than this very poem—this poem *per se,* this poem which is a poem and nothing more—this poem written solely for the poem's sake.

With as deep a reverence for the True as ever inspired the bosom of man, I would nevertheless limit, in some measure, its modes of inculcation. I would limit to enforce them. I would not enfeeble them by dissipation. The demands of Truth are severe. She has no sympathy with the myrtles. All *that* which is so indispensable in Song is precisely all that with which she has nothing whatever to do. It is but making her a flaunting paradox to wreathe her in gems and flowers. In enforcing a truth, we need severity rather than efflorescence of language. We must be simple, precise, terse. We must be cool, calm, unimpassioned. In a word, we must be in that mood which, as nearly as possible, is the exact converse of the poetical. *He* must be blind indeed who does not perceive the radical and chasmal differences between the truthful and the poetical modes of inculcation. He must be theory-mad beyond redemption who, in spite of these differences, shall still persist in attempting to reconcile the obstinate oils and waters of Poetry and Truth.

Dividing the world of mind into its three most immediately obvious distinctions, we have the Pure Intellect, Taste, and the Moral Sense. I place Taste in the middle, because it is just this position which, in the mind, it occupies. It holds intimate relations with either extreme; but from the Moral Sense is separated by so faint a difference that Aristotle has not hesitated to place some of its operations among the virtues themselves. Nevertheless, we find the offices of the trio marked with a sufficient distinction. Just as the Intellect concerns itself with Truth, so Taste informs us of the Beautiful while the Moral Sense is regardful of Duty. Of this latter, while Conscience teaches the obligation, and Reason the expediency, Taste contents herself with displaying the charms:—waging war upon Vice solely on the ground of her deformity, her disproportion, her animosity to the fitting, to the appropriate, to the harmonious, in a word, to Beauty.

An immortal instinct, deep within the spirit of man, is thus plainly a sense of the Beautiful. This it is which administers to his delight in the manifold forms, and sounds, and odors, and sentiments, amid which he exists. And just as the lily is repeated in the lake, or the eyes of Amaryllis in the mirror, so is the mere oral or written repetition of these forms, and sounds, and colors, and odors, and sentiments, a duplicate source of delight. But this mere repetition is not poetry. He who shall simply sing, with however glowing enthusiasm, or with however vivid a truth of description, of the sights, and sounds, and odors, and colors, and sentiments, which greet him in common with all mankind—he, I say, has yet failed to prove his divine title. There is still a something in the distance which he has been unable to attain. We have still a thirst unquenchable, to allay which he has not shown us the crystal springs. This thirst belongs to the immortality of Man. It is at once a consequence and an indication of his perennial existence. It is the desire of the moth for the star. It is no mere appreciation of the Beauty before us—but a wild effort to reach the Beauty above. Inspired by an ecstatic prescience of the glories beyond the grave, we struggle by multiform combinations among the things and thoughts of Time, to attain a portion of that Loveliness whose very elements, perhaps, appertain to eternity alone. And thus when by Poetry—or when by Music, the most entrancing of the Poetic moods—we find ourselves melted into tears—we weep then—not as the Abbate Gravina[4] supposes—through excess of pleasure, but through a certain, petulant, impatient sorrow at our inability to grasp now, wholly, here on earth, at once and forever, those divine and rapturous joys, of which through the poem or through the music, we attain to but brief and indeterminate glimpses.

The struggle to apprehend the supernal Loveliness—this struggle, on the part of souls fittingly constituted—has given to the world all that which it (the world) has ever been enabled at once to understand and to feel as poetic.

The Poetic Sentiment, of course, may develop itself in various modes—in Painting, in Sculpture, in Architecture, in the Dance—very especially in Music—and very peculiarly, and with a wide field, in the composition of the Landscape Garden. Our present theme, however, has regard only to its manifestation in words. And here let me speak briefly on the topic of rhythm. Contenting myself with the certainty that Music, in its various modes of metre, rhythm, and rhyme, is of so vast a moment in Poetry as never to be wisely rejected—is so vitally important an adjunct that he is simply silly who de-

4. Giovanni Gravina (1664–1718), Italian jurist and critic.

clines its assistance, I will not now pause to maintain its absolute essentiality. It is in Music, perhaps, that the soul most nearly attains the great end for which, when inspired by the Poetic Sentiment, it struggles—the creation of supernal Beauty. It may be, indeed, that here this sublime end is, now and then, attained in fact. We are often made to feel, with a shivering delight, that from an earthly harp are stricken notes which cannot have been unfamiliar to the angels. And thus there can be little doubt that in the union of Poetry with Music in its popular sense, we shall find the widest field for the Poetic development. The old Bards and Minnesingers had advantages which we do not possess—and Thomas Moore,[5] singing his own songs, was, in the most legitimate manner, perfecting them as poems.

To recapitulate, then:—I would define, in brief, the Poetry of Words as The Rhythmical Creation of Beauty. Its sole arbiter is Taste. With the Intellect or with the Conscience, it has only collateral relations. Unless incidentally, it has no concern whatever either with Duty or with Truth.

A few words, however, in explanation. That pleasure which is at once the most pure, the most elevating, and the most intense, is derived, I maintain, from the contemplation of the Beautiful. In the contemplation of Beauty we alone find it possible to attain that pleasurable elevation, or excitement, of the soul, which we recognize as the Poetic Sentiment, and which is so easily distinguished from Truth, which is the satisfaction of the Reason, or from Passion, which is the excitement of the heart. I make Beauty, therefore—using the word as inclusive of the sublime—I make Beauty the province of the poem, simply because it is an obvious rule of Art that effects should be made to spring as directly as possible from their causes:—no one as yet having been weak enough to deny that the peculiar elevation in question is at least most readily attainable in the poem. It by no means follows, however, that the incitements of Passion, or the precepts of Duty, or even the lessons of Truth, may not be introduced into a poem, and with advantage; for they may subserve, incidentally, in various ways, the general purposes of the work: —but the true artist will always contrive to tone them down in proper subjection to that Beauty which is the atmosphere and the real essence of the poem.

I cannot better introduce the few poems which I shall present for your consideration, than by the citation of the Proem to Mr. Longfellow's "Waif":[6]

> The day is done, and the darkness
> Falls from the wings of Night,

<hr/>

5. Thomas Moore (1779–1852), Irish poet-composer, was famous for the private performance of his own songs.

6. Title of an anthology edited by Longfellow in 1844.

As a feather is wafted downward
From an eagle in his flight.

I see the lights of the village
Gleam through the rain and the mist,
And a feeling of sadness comes o'er me,
That my soul cannot resist;

A feeling of sadness and longing,
That is not akin to pain,
And resembles sorrow only
As the mist resembles the rain.

Come, read to me some poem,
Some simple and heartfelt lay,
That shall soothe this restless feeling,
And banish the thoughts of day.

Not from the grand old masters,
Not from the bards sublime,
Whose distant footsteps echo
Through the corridors of Time.

For, like strains of martial music,
Their mighty thoughts suggest
Life's endless toil and endeavor;
And to-night I long for rest.

Read from some humbler poet,
Whose songs gushed from his heart,
As showers from the clouds of summer,
Or tears from the eyelids start;

Who through long days of labor,
And nights devoid of ease,
Still heard in his soul the music
Of wonderful melodies.

Such songs have power to quiet
The restless pulse of care,
And come like the benediction
That follows after prayer.

Then read from the treasured volume
The poem of thy choice,
And lend to the rhyme of the poet
The beauty of thy voice.

And the night shall be filled with music,
And the cares, that infest the day,

> Shall fold their tents, like the Arabs,
>   And as silently steal away.

With no great range of imagination, these lines have been justly admired for their delicacy of expression. Some of the images are very effective. Nothing can be better than

> ——The bards sublime,
> Whose distant footsteps echo
> Down the corridors of Time.

The idea of the last quatrain is also very effective. The poem, on the whole, however, is chiefly to be admired for the graceful *insouciance* of its metre, so well in accordance with the character of the sentiments, and especially for the *ease* of the general manner. This "ease" or naturalness, in a literary style, it has long been the fashion to regard as ease in appearance alone—as a point of really difficult attainment. But not so:—a natural manner is difficult only to him who should never meddle with it—to the unnatural. It is but the result of writing with the understanding, or with the instinct, that the *tone*, in composition, should always be that which the mass of mankind would adopt—and must perpetually vary, of course, with the occasion. The author who, after the fashion of "The North American Review," should be, upon all occasions, merely "quiet," must necessarily upon many occasions be simply silly, or stupid; and has no more right to be considered "easy" or "natural" than a Cockney exquisite, or than the sleeping Beauty in the wax-works.

Among the minor poems of Bryant, none has so much impressed me as the one which he entitles "June." I quote only a portion of it:

> There, through the long, long summer hours,
>   The golden light should lie,
> And thick young herbs and groups of flowers
>   Stand in their beauty by.
> The oriole should build and tell
> His love-tale, close beside my cell;
>   The idle butterfly
> Should rest him there, and there be heard
> The housewife-bee and humming bird.
>
> And what, if cheerful shouts, at noon
>   Come, from the village sent,
> Or songs of maids, beneath the moon,
>   With fairy laughter blent?
> And what if, in the evening light,
> Betrothed lovers walk in sight
>   Of my low monument?

I would the lovely scene around
Might know no sadder sight nor sound.

I know, I know I should not see
    The season's glorious show,
Nor would its brightness shine for me,
    Nor its wild music flow;
But if, around my place of sleep,
The friends I love should come to weep,
    They might not haste to go.
Soft airs, and song, and light, and bloom
Should keep them lingering by my tomb.

These to their soften'd hearts should bear
    The thought of what has been,
And speak of one who cannot share
    The gladness of the scene;
Whose part in all the pomp that fills
The circuit of the summer hills,
    Is—that his grave is green;
And deeply would their hearts rejoice
To hear again his living voice.

The rhythmical flow, here, is even voluptuous—nothing could be
more melodious. The poem has always affected me in a remarkable
manner. The intense melancholy which seems to well up, perforce, to
the surface of all the poet's cheerful sayings about his grave, we find
thrilling us to the soul—while there is the truest poetic elevation in
the thrill. The impression left is one of a pleasurable sadness. And
if, in the remaining compositions which I shall introduce to you,
there be more or less of a similar tone always apparent, let me remind
you that (how or why we know not) this certain taint of sadness is
inseparably connected with all the higher manifestations of true
Beauty.[7] * * *

From Alfred Tennyson—although in perfect sincerity I regard
him as the noblest poet that ever lived—I have left myself time to
cite only a very brief specimen. I call him, and think him the noblest
of poets—not because the impressions he produces are, at all times,
the most profound—not because the poetical excitement which he
induces is, at all times, the most intense—but because it is, at all
times, the most ethereal—in other words, the most elevating and
most pure. No poet is so little of the earth, earthy. What I am about
to read is from his last long poem, "The Princess":

Tears, idle tears, I know not what they mean,
Tears from the depth of some divine despair

7. At this point in his lecture Poe read,
without notable constructive comment,
a number of minor poems, then popular,
of Edward Coote Pinkney, Thomas
Moore, Thomas Hood, and Byron.

Rise in the heart, and gather to the eyes,
In looking on the happy Autumn-fields,
And thinking of the days that are no more.

Fresh as the first beam glittering on a sail,
That brings our friends up from the underworld,
Sad as the last which reddens over one
That sinks with all we love below the verge;
So sad, so fresh, the days that are no more.

Ah, sad and strange as in dark summer dawns
The earliest pipe of half-awaken'd birds
To dying ears, when unto dying eyes
The casement slowly grows a glimmering square;
So sad, so strange, the days that are no more.

Dear as remember'd kisses after death,
And sweet as those by hopeless fancy feign'd
On lips that are for others; deep as love,
Deep as first love, and wild with all regret;
O Death in Life, the days that are no more.

Thus, although in a very cursory and imperfect manner, I have endeavoured to convey to you my conception of the Poetic Principle. It has been my purpose to suggest that, while this Principle itself is strictly and simply the Human Aspiration for Supernal Beauty, the manifestation of the Principle is always found in an elevating excitement of the Soul—quite independent of that passion which is the intoxication of the Heart—or of that Truth which is the satisfaction of the Reason. For in regard to Passion, alas! its tendency is to degrade, rather than to elevate the Soul. Love, on the contrary—Love—the true, the divine Eros—the Uranian, as distinguished from the Dionaean Venus—is unquestionably the purest and truest of all poetical themes.[8] And in regard to Truth—if, to be sure, through the attainment of a truth, we are led to perceive a harmony where none was apparent before, we experience, at once, the true poetical effect—but this effect is referable to the harmony alone, and not in the least degree to the truth which merely served to render the harmony manifest.

We shall reach, however, more immediately a distinct conception of what the true Poetry is, by mere reference to a few of the simple elements which induce in the Poet himself the true poetical effect. He recognizes the ambrosia which nourishes his soul, in the bright orbs that shine in Heaven—in the volutes of the flower—in the clustering of low shrubberies—in the waving of the grain-fields—in the slanting of tall, Eastern trees—in the blue distance of moun-

8. Compare with the poem "Ulalume." Here again Poe contrasts celestial love —the Greek god Eros, the Uranian or heavenly one—with the earthly love of Dionæa, or Aphrodite.

tains—in the grouping of clouds—in the twinkling of half-hidden
brooks—in the gleaming of silver rivers—in the repose of sequestered
lakes—in the star-mirroring depths of lonely wells. He perceives it in
the songs of birds—in the harp of Aeolus[9]—in the sighing of the
night-wind—in the repining voice of the forest—in the surf that
complains to the shore—in the fresh breath of the woods—in the
scent of the violet—in the voluptuous perfume of the hyacinth—
in the suggestive odor that comes to him, at eventide, from far-
distant, undiscovered islands, over dim oceans, illimitable and unexplored. He owns it in all noble thoughts—in all unworldly motives
—in all holy impulses—in all chivalrous, generous, and self-sacrificing
deeds. He feels it in the beauty of woman—in the grace of her
step—in the lustre of her eye—in the melody of her voice—in her
soft laughter—in her sigh—in the harmony of the rustling of her
robes. He deeply feels it in her winning endearments—in her burning enthusiasms—in her gentle charities—in her meek and devotional endurances—but above all—ah, far above all—he kneels to
it—he worships it in the faith, in the purity, in the strength, in the
altogether divine majesty—of her love.[1] * * *

1848   1850

9. Aeolus was the Greek god of the
winds; his harp, played by the breezes,
became a romantic symbol of spontaneous song.

1. Poe then concludes the "lecture" with
a brief "recitation," one of the cavalier
ballads of William Motherwell, a Scottish romantic then in vogue.

HERMAN MELVILLE
(1819–1891)

Melville's parents were both of
substantial New York families,
but his father's bankruptcy, soon
followed by his death, left the
mother in financial difficulties
when the boy was only twelve.
She then settled near Albany,
where Melville for a time attended the local academy. Following a brief career as a clerk in
his brother's store and in a bank,
he went to sea at the age of eighteen. His experiences as a merchant sailor on the *Highlander*
and ashore in the slums of Liverpool, later recalled in *Redburn*,
awakened the abhorrence, ex-

pressed throughout his fiction, of
the darkness of man's deeds, and
the evil seemingly inherent in
nature itself. After this first brief
seafaring interlude, he taught
school and began to write sporadically.

In 1841, he shipped once more
before the mast, aboard a New
Bedford whaler, the *Acushnet*,
bound for the Pacific. Altogether,
it was nearly four years before he
returned from the South Seas.
After eighteen months he deserted the whaler, in company
with a close friend, at Nukuhiva,
in the Marquesas Islands. In

Typee, these adventures are embellished by fictional license, but the author and "Toby" Green certainly spent at least a month among the handsome Marquesan Taipis, whose free and idyllic island life was flawed by their regrettable habit of eating their enemies. A passing whaler provided an "escape" to Tahiti. Melville soon shipped on another whaler, *Leviathan,* which carried him finally to the Hawaiian Islands, perhaps by way of Japan. In Honolulu he enlisted for naval service, aboard the U.S.S. *United States,* and was discharged fourteen months later at Boston.

The youth had had a compelling personal experience, and being a natural writer, he at once set to work producing a fiction based in part on his own adventures, employing literary materials which he was the first American writer to exploit. *Typee* (London and New York, 1846) was the first modern novel of South Seas adventure, as the later *Moby-Dick* was the first literary classic of whaling. Indeed, Melville wrote little of significance that was not suggested by his experiences prior to his discharge from the Navy. His impulsive literary energies drove him steadily for eleven years, during which he was the author of ten major volumes; then his fiction writing suddenly ceased, and his life fell into seeming confusion, producing an enigma endlessly intriguing to his critics.

In the beginning he was almost embarrassed by success. *Typee* was at once recognized for the merits which have made it a classic, but its author was notoriously identified as the character

who had lived and eaten with cannibals, and loved the dusky Fayaway—an uncomfortable position for a young New Yorker just married to the daughter of a Boston chief justice. *Omoo* (1847), somewhat inferior to *Typee,* was also a successful novel of Pacific adventures. *Mardi* (1849) began to puzzle a public impatient of symbolic enigmas; but *Redburn* (1849) and *White-Jacket* (1850) were novels of exciting adventure, although the first, as has been suggested above, devotes much of its energy to sociological satire, while the second emphasizes the floggings and other cruelties and degradations then imposed upon enlisted men of the United States Navy.

In 1851, Melville's masterpiece, *Moby-Dick,* was published. A robust and realistic novel of adventure, drawing upon the author's fascination with the whale and whaling, it achieves a compelling symbolism in the character of Captain Ahab, whose monomaniacal fury against the whale, or the evil it represents to him, sends him to his death. This book is now seen as one of a trilogy, including the earlier *Mardi,* and *Pierre* (1852), but neither of the others is wholly comprehensible or successful. Together, however, they represent the struggle of man against his destiny at various levels of experience.

In 1850, Melville had established a residence at Arrowhead, a farm near Pittsfield, Massachusetts. There, completing *Moby-Dick,* with Hawthorne nearby, a stimulating new friend, he was at the height of his career, but curiously near its sudden decline.

After *Moby-Dick*, he published but one more volume of distinguished merit—*The Piazza Tales* (1856), a collection of such smaller masterpieces as "Benito Cereno," "Bartleby the Scrivener," and "The Encantadas." *Pierre* was denounced on moral grounds, and because there was marked confusion of narrative elements and symbolism in that strange novel of incest. *Israel Potter* (1855) and *The Confidence-Man* (1857), both inferior, virtually ended his career as a writer, although he lived for thirty-four years afterward. Readers in general did not understand the symbolic significance of his works, his sales were unsatisfactory, and when the plates of his volumes were destroyed in a publisher's fire, the books were not reprinted. Perhaps he was written out. Four volumes of minor poems, printed chiefly at his uncle's expense, appeared at long intervals.

After some hard and bitter years he settled down humbly in 1866 as a customs inspector in New York, at the foot of Gansevoort Street, which had been named for his mother's distinguished family. Before doing so, however, he launched himself on a pursuit of certainty, a tour to the Holy Land, that inspired *Clarel*. This tedious poem contains a few quite memorable passages, but as in his novels, poetry remained an implicit quality, never satisfactorily expressed. The Civil War involved him deeply in a human cause, and produced a sensitive record, seldom high poetry, in *Battle-Pieces and Aspects of the War* (1866).

In *Billy Budd*, printed below,

the novelist recaptured his highest powers during the very last years of his life. He worked on the novelette from November, 1888, until April, 1891, and the manuscript was not fully prepared for press when he died the following September 28 (see the first note to *Billy Budd*). The story is related to the author's earliest adventures at sea; its theme has obvious relations with that of *Moby-Dick*; yet the essential spirit of the work cancels the infuriated rebellion of Captain Ahab. In its reconciliation of the temporal with the eternal there is a sense of luminous peace and atonement.

Even in Melville's greatest works there are undeniable and glaring defects, and such novels as *Mardi* and *Pierre* are distinguished failures, interesting only to the critic. Melville's greatness is something no commentator has quite explained. It shines above the stylistic awkwardness of many passages, the blurred outlines that result from the confusion of autobiography with invented action, the tendency of the author to lose control of his own symbols, or to set the metaphysical thunderbolt side by side with factual discussion or commonplace realism. Having survived the neglect of his contemporaries and the elaborate attentions of recent critics, he emerges secure in the power and influence of *Typee*, *Moby-Dick*, *The Piazza Tales*, and *Billy Budd*.

Melville's works were collected as *The Works of Herman Melville*, 16 vols., 1922–1924. A projected collected works under scholarly auspices, still without final definition, has resulted in good editions of *Collected Poems*, edited by H. P. Vincent, 1945; *Piazza Tales*, edited by E. S. Oliver, 1948; *Pierre*, edited by H. S. Murray, 1949; *Moby Dick*, edited by Luther S. Mansfield and Howard P. Vincent, 1952. *Moby Dick* was also well edited by Willard Thorp, 1947. Among one-volume collections, see the same editor's *Melville: Representative Selections*, with admirable notes and introduction, American Writers Series, 1938. Popular reprints of *Moby Dick* are legion.

R. M. Weaver, *Herman Melville: Mariner and Mystic*, 1921, was the first full-length biography. Later notable biographies and studies are John Free-

man, *Herman Melville*, 1926; Lewis Mumford, *Herman Melville*, 1929; Charles R. Anderson, *Melville in the South Seas*, 1939; William Braswell, *Melville's Religious Thought*, 1943; W. E. Sedgwick, *Herman Melville: The Tragedy of Mind*, 1944; H. P. Vincent, *The Trying Out of Moby Dick*, 1949; Leon Howard, *Herman Melville: A Biography*, 1951; Jay Leyda, *Melville Log: A Documentary Life of Herman Melville*, 1951; and Eleanor Melville Metcalf, *Herman Melville: Cycle and Epicycle*, 1953.

Billy Budd[1]

Preface[2]

The year 1797, the year of this narrative, belongs to a period which, as every thinker now feels, involved a crisis for Christendom not exceeded in its undetermined momentousness at the time by any other era whereof there is record. The opening proposition made by the Spirit of that Age involved rectification of the Old World's hereditary wrongs. In France, to some extent, this was bloodily effected. But what then? Straightway the Revolution itself became a wrong-

1. *Billy Budd* is fundamentally significant for the interpretation of its enigmatic author and his masterpiece, *Moby-Dick*. From the moment of its dedicatory note, the author's private personality is intricately incorporated with his creative energy and narrative insight. The manuscript title is "Billy Budd / Sailor / (an inside narrative)"; and beneath it appears the following: "Dedicated to Jack Chase, Englishman, wherever that great heart may now be here on earth or harboured in paradise. Captain of the maintop in the year 1843 in the U.S. Frigate 'United States.'" Melville was a shipmate on that cruise, a young sailor experiencing the cruelties and hardships which he soon excoriated in *White-Jacket*, but also laying the foundations for the later acceptance of life which the tale of Billy Budd expresses. This testament of reconciliation provides a clarifying contrast with the novels of the earlier period, with the young novelist's heartbreaking rebellion against the overwhelming capacity for evil in man and the universe, and the inescapable doom, as in *Moby-Dick*, of those who pit themselves against the implacable Leviathan of God. In *Billy Budd* the author has made a truce, perhaps a peace. He is at least reconciled to the enigma represented by Captain Vere's ordeal in sentencing Billy to death for killing, in Claggart, the festering "depravity according to nature." By

"natural law," Billy is guiltless, but not by "[social] law operating through us[.] For that law and the rigour of it, we are not responsible." The novel was posthumously published as *Billy Budd, Foretopman* in 1924, as a supplement to *The Works * * * (1922–1924)*. This was not strictly edited, but all subsequent editions have been based on it. The text below is a new edition, representing a collation with the original manuscript in the Houghton Library of Harvard University by Miss Elizabeth Treeman, an assistant editor of Harvard University Press, and is here published for the first time by special arrangement with Harvard University Press. The present editors recognize that Melville probably did not finally prepare the manuscript for printing. Where additional punctuation is absolutely necessary for clarity, it has been inserted in square brackets. A few interpolated words, and all words not entirely clear in the manuscript have also been placed in square brackets. A few important variant readings left standing in the manuscript are shown in footnotes. Melville's chapter divisions are different from those in the 1924 edition, and we have followed his manuscript in this matter also.

2. The following Preface appeared in the first publication of this work, under the title *Billy Budd, Foretopman*, in 1924.

doer, one more oppressive than the kings. Under Napoleon it enthroned upstart kings, and initiated that prolonged agony of continual war whose final throe was Waterloo. During those years not the wisest could have foreseen that the outcome of all would be what to some thinkers apparently it has since turned out to be—a political advance along nearly the whole line for Europeans.

Now, as elsewhere hinted, it was something caught from the Revolutionary Spirit that at Spithead emboldened the man-of-war's men to rise against real abuses, long-standing ones, and afterwards at the Nore to make inordinate and aggressive demands—successful resistance to which was confirmed only when the ringleaders were hung for an admonitory spectacle to the anchored fleet. Yet in a way analogous to the operation of the Revolution at large—the Great Mutiny, though by Englishmen naturally deemed monstrous at the time, doubtless gave the first latent prompting to most important reforms in the British navy.

1

In the time before steamships, or then more frequently than now, a stroller along the docks of any considerable sea-port would occasionally have his attention arrested by a group of bronzed mariners, man-of-war's men or merchant-sailors in holiday attire ashore on liberty. In certain instances they would flank, or, like a body-guard quite surround some superior figure of their own class, moving along with them like Aldebaran[3] among the lesser lights of his constellation. That signal object was the "Handsome Sailor" of the less prosaic time alike of the military and merchant navies. With no perceptible trace of the vainglorious about him, rather with the off-hand unaffectedness of natural regality, he seemed to accept the spontaneous homage of his shipmates. A somewhat remarkable instance recurs to me. In Liverpool, now half a century ago I saw under the shadow of the great dingy street-wall of Prince's Dock (an obstruction long since removed) a common sailor, so intensely black that he must needs have been a native African of the unadulterate blood of Ham[4] A symmetric figure much above the average height. The two ends of a gay silk handkerchief thrown loose about the neck danced upon the displayed ebony of his chest; in his ears were big hoops of gold, and a Scotch Highland bonnet with a tartan band set off his shapely head.

It was a hot noon in July; and his face, lustrous with perspiration, beamed with barbaric good humor. In jovial sallies right and left[,] his white teeth flashing into view, he rollicked along, the centre of a company of his shipmates. These were made up of such an assort-

3. This large red star was regarded by the ancients as the "eye" of the Bull, the constellation Taurus.
4. In popular superstition, the Negroes, because Noah laid the curse of servitude upon the descendants of his youngest son, Ham, who mocked him; *cf.* Genesis ix: 22–25.

ment of tribes and complexions as would have well fitted them to be marched up by Anacharsis Cloots[5] before the bar of the first French Assembly as Representatives of the Human Race. At each spontaneous tribute rendered by the wayfarers to this black pagod[6] of a fellow—the tribute of a pause and stare, and less frequent an exclamation,—the motley retinue showed that they took that sort of pride in the evoker of it which the Assyrian priests doubtless showed for their grand sculptured Bull when the faithful prostrated themselves.

To return.

If in some cases a bit of a nautical Murat[7] in setting forth his person ashore, the handsome sailor of the period in question evinced nothing of the dandified Billy-be-Damn, an amusing character all but extinct now, but occasionally to be encountered, and in a form yet more amusing than the original, at the tiller of the boats on the tempestuous Erie Canal or, more likely, vaporing in the groggeries along the tow-path. Invariably a proficient in his perilous calling, he was also more or less of a mighty boxer or wrestler. It was strength and beauty. Tales of his prowess were recited. Ashore he was the champion; afloat the spokesman; on every suitable occasion always foremost. Close-reefing topsails in a gale, there he was, astride the weather yard-arm-end, foot in the Flemish horse as "stirrup," both hands tugging at the "earring" as at a bridle, in very much the attitude of young Alexander curbing the fiery Bucephalus.[8] A superb figure, tossed up as by the horns of Taurus[9] against the thunderous sky, cheerily hallooing to the strenuous file along the spar.

The moral nature was seldom out of keeping with the physical make. Indeed, except as toned by the former, the comeliness and power, always attractive in masculine conjunction, hardly could have drawn the sort of honest homage the Handsome Sailor in some examples received from his less gifted associates.

Such a cynosure, at least in aspect, and something such too in nature, though with important variations made apparent as the story proceeds, was welkin-eyed Billy Budd, or Baby Budd as more familiarly under circumstances hereafter to be given he at last came to be called[,] aged twenty-one, a foretopman of the British fleet toward the close of the last decade of the eighteenth century. It was not very long prior to the time of the narration that follows that he had entered the King's Service, having been impressed[1] on the Narrow

---

5. Carlyle, in his *French Revolution* (1837), popularized Cloots's escapade, as here described, by which he claimed the democratic privileges of the Assembly for this group representing various countries and stations.
6. Pagoda.
7. Joachim Murat (1767?–1815); French military adventurer, and con-

spirator with Napoleon. As King of Naples he was called "the Dandy King" for his foppishness.
8. The famous war horse of Alexander the Great (356–323 B.C.)
9. *Cf.* Aldebaran, above.
1. Laws covering British naval recruitment then permitted commanders to complete their crews by forcing, or "im-

Seas from a homeward-bound English merchantman into a seventy-four[2] outward-bound, H.M.S. *Indomitable*; which ship, as was not unusual in those hurried days having been obliged to put to sea short of her proper complement of men. Plump upon Billy at first sight in the gangway the boarding officer Lieutenant Ratcliffe pounced, even before the merchantman's crew was formally mustered on the quarter-deck for his deliberate inspection. And him only he elected. For whether it was because the other men when ranged before him showed to ill advantage after Billy, or whether he had some scruples in view of the merchantman being rather shcrt-handed, however it might be, the officer contented himself with his first spontaneous choice. To the surprise of the ship's company, though much to the Lieutenant's satisfaction Billy made no demur. But, indeed, any demur would have been as idle as the protest of a goldfinch popped into a cage.

Noting this uncomplaining acquiescence, all but cheerful one might say, the shipmates turned a surprised glance of silent reproach at the sailor. The shipmaster was one of those worthy mortals found in every vocation even the humbler ones—the sort of person whom everybody agrees in calling "a respectable man." And—nor so strange to report as it may appear to be—though a ploughman of the troubled waters, life-long contending with the intractable elements, there was nothing this honest soul at heart loved better than simple peace and quiet. For the rest, he was fifty or thereabouts, a little inclined to corpulence, a prepossessing face, unwhiskered, and of an agreeable color—a rather full face, humanely intelligent in expression. On a fair day with a fair wind and all going well, a certain musical chime in his voice seemed to be the veritable unobstructed outcome of the innermost man. He had much prudence, much conscientiousness, and there were occasions when these virtues were the cause of overmuch disquietude in him. On a passage, so long as his craft was in any proximity to land, no sleep for Captain Graveling. He took to heart those serious responsibilities not so heavily borne by some shipmasters.

Now while Billy Budd was down in the forecastle getting his kit together, the *Indomitable's* lieutenant, burly and bluff, nowise disconcerted by Captain Graveling's omitting to proffer the customary hospitalities on an occasion so unwelcome to him, an omission simply caused by preoccupation of thought, unceremoniously invited himself into the cabin, and also to a flask from the spirit-locker, a receptacle which his experienced eye instantly discovered. In fact he was one of those sea-dogs in whom all the hardship and peril of naval life in the great prolonged wars of his time never impaired the

pressing," merchant sailors, on land or sea, into service.

2. *I.e.*, a ship carrying seventy-four guns.

natural instinct for sensuous enjoyment. His duty he always faith-fully did; but duty is sometimes a dry obligation, and he was for irrigating its aridity, whensoever possible, with a fertilizing decoction of strong waters. For the cabin's proprietor there was nothing left but to play the part of the enforced host with whatever grace and alacrity were practicable. As necessary adjuncts to the flask, he silently placed tumbler and water-jug before the irrepressible guest. But excusing himself from partaking just then, [he] dismally watched the unembarrassed officer deliberately diluting his grog a little, then tossing it off in three swallows, pushing the empty tumbler away, yet not so far as to be beyond easy reach, at the same [time] settling himself in his seat and smacking his lips with high satisfaction, look-ing straight at the host.

These proceedings over, the Master broke the silence; and there lurked a rueful reproach in the tone of his voice; "Lieutenant, you are going to take my best man from me, the jewel of 'em."

"Yes, I know" rejoined the other, immediately drawing back the tumbler preliminary to a replenishing; "Yes, I know. Sorry."

"Beg pardon, but you don't understand, Lieutenant. See here now. Before I shipped that young fellow, my forecastle was a rat-pit of quarrels. It was black times, I tell you, aboard the '*Rights*' here. I was worried to that degree my pipe had no comfort for me. But Billy came; and it was like a Catholic priest striking peace in an Irish shindy. Not that he preached to them or said or did anything in particular; but a virtue went out of him, sugaring the sour ones. They took to him like hornets to treacle; all but the buffer of the gang, the big shaggy chap with the fire-red whiskers. He indeed out of envy, perhaps, of the newcomer, and thinking such a 'sweet and pleasant fellow,' as he mockingly designated him to the others, could hardly have the spirit of a game-cock, must needs bestir himself in trying to get up an ugly row with him. Billy forebore with him and reasoned with him in a pleasant way—he is something like myself, lieutenant, to whom aught like a quarrel is hateful—but nothing served. So, in the second dog-watch one day the Red Whiskers in presence of the others, under pretence of showing Billy just whence a sirloin steak was cut—for the fellow had once been a butcher—insultingly gave him a dig under the ribs. Quick as lightning Billy let fly his arm. I dare say he never meant to do quite as much as he did, but anyhow he gave the burly fool a terrible drubbing. It took about half a minute, I should think. And, lord bless you, the lubber was astonished at the celerity. And will you believe it, Lieutenant, the Red Whiskers now really loves Billy—loves him, or is the biggest hypocrite that ever I heard of. But they all love him. Some of 'em do his washing, darn his old trousers for him; the carpenter is at odd times making a pretty little chest of drawers for him. Anybody will do anything for Billy

Budd; and it's the happy family here. But now, Lieutenant, if that young fellow goes—I know how it will be aboard the '*Rights*.' Not again very soon shall I, coming up from dinner, lean over the capstan smoking a quiet pipe—no, not very soon again, I think. Ay, Lieutenant, you are going to take away the jewel of 'em; you are going to take away my peacemaker!" And with that the good soul had really some ado in checking a rising sob.

"Well," said the officer who had listened with amused interest to all this, and now waxing merry with his tipple; "Well, blessed are the peacemakers especially the fighting peacemakers! And such are the seventy-four beauties some of which you see poking their noses out of the port-holes of yonder war-ship lying-to for me" pointing thro' the cabin window at the *Indomitable*. "But courage! don't look so downhearted, man. Why, I pledge you in advance the royal approbation. Rest assured that His Majesty will be delighted to know that in a time when his hard tack is not sought for by sailors with such avidity as should be; a time also when some shipmasters privily resent the borrowing from them a tar or two for the service; His Majesty, I say, will be delighted to learn that *one* shipmaster at least cheerfully surrenders to the King, the flower of his flock, a sailor who with equal loyalty makes no dissent.—But where's my beauty? Ah," looking through the cabin's open door "Here he comes; and, by Jove—lugging along his chest—Apollo with his portmanteau!—My man," stepping out to him, "you can't take that big box aboard a warship. The boxes there are mostly shot-boxes. Put your duds in a bag, lad. Boot and saddle for the cavalryman, bag and hammock for the man-of-war's man."

The transfer from chest to bag was made. And, after seeing his man into the cutter and then following him down, the lieutenant pushed off from the *Rights-of-Man*.[3] That was the merchant-ship's name; tho' by her master and crew abbreviated in sailor fashion into *The Rights*. The hard-headed Dundee owner was a staunch admirer of Thomas Paine whose book in rejoinder to Burke's arraignment of the French Revolution had then been published for some time and had gone everywhere. In christening his vessel after the title of Paine's volume the man of Dundee was something like his contemporary shipowner, Stephen Girard[4] of Philadelphia, whose sympathies, alike with his native land and its liberal philosophers, he evinced by naming his ships after Voltaire, Diderot, and so forth.

But now, when the boat swept under the merchant-man's stern, and officer and oarsmen were noting—some bitterly and others with a grin,—the name emblazoned there; just then it was that the new

3. Title of a work by Thomas Paine, discussed earlier in this volume.
4. Girard (1750–1831), the great Philadelphia merchant and banker, remained in his native France until he was twenty-seven, and read widely among the liberal authors of that period.

recruit jumped up from the bow where the coxswain had directed him to sit, and waving [his] hat to his silent shipmates sorrowfully looking over at him from the taffrail, bade the lads a genial good-bye. Then, making a salutation as to the ship herself, "And good-bye to you too, old *Rights of Man*."

"Down, Sir!" roared the lieutenant, instantly assuming all the rigor of his rank, though with difficulty repressing a smile.

To be sure, Billy's action was a terrible breach of naval decorum. But in that decorum he had never been instructed; in consideration of which the lieutenant would hardly have been so energetic in re-proof but for the concluding farewell to the ship. This he rather took as meant to convey a covert sally on the new recruit's part, a sly slur at impressment in general, and that of himself in especial. And yet, more likely, if satire it was in effect, it was hardly so by in-tention, for Billy tho' happily endowed with the gayety of high health, youth, and a free heart, was yet by no means of a satirical turn. The will to it and the sinister dexterity were alike wanting. To deal in double meanings and insinuations of any sort was quite foreign to his nature.

As to his enforced enlistment, that he seemed to take pretty much as he was wont to take any vicissitude of weather. Like the animals, though no philosopher, he was, without knowing it, practically a fatalist. And, it may be, that he rather liked this adventurous turn in his affairs, which promised an opening into novel scenes and martial excitements.

Aboard the *Indomitable* our merchant-sailor was forthwith rated as an able-seaman and assigned to the starboard watch of the fore-top. He was soon at home in the service, not at all disliked for his un-pretentious good looks and a sort of genial happy-go-lucky air. No merrier man in his mess: in marked contrast to certain other in-dividuals included like himself among the impressed portion of the ship's company; for these when not actively employed were some-times, and more particularly in the last dog-watch when the drawing near of twilight induced revery, apt to fall into a saddish mood which in some partook of sullenness. But they were not so young as our foretopman, and no few of them must have known a hearth of some sort, others may have had wives and children left, too probably, in uncertain circumstances, and hardly any but must have had acknowl-edged kith and kin, while for Billy, as will shortly be seen, his entire family was practically invested in himself.

2

Though our new-made foretopman was well received in the top and on the gun-decks, hardly here was he that cynosure he had pre-viously been among those minor ship's companies of the merchant marine, with which companies only had he hitherto consorted.

He was young; and despite his all but fully developed frame in aspect looked even younger than he really was, owing to a lingering adolescent expression in the as yet smooth face all but feminine in purity of natural complexion but where, thanks to his seagoing, the lily was quite suppressed and the rose had some ado visibly to flush through the tan.

To one essentially such a novice in the complexities of factitious life, the abrupt transition from his former and simpler sphere to the ampler and more knowing world of a great warship; this might well have abashed him had there been any conceit or vanity in his composition. Among her miscellaneous multitude, the *Indomitable* mustered several individuals who however inferior in grade were of no common natural stamp, sailors more signally susceptive of that air which continuous martial discipline and repeated presence in battle can in some degree impart even to the average man. As the *handsome sailor* Billy Budd's position aboard the seventy-four was something analogous to that of a rustic beauty transplanted from the provinces and brought into competition with the highborn dames of the court. But this change of circumstances he scarce noted. As little did he observe that something about him provoked an ambiguous smile in one or two harder faces among the blue-jackets. Nor less unaware was he of the peculiar favorable effect his person and demeanor had upon the more intelligent gentlemen of the quarter-deck. Nor could this well have been otherwise. Cast in a mould peculiar to the finest physical examples of those Englishmen in whom the Saxon strain would seem not at all to partake of any Norman or other admixture, he showed in face that humane look of reposeful good nature which the Greek sculptor in some instances gave to his heroic strong man, Hercules. But this again was subtly modified by another and pervasive quality. The ear, small and shapely, the arch of the foot, the curve in mouth and nostril, even the indurated hand dyed to the orange-tawny of the toucan's[5] bill, a hand telling alike of the halyards and tar-bucket; but, above all, something in the mobile expression, and every chance attitude and movement, something suggestive of a mother eminently favored by Love and the Graces; all this strangely indicated a lineage in direct contradiction to his lot. The mysteriousness here, became less mysterious through a matter-of-fact elicited when Billy at the capstan was being formally mustered into the service. Asked by the officer, a small brisk little gentleman as it chanced among other questions, his place of birth, he replied, "Please, Sir, I don't know."

"Don't know where you were born?—Who was your father?"

"God knows, Sir."

Struck by the straightforward simplicity of these replies, the officer

5. Colorful bird of the American tropics, whose beak is conspicuously large.

next asked "Do you know anything about your beginning?"

"No, Sir. But I have heard that I was found in a pretty silk-lined basket hanging one morning from the knocker of a good man's door in Bristol [.]"

"*Found* say you? Well," throwing back his head and looking up and down the new recruit; "Well[,] it turns out to have been a pretty good find. Hope they'll find some more like you, my man; the fleet sadly needs them."

Yes, Billy Budd was a foundling, a presumable bye-blow,[6] and, evidently, no ignoble one. Noble descent was as evident in him as in a blood horse.

For the rest, with little or no sharpness of faculty or any trace of the wisdom of the serpent, nor yet quite a dove, he possessed that kind and degree of intelligence going along with the unconventional rectitude of a sound human creature, one to whom not yet has been proffered the questionable apple of knowledge. He was illiterate; he could not read, but he could sing, and like the illiterate nightingale was sometimes the composer of his own song.

Of self-consciousness he seemed to have little or none, or about as much as we may reasonably impute to a dog of Saint Bernard's breed.

Habitually living with the elements and knowing little more of the land than as a beach, or, rather, that portion of the terraqueous globe providentially set apart for dance-houses doxies and tapsters, in short what sailors call a "fiddlers' green," his simple nature remained unsophisticated by those moral obliquities which are not in every case incompatible with that manufacturable thing known as respectability. But are sailors, frequenters of "fiddlers'-greens," without vices? No; but less often than with landsmen do their vices, so called, partake of crookedness of heart, seeming less to proceed from viciousness than exuberance of vitality after long constraint; frank manifestations in accordance with natural law. By his original constitution aided by the cooperating influences of his lot, Billy in many respects was little more than a sort of upright barbarian, much such perhaps as Adam presumably might have been ere the urbane Serpent wriggled himself into his company.

And here be it submitted that apparently going to corroborate the doctrine of man's fall, a doctrine now popularly ignored, it is observable that where certain virtues pristine and unadulterate peculiarly characterize anybody in the external uniform of civilization, they will upon scrutiny seem not to be derived from custom or convention, but rather to be out of keeping with these, as if indeed exceptionally transmitted from a period prior to Cain's city and citified man. The character marked by such qualities has to an un-

6. Usually, "by-blow"—an illegitimate child.

vitiated taste an untampered-with flavor like that of berries, while the man thoroughly civilized even in a fair specimen of the breed has to the same moral palate a questionable smack as of a compounded wine. To any stray inheritor of these primitive qualities found, like Caspar Hauser,[7] wandering dazed in any Christian capital of our time the good-natured poet's famous invocation, near two thousand years ago, of the good rustic out of his latitude in the Rome of the Cesars, still appropriately holds:—

> "Honest and poor, faithful in word and thought
> What has thee, Fabian, to the city brought." [8]

Though our Handsome Sailor had as much of masculine beauty as one can expect anywhere to see; nevertheless, like the beautiful woman in one of Hawthorne's minor tales,[9] there was just one thing amiss in him. No visible blemish indeed, as with the lady; no, but an occasional liability to a vocal defect. Though in the hour of elemental uproar or peril, he was everything that a sailor should be, yet under sudden provocation of strong heart-feeling his voice otherwise singularly musical, as if expressive of the harmony within, was apt to develop an organic hesitancy, in fact more or less of a stutter or even worse. In this particular Billy was a striking instance that the arch interferer, the envious marplot of Eden still has more or less to do with every human consignment to this planet of earth. In every case, one way or another he is sure to slip in his little card, as much as to remind us—I too have a hand here.

The avowal of such an imperfection in the Handsome Sailor should be evidence not alone that he is not presented as a conventional hero, but also that the story in which he is the main figure is no romance.

3

At the time of Billy Budd's arbitrary enlistment into the *Indomitable* that ship was on her way to join the Mediterranean fleet. No long time elapsed before the junction was effected. As one of that fleet the seventy-four participated in its movements, tho' at times on account of her superior sailing qualities, in the absence of frigates, despatched on separate duty as a scout and at times on less temporary service. But with all this the story has little concernment, restricted as it is to the inner life of one particular ship and the career of an individual sailor.

It was the summer of 1797. In the April of that year had occurred the commotion at Spithead followed in May by a second and yet

7. Kaspar Hauser (1812?–1833) mysteriously appeared in 1828 in Nuremberg, Germany. Popularly imagined to be of noble birth, he aroused international attention, and was mysteriously assassinated.
8. Martial, *Epigrams*, Book IV, 5.
9. Apparently "The Birthmark"; *cf.* "blemish," below.

more serious outbreak in the fleet at the Nore. The latter is known, and without exaggeration in the epithet, as the Great Mutiny.[1] It was indeed a demonstration more menacing to England than the contemporary manifestoes and conquering and proselyting armies of the French Directory.

To the British Empire the Nore Mutiny was what a strike in the fire-brigade would be to London threatened by general arson. In a crisis when the kingdom might well have anticipated the famous signal that some years later published along the naval line of battle what it was that upon occasion England expected of Englishmen;[2] *that* was the time when at the mast-heads of the three-deckers and seventy-fours moored in her own roadstead—a fleet, the right arm of a Power then all but the sole free conservative one of the Old World, the blue-jackets, to be numbered by thousands [,] ran up with huzzas the British colors with the union and cross wiped out; by that cancellation transmuting the flag of founded law and freedom defined, into the enemy's red meteor of unbridled and unbounded revolt. Reasonable discontent growing out of practical grievances in the fleet had been ignited into irrational combustion as by live cinders blown across the Channel from France in flames.

The event converted into irony for a time those spirited strains of Dibdin[3]—as a song-writer no mean auxiliary to the English Government at the European conjuncture—strains celebrating, among other things, the patriotic devotion of the British tar:

> *"And as for my life, 'tis the King's!"*

Such an episode in the Island's grand naval story her naval historians naturally abridge; one of them (G. P. R. James)[4] candidly acknowledging that fain would he pass it over did not "impartiality forbid fastidiousness." And yet his mention is less a narration than a reference, having to do hardly at all with details. Nor are these readily to be found in the libraries. Like some other events in every age befalling states everywhere including America the Great Mutiny was of such character that national pride along with views of policy would fain shade it off into the historical background. Such events can not be ignored, but there is a considerate way of historically treating them. If a well-constituted individual refrains from blazoning aught amiss or calamitous in his family; a nation in the like circumstance may without reproach be equally discreet.

Though after parleyings between Government and the ringleaders, and concessions by the former as to some glaring abuses, the

1. *Cf.* the Preface, above.
2. In 1805, in the naval battle against the French and Spanish off Trafalgar, where he was killed, Admiral Nelson ran up the famous signal "England expects every man to do his duty."
3. Charles Dibdin (1745–1814) was an English dramatist, but his enduring fame rests on his sailor songs and chanteys.
4. G. P. R. James (1801–1860), a very popular and prolific British novelist.

first uprising—that at Spithead—with difficulty was put down, or matters for the time pacified; yet at the Nore the unforeseen renewal of insurrection on a yet larger scale, and emphasized in the conferences that ensued by demands deemed by the authorities not only inadmissible but aggressively insolent, indicated—if the Red Flag did not sufficiently do so[—]what was the spirit animating the men. Final suppression, however, there was; but only made possible perhaps by the unswerving loyalty of the marine corps a[nd] voluntary resumption of loyalty among influential sections of the crews.

To some extent the Nore Mutiny may be regarded as analogous to the distempering irruption of contagious fever in a frame constitutionally sound, and which anon throws it off.

At all events, of these thousands of mutineers were some of the tars who not so very long afterwards—whether wholly prompted thereto by patriotism, or pugnacious instinct, or by both,—helped to win a coronet for Nelson at the Nile,[5] and the naval crown of crowns for him at Trafalgar. To the mutineers those battles and especially Trafalgar were a plenary absolution and a grand one: For all that goes to make up scenic naval display, heroic magnificence in arms, those battles especially Trafalgar stand unmatched in human annals.

4

Concerning "The greatest sailor since the world began."   Tennyson?[6]

In this matter of writing, resolve as one may to keep to the main road, some by-paths have an enticement not readily to be withstood. I am going to err into such a by-path. If the reader will keep me company I shall be glad. At the least we can promise ourselves that pleasure which is wickedly said to be in sinning, for a literary sin the divergence will be.

Very likely it is no new remark that the inventions of our time have at last brought about a change in sea-warfare in degree corresponding to the revolution in all warfare effected by the original introduction from China into Europe of gunpowder. The first European fire-arm, a clumsy contrivance, was, as is well known, scouted by no few of the knights as a base implement, good enough peradventure for weavers too craven to stand up crossing steel with steel in frank fight. But as ashore knightly valor tho' shorn of its blazonry did not cease with the knights, neither on the seas though nowadays in encounters there a certain kind of displayed gallantry be fallen out of date as hardly applicable under changed circumstances, did the nobler qualities of such naval magnates as Don John of Austria,

5. For his victory at the Nile (1798), Nelson was made a baron; later he became a viscount.
6. Melville's question mark after the quotation suggests his intention to check it before publication. The line, which is line 7 in Tennyson's "Ode on the Death of the Duke of Wellington" (1852), reads: "The greatest sailor since our world began."

Doria, Van Tromp, Jean Bart, the long line of British Admirals and the American Decaturs of 1812 become obsolete with their wooden walls.[7]

Nevertheless, to anybody who can hold the Present at its worth without being inappreciative of the Past, it may be forgiven, if to such an one the solitary old hulk at Portsmouth, Nelson's *Victory*, seems to float there, not alone as the decaying monument of a fame incorruptible, but also as a poetic reproach, softened by its picturesqueness, to the *Monitors*[8] and yet mightier hulls of the European iron-clads. And this not altogether because such craft are unsightly, unavoidably lacking the symmetry and grand lines of the old battle-ships, but equally for other reasons.

There are some, perhaps, who while not altogether inaccessible to that poetic reproach just alluded to, may yet on behalf of the new order, be disposed to parry it; and this to the extent of iconoclasm, if need be. For example, prompted by the sight of the star inserted in the *Victory's* quarter-deck designating the spot where the Great Sailor fell, these martial utilitarians may suggest considerations implying that Nelson's ornate publication of his person in battle was not only unnecessary, but not military, nay, savored of foolhardiness and vanity. They may add, too, that at Trafalgar it was in effect nothing less than a challenge to death; and death came; and that but for his bravado the victorious Admiral might possibly have survived the battle, and so, instead of having his sagacious dying injunctions overruled by his immediate successor in command he himself when the contest was decided might have brought his shattered fleet to anchor, a proceeding which might have averted the deplorable loss of life by shipwreck in the elemental tempest that followed the martial one.

Well, should we set aside the more disputable point whether for various reasons it was possible to anchor the fleet, then plausibly enough the Benthamites[9] of war may urge the above.

But the *might-have-been* is but boggy ground to build on. And, certainly, in foresight as to the larger issue of an encounter, and anxious preparations for it—buoying the deadly way and mapping it

7. All famous "iron admirals" of the wooden ships. Don John of Austria commanded the fleet of the Holy League in the defeat of the Turks at Lepanto (1571); Andrea Doria (1468–1560), Genoese admiral, was the "Liberator of Genoa" from the Turks; Maarten Tromp (1597–1653) commanded the Dutch fleets in struggles for independence from Spain, Portugal, and Britain; Jean Bart, famous French soldier of fortune, commanded privateers against the Dutch (1686–1697); and the American naval hero Stephen Decatur was renowned for daring exploits against the Tripoli pirates (1803–1804) and for victories over British ships in the War of 1812.

8. During the Civil War, the *Monitor's* defeat of the southern *Merrimac* at Hampton Roads (March, 1862), ended the first engagement between ironclad ships.

9. Jeremy Bentham (1748–1832), British jurist and utilitarian philosopher, in *Principles of Morals and Legislation* (1789) propounded his famous dictum that "the greatest happiness of the greatest number is the foundation of morals and legislation."

out, as at Copenhagen[1]—few commanders have been so painstakingly circumspect as this same reckless declarer of his person in fight.

Personal prudence even when dictated by quite other than selfish considerations surely is no special virtue in a military man; while an excessive love of glory, impassioning a less burning impulse, the honest sense of duty, is the first. If the name *Wellington* is not so much of a trumpet to the blood as the simpler name *Nelson*, the reason for this may perhaps be inferred from the above. Alfred[2] in his funeral ode on the victor of Waterloo ventures not to call him the greatest soldier of all time, tho' in the same ode he invokes Nelson as "the greatest sailor since the world began."

At Trafalgar Nelson on the brink of opening the fight sat down and wrote his last brief will and testament. If under the presentiment of the most magnificent of all victories to be crowned by his own glorious death, a sort of priestly motive led him to dress his person in the jewelled vouchers of his own shining deeds; if thus to have adorned himself for the altar and the sacrifice were indeed vainglory, then affectation and fustian is each more heroic line in the great epics and dramas, since in such lines the poet but embodies in verse those exaltations of sentiment that a nature like Nelson, the opportunity being given, vitalizes into acts.

5

Yes, the outbreak at the Nore was put down. But not every grievance was redressed. If the contractors, for example, were no longer permitted to ply some practices peculiar to their tribe everywhere, such as providing shoddy cloth, rations not sound, or false in the measure, not the less impressment, for one thing, went on. By custom sanctioned for centuries, and judicially maintained by a Lord Chancellor as late as Mansfield,[3] that mode of manning the fleet, a mode now fallen into a sort of abeyance but never formally renounced, it was not practicable to give up in those years. Its abrogation would have crippled the indispensable fleet, one wholly under canvas, no steam-power, its innumerable sails and thousands of cannon, everything in short, worked by muscle alone; a fleet the more insatiate in demand for men, because then multiplying its ship[s] of all grades against contingencies present and to come of the convulsed Continent.

Discontent foreran the Two Mutinies, and more or less it lurkingly survived them. Hence it was not unreasonable to apprehend some return of trouble sporadic or general. One instance of such apprehensions: In the same year with this story, Nelson, then Vice Admiral Sir Horatio, being with the fleet off the Spanish coast, was directed by

1. Nelson's seige of Copenhagen (1801) became a famous example of strategy.
2. *I.e.*, Tennyson; *cf.* epigraph to this chapter.

3. William Murray, Baron Mansfield, British parliamentarian, became lord chief justice in 1756, and was later a cabinet minister (1773–1788).

the Admiral in command to shift his pennant from the *Captain* to the *Theseus*; and for this reason: that the latter ship having newly arrived on the station from home where it had taken part in the Great Mutiny, danger was apprehended from the temper of the men; and it was thought that an officer like Nelson was the one, not indeed to terrorize the crew into base subjection, but to win them, by force of his mere presence back to an allegiance if not as enthusiastic as his own, yet as true. So it was that for a time on more than one quarter-deck anxiety did exist. At sea precautionary vigilance was strained against relapse. At short notice an engagement might come on. When it did, the lieutenants assigned to batteries felt it incumbent on them, in some instances, to stand with drawn swords behind the men working the guns.

6

But on board the seventy-four in which Billy now swung his hammock, very little in the manner of the men and nothing obvious in the demeanor of the officers would have suggested to an ordinary observer that the Great Mutiny was a recent event. In their general bearing and conduct the commissioned officers of a war-ship naturally take their tone from the commander, that is if he have that ascendancy of character that ought to be his.

Captain the Honorable Edward Fairfax Vere, to give his full title, was a bachelor of forty or thereabouts, a sailor of distinction even in a time prolific of renowned seamen. Though allied to the higher nobility his advancement had not been altogether owing to influences connected with that circumstance. He had seen much service, been in various engagements, always acquitting himself as an officer mindful of the welfare of his men, but never tolerating an infraction of discipline; thoroughly versed in the science of his profession, and intrepid to the verge of temerity, though never injudiciously so. For his gallantry in the West Indian waters as flag-lieutenant under Rodney in that Admiral's crowning victory over De Grasse,[4] he was made a post-captain.

Ashore in the garb of a civilian scarce anyone would have taken him for a sailor, more especially that he never garnished unprofessional talk with nautical terms, and grave in his bearing, evinced little appreciation of mere humor. It was not out of keeping with these traits that on a passage when nothing demanded his paramount action, he was the most undemonstrative of men. Any landsman observing this gentleman not conspicuous by his stature and wearing no pronounced insignia, emerging from his cabin to the open deck, and noting the silent deference of the officers retiring to leeward, might have taken him for the King's guest, a civilian aboard the

4. The British admiral George Brydges, Baron Rodney (1719–1792) defeated the French admiral DeGrasse in a naval engagement off Dominica, in the Leewards, in 1782.

King's-ship[,] some highly honorable discreet envoy on his way to an important post. But in fact this unobtrusiveness of demeanor may have proceeded from a certain unaffected modesty of manhood sometimes accompanying a resolute nature, a modesty evinced at all times not calling for pronounced action, and which shown in any rank of life suggests a virtue aristocratic in kind.

As with some others engaged in various departments of the world's more heroic activities, Captain Vere though practical enough upon occasion would at times betray a certain dreaminess of mood. Standing alone on the weather-side of the quarter deck, one hand holding by the rigging he would absently gaze off at the blank sea. At the presentation to him then of some minor matter interrupting the current of his thoughts he would show more or less irascibility; but instantly he would control it.

In the navy he was popularly known by the appellation—Starry Vere. How such a designation happened to fall upon one who whatever his sturdy qualities was without any brilliant ones was in this wise: A favorite kinsman, Lord Denton, a free-hearted fellow, had been the first to meet and congratulate him upon his return to England from his West Indian cruise; and but the day previous turning over a copy of Andrew Marvell's[5] poems had lighted, not for the first time however, upon the lines entitled *Appleton House*, the name of one of the seats of their common ancestor, a hero in the German wars of the seventeenth century, in which poem occur the lines,

> "This 'tis to have been from the first
> In a domestic heaven nursed,
> Under the discipline severe
> Of Fairfax and the starry Vere[.]"

And so, upon embracing his cousin fresh from Rodney's great victory wherein he had played so gallant a part, brimming over with just family pride in the sailor of their house, he exuberantly exclaimed, "Give ye joy, Ed; give ye joy, my starry Vere!" This got currency, and the novel prefix serving in familiar parlance readily to distinguish the *Indomitable*'s Captain from another Vere his senior, a distant relative an officer of like rank in the navy, it remained permanently attached to the surname.

7

In view of the part that the commander of the *Indomitable* plays in scenes shortly to follow, it may be well to fill out that sketch of him outlined in the previous chapter.

Aside from his qualities as a sea-officer Captain Vere was an exceptional character. Unlike no few of England's renowned sailors, long

5. British poet (1621–1678), who is still one of the best known of the Caroline writers.

and arduous service with signal devotion to it, had not resulted in absorbing and *salting* the entire man. He had a marked leaning toward everything intellectual. He loved books, never going to sea without a newly replenished library, compact but of the best. The isolated leisure, in some cases so wearisome, falling at intervals to commanders even during a war-cruise, never was tedious to Captain Vere. With nothing of that literary taste which less heeds the thing conveyed than the vehicle, his bias was towards those books to which every serious mind of superior order occupying any active post of authority in the world, naturally inclines: books treating of actual men and events no matter of what era—history, biography and unconventional writers, who, free from cant and convention, like Montaigne, honestly and in the spirit of common sense philosophize upon realities.

In this line of reading he found confirmation of his own more reasoned thoughts—confirmation which he had vainly sought in social converse, so that as touching most fundamental topics, there had got to be established in him some positive convictions, which he forefelt would abide in him essentially unmodified so long as his intelligent part remained unimpaired. In view of the troubled period in which his lot was cast this was well for him. His settled convictions were as a dyke against those invading waters of novel opinion social political and otherwise, which carried away as in a torrent no few minds in those days, minds by nature not inferior to his own. While other members of that aristocracy to which by birth he belonged were incensed at the innovators mainly because their theories were inimical to the privileged classes, not alone Captain Vere disinterestedly opposed them because they seemed to him incapable of embodiment in lasting institutions, but at war with the peace of the world and the true welfare of mankind.

With minds less stored than his and less earnest, some officers of his rank, with whom at times he would necessarily consort, found him lacking in the companionable quality, a dry and bookish gentleman as they deemed. Upon any chance withdrawal from their company one would be apt to say to another, something like this: "Vere is a noble fellow, Starry Vere. Spite the gazettes, Sir Horatio["] meaning him with the Lord title[6] ["]is at bottom scarce a better seaman or fighter. But between you and me now don't you think there is a queer streak of the pedantic running thro' him? Yes, like the King's yarn in a coil of navy-rope?["]

Some apparent ground there was for this sort of confidential criticism; since not only did the Captain's discourse never fall into the jocosely familiar, but in illustrating of any point touching the stirring personages and events of the time he would be as apt to cite

6. *I.e.*, Admiral Horatio Nelson, a viscount.

some historic character or incident of antiquity as that he would cite from the moderns. He seemed unmindful of the circumstance that to his bluff company such remote allusions however pertinent they might really be were altogether alien to men whose reading was mainly confined to the journals. But considerateness in such matters is not easy to natures constituted like Captain Vere's. Their honesty prescribes to them directness, sometimes far-reaching like that of a migratory fowl that in its flight never heeds when it crosses a frontier.

8

The lieutenants and other commissioned gentlemen forming Captain Vere's staff it is not necessary here to particularize, nor needs it to make any mention of any of the warrant-officers. But among the petty-officers was one who having much to do with the story, may as well be forthwith introduced. His portrait I essay, but shall never hit it. This was John Claggart, the Master-at-arms. But that sea-title may to landsmen seem somewhat equivocal. Originally doubtless that petty-officer's function was the instruction of the men in the use of arms, sword or cutlas. But very long ago, owing to the advance in gunnery making hand-to-hand encounters less frequent and giving to nitre and sulphur the preeminence over steel, that function ceased; the master-at-arms of a great war-ship becoming a sort of Chief of Police charged among other matters with the duty of preserving order on the populous lower gun-decks.

Claggart was a man about five and thirty, somewhat spare and tall, yet of no ill figure upon the whole. His hand was too small and shapely to have been accustomed to hard toil. The face was a notable one; the features all except the chin cleanly cut as those on a Greek medallion; yet the chin, beardless as Tecumseh's,[7] had something of strange protuberant heaviness in its make that recalled the prints of the Rev. Dr. Titus Oates, the historic deponent with the clerical drawl in the time of Charles II and the fraud of the alleged Popish Plot.[8] It served Claggart in his office that his eye could cast a tutoring glance. His brow was of the sort phrenologically associated with more than average intellect; silken jet curls partly clustering over it, making a foil to the pallor below, a pallor tinged with a faint shade of amber akin to the hue of time-tinted marbles of old. This complexion, singularly contrasting with the red or deeply bronzed visages of the sailors, and in part the result of his official seclusion from the sunlight, tho it was not exactly displeasing, nevertheless seemed to hint of something defective or abnormal in the constitution and blood. But his general aspect and manner were so suggestive of an

7. Shawnee chieftan (1768?–1813), leader of a western Indian alliance; he joined the British and was killed in the War of 1812.

8. Titus Oates (1649–1705) was fabricator in 1678 of the alleged "Popish Plot" to seize the English crown for Catholicism by assassinating King Charles and terrorizing London.

education and career incongruous with his naval function that when not actively engaged in it he looked like a man of high quality, social and moral, who for reasons of his own was keeping incog.[9] Nothing was known of his former life. It might be that he was an Englishman; and yet there lurked a bit of accent in his speech suggesting that possibly he was not such by birth, but through naturalization in early childhood. Among certain grizzled sea-gossips of the gun-decks and forecastle went a rumor perdue that the master-at-arms was a *chevalier* who had volunteered into the King's navy by way of compounding for some mysterious swindle whereof he had been arraigned at the King's Bench. The fact that nobody could substantiate this report was, of course, nothing against its secret currency. Such a rumor once started on the gun-decks in reference to almost anyone below the rank of a commissioned officer would, during the period assigned to this narrative, have seemed not altogether wanting in credibility to the tarry old wiseacres of a man-of-war crew. And indeed a man of Claggart's accomplishments, without prior nautical experience entering the navy at mature life, as he did, and necessarily allotted at the start to the lowest grade in it; a man too who never made allusion to his previous life ashore; these were circumstances which in the dearth of exact knowledge as to his true antecedents opened to the invidious a vague field for unfavorable surmise.

But the sailors' dog-watch gossip concerning him derived a vague plausibility from the fact that now for some period the British Navy could so little afford to be squeamish in the matter of keeping up the muster-rolls, that not only were press-gangs notoriously abroad both afloat and ashore, but there was little or no secret about another matter, namely that the London police were at liberty to capture any able-bodied suspect, any questionable fellow at large and summarily ship him to the dockyard or fleet. Furthermore, even among voluntary enlistments there were instances where the motive thereto partook neither of patriotic impulse nor yet of a random desire to experience a bit of sea-life and martial adventure. Insolvent debtors of minor grade, together with the promiscuous lame ducks of morality found in the Navy a convenient and secure refuge. Secure, because once enlisted aboard a King's-Ship, they were as much in sanctuary, as the transgressor of the Middle Ages harboring himself under the shadow of the altar. Such sanctioned irregularities, which for obvious reasons the Government would hardly think to parade at the time and which consequently, and as affecting the least influential class of mankind, have all but dropped into oblivion, lend color to something for the truth whereof I do not vouch, and hence have some scruple in stating; something I remember having seen in print though the book I can not recall; but the same thing was per-

9. Then a familiar abbreviation for *incognito,* "unrecognized."

sonally communicated to me now more than forty years ago by an old pensioner in a cocked hat with whom I had a most interesting talk on the terrace at Greenwich, a Baltimore negro, a Trafalgar man.[1] It was to this effect: In the case of a warship short of hands whose speedy sailing was imperative, the deficient quota in lack of any other way of making it good, would be eked out by draughts culled direct from the jails. For reasons previously suggested it would not perhaps be easy at the present day directly to prove or disprove the allegation. But allowed as a verity, how significant would it be of England's straits at the time confronted by those wars which like a flight of harpies rose shrieking from the din and dust of the fallen Bastille. That era appears measurably clear to us who look back at it, and but read of it. But to the grandfathers of us graybeards, the more thoughtful of them, the genius of it presented an aspect like that of Camoen's[2] Spirit of the Cape, an eclipsing menace mysterious and prodigious. Not America was exempt from apprehension. At the height of Napoleon's unexampled conquests, there were Americans who had fought at Bunker Hill who looked forward to the possibility that the Atlantic might prove no barrier against the ultimate schemes of this French upstart from the revolutionary chaos who seemed in act of fulfilling judgment prefigured in the Apocalypse.

But the less credence was to be given to the gun-deck talk touching Claggart, seeing that no man holding his office in a man-of-war can ever hope to be popular with the crew. Besides, in derogatory comments upon anyone against whom they have a grudge, or for any reason or no reason mislike, sailors are much like landsmen, they are apt to exaggerate or romance it.

About as much was really known to the *Indomitable's* tars of the master-at-arms' career before entering the service as an astronomer knows about a comet's travels prior to its first observable appearance in the sky. The verdict of the sea quidnuncs[3] has been cited only by way of showing what sort of moral impression the man made upon rude uncultivated natures whose conceptions of human wickedness were necessarily of the narrowest, limited to ideas of vulgar rascality, —a thief among the swinging hammocks during a night-watch, or the man-brokers and land-sharks of the sea-ports.

It was no gossip, however, but fact, that though, as before hinted, Claggart upon his entrance into the navy was, as a novice, assigned to the least honorable section of a man-of-war's crew, embracing the drudgery, he did not long remain there.

The superior capacity he immediately evinced, his constitutional sobriety, ingratiating deference to superiors, together with a peculiar

---

1. *I.e.*, one who had fought at the Battle of Trafalgar (1805), Nelson's fatal victory.
2. Properly, "Camoëns," English spelling for "Camões," Portuguese-born Spanish poet.
3. Literally, "what now?" Hence, a busybody, a gossip.

ferreting genius manifested on a singular occasion, all this capped by a certain austere patriotism abruptly advanced him to the position of master-at-arms.

Of this maritime Chief of Police the ship's-corporals, so called, were the immediate subordinates, and compliant ones; and this, as is to be noted in some business departments ashore, almost to a degree inconsistent with entire moral volition. His place put various converging wires of underground influence under the Chief's control, capable when astutely worked thro his understrappers of operating to the mysterious discomfort[,] if nothing worse, of any of the sea-commonalty.

9

Life in the fore-top well agreed with Billy Budd. There, when not actually engaged on the yards yet higher aloft, the topmen, who as such had been picked out for youth and activity, constituted an aerial club lounging at ease against the smaller stun'sails rolled up into cushions, spinning yarns like the lazy gods, and frequently amused with what was going on in the busy world of the decks below. No wonder then that a young fellow of Billy's disposition was well content in such society. Giving no cause of offence to anybody, he was always alert at a call. So in the merchant service it had been with him. But now such a punctiliousness in duty was shown that his topmates would sometimes good-naturedly laugh at him for it. This heightened alacrity had its cause, namely, the impression made upon him by the first formal gangway-punishment he had ever witnessed, which befell the day following his impressment. It had been incurred by a little fellow, young, a novice[,] an after-guardsman absent from his assigned post when the ship was being put about; a dereliction resulting in a rather serious hitch to that manœuvre, one demanding instantaneous promptitude in letting go and making fast. When Billy saw the culprit's naked back under the scourge gridironed with red welts, and worse; when he marked the dire expression on the liberated man's face as with his woolen shirt flung over him by the executioner he rushed forward from the spot to bury himself in the crowd, Billy was horrified. He resolved that never through remissness would he make himself liable to such a visitation or do or omit aught that might merit even verbal reproof. What then was his surprise and concern when ultimately he found himself getting into petty trouble occasionally about such matters as the stowage of his bag or something amiss in his hammock, matters under the police oversight of the ship's-corporals of the lower decks, and which brought down on him a vague threat from one of them.

So heedful in all things as he was, how could this be? He could not understand it, and it more than vexed him. When he spoke to his young topmates about it they were either lightly incredulous or found something comical in his unconcealed anxiety. "Is it your bag, Billy?" said one "well, sew yourself up in it, bully boy, and then you'll be sure to know if anybody meddles with it."

Now there was a veteran aboard who because his years began to disqualify him for more active work had been recently assigned duty as main-mast-man in his watch, looking to the gear belayed at the rail roundabout that great spar near the deck. At off-times the fore-topman had picked up some acquaintance with him, and now in his trouble it occurred to him that he might be the sort of person to go to for wise counsel. He was an old Dansker long anglicized in the service, of few words, many wrinkles and some honorable scars. His wizened face, time-tinted and weather-stained to the complexion of an antique parchment, was here and there peppered blue by the chance explosion of a gun-cartridge in action. He was an *Agamemnon*-man; some two years prior to the time of this story having served under Nelson when but Sir Horatio in that ship immortal in naval memory, and which[,] dismantled and in part broken up to her bare ribs[,] is seen a grand skeleton in Haydon's[4] etching. As one of a boarding-party from the *Agamemnon* he had received a cut slantwise along one temple and cheek leaving a long pale scar like a streak of dawn's light falling athwart the dark visage. It was on account of that scar and the affair in which it was known that he had received it, as well as from his blue-peppered complexion that the Dansker went among the *Indomitable's* crew by the name of "Board-her-in-the-smoke."

Now the first time that his small weazel-eyes happened to light on Billy Budd, a certain grim internal merriment set all his ancient wrinkles into antic play. Was it that his eccentric unsentimental old sapience primitive in its kind saw or thought it saw something which in contrast with the war-ship's environment looked oddly in-congruous in the handsome sailor? But after slyly studying him at intervals, the old Merlin's equivocal merriment was modified; for now when the twain would meet, it would start in his face a quizzing sort of look, but it would be but momentary and sometimes replaced by an expression of speculative query as to what might eventually be-fall a nature like that, dropped into a world not without some man-traps and against whose subtleties simple courage lacking experience and address and without any touch of defensive ugliness, is of little avail; and where such innocence as man is capable of does yet in a moral emergency not always sharpen the faculties or enlighten the will.

However it was the Dansker in his ascetic way rather took to Billy.

4. Benjamin Robert Haydon (1786–1846), English historical painter, much praised by contemporary romantic writers.

Nor was this only because of a certain philosophic interest in such a character. There was another cause. While the old man's eccentricities, sometimes bordering on the ursine, repelled the juniors, Billy, undeterred thereby, revering him as a salt hero would make advances, never passing the old Agamemnon-man without a salutation marked by that respect which is seldom lost on the aged however crabbed at times or whatever their station in life.

There was a vein of dry humor, or what not, in the mast-man; and, whether in freak of patriarchal irony touching Billy's youth and athletic frame, or for some other and more recondite reason, from the first in addressing him he always substituted Baby for Billy. The Dansker in fact being the originator of the name by which the foretopman eventually became known aboard ship.

Well then, in his mysterious little difficulty going in quest of the wrinkled one, Billy found him off duty in a dog-watch ruminating by himself seated on a shot-box of the upper gun-deck now and then surveying with a somewhat cynical regard certain of the more swaggering promenaders there. Billy recounted his trouble, again wondering how it all happened. The salt seer attentively listened, accompanying the foretopman's recital with queer twitchings of his wrinkles and problematical little sparkles of his small ferret eyes. Making an end of his story, the foretopman asked, "And now, Dansker, do tell me what you think of it."

The old man, shoving up the front of his tarpaulin and deliberately rubbing the long slant scar at the point where it entered the thin hair, laconically said, "Baby Budd, *Jemmy Legs*"[5] (meaning the master-at-arms) "is down on you[.]"

"*Jemmy Legs!*" ejaculated Billy his welkin eyes expanding; "what for? Why he calls me *the sweet and pleasant young fellow*, they tell me."

"Does he so?" grinned the grizzled one; then said "Ay[,] Baby Lad[,] a sweet voice has *Jemmy Legs*."

"No, not always. But to me he has. I seldom pass him but there comes a pleasant word."

"And that's because he's down upon you, Baby Budd."

Such reiteration along with the manner of it, incomprehensible to a novice, disturbed Billy almost as much as the mystery for which he had sought explanation. Something less unpleasingly oracular he tried to extract; but the old sea-Chiron[6] thinking perhaps that for the nonce he had sufficiently instructed his young Achilles, pursed his lips, gathered all his wrinkles together and would commit himself to nothing further.

5. "Jimmy-Legs" is still a term of disparagement for the master-at-arms in the United States Navy.

6. In Greek myth, the wisest of the centaurs, skilled in healing, who befriended Achilles and other heroes.

Years, and those experiences which befall certain shrewder men subordinated life-long to the will of superiors, all this had developed in the Dansker the pithy guarded cynicism that was his leading characteristic.

10

The next day an incident served to confirm Billy Budd in his incredulity as to the Dansker's strange summing up of the case submitted. The ship at noon going large before the wind was rolling on her course, and he below at dinner and engaged in some sportful talk with the members of his mess, chanced in a sudden lurch to spill the entire contents of his soup-pan upon the new scrubbed deck. Claggart, the Master-at-arms, official rattan in hand, happened to be passing along the battery in a bay of which the mess was lodged, and the greasy liquid streamed just across his path. Stepping over it, he was proceeding on his way without comment, since the matter was nothing to take notice of under the circumstances, when he happened to observe who it was that had done the spilling. His countenance changed. Pausing, he was about to ejaculate something hasty at the sailor, but checked himself, and pointing down to the streaming soup, playfully tapped him from behind with his rattan, saying in a low musical voice peculiar to him at times "Handsomely done, my lad! And handsome is as handsome did it too!" And with that passed on. Not noted by Billy as not coming within his view was the involuntary smile, or rather grimace, that accompanied Claggart's equivocal words. Aridly it drew down the thin corners of his shapely mouth. But everybody taking his remark as meant for humorous, and at which therefore as coming from a superior they were bound to laugh, "with counterfeited glee"[7] acted accordingly; and Billy tickled, it may be, by the allusion to his being the handsome sailor, merrily joined in; then addressing his messmates exclaimed "There now, who says that Jemmy Legs is down on me!" "And who said he was, Beauty?" demanded one Donald with some surprise. Whereat the foretopman looked a little foolish recalling that it was only one person, Board-her-in-the-smoke who had suggested what to him was the smoky idea that this master-at-arms was in any peculiar way hostile to him. Meantime that functionary resuming his path must have momentarily worn some expression less guarded than that of the bitter smile, and usurping the face from the heart, some distorting expression perhaps, for a drummer-boy heedlessly frolicking along from the opposite direction and chancing to come into light collision with his person was strangely disconcerted by his aspect. Nor was the impression lessened when the official impulsively giving him a sharp cut with the rattan, vehemently exclaimed "Look where you go!"

7. *Cf.* Oliver Goldsmith, "The Deserted Village," l. 201, relating to the severe schoolmaster.

11

What was the matter with the master-at-arms? And, be the matter what it might, how could it have direct relation to Billy Budd with whom prior to the affair of the spilled soup he had never come into any special contact official or otherwise? What indeed could the trouble have to do with one so little inclined to give offence as the merchant-ship's *peacemaker*, even him who in Claggart's own phrase was "the sweet and pleasant young fellow? ["] Yes, why should *Jemmy Legs*, to borrow the Dansker's expression, be *down* on the Handsome Sailor? But, at heart and not for nothing, as the late chance encounter may indicate to the discerning, down on him, secretly down on him, he assuredly was.

Now to invent something touching the more private career of Claggart, something involving Billy Budd, of which something the latter should be wholly ignorant, some romantic incident implying that Claggart's knowledge of the young blue-jacket began at some period anterior to catching sight of him on board the seventy-four— all this, not so difficult to do, might avail in a way more or less interesting to account for whatever of enigma may appear to lurk in the case. But in fact there was nothing of the sort. And yet the cause, necessarily to be assumed as the sole one assignable, is in its very realism as much charged with that prime element of Radcliffian[8] romance, *the mysterious*, as any that the ingenuity of the author of the *Mysteries of Udolpho* could devise. For what can more partake of the mysterious than an antipathy spontaneous and profound such as is evoked in certain exceptional mortals by the mere aspect of some other mortal, however harmless he may be? if not called forth by this very harmlessness itself.

Now there can exist no irritating juxtaposition of dissimilar personalities comparable to that which is possible aboard a great war-ship fully manned and at sea. There, every day among all ranks almost every man comes into more or less of contact with almost every other man. Wholly there to avoid even the sight of an aggravating object one must needs give it Jonah's toss[9] or jump overboard himself. Imagine how all this might eventually operate on some peculiar human creature the direct reverse of a saint?

But for the adequate comprehending of Claggart by a normal nature these hints are insufficient. To pass from a normal nature to him one must cross "the deadly space between." And this is best done by indirection.

Long ago an honest scholar my senior, said to me in reference to one who like himself is now no more, a man so unimpeachably respectable that against him nothing was ever openly said tho' among

8. *The Mysteries of Udolfo* (1794), by Anne Radcliffe, was among the most popular of Gothic romances.

9. In the language of seafaring, the putting overboard of an unlucky person or object.

the few something was whispered, "Yes, X—— is a nut not to be cracked by the tap of a lady's fan. You are aware that I am the adherent of no organized religion much less of any philosophy built into a system. Well, for all that, I think that to try and get into X——, enter his labyrinth and get out again, without a clue derived from some source other than what is known as *knowledge of the world*—that were hardly possible, at least for me."

"Why" said I, "X——however singular a study to some, is yet human, and knowledge of the world assuredly implies the knowledge of human nature, and in most of its varieties."

"Yes, but a superficial knowledge of it, serving ordinary purposes. But for anything deeper, I am not certain whether to know the world and to know human nature be not two distinct branches of knowledge, which while they may coexist in the same heart, yet either may exist with little or nothing of the other. Nay, in an average man of the world, his constant rubbing with it blunts that fine spiritual insight indispensable to the understanding of the essential in certain exceptional characters, whether evil ones or good. In a matter of some importance I have seen a girl wind an old lawyer about her little finger. Nor was it the dotage of senile love. Nothing of the sort. But he knew law better than he knew the girl's heart. Coke and Blackstone[1] hardly shed so much light into obscure spiritual places as the Hebrew prophets. And who were they? Mostly recluses."

At the time my inexperience was such that I did not quite see the drift of all this. It may be that I see it now. And, indeed, if that lexicon which is based on Holy Writ were any longer popular, one might with less difficulty define and denominate certain phenomenal men. As it is, one must turn to some authority not liable to the charge of being tinctured with the Biblical element.

In a list of definitions included in the authentic translation of Plato, a list attributed to him, occurs this: "Natural Depravity: a depravity according to nature." A definition which tho' savoring of Calvinism, by no means involves Calvin's dogmas as to total mankind. Evidently its intent makes it applicable but to individuals. Not many are the examples of this depravity which the gallows and jail supply. At any rate for notable instances, since these have no vulgar alloy of the brute in them, but invariably are dominated by intellectuality, one must go elsewhere. Civilization, especially if of the austerer sort, is auspicious to it. It folds itself in the mantle of respectability. It has its certain negative virtues serving as silent auxiliaries. It never allows wine to get within its guard. It is not going too far to say that it is without vices or small sins. There is a phenomenal pride in it that

1. The *Reports* and the *Institutes* of Sir Edward Coke (1552–1634), and the *Commentaries* of Sir William Black- stone (1723–1780) were the foundations of modern British and American jurisprudence.

excludes them from anything mercenary or avaricious. In short the depravity here meant partakes nothing of the sordid or sensual. It is serious, but free from acerbity. Though no flatterer of mankind it never speaks ill of it.

But the thing which in eminent instances signalizes so exceptional a nature is this: though the man's even temper and discreet bearing would seem to intimate a mind peculiarly subject to the law of reason, not the less in his heart he would seem to riot in complete exemption from that law[,] having apparently little to do with reason further than to employ it as an ambidexter implement for effecting the irrational. That is to say: Toward the accomplishment of an aim which in wantonness of malignity would seem to partake of the insane, he will direct a cool judgement sagacious and sound.

These men are true madmen, and of the most dangerous sort, for their lunacy is not continuous but occasional[,] evoked by some special object; it is probably secretive, which is as much to say it is self-contained, so that when moreover, most active[,] it is to the average mind not distinguishable from sanity, and for the reason above suggested that whatever its aims may be, and the aim is never declared—the method and the outward proceeding are always perfectly rational.

Now something such an one was Claggart, in whom was the mania of an evil nature, not engendered by vicious training or corrupting books or licentious living, but born with him and innate, in short "a depravity according to nature."

12
Lawyers, Experts, Clergy
An Episode

By the way, can it be the phenomenon, disowned or at least concealed, that in some criminal cases puzzles the courts? For this cause have our juries at times not only to endure the prolonged contentions of lawyers with their fees, but also the yet more perplexing strife of the medical experts with theirs?—But why leave it to them? why not subpoena as well the clerical proficients? Their vocation bringing them into peculiar contact with so many human beings, and sometimes in their least guarded hour, in interviews very much more confidential than those of physician and patient; this would seem to qualify them to know something about those intricacies involved in the question of moral responsibility; whether in a given case, say, the crime proceeded from mania in the brain or rabies of the heart. As to any differences among themselves these clerical proficients might develop on the stand, these could hardly be greater than the direct contradictions exchanged between the remunerated medical experts.

Dark sayings are these, some will say. But why? Is it because they somewhat savor of Holy Writ in its phrase "mysteries of iniquity"?[2] If they do, such savor was far from being intended for little will it commend these pages to many a reader of to-day.

The point of the present story turning on the hidden nature of the master-at-arms has necessitated this chapter. With an added hint or two in connection with the incident at the mess, the resumed narrative must be left to vindicate, as it may, its own credibility.

13
Pale ire, envy and despair[3]

That Claggart's figure was not amiss, and his face, save the chin, well moulded, has already been said. Of these favorable points he seemed not insensible, for he was not only neat but careful in his dress. But the form of Billy Budd was heroic; and if his face was without the intellectual look of the pallid Claggart's, not the less was it lit, like his, from within, though from a different source. The bonfire in his heart made luminous the rose-tan in his cheek.

In view of the marked contrast between the persons of the twain, it is more than probable that when the master-at-arms in the scene last given applied to the sailor the proverb *Handsome is as handsome does*; he there let escape an ironic inkling, not caught by the young sailors who heard it, as to what it was that had first moved him against Billy, namely, his significant personal beauty.

Now envy and antipathy passions irreconcilable in reason, nevertheless in fact may spring conjoined like Chang and Eng[4] in one birth. Is Envy then such a monster? Well, though many an arraigned mortal has in hopes of mitigated penalty pleaded guilty to horrible actions, did ever anybody seriously confess to envy? Something there is in it universally felt to be more shameful than even felonious crime. And not only does everybody disown it but the better sort are inclined to incredulity when it is in earnest imputed to an intelligent man. But since its lodgement is in the heart not the brain, no degree of intellect supplies a guarantee against it. But Claggart's was no vulgar form of the passion. Nor, as directed toward Billy Budd did it partake of that streak of apprehensive jealousy that marred Saul's visage perturbedly brooding on the comely young David.[5] Claggart's envy struck deeper. If askance he eyed the good looks, cheery health and frank enjoyment of young life in Billy Budd, it was because these [went] along with a nature that as Claggart magnetically felt, had in its simplicity never willed malice or experienced the reactionary bite of that

2. *Cf.* II Thessalonians, ii: 7: "For the mystery of iniquity doth already work * * * " The words that follow recognize a Satanic and active principle of evil in nature.
3. *Cf.* Milton, *Paradise Lost*, Book IV, l. 115. Doomed to be man's evil betrayer, the tortured Satan approached Eden, "his face / Thrice changed with pale—ire, envy, and despair."
4. The original Siamese twins (1811–1874), first exhibited in the United States in 1829.
5. *Cf.* I Samuel xviii: 5–12.

serpent. To him, the spirit lodged within Billy, and looking out from his welkin eyes as from windows, that ineffability it was which made the dimple in his dyed cheek, suppled his joints, and dancing in his yellow curls made him preeminently the Handsome Sailor. One person excepted the master-at-arms was perhaps the only man in the ship intellectually capable of adequately appreciating the moral phenomenon presented in Billy Budd. And the insight but intensified his passion, which assuming various secret forms within him, at times assumed that of cynic disdain—disdain of innocence—To be nothing more than innocent! Yet in an æsthetic way he saw the charm of it, the courageous free-and-easy temper of it, and fain would have shared it, but he despaired of it.

With no power to annul the elemental evil in him, tho readily enough he could hide it; apprehending the good, but powerless to be it; a nature like Claggart's surcharged with energy as such natures almost invariably are, what recourse is left to it but to recoil upon itself and like the scorpion for which the Creator alone is responsible, act out to the end the part allotted it.

14

Passion, and passion in its profoundest, is not a thing demanding a palatial stage whereon to play its part. Down among the groundlings, among the beggars and rakers of the garbage, profound passion is enacted. And the circumstances that provoke it, however trivial or mean, are no measure of its power. In the present instance the stage is a scrubbed gun-deck, and one of the external provocations a man-of-war's-man's spilled soup.

Now when the Master-at-arms noticed whence came that greasy fluid streaming before his feet, he must have taken it—to some extent wilfully, perhaps—not for the mere accident it assuredly was, but for the sly escape of a spontaneous feeling on Billy's part more or less answering to the antipathy on his own. In effect a foolish demonstration he must have thought, and very harmless, like the futile kick of a heifer, which yet were the heifer a shod stallion, would not be so harmless. Even so was it that into the gall of Claggart's envy he infused the vitriol of his contempt. But the incident confirmed to him certain tell-tale reports purveyed to his ear by *Squeak*, one of his more cunning Corporals, a grizzled little man, so nicknamed by the sailors on account of his squeaky voice, and sharp visage ferreting about the dark corners of the lower decks after interlopers, satirically suggesting to them the idea of a rat in a cellar.

From his Chief's employing him as an implicit tool in laying little traps for the worriment of the Foretopman—for it was from the Master-at-arms that the petty persecutions heretofore adverted to had proceeded—the corporal having naturally enough concluded that his master could have no love for the sailor, made it his business, faithful understrapper that he was, to foment the ill blood by perverting to his Chief certain innocent frolics of the good natured Foretopman, besides inventing for his mouth sundry contumelious epithets he claimed to have overheard him let fall. The Master-at-arms never suspected the veracity of these reports, more especially as to the epithets, for he well knew how secretly unpopular may become a master-at-arms[,] at least a master-at-arms of those days zealous in his function, and how the blue-jackets shoot at him in private their raillery and wit; the nickname by which he goes among them (*Jemmy Legs*) implying under the form of merriment their cherished disrespect and dislike.

But in view of the greediness of hate for patrolmen it hardly needed a purveyor to feed Claggart's passion. An uncommon prudence is habitual with the subtler depravity, for it has everything to hide. And in case of an injury but suspected, its secretiveness voluntarily cuts it off from enlightenment or disillusion; and, not unreluctantly, action is taken upon surmise as upon certainty. And the retaliation is apt to be in monstrous disproportion to the supposed offence; for when in anybody was revenge in its exactions aught else but an inordinate usurer. But how with Claggart's conscience? For though consciences are unlike as foreheads, every intelligence, not excluding the Scriptural devils who "believe and tremble," has one. But Claggart's conscience being but the lawyer to his will, made ogres of trifles, probably arguing that the motive imputed to Billy in spilling the soup just when he did, together with the epithets alleged, these, if nothing more, made a strong case against him; nay, justified animosity into a sort of retributive righteousness. The Pharisee is the Guy Fawkes[6] prowling in the hid chambers underlying the Claggarts. And they can really form no conception of an unreciprocated malice. Probably, the master-at-arms' clandestine persecution of Billy was started to try the temper of the man; but it had not developed any quality in him that enmity could make official use of or even pervert into plausible self-justification; so that the occurrence at the mess, petty if it were, was a welcome one to that peculiar conscience assigned to be the private mentor of Claggart; And, for the rest, not improbably it put him upon new experiments.

15

Not many days after the last incident narrated something befell Billy Budd that more gravelled him than aught that had previously occurred.

It was a warm night for the latitude; and the Foretopman, whose watch at the time was properly below, was dozing on the uppermost deck whither he had ascended from his hot hammock one of hundreds suspended so closely wedged together over a lower gun-deck

6. Principal conspirator in the Gunpowder Plot (1604–1605) to blow up the British Houses of Parliament.

that there was little or no swing to them. He lay as in the shadow of a hill-side, stretched under the lee of the booms, a piled ridge of spare spars amidships between foremast and mainmast and among which the ship's largest boat, the launch, was stowed. Alongside of three other slumberers from below, he lay near that end of the booms which approaches the foremast; his station aloft on duty as a foretopman being just over the deck-station of the forecastlemen, entitling him according to usage to make himself more or less at home in that neighborhood.

Presently he was stirred into semi-consciousness by somebody, who must have previously sounded the sleep of the others, touching his shoulder, and then as the Foretopman raised his head, breathing into his ear in a quick whisper, "Slip into the lee forechains, Billy; there is something in the wind. Don't speak. Quick, I will meet you there;" and disappeared.

Now Billy like sundry other essentially good-natured ones had some of the weaknesses inseparable from essential good nature; and among these was a reluctance, almost an incapacity of plumply saying *no* to an abrupt proposition not obviously absurd, on the face of it, nor obviously unfriendly, nor iniquitous. And being of warm blood he had not the phlegm tacitly to negative any proposition by unresponsive inaction. Like his sense of fear, his apprehension as to aught outside of the honest and natural was seldom very quick. Besides, upon the present occasion, the drowse from his sleep still hung upon him.

However it was, he mechanically rose, and sleepily wondering what could be in the wind, betook himself to the designated place, a narrow platform, one of six, outside of the high bulwarks and screened by the great dead-eyes and multiple columned lanyards of the shrouds and back-stays; and, in a great war-ship of that time, of dimensions commensurate [with the] hull's magnitude; a tarry balcony in short overhanging the sea, and so secluded that one mariner of the *Indomitable*, a non-conformist old tar of a serious turn, made it even in daytime his private oratory.

In this retired nook the stranger soon joined Billy Budd. There was no moon as yet; a haze obscured the star-light. He could not distinctly see the stranger's face. Yet from something in the outline and carriage, Billy took him to be, and correctly, for one of the afterguard.

"Hist! Billy," said the man in the same quick cautionary whisper as before; "You were impressed, weren't you? Well, so was I"; and he paused, as to mark the effect. But Billy not knowing exactly what to make of this said nothing. Then the other: "We are not the only impressed ones, Billy. There's a gang of us.—Couldn't you—help—at a pinch?["]

"What do you mean?["] demanded Billy here thoroughly shaking off his drowse.

"Hist, hist!["] the hurried whisper now growing husky, ["]see here"; and the man held up two small objects faintly twinkling in the nightlight; "see, they are yours, Billy, if you'll only—"

But Billy broke in, and in his resentful eagerness to deliver himself his vocal infirmity somewhat intruded: "D-D-Damme, I don't know what you are d-d-driving at, or what you mean, but you had better g-g-go where you belong!" For the moment the fellow, as confounded, did not stir; and Billy springing to his feet, said "If you d-don't start I'll t-t-toss you back over the r-rail!" There was no mistaking this and the mysterious emissary decamped disappearing in the direction of the mainmast in the shadow of the booms.

"Hallo, what's the matter?" here came growling from a forecastle-man awakened from his deck-doze by Billy's raised voice. And as the foretopman reappeared and was recognized by him; "Ah, *Beauty*, is it you? Well, something must have been the matter for you st-st-stuttered."

"O," rejoined Billy, now mastering the impediment; "I found an afterguardsman in our part of the ship here and I bid him be off where he belongs."

"And is that all you did about it, foretopman?" gruffly demanded another, an irascible old fellow of brick-colored visage and hair, and who was known to his associate forecastlemen as *Red Pepper*; "Such sneaks I should like to marry to the gunner's daughter!" by that expression meaning that he would like to subject them to disciplinary castigation over a gun.

However, Billy's rendering of the matter satisfactorily accounted to these inquirers for the brief commotion, since of all the sections of a ship's company the forecastlemen, veterans for the most part and bigoted in their sea-prejudices, are the most jealous in resenting territorial encroachments, especially on the part of any of the afterguard, of whom they have but a sorry opinion, chiefly landsmen, never going aloft except to reef or furl the mainsail, and in no wise competent to handle a marlinspike or turn in a *dead-eye*, say.

16

This incident sorely puzzled Billy Budd. It was an entirely new experience; the first time in his life that he had ever been personally approached in underhand intriguing fashion. Prior to this encounter he had known nothing of the afterguardsman, the two men being stationed wide apart, one forward and aloft during his watch, the other on deck and aft.

What could it mean? And could they really be guineas, those two glittering objects the interloper had held up to his (Billy's)[7]

---

7. The manuscript reads, "up to his (Billy's) eyes," in appearance suggesting the cancellation of "(Billy's)."

eyes? Where could the fellow get guineas? Why even buttons spare buttons[8] are not so plentiful at sea. The more he turned the matter over, the more he was non-plussed, and made uneasy and discomforted. In his disgustful recoil from an overture which tho' he but ill comprehended he instinctively knew must involve evil of some sort, Billy Budd was like a young horse fresh from the pasture suddenly inhaling a vile whiff from some chemical factory and by repeated snortings tries to get it out of his nostrils and lungs. This frame of mind barred all desire of holding further parley with the fellow, even were it but for the purpose of gaining some enlightenment as to his design in approaching him. And yet he was not without natural curiosity to see how such a visitor in the dark would look in broad day.

He espied him the following afternoon in his first dog-watch below one of the smokers on that forward part of the upper gun deck allotted to the pipe.[9] He recognized him by his general cut and build, more than by his round freckled face and glassy eyes of pale blue, veiled with lashes all but white. And yet Billy was a bit uncertain whether indeed it were he—yonder chap about his own age chatting and laughing in free-hearted way, leaning against a gun; a genial young fellow enough to look at, and something of a rattle-brain, to all appearance. Rather chubby too for a sailor even an afterguardsman. In short the last man in the world, one would think, to be overburthened with thoughts, especially those perilous thoughts that must needs belong to a conspirator in any serious project, or even to the underling of such a conspirator.

Altho' Billy was not aware of it, the fellow, with a side-long watchful glance had perceived Billy first, and then noting that Billy was looking at him, thereupon nodded a familiar sort of friendly recognition as to an old acquaintance, without interrupting the talk he was engaged in with the group of smokers. A day or two afterwards chancing in the evening promenade on a gun deck, to pass Billy, he offered a flying word of good-fellowship as it were, which by its unexpectedness, and equivocalness under the circumstances so embarrassed Billy that he knew not how to respond to it, and let it go unnoticed.

Billy was now left more at a loss than before. The ineffectual speculation into which he was led was so disturbingly alien to him that he did his best to smother [it]. It never entered his mind that here was a matter which from its extreme questionableness, it was his duty as a loyal blue-jacket to report in the proper quarter. And, probably, had such a step been suggested to him, he would have been deterred from taking it by the thought, one of novice-magnanimity, that it

8. The manuscript reads, "even buttons spare buttons," in appearance suggesting the cancellation of the first "buttons."

9. The boatswain, who conveys orders to the crew by the blasts of a "bo'sun's" pipe.

would savor overmuch of the dirty work of a tell-tale. He kept the thing to himself. Yet upon one occasion, he could not forbear a little disburthening himself to the old Dansker, tempted thereto perhaps by the influence of a balmy night when the ship lay becalmed; the twain, silent for the most part, sitting together on deck, their heads propped against the bulwarks. But it was only a partial and anonymous account that Billy gave, the unfounded scruples above referred to preventing full disclosure to anybody. Upon hearing Billy's version, the sage Dansker seemed to divine more than he was told; and after a little meditation during which his wrinkles were pursed as into a point, quite effacing for the time that quizzing expression his face sometimes wore,—"Didn't I say so, Baby Budd?"

"Say what?" demanded Billy.

"Why, *Jemmy Legs* is *down* on you."

"And what" rejoined Billy in amazement, "has *Jemmy Legs* to do with that cracked afterguardsman?"

"Ho, it was an afterguardsman then. A cat's-paw, a cat's-paw!" And with that exclamation, which, whether it had reference to a light puff of air just then coming over the calm sea, or subtler relation to the afterguardsman, there is no telling, the old Merlin gave a twisting wrench with his black teeth at his plug of tobacco, vouchsafing no reply to Billy's impetuous question, tho' now repeated, for it was his wont to relapse into grim silence when interrogated in skeptical sort as to any of his sententious oracles, not always very clear ones, rather partaking of that obscurity which invests most Delphic deliverances from any quarter.

Long experience had very likely brought this old man to that bitter prudence which never interferes in aught and never gives advice.

17

Yes, despite the Dansker's pithy insistence as to the Master-at-arms being at the bottom of these strange experiences of Billy on board the *Indomitable*, the young sailor was ready to ascribe them to almost anybody but the man who, to use Billy's own expression, "always had a pleasant word for him." This is to be wondered at. Yet not so much to be wondered at. In certain matters, some sailors even in mature life remain unsophisticated enough. But a young seafarer of the disposition of our athletic Foretopman, is much of a child-man. And yet a child's utter innocence is but its blank ignorance, and the innocence more or less wanes as intelligence waxes. But in Billy Budd intelligence, such as it was, had advanced, while yet his simple mindedness remained for the most part unaffected. Experience is a teacher indeed; yet did Billy's years make his experience small. Besides, he had none of that intuitive knowledge of the bad which in natures not good or incompletely so foreruns experience, and therefore may pertain, as in some instances it too clearly does pertain, even to youth.

And what could Billy know of man except of man as a mere sailor? And the old-fashioned sailor, the veritable man-before-the-mast, the sailor from boyhood up, he, tho' indeed of the same species as a landsman is in some respects singularly distinct from him. The sailor is frankness, the landsman is finesse. Life is not a game with the sailor, demanding the long head; no intricate game of chess where few moves are made in straightforwardness, and ends are attained by indirection; an oblique, tedious, barren game hardly worth that poor candle burnt out in playing it.[1]

Yes, as a class, sailors are in character a juvenile race. Even their deviations are marked by juvenility. And this more especially holding true with the sailors of Billy's time. Then, too, certain things which apply to all sailors, do more pointedly operate here and there, upon the junior one. Every sailor, too is accustomed to obey orders without debating them; his life afloat is externally ruled for him; he is not brought into that promiscuous commerce with mankind where unobstructed free agency on equal terms—equal superficially, at least— soon teaches one that unless upon occasion he exercise a distrust keen in proportion to the fairness of the appearance, some foul turn may be served him. A ruled undemonstrative distrustfulness is so habitual, not with business-men so much, as with men who know their kind in less shallow relations than business, namely, certain men-of-the-world, that they come at last to employ it all but unconsciously; and some of them would very likely feel real surprise at being charged with it as one of their general characteristics.

18

But after the little matter at the mess Billy Budd no more found himself in strange trouble at times about his hammock or his clothes-bag or what not. While, as to that smile that occasionally sunned him, and the pleasant passing word, these were if not more frequent, yet if anything more pronounced than before.

But for all that, there were certain other demonstrations now. When Claggart's unobserved glance happened to light on belted Billy rolling along the upper gun-deck in the leisure of the second dog-watch exchanging passing broadsides of fun with other young promenaders in the crowd; that glance would follow the cheerful sea-Hyperion[2] with a settled meditative and melancholy expression, his eyes strangely suffused with incipient feverish tears. Then would Claggart look like the man of sorrows. Yes, and sometimes the melancholy expression would have in it a touch of soft yearning, as if Claggart could even have loved Billy but for fate and ban. But this was an evanescence, and quickly repented of, as it were, by an immitigable look, pinching and shrivelling the visage into the momentary sem-

1. *Cf.* Shakespeare, *Macbeth*, Act V, Scene 5, ll. 15–17.
2. In early Greek myth, the Titan

Helios, god of the sun; later identified with Apollo, god of manly youth and beauty.

blance of a wrinkled walnut. But sometimes catching sight in advance of the foretopman coming in his direction, he would, upon their nearing, step aside a little to let him pass, dwelling upon Billy for the moment with the glittering dental satire of a Guise.[3] But upon any abrupt unforeseen encounter a red light would [flash] forth from his eye like a spark from an anvil in a dusk smithy. That quick fierce light was a strange one, darted from orbs which in repose were of a color nearest approaching a deeper violet, the softest of shades.

Tho' some of these caprices of the pit could not but be observed by their object, yet were they beyond the construing of such a nature. And the *thews* of Billy were hardly compatible with that sort of sensitive spiritual organisation which in some cases instinctively conveys to ignorant innocence an admonition of the proximity of the malign. He thought the Master-at-arms acted in a manner rather queer at times. That was all. But the occasional frank air and pleasant word went for what they purported to be, the young sailor never having heard as yet of the "too fair-spoken man."

Had the foretopman been conscious of having done or said anything to provoke the ill will of the official, it would have been different with him, and his sight might have been purged if not sharpened. As it was[,] innocence was his blinder.

So was it with him in yet another matter. Two minor officers—the Armorer and Captain of the Hold, with whom he had never exchanged a word, his position in the ship not bringing him into contact with them; these men now for the first began to cast upon Billy when they chanced to encounter him, that peculiar glance which evidences that the man from whom it comes has been some way tampered with and to the prejudice of him upon whom the glance lights. Never did it occur to Billy as a thing to be noted or a thing suspicious, tho' he well knew the fact, that the Armorer and Captain of the Hold, with the ship's-yeoman, apothecary, and others of that grade, were by naval usage, mess-mates of the master-at-arms, men with ears convenient to his confidential tongue.

But the general popularity that our *Handsome Sailor's* manly forwardness upon occasion, and [his] irresistible good nature[,] indicating no mental superiority tending to excite an invidious feeling; this good will on the part of most of his shipmates made him the less to concern himself about such mute aspects toward him as those whereto allusion has just been made.

As to the afterguardsman, tho' Billy for reasons already given necessarily saw little of him, yet when the two did happen to meet, invariably came the fellow's off-hand cheerful recognition, sometimes ac-

3. The Guises, a powerful ducal family of France in the sixteenth and seventeenth centuries, engaged in violent intrigues attractive to romancers, for example Dumas. As for the "glittering dental satire," *cf.* Hamlet's discovery "that one may smile * * * and be a villain" (Act I, Scene 5, ll. 103–105).

companied by a passing pleasant word or two. Whatever that equivocal young person's original design may really have been, or the design
of which he might have been the deputy, certain it was from his
manner upon these occasions, that he had wholly dropped it.

It was as if his precocity of crookedness (and every vulgar villain
is precocious) had for once deceived him, and the man he had sought
to entrap as a simpleton had, through his very simplicity ignorantly
baffled him.

But shrewd ones may opine that it was hardly possible for Billy
to refrain from going up to the afterguardsman and bluntly demanding to know his purpose in the initial interview, so abruptly closed in
the fore-chains. Shrewd ones may also think it but natural in Billy
to set about sounding some of the other impressed men of the ship in
order to discover what basis, if any, there was for the emissary's obscure suggestions as to plotting disaffection aboard. Yes, [the] shrewd
may so think. But something more, or rather, something else than
mere shrewdness is perhaps needful for the due understanding of
such a character as Billy Budd's.

As to Claggart, the monomania in the man—if that indeed it were
—as involuntarily disclosed by starts in the manifestations detailed,
yet in general covered over by his self-contained and rational demeanor; this, like a subterranean fire was eating its way deeper and
deeper in him. Something decisive must come of it.

19

After the mysterious interview in the fore-chains, the one so
abruptly ended there by Billy, nothing especially German[4] to the
story occurred until the events now about to be narrated.

Elsewhere it has been said that in the lack of frigates (of course
better sailers than line-of-battle ships) in the English squadron up the
Straits at that period, the *Indomitable* was occasionally employed not
only as an available substitute for a scout, but at times on detached
service of more important kind. This was not alone because of her
sailing qualities, not common in a ship of her rate, but quite as much,
probably, that the character of her commander, it was thought, spe-
cially adapted him for any duty where under unforeseen difficulties a
prompt initiative might have to be taken in some matter demanding
knowledge and ability in addition to those qualities implied in good
seamanship. It was on an expedition of the latter sort, a somewhat
distant one, and when the *Indomitable* was almost at her furthest
remove from the fleet that in the latter part of an afternoon-watch she
unexpectedly came in sight of a ship of the enemy. It proved to be a
frigate. The latter perceiving thro' the glass that the weight of men
and metal would be heavily against her, invoking her light heels
crowded sail to get away. After a chace urged almost against hope

4. *Cf.* "germane," meaning "akin."

and lasting until about the middle of the first dog-watch, she signally succeeded in effecting her escape.

Not long after the pursuit had been given up, and ere the excitement incident thereto had altogether waned away, the Master-at-Arms ascending from his cavernous sphere made his appearance cap in hand by the mainmast respectfully waiting the notice of Captain Vere then solitary walking the weather-side of the quarter-deck, doubtless somewhat chafed at the failure of the pursuit. The spot where Claggart stood was the place allotted to men of lesser grades seeking some more particular interview either with the officer-of-the-deck or the Captain himself. But from the latter it was not often that a sailor or petty-officer of those days would seek a hearing; only some exceptional cause, would, according to established custom, have warranted that.

Presently, just as the Commander absorbed in his reflections was on the point of turning aft in his promenade, he became sensible of Claggart's presence, and saw the doffed cap held in deferential expectancy. Here be it said that Captain Vere's personal knowledge of this petty-officer had only begun at the time of the ship's last sailing from home, Claggart then for the first, in transfer from a ship detained for repairs, supplying on board the *Indomitable* the place of a previous master-at-arms disabled and ashore.

No sooner did the Commander observe who it was that now deferentially stood awaiting his notice, than a peculiar expression came over him. It was not unlike that which uncontrollably will flit across the countenance of one at unawares encountering a person who though known to him indeed has hardly been long enough known for thorough knowledge, but something in whose aspect nevertheless now for the first provokes a vaguely repellent distaste. But coming to a stand, and resuming much of his wonted official manner, save that a sort of impatience lurked in the intonation of the opening word, he said "Well? what is it, Master-at-Arms?"

With the air of a subordinate grieved at the necessity of being a messenger of ill tidings, and while conscientiously determined to be frank, yet equally resolved upon shunning overstatement, Claggart at this invitation or rather summons to disburthen, spoke up. What he said, conveyed in the language of no uneducated man, was to the effect following if not altogether in these words, namely, that during the chace and preparations for the possible encounter he had seen enough to convince him that at least one sailor aboard was a dangerous character in a ship mustering some who not only had taken a guilty part in the late serious troubles, but others also who, like the man in question, had entered His Majesty's service under another form than enlistment.

At this point Captain Vere with some impatience, interrupted him:

"Be direct, man; say impressed men."

Claggart made a gesture of subservience, and proceeded.

Quite lately he (Claggart) had begun to suspect that on the gun-decks some sort of movement prompted by the sailor in question was covertly going on, but he had not thought himself warranted in reporting the suspicion so long as it remained indistinct. But from what he had that afternoon observed in the man referred to the suspicion of something clandestine going on had advanced to a point less removed from certainty. He deeply felt, he added, the serious responsibility assumed in making a report involving such possible consequences to the individual mainly concerned, besides tending to augment those natural anxieties which every naval commander must feel in view of extraordinary outbreaks so recent as those which, he sorrowfully said it, it needed not to name.

Now at the first broaching of the matter Captain Vere taken by surprise could not wholly dissemble his disquietude. But as Claggart went on, the former's aspect changed into restiveness under something in the witness' manner in giving his testimony. However, he refrained from interrupting him. And Claggart, continuing, concluded with this:

"God forbid, your honor, that the *Indomitable's* should be the experience of the—".

"Never mind that!" here peremptorily broke in the superior, his face altering with anger, instinctively divining the ship that the other was about to name, one in which the Nore Mutiny had assumed a singularly tragical character that for a time jeopardized the life of its commander. Under the circumstances he was indignant at the purposed allusion. When the commissioned officers themselves were on all occasions very heedful how they referred to the recent events, for a petty-officer unnecessarily to allude to them in the presence of his Captain, this struck him as a most immodest presumption. Besides, to his quick sense of self-respect, it even looked under the circumstances something like an attempt to alarm him. Nor at first was he without some surprise that one who so far as he had hitherto come under his notice had shown considerable tact in his function should in this particular evince such lack of it.

But these thoughts and kindred dubious ones flitting across his mind were suddenly replaced by an intuitional surmise which though as yet obscure in form served practically to affect his reception of the ill tidings. Certain it is, that long versed in everything pertaining to the complicated gun-deck life, which like every other form of life, has its secret mines and dubious side, the side popularly disclaimed, Captain Vere did not permit himself to be unduly disturbed by the general tenor of his subordinate's report. Furthermore, if in view of recent events prompt action should be taken at the first palpable sign of recurring insubordination, for all that, not judicious would it be, he thought, to keep the idea of lingering disaffection alive by undue forwardness in crediting an informer even if his own subordinate and charged among other things with police surveillance of the crew. This feeling would not perhaps have so prevailed with him were it not that upon a prior occasion the patriotic zeal officially evinced by Claggart had somewhat irritated him as appearing rather supersensible and strained. Furthermore, something even in the official's self-possessed and somewhat ostentatious manner in making his specifications strangely reminded him of a bandsman, a perjurous witness in a capital case before a court-martial ashore of which when a lieutenant he Captain Vere had been a member.

Now the peremptory check given to Claggart in the matter of the arrested allusion was quickly followed up by this: "You say that there is at least one dangerous man aboard. Name him."

"William Budd. A foretopman, your honor—"

"William Budd" repeated Captain Vere with unfeigned astonishment; "and mean you the man that Lieutenant Ratcliffe took from the merchantman not very long ago—the young fellow who seems to be so popular with the men—Billy, the Handsome Sailor, as they call him?["]

"The same, your honor; but for all his youth and good looks, a deep one. Not for nothing does he insinuate himself into the good will of his shipmates, since at the least all hands will at a pinch say a good word for him at all hazards. Did Lieutenant Ratcliffe happen to tell your honor of that adroit fling of Budd's, jumping up in the cutter's bow under the merchantman's stern when he was being taken off? It is even masqued by that sort of good humored air that at heart he resents his impressment. You have but noted his fair cheek. A man-trap may be under his ruddy-tipped daisies."

Now the *Handsome Sailor* as a signal figure among the crew had naturally enough attracted the Captain's attention from the first. Tho' in general not very demonstrative to his officers, he had congratulated Lieutenant Ratcliffe upon his good fortune in lighting on such a fine specimen of the genus homo, who in the nude might have posed for a statue of young Adam before the Fall.

As to Billy's adieu to the ship *Rights-of-Man*, which the boarding lieutenant had indeed reported to him but in a deferential way more as a good story than aught else, Captain Vere[,] tho mistakenly understanding it as a satiric sally, had but thought so much the better of the impressed man for it; as a military sailor, admiring the spirit that could take an arbitrary enlistment so merrily and sensibly. The foretopman's conduct, too, so far as it had fallen under the Captain's notice had confirmed the first happy augury, while the new recruit's qualities as a *sailor-man* seemed to be such that he had thought of recommending him to the executive officer for promotion to a place that would more frequently bring him under his own observation, namely, the captaincy of the mizzen-top, replacing there in the starboard watch a man not so young whom partly for that reason he deemed less fitted for the post. Be it parenthesized here that since the mizzen-top-men having not to handle such breadths of heavy canvas as the lower sails on the main-mast and fore-mast, a young man if of the right stuff not only seems best adapted to duty there, but in fact is generally selected for the captaincy of that top, and the company under him are light hands and often but striplings. In sum, Captain Vere had from the beginning deemed Billy Budd to be what in the naval parlance of the time was called a *"King's bargain*[,]" that is to say, for His Britannic Majesty's navy a capital investment at small outlay or none at all.

After a brief pause during which the reminiscences above mentioned passed vividly through his mind and he weighed the import of Claggart's last suggestion conveyed in the phrase "pitfall under the clover,"[5] and the more he weighed it the less reliance he felt in the informer's good faith. Suddenly[6] he turned upon him and in a low voice: "Do you come to me, master-at-arms[,] with so foggy a tale? As to Budd, cite me an act or spoken word of his confirmatory of what you in general charge against him. Stay," drawing nearer to him "heed what you speak. Just now, and in a case like this, there is a yard-arm-end for the false-witness."

"Ah, your honor!" sighed Claggart mildly shaking his shapely head as in sad deprecation of such unmerited severity of tone. Then, bridling—erecting himself as in virtuous self-assertion, he circumstantially alleged certain words and acts, which collectively, if credited, led to presumptions mortally inculpating Budd. And for some of these averments, he added, substantiating proof was not far.

With gray eyes impatient and distrustful essaying to fathom to the bottom Claggart's calm violet ones, Captain Vere again heard him out; then for the moment stood ruminating. The mood he evinced, Claggart—himself for the time liberated from the other's scrutiny—steadily regarded with a look difficult to render,—a look curious of the operation of his tactics, a look such as might have been that of the spokesman of the envious children of Jacob deceptively imposing upon the troubled patriarch the blood-dyed coat of young Joseph.[7]

---

5. *Cf.* "A man-trap * * * under his * * * daisies," ending the third paragraph above. There Melville had first written, then canceled, "a pitfall under his ruddy clover," the words that Captain Vere remembers here. The discrepancy might have been corrected had

Melville seen the manuscript through press.
6. The manuscript here reads, "good faith, suddenly * * * ," an obvious comma splice between two sentences, which has been altered for this edition, as in the first edition.
7. Genesis xxxvii: 11–33

Though something exceptional in the moral quality of Captain Vere made him, in earnest encounter with a fellow-man, a veritable touch-stone of that man's essential nature, yet now as to Claggart and what was really going on in him his feeling partook less of intuitional conviction than of strong suspicion clogged by strange dubieties. The perplexity he evinced proceeded less from aught touching the man informed against—as Claggart doubtless opined—than from considerations how best to act in regard to the informer. At first indeed he was naturally for summoning that substantiation of his allegations which Claggart said was at hand. But such a proceeding would result in the matter at once getting abroad, which in the present stage of it, he thought, might undesirably affect the ship's company. If Claggart was a false witness,—that closed the affair. And therefore before trying the accusation, he would first practically test the accuser; and he thought this could be done in a quiet undemonstrative way.

The measure he determined upon involved a shifting of the scene, a transfer to a place less exposed to observation than the broad quarter-deck. For although the few gun-room officers there at the time had, in due observance of naval etiquette, withdrawn to leeward the moment Captain Vere had begun his promenade on the deck's weather-side; and tho' during the colloquy with Claggart they of course ventured not to diminish the distance; and though throughout the interview Captain Vere's voice was far from high, and Claggart's silvery and low; and the wind in the cordage and the wash of the sea helped the more to put them beyond ear-shot; nevertheless, the interview's continuance already had attracted observation from some topmen aloft and other sailors in the waist or further forward.

Having determined upon his measures, Captain Vere forthwith took action. Abruptly turning to Claggart he asked "Master-at-arms, is it now Budd's watch aloft?"

"No, your honor." Whereupon, "Mr. Wilkes!" summoning the nearest midshipman, "tell Albert to come to me." Albert was the Captain's hammock-boy, a sort of sea-valet in whose discretion and fidelity his master had much confidence. The lad appeared. "You know Budd the foretopman?"

"I do, Sir."

"Go find him. It is his watch off. Manage to tell him out of ear-shot that he is wanted aft. Contrive it that he speaks to nobody. Keep him in talk yourself. And not till you get well aft here, not till then let him know that the place where he is wanted is my cabin. You understand. Go.—Master-at-Arms, show yourself on the decks below, and when you think it time for Albert to be coming with his man, stand by quietly to follow the sailor in."

20

Now when the foretopman found himself closeted there, as it were, in the cabin with the Captain and Claggart, he was surprised enough. But it was a surprise unaccompanied by apprehension or distrust. To an immature nature essentially honest and humane, forewarning intimations of subtler danger from one's kind come tardily if at all. The only thing that took shape in the young sailor's mind was this: Yes, the Captain, I have always thought, looks kindly upon me. Wonder if he's going to make me his coxswain. I should like that. And maybe now he is going to ask the master-at-arms about me.

"Shut the door there, sentry," said the commander; "stand without, and let nobody come in.—Now, master-at-arms, tell this man to his face what you told of him to me;" and stood prepared to scrutinize the mutually confronting visages.

With the measured step and calm collected air of an asylum-physician approaching in the public hall some patient beginning to show indications of a coming paroxysm, Claggart deliberately advanced within short range of Billy, and mesmerically looking him in the eye, briefly recapitulated the accusation.

Not at first did Billy take it in. When he did, the rose-tan of his cheek looked struck as by white leprosy. He stood like one impaled and gagged. Meanwhile the accuser's eyes removing not as yet from the blue dilated ones, underwent a phenomenal change, their wonted rich violet color blurring into a muddy purple. Those lights of human intelligence losing human expression, gelidly protruding like the alien eyes of certain uncatalogued creatures of the deep. The first mesmeric glance was one of serpent fascination; the last was as the hungry lurch of the torpedo-fish.

"Speak, man!" said Captain Vere to the transfixed one struck by his aspect even more than by Claggart's, "Speak! defend yourself." Which appeal caused but a strange dumb gesturing and gurgling in Billy; amazement at such an accusation so suddenly sprung on inexperienced nonage; this, and, it may be horror of the accuser, serving to bring out his lurking defect and in this instance for the time intensifying it into a convulsed tongue-tie; while the intent head and entire form straining forward in an agony of ineffectual eagerness to obey the injunction to speak and defend himself, gave an expression to the face like that of a condemned Vestal priestess in the moment of being buried alive, and in the first struggle against suffocation.

Though at the time Captain Vere was quite ignorant of Billy's liability to vocal impediment, he now immediately divined it, since vividly Billy's aspect recalled to him that of a bright young schoolmate of his whom he had once seen struck by much the same startling impotence in the act of eagerly rising in the class to be foremost in response to a testing question put to it by the master. Going close up to the young sailor, and laying a soothing hand on his shoulder, he said[:] "There is no hurry, my boy. Take your time, take your time." Contrary to the effect intended, these words so fatherly in tone, doubtless touching Billy's heart to the quick, prompted yet more violent efforts at utterance—efforts soon ending for the time in confirming the paralysis, and bringing to his face an expression which was as a crucifixion to behold. The next instant, quick as the flame from a discharged cannon at night, his right arm shot out, and Claggart dropped to the deck. Whether intentionally or but owing to the young athlete's superior height, the blow had taken effect full upon the forehead, so shapely and intellectual-looking a feature in the master-at-arms; so that the body fell over lengthwise, like a heavy plank tilted from erectness. A gasp or two, and he lay motionless.

"Fated boy," breathed Captain Vere in tone so low as to be almost a whisper, "what have you done! But here, help me."

The twain raised the felled one from the loins up into a sitting position. The spare form flexibly acquiesced, but inertly. It was like handling a dead snake. They lowered it back. Regaining erectness Captain Vere with one hand covering his face stood to all appearance as impassive as the object at his feet. Was he absorbed in taking in all the bearings of the event and what was best not only now at once to be done, but also in the sequel? Slowly he uncovered his face; and the effect was as if the moon emerging from eclipse should reappear with quite another aspect than that which had gone into hiding. The father in him, manifested towards Billy thus far in the scene, was replaced by the military disciplinarian. In his official tone he bade the foretopman retire to a state-room aft, (pointing it out) and there remain till thence summoned. This order Billy in silence mechanically obeyed. Then going to the cabin-door where it opened on the quarter-deck, Captain Vere said to the sentry without, "Tell somebody to send Albert here." When the lad appeared his master so contrived it that he should not catch sight of the prone one. "Albert," he said to him, "tell the Surgeon I wish to see him. You need not come back till called." When the Surgeon entered— a self-poised character of that grave sense and experience that hardly anything could take him aback,—Captain Vere advanced to meet him, thus unconsciously intercepting his view of Claggart and interrupting the other's wonted ceremonious salutation, said, "Nay, tell me how it is with yonder man," directing his attention to the prostrate one.

The Surgeon looked, and for all his self-command, somewhat

started at the abrupt revelation. On Claggart's always pallid complexion, thick black blood was now oozing from nostril and ear. To the gazer's professional eye it was unmistakably no living man that he saw.

"Is it so then?["] said Captain Vere intently watching him. "I thought it. But verify it." Whereupon the customary tests confirmed the Surgeon's first glance, who now looking up in unfeigned concern, cast a look of intense inquisitiveness upon his superior. But Captain Vere, with one hand to his brow, was standing motionless. Suddenly, catching the Surgeon's arm convulsively, he exclaimed, pointing down to the body—"It is the divine judgment on Ananias![8] Look!"

Disturbed by the excited manner he had never before observed in the *Indomitable's* Captain, and as yet wholly ignorant of the affair, the prudent Surgeon nevertheless held his peace, only again looking an earnest interrogation as to what it was that had resulted in such a tragedy.

But Captain Vere was now again motionless standing absorbed in thought. But again starting, he vehemently exclaimed—"Struck dead by an angel of God! Yet the angel must hang!["]

At these passionate interjections, mere incoherences to the listener as yet unapprised of the antecedents, the Surgeon was profoundly discomposed. But now as recollecting himself, Captain Vere in less harsh tone briefly related the circumstances leading up to the event. ["]But come; we must despatch" he added. ["]Help me to remove him (meaning the body) to yonder compartment,["] designating one opposite that where the foretopman remained immured. Anew disturbed by a request that as implying a desire for secrecy, seemed unaccountably strange to him, there was nothing for the subordinate to do but comply.

"Go now" said Captain Vere with something of his wonted manner—["]Go now. I shall presently call a drum-head court. Tell the lieutenants what has happened, and tell Mr. Mordant," meaning the captain of marines, "and charge them to keep the matter to themselves."

21

Full of disquietude and misgiving the Surgeon left the cabin. Was Captain Vere suddenly affected in his mind, or was it but a transient excitement, brought about by so strange and extraordinary a happening? As to the drum-head court, it struck the Surgeon as impolitic, if nothing more. The thing to do, he thought, was to place Billy Budd in confinement and in a way dictated by usage, and postpone further action in so extraordinary a case, to such time as they should

---

8. Having lied, "not * * * unto men, but unto God," Ananias was stricken dead (Acts v: 1–5).

rejoin the squadron, and then refer it to the Admiral. He recalled the unwonted agitation of Captain Vere and his excited exclamations so at variance with his normal manner. Was he unhinged? But assuming that he is, it is not so susceptible of proof. What then can he do? No more trying situation is conceivable than that of an officer subordinate under a Captain whom he suspects to be, not mad indeed, but yet not quite unaffected in his intellect. To argue his order to him would be insolence. To resist him would be mutiny.

In obedience to Captain Vere he communicated what had happened to the lieutenants & captain of marines; saying nothing as to the Captain's state. They fully shared his own surprise and concern. Like him too they seemed to think that such a matter should be referred to the Admiral.

22

Who in the rainbow can draw the line where the violet tint ends and the orange tint begins? Distinctly we see the difference of the colors, but where exactly does the one first blendingly enter into the other? So with sanity and insanity. In pronounced cases there is no question about them. But in some supposed cases, in various degrees supposedly less pronounced, to draw the exact line of demarkation few will undertake tho for a fee some professional experts will. There is nothing namable but that some men will undertake to do it for pay.

Whether Captain Vere, as the Surgeon professionally and privately surmised, was really the sudden victim of any degree of aberration, one must determine for himself by such light as this narrative may afford.

[That] the unhappy event which has been narrated could not have happened at a worse juncture was but too true. For it was close on the heel of the suppressed insurrections, an aftertime very critical to naval authority, demanding from every English sea-commander two qualities not readily interfusable—prudence and rigor. Moreover there was something crucial in the case.

In the jugglery of circumstances preceding and attending the event on board the *Indomitable* and in the light of that martial code whereby it was formally to be judged, innocence and guilt personified in Claggart and Budd in effect changed places. In a legal view the apparent victim of the tragedy was he who had sought to victimize a man blameless; and the indisputable deed of the latter, navally regarded, constituted the most heinous of military crimes. Yet more. The essential right and wrong involved in the matter, the clearer that might be, so much the worse for the responsibility of a loyal sea-commander inasmuch as he was not authorized to determine the matter on that primitive basis.

Small wonder then that the *Indomitable's* Captain though in general a man of rapid decision, felt that circumspectness not less than promptitude was necessary. Until he could decide upon his course, and in each detail; and not only so, but until the concluding measure was upon the point of being enacted, he deemed it advisable, in view of all the circumstances to guard as much as possible against publicity. Here he may or may not have erred. Certain it is however that subsequently in the confidential talk of more than one or two gun-rooms and cabins he was not a little criticized by some officers, a fact imputed by his friends and vehemently by his cousin Jack Denton to professional jealousy of *Starry Vere*. Some imaginative ground for invidious comment there was. The maintenance of secrecy in the matter, the confining all knowledge of it for a time to the place where the homicide occurred, the quarter-deck cabin; in these particulars lurked some resemblance to the policy adopted in those tragedies of the palace which have occurred more than once in the capital founded by Peter the Barbarian.[9]

The case indeed was such that fain would the *Indomitable's* captain have deferred taking any action whatever respecting it further than to keep the foretopman a close prisoner till the ship rejoined the squadron and then submitting the matter to the judgement of his Admiral.

But a true military officer is in one particular like a true monk. Not with more of self-abnegation will the latter keep his vows of monastic obedience than the former his vows of allegiance to martial duty.

Feeling that unless quick action was taken on it, the deed of the foretopman, so soon as it should be known on the gun-decks would tend to awaken any slumbering embers of the Nore among the crew, a sense of the urgency of the case overruled in Captain Vere every other consideration. But tho' a conscientious disciplinarian he was no lover of authority for mere authority's sake. Very far was he from embracing opportunities for monopolizing to himself the perils of moral responsibility[,] none at least that could properly be referred to an official superior or shared with him by his official equals or even subordinates. So thinking[,] he was glad it would not be at variance with usage to turn the matter over to a summary court of his own officers, reserving to himself as the one on whom the ultimate accountability would rest, the right of maintaining a supervision of it, or formally or informally interposing at need. Accordingly a drum-head court was summarily convened, he electing the individuals composing it, the First Lieutenant, the Captain of marines, and the Sailing Master.

In associating an officer of marines with the sea-lieutenants in a case having to do with a sailor the Commander perhaps deviated

9. Peter I, Czar of Russia (1682–1725), called Peter the Great, founded the new Russian capital of St. Petersburg (1703).

from general custom. He was prompted thereto by the circumstance that he took that soldier to be a judicious person, thoughtful, and not altogether incapable of grappling with a difficult case unprecedented in his prior experience. Yet even as to him he was not without some latent misgiving, for withal he was an extremely good-natured man, an enjoyer of his dinner, a sound sleeper, and inclined to obesity. [A] man who tho' he would always maintain his manhood in battle might not prove altogether reliable in a moral dilemma involving aught of the tragic. As to the First Lieutenant and the Sailing Master Captain Vere could not but be aware that though honest natures, of approved gallantry upon occasion[,] their intelligence was mostly confined to the matter of active seamanship and the fighting demands of their profession. The court was held in the same cabin where the unfortunate affair had taken place. This cabin, the Commander's, embraced the entire area under the poop-deck. Aft, and on either side[,] was a small state-room[;] the one room temporarily a jail & the other a dead-house[,] and a yet smaller compartment leaving a space between, expanding forward into a goodly oblong of length coinciding with the ship's beam. A skylight of moderate dimension was overhead and at each end of the oblong space were two sashed port-hole windows easily convertible back into embrasures for short carronades.

All being quickly in readiness, Billy Budd was arraigned, Captain Vere necessarily appearing as the sole witness in the case, and as such temporarily sinking his rank, though singularly maintaining it in a matter apparently trivial, namely, that he testified from the ship's weather-side[,] with that object having caused the court to sit on the lee-side. Concisely he narrated all that had led up to the catastrophe, omitting nothing in Claggart's accusation and deposing as to the manner in which the prisoner had received it. At this testimony the three officers glanced with no little surprise at Billy Budd, the last man they would have suspected either of the mutinous design alleged by Claggart or the undeniable deed he himself had done.

The First Lieutenant[,] taking judicial primacy and turning toward the prisoner, said, "Captain Vere has spoken. Is it or is it not as Captain Vere says?" In response came syllables not so much impeded in the utterance as might have been anticipated. They were these: "Captain Vere tells the truth. It is just as Captain Vere says, but it is not as the Master-at-Arms said. I have eaten the King's bread and I am true to the King."

"I believe you, my man" said the witness[,] his voice indicating a suppressed emotion not otherwise betrayed.

"God will bless you for that, Your Honor!" not without stammering said Billy, and all but broke down. But immediately was recalled to self-control by another question, to which with the same emotional difficulty of utterance he said "No, there was no malice between us. I never bore malice against the Master-at-arms. I am sorry that he is dead. I did not mean to kill him. Could I have used my tongue I would not have struck him. But he foully lied to my face and in presence of my Captain, and I had to say something, and I could only say it with a blow, God help me!"

In the impulsive above-board manner of the frank one[,] the court saw confirmed all that was implied in words that just previously had perplexed them[,] coming as they did from the testifier to the tragedy and promptly following Billy's impassioned disclaimer of mutinous intent—Captain Vere's words, "I believe you, my man."

Next it was asked of him whether he knew of or suspected aught savoring of incipient trouble (meaning mutiny, tho' the explicit term was avoided) going on in any section of the ship's company.

The reply lingered. This was naturally imputed by the court to the same vocal embarrassment which had retarded or obstructed previous answers. But in main it was otherwise here; the question immediately recalling to Billy's mind the interview with the after-guardsman in the fore-chains. But an innate repugnance to playing a part at all approaching that of an informer against one's own ship-mates—the same erring sense of uninstructed honor which had stood in the way of his reporting the matter at the time though as a loyal man-of-war-man it was incumbent on him[,] and failure so to do if charged against him and proven, would have subjected him to the heaviest of penalties; this, with the blind feeling now his, that nothing really was being hatched, prevailed with him. When the answer came it was a negative.

"One question more," said the officer of marines now first speaking and with a troubled earnestness, "You tell us that what the Master-at-arms said against you was a lie. Now why should he have so lied, so maliciously lied, since you declare there was no malice between you?"

At that question unintentionally touching on a spiritual sphere wholly obscure to Billy's thoughts, he was nonplussed, evincing a confusion indeed that some observers, such as can readily be imagined, would have construed into involuntary evidence of hidden guilt. Nevertheless he strove some way to answer, but all at once relinquished the vain endeavor, at the same time turning an appealing glance towards Captain Vere as deeming him his best helper and friend. Captain Vere who had been seated for a time rose to his feet, addressing the interrogator. "The question you put to him comes naturally enough. But how can he rightly answer it? or anybody else? unless indeed it be he who lies within there" designating the compartment where lay the corpse. "But the prone one there will not rise to our summons. In effect, tho', as it seems to me, the point you make is hardly material. Quite aside from any conceivable motive actuating the Master-at-arms, and irrespective of the provocation to the blow, a martial court must needs in the present case confine its attention to the blow's consequence, which consequence justly is to be deemed not otherwise than as the striker's deed."

This utterance the full significance of which it was not at all likely that Billy took in, nevertheless caused him to turn a wistful interrogative look toward the speaker, a look in its dumb expressiveness not unlike that which a dog of generous breed might turn upon his master seeking in his face some elucidation of a previous gesture ambiguous to the canine intelligence. Nor was the same utterance without marked effect upon the three officers, more especially the soldier. Couched in it seemed to them a meaning unanticipated, involving a prejudgement on the speaker's part. It served to augment a mental disturbance previously evident enough.

The soldier once more spoke; in a tone of suggestive dubiety addressing at once his associates and Captain Vere: "Nobody is present —none of the ship's company, I mean, who might shed lateral light, if any is to be had, upon what remains mysterious in this matter."

"That is thoughtfully put" said Captain Vere; "I see your drift. Ay, there is a mystery; but, to use a Scriptural phrase, it is 'a mystery of iniquity,' a matter for psychologic theologians to discuss. But what has a military court to do with it? Not to add that for us any possible investigation of it is cut off by the lasting tongue-tie of—him—in yonder," again designating the mortuary state-room ["]The prisoner's deed,—with that alone we have to do."

To this, and particularly the closing reiteration, the marine soldier knowing not how aptly to reply, sadly abstained from saying aught. The First Lieutenant who at the outset had not unnaturally assumed primacy in the court, now overrulingly instructed by a glance from Captain Vere, a glance more effective than words, resumed that primacy. Turning to the prisoner, "Budd," he said, and scarce in equable tones, "Budd, if you have aught further to say for yourself, say it now."

Upon this the young sailor turned another quick glance toward Captain Vere; then, as taking a hint from that aspect, a hint confirming his own instinct that silence was now best, replied to the Lieutenant "I have said all, Sir."

The marine—the same who had been the sentinel without the cabin-door at the time that the foretopman followed by the master-at-arms, entered it—he, standing by the sailor throughout these judicial proceedings, was now directed to take him back to the after compartment originally assigned to the prisoner and his custodian. As the twain disappeared from view, the three officers as partially liberated from some inward constraint associated with Billy's mere presence, simultaneously stirred in their seats. They exchanged looks of troubled indecision, yet feeling that decide they must and without long delay. As for Captain Vere, he for the time stood unconsciously with his back toward them, apparently in one of his absent fits, gazing out from a sashed port-hole to windward upon the monotonous blank of the twilight sea. But the court's silence continuing, broken only at moments by brief consultations in low earnest tones, this seemed to arm him and energize him. Turning, he to-and-fro paced the cabin athwart; in the returning ascent to windward, climbing the slant deck in the ship's lee roll; without knowing it symbolizing thus in his action a mind resolute to surmount difficulties even if against primitive instincts strong as the wind and the sea. Presently he came to a stand before the three. After scanning their faces he stood less as mustering his thoughts for expression, than as one inly deliberating how best to put them to well-meaning men not intellectually mature, men with whom it was necessary to demonstrate certain principles that were axioms to himself. Similar impatience as to talking is perhaps one reason that deters some minds from addressing any popular assemblies.

When speak he did, something both in the substance of what he said and his manner of saying it, showed the influence of unshared studies modifying and tempering the practical training of an active career. This, along with his phraseology now and then was suggestive of the grounds whereon rested that imputation of a certain pedantry socially alleged against him by certain naval men of wholly practical cast, captains who nevertheless would frankly concede that His Majesty's navy mustered no more efficient officer of their grade than *Starry Vere*.

What he said was to this effect: "Hitherto I have been but the witness, little more; and I should hardly think now to take another tone, that of your coadjutor, for the time, did I not perceive in you, —at the crisis too—a troubled hesitancy, proceeding, I doubt not from the clash of military duty with moral scruple—scruple vitalized by compassion. For the compassion how can I otherwise than share it. But, mindful of paramount obligations I strive against scruples that may tend to enervate decision. Not, gentlemen, that I hide from myself that the case is an exceptional one. Speculatively regarded, it well might be referred to a jury of casuists. But for us here acting not as casuists or moralists, it is a case practical, and under martial law practically to be dealt with.

"But your scruples: do they move as in a dusk? Challenge them. Make them advance and declare themselves. Come now: do they import something like this: If, mindless of palliating circumstances, we are bound to regard the death of the Master-at-arms as the prisoner's deed, then does that deed constitute a capital crime whereof the penalty is a mortal one. But in natural justice is nothing but the prisoner's overt act to be considered? How can we adjudge to summary and shameful death a fellow-creature innocent before God, and whom we feel to be so?—Does that state it aright? You sign sad assent. Well, I too feel that, the full force of that. It is Nature. But do these buttons that we wear attest that our allegiance is to Nature? No, to the King. Though the ocean, which is inviolate Nature primeval, tho' this be the element where we move and have our being as sailors, yet as the King's officers lies our duty in a sphere correspondingly natural? So little is that true, that in receiving our commissions we in the most important regards ceased to be natural free-agents. When war is declared are we the commissioned fighters previously consulted? We fight at command. If our judgements approve the war, that is but coincidence. So in other particulars. So now. For suppose condemnation to follow these present proceedings. Would it be so much we ourselves that would condemn as it would be martial law operating through us? For that law and the rigour of it, we are not responsible. Our vowed responsibility is in this: That however pitilessly that law may operate, we nevertheless adhere to it and administer it.

[“]But the exceptional in the matter moves the hearts within you. Even so too is mine moved. But let not warm hearts betray heads that should be cool. Ashore in a criminal case will an upright judge allow himself off the bench to be waylaid by some tender kinswoman of the accused seeking to touch him with her tearful plea? Well the heart here denotes the feminine in man[1] is as that piteous woman, and hard tho' it be[,] she must here be ruled out.”

He paused, earnestly studying them for a moment; then resumed.

“But something in your aspect seems to urge that it is not solely the heart that moves in you, but also the conscience, the private conscience. But tell me whether or not, occupying the position we do, private conscience should not yield to that imperial one formulated in the code under which alone we officially proceed?”

Here the three men moved in their seats, less convinced than agitated by the course of an argument troubling but the more the spontaneous conflict within.

Perceiving which, the speaker paused for a moment; then abruptly changing his tone, went on.

“To steady us a bit, let us recur to the facts.—In war-time at sea a man-of-war's-man strikes his superior in grade, and the blow kills. Apart from its effect the blow itself is, according to the Articles of War, a capital crime. Furthermore—”

“Ay, Sir,” emotionally broke in the officer of marines, “in one sense it was. But surely Budd purposed neither mutiny nor homi-

1. Comma in the manuscript here deleted.

cide."

"Surely not, my good man. And before a court less arbitrary and more merciful than a martial one, that plea would largely extenuate. At the Last Assizes[2] it shall acquit. But how here? We proceed under the law of the Mutiny Act. In feature no child can resemble his father more than that Act resembles in spirit the thing from which it derives—War. In His Majesty['s] service—in this ship indeed—there are Englishmen forced to fight for the King against their will. Against their conscience, for aught we know. Tho' as their fellow-creatures some of us may appreciate their position, yet as navy officers, what reck we of it? Still less recks the enemy. Our impressed men he would fain cut down in the same swath with our volunteers. As regards the enemy's naval conscripts, some of whom may even share our own abhorrence of the regicidal French Directory,[3] it is the same on our side. War looks but to the frontage, the appearance. And the Mutiny Act, War's child, takes after the father. Budd's intent or non-intent is nothing to the purpose.

["]But while, put to it by those anxieties in you which I can not but respect, I only repeat myself—while thus strangely we prolong proceedings that should be summary—the enemy may be sighted and an engagement result. We must do; and one of two things must we do—condemn or let go."

"Can we not convict and yet mitigate the penalty?" asked the junior Lieutenant here speaking, and falteringly, for the first.

"Lieutenant, were that clearly lawful for us under the circumstances consider the consequences of such clemency. The people" (meaning the ship's company) "have native-sense; most of them are familiar with our naval usage and tradition; and how would they take it? Even could you explain to them—which our official position forbids—they, long moulded by arbitrary discipline have not that kind of intelligent responsiveness that might qualify them to comprehend and discriminate. No, to the people the foretopman's deed however it be worded in the announcement will be plain homicide committed in a flagrant act of mutiny. What penalty for that should follow, they know. But it does not follow. W*hy?* they will ruminate. You know what sailors are. Will they not revert to the recent outbreak at the Nore? Ay. They know the well-founded alarm—the panic it struck throughout England. Your clement sentence they would account pusillanimous. They would think that we flinch, that we are afraid of them—afraid of practising a lawful rigor singularly demanded at this juncture lest it should provoke new troubles. What

2. Assizes are the highest judicial courts of review of the British counties; here the term refers to the scriptural Judgment Day.

3. The executive council of the French First Republic (1795–1799). This was the enemy against whom the British fleet was engaged in 1797, the year of this story (*cf.* the Preface).

shame to us such a conjecture on their part, and how deadly to discipline. You see then, whither prompted by duty and the law I steadfastly drive. But I beseech you, my friends, do not take me amiss. I feel as you do for this unfortunate boy. But did he know our hearts, I take him to be of that generous nature that he would feel even for us on whom in this military necessity so heavy a compulsion is laid."

With that, crossing the deck he resumed his place by the sashed port-hole, tacitly leaving the three to come to a decision. On the cabin's opposite side the troubled court sat silent. Loyal lieges, plain and practical, though at bottom they dissented from some points Captain Vere had put to them, they were without the faculty, hardly had the inclination to gainsay one whom they felt to be an earnest man, one too not less their superior in mind than in naval rank. But it is not improbable that even such of his words as were not without influence over them, less came home to them than his closing appeal to their instinct as sea-officers in the forethought he threw out as to the practical consequences to discipline, considering the unconfirmed tone of the fleet at the time, should a man-of-war's-man['s] violent killing at sea of a superior in grade be allowed to pass for aught else than a capital crime demanding prompt infliction of the penalty.

Not unlikely they were brought to something more or less akin to that harassed frame of mind which in the year 1842 actuated the commander of the U.S. brig-of-war *Somers* to resolve, under the so-called Articles of War, Articles modelled upon the English Mutiny Act, to resolve upon the execution at sea of a midshipman and two petty-officers as mutineers designing the seizure of the brig. Which resolution was carried out though in a time of peace and within not many days sail of home. An act vindicated by a naval court of inquiry subsequently convened ashore. History, and here cited without comment. True, the circumstances on board the *Somers* were different from those on board the *Indomitable*. But the urgency felt, well-warranted or otherwise, was much the same.

Says a writer whom few know, "Forty years after a battle it is easy for a non-combatant to reason about how it ought to have been fought. It is another thing personally and under fire to direct the fighting while involved in the obscuring smoke of it. Much so with respect to other emergencies involving considerations both practical and moral, and when it is imperative promptly to act. The greater the fog the more it imperils the steamer, and speed is put on tho' at the hazard of running somebody down. Little ween the snug card-players in the cabin of the responsibilities of the sleepless man on the bridge."

In brief, Billy Budd was formally convicted and sentenced to be hung at the yard-arm in the early morning-watch, it being now night. Otherwise, as is customary in such cases, the sentence would forthwith have been carried out. In war-time on the field or in the fleet, a mortal punishment decreed by a drum-head court—on the field sometimes decreed by but a nod from the General—follows without delay on the heel of conviction without appeal.

23

It was Captain Vere himself who of his own motion communicated the finding of the court to the prisoner; for that purpose going to the compartment where he was in custody and bidding the marine there to withdraw for the time.

Beyond the communication of the sentence what took place at this interview was never known. But in view of the character of the twain briefly closeted in that state-room, each radically sharing in the rarer qualities of our nature—so rare indeed as to be all but incredible to average minds however much cultivated—some conjectures may be ventured.

It would have been in consonance with the spirit of Captain Vere should he on this occasion have concealed nothing from the condemned one—should he indeed have frankly disclosed to him the part he himself had played in bringing about the decision, at the same time revealing his actuating motives. On Billy's side it is not improbable that such a confession would have been received in much the same spirit that prompted it. Not without a sort of joy indeed he might have appreciated the brave opinion of him implied in his Captain making such a confidant of him. Nor, as to the sentence itself could he have been insensible that it was imparted to him as to one not afraid to die. Even more may have been. Captain Vere in [the] end may have developed the passion sometimes latent under a[n] exterior stoical or indifferent. He was old enough to have been Billy's father. The austere devotee of military duty letting himself melt back into what remains primeval in our formalized humanity may in [the] end have caught Billy to his heart even as Abraham may have caught young Isaac on the brink of resolutely offering him up in obedience to the exacting behest.[4] But there is no telling the sacrament, seldom if in any case revealed to the gadding world wherever under circumstances at all akin to those here attempted to be set forth two of great Nature's nobler order embrace. There is privacy at the time, inviolable to the survivor, and holy oblivion the sequel to each diviner magnanimity, providentially covers all at last.

The first to encounter Captain Vere in act of leaving the compartment was the senior Lieutenant. The face he beheld, for the moment one expressive of the agony of the strong, was to that officer, tho' a man of fifty, a startling revelation. That the condemned one

4. *Cf.* Genesis xxii: 1–14.

suffered less than he who mainly had effected the condemnation was apparently indicated by the former's exclamation in the scene soon perforce to be touched upon.

24

Of a series of incidents within a brief term rapidly following each other, the adequate narration may take up a term less brief, especially if explanation or comment here and there seem requisite to the better understanding of such incidents. Between the entrance into the cabin of him who never left it alive, and him who when he did leave it left it as one condemned to die; between this and the closeted interview just given less than an hour and a half had elapsed. It was an interval long enough however to awaken speculations among no few of the ship's company as to what it was that could be detaining in the cabin the master-at-arms and the sailor; for a rumor that both of them had been seen to enter it and neither of them had been seen to emerge, this rumor had got abroad upon the gun-decks and in the tops; the people of a great warship being in one respect like villagers taking microscopic note of every outward movement or non-movement going on. When therefore in weather not at all tempestuous all hands were called in the second dog-watch, a summons under such circumstances not usual in those hours, the crew were not wholly unprepared for some announcement extraordinary, one having connection too with the continued absence of the two men from their wonted haunts.

There was a moderate sea at the time; and the moon, newly risen and near to being at its full, silvered the white spar-deck wherever not blotted by the clear-cut shadows horizontally thrown of fixtures and moving men. On either side the quarter-deck the marine guard under arms was drawn up; and Captain Vere standing in his place surrounded by all the ward-room officers, addressed his men. In so doing his manner showed neither more nor less than that property pertaining to his supreme position aboard his own ship. In clear terms and concise he told them what had taken place in the cabin; that the master-at-arms was dead; that he who had killed him had been already tried by a summary court and condemned to death; and that the execution would take place in the early morning watch. The word *mutiny* was not named in what he said. He refrained too from making the occasion an opportunity for any preachment as to the maintenance of discipline, thinking perhaps that under existing circumstances in the navy the consequence of violating discipline should be made to speak for itself.

Their captain's announcement was listened to by the throng of standing sailors in a dumbness like that of a seated congregation of believers in hell listening to the clergyman's announcement of his Calvinistic text.

At the close, however, a confused murmur went up. It began to wax. All but instantly, then, at a sign, it was pierced and suppressed by shrill whistles of the Boatswain and his Mates piping down one watch.

To be prepared for burial Claggart's body was delivered to certain petty-officers of his mess. And here, not to clog the sequel with lateral matters, it may be added that at a suitable hour, the Master-at-arms was committed to the sea with every funeral honor properly belonging to his naval grade.

In this proceeding as in every public one growing out of the tragedy strict adherence to usage was observed. Nor in any point could it have been at all deviated from, either with respect to Claggart or Billy Budd[,] without begetting undesirable speculations in the ship's company, sailors, and more particularly men-of-war's men, being of all men the greatest sticklers for usage.

For similar cause, all communication between Captain Vere and the condemned one ended with the closeted interview already given, the latter being now surrendered to the ordinary routine preliminary to the end. This transfer under guard from the Captain's quarters was effected without unusual precautions—at least no visible ones.

If possible not to let the men so much as surmise that their officers anticipate aught amiss from them is the tacit rule in a military ship. And the more that some sort of trouble should really be apprehended the more do the officers keep that apprehension to themselves; tho' not the less unostentatious vigilance may be augmented.

In the present instance the sentry placed over the prisoner had strict orders to let no one have communication with him but the Chaplain. And certain unobtrusive measures were taken absolutely to insure this point.

25

In a seventy-four of the old order the deck known as the upper gun-deck was the one covered over by the spar-deck which last though not without its armament was for the most part exposed to the weather. In general it was at all hours free from hammocks; those of the crew swinging on the lower gun-deck, and berth-deck, the latter being not only a dormitory but also the place for the stowing of the sailors' bags, and on both sides lined with the large chests or movable pantries of the many messes of the men.

On the starboard side of the *Indomitable's* upper gun-deck, behold Billy Budd under sentry lying prone in irons in one of the bays formed by the regular spacing of the guns comprising the batteries on either side. All these pieces were of the heavier calibre of that period. Mounted on lumbering wooden carriages they were hampered with cumbersome harness of breeching and strong side-tackles for running them out. Guns and carriages, together with the long rammers and shorter lintstocks lodged in loops overhead—all these, as customary, were painted black; and the heavy hempen breechings tarred to the same tint, wore the like livery of the undertakers. In contrast with the funereal hue of these surroundings the prone sailor's exterior apparel, white *jumper* and white duck trousers, each more or less soiled, dimly glimmered in the obscure light of the bay like a patch of discolored snow in early April lingering at some upland cave's black mouth. In effect he is already in his shroud or the garments that shall serve him in lieu of one. Over him but scarce illuminating him, two battle-lanterns swing from two massive beams of the deck above. Fed with the oil supplied by the war-contractors (whose gains, honest or otherwise, are in every land an anticipated portion of the harvest of death) with flickering splashes of dirty yellow light they pollute the pale moonshine[,] all but ineffectually struggling in obstructed flecks thro the open ports from which the tompioned[5] cannon protrude. Other lanterns at intervals serve but to bring out somewhat the obscurer bays which like small confessionals or side-chapels in a cathedral branch from the long dim-vistaed broad aisle between the two batteries of that covered tier.

Such was the deck where now lay the Handsome Sailor. Through the rose-tan of his complexion, no pallor could have shown. It would have taken days of sequestration from the winds and the sun to have brought about the effacement of that. But the skeleton in the cheekbone at the point of its angle was just beginning delicately to be defined under the warm-tinted skin. In fervid hearts self-contained some brief experiences devour our human tissue as secret fire in a ship's hold consumes cotton in the bale.

But now lying between the two guns, as nipped in the vice of fate, Billy's agony, mainly proceeding from a generous young heart's virgin experience of the diabolical incarnate and effective in some men—the tension of that agony was over now. It survived not the something healing in the closeted interview with Captain Vere. Without movement, he lay as in a trance. That adolescent expression previously noted as his, taking on something akin to the look of a slumbering child in the cradle when the warm hearth-glow of the still chamber at night plays on the dimples that at whiles mysteriously form in the cheek, silently coming and going there. For now and then in the gyved one's trance a serene happy light born of some wandering reminiscence or dream would diffuse itself over his face, and then wane away only anew to return.

The Chaplain coming to see him and finding him thus, and perceiving no sign that he was conscious of his presence, attentively regarded him for a space, then slipping aside, withdrew for the time, peradventure feeling that even he the minister of Christ tho' receiving his

---

5. Usually, "tampioned"; plugged with a tampion, as the muzzle of a gun not in use.

stipend from Mars had no consolation to proffer which could result in a peace transcending that which he beheld. But in the small hours he came again. And the prisoner now awake to his surroundings noticed his approach and civilly, all but cheerfully, welcomed him. But it was to little purpose that in the interview following the good man sought to bring Billy Budd to some godly understanding that he must die, and at dawn. True, Billy himself freely referred to his death as a thing close at hand; but it was something in the way that children will refer to death in general, who yet among their other sports will play a funeral with hearse and mourners.

Not that like children Billy was incapable of conceiving what death really is. No, but he was wholly without irrational fear of it, a fear more prevalent in highly civilized communities than those so-called barbarous ones which in all respects stand nearer to unadulterate Nature. And, as elsewhere said, a barbarian Billy radically was; as much so, for all the costume, as his countrymen the British captives, living trophies, made to march in the Roman triumph of Germanicus.[6] Quite as much so as those later barbarians, young men probably, and picked specimens among the earlier British converts to Christianity, at least nominally such and taken to Rome (as today converts from lesser isles of the sea may be taken to London) of whom the Pope of that time, admiring the strangeness of their personal beauty so unlike the Italian stamp, their clear ruddy complexion and curled flaxen locks, exclaimed, "Angles" (meaning *English* the modern derivative) "Angles do you call them? And is it because they look so like angels?" Had it been later in time one would think that the Pope had in mind Fra Angelico's[7] seraphs some of whom, plucking apples in gardens of the Hesperides have the faint rose-bud complexion of the more beautiful English girls.

If in vain the good Chaplain sought to impress the young barbarian with ideas of death akin to those conveyed in the skull, dial, and crossbones on old tombstones; equally futile to all appearance were his efforts to bring home to him the thought of salvation and a Saviour. Billy listened, but less out of awe or reverence perhaps than from a certain natural politeness; doubtless at bottom regarding all that in much the same way that most mariners of his class take any discourse abstract or out of the common tone of the work-a-day world. And this sailor-way of taking clerical discourse is not wholly unlike the way in which the pioneer of Christianity full of transcendent miracles was received long ago on tropic isles by any superior *savage* so called—a Tahitian say of Captain Cook's time or shortly after that time.[8] Out

6. Germanicus Caesar (15 B.C.–1˄ A.D.), Roman general and conqueror, whose triumphs were spectacularly celebrated in Rome in 17 A.D.
7. Italian friar-painter of the fifteenth century, famous for his religious frescoes. The Hesperides, in classical myth, were fabulous gardens where grew golden apples, guarded by a dragon.
8. Captain James Cook (1728–1779), British explorer, made remarkable discoveries in the Pacific, visiting the Marquesas Islands and Tahiti, where Melville adventured in 1842.

of natural courtesy he received, but did not appropriate. It was like a gift placed in the palm of an outreached hand upon which the fingers do not close.

But the *Indomitable's* Chaplain was a discreet man possessing the good sense of a good heart. So he insisted not in his vocation here. At the instance of Captain Vere, a lieutenant had apprised him of pretty much everything as to Billy; and since he felt that innocence was even a better thing than religion wherewith to go to Judgement, he reluctantly withdrew; but in his emotion not without first performing an act strange enough in an Englishman, and under the circumstances yet more so in any regular priest. Stooping over, he kissed on the fair cheek his fellow-man, a felon in martial law, one who though on the confines of death he felt he could never convert to a dogma; nor for all that did he fear for his future.

Marvel not that having been made acquainted with the young sailor's essential innocence (an irruption of heretic thought hard to suppress) the worthy man lifted not a finger to avert the doom of such a martyr to martial discipline. So to do would not only have been as idle as invoking the desert, but would also have been an audacious transgression of the bounds of his function, one as exactly prescribed to him by military law as that of the boatswain or any other naval officer. Bluntly put, a chaplain is the minister of the Prince of Peace serving in the host of the God of War—Mars. As such, he is as incongruous as that musket of Blücher etc.[9] at Christmas. Why then is he there? Because he indirectly subserves the purpose attested by the cannon; because too he lends the sanction of the religion of the meek to that which practically is the abrogation of everything but brute Force.

26

The night so luminous on the spar-deck but otherwise on the cavernous ones below, levels so like the tiered galleries in a coal-mine— the luminous night passed away. But, like the prophet in the chariot disappearing in heaven and dropping his mantle to Elisha, the withdrawing night transferred its pale robe to the breaking day. A meek shy light appeared in the East, where stretched a diaphanous fleece of white furrowed vapor. That light slowly waxed. Suddenly *eight bells* was struck aft, responded to by one louder metallic stroke from forward. It was four o'clock in the morning. Instantly the silver whistles were heard summoning all hands to witness punishment. Up through the great hatchways rimmed with racks of heavy shot, the watch below came pouring overspreading with the watch already on deck the space between the mainmast and foremast including that occupied by the capacious *launch* and the black booms tiered on either side of it, boat and booms making a summit of observation for the

9. The manuscript is illegible; "Blücher etc." is a conjectural reading. Prussian Field Marshal Gebhard von Blücher (1742–1819), who had aided Wellington at Waterloo, was still famous.

powder-boys and younger tars. A different group comprising one watch of topmen leaned over the rail of that sea-balcony, no small one in a seventy-four, looking down on the crowd below. Man or boy none spake but in whisper, and few spake at all. Captain Vere—as before, the central figure among the assembled commissioned officers —stood nigh the break of the poop-deck facing forward. Just below him on the quarter-deck the marines in full equipment were drawn up much as at the scene of the promulgated sentence.

At sea in the old time, the execution by halter of a military sailor was generally from the fore-yard. In the present instance, for special reasons the main-yard was assigned. Under an arm of that lee yard[1] the prisoner was presently brought up, the Chaplain attending him. It was noted at the time and remarked upon afterwards, that in this final scene the good man evinced little or nothing of the perfunctory. Brief speech indeed he had with the condemned one, but the genuine Gospel was less on his tongue than in his aspect and manner towards him. The final preparations personal to the latter being speedily brought to an end by two boatswain's-mates, the consummation impended. Billy stood facing aft. At the penultimate moment, his words, his only ones, words wholly unobstructed in the utterance were these—"God bless Captain Vere!" Syllables so unanticipated coming from one with the ignominious hemp about his neck—a conventional felon's benediction directed aft towards the quarters of honor; syllables too delivered in the clear melody of a singing-bird on the point of launching from the twig, had a phenomenal effect, not unenhanced by the rare personal beauty of the young sailor spiritualized now thro' late experiences so poignantly profound.

Without volition as it were, as if indeed the ship's populace were but the vehicles of some vocal current electric, with one voice from alow and aloft came a resonant sympathetic echo—"God bless Captain Vere!" And yet at that instant Billy alone must have been in their hearts, even as he was in their eyes.

At the pronounced words and the spontaneous echo that voluminously rebounded them, Captain Vere, either thro stoic self-control or a sort of momentary paralysis induced by emotional shock, stood erectly rigid as a musket in the ship-armorer's rack.

The hull deliberately recovering from the periodic roll to leeward was just regaining an even keel, when the last signal[,] a preconcerted dumb one[,] was given. At the same moment it chanced that the vapory fleece hanging low in the East, was shot thro with a soft glory as of the fleece of the Lamb of God seen in mystical vision[,] and simultaneously therewith, watched by the wedged mass of upturned faces, Billy ascended; and, ascending, took the full rose of

1. Melville wrote both "weather" and "lee" above the word "yard," and failed to cancel either of these opposites. The lee yard would be more likely, as being more sheltered.

the dawn.

In the pinioned figure, arrived at the yard-end, to the wonder of all no motion was apparent[,] none save that created by the ship's motion, in moderate weather so majestic in a great ship ponderously cannoned.

End of Chapter

27

A digression

When some days afterward in reference to the singularity just mentioned, the Purser a rather ruddy rotund person more accurate as an accountant than profound as a philosopher, said at mess to the Surgeon, "What testimony to the force lodged in will-power" the latter—saturnine spare and tall, one in whom a discreet causticity went along with a manner less genial than polite, replied, "Your pardon, Mr. Purser. In a hanging scientifically conducted—and under special orders I myself directed how Budd's was to be effected—any movement following the completed suspension and originating in the body suspended, such movement indicates mechanical spasm in the muscular system. Hence the absence of that is no more attributable to will-power as you call it than to horse-power—begging your pardon."

"But this muscular spasm you speak of, is not that in a degree more or less invariable in these cases? ["]

"Assuredly so, Mr. Purser."

"How then, my good sir, do you account for its absence in this instance?"

"Mr. Purser, it is clear that your sense of the singularity in this matter equals not mine. You account for it by what you call will-power a term not yet included in the lexicon of science. For me I do not, with my present knowledge pretend to account for it at all. Even should we assume the hypothesis that at the first touch of the halyards the action of Budd's heart, intensified by extraordinary emotion at its climax, abruptly stopt—much like a watch when in carelessly winding it up you strain at the finish, thus snapping the chain— even under that hypothesis how account for the phenomenon that followed."

"You admit then that the absence of spasmodic movement was phenomenal."

["]It was phenomenal, Mr. Purser, in the sense that it was an appearance the cause of which is not immediately to be assigned."

["]But tell me, my dear Sir,["] pertinaciously continued the other, "was the man's death effected by the halter, or was it a species of euthanasia? ["]

"Euthanasia, Mr. Purser, is something like your will-power: I doubt its authenticity as a scientific term—begging your pardon again. It is at once imaginative and metaphysical,—in short, Greek. But" abruptly changing his tone "there is a case in the sick-bay that I do not care to leave to my assistants. Beg your pardon, but excuse me." And rising from the mess he formally withdrew.

28

The silence at the moment of execution and for a moment or two continuing thereafter, a silence but emphasized by the regular wash of the sea against the hull or the flutter of a sail caused by the helmsman's eyes being tempted astray, this emphasized silence was gradually disturbed by a sound not easily to be verbally rendered. Whoever has heard the freshet-wave of a torrent suddenly swelled by pouring showers in tropical mountains, showers not shared by the plain; whoever has heard the first muffled murmur of its sloping advance through precipitous woods, may form some conception of the sound now heard. The seeming remoteness of its source was because of its murmurous indistinctness since it came from close-by, even from the men massed on the ship's open deck. Being inarticulate, it was dubious in significance further than it seemed to indicate some capricious revulsion of thought or feeling such as mobs ashore are liable to, in the present instance possibly implying a sullen revocation on the men's part of their involuntary echoing of Billy's benediction. But ere the murmur had time to wax into clamor it was met by a strategic command, the more telling that it came with abrupt unexpectedness.

"Pipe down the starboard watch Boatswain, and see that they go."

Shrill as the shriek of the sea-hawk the whistles of the Boatswain and his Mates pierced that ominous low sound, dissipating it; and yielding to the mechanism of discipline the throng was thinned by one half. For the remainder most of them were set to temporary employments connected with trimming the yards and so forth, business readily to be got up to serve occasion by any officer-of-the-deck.

Now each proceeding that follows a mortal sentence pronounced at sea by a drum-head court is characterised by promptitude not perceptibly merging into hurry, tho bordering that. The hammock, the one which had been Billy's bed when alive, having already been ballasted with shot and otherwise prepared to serve for his canvas coffin, the last offices of the sea-undertakers, the Sail-Maker's Mates, were now speedily completed. When everything was in readiness a second call for all hands made necessary by the strategic movement before mentioned was sounded and now to witness burial.

The details of this closing formality it needs not to give. But when the tilted plank let slide its freight into the sea, a second strange human murmur was heard, blended now with another inarticulate sound proceeding from certain larger sea-fowl whose attention having been attracted by the peculiar commotion in the water resulting from the

heavy sloped dive of the shotted hammock into the sea, flew screaming to the spot. So near the hull did they come, that the stridor or
bony creak of their gaunt double-jointed pinions was audible. As the
ship under light airs passed on, leaving the burial-spot astern, they still
kept circling it low down with the moving shadow of their outstretched wings and the croaked requiem of their cries.

Upon sailors as superstitious as those of the age preceding ours,
men-of-war's men too who had just beheld the prodigy of repose in
the form suspended in air and now foundering in the deeps; to such
mariners the action of the sea-fowl tho' dictated by mere animal greed
for prey, was big with no prosaic significance. An uncertain movement began among them, in which some encroachment was made. It
was tolerated but for a moment. For suddenly the drum beat to quarters, which familiar sound happening at least twice every day, had
upon the present occasion a signal peremptoriness in it. True martial
discipline long continued superinduces in average man a sort of
impulse [of] docility whose operation at the official sound of command much resembles in its promptitude the effect of an instinct.

The drum-beat dissolved the multitude, distributing most of them
along the batteries of the two covered gun-decks. There, as wont, the
guns' crews stood by their respective cannon erect and silent. In due
course the First Officer, sword under arm and standing in his place
on the quarter-deck[,] formally received the successive reports of the
sworded Lieutenants commanding the sections of batteries below; the
last of which reports being made[,] the summed report he delivered
with the customary salute to the Commander. All this occupied time,
which in the present case, was the object of beating to quarters at an
hour prior to the customary one. That such variance from usage was
authorized by an officer like Captain Vere, a martinet as some deemed
him, was evidence of the necessity for unusual action implied in what
he deemed to be temporarily the mood of his men. "With mankind"
he would say "forms, measured forms are everything; and that is the
import couched in the story of Orpheus with his lyre spell-binding
the wild denizens of the wood." And this he once applied to the disruption of forms going on across the Channel and the consequences
thereof.

At this unwonted muster at quarters, all proceeded as at the regular
hour. The band on the quarter-deck played a sacred air. After which
the Chaplain went thro' the customary morning service. That done,
the drum beat the retreat, and toned by music and religious rites sub-
serving the discipline & purpose of war, the men in their wonted orderly manner, dispersed to the places allotted them when not at the
guns.

And now it was full day. The fleece of low-hanging vapor had
vanished, licked up by the sun that late had so glorified it. And the

circumambient air in the clearness of its serenity was like smooth white marble in the polished block not yet removed from the marble-dealer's yard.

29

The symmetry of form attainable in pure fiction can not so readily be achieved in a narration essentially having less to do with fable than with fact. Truth uncompromisingly told will always have its ragged edges; hence the conclusion of such a narration is apt to be less finished than an architectural finial.

How it fared with the Handsome Sailor during the year of the Great Mutiny has been faithfully given. But tho' properly the story ends with his life, something in way of sequel will not be amiss. Three brief chapters will suffice.

In the general re-christening under the Directory of the craft originally forming the navy of the French monarchy, the *St. Louis* line-of-battle ship was named the *Athéiste*. Such a name, like some other substituted ones in the Revolutionary fleet while proclaiming the infidel audacity of the ruling power was yet, tho' not so intended to be, the aptest name, if one consider it, ever given to a war-ship; far more so indeed than the *Devastation*, the *Erebus* (the *Hell*) and similar names bestowed upon fighting-ships.

On the return-passage to the English fleet from the detached cruise during which occurred the events already recorded, the *Indomitable* fell in with the *Athéiste*. An engagement ensued; during which Captain Vere in the act of putting his ship alongside the enemy with a view of throwing his boarders across her bulwarks, was hit by a musket-ball from a port-hole of the enemy's main cabin. More than disabled he dropped to the deck and was carried below to the same cock-pit where some of his men already lay. The senior Lieutenant took command. Under him the enemy was finally captured and though much crippled was by rare good fortune successfully taken into Gibraltar, an English port not very distant from the scene of the fight. There, Captain Vere with the rest of the wounded was put ashore. He lingered for some days, but the end came. Unhappily he was cut off too early for the Nile and Trafalgar.[2] The spirit that spite its philosophic austerity may yet have indulged in the most secret of all passions, ambition, never attained to the fulness of fame.

Not long before death while lying under the influence of that magical drug which soothing the physical frame mysteriously operates on the subtler element in man, he was heard to murmur words inexplicable to his attendant—"Billy Budd, Billy Budd." That these were not the accents of remorse, would seem clear from what the attendant said to the *Indomitable*'s senior officer of marines who[,] as the most

2. Admiral Nelson destroyed Napoleon's fleet at the Battle of the Nile (1798); at Trafalgar in 1805 he ended the French naval wars with victory, and was himself killed.

reluctant to condemn of the members of the drum-head court, too well knew[,] tho' here he kept the knowledge to himself, who Billy Budd was.

30

Some few weeks after the execution, among other matters under the head of *News from the Mediterranean*, there appeared in a naval chronicle of the time, an authorized weekly publication, an account of the affair. It was doubtless for the most part written in good faith, tho' the medium, partly rumor, through which the facts must have reached the writer, served to deflect and in part falsify them. The account was as follows:—

"On the tenth of the last month a deplorable occurrence took place on board H.M.S. *Indomitable*. John Claggart, the ship's master-at-arms, discovering that some sort of plot was incipient among an inferior section of the ship's company, and that the ring-leader was one William Budd; he, Claggart in the act of arraigning the man before the Captain was vindictively stabbed to the heart by the suddenly drawn sheath-knife of Budd.

["]The deed and the implement employed, sufficiently suggest that tho' mustered into the service under an English name the assassin was no Englishman, but one of those aliens adopting English cognomens whom the present extraordinary necessities of the Service have caused to be admitted into it in considerable numbers.

["]The enormity of the crime and the extreme depravity of the criminal, appear the greater in view of the character of the victim, a middle-aged man respectable and discreet, belonging to that minor official grade, the petty-officers, upon whom, as none know better than the commissioned gentlemen, the efficiency of His Majesty's navy so largely depends. His function was a responsible one; at once onerous & thankless and his fidelity in it the greater because of his strong patriotic impulse. In this instance as in so many other instances in these days, the character of this unfortunate man signally refutes, if refutation were needed, that peevish saying attributed to the late Dr. Johnson, that patriotism is the last refuge of a scoundrel.

["]The criminal paid the penalty of his crime. The promptitude of the punishment has proved salutary. Nothing amiss is now apprehended aboard H.M.S. *Indomitable*."

The above, appearing in a publication now long ago superannuated and forgotten[,] is all that hitherto has stood in human record to attest what manner of men respectively were John Claggart and Billy Budd[.]

31

Everything is for a term remarkable in navies. Any tangible object associated with some striking incident of the service is converted into a monument. The spar from which the Foretopman was suspended, was for some few years kept trace of by the bluejackets. Their knowledge followed it from ship to dock-yard and again from dock-yard to ship, still pursuing it even when at last reduced to a mere dock-yard boom. To them a chip of it was as a piece of the Cross. Ignorant tho' they were of the secret facts of the tragedy, and not thinking but that the penalty was somehow unavoidably inflicted from the naval point of view, for all that they instinctively felt that Billy was a sort of man as incapable of mutiny as of wilful murder. They recalled the fresh young image of the Handsome Sailor, that face never deformed by a sneer or subtler vile freak of the heart within. Their impression of him was doubtless deepened by the fact that he was gone, and in a measure mysteriously gone. At the time on the gun decks of the *Indomitable* the general estimate of his nature and its unconscious simplicity eventually found rude utterance from another foretop-man[,] one of his own watch[,] gifted, as some sailors are, with an artless poetic temperament; the tarry hands made some lines which after circulating among the shipboard crew for a while, finally got rudely printed at Portsmouth as a ballad. The title given to it was the sailor's.

Billy in the Darbies[3]

Good of the Chaplain to enter Lone Bay
And down on his marrow-bones here and pray
For the likes just o' me, Billy Budd.—But look:
Through the port comes the moon-shine astray!
It tips the guard's cutlas and silvers this nook;
But 'twill die in the dawning of Billy's last day.
A jewel-block they'll make of me tomorrow,
Pendant pearl from the yard-arm-end
Like the ear-drop I gave to Bristol Molly—
O, 'tis me, not the sentence they'll suspend.
Ay, Ay, all is up; and I must up too
Early in the morning, aloft from alow.
On an empty stomach, now, never it would do.
They'll give me a nibble—bit o' biscuit ere I go.
Sure, a messmate will reach me the last parting cup;
But, turning heads away from the hoist and the belay,
Heaven knows who will have the running of me up!
No pipe to those halyards.—But aren't it all sham?
A blur's in my eyes; it is dreaming that I am.
A hatchet to my hawser? all adrift to go?
The drum roll to grog, and Billy never know?
But Donald he has promised to stand by the plank;
So I'll shake a friendly hand ere I sink.

3. Manacles or irons.

Transcendental Idealism

RALPH WALDO EMERSON
(1803–1882)

The durability of Emerson for the general reader is one measure of his genius. Now, a century and a half after his birth, the forum and the market place echo his words and ideas. As Ralph L. Rusk has suggested, this is partly because "he is wise man, wit, and poet, all three," and partly because his speculations proved prophetic, having as firm a practical relationship with the conditions of our present age as with the history of mankind before him. "His insatiable passion for unity resembles Einstein's" as much as Plato's; and this passion unites serenity and practicality, God and science, in a manner highly suggestive for those attempting to solve the twentieth-century dilemmas which have seemed most desperately urgent.

Emerson was born to the clerical tradition; his father was pastor of the First Unitarian Church of Boston, and successor to a line of nonconformist and Puritan clergymen. William Emerson died in 1811, when the boy was eight, leaving his widow to face poverty and to educate their five sons. At Boston Latin School, at the Latin school in Concord, and at Harvard College (where from 1817 to 1821 he enjoyed a "scholarship" in return for services) young Emerson kindled no fires. His slow growth is recorded in his journal for the next eight years. He assisted at his brother William's Boston "School for Young Ladies" (1821–1825), conducting the enterprise alone the last year. In 1825 he entered Harvard Divinity School; in spite of an interval of illness, he was by 1829 associated with the powerful Henry Ware in the pulpit of the Second Unitarian Church of Boston. That year he married Ellen Tucker, whose death, less than two years later, acutely grieved him throughout his life.

In 1832, in the first flush of a genuine success in the pulpit, he resigned from the ministry. At the time, he told his congregation he could no longer find inherent grace in the observation of the Lord's Supper, and later he said that his ideas of self-reliance and the general divinity of man caused him to conclude that "in order to be a good minister it was necessary to leave the ministry." His decision was not the result of hasty judgment. These ideas (as

777

Rusk shows in his excellent *Life of Ralph Waldo Emerson*) had long been available to him in his study of such nonconformists as Fénelon, George Fox, Luther, and Carlyle. They were later made explicit also in his poem "The Problem," printed among the selections in this volume. Six years after his resignation from the ministry, in his "Divinity School Address" (1838), he clarified his position and made permanent his breach with the church. The transcendental law, Emerson believed, was the "moral law," through which man discovers the nature of God, a living spirit; yet it had been the practice of historical Christianity— "as if God were dead"—to formalize Him and to fundamentalize religion through fixed conventions of dogma and scripture. The true nature of life was energetic and fluid; its transcendental unity resulted from the convergence of all forces upon the energetic truth, the heart of the moral law.

Meanwhile, his personal affairs had taken shape again. After resigning his pulpit, he traveled (1832–1833) in France, Italy, and Great Britain, meeting such writers as Landor, Coleridge, Wordsworth, and Carlyle. All of these had been somewhat influenced by the idealism of recent German philosophy, but Carlyle alone was his contemporary, and the two became lasting friends. In 1833, Emerson launched himself upon the career of public lecturer, which thereafter gave him his modest livelihood, made him a familiar figure in many parts of the country, and supported one of his three trips abroad. In 1835,

he made a second marriage, notably successful, and soon settled in his own house, near the ancestral Old Manse in Concord, where his four children were born. The first-born, Waldo (1836), mitigated Emerson's loss of two younger and much-loved brothers in the two previous years; but Waldo, too, died in his sixth year, in the chain of bereavements that Emerson suffered.

The informal Transcendental Club began to meet at the Manse in 1836, including in its association a number of prominent writers of Boston, and others of Concord, such as Bronson Alcott and later, Thoreau, whom Emerson took for a time into his household. Margaret Fuller was selected as first editor of *The Dial*, their famous little magazine, and Emerson succeeded her for two years (1842–1844). He could not personally bring himself to join their co-operative Brook Farm community, although he supported its theory.

After 1850 he gave much of his thought to national politics, social reforms, and the growing contest over slavery. By this time, however, the bulk of his important work had been published, much of the prose resulting from lectures, sometimes rewritten or consolidated in larger forms. *Nature* (1836), his first book, was followed by his first *Essays*, (1841), *Essays: Second Series* (1844), and *Poems* (1847). Emerson wrote and published his poems sporadically, as though they were by-products, but actually they contain the core of his philosophy, which is essentially lyrical, and they are often its best expression. The criticism of the day neglected them, or disparaged them for their alleged formal irregularity in an age of metrical conformity. Today they are read in the light of rhythmic principles recovered by Whitman, whom Emerson first defended almost singlehanded; and their greatness is now evident to a generation newly awakened to the symbolism of ideas which is present in the long tradition from John Donne to T. S. Eliot. Emerson authorized a second volume, *May-Day and Other Poems*, in 1867 and a finally revised *Selected Poems* in 1876.

In 1845, Emerson gave the series of lectures published in 1850 as *Representative Men*. He took this series to England in 1847, and visited Paris again before returning to Concord. His later major works include the remarkable *Journals* and *Letters*, published after his death, the compilation, *Nature, Addresses, and Lectures* (1849), and the provocative essays of *English Traits* (1856) and *The Conduct of Life* (1860).

In 1871 there were evidences that the lofty intellect, now internationally recognized, was beginning to fail. In 1872 his house in Concord was damaged by fire and friends raised a fund to send him abroad and to repair the damage in his absence, but the trip was not sufficient to stem the failing tide of health and memory. He recovered his energies sporadically until 1877, and died in 1882.

It is a familiar truism that Emerson was not an original philosopher, and he fully recognized the fact. "I am too young yet by several ages," he wrote, "to compile a code." Yet confronted by his transcendent vision of the unity of life in the metaphysical Absolute, he declared, "I wish to know the laws of this wonderful power, that I may domesticate it." That he succeeded so well in this mission is the evidence of his true originality and his value for following generations of Americans. In the American soil, and in the common sense of his own mind, he "domesticated" the richest experience of many lands and cultures; he is indeed the "transparent eyeball" through which much of the best light of the ages is brought to a focus of usefulness for the present day.

The most recent and best collection of Emerson is *The Complete Works of Ralph Waldo Emerson* 12 vols., Centenary Edition, 1903–1904. The Concord Edition, 1904, was a reprint of this. Supplementary collections are *Uncollected Writings * * *, edited by C. C. Bigelow, 1912; *The Journals of Ralph Waldo Emerson*, 10 vols., edited by E. W. Emerson and W. E. Forbes, 1909–1914; *The Heart of Emerson's Journals*, edited by Bliss Perry, 1926; *Uncollected Lectures * * *, edited by C. F. Gohdes, 1933; *Young Emerson Speaks * * *, sermons, edited by A. C. McGiffert, 1938; *The Letters of Ralph Waldo Emerson*, 6 vols., edited by R. L. Rusk, 1939, a complete calendar with two thousand new letters.

Available one-volume selections are *The Complete Essays and Other Writings * * *, edited by Brooks Atkinson, 1940; *Ralph Waldo Emerson: Representative Selections*, edited, with a good critical introduction, by F. I. Carpenter, American Writers Series, 1934.

The definitive biography is R. L. Rusk, *The Life of Ralph Waldo Emerson*, 1949. Excellent earlier studies are G. W. Cooke, *Ralph Waldo Emerson * * *, 1881; J. E. Cabot, *A Memoir of Ralph Waldo Emerson*, 2 vols., 1887; G. E. Woodberry, *Ralph Waldo Emerson*, English Men of Letters Series, 1907. A recent study of Emerson's mind is Stephen F. Whicher, *Freedom and Fate*, 1953.

The best introduction to American transcendentalism as a whole and to its literature, is *The Transcendentalists: An Anthology*, compiled by Perry Miller,

1950, containing selections from all leading transcendentalists except Emerson and Thoreau, with historical and biographical notes.

The texts of Emerson reproduced in this volume are based on the last revised edition of each work published during Emerson's lifetime: *Nature, Addresses, and Lectures,* 1849; *Essays,* revised 1847 and 1850; *Representative Men,* first edition, 1850; and *Selected Poems,* 1876. A few obvious textual errors have been corrected by reference to later editions.

Nature[1]

A subtle chain of countless rings
The next unto the farthest brings;
The eye reads omens where it goes,
And speaks all languages the rose;
And, striving to be man, the worm
Mounts through all the spires of form.

Introduction

Our age is retrospective. It builds the sepulchres of the fathers. It writes biographies, histories, and criticism. The fore-going generations beheld God and nature face to face; we, through their eyes. Why should not we also enjoy an original relation to the universe? Why should not we have a poetry and philosophy of insight and not of tradition, and a religion by revelation to us, and not the history of theirs? Embosomed for a season in nature, whose floods of life stream around and through us, and invite us, by the powers they supply, to action proportioned to nature, why should we grope among the dry bones of the past, or put the living generation into masquerade out of its faded wardrobe? The sun shines to-day also. There is more wool and flax in the fields. There are new lands, new men, new thoughts. Let us demand our own works and laws and worship.

Undoubtedly we have no questions to ask which are unanswerable. We must trust the perfection of the creation so far as to believe that whatever curiosity the order of things has awakened in our minds, the order of things can satisfy. Every man's condition is a solution in

1. Emerson's first major work, *Nature,* was also the first comprehensive expression of American transcendentalism. For the student it provides a fresh and lyrical intimation of many of the leading ideas that Emerson developed in various later essays and poems. The author first mentioned this book in a diary entry made in 1833, on his return voyage from the first European visit, during which he had met a number of European writers, especially Carlyle. In 1834, when he settled in the Old Manse, his grandfather's home in Concord, he had already written five chapters. He completed the first draft of the volume there, in the very room in which Hawthorne later wrote his *Mosses from an Old Manse.* The small first edition of *Nature,* published anonymously in 1836, gained critical attention, but few general readers. It was not reprinted until 1849, when it was collected in *Nature, Addresses, and Lectures.* At that time Emerson substituted, as epigraph, the present poem, instead of the quotation from Plotinus which had introduced the first edition: "Nature is but an image or imitation of wisdom, the last thing of the soul; Nature being a thing which doth only do, but not know." The new epigraph supported the concept of evolution presented in *Nature.* Darwin's *Origin of Species* did not appear until 1859, but Emerson had seen the classification of species in 1833 at the Paris Jardin des Plantes, while Lamarck was anticipating Darwin, and Lyell's popular *Geology* emphasized fossil remains. The transcendentalists, and Emerson in particular, regarded theories of evolution as supporting a concept of progress and unity as ancient as the early Greek nature philosophy. These ideas persist throughout *Nature.* The present text is based on the 1849 edition.

hieroglyphic to those inquiries he would put. He acts it as life, before he apprehends it as truth. In like manner, nature is already, in its forms and tendencies, describing its own design. Let us interrogate the great apparition that shines so peacefully around us. Let us inquire, to what end is nature?

All science has one aim, namely, to find a theory of nature. We have theories of races and of functions, but scarcely yet a remote approach to an idea of creation. We are now so far from the road to truth, that religious teachers dispute and hate each other, and speculative men are esteemed unsound and frivolous. But to a sound judgment, the most abstract truth is the most practical. Whenever a true theory appears, it will be its own evidence. Its test is, that it will explain all phenomena. Now many are thought not only un-explained but inexplicable; as language, sleep, madness, dreams, beasts, sex.

Philosophically considered, the universe is composed of Nature and the Soul. Strictly speaking, therefore, all that is separate from us, all which Philosophy distinguishes as the NOT ME, that is, both nature and art, all other men and my own body, must be ranked under this name, NATURE. In enumerating the values of nature and casting up their sum, I shall use the word in both senses;—in its common and in its philosophical import. In inquiries so general as our present one, the inaccuracy is not material; no confusion of thought will occur. *Nature*, in the common sense, refers to essences unchanged by man; space, the air, the river, the leaf. *Art* is applied to the mixture of his will with the same things, as in a house, a canal, a statue, a picture. But his operations taken together are so insignif-icant, a little chipping, baking, patching, and washing, that in an impression so grand as that of the world on the human mind, they do not vary the result.

I. *Nature*

To go into solitude, a man needs to retire as much from his cham-ber as from society. I am not solitary whilst I read and write, though nobody is with me. But if a man would be alone, let him look at the stars. The rays that come from those heavenly worlds will separate between him and what he touches. One might think the atmosphere was made transparent with this design, to give man, in the heavenly bodies, the perpetual presence of the sublime. Seen in the streets of cities, how great they are! If the stars should appear one night in a thousand years, how would men believe and adore; and preserve for many generations the remembrance of the city of God which had been shown! But every night come out these envoys of beauty, and light the universe with their admonishing smile.

The stars awaken a certain reverence, because though always present, they are inaccessible; but all natural objects make a kindred impression, when the mind is open to their influence. Nature never wears a mean appearance. Neither does the wisest man extort her secret, and lose his curiosity by finding out all her perfection. Nature never became a toy to a wise spirit. The flowers, the animals, the mountains, reflected the wisdom of his best hour, as much as they had delighted the simplicity of his childhood.

When we speak of nature in this manner, we have a distinct but most poetical sense in the mind. We mean the integrity of impression made by manifold natural objects. It is this which distinguishes the stick of timber of the wood-cutter from the tree of the poet. The charming landscape which I saw this morning is indubitably made up of some twenty or thirty farms. Miller owns this field, Locke that, and Manning the woodland beyond. But none of them owns the landscape. There is a property in the horizon which no man has but he whose eye can integrate all the parts, that is, the poet. This is the best part of these men's farms, yet to this their warranty-deeds give no title.

To speak truly, few adult persons can see nature. Most persons do not see the sun. At least they have a very superficial seeing. The sun illuminates only the eye of the man, but shines into the eye and the heart of the child. The lover of nature is he whose inward and outward senses are still truly adjusted to each other; who has retained the spirit of infancy even into the era of manhood. His intercourse with heaven and earth becomes part of his daily food. In the presence of nature a wild delight runs through the man, in spite of real sorrows. Nature says,—he is my creature, and maugre[2] all his impertinent griefs, he shall be glad with me. Not the sun or the summer alone, but every hour and season yields its tribute of delight; for every hour and change corresponds to and authorizes a different state of the mind, from breathless noon to grimmest midnight. Nature is a setting that fits equally well a comic or a mourning piece. In good health, the air is a cordial of incredible virtue. Crossing a bare common, in snow puddles, at twilight, under a clouded sky, without having in my thoughts any occurrence of special good fortune, I have enjoyed a perfect exhilaration. I am glad to the brink of fear. In the woods, too, a man casts off his years, as the snake his slough, and at what period soever of life, is always a child. In the woods is perpetual youth. Within these plantations of God, a decorum and sanctity reign, a perennial festival is dressed, and the guest sees not how he should tire of them in a thousand years. In the woods, we return to reason and faith. There I feel that nothing can befall me in life,—no disgrace, no calamity (leaving me my eyes), which nature cannot repair. Standing on the bare ground,—my head

2. Despite.

bathed by the blithe air, and uplifted into infinite space,—all mean egotism vanishes. I become a transparent eyeball; I am nothing; I see all; the currents of the Universal Being circulate through me; I am part or parcel[3] of God. The name of the nearest friend sounds then foreign and accidental: to be brothers, to be acquaintances,—master or servant, is then a trifle and a disturbance. I am the lover of uncontained and immortal beauty. In the wilderness, I find something more dear and connate than in streets or villages. In the tranquil landscape, and especially in the distant line of the horizon, man beholds somewhat as beautiful as his own nature.

The greatest delight which the fields and woods minister is the suggestion of an occult relation between man and the vegetable. I am not alone and unacknowledged. They nod to me, and I to them. The waving of the boughs in the storm is new to me and old. It takes me by surprise, and yet is not unknown. Its effect is like that of a higher thought or a better emotion coming over me, when I deemed I was thinking justly or doing right.

Yet it is certain that the power to produce this delight does not reside in nature, but in man, or in a harmony of both. It is necessary to use these pleasures with great temperance. For nature is not always tricked in holiday attire, but the same scene which yesterday breathed perfume and glittered as for the frolic of the nymphs, is overspread with melancholy to-day. Nature always wears the colors of the spirit. To a man laboring under calamity, the heat of his own fire hath sadness in it. Then there is a kind of contempt of the landscape felt by him who has just lost by death a dear friend.[4] The sky is less grand as it shuts down over less worth in the population.

II. Commodity[5]

Whoever considers the final cause of the world will discern a multitude of uses that enter as parts into that result. They all admit of being thrown into one of the following classes: Commodity; Beauty; Language; and Discipline.

Under the general name of commodity, I rank all those advantages which our senses owe to nature. This, of course, is a benefit which is temporary and mediate, not ultimate, like its service to the soul. Yet although low, it is perfect in its kind, and is the only use of nature which all men apprehend. The misery of man appears like childish petulance, when we explore the steady and prodigal provision that has been made for his support and delight on this green

3. The early editions read "particle." The familiar reading, "parcel," based on a manuscript variant, appeared in the Centenary Edition (1903). *Cf.* "parcel," in the legal phrase, "part and parcel."
4. Writing this at the age of thirty-two,

Emerson already had "lost by death" his first wife, a bride of eighteen months; and, within the last two years, two brothers.
5. In a sense now unfamiliar, a commodity was whatever satisfied man's physical need or convenience.

ball which floats him through the heavens. What angels invented these splendid ornaments, these rich conveniences, this ocean of air above, this ocean of water beneath, this firmament of earth between? this zodiac of lights, this tent of dropping clouds, this striped coat of climates, this fourfold year? Beasts, fire, water, stones, and corn serve him. The field is at once his floor, his work-yard, his playground, his garden, and his bed.

> "More servants wait on man
> Than he'll take notice of."[6]

Nature, in its ministry to man, is not only the material, but is also the process and the result. All the parts incessantly work into each other's hands for the profit of man. The wind sows the seed; the sun evaporates the sea; the wind blows the vapor to the field; the ice, on the other side of the planet, condenses rain on this; the rain feeds the plant; the plant feeds the animal; and thus the endless circulations of the divine charity nourish man.

The useful arts are reproductions or new combinations by the wit of man, of the same natural benefactors. He no longer waits for favoring gales, but by means of steam, he realizes the fable of Æolus's bag,[7] and carries the two and thirty winds in the boiler of his boat. To diminish friction, he paves the road with iron bars, and, mounting a coach with a ship-load of men, animals, and merchandise behind him, he darts through the country, from town to town, like an eagle or a swallow through the air. By the aggregate of these aids, how is the face of the world changed, from the era of Noah to that of Napoleon! The private poor man hath cities, ships, canals, bridges, built for him. He goes to the post-office, and the human race run on his errands; to the book-shop, and the human race read and write of all that happens, for him; to the court-house, and nations repair his wrongs. He sets his house upon the road, and the human race go forth every morning, and shovel out the snow, and cut a path for him.

But there is no need of specifying particulars in this class of uses. The catalogue is endless, and the examples so obvious, that I shall leave them to the reader's reflection, with the general remark, that this mercenary benefit is one which has respect to a farther good. A man is fed, not that he may be fed, but that he may work.

III. Beauty

A nobler want of man is served by nature, namely, the love of Beauty.

6. From "Man," by George Herbert (1593–1633). Emerson quotes most of the poem in Chapter VIII, "Prospects," below.

7. In Greek mythology, Æolus had dominion over the winds, which he was said to keep in a bag.

The ancient Greeks called the world κόσμος,[8] beauty. Such is the constitution of all things, or such the plastic power of the human eye, that the primary forms, as the sky, the mountain, the tree, the animal, give us a delight *in and for themselves*; a pleasure arising from outline, color, motion, and grouping. This seems partly owing to the eye itself. The eye is the best of artists. By the mutual action of its structure and of the laws of light, perspective is produced, which integrates every mass of objects, of what character soever, into a well colored and shaded globe, so that where the particular objects are mean and unaffecting, the landscape which they compose is round and symmetrical. And as the eye is the best composer, so light is the first of painters. There is no object so foul that intense light will not make beautiful. And the stimulus it affords to the sense, and a sort of infinitude which it hath, like space and time, make all matter gay. Even the corpse has its own beauty. But besides this general grace diffused over nature, almost all the individual forms are agreeable to the eye, as is proved by our endless imitations of some of them, as the acorn, the grape, the pine-cone, the wheat-ear, the egg, the wings and forms of most birds, the lion's claw, the serpent, the butterfly, sea-shells, flames, clouds, buds, leaves, and the forms of many trees, as the palm.

For better consideration, we may distribute the aspects of Beauty in a threefold manner.

1. First, the simple perception of natural forms is a delight. The influence of the forms and actions in nature is so needful to man, that, in its lowest functions, it seems to lie on the confines of commodity and beauty. To the body and mind which have been cramped by noxious work or company, nature is medicinal and restores their tone. The tradesman, the attorney comes out of the din and craft of the street and sees the sky and the woods, and is a man again. In their eternal calm, he finds himself. The health of the eye seems to demand a horizon. We are never tired, so long as we can see far enough.

But in other hours, Nature satisfies by its loveliness, and without any mixture of corporeal benefit. I see the spectacle of morning from the hilltop over against my house, from daybreak to sunrise, with emotions which an angel might share. The long slender bars of cloud float like fishes in the sea of crimson light. From the earth, as a shore, I look out into that silent sea. I seem to partake its rapid transformations; the active enchantment reaches my dust, and I dilate and conspire with the morning wind. How does Nature deify us with a few and cheap elements! Give me health and a day, and I will make the pomp of emperors ridiculous. The dawn is my Assyria;[9] the sunset

8. *Kosmos* (cosmos). By this Greek word, meaning essentially "a universal order or harmony of parts," Emerson suggests his own conception of beauty.
9. Here emblematic of an early period of splendor.

and moonrise my Paphos,[1] and unimaginable realms of faerie; broad noon shall be my England of the senses and the understanding; the night shall be my Germany[2] of mystic philosophy and dreams.

Not less excellent, except for our less susceptibility in the afternoon, was the charm, last evening, of a January sunset. The western clouds divided and subdivided themselves into pink flakes modulated with tints of unspeakable softness, and the air had so much life and sweetness that it was a pain to come within doors. What was it that nature would say? Was there no meaning in the live repose of the valley behind the mill, and which Homer or Shakespeare could not re-form for me in words? The leafless trees become spires of flame in the sunset, with the blue east for their background, and the stars of the dead calices[3] of flowers, and every withered stem and stubble rimed with frost, contribute something to the mute music.

The inhabitants of cities suppose that the country landscape is pleasant only half the year. I please myself with the graces of the winter scenery, and believe that we are as much touched by it as by the genial influences of summer. To the attentive eye, each moment of the year has its own beauty, and in the same field, it beholds, every hour, a picture which was never seen before, and which shall never be seen again. The heavens change every moment, and reflect their glory or gloom on the plains beneath. The state of the crop in the surrounding farms alters the expression of the earth from week to week. The succession of native plants in the pastures and road-sides, which makes the silent clock by which time tells the summer hours, will make even the divisions of the day sensible to a keen observer. The tribes of birds and insects, like the plants punctual to their time, follow each other, and the year has room for all. By watercourses, the variety is greater. In July, the blue pontederia or pickerel-weed blooms in large beds in the shallow parts of our pleasant river,[4] and swarms with yellow butterflies in continual motion. Art cannot rival this pomp of purple and gold. Indeed the river is a perpetual gala, and boasts each month a new ornament.

But this beauty of Nature which is seen and felt as beauty, is the least part. The shows of day, the dewy morning, the rainbow, mountains, orchards in blossom, stars, moonlight, shadows in still water, and the like, if too eagerly hunted, become shows merely, and mock us with their unreality. Go out of the house to see the moon, and 'tis mere tinsel; it will not please as when its light shines upon your necessary journey. The beauty that shimmers in the yellow after-

1. Ancient city of Cyprus, noted for its worship of Aphrodite, Greek goddess of sensual love.
2. The rational empiricism of English thinkers, especially Hume and the Scottish "common-sense" school, is compared with German idealism, *e.g.*, Hegel and Kant.
3. Now usually "calyxes" or "calyces," plural of "calyx," the outer perianth of a flower.
4. The Concord River, a meandering branch of the Merrimack.

noons of October, who ever could clutch it? Go forth to find it, and it is gone; 'tis only a mirage as you look from the windows of diligence.

2. The presence of a higher, namely, of the spiritual element is essential to its perfection. The high and divine beauty which can be loved without effeminacy, is that which is found in combination with the human will. Beauty is the mark God sets upon virtue. Every natural action is graceful. Every heroic act is also decent, and causes the place and the bystanders to shine. We are taught by great actions that the universe is the property of every individual in it. Every rational creature has all nature for his dowry and estate. It is his, if he will. He may divest himself of it; he may creep into a corner, and abdicate his kingdom, as most men do, but he is entitled to the world by his constitution. In proportion to the energy of his thought and will, he takes up the world into himself. "All those things for which men plough, build, or sail, obey virtue;" said Sallust.[5] "The winds and waves," said Gibbon,[6] "are always on the side of the ablest navigators." So are the sun and moon and all the stars of heaven. When a noble act is done,—perchance in a scene of great natural beauty; when Leonidas and his three hundred martyrs consume one day in dying, and the sun and moon come each and look at them once in the steep defile of Thermoplylæ;[7] when Arnold Winkelried,[8] in the high Alps, under the shadow of the avalanche, gathers in his side a sheaf of Austrian spears to break the line for his comrades; are not these heroes entitled to add the beauty of the scene to the beauty of the deed? When the bark of Columbus nears the shore of America;—before it, the beach lined with savages, fleeing out of all their huts of cane; the sea behind; and the purple mountains of the Indian Archipelago around, can we separate the man from the living picture? Does not the New World clothe his form with her palm-groves and savannahs as fit drapery? Ever does natural beauty steal in like air, and envelope great actions. When Sir Harry Vane[9] was dragged up the Tower-hill, sitting on a sled, to suffer death as the champion of the English laws, one of the multitude cried out to him, "You never sate on so glorious a seat!" Charles II., to intimidate the citizens of London, caused the patriot Lord Russell[1] to be drawn in an open coach through the principal streets

5. Gaius Sallustius Crispus Sallust (86–34 B.C.), Roman historian; from *The Conspiracy of Cataline.*
6. Edward Gibbon (1737–1794); from *The History of the Decline and Fall of the Roman Empire* (1776–1788), Volume II, Chapter 68.
7. King Leonidas and his three hundred Spartans in 480 B.C. gave their lives in the defense of this pass against the entire Persian army.
8. The traditional hero of Swiss independence, Arnold von Winkelried, at the

Battle of Sempach (1386), exposed himself to the volley of Austrian spears, thus providing a breach through which the ready Swiss rushed to victory.
9. Puritan statesman, once colonial governor of Massachusetts, who opposed the restoration of Charles II (1660) and was executed for treason.
1. William, Lord Russell (1639–1683), strongly opposed the corrupt court and the Catholic party, and was executed for treason in 1683 on perjured testimony connecting him with the Rye House Plot.

of the city on his way to the scaffold. "But," his biographer[2] says, "the multitude imagined they saw liberty and virtue sitting by his side." In private places, among sordid objects, an act of truth or heroism seems at once to draw to itself the sky as its temple, the sun as its candle. Nature stretches out her arms to embrace man, only let his thoughts be of equal greatness. Willingly does she follow his steps with the rose and the violet, and bend her lines of grandeur and grace to the decoration of her darling child. Only let his thoughts be of equal scope, and the frame will suit the picture. A virtuous man is in unison with her works, and makes the central figure of the visible sphere. Homer, Pindar, Socrates, Phocion,[3] associate themselves fitly in our memory with the geography and climate of Greece. The visible heavens and earth sympathize with Jesus. And in common life whosoever has seen a person of powerful character and happy genius, will have remarked how easily he took all things along with him,—the persons, the opinions, and the day, and nature became ancillary to a man.

3. There is still another aspect under which the beauty of the world may be viewed, namely, as it becomes an object of the intellect. Beside the relation of things to virtue, they have a relation to thought. The intellect searches out the absolute order of things as they stand in the mind of God, and without the colors of affection. The intellectual and the active powers seem to succeed each other, and the exclusive activity of the one generates the exclusive activity of the other. There is something unfriendly in each to the other, but they are like the alternate periods of feeding and working in animals; each prepares and will be followed by the other. Therefore does beauty, which, in relation to actions, as we have seen, comes unsought, and comes because it is unsought, remain for the apprehension and pursuit of the intellect; and then again, in its turn, of the active power. Nothing divine dies. All good is eternally reproductive. The beauty of nature re-forms itself in the mind, and not for barren contemplation, but for new creation.

All men are in some degree impressed by the face of the world; some men even to delight. This love of beauty is Taste. Others have the same love in such excess, that, not content with admiring, they seek to embody it in new forms. The creation of beauty is Art.

The production of a work of art throws a light upon the mystery of humanity. A work of art is an abstract or epitome of the world. It is the result or expression of nature, in miniature. For although the works of nature are innumerable and all different, the result or the

2. The excellent *Life of William Lord Russell* (1819), by Lord John Russell, was still current.
3. Great figures of ancient Greece. Homer was traditionally regarded as the author of the heroic epics; Pindar was the great lyrist of heroic themes; Socrates brought philosophical inquiry into the streets, and died in defense of it; Phocion, general and statesman, negotiated successfully to retain limited Athenian nationalism under the Macedonian conquerors, but was condemned to death as a "collaborator."

expression of them all is similar and single. Nature is a sea of forms radically alike and even unique. A leaf, a sunbeam, a landscape, the ocean, make an analogous impression on the mind. What is common to them all,—that perfectness and harmony, is beauty. The standard of beauty is the entire circuit of natural forms,—the totality of nature; which the Italians expressed by defining beauty "il più nell' uno."[4] Nothing is quite beautiful alone; nothing but is beautiful in the whole. A single object is only so far beautiful as it suggests this universal grace. The poet, the painter, the sculptor, the musician, the architect, seek each to concentrate this radiance of the world on one point, and each in his several work to satisfy the love of beauty which stimulates him to produce. Thus is Art a nature passed through the alembic of man. Thus in art does Nature work through the will of a man filled with the beauty of her first works.

The world thus exists to the soul to satisfy the desire of beauty. This element I call an ultimate end. No reason can be asked or given why the soul seeks beauty. Beauty, in its largest and profoundest sense, is one expression for the universe. God is the all-fair. Truth, and goodness, and beauty, are but different faces of the same All. But beauty in nature is not ultimate. It is the herald of inward and eternal beauty, and is not alone a solid and satisfactory good. It must stand as a part, and not as yet the last or highest expression of the final cause of Nature.

IV. *Language*

Language is a third use which Nature subserves to man. Nature is the vehicle of thought, and in a simple, double, and threefold degree.

1. Words are signs of natural facts.
2. Particular natural facts are symbols of particular spiritual facts.
3. Nature is the symbol of spirit.

1. Words are signs of natural facts. The use of natural history is to give us aid in supernatural history: the use of the outer creation, to give us language for the beings and changes of the inward creation. Every word which is used to express a mortal or intellectual fact, if traced to its root, is found to be borrowed from some material appearance. *Right*[5] means *straight; wrong* means *twisted. Spirit* primarily means *wind; transgression*, the crossing of a *line; supercilious*, the *raising of the eyebrow.* We say the *heart* to express emotion, the *head* to denote thought; and *thought* and *emotion* are words borrowed from sensible things, and now appropriated to spiritual nature. Most of the process by which this transformation is made, is hidden from us in the remote time when language was framed; but

4. "The many in one." *Cf.* the poem "Each and All," below.

5. Emerson refers to the etymological derivations of the following five words.

the same tendency may be daily observed in children. Children and savages use only nouns or names of things, which they convert into verbs, and apply to analogous mental acts.

2. But this origin of all words that convey a spiritual import,—so conspicuous a fact in the history of language,—is our least debt to nature. It is not words only that are emblematic; it is things which are emblematic. Every natural fact is a symbol of some spiritual fact. Every appearance in nature corresponds to some state of the mind, and that state of the mind can only be described by presenting that natural appearance as its picture. An enraged man is a lion, a cunning man is a fox, a firm man is a rock, a learned man is a torch. A lamb is innocence; a snake is subtle spite; flowers express to us the delicate affections. Light and darkness are our familiar expression for knowledge and ignorance; and heat for love. Visible distance behind and before us, is respectively our image of memory and hope.

Who looks upon a river in a meditative hour and is not reminded of the flux of all things? Throw a stone into the stream, and the circles that propagate themselves are the beautiful type of all influence. Man is conscious of a universal soul within or behind his individual life, wherein, as in a firmament, the natures of Justice, Truth, Love, Freedom, arise and shine. This universal soul, he calls Reason: it is not mine, or thine, or his, but we are its; we are its property and men. And the blue sky in which the private earth is buried, the sky with its eternal calm, and full of everlasting orbs, is the type of Reason. That which, intellectually considered, we call Reason, considered in relation to nature, we call Spirit. Spirit is the Creator. Spirit hath life in itself. And man in all ages and countries, embodies it in his language, as the FATHER.

It is easily seen that there is nothing lucky or capricious in these analogies, but that they are constant, and pervade nature. These are not the dreams of a few poets, here and there, but man is an analogist, and studies relations in all objects. He is placed in the centre of beings, and a ray of relation passes from every other being to him. And neither can man be understood without these objects, nor these objects without man. All the facts in natural history taken by themselves, have no value, but are barren, like a single sex. But marry it to human history, and it is full of life. Whole Floras, all Linnaeus' and Buffon's[6] volumes, are dry catalogues of facts; but the most trivial of these facts, the habit of a plant, the organs, or work, or noise of an insect, applied to the illustration of a fact in intellectual philosophy,

---

6. Linnaeus (Carl von Linné, 1707–1778), Swedish botanist, founded the modern system of plant classification; Comte de Buffon (Georges Louis Le Clerc, 1707–1788), French naturalist, initiated and was an important collaborator on the forty-four-volume *Histoire Naturelle* (finished in 1804), a comprehensive formulation of the science of botany.

or, in any way associated to human nature, affects us in the most lively and agreeable manner. The seed of a plant,—to what affecting analogies in the nature of man, is that little fruit made use of, in all discourse, up to the voice of Paul, who calls the human corpse a seed,[7]—"It is sown a natural body; it is raised a spiritual body." The motion of the earth round its axis, and round the sun, makes the day, and the year. These are certain amounts of brute light and heat. But is there no intent of an analogy between man's life and the seasons? And do the seasons gain no grandeur or pathos from that analogy? The instincts of the ant are very unimportant, considered as the ant's; but the moment a ray of relation is seen to extend from it to man, and the little drudge is seen to be a monitor, a little body with a mighty heart, then all its habits, even that said to be recently observed, that it never sleeps, become sublime.

Because of this radical[8] correspondence between visible things and human thoughts, savages, who have only what is necessary, converse in figures. As we go back in history, language becomes more picturesque, until its infancy, when it is all poetry; or all spiritual facts are represented by natural symbols.[9] The same symbols are found to make the original elements of all languages. It has moreover been observed, that the idioms of all languages approach each other in passages of the greatest eloquence and power. And as this is the first language, so is it the last. This immediate dependence of language upon nature, this conversion of an outward phenomenon into a type of somewhat in human life, never loses its power to affect us. It is this which gives that piquancy to the conversation of a strong-natured farmer or back-woodsman, which all men relish.

A man's power to connect his thought with its proper symbol, and so to utter it, depends on the simplicity of his character, that is, upon his love of truth, and his desire to communicate it without loss. The corruption of man is followed by the corruption of language. When simplicity of character and the sovereignty of ideas is broken up by the prevalence of secondary desires, the desire of riches, of pleasure, of power, and of praise,—and duplicity and falsehood take place of simplicity and truth, the power over nature as an interpreter of the will, is in a degree lost; new imagery ceases to be created, and old words are perverted to stand for things which are not; a paper currency is employed, when there is no bullion in the vaults. In due time, the fraud is manifest, and words lose all power to stimulate the understanding or the affections. Hundreds of writers may be found in every long-civilized nation, who for a short time believe, and make others believe, that they see and utter truths, who do not of themselves clothe one thought in its natural garment, but who feed un-

7. *Cf*. I Corinthians xv: 42–44.
8. In the etymological sense: from the Latin *radix*, "a root."

9. This romantic theory of primitive word symbolism, then accepted, has now been superseded.

consciously on the language created by the primary writers of the country, those, namely, who hold primarily on nature.

But wise men pierce this rotten diction and fasten words again to visible things; so that picturesque language is at once a commanding certificate that he who employs it, is a man in alliance with truth and God. The moment our discourse rises above the ground line of familiar facts, and is inflamed with passion or exalted by thought, it clothes itself in images. A man conversing in earnest, if he watch his intellectual processes, will find that a material image, more or less luminous, arises in his mind, contemporaneous with every thought, which furnishes the vestment of the thought. Hence, good writing and brilliant discourse are perpetual allegories. This imagery is spontaneous. It is the blending of experience with the present action of the mind. It is proper creation. It is the working of the Original Cause through the instruments he has already made.

These facts may suggest the advantage which the country-life possesses for a powerful mind, over the artificial and curtailed life of cities. We know more from nature than we can at will communicate. Its light flows into the mind evermore, and we forget its presence. The poet, the orator, bred in the woods, whose senses have been nourished by their fair and appeasing changes, year after year, without design and without heed,—shall not lose their lesson altogether, in the roar of cities or the broil of politics. Long hereafter, amidst agitation and terror in national councils,—in the hour of revolution,—these solemn images shall reappear in their morning lustre, as fit symbols and words of the thoughts which the passing events shall awaken. At the call of a noble sentiment, again the woods wave, the pines murmur, the river rolls and shines, and the cattle low upon the mountains, as he saw and heard them in his infancy. And with these forms, the spells of persuasion, the keys of power are put into his hands.

3. We are thus assisted by natural objects in the expression of particular meanings. But how great a language to convey such peppercorn[1] informations! Did it need such noble races of creatures, this profusion of forms, this host of orbs in heaven, to furnish man with the dictionary and grammar of his municipal[2] speech? Whilst we use this grand cipher to expedite the affairs of our pot and kettle, we feel that we have not yet put it to its use, neither are able. We are like travellers using the cinders of a volcano to roast their eggs. Whilst we see that it always stands ready to clothe what we would say, we cannot avoid the question whether the characters are not significant of themselves. Have mountains, and waves, and skies, no significance but what we consciously give them, when we employ them as em-

1. Petty; a meaning derived from the ancient use of a peppercorn for the nomi-

2. In its earlier meaning, "local."

nal payment of an obligation.

blems of our thoughts? The world is emblematic. Parts of speech are metaphors, because the whole of nature is a metaphor of the human mind. The laws of moral nature answer to those of matter as face to face in a glass. "The visible world and the relation of its parts, is the dial plate of the invisible." The axioms of physics translate the laws of ethics. Thus, "the whole is greater than its part;" "reaction is equal to action;" "the smallest weight may be made to lift the greatest, the difference of weight being compensated by time;" and many the like propositions, which have an ethical as well as physical sense. These propositions have a much more extensive and universal sense when applied to human life, than when confined to technical use.

In like manner, the memorable words of history, and the proverbs of nations, consists usually of a natural fact, selected as a picture or parable of a moral truth. Thus; A rolling stone gathers no moss; A bird in the hand is worth two in the bush; A cripple in the right way, will beat a racer in the wrong; Make hay while the sun shines; 'Tis hard to carry a full cup even; Vinegar is the son of wine; The last ounce broke the camel's back; Long-lived trees make roots first;— and the like. In their primary sense these are trivial facts, but we repeat them for the value of their analogical import. What is true of proverbs, is true of all fables, parables, and allegories.

This relation between the mind and matter is not fancied by some poet, but stands in the will of God, and so is free to be known by all men. It appears to men, or it does not appear. When in fortunate hours we ponder this miracle, the wise man doubts, if, at all other times, he is not blind and deaf;

> ———"Can these things be,
> And overcome us like a summer's cloud,
> Without our special wonder?"[3]

for the universe becomes transparent, and the light of higher laws than its own shines through it. It is the standing problem which has exercised the wonder and the study of every fine genius since the world began; from the era of the Egyptians and the Brahmins to that of Pythagoras, of Plato, of Bacon, of Leibnitz, of Swedenborg.[4] There sits the Sphinx at the road-side, and from age to age, as each

3. *Macbeth*, Act III, Scene iv, ll. 110–112. The first two editions read, erroneously, "Can these things be," for, "Can such things be."
4. All these taught, in one way or another, a universe "transparent" in Emerson's meaning above. The Greek Pythagoras (sixth century B.C.), like the Egyptian and Brahmin mystics, taught the transmigration of souls; the Greek Plato (428–347 B.C.) was the father of western philosophical idealism; Francis Bacon (1561–1626) British founder of inductive science, was mystical in his religious philosophy; the German Gottfried Wilhelm von Leibnitz (1646–1716) promulgated a philosophical optimism later satirized by such determinists as Voltaire; and Emanuel Swedenborg (1688–1772) was a Swedish religious thinker who later became Emerson's example for "The Mystic" in *Representative Men*.

prophet comes by, he tries his fortune at reading her riddle.[5] There seems to be a necessity in spirit to manifest itself in material forms; and day and night, river and storm, beast and bird, acid and alkali, preëxist in necessary Ideas in the mind of God, and are what they are by virtue of preceding affections in the world of spirit. A Fact is the end or last issue of spirit. The visible creation is the terminus or the circumference of the invisible world. "Material objects," said a French philosopher, "are necessarily kinds of *scoriae*[6] of the substantial thoughts of the Creator, which must always preserve an exact relation to their first origin; in other words, visible nature must have a spiritual and moral side."

This doctrine is abstruse, and though the images of "garment," "scoriae," "mirror," &c., may stimulate the fancy, we must summon the aid of subtler and more vital expositors to make it plain. "Every scripture is to be interpreted by the same spirit which gave it forth," —is the fundamental law of criticism. A life in harmony with nature, the love of truth and of virtue, will purge the eyes to understand her text. By degrees we may come to know the primitive sense of the permanent objects of nature, so that the world shall be to us an open book, and every form significant of its hidden life and final cause.

A new interest surprises us, whilst, under the view now suggested, we contemplate the fearful extent and multitude of objects; since "every object rightly seen, unlocks a new faculty of the soul." That which was unconscious truth, becomes, when interpreted and defined in an object, a part of the domain of knowledge,—a new weapon in the magazine of power.

V. *Discipline*

In view of the significance of nature, we arrive at once at a new fact, that nature is a discipline.[7] This use of the world includes the preceding uses, as parts of itself.

Space, time, society, labor, climate, food, locomotion, the animals, the mechanical forces, give us sincerest lessons, day by day, whose meaning is unlimited. They educate both the Understanding and the Reason. Every property of matter is a school for the understanding.—its solidity or resistance, its inertia, its extension, its figure, its divisibility. The understanding adds, divides, combines, measures, and finds nutriment and room for its activity in this worthy scene. Meantime, Reason transfers all these lessons into its own world of

---

5. In classic myth, the Sphinx of Thebes slew all travelers unable to solve her riddle. At last Oedipus did so; whereupon, as predicted, she killed herself and he became king, with tragic consequences immortalized in Sophocles' trilogy of *Oedipus*. *Cf.* "The Sphinx," below.
6. Slag from the smelting of metals.

7. A trained ecclesiastic, Emerson utilizes the dualism of this word, signifying at once a controlled obedience to the absolute, and, secondly, the ecclesiastical discipline of practical rules affecting conduct. *Cf.*, following, his transcendentalist's distinction between Understanding, an agent of conduct, and Reason, an agent of truth.

thought, by perceiving the analogy that marries Matter and Mind.

1. Nature is a discipline of the understanding in intellectual truths. Our dealing with sensible objects is a constant exercise in the necessary lessons of difference, of likeness, of order, of being and seeming, of progressive arrangement; of ascent from particular to general; of combination to one end of manifold forces. Proportioned to the importance of the organ to be formed, is the extreme care with which its tuition[8] is provided,—a care pretermitted in no single case. What tedious training, day after day, year after year, never ending, to form the common sense; what continual reproduction of annoyances, inconveniences, dilemmas; what rejoicing over us of little men; what disputing of prices, what reckonings of interest,—and all to form the Hand of the mind;—to instruct us that "good thoughts are no better than good dreams, unless they be executed!"

The same good office is performed by Property and its filial systems of debt and credit. Debt, grinding debt, whose iron face the widow, the orphan, and the sons of genius fear and hate;—debt, which consumes so much time, which so cripples and disheartens a great spirit with cares that seem so base, is a preceptor whose lessons cannot be forgone, and is needed most by those who suffer from it most. Moreover, property, which has been well compared to snow,—"if it fall level to-day, it will be blown into drifts to-morrow,"—is the surface action of internal machinery, like the index on the face of a clock. Whilst now it is the gymnastics of the understanding, it is hiving in the foresight of the spirit, experience in profounder laws.

The whole character and fortune of the individual are affected by the least inequalities in the culture of the understanding; for example, in the perception of differences. Therefore is Space, and therefore Time, that man may know that things are not huddled and lumped, but sundered and individual. A bell and a plough have each their use, and neither can do the office of the other. Water is good to drink, coal to burn, wool to wear; but wool cannot be drunk, nor water spun, nor coal eaten. The wise man shows his wisdom in separation, in gradation, and his scale of creatures and of merits is as wide as nature. The foolish have no range in their scale, but suppose every man is as every other man. What is not good they call the worst, and what is not hateful, they call the best.

In like manner, what good heed nature forms in us! She pardons no mistakes. Her yea is yea, and her nay, nay.

The first steps in Agriculture, Astronomy, Zoölogy, (those first steps which the farmer, the hunter, and the sailor take,) teach that nature's dice are always loaded;[9] that in her heaps and rubbish are

8. Here in its primitive sense of "guardianship," as well as "instruction."
9. E. W. Emerson found the source of this in Fragment 763, from a lost play by Sophocles, reading, "The dice of Zeus ever fall aright" (Centenary Edition, Vol. I, p. 409).

concealed sure and useful results.)

How calmly and genially the mind apprehends one after another the laws of physics! What noble emotions dilate the mortal as he enters into the counsels of the creation, and feels by knowledge the privilege to BE! His insight refines him. The beauty of nature shines in his own breast. Man is greater that[1] he can see this, and the universe less, because Time and Space relations vanish as laws are known.

Here again we are impressed and even daunted by the immense Universe to be explored. "What we know, is a point to what we do not know." Open any recent journal of science, and weigh the problems suggested concerning Light, Heat, Electricity, Magnetism, Physiology, Geology, and judge whether the interest of natural science is likely to be soon exhausted.

Passing by many particulars of the dicipline of nature, we must not omit to specify two.

The exercise of the Will or the lesson of power is taught in every event. From the child's successive possession of his several senses up to the hour when he saith, "Thy will be done!"[2] he is learning the secret, that he can reduce under his will, not only particular events, but great classes, nay the whole series of events, and so conform all facts to his character. Nature is thoroughly mediate. It is made to serve. It receives the dominion of man as meekly as the ass on which the Savior rode.[3] It offers all its kingdoms[4] to man as the raw material which he may mould into what is useful. Man is never weary of working it up. He forges the subtile and delicate air into wise and melodious words, and gives them wing as angels of persuasion and command. One after another, his victorious thought comes up with and reduces all things, until the world becomes at last only a realized will,—the double of the man.

2. Sensible objects conform to the premonitions of Reason and reflect the conscience. All things are moral; and in their boundless changes have an unceasing reference to spiritual nature. Therefore is nature glorious with form, color, and motion, that every globe in the remotest heaven; every chemical change from the rudest crystal up to the laws of life; every change of vegetation from the first principle of growth in the eye of a leaf, to the tropical forest and antediluvian coal-mine;[5] every animal function from the sponge up to Hercules, shall hint or thunder to man the laws of right and wrong, and echo the Ten Commandments. Therefore is nature ever the ally of Religion: lends all her pomp and riches to the religious sentiment.)

1. Reads "than" in 1849; corrected in the Centenary Edition.
2. See the Lord's Prayer, Matthew vi: 9; and *cf.* Acts xxi: 14.
3. See John xii: 12–15; and *cf.* Zechariah ix: 9.
4. *Cf.* Matthew iv: 8.
5. *I.e.*, coal results from the deep burial of forests by geomorphic upheaval.

Prophet and priest, David, Isaiah, Jesus, have drawn deeply from this source. This ethical character so penetrates the bone and marrow of nature, as to seem the end for which it was made. Whatever private purpose is answered by any member or part, this is its public and universal function, and is never omitted. Nothing in nature is exhausted in its first use. When a thing has served an end to the uttermost, it is wholly new for an ulterior service. In God, every end is converted into a new means. Thus the use of commodity, regarded by itself, is mean and squalid. But it is to the mind an education in the doctrine of Use, namely, that a thing is good only so far as it serves; that a conspiring of parts and efforts to the production of an end is essential to any being. The first and gross manifestations of this truth is our inevitable and hated training in values and wants, in corn and meat.

It has already been illustrated, that every natural process is a version of a moral sentence. The moral law lies at the centre of nature and radiates to the circumference. It is the pith and marrow of every substance, every relation, and every process. All things with which we deal, preach to us. What is a farm but a mute gospel? The chaff and the wheat, weeds and plants, blight, rain, insects, sun,—it is a sacred emblem from the first furrow of spring to the last stack which the snow of winter overtakes in the fields. But the sailor, the shepherd, the miner, the merchant, in their several resorts, have each an experience precisely parallel, and leading to the same conclusion: because all organizations are radically alike. Nor can it be doubted that this moral sentiment which thus scents the air, grows in the grain, and impregnates the waters of the world, is caught by man and sinks into his soul. The moral influence of nature upon every individual is that amount of truth which it illustrates to him. Who can estimate this? Who can guess how much firmness the sea-beaten rock has taught the fisherman? how much tranquillity has been reflected to man from the azure sky, over whose unspotted deeps the winds forevermore drive flocks of stormy clouds, and leave no wrinkle or stain? how much industry and providence and affection we have caught from the pantomime of brutes? What a searching preacher of self-command is the varying phenomenon of Health!

Herein is especially apprehended the unity of Nature,—the unity in variety,—which meets us everywhere. All the endless variety of things make an identical impression. Xenophanes[6] complained in his old age, that, look where he would, all things hastened back to Unity. He was weary of seeing the same entity in the tedious variety of forms. The fable of Proteus[7] has a cordial truth. A leaf, a drop, a crystal, a moment of time, is related to the whole, and partakes

---

6. Greek pre-Socratic philosopher (sixth century B.C.), who taught the unity of all existence—"All is one."

7. Proteus, in Greek fable, could elusively change his form to escape having to prophesy.

of the perfection of the whole. Each particle is a microcosm, and faithfully renders the likeness of the world.[8] Not only resemblances exist in things whose analogy is obvious, as when we detect the type of the human hand in the flipper of the fossil saurus,[9] but also in objects wherein there is great superficial unlikeness. Thus architecture is called "frozen music," by De Staël and Goethe.[1] Vitruvius[2] thought an architect should be a musician. "A Gothic church," said Coleridge,[3] "is a petrified religion." Michael Angelo maintained, that, to an architect, a knowledge of anatomy is essential. In Haydn's oratorios,[4] the notes present to the imagination not only motions, as, of the snake, the stag, and the elephant, but colors also; as the green grass. The law of harmonic sounds reappears in the harmonic colors. The granite is differenced in its laws only by the more or less of heat from the river that wears it away. The river, as it flows, resembles the air that flows over it; the air resembles the light which traverses it with more subtile currents; the light resembles the heat which rides with it through Space. Each creature is only a modification of the other; the likeness in them is more than the difference, and their radical law is one and the same. A rule of one art, or a law of one organization, holds true throughout nature. So intimate is this Unity, that, it is easily seen, it lies under the undermost garment of nature, and betrays its source in Universal Spirit. For it pervades Thought also. Every universal truth which we express in words, implies or supposes every other truth. *Omne verum vero consonat.*[5] It is like a great circle on a sphere, comprising all possible circles; which, however, may be drawn and comprise it in like manner. Every such truth is the absolute Ens[6] seen from one side. But it has innumerable sides.

The central Unity is still more conspicuous in actions. Words are finite organs of the infinite mind. They cannot cover the dimensions of what is in truth. They break, chop, and impoverish it. An action is the perfection and publication of thought. A right action seems to fill the eye, and to be related to all nature. "The wise man, in doing one thing, does all; or, in the one thing he does rightly, he sees the

8. The idea that the microcosm recapitulates the universal macrocosm recurs throughout transcendentalism and in Emerson's writing; the pantheism of Xenophanes, just mentioned, suggests it here.

9. A suffix, used in paleontology, for names of various families of extinct reptilian mammoths.

1. Madame de Staël (1766–1817), see *Corinne ou l'Italie* (1807), Book IV, Chapter 3; Johann W. von Goethe (1749–1832), see *Conversations with Eckermann,* the passage dated March 23, 1829. *Cf.* Emerson's *Journals,* Vol. III, p. 363.

2. Marcus Vitruvius Pollio, Roman

architect (first century B.C.), *De Architectura,* Book I, Chapter i, Section 8.

3. Samuel Taylor Coleridge, in "A Lecture on the General Characteristics of the Gothic Mind in the Middle Ages" (*Literary Remains,* 1836): "a Gothic cathedral is the petrification of our religion."

4. Joseph Haydn (1732–1809). His two greatest oratorios, *The Creation* and *The Seasons,* are especially rich in such natural description as Emerson suggests here.

5. Every truth harmonizes with all other truth.

6. "Being" in the most general sense of the term.

likeness of all which is done rightly."

Words and actions are not the attributes of brute nature. They introduce us to the human form, of which all other organizations appear to be degradations. When this appears among so many that surround it, the spirit prefers it to all others. It says, "From such as this, have I drawn joy and knowledge; in such as this, have I found and beheld myself; I will speak to it; it can speak again; it can yield me thought already formed and alive." In fact, the eye,—the mind,—is always accompanied by these forms, male and female; and these are incomparably the richest informations of the power and order that lie at the heart of things. Unfortunately every one of them bears the marks as of some injury; is marred and superficially defective. Nevertheless, far different from the deaf and dumb nature around them, these all rest like fountain-pipes on the unfathomed sea of thought and virtue whereto they alone, of all organizations, are the entrances.

It were a pleasant inquiry to follow into detail their ministry to our education, but where would it stop? We are associated in adolescent and adult life with some friends, who, like skies and waters, are co-extensive with our idea; who, answering each to a certain affection of the soul, satisfy our desire on that side; whom we lack power to put at such focal distance from us, that we can mend or even analyze them. We cannot choose but love them. When much intercourse with a friend has supplied us with a standard of excellence, and has increased our respect for the resources of God who thus sends a real person to outgo our ideal; when he has, moreover, become an object of thought, and, whilst his character retains all its unconscious effect, is converted in the mind into solid and sweet wisdom,—it is a sign to us that his office is closing, and he is commonly withdrawn from our sight in a short time.[7]

VI. *Idealism*

Thus is the unspeakable but intelligible and practicable meaning of the world conveyed to man, the immortal pupil, in every object of sense. To this one end of Discipline, all parts of nature conspire.

A noble doubt perpetually suggests itself,—whether this end be not the Final Cause of the Universe; and whether nature outwardly exists. It is a sufficient account of that Appearance we call the World, that God will teach a human mind, and so makes it the receiver of a certain number of congruent sensations, which we call sun and moon, man and woman, house and trade. In my utter impotence to test the authenticity of the report of my senses, to know whether

7. According to E. W. Emerson (Centenary Edition, Vol. I, p. 410), this thought relates to the death, within the previous two years, of Emerson's brothers Edward and Charles, the latter of whom he called "a brother and a friend in one."

the impressions they make on me correspond with outlying objects, what difference does it make, whether Orion is up there in heaven, or some god paints the image in the firmament of the soul? The relations of parts and the end of the whole remaining the same, what is the difference, whether land and sea interact, and worlds revolve and intermingle without number or end,—deep yawning under deep,[8] and galaxy balancing galaxy, throughout absolute space,—or whether, without relations of time and space, the same appearances are inscribed in the constant faith of man? Whether nature enjoy a substantial existence without, or is only in the apocalypse[9] of the mind, it is alike useful and alike venerable to me. Be it what it may, it is ideal to me so long as I cannot try the accuracy of my senses.

The frivolous make themselves merry with the Ideal theory,[1] as if its consequences were burlesque; as if it affected the stability of nature. It surely does not. God never jests with us, and will not compromise the end of nature by permitting any inconsequence in its procession. Any distrust of the permanence of laws would paralyze the faculties of man. Their permanence is sacredly respected, and his faith therein is perfect. The wheels and springs of man are all set to the hypothesis of the permanence of nature. We are not built like a ship to be tossed, but like a house to stand. It is a natural consequence of this structure, that so long as the active powers predominate over the reflective, we resist with indignation any hint that nature is more short-lived or mutable than spirit. The broker, the wheelwright, the carpenter, the tollman, are much displeased at the intimation.

But whilst we acquiesce entirely in the permanence of natural laws, the question of the absolute existence of nature still remains open. It is the uniform effect of culture on the human mind, not to shake our faith in the stability of particular phenomena, as of heat, water, azote;[2] but to lead us to regard nature as phenomenon, not a substance; to attribute necessary existence to spirit; to esteem nature as an accident and an effect.

To the senses and the unrenewed understanding, belongs a sort of instinctive belief in the absolute existence of nature. In their view man and nature are indissolubly joined. Things are ultimates, and they never look beyond their sphere. The presence of Reason mars this faith. The first effort of thought tends to relax this despotism of the senses which binds us to nature as if we were a part of it, and shows us nature aloof, and, as it were, afloat. Until this higher agency intervened, the animal eye sees, with wonderful accuracy, sharp outlines and colored surfaces. When the eye of

8. *Cf.* Psalms xlii: 7.
9. A prophetic revelation.
1. That is, they make a jest of the transcendental belief (suggested in the two previous paragraphs) that the essential reality of the thing inheres in the idea, to be sought in the mind.
2. Nitrogen.

Reason opens, to outline and surface are at once added grace and expression. These proceed from imagination and affection, and abate somewhat of the angular distinctness of objects. If the Reason be stimulated to more earnest vision, outlines and surfaces become transparent, and are no longer seen; causes and spirits are seen through them. The best moments of life are these delicious awakenings of the higher powers, and the reverential withdrawing of nature before its God.

Let us proceed to indicate the effects of culture.

1. Our first institution in the Ideal philosophy is a hint from Nature herself.

Nature is made to conspire with spirit to emancipate us. Certain mechanical changes, a small alteration in our local position, apprises us of a dualism. We are strangely affected by seeing the shore from a moving ship, from a balloon, or through the tints of an unusual sky. The least change in our point of view gives the whole world a pictorial air. A man who seldom rides, needs only to get into a coach and traverse his own town, to turn the street into a puppet-show. The men, the women,—talking, running, bartering, fighting,—the earnest mechanic, the lounger, the beggar, the boys, the dogs, are unrealized[3] at once, or, at least, wholly detached from all relation to the observer, and seen as apparent, not substantial beings. What new thoughts are suggested by seeing a face[4] of country quite familiar, in the rapid movement of the railroad car! Nay, the most wonted objects, (make a very slight change in the point of vision,) please us most. In a camera obscura,[5] the butcher's cart, and the figure of one of our own family amuse us. So a portrait of a well-known face gratifies us. Turn the eyes upside down, by looking at the landscape through your legs, and how agreeable is the picture, though you have seen it any time these twenty years!

In these cases, by mechanical means, is suggested the difference between the observer and the spectacle—between man and nature. Hence arises a pleasure mixed with awe; I may say, a low degree of the sublime is felt, from the fact, probably, that man is hereby apprised that whilst the world is a spectacle, something in himself is stable.

2. In a higher manner the poet communicates the same pleasure. By a few strokes he delineates, as on air, the sun, the mountain, the camp, the city, the hero, the maiden, not different from what we know them, but only lifted from the ground and afloat before the eye. He unfixes the land and the sea, makes them revolve around the axis of his primary thought, and disposes them anew. Possessed himself by a heroic passion, he uses matter as symbols of it. The

3. *I.e.*, deprived of reality.
4. In the archaic sense, meaning "view."

5. An optical instrument, the ancestor of the camera.

sensual man conforms thoughts to things; the poet conforms things to his thoughts. The one esteems nature as rooted and fast; the other, as fluid, and impresses his being thereon. To him, the refractory world is ductile and flexible; he invests dust and stones with humanity, and makes them the words of the Reason. The Imagination may be defined to be the use which the Reason makes of the material world. Shakespeare possesses the power of subordinating nature for the purposes of expression, beyond all poets. His imperial muse tosses the creation like a bauble from hand to hand, and uses it to embody any caprice of thought that is uppermost in his mind. The remotest spaces of nature are visited, and the farthest sundered things are brought together, by a subtile spiritual connection. We are made aware that magnitude of material things is relative, and all objects shrink and expand to serve the passion of the poet. Thus in his sonnets, the lays of birds, the scents and dyes of flowers he finds to be the *shadow* of his beloved;[6] time, which keeps her from him, is his *chest*;[7] the suspicion she has awakened, is her *ornament*;

> The ornament of beauty is Suspect,
> A crow which flies in heaven's sweetest air.[8]

His passion is not the fruit of chance; it swells, as he speaks, to a city, or a state,

> No, it was builded far from accident;
> It suffers not in smiling pomp, nor falls
> Under the brow of thralling discontent;
> It fears not policy, that heretic,
> That works on leases of short numbered hours,
> But all alone stands hugely politic.[9]

In the strength of his constancy, the Pyramids[1] seem to him recent and transitory. The freshness of youth and love dazzles him with its resemblance to morning;

> Take those lips away
> Which so sweetly were forsworn;
> And those eyes,—the break of day,
> Lights that do mislead the morn.[2]

The wild beauty of this hyperbole, I may say in passing, it would not be easy to match in literature.

This transfiguration which all material objects undergo through

6. *Cf.* Shakespeare, Sonnet XCVIII.
7. *Cf.* Shakespeare, Sonnet LXV, l. 10.
8. Shakespeare, Sonnet LXX, ll. 3–4. For "which" read "that."
9. From Shakespeare, Sonnet CXXIV, with slight alteration.

1. *Cf.* Shakespeare, Sonnet CXXIII, l. 2.
2. See Shakespeare's *Measure For Measure*, the song opening Act IV, Scene 1. Lines 1–4 are here slightly altered.

the passion of the poet,—this power which he exerts to dwarf the great, to magnify the small,—might be illustrated by a thousand examples from his Plays. I have before me the Tempest, and will cite only these few lines.

> ARIEL. The strong based promontory
> Have I made shake, and by the spurs plucked up
> The pine and cedar.[3]

Prospero calls for music to soothe the frantic Alonzo, and his companions;

> A solemn air, and the best comforter
> To an unsettled fancy, cure my brains
> Now useless, boiled within thy skull.[4]

Again;

> The charm dissolves apace,
> And, as the morning steals upon the night,
> Melting the darkness, so their rising senses
> Begin to chase the ignorant fumes that mantle
> Their clearer reason. Their understanding
> Begins to swell: and the approaching tide
> Will shortly fill the reasonable shores
> That now lie foul and muddy.[5]

The perception of real affinities between events (that is to say, of *ideal* affinities, for those only are real), enables the poet thus to make free with the most imposing forms and phenomena of the world, and to assert the predominance of the soul.

3. Whilst thus the poet animates nature with his own thoughts, he differs from the philosopher only herein, that the one proposes Beauty as his main end; the other Truth. But the philosopher, not less than the poet, postpones the apparent order and relations of things to the empire of thought. "The problem of philosophy," according to Plato, "is, for all that exists conditionally, to find a ground unconditioned and absolute."[6] It proceeds on the faith that a law determines all phenomena, which being known, the phenomena can be predicted. That law, when in the mind, is an idea. Its beauty is infinite. The true philosopher and the true poet are one, and a beauty, which is truth, and a truth, which is beauty, is the aim of both. Is not the charm of one of Plato's or Aristotle's definitions strictly like that of the Antigone of Sophocles?[7] It is, in both cases, that a spirit-

---

3. *The Tempest*, Act V, Scene 1, ll. 46–48; but the speaker is Prospero, not Ariel.
4. *Ibid*. Act V, Scene 1, ll. 58–60.
5. *Ibid*. Act V, Scene 1, ll. 64–68, 79–82.

6. See the *Republic*, Book V.
7. Sophocles (496?–406 B.C.) produced in the *Antigone* one of the most moving of the great Greek tragedies.

ual life has been imparted to nature; that the solid seeming block of matter has been pervaded and dissolved by a thought; that this feeble human being has penetrated the vast masses of nature with an informing soul, and recognized itself in their harmony, that is, seized their law. In physics, when this is attained, the memory disburthens itself of its cumbrous catalogues of particulars, and carries centuries of observation in a single formula.

Thus even in physics, the material is degraded before the spiritual. The astronomer, the geometer, rely on their irrefragable analysis, and disdain the results of observation. The sublime remark of Euler[8] on his law of arches, "This will be found contrary to all experience, yet is true;" had already transferred nature into the mind, and left matter like an outcast corpse.

4. Intellectual science has been observed to beget invariably a doubt of the existence of matter. Turgot[9] said, "He that has never doubted the existence of matter, may be assured he has no aptitude for metaphysical inquiries." It fastens the attention upon immortal necessary uncreated natures, that is, upon Ideas; and in their presence we feel that the outward circumstance is a dream and a shade. Whilst we wait in this Olympus of gods, we think of nature as an appendix to the soul. We ascend into their region, and know that these are the thoughts of the Supreme Being. "These are they who were set up from everlasting, from the beginning, or even the earth was. When he prepared the heavens, they were there; when he established the clouds above, when he strengthened the fountains of the deep. Then they were by him, as one brought up with him. Of them took he counsel."[1]

Their influence is proportionate. As objects of science they are accessible to few men. Yet all men are capable of being raised by piety or by passion, into their region. And no man touches these divine natures, without becoming, in some degree, himself divine. Like a new soul, they renew the body. We become physically nimble and lightsome; we tread on air; life is no longer irksome, and we think it will never be so. No man fears age or misfortune or death in their serene company, for he is transported out of the district of change. Whilst we behold unveiled the nature of Justice and Truth, we learn the difference between the absolute and the conditional or relative. We apprehend the absolute. As it were, for the first time, *we exist*. We become immortal, for we learn that time and space are relations of matter; that with a perception of truth or a virtuous will they have no affinity.

8. Leonhard Euler (1707–1783), Swiss mathematician.
9. Anne Robert Jacques Turgot (1727–1781), French liberal, statesman and economist.
1. Condensed paraphrase of Proverbs viii: 23, 27, 28, 30

5. Finally, religion and ethics, which may be fitly called the practice of ideas, or the introduction of ideas into life, have an analogous effect with all lower culture, in degrading nature and suggesting its dependence on spirit. Ethics and religion differ herein; that the one is the system of human duties commencing from man; the other, from God. Religion includes the personality of God; Ethics does not. They are one to our present design. They both put nature under foot. The first and last lesson of religion is, "The things that are seen, are temporal; the things that are unseen, are eternal."[2] It puts an affront upon nature. It does that for the unschooled, which philosophy does for Berkeley and Viasa.[3] The uniform language that may be heard in the churches of the most ignorant sects is,—"Contemn the unsubstantial shows of the world; they are vanities, dreams, shadows, unrealities; seek the realities of religion." The devotee flouts nature. Some theosophists[4] have arrived at a certain hostility and indignation towards nature, as the Manichean [5] and Plotinus.[6] They distrusted in themselves any looking back to these flesh-pots of Egypt.[7] Plotinus was ashamed of his body. In short, they might all say of matter, what Michael Angelo said of external beauty, "It is the frail and weary weed, in which God dresses the soul which he has called into time."

It appears that motion, poetry, physical and intellectual science, and religion, all tend to affect our convictions of the reality of the external world. But I own there is something ungrateful in expanding too curiously the particulars of the general proposition, that all culture tends to imbue us with idealism. I have no hostility to nature, but a child's love to it. I expand and live in the warm day like corn and melons. Let us speak her fair. I do not wish to fling stones at my beautiful mother, nor soil my gentle nest. I only wish to indicate the true position of nature in regard to man, wherein to establish man all right education tends; as the ground which to attain is the object of human life, that is, of man's connection with nature. Culture inverts the vulgar views of nature, and brings the mind to call that apparent which it uses to call real, and that real which it uses to call visionary. Children, it is true, believe in the external world. The belief that it appears only, is an afterthought, but with culture this faith will as surely arise on the mind as did the first.

2. *Cf.* II Corinthians iv: 18.
3. George Berkeley (1685–1753), English churchman and thinker, whose idealistic philosophy is here associated with the spirit of Viasa, a legendary Hindu personage credited with the authorship of a substantial part of the Sanskrit scriptures.
4. The term is here broadly applied to theologians who claim direct knowledge of God by mystical revelation.

5. An adherent to the doctrine of Mani, or Manes, a third century Persian sage who asserted that the body was produced by evil or darkness, but the soul streams from the principle of goodness or light.
6. Plotinus (204?–270? A.D.), a Roman Platonist of Egyptian origin, gave a mystical and symbolic interpretation to the doctrines of Plato.
7. *Cf.* Exodus xvi: 3.

The advantage of the ideal theory over the popular faith is this, that it presents the world in precisely that view which is most desirable to the mind. It is, in fact, the view which Reason, both speculative and practical,[8] that is, philosophy and virtue, take. For seen in the light of thought, the world always is phenomenal; and virtue subordinates it to the mind. Idealism sees the world in God. It beholds the whole circle of persons and things, of actions and events, of country and religion, not as painfully accumulated, atom after atom, act after act, in an aged creeping Past, but as one vast picture which God paints on the instant eternity for the contemplation of the soul. Therefore the soul holds itself off from a too trivial and microscopic study of the universal tablet. It respects the end too much to immerse itself in the means. It sees something more important in Christianity than the scandals of ecclesiastical history or the niceties of criticism; and, very incurious concerning persons or miracles, and not at all disturbed by chasms of historical evidence, it accepts from God the phenomenon, as it finds it, as the pure and awful form of religion in the world. It is not hot and passionate at the appearance of what it calls its own good or bad fortune, at the union or opposition of other persons. No man is its enemy. It accepts whatsoever befalls, as part of its lesson. It is a watcher more than a doer, and it is a doer, only that it may the better watch.

VII. *Spirit*

It is essential to a true theory of nature and of man, that it should contain somewhat progressive. Uses that are exhausted or that may be, and facts that end in the statement, cannot be all that is true of this brave lodging wherein man is harbored, and wherein all his faculties find appropriate and endless exercise. And all the uses of nature admit of being summed in one, which yields the activity of man an infinite scope. Through all its kingdoms, to the suburbs and outskirts of things, it is faithful to the cause whence it had its origin. It always speaks of Spirit. It suggests the absolute. It is a perpetual effect. It is a great shadow pointing always to the sun behind us.

The aspect of Nature is devout. Like the figure of Jesus, she stands with bended head, and hands folded upon the breast. The happiest man is he who learns from nature the lesson of worship.

Of that ineffable essence which we call Spirit, he that thinks most, will say least. We can foresee God in the coarse, and, as it were, distant phenomena of matter; but when we try to define and describe himself, both language and thought desert us, and we are as helpless as fools and savages. That essence refuses to be recorded in proposi-

8. Kant's distinction between the practical Reason (understanding), which regulates behavior, and speculative Reason, which supports metaphysical thought, was a familiar concept among transcendentalists.

tions, but when man has worshipped him intellectually, the noblest ministry of nature is to stand as the apparition of God. It is the organ through which the universal spirit speaks to the individual, and strives to lead back the individual to it.

When we consider Spirit, we see that the views already presented do not include the whole circumference of man. We must add some related thoughts.

Three problems are put by nature to the mind: What is matter? Whence is it? and Whereto? The first of these questions only, the ideal theory answers. Idealism saith: matter is a phenomenon, not a substance. Idealism acquaints us with the total disparity between the evidence of our own being and the evidence of the world's being. The one is perfect; the other, incapable of any assurance; the mind is a part of the nature of things; the world is a divine dream, from which we may presently awake to the glories and certainties of day. Idealism is a hypothesis to account for nature by other principles than those of carpentry and chemistry. Yet, if it only deny the existence of matter, it does not satisfy the demands of the spirit. It leaves God out of me. It leaves me in the splendid labyrinth of my perceptions, to wander without end. Then the heart resists it, because it balks the affections in denying substantive being to men and women. Nature is so pervaded with human life that there is something of humanity in all and in every particular. But this theory makes nature foreign to me, and does not account for that consanguinity which we acknowledge to it.

Let it stand then, in the present state of our knowledge, merely as a useful introductory hypothesis, serving to apprise us of the eternal distinction between the soul and the world.

But when, following the invisible steps of thought, we come to inquire, Whence is matter? and Whereto? many truths arise to us out of the recesses of consciousness. We learn that the highest is present to the soul of man; that the dread universal essence, which is not wisdom, or love, or beauty, or power, but all in one, and each entirely, is that for which all things exist, and that by which they are; that spirit creates; that behind nature, throughout nature, spirit is present; one and not compound it does not act upon us from without, that is, in space and time, but spiritually, or through ourselves: therefore, that spirit, that is, the Supreme Being, does not build up nature around us, but puts it forth through us, as the life of the tree puts forth new branches and leaves through the pores of the old. As a plant upon the earth, so a man rests upon the bosom of God; he is nourished by unfailing fountains, and draws at his need inexhaustible power. Who can set bounds to the possibilities of man? Once inhale the upper air, being admitted to behold the absolute natures of justice and truth, and we learn that man has access to the entire mind of the Creator, is himself the creator in the finite. This view, which admonishes me where the sources of wisdom and power lie, and points to virtue as to

> "The golden key
> Which opes the palace of eternity,"[9]

carries upon its face the highest certificate of truth, because it animates me to create my own world through the purification of my soul.

The world proceeds from the same spirit as the body of man. It is a remoter and inferior incarnation of God, a projection of God in the unconscious. But it differs from the body in one important respect. It is not, like that, now subjected to the human will. Its serene order is inviolable by us. It is, therefore, to us, the present expositor of the divine mind. It is a fixed point whereby we may measure our departure. As we degenerate, the contrast between us and our house is more evident. We are as much strangers in nature as we are aliens from God. We do not understand the notes of birds. The fox and the deer run away from us; the bear and tiger rend us. We do not know the uses of more than a few plants, as corn and the apple, the potato and the vine. Is not the landscape, every glimpse of which hath a grandeur, a face of him? Yet this may show us what discord is between man and nature, for you cannot freely admire a noble landscape if laborers are digging in the field hard by. The poet finds something ridiculous in his delight until he is out of the sight of men.

VIII. Prospects

In inquiries respecting the laws of the world and the frame of things, the highest reason is always the truest. That which seems faintly possible—it is so refined, is often faint and dim because it is deepest seated in the mind among the eternal verities. Empirical[1] science is apt to cloud the sight, and by the very knowledge of functions and processes, to bereave the student of the manly contemplation of the whole. The savant[2] becomes unpoetic. But the best read naturalist who lends an entire and devout attention to truth, will see that there remains much to learn of his relation to the world, and that it is not to be learned by any addition or subtraction or other comparison of known quantities, but is arrived at by untaught sallies of the spirit, by a continual self-recovery, and by entire humility. He will perceive that there are far more excellent qualities in the student than preciseness and infallibility; that a guess is often more fruitful than an indisputable affirmation, and that a dream may let us deeper

9. John Milton, *Comus*, ll. 13–14.
1. Experimental, based on systematized observation, as contrasted with intuitive cognition.

2. By derivation, "one who knows," a scholar; but here suggesting a dogmatist.

into the secret of nature than a hundred concerted experiments.

For the problems to be solved are precisely those which the physiologist and the naturalist omit to state. It is not so pertinent to man to know all the individuals of the animal kingdom, as it is to know whence and whereto is this tyrannizing unity in his constitution, which evermore separates and classifies things, endeavoring to reduce the most diverse to one form. When I behold a rich landscape, it is less to my purpose to recite correctly the order and superposition of the strata, than to know why all thought of multitude is lost in a tranquil sense of unity. I cannot greatly honor minuteness in details, so long as there is no hint to explain the relation between things and thoughts; no ray upon the *metaphysics* of conchology, of botany, of the arts, to show the relation of the forms of flowers, shells, animals, architecture, to the mind, and build science upon ideas. In a cabinet of natural history,[3] we become sensible of a certain occult recognition and sympathy in regard to the most unwieldy and eccentric forms of beast, fish, and insect. The American who has been confined, in his own country, to the sight of buildings designed after foreign models, is surprised on entering York Minster [4] or St. Peter's at Rome,[5] by the feeling that these structures are imitations also,—faint copies of an invisible archetype. Nor has science sufficient humanity, so long as the naturalist overlooks that wonderful congruity which subsists between man and the world; of which he is lord, not because he is the most subtile inhabitant, but because he is its head and heart, and finds something of himself in every great and small thing, in every mountain stratum, in every new law of color, fact of astronomy, or atmospheric influence which observation or analysis lays open. A perception of this mystery inspires the muse of George Herbert,[6] the beautiful psalmist of the seventeenth century. The following lines are part of his little poem on Man.

> "Man is all symmetry,
>   Full of proportions, one limb to another,
>   And to all the world besides.
>   Each part may call the farthest, brother;
> For head with foot hath private amity,
>   And both with moons and tides.
>
> "Nothing hath got so far
> But man hath caught and kept it as his prey;
>   His eyes dismount the highest star:

---

3. The "cabinet," or display case of classified specimens, was then a principal pedagogical instrument for biological science.
4. The stately minster (cathedral) at York, England, replacing a church dating from 627, was under construction from 1230 to 1474.

5. Saint Peter's at Rome, like York Minster, was long under construction (1445–1626). It was the work of many creators, of whom Michelangelo was the most important.
6. British metaphysical poet (1593–1633). The lines quoted are from "Man," stanzas 3–6 and 8.

He is in little all the sphere.
Herbs gladly cure our flesh, because that they
Find their acquaintance there.

"For us, the winds do blow,
The earth doth rest, heaven move, and fountains flow;
Nothing we see, but means our good,
As our delight, or as our treasure;
The whole is either our cupboard of food,
Or cabinet of pleasure.

"The stars have us to bed:
Night draws the curtain; which the sun withdraws.
Music and light attend our head.
All things unto our flesh are kind,
In their descent and being; to our mind,
In their ascent and cause.

"More servants wait on man
Than he'll take notice of. In every path,
He treads down that which doth befriend him
When sickness makes him pale and wan.
Oh mighty love! Man is one world, and hath
Another to attend him."

The perception of this class of truths makes the attraction which draws men to science, but the end is lost sight of in attention to the means. In view of this half-sight of science, we accept the sentence of Plato, that "poetry comes nearer to vital truth than history." Every surmise and vaticination[7] of the mind is entitled to a certain respect, and we learn to prefer imperfect theories, and sentences which contain glimpses of truth, to digested systems which have no one valuable suggestion. A wise writer will feel that the ends of study and composition are best answered by announcing undiscovered regions of thought, and so communicating, through hope, new activity to the torpid spirit.

I shall therefore conclude this essay with some traditions of man and nature, which a certain poet[8] sang to me; and which, as they have always been in the world, and perhaps reappear to every bard, may be both history and prophecy.

"The foundations of man are not in matter, but in spirit. But the element of spirit is eternity. To it, therefore, the longest series of

---

7. Ordinarily, prophecy; here, as a mental process, revelation.

8. [Amos] Bronson Alcott (1799–1888), transcendentalist and educational pioneer, employed conversation as the medium for his philosophy. E. W. Emerson (Centenary Edition, Vol. I, p.

412) notes that his father here attempted to reproduce the style of Alcott's "conversations" (*cf.* "Orphic Sayings," *The Dial*, 1840). See Emerson's phrase "my Orphic poet," below. Orpheus was a poet-musician of Greek myth, at whose song all Nature followed.

events, the oldest chronologies are young and recent. In the cycle of the universal man, from whom the known individuals proceed, centuries are points, and all history is but the epoch of one degradation.

"We distrust and deny inwardly our sympathy with nature. We own and disown our relation to it, by turns. We are, like Nebuchadnezzar,[9] dethroned, bereft of reason, and eating grass like an ox. But who can set limits to the remedial force of spirit?

"A man is a god in ruins. When men are innocent, life shall be longer, and shall pass into the immortal, as gently as we awake from dreams. Now, the world would be insane and rabid, if these disorganizations should last for hundreds of years. It is kept in check by death and infancy. Infancy is the perpetual Messiah, which comes into the arms of fallen men, and pleads with them to return to paradise.

"Man is the dwarf of himself. Once he was permeated and dissolved by spirit. He filled nature with his overflowing currents. Out from him sprang the sun and moon; from man the sun; from woman, the moon. The laws of his mind, the periods of his actions externized themselves into day and night, into the year and the seasons. But, having made for himself this huge shell, his waters retired; he no longer fills the veins and veinless; he is shrunk to a drop. He sees, that the structure still fits him, but fits him colossally. Say, rather, once it fitted him, now it corresponds to him from far and on high. He adores timidly his own work. Now is man the follower of the sun, and woman the follower of the moon. Yet sometimes he starts in his slumber, and wonders at himself and his house, and muses strangely at the resemblance betwixt him and it. He perceives that if his law is still paramount, if still he have elemental power, if his word is sterling yet in nature, it is not conscious power, it is not inferior but superior to his will. It is instinct." Thus my Orphic poet sang.

At present, man applies to nature but half his force. He works on the world with his understanding alone. He lives in it, and masters it by a penny-wisdom; and he that works most in it, is but a half-man and whilst his arms are strong and his digestion good, his mind is imbruted, and he is a selfish savage. His relation to nature, his power over it, is through the understanding; as by manure; the economic use of fire, wind, water, and the mariner's needle; steam, coal, chemical agriculture; the repairs of the human body by the dentist and the surgeon. This is such a resumption of power, as if a banished king should buy his territories inch by inch, instead of vaulting at once into his throne. Meantime, in the thick darkness, there are not wanting gleams of a better light,—occasional examples of the action of man upon nature with his entire force,—with reason as well as under-

9. Daniel iv: 31–33.

standing. Such examples are[:] the traditions of miracles in the earliest antiquity of all nations; the history of Jesus Christ; the achievements of a principle, as in religious and political revolutions, and in the abolition of the Slave-trade; the miracles of enthusiasm,[1] as those reported of Swedenborg, Hohenlohe, and the Shakers; many obscure and yet contested facts, now arranged under the name of Animal Magnetism; [2] prayer; eloquence; self-healing; and the wisdom of children. These are examples of Reason's momentary grasp of the sceptre; the exertions of a power which exists not in time or space, but an instantaneous instreaming causing power. The difference between the actual and the ideal force of man is happily figured by the schoolmen, in saying that the knowledge of man is an evening knowledge, *vespertina cognitio*, but that of God is a morning knowledge, *matutina cognitio*.[3]

The problem of restoring to the world original and eternal beauty, is solved by the redemption of the soul. The ruin or the blank that we see when we look at nature, is in our own eye. The axis of vision is not coincident with the axis of things, and so they appear not transparent but opaque.[4] The reason why the world lacks unity, and lies broken, and in heaps, is, because man is disunited with himself. He cannot be a naturalist, until he satisfies all the demands of the spirit. Love is as much its demand as perception. Indeed, neither can be perfect without the other. In the uttermost meaning of the words, thought is devout, and devotion is thought. Deep calls unto deep.[5] But in actual life, the marriage is not celebrated. There are innocent men who worship God after the tradition of their fathers, but their sense of duty has not yet extended to the use of all their faculties. And there are patient naturalists, but they freeze their subject under the wintry light of the understanding. Is not prayer also a study of truth, —a sally of the soul into the unfound infinite? No man ever prayed heartily without learning something. But when a faithful thinker, resolute to detach every object from personal relations and see it in the light of thought, shall, at the same time, kindle science with the fire of the holiest affections, then will God go forth anew into the creation.

It will not need, when the mind is prepared for study, to search for

1. In the historical sense, inspiration or possesion by the god. Alexander Leopold, Prince of Hohenlohe (1794–1849), German Catholic priest, caused a sensational controversy by his "miracles"; the Shakers prophesied the millennium and exhibited hysterical manifestations of "possession."
2. The term given to hypnosis by the pioneer experimenter, Franz Anton Mesmer (1734–1815), Austrian physician.
3. These Latin phrases, translated in the sentence, belonged to the logic of the Schoolmen—the scholastic philosophers of the Middle Ages. See Centenary Edition, Vol. I, pp. 413–414, for particular reference to St. Augustine and St. Thomas Aquinas.
4. Spelled "opake" in 1849; corrected in later editions.
5. *Cf.* Psalms xlii: 7: "Deep calleth unto deep at the noise of thy waterspouts: all thy waves and thy billows are gone over me."

objects. The invariable mark of wisdom is to see the miraculous in the common. What is a day? What is a year? What is summer? What is woman? What is a child? What is sleep? To our blindness, these things seem unaffecting. We make fables to hide the baldness of the fact and conform it, as we say, to the higher law of the mind. But when the fact is seen under the light of an idea, the gaudy fable fades and shrivels. We behold the real higher law. To the wise, therefore, a fact is true poetry, and the most beautiful of fables. These wonders are brought to our own door. You also are a man. Man and woman and their social life, poverty, labor, sleep, fear, fortune, are known to you. Learn that none of these things is superficial, but that each phenomenon has its roots in the faculties and affections of the mind. Whilst the abstract question occupies your intellect, nature brings it in the concrete to be solved by your hands. It were a wise inquiry for the closet, to compare, point by point, especially at remarkable crises in life, our daily history with the rise and progress of ideas in the mind.

So shall we come to look at the world with new eyes. It shall answer the endless inquiry of the intellect,—What is truth? and of the affections,—What is good? by yielding itself passive to the educated Will. Then shall come to pass what my poet said; "Nature is not fixed but fluid. Spirit alters, moulds, makes it. The immobility or bruteness of nature, is the absence of spirit; to pure spirit, it is fluid, it is volatile, it is obedient. Every spirit builds itself a house; and beyond its house a world; and beyond its world, a heaven. Know then, that the world exists for you. For you is the phenomenon perfect. What we are, that only can we see. All that Adam had, all that Caesar could, you have and can do. Adam called his house, heaven and earth; Caesar called his house, Rome; you perhaps call yours, a cobler's trade; a hundred acres of ploughed land; or a scholar's garret. Yet line for line and point for point, your dominion is as great as theirs, though without fine names. Build, therefore, your own world. As fast as you conform your life to the pure idea in your mind, that will unfold its great proportions. A correspondent revolution in things will attend the influx of the spirit. So fast will disagreeable appearances, swine, spiders, snakes, pests, mad-houses, prisons, enemies, vanish; they are temporary and shall be no more seen. The sordor and filths of nature, the sun shall dry up, and the wind exhale. As when the summer comes from the south; the snow-banks melt, and the face of the earth becomes green before it, so shall the advancing spirit create its ornaments along its path, and carry with it the beauty it visits and the song which enchants it; it shall draw beautiful faces, warm hearts, wise discourse, and heroic acts, around its way, until evil is no more seen. The kingdom of man over nature, which cometh not with observation,—a dominion such as now is beyond his dream of God,—he shall enter without more wonder than the blind man feels who is gradually restored to perfect sight."

1833–1836   1836

The American Scholar[6]

MR. PRESIDENT AND GENTLEMEN,

I greet you on the re-commencement of our literary year.[7] Our anniversary is one of hope, and, perhaps, not enough of labor. We do not meet for games of strength or skill, for the recitation of histories, tragedies, and odes, like the ancient Greeks; for parliaments of love and poesy, like the Troubadours; nor for the advancement of science,[8] like our contemporaries[9] in the British and European capitals. Thus far, our holiday has been simply a friendly sign of the survival of the love of letters amongst a people too busy to give to letters any more. As such, it is precious as the sign of an indestructible instinct. Perhaps the time is already come, when it ought to be, and will be, something else; when the sluggard intellect of this continent will look from under its iron lids, and fill the postponed expectation of the world with something better than the exertions of mechanical skill. Our day of dependence, our long apprenticeship to the learning of other lands, draws to a close. The millions, that around us are rushing into life, cannot always be fed on the sere remains of foreign harvests. Events, actions arise, that must be sung, that will sing themselves. Who can doubt, that poetry will revive and lead in a new age, as the star in the constellation Harp,[1] which now flames in our zenith, astronomers announce, shall one day be the pole-star for a thousand years?

In this hope I accept the topic which not only usage, but the

6. The Phi Beta Kappa address at Harvard College on August 31, 1837, like the guns of its author's "embattled farmers," was "heard round the world," the first clarion of an American literary renaissance. Emerson had no such heroic expectations; he had modestly recorded his compact with his destiny in his journal a month before: "If the All-wise would give me light, I should write for the Cambridge men a theory of the Scholar's office." But Lowell, remembering thirty-four years later the "enthusiasm of approval" (in "Thoreau," *My Study Windows*, 1871), saw the awakening of a spiritual epoch: "The * * * Revolution [had made us] politically independent, but we were still socially and intellectually moored to English thought till Emerson cut the cable. * * * "

Holmes's *obiter dictum*, "Our intellectual Declaration of Independence," however familiar, is still final. The address was published in 1837 and again in 1838; as *Man Thinking: An Oration*, in London in 1844; and as one of the essays in the collection, *Nature, Addresses, and Lectures* (1849). The present text is based on the 1849 edition.
7. *I.e.*, "our college year," then customarily beginning about September 1.
8. The development of learned associations abroad and the research of European universities had then no parallel in America.
9. The 1849 text read "co-temporaries"; corrected in later editions.
1. The constellation Lyra, containing Vega, the fourth brightest star of the heavens, to which Emerson refers.

nature of our association, seem to prescribe to this day,—the AMERI-CAN SCHOLAR. Year by year, we come up hither to read one more chapter of his biography. Let us inquire what light new days and events have thrown on his character and his hopes.

It is one of those fables which, out of an unknown antiquity, convey an unlooked-for wisdom, that the gods, in the beginning, divided Man into men, that he might be more helpful to himself;[2] just as the hand was divided into fingers, the better to answer its end.

The old fable covers a doctrine ever new and sublime; that there is One Man,—present to all particular men only partially, or through one faculty; and that you must take the whole society to find the whole man. Man is not a farmer, or a professor, or an engineer, but he is all. Man is priest, and scholar, and statesman, and producer, and soldier. In the *divided* or social state, these functions are parcelled out to individuals, each of whom aims to do his stint of the joint work, whilst each other performs his. The fable implies, that the individual, to possess himself, must sometimes return from his own labor to embrace all the other laborers. But unfortunately, this original unit, this fountain of power, has been so distributed to multitudes, has been so minutely subdivided and peddled out, that it is spilled into drops, and cannot be gathered. The state of society is one in which the members have suffered amputation from the trunk, and strut about so many walking monsters,—a good finger, a neck, a stomach, an elbow, but never a man.

Man is thus metamorphosed into a thing, into many things. The planter, who is Man sent out into the field to gather food, is seldom cheered by any idea of the true dignity of his ministry. He sees his bushel and his cart, and nothing beyond, and sinks into the farmer, instead of Man on the farm. The tradesman scarcely ever gives an ideal worth to his work, but is ridden by the routine of his craft, and the soul is subject to dollars. The priest becomes a form; the attorney, a statute-book; the mechanic, a machine; the sailor, a rope of a ship.

In this distribution of functions, the scholar is the delegated intellect. In the right state, he is *Man Thinking*. In the degenerate state, when the victim of society, he tends to become a mere thinker, or, still worse, the parrot of other men's thinking.

In this view of him, as Man Thinking, the theory of his office is contained. Him nature solicits with all her placid, all her monitory pictures; him the past instructs; him the future invites. Is not, indeed, every man a student, and do not all things exist for the student's behoof? And, finally, is not the true scholar the only true master? But the old oracle said, "All things have two handles: beware of the wrong one." In life, too often, the scholar errs with mankind and

2. Emerson was familiar with a version of this fable in Plato, the *Symposium;* and with another, "Of Brotherly Love," in Plutarch's *Morals* (E. W. Emerson, Centenary Edition, Vol. I, p. 417).

forfeits his privilege. Let us see him in his school, and consider him in reference to the main influences he receives.

I. The first in time and the first in importance of the influences upon the mind is that of nature. Every day, the sun; and, after sunset, night and her stars. Ever the winds blow; ever the grass grows. Every day, men and women, conversing, beholding and beholden. The scholar is he of all men whom this spectacle most engages. He must settle its value in his mind. What is nature to him? There is never a beginning, there is never an end, to the inexplicable continuity of this web of God, but always circular power returning into itself. Therein it resembles his own spirit, whose beginning, whose ending, he never can find,—so entire, so boundless. Far, too, as her splendors shine, system on system shooting like rays, upward, downward, without centre, without circumference,—in the mass and in the particle, nature hastens to render account of herself to the mind. Classification begins. To the young mind, every thing is individual, stands by itself. By and by, it finds how to join two things, and see in them one nature; then three, then three thousand; and so, tyrannized over by its own unifying instinct, it goes on tying things together, diminishing anomalies, discovering roots running under ground, whereby contrary and remote things cohere, and flower out from one stem. It presently learns, that since the dawn of history, there has been a constant accumulation and classifying of facts. But what is classification but the perceiving that these objects are not chaotic, and are not foreign, but have a law which is also a law of the human mind? The astronomer discovers that geometry, a pure abstraction of the human mind, is the measure of planetary motion. The chemist finds proportions and intelligible method throughout matter; and science is nothing but the finding of analogy, identity, in the most remote parts. The ambitious soul sits down before each refractory fact; one after another, reduces all strange constitutions, all new powers, to their class and their law, and goes on for ever to animate the last fibre of organization, the outskirts of nature, by insight.

Thus to him, to this school-boy under the bending dome of day, is suggested, that he and it proceed from one root; one is leaf and one is flower; relation, sympathy, stirring in every vein. And what is that Root? Is not that the soul of his soul?—A thought too bold,—a dream too wild. Yet when this spiritual light shall have revealed the law of more earthly natures,—when he has learned to worship the soul, and to see that the natural philosophy that now is, is only the first gropings of its gigantic hand, he shall look forward to an ever expanding knowledge as to a becoming creator.[3] He shall see, that nature is the opposite of the soul, answering to it part for part. One

---

3. "Whether or no there be a God, it is certain that there will be." Translation in Emerson's *Journals* from a French source. (Centenary Edition, Vol. I, p. 418).

is seal, and one is print. Its beauty is the beauty of his own mind. Its laws are the laws of his own mind. Nature then becomes to him the measure of his attainments. So much of nature as he is ignorant of, so much of his own mind does he not yet possess. And, in fine, the ancient precept, "Know thyself," and the modern precept, "Study nature," become at last one maxim.

II. The next great influence[4] into the spirit of the scholar, is, the mind of the Past,—in whatever form, whether of literature, of art, of institutions, that mind is inscribed. Books are the best type of the influence of the past, and perhaps we shall get at the truth,—learn the amount of this influence more conveniently,—by considering their value alone.

The theory of books is noble. The scholar of the first age received into him the world around; brooded thereon; gave it the new arrangement of his own mind, and uttered it again. It came into him, life; it went out from him, truth. It came to him, short-lived actions; it went out from him, immortal thoughts. It came to him, business; it went from him, poetry. It was dead fact; now, it is quick thought. It can stand, and it can go. It now endures, it now flies, it now inspires. Precisely in proportion to the depth of mind from which it issued, so high does it soar, so long does it sing.

Or, I might say, it depends on how far the process had gone, of transmuting life into truth. In proportion to the completeness of the distillation, so will the purity and imperishableness of the product be. But none is quite perfect. As no air-pump can by any means make a perfect vacuum, so neither can any artist entirely exclude the conventional, the local, the perishable from his book, or write a book of pure thought, that shall be as efficient, in all respects, to a remote posterity, as to contemporaries, or rather to the second age. Each age, it is found, must write its own books; or rather, each generation for the next succeeding. The books of an older period will not fit this.

Yet hence arises a grave mischief. The sacredness which attaches to the act of creation,—the act of thought,—is transferred to the record. The poet chanting, was felt to be a divine man: henceforth the chant is divine also. The writer was a just and wise spirit: henceforward it is settled, the book is perfect; as love of the hero corrupts into worship of his statue. Instantly, the book becomes noxious: the guide is a tyrant. The sluggish and perverted mind of the multitude, slow to open to the incursions of Reason, having once so opened, having once received this book, stands upon it, and makes an outcry, if it is disparaged. Colleges are built on it. Books are written on it by thinkers, not by Man Thinking; by men of talent, that is, who start wrong, who set out from accepted dogmas, not from their own sight of prin-

4. As by Latin derivation, "inflowing."

ciples. Meek young men grow up in libraries, believing it their duty to accept the views which Cicero, which Locke, which Bacon,[5] have given, forgetful that Cicero, Locke, and Bacon were only young men in libraries, when they wrote these books.

Hence, instead of Man Thinking, we have the bookworm. Hence, the book-learned class, who value books, as such; not as related to nature and the human constitution, but as making a sort of Third Estate[6] with the world and the soul. Hence, the restorers of readings, the emendators, the bibliomaniacs of all degrees.

Books are the best of things, well used; abused, among the worst. What is the right use? What is the one end which all means go to effect? They are for nothing but to inspire. I had better never see a book, than to be warped by its attraction clean out of my own orbit, and made a satellite instead of a system. The one thing in the world, of value, is the active soul. This every man is entitled to; this every man contains within him, although, in almost all men, obstructed, and as yet unborn. The soul active sees absolute truth; and utters truth, or creates. In this action, it is genius; not the privilege of here and there a favorite, but the sound estate of every man. In its essence, it is progressive. The book, the college, the school of art, the institution of any kind, stop with some past utterance of genius. This is good, say they,—let us hold by this. They pin me down. They look backward and not forward. But genius looks forward: the eyes of man are set in his forehead, not in his hind-head: man hopes: genius creates. Whatever talents may be, if the man create not, the pure efflux[7] of the Deity is not his;—cinders and smoke there may be, but not yet flame. There are creative manners, there are creative actions, and creative words; manners, actions, words, that is indicative of no custom or authority, but springing spontaneous from the mind's own sense of good and fair.

On the other part, instead of being its own seer, let it receive from another mind its truth, though it were in torrents of light, without periods of solitude, inquest, and self-recovery, and a fatal disservice is done. Genius is always sufficiently the enemy of genius by over influence. The literature of every nation bears me witness. The English dramatic poets have Shakspearized now for two hundred years.

Undoubtedly there is a right way of reading, so it be sternly subordinated. Man Thinking must not be subdued by his instruments.

5. These were then standard authorities for the young student: Marcus Tullius Cicero (106–43 B.C.), both for his orations and his moral philosophy; John Locke (1632–1704), whose theory of knowledge dominated eighteenth-century thought; and Francis Bacon (1561–1626), British pioneer of inductive science.
6. Under the French monarchy, the "common" people; therefore, a term in bad odor with democrats (the clergy and nobles formed the first two estates).
7. "Outflowing;" *cf.* "influence," above. Emerson may be alluding to the ancient theory of "effluxes" or "simulacra" propounded by Empedocles, which holds that only like perceives like. Here the interpretation would be that only the creative man understands the Diety.

Books are for the scholar's idle times. When he can read God directly, the hour is too precious to be wasted in other men's transcripts of their readings. But when the intervals of darkness come, as come they must,—when the sun is hid and the stars withdraw their shining,—we repair to the lamps which were kindled by their ray, to guide our steps to the East again, where the dawn is. We hear, that we may speak. The Arabian proverb says, "A fig tree, looking on a fig tree, becometh fruitful."

It is remarkable, the character of the pleasure we derive from the best books. They impress us with the conviction, that one nature wrote and the same reads. We read the verses of one of the great English poets, of Chaucer, of Marvell, of Dryden, with the most modern joy,[8]—with a pleasure, I mean, which is in great part caused by the abstraction of all *time* from their verses. There is some awe mixed with the joy of our surprise, when this poet, who lived in some past world, two or three hundred years ago, says that which lies close to my own soul, that which I also had well nigh thought and said. But for the evidence thence afforded to the philosophical doctrine of the identity of all minds, we should suppose some preëstablished harmony, some foresight of souls that were to be, and some preparation of stores for their future wants, like the fact observed in insects, who lay up food before death for the young grub they shall never see.

I would not be hurried by any love of system, by any exaggeration of instincts, to underrate the Book. We all know, that, as the human body can be nourished on any food, though it were boiled grass and the broth of shoes, so the human mind can be fed by any knowledge. And great and heroic men have existed, who had almost no other information than by the printed page. I only would say that it needs a strong head to bear that diet. One must be an inventor to read well. As the proverb says, "He that would bring home the wealth of the Indies, must carry out the wealth of the Indies."[9] There is then creative reading as well as creative writing. When the mind is braced by labor and invention, the page of whatever book we read becomes luminous with manifold allusion. Every sentence is doubly significant, and the sense of our author is as broad as the world.[1] We then see, what is always true, that, as the seer's hour of vision is short and rare among heavy days and months, so is its record, perchance, the least part of his volume. The discerning will read, in his Plato or Shakspeare, only that least part,—only the authentic utterances

8. The timeless appeal of Chaucer and Dryden is self-evident, but a revival of interest in the poetry of Andrew Marvell (1621–1678) did not occur until the 1920's.
9. Boswell had reported Dr. Johnson as repeating this "Spanish" proverb in almost the same words and context (*Life of Dr. Johnson*, Everyman edition, Vol. II, p. 216).
1. Emerson had written the three previous sentences in his *Journal* ten months earlier (October 29, 1836; *Journals*, Vol. IV, p. 254).

of the oracle;—all the rest he rejects, were it never so many times Plato's and Shakspeare's.

Of course, there is a portion of reading quite indispensable to a wise man. History and exact science he must learn by laborious reading. Colleges, in like manner, have their indispensable office,—to teach elements. But they can only highly serve us, when they aim not to drill, but to create; when they gather from far every ray of various genius to their hospitable halls, and by the concentrated fires, set the hearts of their youth on flame. Thought and knowledge are natures in which apparatus and pretension avail nothing. Gowns, and pecuniary foundations, though of towns of gold, can never countervail the least sentence or syllable of wit.[2] Forget this, and our American colleges will recede in their public importance, whilst they grow richer every year.

III. There goes in the world a notion, that the scholar should be a recluse, a valetudinarian,—as unfit for any handiwork or public labor as a penknife for an axe. The so-called "practical men" sneer at speculative men, as if, because they speculate or *see*, they could do nothing. I have heard it said that the clergy,—who are always, more universally than any other class, the scholars of their day,—are addressed as women; that the rough, spontaneous conversation of men they do not hear, but only a mincing and diluted speech. They are often virtually disfranchised; and, indeed, there are advocates for their celibacy. As far as this is true of the studious classes, it is not just and wise. Action is with the scholar subordinate, but it is essential. Without it, he is not yet man. Without it, thought can never ripen into truth. Whilst the world hangs before the eye as a cloud of beauty, we cannot even see its beauty. Inaction is cowardice, but there can be no scholar without the heroic mind. The preamble of thought, the transition through which it passes from the unconscious to the conscious, is action. Only so much do I know, as I have lived. Instantly we know whose words are loaded with life, and whose not.

The world,—this shadow of the soul, or *other me*, lies wide around. Its attractions are the keys which unlock my thoughts and make me acquainted with myself. I run eagerly into this resounding tumult. I grasp the hands of those next me, and take my place in the ring to suffer and to work, taught by an instinct, that so shall the dumb abyss be vocal with speech. I pierce its order; I dissipate its fear; I dispose of it within the circuit of my expanding life. So much only of life as I know by experience, so much of the wilderness have I vanquished and planted, or so far have I extended my being, my dominion. I do not see how any man can afford, for the sake of his nerves and his nap, to spare any action in which he can partake. It

2. In the archaic but fundamental meaning: "knowledge," "intellect."

is pearls and rubies to his discourse. Drudgery, calamity, exasperation, want, are instructors in eloquence and wisdom. The true scholar grudges every opportunity of action past by, as a loss of power.

It is the raw material out of which the intellect moulds her splendid products. A strange process too, this, by which experience is converted into thought, as a mulberry leaf is converted into satin.[3] The manufacture goes forward at all hours.

The actions and events of our childhood and youth, are now matters of calmest observation. They lie like fair pictures in the air. Not so with our recent actions,—with the business which we now have in hand. On this we are quite unable to speculate. Our affections as yet circulate through it. We no more feel or know it, than we feel the feet, or the hand, or the brain of our body. The new deed is yet a part of life,—remains for a time immersed in our unconscious life. In some contemplative hour, it detaches itself from the life like a ripe fruit, to become a thought of the mind. Instantly it is raised, transfigured; the corruptible has put on incorruption.[4] Henceforth it is an object of beauty, however base its origin and neighborhood. Observe, too, the impossibility of antedating this act. In its grub state, it cannot fly, it cannot shine, it is a dull grub. But suddenly, without observation, the selfsame thing unfurls beautiful wings, and is an angel of wisdom. So is there no fact, no event, in our private history, which shall not, sooner or later, lose its adhesive, inert form, and astonish us by soaring from our body into the empyrean. Cradle and infancy, school and playground, the fear of boys, and dogs, and ferules, the love of little maids and berries, and many another fact that once filled the whole sky, are gone already; friend and relative, profession and party, town and country, nation and world, must also soar and sing.

Of course, he who has put forth his total strength in fit actions, has the richest return of wisdom. I will not shut myself out of this globe of action, and transplant an oak into a flower-pot, there to hunger and pine; nor trust the revenue of some single faculty, and exhaust one vein of thought, much like those Savoyards,[5] who, getting their livelihood by carving shepherds, shepherdesses, and smoking Dutchmen, for all Europe, went out one day to the mountain to find stock, and discovered that they had whittled up the last of their pine-trees. Authors we have, in numbers, who have written out their vein, and who, moved by a commendable prudence, sail for Greece or Palestine, follow the trapper into the prairie, or ramble round Algiers, to replenish their merchantable stock.

If it were only for a vocabulary, the scholar would be covetous of action. Life is our dictionary. Years are well spent in country labors;

3. *I.e.*, silkworms feed on mulberry leaves.
4. *Cf.* I Corinthians xv: 54.
5. Inhabitants of Savoy, now a province of southeast France, then still divided with Italy.

in town,—in the insight into trades and manufactures; in frank intercourse with many men and women; in science; in art; to the one end of mastering in all their facts a language by which to illustrate and embody our perceptions. I learn immediately from any speaker how much he has already lived, through the poverty or the splendor of his speech. Life lies behind us as the quarry from whence we get tiles and copestones for the masonry of to-day. This is the way to learn grammar. Colleges and books only copy the language which the field and the work-yard made.

But the final value of action, like that of books, and better than books, is, that it is a resource. That great principle of Undulation in nature, that shows itself in the inspiring and expiring of the breath; in desire and satiety; in the ebb and flow of the sea; in day and night; in heat and cold; and, as yet more deeply ingrained in every atom and every fluid, is known to us under the name of Polarity,—these "fits of easy transmission and reflection," as Newton[6] called them, are the law of nature because they are the law of spirit.

The mind now thinks; now acts; and each fit reproduces the other. When the artist has exhausted his materials, when the fancy no longer paints, when thoughts are no longer apprehended and books are a weariness,—he has always the resource to *live*. Character is higher than intellect. Thinking is the function. Living is the functionary. The stream retreats to its source. A great soul will be strong to live, as well as strong to think. Does he lack organ or medium to impart his truths? He can still fall back on this elemental force of living them. This is a total act. Thinking is a partial act. Let the grandeur of justice shine in his affairs. Let the beauty of affection cheer his lowly roof. Those "far from fame," who dwell and act with him, will feel the force of his constitution in the doings and passages of the day better than it can be measured by any public and designed display. Time shall teach him, that the scholar loses no hour which the man lives. Herein he unfolds the sacred germ of his instinct, screened from influence. What is lost in seemliness is gained in strength. Not out of those, on whom systems of education have exhausted their culture, comes the helpful giant to destroy the old or to build the new, but out of unhandselled[7] savage nature, out of terrible Druids and Berserkirs come at last Alfred[8] and Shakspeare.

I hear therefore with joy whatever is beginning to be said of the dignity and necessity of labor to every citizen. There is virtue yet in the hoe and the spade, for learned as well as for unlearned hands.

6. Sir Isaac Newton (1642–1727), English mathematician, the pioneer of modern physical science. The phrase is from *Optics* (1704), the summation of his researches in light.

7. A "handsel" was an inaugural gift for good luck. Here the word is used in its figurative meaning: "unencouraged," "unappreciated."

8. Druids were prehistoric Celtic priests; berserkers, incredibly savage warriors of Norse mythology. Alfred (849–899), greatest of the Saxon kings, was a patriot, lawgiver, and father of English prose.

And labor is everywhere welcome; always we are invited to work; only be this limitation observed, that a man shall not for the sake of wider activity sacrifice any opinion to the popular judgments and modes of action.

I have now spoken of the education of the scholar by nature, by books, and by action. It remains to say somewhat of his duties.

They are such as become Man Thinking. They may all be comprised in self-trust. The office of the scholar is to cheer, to raise, and to guide men by showing them facts amidst appearances. He plies the slow, unhonored, and unpaid task of observation. Flamsteed and Herschel,[9] in their glazed observatories, may catalogue the stars with the praise of all men, and, the results being splendid and useful, honor is sure. But he, in his private observatory, cataloguing obscure and nebulous stars of the human mind, which as yet no man has thought of as such,—watching days and months, sometimes, for a few facts; correcting still his old records;—must relinquish display and immediate fame. In the long period of his preparation, he must betray often an ignorance and shiftlessness in popular arts, incurring the disdain of the able who shoulder him aside. Long he must stammer in his speech; often forego the living for the dead. Worse yet, he must accept,—how often! poverty and solitude. For the ease and pleasure of treading the old road, accepting the fashions, the education, the religion of society, he takes the cross of making his own, and, of course, the self-accusation, the faint heart, the frequent uncertainty and loss of time, which are the nettles and tangling vines in the way of the self-relying and self-directed; and the state of virtual hostility in which he seems to stand to society, and especially to educated society. For all this loss and scorn, what offset? He is to find consolation in exercising the highest functions of human nature. He is one, who raises himself from private considerations, and breathes and lives on public and illustrious thoughts. He is the world's eye. He is the world's heart. He is to resist the vulgar prosperity that retrogrades ever to barbarism, by preserving and communicating heroic sentiments, noble biographies, melodious verse, and the conclusions of history. Whatsoever oracles the human heart, in all emergencies, in all solemn hours, has uttered as its commentary on the world of actions,—these he shall receive and impart. And whatsoever new verdict Reason from her inviolable seat pronounces on the passing men and events of to-day,—this he shall hear and promulgate.

These being his functions, it becomes him to feel all confidence in himself, and to defer never to the popular cry. He and he only

9. John Flamsteed (1646–1719), British astronomer; Sir [Frederick] William Herschel (1738–1822), his sister, Caro-line, and his son, John Frederick William, were also astronomers, prominent during Emerson's lifetime.

knows the world. The world of any moment is the merest appearance. Some great decorum,[1] some fetish of a government, some ephemeral trade, or war, or man, is cried up by half mankind and cried down by the other half, as if all depended on this particular up or down. The odds are that the whole question is not worth the poorest thought which the scholar has lost in listening to the controversy. Let him not quit his belief that a popgun is a popgun, though the ancient and honorable of the earth affirm it to be the crack of doom. In silence, in steadiness, in severe abstraction, let him hold by himself; add observation to observation, patient of neglect, patient of reproach, and bide his own time,—happy enough, if he can satisfy himself alone, that this day he has seen something truly. Success treads on every right step. For the instinct is sure, that prompts him to tell his brother what he thinks. He then learns, that in going down into the secrets of his own mind, he has descended into the secrets of all minds. He learns that he who has mastered any law in his private thoughts, is master to that extent of all men whose language he speaks, and of all into whose language his own can be translated. The poet, in utter solitude remembering his spontaneous thoughts and recording them, is found to have recorded that, which men in crowded cities find true for them also. The orator distrusts at first the fitness of his frank confessions,—his want of knowledge of the persons he addresses,—until he finds that he is the complement of his hearers;—that they drink his words because he fulfils for them their own nature; the deeper he dives into his privatest, secretest presentiment, to his wonder he finds, this is the most acceptable, most public, and universally true. The people delight in it; the better part of every man feels, This is my music; this is myself.

In self-trust, all the virtues are comprehended. Free should the scholar be,—free and brave. Free even to the definition of freedom, "without any hindrance that does not arise out of his own constitution." Brave; for fear is a thing, which a scholar by his very function puts behind him. Fear always springs from ignorance. It is a shame to him if his tranquillity, amid dangerous times, arise from the presumption that, like children and women, his is a protected class; or if he seek a temporary peace by the diversion of his thoughts from politics or vexed questions, hiding his head like an ostrich in the flowering bushes, peeping into microscopes, and turning rhymes, as a boy whistles to keep his courage up. So is the danger a danger still; so is the fear worse. Manlike let him turn and face it. Let him look into its eye and search its nature, inspect its origin,—see the whelping of this lion,—which lies no great way back; he will then find in himself a perfect comprehension of its nature and extent;

1. In the Latin sense: a critical code or standard.

he will have made his hands meet on the other side, and can hence-forth defy it, and pass on superior. The world is his, who can see through its pretension. What deafness, what stone-blind custom, what overgrown error you behold, is there only by sufferance,—by your sufferance. See it to be a lie, and you have already dealt it its mortal blow.

Yes, we are the cowed,—we the trustless. It is a mischievous no-tion that we are come late into nature; that the world was finished a long time ago. As the world was plastic and fluid in the hands of God, so it is ever to so much of his attributes as we bring to it. To ignorance and sin, it is flint. They adapt themselves to it as they may; but in proportion as a man has any thing in him divine, the firma-ment flows before him and takes his signet and form. Not he is great who can alter matter, but he who can alter my state of mind. They are the kings of the world who give the color of their present thought to all nature and all art, and persuade men by the cheerful serenity of their carrying the matter, that this thing which they do, is the apple which the ages have desired to pluck, now at last ripe, and inviting nations to the harvest. The great man makes the great thing. Where-ever Macdonald sits, there is the head of the table.[2] Linnaeus makes botany the most alluring of studies, and wins it from the farmer and the herb-woman; Davy, chemistry; and Cuvier, fossils.[3] The day is always his who works in it with serenity and great aims. The unstable estimates of men crowd to him whose mind is filled with a truth, as the heaped waves of the Atlantic follow the moon.

For this self-trust, the reason is deeper than can be fathomed,— darker than can be enlightened. I might not carry with me the feel-ing of my audience in stating my own belief. But I have already shown the ground of my hope, in adverting to the doctrine that man is one. I believe man has been wronged; he has wronged himself. He has almost lost the light that can lead him back to his prerogatives. Men are become of no account. Men in history, men in the world of to-day, are bugs, are spawn, and are called "the mass" and "the herd." In a century, in a millennium, one or two men; that is to say,—one or two approximations to the right state of every man. All the rest behold in the hero or the poet their own green and crude being,— ripened; yes, and are content to be less, so *that* may attain to its full stature. What a testimony,—full of grandeur, full of pity, is borne to the demands of his own nature, by the poor clansman, the poor partisan, who rejoices in the glory of his chief. The poor and the low find some amends to their immense moral capacity, for their

2. The source is obscure, perhaps pro-verbial, since the same aphorism appears in Cervantes' *Don Quixote* (Part II, Chapter 31). There it is a boorish jest, not an epigram as here, and the char-acter is not named MacDonald.

3. Sir Humphrey Davy (1778–1829), English chemist, pioneer in electrolysis; Baron Georges Léopold Chrétien Fré-déric Dagobert Cuvier (1769–1832), French naturalist, founder of compara-tive anatomy and paleontology.

acquiescence in a political and social inferiority. They are content to be brushed like flies from the path of a great person, so that justice shall be done by him to that common nature which it is the dearest desire of all to see enlarged and glorified. They sun themselves in the great man's light, and feel it to be their own element. They cast the dignity of man from their downtrod selves upon the shoulders of a hero, and will perish to add one drop of blood to make that great heart beat, those giant sinews combat and conquer. He lives for us, and we live in him.

Men such as they are, very naturally seek money or power; and power because it is as good as money,—the "spoils," so called, "of office." And why not? For they aspire to the highest, and this, in their sleep-walking, they dream is highest. Wake them, and they shall quit the false good, and leap to the true, and leave governments to clerks and desks. This revolution is to be wrought by the gradual domestication of the idea of Culture. The main enterprise of the world for splendor, for extent, is the upbuilding of a man. Here are the materials strown along the ground. The private life of one man shall be a more illustrious monarchy,—more formidable to its enemy, more sweet and serene in its influence to its friend, than any kingdom in history. For a man, rightly viewed, comprehendeth the particular natures of all men. Each philosopher, each bard, each actor has only done for me, as by a delegate, what one day I can do for myself. The books which once we valued more than the apple of the eye, we have quite exhausted. What is that but saying, that we have come up with the point of view which the universal mind took through the eyes of one scribe; we have been that man, and have passed on. First, one; then, another; we drain all cisterns, and, waxing greater by all these supplies, we crave a better and more abundant food. The man has never lived that can feed us ever. The human mind cannot be enshrined in a person, who shall set a barrier on any one side to this unbounded, unboundable empire. It is one central fire, which, flaming now out of the lips of Etna, lightens the capes of Sicily; and, now out of the throat of Vesuvius, illuminates the towers and vineyards of Naples. It is one light which beams out of a thousand stars. It is one soul which animates all men.

But I have dwelt perhaps tediously upon this abstraction of the Scholar. I ought not to delay longer to add what I have to say, of nearer reference to the time and to this country.

Historically, there is thought to be a difference in the ideas which predominate over successive epochs, and there are data for marking the genius of the Classic, of the Romantic, and now of the Reflective or Philosophical age. With the views I have intimated of the oneness or the identity of the mind through all individuals, I do not much dwell on these differences. In fact, I believe each individual passes through all three. The boy is a Greek; the youth, romantic; the adult, reflective. I deny not, however, that a revolution in the leading idea may be distinctly enough traced.

Our age is bewailed as the age of Introversion. Must that needs be evil? We, it seems, are critical; we are embarrassed with second thoughts; we cannot enjoy any thing for hankering to know whereof the pleasure consists; we are lined with eyes; we see with our feet; the time is infected with Hamlet's unhappiness, —

> "Sicklied o'er with the pale cast of thought."[4]

It is so bad then? Sight is the last thing to be pitied. Would we be blind? Do we fear lest we should outsee nature and God, and drink truth dry? I look upon the discontent of the literary class, as a mere announcement of the fact, that they find themselves not in the state of mind of their fathers, and regret the coming state as untried; as a boy dreads the water before he has learned that he can swim. If there is any period one would desire to be born in,—is it not the age of Revolution; when the old and the new stand side by side, and admit of being compared; when the energies of all men are searched by fear and by hope; when the historic glories of the old, can be compensated by the rich possibilities of the new era? This time, like all times, is a very good one, if we but know what to do with it.

I read with some joy of the auspicious signs of the coming days, as they glimmer already through poetry and art, through philosophy and science, through church and state.

One of these signs is the fact, that the same movement which effected the elevation of what was called the lowest class in the state, assumed in literature a very marked and as benign an aspect. Instead of the sublime and beautiful, the near, the low, the common was explored and poetized. That, which had been negligently trodden under foot by those who were harnessing and provisioning themselves for long journeys into far countries, is suddenly found to be richer than all foreign parts. The literature of the poor, the feelings of the child, the philosophy of the street, the meaning of household life, are the topics of the time. It is a great stride. It is a sign—is it not? of new vigor when the extremities are made active, when currents of warm life run into the hands and the feet. I ask not for the great, the remote, the romantic; what is doing in Italy or Arabia; what is Greek art, or Provençal minstrelsy;[5] I embrace the common, I explore and sit at the feet of the familiar, the low. Give me insight into to-day, and you may have the antique and future worlds. What would we really know the meaning of? The meal in

4. *Hamlet*, Act III, Scene i, l. 85.
5. Provence, ancient province in southeast France, was the cultural center of the troubadours, traveling minstrels, (*fl.* 1200–1400).

the firkin; the milk in the pan; the ballad in the street; the news of the boat; the glance of the eye; the form and the gait of the body;—show me the ultimate reason of these matters; show me the sublime presence of the highest spiritual cause lurking, as always it does lurk, in these suburbs and extremities of nature; let me see every trifle bristling with the polarity that ranges it instantly on an eternal law; and the shop, the plough, and the ledger, referred to the like cause by which light undulates and poets sing;—and the world lies no longer a dull miscellany and lumber-room, but has form and order; there is no trifle; there is no puzzle; but one design unites and animates the farthest pinnacle and the lowest trench.

This idea has inspired the genius of Goldsmith, Burns, Cowper, and, in a newer time, of Goethe,[6] Wordsworth, and Carlyle. This idea they have differently followed and with various success. In contrast with their writing, the style of Pope, of Johnson, of Gibbon, looks cold and pedantic. This writing is bloodwarm. Man is surprised to find that things near are not less beautiful and wondrous than things remote. The near explains the far. The drop is a small ocean. A man is related to all nature. This perception of the worth of the vulgar is fruitful in discoveries. Goethe, in this very thing the most modern of the moderns, has shown us, as none ever did, the genius of the ancients.

There is one man of genius, who has done much for this philosophy of life, whose literary value has never yet been rightly estimated;—I mean Emanuel Swedenborg. The most imaginative of men, yet writing with the precision of a mathematician, he endeavored to engraft a purely philosophical Ethics on the popular Christianity of his time. Such an attempt, of course, must have difficulty, which no genius could surmount. But he saw and showed the connection between nature and the affections of the soul. He pierced the emblematic or spiritual character of the visible, audible, tangible world. Especially did his shade-loving muse hover over and interpret the lower parts of nature; he showed the mysterious bond that allies moral evil to the foul material forms, and has given in epical parables a theory of insanity, of beasts, of unclean and fearful things.

Another sign of our times, also marked by an analogous political movement, is the new importance given to the single person. Every thing that tends to insulate the individual,—to surround him with barriers of natural respect, so that each man shall feel the world is his, and man shall treat with man as a sovereign state with a sovereign state;—tends to true union as well as greatness. "I learned," said the melancholy Pestalozzi,[7] "that no man in God's wide earth is

6. Emerson used Goethe as his arche-type for "The Writer" in *Representative Men*.
7. Johann Heinrich Pestalozzi (1746–1827), Swiss educator, "melancholy" at the apparent failure of his theories, had a posthumous triumph. Bronson Alcott introduced his methods, hence Emerson's interest.

either willing or able to help any other man." Help must come from the bosom alone. The scholar is that man who must take up into himself all the ability of the time, all the contributions of the past, all the hopes of the future. He must be an university of knowledges. If there be one lesson more than another, which should pierce his ear, it is, The world is nothing, the man is all; in yourself is the law of all nature, and you know not yet how a globule of sap ascends; in yourself slumbers the whole of Reason; it is for you to know all; it is for you to dare all. Mr. President and Gentlemen, this confidence in the unsearched might of man belongs, by all motives, by all prophecy, by all preparation, to the American Scholar. We have listened too long to the courtly muses of Europe. The spirit of the American freeman is already suspected to be timid, imitative, tame. Public and private avarice make the air we breathe thick and fat. The scholar is decent, indolent, complaisant. See already the tragic consequence. The mind of this country, taught to aim at low objects, eats upon itself. There is no work for any but the decorous and the complaisant. Young men of the fairest promise, who begin life upon our shores, inflated by the mountain winds, shined upon by all the stars of God, find the earth below not in unison with these,—but are hindered from action by the disgust which the principles on which business is managed inspire, and turn drudges, or die of disgust, —some of them suicides. What is the remedy? They did not yet see, and thousands of young men as hopeful now crowding to the barriers for the career, do not yet see, that, if the single man plant himself indomitably on his instincts, and there abide, the huge world will come round to him. Patience,—patience;—with the shades of all the good and great for company; and for solace, the perspective of your own infinite life; and for work, the study and the communication of principles, the making those instincts prevalent, the conversion of the world. Is it not the chief disgrace in the world, not to be an unit;—not to be reckoned one character;—not to yield that peculiar fruit which each man was created to bear, but to be reckoned in the gross, in the hundred, or the thousand, of the party, the section, to which we belong; and our opinion predicted geographically, as the north, or the south? Not so, brothers and friends,— please God, ours shall not be so. We will walk on our own feet; we will work with our own hands; we will speak our own minds. The study of letters shall be no longer a name for pity, for doubt, and for sensual indulgence. The dread of man and the love of man shall be a wall of defence and a wreath of joy around all. A nation of men will for the first time exist, because each believes himself inspired by the Divine Soul which also inspires all men.

1837

Letter to the Reverend Henry Ware, Jr.[8]

CONCORD, October 8, 1838.

MY DEAR SIR,—

I ought sooner to have acknowledged your kind letter of last week, and the Sermon it accompanied. The letter was right manly and noble. The Sermon, too, I have read with attention. If it assails any doctrines of mine, perhaps I am not so quick to see it as writers generally—certainly I did not feel any disposition to depart from my habitual contentment that you should say your thought, whilst I say mine.

I believe I must tell you what I think of my new position. It strikes me very oddly that good and wise men at Cambridge and Boston should think of raising me into an object of criticism. I have always been, from my very incapacity of methodical writing, "a chartered libertine," free to worship and free to rail; lucky when I could make myself understood, but never esteemed near enough to the institutions and mind of society to deserve the notice of the masters of literature and religion. I have appreciated fully the advantage of my position; for I well know that there is no scholar less willing or less able to be a polemic. I could not give account of myself, if challenged. I could not possibly give you one of the "arguments" you cruelly hint at, on which any doctrine of mine stands. For I do not know what arguments mean in reference to any expression of a thought. I delight in telling what I think, but if you ask how I dare say so, or why it is so, I am the most helpless of mortal men. I do not even see that either of these questions admits of an answer. So that, in the present droll posture of my affairs, when I see myself suddenly raised into the importance of a heretic, I am very uneasy when I advert to the supposed duties of such a personage, who is expected to make good his thesis against all comers.

I certainly shall do no such thing. I shall read what you and other good men write, as I have always done,—glad when you speak my thought, and skipping the page that has nothing for me. I shall go on, just as before, seeing whatever I can, and telling what I see; and,

8. The Reverend Henry Ware, Jr. (1794–1843), Emerson's distinguished predecessor as pastor of the Boston Second Church, was now a professor at Harvard Divinity School. His letter, to which Emerson here replies, protested against Emerson's advanced religious modernism in his "Divinity School Address," delivered July 15, 1838. Following the pattern of *The American Scholar*, Emerson had condemned historical Christianity for its servitude to canonical authority and scripture. The higher authority was intuition, the immediate revelation of truth; the moral nature of man and God was revealed in our experience, not in *a priori* Biblical dogmatism. This was outright transcendentalism, beyond the liberal limits of his Unitarian college, from which Emerson was outcast for a generation. (For fuller development of this theology, *cf.* "The Over-Soul.") The letter to Ware is itself a convincing illustration of the transcendental process as opposed to logical argument; it is one of the best revelations of Emerson's character.

I suppose, with the same fortune that has hitherto attended me,—the joy of finding that my abler and better brothers, who work with the sympathy of society, loving and beloved, do now and then unexpectedly confirm my perceptions, and find my nonsense is only their own thought in motley. And so I am

Your affectionate servant,

R. W. EMERSON.

Self-Reliance[9]

"Ne te quæsiveris extra." [1]

"Man is his own star; and the soul that can
Render an honest and a perfect man
Commands all light, all influence, all fate;
Nothing to him falls early or too late.
Our acts our angels are, or good or ill,
Our fatal shadows that walk by us still."
—EPILOGUE TO BEAUMONT AND
FLETCHER'S HONEST MAN'S FORTUNE

Cast the bantling on the rocks,
Suckle him with the she-wolf's teat,
Wintered with the hawk and fox,
Power and speed be hands and feet.

I read the other day some verses written by an eminent painter[2] which were original and not conventional. The soul always hears an admonition in such lines, let the subject be what it may. The sentiment they instil is of more value than any thought they may contain. To believe your own thought, to believe that what is true for you in your private heart is true for all men,—that is genius. Speak your latent conviction, and it shall be the universal sense; for the inmost in due time becomes the outmost,—and our first thought is rendered back to us by the trumpets of the Last Judgment. Familiar as the voice of the mind is to each, the highest merit we ascribe to Moses, Plato, and Milton is that they set at naught books and traditions, and spoke not what men, but what they thought. A man should

9. "Self-Reliance" is generally regarded as indispensable for the clear understanding of Emerson's matured philosophy of individualism. This individualism functions through the relations of the "self" with God, or the "Over-Soul" —which is another name for the moral law inherent in nature. But these relations are not automatic; the individual is accorded the responsibility of freedom of choice, guided by intuition and experience. Apart from its ideas, "Self-Reliance" is regarded by many as the high tide of Emerson's prose; it is compact and cogent in its logic, and its style is a perfect instrument for its emotional intensity and its wit. The ideas of this essay took shape over a long period. It contains a passage from a journal entry of 1832, and others from various lec-

tures delivered between 1836 and 1839 (Centenary Edition, Vol. II, pp. 389–390). It was first published in *Essays* [First Series] (1841), which Emerson revised for the edition of 1847, on which the present text is based.
1. "Do not seek [answers] outside yourself." The first edition of "Self-Reliance" bore all three epigraphs as printed here. Emerson composed the quatrain himself, and dropped it from the second edition (1847). It was restored by later editors of the essay and also appears in the *Poems* as "Power."
2. The painter-poet may be the American Washington Allston (1779–1843), or the English William Blake (1757–1827), according to E. W. Emerson (Centenary Edition, Vol. II, p. 390).

learn to detect and watch that gleam of light which flashes across his mind from within, more than the lustre of the firmament of bards and sages. Yet he dismisses without notice his thought, because it is his. In every work of genius we recognize our own rejected thoughts: they come back to us with a certain alienated majesty. Great works of art have no more affecting lesson for us than this. They teach us to abide by our spontaneous impression with good-humored inflexibility then most when the whole cry of voices is on the other side. Else, to-morrow a stranger will say with masterly good sense precisely what we have thought and felt all the time, and we shall be forced to take with shame our own opinion from another.

There is a time in every man's education when he arrives at the conviction that envy is ignorance; that imitation is suicide; that he must take himself for better for worse as his portion; that though the wide universe is full of good, no kernel of nourishing corn can come to him but through his toil bestowed on that plot of ground which is given to him to till. The power which resides in him is new in nature, and none but he knows what that is which he can do, nor does he know until he has tried. Not for nothing one face, one character, one fact, makes much impression on him, and another none. This sculpture in the memory is not without preëstablished harmony. The eye was placed where one ray should fall, that it might testify of that particular ray. We but half express ourselves, and are ashamed of that divine idea which each of us represents. It may be safely trusted as proportionate and of good issues, so it be faithfully imparted, but God will not have his work made manifest by cowards. A man is relieved and gay when he has put his heart into his work and done his best; but what he has said or done otherwise shall give him no peace. It is a deliverance which does not deliver. In the attempt his genius deserts him; no muse befriends; no invention, no hope.

Trust thyself: every heart vibrates to that iron string. Accept the place the divine providence has found for you, the society of your contemporaries, the connection of events. Great men have always done so, and confided themselves childlike to the genius of their age, betraying their perception that the absolutely trustworthy was seated at their heart, working through their hands, predominating in all their being. And we are now men, and must accept in the highest mind the same transcendent destiny; and not minors and invalids in a protected corner, not cowards fleeing before a revolution, but guides, redeemers, and benefactors, obeying the Almighty effort, and advancing on Chaos and the Dark.[3]

What pretty oracles nature yields us on this text, in the face and behaviour of children, babes, and even brutes! That divided and

3. *Cf.* Milton, *Paradise Lost*, Book I, l. 543.

rebel mind, that distrust of a sentiment because our arithmetic has computed the strength and means opposed to our purpose, these have not. Their mind being whole, their eye is as yet unconquered, and when we look in their faces, we are disconcerted. Infancy conforms to nobody: all conform to it, so that one babe commonly makes four or five out of the adults who prattle and play to it. So God has armed youth and puberty and manhood no less with its own piquancy and charm, and made it enviable and gracious and its claims not to be put by, if it will stand by itself. Do not think the youth has no force, because he cannot speak to you and me. Hark! in the next room his voice is sufficiently clear and emphatic. It seems he knows how to speak to his contemporaries. Bashful or bold, then, he will know how to make us seniors very unnecessary.

The nonchalance of boys who are sure of a dinner, and would disdain as much as a lord to do or say aught to conciliate one, is the healthy attitude of human nature. A boy is in the parlour what the pit[4] is in the playhouse; independent, irresponsible, looking out from his corner on such people and facts as pass by, he tries and sentences them on their merits, in the swift, summary ways of boys, as good, bad, interesting, silly, eloquent, troublesome. He cumbers himself never about consequences, about interests: he gives an independent, genuine verdict. You must court him: he does not court you. But the man is, as it were, clapped into jail by his consciousness. As soon as he has once acted or spoken with éclat, he is a committed person, watched by the sympathy or the hatred of hundreds, whose affections must now enter into his account. There is no Lethe[5] for this. Ah, that he could pass again into his neutrality! Who can thus avoid all pledges, and having observed, observe again from the same unaffected, unbiased, unbribable, unaffrighted innocence, must always be formidable. He would utter opinions on all passing affairs, which being seen to be not private, but necessary, would sink like darts into the ear of men, and put them in fear.

These are the voices which we hear in solitude, but they grow faint and inaudible as we enter into the world. Society everywhere is in conspiracy against the manhood of every one of its members. Society is a joint-stock company, in which the members agree, for the better securing of his bread to each shareholder, to surrender the liberty and culture of the eater. The virtue in most request is conformity. Self-reliance is its aversion. It loves not realities and creators, but names and customs.

Whoso would be a man, must be a nonconformist. He who would gather immortal palms must not be hindered by the name of goodness, but must explore if it be goodness. Nothing is at last sacred but

4. In old theaters, the cheaper seats behind the orchestra, below the level of the stage.

5. In Greek myth, a river of forgetfulness in the nether world.

the integrity of your own mind. Absolve you to yourself, and you shall have the suffrage of the world. I remember an answer which when quite young I was prompted to make to a valued adviser, who was wont to importune me with the dear old doctrines of the church. On my saying, What have I to do with the sacredness of traditions, if I live wholly from within? my friend suggested,—"But these impulses may be from below, not from above." I replied, "They do not seem to me to be such; but if I am the Devil's child, I will live then from the Devil." No law can be sacred to me but that of my nature. Good and bad are but names very readily transferable to that or this; the only right is what is after my constitution, the only wrong what is against it. A man is to carry himself in the presence of all opposition as if everything were titular and ephemeral but he. I am ashamed to think how easily we capitulate to badges and names, to large societies and dead institutions. Every decent and well-spoken individual affects and sways me more than is right. I ought to go upright and vital, and speak the rude truth in all ways. If malice and vanity wear the coat of philanthropy, shall that pass? If an angry bigot assumes this bountiful cause of Abolition, and comes to me with his last news from Barbadoes,[6] why should I not say to him, "Go love thy infant; love thy wood-chopper; be good-natured and modest: have that grace; and never varnish your hard, uncharitable ambition with this incredible tenderness for black folk a thousand miles off. Thy love afar is spite at home." Rough and graceless would be such greeting, but truth is handsomer than the affectation of love. Your goodness must have some edge to it,—else it is none. The doctrine of hatred must be preached as the counteraction of the doctrine of love when that pules and whines. I shun father and mother and wife and brother, when my genius calls me.[7] I would write on the lintels of the door-post, Whim.[8] I hope it is somewhat better than whim at last, but we cannot spend the day in explanation. Expect me not to show cause why I seek or why I exclude company. Then, again, do not tell me, as a good man did to-day, of my obligation to put all poor men in good situations. Are they *my* poor? I tell thee, thou foolish philanthropist, that I grudge the dollar, the dime, the cent I give to such men as do not belong to me and to whom I do not belong. There is a class of persons to whom by all spiritual affinity I am bought and sold; for them I will go to prison, if need be; but your miscellaneous popular charities; the education at college of fools; the building of meeting-houses to the vain end to which many now stand; alms to sots; and the thousandfold Relief Societies;

6. British legislation abolished slavery in the West Indies, including Barbadoes, in 1833.
7. *Cf.* Matthew x: 34–37.
8. *Cf.* Exodus xii: 17. In Hebrew and other Eastern cultures, a mark on the lintel or doorframe characterized the resident. Emerson's "Whim" signifies individualism, not capriciousness.

—though I confess with shame I sometimes succumb and give the dollar, it is a wicked dollar, which by and by I shall have the manhood to withhold.

Virtues are, in the popular estimate, rather the exception than the rule. There is the man *and* his virtues. Men do what is called a good action, as some piece of courage or charity, much as they would pay a fine in expiation of daily nonappearance on parade. Their works are done as an apology or extenuation of their living in the world,—as invalids and the insane pay a high board. Their virtues are penances. I do not wish to expiate, but to live. My life is for itself and not for a spectacle. I much prefer that it should be of a lower strain, so it be genuine and equal, than that it should be glittering and unsteady. I wish it to be sound and sweet, and not to need diet and bleeding. I ask primary evidence that you are a man, and refuse this appeal from the man to his actions. I know that for myself it makes no difference whether I do or forbear those actions which are reckoned excellent. I cannot consent to pay for a privilege where I have intrinsic right. Few and mean as my gifts may be, I actually am, and do not need for my own assurance or the assurance of my fellows any secondary testimony.

What I must do is all that concerns me, not what the people think. This rule, equally arduous in actual and in intellectual life, may serve for the whole distinction between greatness and meanness. It is the harder, because you will always find those who think they know what is your duty better than you know it. It is easy in the world to live after the world's opinion; it is easy in solitude to live after our own; but the great man is he who in the midst of the crowd keeps with perfect sweetness the independence of solitude.

The objection to conforming to usages that have become dead to you is, that it scatters your force. It loses your time and blurs the impression of your character. If you maintain a dead church, contribute to a dead Bible-society, vote with a great party either for the government or against it, spread your table like base housekeepers,—under all these screens I have difficulty to detect the precise man you are. And, of course, so much force is withdrawn from all your proper life. But do your work, and I shall know you. Do your work, and you shall reinforce yourself. A man must consider what a blind man's-buff is this game of conformity. If I know your sect, I anticipate your argument. I hear a preacher announce for his text and topic the expediency of one of the institutions of his church. Do I not know beforehand that not possibly can he say a new and spontaneous word? Do I not know that, with all this ostentation of examining the grounds of the institution, he will do no such thing? Do I not know that he is pledged to himself not to look but at one side,—the permitted side, not as a man, but as a parish minister? He is a re-

tained attorney, and these airs of the bench are the emptiest affectation. Well, most men have bound their eyes with one or another
handkerchief, and attached themselves to some one of these communities of opinion. This conformity makes them not false in a few
particulars, authors of a few lies, but false in all particulars. Their
every truth is not quite true. Their two is not the real two, their
four not the real four; so that every word they say chagrins us, and
we know not where to begin to set them right. Meantime nature is
not slow to equip us in the prison-uniform of the party to which we
adhere. We come to wear one cut of face and figure, and acquire by
degrees the gentlest asinine expression. There is a mortifying experience in particular, which does not fail to wreak itself also in the general history; I mean "the foolish face of praise,"[9] the forced smile
which we put on in company where we do not feel at ease in answer
to conversation which does not interest us. The muscles, not spontaneously moved, but moved by a low usurping wilfulness, grow
tight about the outline of the face, with the most disagreeable
sensation.

For nonconformity the world whips you with its displeasure. And
therefore a man must know how to estimate a sour face. The by-
standers look askance on him in the public street or in the friend's
parlour. If this aversion had its origin in contempt and resistance like
his own, he might well go home with a sad countenance; but the
sour faces of the multitude, like their sweet faces, have no deep
cause, but are put on and off as the wind blows and a newspaper
directs. Yet is the discontent of the multitude more formidable than
that of the senate and the college. It is easy enough for a firm man
who knows the world to brook the rage of the cultivated classes. Their
rage is decorous and prudent, for they are timid as being very vulnerable themselves. But when to their feminine rage the indignation
of the people is added, when the ignorant and the poor are aroused,
when the unintelligent brute force that lies at the bottom of society
is made to growl and mow,[1] it needs the habit of magnanimity and
religion to treat it godlike as a trifle of no concernment.

The other terror that scares us from self-trust is our consistency;
a reverence for our past act or word, because the eyes of others have
no other data for computing our orbit than our past acts, and we
are loth to disappoint them.

But why should you keep your head over your shoulder? Why
drag about this corpse of your memory, lest you contradict somewhat you have stated in this or that public place? Suppose you should
contradict yourself; what then? It seems to be a rule of wisdom never
to rely on your memory alone, scarcely even in acts of pure memory,

9. *Cf.* Alexander Pope, "Epistle to Dr.   1. To mock or grimace.
Arbuthnot," l. 212.

but to bring the past for judgment into the thousand-eyed present, and live ever in a new day. In your metaphysics you have denied personality to the Deity: yet when the devout motions of the soul come, yield to them heart and life, though they should clothe God with shape and color. Leave your theory, as Joseph his coat in the hand of the harlot,[2] and flee.

A foolish consistency is the hobgoblin of little minds, adored by little statesmen and philosophers and divines. With consistency a great soul has simply nothing to do. He may as well concern himself with his shadow on the wall. Speak what you think now in hard words, and to-morrow speak what to-morrow thinks in hard words again, though it contradict every thing you said to-day.—"Ah, so you shall be sure to be misunderstood."—Is it so bad, then, to be misunderstood? Pythagoras was misunderstood, and Socrates, and Jesus, and Luther, and Copernicus, and Galileo,[3] and Newton, and every pure and wise spirit that ever took flesh. To be great is to be misunderstood.

I suppose no man can violate his nature. All the sallies of his will are rounded in by the law of his being, as the inequalities of Andes and Himmaleh are insignificant in the curve of the sphere. Nor does it matter how you gauge and try him. A character is like an acrostic or Alexandrian stanza;[4]—read it forward, backward, or across, it still spells the same thing. In this pleasing, contrite wood-life which God allows me, let me record day by day my honest thought without prospect or retrospect, and, I cannot doubt, it will be found symmetrical, though I mean it not, and see it not. My book should smell of pines and resound with the hum of insects. The swallow over my window should interweave that thread or straw he carries in his bill into my web also. We pass for what we are. Character teaches above our wills. Men imagine that they communicate their virtue or vice only by overt actions, and do not see that virtue or vice emit a breath every moment.

There will be an agreement in whatever variety of actions, so they be each honest and natural in their hour. For of one will, the actions will be harmonious, however unlike they seem. These varieties are lost sight of at a little distance, at a little height of thought. One tendency unites them all. The voyage of the best ship is a zigzag line of a hundred tacks. See the line from a sufficient distance, and it straightens itself to the average tendency. Your genuine action will

2. *Cf.* Joseph and Potiphar's wife, Genesis xxxix. 12.
3. Pythagoras, Greek thinker of the fifth century B.C., aroused controversy by his revolutionary ideas and mathematical discoveries; Copernicus (1473–1543) risked charges of impiety in promulgating the theory of the solar system now accepted; Galileo (1564–1642) was tried by the Inquisition and condemned to retirement for supporting the theories of Copernicus. The remainder of these names suggest familiar controversies.
4. An Alexandrian stanza is a palindrome, or an arrangement of words which read the same backward as forward.

explain itself, and will explain your other genuine actions. Your conformity explains nothing. Act singly, and what you have already done singly will justify you now. Greatness appeals to the future. If I can be firm enough to-day to do right, and scorn eyes, I must have done so much right before as to defend me now. Be it how it will, do right now. Always scorn appearances, and you always may. The force of character is cumulative. All the foregone days of virtue work their health into this. What makes the majesty of the heroes of the senate and the field, which so fills the imagination? The consciousness of a train of great days and victories behind. They shed a united light on the advancing actor. He is attended as by a visible escort of angels. That is it which throws thunder into Chatham's[5] voice, and dignity into Washington's port, and America into Adams's[6] eye. Honor is venerable to us because it is no ephemera. It is always ancient virtue. We worship it to-day because it is not of to-day. We love it and pay it homage, because it is not a trap for our love and homage, but is self-dependent, self-derived, and therefore of an old immaculate pedigree, even if shown in a young person.

I hope in these days we have heard the last of conformity and consistency. Let the words be gazetted[7] and ridiculous henceforward. Instead of the gong for dinner, let us hear a whistle from the Spartan fife.[8] Let us never bow and apologize more. A great man is coming to eat at my house. I do not wish to please him; I wish that he should wish to please me. I will stand here for humanity, and though I would make it kind, I would make it true. Let us affront and reprimand the smooth mediocrity and squalid contentment of the times, and hurl in the face of custom, and trade, and office, the fact which is the upshot of all history, that there is a great responsible Thinker and Actor working wherever a man works; that a true man belongs to no other time or place, but is the centre of things. Where he is, there is nature. He measures you, and all men, and all events. Ordinarily, every body in society reminds us of somewhat else, or of some other person. Character, reality, reminds you of nothing else; it takes place of the whole creation. The man must be so much, that he must make all circumstances indifferent. Every true man is a cause, a country, and an age; requires infinite spaces and numbers and time fully to accomplish his design;—and posterity seem to follow his steps as a train of clients. A man Caesar is born, and for ages after we have a Roman Empire. Christ is born, and millions of

---

5. The Earl of Chatham, William Pitt (1708–1778), greatest English orator of his day; he supported the American colonists in Parliament.
6. By 1841 there had been three Adamses to whom this reference might apply: Samuel, a leader of the Revolution; John, who became the second

president; and John Quincy, the sixth president.
7. *I.e.*, "dismissed." The British official "gazettes" announced dismissals, bankruptcies, and the like, as well as honors.
8. The strict discipline of the Spartans extended to musical instruments.

minds so grow and cleave to his genius that he is confounded with virtue and the possible of man. An institution is the lengthened shadow of one man; as, Monachism, of the Hermit Antony;[9] the Reformation, of Luther; Quakerism, of Fox;[1] Methodism, of Wesley; Abolition, of Clarkson.[2] Scipio, Milton called "the height of Rome;"[3] and all history resolves itself very easily into the biography of a few stout and earnest persons.

Let a man then know his worth, and keep things under his feet. Let him not peep or steal, or skulk up and down with the air of a charity-boy, a bastard, or an interloper, in the world which exists for him. But the man in the street, finding no worth in himself which corresponds to the force which built a tower or sculptured a marble god, feels poor when he looks on these. To him a palace, a statue, or a costly book have an alien and forbiddding air, much like a gay equipage, and seem to say like that, "Who are you, Sir?" Yet they all are his, suitors for his notice, petitioners to his faculties that they will come out and take possession. The picture waits for my verdict: it is not to command me, but I am to settle its claims to praise. That popular fable[4] of the sot who was picked up dead drunk in the street, carried to the duke's house, washed and dressed and laid in the duke's bed, and, on his waking, treated with all obsequious ceremony like the duke, and assured that he had been insane, owes its popularity to the fact, that it symbolizes so well the state of man, who is in the world a sort of sot, but now and then wakes up, exercises his reason and finds himself a true prince.

Our reading is mendicant and sycophantic. In history, our imagination plays us false. Kingdom and lordship, power and estate, are a gaudier vocabulary than private John and Edward in a small house and common day's work; but the things of life are the same to both; the sum total of both is the same. Why all this deference to Alfred,[5] and Scanderbeg,[6] and Gustavus?[7] Suppose they were virtuous; did they wear out virtue? As great a stake depends on your private act to-day, as followed their public and renowned steps. When private men shall act with original views, the lustre will be transferred from the actions of kings to those of gentlemen.

9. The hermitages of St. Anthony (ca. 250–350) were the beginnings of Christian monasticism.

1. George Fox (1624–1691) founded the Society of Friends in England (1647).

2. Thomas Clarkson (1760–1846) was the pioneer of the British antislavery movement.

3. *Cf.* John Milton, *Paradise Lost*, Book IX, l. 510. Scipio Africanus "the Elder" (237–183 B.C.), conqueror of Hannibal, was the greatest Roman general before Julius Caesar.

4. *Cf.* the same story in Shakespeare's "Induction," *The Taming of the Shrew* (Centenary Edition, Vol. II, p. 392).

5. Alfred (849–899), called "the Great" among Saxon kings of Britain.

6. Scanderbeg (Turkish title, "Iskander Bey") was George Castriota (1403?–1468), national hero of the Albanians, whom he led against the Turks.

7. Sweden's King Gustavus I (Gustavus Vasa, 1496–1560) defeated the Danes, and proclaimed Christianity; Gustavus II (Gustavus Adolphus, 1594–1632) freed Swedish territories occupied by Denmark, Russia, and Poland.

The world has been instructed by its kings, who have so magnetized the eyes of nations. It has been taught by this colossal symbol the mutual reverence that is due from man to man. The joyful loyalty with which men have everywhere suffered the king, the noble, or the great proprietor to walk among them by a law of his own, make his own scale of men and things, and reverse theirs, pay for benefits not with money but with honor, and represent the law in his person, was the hieroglyphic by which they obscurely signified their consciousness of their own right and comeliness, the right of every man.

The magnetism which all original action exerts is explained when we inquire the reason of self-trust. Who is the Trustee? What is the aboriginal Self, on which a universal reliance may be grounded? What is the nature and power of that science-baffling star, without parallax,[8] without calculable elements, which shoots a ray of beauty even into trivial and impure actions, if the least mark of independence appear? The inquiry leads us to that source, at once the essence of genius, of virtue, and of life, which we call Spontaneity or Instinct. We denote this primary wisdom as Intuition, whilst all later teachings are tuitions. In that deep force, the last fact behind which analysis cannot go, all things find their common origin. For the sense of being which in calm hours rises, we know not how, in the soul, is not diverse from things, from space, from light, from time, from man, but one with them, and proceeds obviously from the same source whence their life and being also proceed. We first share the life by which things exist, and afterwards see them as appearances in nature, and forget that we have shared their cause. Here is the fountain of action and of thought. Here are the lungs of that inspiration which giveth man wisdom, and which cannot be denied without impiety and atheism. We lie in the lap of immense intelligence, which makes us receivers of its truth and organs of its activity. When we discern justice, when we discern truth, we do nothing of ourselves, but allow a passage to its beams. If we ask whence this comes, if we seek to pry into the soul that causes, all philosophy is at fault. Its presence or its absence is all we can affirm. Every man discriminates between the voluntary acts of his mind, and his involuntary perceptions, and knows that to his involuntary perceptions a perfect faith is due. He may err in the expression of them, but he knows that these things are so, like day and night, not to be disputed. My wilful actions and acquisitions are but roving;—the idlest reverie, the faintest native emotion, command my curiosity and respect. Thoughtless people contradict as readily the statement of perceptions as of opinions, or rather much more readily; for they do not distinguish between perception and notion. They fancy that

8. *I.e.*, "incalculable."

I choose to see this or that thing. But perception is not whimsical, but fatal. If I see a trait, my children will see it after me, and in course of time, all mankind,—although it may chance that no one has seen it before me. For my perception of it is as much a fact as the sun.

The relations of the soul to the divine spirit are so pure, that it is profane to seek to interpose helps. It must be that when God speaketh he should communicate, not one thing, but all things; should fill the world with his voice; should scatter forth light, nature, time, souls, from the centre of the present thought; and new date and new create the whole. Whenever a mind is simple, and receives a divine wisdom, old things pass away,—means, teachers, texts, temples fall; it lives now, and absorbs past and future into the present hour. All things are made sacred by relation to it,—one as much as another. All things are dissolved to their centre by their cause, and, in the universal miracle, petty and particular miracles disappear. If, therefore, a man claims to know and speak of God, and carries you backward to the phraseology of some old mouldered nation in another country, in another world, believe him not. Is the acorn better than the oak which is its fulness and completion? Is the parent better than the child into whom he has cast his ripened being? Whence, then, this worship of the past? The centuries are conspirators against the sanity and authority of the soul. Time and space are but physiological colors which the eye makes, but the soul is light; where it is, is day; where it was, is night; and history is an impertinence and an injury, if it be anything more than a cheerful apologue or parable of my being and becoming.

Man is timid and apologetic; he is no longer upright; he dares not say "I think," "I am," but quotes some saint or sage. He is ashamed before the blade of grass or the blowing rose. These roses under my window make no reference to former roses or to better ones; they are for what they are; they exist with God to-day. There is no time to them. There is simply the rose; it is perfect in every moment of its existence. Before a leaf-bud has burst, its whole life acts; in the full-blown flower there is no more; in the leafless root there is no less. Its nature is satisfied, and it satisfies nature, in all moments alike. But man postpones or remembers; he does not live in the present, but with reverted eye laments the past, or, heedless of the riches that surround him, stands on tiptoe to foresee the future. He cannot be happy and strong until he too lives with nature in the present, above time.

This should be plain enough. Yet see what strong intellects dare not yet hear God himself, unless he speaks the phraseology of I know not what David, or Jeremiah, or Paul. We shall not always set so great a price on a few texts, on a few lives. We are like children who repeat by rote the sentences of grandames and tutors, and, as they grow older, of the men of talents and character they chance to see,—painfully recollecting the exact words they spoke; afterwards, when they come into the point of view which those had who uttered these sayings, they understand them, and are willing to let the words go; for, at any time, they can use words as good when occasion comes. If we live truly, we shall see truly. It is as easy for the strong man to be strong, as it is for the weak to be weak. When we have new perception, we shall gladly disburden the memory of its hoarded treasures as old rubbish. When a man lives with God, his voice shall be as sweet as the murmur of the brook and the rustle of the corn.

And now at last the highest truth on this subject remains unsaid; probably cannot be said; for all that we say is the far-off remembering of the intuition. That thought, by what I can now nearest approach to say it, is this. When good is near you, when you have life in yourself, it is not by any known or accustomed way; you shall not discern the foot-prints of any other; you shall not see the face of man; you shall not hear any name;—the way, the thought, the good, shall be wholly strange and new. It shall exclude example and experience. You take the way from man, not to man. All persons that ever existed are its forgotten ministers. Fear and hope are alike beneath it. There is somewhat low even in hope. In the hour of vision, there is nothing that can be called gratitude, nor properly joy. The soul raised over passion beholds identity and eternal causation, perceives the self-existence of Truth and Right, and calms itself with knowing that all things go well. Vast spaces of nature, the Atlantic Ocean, the South Sea,—long intervals of time, years, centuries,—are of no account. This which I think and feel underlay every former state of life and circumstances, as it does underlie my present, and what is called life, and what is called death.

Life only avails, not the having lived. Power ceases in the instant of repose; it resides in the moment of transition from a past to a new state, in the shooting of the gulf, in the darting to an aim. This one fact the world hates, that the soul *becomes*; for that forever degrades the past, turns all riches to poverty, all reputation to a shame, confounds the saint with the rogue, shoves Jesus and Judas equally aside. Why, then, do we prate of self-reliance? Inasmuch as the soul is present, there will be power not confident but agent. To talk of reliance is a poor external way of speaking. Speak rather of that which relies, because it works and is. Who has more obedience than I masters me, though he should not raise his finger. Round him I must revolve by the gravitation of spirits. We fancy it rhetoric, when we speak of eminent virtue. We do not yet see that virtue is Height, and that a man or a company of men, plastic and permeable to principles, by the law of nature must overpower and ride all cities, nations, kings, rich men, poets, who are not.

This is the ultimate fact which we so quickly reach on this, as on every topic, the resolution of all into the ever-blessed ONE. Self-existence is the attribute of the Supreme Cause, and it constitutes the measure of good by the degree in which it enters into all lower forms. All things real are so by so much virtue as they contain. Commerce, husbandry, hunting, whaling, war, eloquence, personal weight, are somewhat, and engage my respect as examples of its presence and impure action. I see the same law working in nature for conservation and growth. Power is in nature the essential measure of right. Nature suffers nothing to remain in her kingdoms which cannot help itself. The genesis and maturation of a planet, its poise and orbit, the bended tree recovering itself from the strong wind, the vital resources of every animal and vegetable, are demonstrations of the self-sufficing, and therefore self-relying soul.

Thus all concentrates: let us not rove; let us sit at home with the cause. Let us stun and astonish the intruding rabble of men and books and institutions, by a simple declaration of the divine fact. Bid the invaders take the shoes from off their feet, for God is here within.[9] Let our simplicity judge them, and our docility to our own law demonstrate the poverty of nature and fortune beside our native riches.

But now we are a mob. Man does not stand in awe of man, nor is his genius admonished to stay at home, to put itself in communication with the internal ocean, but it goes abroad to beg a cup of water of the urns of other men. We must go alone. I like the silent church before the service begins, better than any preaching. How far off, how cool, how chaste the persons look, begirt each one with a precinct or sanctuary! So let us always sit. Why should we assume the faults of our friends, or wife, or father, or child, because they sit around our hearth, or are said to have the same blood? All men have my blood, and I all men's. Not for that will I adopt their petulance or folly, even to the extent of being ashamed of it. But your isolation must not be mechanical, but spiritual, that is, must be elevation. At times the whole world seems to be in conspiracy to importune you with emphatic trifles. Friend, client, child, sickness, fear, want, charity, all knock at once at thy closet door, and say,—"Come out unto us." But keep thy state; come not into their confusion. The power men possess to annoy me, I give them by a weak curiosity. No man can come near me but through my act. "What we love that we have, but by desire we bereave ourselves of the love."

If we cannot at once rise to the sanctities of obedience and faith, let us at least resist our temptations; let us enter into the state of

9. *Cf.* Joshua v: 15; Exodus iii: 5.

war, and wake Thor[1] and Woden,[2] courage and constancy, in our Saxon breasts. This is to be done in our smooth times by speaking the truth. Check this lying hospitality and lying affection. Live no longer to the expectation of these deceived and deceiving people with whom we converse. Say to them, "O father, O mother, O wife, O brother, O friend, I have lived with you after appearances hitherto. Henceforward I am the truth's. Be it known unto you that henceforward I obey no law less than the eternal law. I will have no covenants but proximities. I shall endeavor to nourish my parents, to support my family, to be the chaste husband of one wife,—but these relations I must fill after a new and unprecedented way. I appeal from your customs. I must be myself. I cannot break myself any longer for you, or you. If you can love me for what I am, we shall be the happier. If you cannot, I will still seek to deserve that you should. I will not hide my tastes or aversions. I will so trust that what is deep is holy, that I will do strongly before the sun and moon whatever inly rejoices me, and the heart appoints. If you are noble, I will love you; if you are not, I will not hurt you and myself by hypocritical attentions. If you are true, but not in the same truth with me, cleave to your companions; I will seek my own. I do this not selfishly but humbly and truly. It is alike your interest, and mine, and all men's, however long we have dwelt in lies, to live in truth. Does this sound harsh to-day? You will soon love what is dictated by your nature as well as mine, and if we follow the truth, it will bring us out safe at last."—But so you may give these friends pain. Yes, but I cannot sell my liberty and my power, to save their sensibility. Besides, all persons have their moments of reason, when they look out into the region of absolute truth; then will they justify me, and do the same thing.

The populace think that your rejection of popular standards is a rejection of all standard, and mere antinomianism;[3] and the bold sensualist will use the name of philosophy to gild his crimes. But the law of consciousness abides. There are two confessionals, in one or the other of which we must be shriven. You may fulfil your round of duties by clearing yourself in the *direct*, or in the *reflex* way. Consider whether you have satisfied your relations to father, mother, cousin, neighbour, town, cat and dog; whether any of these can upbraid you. But I may also neglect this reflex standard, and absolve me to myself. I have my own stern claims and perfect circle. It denies the name of duty to many offices that are called duties. But if I can discharge its debts, it enables me to dispense with the popular code. If any one imagines that this law is lax, let him keep its command-

---

1. In Norse myth, "the Thunderer," god of war.
2. Anglo-Saxon form of the name of Odin—in Teutonic myth the god of war

but also the patron of the slain.
3. The doctrine of salvation by faith alone, without reference to breaches of the moral law.

ment one day.

And truly it demands something godlike in him who has cast off the common motives of humanity, and has ventured to trust himself for a taskmaster. High be his heart, faithful his will, clear his sight, that he may in good earnest be doctrine, society, law, to himself, that a simple purpose may be to him as strong as iron necessity is to others!

If any man consider the present aspects of what is called by distinction *society*, he will see the need of these ethics. The sinew and heart of man seem to be drawn out, and we are become timorous, desponding whimperers. We are afraid of truth, afraid of fortune, afraid of death, and afraid of each other. Our age yields no great and perfect persons. We want men and women who shall renovate life and our social state, but we see that most natures are insolvent, cannot satisfy their own wants, have an ambition out of all proportion to their practical force and do lean and beg day and night continually. Our housekeeping is mendicant, our arts, our occupations, our marriages, our religion, we have not chosen, but society has chosen for us. We are parlour soldiers. We shun the rugged battle of fate, where strength is born.

If our young men miscarry in their first enterprises, they lose all heart. If the young merchant fails, men say he is *ruined*. If the finest genius studies at one of our colleges, and is not installed in an office within one year afterwards in the cities or suburbs of Boston or New York, it seems to his friends and to himself that he is right in being disheartened, and in complaining the rest of his life. A sturdy lad from New Hampshire or Vermont, who in turn tries all the professions, who *teams it, farms it, peddles*, keeps a school, preaches, edits a newspaper, goes to Congress, buys a township, and so forth, in successive years, and always, like a cat, falls on his feet, is worth a hundred of these city dolls. He walks abreast with his days, and feels no shame in not "studying a profession," for he does not postpone his life, but lives already. He has not one chance, but a hundred chances. Let a Stoic[4] open the resources of man, and tell men they are not leaning willows, but can and must detach themselves; that with the exercise of self-trust, new powers shall appear; that a man is the word made flesh,[5] born to shed healing to the nations, that he should be ashamed of our compassion, and that the moment he acts from himself, tossing the laws, the books, idolatries, and customs out of the window, we pity him no more, but thank and revere him,—and that teacher shall restore the life of man to splendor, and make his name dear to all history.

It is easy to see that a greater self-reliance must work a revolution

4. The original Stoics, led by Zeno of Athens after 300 B.C., taught passionless self-reliance and submission to natural law.
5. *Cf.* John i: 14.

in all the offices and relations of men; in their religion; in their education; in their pursuits; their modes of living; their association; in their property; in their speculative views.

1. In what prayers do men allow themselves! That which they call a holy office is not so much as brave and manly. Prayer looks abroad and asks for some foreign addition to come through some foreign virtue, and loses itself in endless mazes of natural and supernatural, and mediatorial and miraculous. Prayer that craves a particular commodity,—anything less than all good,—is vicious. Prayer is the contemplation of the facts of life from the highest point of view. It is the soliloquy of a beholding and jubilant soul. It is the spirit of God pronouncing his works good.[6] But prayer as a means to effect a private end is meanness and theft. It supposes dualism and not unity in nature and consciousness. As soon as the man is at one with God, he will not beg. He will then see prayer in all action. The prayer of the farmer kneeling in his field to weed it, the prayer of the rower kneeling with the stroke of his oar, are true prayers heard throughout nature, though for cheap ends. Caratach, in Fletcher's Bonduca,[7] when admonished to inquire the mind of the god Audate, replies,—

> "His hidden meaning lies in our endeavours;
> Our valors are our best gods."

Another sort of false prayers are our regrets. Discontent is the want of self-reliance: it is infirmity of will. Regret calamities, if you can thereby help the sufferer; if not, attend your own work, and already the evil begins to be repaired. Our sympathy is just as base. We come to them who weep foolishly, and sit down and cry for company, instead of imparting to them truth and health in rough electric shocks, putting them once more in communication with their own reason. The secret of fortune is joy in our hands. Welcome evermore to gods and men is the self-helping man. For him all doors are flung wide: him all tongues greet, all honors crown, all eyes follow with desire. Our love goes out to him and embraces him, because he did not need it. We solicitously and apologetically caress and celebrate him, because he held on his way and scorned our disapprobation. The gods love him because men hated him. "To the persevering mortal," said Zoroaster,[8] "the blessed Immortals are swift."

As men's prayers are a disease of the will, so are their creeds a disease of the intellect. They say with those foolish Israelites, "Let not God speak to us, lest we die. Speak thou, speak any man with us, and we will obey."[9] Everywhere I am hindered of meeting God in

6. *Cf.* Genesis i: 25.
7. The Elizabethan playwright John Fletcher wrote *Bonduca* (1618) perhaps in collaboration with Francis Beaumont.
8. Reputed founder (sixth century B.C.?) of ancient Persian religion, recorded in the Avesta, here quoted.
9. *Cf.* the words of the Israelites to Moses concerning the Ten Commandments: Exodus xx: 19.

my brother, because he has shut his own temple doors, and recites fables merely of his brother's, or his brother's brother's God. Every new mind is a new classification.[1] If it prove a mind of uncommon activity and power, a Locke, a Lavoisier, a Hutton, a Bentham, a Fourier, it imposes its classification on other men, and lo! a new system. In proportion to the depth of the thought, and so to the number of the objects it touches and brings within reach of the pupil, is his complacency. But chiefly is this apparent in creeds and churches, which are also classifications of some powerful mind acting on the elemental thought of duty, and man's relation to the Highest. Such is Calvinism, Quakerism, Swedenborgism. The pupil takes the same delight in subordinating every thing to the new terminology, as a girl who has just learned botany in seeing a new earth and new seasons thereby. It will happen for a time, that the pupil will find his intellectual power has grown by the study of his master's mind. But in all unbalanced minds, the classification is idolized, passes for the end, and not for a speedily exhaustible means, so that the walls of the system blend to their eye in the remote horizon with the walls of the universe; the luminaries of heaven seem to them hung on the arch their master built. They cannot imagine how you aliens have any right to see,—how you can see; "It must be somehow that you stole the light from us." They do not yet perceive that light, unsystematic, indomitable, will break into any cabin, even into theirs. Let them chirp awhile and call it their own. If they are honest and do well, presently their neat new pinfold will be too strait and low, will crack, will lean, will rot and vanish, and the immortal light, all young, and joyful, million-orbed, million-colored, will beam over the universe as on the first morning.

2. It is for want of self-culture that the superstition of Travelling, whose idols are Italy, England, Egypt, retains its fascination for all educated Americans. They who made England, Italy, or Greece venerable in the imagination did so by sticking fast where they were, like an axis of the earth. In manly hours, we feel that duty is our place. The soul is no traveller; the wise man stays at home, and when his necessities, his duties, on any occasion call him from his house, or into foreign lands, he is at home still, and shall make men sensible by the expression of his countenance, that he goes the missionary of wisdom and virtue, and visits cities and men like a sovereign, and not like an interloper or a valet.

I have no churlish objection to the circumnavigation of the globe, for the purposes of art, of study, and benevolence, so that the man

---

1. Each of the following was a pioneer of the "systematic" science: John Locke (1632–1704) developed a theory of knowledge; Antoine Laurent Lavoisier (1743–1794) pioneered in chemistry and James Hutton (1726–1797) in geology; Jeremy Bentham (1748–1832) formulated utilitarian concepts of law and government; François Marie Charles Fourier (1772–1837) originated plans for the co-operative organization of society.

is first domesticated, or does not go abroad with the hope of finding somewhat greater than he knows. He who travels to be amused, or to get somewhat which he does not carry, travels away from himself, and grows old even in youth among old things. In Thebes, in Palmyra, his will and mind have become old and dilapidated as they. He carries ruins to ruins.

Travelling is a fool's paradise. Our first journeys discover to us the indifference of places. At home I dream that at Naples, at Rome, I can be intoxicated with beauty, and lose my sadness. I pack my trunk, embrace my friends, embark on the sea and at last wake up in Naples, and there beside me is the stern fact, the sad self, unrelenting, identical, that I fled from. I seek the Vatican, and the palaces. I affect to be intoxicated with sights and suggestions, but I am not intoxicated. My giant goes with me wherever I go.

3. But the rage of travelling is a symptom of a deeper unsoundness affecting the whole intellectual action. The intellect is vagabond, and our system of education fosters restlessness. Our minds travel when our bodies are forced to stay at home. We imitate; and what is imitation but the travelling of the mind? Our houses are built with foreign taste; our shelves are garnished with foreign ornaments; our opinions, our tastes, our faculties, lean, and follow the Past and the Distant. The soul created the arts wherever they have flourished. It was in his own mind that the artist sought his model. It was an application of his own thought to the thing to be done and the conditions to be observed. And why need we copy the Doric or the Gothic model? Beauty, convenience, grandeur of thought, and quaint expression are as near to us as to any, and if the American artist will study with hope and love the precise thing to be done by him, considering the climate, the soil, the length of the day, the wants of the people, the habit and form of the government, he will create a house in which all these will find themselves fitted, and taste and sentiment will be satisfied also.

Insist on yourself; never imitate. Your own gift you can present every moment with the cumulative force of a whole life's cultivation; but of the adopted talent of another, you have only an extemporaneous, half possession. That which each can do best, none but his Maker can teach him. No man yet knows what it is, nor can, till that person has exhibited it. Where is the master who could have taught Shakspeare? Where is the master who could have instructed Franklin, or Washington, or Bacon, or Newton? Every great man is a unique. The Scipionism of Scipio is precisely that part he could not borrow.[2] Shakspeare will never be made by the study of Shakspeare. Do that which is assigned you, and you cannot hope too much or dare too

2. The essay "Self-Reliance" originated as a development of the preceding portion of this paragraph, which formed an entry in Emerson's journal for 1832 (*cf.* Centenary Edition, Vol. II, p. 395).

much. There is at this moment for you an utterance brave and grand as that of the colossal chisel of Phidias,[3] or trowel of the Egyptians, or the pen of Moses, or Dante, but different from all these. Not possibly will the soul, all rich, all eloquent, with thousand-cloven tongue, deign to repeat itself but if you can hear what these patriarchs say, surely you can reply to them in the same pitch of voice; for the ear and the tongue are two organs of one nature. Abide in the simple and noble regions of thy life, obey thy heart, and thou shall reproduce the Foreworld again.

4. As our Religion, our Education, our Art look abroad, so does our spirit of society. All men plume themselves on the improvement of society, and no man improves.

Society never advances. It recedes as fast on one side as it gains on the other. It undergoes continual changes; it is barbarous, it is civilized, it is christianized, it is rich, it is scientific; but this change is not amelioration. For every thing that is given, something is taken. Society acquires new arts, and loses old instincts. What a contrast between the well-clad, reading, writing, thinking American, with a watch, a pencil, and a bill of exchange in his pocket, and the naked New Zealander, whose property is a club, a spear, a mat, and an undivided twentieth of a shed to sleep under! But compare the health of the two men, and you shall see that the white man has lost his aboriginal strength. If the traveller tell us truly, strike the savage with a broad-axe and in a day or two the flesh shall unite and heal as if you struck the blow into soft pitch, and the same blow shall send the white to his grave.

The civilized man has built a coach, but has lost the use of his feet. He is supported on crutches, but lacks so much support of muscle. He has a fine Geneva watch, but he fails of the skill to tell the hour by the sun. A Greenwich nautical almanac he has, and so being sure of the information when he wants it, the man in the street does not know a star in the sky. The solstice he does not observe; the equinox he knows as little; and the whole bright calendar of the year is without a dial in his mind. His note-books impair his memory; his libraries overload his wit; the insurance-office increases the number of accidents; and it may be a question whether machinery does not encumber; whether we have not lost by refinement some energy, by a Christianity, entrenched in establishments and forms, some vigor of wild virtue. For every Stoic was a Stoic; but in Christendom where is the Christian?

There is no more deviation in the moral standard than in the standard of height or bulk. No greater men are now than ever were. A singular equality may be observed between the great men of the first and of the last ages; nor can all the science, art, religion, and

3. The greatest of ancient Greek sculptors (*fl.* fifth century B.C.).

philosophy of the nineteenth century avail to educate greater men than Plutarch's[4] heroes, three or four and twenty centuries ago. Not in time is the race progressive. Phocion, Socrates, Anaxagoras, Diogenes, are great men, but they leave no class. He who is really of their class will not be called by their name, but will be his own man, and in his turn the founder of a sect. The arts and inventions of each period are only its costume, and do not invigorate men. The harm of the improved machinery may compensate its good. Hudson and Behring accomplished so much in their fishing-boats, as to astonish Parry and Franklin,[5] whose equipment exhausted the resources of science and art. Galileo, with an opera-glass,[6] discovered a more splendid series of celestial phenomena than any one since. Columbus found the New World in an undecked boat. It is curious to see the periodical disuse and perishing of means and machinery, which were introduced with loud laudation a few years or centuries before. The great genius returns to essential man. We reckoned the improvements of the art of war among the triumphs of science, and yet Napoleon conquered Europe by the bivouac, which consisted of falling back on naked valor, and disencumbering it of all aids. The Emperor held it impossible to make a perfect army, says Las Casas,[7] "without abolishing our arms, magazines, commissaries, and carriages, until, in imitation of the Roman custom, the soldier should receive his supply of corn, grind it in his hand-mill, and bake his bread himself."

Society is a wave. The wave moves onward, but the water of which it is composed does not. The same particle does not rise from the valley to the ridge. Its unity is only phenomenal. The persons who make up a nation to-day, next year die, and their experience dies with them.

And so the reliance on Property, including the reliance on governments which protect it, is the want of self-reliance. Men have looked away from themselves and at things so long, that they have come to esteem the religious, learned, and civil institutions as guards of property, and they deprecate assaults on these, because they feel them to be assaults on property. They measure their esteem of each other by what each has, and not by what each is. But a cultivated man becomes ashamed of his property, out of new respect for his nature.

4. Graeco-Roman biographer (46?–120?), whose *Lives* became a source book for Renaissance literature, especially the Elizabethan.
5. The earlier explorers, Henry Hudson (died 1611) and Vitus Bering (Behring) (1680–1741), left their names on the map of North America; Sir William E. Parry (1790–1855) and Sir John Franklin (1786–1847) were English Arctic explorers famous in Emerson's day.
6. The "opera-glass" of Galileo (1564–1642), Italian astronomer, was the first modern refracting telescope.
7. Properly Las Cases (Comte Emmanuel Augustin Dieudonné de, 1766–1842), Napoleon's secretary during his exile on St. Helena, who compiled from the Emperor's conversations the *Mémorial de Sainte Hélène* (1818, revised 1823) which Emerson here paraphrases.

Especially he hates what he has, if he sees that it is accidental,—came to him by inheritance, or gift, or crime; then he feels that it is not having, it does not belong to him, has no root in him, and merely lies there, because no revolution or no robber takes it away. But that which a man is, does always by necessity acquire, and what the man acquires is living property, which does not wait the beck of rulers, or mobs, or revolutions, or fire, or storm, or bankruptcies, but perpetually renews itself wherever the man breathes. "Thy lot or portion of life," said the Caliph Ali,[8] "is seeking after thee; therefore be at rest from seeking after it." Our dependence on these foreign goods leads us to our slavish respect for numbers. The political parties meet in numerous conventions; the greater the concourse, and with each new uproar of announcement, The delegation from Essex! The Democrats from New Hampshire! The Whigs of Maine! the young patriot feels himself stronger than before by a new thousand of eyes and arms. In like manner the reformers summon conventions, and vote and resolve in multitude. Not so, O friends! will the God deign to enter and inhabit you, but by a method precisely the reverse. It is only as a man puts off all foreign support, and stands alone, that I see him to be strong and to prevail. He is weaker by every recruit to his banner. Is not a man better than a town? Ask nothing of men, and, in the endless mutation, thou only firm column must presently appear the upholder of all that surrounds thee. He who knows that power is inborn, that he is weak because he has looked for good out of him and elsewhere, and so perceiving, throws himself unhesitatingly on his thought, instantly rights himself, stands in the erect position, commands his limbs, works miracles; just as a man who stands on his feet is stronger than a man who stands on his head.

So use all that is called Fortune. Most men gamble with her, and gain all, and lose all, as her wheel rolls.[9] But do thou leave as unlawful these winnings, and deal with Cause and Effect, the chancellors of God. In the Will work and acquire, and thou hast chained the wheel of Chance, and shalt sit hereafter out of fear from her rotations. A political victory, a rise of rents, the recovery of your sick, or the return of your absent friend, or some other favorable event, raises your spirits, and you think good days are preparing for you. Do not believe it. Nothing can bring you peace but yourself. Nothing can bring you peace but the triumph of principles.

1841

8. Ali ibn-abu-Talib (600?–661), the fourth Moslem Caliph and son-in-law of the Prophet; his reputed sayings, surviving as proverbs, had appeared in English translation (1832).

9. The ancients sometimes pictured Fortuna as dispensing her gifts at the whim of a wheel of chance.

The Over-Soul[1]

"But souls that of his own good life partake,
He loves as his own self; dear as his eye
They are to Him: He'll never them forsake:
When they shall die, then God himself shall die:
They live, they live in blest eternity."
—HENRY MORE [2]

Space is ample, east and west,
But two cannot go abreast,
Cannot travel in it two:
Yonder masterful cuckoo
Crowds every egg out of the nest,
Quick or dead, except its own;
A spell is laid on sod and stone,
Night and Day've been tampered with,
Every quality and pith
Surcharged and sultry with a power
That works its will on age and hour.

There is a difference between one and another hour of life, in their authority and subsequent effect. Our faith comes in moments; our vice is habitual. Yet there is a depth in those brief moments which constrains us to ascribe more reality to them than to all other experiences. For this reason, the argument which is always forthcoming to silence those who conceive extraordinary hopes of man, namely, the appeal to experience, is forever invalid and vain. We give up the past to the objector, and yet we hope. He must explain this hope. We grant that human life is mean; but how did we find out that it was mean? What is the ground of this uneasiness of ours; of this old discontent? What is the universal sense of want and ignorance, but the fine innuendo by which the soul makes its enormous claim? Why do men feel that the natural history of man has never been written, but he is always leaving behind what you have said of him, and it becomes old, and books of metaphysics worthless? The philosophy of six thousand years has not searched the chambers and magazines of the soul. In its experiments there has always remained, in the last analysis, a residuum it could not resolve. Man is a stream whose source is hidden. Our being is descending into us from we know not whence. The most exact calculator has no prescience that somewhat incalculable may not balk the very next moment. I am constrained every moment to acknowledge a higher origin for events than the will I call mine.

As with events, so is it with thoughts. When I watch that flowing

1. As "Self-Reliance" broadens the social concepts which Emerson first suggested in "The American Scholar," so "The Over-Soul" intensifies the spiritual idealism of the earlier essay *Nature*. In this sense it is Emerson's most "transcendental" pronouncement. It has also been his most controversial, ever since its first appearance in *Essays* [First Series] (1841). Yet many readers who cannot accept its extreme idealism or its theological implications have found delight in the art of its expression. The present text is based on Emerson's last revision, for the edition of 1847. The second epigraph, Emerson's own composition, was added in the 1847 edition and retained by later editors.
2. English Cambridge Platonist; from his *Psychozoia Platonica* (1642), Canto II, l. 19.

river, which, out of regions I see not, pours for a season its streams into me, I see that I am a pensioner; not a cause but a surprised spectator of this ethereal water; that I desire and look up and put myself in the attitude of reception, but from some alien energy the visions come.

The Supreme Critic on the errors of the past and the present, and the only prophet of that which must be, is that great nature in which we rest, as the earth lies in the soft arms of the atmosphere; that Unity, that Over-Soul, within which every man's particular being is contained and made one with all other; that common heart, of which all sincere conversation is the worship, to which all right action is submission; that overpowering reality which confutes our tricks and talents, and constrains every one to pass for what he is, and to speak from his character, and not from his tongue, and which evermore tends to pass into our thought and hand, and become wisdom, and virtue, and power, and beauty. We live in succession, in division, in parts, in particles. Meantime within man is the soul of the whole; the wise silence; the universal beauty, to which every part and particle is equally related; the eternal ONE. And this deep power in which we exist, and whose beatitude is all accessible to us, is not only self-sufficing and perfect in every hour, but the act of seeing and the thing seen, the seer and the spectacle, the subject and the object, are one. We see the world piece by piece, as the sun, the moon, the animal, the tree; but the whole, of which these are the shining parts, is the soul. Only by the vision of that Wisdom can the horoscope of the ages be read, and by falling back on our better thoughts, by yielding to the spirit of prophecy which is innate in every man, we can know what is saith. Every man's words, who speaks from that life, must sound vain to those who do not dwell in the same thought on their own part. I dare not speak for it. My words do not carry its august sense; they fall short and cold. Only itself can inspire whom it will, and behold! their speech shall be lyrical, and sweet, and universal as the rising of the wind. Yet I desire, even by profane words, if I may not use sacred, to indicate the heaven of this deity, and to report what hints I have collected of the transcendent simplicity and energy of the Highest Law.

If we consider what happens in conversation, in reveries, in remorse, in times of passion, in surprises, in the instructions of dreams, wherein often we see ourselves in masquerade,—the droll disguises only magnifying and enhancing a real element, and forcing it on our distant notice,—we shall catch many hints that will broaden and lighten into knowledge of the secret of nature. All goes to show that the soul in man is not an organ, but animates and exercises all the organs; is not a function, like the power of memory, of calculation, of comparison, but uses these as hands and feet; is not a faculty, but a light; is not the intellect or the will, but the master of the intellect and the will; is the background of our being, in which they lie,—an immensity not possessed and that cannot be possessed. From within or from behind, a light shines through us upon things, and makes us aware that we are nothing, but the light is all. A man is the façade of a temple wherein all wisdom and all good abide. What we commonly call man, the eating, drinking, planting, counting man, does not, as we know him, represent himself, but misrepresents himself. Him we do not respect, but the soul, whose organ he is, would he let it appear through his action, would make our knees bend. When it breathes through his intellect, it is genius; when it breathes through his will, it is virtue; when it flows through his affection, it is love. And the blindness of the intellect begins, when it would be something of itself. The weakness of the will begins when the individual would be something of himself. All reform aims, in some one particular, to let the soul have its way through us; in other words, to engage us to obey.

Of this pure nature every man is at some time sensible. Language cannot paint it with his colors. It is too subtile. It is undefinable, unmeasurable, but we know that it pervades and contains us. We know that all spiritual being is in man. A wise old proverb says, "God comes to see us without bell";[3] that is, as there is no screen or ceiling between our heads and the infinite heavens, so is there no bar or wall in the soul where man, the effect, ceases, and God, the cause, begins. The walls are taken away. We lie open on one side to the deeps of spiritual nature, to the attributes of God. Justice we see and know, Love, Freedom, Power. These natures no man ever got above, but they tower over us, and most in the moment when our interests tempt us to wound them.

The sovereignty of this nature whereof we speak is made known by its independency of those limitations which circumscribe us on every hand. The soul circumscribes all things. As I have said, it contradicts all experience. In like manner it abolishes time and space. The influence of the senses has, in most men, overpowered the mind to that degree, that the walls of time and space have come to look real and insurmountable; and to speak with levity of these limits is, in the world, the sign of insanity. Yet time and space are but inverse measures of the force of the soul. The spirit sports with time,—

> "Can crowd eternity into an hour,
> Or stretch an hour to eternity."[4]

We are often made to feel that there is another youth and age than that which is measured from the year of our natural birth. Some

3. Among the "Spanish proverbs" listed in Emerson's *Journals*, Vol. II, p. 480 (noted in the Centenary Edition, Vol. II, p. 429).

4. From the poem "Auguries of Innocence," by William Blake (1757–1827).

thoughts always find us young, and keep us so. Such a thought is the love of the universal and eternal beauty. Every man parts from that contemplation with the feeling that it rather belongs to ages than to mortal life. The least activity of the intellectual powers redeems us in a degree from the conditions of time. In sickness, in languor, give us a strain of poetry, or a profound sentence, and we are refreshed; or produce a volume of Plato, or Shakspeare, or remind us of their names, and instantly we come into a feeling of longevity. See how the deep divine thought reduces centuries, and millenniums, and makes itself present through all ages. Is the teaching of Christ less effective now than it was when first his mouth was opened? The emphasis of facts and persons in my thought has nothing to do with time. And so, always, the soul's scale is one; the scale of the senses and the understanding is another. Before the revelations of the soul, Time, Space, and Nature shrink away. In common speech, we refer all things to time, as we habitually refer the immensely sundered stars to one concave sphere. And so we say that the Judgment is distant or near, that the Millennium approaches,[5] that a day of certain political, moral, social reforms is at hand, and the like, when we mean, that, in the nature of things, one of the facts we contemplate is external and fugitive, and the other is permanent and connate with the soul. The things we now esteem fixed shall, one by one, detach themselves, like ripe fruit, from our experience, and fall. The wind shall blow them none knows whither.[6] The landscape, the figures, Boston, London, are facts as fugitive as any institution past, or any whiff of mist or smoke, and so is society, and so is the world. The soul looketh steadily forwards, creating a world before her, leaving worlds behind her. She has no dates, nor rites, nor persons, nor specialties, nor men. The soul knows only the soul; the web of events is the flowing robe in which she is clothed.

After its own law and not by arithmetic is the rate of its progress to be computed. The soul's advances are not made by gradation, such as can be represented by motion in a straight line; but rather by ascension of state, such as can be represented by metamorphosis,— from the egg to the worm, from the worm to the fly. The growths of genius are of a certain *total* character, that does not advance the elect individual first over John, then Adam, then Richard, and give to each the pain of discovered inferiority, but by every throe of growth the man expands there where he works, passing, at each pulsation, classes, populations, of men. With each divine impulse the mind rends the thin rinds of the visible and finite, and comes out into eternity, and inspires and expires its air. It converses with truths that have always been spoken in the world, and becomes conscious of a

5. William Miller, founder of the Millerites, was then predicting the second advent of Christ for 1843.
6. *Cf.* John iii: 8.

closer sympathy with Zeno[7] and Arrian,[8] than with persons in the house.

This is the law of moral and of mental gain. The simple rise as by specific levity,[9] not into a particular virtue, but into the region of all the virtues. They are in the spirit which contains them all. The soul requires purity, but purity is not it; requires justice, but justice is not that; requires beneficence, but is somewhat better; so that there is a kind of descent and accommodation felt when we leave speaking of moral nature to urge a virtue which it enjoins. To the well-born child, all the virtues are natural, and not painfully acquired. Speak to his heart, and the man becomes suddenly virtuous.

Within the same sentiment is the germ of intellectual growth, which obeys the same law. Those who are capable of humility, of justice, of love, of aspiration, stand already on a platform that commands the sciences and arts, speech and poetry, action and grace. For whoso dwells in this moral beatitude already anticipates those special powers which men prize so highly. The lover has no talent, no skill, which passes for quite nothing with his enamored maiden, however little she may possess of related faculty; and the heart which abandons itself to the Supreme Mind finds itself related to all its works, and will travel a royal road to particular knowledges and powers. In ascending to this primary and aboriginal sentiment, we have come from our remote station on the circumference instantaneously to the centre of the world, where, as in the closet of God, we see causes, and anticipate the universe, which is but a slow effect.

One mode of the divine teaching is the incarnation of the spirit in a form,—in forms, like my own. I live in society; with persons who answer to thoughts in my own mind, or express a certain obedience to the great instincts to which I live. I see its presence to them. I am certified of a common nature; and these other souls, these separated selves, draw me as nothing else can. They stir in me the new emotions we call passion; of love, hatred, fear, admiration, pity; thence come conversation, competition, persuasion, cities, and war. Persons are supplementary to the primary teaching of the soul. In youth we are mad for persons. Childhood and youth see all the world in them. But the larger experience of man discovers the identical nature appearing through them all. Persons themselves acquaint us with the impersonal. In all conversation between two persons, tacit reference is made, as to a third party, to a common nature. That third party or common nature is not social; it is impersonal; is God. And so in groups where debate is earnest, and especially on high questions, the company become aware that the thought rises to an equal level

7. Founder of the Stoic philosophy.
8. Greek historian (died 180 A.D.), whose *Discourses* and *Enchiridion* are the source of our knowledge of the philosophy of his teacher Epictetus, a Stoic.
9. *I.e.*, lightness by nature; a coinage contrasting with "specific gravity."

in all bosoms, that all have a spiritual property in what was said, as well as the sayer. They all become wiser than they were. It arches over them like a temple, this unity of thought in which every heart beats with nobler sense of power and duty, and thinks and acts with unusual solemnity. All are conscious of attaining to a higher self-possession. It shines for all. There is a certain wisdom of humanity which is common to the greatest men with the lowest, and which our ordinary education often labors to silence and obstruct. The mind is one, and the best minds, who love truth for its own sake, think much less of property in truth. They accept it thankfully everywhere, and do not label or stamp it with any man's name, for it is theirs long beforehand, and from eternity. The learned and the studious of thought have no monopoly of wisdom. Their violence of direction in some degree disqualifies them to think truly. We owe many valuable observations to people who are not very acute or profound, and who say the thing without effort, which we want and have long been hunting in vain. The action of the soul is oftener in that which is felt and left unsaid, than in that which is said in any conversation. It broods over every society, and they unconsciously seek for it in each other. We know better than we do. We do not yet possess ourselves, and we know at the same time that we are much more. I feel the same truth how often in my trivial conversation with my neighbours, that somewhat higher in each of us overlooks this by-play, and Jove nods to Jove from behind each of us.

Men descend to meet. In their habitual and mean service to the world, for which they forsake their native nobleness, they resemble those Arabian sheiks, who dwell in mean houses, and affect an external poverty, to escape the rapacity of the Pacha,[1] and reserve all their display of wealth for their interior and guarded retirements.

As it is present in all persons, so it is in every period of life. It is adult already in the infant man. In my dealing with my child, my Latin and Greek, my accomplishments and my money stead me nothing; but as much soul as I have avails. If I am wilful, he sets his will against mine, one for one, and leaves me, if I please, the degradation of beating him by my superiority of strength. But if I renounce my will, and act for the soul, setting that up as umpire between us two, out of his young eyes looks the same soul; he reveres and loves with me.

The soul is the perceiver and revealer of truth. We know truth when we see it, let skeptic and scoffer say what they choose. Foolish people ask you, when you have spoken what they do not wish to hear, "How do you know it is truth, and not an error of your own?" We know truth when we see it, from opinion, as we know when we are awake that we are awake. It was a grand sentence of Emanuel Swe-

1. The Turkish governor, who levied taxes upon these Arabs.

denborg,[2] which would alone indicate the greatness of that man's perception,—"It is no proof of a man's understanding to be able to affirm whatever he pleases; but to be able to discern that what is true is true, and that what is false is false, this is the mark and character of intelligence." In the book I read, the good thought returns to me, as every truth will, the image of the whole soul. To the bad thought which I find in it, the same soul becomes a discerning, separating sword, and lops it away. We are wiser than we know. If we will not interfere with our thought, but will act entirely, or see how the thing stands in God, we know the particular thing, and every thing, and every man. For the Maker of all things and all persons stands behind us, and casts his dread omniscience through us over things.

But beyond this recognition of its own in particular passages of the individual's experience, it also reveals truth. And here we should seek to reinforce ourselves by its very presence, and to speak with a worthier, loftier strain of that advent. For the soul's communication of truth is the highest event in nature, since it then does not give somewhat from itself, but it gives itself, or passes into and becomes that man whom it enlightens; or, in proportion to that truth he receives, it takes him to itself.

We distinguish the announcements of the soul, its manifestations of its own nature, by the term *Revelation*. These are always attended by the emotion of the sublime. For this communication is an influx of the Divine mind into our mind. It is an ebb of the individual rivulet before the flowing surges of the sea of life. Every distinct apprehension of this central commandment agitates men with awe and delight. A thrill passes through all men at the reception of new truth, or at the performance of a great action, which comes out of the heart of nature. In these communications, the power to see is not separated from the will to do, but the insight proceeds from obedience, and the obedience proceeds from a joyful perception. Every moment when the individual feels himself invaded by it is memorable. By the necessity of our constitution, a certain enthusiasm attends the individual's consciousness of that divine presence. The character and duration of this enthusiasm varies with the state of the individual, from an ecstasy and trance and prophetic inspiration,—which is its rarer appearance,—to the faintest glow of virtuous emotion, in which form it warms, like our household fires, all the families and associations of men, and makes society possible. A certain tendency to insanity has always attended the opening of the religious sense in men, as if they had been "blasted with excess of light."[3] The trances of Socrates, the "union" of Plotinus, the vision of Porphyry,[4] the con-

2. Swedish religious thinker who later became Emerson's example for "The Mystic" in *Representative Men*.
3. Thomas Gray (1716–1771), "The Progress of Poesy," III. ii, l. 7.
4. Plotinus (205?–270?), principal formulator of Neo-platonic philosophy, emphasized the soul's capacity for mys-

version of Paul,[5] the aurora of Behmen,[6] the convulsions of George Fox and his Quakers, the illumination of Swedenborg,[7] are of this kind. What was in the case of these remarkable persons a ravishment, has, in innumerable instances in common life, been exhibited in less striking manner. Everywhere the history of religion betrays a tendency to enthusiasm. The rapture of the Moravian and Quietist; the opening of the eternal sense of the Word, in the language of the New Jerusalem Church; the *revival* of the Calvinistic churches; the *experiences* of the Methodists, are varying forms of that shudder of awe and delight with which the individual soul always mingles with the universal soul.

The nature of these revelations is the same; they are perceptions of the absolute law. They are solutions of the soul's own questions. They do not answer the questions which the understanding asks. The soul answers never by words, but by the thing itself that is inquired after.

Revelation is the disclosure of the soul. The popular notion of a revelation is, that it is a telling of fortunes. In past oracles of the soul, the understanding seeks to find answers to sensual questions, and undertakes to tell from God how long men shall exist, what their hands shall do, and who shall be their company, adding names, and dates, and places. But we must pick no locks. We must check this low curiosity. An answer in words is delusive; it is really no answer to the questions you ask. Do not require a description of the countries towards which you sail. The description does not describe them to you, and to-morrow you arrive there, and know them by inhabiting them. Men ask concerning the immortality of the soul, the employments of heaven, the state of the sinner, and so forth. They even dream that Jesus has left replies to precisely these interrogatories. Never a moment did that sublime spirit speak in their *patois*.[8] To truth, justice, love, the attributes of the soul, the idea of immutableness is essentially associated. Jesus, living in these moral sentiments, heedless of sensual fortunes, heeding only the manifestations of these, never made the separation of the idea of duration from the essence of these attributes, nor uttered a syllable concerning the duration of the soul. It was left to his disciples to sever duration from the moral elements, and to teach the immortality of the soul as a doctrine, and maintain it by evidences. The moment the doctrine of the im-

tical "unification" with the Highest. Porphyry (233–304?), his visionary pupil, preserved Plotinus' teachings.

5. See Paul's miraculous conversion (Acts ix: 1–18).

6. Jakob Böhme (1575–1624), German theosophist, whose *Aurora, oder die Morgenröte im Aufgang,* was banned as heretical.

7. These mystics and their followers experienced trances, tremors, and illumina-tions which Emerson compares with various manifestations later named. The Moravians, originally fifteenth-century Bohemian Hussites, were evangelical mystics; while the Quietists, Catholic dissenters in the seventeenth century, sought the mystical union by passive selflessness.

8. Literally "dialect"; here signifying limited communication.

mortality is separately taught, man is already fallen.[9] In the flowing of love, in the adoration of humility, there is no question of continuance. No inspired man ever asks this question, or condescends to these evidences. For the soul is true to itself, and the man in whom it is shed abroad cannot wander from the present, which is infinite, to a future which would be finite.

These questions which we lust to ask about the future are a confession of sin. God has no answer for them. No answer in words can reply to a question of things. It is not in an arbitrary "decree of God," but in the nature of man, that a veil shuts down on the facts of to-morrow; for the soul will not have us read any other cipher than that of cause and effect. By this veil, which curtains events, it instructs the children of men to live in to-day. The only mode of obtaining an answer to these questions of the senses is to forego all low curiosity, and, accepting the tide of being which floats us into the secret of nature, work and live, work and live, and all unawares the advancing soul has built and forged for itself a new condition, and the question and the answer are one.

By the same fire, vital, consecrating, celestial, which burns until it shall dissolve all things into the waves and surges of an ocean of light, we see and know each other, and what spirit each is of. Who can tell the grounds of his knowledge of the character of the several individuals in his circle of friends? No man. Yet their acts and words do not disappoint him. In that man, though he knew no ill of him, he put no trust. In that other, though they had seldom met, authentic signs had yet passed, to signify that he might be trusted as one who had an interest in his own character. We know each other very well,—which of us has been just to himself, and whether that which we teach or behold is only an aspiration, or is our honest effort also.

We are all discerners of spirits. That diagnosis lies aloft in our life or unconscious power. The intercourse of society,—its trade, its religion, its friendships, its quarrels,—is one wide, judicial investigation of character. In full court, or in small committee, or confronted face to face, accuser and accused, men offer themselves to be judged. Against their will they exhibit those decisive trifles by which character is read. But who judges? and what? Not our understanding. We do not read them by learning or craft. No; the wisdom of the wise man consists herein, that he does not judge them; he lets them judge themselves, and merely reads and records their own verdict.

By virtue of this inevitable nature, private will is overpowered, and, maugre our efforts or our imperfections, your genius will speak from you, and mine from me. That which we are, we shall teach, not voluntarily but involuntarily. Thoughts come into our minds by avenues which we never left open, and thoughts go out of our minds

---

9. *Cf.* the New England Puritan tradition of cleavage between the mortal earth of "fallen man" and the heaven of the "saved."

through avenues which we never voluntarily opened. Character teaches over our head. The infallible index of true progress is found in the tone the man takes. Neither his age, nor his breeding, nor company, nor books, nor actions, nor talents, nor all together, can hinder him from being deferential to a higher spirit than his own. If he have not found his home in God, his manners, his forms of speech, the turn of his sentences, the build, shall I say, of all his opinions will involuntarily confess it, let him brave it out how he will. If he have found his centre, the Deity will shine through him, through all the disguises of ignorance, of ungenial temperament, of unfavorable circumstance. The tone of seeking is one, and the tone of having is another.

The great distinction between teachers sacred or literary,—between poets like Herbert, and poets like Pope,[1]—between philosophers like Spinoza, Kant, and Coleridge, and philosophers like Locke, Paley, Mackintosh, and Stewart,[2]—between men of the world who are reckoned accomplished talkers, and here and there a fervent mystic, prophesying, half insane under the infinitude of his thought, —is that one class speak *from within*, or from experience, as parties and possessors of the fact; and the other class, *from without*, as spectators merely, or perhaps as acquainted with the fact on the evidence of third persons. It is of no use to preach to me from without. I can do that too easily myself. Jesus speaks always from within, and in a degree that transcends all others. In that is the miracle. I believe beforehand that it ought so to be. All men stand continually in the expectation of the appearance of such a teacher. But if a man do not speak from within the veil, where the word is one with that it tells of, let him lowly confess it.

The same Omniscience flows into the intellect, and makes what we call genius. Much of the wisdom of the world is not wisdom, and the most illuminated class of men are no doubt superior to literary fame, and are not writers. Among the multitude of scholars and authors, we feel no hallowing presence; we are sensible of a knack and skill rather than of inspiration; they have a light, and know not whence it comes, and call it their own; their talent is some exaggerated faculty, some overgrown member, so that their strength is a disease. In these instances the intellectual gifts do not make the impression of virtue, but almost of vice; and we feel that a man's talents stand in the way of his advancement in truth. But genius is religious.

1. George Herbert (1593–1633), whose poems of religious mysticism had recently been praised by Coleridge, is contrasted with Alexander Pope (1688–1744), whose satires were pointed with worldly sophistication.
2. Spinoza employed the Cartesian metaphysics to expound his pantheism; Kant was the German founder of idealism; Coleridge's writings had popularized transcendental concepts. These are contrasted with the empiricism of Locke; with the utilitarianism of William Paley (1743–1805), who in *Natural Theology* (1802) "proved" the existence of God by the argument from design in nature; with the rationalism of the contemporary historian Sir James Mackintosh (1765–1832); and with the materialism of the "Common-Sense" Scottish philosopher Dugald Stewart (1753–1828).

It is a larger imbibing of the common heart. It is not anomalous, but more like and not less like other men. There is, in all great poets, a wisdom of humanity which is superior to any talents they exercise. The author, the wit, the partisan, the fine gentleman, does not take place of the man. Humanity shines in Homer, in Chaucer, in Spenser, in Shakspeare, in Milton. They are content with truth. They use the positive degree. They seem frigid and phlegmatic to those who have been spiced with the frantic passion and violent coloring of inferior, but popular writers. For they are poets by the free course which they allow to the informing soul, which through their eyes beholds again, and blesses the things which it hath made. The soul is superior to its knowledge; wiser than any of its works. The great poet makes us feel our own wealth, and then we think less of his compositions. His best communication to our mind is to teach us to despise all he has done. Shakspeare carries us to such a lofty strain of intelligent activity, as to suggest a wealth which beggars his own; and we then feel that the splendid works which he has created, and which in other hours we extol as a sort of self-existent poetry, take no stronger hold of real nature than the shadow of a passing traveller on the rock. The inspiration which uttered itself in Hamlet and Lear could utter things as good from day to day for ever. Why, then, should I make account of Hamlet and Lear, as if we had not the soul from which they fell as syllables from the tongue?

This energy does not descend into individual life on any other condition than entire possession. It comes to the lowly and simple; it comes to whomsoever will put off what is foreign and proud; it comes as insight; it comes as serenity and grandeur. When we see those whom it inhabits, we are apprised of new degrees of greatness. From that inspiration the man comes back with a changed tone. He does not talk with men with an eye to their opinion. He tries them. It requires of us to be plain and true. The vain traveller attempts to embellish his life by quoting my lord, and the prince, and the countess, who thus said or did to *him*. The ambitious vulgar show you their spoons, and brooches, and rings, and preserve their cards and compliments. The more cultivated, in their account of their own experience, cull out the pleasing, poetic circumstance,—the visit to Rome, the man of genius they saw, the brilliant friend they know; still further on, perhaps, the gorgeous landscape, the mountain lights, the mountain thoughts, they enjoyed yesterday,—and so seek to throw a romantic color over their life. But the soul that ascends to worship the great God is plain and true; has no rose-color, no fine friends, no chivalry, no adventures; does not want admiration; dwells in the hour that now is, in the earnest experience of the common day,—by reason of the present moment and the mere trifle having become porous to thought, and bibulous of the sea of light.

Converse with a mind that is grandly simple, and literature looks like word-catching. The simplest utterances are worthiest to be written, yet are they so cheap, and so things of course, that, in the infinite riches of the soul, it is like gathering a few pebbles off the ground, or bottling a little air in a phial, when the whole earth and the whole atmosphere are ours. Nothing can pass there, or make you one of the circle, but the casting aside your trappings, and dealing man to man in naked truth, plain confession, and omniscient affirmation.

Souls such as these treat you as gods would; walk as gods in the earth, accepting without any admiration your wit, your bounty, your virtue even,—say rather your act of duty, for your virtue they own as their proper blood, royal as themselves, and over-royal, and the father of the gods. But what rebuke their plain fraternal bearing casts on the mutual flattery with which authors solace each other and wound themselves! These flatter not. I do not wonder that these men go to see Cromwell, and Christina,[3] and Charles the Second, and James the First, and the Grand Turk.[4] For they are, in their own elevation, the fellows of kings, and must feel the servile tone of conversation in the world. They must always be a godsend to princes, for they confront them, a king to a king, without ducking or concession, and give a high nature the refreshment and satisfaction of resistance, of plain humanity, of even companionship, and of new ideas. They leave them wiser and superior men. Souls like these make us feel that sincerity is more excellent than flattery. Deal so plainly with man and woman, as to constrain the utmost sincerity, and destroy all hope of trifling with you. It is the highest compliment you can pay. Their "highest praising," said Milton, "is not flattery, and their plainest advice is a kind of praising."[5]

Ineffable is the union of man and God in every act of the soul. The simplest person, who in his integrity worships God, becomes God; yet for ever and ever the influx of this better and universal self is new and unsearchable. It inspires awe and astonishment. How dear, how soothing to man, arises the idea of God, peopling the lonely place, effacing the scars of our mistakes and disappointments! When we have broken our god of tradition, and ceased from our god of rhetoric, then may God fire the heart with his presence. It is the doubling of the heart itself, nay, the infinite enlargement of the heart with a power of growth to a new infinity on every side. It inspires in man an infallible trust. He has not the conviction, but the sight, that the best is the true, and may in that thought easily dismiss all particular uncertainties and fears, and adjourn to the

3. Queen of Sweden. Descartes was notable among many writers and artists who enjoyed the hospitality of her court.
4. Then a familiar reference to the former magnificence of the Turkish sultans.
5. Milton, *Areopagitica* (1644), paragraph 4, sentence 2.

sure revelation of time, the solution of his private riddles. He is sure that his welfare is dear to the heart of being. In the presence of law to his mind, he is overflowed with a reliance so universal, that it sweeps away all cherished hopes and the most stable projects of mortal condition in its flood. He believes that he cannot escape from his good. The things that are really for thee gravitate to thee. You are running to seek your friend. Let your feet run, but your mind need not. If you do not find him, will you not acquiesce that it is best you should not find him? for there is a power, which, as it is in you, is in him also, and could therefore very well bring you together, if it were for the best. You are preparing with eagerness to go and render a service to which your talent and your taste invite you, the love of men and the hope of fame. Has it not occurred to you, that you have no right to go, unless you are equally willing to be prevented from going?[6] O, believe, as thou livest, that every sound that is spoken over the round world, which thou oughtest to hear, will vibrate on thine ear! Every proverb, every book, every byword that belongs to thee for aid or comfort, shall surely come home through open or winding passages. Every friend whom not thy fantastic will, but the great and tender heart in thee craveth, shall lock thee in his embrace. And this, because the heart in thee is the heart of all; not a valve, not a wall, not an intersection is there anywhere in nature, but one blood rolls uninterruptedly an endless circulation through all men, as the water of the globe is all one sea, and, truly seen, its tide is one.

Let man, then, learn the revelation of all nature and all thought to his heart; this, namely; that the Highest dwells with him; that the sources of nature are in his own mind, if the sentiment of duty is there. But if he would know what the great God speaketh, he must "go into his closet and shut the door,"[7] as Jesus said. God will not make himself manifest to cowards. He must greatly listen to himself, withdrawing himself from all the accents of other men's devotion. Even their prayers are hurtful to him, until he have made his own. Our religion vulgarly stands on numbers of believers. Whenever the appeal is made—no matter how indirectly—to numbers, proclamation is then and there made, that religion is not. He that finds God a sweet, enveloping thought to him never counts his company. When I sit in that presence, who shall dare to come in? When I rest in perfect humility, when I burn with pure love, what can Calvin[8] or Swedenborg say?

6. The sentence appears as Emerson's journal entry on the eve of his "Divinity School Address" (July 15, 1838); the entire paragraph was developed in a sermon the following winter.
7. *Cf.* Matthew vi: 6.

8. John Calvin (1509–1564), whose theology supported the authoritarianism of the Puritans, is contrasted with the mystical Swedenborg; see the following paragraph.

It makes no difference whether the appeal is to numbers or to one. The faith that stands on authority is not faith. The reliance on authority measures the decline of religion, the withdrawal of the soul. The position men have given to Jesus, now for many centuries of history, is a position of authority. It characterizes themselves. It cannot alter the eternal facts. Great is the soul, and plain. It is no flatterer, it is no follower; it never appeals from itself. It believes in itself. Before the immense possibilities of man, all mere experience, all past biography, however spotless and sainted, shrinks away. Before that heaven which our presentiments foreshow us, we cannot easily praise any form of life we have seen or read of. We not only affirm that we have few great men, but, absolutely speaking, that we have none; that we have no history, no record of any character or mode of living, that entirely contents us. The saints and demigods whom history worships we are constrained to accept with a grain of allowance. Though in our lonely hours we draw a new strength out of their memory, yet, pressed on our attention, as they are by the thoughtless and customary, they fatigue and invade. The soul gives itself, alone, original, and pure, to the Lonely, Original, and Pure, who, on that condition, gladly inhabits, leads, and speaks through it. Then is it glad, young, and nimble. It is not wise, but it sees through all things. It is not called religious, but it is innocent. It calls the light its own, and feels that the grass grows and the stone falls by a law inferior to, and dependent on, its nature. Behold, it saith, I am born into the great, the universal mind. I, the imperfect, adore my own Perfect. I am somehow receptive of the great soul, and thereby I do overlook the sun and the stars, and feel them to be the fair accidents and effects which change and pass. More and more the surges of everlasting nature enter into me, and I become public and human in my regards and actions. So come I to live in thoughts, and act with energies, which are immortal. Thus revering the soul, and learning, as the ancient said, that "its beauty is immense," man will come to see that the world is the perennial miracle which the soul worketh, and be less astonished at particular wonders; he will learn that there is no profane history; that all history is sacred; that the universe is represented in an atom, in a moment of time. He will weave no longer a spotted life of shreds and patches,[9] but he will live with a divine unity. He will cease from what is base and frivolous in his life, and be content with all places and with any service he can render. He will calmly front the morrow in the negligency of that trust which carries God with it and so hath already the whole future in the bottom of the heart.

1841

9. *Cf.* Shakespeare, *Hamlet*, Act III, Scene 4, l. 102.

Experience[1]

The lords of life, the lords of life,—
I saw them pass,
In their own guise,
Like and unlike,
Portly and grim,
Use and Surprise,
Surface and Dream,
Succession swift, and spectral Wrong,
Temperament without a tongue,
And the inventor of the game
Omnipresent without name;—
Some to see, some to be guessed.
They marched from east to west:
Little man, least of all,
Among the legs of his guardians tall,
Walked about with puzzled look:—
Him by the hand dear Nature took;
Dearest Nature, strong and kind,
Whispered, "Darling, never mind!
To-morrow they will wear another face,
The founder thou! these are thy race!"

Where do we find ourselves? In a series of which we do not know
the extremes,[2] and believe that it has none. We wake and find ourselves on a stair; there are stairs below us, which we seem to have
ascended; there are stairs above us, many a one, which go upward and
out of sight. But the Genius[3] which according to the old belief stands
at the door by which we enter, and gives us the lethe to drink, that
we may tell no tales, mixed the cup too strongly, and we cannot shake
off the lethargy now at noonday. Sleep lingers all our lifetime about
our eyes, as night hovers all day in the boughs of the fir-tree. All
things swim and glitter. Our life is not so much threatened as our perception. Ghostlike we glide through nature, and should not know
our place again. Did our birth fall in some fit of indigence and frugality in nature, that she was so sparing of her fire and so liberal of

1. The death of Waldo Emerson, not yet
six, in 1842, may have compelled his
father to explore the nature of experience. The result is a difficult essay,
which has not been a popular favorite,
but which sturdy minds have repeatedly
approved as original, bold, and brilliant.
That the essay should be toughly reasoned and difficult reading is inherent in
its purpose: to define the ultimate
reality in our earthly experience, enmeshed, as it is, in a web of illusions,
moods, and seemingly blind chance.
Emerson's austere reference to his son's
death, repellent to some critics, actually
demonstrates the disciplined character
of the essay; for the man Emerson, as
contrasted with the philosopher, was an
anguished man, as revealed in his journal and in the poem "Threnody." "I
have set my heart on honesty in this
chapter," he wrote in the journal, and
echoed the words here. Just as he had
found an abiding unity in the spiritual
universe, so there must be, in the world

of concrete phenomena, some harmonious unity of experience, if only in the
selfhood of the individual daily confronted with the welter of cash and
plowshares and bread and begetting. Not
having been compiled from lectures, this
writing gives more the impression of
homogeneous construction than most of
Emerson's essays. Included in *Essays:
Second Series* (1844), it also appeared
in the revised *Essays* (1850), on which
the present text is based. Emerson wrote
the poem later than the essay (Centenary
Edition, Vol. III, p. 303). Compare the
"lords of life" passage, in the third paragraph from the end of the essay, with
the epigraph.
2. In mathematics, the initial and the
ultimate terms of a series or progression,
which therefore limit its finite extension.
3. In classical mythology, a personal
guardian spirit (Greek *dæmon*) assigned
to each person at birth, whose first gift
was a cup of the waters of forgetfulness
(here "lethe").

her earth that it appears to us that we lack the affirmative principle, and though we have health and reason, yet we have no superfluity of spirit for new creation? We have enough to live and bring the year about, but not an ounce to impart or to invest. Ah that our Genius were a little more of a genius! We are like millers on the lower levels of a stream, when the factories above them have exhausted the water. We too fancy that the upper people must have raised their dams.

If any of us knew what we were doing, or where we are going, then when we think we best know! We do not know to-day whether we are busy or idle. In times when we thought ourselves indolent, we have afterwards discovered that much was accomplished and much was begun in us. All our days are so unprofitable while they pass, that 't is wonderful where or when we ever got anything of this which we call wisdom, poetry, virtue. We never got it on any dated calendar day. Some heavenly days must have been intercalated somewhere, like those that Hermes won with dice of the Moon, that Osiris might be born.[4] It is said all martyrdoms looked mean when they were suffered. Every ship is a romantic object, except that we sail in. Embark, and the romance quits our vessel and hangs on every other sail in the horizon. Our life looks trivial, and we shun to record it. Men seem to have learned of the horizon the art of perpetual retreating and reference. "Yonder uplands are rich pasturage, and my neighbor has fertile meadow, but my field," says the querulous farmer, "only holds the world together." I quote another man's saying; unluckily that other withdraws himself in the same way, and quotes me. 'T is the trick of nature thus to degrade to-day; a good deal of buzz, and somewhere a result slipped magically in. Every roof is agreeable to the eye until it is lifted; then we find tragedy and moaning women and hard-eyed husbands and deluges of lethe, and the men ask, "What's the news?" as if the old were so bad. How many individuals can we count in society? how many actions? how many opinions? So much of our time is preparation, so much is routine, and so much retrospect, that the pith of each man's genius contracts itself to a very few hours. The history of literature—take the net result of Tiraboschi, Warton, or Schlegel[5]—is a sum of very few ideas and of very few original tales; all the rest being variation of these. So in this great society wide lying around us, a critical analysis would find very few spontaneous actions. It is almost all custom and gross sense. There are even few opinions, and these seem organic in the

4. Cronus had decreed that Rhea, his wife, should not be delivered of her lover's child on any day; but Hermes, by defeating the Moon at dice, won five extra days for the calendar, on the first of which Rhea bore Osiris, the greatest Egyptian divinity.
5. Girolamo Tiraboschi (1731–1794)

wrote an encyclopedic history of Italian literature; Thomas Warton (1728–1790), in a learned history of earlier British poetry, shook the authority of the reigning classicists; August Wilhelm von Schlegel (1767–1845) wrote voluminously of oriental and European literature.

speakers, and do not disturb the universal necessity.

What opium is instilled into all disaster! It shows formidable as we approach it, but there is at last no rough rasping friction, but the most slippery sliding surfaces; we fall soft on a thought; *Ate Dea*[6] is gentle,—

> "Over men's heads walking aloft,
> With tender feet treading so soft."

People grieve and bemoan themselves, but it is not half so bad with them as they say. There are moods in which we court suffering, in the hope that here at least we shall find reality, sharp peaks and edges of truth. But it turns out to be scene-painting and counterfeit. The only thing grief has taught me is to know how shallow it is. That, like all the rest, plays about the surface, and never introduces me into the reality, for contact with which we would even pay the costly price of sons and lovers. Was it Boscovich who found out that bodies never come in contact?[7] Well, souls never touch their objects. An innavigable sea washes with silent waves between us and the things we aim at and converse with. Grief too will make us idealists. In the death of my son, now more than two years ago, I seem to have lost a beautiful estate,—no more. I cannot get it nearer to me. If to-morrow I should be informed of the bankruptcy of my principal debtors, the loss of my property would be a great inconvenience to me, perhaps, for many years; but it would leave me as it found me, —neither better nor worse. So is it with this calamity; it does not touch me; something which I fancied was a part of me, which could not be torn away without tearing me nor enlarged without enriching me, falls off from me and leaves no scar. It was caducous. I grieve that grief can teach me nothing, nor carry me one step into real nature. The Indian who was laid under a curse that the wind should not blow on him, nor water flow to him, nor fire burn him,[8] is a type of us all. The dearest events are summer-rain, and we the Para[9] coats that shed every drop. Nothing is left us now but death. We look to that with a grim satisfaction, saying, There at least is reality that will not dodge us.

I take this evanescence and lubricity of all objects, which lets them slip through our fingers then when we clutch hardest, to be the most unhandsome part of our condition. Nature does not like to be observed, and likes that we should be her fools and playmates. We may have the sphere for our cricket-ball, but not a berry for

6. Goddess Ate; The Greek divinity of rashness, hence "disaster." The following verses are not identified.
7. *I.e.*, according to the molecular theory of matter, advanced by Ruggiero Guiseppe Boscovich (1711–1787), Italian apostle of Newtonian physics.
8. *Cf.* "The *Curse of Kehama*" (1810) by Robert Southey, English poet.
9. Abbreviation for "Para rubber," then coming into use.

our philosophy. Direct strokes she never gave us power to make; all our blows glance, all our hits are accidents. Our relations to each other are oblique and casual.

Dream delivers us to dream, and there is no end to illusion.[1] Life is a train of moods like a string of beads, and as we pass through them they prove to be many-colored lenses which paint the world their own hue, and each shows only what lies in its focus. From the mountain you see the mountain. We animate what we can, and we see only what we animate. Nature and books belong to the eyes that see them. It depends on the mood of the man whether he shall see the sunset or the fine poem. There are always sunsets, and there is always genius; but only a few hours so serene that we can relish nature or criticism. The more or less depends on structure or temperament. Temperament is the iron wire on which the beads are strung. Of what use is fortune or talent to a cold and defective nature? Who cares what sensibility or discrimination a man has at some time shown, if he falls asleep in his chair? or if he laugh and giggle? or if he apologize? or is infected with egotism? or thinks of his dollar? or cannot go by food? or has gotten a child in his boyhood? Of what use is genius, if the organ is too convex or too concave and cannot find a focal distance within the actual horizon of human life? Of what use, if the brain is too cold or too hot, and the man does not care enough for results to stimulate him to experiment, and hold him up in it? or if the web is too finely woven, too irritable by pleasure and pain, so that life stagnates from too much reception without due outlet? Of what use to make heroic vows of amendment, if the same old law-breaker is to keep them? What cheer can the religious sentiment yield, when that is suspected to be secretly dependent on the seasons of the year and the state of the blood? I knew a witty physician[2] who found the creed in the biliary duct, and used to affirm that if there was disease in the liver, the man became a Calvinist, and if that organ was sound, he became a Unitarian. Very mortifying is the reluctant experience that some unfriendly excess or imbecility neutralizes the promise of genius. We see young men who owe us a new world, so readily and lavishly they promise, but they never acquit the debt; they die young and dodge the account; or if they live they lose themselves in the crowd.

Temperament also enters fully into the system of illusions and shuts us in a prison of glass which we cannot see. There is an optical illusion about every person we meet. In truth they are all creatures of given temperament, which will appear in a given character, whose

---

1. *Cf.* "Dream" in the introductory poem. Emerson associated "illusion" with the concept of "Maya" in the ancient scriptures of India. See "Illusions," in *The Conduct of Life*.
2. Dr. Gamaliel Bradford (Centenary Edition, Vol. III, p. 305).

boundaries they will never pass; but we look at them, they seem alive, and we presume there is impulse in them. In the moment it seems impulse; in the year, in the lifetime, it turns out to be a certain uniform tune which the revolving barrel of the music-box must play. Men resist the conclusion in the morning, but adopt it as the evening wears on, that temper prevails over everything of time, place and condition, and is inconsumable in the flames of religion. Some modifications the moral sentiment avails to impose, but the individual texture holds its dominion, if not to bias the moral judgments, yet to fix the measure of activity and of enjoyment.

I thus express the law as it is read from the platform of ordinary life, but must not leave it without noticing the capital exception. For temperament is a power which no man willingly hears any one praise but himself. On the platform of physics we cannot resist the contracting influences of so-called science. Temperament puts all divinity to rout. I know the mental proclivity of physicians. I hear the chuckle of the phrenologists.[3] Theoretic kidnappers and slave-drivers, they esteem each man the victim of another, who winds him round his finger by knowing the law of his being; and, by such cheap signboards as the color of his beard or the slope of his occiput, reads the inventory of his fortunes and character. The grossest ignorance does not disgust like this impudent knowingness. The physicians say they are not materialists; but they are:—Spirit is matter reduced to an extreme thinness: O *so* thin!—But the definition of *spiritual* should be, *that which is its own evidence.* What notions do they attach to love! what to religion! One would not willingly pronounce these words in their hearing, and give them the occasion to profane them. I saw a gracious gentleman who adapts his conversation to the form of the head of the man he talks with! I had fancied that the value of life lay in its inscrutable possibilities; in the fact that I never know, in addressing myself to a new individual, what may befall me. I carry the keys of my castle in my hand, ready to throw them at the feet of my lord, whenever and in what disguise soever he shall appear. I know he is in the neighborhood, hidden among vagabonds. Shall I preclude my future by taking a high seat and kindly adapting my conversation to the shape of heads? When I come to that, the doctors shall buy me for a cent.—"But, sir, medical history; the report to the Institute; the proven facts!"—I distrust the facts and the inferences. Temperament is the veto or limitation-power in the constitution, very justly applied to restrain an opposite excess in the constitution, but absurdly offered as a bar to original equity. When virtue is in presence, all subordinate powers sleep. On its own level, or in view of nature, temperament is final. I see not, if one be once caught in this trap of so-called sciences, any escape for the man from

3. Phrenology was then seriously re-garded by many. Emerson condemned its glib materialism in a contemporary lecture.

the links of the chain of physical necessity. Given such an embryo, such a history must follow. On this platform one lives in a sty of sensualism, and would soon come to suicide. But it is impossible that the creative power should exclude itself. Into every intelligence there is a door which is never closed, through which the creator passes. The intellect, seeker of absolute truth, or the heart, lover of absolute good, intervenes for our succor, and at one whisper of these high powers we awake from ineffectual struggles with this nightmare. We hurl it into its own hell, and cannot again contract ourselves to so base a state.

The secret of the illusoriness is in the necessity of a succession of moods or objects. Gladly we would anchor, but the anchorage is quicksand. This onward trick of nature is too strong for us: *Pero si muove.*[4] When at night I look at the moon and stars, I seem stationary, and they to hurry. Our love of the real draws us to permanence, but health of body consists in circulation, and sanity of mind in variety or facility of association. We need change of objects. Dedication to one thought is quickly odious. We house with the insane, and must humor them; then conversation dies out. Once I took such delight in Montaigne that I thought I should not need any other book; before that, in Shakespeare; then in Plutarch; then in Plotinus; at one time in Bacon; afterwards in Goethe; even in Bettine; but now I turn the pages of either of them languidly, whilst I still cherish their genius. So with pictures; each will bear an emphasis of attention once, which it cannot retain, though we fain would continue to be pleased in that manner. How strongly I have felt of pictures that when you have seen one well, you must take your leave of it; you shall never see it again. I have had good lessons from pictures which I have since seen without emotion or remark. A deduction must be made from the opinion which even the wise express on a new book or occurrence. Their opinion gives me tidings of their mood, and some vague guess at the new fact, but is nowise to be trusted as the lasting relation between that intellect and that thing. The child asks, "Mamma, why don't I like the story as well as when you told it me yesterday?" Alas! child, it is even so with the oldest cherubim of knowledge. But will it answer thy question to say, Because thou wert born to a whole and this story is a particular? The reason of the pain this discovery causes us (and we make it late in respect to works of art and intellect) is the plaint of tragedy which murmurs from it in regard to persons, to friendship and love.

That immobility and absence of elasticity which we find in the arts, we find with more pain in the artist. There is no power of expansion in men. Our friends early appear to us as representatives of

---

4. "Still, it moves." Having obeyed the command of the Inquisition to kneel and retract his "heresy" that the earth re- volves about the sun, Galileo arose, and uttered these words.

certain ideas which they never pass or exceed. They stand on the brink of the ocean of thought and power, but they never take the single step that would bring them there. A man is like a bit of Labrador spar,[5] which has no lustre as you turn it in your hand until you come to a particular angle; then it shows deep and beautiful colors. There is no adaptation or universal applicability in men, but each has his special talent, and the mastery of successful men consists in adroitly keeping themselves where and when that turn shall be oftenest to be practised. We do what we must, and call it by the best names we can, and would fain have the praise of having intended the result which ensues. I cannot recall any form of man who is not superfluous sometimes. But is not this pitiful? Life is not worth the taking, to do tricks in.

Of course it needs the whole society to give the symmetry we seek. The party-colored wheel must revolve very fast to appear white. Something is earned too by conversing with so much folly and defect. In fine, whoever loses, we are always of the gaining party. Divinity is behind our failures and follies also. The plays of children are nonsense, but very educative nonsense. So it is with the largest and solemnest things, with commerce, government, church, marriage, and so with the history of every man's bread, and the ways by which he is to come by it. Like a bird which alights nowhere, but hops perpetually from bough to bough, is the Power which abides in no man and in no woman, but for a moment speaks from this one, and for another moment from that one.

But what help from these fineries or pedantries? What help from thought? Life is not dialectics. We, I think, in these times, have had lessons enough of the futility of criticism. Our young people have thought and written much on labor and reform, and for all that they have written, neither the world nor themselves have got on a step. Intellectual tasting of life will not supersede muscular activity. If a man should consider the nicety of the passage of a piece of bread down his throat, he would starve. At Education Farm[6] the noblest theory of life sat on the noblest figures of young men and maidens, quite powerless and melancholy. It would not rake or pitch a ton of hay; it would not rub down a horse; and the men and maidens it left pale and hungry. A political orator wittily compared our party promises to western roads, which opened stately enough, with planted trees on either side to tempt the traveller, but soon became narrow and narrower and ended in a squirrel-track and ran up a tree. So does culture with us; it ends in headache. Unspeakably sad and barren does life look to those who a few months ago were dazzled with the splendor of the promise of the times. "There is now no

5. *I.e.,* labradorite, a crystalline rock.
6. Brook Farm (1841–1847), the co-operative agrarian community of the transcendentalists.

longer any right course of action nor any self-devotion left among the Iranis."[7] Objections and criticism we have had our fill of. There are objections to every course of life and action, and the practical wisdom infers an indifferency, from the omnipresence of objection. The whole frame of things preaches indifferency. Do not craze yourself with thinking, but go about your business anywhere. Life is not intellectual or critical, but sturdy. Its chief good is for well-mixed people who can enjoy what they find, without question. Nature hates peeping, and our mothers speak her very sense when they say, "Children, eat your victuals, and say no more of it." To fill the hour,— that is happiness; to fill the hour and leave no crevice for a repentance or an approval. We live amid surfaces, and the true art of life is to skate well on them. Under the oldest mouldiest conventions a man of native force prospers just as well as in the newest world, and that by skill of handling and treatment. He can take hold anywhere. Life itself is a mixture of power and form, and will not bear the least excess of either. To finish the moment, to find the journey's end in every step of the road, to live the greatest number of good hours, is wisdom. It is not the part of men, but of fanatics, or of mathematicians if you will, to say that, the shortness of life considered, it is not worth caring whether for so short a duration we were sprawling in want or sitting high. Since our office is with moments, let us husband them. Five minutes of to-day are worth as much to me as five minutes in the next millennium. Let us be poised, and wise, and our own, to-day. Let us treat the men and women well; treat them as if they were real; perhaps they are. Men live in their fancy, like drunkards whose hands are too soft and tremulous for successful labor. It is a tempest of fancies, and the only ballast I know is a respect to the present hour. Without any shadow of doubt, amidst this vertigo of shows and politics, I settle myself ever the firmer in the creed that we should not postpone and refer and wish, but do broad justice where we are, by whomsoever we deal with, accepting our actual companions and circumstances, however humble or odious, as the mystic officials to whom the universe has delegated its whole pleasure for us. If these are mean and malignant, their contentment, which is the last victory of justice, is a more satisfying echo to the heart than the voice of poets and the casual sympathy of admirable persons. I think that however a thoughtful man may suffer from the defects and absurdities of his company, he cannot without affectation deny to any set of men and women a sensibility to extraordinary merit. The coarse and frivolous have an instinct of superiority, if they have not a sympathy, and honor it in their blind capricious way with sincere homage.

7. Ascribed to Zoroaster (sixth century B.C.?), founder of the Persian religion (Centenary Edition, Vol. III, p. 306).

The fine young people despise life, but in me, and in such as with me are free from dyspepsia, and to whom a day is a sound and solid good, it is a great excess of politeness to look scornful and to cry for company. I am grown by sympathy a little eager and sentimental, but leave me alone and I should relish every hour and what it brought me, the potluck of the day, as heartily as the oldest gossip in the bar-room. I am thankful for small mercies. I compared notes with one of my friends who expects everything of the universe and is disappointed when anything is less than the best, and I found that I begin at the other extreme, expecting nothing, and am always full of thanks for moderate goods. I accept the clangor and jangle of contrary tendencies. I find my account in sots and bores also. They give a reality to the circumjacent picture which such a vanishing meteorous appearance can ill spare. In the morning I awake and find the old world, wife, babes and mother, Concord and Boston, the dear old spiritual world and even the dear old devil not far off. If we will take the good we find, asking no questions, we shall have heaping measures. The great gifts are not got by analysis. Everything good is on the highway. The middle region of our being is the temperate zone. We may climb into the thin and cold realm of pure geometry and lifeless science, or sink into that of sensation. Between these extremes is the equator of life, of thought, of spirit, of poetry,—a narrow belt. Moreover, in popular experience everything good is on the highway. A collector peeps into all the picture-shops of Europe for a landscape of Poussin, a crayon-sketch of Salvator;[8] but the Transfiguration, the Last Judgment, the Communion of Saint Jerome, and what are as transcendent as these, are on the walls of the Vatican, the Uffizi, or the Louvre,[9] where every footman may see them; to say nothing of Nature's pictures in every street, of sunsets and sunrises every day, and the sculpture of the human body never absent. A collector recently bought at public auction, in London, for one hundred and fifty-seven guineas, an autograph of Shakspeare; but for nothing a school-boy can read Hamlet and can detect secrets of highest concernment yet unpublished therein. I think I will never read any but the commonest books,—the Bible, Homer, Dante, Shakspeare and Milton. Then we are impatient of so public a life and planet, and run hither and thither for nooks and secrets. The imagination delights in the woodcraft of Indians, trappers and bee-hunters. We fancy that we are strangers, and not so intimately domesticated in the planet as the wild man and the wild beast and bird.

---

8. Contemporaries in Italy, the French-man Nicolas Poussin (1594–1665) and the Italian Salvator Rosa (1615–1673) were remembered chiefly for their landscapes and historical paintings.

9. The Vatican Gallery, in Rome, contains the famous "Transfiguration,"

painted by Raphael; the best known "Last Judgment" in Florence is that of Fra Angelico, not at the Uffizi, but in the Academy; of the several paintings of St. Jerome in the Louvre, in Paris, Emerson may refer to that by Titian.

But the exclusion reaches them also; reaches the climbing, flying, gliding, feathered and four-footed man. Fox and woodchuck, hawk and snipe and bittern, when nearly seen, have no more root in the deep world than man, and are just such superficial tenants of the globe. Then the new molecular philosophy shows astronomical interspaces betwixt atom and atom, shows that the world is all outside; it has no inside.

The mid-world is best. Nature, as we know her, is no saint. The lights of the church, the ascetics, Gentoos[1] and corn-eaters, she does not distinguish by any favor. She comes eating and drinking and sinning. Her darlings, the great, the strong, the beautiful, are not children of our law; do not come out of the Sunday School, nor weigh their food, nor punctually keep the commandments. If we will be strong with her strength we must not harbor such disconsolate consciences, borrowed too from the consciences of other nations. We must set up the strong present tense against all the rumors of wrath, past or to come. So many things are unsettled which it is of the first importance to settle;—and, pending their settlement, we will do as we do. Whilst the debate goes forward on the equity of commerce, and will not be closed for a century or two, New and Old England may keep shop. Law of copyright and international copyright is to be discussed, and in the interim we will sell our books for the most we can. Expediency of literature, reason of literature, lawfulness of writing down a thought, is questioned; much is to say on both sides, and, while the fight waxes hot, thou, dearest scholar, stick to thy foolish task, add a line every hour, and between whiles add a line. Right to hold land, right of property, is disputed, and the conventions convene, and before the vote is taken, dig away in your garden, and spend your earnings as a waif or godsend to all serene and beautiful purposes. Life itself is a bubble and a scepticism, and a sleep within a sleep. Grant it, and as much more as they will,—but thou, God's darling! heed thy private dream; thou wilt not be missed in the scorning and scepticism; there are enough of them; stay there in thy closet and toil until the rest are agreed what to do about it. Thy sickness, they say, and thy puny habit require that thou do this or avoid that, but know that thy life is a fitting state, a tent for a night, and do thou, sick or well, finish that stint. Thou art sick, but shalt not be worse, and the universe, which holds thee dear, shall be the better.

Human life is made up of the two elements, power and form, and the proportion must be invariably kept if we would have it sweet and sound. Each of these elements in excess makes a mischief as hurtful as its defect. Everything runs to excess; every good quality is noxious if unmixed, and, to carry the danger to the edge of ruin, nature

1. A Hindu sect.

causes each man's peculiarity to superabound. Here, among the farms, we adduce the scholars as examples of this treachery. They are nature's victims of expression. You who see the artist, the orator, the poet, too near, and find their life no more excellent than that of mechanics or farmers, and themselves victims of partiality, very hollow and haggard, and pronounce them failures, not heroes, but quacks,—conclude very reasonably that these arts are not for man, but are disease. Yet nature will not bear you out. Irresistible nature made men such, and makes legions more of such, every day. You love the boy reading in a book, gazing at a drawing or a cast; yet what are these millions who read and behold, but incipient writers and sculptors? Add a little more of that quality which now reads and sees, and they will seize the pen and chisel. And if one remembers how innocently he began to be an artist, he perceives that nature joined with his enemy. A man is a golden impossibility. The line he must walk is a hair's breadth. The wise through excess of wisdom is made a fool.

How easily, if fate would suffer it, we might keep forever these beautiful limits, and adjust ourselves, once for all, to the perfect calculation of the kingdom of known cause and effect. In the street and in the newspapers, life appears so plain a business that manly resolution and adherence to the multiplication-table through all weathers will insure success. But ah! presently comes a day, or is it only a half-hour, with its angel-whispering,—which discomfits the conclusions of nations and of years! To-morrow again every thing looks real and angular, the habitual standards are reinstated, common-sense is as rare as genius,—is the basis of genius, and experience is hands and feet to every enterprise;—and yet, he who should do his business on this understanding would be quickly bankrupt. Power keeps quite another road than the turnpikes of choice and will; namely the subterranean and invisible tunnels and channels of life. It is ridiculous that we are diplomatists, and doctors, and considerate people; there are no dupes like these. Life is a series of surprises, and would not be worth taking or keeping if it were not. God delights to isolate us every day, and hide from us the past and the future. We would look about us, but with grand politeness he draws down before us an impenetrable screen of purest sky, and another behind us of purest sky. "You will not remember," he seems to say, "and you will not expect." All good conversation, manners and action come from a spontaneity which forgets usages and makes the moment great. Nature hates calculators; her methods are saltatory and impulsive. Man lives by pulses; our organic movements are such; and the chemical and ethereal agents are undulatory and alternate; and the mind goes antagonizing on, and never prospers but by fits. We thrive by casualties. Our chief experiences have been casual. The most attractive class of people are those who are powerful obliquely and not by the direct stroke; men of genius, but not yet accredited; one gets the cheer of their light without paying too great a tax. Theirs is the beauty of the bird or the morning light, and not of art. In the thought of genius there is always a surprise; and the moral sentiment is well called "the newness," for it is never other; as new to the oldest intelligence as to the young child;—"the kingdom that cometh without observation."[2] In like manner, for practical success, there must not be too much design. A man will not be observed in doing that which he can do best. There is a certain magic about his properest action which stupefies your powers of observation, so that though it is done before you, you wist not of it. The art of life has a pudency, and will not be exposed. Every man is an impossibility until he is born; every thing impossible until we see a success. The ardors of piety agree at last with the coldest scepticism,—that nothing is of us or our works,—that all is of God. Nature will not spare us the smallest leaf of laurel. All writing comes by the grace of God, and all doing and having. I would gladly be moral and keep due metes and bounds, which I dearly love, and allow the most to the will of man; but I have set my heart on honesty in this chapter, and I can see nothing at last, in success or failure, than more or less of vital force supplied from the Eternal. The results of life are uncalculated and uncalculable. The years teach much which the days never know. The persons who compose our company converse, and come and go, and design and execute many things, and somewhat comes of it all, but an unlooked-for result. The individual is always mistaken. He designed many things, and drew in other persons as coadjutors, quarrelled with some or all, blundered much, and something is done; all are a little advanced, but the individual is always mistaken. It turns out somewhat new and very unlike what he promised himself.

The ancients, struck with this irreducibleness of the elements of human life to calculation, exalted Chance into a divinity; but that is to stay too long at the spark, which glitters truly at one point, but the universe is warm with the latency of the same fire. The miracle of life which will not be expounded but will remain a miracle, introduces a new element. In the growth of the embryo, Sir Everard Home[3] I think noticed that the evolution was not from one central point, but coactive from three or more points. Life has no memory. That which proceeds in succession might be remembered, but that which is coexistent, or ejaculated from a deeper cause, as yet far from being conscious, knows not its own tendency. So is it with us, now sceptical or without unity, because immersed in forms and effects all seeming to be of equal yet hostile value, and now religious,

2. *I.e.,* the kingdom of God; *cf.* Luke xvii: 20.   3. Scottish surgeon and scientist (1756–1832).

whilst in the reception of spiritual law. Bear with these distractions, with this coetaneous growth of the parts; they will one day be *members*, and obey one will. On that one will, on that secret cause, they nail our attention and hope. Life is hereby melted into an expectation or a religion. Underneath the inharmonious and trivial particulars, is a musical perfection; the Ideal journeying always with us, the heaven without rent or seam. Do but observe the mode of our illumination. When I converse with a profound mind, or if at any time being alone I have good thoughts, I do not at once arrive at satisfactions, as when, being thirsty, I drink water; or go to the fire, being cold; no! but I am at first apprised of my vicinity to a new and excellent region of life. By persisting to read or to think, this region gives further sign of itself, as it were in flashes of light, in sudden discoveries of its profound beauty and repose, as if the clouds that covered it parted at intervals and showed the approaching traveller the inland mountains, with the tranquil eternal meadows spread at their base, whereon flocks graze and shepherds pipe and dance. But every insight from this realm of thought is felt as initial, and promises a sequel. I do not make it; I arrive there, and behold what was there already. I make! O no! I clap my hands in infantine joy and amazement before the first opening to me of this august magnificence, old with the love and homage of innumerable ages, young with the life of life, the sunbright Mecca of the desert. And what a future it opens! I feel a new heart beating with the love of the new beauty. I am ready to die out of nature and be born again into this new yet unapproachable America I have found in the West:—

> "Since neither now nor yesterday began
> These thoughts, which have been ever, nor yet can
> A man be found who their first entrance knew."[4]

If I have described life as a flux of moods, I must now add that there is that in us which changes not and which ranks all sensations and states of mind. The consciousness in each man is a sliding scale, which identifies him now with the First Cause, and now with the flesh of his body; life above life, in infinite degrees. The sentiment from which it sprung determines the dignity of any deed, and the question ever is, not what you have done or forborne, but at whose command you have done or forborne it.

Fortune, Minerva, Muse, Holy Ghost,—these are quaint names, too narrow to cover this unbounded substance. The baffled intellect must still kneel before this cause, which refuses to be named,—ineffable cause, which every fine genius has essayed to represent by some emphatic symbol, as, Thales by water, Anaximenes by air,

---

4. Attributed to a source in Sophocles' *Antigone* (Centenary Edition, Vol. III, p. 308).

Anaxagoras by (Νοῦς) thought, Zoroaster[5] by fire, Jesus and the moderns by love; and the metaphor of each has become a national religion. The Chinese Mencius[6] has not been the least successful in his generalization. "I fully understand language," he said, "and nourish well my vast-flowing vigor."—"I beg to ask what you call vast-flowing vigor?" said his companion. "The explanation," replied Mencius, "is difficult. This vigor is supremely great, and in the highest degree unbending. Nourish it correctly and do it no injury, and it will fill up the vacancy between heaven and earth. This vigor accords with and assists justice and reason, and leaves no hunger."— In our more correct writing we give to this generalization the name of Being, and thereby confess that we have arrived as far as we can go. Suffice it for the joy of the universe that we have not arrived at a wall, but at interminable oceans. Our life seems not present so much as prospective; not for the affairs on which it is wasted, but as a hint of this vast-flowing vigor. Most of life seems to be mere advertisement of faculty; information is given us not to sell ourselves cheap; that we are very great. So, in particulars, our greatness is always in a tendency or direction, not in an action. It is for us to believe in the rule, not in the exception. The noble are thus known from the ignoble. So in accepting the leading of the sentiments, it is not what we believe concerning the immortality of the soul or the like, but *the universal impulse to believe,* that is the material circumstance and is the principal fact in the history of the globe. Shall we describe this cause as that which works directly? The spirit is not helpless or needful of mediate organs. It has plentiful powers and direct effects. I am explained without explaining, I am felt without acting, and where I am not. Therefore all just persons are satisfied with their own praise. They refuse to explain themselves, and are content that new actions should do them that office. They believe that we communicate without speech and above speech, and that no right action of ours is quite unaffecting to our friends, at whatever distance; for the influence of action is not to be measured by miles. Why should I fret myself because a circumstance has occurred which hinders my presence where I was expected? If I am not at the meeting, my presence where I am should be as useful to the commonwealth of friendship and wisdom, as would be my presence in that place. I exert the same quality of power in all places. Thus journeys the mighty Ideal before us; it never was known to fall into the rear. No man ever came to an experience which was satiating, but his good is tidings of a better. Onward and onward! In liberated moments we

5. Zoroaster, a Persian, and the others, all Greeks, philosophers of the sixth and fifth centuries B.C., taught that the universe was derived from a primary substance.

6. Mencius, Chinese Meng-tse (372?– 289? B.C.), compiled, in the *Book of Mencius,* the earliest classic of Chinese Confucianism.

know that a new picture of life and duty is already possible; the elements already exist in many minds around you of a doctrine of life which shall transcend any written record we have. The new statement will comprise the scepticisms as well as the faiths of society, and out of unbeliefs a creed shall be formed. For scepticisms are not gratuitous or lawless, but are limitations of the affirmative statement, and the new philosophy must take them in and make affirmations outside of them, just as much as it must include the oldest beliefs.

It is very unhappy, but too late to be helped, the discovery we have made that we exist. That discovery is called the Fall of Man. Ever afterwards we suspect our instruments. We have learned that we do not see directly, but mediately, and that we have no means of correcting these colored and distorting lenses which we are, or of computing the amount of their errors. Perhaps these subject-lenses have a creative power; perhaps there are no objects. Once we lived in what we saw; now, the rapaciousness of this new power, which threatens to absorb all things, engages us. Nature, art, persons, letters, religions, objects, successively tumble in, and God is but one of its ideas. Nature and literature are subjective phenomena; every evil and every good thing is a shadow which we cast. The street is full of humiliations to the proud. As the fop contrived to dress his bailiffs in his livery and make them wait on his guests at table, so the chagrins which the bad heart gives off as bubbles, at once take form as ladies and gentlemen in the street, shopmen or bar-keepers in hotels, and threaten or insult whatever is threatenable and insultable in us. 'Tis the same with our idolatries. People forget that it is the eye which makes the horizon, and the rounding mind's eye which makes this or that man a type or representative of humanity, with the name of hero or saint. Jesus, the "providential man," is a good man on whom many people are agreed that these optical laws shall take effect. By love on one part and by forbearance to press objection on the other part, it is for a time settled that we will look at him in the center of the horizon, and ascribe to him the properties that will attach to any man so seen. But the longest love or aversion has a speedy term. The great and crescive self, rooted in absolute nature, supplants all relative existence and ruins the kingdom of mortal friendship and love. Marriage (in what is called the spiritual world) is impossible, because of the inequality between every subject and every object. The subject is the receiver of Godhead, and at every comparison must feel his being exhanced by that cryptic might. Though not in energy, yet by presence, this magazine of substance cannot be otherwise than felt; nor can any force of intellect attribute to the object the proper deity which sleeps or wakes forever in every subject. Never can love make consciousness and ascription equal in force. There will be the same gulf between every me and thee as between the original and the picture. The universe is the bride of the soul. All private sympathy is partial. Two human beings are like globes, which can touch only in a point, and whilst they remain in contact all other points of each of the spheres are inert; their turn must also come, and the longer a particular union lasts the more energy of appetency the parts not in union acquire.

Life will be imagined, but cannot be divided nor doubled. Any invasion of its unity would be chaos. The soul is not twin-born but the only begotten, and though revealing itself as child in time, child in appearance, is of a fatal and universal power, admitting no co-life. Every day, every act betrays the ill-concealed deity. We believe in ourselves as we do not believe in others. We permit all things to ourselves, and that which we call sin in others is experiment for us. It is an instance of our faith in ourselves that men never speak of crime as lightly as they think; or every man thinks a latitude safe for himself which is nowise to be indulged to another. The act looks very differently on the inside and on the outside; in its quality and in its consequences. Murder in the murderer is no such ruinous thought as poets and romancers will have it; it does not unsettle him or fright him from his ordinary notice of trifles; it is an act quite easy to be contemplated; but in its sequel it turns out to be a horrible jangle and confounding of all relations. Especially the crimes that spring from love seem right and fair from the actor's point of view, but when acted are found destructive of society. No man at last believes that he can be lost, or that the crime in him is as black as in the felon. Because the intellect qualifies in our own case the moral judgments. For there is no crime to the intellect. That is antinomian or hypernomian,[7] and judges law as well as fact. "It is worse than a crime, it is a blunder," said Napoleon, speaking the language of the intellect. To it, the world is a problem in mathematics or the science of quantity, and it leaves out praise and blame and all weak emotions. All stealing is comparative. If you come to absolutes, pray who does not steal? Saints are sad, because they behold sin (even when they speculate) from the point of view of the conscience, and not of the intellect; a confusion of thought. Sin, seen from the thought, is a diminution, or *less*; seen from the conscience or will, it is pravity or *bad*. The intellect names it shade, absence of light, and no essence. The conscience must feel it as essence, essential evil. This it is not; it has an objective existence, but no subjective.

Thus inevitably does the universe wear our color, and every object fall successively into the subject itself. The subject exists, the subject

7. *I.e.*, "against the law or above the law"; antinomians were then preaching salvation by faith rather than by adherence to moral law.

enlarges; all things sooner or later fall into place. As I am, so I see; use what language we will, we can never say anything but what we are; Hermes, Cadmus, Columbus, Newton, Bonaparte,[8] are the mind's ministers. Instead of feeling a poverty when we encounter a great man, let us treat the newcomer like a travelling geologist who passes through our estate and shows us good slate, or limestone, or anthracite, in our brush pasture. The partial action of each strong mind in one direction is a telescope for the objects on which it is pointed. But every other part of knowledge is to be pushed to the same extravagance, ere the soul attains her due sphericity. Do you see that kitten chasing so prettily her own tail? If you could look with her eyes you might see her surrounded with hundreds of figures performing complex dramas, with tragic and comic issues, long conversations, many characters, many ups and downs of fate,—and meantime it is only puss and her tail. How long before our masquerade will end its noise of tambourines, laughter and shouting, and we shall find it was a solitary performance? A subject and an object,—it takes so much to make the galvanic circuit complete, but magnitude adds nothing. What imports it whether it is Kepler and the sphere,[9] Columbus and America, a reader and his book, or puss with her tail?

It is true that all the muses and love and religion hate these developments, and will find a way to punish the chemist who publishes in the parlor the secrets of the laboratory. And we cannot say too little of our constitutional necessity of seeing things under private aspects, or saturated with our humors. And yet is the God the native of these bleak rocks. That need makes in morals the capital virtue of self-trust. We must hold hard to this poverty, however scandalous, and by more vigorous self-recoveries, after the sallies of action, possess our axis more firmly. The life of truth is cold and so far mournful; but it is not the slave of tears, contritions and perturbations. It does not attempt another's work, nor adopt another's facts. It is a main lesson of wisdom to know your own from another's. I have learned that I cannot dispose of other people's facts; but I possess such a key to my own as persuades me, against all their denials, that they also have a key to theirs. A sympathetic person is placed in the dilemma of a swimmer among drowning men, who all catch at him, and if he give so much as a leg or a finger they will drown him. They wish to be saved from the mischiefs of their vices, but not from their vices. Charity would be wasted on this poor waiting on the symp-

8. In Greek legend, Hermes was the messenger of the gods, and the god of invention; Cadmus introduced the alphabet, and created the history-making Thebans by sowing the dragon's teeth; the later and familiar figures on this list were also "the mind's ministers."
9. Johannes Kepler (1571–1630), German physicist, discovered the three fundamental laws of planetary motion.

toms. A wise and hardy physician will say, *Come out of that*, as the first condition of advice.

In this our talking America we are ruined by our good nature and listening on all sides. This compliance takes away the power of being greatly useful. A man should not be able to look other than directly and forthright. A preoccupied attention is the only answer to the importunate frivolity of other people; an attention, and to an aim which makes their wants frivolous. This is a divine answer, and leaves no appeal and no hard thoughts. In Flaxman's[1] drawing of the Eumenides of Æschylus, Orestes supplicates Apollo, whilst the Furies sleep on the threshold. The face of the god expresses a shade of regret and compassion, but is calm with the conviction of the irreconcilableness of the two spheres. He is born into other politics, into the eternal and beautiful. The man at his feet asks for his interest in turmoils of the earth, into which his nature cannot enter. And the Eumenides there lying express pictorially this disparity. The god is surcharged with his divine destiny.

Illusion, Temperament, Succession, Surface, Surprise, Reality, Subjectiveness,—these are threads on the loom of time, these are the lords of life. I dare not assume to give their order, but I name them as I find them in my way. I know better than to claim any completeness for my picture. I am a fragment, and this is a fragment of me. I can very confidently announce one or another law, which throws itself into relief and form, but I am too young yet by some ages to compile a code. I gossip for my hour concerning the eternal politics. I have seen many fair pictures not in vain. A wonderful time I have lived in. I am not the novice I was fourteen, nor yet seven years ago. Let who will ask, Where is the fruit? I find a private fruit sufficient. This is a fruit,—that I should not ask for a rash effect from meditations, counsels and the hiving of truths. I should feel it pitiful to demand a result on this town and county, an overt effect on the instant month and year. The effect is deep and secular as the cause. It works on periods in which mortal lifetime is lost. All I know is reception; I am and I have: but I do not get, and when I have fancied I had gotten anything, found I did not. I worship with wonder the great Fortune. My reception has been so large, that I am not annoyed by receiving this or that superabundantly. I say to the Genius, if he will pardon the proverb, *In for a mill, in for a million*. When I receive a new gift, I do not macerate my body to make the account square, for if I should die I could not make the account square. The benefit overran the merit the first day, and has overrun the merit ever since. The merit itself, so-called, I reckon part of the receiving.

1. John Flaxman (1755–1826), English sculptor and illustrator; his drawings were popularly reproduced in American magazines.

Also that hankering after an overt or practical effect seems to me an apostasy. In good earnest I am willing to spare this most unnecessary deal of doing. Life wears to me a visionary face. Hardest roughest action is visionary also. It is but a choice between soft and turbulent dreams. People disparage knowing and the intellectual life, and urge doing. I am very content with knowing, if only I could know. That is an august entertainment, and would suffice me a great while. To know a little would be worth the expense of this world. I hear always the law of Adrastia,[2] "that every soul which had acquired any truth, should be safe from harm until another period."

I know that the world I converse with in the city and in the farms, is not the world I *think*. I observe that difference, and shall observe it. One day I shall know the value and law of this discrepance. But I have not found that much was gained by manipular attempts to realize the world of thought. Many eager persons successively make an experiment in this way, and make themselves ridiculous. They acquire democratic manners, they foam at the mouth, they hate and deny. Worse, I observe that in the history of mankind there is never a solitary example of success,—taking their own tests of success. I say this polemically, or in reply to the inquiry, Why not realize your world? But far be from me the despair which prejudges the law by a paltry empiricism;—since there never was a right endeavor but it succeeded. Patience and patience, we shall win at the last. We must be very suspicious of the deceptions of the element of time. It takes a good deal of time to eat or to sleep, or to earn a hundred dollars, and a very little time to entertain a hope and an insight which becomes the light of our life. We dress our garden, eat our dinners, discuss the household with our wives, and these things make no impression, are forgotten next week; but, in the solitude to which every man is always returning, he has a sanity and revelations which in his passage into new worlds he will carry with him. Never mind the ridicule, never mind the defeat; up again, old heart![3]—it seems to say,—there is victory yet for all justice; and the true romance which the world exists to realize will be the transformation of genius into practical power.

1842?   1844

---

2. Nemesis, the Greek goddess of retributive justice. She spared only those who fulfilled the requirement here quoted by Emerson from Plato's *Phaedrus* (Centenary Edition, Vol. III, p. 308).

3. *Cf.* the familiar Latin from the Mass—*sursum corda* ("upward, hearts") —used as a title for one of Emerson's poems.

Concord Hymn

SUNG AT THE COMPLETION OF THE BATTLE MONUMENT,[4]
JULY 4, 1837

By the rude bridge that arched the flood,
    Their flag to April's breeze unfurled,
Here once the embattled farmers stood
    And fired the shot heard round the world.

The foe long since in silence slept;   5
    Alike the conqueror silent sleeps;
And Time the ruined bridge has swept
    Down the dark stream which seaward creeps.

On this green bank, by this soft stream,
    We set to-day a votive stone;   10
That memory may their deed redeem,
    When, like our sires, our sons are gone.

Spirit, that made those heroes dare
    To die, and leave their children free,
Bid Time and Nature gently spare
    The shaft we raise to them and thee.   15

1837, 1876

Each and All[5]

Little thinks, in the field, yon red-cloaked clown
Of thee from the hill-top looking down;
The heifer that lows in the upland farm,
Far-heard, lows not thine ear to charm;
The sexton, tolling his bell at noon,   5
Deems not that great Napoleon
Stops his horse, and lists with delight,
Whilst his files sweep round yon Alpine height;
Nor knowest thou what argument
Thy life to thy neighbor's creed has lent.   10

4. The monument commemorates the battles of Lexington and Concord, April 19, 1775. At the dedication, this poem was distributed as a printed leaflet; it was not collected until the *Selected Poems* of 1876, for which Emerson made slight revisions, here retained. He also changed the title to "Concord Fight," and wrongly dated the commemoration as "April 19, 1836." The editors of the Centenary Edition restored the now familiar title, and corrected the date to July 4, 1837. We have followed them in these respects.

5. The transcendent unity of the many and the one, presented from various angles in the essays, from *Nature* to "Plato," here begets one of Emerson's most characteristic poems. At least the episode of the sea shells is actual; Emerson recorded it in his Journal for May 16, 1834. The poem appeared in the *Western Messenger* for February, 1839, and in the collections of 1847 and 1876.

All are needed by each one;
Nothing is fair or good alone.
I thought the sparrow's note from heaven,
Singing at dawn on the alder bough;
I brought him home, in his nest, at even;   15
He sings the song, but it cheers not now,
For I did not bring home the river and sky;—
He sang to my ear,—they sang to my eye.
The delicate shells lay on the shore;
The bubbles of the latest wave   20
Fresh pearls to their enamel gave,
And the bellowing of the savage sea
Greeted their safe escape to me.
I wiped away the weeds and foam,
I fetched my sea-born treasures home;   25
But the poor, unsightly, noisome things
Had left their beauty on the shore
With the sun and the sand and the wild uproar.
The lover watched his graceful maid,
As 'mid the virgin train she strayed,   30
Nor knew her beauty's best attire
Was woven still by the snow-white choir.
At last she came to his hermitage,
Like the bird from the woodlands to the cage:—
The gay enchantment was undone,   35
A gentle wife, but fairy none.
Then I said, "I covet truth;
Beauty is unripe childhood's cheat;
I leave it behind with the games of youth:"—
As I spoke, beneath my feet   40
The ground-pine curled its pretty wreath,
Running over the club-moss burrs;
I inhaled the violet's breath;
Around me stood the oaks and firs;
Pine-cones and acorns lay on the ground;   45
Over me soared the eternal sky,
Full of light and of deity;
Again I saw, again I heard,
The rolling river, the morning bird;—
Beauty through my senses stole;   50
I yielded myself to the perfect whole.

                                            1839, 1847

The Rhodora:

ON BEING ASKED, WHENCE IS THE FLOWER?[6]

In May, when sea-winds pierced our solitudes,
I found the fresh Rhodora in the woods,
Spreading its leafless blooms in a damp nook,
To please the desert and the sluggish brook.
The purple petals, fallen in the pool,   5
Made the black water with their beauty gay;
Here might the red-bird come his plumes to cool,
And court the flower that cheapens his array.
Rhodora! if the sages ask thee why
This charm is wasted on the earth and sky,   10
Tell them, dear, that if eyes were made for seeing,
Then Beauty is its own excuse for being:
Why thou wert there, O rival of the rose!
I never thought to ask, I never knew;
But, in my simple ignorance, suppose   15
The self-same Power that brought me there brought you.

1834   1839, 1847

The Problem[1]

I like a church; I like a cowl;
I love a prophet of the soul;
And on my heart monastic aisles
Fall like sweet strains, or pensive smiles;
Yet not for all his faith can see   5
Would I that cowled churchman be.

Why should the vest on him allure,
Which I could not on me endure?

Not from a vain or shallow thought
His awful Jove young Phidias[2] brought,   10
Never from lips of cunning fell

---

6. Like "Each and All," this is one of the four lyrics which, in 1839, were the first of Emerson's poems to be published in periodicals. "The Rhodora" first appeared in the *Western Messenger* for July, 1839, and was collected in the volumes of 1847 and 1876.

1. Soon after the "Divinity School Address," in his *Journal* for August 28, 1838, Emerson entered his objection to the "division of labor" that sets the clergyman apart from those who express in other ways the wholeness and holiness

of the divine unity. In "The Problem," the artist, poet, thinker, prophet, all the genuine Makers among men, reaffirm the same Pentecost, as priests of the God made manifest in nature. First published in the *Dial* for July, 1840, the poem was collected in the volumes of 1847 and 1876.

2. Phidias was the great sculptor of Pericles' Athens. However, his masterpiece, the Zeus ("Jove") described by Pausanias, was in the temple at Olympia.

The thrilling Delphic oracle;[3]
Out from the heart of nature rolled
The burdens of the Bible old;
The litanies of nations came,   15
Like the volcano's tongue of flame,
Up from the burning core below,—
The canticles of love and woe;
The hand that rounded Peter's dome[4]
And groined the aisles of Christian Rome   20
Wrought in a sad sincerity;
Himself from God he could not free;
He builded better than he knew;—
The conscious stone to beauty grew.

Know'st thou what wove yon woodbird's nest   25
Of leaves, and feathers from her breast?
Or how the fish outbuilt her shell,
Painting with morn each annual cell?
Or how the sacred pine-tree adds
To her old leaves new myriads?   30
Such and so grew these holy piles,
Whilst love and terror laid the tiles.
Earth proudly wears the Parthenon,[5]
As the best gem upon her zone;
And Morning opes with haste her lids,   35
To gaze upon the Pyramids;
O'er England's abbeys bends the sky,
As on its friends, with kindred eye;
For out of Thought's interior sphere,
These wonders rose to upper air;   40
And Nature gladly gave them place,
Adopted them into her race,
And granted them an equal date
With Andes and with Ararat.

These temples grew as grows the grass;   45
Art might obey, but not surpass.
The passive Master lent his hand
To the vast soul that o'er him planned;
And the same power that reared the shrine
Bestrode the tribes that knelt within.   50
Ever the fiery Pentecost[6]

3. The Delphic oracle communicated the revelations of Apollo, the loftiest embodiment of the Greek mind and creativeness.
4. Michelangelo designed and engineered the great dome of St. Peter's at Rome, nearly completed when he died in 1564.

5. Greatest architectural monument of Greek culture, it honored Athena, goddess of wisdom.
6. The miraculous descent of the Holy Ghost upon the disciples of Jesus after his resurrection. *Cf.* Acts ii: 1–36.

Girds with one flame the countless host,
Trances the heart through chanting choirs,
And through the priest the mind inspires.
The word unto the prophet spoken
Was writ on tables yet unbroken;[7]   55
The word by seers or sibyls told,
In groves of oak, or fanes of gold,
Still floats upon the morning wind,
Still whispers to the willing mind.   60
One accent of the Holy Ghost
The heedless world hath never lost.
I know what say the fathers wise,—
The Book itself before me lies,
Old Crysostom,[8] best Augustine,[9]   65
And he who blent both in his line,
The younger *Golden Lips* or mines,
Taylor,[1] the Shakspeare of divines.
His words are music in my ear,
I see his cowled portrait dear;   70
And yet, for all his faith could see,
I would not the good bishop be.

1839   1840, 1847

The Sphinx[2]

The Sphinx is drowsy,
    Her wings are furled;
Her ear is heavy,
    She broods on the world.
'Who'll tell me my secret,   5
    The ages have kept?—
I awaited the seer,
    While they slumbered and slept;—

7. *Cf.* Exodus xxxii: 19.
8. John of Antioch (347?–407), Greek Church Father and saint, later called Chrysostom ("Golden Mouth") in honor of his *Homilies*.
9. St. Augustine (354–430), whose *Confessions* Emerson once called "golden words" (*cf.* l. 67, and Centenary Edition, Vol. IX, p. 406).
1. Jeremy Taylor (1613–1667), English churchman, author of *Holy Living* and *Holy Dying*.
2. The Sphinx of Thebes was known in legend for her riddle, whose answer symbolized the rise and fall of man. The inscrutable Great Sphinx near the pyramids of Giza, Egypt, combines various animal and human characteristics. The association of these ideas is clarified by Emerson's note on the meaning of the poem, in his notebooks (1859): "The perception of identity unites all things and explains one by another, and the most rare and strange is equally facile as the most common. But if the mind live only in particulars, and see only differences (wanting the power to see the whole—all in each), then the world addresses to this mind a question it cannot answer, and each new fact tears it in pieces." The poem appeared in *The Dial* for January, 1841, and in the volumes of 1847 and 1876.

'The fate of the man-child;
    The meaning of man;   10
Known fruit of the Unknown;
    Daedalian³ plan;
Out of sleeping a waking,
    Out of waking a sleep;
Life death overtaking;   15
    Deep underneath deep?

'Erect as a sunbeam,
    Upspringeth the palm;
The elephant browses,
    Undaunted and calm;   20
In beautiful motion
    The thrush plies his wings;
Kind leaves of his covert
    Your silence he sings.

'The waves, unashamed,   25
    In difference sweet,
Play glad with the breezes,
    Old playfellows meet;
The journeying atoms,
    Primordial wholes,   30
Firmly draw, firmly drive,
    By their animate poles.

'Sea, earth, air, sound, silence,
    Plant, quadruped, bird,
By one music enchanted,   35
    One deity stirred,—
Each the other adorning
    Accompany still;
Night veileth the morning,
    The vapor the hill.   40

'The babe by its mother
    Lies bathed in joy;
Glide its hours uncounted,—
    The sun is its toy;
Shines the peace of all being,   45
    Without cloud, in its eyes;
And the sum of the world
    In soft miniature lies.

---

3. Daedalus, in Greek mythology, personified the development of craftsmanship among mortals, and finally devised wings to escape the vengeance of a god.

'But man crouches and blushes,
　　Absconds and conceals;
He creepeth and peepeth,
　　He palters and steals;
Infirm, melancholy,
　　Jealous glancing around,
An oaf, an accomplice,
　　He poisons the ground.　　　　　　　　　　50

'Out spoke the great mother,
　　Beholding his fear;—
At the sound of her accents
　　Cold shuddered the sphere:—　　　　　　　60
"Who has drugged my boy's cup?
　　Who has mixed my boy's bread?
Who, with sadness and madness,
　　Has turned my child's head?"'

I heard a poet answer　　　　　　　　　　　65
　　Aloud and cheerfully,
'Say on, sweet Sphinx! thy dirges
　　Are pleasant songs to me.
Deep love lieth under
　　These pictures of time;　　　　　　　　　70
They fade in the light of
　　Their meaning sublime.

'The fiend that man harries
　　Is love of the Best;
Yawns the pit of the Dragon,[4]
　　Lit by rays from the Blest.[5]　　　　　　75
The Lethe of Nature
　　Can't trance him again,
Whose soul sees the perfect,
　　Which his eyes seek in vain.　　　　　　80

'To vision profounder
　　Man's spirit must dive;
His aye-rolling orb
　　At no goal will arrive;
The heavens that now draw him
　　With sweetness untold,　　　　　　　　85
Once found,—for new heavens
　　He spurneth the old.

---

4. Where an angel chained "the dragon, that old serpent, which is the Devil"; *cf*. Revelation xx: 1–3.

5. General term in hymnology and Scripture for God's heaven of redemption.

'Pride ruined the angels,
   Their shame them restores;   90
And the joy that is sweetest
   Lurks in stings of remorse.[6]
Have I a lover
   Who is noble and free?—
I would he were nobler   95
   Than to love me.

'Eterne alternation
   Now follows, now flies;
And under pain, pleasure,—
   Under pleasure, pain lies.   100
Love works at the centre,
   Heart-heaving alway;
Forth speed the strong pulses
   To the borders of day.

'Dull Sphinx, Jove keep thy five wits: 105
   Thy sight is growing blear;
Rue, myrrh and cummin[7] for the Sphinx,——
   Her muddy eyes to clear!'——
The old Sphinx bit her thick lip,—
   Said, 'Who taught thee me to name?   110
I am thy spirit, yoke-fellow,
   Of thine eye I am eyebeam.[8]

'Thou art the unanswered question;
   Couldst see thy proper eye
Alway it asketh, asketh;   115
   And each answer is a lie.
So take thy quest through nature,
   It through thousand natures ply;
Ask on, thou clothed eternity;
   Time is the false reply.'   120

Uprose the merry Sphinx,
   And crouched no more in stone;
She melted into purple cloud,
   She silvered in the moon;

6. Ll. 91–92 were changed in the posthumous Centenary Edition to read: "Lurks the joy that is sweetest / In stings of remorse."
7. In the ancient tradition of the herbalist, rue was medicine for remorse (*cf.* l. 92); myrrh was the Hebrew aromatic for anointment or purification, brought to the infant Jesus by the Magi, and offered Him upon the Cross (*cf.* ll. 76–80); cummin was a Palestinian spice, a relish for food (*cf.* ll. 99–104).
8. Thus the poet is the prophet of the riddle of the Sphinx or of nature. See *Nature*, Chapter I, paragraph 4: "I become a transparent eyeball."

She spired into a yellow flame;   125
  She flowered in blossoms red;
She flowed into a foaming wave:
  She stood Monadnoc's[9] head.

Thorough a thousand voices
  Spoke the universal dame: 130
'Who telleth one of my meanings,
  Is master of all I am.'

                                        1841, 1847

Compensation[1]

I

The wings of Time are black and white,
Pied with morning and with night.
Mountain tall and ocean deep
Trembling balance duly keep.
In changing moon and tidal wave   5
Glows the feud of Want and Have.
Gauge of more and less through space,
Electric star or pencil plays,
The lonely Earth amid the balls
That hurry through the eternal halls,   10
A makeweight flying to the void,
Supplemental asteroid,
Or compensatory spark,
Shoots across the neutral Dark.

II

Man's the elm, and Wealth the vine;   15
Stanch and strong the tendrils twine:
Though the frail ringlets thee deceive,
None from its stock that vine can reave.
Fear not, then, thou child infirm,
There's no god dare wrong a worm;   20
Laurel crowns cleave to deserts,
And power to him who power exerts.
Hast not thy share? On winged feet,
Lo! it rushes thee to meet;
And all that Nature made thy own,   25
Floating in air or pent in stone,

9. A peak that dominates the mountain scenery of southwest New Hampshire.
1. "Compensation" was Emerson's poetical motto for the essay of the same name, published in *Essays* [First Series] (1841). Together with other such "Elements and Mottoes" it was collected in *May-Day and Other Pieces* (1867).

Will rive the hills, and swim the sea,
And, like thy shadow, follow thee.[2]

1841, 1867

Ode to Beauty[3]

Who gave thee, O Beauty,
The keys of this breast,—
Too credulous lover
Of blest and unblest?
Say, when in lapsed ages   5
Thee knew I of old?
Or what was the service
For which I was sold?
When first my eyes saw thee,
I found me thy thrall,   10
By magical drawings,
Sweet tyrant of all!
I drank at thy fountain
False waters of thirst;
Thou intimate stranger,   15
Thou latest and first!
Thy dangerous glances
Make women of men;
New-born, we are melting
Into nature again.   20

Lavish, lavish promiser,
Nigh persuading gods to err!
Guest of million painted forms,
Which in turn thy glory warms!
The frailest leaf, the mossy bark,   25
The acorn's cup, the rain-drop's arc,
The swinging spider's silver line,
The ruby of the drop of wine,
The shining pebble of the pond,
Thou inscribest with a bond,   30
In thy momentary play,
Would bankrupt nature to repay.

Ah, what avails it
To hide or to shun

2. Ll. 23–28 are an enlarged paraphrase from "a noble sentence of Ali," cousin and son-in-law of Mohammed (Centenary Edition, Vol. IX, p. 494).
3. The "Ode to Beauty," distinguished among Emerson's poems for a lyric grace that responds to feeling more than to idea, was published in *The Dial* for October, 1843. It was revised slightly for the *Poems* (1847), and finally, for the *Selected Poems* (1876), as given here.

Whom the Infinite One   35
Hath granted his throne?
The heaven high over
Is the deep's lover;
The sun and sea,
Informed by thee,   40
Before me run
And draw me on,
Yet fly me still,
As Fate refuses
To me the heart Fate for me chooses.   45
Is it that my opulent soul
Was mingled from the generous whole;
Sea-valleys and the deep of skies
Furnished several supplies;
And the sands whereof I'm made   50
Draw me to them, self-betrayed?
I turn the proud portfolio
Which holds the grand designs
Of Salvator, of Guercino,
And Piranesi's lines.[4]   55
I hear the lofty paeans
Of the masters of the shell,[5]
Who heard the starry music
And recount the numbers well;
Olympian bards who sung   60
Divine Ideas below,[6]
Which always find us young
And always keep us so.
Oft, in streets or humblest places,
I detect far-wandered graces,   65
Which, from Eden wide astray,
In lowly homes have lost their way.

Thee gliding through the sea of form,
Like the lightning through the storm,
Somewhat not to be possessed,
Somewhat not to be caressed,   70

4. According to Emerson's editors (Centenary Edition, Vol. IX, p. 432), Margaret Fuller had sent him the "portfolio" (l. 52). Salvator Rosa (1615–1673) was leader of the Neapolitan revival of landscape painting; Guercino (Giovanni Francesco Barbieri, 1591–1666) was a Bolognese Eclectic painter; Giambattista Piranesi (1720–1778), Italian architect and painter, influenced both neoclassical architects and later romantic writers by his engravings of classical antiquity.

5. According to Greek myth, it was from a turtle shell that Apollo formed the lyre, instrument of the twin arts of music and poetry; hence poets are "masters of the shell."

6. The Greek gods, dwelling on Mount Olympus, heard daily the poetry of divine bards; Orpheus, a mortal, taught by Apollo, "sung / Divine Ideas below."

No feet so fleet could ever find,
No perfect form could ever bind.
Thou eternal fugitive,
Hovering over all that live, 75
Quick and skilful to inspire
Sweet, extravagant desire,
Starry space and lily-bell
Filling with thy roseate smell,
Wilt not give the lips to taste 80
Of the nectar which thou hast.

All that's good and great with thee
Works in close conspiracy;
Thou hast bribed the dark and lonely
To report thy features only, 85
And the cold and purple morning
Itself with thoughts of thee adorning;
The leafy dell, the city mart,
Equal trophies of thine art;
E'en the flowing azure air 90
Thou hast touched for my despair;
And, if I languish into dreams,
Again I meet the ardent beams.
Queen of things! I dare not die
In Being's deeps past ear and eye; 95
Lest there I find the same deceiver
And be the sport of Fate forever.
Dread Power, but dear! if God thou be,
Unmake me quite, or give thyself to me!

1843, 1847

Hamatreya[7]

Bulkeley, Hunt, Willard, Hosmer, Meriam, Flint,[8]
Possessed the land which rendered to their toil
Hay, corn, roots, hemp, flax, apples, wool and wood.
Each of these landlords walked amidst his farm,
Saying, ' 'T is mine, my children's and my name's. 5

7. In Emerson's journal (1845) appears a long passage from the Hindu *Vishnu Purana*. The gist of this poem is found in the following extract: "Kings who with perishable frames have possessed this ever-enduring world, and who * * * have indulged the feeling that suggests 'This earth is mine,—it is my son's,—it belongs to my dynasty,'— have all passed away. * * * Earth laughs, as if smiling with autumnal flowers to behold her kings unable to effect the subjugation of themselves." The song of the Earth (on which Emerson based the "Earth-Song" in this poem) is then recited to Maitreya, but Emerson rejected that name for his title in favor of the variant "Hamatreya." The poem was published in the *Poems* (1847) and in the *Selected Poems* (1876), as here printed.
8. Names of first settlers of Concord, Massachusetts, including Peter Bulkeley, an ancestor of Emerson.

How sweet the west wind sounds in my own trees!
How graceful climb those shadows on my hill!
I fancy these pure waters and the flags
Know me, as does my dog: we sympathize;
And, I affirm, my actions smack of the soil.'   10

Where are these men? Asleep beneath their grounds:
And strangers, fond as they, their furrows plough.
Earth laughs in flowers, to see her boastful boys
Earth-proud, proud of the earth which is not theirs;
Who steer the plough, but cannot steer their feet   15
Clear of the grave.
They added ridge to valley, brook to pond,
And sighed for all that bounded their domain;
'This suits me for a pasture; that's my park;
We must have clay, lime, gravel, granite-ledge,   20
And misty lowland, where to go for peat.
The land is well,—lies fairly to the south.
'T is good, when you have crossed the sea and back,
To find the sitfast acres where you left them.'
Ah! the hot owner sees not Death, who adds   25
Him to his land, a lump of mould the more.
Hear what the Earth says:—

EARTH-SONG

Mine and yours;
Mine, not yours.
Earth endures;
Stars abide—   30
Shine down in the old sea;
Old are the shores;
But where are old men?
I who have seen much,   35
Such have I never seen.

The lawyer's deed
Ran sure,
In tail,[9]
To them, and to their heirs   40
Who shall succeed,
Without fail,
Forevermore.

Here is the land,
Shaggy with wood,   45

9. *I.e.*, "entailed"; legal term applied to an estate irrevocably settled upon designated descendants.

With its old valley,
Mound and flood.
But the heritors?—
Fled like the flood's foam.
The lawyer, and the laws,   50
And the kingdom,
Clean swept herefrom.

They called me theirs,
Who so controlled me;
Yet every one   55
Wished to stay, and is gone,
How am I theirs,
If they cannot hold me,
But I hold them?

When I heard the Earth-song,   60
I was no longer brave;
My avarice cooled
Like lust in the chill of the grave.

1847

Give All to Love[1]

Give all to love;
Obey thy heart;
Friends, kindred, days,
Estate, good-fame,
Plans, credit and the Muse,—   5
Nothing refuse.

'T is a brave master;
Let it have scope:
Follow it utterly,
Hope beyond hope: 10
High and more high
It dives into noon,
With wing unspent,
Untold intent;
But it is a god,   15
Knows its own path
And the outlets of the sky.

1. "Give All to Love" is puzzling to
readers who have not understood Emerson's toughness of mind in pushing his
ideas to their logical limits of social
application. If his theory of individualism is sound, it must function also between lovers. Thus he ends another poem,
"The Initial Love": "So lovers melt
their sundered selves, / Yet melted
would be twain."

It was never for the mean;
It requireth courage stout.
Souls above doubt,   20
Valor unbending,
It will reward,—
They shall return
More than they were,
And ever ascending.   25

Leave all for love;
Yet, hear me, yet,
One word more thy heart behoved,
One pulse more of firm endeavor,—
Keep thee to-day,   30
To-morrow, forever,
Free as an Arab
Of thy beloved.

Cling with life to the maid;
But when the surprise,   35
First vague shadow of surmise
Flits across her bosom young,
Of a joy apart from thee,
Free be she, fancy-free;
Nor thou detain her vesture's hem,   40
Nor the palest rose she flung
From her summer diadem.

Though thou loved her as thyself,
As a self of purer clay,
Though her parting dims the day,   45
Stealing grace from all alive;
Heartily know,
When half-gods go,
The gods arrive.

                                                1847

Ode

INSCRIBED TO W. H. CHANNING[2]

Though loath to grieve
The evil time's sole patriot,

2. The so-called Channing Ode was published in the *Poems* (1847), in the midst of the Mexican War, which Emerson had opposed both on pacific grounds and because the war was presumably fomented to achieve the extension of slave territory. William Henry Channing (1810–1884) was a Unitarian clergyman and active transcendentalist. Whether or not he had urged Emerson to give concrete support to the mounting abolition movement, Channing was so fully identified

I cannot leave
My honied thought
For the priest's cant,   5
Or statesman's rant.

If I refuse
My study for their politique,
Which at the best is trick,
The angry Muse   10
Puts confusion in my brain.

But who is he that prates
Of the culture of mankind,
Of better arts and life?
Go, blindworm, go,   15
Behold the famous States
Harrying Mexico
With rifle and with knife!

Or who, with accent bolder,
Dare praise the freedom-loving mountaineer?   20
I found by thee, O rushing Contoocook![3]
And in thy valleys, Agiochook![4]
The jackals of the negro-holder.[5]

The God who made New Hampshire
Taunted the lofty land   25
With little men;—
Small bat and wren
House in the oak:—
If earth-fire cleave
The upheaved land, and bury the folk,   30
The southern crocodile would grieve.
Virtue palters; Right is hence;
Freedom praised, but hid;
Funeral eloquence
Rattles the coffin-lid.   35

What boots thy zeal,
O glowing friend,
That would indignant rend
The northland from the south?

with such humanitarian causes that the
poet was justified in using his friend's
name to establish his argument, which
strikingly illustrates the application of
his philosophy to social action.
3. A branch of the Merrimack River in
New Hampshire.

4. Indian name for the White Mountains of New Hampshire.
5. *I.e.*, those who hounded escaped slaves under sanction of the fugitive-slave laws; the jackal is a mean and cowardly wild dog.

Wherefore? to what good end?
Boston Bay and Bunker Hill
Would serve things still;—
Things are of the snake.

The horseman serves the horse,
The neatherd serves the neat,[6]
The merchant serves the purse,
The eater serves his meat;
'T is the day of the chattel,
Web to weave, and corn to grind;
Things are in the saddle,
And ride mankind.

There are two laws discrete.
Not reconciled,—
Law for man, and law for things;
The last builds town and fleet,
But it runs wild,
And doth the man unking.

'T is fit the forest fall,
The steep be graded,
The mountain tunnelled,
The sand shaded,
The orchard planted,
The glebe tilled,
The prairie granted,
The steamer built.

Let man serve law for man;
Live for friendship, live for love,
For truth's and harmony's behoof;
The state may follow how it can,
As Olympus follows Jove.[7]

Yet do not I implore
The wrinkled shopman to my sounding woods,
Nor bid the unwilling senator
Ask votes of thrushes in the solitudes.
Every one to his chosen work;—
Foolish hands may mix and mar;
Wise and sure the issues are.
Round they roll till dark is light,
Sex to sex, and even to odd;—

6. Obsolete term for oxen.
7. Jove (Jupiter, or Zeus) was the father-god of the Greek deities on Olympus.

The over-god   80
Who marries Right to Might,
Who peoples, unpeoples,—
He who exterminates
Races by stronger races,
Black by white faces,—   85
Knows to bring honey
Out of the lion;[8]
Grafts gentlest scion
On pirate and Turk.

The Cossack eats Poland,[9]   90
Like stolen fruit;
Her last noble is ruined,
Her last poet mute:
Straight, into double band
The victors divide;   95
Half for freedom strike and stand;—
The astonished Muse finds thousands at her side.

1847

Fable[1]

The mountain and the squirrel
Had a quarrel,
And the former called the latter "Little Prig;"
Bun replied,
"You are doubtless very big;   5
But all sorts of things and weather
Must be taken in together,
To make up a year
And a sphere.
And I think it no disgrace   10
To occupy my place.
If I'm not so large as you,
You are not so small as I,
And not half so spry.
I'll not deny you make   15
A very pretty squirrel track;
Talents differ; all is well and wisely put;

8. *Cf.* Samson's exploit (Judges xiv: 9).
9. In spite of the Russian military despotism in Poland after the popular insurrections of 1830–1831, a new Polish generation was striking for liberty in 1846 (*cf.* ll. 94–96).
1. "Fable" first appeared in *The Diadem* in 1846, and was collected in the volumes of 1847 and 1876.

If I cannot carry forests on my back,
Neither can you crack a nut."

1845   1846, 1847

Brahma[2]

If the red slayer think he slays,
    Or if the slain think he is slain,
They know not well the subtle ways
    I keep, and pass, and turn again.

Far or forgot to me is near;   5
    Shadow and sunlight are the same;
The vanished gods to me appear;
    And one to me are shame and fame.

They reckon ill who leave me out;
    When me they fly, I am the wings;   10
I am the doubter and the doubt,
    And I the hymn the Brahmin sings.

The strong gods pine for my abode,
    And pine in vain the sacred Seven,[3]
But thou, meek lover of the good!   15
    Find me, and turn thy back on heaven.

1856   1857, 1867

Days[4]

Daughters of Time, the hypocritic Days,
Muffled and dumb like barefoot dervishes,
And marching single in an endless file,
Bring diadems and fagots in their hands.
To each they offer gifts after his will,   5
Bread, kingdoms, stars, and sky that holds them all.

2. Brahma is the Hindu supreme soul of the universe—an uncreated, illimitable, and timeless essence or being. Emerson, discussing with his daughter the perplexity into which his poem had thrown many, said "tell them to say Jehovah instead of Brahma." The poem is an exposition of the erroneous relativity of human and temporal perception, as compared with the sublime harmony of cosmic divinity. The images of the poem are presumably based on certain extracts in Emerson's *Journals* from the *Vishnu Purana*, extensively discussed in the Centenary Edition (Vol. IX, pp. 464–467). "Brahma" was one of four poems by Emerson in the first number of the *Atlantic Monthly*, November, 1857; it then took its place in the volumes of 1867 and 1876.

3. The seven high saints of the Brahmin faith.

4. One of the most perfect of Emerson's lyrics, "Days" appeared with "Brahma" in the *Atlantic Monthly* for November, 1857 and in the volumes of 1867 and 1876.

I, in my pleached garden, watched the pomp,
Forgot my morning wishes, hastily
Took a few herbs and apples, and the Day
Turned and departed silent. I, too late,   10
Under her solemn fillet saw the scorn.

1857, 1867

Waldeinsamkeit[5]

I do not count the hours I spend
In wandering by the sea;
The forest is my loyal friend,
Like God it useth me.

In plains that room for shadows make   5
Of skirting hills to lie,
Bound in by streams which give and take
Their colors from the sky;

Or on the mountain-crest sublime,
Or down the oaken glade,   10
O what have I to do with time?
For this the day was made.

Cities of mortals woe-begone
Fantastic care derides,
But in the serious landscape lone   15
Stern benefit abides.

Sheen will tarnish, honey cloy,
And merry is only a mask of sad,
But, sober on a fund of joy,
The woods at heart are glad.   20

There the great Planter plants
Of fruitful worlds the grain,
And with a million spells enchants
The souls that walk in pain.

Still on the seeds of all he made   25
The rose of beauty burns;
Through times that wear and forms that fade,
Immortal youth returns.

5. Emerson's son and editor translated
this German title as "Forest Solitude,"
and associated it with the woods of
Walden, Thoreau's hermitage. The poem
appeared in the *Atlantic Monthly* for
October, 1858, and in the volume of
1867.

The black ducks mounting from the lake,
The pigeon in the pines,
The bittern's boom, a desert make   30
Which no false art refines.

Down in yon watery nook,
Where bearded mists divide,
The gray old gods whom Chaos knew,   35
The sires of Nature, hide.

Aloft, in secret veins of air,
Blows the sweet breath of song,
O, few to scale those uplands dare,
Though they to all belong!   40

See thou bring not to field or stone
The fancies found in books;
Leave authors' eyes, and fetch your own,
To brave the landscape's looks.

Oblivion here thy wisdom is,   45
Thy thrift, the sleep of cares;
For a proud idleness like this
Crowns all thy mean affairs.

1858, 1867

Terminus[6]

It is time to be old,
To take in sail:—
The god of bounds,
Who sets to seas a shore,
Came to me in his fatal rounds,   5
And said: 'No more!
No farther shoot
Thy broad ambitious branches, and thy root,
Fancy departs: no more invent,
Contract thy firmament   10
To compass of a tent.
There's not enough for this and that,
Make thy option which of two;
Economize the failing river,
Nor the less revere the Giver,   15

6. Terminus was the Roman deity of boundaries; the poem, of course, has autobiographical significance. It ap-peared in the *Atlantic Monthly* for January, 1867, and the same year in the *May-Day* volume.

Leave the many and hold the few.
Timely wise accept the terms,
Soften the fall with wary foot;
A little while
Still plan and smile,   20
And, fault of novel germs,
Mature the unfallen fruit.
Curse, if thou wilt, thy sires,
Bad husbands of their fires,
Who, when they gave thee breath,   25
Failed to bequeath
The needful sinew stark as once,
The Baresark[7] marrow to thy bones,
But left a legacy of ebbing veins,
Inconstant heat and nerveless reins,—   30
Amid the Muses, left thee deaf and dumb,
Amid the gladiators, halt and numb.'

   As the bird trims her to the gale,
I trim myself to the storm of time,
I man the rudder, reef the sail,   35
Obey the voice at eve obeyed at prime:
'Lowly faithful, banish fear,
Right onward drive unharmed;
The port well worth the cruise, is near,
And every wave is charmed.'   40

1867

7. *I.e.*, berserk ("bare of shirt"); said of the ancient Germanic warriors who fought
without armor.

HENRY DAVID THOREAU
(1817–1862)

Thoreau died at forty-four, having published relatively little of what he had written. He expressed his characteristic dilemma when he declared: "My life has been the poem I would have writ, / But I could not both live and utter it." At his best, perhaps he succeeded in doing just that.

   Thoreau's outward life reflected his inward stature as a small and quiet pond reflects the diminished outline of a mountain. Concord, the place where he lived and died, was tiny, but it was the center of an exciting intellectual world, and the poverty of his family did not prevent him from getting a good start in the classics at the local academy. At Harvard College in Cambridge, a few miles away, he maintained himself frugally with the help of his aunts, and by doing chores and teaching during leisure hours and vacations. There he began his *Journals*, ultimately to become the largest of his works, a storehouse of his observations and ideas. Upon graduation he tried teaching, and for a time conducted a private school in Concord with his brother, John; but he had no inclination toward a career in the ordinary sense. Living was the object of life, and work was never an end in itself, but merely the self-respecting means by which one paid his way in the world. While he made his home with his father, he assisted him in his trade of pencil maker, but he lost interest as soon as they had learned to make the best pencil to be had. When he lived with Emerson (1841–1843 and 1847–1848) he did the chores, and he kept the house while Emerson was abroad. At the home of Emerson's brother William on Staten Island, in 1843, he tutored the children. In Concord village, he did odd jobs, hired himself out, and surveyed other men's lands without coveting them.

Meanwhile, his inward life, as recorded in the *Journals*, was vastly enriched by experience and steady reading. In the year of his graduation from Harvard (1837), his Concord neighbor, Emerson, made his address on *The American Scholar*, and both the man and the essay became Thoreau's early guide. The next year he delivered his first lecture, at the Concord Lyceum; he later gave lectures from Bangor, Maine, to Philadelphia, but never acquired Emerson's skill in communicating to his audience.

On his journeys he made friends as various as Orestes Brownson, Horace Greeley, John Brown, and Walt Whitman; he and Emerson were the two who recognized Whitman's genius from the beginning. At home in Concord he attended Alcott's "conversations," and shared the intellectual excitements and stimulation of the informal Transcendental Club which met at Concord and Boston. The Club sponsored *The Dial* (1840–1844), to which he contributed essays drawn from his *Journals* and his study of natural history and philosophy.

A number of his best poems also appeared in *The Dial*, and the bulk of his poetry was written in the earlier years. Although Emerson overshot the mark in declaring that "his biography is in his verses," it is true that the same lyrical response to ideas pervades his poetry, his prose, and his life. Thoreau tacitly recognized this by incorporating much of his poetry in *A Week on the Concord and Merrimack Rivers* (1849) and *Walden* (1854), the two volumes which were published before his death. But it is a mistake to suppose that the serene individualism of his writings reflects only an unbroken serenity of life. Many Massachusetts neighbors, and even some transcendentalists, regarded Thoreau as an extremist, especially on public and economic issues. There were painful clashes of temperament with Emerson. In his personal life he suffered deep bereavements. His older brother, John, who was also his best friend, revealed his love for the girl whom Henry hoped to marry, and Ellen Sewall refused them both. Two years later, John died at twenty-seven, first victim of the family frailty which removed the beloved sister Helen at thirty-six, and caused Thoreau's death, after seven years of tuberculosis, at the age of forty-four.

Two aspects of Thoreau's life provided the bulk of his literary materials: his active concern with social issues and his feeling for the unity of man and nature. He took an early interest in abolition, appearing as speaker at anti-slavery conventions, once in company with John Brown, whom he later publicly defended after the terrifying and bloody raid at Harpers Ferry. (See "Slavery in Massachusetts," 1854, and "A Plea for John Brown," 1859.) He was able also to associate his private rebellion with large social issues, as in his resistance to taxation. He refused to pay the church taxes (1838) because they were levied on all alike, as for an "established" church. In his refusal to pay the poll tax, which cost him a jail sentence (1845), he was resisting the "constitutional" concept which led Massachusetts to give support in Congress to southern leadership, as represented by the Mexican War and repugnant laws concerning slave "property." Four years later he formalized his theory of social action in the essay "Civil Disobedience," the origin of the modern concept of pacific resistance as the final instrument of minority opinion, which found its spectacular demonstration in the life of Mahatma Gandhi of India.

Thoreau's works at all points reveal his economic and social individualism, but until recently his readers responded chiefly to his accurate and sympathetic reporting of nature, his interesting use of the stored learning of the past, and the wit, grace, and power of his style. His description of nature was based on his journals of his various "excursions," as he called them. A Week on the Concord and Merrimack Rivers, his first published volume, described a canoe trip with his brother John in 1839. Other trips of literary significance were his explorations of the Penobscot forests of Maine (1846, 1853, and 1857), and his walking tours on Cape Cod (1849, 1850, 1855, and 1857) and in Canada. Certain essays on these adventures were published in magazines before his death; later his friends published Cape Cod (1863), The Maine Woods (1864), and A Yankee in Canada (1866), which resulted from a trip to Canada with W. E. Channing in 1850.

In his revelation of the simplicity and divine unity of nature, in his faith in man, in his own sturdy individualism, in his deep-rooted love for one place as an epitome of the universe, Thoreau reminds us of what we are and what we yet may be.

Posthumously collected volumes of Thoreau, in addition to those mentioned in the text, were Excursions, 1863, Early Spring in Massachusetts, 1881, Summer, 1884, Winter, 1888, and Autumn, 1892. Emerson included some poems, not strictly edited, in a collection of Letters to Various Persons, 1865, but a more reliable and inclusive edition, collated with manuscripts, is the Poems of Nature, 1895. A recent critical edition of the poems is Collected Poems, edited by Carl Bode, 1943.

The first major collection was the

Riverside Edition, 10 vols., 1894, now superseded by the Manuscript Edition and the standard Walden Edition (from the same plates), *The Writings of Henry David Thoreau*, 20 vols., 1906. The bulk of the published letters are in *Familiar Letters of Henry David Thoreau*, 1894, included as Vol. VI of the Walden Edition. The *Journals* (1837–1861), edited by Bradford Torrey, are available as Vols., VII–XX of the Walden Edition, and were reprinted, with an introduction by H. S. Canby, 1951. A good selection is *The Heart of Thoreau's Journals*, edited by Odell Shepard, 1927. An available modern collection is *The Works of Thoreau*, Cambridge Edition, edited by H. S. Canby, 1947; standard selections are *Henry David Thoreau: Representative Selections*, edited by B. V. Crawford,

American Writers Series, 1934, and *The Portable Thoreau*, edited by Carl Bode, 1947.

Standard biographies of Thoreau are those of F. B. Sanborn, 1882, H. S. Salt, 1896, and Mark Van Doren, 1916. Recent scholarship and criticism is reflected in J. B. Atkinson, *Henry Thoreau, the Cosmic Yankee*, 1927; H. S. Canby, *Thoreau*, 1939; and J. W. Krutch, *Henry David Thoreau*, 1948.

In the present edition, the prose texts are those of the first appearance in a volume, unless otherwise noted; the poems represent a collation of *Poems of Nature*, with the excerpts in *A Week on the Concord and Merrimack Rivers* and *Walden*. The prose selections are reprinted in the order of composition, verse in the order of first publication.

From A Week on the Concord and Merrimack Rivers

[*Nature, Poetry, and the Poet*][1]

If one doubts whether Grecian valor and patriotism are not a fiction of the poets, he may go to Athens and see still upon the walls of the temple of Minerva[2] the circular marks made by the shields taken from the enemy in the Persian war, which were suspended there. We have not far to seek for living and unquestionable evidence. The very dust takes shape and confirms some story which we had read. As Fuller said, commenting on the zeal of Camden,[3] "A broken urn is a whole evidence; or an old gate still surviving out of which the city is run out." When Solon[4] endeavored to prove that Salamis had formerly belonged to the Athenians, and not to the Megareans, he caused the tombs to be opened, and showed that the inhabitants of Salamis turned the faces of their dead to the same side with the Athenians, but the Megareans to the opposite side. There they were to be interrogated.

1. *A Week on the Concord and Merrimack Rivers* (1849) was Thoreau's first book, the miscellany of an already learned young poet and meditative thinker. While describing his "fluvial excursions" with his brother, John, on these rivers in 1839, he makes observant comments on nature, man, society, and literature, occasionally introducing a poem of his own. *Walden* has a more finished style, but *A Week * * ** is distinguished among Thoreau's works for its unique morning-charm, as whimsical as the naming of chapters for days of the week. The scattered passages here assembled express a theory of art and poetry, transcendental in nature, which Thoreau consistently supported. A number of the poems of *A Week * * ** are

also reprinted below, as noted.
2. Known to the Greeks as Athena, goddess of wisdom, protectress of Athens, to whom were dedicated the spoils of battle, as here mentioned.
3. Thomas Fuller (1608–1661), churchman and writer, in his famous *History of the Worthies of England*, praised William Camden (1551–1623), a learned schoolmaster whose history, *Britannia*, treated British antiquities; but Thoreau, as he says in the following paragraphs, would rather draw the poet's attention to the antiquities of nature.
4. Greek statesman (638?–559? B.C.), called "the lawgiver," who made his advent as one of the Seven Wise Men of Greece by this recovery of Salamis.

Some minds are as little logical or argumentative as nature; they can offer no reason or "guess," but they exhibit the solemn and incontrovertible fact. If a historical question arises, they cause the tombs to be opened. Their silent and practical logic convinces the reason and the understanding at the same time. Of such sort is always the only pertinent question and the only unanswerable reply.

Our own country furnishes antiquities as ancient and durable, and as useful, as any; rocks at least as well covered with moss, and a soil which if it is virgin, is but virgin mould, the very dust of nature. What if we cannot read Rome, or Greece, Etruria, or Carthage, or Egypt, or Babylon, on these; are our cliffs bare? The lichen on the rocks is a rude and simple shield which beginning and imperfect Nature suspended there. Still hangs her wrinkled trophy. And here too the poet's eye may still detect the brazen nails which fastened Time's inscriptions, and if he has the gift, decipher them by this clue. The walls that fence our fields, as well as modern Rome, and not less the Parthenon itself, are all built of *ruins*. Here may be heard the din of rivers, and ancient winds which have long since lost their names sough through our woods;—the first faint sounds of spring, older than the summer of Athenian glory, the titmouse lisping in the wood, the jay's scream, and blue-bird's warble, and the hum of

> "bees that fly
> About the laughing blossoms of sallowy."

Here is the gray dawn for antiquity, and our to-morrow's future should be at least paulo-post[5] to theirs which we have put behind us. There are the red-maple and birchen leaves, old runes which are not yet deciphered; catkins, pine-cones, vines, oak-leaves, and acorns; the very things themselves, and not their forms in stone,—so much the more ancient and venerable. And even to the current summer there has come down tradition of a hoary-headed master of all art, who once filled every field and grove with statues and god-like architecture, of every design which Greece has lately copied; whose ruins are now mingled with the dust, and not one block remains upon another. The century sun and unwearied rain have wasted them, till not one fragment from that quarry now exists; and poets perchance will feign that gods sent down the material from heaven. * * *

Poetry is the mysticism of mankind.

The expressions of the poet cannot be analyzed; his sentence is one word, whose syllables are words. There are indeed no *words* quite worthy to be set to his music. But what matter if we do not hear the words always, if we hear the music?

5. Latin, "a little bit afterward"; hence, "at the least interval succeeding to theirs."

Much verse fails of being poetry because it was not written exactly at the right crisis, though it may have been inconceivably near to it. It is only by a miracle that poetry is written at all. It is not recoverable thought, but a hue caught from a vaster receding thought.

A poem is one undivided, unimpeded expression fallen ripe into literature, and it is undividedly and unimpededly received by those for whom it was matured.

If you can speak what you will never hear,—if you can write what you will never read, you have done rare things.

There are two classes of men called poets. The one cultivates life, the other art,—one seeks food for nutriment, the other for flavor; one satisfies hunger, the other gratifies the palate. There are two kinds of writing, both great and rare; one that of genius, or the inspired, the other of intellect and taste, in the intervals of inspiration. The former is above criticism, always correct, giving the law to criticism. It vibrates and pulsates with life forever. It is sacred, and to be read with reverence, as the works of nature are studied. There are few instances of a sustained style of this kind; perhaps every man has spoken words, but the speaker is then careless of the record. Such a style removes us out of personal relations with its author, we do not take his words on our lips, but his sense into our hearts. It is the stream of inspiration, which bubbles out, now here, now there, now in this man, now in that. It matters not through what ice-crystals it is seen, now a fountain, now the ocean stream running under ground. It is in Shakspeare, Alpheus, in Burns, Arethuse;[6] but ever the same. —The other is self-possessed and wise. It is reverent of genius, and greedy of inspiration. It is conscious in the highest and the least degree. It consists with the most perfect command of the faculties. It dwells in a repose as of the desert, and objects are as distinct in it as oases or palms in the horizon of sand. The train of thought moves with subdued and measured step, like a caravan. But the pen is only an instrument in its hand, and not instinct with life, like a longer arm. It leaves a thin varnish or glaze over all its work. The works of Goethe furnish remarkable instances of the latter.

There is no just and serene criticism as yet. Nothing is considered simply as it lies in the lap of eternal beauty, but our thoughts, as well as our bodies, must be dressed after the latest fashions. Our taste is too delicate and particular. It says nay to the poet's work, but never yea to his hope. It invites him to adorn his deformities, and not to cast them off by expansion, as the tree its bark. We are a people who live in a bright light, in houses of pearl and porcelain, and drink only light wines, whose teeth are easily set on edge by the least natural

6. Alpheus, fabled god of a Greek river, pursued the nymph Arethusa, who was changed into a Sicilian fountain; but Alpheus followed her undersea in order to mingle their waters (see Thoreau's previous sentence).

sour. If we had been consulted, the backbone of the earth would have been made, not of granite, but of Bristol spar.[7] A modern author would have died in infancy in a ruder age. But the poet is something more than a scald,[8] "a smoother and polisher of language;" he is a Cincinnatus[9] in literature, and occupies no west end of the world. Like the sun, he will indifferently select his rhymes, and with a liberal taste weave into his verse the planet and the stubble.

In these old books the stucco has long since crumbled away, and we read what was sculptured in the granite. They are rude and massive in their proportions, rather than smooth and delicate in their finish. The workers in stone polish only their chimney ornaments, but their pyramids are roughly done. There is a soberness in a rough aspect, as of unhewn granite, which addresses a depth in us, but a polished surface hits only the ball of the eye. The true finish is the work of time and the use to which a thing is put. The elements are still polishing the pyramids. Art may varnish and gild, but it can do no more. A work of genius is rough-hewn from the first, because it anticipates the lapse of time, and has an ingrained polish, which still appears when fragments are broken off, an essential quality of its substance. Its beauty is at the same time its strength, and it breaks with a lustre.

1839   1849

From Walden[1]

I. Economy

When I wrote the following pages, or rather the bulk of them, I lived alone, in the woods, a mile from any neighbor, in a house which I had built myself, on the shore of Walden Pond,[2] in Concord, Massa-

7. The spars are lustrous rocks, readily broken; granite, though less eye-catching, is hard and durable.

8. The ancient Norse *skald* generally recited poems already traditional.

9. Lucius Quintus Cincinnatus (519–439? B.C.), legendary symbol of virtuous power, was twice appointed dictator of Rome in military crises, and promptly defeating his country's enemies, resigned his powers in favor of his farm.

1. The earliest manuscript of this famous book, entitled "Walden, or Life in the Woods," was prepared, as Thoreau there states, "about 1846." It was later much revised in the preparation of portions for reading at meetings of the Concord Lyceum, and for the publication of the volume in 1854. The present text is based on this 1854 edition. Of the selections below, Chapter I is Thoreau's analysis of the economy of individualism and the details of the experiment at Walden Pond, by which he

sought to test his theories; Chapter II discusses the values which a free individual may win by self-reliance in society or solitude; Chapter XII is a collection of sketches of the wild life of the woods, of which the wonderful narrative of the battle of the ants is included in this volume; and Chapter XVIII, the "Conclusion," summarizes Thoreau's transcendental concept of the human personality, of man's relations with the Timeless rather than with Time, and other ideas which have been suggested in chapters which, from considerations of space, have been omitted.

2. Thoreau later describes Walden Pond as half a mile wide and located about a mile and a half south of Concord, in a large wood between Concord and Lincoln. He resided there from July 4, 1845 until September 6, 1847, building his house on land belonging to Emerson, on the north shore.

chusetts, and earned my living by the labor of my hands only. I lived there two years and two months. At present I am a sojourner in civilized life again.

I should not obtrude my affairs so much on the notice of my readers if very particular inquiries had not been made by my townsmen concerning my mode of life, which some would call impertinent, though they do not appear to me at all impertinent, but, considering the circumstances, very natural and pertinent. Some have asked what I got to eat; if I did not feel lonesome; if I was not afraid; and the like. Others have been curious to learn what portion of my income I devoted to charitable purposes; and some, who have large families, how many poor children I maintained. I will therefore ask those of my readers who feel no particular interest in me to pardon me if I undertake to answer some of these questions in this book. In most books, the I, or first person, is omitted; in this it will be retained; that, in respect to egotism, is the main difference. We commonly do not remember that it is, after all, always the first person that is speaking. I should not talk so much about myself if there were anybody else whom I knew as well. Unfortunately, I am confined to this theme by the narrowness of my experience. Moreover, I, on my side, require of every writer, first or last, a simple and sincere account of his own life, and not merely what he has heard of other men's lives; some such account as he would send to his kindred from a distant land; for if he has lived sincerely, it must have been in a distant land to me. Perhaps these pages are more particularly addressed to poor students. As for the rest of my readers, they will accept such portions as apply to them. I trust that none will stretch the seams in putting on the coat, for it may do good service to him whom it fits.

I would fain say something, not so much concerning the Chinese and Sandwich Islanders as you who read these pages, who are said to live in New England; something about your condition, especially your outward condition or circumstances in this world, in this town, what it is, whether it is necessary that it be as bad as it is, whether it cannot be improved as well as not. I have travelled a good deal in Concord; and everywhere, in shops, and offices, and fields, the inhabitants have appeared to me to be doing penance in a thousand remarkable ways. What I have heard of Bramins sitting exposed to four fires and looking in the face of the sun; or hanging suspended, with their heads downward, over flames; or looking at the heavens over their shoulders "until it becomes impossible for them to resume their natural position, while from the twist of the neck nothing but liquids can pass into the stomach;" or dwelling, chained for life, at the foot of a tree; or measuring with their bodies, like caterpillars, the breadth of vast empires; or standing on one leg on the tops of pillars,—even these forms of conscious penance are hardly more incredible and astonishing than the scenes which I daily witness. The twelve labors of Hercules[3] were trifling in comparison with those which my neighbors have undertaken; for they were only twelve, and had an end; but I could never see that these men slew or captured any monster or finished any labor. They have no friend Iolaus to burn with a hot iron the root of the hydra's head, but as soon as one head is crushed, two spring up.

I see young men, my townsmen, whose misfortune it is to have inherited farms, houses, barns, cattle, and farming tools; for these are more easily acquired than got rid of. Better if they had been born in the open pasture and suckled by a wolf, that they might have seen with clearer eyes what field they were called to labor in. Who made them serfs of the soil? Why should they eat their sixty acres, when man is condemned to eat only his peck of dirt? Why should they begin digging their graves as soon as they are born? They have got to live a man's life, pushing all these things before them, and get on as well as they can. How many a poor immortal soul have I met well-nigh crushed and smothered under its load, creeping down the road of life, pushing before it a barn seventy-five feet by forty, its Augean stables never cleansed,[4] and one hundred acres of land, tillage, mowing, pasture, and wood-lot! The portionless, who struggle with no such unnecessary inherited encumbrances, find it labor enough to subdue and cultivate a few cubic feet of flesh.

But men labor under a mistake. The better part of the man is soon plowed into the soil for compost. By a seeming fate, commonly called necessity, they are employed, as it says in an old book, laying up treasures which moth and rust will corrupt and thieves break through and steal.[5] It is a fool's life, as they will find when they get to the end of it, if not before. It is said that Deucalion and Pyrrha created men by throwing stones over their heads behind them:—[6]

> Inde genus durum sumus, experiensque laborum,
> Et documenta damus quâ simus origine nati.

Or, as Raleigh rhymes it in his sonorous way,—

> "From thence our kind hard-hearted is, enduring pain and care,
> Approving that our bodies of a stony nature are."

3. The fabulous strong man of the Greeks, the son of Jupiter by a mortal. The goddess Juno, jealous, set him the almost impossible "twelve labors." Iolaus, as here mentioned, helped him to subdue the hydra; another of his tasks was to cleanse the Augean stables, mentioned in the following paragraph.
4. The stables of Augeus had housed three thousand oxen for thirty years, but Hercules cleansed them in one day by turning the course of a river through the stalls.
5. Matthew vi: 19–20.
6. This story of the creation occurs in Ovid, *Metamorphoses*, Book I. The Latin lines 414–415 are well represented in the English translation of Raleigh, an Elizabethan whom Thoreau praised as poet and man of action in "Sir Walter Raleigh," an essay.

So much for a blind obedience to a blundering oracle, throwing the stones over their heads behind them, and not seeing where they fell.

Most men, even in this comparatively free country, through mere ignorance and mistake, are so occupied with the factitious cares and superfluously coarse labors of life that its finer fruits cannot be plucked by them. Their fingers, from excessive toil, are too clumsy and tremble too much for that. Actually, the laboring man has not leisure for a true integrity day by day; he cannot afford to sustain the manliest relations to men; his labor would be depreciated in the market. He has no time to be anything but a machine. How can he remember well his ignorance—which his growth requires—who has so often to use his knowledge? We should feed and clothe him gratuitously sometimes, and recruit him with our cordials, before we judge of him. The finest qualities of our nature, like the bloom on fruits, can be preserved only by the most delicate handling. Yet we do not treat ourselves nor one another thus tenderly.

Some of you, we all know, are poor, find it hard to live, are sometimes, as it were, gasping for breath. I have no doubt that some of you who read this book are unable to pay for all the dinners which you have actually eaten, or for the coats and shoes which are fast wearing or are already worn out, and have come to this page to spend borrowed or stolen time, robbing your creditors of an hour. It is very evident what mean and sneaking lives many of you live, for my sight has been whetted by experience; always on the limits, trying to get into business and trying to get out of debt, a very ancient slough, called by the Latins *aes alienum*,[7] another's brass, for some of their coins were made of brass; still living, and dying, and buried by this other's brass; always promising to pay, promising to pay, to-morrow, and dying to-day, insolvent; seeking to curry favor, to get custom, by how many modes, only not state-prison offences; lying, flattering, voting, contracting yourselves into a nutshell of civility or dilating into an atmosphere of thin and vaporous generosity, that you may persuade your neighbor to let you make his shoes, or his hat, or his coat, or his carriage, or import his groceries for him; making yourselves sick, that you may lay up something against a sick day, something to be tucked away in an old chest, or in a stocking behind the plastering, or, more safely, in the brick bank; no matter where, no matter how much or how little.

I sometimes wonder that we can be so frivolous, I may almost say, as to attend to the gross but somewhat foreign form of servitude called Negro Slavery, there are so many keen and subtle masters that enslave both North and South. It is hard to have a Southern overseer; it is worse to have a Northern one; but worst of all when you are the slave-driver of yourself. Talk of a divinity in man! Look at

---

7. Latin *aes*, "bronze" (brass) or "copper," signified also metal coinage or money; hence *aes alienum*, "another's money," meant "debt."

the teamster on the highway, wending to market by day or night; does any divinity stir within him?[8] His highest duty to fodder and water his horses! What is his destiny to him compared with the shipping interests? Does not he drive for Squire Make-a-stir? How godlike, how immortal, is he? See how he cowers and sneaks, how vaguely all the day he fears, not being immortal nor divine, but the slave and prisoner of his own opinion of himself, a fame won by his own deeds. Public opinion is a weak tyrant compared with our own private opinion. What a man thinks of himself, that it is which determines, or rather indicates, his fate. Self-emancipation even in the West Indian provinces of the fancy and imagination,—what Wilberforce[9] is there to bring that about? Think, also, of the ladies of the land weaving toilet cushions against the last day, not to betray too green an interest in their fates! As if you could kill time without injuring eternity.

The mass of men lead lives of quiet desperation. What is called resignation is confirmed desperation. From the desperate city you go into the desperate country, and have to console yourself with the bravery of minks and muskrats. A stereotyped but unconscious despair is concealed even under what are called the games and amusements of mankind. There is no play in them, for this comes after work. But it is a characteristic of wisdom not to do desperate things.

When we consider what, to use the words of the catechism, is the chief end of man,[1] and what are the true necessaries and means of life, it appears as if men had deliberately chosen the common mode of living because they preferred it to any other. Yet they honestly think there is no choice left. But alert and healthy natures remember that the sun rose clear. It is never too late to give up our prejudices. No way of thinking or doing, however ancient, can be trusted without proof. What everybody echoes or in silence passes by as true to-day may turn out to be falsehood to-morrow, mere smoke of opinion, which some had trusted for a cloud that would sprinkle fertilizing rain on their fields. What old people say you cannot do, you try and find that you can. Old deeds for old people, and new deeds for new. Old people did not know enough once, perchance, to fetch fresh fuel to keep the fire a-going; new people put a little dry wood under a pot, and are whirled round the globe with the speed of birds, in a way to kill old people, as the phrase is. Age is no better, hardly so well, qualified for an instructor as youth, for

8. A leading tenet of transcendentalism, but he may also have remembered Joseph Addison's *Cato*, Act V, Scene 1: " 'Tis the divinity that stirs within us"; this divinity was seemingly defeated by economic hardships and slaveholding in Massachusetts (see *Journals*, Vol. VIII, p. 175 and Vol. XII, pp. 313, 355–8).
9. William Wilberforce (1759–1833),

British parliamentarian, was a prominent leader in the British abolition movement which secured laws abolishing the slave trade (1807) and emancipating the slaves in British territories (1833).
1. In the *Westminster Shorter Catechism*, the response to this question is: "To glorify God, and to enjoy Him forever."

it has not profited so much as it has lost. One may almost doubt if the wisest man has learned anything of absolute value by living. Practically, the old have no very important advice to give the young, their own experience has been so partial, and their lives have been such miserable failures, for private reasons, as they must believe; and it may be that they have some faith left which belies that experience, and they are only less young than they were. I have lived some thirty years on this planet, and I have yet to hear the first syllable of valuable or even earnest advice from my seniors. They have told me nothing, and probably cannot tell me anything to the purpose. Here is life, an experiment to a great extent untried by me; but it does not avail me that they have tried it. If I have any experience which I think valuable, I am sure to reflect that this my Mentors said nothing about.

One farmer says to me, "You cannot live on vegetable food solely, for it furnishes nothing to make bones with;" and so he religiously devotes a part of his day to supplying his system with the raw material of bones; walking all the while he talks behind his oxen, which, with vegetable-made bones, jerk him and his lumbering plow along in spite of every obstacle. Some things are really necessaries of life in some circles, the most helpless and diseased, which in others are luxuries merely, and in others still are entirely unknown.

The whole ground of human life seems to some to have been gone over by their predecessors, both the heights and the valleys, and all things to have been cared for. According to Evelyn,[2] "the wise Solomon prescribed ordinances for the very distances of trees; and the Roman prætors have decided how often you may go into your neighbor's land to gather the acorns which fall on it without trespass, and what share belongs to that neighbor." Hippocrates[3] has even left directions how we should cut our nails; that is, even with the ends of the fingers, neither shorter nor longer. Undoubtedly the very tedium and ennui which presume to have exhausted the variety and the joys of life are as old as Adam. But man's capacities have never been measured; nor are we to judge of what he can do by any precedents, so little has been tried. Whatever have been thy failures hitherto, "be not afflicted, my child, for who shall assign to thee what thou hast left undone?"

We might try our lives by a thousand simple tests; as, for instance, that the same sun which ripens my beans illumines at once a system of earths like ours. If I had remembered this it would have prevented some mistakes. This was not the light in which I hoed them. The

2. John Evelyn (1620–1706), British official famous for his *Diary*, wrote many technical works, including a book on arboriculture, *Sylva* (1664), the source of this quotation.

3. Hippocrates (460?–377? B.C.) Greek "father of medicine," reputed author of eighty-seven treatises and the Hippocratic Oath.

stars are the apexes of what wonderful triangles! What distant and different beings in the various mansions of the universe are contemplating the same one at the same moment! Nature and human life are as various as our several constitutions. Who shall say what prospect life offers to another? Could a greater miracle take place than for us to look through each other's eyes for an instant? We should live in all the ages of the world in an hour; ay, in all the worlds of the ages. History, Poetry, Mythology!—I know of no reading of another's experience so startling and informing as this would be.

The greater part of what my neighbors call good I believe in my soul to be bad, and if I repent of anything, it is very likely to be my good behavior. What demon possessed me that I behaved so well? You may say the wisest thing you can, old man,—you who have lived seventy years, not without honor of a kind,—I hear an irresistible voice which invites me away from all that. One generation abandons the enterprises of another like stranded vessels. * * *

If I should attempt to tell how I have desired to spend my life in years past, it would probably surprise those of my readers who are somewhat acquainted with its actual history; it would certainly astonish those who know nothing about it. I will only hint at some of the enterprises which I have cherished.

In any weather, at any hour of the day or night, I have been anxious to improve the nick of time, and notch it on my stick too; to stand on the meeting of two eternities, the past and future, which is precisely the present moment; to toe that line. You will pardon some obscurities, for there are more secrets in my trade than in most men's, and yet not voluntarily kept, but inseparable from its very nature. I would gladly tell all that I know about it, and never paint "No Admittance" on my gate.

I long ago lost a hound, a bay horse, and a turtledove, and am still on their trail. Many are the travellers I have spoken concerning them, describing their tracks and what calls they answered to. I have met one or two who had heard the hound, and the tramp of the horse, and even seen the dove disappear behind a cloud, and they seemed as anxious to recover them as if they had lost them themselves.

To anticipate, not the sunrise and the dawn merely, but, if possible, Nature herself! How many mornings, summer and winter, before yet any neighbor was stirring about his business, have I been about mine! No doubt, many of my townsmen have met me returning from this enterprise, farmers starting for Boston in the twilight, or woodchoppers going to their work. It is true, I never assisted the sun materially in his rising, but, doubt not, it was of the last importance only to be present at it.

So many autumn, ay, and winter days, spent outside the town, trying to hear what was in the wind, to hear and carry it express! I well-nigh sunk all my capital in it, and lost my own breath into the bargain, running in the face of it. If it had concerned either of the political parties, depend upon it, it would have appeared in the Gazette with the earliest intelligence. At other times watching from the observatory of some cliff or tree, to telegraph any new arrival; or waiting at evening on the hill-tops for the sky to fall, that I might catch something, though I never caught much, and that, manna-wise, would dissolve again in the sun.

For a long time I was reporter to a journal,[4] of no very wide circulation, whose editor has never yet seen fit to print the bulk of my contributions, and, as it is too common with writers, I got only my labor for my pains. However, in this case my pains were their own reward.

For many years I was self-appointed inspector of snow-storms and rain-storms, and did my duty faithfully; surveyor, if not of highways, then of forest paths and all across-lot routes, keeping them open, and ravines bridged and passable at all seasons, where the public heel had testified to their utility.

I have looked after the wild stock of the town, which give a faithful herdsman a good deal of trouble by leaping fences; and I have had an eye to the unfrequented nooks and corners of the farm; though I did not always know whether Jonas or Solomon worked in a particular field to-day; that was none of my business. I have watered the red huckleberry, the sand cherry and the nettle tree, the red pine and the black ash, the white grape and the yellow violet, which might have withered else in dry seasons.

In short, I went on thus for a long time (I may say it without boasting), faithfully minding my business, till it became more and more evident that my townsmen would not after all admit me into the list of town officers, nor make my place a sinecure with a moderate allowance. My accounts, which I can swear to have kept faithfully, I have, indeed, never got audited, still less accepted, still less paid and settled. However, I have not set my heart on that. * * *

Finding that my fellow-citizens were not likely to offer me any room in the court house, or any curacy or living anywhere else, but I must shift for myself, I turned my face more exclusively than ever to the woods, where I was better known. I determined to go into business at once, and not wait to acquire the usual capital, using such slender means as I had already got. My purpose in going to Walden Pond was not to live cheaply nor to live dearly there, but to transact some private business with the fewest obstacles; to be

4. Probably a reference to his extensive *Journals*, not to be published until 1906; but the circumstances also fit *The Dial* and other magazines which occasionally published his writing.

hindered from accomplishing which for want of a little common sense, a little enterprise and business talent, appeared not so sad as foolish. * * *

The farmer is endeavoring to solve the problem of a livelihood by a formula more complicated than the problem itself. To get his shoestrings he speculates in herds of cattle. With consummate skill he has set his trap with a hair springe to catch comfort and independence, and then, as he turned away, got his own leg into it. This is the reason he is poor; and for a similar reason we are all poor in respect to a thousand savage comforts, though surrounded by luxuries. As Chapman[5] sings,—

> "The false society of men—
>   —for earthly greatness
> All heavenly comforts rarefies to air."

And when the farmer has got his house, he may not be the richer but the poorer for it, and it be the house that has got him. As I understand it, that was a valid objection urged by Momus against the house which Minerva made, that she "had not made it movable, by which means a bad neighborhood might be avoided;" and it may still be urged, for our houses are such unwieldy property that we are often imprisoned rather than housed in them; and the bad neighborhood to be avoided is our own scurvy selves. I know one or two families, at least, in this town, who, for nearly a generation, have been wishing to sell their houses in the outskirts and move into the village, but have not been able to accomplish it, and only death will set them free.

Granted that the *majority* are able at last either to own or hire the modern house with all its improvements. While civilization has been improving our houses, it has not equally improved the men who are to inhabit them. It has created palaces, but it was not so easy to create noblemen and kings. And *if the civilized man's pursuits are no worthier than the savage's, if he is employed the greater part of his life in obtaining gross necessaries and comforts merely, why should he have a better dwelling than the former?*

But how do the poor *minority* fare? Perhaps it will be found that just in proportion as some have been placed in outward circumstances above the savage, others have been degraded below him. The luxury of one class is counterbalanced by the indigence of another. On the one side is the palace, on the other are the almshouse and "silent poor." The myriads who built the pyramids to be the tombs of the Pharaohs were fed on garlic, and it may be were not decently buried themselves. The mason who finishes the cornice of the palace

5. George Chapman (1559?–1634), Elizabethan playwright, remembered chiefly for his translations of Homer.

returns at night perchance to a hut not so good as a wigwam. It is a mistake to suppose that, in a country where the usual evidences of civilization exist, the condition of a very large body of the inhabitants may not be as degraded as that of savages. I refer to the degraded poor, not now to the degraded rich. To know this I should not need to look farther than to the shanties which everywhere border our railroads, that last improvement in civilization; where I see in my daily walks human beings living in sties, and all winter with an open door, for the sake of light, without any visible, often imaginable, wood-pile, and the forms of both old and young are permanently contracted by the long habit of shrinking from cold and misery, and the development of all their limbs and faculties is checked. It certainly is fair to look at that class by whose labor the works which distinguish this generation are accomplished. Such too, to a greater or less extent, is the condition of the operatives of every denomination in England, which is the great workhouse of the world. Or I could refer you to Ireland, which is marked as one of the white or enlightened spots on the map. Contrast the physical condition of the Irish with that of the North American Indian, or the South Sea Islander, or any other savage race before it was degraded by contact with the civilized man. Yet I have no doubt that that people's rulers are as wise as the average of civilized rulers. Their condition only proves what squalidness may consist with civilization. I hardly need refer now to the laborers in our Southern States who produce the staple exports of this country, and are themselves a staple production of the South. But to confine myself to those who are said to be in *moderate* circumstances.

Most men appear never to have considered what a house is, and are actually though needlessly poor all their lives because they think that they must have such a one as their neighbors have. As if one were to wear any sort of coat which the tailor might cut out for him, or, gradually leaving off palmleaf hat or cap of woodchuck skin, complain of hard times because he could not afford to buy him a crown! It is possible to invent a house still more convenient and luxurious than we have, which yet all would admit that man could not afford to pay for. Shall we always study to obtain more of these things, and not sometimes to be content with less? Shall the respectable citizen thus gravely teach, by precept and example, the necessity of the young man's providing a certain number of superfluous glowshoes, and umbrellas, and empty guest chambers for empty guests, before he dies? Why should not our furniture be as simple as the Arab's or the Indian's? When I think of the benefactors of the race, whom we have apotheosized as messengers from heaven, bearers of divine gifts to man, I do not see in my mind any retinue at their heels, any carload of fashionable furniture. Or what if I were to allow—would it not be a singular allowance?—that our furniture should be more complex than the Arab's, in proportion as we are morally and intellectually his superiors! At present our houses are cluttered and defiled with it, and a good housewife would sweep out the greater part into the dust hole, and not leave her morning's work undone. Morning work! By the blushes of Aurora and the music of Memnon,[6] what should be man's *morning work* in this world? I had three pieces of limestone on my desk, but I was terrified to find that they required to be dusted daily, when the furniture of my mind was all undusted still, and I threw them out the window in disgust. How, then, could I have a furnished house? I would rather sit in the open air, for no dust gathers on the grass, unless where man has broken ground. * * *

Near the end of March, 1845, I borrowed an axe and went down to the woods by Walden Pond, nearest to where I intended to build my house, and began to cut down some tall arrowy white pines, still in their youth, for timber. It is difficult to begin without borrowing, but perhaps it is the most generous course thus to permit your fellow-men to have an interest in your enterprise. The owner of the axe, as he released his hold on it, said that it was the apple of his eye; but I returned it sharper than I received it. It was a pleasant hillside where I worked, covered with pine woods, through which I looked out on the pond, and a small open field in the woods where pines and hickories were springing up. The ice in the pond was not yet dissolved, though there were some open spaces, and it was all dark colored and saturated with water. There were some slight flurries of snow during the days that I worked there; but for the most part when I came out on to the railroad, on my way home, its yellow sand heap stretched away gleaming in the hazy atmosphere, and the rails shone in the spring sun, and I heard the lark and pewee and other birds already come to commence another year with us. They were pleasant spring days, in which the winter of man's discontent[7] was thawing as well as the earth, and the life that had lain torpid began to stretch itself. One day, when my axe had come off and I had cut a green hickory for a wedge, driving it with a stone, and had placed the whole to soak in a pond hole in order to swell the wood, I saw a striped snake run into the water, and he lay on the bottom, apparently without inconvenience, as long as I staid there, or more than a quarter of an hour; perhaps because he had not yet fairly come out of the torpid state. It appeared to me that for a like reason men remain in their present low and primitive condition; but if they should feel the influence of the spring of springs arousing them, they would

6. Aurora was the Roman goddess of morning; according to legend, the colossal statue at Thebes of Memnon, her son, gave off music at dawn.

7. *Cf.* Shakespeare, *Richard III*, Act I, Scene 1, l. 1: "Now is the winter of our discontent / Made glorious summer * * * "

of necessity rise to a higher and more ethereal life. I had previously seen the snakes in frosty mornings in my path with portions of their bodies still numb and inflexible, waiting for the sun to thaw them. On the 1st of April it rained and melted the ice, and in the early part of the day, which was very foggy, I heard a stray goose groping about over the pond and cackling as if lost, or like the spirit of the fog.

So I went on for some days cutting and hewing timber, and also studs and rafters, all with my narrow axe, not having many communicable or scholar-like thoughts, singing to myself,—

> Men say they know many things;
> But lo! they have taken wings,—
> The arts and sciences,
> And a thousand appliances;
> The wind that blows
> Is all that any body knows.

I hewed the main timbers six inches square, most of the studs on two sides only, and the rafters and floor timbers on one side, leaving the rest of the bark on, so that they were just as straight and much stronger than sawed ones. Each stick was carefully mortised or tenoned by its stump, for I had borrowed other tools by this time. My days in the woods were not very long ones; yet I usually carried my dinner of bread and butter, and read the newspaper in which it was wrapped, at noon, sitting amid the green pine boughs which I had cut off, and to my bread was imparted some of their fragrance, for my hands were covered with a thick coat of pitch. Before I had done I was more the friend than the foe of the pine tree, though I had cut down some of them, having become better acquainted with it. Sometimes a rambler in the wood was attracted by the sound of my axe, and we chatted pleasantly over the chips which I had made.

By the middle of April, for I made no haste in my work, but rather made the most of it, my house was framed and ready for the raising. I had already bought the shanty of James Collins, an Irishman who worked on the Fitchburg Railroad, for boards. James Collins' shanty was considered an uncommonly fine one. When I called to see it he was not at home. I walked about the outside, at first unobserved from within, the window was so deep and high. It was of small dimensions, with a peaked cottage roof, and not much else to be seen, the dirt being raised five feet all around as if it were a compost heap. The roof was the soundest part, though a good deal warped and made brittle by the sun. Doorsill there was none, but a perennial passage for the hens under the door board. Mrs. C. came to the door and asked me to view it from the inside. The hens were driven in by my approach. It was dark, and had a dirt floor for the most part, dank, clammy, and aguish, only here a board and there a board which would not bear removal. She lighted a lamp to show me the inside of the roof and the walls, and also that the board floor extended under the bed, warning me not to step into the cellar, a sort of dust hole two feet deep. In her own words, they were "good boards overhead, good boards all around, and a good window,"—of two whole squares originally, only the cat had passed out that way lately. There was a stove, a bed, and a place to sit, an infant in the house where it was born, a silk parasol, gilt-framed looking-glass, and a patent new coffee mill nailed to an oak sapling, all told. The bargain was soon concluded, for James had in the mean while returned. I to pay four dollars and twenty-five cents to-night, he to vacate at five to-morrow morning, selling to nobody else meanwhile; I to take possession at six. It were well, he said, to be there early, and anticipate certain indistinct but wholly unjust claims on the score of ground rent and fuel. This he assured me was the only encumbrance. At six I passed him and his family on the road. One large bundle held their all,—bed, coffee-mill, looking-glass, hens,—all but the cat, she took to the woods and became a wild cat, and, as I learned afterward, trod in a trap set for woodchucks, and so became a dead cat at last.

I took down this dwelling the same morning, drawing the nails, and removed it to the pond side by small cartloads, spreading the boards on the grass there to bleach and warp back again in the sun. One early thrush gave me a note or two as I drove along the woodland path. I was informed treacherously by a young Patrick that neighbor Seeley, an Irishman, in the intervals of the carting, transferred the still tolerable, straight, and drivable nails, staples, and spikes to his pocket, and then stood when I came back to pass the time of day, and look freshly up, unconcerned, with spring thoughts, at the devastation; there being a dearth of work, as he said. He was there to represent spectatordom, and help make this seemingly insignificant event one with the removal of the gods of Troy.[8]

I dug my cellar in the side of a hill sloping to the south, where a woodchuck had formerly dug his burrow, down through sumach and blackberry roots, and the lowest stain of vegetation, six feet square by seven deep, to a fine sand where potatoes would not freeze in any winter. The sides were left shelving, and not stoned; but the sun having never shone on them, the sand still keeps its place. It was but two hours' work. I took particular pleasure in this breaking of ground, for in almost all latitudes men dig into the earth for an equable temperature. Under the most splendid house in the city is still to be found the cellar where they store their roots as of old,

8. At the fall of Troy (in Homer's *Iliad*) Ulysses and Diomede, Greek conquerors, carried off the images of the gods, including the Palladium (Pallas was protectress of the city), while Helen watched and encouraged them.

and long after the superstructure has disappeared posterity remark its dent in the earth. The house is still but a sort of porch at the entrance of a burrow.

At length, in the beginning of May, with the help of some of my acquaintances, rather to improve so good an occasion for neighborliness than from any necessity, I set up the frame of my house. No man was ever more honored in the character of his raisers than I.[9] They are destined, I trust, to assist at the raising of loftier structures one day. I began to occupy my house on the 4th of July, as soon as it was boarded and roofed, for the boards were carefully feather-edged and lapped, so that it was perfectly impervious to rain; but before boarding I laid the foundation of a chimney at one end, bringing two cartloads of stones up the hill from the pond in my arms. I built the chimney after my hoeing in the fall, before a fire became necessary for warmth, doing my cooking in the mean while out of doors on the ground, early in the morning: which mode I still think is in some respects more convenient and agreeable than the usual one. When it stormed before my bread was baked, I fixed a few boards over the fire, and sat under them to watch my loaf, and passed some pleasant hours in that way. In those days, when my hands were much employed, I read but little, but the least scraps of paper which lay on the ground, my holder, or tablecloth, afforded me as much entertainment, in fact answered the same purpose as the Iliad. * * *

Before winter I built a chimney, and shingled the sides of my house, which were already impervious to rain, with imperfect and sappy shingles made of the first slice of the log, whose edges I was obliged to straighten with a plane.

I have thus a tight shingled and plastered house, ten feet wide by fifteen long, and eight-feet posts, with a garret and a closet, a large window on each side, two trap-doors, one door at the end, and a brick fireplace opposite. The exact cost of my house, paying the usual price for such materials as I used, but not counting the work, all of which was done by myself, was as follows; and I give the details because very few are able to tell exactly what their houses cost, and fewer still, if any, the separate cost of the various materials which compose them:—

Boards	$8 03½,	mostly shanty boards.
Refuse shingles for roof and sides	4 00	
Laths	1 25	
Two second-hand windows with glass	2 43	
One thousand old brick	4 00	

9. According to tradition, nine friends were his house-raisers, including Emerson, Bronson Alcott, and W. E. Channing.

Two casks of lime	2 40	That was high.
Hair	0 31	More than I needed.
Mantle-tree iron	0 15	
Nails	3 90	
Hinges and screws	0 14	
Latch	0 10	
Chalk	0 01	
Transportation	1 40	{ I carried a good part on my back.
In all	$28 12½	

These are all the materials, excepting the timber, stones, and sand, which I claimed by squatter's right. I have also a small woodshed adjoining, made chiefly of the stuff which was left after building the house.

I intend to build me a house which will surpass any on the main street in Concord in grandeur and luxury, as soon as it pleases me as much and will cost me no more than my present one.

I thus found that the student who wishes for a shelter can obtain one for a lifetime at an expense not greater than the rent which he now pays annually. If I seem to boast more than is becoming, my excuse is that I brag for humanity rather than for myself; and my shortcomings and inconsistencies do not affect the truth of my statement. Notwithstanding much cant and hypocrisy,—chaff which I find it difficult to separate from my wheat, but for which I am as sorry as any man,—I will breathe freely and stretch myself in this respect, it is such a relief to both the moral and physical system; and am resolved that I will not through humility become the devil's attorney. I will endeavor to speak a good word for the truth. At Cambridge College the mere rent of a student's room, which is only a little larger than my own, is thirty dollars each year, though the corporation had the advantage of building thirty-two side by side and under one roof, and the occupant suffers the inconvenience of many and noisy neighbors, and perhaps a residence in the fourth story.[1] I cannot but think that if we had more true wisdom in these respects, not only less education would be needed, because, forsooth, more would already have been acquired, but the pecuniary expense of getting an education would in a great measure vanish. Those conveniences which the student requires at Cambridge or elsewhere cost him or somebody else ten times as great a sacrifice of life as they would with proper management on both sides. Those things for which the most money is demanded are never the things which the student most wants. Tuition, for instance, is an important item

1. Thoreau's Harvard room was on the fourth floor of Hollis Hall; he defrayed expenses by part-time work, and relatives managed to give him some financial assistance.

in the term bill, while for the far more valuable education which he gets by associating with the most cultivated of his contemporaries no charge is made. The mode of founding a college is, commonly, to get up a subscription of dollars and cents, and then, following blindly the principles of a division of labor to its extreme,—a principle which should never be followed but with circumspection,—to call in a contractor who makes this a subject of speculation, and he employs Irishmen or other operatives actually to lay the foundations, while the students that are to be are said to be fitting themselves for it; and for these oversights successive generations have to pay. I think that it would be *better than this*, for the students, or those who desire to be benefited by it, even to lay the foundation themselves. The student who secures his coveted leisure and retirement by systematically shirking any labor necessary to man obtains but an ignoble and unprofitable leisure, defrauding himself of the experience which alone can make leisure fruitful. "But," says one, "you do not mean that the students should go to work with their hands instead of their heads?" I do not mean that exactly, but I mean something which he might think a good deal like that; I mean that they should not *play* life, or *study* it merely, while the community supports them at this expensive game, but earnestly *live* it from beginning to end. How could youths better learn to live than by at once trying the experiment of living? Methinks this would exercise their minds as much as mathematics. If I wished a boy to know something about the arts and sciences, for instance, I would not pursue the common course, which is merely to send him into the neighborhood of some professor, where anything is professed and practised but the art of life;—to survey the world through a telescope or a microscope, and never with his natural eye; to study chemistry, and not learn how his bread is made, or mechanics, and not learn how it is earned; to discover new satellites to Neptune, and not detect the motes in his eyes, or to what vagabond he is a satellite himself; or to be devoured by the monsters that swarm all around him, while contemplating the monsters in a drop of vinegar. Which would have advanced the most at the end of a month,—the boy who had made his own jackknife from the ore which he had dug and smelted, reading as much as would be necessary for this—or the boy who had attended the lectures on metallurgy at the Institute in the meanwhile, and had received a Rodgers penknife[2] from his father? Which would be most likely to cut his fingers? . . . To my astonishment I was informed on leaving college that I had studied navigation!—why, if I had taken one turn down the harbor I should have known more about it. Even the *poor* student studies and is taught only *political* economy, while that economy of living which

2. The knives of James Rodgers and Sons, Sheffield, England, were then famous.

is synonymous with philosophy is not even sincerely professed in our colleges. The consequence is, that while he is reading Adam Smith, Ricardo, and Say,[3] he runs his father in debt irretrievably.

As with our colleges, so with a hundred "modern improvements;" there is an illusion about them; there is not always a positive advance. The devil goes on exacting compound interest to the last for his early share and numerous succeeding investments in them. Our inventions are wont to be pretty toys, which distract our attention from serious things. They are but improved means to an unimproved end, an end which it was already but too easy to arrive at; as railroads lead to Boston or New York. We are in great haste to construct a magnetic telegraph from Maine to Texas;[4] but Maine and Texas, it may be, have nothing important to communicate. Either is in such a predicament as the man who was earnest to be introduced to a distinguished deaf woman,[5] but when he was presented, and one end of her ear trumpet was put into his hand, had nothing to say. As if the main object were to talk fast and not to talk sensibly. We are eager to tunnel under the Atlantic and bring the Old World some weeks nearer to the New; but perchance the first news that will leak through into the broad, flapping American ear will be that the Princess Adelaide[6] has the whooping cough. After all, the man whose horse trots a mile in a minute does not carry the most important messages; he is not an evangelist, nor does he come round eating locusts and wild honey.[7] I doubt if Flying Childers[8] ever carried a peck of corn to mill. * * *

Before I finished my house, wishing to earn ten or twelve dollars by some honest and agreeable method, in order to meet my unusual expenses, I planted about two acres and a half of light and sandy soil near it chiefly with beans, but also a small part with potatoes, corn, peas, and turnips. The whole lot contains eleven acres, mostly growing up to pines and hickories, and was sold the preceding season for eight dollars and eight cents an acre. One farmer said that it was "good for nothing but to raise cheeping squirrels on." I put no manure whatever on this land, not being the owner, but merely a squatter,[9] and not expecting to cultivate so much again, and I did

3. Adam Smith (1723–1790), Scottish economist, in *The Wealth of Nations* founded "classical" economics; David Ricardo (1772–1823) an Englishman, broadened its applications; Jean Baptiste Say (1767–1832) was a French economic thinker of the same school.
4. Samuel F. B. Morse first succeeded in transmitting a message by telegraph in 1844; by 1850 nearly fifty commercial companies had been established.
5. Harriet Martineau, then famous British novelist and economist, who visited Concord in 1836.

6. Adelaide, Princess of Orleans, sister of King Louis Philippe of France; she died in 1847.
7. *Cf.* the evangelist, John the Baptist (Matthew iii: 1–4).
8. An English race horse, born 1715, then the fastest on record.
9. Thoreau's failure to mention rent among his expenses impairs his economic argument; but the "squatter," then widely tolerated, cleared and improved the abundant land. Emerson owned the land occupied by Thoreau, who may have repaid him in produce, and certainly set out young trees by request.

not quite hoe it all once. I got out several cords of stumps in plowing, which supplied me with fuel for a long time, and left small circles of virgin mould, easily distinguishable through the summer by the greater luxuriance of the beans there. The dead and for the most part unmerchantable wood behind my house, and the driftwood from the pond, have supplied the remainder of my fuel. I was obliged to hire a team and a man for the plowing, though I held the plow myself. My farm outgoes for the first season were, for implements, seed, work, etc., $14.72½. The seed corn was given me. This never costs anything to speak of, unless you plant more than enough. I got twelve bushels of beans, and eighteen bushels of potatoes, beside some peas and sweet corn. The yellow corn and turnips were too late to come to anything. My whole income from the farm was

$$\begin{array}{lr} & \$23 \ 44 \\ \text{Deducting the outgoes} & 14 \ 72\frac{1}{2} \\ \hline \text{There are left} & \$8 \ 71\frac{1}{2}, \end{array}$$

beside produce consumed and on hand at the time this estimate was made of the value of $4.50,—the amount on hand much more than balancing a little grass which I did not raise. All things considered, that is, considering the importance of a man's soul and of to-day, notwithstanding the short time occupied by my experiment, nay, partly even because of its transient character, I believe that that was doing better than any farmer in Concord did that year. * * * Beside being better off than they already, if my house had been burned or my crops had failed, I should have been nearly as well off as before.

I am wont to think that men are not so much the keepers of herds as herds are the keepers of men, the former are so much the freer. Men and oxen exchange work; but if we consider necessary work only, the oxen will be seen to have greatly the advantage, their farm is so much the larger. Man does some of his part of the exchange work in his six weeks of haying, and it is no boy's play. Certainly no nation that lived simply in all respects, that is, no nation of philosophers, would commit so great a blunder as to use the labor of animals. True, there never was and is not likely soon to be a nation of philosophers, nor am I certain it is desirable that there should be. However, I should never have broken a horse or bull and taken him to board for any work he might do for me, for fear I should become a horse-man or a herdsman merely; and if society seems to be the gainer by so doing, are we certain that what is one man's gain is not another's loss, and that the stable-boy has equal cause with his master to be satisfied? Granted that some public works would not have been constructed without this aid, and let man share the glory of such with the ox and horse; does it follow that he could not have accomplished works yet more worthy of himself in that case? When men begin to do, not merely unnecessary or artistic, but luxurious and idle work, with their assistance, it is inevitable that a few do all the exchange work with the oxen, or, in other words, become the slaves of the strongest. Man thus not only works for the animal within him, but, for a symbol of this, he works for the animal without him. Though we have many substantial houses of brick or stone, the prosperity of the farmer is still measured by the degree to which the barn overshadows the house. This town is said to have the largest houses for oxen, cows, and horses hereabouts, and it is not behindhand in its public buildings; but there are very few halls for free worship or free speech in this county. It should not be by their architecture, but why not even by their power of abstract thought, that nations should seek to commemorate themselves? How much more admirable the Bhagvat-Geeta[1] than all the ruins of the East! Towers and temples are the luxury of princes. A simple and independent mind does not toil at the bidding of any prince. Genius is not a retainer to any emperor, nor is its material silver, or gold, or marble, except to a trifling extent. To what end, pray, is so much stone hammered? In Arcadia, when I was there, I did not see any hammering stone. Nations are possessed with an insane ambition to perpetuate the memory of themselves by the amount of hammered stone they leave. What if equal pains were taken to smooth and polish their manners? One piece of good sense would be more memorable than a monument as high as the moon. I love better to see stones in place. The grandeur of Thebes was a vulgar grandeur.[2] More sensible is a rod of stone wall that bounds an honest man's field than a hundred-gated Thebes that has wandered farther from the true end of life. The religion and civilization which are barbaric and heathenish build splendid temples; but what you might call Christianity does not. Most of the stone a nation hammers goes toward its tomb only. It buries itself alive. As for the Pyramids, there is nothing to wonder at in them so much as the fact that so many men could be found degraded enough to spend their lives constructing a tomb for some ambitious booby, whom it would have been wiser and manlier to have drowned in the Nile, and then given his body to the dogs. I might possibly invent some excuse for them and him, but I have no time for it. As for the religion and love of art of the builders, it is much the same all the world over, whether the building be an Egyptian temple or the United States Bank. It costs more than it comes to. The mainspring is vanity, assisted by the love of garlic and bread and butter. Mr. Balcom, a promising young architect, designs it on the back of his Vitruvius,[3] with hard pencil

---

1. Usually *Bhagavad-Gita;* the cardinal devotional scripture of Indian Hinduism, a divine revelation from Krishna, inserted in the *Mahabharata.*
2. Thoreau follows the Greek poets, especially Homer, in references to the barbaric splendors of this culture of Ammon in the Upper Nile valley about 1600 B.C.
3. Marcus Vitruvius Pollio, Roman architect (first century B.C.), whose

and ruler, and the job is let out to Dobson & Sons, stonecutters. When the thirty centuries begin to look down on it,[4] mankind begin to look up at it. As for your high towers and monuments, there was a crazy fellow once in this town who undertook to dig through to China, and he got so far that, as he said, he heard the Chinese pots and kettles rattle; but I think that I shall not go out of my way to admire the hole which he made. Many are concerned about the monuments of the West and the East,—to know who built them. For my part, I should like to know who in those days did not build them,—who were above such trifling. But to proceed with my statistics.

By surveying, carpentry, and day-labor of various other kinds in the village in the meanwhile, for I have as many trades as fingers, I had earned $13.34. The expense of food for eight months, namely, from July 4th to March 1st, the time when these estimates were made, though I lived there more than two years,—not counting potatoes, a little green corn, and some peas, which I had raised, nor considering the value of what was on hand at the last date,—was

Rice	$1 73½	
Molasses	1 73	Cheapest form of the saccharine.
Rye meal	1 04¾	
Indian meal	0 99¾	Cheaper than rye.
Pork	0 22	Costs more than Indian meal, both money and trouble.
Flour	0 88	
Sugar	0 80	
Lard	0 65	
Apples	0 25	
Dried apple	0 22	
Sweet potatoes	0 10	
One pumpkin	0 6	
One watermelon	0 2	
Salt	0 3	

All experiments which failed.

Yes, I did eat $8.74, all told; but I should not thus unblushingly publish my guilt, if I did not know that most of my readers were equally guilty with myself, and that their deeds would look no better in print. The next year I sometimes caught a mess of fish for my dinner, and once I went so far as to slaughter a woodchuck which ravaged my bean-field,—effect his transmigration, as a Tartar would say,—and devour him, partly for experiment's sake; but though it afforded me a momentary enjoyment, notwithstanding a musky flavor, I saw that the longest use would not make that a good prac-

writings and drawings still survived as the classical textbook of the young architect.

4. Recalling that Napoleon, having won his first battle against the British in Egypt (July, 1798), told his troops at the Pyramids that forty centuries (not "thirty") were looking down on them.

tice, however it might seem to have your woodchucks ready dressed by the village butcher.

Clothing and some incidental expenses within the same dates, though little can be inferred from this item, amounted to

	$8 40¾
Oil and some household utensils	2 00

So that all the pecuniary outgoes, excepting for washing and mending, which for the most part were done out of the house, and their bills have not yet been received,—and these are all and more than all the ways by which money necessarily goes out in this part of the world,—were

House	$28 12½
Farm one year	14 72½
Food eight months	8 74
Clothing, etc., eight months	8 40¾
Oil, etc., eight months	2 00
In all	$61 99¾

I address myself now to those of my readers who have a living to get. And to meet this I have for farm produce sold

	$23 44
Earned by day-labor	13 34
In all	$36 78,

which subtracted from the sum of the outgoes leaves a balance of $25.21¾ on the one side,—this being very nearly the means with which I started, and the measure of expenses to be incurred,—and on the other, beside the leisure and independence and health thus secured, a comfortable house for me as long as I choose to occupy it.

These statistics, however accidental and therefore uninstructive they may appear, as they have a certain completeness, have a certain value also. Nothing was given me of which I have not rendered some account. It appears from the above estimate, that my food alone cost me in money about twenty-seven cents a week. It was, for nearly two years after this, rye and Indian meal without yeast, potatoes, rice, a very little salt pork, molasses, and salt; and my drink, water. It was fit that I should live on rice, mainly, who loved so well the philosophy of India. To meet the objections of some inveterate cavillers, I may as well state, that if I dined out occasionally, as I always had done, and I trust shall have opportunities to do again, it was frequently to the detriment of my domestic arrangements. But the dining out, being, as I have stated, a constant element, does not in the least affect a comparative statement like this.

I learned from my two years' experience that it would cost incredibly little trouble to obtain one's necessary food, even in this latitude; that a man may use as simple a diet as the animals, and yet retain health and strength. I have made a satisfactory dinner, satisfactory on several accounts, simply off a dish of purslane (*Portulaca oleracea*) which I gathered in my cornfield, boiled and salted. I give the Latin on account of the savoriness of the trivial name. And pray what more can a reasonable man desire, in peaceful times, in ordinary noons, than a sufficient number of ears of green sweet corn boiled, with the addition of salt? Even the little variety which I used was a yielding to the demands of appetite, and not of health. Yet men have come to such a pass that they frequently starve, not for want of necessaries, but for want of luxuries; and I know a good woman who thinks that her son lost his life because he took to drinking water only. * * *

For more than five years I maintained myself thus solely by the labor of my hands, and I found, that by working about six weeks in a year, I could meet all the expenses of living. The whole of my winters, as well as most of my summers, I had free and clear for study. I have thoroughly tried school-keeping, and found that my expenses were in proportion, or rather out of proportion, to my income, for I was obliged to dress and train, not to say think and believe, accordingly, and I lost my time into the bargain. As I did not teach for the good of my fellow-men, but simply for a livelihood, this was a failure. I have tried trade; but I found that it would take ten years to get under way in that, and that then I should probably be on my way to the devil. I was actually afraid that I might by that time be doing what is called a good business. When formerly I was looking about to see what I could do for a living, some sad experience in conforming to the wishes of friends being fresh in my mind to tax my ingenuity, I thought often and seriously of picking huckleberries; that surely I could do, and its small profits might suffice,—for my greatest skill has been to want but little,—so little capital it required, so little distraction from my wonted moods, I foolishly thought. While my acquaintances went unhesitatingly into trade or the professions, I contemplated this occupation as most like theirs; ranging the hills all summer to pick the berries which came in my way, and thereafter carelessly dispose of them; so, to keep the flocks of Admetus. I also dreamed that I might gather the wild herbs, or carry evergreens to such villagers as loved to be reminded of the woods, even to the city, by hay-cart loads. But I have since learned that trade curses every thing it handles; and though you trade in messages from heaven, the whole curse of trade attaches to the business.

As I preferred some things to others, and especially valued my freedom, as I could fare hard and yet succeed well, I did not wish to spend my time in earning rich carpets or other fine furniture, or delicate cookery, or a house in the Grecian or the Gothic style just yet. If there are any to whom it is no interruption to acquire these things, and who know how to use them when acquired, I relinquish to them the pursuit. Some are "industrious," and appear to love labor for its own sake, or perhaps because it keeps them out of worse mischief; to such I have at present nothing to say. Those who would not know what to do with more leisure than they now enjoy, I might advise to work twice as hard as they do,—work till they pay for themselves, and get their free papers. For myself I found that the occupation of a day-laborer was the most independent of any, especially as it required only thirty or forty days in a year to support one. The laborer's day ends with the going down of the sun, and he is then free to devote himself to his chosen pursuit, independent of his labor; but his employer, who speculates from month to month, has no respite from one end of the year to the other.

In short, I am convinced, both by faith and experience, that to maintain one's self on this earth is not a hardship but a pastime,[5] if we will live simply and wisely; as the pursuits of the simpler nations are still the sports of the more artificial. It is not necessary that a man should earn his living by the sweat of his brow, unless he sweats easier than I do.

One young man of my acquaintance, who has inherited some acres, told me that he thought he should live as I did, *if he had the means*. I would not have any one adopt *my* mode of living on any account; for, beside that before he has fairly learned it I may have found out another for myself, I desire that there may be as many different persons in the world as possible; but I would have each one be very careful to find out and pursue *his own* way, and not his father's or his mother's or his neighbor's instead. The youth may build or plant or sail, only let him not be hindered from doing that which he tells me he would like to do. It is by a mathematical point only that we are wise, as the sailor or the fugitive slave keeps the polestar in his eye; but that is sufficient guidance for all our life. We may not arrive at our port within a calculable period, but we would preserve the true course.

Undoubtedly, in this case, what is true for one is truer still for a thousand, as a large house is not proportionally more expensive than a small one, since one roof may cover, one cellar underlie, and

---

5. A familiar theory of Charles Fourier (1772–1837), French founder of the agrarian co-operative movement which was then attractive to American intellectuals, and represented, among transcendentalists, by Brook Farm (1841–1847) and Fruitlands (1842), before Thoreau tested the agrarian hypothesis on an *individualistic* basis.

one wall separate several apartments. But for my part, I preferred the solitary dwelling. Moreover, it will commonly be cheaper to build the whole yourself than to convince another of the advantage of the common wall; and when you have done this, the common partition, to be much cheaper, must be a thin one, and that other may prove a bad neighbor, and also not keep his side in repair. The only coöperation which is commonly possible is exceedingly partial and superficial; and what little true coöperation there is, is if it were not, being a harmony inaudible to men. If a man has faith he will coöperate with equal faith every where, if he has not faith, he will continue to live like the rest of the world, whatever company he is joined to. To coöperate, in the highest as well as the lowest sense, means *to get our living together.* I heard it proposed lately that two young men should travel together over the world, the one without money, earning his means as he went, before the mast and behind the plough, the other carrying a bill of exchange in his pocket. It was easy to see that they could not long be companions or coöperate, since one would not *operate* at all. They would part at the first interesting crisis in their adventures. Above all, as I have implied, the man who goes alone can start to-day; but he who travels with another must wait till that other is ready, and it may be a long time before they get off.

But all this is very selfish, I have heard some of my townsmen say. I confess that I have hitherto indulged very little in philanthropic enterprises. I have made some sacrifices to a sense of duty, and among others have sacrificed this pleasure also. There are those who have used all their arts to persuade me to undertake the support of some poor family in the town; and if I had nothing to do,—for the devil finds employment for the idle,[6]—I might try my hand at some such pastime as that. However, when I have thought to indulge myself in this respect, and lay their Heaven under an obligation by maintaining certain poor persons in all respects as comfortably as I maintain myself, and have even ventured so far as to make them the offer, they have one and all unhesitatingly preferred to remain poor. While my townsmen and women are devoted in so many ways to the good of their fellows, I trust that one at least may be spared to other and less humane pursuits. You must have a genius for charity as well as for any thing else. As for Doing-good, that is one of the professions which are full. Moreover, I have tried it fairly, and, strange as it may seem, am satisfied that it does not agree with my constitution. Probably I should not consciously and deliberately forsake my particular calling to do the good which society demands of me, to save the universe from annihilation; and I believe that a like but infinitely greater

6. Restatement from a hymn then very familiar (Isaac Watts, *Divine Songs*, No. XX).

steadfastness elsewhere is all that now preserves it. But I would not stand between any man and his genius; and to him who does this work, which I decline, with his whole heart and soul and life, I would say, Persevere, even if the world call it doing evil, as it is most likely they will.[7]

I am far from supposing that my case is a peculiar one; no doubt many of my readers would make a similar defence. At doing something,—I will not engage that my neighbors shall pronounce it good, —I do not hesitate to say that I should be a capital fellow to hire; but what that is, it is for my employer to find out. What good I do, in the common sense of that word, must be aside from my main path, and for the most part wholly unintended. Men say, practically, Begin where you are and such as you are, without aiming mainly to become of more worth, and with kindness aforethought go about doing good. If I were to preach at all in this strain, I should say rather, Set about being good. As if the sun should stop when he had kindled his fires up to the splendor of a moon or a star of the sixth magnitude, and go about like a Robin Goodfellow,[8] peeping in at every cottage window, inspiring lunatics, and tainting meats, and making darkness visible, instead of steadily increasing his genial heat and beneficence till he is of such brightness that no mortal can look him in the face, and then, and in the mean while too, going about the world in his own orbit, doing it good, or rather, as a truer philosophy has discovered, the world going about him getting good. When Phaeton,[9] wishing to prove his heavenly birth by his beneficence, had the sun's chariot but one day, and drove out of the beaten track, he burned several blocks of houses in the lower streets of heaven, and scorched the surface of the earth, and dried up every spring, and made the great desert of Sahara, till at length Jupiter hurled him headlong to the earth with a thunderbolt, and the sun, through grief at his death, did not shine for a year.

There is no odor so bad as that which arises from goodness tainted. It is human, it is divine, carrion. If I knew for a certainty that a man was coming to my house with the conscious design of doing me good, I should run for my life, as from that dry and parching wind of the African deserts called the simoom, which fills the mouth and nose and ears and eyes with dust till you are suffocated, for fear that I should get some of his good done to me,—some of its virus mingled with my blood. No,—in this case I would rather suffer evil the natural way. A man is not a good *man* to me because he will feed me if I

7. Numerous instances of Thoreau's charitable generosity are recorded, yet his ideal convictions, as stated in the following paragraphs, seem contrary to the philanthropic spirit of his age. But note his emphasis on individualism, which resists, as of doubtful benefit, "an-

other man's good"; (cf. *Journals*, Vol, VII, p. 211, February 11, 1841).
8. A mischievous elf of British folklore; sometimes "Puck."
9. The son of Helios (the sun) in Greek myth, actuated by presumptuous vanity in the episode here narrated.

should be starving, or warm me if I should be freezing, or pull me out of a ditch if I should ever fall into one. I can find you a New-foundland dog that will do as much. Philanthropy is not love for one's fellow-man in the broadest sense. Howard[1] was no doubt an ex-ceedingly kind and worthy man in his way, and has his reward; but, comparatively speaking, what are a hundred Howards to *us*, if their philanthropy do not help *us* in our best estate, when we are most worthy to be helped? I never heard of a philanthropic meeting in which it was sincerely proposed to do any good to me, or the like of me.

The Jesuits were quite balked by those Indians who, being burned at the stake, suggested new modes of torture to their tormentors. Being superior to physical suffering, it sometimes chanced that they were superior to any consolation which the missionaries could offer; and the law to do as you would be done by fell with less persuasive-ness on the ears of those, who, for their part, did not care how they were done by, who loved their enemies after a new fashion, and came very near freely forgiving them all they did.

Be sure that you give the poor the aid they most need, though it be your example which leaves them far behind. If you give money, spend yourself with it, and do not merely abandon it to them. We make curious mistakes sometimes. Often the poor man is not so cold and hungry as he is dirty and ragged and gross. It is partly his taste, and not merely his misfortune. If you give him money, he will perhaps buy more rags with it. I was wont to pity the clumsy Irish laborers who cut ice on the pond, in such mean and ragged clothes, while I shiv-ered in my more tidy and somewhat more fashionable garments, till, one bitter cold day, one who had slipped into the water came to my house to warm him, and I saw him strip off three pairs of pants and two pairs of stockings ere he got down to the skin, though they were dirty and ragged enough, it is true, and that he could afford to refuse the *extra* garments which I offered him, he had so many *intra* ones. This ducking was the very thing he needed. Then I began to pity myself, and I saw that it would be a greater charity to bestow on me a flannel shirt than a whole slop-shop on him. There are a thousand hacking at the branches of evil to one who is striking at the root, and it may be that he who bestows the largest amount of time and money on the needy is doing the most by his mode of life to produce that misery which he strives in vain to relieve. It is the pious slave-breeder devoting the proceeds of every tenth slave to buy a Sunday's liberty for the rest. Some show their kindness to the poor by employing them in their kitchens. Would they not be kinder if they employed themselves there? You boast of spending a tenth part of your income in charity; may be you should spend the nine tenths so,

1. John Howard (1726?–1790), British leader of the prison-reform movement.

and done with it. Society recovers only a tenth part of the property then. Is this owing to the generosity of him in whose possession it is found, or to the remissness of the officers of justice?

Philanthropy is almost the only virtue which is sufficiently appreciated by mankind. Nay, it is greatly overrated; and it is our selfishness which overrates it. A robust poor man, one sunny day here in Concord, praised a fellow-townsman to me, because, as he said, he was kind to the poor; meaning himself. The kind uncles and aunts of the race are more esteemed than its true spiritual fathers and mothers. I once heard a reverend lecturer on England, a man of learning and intelligence, after enumerating her scientific, literary, and political worthies, Shakspeare, Bacon, Cromwell, Milton, Newton, and others, speak next of her Christian heroes, whom, as if his profession required it of him, he elevated to a place far above all the rest, as the greatest of the great. They were Penn, Howard, and Mrs. Fry.[2] Every one must feel the falsehood and cant of this. The last were not England's best men and women; only, perhaps, her best philanthropists.

I would not subtract any thing from the praise that is due to philanthropy, but merely demand justice for all who by their lives and works are a blessing to mankind. I do not value chiefly a man's uprightness and benevolence, which are, as it were, his stem and leaves. Those plants of whose greenness withered we make herb tea for the sick, serve but a humble use, and are most employed by quacks. I want the flower and fruit of a man; that some fragrance be wafted over from him to me, and some ripeness flavor our intercourse. His goodness must not be a partial and transitory act, but a constant superfluity, which costs him nothing and of which he is unconscious. This is a charity that hides a multitude of sins. The philanthropist too often surrounds mankind with the remembrance of his own cast-off griefs as an atmosphere, and calls it sympathy. We should impart our courage, and not our despair, our health and ease, and not our disease, and take care that this does not spread by contagion. From what southern plains comes up the voice of wailing? Under what latitudes reside the heathen to whom we would send light? Who is that intemperate and brutal man whom we would redeem? If any thing ail a man, so that he does not perform his functions, if he have a pain in his bowels even,—for that is the seat of sympathy,—he forthwith sets about reforming—the world. Being a microcosm himself, he discovers, and it is a true discovery, and he is the man to make it,—that the world has been eating green apples; to his eyes, in fact, the globe itself is a great green apple, which there is danger awful to think of that the children of men will nibble before it is ripe; and

2. Elizabeth Fry (1780–1845) a Quaker evangelist, followed in Howard's footsteps and founded an international organization for prison reform. The other reference is to William Penn, whose "Holy Experiment" in Pennsylvania was a practical expression of Quaker philanthropy.

straightway his drastic philanthropy seeks out the Esquimaux and the Patagonian, and embraces the populous Indian and Chinese villages; and thus, by a few years of philanthropic activity, the powers in the mean while using him for their own ends, no doubt, he cures himself of his dyspepsia, the globe acquires a faint blush on one or both of its cheeks, as if it were beginning to be ripe, and life loses its crudity and is once more sweet and wholesome to live. I never dreamed of any enormity greater than I have committed. I never knew, and never shall know, a worse man than myself.

I believe that what so saddens the reformer is not his sympathy with his fellows in distress, but, though he be the holiest son of God, is his private ail. Let this be righted, let the spring come to him, the morning rise over his couch, and he will forsake his generous companions without apology. My excuse for not lecturing against the use of tobacco is, that I never chewed it; that is a penalty which reformed tobacco-chewers have to pay; though there are things enough I have chewed, which I could lecture against. If you should ever be betrayed into any of these philanthropies, do not let your left hand know what your right hand does,[3] for it is not worth knowing. Rescue the drowning and tie your shoe-strings. Take your time, and set about some free labor.

Our manners have been corrupted by communication with the saints. Our hymn-books resound with a melodious cursing of God and enduring him forever.[4] One would say that even the prophets and redeemers had rather consoled the fears than confirmed the hopes of man. There is nowhere recorded a simple and irrepressible satisfaction with the gift of life, any memorable praise of God. All health and success does me good, however far off and withdrawn it may appear; all disease and failure helps to make me sad and does me evil, however much sympathy it may have with me or I with it. If, then, we would indeed restore mankind by truly Indian, botanic, magnetic, or natural means, let us first be as simple and well as Nature ourselves, dispel the clouds which hang over our own brows, and take up a little life into our pores. Do not stay to be an overseer of the poor, but endeavor to become one of the worthies of the world.

I read in the Gulistan, or Flower Garden, of Sheik Sadi[5] of Shiraz, that "They asked a wise man, saying; Of the many celebrated trees which the Most High God has created lofty and umbrageous, they call none azad, or free, excepting the cypress, which bears no fruit; what mystery is there in this? He replied; Each has its appropriate produce,

---

3. *Cf.* Matthew vi: 3.
4. *Cf.* the *Westminster Shorter Catechism*, in which the first response is: "To glorify God, and to enjoy Him forever."
5. Saadi, named Muslik-ud-Din, Persian poet, survives in three famous collections, of which the *Gulistān* (1258) is the second. Thoreau read much oriental literature in translation, but acknowledged a particular kinship with Saadi (*Journals*, Vol. X, pp. 289–290, August 8, 1852).

and appointed season, during the continuance of which it is fresh and blooming, and during their absence dry and withered; to neither of which states is the cypress exposed, being always flourishing; and of this nature are the azads, or religious independents.—Fix not thy heart on that which is transitory; for the Dijlah, or Tigris, will continue to flow through Bagdad after the race of caliphs is extinct: if thy hand has plenty, be liberal as the date tree; but if it affords nothing to give away, be an azad, or free man, like the cypress."

II. Where I Lived, and What I Lived For

At a certain season of our life we are accustomed to consider every spot as the possible site of a house. I have thus surveyed the country on every side within a dozen miles of where I live. In imagination I have bought all the farms in succession, for all were to be bought, and I knew their price. I walked over each farmer's premises, tasted his wild apples, discoursed on husbandry with him, took his farm at his price, at any price, mortgaging it to him in my mind; even put a higher price on it,—took everything but a deed of it,—took his word for his deed, for I dearly love to talk,—cultivated it, and him too to some extent, I trust, and withdrew when I had enjoyed it long enough, leaving him to carry it on. This experience entitled me to be regarded as a sort of real-estate broker by my friends. Wherever I sat, there I might live, and the landscape radiated from me accordingly. What is a house but a *sedes*, a seat?[6]—better if a country seat. I discovered many a site for a house not likely to be soon improved, which some might have thought too far from the village, but to my eyes the village was too far from it. Well, there I might live, I said; and there I did live, for an hour, a summer and a winter life; saw how I could let the years run off, buffet the winter through, and see the spring come in. The future inhabitants of this region, wherever they may place their houses, may be sure that they have been anticipated. An afternoon sufficed to lay out the land into orchard, wood-lot, and pasture, and to decide what fine oaks or pines should be left to stand before the door, and whence each blasted tree could be seen to the best advantage; and then I let it lie, fallow perchance, for a man is rich in proportion to the number of things which he can afford to let alone.

My imagination carried me so far that I even had the refusal of several farms,—the refusal was all I wanted,—but I never got my fingers burned by actual possession. The nearest that I came to actual possession was when I bought the Hollowell place,[7] and had begun

6. The double meaning is inherent in the Latin *sedes*, which means either "a seat" or "a dwelling place."
7. Associated with his boyhood memories, this house, off the road near Con-

cord, faced the Concord River, which Thoreau, in *A Week* * * * , called Musketaquid ("grass-ground"), remembering the Indian village that preceded Concord.

to sort my seeds, and collected materials with which to make a wheelbarrow to carry it on or off with; but before the owner gave me a deed of it, his wife—every man has such a wife—changed her mind and wished to keep it, and he offered me ten dollars to release him. Now, to speak the truth, I had but ten cents in the world, and it surpassed my arithmetic to tell, if I was that man who had ten cents, or who had a farm, or ten dollars, or all together. However, I let him keep the ten dollars and the farm too, for I had carried it far enough; or rather, to be generous, I sold him the farm for just what I gave for it, and, as he was not a rich man, made him a present of ten dollars, and still had my ten cents, and seeds, and materials for a wheelbarrow left. I found thus that I had been a rich man without any damage to my poverty. But I retained the landscape, and I have since annually carried off what it yielded without a wheelbarrow. With respect to landscapes,—

> "I am monarch of all I *survey*,
> My right there is none to dispute."[8]

I have frequently seen a poet withdraw, having enjoyed the most valuable part of a farm, while the crusty farmer supposed that he had got a few wild apples only. Why, the owner does not know it for many years when a poet has put his farm in rhyme, the most admirable kind of invisible fence, has fairly impounded it, milked it, skimmed it, and got all the cream, and left the farmer only the skimmed milk.

The real attractions of the Hollowell farm, to me, were: its complete retirement, being about two miles from the village, half a mile from the nearest neighbor, and separated from the highway by a broad field; its bounding on the river, which the owner said protected it by its fogs from frosts in the spring, though that was nothing to me; the gray color and ruinous state of the house and barn, and the dilapidated fences, which put such an interval between me and the last occupant; the hollow and lichen-covered apple trees, gnawed by rabbits, showing what kind of neighbors I should have; but above all, the recollection I had of it from my earliest voyages up the river, when the house was concealed behind a dense grove of red maples, through which I heard the housedog bark. I was in haste to buy it, before the proprietor finished getting out some rocks, cutting down the hollow apple trees, and grubbing up some young birches which had sprung up in the pasture, or, in short, had made any more of his improvements. To enjoy these advantages I was ready to carry it on;

8. From stanza 1 of "Verses Supposed to be Written by Alexander Selkirk," by William Cowper (1731–1800). Selkirk, a famous castaway, was the original for Defoe's *Robinson Crusoe;* thus Thoreau suggested a comparison with his own situation at Walden. He italicized the *survey* because he had worked as a surveyor of land.

like Atlas, to take the world on my shoulders,—I never heard what compensation he received for that,—and do all those things which had no other motive or excuse but that I might pay for it and be unmolested in my possession of it; for I knew all the while that it would yield the most abundant crop of the kind I wanted, if I could only afford to let it alone. But it turned out as I have said.

All that I could say, then, with respect to farming on a large scale —I have always cultivated a garden—was, that I had had my seeds ready. Many think that seeds improve with age. I have no doubt that time discriminates between the good and the bad; and when at last I shall plant, I shall be less likely to be disappointed. But I would say to my fellows, once for all, As long as possible live free and uncommitted. It makes but little difference whether you are committed to a farm or the county jail.

Old Cato,[9] whose "De Re Rusticâ" is my "Cultivator," says,— and the only translation I have seen makes sheer nonsense of the passage,—"When you think of getting a farm turn it thus in your mind, not to buy greedily; nor spare your pains to look at it, and do not think it enough to go round it once. The oftener you go there the more it will please you, if it is good." I think I shall not buy greedily, but go round and round it as long as I live, and be buried in it first, that it may please me the more at last.

The present was my next experiment of this kind, which I purpose to describe more at length, for convenience putting the experience of two years into one. As I have said, I do not propose to write an ode to dejection,[1] but to brag as lustily as chanticleer in the morning, standing on his roost, if only to wake my neighbors up.

When first I took up my abode in the woods, that is, began to spend my nights as well as days there, which, by accident, was on Independence Day, or the Fourth of July, 1845, my house was not finished for winter, but was merely a defence against the rain, without plastering or chimney, the walls being of rough, weather-stained boards, with wide chinks, which made it cool at night. The upright white hewn studs and freshly planed door and window casings gave it a clean and airy look, especially in the morning, when its timbers were saturated with dew, so that I fancied that by noon some sweet gum would exude from them. To my imagination it retained throughout the day more or less of this auroral character, reminding me of a certain house on a mountain which I had visited a year before. This was an airy and unplastered cabin, fit to entertain a travelling god, and where a goddess might trail her garments. The winds which

9. Marcus Porcius Cato (234–149 B.C.), Roman statesman and author, urged a return to agrarian simplicity and high thinking. The quotation is from Chapter

1 of *De Re Rustica*, his only surviving work.
1. Coleridge's "Dejection: An Ode" was then generally familiar.

passed over my dwelling were such as sweep over the ridges of mountains, bearing the broken strains, or celestial parts only, of terrestrial music. The morning wind forever blows, the poem of creation is uninterrupted; but few are the ears that hear it. Olympus is but the outside of the earth everywhere.

The only house I had been the owner of before, if I except a boat, was a tent, which I used occasionally when making excursions in the summer, and this is still rolled up in my garret; but the boat, after passing from hand to hand, has gone down the stream of time. With this more substantial shelter about me, I had made some progress toward settling in the world. This frame, so slightly clad, was a sort of crystallization around me, and reacted on the builder. It was suggestive somewhat as a picture in outlines. I did not need to go outdoors to take the air, for the atmosphere within had lost none of its freshness. It was not so much within-doors as behind a door where I sat, even in the rainiest weather. The Harivansa[2] says, "An abode without birds is like a meat without seasoning." Such was not my abode, for I found myself suddenly neighbor to the birds; not by having imprisoned one, but having caged myself near them. I was not only nearer to some of those which commonly frequent the garden and the orchard, but to those wilder and more thrilling songsters of the forest which never, or rarely, serenade a villager,—the wood thrush, the veery, the scarlet tanager, the field sparrow, the whippoor-will, and many others.

I was seated by the shore of a small pond, about a mile and a half south of the village of Concord and somewhat higher than it, in the midst of an extensive wood between that town and Lincoln,[3] and about two miles south of that our only field known to fame, Concord Battle Ground;[4] but I was so low in the woods that the opposite shore, half a mile off, like the rest, covered with wood, was my most distant horizon. For the first week, whenever I looked out on the pond it impressed me like a tarn high up on the side of a mountain, its bottom far above the surface of other lakes, and, as the sun arose, I saw it throwing off its nightly clothing of mist, and here and there, by degrees, its soft ripples or its smooth reflecting surface was revealed, while the mists, like ghosts, were stealthily withdrawing in every direction into the woods, as at the breaking up of some nocturnal conventicle. The very dew seemed to hang upon the trees later into the day than usual, as on the sides of mountains.

This small lake was of most value as a neighbor in the intervals of a gentle rain-storm in August, when, both air and water being

---

2. The *Harivansa,* a Hindu religious epic of the fifth century (associated with the earlier *Mahabharata*), recorded the deeds and religious teachings of Krishna, incarnation of the god Vishnu.

Langois' French translation (1834–1835) influenced the transcendentalists.
3. On the road to Sudbury.
4. See "Concord Hymn" (1837), in the selections from Emerson, above.

perfectly still, but the sky overcast, mid-afternoon had all the serenity of evening, and the wood thrush sang around, and was heard from shore to shore. A lake like this is never smoother than at such a time; and the clear portion of the air above it being shallow and darkened by clouds, the water, full of light and reflections, becomes a lower heaven itself so much the more important. From a hill-top near by, where the wood had been recently cut off, there was a pleasing vista southward across the pond, through a wide indentation in the hills which form the shore there, where their opposite sides sloping toward each other suggested a stream flowing out in that direction through a wooded valley, but stream there was none. That way I looked between and over the near green hills to some distant and higher ones in the horizon, tinged with blue. Indeed, by standing on tiptoe I could catch a glimpse of some of the peaks of the still bluer and more distant mountain ranges in the northwest, those true-blue coins from heaven's own mint, and also of some portion of the village. But in other directions, even from this point, I could not see over or beyond the woods which surrounded me. It is well to have some water in your neighborhood, to give buoyancy to and float the earth. One value even of the smallest well is, that when you look into it you see that earth is not continent but insular. This is as important as that it keeps butter cool. When I looked across the pond from this peak toward the Sudbury meadows,[5] which in time of flood I distinguished elevated perhaps by a mirage in their seething valley, like a coin in a basin, all the earth beyond the pond appeared like a thin crust insulated and floated even by this small sheet of intervening water, and I was reminded that this on which I dwelt was but *dry land*.

Though the view from my door was still more contracted, I did not feel crowded or confined in the least. There was pasture enough for my imagination. The low shrub oak plateau to which the opposite shore arose stretched away toward the prairies of the West and the steppes of Tartary,[6] affording ample room for all the roving families of men. "There are none happy in the world but beings who enjoy freely a vast horizon,"—said Damodara,[7] when his herds required new and larger pastures.

Both place and time were changed, and I dwelt nearer to those parts of the universe and to those eras in history which had most attracted me. Where I lived was as far off as many a region viewed nightly by astronomers. We are wont to imagine rare and delectable places in some remote and more celestial corner of the system, be-

5. As a hiker Thoreau had often gone to the Sudbury meadows, the thickly wooded area at the confluence of two forks of the Concord River.
6. Preferably "Tatary"; formerly designating the great plains of northern Asia

and Europe, irrespective of national borders, from the Sea of Japan westward to the Dnieper River.
7. Another name for the Hindu divinity Krishna.

hind the constellation of Cassiopeia's Chair,[8] far from noise and disturbance. I discovered that my house actually had its site in such a withdrawn, but forever new and unprofaned, part of the universe. If it were worth the while to settle in those parts near to the Pleiades or the Hyades, to Aldebaran or Altair,[9] then I was really there, or at an equal remoteness from the life which I had left behind, dwindled and twinkling with as fine a ray to my nearest neighbor, and to be seen only in moonless nights by him. Such was that part of creation where I had squatted;—

> "There was a shepherd that did live,
> And held his thoughts as high
> As were the mounts whereon his flocks
> Did hourly feed him by."

What should we think of the shepherd's life if his flocks always wandered to higher pastures than his thoughts?

Every morning was a cheerful invitation to make my life of equal simplicity, and I may say innocence, with Nature herself. I have been as sincere a worshipper of Aurora as the Greeks. I got up early and bathed in the pond; that was a religious exercise, and one of the best things which I did. They say that characters were engraven on the bathing tub of King Tching-thang to this effect: "Renew thyself completely each day; do it again, and again, and forever again." I can understand that. Morning brings back the heroic ages. I was as much affected by the faint hum of a mosquito making its invisible and unimaginable tour through my apartment at earliest dawn, when I was sitting with door and windows open, as I could be by any trumpet that ever sang of fame. It was Homer's requiem; itself an Iliad and Odyssey in the air, singing its own wrath and wanderings.[1] There was something cosmical about it; a standing advertisement, till forbidden, of the everlasting vigor and fertility of the world. The morning, which is the most memorable season of the day, is the awakening hour. Then there is least somnolence in us; and for an hour, at least, some part of us awakes which slumbers all the rest of the day and night. Little is to be expected of that day, if it can be called a day, to which we are not awakened by our Genius,[2] but by the mechanical nudgings of some servitor, are not awakened by our own newly acquired force and aspirations from within, accompanied by the undulations of celestial music, instead of factory bells, and a fragrance filling the air—to a higher life than we fell asleep from;

8. A star cluster in the constellation of Cassiopeia.
9. The Pleiades and Hyades are star clusters in the constellation Taurus (the Bull); the Hyades include Aldebaran, the bull's bright eye. Altair is another star of the first magnitude.

1. The "wrath" of Achilles underlies important episodes in the *Iliad;* the "wanderings" of Odysseus are the subject of the *Odyssey.*
2. In classical mythology, the guardian spirit assigned to each person at birth.

and thus the darkness bear its fruit, and prove itself to be good, no less than the light. That man who does not believe that each day contains an earlier, more sacred, and auroral hour than he has yet profaned, has despaired of life, and is pursuing a descending and darkening way. After a partial cessation of his sensuous life, the soul of man, or its organs rather, are reinvigorated each day, and his Genius tries again what noble life it can make. All memorable events, I should say, transpire in morning time and in a morning atmosphere. The Vedas[3] say, "All intelligences awake with the morning." Poetry and art, and the fairest and most memorable of the actions of men, date from such an hour. All poets and heroes, like Memnon, are the children of Aurora, and emit their music at sunrise. To him whose elastic and vigorous thought keeps pace with the sun, the day is a perpetual morning. It matters not what the clocks say or the attitudes and labors of men. Morning is when I am awake and there is a dawn in me. Moral reform is the effort to throw off sleep. Why is it that men give so poor an account of their day if they have not been slumbering? They are not such poor calculators. If they had not been overcome with drowsiness, they would have performed something. The millions are awake enough for physical labor; but only one in a million is awake enough for effective intellectual exertion, only one in a hundred millions to a poetic or divine life. To be awake is to be alive. I have never yet met a man who was quite awake. How could I have looked him in the face?

We must learn to reawaken and keep ourselves awake, not by mechanical aids, but by an infinite expectation of the dawn, which does not forsake us in our soundest sleep. I know of no more encouraging fact than the unquestionable ability of man to elevate his life by a conscious endeavor. It is something to be able to paint a particular picture, or to carve a statue, and so to make a few objects beautiful; but it is far more glorious to carve and paint the very atmosphere and medium through which we look, which morally we can do. To affect the quality of the day, that is the highest of arts. Every man is tasked to make his life, even in its details, worthy of the contemplation of his most elevated and critical hour. If we refused, or rather used up, such paltry information as we get, the oracles would distinctly inform us how this might be done.

I went to the woods because I wished to live deliberately, to front only the essential facts of life, and see if I could not learn what it had to teach, and not, when I came to die, discover that I had not lived. I did not wish to live what was not life, living is so dear; nor did I wish to practise resignation, unless it was quite necessary. I wanted to live deep and suck out all the marrow of life, to live so sturdily and Spartan-like as to put to rout all that was not life, to cut a broad

3. Ancient devotional books of Hindu religious literature.

swath and shave close, to drive life into a corner, and reduce it to its lowest terms, and, if it proved to be mean, why then to get the whole and genuine meanness of it, and publish its meanness to the world; or if it were sublime, to know it by experience, and be able to give a true account of it in my next excursion. For most men, it appears to me, are in a strange uncertainty about it, whether it is of the devil or of God, and have *somewhat hastily* concluded that it is the chief end of man here to "glorify God and enjoy him forever."[4]

Still we live meanly, like ants; though the fable tells us that we were long ago changed into men; like pygmies[5] we fight with cranes; it is error upon error, and clout upon clout, and our best virtue has for its occasion a superfluous and evitable wretchedness. Our life is frittered away by detail. An honest man has hardly need to count more than his ten fingers, or in extreme cases he may add his ten toes, and lump the rest. Simplicity, simplicity, simplicity! I say, let your affairs be as two or three, and not a hundred or a thousand; instead of a million count half a dozen, and keep your accounts on your thumb-nail. In the midst of this chopping sea of civilized life, such are the clouds and storms and quicksands and thousand-and-one items to be allowed for, that a man has to live, if he would not founder and go to the bottom and not make his port at all, by dead reckoning,[6] and he must be a great calculator indeed who succeeds. Simplify, simplify. Instead of three meals a day, if it be necessary eat but one; instead of a hundred dishes, five; and reduce other things in proportion. Our life is like a German Confederacy,[7] made up of petty states, with its boundary forever fluctuating, so that even a German cannot tell you how it is bounded at any moment. The nation itself, with all its so-called internal improvements, which, by the way are all external and superficial, is just such an unwieldy and overgrown establishment, cluttered with furniture and tripped up by its own traps, ruined by luxury and heedless expense, by want of calculation and a worthy aim, as the million households in the land; and the only cure for it, as for them, is in a rigid economy, a stern and more than Spartan simplicity of life and elevation of purpose. It lives too fast. Men think that it is essential that the *Nation* have commerce, and export ice, and talk through a telegraph, and ride thirty miles an hour, without a doubt, whether *they* do or not; but whether we should live like baboons or like men, is a little uncertain. If we do not get out sleepers,[8] and forge rails, and devote days and nights to the work, but go to tinkering upon our *lives* to improve *them*, who will

4. As stated in the *Westminster Shorter Catechism.*
5. Homer (*Iliad*, Book III, l. 5) first told of the pygmies, people so tiny that they were attacked by flights of cranes.
6. In dead reckoning, a ship's position is determined by the calculation of speed, distances, and directions sailed, rather than by the more accurate method of astronomical observation.
7. The first modern confederacy of German states (1815) was too loosely organized for effectiveness.
8. Railroad ties.

build railroads? And if railroads are not built, how shall we get to heaven in season? But if we stay at home and mind our business, who will want railroads? We do not ride on the railroad; it rides upon us. Did you ever think what those sleepers are that underlie the railroad? Each one is a man, an Irishman, or a Yankee man. The rails are laid on them, and they are covered with sand, and the cars run smoothly over them. They are sound sleepers, I assure you. And every few years a new lot is laid down and run over; so that, if some have the pleasure of riding on a rail, others have the misfortune to be ridden upon. And when they run over a man that is walking in his sleep, a supernumerary sleeper in the wrong position, and wake him up, they suddenly stop the cars, and make a hue and cry about it, as if this were an exception. I am glad to know that it takes a gang of men for every five miles to keep the sleepers down and level in their beds as it is, for this is a sign that they may sometime get up again.

Why should we live with such hurry and waste of life? We are determined to be starved before we are hungry. Men say that a stitch in time saves nine, and so they take a thousand stitches to-day to save nine to-morrow. As for *work*, we haven't any of any consequence. We have the Saint Vitus' dance, and cannot possibly keep our heads still. If I should only give a few pulls at the parish bell-rope, as for a fire, that is, without setting the bell,[9] there is hardly a man on his farm in the outskirts of Concord, notwithstanding that press of engagements which was his excuse so many times this morning, nor a boy, nor a woman, I might almost say, but would forsake all and follow that sound, not mainly to save property from the flames, but, if we will confess the truth, much more to see it burn, since burn it must, and we, be it known, did not set it on fire,—or to see it put out, and have a hand in it, if that is done as handsomely; yes, even if it were the parish church itself. Hardly a man takes a half-hour's nap after dinner, but when he wakes he holds up his head and asks, "What's the news?" as if the rest of mankind had stood his sentinels. Some give directions to be waked every half-hour, doubtless for no other purpose; and then, to pay for it, they tell what they have dreamed. After a night's sleep the news is as indispensable as the breakfast. "Pray tell me anything new that has happened to a man anywhere on this globe,"—and he reads it over his coffee and rolls, that a man has had his eyes gouged out this morning on the Wachito River;[1] never dreaming the while that he lives in the dark unfathomed mammoth cave of this world,[2] and has but

9. Without giving the alarm bell a complete rotation instead of a pendulum swing.
1. Properly, the Ouachita River, in southwest Arkansas; "gouging" was a form of mayhem then prevalent in the physical combat of the frontier.
2. *Cf.* "the dark unfathomed caves of ocean" in Gray's "Elegy"; here combined with Kentucky's famous Mammoth Cave.

the rudiment of an eye himself.

For my part, I could easily do without the post-office. I think that there are very few important communications made through it. To speak critically, I never received more than one or two letters in my life—I wrote this some years ago—that were worth the postage. The penny-post is, commonly, an institution through which you seriously offer a man that penny for his thoughts which is so often safely offered in jest. And I am sure that I never read any memorable news in a newspaper. If we read of one man robbed, or murdered, or killed by accident, or one house burned, or one vessel wrecked, or one steamboat blown up, or one cow run over on the Western Railroad,[3] or one mad dog killed, or one lot of grasshoppers in the winter,—we never need read of another. One is enough. If you are acquainted with the principle, what do you care for a myriad instances and applications? To a philosopher all *news*, as it is called, is gossip, and they who edit and read it are old women over their tea. Yet not a few are greedy after this gossip. There was such a rush, as I hear, the other day at one of the offices to learn the foreign news by the last arrival, that several large squares of plate glass belonging to the establishment were broken by the pressure,—news which I seriously think a ready wit might write a twelvemonth, or twelve years, beforehand with sufficient accuracy. As for Spain,[4] for instance, if you know how to throw in Don Carlos and the Infanta, and Don Pedro and Seville and Granada, from time to time in the right proportions,—they may have changed the names a little since I saw the papers,—and serve up a bull-fight when other entertainments fail, it will be true to the letter, and give us as good an idea of the exact state or ruin of things in Spain as the most succinct and lucid reports under this head in the newspapers: and as for England, almost the last significant scrap of news from that quarter was the revolution[5] of 1649; and if you have learned the history of her crops for an average year, you never need attend to that thing again, unless your speculations are of a merely pecuniary character. If one may judge who rarely looks into the newspapers, nothing new does ever happen in foreign parts, a French revolution not excepted.[6]

What news! how much more important to know what that is which was never old! "Kieou-he-yu (great dignitary of the state of Wei) sent a man to Khoung-tseu to know his news. Khoung-tseu caused the messenger to be seated near him, and questioned him in

3. From Boston to Troy; later a branch of the Boston and Maine system.
4. What follows refers to the contemporary disorders between the Carlists (who recognized Don Carlos II as King Charles VI) and supporters of the Infanta, who had been proclaimed Queen Isabella II in 1843.

5. The English Civil War (1642–1649), indeed a "revolution," resulted in the execution of Charles I, the victory of Cromwell and the temporary abolition of the monarchy (1649–1660).
6. On his manuscript Thoreau noted that he wrote this before "the last Revolution broke out" (1848).

these terms: What is your master doing? The messenger answered with respect: My master desires to diminish the number of his faults, but he cannot come to the end of them. The messenger being gone, the philosopher remarked: What a worthy messenger! What a worthy messenger!"[7] The preacher, instead of vexing the ears of drowsy farmers on their day of rest at the end of the week,—for Sunday is the fit conclusion of an ill-spent week, and not the fresh and brave beginning of a new one,—with this one other draggle-tail of a sermon, should shout with thundering voice, "Pause! Avast! Why so seeming fast, but deadly slow?"

Shams and delusions are esteemed for soundest truths, while reality is fabulous. If men would steadily observe realities only, and not allow themselves to be deluded, life, to compare it with such things as we know, would be like a fairy tale and the Arabian Nights' Entertainments. If we respected only what is inevitable and has a right to be, music and poetry would resound along the streets. When we are unhurried and wise, we perceive that only great and worthy things have any permanent and absolute existence, that petty fears and petty pleasures are but the shadow of the reality. This is always exhilarating and sublime. By closing the eyes and slumbering, and consenting to be deceived by shows,[8] men establish and confirm their daily life of routine and habit everywhere, which still is built on purely illusory foundations. Children, who play life, discern its true law and relations more clearly than men, who fail to live it worthily, but who think that they are wiser by experience, that is, by failure. I have read in a Hindoo book, that "there was a king's son, who, being expelled in infancy from his native city, was brought up by a forester, and, growing up to maturity in that state, imagined himself to belong to the barbarous race with which he lived. One of his father's ministers having discovered him, revealed to him what he was, and the misconception of his character was removed, and he knew himself to be a prince. So soul," continues the Hindoo philosopher, "from the circumstances in which it is placed, mistakes its own character, until the truth is revealed to it by some holy teacher, and then it knows itself to be *Brahme*."[9] I perceive that we inhabitants of New England live this mean life that we do because our vision does not penetrate the surface of things. We think that that *is* which *appears* to be. If a man should walk through this town and see only the reality, where, think you, would the "Mill-dam" go to?[1] If he should give us an account of the realities he beheld there,

---

7. *Cf. Analects* of Confucius, XIV, 26, 1–2.
8. In the sense of pretense or mere appearance.
9. To the Hindu, God the Creator; but also, as here, the supreme essence or intelligence. *Cf.* the Oversoul of transcendentalism, and see Emerson's

"Brahma" and the footnote to that poem.
1. One manuscript version reads "State Street," another place common to every town; the transcendentalist sought a transcendent reality behind the actual or familiar object.

we should not recognize the place in his description. Look at a meeting-house, or a court-house, or a jail, or a shop, or a dwelling-house, and say what that thing really is before a true gaze, and they would all go to pieces in your account of them. Men esteem truth remote, in the outskirts of the system, behind the farthest star, before Adam and after the last man. In eternity there is indeed something true and sublime. But all these times and places and occasions are now and here. God himself culminates in the present moment, and will never be more divine in the lapse of all the ages. And we are enabled to apprehend at all what is sublime and noble only by the perpetual instilling and drenching of the reality that surrounds us. The universe constantly and obediently answers to our conceptions; whether we travel fast or slow, the track is laid for us. Let us spend our lives in conceiving then. The poet or the artist never yet had so fair and noble a design but some of his posterity at least could accomplish it.

Let us spend one day as deliberately as Nature, and not be thrown off the track by every nutshell and mosquito's wing that falls on the rails. Let us rise early and fast, or break fast, gently and without perturbation; let company come and let company go, let the bells ring and the children cry,—determined to make a day of it. Why should we knock under and go with the stream? Let us not be upset and overwhelmed in that terrible rapid and whirlpool called a dinner, situated in the meridian shallows. Weather this danger and you are safe, for the rest of the way is down hill. With unrelaxed nerves, with morning vigor, sail by it, looking another way, tied to the mast like Ulysses.[2] If the engine whistles, let it whistle till it is hoarse for its pains. If the bell rings, why should we run? We will consider what kind of music they are like. Let us settle ourselves, and work and wedge our feet downward through the mud and slush of opinion, and prejudice, and tradition, and delusion, and appearance, that alluvion which covers the globe, through Paris and London, through New York and Boston and Concord, through Church and State, through poetry and philosophy and religion, till we come to a hard bottom and rocks in place, which we can call *reality*, and say, This is, and no mistake; and then begin, having a *point d'appui*,[3] below freshet and frost and fire, a place where you might found a wall or a state, or set a lamp-post safely, or perhaps a gauge, not a Nilometer,[4] but a Realometer, that future ages might know how deep a freshet of shams and appearances had gathered from time to time. If you stand right fronting and face to face to a fact, you will see the sun

2. Mariners bewitched by the Sirens' songs often leaped to destruction; but Ulysses (Odysseus) had himself bound to the mast, having avoided Charybdis, the "whirlpool" above (*Odyssey*, Book XII).

3. Literally, a "point of support"; a firm base.

4. Ancient instrument devised to record the rise and fall of the great floods of the Nile; the associated coinage of "Realometer" contrasts the relative with the absolute.

glimmer on both its surfaces, as if it were a cimeter,[5] and feel its sweet edge dividing you through the heart and marrow, and so you will happily conclude your mortal career. Be it life or death, we crave only reality. If we are really dying, let us hear the rattle in our throats and feel cold in the extremities; if we are alive, let us go about our business.

Time is but the stream I go a-fishing in.[6] I drink at it; but while I drink I see the sandy bottom and detect how shallow it is. Its thin current slides away, but eternity remains. I would drink deeper; fish in the sky, whose bottom is pebbly with stars. I cannot count one. I know not the first letter of the alphabet. I have always been regretting that I was not as wise as the day I was born. The intellect is a cleaver; it discerns and rifts its way into the secret of things. I do not wish to be any more busy with my hands than is necessary. My head is hands and feet. I feel all my best faculties concentrated in it. My instinct tells me that my head is an organ for burrowing, as some creatures use their snout and fore-paws, and with it I would mine and burrow my way through these hills. I think that the richest vein is somewhere hereabouts; so by the divining-rod and thin rising vapors I judge; and here I will begin to mine.

XII. Brute Neighbors

* * * The mice which haunted my house were not the common ones, which are said to have been introduced into the country, but a wild native kind not found in the village. I sent one to a distinguished naturalist, and it interested him much. When I was building, one of these had its nest underneath the house, and before I had laid the second floor, and swept out the shavings, would come out regularly at lunch time and pick up the crumbs at my feet. It probably had never seen a man before; and it soon became quite familiar, and would run over my shoes and up my clothes. It could readily ascend the sides of the room by short impulses, like a squirrel, which it resembled in its motions. At length, as I leaned with my elbow on the bench one day, it ran up my clothes, and along my sleeve, and round and round the paper which held my dinner, while I kept the latter close, and dodged and played at bo-peep with it; and when at last I held still a piece of cheese between my thumb and finger, it came and nibbled it, sitting in my hand, and afterward cleaned its face and paws, like a fly, and walked away.

A phoebe soon built in my shed, and a robin for protection in a pine which grew against the house. In June the partridge (*Tetrao umbellus*,) which is so shy a bird, led her brood past my windows,

5. Properly, "scimitar" or "scimiter."
6. *Cf. The Pleasures of Memory* (Part II, i, ll. 1–2), a poem then familiar, in which Samuel Rogers (1763–1855)
spoke of sailing "the stream of Time" for Memory's sake; compare Thoreau's "eternity" below.

from the woods in the rear to the front of my house, clucking and calling to them like a hen, and in all her behavior proving herself the hen of the woods. The young suddenly disperse on your approach, at a signal from the mother, as if a whirlwind had swept them away, and they so exactly resemble the dried leaves and twigs that many a traveller has placed his foot in the midst of a brood, and heard the whir of the old bird as she flew off, and her anxious calls and mewing, or seen her trail her wings to attract his attention, without suspecting their neighborhood. The parent will sometimes roll and spin round before you in such a dishabille, that you cannot, for a few moments, detect what kind of creature it is. The young squat still and flat, often running their heads under a leaf, and mind only their mother's directions given from a distance, nor will your approach make them run again and betray themselves. You may even tread on them, or have your eyes on them for a minute, without discovering them. I have held them in my open hand at such a time, and still their only care, obedient to their mother and their instinct, was to squat there without fear or trembling. So perfect is this instinct, that once, when I had laid them on the leaves again, and one accidentally fell on its side, it was found with the rest in exactly the same position ten minutes afterward. They are not callow like the young of most birds, but more perfectly developed and precocious even than chickens. The remarkable adult yet innocent expression of their open and serene eyes is very memorable. All intelligence seems reflected in them. They suggest not merely the purity of infancy, but a wisdom clarified by experience. Such an eye was not born when the bird was, but is coeval with the sky it reflects. The woods do not yield another such a gem. The traveller does not often look into such a limpid well. The ignorant or reckless sportsman often shoots the parent at such a time, and leaves these innocents to fall a prey to some prowling beast or bird, or gradually mingle with the decaying leaves which they so much resemble. It is said that when hatched by a hen they will directly disperse on some alarm, and so are lost, for they never hear the mother's call which gathers them again. These were my hens and chickens.

It is remarkable how many creatures live wild and free though secret in the woods, and still sustain themselves in the neighborhood of towns, suspected by hunters only. How retired the otter manages to live here! He grows to be four feet long, as big as a small boy, perhaps without any human being getting a glimpse of him. I formerly saw the raccoon in the woods behind where my house is built, and probably still heard their whinnering at night. Commonly I rested an hour or two in the shade at noon, after planting, and ate my lunch, and read a little by a spring which was the source of a swamp and of a brook, oozing from under Brister's Hill, half a mile from my field. The approach to this was through a succession of descending grassy hollows, full of young pitch-pines, into a larger wood about the swamp. There, in a very secluded and shaded spot, under a spreading white-pine, there was yet a clean firm sward to sit on. I had dug out the spring and made a well of clear gray water, where I could dip up a pailful without roiling it, and thither I went for this purpose almost every day in midsummer, when the pond was warmest. Thither too the woodcock led her brood, to probe the mud for worms, flying but a foot above them down the bank, while they ran in a troop beneath; but at last, spying me, she would leave her young and circle round and round me, nearer and nearer till within four or five feet, pretending broken wings and legs, to attract my attention, and get off her young, who would already have taken up their march, with faint wiry peep, single file through the swamp, as she directed. Or I heard the peep of the young when I could not see the parent bird. There too the turtle-doves sat over the spring, or fluttered from bough to bough of the soft white-pines over my head; or the red squirrel, coursing down the nearest bough, was particularly familiar and inquisitive. You only need sit still long enough in some attractive spot in the woods that all its inhabitants may exhibit themselves to you by turns.

I was witness to events of a less peaceful character. One day when I went out to my wood-pile, or rather my pile of stumps, I observed two large ants, the one red, the other much larger, nearly half an inch long, and black, fiercely contending with one another. Having once got hold they never let go, but struggled and wrestled and rolled on the chips incessantly. Looking farther, I was surprised to find that the chips were covered with such combatants, that it was not a *duellum*, but a *bellum*,[7] a war between two races of ants, the red always pitted against the black, and frequently two red ones to one black. The legions of these Myrmidons[8] covered all the hills and vales in my woodyard, and the ground was already strewn with the dead and dying, both red and black. It was the only battle-field I have ever witnessed, the only battle-field I ever trod while the battle was raging; internecine war; the red republicans on the one hand, and the black imperialists on the other. On every side they were engaged in deadly combat, yet without any noise that I could hear, and human soldiers never fought so resolutely. I watched a couple that were fast locked in each other's embraces, in a little sunny valley amid the chips, now at noon-day prepared to fight till the sun went down, or life went out. The smaller red champion had fastened himself like a vice to his adversary's front, and through all the tumblings on that field never for an instant ceased to gnaw at one of his feelers near

7. Not a duel, but a war. Compare this battle of the ants with that in the poem, "The Summer Rain," below.

8. The soldiers who followed the Greek Achilles in the Trojan War were Myrmidons (*Iliad*).

the root, having already caused the other to go by the board; while the stronger black one dashed him from side to side, and as I saw on looking nearer, had already divested him of several of his members. They fought with more pertinacity than bulldogs. Neither manifested the least disposition to retreat. It was evident that their battle-cry was Conquer or die. In the mean while there came along a single red ant on the hill-side of this valley, evidently full of excitement, who either had despatched his foe, or had not yet taken part in the battle; probably the latter, for he had lost none of his limbs; whose mother had charged him to return with his shield or upon it.[9] Or perchance he was some Achilles,[1] who had nourished his wrath apart, and had now come to avenge or rescue his Patroclus. He saw this unequal combat from afar—for the blacks were nearly twice the size of the red,—he drew near with rapid pace till he stood on his guard within half an inch of the combatants; then, watching his opportunity, he sprang upon the black warrior and commenced his operations near the root of his right fore-leg, leaving the foe to select among his own members; and so there were three united for life, as if a new kind of attraction had been invented which put all other locks and cements to shame. I should not have wondered by this time to find that they had their respective musical bands stationed on some eminent chip, and playing their national airs the while, to excite the slow and cheer the dying combatants. I was myself excited somewhat even as if they had been men. The more you think of it, the less the difference. And certainly there is not the fight recorded in Concord history, at least, if in the history of America, that will bear a moment's comparison with this, whether for the numbers engaged in it, or for the patriotism and heroism displayed. For numbers and for carnage it was an Austerlitz or Dresden.[2] Concord Fight! Two killed on the patriots' side, and Luther Blanchard wounded! Why here every ant was a Buttrick,—"Fire! for God's sake fire!"—and thousands shared the fate of Davis and Hosmer. There was not one hireling there.[3] I have no doubt that it was a principle they fought for, as much as our ancestors, and not to avoid a three-penny tax on their tea; and the results of this battle will be as important and memorable to those whom it concerns as those of the battle of Bunker Hill at least.

I took up the chip on which the three I have particularly described were struggling, carried it into my house, and placed it under a tum-

9. The legendary command of the Spartan mothers to their warrior sons.
1. Achilles had retired from battle, sulking at a slight; but at the death of his friend Patroclus he leaped into the fray and killed the Trojan Hector (*Iliad*).
2. Two bloody battles of the Napoleonic Wars.

3. Five hundred minutemen, led by Major John Buttrick, successfully repelled the British (including "hirelings") at Concord, April 19, 1775. Captain Isaac Davis and David Hosmer were killed. The tax on tea mentioned in the next sentence was an abominated British mercantile tax. *Cf.* Emerson's "Concord Hymn."

bler on my window-sill, in order to see the issue. Holding a microscope to the first-mentioned red ant, I saw that, though he was assiduously gnawing at the near fore-leg of his enemy, having severed his remaining feeler, his own breast was all torn away, exposing what vitals he had there to the jaws of the black warrior, whose breast-plate was apparently too thick for him to pierce; and the dark carbuncles of the sufferer's eyes shone with ferocity such as war only could excite. They struggled half an hour longer under the tumbler, and when I looked again the black soldier had severed the heads of his foes from their bodies, and the still living heads were hanging on either side of him like ghastly trophies at his saddlebow, still apparently as firmly fastened as ever, and he was endeavoring with feeble struggles, being without feelers and with only the remnant of a leg, and I know not how many other wounds, to divest himself of them; which at length, after half an hour more, he accomplished. I raised the glass, and he went off over the window-sill in that crippled state. Whether he finally survived that combat, and spent the remainder of his days in some Hotel des Invalides,[4] I do not know; but I thought that his industry would not be worth much thereafter. I never learned which party was victorious, nor the cause of the war; but I felt for the rest of that day as if I had my feelings excited and harrowed by witnessing the struggle, the ferocity and carnage, of a human battle before my door.

Kirby and Spence tell us that the battles of ants have long been celebrated and the date of them recorded, though they say that Huber[5] is the only modern author who appears to have witnessed them. "Aeneas Sylvius,"[6] say they, "after giving a very circumstantial account of one contested with great obstinacy by a great and small species on the trunk of a pear tree," adds that " 'This action was fought in the pontificate of Eugenius the Fourth, in the presence of Nicholas Pistoriensis, an eminent lawyer, who related the whole history of the battle with the greatest fidelity.' A similar engagement between great and small ants is recorded by Olaus Magnus,[7] in which the small ones, being victorious, are said to have buried the bodies of their own soldiers, but left those of their giant enemies a prey to the birds. This event happened previous to the expulsion of the tyrant Christiern the Second from Sweden." The battle which I witnessed

4. A famous veteran's hospital in Paris.
5. Then standard authorities on entomology: the British William Kirby (1759–1850) and William Spence (1783–1860), joint authors of *An Introduction to Entomology* (4 vols., 1815–1826); and François Huber (1750–1831), great Swiss authority on bees, who "witnessed" insect behavior chiefly through the eyes of his wife and son, for he began to go blind in youth.
6. Literary name of Pope Pius II (1405–1464), a prolific poet, geographer, and historian.
7. Swedish-born ecclesiastic (1490–1558), brother of the Archbishop of Uppsala, entered a Roman monastery at thirty-seven and produced a history of Sweden, long accepted.

took place in the Presidency of Polk, five years before the passage of Webster's Fugitive-Slave Bill.[8] * * *

XVIII. Conclusion

To the sick the doctors wisely recommend a change of air and scenery. Thank Heaven, here is not all the world. The buckeye does not grow in New England, and the mockingbird is rarely heard here. The wild goose is more of a cosmopolite than we; he breaks his fast in Canada, takes a luncheon in the Ohio, and plumes himself for the night in a southern bayou. Even the bison, to some extent, keeps pace with the seasons, cropping the pastures of the Colorado only till a greener and sweeter grass awaits him by the Yellowstone. Yet we think that if rail fences are pulled down, and stone walls piled up on our farms, bounds are henceforth set to our lives and our fates decided. If you are chosen town clerk, forsooth, you cannot go to Tierra del Fuego[9] this summer: but you may go to the land of infernal fire nevertheless. The universe is wider than our views of it.

Yet we should oftener look over the tafferel[1] of our craft, like curious passengers, and not make the voyage like stupid sailors picking oakum. The other side of the globe is but the home of our correspondent. Our voyaging is only great-circle sailing, and the doctors prescribe for diseases of the skin merely. One hastens to southern Africa to chase the giraffe; but surely that is not the game he would be after. How long, pray, would a man hunt giraffes if he could? Snipes and woodcocks also may afford rare sport; but I trust it would be nobler game to shoot one's self.—

> "Direct your eye right inward, and you'll find
> A thousand regions in your mind
> Yet undiscovered. Travel them, and be
> Expert in home-cosmography."

What does Africa,—what does the West stand for? Is not our own interior white on the chart? black though it may prove, like the coast, when discovered. Is it the source of the Nile, or the Niger, or the Missipissippi, or a Northwest Passage around this continent, that we would find? Are these the problems which most concern mankind? Is Franklin[2] the only man who is lost, that his wife should be so earnest to find him? Does Mr. Grinnell[3] know where he him-

---

8. *I.e.,* 1845. James K. Polk was president from 1845 to 1849. Daniel Webster, then senator from Massachusetts, gave support to the Compromises of 1850, reaffirming the fugitive-slave laws.
9. Group of islands, the remotest extremity of South America; the name means "Land of Fire" (*cf.* "infernal fire," following).

1. Obsolete for "taffrail," the rail, or (rarely) the upper part of a ship's stern.
2. Sir John Franklin (1786–1847), English explorer of the Arctic, lost while seeking the Northwest Passage (1845–1847); several rescue parties failed to find him.
3. Henry Grinnell, American merchant, financed two of the expeditions to relieve Franklin.

self is? Be rather the Mungo Park, the Lewis and Clark and Frobisher,[4] of your own streams and oceans; explore your own higher latitudes,—with shiploads of preserved meats to support you, if they be necessary; and pile the empty cans sky-high for a sign. Were preserved meats invented to preserve meat merely? Nay, be a Columbus to whole new continents and worlds within you, opening new channels, not of trade, but of thought. Every man is the lord of a realm beside which the earthly empire of the Czar is but a petty state, a hummock left by the ice. Yet some can be patriotic who have no *self*-respect, and sacrifice the greater to the less. They love the soil which makes their graves, but have no sympathy with the spirit which may still animate their clay. Patriotism is a maggot in their heads. What was the meaning of that South-Sea Exploring Expedition,[5] with all its parade and expense, but an indirect recognition of the fact that there are continents and seas in the moral world to which every man is an isthmus or an inlet, yet unexplored by him, but that it is easier to sail many thousand miles through cold and storm and cannibals, in a government ship, with five hundred men and boys to assist one, than it is to explore the private sea, the Atlantic and Pacific Ocean of one's being alone.—

"Erret, et extremos alter scrutetur Iberos.
Plus habet hic vitae, plus habet ille viae."[6]
Let them wander and scrutinize the out-
            landish Australians.
I have more of God, they more of the road.

It is not worth the while to go round the world to count the cats in Zanzibar.[7] Yet do this even till you can do better, and you may perhaps find some "Symmes' Hole"[8] by which to get at the inside at last. England and France, Spain and Portugal, Gold Coast and Slave Coast, all front on this private sea; but no bark from them has ventured out of sight of land, though it is without doubt the direct way to India. If you would learn to speak all tongues and conform to the customs of all nations, if you would travel farther than all travellers, be naturalized in all climes, and cause the Sphinx to dash her head against a stone,[9] even obey the precept of the old philos-

4. Explorers all: Mungo Park (1771–1806), English pioneer of West Africa and the Niger, killed by natives; Meriwether Lewis and George Rogers Clark mapped a route from Illinois to the Pacific (1804–1806); Martin Frobisher (1535?–1594), Elizabethan navigator, sought the Northwest Passage and explored various areas of Canada and the West Indies.
5. Explorations in the Antarctic and South Pacific by the United States Navy (1838–1842).
6. The concluding lines of *De Sene*

Veronensi by Claudian (Claudius Claudianus, late Roman classical poet, fourth century). To suit his purpose, Thoreau whimsically translates *extremos Iberos* ("farthest Spain") as "the outlandish Australians," and *vitae* ("of life" or "vitality") as "of God"—in defiance of the original pun of *vitae* and *viae*.
7. An island off the coast of East Africa; hence, "a very distant place."
8. John Cleve Symmes in 1826 published the theory that the earth is hollow, with an opening at each pole.
9. Thus behaved the Sphinx of Thebes

opher,[1] and Explore thyself. Herein are demanded the eye and the nerve. Only the defeated and deserters go to the wars, cowards that run away and enlist. Start now on that farthest western way, which does not pause at the Mississippi or the Pacific, nor conduct toward a worn-out China or Japan, but leads on direct, a tangent to this sphere, summer and winter, day and night, sun down, moon down, and at last earth down too.

It is said that Mirabeau[2] took to highway robbery "to ascertain what degree of resolution was necessary in order to place one's self in formal opposition to the most sacred laws of society." He declared that "a soldier who fights in the ranks does not require half so much courage as a foot-pad,"—"that honor and religion has never stood in the way of a well-considered and a firm resolve." This was manly, as the world goes; and yet it was idle, if not desperate. A saner man would have found himself often enough "in formal opposition" to what are deemed "the most sacred laws of society," through obedience to yet more sacred laws, and so have tested his resolution without going out of his way. It is not for a man to put himself in such an attitude to society, but to maintain himself in whatever attitude he find himself through obedience to the laws of his being, which will never be one of opposition to a just government, if he should chance to meet with such.

I left the woods for as good a reason as I went there. Perhaps it seemed to me that I had several more lives to live, and could not spare any more time for that one. It is remarkable how easily and insensibly we fall into a particular route, and make a beaten track for ourselves. I had not lived there a week before my feet wore a path from my door to the pond-side; and though it is five or six years since I trod it, it is still quite distinct. It is true, I fear, that others may have fallen into it, and so helped to keep it open. The surface of the earth is soft and impressible by the feet of men; and so with the paths which the mind travels. How worn and dusty, then, must be the highways of the world, how deep the ruts of tradition and conformity! I did not wish to take a cabin passage, but rather to go before the mast and on the deck of the world, for there I could best see the moonlight amid the mountains. I do not wish to go below now.

I learned this, at least, by my experiment: that if one advances confidently in the direction of his dreams, and endeavors to live the life which he has imagined, he will meet with a success unexpected in common hours. He will put some things behind, will pass

when the traveler, Oedipus, guessed her riddle (Sophocles, *Oedipus Rex*).
1. Bias of Priene (sixth century B.C.), one of the Seven Wise Men, famous for his maxims (*cf.* Thoreau's *Journals,*

Vol. VII, pp. 169–170, July 12, 1840).
2. Victor Riqueti, Marquis de Mirabeau (1715–1789), radical French economist and physiocrat.

an invisible boundary; new, universal, and more liberal laws will begin to establish themselves around and within him; or the old laws be expanded, and interpreted in his favor in a more liberal sense, and he will live with the license of a higher order of beings. In proportion as he simplifies his life, the laws of the universe will appear less complex, and solitude will not be solitude, nor poverty poverty, nor weakness weakness. If you have built castles in the air,[3] your work need not be lost; that is where they should be. Now put the foundations under them.

It is a ridiculous demand which England and America make, that you shall speak so that they can understand you. Neither men nor toadstools grow so. As if that were important, and there were not enough to understand you without them. As if Nature could support but one order of understandings, could not sustain birds as well as quadrupeds, flying as well as creeping things, and *hush* and *whoa*, which Bright[4] can understand, were the best English. As if there were safety in stupidity alone. I fear chiefly lest my expression may not be *extra-vagant*[5] enough, may not wander far enough beyond the narrow limits of my daily experience, so as to be adequate to the truth of which I have been convinced. *Extra vagance!* it depends on how you are yarded. The migrating buffalo, which seeks new pastures in another latitude, is not extravagant like the cow which kicks over the pail, leaps the cowyard fence, and runs after her calf, in milking time. I desire to speak somewhere *without* bounds; like a man in a waking moment, to men in their waking moments; for I am convinced that I cannot exaggerate enough even to lay the foundation of a true expression. Who that has heard a strain of music feared then lest he should speak extravagantly any more forever? In view of the future or possible, we should live quite laxly and undefined in front, our outlines dim and misty on that side; as our shadows reveal an insensible perspiration toward the sun. The volatile truth of our words should continually betray the inadequacy of the residual statement. Their truth is instantly *translated;*[6] its literal monument alone remains. The words which express our faith and piety are not definite; yet they are significant and fragrant like frankincense to superior natures.

Why level downward to our dullest perception always, and praise that as common sense? The commonest sense is the sense of men

3. The original source of this familiar saying is probably Cervantes' *Don Quixote* (1605, 1615), well-known to Thoreau. (*Cf.* Part II, Book III, Chapter 31.)
4. Probably John Bright (1811–1889), British parliamentarian, whose liberal oratory had been a deterrent (*"hush* and *whoa"*) to the conservative majority.
5. "Extravagant" is derived from two Latin roots: *vagari,* "to roam about"; and *extra,* "outside" or "outside of." Thoreau plays on these words to the end of this paragraph.
6. In earlier usage, and by derivation, the word often signified an exaltation into a higher condition or state; hence the contrast here, between the ideal "truth" of words and their "literal monument" (mere letters).

asleep, which they express by snoring. Sometimes we are inclined to class those who are once-and-a-half-witted with the half-witted, because we appreciate only a third part of their wit. Some would find fault with the morning red, if they ever got up early enough. "They pretend," as I hear, "that the verses of Kabir[7] have four different senses; illusion, spirit, intellect, and the exoteric doctrine of the Vedas;" but in this part of the world it is considered a ground for complaint if a man's writings admit of more than one interpretation. While England endeavors to cure the potato-rot, will not any endeavor to cure the brain-rot, which prevails so much more widely and fatally?

I do not suppose that I have attained to obscurity, but I should be proud if no more fatal fault were found with my pages on this score than was found with the Walden ice. Southern customers objected to its blue color, which is the evidence of its purity, as if it were muddy, and preferred the Cambridge ice, which is white, but tastes of weeds. The purity men love is like the mists which envelop the earth, and not like the azure ether beyond.

Some are dinning in our ears that we Americans, and moderns generally, are intellectual dwarfs compared with the ancients, or even the Elizabethan men. But what is that to the purpose? A living dog is better than a dead lion.[8] Shall a man go and hang himself because he belongs to the race of pygmies, and not be the biggest pygmy that he can? Let every one mind his own business, and endeavor to be what he was made.

Why should we be in such desperate haste to succeed and in such desperate enterprises? If a man does not keep pace with his companions, perhaps it is because he hears a different drummer. Let him step to the music which he hears, however measured or far away. It is not important that he should mature as soon as an apple tree or an oak. Shall he turn his spring into summer? If the condition of things which we were made for is not yet, what were any reality which we can substitute? We will not be shipwrecked on a vain reality. Shall we with pains erect a heaven of blue glass over ourselves, though when it is done we shall be sure to gaze still at the true ethereal heaven far above, as if the former were not?

There was an artist in the city of Kouroo[9] who was disposed to strive after perfection. One day it came into his mind to make a staff. Having considered that in an imperfect work time is an ingredient, but into a perfect work time does not enter, he said to himself, It shall be perfect in all respects, though I should do nothing

7. Indian poet and mystic (1450–1518), regarded as a saint by both Hindus and Moslems, taught monotheism and the abolition of caste, influencing the nascent creed of the Sikh.

8. *Cf.* Ecclesiastes ix: 4.

9. There is an ancient city of this name in French Equatorial Africa. The legend is not identified.

else in my life. He proceeded instantly to the forest for wood, being resolved that it should not be made of unsuitable material; and as he searched for and rejected stick after stick, his friends gradually deserted him, for they grew old in their works and died, but he grew not older by a moment. His singleness of purpose and resolution, and his elevated piety, endowed him, without his knowledge, with perennial youth. As he made no compromise with Time, Time kept out of his way, and only sighed at a distance because he could not overcome him. Before he had found a stick in all respects suitable the city of Kouroo was a hoary ruin, and he sat on one of its mounds to peel the stick. Before he had given it the proper shape the dynasty of the Candahars was at an end, and with the point of the stick he wrote the name of the last of that race in the sand, and then resumed his work. By the time he had smoothed and polished the staff Kalpa was no longer the pole-star; and ere he had put on the ferule and the head adorned with precious stones, Brahma had awoke and slumbered many times. But why do I stay to mention these things? When the finishing stroke was put to his work, it suddenly expanded before the eyes of the astonished artist into the fairest of all the creations of Brahma. He had made a new system in making a staff, a world with full and fair proportions; in which, though the old cities and dynasties had passed away, fairer and more glorious ones had taken their places. And now he saw by the heap of shavings still fresh at his feet, that, for him and his work, the former lapse of time had been an illusion, and that no more time had elapsed than is required for a single scintillation from the brain of Brahma to fall on and inflame the tinder of a mortal brain. The material was pure, and his art was pure; how could the result be other than wonderful?

No face which we can give to a matter will stead us so well at last as the truth. This alone wears well. For the most part, we are not where we are, but in a false position. Through an infirmity of our natures, we suppose a case, and put ourselves into it, and hence are in two cases at the same time, and it is doubly difficult to get out. In sane moments we regard only the facts, the case that is. Say what you have to say, not what you ought. Any truth is better than make-believe. Tom Hyde, the tinker, standing on the gallows, was asked if he had anything to say. "Tell the tailors," said he, "to remember to make a knot in their thread before they take the first stitch." His companion's prayer is forgotten.

However mean your life is, meet it and live it; do not shun it and call it hard names. It is not so bad as you are. It looks poorest when you are richest. The faultfinder will find faults even in paradise. Love your life, poor as it is. You may perhaps have some pleasant, thrilling, glorious hours, even in a poor-house. The setting sun is reflected from the windows of the almshouse as brightly as from the rich man's abode; the snow melts before its door as early in the spring. I do not see but a quiet mind may live as contentedly there, and have as cheering thoughts, as in a palace. The town's poor seem to me often to live the most independent lives of any.[1] Maybe they are simply great enough to receive without misgiving. Most think that they are above being supported by the town; but it oftener happens that they are not above supporting themselves by dishonest means, which should be more disreputable. Cultivate poverty like a garden herb, like sage. Do not trouble yourself much to get new things, whether clothes or friends. Turn the old; return to them. Things do not change; we change. Sell your clothes and keep your thoughts. God will see that you do not want society. If I were confined to a corner of a garret all my days, like a spider, the world would be just as large to me while I had my thoughts about me. The philosopher said: "From an army of three divisions one can take away its general, and put it in disorder; from the man the most abject and vulgar one cannot take away his thought." Do not seek so anxiously to be developed, to subject yourself to many influences to be played on; it is all dissipation. Humility like darkness reveals the heavenly lights. The shadows of poverty and meanness gather around us, "and lo! creation widens to our view."[2] We are often reminded that if there were bestowed on us the wealth of Crœsus, our aims must still be the same, and our means essentially the same. Moreover, if you are restricted in your range by poverty, if you cannot buy books and newspapers, for instance, you are but confined to the most significant and vital experiences; you are compelled to deal with the material which yields the most sugar and the most starch. It is life near the bone where it is sweetest. You are defended from being a trifler. No man loses ever on a lower level by magnanimity on a higher. Superfluous wealth can buy superfluities only. Money is not required to buy one necessary of the soul.

I live in the angle of a leaden wall, into whose composition was poured a little alloy of bell-metal. Often, in the repose of my midday, there reaches my ears a confused *tintinnabulum*[3] from without. It is the noise of my contemporaries. My neighbors tell me of their adventures with famous gentlemen and ladies, what notabilities they met at the dinner-table; but I am no more interested in such things than in the contents of the Daily Times. The interest and the conversation are about costume and manners chiefly; but a goose is a goose still, dress it as you will. They tell me of California and Texas, of England and the Indies, of the Hon. Mr. —— of Georgia or of

1. The town poor farm was on the road from Concord to Walden, a familiar walk for Thoreau.
2. The original (by Joseph Blanco White, 1775–1818) reads: "And lo! creation widened in man's view." It is

l. 8 of "Night," a sonnet praised by Coleridge, and much quoted, but its author's only success.
3. Latin, meaning "a ringing of little bells."

Massachusetts, all transient and fleeting phenomena, till I am ready to leap from their court-yard like the Mameluke bey.[4] I delight to come to my bearings,—not walk in procession with pomp and parade, in a conspicuous place, but to walk even with the Builder of the universe, if I may,—not to live in this restless, nervous, bustling, trivial Nineteenth Century, but stand or sit thoughtfully while it goes by. What are men celebrating? They are all on a committee of arrangements, and hourly expect a speech from somebody. God is only the president of the day, and Webster[5] is his orator. I love to weigh, to settle, to gravitate toward that which most strongly and rightfully attracts me;—not hang by the beam of the scale and try to weigh less,—not suppose a case, but take the case that is; to travel the only path I can, and that on which no power can resist me. It affords me no satisfaction to commence to spring an arch before I have got a solid foundation. Let us not play at kittly-benders.[6] There is a solid bottom everywhere. We read that the traveller asked the boy if the swamp before him had a hard bottom. The boy replied that it had. But presently the traveller's horse sank in up to the girths, and he observed to the boy, "I thought you said that this bog had a hard bottom." "So it has," answered the latter, "but you have not got half way to it yet." So it is with the bogs and quicksands of society; but he is an old boy that knows it. Only what is thought, said, or done at a certain rare coincidence is good. I would not be one of those who will foolishly drive a nail into mere lath and plastering; such a deed would keep me awake nights. Give me a hammer, and let me feel for the furring.[7] Do not depend on the putty. Drive a nail home and clinch it so faithfully that you can wake up in the night and think of your work with satisfaction,—a work at which you would not be ashamed to invoke the Muse. So will help you God, and so only. Every nail driven should be as another rivet in the machine of the universe, you carrying on the work.

Rather than love, than money, than fame, give me truth. I sat at a table where were rich food and wine in abundance, and obsequious attendance, but sincerity and truth were not; and I went away hungry from the inhospitable board. The hospitality was as cold as the ices. I thought that there was no need of ice to freeze them. They talked to me of the age of the wine and the fame of the vintage; but I thought of an older, a newer, and purer wine, of a more glorious vintage, which they had not got, and could not buy. The style, the house and grounds and "entertainment" pass for nothing with me. I called on the king, but he made me wait in his hall, and conducted like a man incapacitated for hospitality. There was

---

4. One of the leaders of the Mamelukes, warlike Egyptian sectaries noted for agility, exterminated (1811) by Mehemet Ali in his unification of Egypt.
5. Satirical reference to Daniel Webster.

6. A game involving skill in skating over thin ice.
7. The substantial wooden supports beneath the lathwork.

a man in my neighborhood who lived in a hollow tree. His manners were truly regal. I should have done better had I called on him.

How long shall we sit in our porticoes practising idle and musty virtues, which any work would make impertinent? As if one were to begin the day with long-suffering, and hire a man to hoe his potatoes; and in the afternoon go forth to practise Christian meekness and charity with goodness aforethought! Consider the China pride and stagnant self-complacency of mankind. This generation inclines a little to congratulate itself on being the last of an illustrious line; and in Boston and London and Paris and Rome, thinking of its long descent, it speaks of its progress in art and science and literature with satisfaction. There are the Records of the Philosophical Societies, and the public Eulogies of *Great Men!* It is the good Adam contemplating his own virtue. "Yes, we have done great deeds, and sung divine songs, which shall never die,"—that is, as long as *we* can remember them. The learned societies and great men of Assyria,—where are they? What youthful philosophers and experimentalists we are! There is not one of my readers who has yet lived a whole human life. These may be but the spring months in the life of the race. If we have had the seven-years' itch, we have not seen the seventeen-year locust yet in Concord. We are acquainted with a mere pellicle of the globe on which we live. Most have not delved six feet beneath the surface, nor leaped as many above it. We know not where we are. Beside, we are sound asleep nearly half our time. Yet we esteem ourselves wise, and have an established order on the surface. Truly, we are deep thinkers, we are ambitious spirits! As I stand over the insect crawling amid the pine needles on the forest floor, and endeavoring to conceal itself from my sight, and ask myself why it will cherish those humble thoughts, and hide its head from me who might, perhaps, be its benefactor, and impart to its race some cheering information, I am reminded of the greater Benefactor and Intelligence that stands over me the human insect.

There is an incessant influx of novelty into the world, and yet we tolerate incredible dulness. I need only suggest what kind of sermons are still listened to in the most enlightened countries. There are such words as joy and sorrow, but they are only the burden of a psalm, sung with a nasal twang, while we believe in the ordinary and mean. We think that we can change our clothes only. It is said that the British Empire is very large and respectable, and that the United States are a first-rate power. We do not believe that a tide rises and falls behind every man which can float the British Empire like a chip, if he should ever harbor it in his mind. Who knows what sort of seventeen-year locust will next come out of the ground? The government of the world I live in was not framed, like that of Britain, in after-dinner conversations over the wine.

The life in us is like the water in the river. It may rise this year

and systematically. Carried out, it finally amounts to this, which also I believe,—"That government is best which governs not at all;" and when men are prepared for it, that will be the kind of government which they will have. Government is at best but an expedient; but most governments are usually, and all governments are sometimes, inexpedient. The objections which have been brought against a standing army, and they are many and weighty, and deserve to prevail, may also at last be brought against a standing government. The standing army is only an arm of the standing government. The government itself, which is only the mode which the people have chosen to execute their will, is equally liable to be abused and perverted before the people can act through it. Witness the present Mexican war, the work of comparatively a few individuals[3] using the standing government as their tool; for, in the outset, the people would not have consented to this measure.

This American government,—what is it but a tradition, though a recent one, endeavoring to transmit itself unimpaired to posterity, but each instant losing some of its integrity? It has not the vitality and force of a single living man; for a single man can bend it to his will. It is a sort of wooden gun to the people themselves. But it is not the less necessary for this; for the people must have some complicated machinery or other, and hear its din, to satisfy that idea of government which they have. Governments show thus how successfully men can be imposed on, even impose on themselves, for their own advantage. It is excellent, we must all allow. Yet this government never of itself furthered any enterprise, but by the alacrity with which it got out of its way. *It* does not keep the country free. *It* does not settle the West. *It* does not educate. The character inherent in the American people has done all that has been accomplished; and it would have done somewhat more, if the government had not sometimes got in its way. For government is an expedient by which men would fain succeed in letting one another alone; and, as has been said, when it is most expedient, the governed are most let alone by it. Trade and commerce, if they were not made of india-rubber, would never manage to bounce over the obstacles which legislators are continually putting in their way; and, if one were to judge these men wholly by the effects of their actions and not partly by their intentions, they would deserve to be classed and punished with those mischievous persons who put obstructions on the railroads.

But, to speak practically and as a citizen, unlike those who call

social contract sanctioned only by necessity was an active influence during the Revolution and the Constitutional Convention.

3. The war was regarded by northern reformers as resulting primarily from the selfish interest of southern politicians and northern cotton merchants in extending slave territory.

themselves no-government men, I ask for, not at once no government, but at once a better government. Let every man make known what kind of government would command his respect, and that will be one step toward obtaining it.

After all, the practical reason why, when the power is once in the hands of the people, a majority are permitted, and for a long period continue, to rule is not because they are most likely to be in the right, nor because this seems fairest to the minority, but because they are physically the strongest. But a government in which the majority rule in all cases cannot be based on justice, even as far as men understand it.[4] Can there be a government in which majorities do not virtually decide right and wrong, but conscience?—in which majorities decide only those questions to which the rule of expediency is applicable? Must the citizen ever for a moment, or in the least degree, resign his conscience to the legislator? Why has every man a conscience, then? I think that we should be men first, and subjects afterward. It is not desirable to cultivate a respect for the law, so much as for the right. The only obligation which I have a right to assume is to do at any time what I think right. It is truly enough said that a corporation has no conscience; but a corporation of conscientious men is a corporation *with* a conscience. Law never made men a whit more just; and, by means of their respect for it, even the well-disposed are daily made the agents of injustice. A common and natural result of an undue respect for law is, that you may see a file of soldiers, colonel, captain, corporal, privates, powder-monkeys, and all, marching in admirable order over hill and dale to the wars, against their wills, ay, against their common sense and consciences, which makes it very steep marching indeed, and produces a palpitation of the heart. They have no doubt that it is a damnable business in which they are concerned; they are all peaceably inclined. Now, what are they? Men at all? or small movable forts and magazines, at the service of some unscrupulous man in power? Visit the Navy-Yard, and behold a marine, such a man as an American government can make, or such as it can make a man with its black arts,—a mere shadow and reminiscence of humanity, a man laid out alive and standing, and already, as one may say, buried under arms with funeral accompaniments, though it may be,—

> "Not a drum was heard, not a funeral note,
> As his corse to the rampart we hurried;
> Not a soldier discharged his farewell shot
> O'er the grave where our hero we buried."[5]

4. Recalling a principal controversy of the Constitutional Convention, where the conservative minority, represented by Hamilton and Adams, were overcome by the Jeffersonians, who favored majority rule.
5. Charles Wolfe (1791–1823), Irish clergyman who died at thirty-two, won

The mass of men serve the state thus, not as men mainly, but as machines, with their bodies. They are the standing army, and the militia, jailers, constables, *posse comitatus*,[6] etc. In most cases there is no free exercise whatever of the judgment or of the moral sense; but they put themselves on a level with wood and earth and stones; and wooden men can perhaps be manufactured that will serve the purpose as well. Such command no more respect than men of straw or a lump of dirt. They have the same sort of worth only as horses and dogs. Yet such as these even are commonly esteemed good citizens. Others—as most legislators, politicians, lawyers, ministers, and office-holders—serve the state chiefly with their heads; and, as they rarely make any moral distinctions, they are as likely to serve the devil, without *intending* it, as God. A very few,—as heroes, patriots, martyrs, reformers in the great sense, and *men*—serve the state with their consciences also, and so necessarily resist it for the most part; and they are commonly treated as enemies by it. A wise man will only be useful as a man, and will not submit to be "clay," and "stop a hole to keep the wind away,"[7] but leave that office to his dust at least:—

> "I am too high-born to be propertied,
> To be a secondary at control,
> Or useful serving-man and instrument
> To any sovereign state throughout the world."[8]

He who gives himself entirely to his fellow-men appears to them useless and selfish; but he who gives himself partially to them is pronounced a benefactor and philanthropist.

How does it become a man to behave toward this American government to-day? I answer, that he cannot without disgrace be associated with it.[9] I cannot for an instant recognize that political organization as *my* government which is the *slave's* government also.

All men recognize the right of revolution; that is, the right to refuse allegiance to, and to resist, the government, when its tyranny or its inefficiency are great and unendurable. But almost all say that such is not the case now. But such was the case, they think, in the Revolution of '75. If one were to tell me that this was a bad government because it taxed certain foreign commodities brought to its ports, it is most probable that I should not make an ado about it, for I can do without them. All machines have their friction; and possibly this does enough good to counterbalance the evil. At any

several decades of remembrance by his "Burial of Sir John Moore at Corunna" (1817), of which this is the opening.
6. Legal Latin, meaning "having the authority of the county"; *cf.* the sheriff's "posse."
7. *Cf.* Shakespeare, *Hamlet*, Act V,

Scene 1, ll. 236–237.
8. *Cf.* Shakespeare, *King John*, Act V, Scene 2, ll. 79–82.
9. Many accused Polk's administration (1845–1849) of strengthening slavery through fugitive-slave laws and the Mexican War.

rate, it is a great evil to make a stir about it. But when the friction comes to have its machine, and oppression and robbery are organized, I say, let us not have such a machine any longer. In other words, when a sixth of the population of a nation which has undertaken to be the refuge of liberty are slaves, and a whole country[1] is unjustly overrun and conquered by a foreign army, and subjected to military law, I think that it is not too soon for honest men to rebel and revolutionize. What makes this duty the more urgent is the fact that the country so overrun is not our own, but ours is the invading army.

Paley,[2] a common authority with many on moral questions, in his chapter on the "Duty of Submission to Civil Government," resolves all civil obligation into expediency; and he proceeds to say "that so long as the interest of the whole society requires it, that is, so long as the established government cannot be resisted or changed without public inconveniency, it is the will of God . . . that the established government be obeyed,—and no longer. This principle being admitted, the justice of every particular case of resistance is reduced to a computation of the quantity of the danger and grievance on the one side, and of the probability and expense of redressing it on the other." Of this, he says, every man shall judge for himself. But Paley appears never to have contemplated those cases to which the rule of expediency does not apply, in which a people, as well as an individual, must do justice, cost what it may. If I have unjustly wrested a plank from a drowning man, I must restore it to him though I drown myself. This, according to Paley, would be inconvenient. But he that would save his life, in such a case, shall lose it.[3] This people must cease to hold slaves, and to make war on Mexico, though it cost them their existence as a people.

In their practice, nations agree with Paley; but does any one think that Massachusetts does exactly what is right at the present crisis?

"A drab of state, a cloth-o'-silver slut,
  To have her train borne up, and her soul trail in the dirt."

Practically speaking, the opponents to a reform in Massachusetts are not a hundred thousand politicians at the South, but a hundred thousand merchants and farmers here, who are more interested in commerce and agriculture than they are in humanity, and are not prepared to do justice to the slave and to Mexico, *cost what it may.* I quarrel not with far-off foes, but with those who, near at home, coöperate with, and do the bidding of, those far away, and without whom the latter would be harmless. We are accustomed to say, that the mass of men are unprepared; but improvement is slow, because the few are not materially wiser or better than the many. It is not

1. Mexico.
2. William Paley (1743–1805), British thinker, whose utilitarianism motivates

this quotation from his *Principles of Moral and Political Philosophy,* (1785).
3. *Cf.* Luke ix: 24.

so important that many should be as good as you, as that there be some absolute goodness somewhere; for that will leaven the whole lump.[4] There are thousands who are *in opinion* opposed to slavery and to the war, who yet in effect do nothing to put an end to them; who, esteeming themselves children of Washington and Franklin, sit down with their hands in their pockets, and say that they know not what to do, and do nothing; who even postpone the question of freedom to the question of free trade, and quietly read the prices-current along with the latest advices from Mexico, after dinner, and, it may be, fall asleep over them both. What is the price-current of an honest man and patriot to-day? They hesitate, and they regret, and sometimes they petition; but they do nothing in earnest and with effect. They will wait, well disposed, for others to remedy the evil, that they may no longer have it to regret. At most, they give only a cheap vote, and a feeble countenance and God-speed, to the right, as it goes by them. There are nine hundred and ninety-nine patrons of virtue to one virtuous man. But it is easier to deal with the real possessor of a thing than with the temporary guardian of it.

All voting is a sort of gaming, like checkers or backgammon, with a slight moral tinge to it, a playing with right and wrong, with moral questions; and betting naturally accompanies it. The character of the voters is not staked. I cast my vote, perchance, as I think right; but I am not vitally concerned that that right should prevail. I am willing to leave it to the majority. Its obligation, therefore, never exceeds that of expediency. Even voting *for the right* is *doing* nothing for it. It is only expressing to men feebly your desire that it should prevail. A wise man will not leave the right to the mercy of chance, nor wish it to prevail through the power of the majority. There is but little virtue in the action of masses of men. When the majority shall at length vote for the abolition of slavery, it will be because they are indifferent to slavery, or because there is but little slavery left to be abolished by their vote. *They* will then be the only slaves. Only *his* vote can hasten the abolition of slavery who asserts his own freedom by his vote.

I hear of a convention to be held at Baltimore,[5] or elsewhere, for the selection of a candidate for the Presidency, made up chiefly of editors, and men who are politicians by profession; but I think, what is it to any independent, intelligent, and respectable man what decision they may come to? Shall we not have the advantage of his wisdom and honesty, nevertheless? Can we not count upon some independent votes? Are there not many individuals in the country who do not attend conventions? But no: I find that the respectable man, so called, has immediately drifted from his position, and despairs

4. *Cf.* I Corinthians v: 6.
5. The Democratic convention at Baltimore, in May, 1848, fulfilled Thoreau's prediction of expediency in its platform, and in its man, Lewis Cass, "a northern man with southern principles."

of his country, when his country has more reason to despair of him. He forthwith adopts one of the candidates thus selected as the only *available* one, thus proving that he is himself *available* for any purposes of the demagogue. His vote is of no more worth than that of any unprincipled foreigner or hireling native, who may have been bought. O for a man who is a *man*, and, as my neighbor says, has a bone in his back which you cannot pass your hand through! Our statistics are at fault: the population has been returned too large. How many *men* are there to a square thousand miles in this country? Hardly one. Does not America offer any inducement for men to settle here? The American has dwindled into an Odd Fellow,⁶—one who may be known by the development of his organ of gregariousness, and a manifest lack of intellect and cheerful self-reliance; whose first and chief concern, on coming into the world, is to see that the almshouses are in good repair; and, before yet he has lawfully donned the virile garb,⁷ to collect a fund for the support of the widows and orphans that may be; who, in short, ventures to live only by the aid of the Mutual Insurance company, which has promised to bury him decently.

It is not a man's duty, as a matter of course, to devote himself to the eradication of any, even the most enormous, wrong; he may still properly have other concerns to engage him; but it is his duty, at least, to wash his hands of it, and, if he gives it no thought longer, not to give it practically his support. If I devote myself to other pursuits and contemplations, I must first see, at least, that I do not pursue them sitting upon another man's shoulders. I must get off him first, that he may pursue his contemplations too. See what gross inconsistency is tolerated. I have heard some of my townsmen say, "I should like to have them order me out to help put down an insurrection of the slaves, or to march to Mexico;—see if I would go;" and yet these very men have each, directly by their allegiance, and so indirectly, at least, by their money, furnished a substitute. The soldier is applauded who refuses to serve in an unjust war by those who do not refuse to sustain the unjust government which makes the war; is applauded by those whose own act and authority he disregards and sets at naught; as if the state were penitent to that degree that it hired one to scourge it while it sinned, but not to that degree that it left off sinning for a moment. Thus, under the name of Order and Civil Government, we are all made at last to pay homage to and support our own meanness. After the first blush of sin comes its indifference; and from immoral it becomes, as it were, *unmoral*, and not quite unnecessary to that life which we have made.

---

6. The Independent Order of Odd Fellows, one of numerous secret fraternal societies then being developed for social diversion and mutual insurance.

7. Cf. the *toga virilis*, which the Roman boy was permitted to wear on attaining the age of fourteen.

The broadest and most prevalent error requires the most disinterested virtue to sustain it. The slight reproach to which the virtue of patriotism is commonly liable, the noble are most likely to incur. Those who, while they disapprove of the character and measures of a government, yield to it their allegiance and support are undoubtedly its most conscientious supporters, and so frequently the most serious obstacles to reform. Some are petitioning the State to dissolve the Union, to disregard the requisitions of the President. Why do they not dissolve it themselves,—the union between themselves and the State,—and refuse to pay their quota into its treasury? Do not they stand in the same relation to the State that the State does to the Union? And have not the same reasons prevented the State from resisting the Union which have prevented them from resisting the State?

How can a man be satisfied to entertain an opinion merely, and enjoy *it*? Is there any enjoyment in it, if his opinion is that he is aggrieved? If you are cheated out of a single dollar by your neighbor, you do not rest satisfied with knowing that you are cheated, or with saying that you are cheated, or even with petitioning him to pay you your due; but you take effectual steps at once to obtain the full amount, and see that you are never cheated again. Action from principle, the perception and the performance of right, changes things and relations; it is essentially revolutionary, and does not consist wholly with anything which was. It not only divides States and churches, it divides families; ay, it divides the *individual*, separating the diabolical in him from the divine.

Unjust laws exist: shall we be content to obey them, or shall we endeavor to amend them, and obey them until we have succeeded, or shall we transgress them at once? Men generally, under such a government as this, think that they ought to wait until they have persuaded the majority to alter them. They think that, if they should resist, the remedy would be worse than the evil. But it is the fault of the government itself that the remedy *is* worse than the evil. *It* makes it worse. Why is it not more apt to anticipate and provide for reform? Why does it not cherish its wise minority? Why does it cry and resist before it is hurt? Why does it not encourage its citizens to be on the alert to point out its faults, and *do* better than it would have them? Why does it always crucify Christ, and excommunicate Copernicus and Luther,[8] and pronounce Washington and Franklin rebels?

One would think, that a deliberate and practical denial of its authority was the only offense never contemplated by government;

8. Copernicus was on his deathbed (1543) when his description of the solar system was published, later to come under the ban of the Church; but Luther, the founder of the German Reformation, was officially excommunicated in 1521, twenty-five years before his death.

else, why has it not assigned its definite, its suitable and proportionate penalty? If a man who has no property refuses but once to earn nine shillings for the State, he is put in prison for a period unlimited by any law that I know, and determined only by the discretion of those who placed him there; but if he should steal ninety times nine shillings from the State, he is soon permitted to go at large again.

If the injustice is part of the necessary friction of the machine of government, let it go, let it go: perchance it will wear smooth,—certainly the machine will wear out. If the injustice has a spring, or a pulley, or a rope, or a crank, exclusively for itself, then perhaps you may consider whether the remedy will not be worse than the evil; but if it is of such a nature that it requires you to be the agent of injustice to another, then, I say, break the law. Let your life be a counter friction to stop the machine. What I have to do is to see, at any rate, that I do not lend myself to the wrong which I condemn.

As for adopting the ways which the State has provided for remedying the evil, I know not of such ways. They take too much time, and a man's life will be gone. I have other affairs to attend to. I came into this world, not chiefly to make this a good place to live in, but to live in it, be it good or bad. A man has not everything to do, but something; and because he cannot do *everything*, it is not necessary that he should do *something* wrong. It is not my business to be petitioning the Governor or the Legislature any more than it is theirs to petition me; and if they should not hear my petition, what should I do then? But in this case the State has provided no way: its very Constitution is the evil. This may seem to be harsh and stubborn and unconciliatory; but it is to treat with the utmost kindness and consideration the only spirit that can appreciate or deserves it. So is all change for the better, like birth and death, which convulse the body.

I do not hesitate to say, that those who call themselves Abolitionists should at once effectually withdraw their support, both in person and property, from the government of Massachusetts, and not wait till they constitute a majority of one, before they suffer the right to prevail through them. I think that it is enough if they have God on their side, without waiting for that other one.[9] Moreover, any man more right than his neighbors constitutes a majority of one already.

I meet this American government, or its representative, the State government, directly, and face to face, once a year—no more—in the person of its tax-gatherer; this is the only mode in which a man situated as I am necessarily meets it; and it then says distinctly, Recognize me; and the simplest, the most effectual, and, in the present posture of affairs, the indispensablest mode of treating with it on this head, of expressing your little satisfaction with and love

9. *Cf.* the proverb "One on God's side is a majority."

for it, is to deny it then. My civil neighbor, the tax-gatherer, is the very man I have to deal with,—for it is, after all, with men and not with parchment that I quarrel,—and he has voluntarily chosen to be an agent of the government. How shall he ever know well what he is and does as an officer of the government, or as a man, until he is obliged to consider whether he shall treat me, his neighbor, for whom he has respect, as a neighbor and well-disposed man, or as a maniac and disturber of the peace, and see if he can get over this obstruction to his neighborliness without a ruder and more impetuous thought or speech corresponding with his action. I know this well, that if one thousand, if one hundred, if ten men whom I could name,—if ten *honest* men only,—ay, if *one* HONEST man, in this State of Massachusetts, *ceasing to hold slaves,* were actually to withdraw from this copartnership, and be locked up in the county jail therefor, it would be the abolition of slavery in America.[1] For it matters not how small the beginning may seem to be: what is once well done is done forever. But we love better to talk about it: that we say is our mission. Reform keeps many scores of newspapers in its service, but not one man. If my esteemed neighbor, the State's ambassador,[2] who will devote his days to the settlement of the question of human rights in the Council Chamber, instead of being threatened with the prisons of Carolina, were to sit down the prisoner of Massachusetts, that State which is so anxious to foist the sin of slavery upon her sister,—though at present she can discover only an act of inhospitality to be the ground of a quarrel with her, —the Legislature would not wholly waive the subject the following winter.

Under a government which imprisons any unjustly, the true place for a just man is also a prison. The proper place to-day, the only place which Massachusetts has provided for her freer and less desponding spirits, is in her prisons, to be put out and locked out of the State by her own act, as they have already put themselves out by their principles. It is there that the fugitive slave, and the Mexican prisoner on parole, and the Indian come to plead the wrongs of his race should find them; on that separate, but more free and honorable ground, where the State places those who are not *with* her, but *against* her,—the only house in a slave State in which a free man can abide with honor. If any think that their influence would be lost there, and their voices no longer afflict the ear of the State, that they would not be as an enemy within its walls, they do not know

1. An example of the operation of passive resistance, the doctrine for which Gandhi acknowledged indebtedness to Thoreau.
2. Samuel Hoar (1778–1856), distinguished Concord lawyer and congressman, was officially delegated to South Carolina to test certain laws denying the ports to Negro seamen on Massachusetts ships, under penalty of arrest and possible enslavement. Hoar was forcibly expelled from South Carolina by action of the legislature.

by how much truth is stronger than error, nor how much more eloquently and effectively he can combat injustice who has experienced a little in his own person. Cast your whole vote, not a strip of paper merely, but your whole influence. A minority is powerless while it conforms to the majority; it is not even a minority then; but it is irresistible when it clogs by its whole weight. If the alternative is to keep all just men in prison, or give up war and slavery, the State will not hesitate which to choose. If a thousand men were not to pay their tax-bills this year, that would not be a violent and bloody measure, as it would be to pay them, and enable the State to commit violence and shed innocent blood. This is, in fact, the definition of a peaceable revolution, if any such is possible. If the tax-gatherer, or any other public officer, asks me, as one has done, "But what shall I do?" my answer is, "If you really wish to do anything, resign your office." When the subject has refused allegiance, and the officer has resigned his office, then the revolution is accomplished. But even suppose blood should flow. Is there not a sort of blood shed when the conscience is wounded? Through this wound a man's real manhood and immortality flow out, and he bleeds to an everlasting death. I see this blood flowing now.

I have contemplated the imprisonment of the offender, rather than the seizure of his goods,—though both will serve the same purpose,—because they who assert the purest right, and consequently are most dangerous to a corrupt State, commonly have not spent much time in accumulating property. To such the State renders comparatively small service, and a slight tax is wont to appear exorbitant, particularly if they are obliged to earn it by special labor[3] with their hands. If there were one who lived wholly without the use of money, the State itself would hesitate to demand it of him. But the rich man—not to make any invidious comparison—is always sold to the institution which makes him rich. Absolutely speaking, the more money, the less virtue; for money comes between a man and his objects, and obtains them for him; and it was certainly no great virtue to obtain it. It puts to rest many questions which he would otherwise be taxed to answer; while the only new question which it puts is the hard but superfluous one, how to spend it. Thus his moral ground is taken from under his feet. The opportunities of living are diminished in proportion as what are called the "means" are increased. The best thing a man can do for his culture when he is rich is to endeavor to carry out those schemes which he entertained when he was poor. Christ answered the Herodians according to their condition. "Show me the tribute-money," said he;—and took one penny out of his pocket;—if you use money which has the image

3. Referring to his stand against the Massachusetts church tax and poll tax, assessed against all males.

of Caesar on it and which he has made current and valuable, that is, *if you are men of the State*, and gladly enjoy the advantages of Caesar's government, then pay him back some of his own when he demands it. "Render therefore to Caesar that which is Caesar's, and to God those things which are God's,"[4]—leaving them no wiser than before as to which was which; for they did not wish to know.

When I converse with the freest of my neighbors, I perceive that, whatever they may say about the magnitude and seriousness of the question, and their regard for the public tranquillity, the long and the short of the matter is, that they cannot spare the protection of the existing government, and they dread the consequences to their property and families of disobedience to it. For my own part, I should not like to think that I ever rely on the protection of the State. But, if I deny the authority of the State when it presents its tax-bill, it will soon take and waste all my property, and so harass me and my children without end. This is hard. This makes it impossible for a man to live honestly, and at the same time comfortably, in outward respects. It will not be worth the while to accumulate property; that would be sure to go again. You must hire or squat somewhere, and raise but a small crop, and eat that soon. You must live within yourself, and depend upon yourself always tucked up and ready for a start, and not have many affairs. A man may grow rich in Turkey even, if he will be in all respects a good subject of the Turkish government. Confucius[5] said: "If a state is governed by the principles of reason, poverty and misery are subjects of shame; if a state is not governed by the principles of reason, riches and honors are the subjects of shame." No: until I want the protection of Massachusetts to be extended to me in some distant Southern port, where my liberty is endangered, or until I am bent solely on building up an estate at home by peaceful enterprise, I can afford to refuse allegiance to Massachusetts, and her right to my property and life. It costs me less in every sense to incur the penalty of disobedience to the State than it would to obey. I should feel as if I were worth less in that case.

Some years ago, the State met me in behalf of the Church, and commanded me to pay a certain sum toward the support of a clergyman whose preaching my father attended, but never I myself. "Pay," it said, "or be locked up in the jail."[6] I declined to pay. But, unfortunately, another man saw fit to pay it. I did not see why the schoolmaster should be taxed to support the priest, and not the priest the schoolmaster; for I was not the State's schoolmaster, but I sup-

---

4. *Cf.* Matthew xxii: 16–21.
5. Confucius (551?–479? B.C.) was primarily a utilitarian and social philosopher; his formulation of Chinese "wisdom," preserved in the *Analects*, was familiar in translation to the transcendentalists.

6. Thoreau's resistance to compulsory church taxes occured in 1838, and he was not jailed. The failure to comply with the poll tax probably began in 1840 (see the next paragraph).

ported myself by voluntary subscription. I did not see why the lyceum should not present its tax-bill, and have the State to back its demand, as well as the Church. However, at the request of the selectmen, I condescended to make some such statement as this in writing:— "Know all men by these presents, that I, Henry Thoreau, do not wish to be regarded as a member of any incorporated society which I have not joined." This I gave to the town clerk; and he has it. The State, having thus learned that I did not wish to be regarded as a member of that church, has never made a like demand on me since; though it said that it must adhere to its original presumption that time. If I had known how to name them, I should then have signed off in detail from all the societies which I never signed on to; but I did not know where to find a complete list.

I have paid no poll-tax for six years. I was put into a jail once on this account, for one night;[7] and, as I stood considering the walls of solid stone, two or three feet thick, the door of wood and iron, a foot thick, and the iron grating which strained the light, I could not help being struck with the foolishness of that institution which treated me as if I were mere flesh and blood and bones, to be locked up. I wondered that it should have concluded at length that this was the best use it could put me to, and had never thought to avail itself of my services in some way. I saw that, if there was a wall of stone between me and my townsmen, there was a still more difficult one to climb or break through before they could get to be as free as I was. I did not for a moment feel confined, and the walls seemed a great waste of stone and mortar. I felt as if I alone of all my townsmen had paid my tax. They plainly did not know how to treat me, but behaved like persons who are underbred. In every threat and in every compliment there was a blunder; for they thought that my chief desire was to stand the other side of that stone wall. I could not but smile to see how industriously they locked the door on my meditations, which followed them out again without let or hindrance, and *they* were really all that was dangerous. As they could not reach me, they had resolved to punish my body; just as boys, if they cannot come at some person against whom they have a spite, will abuse his dog. I saw that the State was half-witted, that it was timid as a lone woman with her silver spoons, and that it did not know its friends from its foes, and I lost all my remaining respect for it, and pitied it.

Thus the State never intentionally confronts a man's sense, intellectual or moral, but only his body, his senses. It is not armed with superior wit or honesty, but with superior physical strength. I was not born to be forced. I will breathe after my own fashion. Let us

7. Bronson Alcott had resisted the tax and been jailed for one night in 1843. The fundamental reason for resistance, for both men, was repugnance at supporting a state that recognized slavery, as Massachusetts still did in legal fact. H. S. Canby in his *Thoreau* (p. 473) dates Thoreau's experience in jail as July 23 or 24, 1846.

see who is the strongest. What force has a multitude? They only can force me who obey a higher law than I. They force me to become like themselves. I do not hear of *men* being *forced* to live this way or that by masses of men. What sort of life were that to live? When I meet a government which says to me, "Your money or your life," why should I be in haste to give it my money? It may be in a great strait, and not know what to do: I cannot help that. It must help itself; do as I do. It is not worth the while to snivel about it. I am not responsible for the successful working of the machinery of society. I am not the son of the engineer. I perceive that, when an acorn and a chestnut fall side by side, the one does not remain inert to make way for the other, but both obey their own laws, and spring and grow and flourish as best they can, till one, perchance, over-shadows and destroys the other. If a plant cannot live according to its nature, it dies; and so a man.

The night in prison was novel and interesting enough. The prisoners in their shirt-sleeves were enjoying a chat and the evening air in the doorway, when I entered. But the jailer said, "Come, boys, it is time to lock up;" and so they dispersed, and I heard the sound of their steps returning into the hollow apartments. My room-mate was introduced to me by the jailer as "a first-rate fellow and a clever[8] man." When the door was locked, he showed me where to hang my hat, and how he managed matters there. The rooms were white-washed once a month; and this one, at least, was the whitest, most simply furnished, and probably the neatest apartment in the town. He naturally wanted to know where I came from, and what brought me there; and, when I had told him, I asked him in my turn how he came there, presuming him to be an honest man, of course; and, as the world goes, I believe he was. "Why," said he, "they accuse me of burning a barn; but I never did it." As near as I could discover, he had probably gone to bed in a barn when drunk, and smoked his pipe there; and so a barn was burnt. He had the reputation of being a clever man, had been there some three months waiting for his trial to come on, and would have to wait as much longer; but he was quite domesticated and contented, since he got his board for nothing, and thought that he was well treated.

He occupied one window, and I the other; and I saw that if one stayed there long, his principal business would be to look out the window. I had soon read all the tracts that were left there, and examined where former prisoners had broken out, and where a grate had been sawed off, and heard the history of the various occupants of that room; for I found that even here there was a history and a gossip which never circulated beyond the walls of the jail. Probably this is the only house in the town where verses are composed, which are afterward printed in circular form, but not published. I was shown

8. American dialect for "honest," "kind."

quite a long list of verses which were composed by some young men who had been detected in an attempt to escape, who avenged themselves by singing them.

I pumped my fellow-prisoner as dry as I could, for fear I should never see him again; but at length he showed me which was my bed, and left me to blow out the lamp.

It was like traveling into a far country, such as I had never expected to behold, to lie there for one night. It seemed to me that I never had heard the town clock strike before, nor the evening sounds of the village; for we slept with the windows open, which were inside the grating. It was to see my native village in the light of the Middle Ages, and our Concord was turned into a Rhine stream, and visions of knights and castles passed before me. They were the voices of old burghers that I heard in the streets. I was an involuntary spectator and auditor of whatever was done and said in the kitchen of the adjacent village-inn,—a wholly new and rare experience to me. It was a closer view of my native town. I was fairly inside of it. I never had seen its institutions before. This is one of the peculiar institutions; for it is a shire town. I began to comprehend what its inhabitants were about.

In the morning, our breakfasts were put through the hole in the door, in small oblong-square tin pans, made to fit, and holding a pint of chocolate, with brown bread, and an iron spoon. When they called for the vessels again, I was green enough to return what bread I had left; but my comrade seized it, and said that I should lay that up for lunch or dinner. Soon after he was let out to work at haying in a neighboring field, whither he went every day, and would not be back till noon; so he bade me good-day, saying that he doubted if he should see me again.

When I came out of prison,—for some one interfered, and paid that tax,[9]—I did not perceive that great changes had taken place on the common, such as he observed who went in a youth and emerged a tottering and gray-headed man; and yet a change had to my eyes come over the scene,—the town, and State, and country,— greater than any that mere time could effect. I saw yet more distinctly the State in which I lived. I saw to what extent the people among whom I lived could be trusted as good neighbors and friends; that their friendship was for summer weather only; that they did not greatly propose to do right; that they were a distinct race from me by their prejudices and superstitions, as the Chinamen and Malays are; that in their sacrifices to humanity they ran no risks, not even to their property; that after all they were not so noble but they treated the thief as he had treated them, and hoped, by a certain outward observance and a few prayers, and by walking in a particular straight

9. It is legendary but unlikely that Emerson paid the tax. Family reminiscence ascribed the deed to his Aunt Maria.

though useless path from time to time, to save their souls. This may be to judge my neighbors harshly; for I believe that many of them are not aware that they have such an institution as the jail in their village.

It was formerly the custom in our village, when a poor debtor came out of jail, for his acquaintances to salute him, looking through their fingers, which were crossed to represent the grating of a jail window, "How do ye do?" My neighbors did not thus salute me, but first looked at me, and then at one another, as if I had returned from a long journey. I was put into jail as I was going to the shoemaker's to get a shoe which was mended. When I was let out the next morning, I proceeded to finish my errand, and, having put on my mended shoe, joined a huckleberry party, who were impatient to put themselves under my conduct; and in half an hour,—for the horse was soon tackled,—was in the midst of a huckleberry field, on one of our highest hills, two miles off, and then the State was nowhere to be seen. This is the whole history of "My Prisons."[1]

I have never declined paying the highway tax, because I am as desirous of being a good neighbor as I am of being a bad subject; and as for supporting schools, I am doing my part to educate my fellow-countrymen now. It is for no particular item in the tax-bill that I refuse to pay it. I simply wish to refuse allegiance to the State, to withdraw and stand aloof from it effectually. I do not care to trace the course of my dollar, if I could, till it buys a man or a musket to shoot one with,—the dollar is innocent,—but I am concerned to trace the effects of my allegiance. In fact, I quietly declare war with the State, after my fashion, though I will still make what use and get what advantage of her I can, as is usual in such cases.

If others pay the tax which is demanded of me, from a sympathy with the State, they do but what they have already done in their own case, or rather they abet injustice to a greater extent than the State requires. If they pay the tax from a mistaken interest in the individual taxed, to save his property, or prevent his going to jail, it is because they have not considered wisely how far they let their private feelings interfere with the public good.

This, then, is my position at present. But one cannot be too much on his guard in such a case, lest his action be biased by obstinacy or an undue regard for the opinions of men. Let him see that he does only what belongs to himself and to the hour.

I think sometimes, Why, this people mean well, they are only ignorant; they would do better if they knew how: why give your neighbors this pain to treat you as they are not inclined to? But I think again, This is no reason why I should do as they do, or per-

1. English translation of the title *Le mie prigioni* (1832), a record of his years of hard labor in Austrian prisons by Silvio Pellico (1789–1854), Italian poet, playwright, and patriot.

mit others to suffer much greater pain of a different kind. Again, I sometimes say to myself, When many millions of men, without heat, without ill will, without personal feeling of any kind, demand of you a few shillings only, without the possibility, such is their constitution, of retracting or altering their present demand, and without the possibility, on your side, of appeal to any other millions, why expose yourself to this overwhelming brute force? You do not resist cold and hunger, the winds and the waves, thus obstinately; you quietly submit to a thousand similar necessities. You do not put your head into the fire. But just in proportion as I regard this as not wholly a brute force, but partly a human force, and consider that I have relations to those millions as to so many millions of men, and not of mere brute or inanimate things, I see that appeal is possible, first and instantaneously, from them to the Maker of them, and, secondly, from them to themselves. But if I put my head deliberately into the fire, there is no appeal to fire or to the Maker of fire, and I have only myself to blame. If I could convince myself that I have any right to be satisfied with men as they are, and to treat them accordingly, and not according, in some respects, to my requisitions and expectations of what they and I ought to be, then, like a good Mussulman and fatalist, I should endeavor to be satisfied with things as they are, and say it is the will of God. And, above all, there is this difference between resisting this and a purely brute or natural force, that I can resist this with some effect; but I cannot expect, like Orpheus,[2] to change the nature of the rocks and trees and beasts.

I do not wish to quarrel with any man or nation. I do not wish to split hairs, to make fine distinctions, or set myself up as better than my neighbors. I seek rather, I may say, even an excuse for conforming to the laws of the land. I am but too ready to conform to them. Indeed, I have reason to suspect myself on this head; and each year, as the tax-gatherer comes round, I find myself disposed to review the acts and position of the general and State governments, and the spirit of the people, to discover a pretext for conformity.

> "We must affect our country as our parents,
>   And if at any time we alienate
>   Our love or industry from doing it honor,
>   We must respect effects and teach the soul
>   Matter of conscience and religion,
>   And not desire of rule or benefit."

I believe that the State will soon be able to take all my work of this sort out of my hands, and then I shall be no better a patriot than

2. Orpheus, a mythical Greek poet-musician, caused "rocks and trees and beasts" to follow the music of his lute.

my fellow-countrymen. Seen from a lower point of view, the Constitution, with all its faults, is very good; the law and the courts are very respectable; even this State and this American government are, in many respects, very admirable, and rare things, to be thankful for, such as a great many have described them; but seen from a point of view a little higher, they are what I have described them; seen from a higher still, and the highest, who shall say what they are, or that they are worth looking at or thinking of at all?

However, the government does not concern me much, and I shall bestow the fewest possible thoughts on it. It is not many moments that I live under a government, even in this world. If a man is thought-free, fancy-free, imagination-free, that which *is not* never for a long time appearing *to be* to him, unwise rulers or reformers cannot fatally interrupt him.

I know that most men think differently from myself; but those whose lives are by profession devoted to the study of these or kindred subjects content me as little as any. Statesmen and legislators, standing so completely within the institution, never distinctly and nakedly behold it. They speak of moving society, but have no resting-place without it. They may be men of a certain experience and discrimination, and have no doubt invented ingenious and even useful systems, for which we sincerely thank them; but all their wit and usefulness lie within certain not very wide limits. They are wont to forget that the world is not governed by policy and expediency. Webster[3] never goes behind government, and so cannot speak with authority about it. His words are wisdom to those legislators who contemplate no essential reform in the existing government; but for thinkers, and those who legislate for all time, he never once glances at the subject. I know of those whose serene and wise speculations on this theme would soon reveal the limits of his mind's range and hospitality. Yet, compared with the cheap professions of most reformers, and the still cheaper wisdom and eloquence of politicians in general, his are almost the only sensible and valuable words, and we thank Heaven for him. Comparatively, he is always strong, original, and, above all, practical. Still, his quality is not wisdom, but prudence. The lawyer's truth is not Truth, but consistency or a consistent expediency. Truth is always in harmony with herself, and is not concerned chiefly to reveal the justice that may consist with wrong-doing. He well deserves to be called, as he has been called, the Defender of the Constitution. There are really no blows to be given by him but defensive ones. He is not a leader, but a follower. His leaders are the men of '87.[4] "I

3. Daniel Webster's respect for authority won him the title (mentioned later in this paragraph) "Defender of the Constitution"; he was therefore willing to compromise about slavery while it was "constitutional," thus losing many northern supporters.

4. *I.e.*, the framers of the Constitution, which was sent to the states for ratification in 1787.

have never made an effort," he says, "and never propose to make an effort; I have never countenanced an effort, and never mean to countenance an effort, to disturb the arrangement as originally made, by which the various States came into the Union." Still thinking of the sanction which the Constitution gives to slavery, he says, "Because it was a part of the original compact,—let it stand." Notwithstanding his special acuteness and ability, he is unable to take a fact out of its merely political relations, and behold it as it lies absolutely to be disposed of by the intellect,—what, for instance, it behooves a man to do here in America to-day with regard to slavery,—but ventures, or is driven, to make some such desperate answer as the following, while professing to speak absolutely, and as a private man,—from which what new and singular code of social duties might be inferred? "The manner," says he, "in which the governments of those States where slavery exists are to regulate it is for their own consideration, under their responsibility to their constituents, to the general laws of propriety, humanity, and justice, and to God. Associations formed elsewhere, springing from a feeling of humanity, or any other cause, have nothing whatever to do with it. They have never received any encouragement from me, and they never will."

They who know of no purer sources of truth, who have traced up its stream no higher, stand, and wisely stand, by the Bible and the Constitution, and drink at it there with reverence and humility; but they who behold where it comes trickling into this lake or that pool, gird up their loins once more, and continue their pilgrimage toward its fountain-head.

No man with a genius for legislation has appeared in America. They are rare in the history of the world. There are orators, politicians, and eloquent men, by the thousand; but the speaker has not yet opened his mouth to speak who is capable of settling the much-vexed questions of the day. We love eloquence for its own sake, and not for any truth which it may utter, or any heroism it may inspire. Our legislators have not yet learned the comparative value of free trade and of freedom, of union, and of rectitude, to a nation. They have no genius or talent for comparatively humble questions of taxation and finance, commerce and manufactures and agriculture. If we were left solely to the wordy wit of legislators in Congress for our guidance, uncorrected by the seasonable experience and the effectual complaints of the people, America would not long retain her rank among the nations. For eighteen hundred years, though perchance I have no right to say it, the New Testament has been written; yet where is the legislator who has wisdom and practical talent enough to avail himself of the light which it sheds on the science of legislation?

The authority of government, even such as I am willing to submit to,—for I will cheerfully obey those who know and can do better than I, and in many things even those who neither know nor can do so well,—is still an impure one: to be strictly just, it must have the sanction and consent of the governed. It can have no pure right over my person and property but what I concede to it. The progress from an absolute to a limited monarchy, from a limited monarchy to a democracy, is a progress toward a true respect for the individual. Even the Chinese philosopher was wise enough to regard the individual as the basis of the empire. Is a democracy, such as we know it, the last improvement possible in government? Is it not possible to take a step further towards recognizing and organizing the rights of man? There will never be a really free and enlightened State until the State comes to recognize the individual as a higher and independent power, from which all its own power and authority are derived, and treats him accordingly. I please myself with imagining a State at last which can afford to be just to all men, and to treat the individual with respect as a neighbor; which even would not think it inconsistent with its own repose if a few were to live aloof from it, not meddling with it, nor embraced by it, who fulfilled all the duties of neighbors and fellow-men. A State which bore this kind of fruit, and suffered it to drop off as fast as it ripened, would prepare the way for a still more perfect and glorious State, which also I have imagined, but not yet anywhere seen.

1848

1849, 1866

From The Maine Woods

IV. The Moose Hunt[5]

We concluded merely to prepare our camp, and leave our baggage here, that all might be ready when we returned from moose-

5. *The Maine Woods* resulted from three expeditions into the forest around the upper Penobscot River. During the summer of 1846 Thoreau explored the river by "bateau," and climbed Mount Katahdin (here called Ktaadn). In September, 1853, a canoe trip on Moosehead Lake and the Penobscot "West Branch" included the moose hunt here described. As before, Thoreau took along a relative, George A. Thatcher. They had an Indian guide, Joe Aitteon, who is mentioned in the account. On a third expedition, in the summer of 1857, Thoreau encircled Katahdin by way of the chain of lakes and the Penobscot River. His journals of the first two trips were published serially before his death; the first, entitled "Ktaadn," in the *Union Magazine*, Vol. III, Nos. 1–5, 1848; the second, "Chesuncook," in the *Atlantic Monthly*, Vol. II, Nos. 1–3 (June, July, August, 1858). The selections from "A Moose Hunt" were in the June number of the *Atlantic*. After Thoreau's death the three essays were reprinted as a volume, *The Maine Woods* (1864), but without editorial rearrangement to exclude overlapping passages and repetitive introductions. In a modern edition, edited by Dudley C. Lunt (New York, Norton, 1950) such passages have been consigned to the Appendix, leaving a continuous narrative.

hunting. Though I had not come a-hunting, and felt some com-
punctions about accompanying the hunters, I wished to see a moose
near at hand, and was not sorry to learn how the Indian managed
to kill one. I went as reporter or chaplain to the hunters,—and the
chaplain has been known to carry a gun himself. After clearing a
small space amid the dense spruce and fir trees, we covered the
damp ground with a shingling of fir-twigs, and, while Joe[6] was preparing his birch horn and pitching his canoe,—for this had to be
done whenever we stopped long enough to build a fire, and was the
principal labor which he took upon himself at such times,—we collected fuel for the night, large, wet, and rotting logs, which had
lodged at the head of the island, for our hatchet was too small for
effective chopping; but we did not kindle a fire, lest the moose
should smell it. Joe set up a couple of forked stakes, and prepared
half a dozen poles, ready to cast one of our blankets over in case
it rained in the night, which precaution, however, was omitted the
next night. We also plucked the ducks which had been killed for
breakfast. * * *

At starlight we dropped down the stream, which was a dead-
water for three miles, or as far as the Moosehorn; Joe telling us that
we must be very silent, and he himself making no noise with his
paddle, while he urged the canoe along with effective impulses. It
was a still night, and suitable for this purpose,—for if there is wind,
the moose will smell you,—and Joe was very confident that he
should get some. The harvest moon had just risen, and its level
rays began to light up the forest on our right, while we glided
downward in the shade on the same side, against the little breeze
that was stirring. The lofty, spiring tops of the spruce and fir were
very black against the sky, and more distinct than by day, close
bordering this broad avenue on each side; and the beauty of the
scene, as the moon rose above the forest, it would not be easy to
describe. * * *

The moose venture out to the river-side to feed and drink at night.
Earlier in the season the hunters do not use a horn to call them out,
but steal upon them as they are feeding along the sides of the
stream, and often the first notice they have of one is the sound of
the water dropping from its muzzle. An Indian whom I heard
imitate the voice of the moose, and also that of the caribou and
the deer, using a much longer horn than Joe's, told me that the
first could be heard eight or ten miles, sometimes; it was a loud
sort of bellowing sound, clearer and more sonorous than the lowing
of cattle,—the caribou's a sort of snort,—and the small deer's like
that of a lamb.

6. The Indian guide, Joe Aitteon.

At length we turned up the Moosehorn, where the Indians at the carry had told us that they killed a moose the night before. This is a very meandering stream, only a rod or two in width, but comparatively deep, coming in on the right, fitly enough named Moosehorn, whether from its windings or its inhabitants. It was bordered here and there by narrow meadows between the stream and the endless forest, affording favorable places for the moose to feed, and to call them out on. We proceeded half a mile up this, as through a narrow, winding canal, where the tall, dark spruce and firs and arbor-vitæ towered on both sides in the moonlight, forming a perpendicular forest-edge of great height, like the spires of a Venice in the forest. In two places stood a small stack of hay on the bank, ready for the lumberer's use in the winter, looking strange enough there. We thought of the day when this might be a brook winding through smooth-shaven meadows on some gentleman's grounds; and seen by moonlight then, excepting the forest that now hems it in, how little changed it would appear!

Again and again Joe called the moose, placing the canoe by some favorable point of meadow for them to come out on, but listened in vain to hear one come rushing through the woods, and concluded that they had been hunted too much thereabouts. We saw, many times, what to our imaginations looked like a gigantic moose, with his horns peering from out the forest edge; but we saw the forest only, and not its inhabitants, that night. So at last we turned about. There was now a little fog on the water, though it was a fine, clear night above. There were very few sounds to break the stillness of the forest. Several times we heard the hooting of a great horned-owl, as at home, and told Joe that he would call out the moose for him, for he made a sound considerably like the horn,— but Joe answered, that the moose had heard that sound a thousand times, and knew better; and oftener still we were startled by the plunge of a musquash.

Once, when Joe had called again, and we were listening for moose, we heard, come faintly echoing, or creeping from far, through the moss-clad aisles, a dull, dry, rushing sound, with a solid core to it, yet as if half smothered under the grasp of the luxuriant and fungus-like forest, like the shutting of a door in some distant entry of the damp and shaggy wilderness. If we had not been there, no mortal had heard it. When we asked Joe in a whisper what it was, he answered, "Tree fall."

There is something singularly grand and impressive in the sound of a tree falling in a perfectly calm night like this, as if the agencies which overthrow it did not need to be excited, but worked with a subtle, deliberate, and conscious force, like a boa-constrictor, and more effectively then than even in a windy day. If there is any such difference, perhaps it is because trees with the dews of the night on them are heavier than by day.

Having reached the camp, about ten o'clock, we kindled our fire and went to bed. Each of us had a blanket, in which he lay on the fir-twigs, with his extremities toward the fire, but nothing over his head. It was worth the while to lie down in a country where you could afford such great fires; that was one whole side, and the bright side, of our world. We had first rolled up a large log some eighteen inches through and ten feet long, for a backlog, to last all night, and then piled on the trees to the height of three or four feet, no matter how green or damp. In fact, we burned as much wood that night as would, with economy and an air-tight stove, last a poor family in one of our cities all winter.

It was very agreeable, as well as independent, thus lying in the open air, and the fire kept our uncovered extremities warm enough. The Jesuit missionaries used to say, that, in their journeys with the Indians in Canada, they lay on a bed which had never been shaken up since the creation, unless by earthquakes. It is surprising with what impunity and comfort one who has always lain in a warm bed in a close apartment, and studiously avoided drafts of air, can lie down on the ground without a shelter, roll himself in a blanket, and sleep before a fire, in a frosty, autumn night just after a long rainstorm, and even come soon to enjoy and value the fresh air.

I lay awake awhile, watching the ascent of the sparks through the firs, and sometimes their descent in half-extinguished cinders on my blanket. They were as interesting as fireworks, going up in endless, successive crowds, each after an explosion, in an eager, serpentine course, some to five or six rods above the treetops before they went out. We do not suspect how much our chimneys have concealed; and now air-tight stoves have come to conceal all the rest. In the course of the night, I got up once or twice and put fresh logs on the fire, making my companions curl up their legs.

When we awoke in the morning (Saturday, September 17), there was considerable frost whitening the leaves. We heard the sound of the chickadee, and a few faintly lisping birds, and also of ducks in the water about the island. I took a botanical account of stock of our domains before the dew was off, and found that the ground hemlock, or American yew, was the prevailing under-shrub. We breakfasted on tea, hard bread, and ducks.

Before the fog had fairly cleared away we paddled down the stream again, and were soon past the mouth of the Moosehorn. These twenty miles of the Penobscot, between Moosehead and Chesuncook lakes, are comparatively smooth, and a great part dead-water; but from time to time it is shallow and rapid, with rocks or gravel beds, where you can wade across. There is no expanse of water, and no break in the forest, and the meadow is a mere edging here and there. There are no hills near the river nor within sight, except one or two distant mountains seen in a few places. The banks are from six to ten feet high, but once or twice rise gently to higher ground. In many places the forest on the bank was but a thin strip, letting the light through from some alder swamp or meadow behind.

The conspicuous berry-bearing bushes and trees along the shore were the red osier, with its whitish fruit, hobble-bush, mountain-ash, tree-cranberry, choke-cherry, now ripe, alternate cornel, and naked viburnum. Following Joe's example, I ate the fruit of the last, and also of the hobble-bush, but found them rather insipid and seedy. I looked very narrowly at the vegetation, as we glided along close to the shore, and frequently made Joe turn aside for me to pluck a plant, that I might see by comparison what was primitive about my native river. Horehound, horsemint, and the sensitive fern grew close to the edge, under the willows and alders, and wool-grass on the islands, as along the Assabet River in Concord. It was too late for flowers, except a few asters, goldenrods, etc. In several places we noticed the slight frame of a camp, such as we had prepared to set up, amid the forest by the river-side, where some lumberers or hunters had passed a night,—and sometimes steps cut in the muddy or clayey bank in front of it. * * *

At one place below this, on the east side, where the bank was higher and drier than usual, rising gently from the shore to a slight elevation, some one had felled the trees over twenty or thirty acres, and left them dying in order to burn. This was the only preparation for a house between the Moosehead carry and Chesuncook, but there was no hut nor inhabitants there yet. The pioneer thus selects a site for his house, which will, perhaps, prove the germ of a town.

My eyes were all the while on the trees, distinguishing between the black and white spruce and the fir. You paddle along in a narrow canal through an endless forest, and the vision I have in my mind's eye, still, is of the small, dark, and sharp tops of tall fir and spruce trees, and pagoda-like arbor-vitæs, crowded together on each side, with various hard woods inter-mixed. Some of the arbor-vitæs were at least sixty feet high. The hard woods, occasionally occurring exclusively, were less wild to my eye. I fancied them ornamental grounds, with farm-houses in the rear. The canoe and yellow birch, beech, maple, and elm are Saxon and Norman, but the spruce and fir, and pines generally, are Indian. The soft engravings which adorn the annuals[7] give no idea of a stream in such a wilderness as this. The rough sketches in Jackson's Reports on the Geology of

7. Also known as gift books, annual miscellanies of the best literature, art, and engravings, of which more than a thousand different volumes appeared between 1825 and 1865.

Maine answer much better.

At one place we saw a small grove of slender sapling white-pines, the only collection of pines that I saw on this voyage. Here and there, however, was a full-grown, tall, and slender, but defective one, what lumbermen call a *konchus* tree, which they ascertain with their axes, or by the knots. I did not learn whether this word was Indian or English. It reminded me of the Greek κόγχη, a conch or shell, and I amused myself with fancying that it might signify the dead sound which the trees yield when struck. All the rest of the pines had been driven off.

How far men go for the materials of their houses! The inhabitants of the most civilized cities, in all ages, send into far, primitive forests, beyond the bounds of their civilization, where the moose and bear and savage dwell, for their pine boards for ordinary use. And, on the other hand, the savage soon receives from cities iron arrow-points, hatchets, and guns, to point his savageness with.

The solid and well-defined fir-tops, like sharp and regular spear-heads, black against the sky, gave a peculiar, dark, and sombre look to the forest. The spruce-tops have a similar but more ragged outline, —their shafts also merely feathered below. The firs were somewhat oftener regular and dense pyramids. I was struck by this universal spiring upward of the forest evergreens. The tendency is to slender, spiring tops, while they are narrower below. Not only the spruce and fir, but even the arbor-vitæ and white-pine, unlike the soft, spreading, second-growth, of which I saw none; all spire upwards, lifting a dense spear-head of cones to the light and air, at any rate, while their branches straggle after as they may; as Indians lift the ball over the heads of the crowd in their desperate game. In this they resemble grasses, as also palms somewhat. The hemlock is commonly a tent-like pyramid from the ground to its summit.

After passing through some long rips, and by a large island, we reached an interesting part of the river called the Pine Stream Dead-Water, about six miles below Ragmuff, where the river expanded to thirty rods in width and had many islands in it, with elms and canoe-birches, now yellowing, along the shore, and we got our first sight of Ktaadn.[8]

Here, about two o'clock, we turned up a small branch three or four rods wide, which comes in on the right from the south, called Pine Stream, to look for moose signs. We had gone but a few rods before we saw very recent signs along the water's edge, the mud lifted up by their feet being quite fresh, and Joe declared that they had gone along there but a short time before. We soon reached a

8. Mount Katahdin, in north-central Maine, is a spectacular peak, 5,268 feet in height, often mentioned by New England authors.

small meadow on the east side, at an angle in the stream, which was, for the most part, densely covered with alders. As we were advancing along the edge of this, rather more quietly than usual, perhaps, on account of the freshness of the signs,—the design being to camp up this stream, if it promised well,—I heard a slight crackling of twigs deep in the alders, and turned Joe's attention to it; whereupon he began to push the canoe back rapidly; and we had receded thus half a dozen rods, when we suddenly spied two moose standing just on the edge of the open part of the meadow which we had passed, not more than six or seven rods distant, looking round the alders at us.

They made me think of great frightened rabbits, with their long ears and half-inquisitive, half-frightened looks; the true denizens of the forest (I saw at once), filling a vacuum which now first I discovered had not been filled for me,—*moose*-men, *wood-eaters*, the word is said to mean,—clad in a sort of Vermont gray, or home-spun. Our Nimrod, owing to the retrograde movement, was now the farthest from the game; but being warned of its neighborhood, he hastily stood up, and, while we ducked, fired over our heads one barrel at the foremost, which alone he saw, though he did not know what kind of creature it was; whereupon this one dashed across the meadow and up a high bank on the northeast, so rapidly as to leave but an indistinct impression of its outlines on my mind.

At the same instant, the other, a young one, but as tall as a horse, leaped out into the stream, in full sight, and there stood cowering for a moment, or rather its disproportionate lowness behind gave it that appearance, and uttering two or three trumpeting squeaks. I have an indistinct recollection of seeing the old one pause an instant on the top of the bank in the woods, look toward its shivering young, and then dash away again. The second barrel was leveled at the calf, and when we expected to see it drop in the water, after a little hesitation, it, too, got out of the water, and dashed up the hill, though in a somewhat different direction.

All this was the work of a few seconds, and our hunter, having never seen a moose before, did not know but they were deer, for they stood partly in the water, nor whether he had fired at the same one twice or not. From the style in which they went off, and the fact that he was not used to standing up and firing from a canoe, I judged that we should not see anything more of them. The Indian said that they were a cow and her calf,—a yearling, or perhaps two years old, for they accompany their dams so long; but, for my part, I had not noticed much difference in their size. It was but two or three rods across the meadow to the foot of the bank, which, like all the world thereabouts, was densely wooded; but I was surprised to notice, that, as soon as the moose had passed behind the veil of the woods, there was no sound of footsteps to be heard from the soft, damp moss which carpets that forest, and long before we landed, perfect silence reigned. Joe said, "If you wound 'em moose, me sure get 'em."

We all landed at once. My companion reloaded; the Indian fastened his birch,[9] threw off his hat, adjusted his waistband, seized the hatchet, and set out. He told me afterward, casually, that before we landed he had seen a drop of blood on the bank, when it was two or three rods off. He proceeded rapidly up the bank and through the woods, with a peculiar, elastic, noiseless, and stealthy tread, looking to right and left on the ground, and stepping in the faint tracks of the wounded moose, now and then pointing in silence to a single drop of blood on the handsome, shining leaves of the Clintonia borealis, which, on every side, covered the ground, or to a dry fern-stem freshly broken, all the while chewing some leaf or else the spruce gum. I followed, watching his motions more than the trail of the moose. After following the trail about forty rods in a pretty direct course, stepping over fallen trees and winding between standing ones, he at length lost it, for there were many other moose tracks there, and, returning once more to the last bloodstain, traced it a little way and lost it again, and, too soon, I thought, for a good hunter, gave it up entirely. He traced a few steps, also, the tracks of the calf; but, seeing no blood, soon relinquished the search.

I observed, while he was tracking the moose, a certain reticence or moderation in him. He did not communicate several observations of interest which he made, as a white man would have done, though they may have leaked out afterward. At another time, when we heard a slight crackling of twigs and he landed to reconnoitre, he stepped lightly and gracefully, stealing through the bushes with the least possible noise, in a way in which no white man does,—as it were, finding a place for his foot each time.

About half an hour after seeing the moose, we pursued our voyage up Pine Stream, and soon, coming to a part which was very shoal and also rapid, we took out the baggage, and proceeded to carry it round, while Joe got up with the canoe alone. We were just completing our portage and I was absorbed in the plants, admiring the leaves of the Aster macrophyllus, ten inches wide, and plucking the seeds of the great round-leaved orchis, when Joe exclaimed from the stream that he had killed a moose. He had found the cow-moose lying dead, but quite warm, in the middle of the stream, which was so shallow that it rested on the bottom, with hardly a third of its body above water. It was about an hour after it was shot, and it was

9. Then the familiar designation for a birch-bark canoe.

swollen with water. It had run about a hundred rods and sought the stream again, cutting off a slight bend. No doubt a better hunter would have tracked it to this spot at once.

I was surprised at its great size, horse-like, but Joe said it was not a large cow-moose. My companion went in search of the calf again. I took hold of the ears of the moose, while Joe pushed his canoe down-stream toward a favorable shore, and so we made out, though with some difficulty, its long nose frequently sticking in the bottom, to drag it into still shallower water. It was a brownish black, or perhaps a dark iron-gray, on the back and sides, but lighter beneath and in front. I took the cord which served for the canoe's painter, and with Joe's assistance measured it carefully, the greatest distances first, making a knot each time. The painter being wanted, I reduced these measures that night with equal care to lengths and fractions of my umbrella, beginning with the smallest measures, and untying the knots as I proceeded; and when we arrived at Chesuncook the next day, finding a two-foot rule there, I reduced the last to feet and inches; and, moreover, I made myself a two-foot rule of a thin and narrow strip of black ash, which would fold up conveniently to six inches.

All this pains I took because I did not wish to be obliged to say merely that the moose was very large. Of the various dimensions which I obtained I will mention only two. The distance from the tips of the hoofs of the fore-feet, stretched out, to the top of the back between the shoulders, was seven feet and five inches. I can hardly believe my own measure, for this is about two feet greater than the height of a tall horse. (Indeed, I am now satisfied that this measurement was incorrect, but the other measures given here I can warrant to be correct, having proved them in a more recent visit to those woods.) The extreme length was eight feet and two inches. Another cow-moose, which I have since measured in those woods with a tape, was just six feet from the tip of the hoof to the shoulders, and eight feet long as she lay.

When afterward I asked an Indian at the carry how much taller the male was, he answered, "Eighteen inches," and made me observe the height of a cross-stake over the fire, more than four feet from the ground, to give me some idea of the depth of his chest. Another Indian, at Oldtown, told me that they were nine feet high to the top of the back, and that one which he tried weighed eight hundred pounds. The length of the spinal projections between the shoulders is very great. A white hunter, who was the best authority among hunters that I could have, told me that the male was *not* eighteen inches taller than the female; yet he agreed that he was sometimes nine feet high to the top of the back, and weighed a thousand pounds.

Only the male has horns, and they rise two feet or more above the shoulders,—spreading three or four, and sometimes six feet,—which would make him in all, sometimes, eleven feet high! According to this calculation, the moose is as tall, though it may not be as large, as the great Irish elk, Megaceros Hibernicus, of a former period, of which Mantell[1] says that it "very far exceeded in magnitude any living species, the skeleton" being "upward of ten feet high from the ground to the highest point of the antlers." Joe said, that, though the moose shed the whole horn annually, each new horn has an additional prong; but I have noticed that they sometimes have more prongs on one side than on the other. I was struck with the delicacy and tenderness of the hoofs, which divide very far up, and the one half could be pressed very much behind the other, thus probably making the animal surer-footed on the uneven ground and slippery moss-covered logs of the primitive forest. They were very unlike the stiff and battered feet of our horses and oxen. The bare, horny part of the fore-foot was just six inches long, and the two portions could be separated four inches at the extremities.

The moose is singularly grotesque and awkward to look at. Why should it stand so high at the shoulders? Why have so long a head? Why have no tail to speak of? for in my examination I overlooked it entirely. Naturalists say it is an inch and a half long. It reminded me at once of the camelopard, high before and low behind,—and no wonder, for, like it, it is fitted to browse on trees. The upper lip projected two inches beyond the lower for this purpose. This was the kind of man that was at home there; for, as near as I can learn, that has never been the residence, but rather the hunting-ground of the Indian. The moose will, perhaps, one day become extinct; but how naturally then, when it exists only as a fossil relic, and unseen as that, may the poet or sculptor invent a fabulous animal with similar branching and leafy horns,—a sort of fucus or lichen in bone,—to be the inhabitant of such a forest as this!

Here, just at the head of the murmuring rapids, Joe now proceeded to skin the moose with a pocket-knife, while I looked on; and a tragical business it was,—to see that still warm and palpitating body pierced with a knife, to see the warm milk stream from the rent udder, and the ghastly naked red carcass appearing from within its seemly robe, which was made to hide it. The ball had passed through the shoulder-blade diagonally and lodged under the skin on the opposite side, and was partially flattened. My companion keeps it to show to his grandchildren. He has the shanks of another moose which he has since shot, skinned and stuffed, ready to be

1. Gideon Algernon Mantell (1790–1852), English geologist and paleontologist.

made into boots by putting in a thick leather sole. Joe said, if a moose stood fronting you, you must not fire, but advance toward him, for he will turn slowly and give you a fair shot. * * *

This afternoon's experience suggested to me how base or coarse are the motives which commonly carry men into the wilderness. The explorers and lumberers generally are all hirelings, paid so much a day for their labor, and as such they have no more love for wild nature than wood-sawyers have for forests. Other white men and Indians who come here are for the most part hunters, whose object is to slay as many moose and other wild animals as possible. But, pray, could not one spend some weeks or years in the solitude of this vast wilderness with other employments than these—employments perfectly sweet and innocent and ennobling? For one that comes with a pencil to sketch or sing, a thousand come with an axe or rifle. What a coarse and imperfect use Indians and hunters make of Nature! No wonder that their race is so soon exterminated. I already, and for weeks afterward, felt my nature the coarser for this part of my woodland experience, and was reminded that our life should be lived as tenderly and daintily as one would pluck a flower.

With these thoughts, when we reached our camping-ground, I decided to leave my companions to continue moose-hunting down the stream, while I prepared the camp, though they requested me not to chop much nor make a large fire, for fear I should scare their game. In the midst of the damp fir-wood, high on the mossy bank, about nine o'clock of this bright moonlight night, I kindled a fire, when they were gone, and, sitting on the fir-twigs, within sound of the falls, examined by its light the botanical specimens which I had collected that afternoon, and wrote down some of the reflections which I have here expanded; or I walked along the shore and gazed up the stream, where the whole space above the falls was filled with mellow light. As I sat before the fire on my fir-twig seat, without walls above or around me, I remembered how far on every hand that wilderness stretched, before you came to cleared or cultivated fields, and wondered if any bear or moose was watching the light of my fire; for Nature looked sternly upon me on account of the murder of the moose.

Strange that so few ever came to the woods to see how the pine lives and grows and spires, lifting its evergreen arms to the light,— to see its perfect success; but most are content to behold it in the shape of many broad boards brought to market, and deem *that* its true success! But the pine is no more lumber than man is, and to be made into boards and houses is no more its true and highest use than the truest use of a man is to be cut down and made into manure. There is a higher law affecting our relation to pines as well as to men.

A pine cut down, a dead pine, is no more a pine than a dead human carcass is a man. Can he who has discovered only some of the values of whalebone and whale oil be said to have discovered the true use of the whale? Can he who slays the elephant for his ivory be said to have "seen the elephant"? These are petty and accidental uses; just as if a stronger race were to kill us in order to make buttons and flageolets of our bones; for everything may serve a lower as well as a higher use. Every creature is better alive than dead, men and moose and pine-trees, and he who understands it aright will rather preserve its life than destroy it.

Is it the lumberman, then, who is the friend and lover of the pine, stands nearest to it, and understands its nature best? Is it the tanner who has barked it, or he who has boxed it for turpentine, whom posterity will fable to have been changed into a pine at last? No! no! it is the poet; he it is who makes the truest use of the pine, —who does not fondle it with an axe, nor tickle it with a saw, nor stroke it with a plane,—who knows whether its heart is false without cutting into it,—who has not bought the stumpage of the township on which it stands. All the pines shudder and heave a sigh when *that* man steps on the forest floor. No, it is the poet, who loves them as his own shadow in the air, and lets them stand.

I have been into the lumber-yard, and the carpenter's shop, and the tannery, and the lampblack factory, and the turpentine clearing; but when at length I saw the tops of the pines waving and reflecting the light at a distance high over all the rest of the forest, I realized that the former were not the highest uses of the pine. It is not their bones or hide or tallow that I love most. It is the living spirit of the tree, not its spirit of turpentine, with which I sympathize, and which heals my cuts. It is as immortal as I am, and perchance will go to as high a heaven, there to tower above me still.[2]

Erelong, the hunters returned, not having seen a moose, but, in consequence of my suggestions, bringing a quarter of the dead one, which, with ourselves, made quite a load for the canoe.

1853–1858   1858, 1864

My Prayer[3]

Great God, I ask thee for no meaner pelf
Than that I may not disappoint myself;

2. Lowell, editor of the *Atlantic*, excluded this sentence without the consent of Thoreau, whose extreme flights he regarded as fantastic. But Thoreau meant what he wrote, and declined again to trust Lowell's editorial pencil.
3. The first appearance of this poem was its quotation, without title, in an article,

That in my action I may soar as high
As I can now discern with this clear eye.

And next in value, which thy kindness lends,   5
That I may greatly disappoint my friends,
Howe'er they think or hope that it may be,
They may not dream how thou'st distinguished me;

That my weak hand may equal my firm faith,
And my life practice more than my tongue saith;   10
   That my low conduct may not show,
     Nor my relenting lines,
   That I thy purpose did not know,
     Or overrated thy designs.

1842, 1866

Rumors from an Aeolian Harp[4]

There is a vale which none hath seen,
Where foot of man has never been,
Such as here lives with toil and strife,
An anxious and a sinful life.

There every virtue has its birth,   5
Ere it descends upon the earth,
And thither every deed returns,
Which in the generous bosom burns.

There love is warm, and youth is young,
And poetry is yet unsung,   10
For Virtue still adventures there,
And freely breathes her native air.

And ever, if you hearken well,
You still may hear its vesper bell,
And tread of high-souled men go by,   15
Their thoughts conversing with the sky.

1842, 1849

"Prayers," by Emerson in *The Dial* for July, 1842. It reappeared in periodicals as "A Prayer" and "My Prayer" before Thoreau's death, and was first collected in the posthumous *A Yankee in Canada* (1866) as "Prayer." The following is the text of *Poems of Nature* (1895).

4. In the Greek myth, Aeolus possessed a harp played by the movement of the winds of heaven, over which the gods had granted him dominion. The symbolic idea—that nature is the source of the artist's inspiration, is recalled in Thoreau's introductory comment for the poem: "Music is the sound of the universal laws promulgated. It is the only assured tone" ("Monday," in *A Week on the Concord and Merrimack Rivers*, 1849). The poem first appeared, without the comment, in *The Dial* for October, 1842. The text is identical in *Poems of Nature* (1895) and *A Week* * * * , as given here.

The Inward Morning[5]

Packed in my mind lie all the clothes
    Which outward nature wears,
And in its fashion's hourly change
    It all things else repairs.

In vain I look for change abroad,   5
    And can no difference find,
Till some new ray of peace uncalled
    Illumes my inmost mind.

What is it gilds the trees and clouds,
    And paints the heavens so gay,   10
But yonder fast-abiding light
    With its unchanging ray?

Lo, when the sun streams through the wood,
    Upon a winter's morn,
Where'er his silent beams intrude   15
    The murky night is gone.

How could the patient pine have known
    The morning breeze would come,
Or humble flowers anticipate
    The insect's noonday hum,—   20

Till the new light with morning cheer
    From far streamed through the aisles,
And nimbly told the forest trees
    For many stretching miles?

I've heard within my inmost soul   25
    Such cheerful morning news,
In the horizon of my mind
    Have seen such orient hues,

As in the twilight of the dawn,
    When the first birds awake,   30
Are heard within some silent wood,
    Where they the small twigs break,

Or in the eastern skies are seen,
    Before the sun appears,
The harbingers of summer heats   35
    Which from afar he bears.

1842, 1849

5. First published in *The Dial* for October, 1842, and reprinted in Thoreau's "Wednesday" chapter of *A Week on the Concord and Merrimack Rivers* (1849), where the text is identical with that of *Poems of Nature* (1895) and that given here.

The Summer Rain[6]

My books I'd fain cast off, I cannot read;
'Twixt every page my thoughts go stray at large
Down in the meadow, where is richer feed,
And will not mind to hit their proper targe.

Plutarch was good, and so was Homer too,   5
Our Shakespeare's life were rich to live again;
What Plutarch read, that was not good nor true,
Nor Shakespeare's books, unless his books were men.

Here while I lie beneath this walnut bough,
What care I for the Greeks or for Troy town,   10
If juster battles are enacted now
Between the ants upon this hummock's crown?

Bid Homer wait till I the issue learn,
If red or black[7] the gods will favor most,
Or yonder Ajax will the phalanx turn,   15
Struggling to heave some rock against the host.

Tell Shakespeare to attend some leisure hour,
For now I've business with this drop of dew,
And see you not, the clouds prepare a shower,—
I'll meet him shortly when the sky is blue.   20

This bed of herd's-grass and wild oats was spread
Last year with nicer skill than monarchs use,
A clover tuft is pillow for my head,
And violets quite overtop my shoes.

And now the cordial clouds have shut all in,   25
And gently swells the wind to say all's well,
The scattered drops are falling fast and thin,
Some in the pool, some in the flower-bell.

I am well drenched upon my bed of oats;
But see that globe come rolling down its stem;   30
Now like a lonely planet there it floats,
And now it sinks into my garment's hem.

Drip, drip the trees for all the country round,
And richness rare distills from every bough,

6. First published in *The Dial* for October, 1842, and reprinted in Thoreau's "Thursday" chapter of *A Week on the Concord and Merrimack Rivers* (1849), as given here. The version in *The Poems of Nature* (1895) shows slight variants in punctuation and indentation.
7. *Cf.* the battle of the red and black ants in "Brute Neighbors," in *Walden,* also described in Homeric terms. There the champion ant is called Achilles; in the present passage the hero is Ajax.

The wind alone it is makes every sound, 35
Shaking down crystals on the leaves below.

For shame the sun will never show himself,
Who could not with his beams e'er melt me so,
My dripping locks,—they would become an elf,
Who in a beaded coat does gayly go. 40

1842, 1849

Haze[8]

Woof of the sun, ethereal gauze,
Woven of Nature's richest stuffs,
Visible heat, air-water, and dry sea,
Last conquest of the eye;
Toil of the day displayed, sun-dust, 5
Aerial surf upon the shores of earth,
Ethereal estuary, frith of light,
Breakers of air, billows of heat,
Fine summer spray on inland seas;
Bird of the sun, transparent-winged 10
Owlet of noon, soft-pinioned,
From heath or stubble rising without song,—
Established thy serenity o'er the fields.

1843, 1849

Smoke[9]

Light-winged Smoke, Icarian bird,[1]
Melting thy pinions in thy upward flight;
Lark without song, and messenger of dawn,
Circling above the hamlets as thy nest;
Or else, departing dream, and shadowy form 5
Of midnight vision, gathering up thy skirts;

8. One of the vignettes captioned "Orphics" published in *The Dial* for April, 1843, this was reprinted without title in Thoreau's "Tuesday" chapter of *A Week on the Concord and Merrimack Rivers* (1849). In reprinting this, with other poems, in *Letters * * * * (1865), Emerson changed "fen" to "sun" in the first line, and this reading occurs in numerous later editions, but not in *Poems of Nature* (1895).
9. One of the vignettes captioned "Orphics" published in *The Dial* for April, 1843, this was reprinted in "House-warming" in *Walden* (1854), following the sentence: "When the villagers were lighting their fires beyond the horizon, I too gave notice to the various wild inhabitants of Walden vale, by a smoky streamer from my chimney, that I was awake." The *Walden* text is identical with that of *Poems of Nature*, except for a comma at the end of l. 2.
1. Daedalus, mythical artisan of the Greeks, escaped his enemies on wings made of feathers and wax, but Icarus, his son, melted his by flying too near the sun, and plunged to his death.

By night star-veiling, and by day
Darkening the light and blotting out the sun;
Go thou my incense upward from this hearth,
And ask the gods to pardon this clear flame.   10

                                              1843, 1854

Inspiration[2]

Whate'er we leave to God, God does,
    And blesses us;
The work we choose should be our own,
    God leaves alone.

If with light head erect I sing,   5
    Though all the Muses lend their force,
From my poor love of anything,
    The verse is weak and shallow as its source.

But if with bended neck I grope
    Listening behind me for my wit,   10
With faith superior to hope,
    More anxious to keep back than forward it;

Making my soul accomplice there
    Unto the flame my heart hath lit,
Then will the verse forever wear—   15
    Time cannot bend the line which God hath writ.

Always the general show of things
    Floats in review before my mind,
And such true love and reverence brings,
    That sometimes I forget that I am blind.   20

But now there comes unsought, unseen,
    Some clear divine electuary,

2. "Inspiration," one of Thoreau's best poems, is also important because it reflects his transcendental ideas as applied to creative expression, especially poetry. Not published in its entirety during Thoreau's life, this poem was conceived early—fragments of it appear in *A Week on the Concord and Merrimack Rivers* (1849) as a kind of commentary on the ideas of this first prose volume. In his "Monday" chapter the reader will find ll. 29–30, ll. 39–40, and also a curious six-line combination of ll. 45–46 with the stanza beginning l. 69. In "Friday" one finds the quatrain beginning l. 25; all of these passages emphasize the transcendentalist's reliance on revealed or intuitional truth. Modern anthologies give several abbreviated versions of the poem, resulting from the publication of two different abbreviated texts soon after Thoreau's death. The first was of seven stanzas, not consecutive, in the Boston *Commonwealth* for June 19, 1863. The second, consisting of the first six of these stanzas, was included by Emerson in the *Letters * * ** (1865). Our text reprints the twenty-one stanzas as they were printed (from a manuscript) in *Poems of Nature* (1895).

And I, who had but sensual been,
   Grow sensible, and as God is, am wary.

I hearing get, who had but ears,   25
   And sight, who had but eyes before,
I moments live, who lived but years,
   And truth discern, who knew but learning's lore.

I hear beyond the range of sound,
   I see beyond the range of sight,   30
New earths and skies and seas around,
   And in my day the sun doth pale his light.

A clear and ancient harmony
   Pierces my soul through all its din,
As through its utmost melody,—   35
   Farther behind than they, farther within.

More swift its bolt than lightning is,
   Its voice than thunder is more loud,
It doth expand my privacies
   To all, and leave me single in the crowd.   40

It speaks with such authority,
   With so serene and lofty tone,
That idle Time runs gadding by,
   And leaves me with Eternity alone.

Now chiefly is my natal hour,   45
   And only now my prime of life,
Of manhood's strength it is the flower,
   'Tis peace's end and war's beginning strife.

It comes in summer's broadest noon,
   By a grey wall or some chance place,   50
Unseasoning Time, insulting June,
   And vexing day with its presuming face.

Such fragrance round my couch it makes,
   More rich than are Arabian drugs,
That my soul scents its life and wakes   55
   The body up beneath its perfumed rugs.

Such is the Muse, the heavenly maid,
   The star that guides our mortal course,
Which shows where life's true kernel's laid,
   Its wheat's fine flour, and its undying force.   60

She with one breath attunes the spheres,
   And also my poor human heart,

With one impulse propels the years
    Around, and gives my throbbing pulse its start.

I will not doubt for evermore,   65
    Nor falter from a steadfast faith,
For though the system be turned o'er,
    God takes not back the word which once He saith.

I will not doubt the love untold
    Which not my worth nor want has bought,   70
Which wooed me young, and wooes me old,
    And to this evening hath me brought.

My memory I'll educate
    To know the one historic truth,
Remembering to the latest date   75
    The only true and sole immortal youth.

Be but thy inspiration given,
    No matter through what danger sought,
I'll fathom hell or climb to heaven,
    And yet esteem that cheap which love has bought.   80

Fame cannot tempt the bard
    Who's famous with his God,
Nor laurel him reward
    Who has his Maker's nod.

1848   1849, 1895

The Fall of the Leaf[3]

Thank God who seasons thus the year,
And sometimes kindly slants his rays;
For in his winter he's most near
And plainest seen upon the shortest days.

Who gently tempers now his heats,   5
And then his harsher cold, lest we
Should surfeit on the summer's sweets,
Or pine upon the winter's crudity.

3. This serene and genuinely inspired poem of reflection, notable among Thoreau's poems for its unity of mood and form, was actually dismembered in its first publication, in the Boston *Commonwealth* in 1863. In the issue for October 9, stanzas 5–13 appeared as "The Fall of the Leaf." Nearly a month later, on November 6, the first four stanzas were printed as "The Soul's Season," but the *Commonwealth* did not print the last three stanzas of the present version. The entire sixteen stanzas appeared in *Poems of Nature* (1895), whose editor had access to a manuscript which has not been recovered.

A sober mind will walk alone,
Apart from nature, if need be, 10
And only its own seasons own;
For nature leaving its humanity.

Sometimes a late autumnal thought
Has crossed my mind in green July,
And to its early freshness brought 15
Late ripened fruits, and an autumnal sky.

The evening of the year draws on,
The fields a later aspect wear;
Since Summer's garishness is gone,
Some grains of night tincture the noontide air. 20

Behold! the shadows of the trees
Now circle wider 'bout their stem,
Like sentries that by slow degrees
Perform their rounds, gently protecting them.

And as the year doth decline, 25
The sun allows a scantier light;
Behind each needle of the pine
There lurks a small auxiliar to the night.

I hear the cricket's slumbrous lay
Around, beneath me, and on high; 30
It rocks the night, it soothes the day,
And everywhere is Nature's lullaby.

But most he chirps beneath the sod,
When he has made his winter bed;
His creak grown fainter but more broad, 35
A film of autumn o'er the summer spread.

Small birds, in fleets migrating by,
Now beat across some meadow's bay,
And as they tack and veer on high,
With faint and hurried click beguile the way. 40

Far in the woods, these golden days,
Some leaf obeys its Maker's call;
And through their hollow aisles it plays
With delicate touch the prelude of the Fall.

Gently withdrawing from its stem, 45
It lightly lays itself along
Where the same hand hath pillowed them,
Resigned to sleep upon the old year's throng.

The loneliest birch is brown and sere,
The furthest pool is strewn with leaves,
Which float upon their watery bier,
Where is no eye that sees, no heart that grieves. 50

The jay screams through the chestnut wood;
The crisped and yellow leaves around
Are hue and texture of my mood—
And these rough burrs my heirlooms on the ground. 55

The threadbare trees, so poor and thin—
They are no wealthier than I;
But with as brave a core within
They rear their boughs to the October sky. 60

Poor knights they are which bravely wait
The charge of Winter's cavalry,
Keeping a simple Roman state,
Discumbered of their Persian luxury.

1863, 1895

The Humanitarian and Critical Temper

FRONTIERS OF HUMOR

Americans have produced humor almost as abundantly as manufactured goods, and much of it has been successfully exported. Characteristics common to American humor are found as far back as Thomas Morton of Merrymount, who deflated the Puritans by calling their warrior, Myles Standish, "Captain Shrimp"; William Byrd, whose observations on Carolina backwoodsmen suggest the exaggerated buffoonery of the tall tale; and the early caricatures of the British John Bull and the American Brother Jonathan.

In the new United States, by 1830, such humor rose to flood tide. The writings of Irving and the Knickerbockers suggest that established authors were only mildly influenced; but a comic American Gargantua laughed with the masses—in the popular theater and journalism, folklore and oral story, minstrelsy and song. To the new fiction, as here represented, many frontier experiences gave an original energy: the tall tales of hunters and squatters in Kentucky and Tennessee, boisterous adventures of Georgia "crackers," exploits—sentimental or savage—of Mississippi boatmen, ribald extravagance from the lower Mississippi, mingled with the droll laconism of the earlier Yankee wit and homely aphorisms such as Poor Richard wrote in Philadelphia.

The four authors represented here are best understood against this background. Seba Smith and Longstreet, Hooper and Harris, all had intrinsic merits as writers, and were widely read and influential. Each reached the public first by way of the flourishing popular journalism, particularly the newspapers which sprang up everywhere, even in the new frontiers. These writers have outlived many other humorists of their day. In addition they recall a forgotten past in American life. They were progenitors of the new everyday realism in fiction, and of a more precise and comically effective use of dialect of which Lowell's *Biglow Papers* remains the earliest great example; they helped to develop humor and dialect as satirical instruments in a great American tradition extending from Lowell and Seba Smith, through Mark Twain and Joel Chandler Harris, Josh Billings, Artemus Ward, Mr. Dooley, and O. Henry, down to the recent days of Ring Lardner, Will Rogers, and beyond.

The four authors included in this section are also the best illustrations, in the earlier period, of four comic types and tendencies which have prevailed in American literature. Seba Smith, one of the most successful of the early Yankee humorists, homespun commentators, and crackerbox philosophers, created Major Jack Downing as a scourge against political folly in the age of Andrew Jackson, but Jack continued his work long enough to become one of Lincoln's favorite humorists. He begot several imitators; and cartoonists, endeavoring to compound Jack with the earlier Brother Jonathan, created the beloved but vinegary caricature, Uncle Sam. Augustus Baldwin Longstreet, in *Georgia Scenes*, provided an early classic of humorous and bucolic realism which influenced not only his southwestern followers but even Mark Twain, the master of this American tradition. Captain Simon Suggs is at once the creation of an individual author, Johnson J. Hooper, and the best summation of a character familiar in the oral tradition and newspaper realism of the frontier. He is the product of "flush times," and he takes advantage of the fact that "it's good to be shifty in a new country." He is a sharper and thief, a liar and braggart, sometimes ruthless or even cruel; but his misadventures always contain that caustic and retributive irony of nature which Zinc Barnes had in mind when he told Mark Twain, in the Washoe country, "out here, an honest politician is a son of a —— who will *stay* bought." George Washington Harris, in Sut Lovingood, also provided the epitome of a prevalent type, the comically irresponsible Hallowe'en prankster, the backwoods Til Eulenspiegel, whose escapades permeate so much of the oral humor of the frontier, and are reflected, again, in some of the experiences of Mark Twain's urchins.

General references for these authors and the American humor of their times are: Constance Rourke, *American Humor*, 1931; Walter Blair, *Native American Humor*, 1937, and *Horse Sense in American Humor*, 1942; Jennette Tandy, *Crackerbox Philosophers*, 1925; Franklin J. Meine, *Tall Tales of the Southwest*, 1930; Bernard De Voto, *Mark Twain's America*, 1934; and *Literary History of the United States*, edited by Robert E. Spiller, Willard Thorp, Thomas H. Johnson, and Henry Seidel Canby, 1948, Chapter 44, and Bibliography, pp. 202–212. Further brief notes concerning each author are given below:

SEBA SMITH (1792–1868). His principal volumes are *The Life and Writings of Major Jack Downing of Downingville*, 1833; *John Smith's Letters with Picters to Match*, 1839; *Jack Downing's Letters*, 1845; *'Way Down East, or Portraitures of Yankee Life*, 1854; and *My Thirty Years Out of the Senate*, 1850. See Mary Alice Wyman, *Two American Pioneers*, 1927; and "Seba Smith," *Dictionary of American Biography*, 1935.

AUGUSTUS BALDWIN LONGSTREET (1790–1870). His anonymous Georgia sketches first appeared in 1827, in a Milledgeville, Georgia, newspaper, and later in the Augusta *States Rights Sentinel*, which he owned. In 1835 they were collected, anonymously, as *Georgia Scenes, Characters, Incidents, Etc. in the First Half Century of the Republic*. John Donald Wade's biography, 1924, is reliable.

JOHNSON JONES HOOPER (1815–1862). His tales of Captain Simon Suggs were published in southern papers, and then collected as *Some Adventures of Captain Simon Suggs, Late of the Tallapoosa Volunteers*, 1845. Other sketches by Hooper, similar to the Suggs stories, were collected as *A Ride with Old Kit Kuncker*, 1849, reprinted as *The Widow Rugby's Husband * * * *, 1851. Stanley Hoole's *Johnson Jones Hooper*, 1952, is the only biography.

GEORGE WASHINGTON HARRIS (1814–1869). A collection of twenty-five of his

tales, entitled *Sut Lovingood's Yarns*, appeared in 1867. *Sut Lovingood's Travels with Old Abe Linkhorn*, first published in the Nashville *American*, was edited by Edd Winfield Parks, 1937. Franklin J. Meine, "George Washington Harris," *Dictionary of American Biography*, 1932, is the only recent account.

SEBA SMITH: *From* The Life and Writings of Major Jack Downing of Downingville[1]

[*The Maine Legislature Chooses a Speaker*]

TO COUSIN EPHRAIM DOWNING, UP IN DOWNINGVILLE

PORTLAND, Monday, Jan. 18, 1830.

DEAR COUSIN EPHRAIM:—

I now take my pen in hand to let you know that I am well, hoping these few lines will find you enjoying the same blessing. When I come down to Portland I didn't think o' staying more than three or four days, if I could sell my load of ax handles, and mother's cheese, and Cousin Nabby's bundle of footings;[2] but when I got here I found Uncle Nat was gone a freighting down to Quoddy,[3] and Aunt Sally said as how I shouldn't stir a step home till he come back agin, which won't be this month. So here I am, loitering about this great town, as lazy as an ox. Ax handles don't fetch nothing; I couldn't hardly give 'em away. Tell Cousin Nabby I sold her footings for nine-pence a pair, and took it all in cotton cloth. Mother's cheese come to seven and six-pence; I got her half a pound of shushon,[4] and two ounces of snuff, and the rest in sugar. When Uncle Nat comes home I shall put my ax handles aboard of him, and let him take 'em to Boston next time he goes; I saw a feller tother day, that told me they'd fetch a good price there. I've been

1. The first Jack Downing letters appeared in 1830, in the Portland, Maine, *Daily Courier*, of which their author was editor. They established a pattern which survived for a century in comic journalism and political satire. A succession of cracker-box philosophers intensified their witty criticism of American life by assuming the pose of naïve illiteracy and homely dialect. The classic example was provided by Lowell in the *Biglow Papers*, a satirical commentary on the Mexican War and the Civil War. Later Artemus Ward and Josh Billings won an international audience. Toward the end of the century, Mr. Dooley, with his Irish brogue, became the political commentator of the age of expansionism, and illustrated the comic use of various immigrant dialects. Will Rogers (died 1935), the last avatar of the type, spoke

with the lariat tongue of the cowboy. Seba Smith's Jack Downing posed as nonpartisan, thus increasing the range and usefulness of his satire. At first a rustic trader in Portland (*cf.* the "letter" here reprinted) he soon moved from Maine to the national capital, pretending intimacy with President Jackson and later figures, flailing incompetence, stupidity, and graft wherever he saw them, until the beginnings of the Civil War. His homely good nature and wit, his simple audacity and shrewdness in exploring men and motives, gave him an enormous audience and influence.

2. Hand-knit stocking feet.
3. Passamaquoddy Bay, at the extreme eastern end of Maine.
4. A Chinese tea then common, named from its origin in Chu Shan.

here now a whole fortnight, and if I could tell ye one half I've seen, I guess you'd stare worse than if you'd seen a catamount. I've been to meeting, and to the museum, and to both Legislaters, the one they call the House, and the one they call the Sinnet. I spose Uncle Joshua is in a great hurry to hear something about these Legislaters; for you know he's always reading newspapers, and talking politics, when he can get anybody to talk with him. I've seen him when he had five tons of hay in the field well made, and a heavy shower coming up, stand two hours disputing with Squire W. about Adams and Jackson[5]—one calling Adams a tory and a fed, and the other saying Jackson was a murderer and a fool;[6] so they kept it up, till the rain began to pour down, and about spoilt all his hay.

Uncle Joshua may set his heart at rest about the bushel of corn that he bet 'long with the postmaster, that Mr. Ruggles would be Speaker of that Legislater they call the House; for he's lost it, slick as a whistle. As I hadn't much to do, I've been there every day since they've been a setting. A Mr. White, of Monmouth, was the Speaker the first two days; and I can't see why they didn't keep him in all the time; for he seemed to be a very clever, good-natured sort of man, and he had such a smooth, pleasant way with him, that I couldn't help feeling sorry when they turned him out and put in another. But some said he wasn't put in hardly fair; and I don't know as he was, for the first day, when they were all coming in and crowding round, there was a large, fat man, with a round, full, jolly sort of a face. I suppose he was the captain, for he got up and commanded them to come to order, and then he told this Mr. White to whip into the chair quicker than you could say Jack Robinson. Some of 'em scolded about it, and I heard some, in a little room they called the lobby, say 'twas a mean trick; but I couldn't see why, for I thought Mr. White made a capital Speaker, and when *our* company turns out, the cap'n always has a right to do as he's a mind to.[7]

They kept disputing most all the time for the first two days about a poor Mr. Roberts, from Waterborough. Some said he shouldn't have a seat because he adjourned the town meeting and wasn't fairly elected. Others said it was no such thing, and that he was elected as fairly as any of 'em. And Mr. Roberts himself said he was, and said he could bring men that would swear to it, and good men too. But, notwithstanding all this, when they came to vote, they got three or four majority that he shouldn't have a seat. And I thought

5. Current differences of political opinion were represented by John Quincy Adams, president from 1825 to 1829, and his successor, Andrew Jackson, president from 1829 to 1837.
6. In youth Adams was only a mild "fed" (Federalist) but he led the conservative ("tory") National Republicans after 1823. Jackson was presumably the military "murderer" of certain British and Seminole enemies.
7. Volunteer militia companies, especially in rural areas, provided a frequent subject for contemporary humor.

it a needless piece of cruelty, for they wan't crowded, and there was a number of seats empty. But they would have it so, and the poor man had to go and stand up in the lobby.

Then they disputed about a Mr. Fowler's having a seat. Some said he shouldn't have a seat, because when he was elected some of his votes were given for his father. But they were more kind to him than they were to Mr. Roberts, for they voted that he *should* have a seat; and I suppose it was because they thought he had a lawful right to inherit whatever was his father's. They all declared there was no party politics about it, and I don't think there was; for I noticed that all who voted that Mr. Roberts should *not* have a seat, voted that Mr. Fowler should. So, as they all voted *both* ways, they must have been conscientious, and I don't see how there could be any party about it.

It's a pity they couldn't be allowed to have two Speakers, for they seemed to be very anxious to choose Mr. Ruggles and Mr. Goodenow. They two had every vote except one, and if they had had *that*, I believe they would both have been chosen;[8] as it was, however, they both came within a humbird's eye of it. Whether it was Mr. Ruggles voted for Mr. Goodenow, or Mr. Goodenow for Mr. Ruggles, I can't exactly tell; but I rather guess it was Mr. Ruggles voted for Mr. Goodenow; for he appeared to be very glad to see Mr. Goodenow in the chair, and shook hands with him as good-natured as could be. I would have given half my load of ax handles if they could both have been so happy. But as they can't have but one Speaker at a time, and as Mr. Goodenow appears to understand the business very well, it is not likely Mr. Ruggles will be Speaker any this winter. So Uncle Joshua will have to shell out his bushel of corn, and I hope it will learn him better than to bet about politics again. Before I came from home, some of the papers said how there was a majority of ten or fifteen *National Republicans* in the Legislater, and the other party said there was a pretty clever little majority of *Democratic Republicans*. Well, now everybody says it has turned out jest as that queer little paper, called the Daily Courier, said 'twould. That paper said it was such a close rub it couldn't hardly tell which side would beat. And it's jest so, for they've been here now most a fortnight acting jest like two boys playin see-saw on a rail. First one goes up, and then 'tother; but I reckon one of the boys is rather heaviest, for once in a while he comes down chuck, and throws the other up into the air as though he would pitch him heads over heels. Your loving cousin till death.

JACK DOWNING.

1830, 1833

8. *Cf.* below, the reference to the very evenly divided legislature.

SEBA SMITH: *From* My Thirty Years Out
of the Senate

[*Jack Downing Shakes Hands for President Jackson*][9]

TO UNCLE JOSHUA DOWNING, POSTMASTER, UP IN DOWNINGVILLE,
IN THE STATE OF MAINE, WITH CARE AND SPEED

PHILADELPHIA, June 10, 1833

DEAR UNCLE JOSHUA:—We are coming on, full chisel. I've been
trying, ever since we started, to get a chance to write a little to you;
but when we've been on the road I couldn't catch my breath hardly
long enough to write my name, we kept flying so fast; and when
we made any stop, there was such a jam around us there wasn't
elbow room enough for a miskeeter to turn round without knocking
his wings off.

I'm most afraid now we shall get to Downingville before this
letter does, so that we shall be likely to catch you all in the suds
before you think of it. But I understand there is a *fast mail* goes
on that way, and I mean to send it by that, so I'm in hopes you'll
get it time enough to have the children's faces washed and their
heads combed, and the gals get on their clean gowns. And if Sargent
Joel *could* have time enough to call out my old Downingville company and get their uniforms brushed up a little, and come down
the road as fur as your new barn to meet us, there's nothing that
would please the President better. As for victuals, most anything
won't come amiss; we are as hungry as bears after traveling a hundred miles a day. A little fried pork and eggs, or a pot of baked
beans and an Indian pudding would suit us much better than the
soft stuff they give here in these great cities.

The President wouldn't miss of seeing you for anything in the
world, and he will go to Downingville if he has legs and arms
enough left when he goes to Portland to carry him there. But, for
fear that anything should happen that he shouldn't be able to come,
you had better meet us in Portland, say about the 22d; and then
you can go up to Downingville with us.

This traveling with the President is capital fun, after all, if it
wasn't so plaguy tiresome. We come into Baltimore on a railroad,
and we flew over the ground like a harrycane. There isn't a horse in
this country that could keep up with us, if he should go upon the

9. Having been re-elected in 1832 in
spite of strong resistance from conservative and banking interests, Jackson, in
the summer of 1833, took an impressive
group of officials and politicians on a
visit to several northern cities. Having
recently threatened armed resistance
against South Carolina's threat of nullification, he was sensationally popular
with antislavery forces, while conservatives muttered of extravagance and vulgarity. Seba Smith exploited the humorous potentialities of this situation in
several cities, as in this account by Jack
Downing of the Philadelphia visit.

clean clip. When we got to Baltimore, the streets were filled with folks as thick as the spruce trees down in your swamp. There we found Black Hawk,[1] a little, old, dried up Indian king. And I thought the folks looked at him and the prophet about as much as they did at me and the President. I gave the President a wink that this Indian fellow was taking the shine off us a little; so we concluded we wouldn't have him with us any more, but go on without him.

I can't stop to tell you, in this letter, how we got along to Philadelphy, though we had a pretty easy time some of the way in the steamboats. And I can't stop to tell you of half of the fine things I have seen here. They took us up into a great hall this morning, as big as a meeting-house, and then the folks begun to pour in by thousands to shake hands with the President—Federalists and all, it made no difference. There was such a stream of 'em coming in that the hall was full in a few minutes, and it was so jammed up around the door that they couldn't get out again if they were to die. So they had to knock out some of the windows, and go out t'other way.

The President shook hands with all his might an hour or two, 'till he got so tired he couldn't hardly stand it. I took hold and shook for him once in a while to help him along, but at last he got so tired he had to lay down on a soft bench, covered with cloth, and shake as well as he could; and when he couldn't shake, he'd nod to 'em as they come along. And at last he got so beat out, he couldn't only wrinkle his forehead and wink. Then I kind of stood behind him, and reached my arm round under his, and shook for him for about half an hour as tight as I could spring. Then we concluded it was best to adjourn for to-day.

And I've made out to get away up into the garret in the tavern long enough to write this letter. We shall be off tomorrow or next day for York; and if I can possibly get breathing time enough there, I shall write to you again.

Give my love to all the folks in Downingville, and believe me your loving neffu,

MAJOR JACK DOWNING

1833, 1859

1. The Sauk chieftain's *Autobiography* had just appeared. The so-called Black Hawk War, the year before, represented his armed rebellion against the resettlement of his people.

AUGUSTUS BALDWIN LONGSTREET:
From Georgia Scenes[1]
The Horse Swap

During the session of the Superior Court in the village of——,
about three weeks ago, when a number of people were collected
in the principal street of the village, I observed a young man riding
up and down the street, as I supposed, in a violent passion. He
galloped this way, then that, and then the other; spurred his horse
to one group of citizens, then to another; then dashed off at half-
speed, as if fleeing from danger; and, suddenly checking his horse,
returned—first in a pace, then in a trot, and then in a canter. While
he was performing these various evolutions he cursed, swore,
whooped, screamed, and tossed himself in every attitude which man
could assume on horseback. In short, he cavorted most magnanimously (a term which, in our tongue, expresses all that I have described, and a little more), and seemed to be setting all creation at
defiance. As I like to see all that is passing, I determined to take a
position a little nearer to him, and to ascertain, if possible, what it
was that affected him so sensibly. Accordingly I approached a crowd
before which he had stopped for a moment, and examined it with
the strictest scrutiny. But I could see nothing in it that seemed to
have anything to do with the cavorter. Every man appeared to be in
good humor, and all minding their own business. Not one so much
as noticed the principal figure. Still he went on. After a semicolon
pause, which my appearance seemed to produce (for he eyed me
closely as I approached), he fetched a whoop, and swore that "he
could out-swap any live man, woman, or child that ever walked
these hills, or that ever straddled horseflesh since the days of old
daddy Adam." "Stranger," said he to me, "did you ever see the
Yellow Blossom from Jasper?"

"No," said I, "but I have often heard of him."

"I'm the boy," continued he; "perhaps a *leetle,* jist a *leetle* of the
best man at a horse-swap that ever trod shoe-leather."

1. Edgar Allan Poe especially admired
"The Horse Swap." In reviewing *Georgia
Scenes* (*Southern Literary Messenger,*
March 1836, pp. 287–292), he singled
out this "vivid encounter between the
wits of two Georgian horse-jockies. This
is most excellent in every respect, but
especially so in its delineation of Southern bravado, and the keen sense of the
ludicrous evinced in the portraiture of
the steeds. We think parts of this free
and easy sketch of a *hoss* superior, in
point of humor and verisimilitude, to
anything of the kind we have ever seen
* * * [The author has] penetrative
understanding of Southern character
* * * and of good-for-nothing horses."
The eighteen sketches of the volume had
appeared under pseudonyms from 1832
to 1835, in the author's newspaper, *The
States Rights Sentinel,* Augusta, Georgia,
and the first collection, still anonymous
("By a Native Georgian") came in 1835
from the same press. There have been
twelve later editions. The text here given
is that of the first edition, with the correction of a typographical error noted
and the silent correction of a few errors
in punctuation.

I began to feel my situation a little awkward, when I was relieved by a man somewhat advanced in years, who stepped up and began to survey the Yellow Blossom's horse with much apparent interest. This drew the rider's attention, and he turned the conversation from me to the stranger.

"Well, my old coon," said he, "do you want to swap *hosses?*"

"Why, I don't know," replied the stranger; "I believe I've got a beast I'd trade with you for that one, if you like him."

"Well, fetch up your nag, my old cock; you're jist the lark I wanted to get hold of. I am perhaps a *leetle*, jist a *leetle*, of the best man at a horse swap that ever stole *cracklins*[2] out of his mammy's fat gourd. Where's your *hoss?*"

"I'll bring him presently; but I want to examine your horse a little."

"Oh, look at him," said the Blossom, alighting and hitting him a cut—"look at him! He's the best piece of *hoss*flesh in the thirteen united universal worlds. There's no sort o' mistake in little Bullet. He can pick up miles on his feet, and fling 'em behind him as fast as the next man's *hoss*, I don't care where he comes from. And he can keep at it as long as the sun can shine without resting."

During this harangue little Bullet looked as if he understood it all, believed it, and was ready at any moment to verify it. He was a horse of goodly countenance, rather expressive of vigilance than fire; though an unnatural appearance of fierceness was thrown into it by the loss of his ears, which had been cropped pretty close to his head. Nature had done but little for Bullet's head and neck; but he managed, in a great measure, to hide their defects by bowing perpetually. He had obviously suffered severely for corn; but if his ribs and hip bones had not disclosed the fact, *he* never would have done it; for he was in all respects as cheerful and happy as if he commanded all the corn-cribs and fodder-stacks in Georgia. His height was about twelve hands; but as his shape partook somewhat of that of the giraffe, his haunches stood much lower. They were short, strait, peaked, and concave. Bullet's tail, however, made amends for all his defects. All that the artist could do to beautify it had been done; and all that horse could do to compliment the artist, Bullet did. His tail was nicked in superior style, and exhibited the line of beauty in so many directions that it could not fail to hit the most fastidious taste in some of them. From the root it dropped into a graceful festoon, then rose in a handsome curve, then resumed its first direction, and then mounted suddenly upward like a cypress knee to a perpendicular of about two and a half inches. The whole had a careless and bewitching inclination to the right. Bullet obvi-

2. Properly, "cracklings"; the crisp rinds and meaty residue from the boiling of lard.

ously knew where his beauty lay, and took all occasions to display it to the best advantage. If a stick cracked, or if any one moved suddenly about him, or coughed, or hawked, or spoke a little louder than common, up went Bullet's tail like lightning; and if the *going up* did not please, the *coming down* must of necessity, for it was as different from the other movement as was its direction. The first was a bold and rapid flight upward, usually to an angle of forty-five degrees. In this position he kept his interesting appendage until he satisfied himself that nothing in particular was to be done; when he commenced dropping it by half inches, in second beats, then in triple time, then faster and shorter, and faster and shorter still, until it finally died away imperceptibly into its natural position. If I might compare sights to sounds, I should say its *settling* was more like the note of a locust than anything else in nature.

Either from native sprightliness of disposition, from uncontrollable activity, or from an unconquerable habit of removing flies by the stamping of the feet, Bullet never stood still, but always kept up a gentle fly-scaring movement of his limbs, which was peculiarly interesting.

"I tell you, man," proceeded the Yellow Blossom, "he's the best live hoss that ever trod the grit of Georgia. Bob Smart knows the hoss. Come here, Bob, and mount this hoss, and show Bullet's motions." Here Bullet bristled up, and looked as if he had been hunting for Bob all day long, and had just found him. Bob sprang on his back. "Boo-oo-oo!" said Bob, with a fluttering noise of the lips, and away went Bullet as if in a quarter race, with all his beauties spread in handsome style.

"Now fetch him back," said Blossom. Bullet turned and came in pretty much as he went out.

"Now trot him by." Bullet reduced his tail to *customary*, sidled to the right and left airily, and exhibited at least three varieties of trot in the short space of fifty yards.

"Make him pace!" Bob commenced twitching the bridle and kicking at the same time. These inconsistent movements obviously (and most naturally) disconcerted Bullet; for it was impossible for him to learn from them whether he was to proceed or stand still. He started to trot, and was told that wouldn't do. He attempted a canter, and was checked again. He stopped, and was urged to go on. Bullet now rushed into the wide field of experiment, and struck out a gait of his own that completely turned the tables upon his rider, and certainly deserved a patent. It seemed to have derived its elements from the jig, the minuet, and the cotillion. If it was not a pace, it certainly had *pace* in it, and no man would venture to call it anything else; so it passed off to the satisfaction of the owner.

"Walk him!" Bullet was now at home again, and he walked as if money were staked on him.

The stranger, whose name I afterwards learned was Peter Ketch, having examined Bullet to his heart's content, ordered his son Neddy to go and bring up Kit. Neddy soon appeared upon Kit, a well-formed sorrel of the middle size, and in good order. His *tout-ensemble* threw Bullet entirely in the shade, though a glance was sufficient to satisfy any one that Bullet had the decided advantage of him in point of intellect.

"Why, man," said Blossom, "do you bring such a hoss as that to trade for Bullet? Oh, I see, you've no notion of trading!"

"Ride him off, Neddy!" said Peter. Kit put off at a handsome lope.

"Trot him back!" Kit came in at a long sweeping trot, and stopped suddenly at the crowd.

"Well," said Blossom, "let me look at him; maybe he'll do to plough."

"Examine him," said Peter, taking hold the bridle close to the mouth; "he's nothing but a tacky. He ain't as *pretty* a horse as Bullet, I know, but he'll do. Start 'em together for a hundred and fifty *mile*, and if Kit ain't twenty *mile* ahead of him at the coming out, any man may take Kit for nothing. But he's a monstrous mean horse, gentlemen; any man may see that. He's the scariest horse, too, you ever saw. He won't do to hunt on, nohow. Stranger, will you let Neddy have your rifle to shoot off him? Lay the rifle between his ears, Neddy, and shoot at the blaze[3] in that stump. Tell me when his head is high enough."

Ned fired and hit the blaze, and Kit did not move a hair's breadth.

"Neddy, take a couple of sticks, and beat on that hogshead at Kit's tail."

Ned made a tremendous rattling, at which Bullet took fright, broke his bridle, and dashed off in grand style, and would have stopped all farther negotiations by going home in disgust, had not a traveller arrested him and brought him back; but Kit did not move.

"I tell you, gentlemen," continued Peter, "he's the scariest horse you ever saw. He ain't as gentle as Bullet, but he won't do any harm if you watch him. Shall I put him in a cart, gig, or wagon for you, stranger? He'll cut the same capers there he does here. He's a monstrous mean horse."

During all this time Blossom was examining him with the nicest scrutiny. Having examined his frame and limbs, he now looked at his eyes.

"He's got a curious look out of his eyes," said Blossom.

"Oh yes, sir," said Peter, "just as blind as a bat. Blind horses

3. The mark of an ax on a tree.

always have clear eyes. Make a motion at his eyes, if you please, sir."

Blossom did so, and Kit threw up his head rather as if something pricked him under the chin than as if fearing a blow. Blossom repeated the experiment, and Kit jerked back in considerable astonishment.

"Stone-blind, you see, gentlemen," proceeded Peter; "but he's just as good to travel of a dark night as if he had eyes."

"Blame my buttons," said Blossom, "if I like them eyes!"

"No," said Peter, "nor I neither. I'd rather have 'em made of diamonds; but they'll do—if they don't show as much white as Bullet's."

"Well," said Blossom, "make a pass at me."

"No," said Peter, "you made the banter, now make your pass."

"Well, I'm never afraid to price my hosses. You must give me twenty-five dollars boot."[4]

"Oh, certainly; say fifty, and my saddle and bridle in. Here, Neddy, my son, take away daddy's horse."

"Well," said Blossom, "I've made my pass, now you make yours."

"I'm for short talk in a horse swap, and therefore always tell a gentleman at once what I mean to do. You must give me ten dollars."

Blossom swore absolutely, roundly, and profanely that he never would give boot.

"Well," said Peter, "I didn't care about trading; but you cut such high shines that I thought I'd like to back you out, and I've done it. Gentlemen, you see I've brought him to a back."[5]

"Come, old man," said Blossom, "I've been joking with you. I begin to think you do want to trade; therefore, give me five dollars and take Bullet. I'd rather lose ten dollars any time than not make a trade, though I hate to fling away a good hoss."

"Well," said Peter, "I'll be as clever as you are. Just put the five dollars on Bullet's back, and hand him over; it's a trade."

Blossom swore again, as roundly as before, that he would not give boot; and, said he, "Bullet wouldn't hold five dollars on his back, no how. But, as I bantered you, if you say an even swap, here's at you."

"I told you," said Peter, "I'd be as clever as you; therefore, here goes two dollars more, just for trade sake. Give me three dollars, and it's a bargain."

Blossom repeated his former assertion; and here the parties stood for a long time, and the by-standers (for many were now collected) began to taunt both parties. After some time, however, it was pretty

---

4. An extra consideration, paid to equalize an exchange of goods.   5. First edition reads "hack," in error.

unanimously decided that the old man had backed Blossom out.

At length Blossom swore he "never should be backed out for three dollars after bantering a man"; and, accordingly, they closed the trade.

"Now," said Blossom, as he handed Peter the three dollars, "I'm a man that, when he makes a bad trade, makes the most of it until he can make a better. I'm for no rues and after-claps."

"That's just my way," said Peter; "I never goes to law to mend my bargains."

"Ah, you're the kind of boy I love to trade with. Here's your hoss, old man. Take the saddle and bridle off him, and I'll strip yours; but lift up the blanket easy from Bullet's back, for he's a mighty tender-backed hoss."

The old man removed the saddle, but the blanket stuck fast. He attempted to raise it, and Bullet bowed himself, switched his tail, danced a little, and gave signs of biting.

"Don't hurt him, old man," said Blossom, archly; "take it off easy. I am, perhaps, a leetle of the best man at a horse-swap that ever catched a coon."

Peter continued to pull at the blanket more and more roughly, and Bullet became more and more *cavortish*, insomuch that, when the blanket came off, he had reached the *kicking* point in good earnest.

The removal of the blanket disclosed a sore on Bullet's back that seemed to have defied all medical skill. It measured six full inches in length and four in breadth, and had as many features as Bullet had motions. My heart sickened at the sight; and I felt that the brute who had been riding him in that situation deserved the halter.

The prevailing feeling, however, was that of mirth. The laugh became loud and general at the old man's expense, and rustic witticisms were liberally bestowed upon him and his late purchase. These Blossom continued to provoke by various remarks. He asked the old man "if he thought Bullet would let five dollars lie on his back." He declared most seriously that he had owned that horse three months, and had never discovered before that he had a sore back, "or he never should have thought of trading him," etc., etc.

The old man bore it all with the most philosophic composure. He evinced no astonishment at his late discovery, and made no replies. But his son Neddy had not disciplined his feelings quite so well. His eyes opened wider and wider from the first to the last pull of the blanket, and when the whole sore burst upon his view, astonishment and fright seemed to contend for the mastery of his countenance. As the blanket disappeared, he stuck his hands in his breeches pockets, heaved a deep sigh, and lapsed into a profound reverie, from which he was only roused by the cuts at his father.

He bore them as long as he could; and, when he could contain himself no longer, he began, with a certain wildness of expression which gave a peculiar interest to what he uttered: "His back's mighty bad off; but dod drot my sould[6] if he's put it to daddy as bad as he thinks he has, for old Kit's both blind and *deef*, I'll be dod drot if he eint!"

"The devil he is!" said Blossom.

"Yes, dod drot my soul if he *eint!*" You walk him, and see if he *eint*. His eyes don't look like it; but he's *jist as leve go agin the* house with you, or in a ditch, as anyhow. Now you go try him." The laugh was now turned on Blossom, and many rushed to test the fidelity of the little boy's report. A few experiments established its truth beyond controversy.

"Neddy," said the old man, "you oughtn't to try and make people discontented with their things. Stranger, don't mind what the little boy says. If you can only get Kit rid of them little failings you'll find him all sorts of a horse. You are a *leetle* the best man at a horse-swap that ever I got hold of but don't fool away Kit. Come, Neddy, my son, let's be moving; the stranger seems to be getting snappish."

1835

JOHNSON JONES HOOPER: *From* Some Adventures of Captain Simon Suggs[1]

Chapter the Tenth. The Captain Attends a Camp-Meeting

Captain Suggs found himself as poor at the conclusion of the Creek war,[2] as he had been at its commencement. Although no "arbitrary," "despotic," "corrupt," and "unprincipled" judge had fined him a thousand dollars for his proclamation of martial law at

6. Euphemism for "God rot my soul."

1. *Some Adventures of Captain Simon Suggs* recalls the European picaresque tradition of the engaging rascal, present in writers ranging from Cervantes to Fielding and Smollett. But more closely the book derives from the actualities of the American frontier and Mississippi River life, which produced a roguish literature of oral anecdote. In the "flush times" of frontier Alabama, Suggs is so completely the rogue and the cheat that his wholehearted devotion to rascality is fundamentally comic. A little later Mark Twain, on the Mississippi, knew the same oral literature as Hooper, but there must be more than coincidence in the resemblance between his "King" and "Duke," in *Huckleberry Finn*, and the Captain Suggs of the camp-meeting episode, below. Hooper published a con-

siderable number of Suggs stories, and other frontier sketches, in periodicals, and was well known before he collected the volume of *Adventures* in 1845. The book was often reprinted, even as late as 1928. In the collection, the tales were given the loose continuity of picaresque biography, emphasizing Suggs's campaigns for political office—and of all imaginable offices, that of sheriff. The text reprinted here is that of the first edition.

2. The Creeks were a confederacy of Indian tribes in Alabama and Georgia. Traditional allies of the English against the oppressive Spanish colonists, they gave the Americans trouble after the war with the British in 1812. Sugg's "exploits" against the Creeks were the subject of the previous chapter.

Fort Suggs, or the enforcement of its rules in the case of Mrs. Haycock; yet somehow—the thing is alike inexplicable to him and to us—the money which he had contrived, by various shifts to obtain, melted away and was gone for ever. To a man like the Captain, of intense domestic affections, this state of destitution was most distressing. "He could stand it himself—didn't care a d——n for it, no way," he observed, "but the old woman and the children; *that* bothered him!"

As he sat one day, ruminating upon the unpleasant condition of his "financial concerns," Mrs. Suggs informed him that "the sugar and coffee was nigh about out," and that there were not "a dozen j'ints and middlins, *all put together*, in the smoke-house." Suggs bounced up on the instant, exclaiming, "D——n it! *somebody* must suffer!" But whether this remark was intended to convey the idea that he and his family were about to experience the want of the necessaries of life; or that some other, and as yet unknown, individual should "suffer" to prevent that prospective exigency, must be left to the commentators, if perchance any of that ingenious class of persons should hereafter see proper to write notes for this history. It is enough for us that we give all the facts in this connection, so that ignorance of the subsequent conduct of Captain Suggs may not lead to an erroneous judgment in respect to his words.

Having uttered the exclamation we have repeated—and perhaps, hurriedly walked once or twice across the room—Captain Suggs drew on his famous old green-blanket overcoat, and ordered his horse, and within five minutes was on his way to a camp-meeting, then in full blast on Sandy creek, twenty miles distant, where he hoped to find amusement, at least. When he arrived there, he found the hollow square of the encampment filled with people, listening to the mid-day sermon and its dozen accompanying "exhortations." A half-dozen preachers were dispensing the word; the one in the pulpit, a meek-faced old man, of great simplicity and benevolence. His voice was weak and cracked, notwithstanding which, however, he contrived to make himself heard occasionally, above the din of the exhorting, the singing, and the shouting which were going on around him. The rest were walking to and fro (engaged in the other exercises we have indicated) among the "mourners"—a host of whom occupied the seat set apart for their especial use—or made personal appeals to the mere spectators. The excitement was intense. Men and women rolled about on the ground, or lay sobbing or shouting in promiscuous heaps. More than all, the negroes sang and screamed and prayed. Several, under the influence of what is technically called "the jerks," were plunging and pitching about with convulsive energy. The great object of all seemed to be, to see who could make the greatest noise—

> "And each—for madness ruled the hour—
> Would try his own expressive power."[3]

"Bless my poor old soul!" screamed the preacher in the pulpit; "ef yonder aint a squad in that corner that we aint got one outen yet! It'll never do"—raising his voice—"you must come outen that! Brother Fant, fetch up that youngster in the blue coat! I see the Lord's a-workin' upon him! Fetch him along—glory yes!—hold to him!"

"Keep the thing warm!" roared a sensual seeming man, of stout mould and florid countenance, who was exhorting among a bevy of young women, upon whom he was lavishing caresses. "Keep the thing warm, breethring!—come to the Lord, honey!" he added, as he vigorously hugged one of the damsels he sought to save.

"Oh, I've got him!" said another in exulting tones, as he led up a gawky youth among the mourners—"I've got him—he tried to git off, but—ha! Lord!"—shaking his head as much as to say, it took a smart fellow to escape him—"ha! Lord!"—and he wiped the perspiration from his face with one hand, and with the other, patted his neophyte on the shoulder—"he couldn't do it! No! Then he tried to argy wi' me—but bless the Lord!—he couldn't do that nother! Ha! Lord! I tuk him, fust in the Old Testament— bless the Lord!—and I argyed him all thro' Kings—then I throwed him into Proverbs—and from that, here we had it up and down, kleer down to the New Testament, and then I begun to see it work him!—then we got into Matthy, and from Matthy right straight along to Acts; and *thar* I throwed him! Y-e-s L-o-r-d!"—assuming the nasal twang and high pitch which are, in some parts, considered the perfection of rhetorical art—"Y-e-s L-o-r-d! and h-e-r-e he is! Now g-i-t down thar," addressing the subject, "and s-e-e ef the L-o-r-d won't do somethin' f-o-r you!" Having thus deposited his charge among the mourners, he started out, summarily to convert another soul!

"Gl-o-*ree*!" yelled a huge, greasy negro woman, as in a fit of the jerks, she threw herself convulsively from her feet, and fell "like a thousand of bricks," across a diminutive old man in a little round hat, who was speaking consolation to one of the mourners.

"Good Lord, have mercy!" ejaculated the little man earnestly and unaffectedly, as he strove to crawl from under the sable mass which was crushing him.

---

3. From "The Passions" (1747), one of the best-known odes of William Collins (1721–1759), a British preromantic poet.

In another part of the square a dozen old women were singing. They were in a state of absolute extasy, as their shrill pipes gave forth,

> "I rode on the sky,
> Quite ondestified[4] I,
> And the moon it was under my feet!"

Near these last, stood a delicate woman in that hysterical condition in which the nerves are incontrollable, and which is vulgarly —and almost blasphemously—termed the "holy laugh." A hideous grin distorted her mouth, and was accompanied with a maniac's chuckle; while every muscle and nerve of her face twitched and jerked in horrible spasms.[5]

Amid all this confusion and excitement Suggs stood unmoved. He viewed the whole affair as a grand deception—a sort of "opposition line" running against his own, and looked on with a sort of professional jealousy. Sometimes he would mutter running comments upon what passed before him.

"Well, now," said he, as he observed the full-faced brother who was "officiating," among the women, "that ere feller takes *my* eye! —thar he's been this half-hour, a-figurin amongst them galls, and's never said the fust word to nobody else. Wonder what's the reason these here preachers never hugs up the old, ugly women? Never seed one do it in my life—the sperrit never moves 'em that way! It's nater tho'; and the women, *they* never flocks round one o' the old dried-up breethring—bet two to one old splinter-legs thar,"— nodding at one of the ministers—"won't git a chance to say turkey to a good-lookin gall to-day! Well! who blames 'em? Nater will be nater, all the world over; and I judge ef I was a preacher, I should save the purtiest souls fust, myself!"

While the Captain was in the middle of this conversation with himself, he caught the attention of the preacher in the pulpit, who inferring from an indescribable something about his appearance that he was a person of some consequence, immediately determined to add him at once to the church if it could be done; and to that end began a vigorous, direct personal attack.

"Breethring," he exclaimed, "I see yonder a man that's a sinner;

---

4. An example of the picturesque word coinage of the American frontier; here a combination of "unsanctified" with "predestined."

5. "The reader is requested to bear in mind, that the scenes described in this chapter are not *now* to be witnessed. Eight or ten years ago, all classes of population of the Creek country were very different from what they now are. Of course, no disrespect is intended to any denomination of Christians. We believe that camp-meetings are not peculiar to any church, though most usual in the Methodist—a denomination whose respectability in Alabama is attested by the fact, that *very many* of its worthy clergymen and lay members, hold honourable and profitable offices in the gift of the state legislature; of which, indeed, almost a controlling portion are themselves Methodists" [Hooper's note].

I *know* he's a sinner! Thar he stands," pointing at Simon, "a mis-subble old crittur, with his head a-blossomin for the grave! A few more short years, and d-o-w-n he'll go to perdition, lessen the Lord have mer-cy on him! Come up here, you old hoary-headed sinner, a-n-d git down upon your knees, a-n-d put up your cry for the Lord to snatch you from the bottomless pit! Your're ripe for the devil—you're b-o-u-n-d for hell, and the Lord only knows what'll become on you!"

"D——n it," thought Suggs, "*ef* I only had you down in the krick swamp for a minit or so, *I'd* show you who's *old! I'd* alter your tune *mighty* sudden, you sassy, 'saitful[6] old rascal!'" But he judiciously held his tongue and gave no utterance to the thought.

The attention of many having been directed to the Captain by the preacher's remarks, he was soon surrounded by numerous well-meaning, and doubtless very pious persons, each one of whom seemed bent on the application of his own particular recipe for the salvation of souls. For a long time the Captain stood silent, or answered the incessant stream of exhortation only with a sneer; but at length, his countenance began to give token of inward emotion. First his eye-lids twitched—then his upper lip quivered—next a transparent drop formed on one of his eyelashes and a similar one on the tip of his nose—and, at last, a sudden bursting of air from nose and mouth, told that Captain Suggs was overpowered by his emotions. At the moment of the explosion, he made a feint as if to rush from the crowd, but he was in experienced hands, who well knew that the battle was more than half won.

"Hold to him!" said one—"it's a-working in him as strong as a Dick horse!"

"Pour it into him," said another, "it'll all come right directly!"

"That's the way I love to see 'em do," observed a third; "when you begin to draw water from their eyes, taint gwine to be long afore you'll have 'em on their knees!"

And so they clung to the Captain manfully, and half dragged, half led him to the mourner's bench; by which he threw himself down, altogether unmanned, and bathed in tears. Great was the rejoicing of the brethren, as they sang, shouted, and prayed around him—for by this time it had come to be generally known that the "convicted" old man was Captain Simon Suggs, the very "chief of sinners" in all that region.

The Captain remained grovelling in the dust during the usual time, and gave vent to even more than the requisite number of sobs, and groans, and heart-piercing cries. At length, when the proper time had arrived, he bounced up, and with a face radiant with joy commenced a series of vaultings and tumblings, which

6. Deceitful.

"laid in the shade" all previous performances of the sort at that camp-meeting. The brethren were in extasies at this demonstrative evidence of completion of the work; and whenever Suggs shouted "Gloree!" at the top of his lungs, every one of them shouted it back, until the woods rang with echoes.

The effervescence having partially subsided, Suggs was put upon his pins to relate his experience, which he did somewhat in this style—first brushing the tear-drops from his eyes, and giving the end of his nose a preparatory wring with his fingers, to free it of the superabundant moisture:

"Friends," he said, "it don't take long to curry a short horse, accordin' to the old saying', and I'll give you the perticklers of the way I was brought to a knowledge"—here the Captain wiped his eyes, brushed the tip of his nose and snuffled a little—"in less'n no time."

"Praise the Lord!" ejaculated a bystander.

"You see I come here full o' romancin' and devilment, and jist to make game of all the purceedins. Well, sure enough, I done so for some time, and was a-thinkin how I should play some trick——"

"Dear soul alive! *don't* he talk sweet!" cried an old lady in black silk—"Whar's John Dobbs? You Sukey!" screaming at a negro woman on the other side of the square—"ef you don't hunt up your mass John in a minute, and have him here to listen to this 'sperience, I'll tuck you up when I git home and give you a hundred and fifty lashes, madam!—see ef I don't! Blessed Lord!"—referring again to the Captain's relation—"aint it a *precious* 'scource!"[7]

"I was jist a-thinkin' how I should play some trick to turn it all into redecule, when they began to come round me and talk. Long at fust I didn't mind it, but arter a little that brother"—pointing to the reverend gentleman who had so successfully carried the un-believer through the Old and New Testaments, and who Simon was convinced was the "big dog of the tanyard"—"that brother spoke a word that struck me kleen to the heart, and run all over me, like fire in dry grass——"

"I-I-I can bring 'em!" cried the preacher alluded to, in a tone of exultation—"Lord thou knows ef thy servant can't stir 'em up, no-body else needn't try—but the glory aint mine! I'm a poor worrum of the dust," he added, with ill-managed affectation.

"And so from that I felt somethin' a-pullin' me inside——"

"Grace! grace! nothin' but grace!" exclaimed one; meaning that "grace" had been operating in the Captain's gastric region.[8]

"And then," continued Suggs, "I wanted to git off, but they hilt me, and bimeby I felt so missuble, I had to go yonder"—pointing

7. Discourse.
8. The object of the camp-meeting "revival" was conversion—the recognition of grace, the divine love of God extended to fallen man.

to the mourners' seat—"and when I lay down thar it got wuss and wuss, and 'peared like somethin' was a-mashin' down on my back——"

"That was his load o' sin," said one of the brethren—"never mind, it'll tumble off presently, see ef it don't!" and he shook his head professionally and knowingly.

"And it kept a-gittin heavier and heavier, ontwell it looked like it might be a four year old steer, or a big pine log, or somethin' of that sort——"

"Glory to my soul," shouted Mrs. Dobbs, "it's the sweetest talk I *ever* hearn! You Sukey! aint you got John yit? Never mind, my lady, I'll settle wi' you!" Sukey quailed before the finger which her mistress shook at her.

"And arter awhile," Suggs went on, "'peared like I fell into a trance, like, and I seed——"

"Now we'll git the good on it" cried one of the sanctified.

"And I seed the biggest, longest, rip-roarenest, blackest, scaliest—" Captain Suggs paused, wiped his brow, and ejaculated "Ah, L-o-r-d!" so as to give full time for curiosity to become impatience to know what he saw.

"*Sarpent!* warn't it?" asked one of the preachers.

"No, not a sarpent," replied Suggs, blowing his nose.

"Do tell us *what* it war, soul alive!—whar *is* John?" said Mrs. Dobbs.

"Allegator!" said the Captain.

"Alligator!" repeated every woman present, and screamed for very life.

Mrs. Dobbs' nerves were so shaken by the announcement, that after repeating the horrible word, she screamed to Sukey, "You Sukey, I say, you Su-u-ke-e-y! ef you let John come a-nigh this way, whar the dreadful alliga—shaw! what am I thinkin' 'bout? 'Twarn't nothin' but a vishin!"

"Well," said the Captain in continuation, "the allegator kept a-comin' and a-comin' to'ards me, with his great long jaws a-gapin' open like a ten-foot pair o' tailors' shears——"

"Oh! oh! oh! Lord! gracious above!" cried the women.

"SATAN!" was the laconic ejaculation of the oldest preacher present, who thus informed the congregation that it was the devil which had attacked Suggs in the shape of an alligator.

"And then I concluded the jig was up, 'thout I could block his game some way; for I seed his idee was to snap off my head——"

The women screamed again.

"So I fixed myself jist like I was purfectly willin' for him to take my head, and rather he'd do it as not"—here the women shuddered perceptibly—"and so I hilt my head straight out"—the Captain illustrated by elongating his neck—"and when he come up and was a gwine to *shet down* on it, I jist pitched in a big rock which choked him to death, and that minit I felt the weight slide off, and I had the best feelins—sorter like you'll have from *good* sperrits— any body ever had!"

"Didn't I *tell* you so? Didn't I *tell* you so?" asked the brother who had predicted the off-tumbling of the load of sin. "Ha, Lord! fool *who?* I've been *all* along thar!—yes, *all along thar!* and I know every inch of the way jist as good as I do the road home!" and then he turned round and round, and looked at all, to receive a silent tribute to his superior penetration.

Captain Suggs was now the "lion of the day." Nobody could pray so well, or exhort so movingly, as "brother Suggs." Nor did his natural modesty prevent the performance of appropriate exercises. With the reverend Bela Bugg (him to whom, under providence, he ascribed his conversion) he was a most especial favourite. They walked, sang, and prayed together for hours.

"Come, come up; thar's room for all!" cried brother Bugg, in his evening exhortation. "Come to the 'seat,' and ef you won't pray yourselves, let *me* pray for you!"

"Yes!" said Simon, by way of assisting his friend; "it's a game that all can win at! Ante up! ante up, boys—friends, I mean— don't back out!"

"Thar aint a sinner here," said Bugg, "no matter ef his soul's black as a nigger, but what thar's room for him!"

"No matter what sort of a hand you've got," added Simon in the fulness of his benevolence; "take stock! Here am *I*, the wickedest and blindest of sinners—has spent my whole life in the sarvice of the devil—has now come in on *narry pair* and won a *pile!*" and the Captain's face beamed with holy pleasure.

"D-o-n-'t be afeard!" cried the preacher; "come along! the meanest won't be turned away! humble yourselves and come!"

"No!" said Simon, still indulging in his favourite style of metaphor; "the bluff game aint played here! No runnin' of a body off! every body holds four aces, and when you bet, you win!"

And thus the Captain continued, until the services were concluded, to assist in adding to the number at the mourners' seat; and up to the hour of retiring, he exhibited such enthusiasm in the cause, that he was unanimously voted to be the most efficient addition the church had made during that meeting.

The next morning, when the preacher of the day first entered the pulpit, he announced that "brother Simon Suggs," mourning over his past iniquities, and desirous of going to work in the cause as speedily as possible, would take up a collection to found a church in his own neighborhood, at which he hoped to make himself useful as soon as he could prepare himself for the ministry, which the preacher didn't doubt, would be in a very few weeks, as brother Suggs was "a man of mighty good *judgment,* and of a *great discorse.*" The funds were to be collected by "brother Suggs," and held in trust by brother Bela Bugg, who was the financial officer of the circuit, until some arrangement could be made to build a suitable house.

"Yes, breethring," said the Captain, rising to his feet; "I want to start a little 'sociation close to me, and I want you all to help. I'm mighty poor myself, as poor as any of you—don't leave breethring"—observing that several of the well-to-do were about to go off—"don't leave; ef you aint able to afford any thing, jist give us your blessin' and it'll be all the same!"

This insinuation did the business, and the sensitive individuals re-seated themselves.

"It's mighty little of this world's goods I've got," resumed Suggs, pulling off his hat and holding it before him; "but I'll bury *that* in the cause any how," and he deposited his last five-dollar bill in the hat.

There was a murmur of approbation at the Captain's liberality throughout the assembly.

Suggs now commenced collecting, and very prudently attacked first the gentlemen who had shown a disposition to escape. These, to exculpate themselves from any thing like poverty, contributed handsomely.

"Look here, breethring," said the Captain, displaying the banknotes thus received, "brother Snooks has drapt a five wi' me, and brother Snodgrass a ten! In course 'taint expected that you *that aint as well off as them,* will give *as much;* let every one give *accordin'* to ther means."

This was another chain-shot that raked as it went! "Who so low" as not to be able to contribute as much as Snooks and Snodgrass?

"Here's all the *small* money I've got about me," said a burly old fellow, ostentatiously handing to Suggs, over the heads of a half dozen, a ten dollar bill.

"That's what I call maganimus!" exclaimed the Captain; "that's the way *every* rich man ought to do!"

These examples were followed, more or less closely, by almost all present, for Simon had excited the pride of purse of the congregation, and a very handsome sum was collected in a very short time.

The reverend Mr. Bugg, as soon as he observed that our hero had obtained all that was to be had at that time, went to him and inquired what amount had been collected. The Captain replied that it was still uncounted, but that it couldn't be much under a hundred.

"Well, brother Suggs, you'd better count it and turn it over to me now. I'm goin' to leave presently."

"No!" said Suggs—"can't do it!"

"Why?—what's the matter?" inquired Bugg.

"It's got to be *prayed over*, fust!" said Simon, a heavenly smile illuminating his whole face.

"Well," replied Bugg, "less go one side and do it!"

"No!" said Simon, solemnly.

Mr. Bugg gave a look of inquiry,

"You see that krick swamp?" asked Suggs—"I'm gwine down in *thar*, and I'm gwine to lay this money down *so*"—showing how he would place it on the ground—"and I'm gwine to git on these here knees"—slapping the right one—"and I'm *n-e-v-e-r* gwine to quit the grit ontwell I feel it's got the blessin'! And nobody aint got to be thar but me!"

Mr. Bugg greatly admired the Captain's fervent piety, and bidding him God-speed, turned off.

Captain Suggs "struck for" the swamp sure enough, where his horse was already hitched. "Ef them fellers aint done to a cracklin'," he muttered to himself as he mounted, "*I'll* never bet on two pair agin! They're peart at the snap game, theyselves; but they're badly lewed[9] this hitch! Well, Live and let live is a good old motter, and it's my sentiments adzactly!" And giving the spur to his horse, off he cantered.

1845

GEORGE WASHINGTON HARRIS:
From Sut Lovingood's Yarns[1]

Sicily Burns's Wedding

"HEY GE-ORGE!" rang among the mountain slopes; and looking up to my left, I saw "Sut," tearing along down a steep point, heading me off, in a long kangaroo lope, holding his flask high above his head, and hat in hand. He brought up near me, banter-

9. Brought low or outwitted.

1. In *Sut Lovingood's Yarns* the early humor of the South reached its highest level before Mark Twain and Joel Chandler Harris. Although some of the sketches were first printed in periodicals, the book has the anecdotal continuity of the picaresque novel, made familiar in English by Fielding and Smollett. Here literary analogies cease, for Sut rises from the soil of Tennessee like a folk hero, and indeed represents Harris' summation of the mountain legendry of his beloved simple neighbors among "the knobs of Old Knox." But the coarse and earthy anecdotes somehow blend with the unearthly fantasy that the visitor still finds in the scenery of the Great Smokies, and this is the way of all genuine folk legend. Harris caught not only the stamp of character and the pace of incident, but also the indigenous luxuriance of language on this frontier, almost Elizabethan in its combination of the precise with the extravagant. Like Simon Suggs, Sut is a rogue and a wastrel, but Suggs is merely comic, while Sut is also lovable in the Falstaffian sense.

ingly shaking the half-full "tickler," within an inch of my face.

"Whar am yu gwine? take a suck, hoss? This yere truck's *ole*. I kotch hit myse'f, hot this mornin frum the still wum.[2] Nara durn'd bit ove strike-nine[3] in hit—I put that ar piece ove burnt dried peach in myse'f tu gin hit color—better nur ole Bullen's plan: he puts in tan ooze, in what he sells, an' when that haint handy, he uses the red warter outen a pon' jis' below his barn;—makes a pow'ful natral color, but don't help the taste much. Then he corrects that wif red pepper; hits an orful mixtry, that whisky ole Bullen makes; no wonder he seed 'Hell-sarpints.' He's pisent ni ontu three quarters ove the b'levin parts ove his congregashun wif hit, an' tuther quarter he's sot intu ruff stealin an' cussin. Ef his still-'ous don't burn down, ur he peg out hisse'f, the neighborhood am ruinated a-pas' salvashun. Haint he the durndes sampil ove a passun[4] yu ever seed enyhow?

"Say George, du yu see these yere well-poles what I uses fur laigs? Yu sez yu sees em, dus yu?"

"Yes."

"Very well; I passed 'em a-pas' each uther tuther day, right peart. I put one out a-head jis' so, an' then tuther 'bout nine feet a-head ove hit agin jis' so, an' then kep on a-duin hit. I'll jis' gin yu leave tu go tu the devil ha'f hamon,[5] ef I didn't make fewer tracks tu the mile, an' more tu the minit, than wer ever made by eny human man body, since Bark Wilson beat the saw-log frum the top ove the Frog Mountin intu the Oconee River, an' dove, an' dodged hit at las'. I hes allers look'd ontu that performince ove Bark's as onekel'd in histery, allers givin way tu dad's ho'net race, however.

"George, every livin thing hes hits pint, a pint ove sum sort. Ole Bullen's pint is a durn'ed fust rate, three bladed, dubbil barril'd, warter-proof, hypockracy, an' a never-tirein appertite fur bal'face.[6] Sicily Burns's pint am tu drive men folks plum crazy, an' then bring em too agin. Gin em a rale Orleans fever in five minits, an' then in five minits more, gin them a Floridy ager.[7] Durn her, she's down on her heels flat-footed now. Dad's pint is tu be king ove all durn'd fools, ever since the day ove that feller what cribb'd up so much co'n down in Yegipt,[8] long time ago, (he run outen his coat yu minds.) The Bibil tells us hu wer the stronges' man—hu wer

---

2. Still worm; the curled tube condenser in a whisky still.
3. A popular plug tobacco. Of the other alternatives that Sut rejected (below) for coloring his whisky, "tan ooze" would be the liquor from tanning hides, and "red warter" the cedar water from a swamp.
4. Parson.
5. Probably Haman, whose biblical story, then familiar, made his name the byword for a scamp.

6. The colloquialism "a bald-face lie," was often abbreviated as the noun "bald-face."
7. Ague, malaria.
8. Egypt. In the following passage Sut gives a new interpretation of Joseph, as the Bible's "bigges' durn fool"—whether for resisting the seduction of Potiphar's wife, or leaving his "coat" behind for her "evidence" in accusing him is not clear. *Cf.* Genesis xxxix: 7–20.

the bes' man—hu wer the meekis' man, an' hu the wises' man, but leaves yu tu guess hu wer the bigges' fool.

"Well eny man what cudent guess arter readin that ar scrimmage wif an' 'oman 'bout the coat, haint sense enuf tu run intu the hous', ef hit wer rainin ded cats, that's all. Mam's pint am in kitchen insex, baking hoe-cake, bilin greens, an' runnin bar laiged.[9] My pint am in takin aboard big skeers, an' then beatin enbody's hoss, ur skared dorg, a-runnin frum onder em agin. I used tu think my pint an' dad's wer jis' the same, sulky, unmix'd king durn'd fool; but when he acted hoss, an' mistook hossflies fur ho'nets, I los' heart. Never mine, when I gits his 'sperence, I may be king fool, but yet great golly, he gets frum bad tu wus, monstrus fas'.

"Now ef a feller happens tu know what his pint am, he kin allers git along, sumhow, purvided he don't swar away his liberty tu a temprins s'ciety, live tu fur frum a still-'ous, an' too ni a chu'ch ur a jail. Them's my sentimints on 'pints,'—an' yere's my sentimints ontu folks: Men wer made a-purpus jis' tu eat, drink, an' fur stayin awake in the yearly part ove the nites: an' wimen wer made tu cook the vittils, mix the sperits, an' help the men du the stayin awake. That's all, an' nuthin more, onless hits fur the wimen tu raise the devil atwix meals, an' knit socks atwix drams, an' the men tu play short kerds, swap hosses wif fools, an' fite fur exersise, at odd spells.

"George, yu don't onderstan life yet scarcely at all, got a heap tu larn, a heap. But 'bout my swappin my laigs so fas'—these yere very par ove laigs. I hed got about a fox squirril skin full ove biled co'n juice packed onder my shut, an' onder my hide too, I mout es well add, an' wer aimin fur Bill Carr's on foot. When I got in sight ove ole man Burns's, I seed ni ontu fifty hosses an' muels hitch'd tu the fence. Durnatshun! I jis' then tho't ove hit, 'twer Sicily's wedding day. She married ole Clapshaw, the suckit-rider.[1] The very feller hu's faith gin out when he met me sendin sody[2] all over creashun. Suckit-riders am surjestif things tu me. They preaches agin me, an' I hes no chance tu preach back at them. Ef I cud I'd make the institushun behave hitsef better nur hit dus. They hes sum wunderful pints, George. Thar am two things nobody never seed: wun am a dead muel, an' tuther is a suckit-rider's grave. Kaze why, the he muels all turn intu old field school-masters, an' the she ones intu strong minded wimen, an' then when thar time cums, they dies sorter like uther folks. An' the suckit-riders ride intil they marry; ef they marrys money, they turns intu store-keepers, swaps hosses, an' stays away ove colleckshun Sundays. Them what marrys, an' by sum orful mistake *misses the money*, jis' turns intu polertishuns, sells 'ile well stock,' an' dies sorter in the human way too.

---

9. Barelegged.
1. Circuit rider. An itinerant preacher on an established "circuit."

2. Soda. Referring to a previous episode in which he doused Clapshaw and Sicily with soda water.

"But 'bout the wedding. Ole Burns hed a big black an' white bull, wif a ring in his snout, an' the rope tied up roun his ho'ns. They rid 'im tu mill, an' sich like wif a saddil made outen two dorgwood forks, an' two clapboards, kivered wif a ole piece ove carpet, rope girth, an' rope stirrups wif a loop in hit fur the foot. Ole 'Sock,' es they call'd the bull, hed jis' got back from mill, an' wer turn'd into the yard, saddil an' all, tu solace hissef a-pickin grass. I wer slungin roun the outside ove the hous', fur they hedn't hed the manners tu ax me in, when they sot down tu dinner. I wer pow'fully hurt 'bout hit, an' happen'd tu think—SODY.[3] So I sot in a-watchin fur a chance tu du sumthin. I fus' tho't I'd shave ole Clapshaw's hoss's tail, go tu the stabil an' shave Sicily's mare's tail, an' ketch ole Burns out, an' shave his tail too. While I wer a-studyin 'bout this, ole Sock wer a-nosin 'roun, an' cum up ontu a big baskit what hilt a littil shattered co'n; he dipp'd in his head tu git hit, an' I slipp'd up an' jerked the handil over his ho'ns.

"Now, George, ef yu knows the nater ove a cow brute, they is the durndes' fools amung all the beastes, ('scept the Lovingoods); when they gits intu tribulashun, they knows nuffin but tu shot thar eyes, beller, an' back, an' keep a-backin. Well, when ole Sock raised his head an' foun hissef in darkness, he jis' twisted up his tail, snorted the shatter'd co'n outen the baskit, an' made a tremenjus lunge agin the hous'. I hearn the picters a-hangin agin the wall on the inside a-fallin. He fotch a deep loud rusty beller, mout been hearn a mile, an' then sot intu a onendin sistem ove backin. A big craw-fish wif a hungry coon a-reachin fur him, wer jus' nowhar. Fust agin one thing, then over anuther, an' at las' agin the bee-bainch, knockin hit an' a dozen stan[4] ove bees heads over heels, an' then stompin back'ards thru the mess. Hit haint much wuf while tu tell what the bees did, ur how soon they sot intu duin hit. They am pow'ful quick-tempered littil critters, enyhow. The air wer dark wif 'em, an' Sock wer kivered all over, frum snout tu tail, so clost yu cudent a-sot down a grain ove wheat fur bees, an' they were a-fitin one another in the air, fur a place on the bull. The hous' stood on sidelin groun, an' the back door wer even wif hit. So Sock happen tu hit hit plum, jis' backed into the hous' onder 'bout two hundred an' fifty pouns ove steam, bawlin orful, an' every snort he fotch he snorted away a quart ove bees ofen his sweaty snout. He wer the leader ove the bigges' an' the madest army ove bees in the worild. Thar wer at leas' five solid bushels ove 'em. They hed filled the baskit, an' hed lodged ontu his tail, ten deep, ontil hit were es thick es a waggin tung.[5] He hed hit stuck strait up in the air, an' hit looked adzackly like a dead pine kivered wif ivey.

3. Here the memory of a former prank suggests another.
4. Stands, or hives, of bees.
5. Wagon tongue, the shaft between the horses.

I think he wer the hottes' and wus hurtin bull then livin; his temper, too, seemed tu be pow'fully flustrated. Ove *all* the durn'd times an' kerryins on yu *ever* hearn tell on wer thar an' thar abouts. He cum tail fust agin the ole two story Dutch clock, an' fotch hit, bustin hits runnin geer outen hit, the littil wheels a-trundlin over the floor, an' the bees even chasin them. Nex pass, he fotch up agin the foot ove a big dubbil ingine bedstead, rarin hit on aind, an' punchin one ove the posts thru a glass winder. The nex tail fus' experdishun wer made aginst the cati-corner'd cupboard, outen which he made a perfeck momox.[6] Fus' he upsot hit, smashin in the glass doors, an' then jis sot in an' stomp'd everything on the shelves intu giblits, a-tryin tu back furder in that direckshun, an' tu git the bees ofen his laigs.

"Pickil crocks, preserves jars, vinegar jugs, seed bags, yarb bunches, paragorick bottils, aig baskits, an' delf war—all mix'd dam permiskusly, an' not worth the sortin, by a duller an' a 'alf. Nex he got a far back acrost the room agin the board pertishun; he went thru hit like hit hed been paper, takin wif him 'bout six foot squar ove hit in splinters, an' broken boards, intu the nex room, whar they wer eatin dinner, an' rite yere the fitin becum gineral, an' the dancin, squawkin, cussin, an' dodgin begun.

"Clapshaw's ole mam wer es deaf es a dogiron,[7] an sot at the aind ove the tabil, nex tu whar ole Sock busted thru the wall; tail fus' he cum agin her cheer, ahistin her an' hit ontu the tabil. Now, the smashin ove delf, an' the mixin ove vittils begun. They hed sot severil tabils tugether tu make hit long enuf. So he jis' rolled 'em up a-top ove one anuther, an' thar sot ole Missis Clapshaw, a-straddil ove the top ove the pile, a-fitin bees like a mad wind-mill, wif her calliker cap in one han, fur a wepun, an' a cract frame in tuther, an' a-kickin, an' a-spurrin like she wer ridin a lazy hoss arter the doctor, an' a-screamin rape, fire, an' murder, es fas' es she cud name 'em over.

"Taters, cabbige, meat, soup, beans, sop, dumplins, an' the truck what yu wallers 'em in; milk, plates, pies, puddins, an' every durn fixin yu cud think ove in a week, wer thar, mix'd an' mashed, like hit had been thru a thrashin-meesheen. Ole Sock still kep a-backin, an' backed the hole pile, ole 'oman an' all, also sum cheers, outen the frunt door, an' down seven steps intu the lane, an' then by golly, turn'd a fifteen hundred poun summerset hissef arter em, lit a-top ove the mix'd up mess, flat ove his back, an' then kicked hissef ontu his feet agin. About the time he ris, ole man Burns—yu know how fat, an' stumpy, an' cross-grained he is, enyhow—made a vigrus mad snatch at the baskit, an' got a savin holt ontu hit, but cudent

6. Usually "mommix"; dialect term for "a mess."

7. A lumberman's tool for rolling logs; *cf.* the peavey.

let go quick enuf; fur ole Sock jis' snorted, bawled, an' histed the
ole cuss heels fust up intu the air, an' he lit on the bull's back, an'
hed the baskit in his han.

"Jis' es soon es ole Blackey got the use ove his eyes, he tore off
down the lane tu out-run the bees, so durn'd fas' that ole Burns
wer feard tu try tu git off. So he jus' socked his feet intu the rope
loops, an' then cummenc'd the durndes' bull-ride ever mortal man
ondertuck. Sock run atwix the hitched critters[8] an' the railfence, ole
Burns fust fitin him over the head wif the baskit tu stop him, an'
then fitin the bees wif hit. I'll jis' be durn'd ef I didn't think he
hed four ur five baskits, hit wer in so meny places at onst. Well,
Burns, baskit, an' bull, an' bees, skared every durn'd hoss an' muel
loose frum that fence—bees ontu all ove 'em, bees, by golly, every-
whar. Mos' on 'em, too, tuck a fence rail along, fas' tu the bridil
reins. Now I'll jis gin yu leave tu kiss my sister Sall till she squalls,
ef ever sich a sight wer seed ur sich noises hearn, es filled up that
long lane. A heavy cloud ove dus', like a harycane hed been blowin,
hid all the hosses, an' away abuv hit yu cud see tails, an' ainds ove
fence-rails a-flyin about; now an' then a par ove bright hine shoes
wud flash in the sun like two sparks, an' away ahead wer the baskit
a-sirklin roun an' about at randum. Brayin, nickerin, the bellerin
ove the bull, clatterin ove runnin hoofs, an' a mons'ous rushin soun,
made up the noise. Lively times in that lane jus' then, warn't thar?

"I swar ole Burns kin beat eny man on top ove the yeath[9] a-fitin
bees wif a baskit. Jis' set 'im a-straddil ove a mad bull, an' let thar
be bees enuf tu exhite the ole man, an' the man what beats him kin
break me. Hosses an' muels wer tuck up all over the county, an'
sum wer forever los'. Yu cudent go eny course, in a cirkil ove a
mile, an' not find buckils, stirrups, straps, saddil blankits, ur sumthin belongin tu a saddil hoss. Now don't forgit that about that
hous' thar wer a good time bein had ginerally. Fellers an' gals
loped outen windows, they rolled outen the doors in bunches, they
clomb the chimleys, they darted onder the house jis' tu dart out
agin, they tuck tu the thicket, they rolled in the wheat field, lay
down in the krick, did everything but stan still. Sum made a strait
run *fur* home, an' sum es strait a run *frum* home; livelyest folks I
ever did see. Clapshaw crawled onder a straw pile in the barn, an'
sot intu prayin—yu cud a-hearn him a mile—sumthin 'bout the
plagues ove Yegipt, an' the pains ove the secon death. I tell yu now
he lumbered.

"Sicily, she squatted in the cold spring, up tu her years,[1] an'
turn'd a milk crock over her head, while she were a drownin a mess
ove bees onder her coats.[2] I went tu her, an' sez I, 'Yu hes got an-

8. Creatures; the horses of the guests.
9. Earth.
1. Ears.
2. Petticoats.

uther new sensashun haint yu?' Sez she—

" 'Shet yer mouth, yu cussed fool!'

"Sez I, 'Power'ful sarchin feelin bees gins a body, don't they?'

" 'Oh, lordy, lordy, Sut, these yere 'bominabil insex is jis' burnin me up!'

" 'Gin 'em a mess ove SODY,' sez I, 'that'll cool 'em off, an' 'skeer the las' durn'd one ofen the place.'

"She lifted the crock, so she cud flash her eyes at me, an' sed, 'Yu go tu hell!' *jis es plain.* I thought, takin all things together, that p'raps I mout es well put the mountain atwix me an' that plantashun; an' I did hit.

"Thar warnt an' 'oman, ur a gal at that weddin, but what thar frocks, an' stockins wer too tite fur a week. Bees am wus on wimin than men, enyhow. They hev a farer chance at 'em. Nex day I passed ole Hawley's, an' his gal Betts wer sittin in the porch, wif a white hankerchef tied roun her jaws; her face wer es red es a beet, an' her eyebrows hung 'way over heavy. Sez I, 'Hed a fine time at the weddin, didn't yu?' 'Yu mus' be a durn'd fool,' wer every word she sed. I hadent gone a hundred yards, ontil I met Missis Brady, her hans fat, an' her ankils swelled ontil they shined. Sez she,—

" 'Whar yu gwine, Sut?'

" 'Bee huntin,' sez I.

" 'Yu jis' say bees agin, yu infunel gallinipper, an' I'll scab yer head wif a rock.'

"Now haint hit strange how tetchus they am, on the subjick ove bees?

"Ove all the durn'd misfortinit weddins ever since ole Adam married that heifer, what wer so fon' ove talkin tu snaix, an' eatin appils, down ontil now, that one ove Sicily's an' Clapshaw's wer the worst one fur noise, disappintment, skeer, breakin things, hurtin, trubbil, vexashun ove spirrit, an' gineral swellin. Why, George, her an' him cudent sleep together fur ni ontu a week, on account ove the doins ove them ar hot-footed, 'vengeful 'bominabil littil insex. They never will gee together, got tu bad a start, mine[3] what I tell yu. Yu haint time now tu hear how ole Burns finished his bull-ride, an' how I cum tu du that lofty, topliftical speciment ove fas' runnin. I'll tell yu all that, sum uther time. Ef eny ove 'em axes after me, tell 'em that I'm over in Fannin, on my way tu Dahlonega. They is huntin me tu kill me, I is fear'd.

"Hit am an orful thing, George, tu be a natral born durn'd fool. Yu'se never 'sperienced hit pussonally, hev yu? Hits made pow'fully agin our famerly, an all owin tu dad. I orter bust my head open agin a bluff ove rocks, an' jis' wud du hit, ef I warnt a cussed coward. All my yeathly 'pendence is in these yere laigs—

3. Mind.

d'ye see 'em? Ef they don't fail, I may turn human sum day, that is sorter human, enuf tu be a Squire or school commisiner. Ef I wer jis' es smart es I am mean, an' ornary, I'd be President ove a Wild Cat Bank in less nor a week. Is sperrits⁴ plenty over wif yu?"

1867

4. Spirits, whisky.

HENRY WADSWORTH LONGFELLOW
(1807–1882)

Longfellow was one of the most serious writers of his age, and although a poet, enormously popular. He combined considerable learning with an enlightened understanding of the people, and he expressed the lives and ideals of humbler Americans in poems that they could not forget. Amid the rising democracy of his day, Longfellow became the national bard. His more popular poems strongly reflected the optimistic sentiment and the love of a good lesson that characterized the humanitarian spirit of the people. Unfortunately for his reputation in the twentieth century, the surviving picture has been that of the gray old poet of "The Children's Hour," seated by the fireside in the armchair made from "the spreading chestnut tree," a present from the children of Cambridge. Recent criticism has again emphasized the other Longfellow, well known to more discerning readers of his own day as the poet of "The Saga of King Olaf" and *Christus*, the author of great ballads and of many sonnets and reflective lyrics remarkable for imaginative propriety and constructive skill. To be sure, the familiar spirit is always present in his work, and this is not the tradition admired today, but it too contributes to what in his writing is genuine, large, and enduring.

Longfellow was born in Portland, Maine, on February 27, 1807, into a family of established tradition and moderate means. He attended Portland Academy and was tutored for admission to nearby Bowdoin College, which he entered in the sophomore class, a fellow student of Hawthorne. Having published his first poem at thirteen, two years earlier, he dreamed of "future eminence in literature." Upon his graduation in 1825, he accepted a professorship of foreign languages at Bowdoin, which included a provision for further preparatory study abroad. He visited France, Spain, Italy, and Germany, returning to Bowdoin in the autumn of 1829. There he taught for six years, edited textbooks, and wrote articles on European literatures in the tradition of his profession. His reward was the offer of the Smith professorship at Harvard, which George Ticknor was vacating; and a leave of absence for further study of German. Meanwhile he had married

(1831), and published in the *New England Magazine* the travel sketches which appeared as his first volume, *Outre Mer*, in 1835. The twenty months abroad (1835–1836), increased Longfellow's knowledge of Germanic and Scandinavian literatures, soon to become a deep influence upon his writing.

His young wife died during the journey, in November, 1835. With renewed dedication to the combined responsibilities of teacher and creative writer, at the dawn of the well-named "flowering of New England," Longfellow soon became a leading figure among the writers and scholars of that region. Hawthorne was now an intimate friend. Within three years he entered upon the decade of remarkable production (1839–1849) which gave him national prominence and the affection of his countrymen.

Hyperion, a prose romance, and *Voices of the Night*, his first collection of poems, both appeared in 1839. *Ballads and Other Poems* (December, 1841, dated 1842), containing "The Skeleton in Armor," "The Wreck of the Hesperus," and "The Village Blacksmith," exactly expressed the popular spirit of the day. *Poems on Slavery* (1842) was followed by *The Spanish Student* (1843), his first large treatment of a foreign theme.

Of more importance was *The Belfry of Bruges and Other Poems* (1845, dated 1846). Such poems as "Nuremberg" illustrate how the poet familiarized untraveled Americans with the European scene and culture.

At the same time he was acquainting his countrymen with themselves in such poems as "The Arsenal at Springfield," "The Old Clock on the Stairs," and "The Arrow and the Song." His contribution to the epic of his country found its first large expression in *Evangeline* (1847), which aroused national enthusiasm for its pictorial vividness and narrative skill. *The Seaside and the Fireside* (1849, dated 1850) contained "The Building of the Ship," a powerful plea for national unity in the face of the mounting crises before the Civil War. Minor works of this period include a prose tale, *Kavanagh* (1849), and several anthologies of poetry and criticism.

After two decades of conflict between the writer and the teacher, he resigned his Harvard professorship to James Russell Lowell in 1854. But Craigie House, his home in Cambridge, remained no less a sort of literary capitol. Longfellow had lodged there on first going to Harvard, and it became his as a gift from Nathan Appleton, the Lowell industrialist whose daughter the poet had married in 1843.

In 1855, he published *The Song of Hiawatha*, based on American Indian legends, and in 1858 *The Courtship of Miles Standish*, which popularized the legend of Plymouth Colony. These poems gave him an impregnable position in the affections of his countrymen, and increased his already wide recognition abroad. It is to be remembered that his appeal for the common reader in England was as great as at home, and rivaled that of Tennyson; a bust of Longfellow, the only American so honored, occupies a niche in Westminster Abbey's Poets' Corner.

In 1861, his beloved Frances Appleton, reputed heroine of *Hyperion* and eighteen years his wife, was burned to death. His deep religious feeling and his reflective spirit, present in his work from the beginning, now became dominant. He bent his energies upon two large works, earlier begun and laid aside. To the translation of Dante's *Divine Comedy* he brought both a scholar's love and religious devotion. It appeared in three volumes (1865–1867), principally in unrimed triplets, and it long remained a useful translation, although in most respects not an inspired one. However, *Christus, A Mystery* (1872) reveals at many points his highest inspiration. *The Golden Legend*, a cycle of religious miracle plays, ultimately Part II of *Christus*, had appeared in 1851. He now added Part III, *The New England Tragedies* (1868), two fine closet dramas dealing with the Puritan themes of "John Endicott" and "Giles Corey." Part I, published in 1871 as *The Divine Tragedy*, dealt with Christ's life and Passion.

During these last twenty years the poet published several additional volumes, containing many of his most mature reflective lyrics. When *Tales of a Wayside Inn* appeared in 1863, his publishers prepared an unprecedented first edition of fifteen thousand copies. A second group of the *Tales* appeared in *Three*

Books of Song (1872), and a third in *Aftermath* (1873). These famous *Tales* ranged from the level of "Paul Revere's Ride" to "The Saga of King Olaf," a high point of accomplishment. Among other volumes were *Flower-de-Luce* (1867), in which the sonnets "Divina Commedia" appeared as a sequence; *The Masque of Pandora* (1875); *Keramos and Other Poems* (1878); *Ultima Thule* (1880); and *In the Harbor*, published in 1882, the year of his death.

Longfellow's lapses into didacticism and sentimentality reflected the flabbier romanticism of his age, but he has remained in the tradition and memory of the American people. Admiration for Longfellow today rests on his gift for narrative and his daring experiments in narrative verse, on his balladry, his popularization of the national epic, his naturalization of foreign themes and poetic forms, his ability to bring his erudition within the range of general understanding, his versatile and sensitive craftsmanship, and, perhaps beyond all else, on the large and endearing qualities of the man himself.

The standard text is the Riverside Edition of the *Complete Poetical and Prose Works*, 11 vols., edited by H. E. Scudder, 1886, with valuable notes, based in part on Samuel Longfellow's *Life*. The one-volume *Complete Poetical Works*, Cambridge Edition, 1893, is excellent, and available. More recent collections are the Craigie Edition, 11 vols., 1904, and the De Luxe Edition, 10 vols., 1909.

The Life of Henry Wadsworth Longfellow, 2 vols., 1886, by the poet's brother, Samuel Longfellow, is still the standard biography. The same author added a third volume, *Final Memorials*, in 1887. The best shorter biographies

Footprints, that perhaps another,
  Sailing o'er life's solemn main,
A forlorn and shipwrecked brother,
  Seeing, shall take heart again.

Let us, then, be up and doing,
  With a heart for any fate;
Still achieving, still pursuing,
  Learn to labor and to wait.

1838   1838, 1839

Hymn to the Night[3]

'Ασπασίη, τρίλλιστος

I heard the trailing garments of the Night
  Sweep through her marble halls!
I saw her sable skirts all fringed with light
  From the celestial walls!

I felt her presence, by its spell of might,
  Stoop o'er me from above;
The calm, majestic presence of the Night,
  As of the one I love.

I heard the sounds of sorrow and delight,
  The manifold, soft chimes,
That fill the haunted chambers of the Night,
  Like some old poet's rhymes.

From the cool cisterns of the midnight air
  My spirit drank repose;
The fountain of perpetual peace flows there,—
  From those deep cisterns flows.

O holy Night! from thee I learn to bear
  What man has borne before!
Thou layest thy finger on the lips of Care,
  And they complain no more.

Peace! Peace! Orestes-like[4] I breathe this prayer!
  Descend with broad-winged flight,

3. Written "in the summer of 1839," and published in December as the leading poem of the poet's first volume, *Voices of the Night*. The epigraph, translated "Welcome, thrice prayed for" (*cf.* l. 23), is from Homer's *Iliad*, Book VIII,

l. 488.
4. Orestes was pursued by the Furies for having killed his mother to avenge his father's murder. His discovery of "peace" is the subject of Aeschylus' *Eumenides*.

The welcome, the thrice-prayed for, the most fair,
The best-beloved Night!

1839   1839

The Wreck of the Hesperus[5]

It was the schooner Hesperus,
    That sailed the wintry sea;
And the skipper had taken his little daughtèr,
    To bear him company.

Blue were her eyes as the fairy-flax,   5
    Her cheeks like the dawn of day,
And her bosom white as the hawthorn buds,
    That ope in the month of May.

The skipper he stood beside the helm,
    His pipe was in his mouth,   10
And he watched how the veering flaw did blow
    The smoke now West, now South.

Then up and spake an old Sailòr,
    Had sailed to the Spanish Main,
"I pray thee, put into yonder port,   15
    For I fear a hurricane.

"Last night, the moon had a golden ring,
    And to-night no moon we see!"
The skipper, he blew a whiff from his pipe,
    And a scornful laugh laughed he.   20

Colder and louder blew the wind,
    A gale from the Northeast,
The snow fell hissing in the brine,
    And the billows frothed like yeast.

Down came the storm, and smote amain   25
    The vessel in its strength;
She shuddered and paused, like a frightened steed,
    Then leaped her cable's length.

"Come hither! come hither! my little daughtèr,
    And do not tremble so;   30

5. This is Longfellow's most successful effort—and one of the best in the language—to employ the traditional ballad form, with its simple construction, naïve sentiment, phrases from the common stock of folk tradition and superstition, and archaic rhymes. Written on December 30, 1839, it appeared in a newspaper before being collected in *Ballads and Other Poems*.

For I can weather the roughest gale
  That ever wind did blow."

He wrapped her warm in his seaman's coat
  Against the stinging blast;
He cut a rope from a broken spar,   35
  And bound her to the mast.

"O father! I hear the church-bells ring,
  Oh say, what may it be?"
" 'Tis a fog-bell on a rock-bound coast!"—
  And he steered for the open sea.   40

"O father! I hear the sound of guns,
  Oh say, what may it be?"
"Some ship in distress, that cannot live
  In such an angry sea!"

"O father! I see a gleaming light,   45
  Oh say, what may it be?"
But the father answered never a word,
  A frozen corpse was he.

Lashed to the helm, all stiff and stark,
  With his face turned to the skies,
The lantern gleamed through the gleaming snow   50
  On his fixed and glassy eyes.

Then the maiden clasped her hands and prayed
  That savèd she might be;
And she thought of Christ, who stilled the wave,
  On the Lake of Galilee.[6]   55

And fast through the midnight dark and drear,
  Through the whistling sleet and snow,
Like a sheeted ghost, the vessel swept
  Tow'rds the reef of Norman's Woe.   60

And ever the fitful gusts between
  A sound came from the land;
It was the sound of the trampling surf
  On the rocks and the hard sea-sand.

The breakers were right beneath her bows,   65
  She drifted a dreary wreck,
And a whooping billow swept the crew
  Like icicles from her deck.

She struck where the white and fleecy waves
  Looked soft as carded wool,   70

6. Matthew viii: 23–27.

But the cruel rocks, they gored her side
  Like the horns of an angry bull.

Her rattling shrouds, all sheathed in ice,
  With the masts went by the board;
Like a vessel of glass, she stove and sank,   75
  Ho! ho! the breakers roared!

At daybreak, on the bleak sea-beach,
  A fisherman stood aghast,
To see the form of a maiden fair,
  Lashed close to a drifting mast.   80

The salt sea was frozen on her breast,
  The salt tears in her eyes;
And he saw her hair, like the brown sea-weed,
  On the billows fall and rise.

Such was the wreck of the Hesperus,   85
  In the midnight and the snow!
Christ save us all from a death like this,
  On the reef of Norman's Woe!

1839   1841

The Skeleton in Armor[1]

"Speak! speak! thou fearful guest
Who, with thy hollow breast
Still in rude armor drest,
  Comest to daunt me!
Wrapt not in Eastern balms,   5
But with thy fleshless palms
Stretched, as if asking alms,
  Why dost thou haunt me?"

Then, from those cavernous eyes
Pale flashes seemed to rise,   10
As when the Northern skies
  Gleam in December;
And, like the water's flow

---

1. This, like "The Wreck of the Hesperus," is an experiment in balladry. Its sources are older, representing the rough, two-beat measures of the verse of the Old English, Icelandic, and Norse skalds, or poets (*cf.* l. 19), which Longfellow had been studying, and used again in "The Saga of King Olaf." The story was Longfellow's response to the debated theories that an ancient stone tower in Newport, and an "armored" skeleton unearthed and destroyed at Fall River, were relics of prehistoric Scandinavian settlement. Written in 1840, the poem appeared in the *Knickerbocker Magazine* for January, 1841, before being collected in *Ballads and Other Poems* that year.

Under December's snow,
Came a dull voice of woe
    From the heart's chamber.   15

"I was a Viking old!
My deeds, though manifold,
No Skald in song has told,
    No Saga taught thee!   20
Take heed, that in thy verse
Thou dost the tale rehearse,
Else dread a dead man's curse;
    For this I sought thee.

"Far in the Northern Land,   25
By the wild Baltic's strand,
I, with my childish hand,
    Tamed the gerfalcon;²
And, with my skates fast-bound,
Skimmed the half-frozen Sound,   30
That the poor whimpering hound
    Trembled to walk on.

"Oft to his frozen lair
Tracked I the grisly bear,
While from my path the hare   35
    Fled like a shadow;
Oft through the forest dark
Followed the were-wolf's bark,
Until the soaring lark
    Sang from the meadow.   40

"But when I older grew,
Joining a corsair's crew,
O'er the dark sea I flew
    With the marauders.
Wild was the life we led;   45
Many the souls that sped,
Many the hearts that bled,
    By our stern orders.

"Many a wassail-bout
Wore the long Winter out;   50
Often our midnight shout
    Set the cocks crowing,
As we the Berserk's³ tale

2. A large Arctic falcon used in hunting.

3. Berserkers were mythological Norse warriors of invulnerable fury in battle.

Measured in cups of ale,
Draining the oaken pail,
   Filled to o'erflowing.   55

"Once as I told in glee
Tales of the stormy sea,
Soft eyes did gaze on me,
   Burning yet tender;   60
And as the white stars shine
On the dark Norway pine,
On that dark heart of mine
   Fell their soft splendor.

"I wooed the blue-eyed maid,   65
Yielding, yet half afraid,
And in the forest's shade
   Our vows were plighted.
Under its loosened vest
Fluttered her little breast,   70
Like birds within their nest
   By the hawk frighted.

"Bright in her father's hall
Shields gleamed upon the wall,
Loud sang the minstrels all,   75
   Chanting his glory;
When of old Hildebrand
I asked his daughter's hand,
Mute did the minstrels stand.
   To hear my story.   80

"While the brown ale he quaffed,
Loud then the champion laughed,
And as the wind-gusts waft
   The sea-foam brightly,
So the loud laugh of scorn,   85
Out of those lips unshorn,
From the deep drinking-horn
   Blew the foam lightly.

"She was a Prince's child,
I but a Viking wild,   90
And though she blushed and smiled,
   I was discarded!
Should not the dove so white
Follow the sea-mew's[4] flight,

---

4. A species of European sea gull.

Why did they leave that night
Her nest unguarded?   95

"Scarce had I put to sea,
Bearing the maid with me,
Fairest of all was she
    Among the Norsemen!   100
When on the white sea-strand,
Waving his armèd hand,
Saw we old Hildebrand,
    With twenty horsemen.

"Then launched they to the blast,   105
Bent like a reed each mast,
Yet we were gaining fast,
    When the wind failed us;
And with a sudden flaw
Came round the gusty Skaw,[5]   110
So that our foe we saw
    Laugh as he hailed us.

"And as to catch the gale
Round veered the flapping sail,
'Death!' was the helmsman's hail,   115
    'Death without quarter!'
Mid-ships with iron keel
Struck we her ribs of steel;
Down her black hulk did reel
    Through the black water!   120

"As with his wings aslant,
Sails the fierce cormorant,
Seeking some rocky haunt,
    With his prey laden,—
So toward the open main,   125
Beating to sea again,
Through the wild hurricane,
    Bore I the maiden.

"Three weeks we westward bore,
And when the storm was o'er
Cloud-like we saw the shore   130
    Stretching to leeward;
There for my lady's bower
Built I the lofty tower,[6]

5. The northernmost cape of Jutland,   6. *I.e.*, the Newport tower.
Denmark.

Which, to this very hour,   135
   Stands looking seaward.

"There lived we many years;
Time dried the maiden's tears;
She had forgot her fears,
   She was a mother;   140
Death closed her mild blue eyes,
Under that tower she lies;
Ne'er shall the sun arise
   On such another!

"Still grew my bosom then,   145
Still as a stagnant fen!
Hateful to me were men,
   The sunlight hateful!
In the vast forest here,
Clad in my warlike gear,   150
Fell I upon my spear,
   Oh, death was grateful!

"Thus, seamed with many scars,
Bursting these prison bars,
Up to its native stars   155
   My soul ascended!
There from the flowing bowl
Deep drinks the warrior's soul,
Skoal![7] to the Northland! *skoal!*"
   Thus the tale ended.   160

1840   1841

Serenade[8]

Stars of the summer night!
   Far in yon azure deeps,
Hide, hide your golden light!
   She sleeps!
   My lady sleeps!   5
   Sleeps!

Moon of the summer night!
   Far down yon western steeps,

7. "In Scandinavia, this is the customary salutation when drinking a health. * * * " [Longfellow's note].
8. This famous song, written in 1840, was published in September, 1842, in *Graham's Magazine,* and in 1843 as part of the drama *The Spanish Student* (Act I, Scene 3, ll. 8 ff.), where it is sung below the bedroom balcony of Preciosa, by her lover, Victorian.

Sink, sink in silver light!
She sleeps!   10
My lady sleeps!
Sleeps!

Wind of the summer night!
Where yonder woodbine creeps,
Fold, fold thy pinions light!   15
She sleeps!
My lady sleeps!
Sleeps!

Dreams of the summer night!
Tell her, her lover keeps   20
Watch! while in slumbers light
She sleeps!
My lady sleeps!
Sleeps!

1840   1842, 1843

Mezzo Cammin[9]

Half of my life is gone, and I have let
The years slip from me and have not fulfilled
The aspiration of my youth, to build
Some tower of song with lofty parapet.
Not indolence, nor pleasure, nor the fret   5
Of restless passions that would not be stilled,
But sorrow, and a care that almost killed,[1]
Kept me from what I may accomplish yet;
Though, half-way up the hill, I see the Past
Lying beneath me with its sounds and sights,—   10
A city in the twilight dim and vast,
With smoking roofs, soft bells, and gleaming lights,—
And hear above me on the autumnal blast
The cataract of Death far thundering from the heights.

1842   [1845] 1846

9. Among Longfellow's sonnets, this is
notable for the effective irregularity of
its extended last line. The words of the
title appear in the first line of Dante's
*Divine Comedy: Nel mezzo del cammin
di nostra vita,* translated, "Midway
upon the journey of our life." Like
Dante when he wrote these lines, Longfellow had reached the mid-point of the
biblical three score and ten years. The
poem was collected in *The Belfry of
Bruges,* dated 1846, but published on
December 23, 1845.
1. Longfellow's first wife had died in
1835, during his previous trip abroad.

The Arsenal at Springfield[2]

This is the Arsenal. From floor to ceiling,
  Like a huge organ, rise the burnished arms;
But from their silent pipes no anthem pealing
  Startles the villages with strange alarms.

Ah! what a sound will rise, how wild and dreary,   5
  When the death-angel touches those swift keys!
What loud lament and dismal Miserere[3]
  Will mingle with their awful symphonies!

I hear even now the infinite fierce chorus,
  The cries of agony, the endless groan,   10
Which, through the ages that have gone before us,
  In long reverberations reach our own.

On helm and harness rings the Saxon hammer,
  Through Cimbric[4] forest roars the Norseman's song,
And loud, amid the universal clamor,   15
  O'er distant deserts sounds the Tartar gong.

I hear the Florentine, who from his palace
  Wheels out his battle-bell with dreadful din,
And Aztec priests upon their teocallis[5]
  Beat the wild war-drums made of serpent's skin;   20

The tumult of each sacked and burning village;
  The shout that every prayer for mercy drowns;
The soldiers' revels in the midst of pillage;
  The wail of famine in beleaguered towns;

The bursting shell, the gateway wrenched asunder,   25
  The rattling musketry, the clashing blade;
And ever and anon, in tones of thunder,
  The diapason of the cannonade.

Is it, O man, with such discordant noises,
  With such accursed instruments as these,   30

2. Longfellow and his second wife on their wedding journey in 1843 visited Springfield, Massachusetts, where the rows of guns on the walls of the arsenal suggested to the bride the organ pipes of death. The first International Peace Conference was meeting in London that year, and the next year, 1844, saw the birth of the *Christian Citizen*, the first periodical devoted to the cause of peace. Longfellow responded with this poem in *Graham's Magazine*, April, 1844, and the next year collected it in *The Belfry of Bruges*.
3. A lyrical supplication for mercy; specifically, the first line of Psalm L, in the Latin Vulgate, used in the Catholic service: *Miserere mei Domine* ("Have mercy on me, Lord").
4. The Cimbri, originally Danish, long opposed the Roman Empire.
5. Places of worship of Mexican and Central American Indians, the temple surmounting a truncated pyramidal mound.

Thou drownest Nature's sweet and kindly voices,
And jarrest the celestial harmonies?

Were half the power that fills the world with terror,
Were half the wealth bestowed on camps and courts,
Given to redeem the human mind from error,
There were no need of arsenals or forts: 35

The warrior's name would be a name abhorrèd!
And every nation, that should lift again
Its hand against a brother, on its forehead
Would wear forevermore the curse of Cain!   40

Down the dark future, through long generations,
The echoing sounds grow fainter and then cease;
And like a bell, with solemn, sweet vibrations,
I hear once more the voice of Christ say, "Peace!"

Peace! and no longer from its brazen portals   45
The blast of War's great organ shakes the skies!
But beautiful as songs of the immortals,
The holy melodies of love arise.

1844   1844, [1845] 1846

Nuremberg[6]

In the valley of the Pegnitz, where across broad meadow-lands
Rise the blue Franconian mountains, Nuremberg, the ancient, stands.

Quaint old town of toil and traffic, quaint old town of art and song,
Memories haunt thy pointed gables, like the rooks that round them throng:

Memories of the Middle Ages, when the emperors, rough and bold,
Had their dwelling in thy castle,[7] time-defying, centuries old;   5

And thy brave and thrifty burghers boasted, in their uncouth rhyme,
That their great imperial city stretched its hand through every clime.[8]

6. In "Nuremberg," and many other poems, Longfellow the teacher communicated his enthusiasm for the culture of the past to a middle-class audience largely untraveled. However, although he here recalls the romantic history of a medieval cathedral city, he emphasizes its democratic tradition, and, in the last line, reflects a dominant American attitude. The poem, inspired by the poet's visit in 1842, was written in 1844, appearing in *Graham's Maga-*zine in June, and in *The Belfry of Bruges* the following year.

7. Nuremberg became a free imperial city in 1219, and for more than four hundred years its princes fostered traditions of freedom, providing a German Gothic Renaissance in the fifteenth and sixteenth centuries, and a favorable soil for the Protestant Reformation of Luther (1483–1546).

8. Paraphrase of an ancient German proverb.

In the court-yard of the castle, bound with many an iron band,
Stands the mighty linden planted by Queen Cunigunde's[9] hand;   10

On the square the oriel window, where in old heroic days
Sat the poet Melchior[1] singing Kaiser Maximilian's praise,

Everywhere I see around me rise the wondrous world of Art:
Fountains wrought with richest sculpture standing in the common
    mart;

And above the cathedral doorways saints and bishops carved in
    stone,   15
By a former age commissioned as apostles to our own.

In the church of sainted Sebald sleeps enshrined his holy dust,
And in bronze the Twelve Apostles guard from age to age their
    trust;[2]

In the church of sainted Lawrence stands a pix of sculpture rare,
Like the foamy sheaf of fountains, rising through the painted
    air.[3]   20

Here, when Art was still religion, with a simple, reverent heart,
Lived and labored Albrecht Dürer, the Evangelist of Art;[4]

Hence in silence and in sorrow, toiling still with busy hand,
Like an emigrant he wandered, seeking for the Better Land.

Emigravit[5] is the inscription on the tombstone where he lies;   25
Dead he is not, but departed,—for the artist never dies.

Fairer seems the ancient city, and the sunshine seems more fair,
That he once has trod its pavement, that he once has breathed its
    air!

Through these streets so broad and stately, these obscure and dismal
    lanes,
Walked of yore the Mastersingers,[6] chanting rude poetic strains.   30

9. Kunigunde (died about 1039), wife of Henry II. She repudiated false charges by walking barefoot over hot irons, and was canonized as a saint in 1200.
1. "Melchior Pfinzing was one of the most celebrated German poets of the sixteenth century. The hero of his *Tenerdank* was the reigning Emperor, Maximilian * * * " [Longfellow's note].
2. "The tomb of Saint Sebald, in the church which bears his name, is one of the richest works of art in Nuremberg. It is of bronze, and was cast by Peter Vischer and his sons, who labored upon it thirteen years. It is adorned with nearly one hundred figures, among which those of the Twelve Apostles are conspicuous for size and beauty" [Long-

fellow's note].
3. St. Lawrence Justinian (1381–1456), author of the constitution of the Augustinians, an order of monks whose large German following included Luther. In his note, Longfellow describes the "pix" of this church as "a tabernacle for vessels of the sacrament, * * * an exquisite sculpture of white stone," sixty-four feet high, reflecting the rich colors of the choir windows.
4. Albrecht Dürer (1471–1528), most celebrated painter of the German Renaissance, inventor of etching, and an "Evangelist" because of his magnificent woodcuts of biblical subjects, still treasured in old German Bibles.
5. He has gone forth.
6. Meistersingers; guilds of musicians and poets, chiefly from the artisan class,

From remote and sunless suburbs came they to the friendly guild,
Building nests in Fame's great temple, as in spouts the swallows
    build.

As the weaver plied the shuttle, wove he too the mystic rhyme,
And the smith his iron measures hammered to the anvil's chime;

Thanking God, whose boundless wisdom makes the flowers of poesy
    bloom 35
In the forge's dust and cinders, in the tissues of the loom.

Here Hans Sachs,[7] the cobbler-poet, laureate of the gentle craft,
Wisest of the Twelve Wise Masters,[8] in huge folios sang and
    laughed.

But his house is now an ale-house, with a nicely sanded floor,
And a garland in the window, and his face above the door; 40

Painted by some humble artist, as in Adam Puschman's[9] song,
As the old man gray and dove-like, with his great beard white and
    long.

·And at night the swart mechanic comes to drown his cark and care,
Quaffing ale from pewter tankards, in the master's antique chair.

Vanished is the ancient splendor, and before my dreamy eye 45
Wave these mingled shapes and figures, like a faded tapestry.

Not thy Councils, not thy Kaisers, win for thee the world's regard;
But thy painter, Albrecht Dürer, and Hans Sachs thy cobbler bard.

Thus, O Nuremberg, a wanderer from a region far away,
As he paced thy streets and court-yards, sang in thought his careless
    lay: 50

Gathering from the pavement's crevice, as a floweret of the soil,
The nobility of labor,—the long pedigree of toil.

1844   1844, [1845] 1846

which flourished in various German cities from the fourteenth to the sixteenth centuries. That at Nuremberg, the most renowned, included Hans Sachs (*cf.* l. 37, below).
7. Hans Sachs (1494–1576) of Nuremberg, the most talented of the Meistersingers, was also a shoemaker ("the gentle craft"); Wagner later made him the central figure in the opera *Die Meistersinger von Nürnberg* (1867).

8. "The Twelve Wise Masters was the title of the original corporation of the Mastersingers. Hans Sachs, * * * though not one of the original Twelve, was the most renowned of the Mastersingers" [Longfellow's note].
9. In his note, Longfellow translates some lines from this obscure German poet as the source of his description of Sachs, below.

Seaweed[1]

When descends on the Atlantic
    The gigantic
Storm-wind of the equinox,
Landward in his wrath he scourges
    The toiling surges,   5
Laden with seaweed from the rocks:

From Bermuda's reefs; from edges
    Of sunken ledges,
In some far-off, bright Azore;
From Bahama, and the dashing,
    Silver-flashing   10
Surges of San Salvador;

From the tumbling surf, that buries
    The Orkneyan skerries,
Answering the hoarse Hebrides;   15
And from wrecks of ships, and drifting
    Spars, uplifting
On the desolate, rainy seas;—

Ever drifting, drifting, drifting
    On the shifting   20
Currents of the restless main;
Till in sheltered coves, and reaches
    Of sandy beaches,
All have found repose again.

So when storms of wild emotion   25
    Strike the ocean
Of the poet's soul, erelong
From each cave and rocky fastness,
    In its vastness,
Floats some fragment of a song: 30

From the far-off isles enchanted,
    Heaven has planted
With the golden fruit of Truth;
From the flashing surf, whose vision
    Gleams Elysian   35
In the tropic clime of Youth;

---

1. In its earlier stanzas, this poem is remarkable for the poet's command of the imagery and wild music of his theme; in the last three stanzas it shows his surrender to the didactic impulse of his times—here the desire to elaborate, for the common reader, the functions of the poet. The work appeared in *Graham's Magazine* for January, 1845, and again at the end of the year in *The Belfry of Bruges*.

From the strong Will, and the Endeavor
  That forever
Wrestle with the tides of Fate;
From the wreck of Hopes far-scattered,
  Tempest-shattered,
Floating waste and desolate;—   40

Ever drifting, drifting, drifting
  On the shifting
Currents of the restless heart;
Till at length in books recorded,   45
  They, like hoarded
Household words, no more depart.

1844   1845

The Evening Star[2]

Lo! in the painted oriel[3] of the West,
  Whose panes the sunken sun incarnadines,
  Like a fair lady at her casement, shines
The evening star, the star of love and rest!
And then anon she doth herself divest   5
  Of all her radiant garments, and reclines
  Behind the sombre screen of yonder pines,
With slumber and soft dreams of love oppressed.
O my beloved, my sweet Hesperus![4]
  My morning and my evening star of love!
  My best and gentlest lady! even thus,   10
As that fair planet in the sky above,
  Dost thou retire unto thy rest at night,
  And from thy darkened window fades the light.

1845   [1845] 1846

The Old Clock on the Stairs[5]

Somewhat back from the village street
Stands the old-fashioned country-seat.

2. "October 30, 1845 * * * Wrote the sonnet *Hesperus* in the rustic seat of the old apple-tree" [Longfellow's diary]. It was addressed to his second wife. His brother, in the *Life*, called it his "only love-poem." It was collected in *The Belfry of Bruges*.
3. Architectural term for a large bay window, here the western sky.
4. Hesperus was the Roman deity of the evening star, but in classical poetry sometimes the morning star also (*cf.* l. 10). Identified with the planet Venus in modern astronomy.
5. The ancient homestead of the poem, in Pittsfield, was that of the grandparents of his second wife, whom Longfellow visited on his wedding journey in 1843. On beginning the composition (November 12, 1845), he noted in his

Across its antique portico
Tall poplar-trees their shadows throw;
And from its station in the hall   5
An ancient timepiece says to all,—
          "Forever—never!
          Never—forever!"

Half-way up the stairs it stands,
And points and beckons with its hands   10
From its case of massive oak,
Like a monk, who, under his cloak,
Crosses himself, and sighs, alas!
With sorrowful voice to all who pass,—
          "Forever—never!   15
          Never—forever!"

By day its voice is low and light;
But in the silent dead of night,
Distinct as a passing footstep's fall,
It echoes along the vacant hall,   20
Along the ceiling, along the floor,
And seems to say, at each chamber-door,—
          "Forever—never!
          Never—forever!"

Through days of sorrow and of mirth,   25
Through days of death and days of birth,
Through every swift vicissitude
Of changeful time, unchanged it has stood,
And as if, like God, it all things saw,
It calmly repeats those words of awe,—   30
          "Forever—never!
          Never—forever!"

In that mansion used to be
Free-hearted Hospitality;
His great fires up the chimney roared;   35
The stranger feasted at his board;
But, like the skeleton at the feast,
That warning timepiece never ceased,—
          "Forever—never!
          Never—forever!"   40

diary the source of the refrain in a
French passage (which we translate), by
"Bridaine, the old French missionary,
who said of eternity": *It is a clock
whose pendulum endlessly repeats only
these two words in the silence of the
tombs,—Forever, never! Never, forever!
And amid these fearful reverberations
the condemned cries out, "What is the
hour?" and the voice of another outcast
answers him, "Eternity."* The poem was
included in The Belfry of Bruges.

There groups of merry children played,
There youths and maidens dreaming strayed;
O precious hours! O golden prime,
And affluence of love and time!
Even as a miser counts his gold,   45
Those hours the ancient timepiece told,—
    "Forever—never!
    Never—forever!"

From that chamber, clothed in white,
The bride came forth on her wedding night;   50
There, in that silent room below,
The dead lay in his shroud of snow;
And in the hush that followed the prayer,
Was heard the old clock on the stair,—
    "Forever—never!   55
    Never—forever!"

All are scattered now and fled,
Some are married, some are dead;
And when I ask, with throbs of pain,
"Ah! when shall they all meet again?"
As in the days long since gone by,   60
The ancient timepiece makes reply,—
    "Forever—never!
    Never—forever!"

Never here, forever there,   65
Where all parting, pain, and care,
And death, and time shall disappear,—
Forever there, but never here!
The horologe of Eternity
Sayeth this incessantly,—   70
    "Forever—never!
    Never—forever!"

1845   [1845] 1846

Evangeline[6]

A TALE OF ACADIE

This is the forest primeval. The murmuring pines and the hemlocks,
Bearded with moss, and in garments green, indistinct in the twilight,

6. The legend of Evangeline was reported by a friend at dinner to Hawthorne and Longfellow, but the novelist did not wish to use it. Longfellow made of it his first epical tale, later to be rivaled but not surpassed in popularity by *Hiawatha* and *The Courtship of Miles Standish*. Its publication in 1847 revived interest in French Acadia, and historical research corrected certain facts

Stand like Druids[7] of eld, with voices sad and prophetic,
Stand like harpers hoar, with beards that rest on their bosoms.
Loud from its rocky caverns, the deep-voiced neighboring ocean   5
Speaks, and in accents disconsolate answers the wail of the forest.

This is the forest primeval; but where are the hearts that beneath
  it
Leaped like the roe, when he hears in the woodland the voice of
  the huntsman?
Where is the thatch-roofed village, the home of Acadian farmers,—
Men whose lives glided on like rivers that water the woodlands,   10
Darkened by shadows of earth, but reflecting an image of heaven?
Waste are those pleasant farms, and the farmers forever departed!
Scattered like dust and leaves, when the mighty blasts of October
Seize them, and whirl them aloft, and sprinkle them far o'er the
  ocean.   14
Naught but tradition remains of the beautiful village of Grand-Pré.[8]

Ye who believe in affection that hopes, and endures, and is
  patient,
Ye who believe in the beauty and strength of woman's devotion,
List to the mournful tradition, still sung by the pines of the forest;
List to a Tale of Love in Acadie, home of the happy.

Part the First

I

In the Acadian land, on the shores of the Basin of Minas,[9]   20
Distant, secluded, still, the little village of Grand-Pré
Lay in the fruitful valley. Vast meadows stretched to the eastward,
Giving the village its name, and pasture to flocks without number.
Dikes, that the hands of the farmers had raised with labor incessant,
Shut out the turbulent tides; but at stated seasons the flood-gates   25

without altering the spirit of events as Longfellow reported them.

The sources then available were meager, principally T. C. Haliburton's *An Historical and Statistical Account of Nova Scotia* (1829), based in part on Abbé Raynal's chronicle, *Histoire philosophique et politique * * * dans les deux Indes* (1770), Longfellow's immediate source for colonial French folklore and antiquities. Acadia, or Acadie, colonized by the French, who first settled in Port Royal in 1605, included Nova Scotia and the mainland from the St. Lawrence southward into Maine, long the scene of Franco-British imperial conflicts. In 1713, with the Peace of Utrecht, Nova Scotia was ceded to the British; they later used Port Royal (now Annapolis) as a base against French Canada in the French and Indian War (1754–1763), the American phase of the Seven Years' War, occurring at the time of this story. The French farmers of Nova Scotia, seeking neutrality with their French and Indian neighbors, refused to swear British allegiance. The British in 1755 therefore resorted to mass deportation, often separating families, as the betrothed Evangeline and Gabriel were parted. Part I, reprinted here, ends with the separation. In Part II, Evangeline makes her long pilgrimage through the colonies, unsuccessfully seeking Gabriel among the exiles as far off as Louisiana, where the Acadians' present descendants are the "cajuns."

7. Priests of the ancient Celts of northern Europe, who worshiped in groves.
8. Translated "Great Meadow" (*cf.* l. 23).
9. An arm of the Bay of Fundy, on the northwest shore of Nova Scotia, site of Grand-Pré, Evangeline's village.

Opened, and welcomed the sea to wander at will o'er the meadows.
West and south there were fields of flax, and orchards and cornfields
Spreading afar and unfenced o'er the plain; and away to the north-
ward
Blomidon[1] rose, and the forests old, and aloft on the mountains
Sea-fogs pitched their tents, and mists from the mighty Atlantic 30
Looked on the happy valley, but ne'er from their station descended.
There, in the midst of its farms, reposed the Acadian village.
Strongly built were the houses, with frames of oak and of hemlock,
Such as the peasants of Normandy built in the reign of the Henries.[2]
Thatch were the roofs, with dormer-windows; and gables projecting
Over the basement below protected and shaded the doorway. 36
There in the tranquil evenings of summer, when brightly the sunset
Lighted the village street, and gilded the vanes on the chimneys,
Matrons and maidens sat in snow-white caps and in kirtles
Scarlet and blue and green, with distaffs spinning the golden 40
Flax for the gossiping looms, whose noisy shuttles within doors
Mingled their sound with the whir of the wheels and the songs of
the maidens.
Solemnly down the street came the parish priest, and the children
Paused in their play to kiss the hand he extended to bless them.
Reverend walked he among them; and up rose matrons and maidens,
Hailing his slow approach with words of affectionate welcome. 46
Then came the laborers home from the field, and serenely the sun
sank
Down to his rest, and twilight prevailed. Anon from the belfry
Softly the Angelus[3] sounded, and over the roofs of the village
Columns of pale blue smoke, like clouds of incense ascending, 50
Rose from a hundred hearths, the homes of peace and contentment.
Thus dwelt together in love these simple Acadian farmers,—
Dwelt in the love of God and of man. Alike were they free from
Fear, that reigns with the tyrant, and envy, the vice of republics.
Neither locks had they to their doors, nor bars to their windows; 55
But their dwellings were open as day and the hearts of the owners;
There the richest was poor, and the poorest lived in abundance.

Somewhat apart from the village, and nearer the Basin of Minas,
Benedict Bellefontaine, the wealthiest farmer of Grand-Pré,
Dwelt on his goodly acres; and with him, directing his household,
Gentle Evangeline lived, his child, and the pride of the village. 61
Stalworth[4] and stately in form was the man of seventy winters;
Hearty and hale was he, an oak that is covered with snow-flakes;

1. Headland at the entrance to the Basin of Minas.
2. Three "Henries"—Second to Fourth—ruled France between 1547 and 1610.
3. The Angelus (Latin, "messenger"), a devotion commemorating the incarnation of God in Jesus Christ, is announced at morning, noon, and nightfall by the church bell's call to prayer.
4. Stalwart.

White as the snow were his locks, and his cheeks as brown as the
 oak-leaves.
Fair was she to behold, that maiden of seventeen summers.   65
Black were her eyes as the berry that grows on the thorn by the
 wayside,
Black, yet how softly they gleamed beneath the brown shade of her
 tresses!
Sweet was her breath as the breath of kine that feed in the meadows.
When in the harvest heat she bore to the reapers at noontide.
Flagons of home-brewed ale, ah! fair in sooth was the maiden.   70
Fairer was she when, on Sunday morn, while the bell from its turret
Sprinkled with holy sounds the air, as the priest with his hyssop[5]
Sprinkles the congregation, and scatters blessings upon them,
Down the long street she passed, with her chaplet of beads and her
 missal,[6]   74
Wearing her Norman cap and her kirtle of blue, and the ear-rings
Brought in the olden time from France, and since, as an heirloom,
Handed down from mother to child, through long generations.
But a celestial brightness—a more ethereal beauty—
Shone on her face and encircled her form, when, after confession,
Homeward serenely she walked with God's benediction upon
 her.   80
When she had passed, it seemed like the ceasing of exquisite music.

   Firmly builded with rafters of oak, the house of the farmer
Stood on the side of a hill commanding the sea; and a shady
Sycamore grew by the door, with a woodbine wreathing around it.
Rudely carved was the porch, with seats beneath; and a footpath   85
Led through an orchard wide, and disappeared in the meadow.
Under the sycamore-tree were hives overhung by a penthouse,
Such as the traveler sees in regions remote by the roadside,
Built o'er a box for the poor, or the blessed image of Mary.
Farther down, on the slope of the hill, was the well with its moss-
 grown   90
Bucket, fastened with iron, and near it a trough for the horses.
Shielding the house from storms, on the north, were the barns and
 the farmyard.
There stood the broad-wheeled wains and the antique ploughs and
 the harrows;
There were the folds for the sheep; and there, in his feathered
 seraglio,
Strutted the lordly turkey, and crowed the cock, with the selfsame   95
Voice that in ages of old had startled the penitent Peter.[7]

5. Holy water.
6. A book of the Mass, or other formal
devotions.

7. *Cf.* Matthew xxvi: 34, 69–75. Jesus
had prophesied that, before cockcrow,
Peter would deny him.

Bursting with hay were the barns, themselves a village. In each one
Far o'er the gable projected a roof of thatch; and a staircase,
Under the sheltering eaves, led up to the odorous corn-loft.
There too the dove-cot stood, with its meek and innocent inmates
Murmuring ever of love; while above in the variant breezes   101
Numberless noisy weathercocks rattled and sang of mutation.

Thus, at peace with God and the world, the farmer of Grand-Pré
Lived on his sunny farm, and Evangeline governed his household.
Many a youth, as he knelt in the church and opened his missal,   105
Fixed his eyes upon her as the saint of his deepest devotion;
Happy was he who might touch her hand or the hem of her
    garment!
Many a suitor came to her door, by the darkness befriended,
And, as he knocked and waited to hear the sound of her footsteps,
Knew not which beat the louder, his heart or the knocker of iron;
Or, at the joyous feast of the Patron Saint of the village,   111
Bolder grew, and pressed her hand in the dance as he whispered
Hurried words of love, that seemed a part of the music.
But among all who came young Gabriel only was welcome;
Gabriel Lajeunesse, the son of Basil the blacksmith,   115
Who was a mighty man in the village, and honored of all men;
For, since the birth of time, throughout all ages and nations,
Has the craft of the smith been held in repute by the people.
Basil was Benedict's friend. Their children from earliest childhood
Grew up together as brother and sister; and Father Felician,   120
Priest and pedagogue both in the village, had taught them their
    letters
Out of the selfsame book, with the hymns of the church and the
    plain-song.[8]
But when the hymn was sung, and the daily lesson completed,
Swiftly they hurried away to the forge of Basil the blacksmith.
There at the door they stood, with wondering eyes to behold him
Take in his leathern lap the hoof of the horse as a plaything,   126
Nailing the shoe in its place; while near him the tire of the cart-
    wheel
Lay like a fiery snake, coiled round in a circle of cinders.
Oft on autumnal eves, when without in the gathering darkness
Bursting with light seemed the smithy, through every cranny and
    crevice,   130
Warm by the forge within they watched the laboring bellows,
And as its panting ceased, and the sparks expired in the ashes,
Merrily laughed, and said they were nuns going into the chapel.
Oft on sledges in winter, as swift as the swoop of the eagle,

8. Ancient formalized Gregorian chants, simple and usually sung without accompaniment.

Down the hillside bounding, they glided away o'er the meadow.   135
Oft in the barns they climbed to the populous nests on the rafters,
Seeking with eager eyes that wondrous stone, which the swallow
Brings from the shore of the sea to restore the sight of its fledglings;
Lucky was he who found that stone in the nest of the swallow![9]
Thus passed a few swift years, and they no longer were children.   140
He was a valiant youth, and his face, like the face of the morning,
Gladdened the earth with its light, and ripened thought into action.
She was a woman now, with the heart and hopes of a woman.
"Sunshine of St. Eulalie," was she called; for that was the sunshine
Which, as the farmers believed, would load their orchards with
    apples;[1]   145
She too would bring to her husband's house delight and abundance,
Filling it with love and the ruddy faces of children.

II

Now had the season returned, when the nights grow colder and
    longer,
And the retreating sun the sign of the Scorpion enters.[2]
Birds of passage sailed through the air, from the ice-bound,   150
Desolate northern bays to the shores of tropical islands.
Harvests were gathered in; and wild with the winds of September
Wrestled the trees of the forest, as Jacob of old with the angel.[3]
All the signs foretold a winter long and inclement.
Bees, with prophetic instinct of want, had hoarded their honey   155
Till the hives overflowed; and the Indian hunters asserted
Cold would the winter be, for thick was the fur of the foxes.
Such was the advent of autumn. Then followed that beautiful
    season,
Called by the pious Acadian peasants the Summer of All-Saints![4]
Filled was the air with a dreamy and magical light; and the land-
    scape   160
Lay as if new-created in all the freshness of childhood.
Peace seemed to reign upon earth, and the restless heart of the ocean
Was for a moment consoled. All sounds were in harmony blended.
Voices of children at play, the crowing of cocks in the farm-yards,
Whir of wings in the drowsy air, and the cooing of pigeons,   165
All were subdued and low as the murmurs of love, and the great sun
Looked with the eye of love through the golden vapors around him;
While arrayed in its robes of russet and scarlet and yellow,

9. Longfellow's notes indicate that his immediate source for folklore and French antiquities was *Literature and Superstition of England in the Middle Ages,* by Thomas Wright (1810–1877), who translated many French stories from Pluquet's *Contes populaires.*
1. According to Longfellow's note, this superstitition of St. Eulalie's Day (February 12) is from "Pluquet in Wright, I, 131" (see Note 9, directly above).
2. The sun "enters" Scorpio, the eighth sign of the zodiac, in October (*cf.* Longfellow's "September").
3. *Cf.* Genesis xxxii: 24–30.
4. Indian summer. All Saints' Day is November 1.

Bright with the sheen of the dew, each glittering tree of the forest
Flashed like the plane-tree the Persian adorned with mantles and
    jewels.[5]
                                 170

    Now recommenced the reign of rest and affection and stillness.
Day with its burden and heat had departed, and twilight descending
Brought back the evening star to the sky, and the herds of the
    homestead.
Pawing the ground they came, and resting their necks on each other,
And with their nostrils distended inhaling the freshness of evening.
Foremost, bearing the bell, Evangeline's beautiful heifer,   176
Proud of her snow-white hide, and the ribbon that waved from her
    collar,
Quietly paced and slow, as if conscious of human affection.
Then came the shepherd back with his bleating flocks from the
    seaside,
Where was their favorite pasture. Behind them followed the watch-
    dog,
                                 180
Patient, full of importance, and grand in the pride of his instinct,
Walking from side to side with a lordly air, and superbly
Waving his bushy tail, and urging forward the stragglers;
Regent of flocks was he when the shepherd slept; their protector,
When from the forest at night, through the starry silence, the
    wolves howled.
                                 185
Late, with the rising moon, returned the wains from the marshes,
Laden with briny hay, that filled the air with its odor.
Cheerily neighed the steeds, with dew on their manes and their
    fetlocks,
While aloft on their shoulders the wooden and ponderous saddles,
Painted with brilliant dyes, and adorned with tassels of crimson,
Nodded in bright array, like hollyhocks heavy with blossoms.   191
Patiently stood the cows meanwhile, and yielded their udders
Unto the milkmaid's hand; whilst loud and in regular cadence
Into the sounding pails the foaming streamlets descended.
Lowing of cattle and peals of laughter were heard in the farm-yard,
Echoed back by the barns. Anon they sank into stillness;   196
Heavily closed, with a jarring sound, the valves of the barn-doors,
Rattled the wooden bars, and all for a season was silent.

    In-doors, warm by the wide-mouthed fireplace, idly the farmer
Sat in his elbow-chair, and watched how the flames and the smoke-
    wreaths
                                 200
Struggled together like foes in a burning city. Behind him,
Nodding and mocking along the wall, with gestures fantastic,

5. The "Persian" Xerxes bedecked a beloved tree with fine raiment and jewels. Longfellow's acknowledged sources were *Sylva*, II, 53, by John Evelyn (1620–1706), and Herodotus, VII, 31.

Darted his own huge shadow, and vanished away into darkness.
Faces, clumsily carved in oak, on the back of his arm-chair   204
Laughed in the flickering light, and the pewter plates on the dresser
Caught and reflected the flame, as shields of armies the sunshine.
Fragments of song the old man sang, and carols of Christmas,
Such as at home, in the olden time, his fathers before him
Sang in their Norman orchards and bright Burgundian vineyards.
Close at her father's side was the gentle Evangeline seated,   210
Spinning flax for the loom, that stood in the corner behind her,
Silent awhile were its treadles, at rest was its diligent shuttle,
While the monotonous drone of the wheel, like the drone of a bag-
pipe,
Followed the old man's song, and united the fragments together.
As in a church, when the chant of the choir at intervals ceases,   215
Footfalls are heard in the aisles, or words of the priest at the altar,
So, in each pause of the song, with measured motion the clock
clicked.

Thus as they sat, there were footsteps heard, and, suddenly lifted,
Sounded the wooden latch, and the door swung back on its hinges.
Benedict knew by the hob-nailed shoes it was Basil the blacksmith,
And by her beating heart Evangeline knew who was with him.   221
"Welcome!" the farmer exclaimed, as their footsteps paused on the
threshold,
"Welcome, Basil, my friend! Come, take thy place on the settle
Close by the chimney-side, which is always empty without thee;
Take from the shelf overhead thy pipe and the box of tobacco;   225
Never so much thyself art thou as when through the curling
Smoke of the pipe or the forge thy friendly and jovial face gleams,
Round and red as the harvest moon through the mist of the
marshes."
Then, with a smile of content, thus answered Basil the blacksmith,
Taking with easy air the accustomed seat by the fireside:—   230
"Benedict Bellefontaine, thou hast ever thy jest and thy ballad!
Ever in cheerfullest mood art thou, when others are filled with
Gloomy forebodings of ill, and see only ruin before them.
Happy art thou, as if every day thou hadst picked up a horseshoe."
Pausing a moment, to take the pipe that Evangeline brought him,
And with a coal from the embers had lighted, he slowly con-
tinued:—   236
"Four days now are passed since the English ships at their anchors,
Ride in the Gaspereau's[6] mouth, with their cannon pointed against
us.
What their design may be is unknown; but all are commanded

6. A small inlet on the south shore of the Basin of Minas, Nova Scotia, near Grand-
Pré.

On the morrow to meet in the church, where his Majesty's mandate
Will be proclaimed as law in the land. Alas! in the mean time   241
Many surmises of evil alarm the hearts of the people."
Then made answer the farmer: "Perhaps some friendlier purpose
Brings these ships to our shores. Perhaps the harvests in England
By untimely rains or untimelier heat have been blighted,   245
And from our bursting barns they would feed their cattle and
     children."
"Not so thinketh the folk in the village," said warmly the black-
     smith,
Shaking his head as in doubt; then, heaving a sigh, he continued:—
"Louisburg is not forgotten, nor Beau Séjour, nor Port Royal.[7]
Many already have fled to the forest, and lurk on its outskirts,   250
Waiting with anxious hearts the dubious fate of tomorrow.
Arms have been taken from us, and warlike weapons of all kinds;
Nothing is left but the blacksmith's sledge and the scythe of the
     mower."
Then with a pleasant smile made answer the jovial farmer:—
"Safer are we unarmed, in the midst of our flocks and our corn-
     fields,
                                                                          255
Safer within these peaceful dikes besieged by the ocean,
Than our fathers in forts, besieged by the enemy's cannon.
Fear no evil, my friend, and tonight may no shadow of sorrow
Fall on this house and hearth; for this is the night of the contract.
Built are the house and the barn. The merry lads of the village   260
Strongly have built them and well; and, breaking the glebe round
     about them,
Filled the barn with hay, and the house with food for a twelve-
     month.
René Leblanc will be here anon, with his papers and inkhorn.
Shall we not then be glad, and rejoice in the joy of our children?"
As apart by the window she stood, with her hand in her lover's,   265
Blushing Evangeline heard the words that her father had spoken,
And, as they died on his lips, the worthy notary entered.

III

Bent like a laboring oar, that toils in the surf of the ocean,
Bent, but not broken, by age was the form of the notary public;
Shocks of yellow hair, like the silken floss of the maize, hung   270
Over his shoulders; his forehead was high; and glasses with horn
     bows
Sat astride on his nose, with a look of wisdom supernal.
Father of twenty children was he, and more than a hundred
Children's children rode on his knee, and heard his great watch tick.

---

7. Louisburg, Beau Séjour and Port
Royal were localities in Nova Scotia and
Cape Breton, taken by the British from
the French during the colonial wars.

Four long years in the times of the war had he languished a captive,
Suffering much in an old French fort as the friend of the English.
Now, though warier grown, without all guile or suspicion,   277
Ripe in wisdom was he, but patient, and simple, and childlike.
He was beloved by all, and most of all by the children;
For he told them tales[8] of the Loup-garou in the forest,   280
And of the goblin that came in the night to water the horses,
And of the white Létiche, the ghost of a child who unchristened
Died, and was doomed to haunt unseen the chambers of children;
And how on Christmas eve the oxen talked in the stable,
And how the fever was cured by a spider shut up in a nutshell,   285
And of the marvelous powers of four-leaved clover and horseshoes,
With whatsoever else was writ in the lore of the village.
Then up rose from his seat by the fireside Basil the blacksmith,
Knocked from his pipe the ashes, and slowly extending his right
    hand,
"Father Leblanc," he exclaimed, "thou hast heard the talk in the
    village,   290
And, perchance, canst tell us some news of these ships and their
    errand."
Then with modest demeanor made answer the notary public,—
"Gossip enough have I heard, in sooth, yet am never the wiser;
And what their errand may be I know not better than others.
Yet am I not of those who imagine some evil intention   295
Brings them here, for we are at peace; and why then molest us?"
"God's name!" shouted the hasty and somewhat irascible black-
    smith;
"Must we in all things look for the how, and the why, and the
    wherefore?
Daily injustice is done, and might is the right of the strongest!"
But without heeding his warmth, continued the notary public,—
"Man is unjust, but God is just; and finally justice   301
Triumphs; and well I remember a story that often consoled me,
When as a captive I lay in the old French fort at Port Royal."
This was the old man's favorite tale, and he loved to repeat it
When his neighbors complained that any injustic was done them.
"Once in an ancient city, whose name I no longer remember,[9]   306
Raised aloft on a column, a brazen statue of Justice
Stood in the public square, upholding the scales in its left hand,
And in its right a sword, as an emblem that justice presided   309
Over the laws of the land, and the hearts and homes of the people.

8. Longfellow notes that these folk tales were found in Pluquet's *Contes populaires*. The Loup-garou is a werewolf; the Létiche, as Pluquet conjectures, was inspired by the fleet, wraith-like white ermine fox.
9. "This is an old Florentine story; in an altered form it is the theme of Rossini's opera of *La Gazza Ladra*" [Longfellow's note].

Even the birds had built their nests in the scales of the balance,
Having no fear of the sword that flashed in the sunshine above
them.
But in the course of time the laws of the land were corrupted;
Might took the place of right, and the weak were oppressed, and
the mighty
Ruled with an iron rod. Then it chanced in a nobleman's palace
That a necklace of pearls was lost, and erelong a suspicion   316
Fell on an orphan girl who lived as maid in the household.
She, after form of trial condemned to die on the scaffold,
Patiently met her doom at the foot of the statue of Justice.
As to her Father in heaven her innocent spirit ascended,   320
Lo! o'er the city a tempest rose; and the bolts of the thunder
Smote the statue of bronze, and hurled in wrath from its left hand
Down on the pavement below the clattering scales of the balance,
And in the hollow thereof was found the nest of a magpie,   324
Into whose clay-built walls the necklace of pearls was inwoven."
Silenced, but not convinced, when the story was ended, the black-
smith
Stood like a man who fain would speak, but findeth no language;
All his thoughts were congealed into lines on his face, as the vapors
Freeze in fantastic shapes on the window-panes in the winter.

Then Evangeline lighted the brazen lamp on the table,   330
Filled, till it overflowed the pewter tankard with home-brewed
Nut-brown ale, that was famed for its strength in the village of
Grand-Pré;
While from his pocket the notary drew his papers and inkhorn,
Wrote with a steady hand the date and the age of the parties,
Naming the dower of the bride in flocks of sheep and in cattle.   335
Orderly all things proceeded, and duly and well were completed,
And the great seal of the law was set like a sun on the margin.
Then from his leathern pouch the farmer threw on the table
Three times the old man's fee in solid pieces of silver;
And the notary rising, and blessing the bride and the bridegroom,
Lifted aloft the tankard of ale and drank to their welfare.   341
Wiping the foam from his lip, he solemnly bowed and departed,
While in silence the others sat and mused by the fireside,
Till Evangeline brought the draught-board out of its corner.
Soon was the game begun. In friendly contention the old men   345
Laughed at each lucky hit, or unsuccessful manoeuvre,
Laughed when a man was crowned, or a breach was made in the
king-row.
Meanwhile apart, in the twilight gloom of a window's embrasure,
Sat the lovers and whispered together, beholding the moon rise

Over the pallid sea and the silvery mist of the meadows.   350
Silently one by one, in the infinite meadows of heaven,
Blossomed the lovely stars, the forget-me-nots of the angels.

  Thus was the evening passed. Anon the bell from the belfry
Rang out the hour of nine, the village curfew, and straightway
Rose the guests and departed; and silence reigned in the household.
Many a farewell word and sweet good-night on the door-step   356
Lingered long in Evangeline's heart, and filled it with gladness.
Carefully then were covered the embers that glowed on the hearth-
    stone,
And on the oaken stairs resounded the tread of the farmer.
Soon with a soundless step the foot of Evangeline followed.   360
Up to the staircase moved a luminous space in the darkness,
Lighted less by the lamp than the shining face of the maiden.
Silent she passed the hall, and entered the door of her chamber.
Simple that chamber was, with its curtains of white, and its clothes-
    press
Ample and high, on whose spacious shelves were carefully folded
Linen and woollen stuffs, by the hand of Evangeline woven.   366
This was the precious dower she would bring to her husband in
    marriage,
Better than flocks and herds, being proofs of her skill as a house-
    wife.
Soon she extinguished her lamp, for the mellow and radiant moon-
    light
Streamed through the windows, and lighted the room, till the heart
    of the maiden   370
Swelled and obeyed its power, like the tremulous tides of the ocean.
Ah! she was fair, exceeding fair to behold, as she stood with
Naked snow-white feet on the gleaming floor of her chamber!
Little she dreamed that below, among the trees of the orchard,
Waited her lover and watched for the gleam of her lamp and her
    shadow.   375
Yet were her thoughts of him, and at times a feeling of sadness
Passed o'er her soul, as the sailing shade of clouds in the moonlight
Flitted across the floor and darkened the room for a moment.   378
And, as she gazed from the window, she saw serenely the moon pass
Forth from the folds of a cloud, and one star follow her footsteps,
As out of Abraham's tent young Ishmael wandered with Hagar![1]

IV

Pleasantly rose next morn the sun on the village of Grand-Pré.
Pleasantly gleamed in the soft, sweet air the Basin of Minas,
Where the ships, with their wavering shadows, were riding at
    anchor.

1. *Cf.* Genesis xxi: 9–14.

Life had long been astir in the village, and clamorous labor   385
Knocked with its hundred hands at the golden gates of the morn-
  ing.
Now from the country around, from the farms and neighboring
  hamlets,
Came in their holiday dresses the blithe Acadian peasants.
Many a glad good-morrow and jocund laugh from the young folk
Made the bright air brighter, as up from the numerous meadows,
Where no path could be seen but the track of wheels in the green-
  sward,   391
Group after group appeared, and joined, or passed on the highway.
Long ere noon, in the village all sounds of labor were silenced.
Thronged were the streets with people; and noisy groups at the
  house-doors
Sat in the cheerful sun, and rejoiced and gossiped together.   395
Every house was an inn, where all were welcomed and feasted;
For with this simple people, who lived like brothers together,
All things were held in common, and what one had was another's.
Yet under Benedict's roof hospitality seemed more abundant:
For Evangeline stood among the guests of her father;   400
Bright was her face with smiles, and words of welcome and gladness
Fell from her beautiful lips, and blessed the cup as she gave it.

  Under the open sky, in the odorous air of the orchard,
Stript of its golden fruit, was spread the feast of betrothal.
There in the shade of the porch were the priest and the notary
  seated;   405
There good Benedict sat, and sturdy Basil the blacksmith.
Not far withdrawn from these, by the cider-press and the beehives,
Michael the fiddler was placed, with the gayest of hearts and of
  waistcoats.
Shadow and light from the leaves alternately played on his snow-
  white
Hair, as it waved in the wind; and the jolly face of the fiddler   410
Glowed like a living coal when the ashes are blown from the embers.
Gayly the old man sang to the vibrant sound of his fiddle,
Tous les Bourgeois de Chartres, and *Le Carillon de Dunkerque*,[2]
And anon with his wooden shoes beat time to the music.
Merrily, merrily whirled the wheels of the dizzying dances   415
Under the orchard-trees and down the path to the meadows;
Old folk and young together, and children mingled among them.
Fairest of all the maids was Evangeline, Benedict's daughter!
Noblest of all the youths was Gabriel, son of the blacksmith!

2. Translated, "All the People of Char-   *lection of Mission Songs* (Quebec,
tres," and "The Chimes of Dunkirk";   1833).
Longfellow found them in a French *Col-*

So passed the morning away. And lo! with a summons sonorous
Sounded the bell from its tower, and over the meadows a drum
    beat. 421
Thronged ere long was the church with men. Without, in the
    churchyard,
Waited the women. They stood by the graves, and hung on the
    headstones
Garlands of autumn-leaves and evergreens fresh from the forest.
Then came the guard from the ships, and marching proudly among
    them 425
Entered the sacred portal. With loud and dissonant clangor
Echoed the sound of their brazen drums from ceiling and case-
    ment,—
Echoed a moment only, and slowly the ponderous portal
Closed, and in silence the crowd awaited the will of the soldiers.
Then uprose their commander,[3] and spake from the steps of the
    altar, 430
Holding aloft in his hands, with its seals, the royal commission.
"You are convened this day," he said, "by His Majesty's orders.
Clement and kind has he been; but how you have answered his
    kindness
Let your own hearts reply! To my natural make and my temper
Painful the task is I do, which to you I know must be grievous. 435
Yet must I bow and obey, and deliver the will of our monarch:[4]
Namely, that all your lands, and dwellings, and cattle of all kinds
Forfeited be to the crown; and that you yourselves from this
    province
Be transported to other lands. God grant you may dwell there
Ever as faithful subjects, a happy and peaceable people! 440
Prisoners now I declare you, for such is His Majesty's pleasure!"
As, when the air is serene in the sultry solstice of summer,
Suddenly gathers a storm, and the deadly sling of the hailstones
Beats down the farmer's corn in the field, and shatters his windows,
Hiding the sun, and strewing the ground with thatch from the
    house-roofs, 445
Bellowing fly the herds, and seek to break their enclosures;
So on the hearts of the people descended the words of the speaker.
Silent a moment they stood in speechless wonder, and then rose
Louder and ever louder a wail of sorrow and anger,
And, by one impulse moved, they madly rushed to the door-way.
Vain was the hope of escape; and cries and fierce imprecations 451

3. The "commander," whose orders for
the deportation came, not from Great
Britain, but only from the British
Governor Monckton of Nova Scotia, was
General John Winslow, great-grandson
of Edward Winslow, a founder of Plymouth Colony.
4. The following speech of the "commander" is Longfellow's close metrical
adaptation of the actual *Proclamation,*
as reported in Haliburton.

Rang through the house of prayer; and high o'er the head of the
others

Rose, with his arms uplifted, the figure of Basil the blacksmith,

As, on a stormy sea, a spar is tossed by the billows.

Flushed was his face and distorted with passion; and wildly he
shouted,— 455

"Down with the tyrants of England! we never have sworn them
allegiance!

Death to these foreign soldiers, who seize on our homes and our
harvests!"

More he fain would have said, but the merciless hand of a soldier

Smote him upon the mouth, and dragged him down to the pavement.

In the midst of the strife and tumult of angry contention, 460

Lo! the door of the chancel opened, and Father Felician

Entered, with serious mien, and ascended the steps of the altar.

Raising his reverend hand, with a gesture he awed into silence

All that clamorous throng; and thus he spake to his people; 464

Deep were his tones and solemn; in accents measured and mournful

Spake he, as, after the tocsin's alarum, distinctly the clock strikes.

"What is this that ye do, my children? what madness has seized
you?

Forty years of my life have I labored among you, and taught you,

Not in word alone, but in deed, to love one another?[5]

Is this the fruit of my toils, of my vigils and prayers and privations?

Have you so soon forgotten all lessons of love and forgiveness? 471

This is the house of the Prince of Peace, and would you profane it[6]

Thus with violent deeds and hearts overflowing with hatred?

Lo! where the crucified Christ from his cross is gazing upon you!

See! in those sorrowful eyes what meekness and holy compassion!

Hark! how those lips still repeat the prayer, 'O Father, forgive
them!'[7]

Let us repeat that prayer in the hour when the wicked assail us, 476

Let us repeat it now, and say, 'O Father, forgive them!'"

Few were his words of rebuke, but deep in the hearts of his people

Sank they, and sobs of contrition succeeded the passionate outbreak,

While they repeated his prayer, and said, "O Father, forgive them!" 480

Then came the evening service. The tapers gleamed from the
altar.

5. Father Felician refers at once to three texts of countless sermons—John xiii: 34 (Jesus' "new commandment, * * * that ye love one another"), I John iii: 18, and James i: 22.

6. *Cf.* Luke xix: 45–46.

7. The words of the crucified Jesus (Luke xxiii: 34).

Fervent and deep was the voice of the priest, and the people re-
    sponded,
Not with their lips alone, but their hearts; and the Ave Maria[8]
Sang they, and fell on their knees, and their souls, with devotion
    translated,   485
Rose on the ardor of prayer, like Elijah ascending to heaven.[9]

  Meanwhile had spread in the village the tidings of ill, and on all
    sides
Wandered, wailing, from house to house the women and children.
Long at her father's door Evangeline stood, with her right hand   489
Shielding her eyes from the level rays of the sun, that, descending,
Lighted the village street with mysterious splendor, and roofed each
Peasant's cottage with golden thatch, and emblazoned its windows.
Long within had been spread the snow-white cloth on the table;
There stood the wheaten loaf, and the honey fragrant with wild-
    flowers;
There stood the tankard of ale, and the cheese fresh brought from
    the dairy,   495
And, at the head of the board, the great arm-chair of the farmer.
Thus did Evangeline wait at her father's door, as the sunset
Threw the long shadows of trees o'er the broad ambrosial[1] meadows.
Ah! on her spirit within a deeper shadow had fallen,
And from the fields of her soul a fragrance celestial ascended,—   500
Charity, meekness, love, and hope, and forgiveness, and patience!
Then, all-forgetful of self, she wandered into the village,
Cheering with looks and words the mournful hearts of the women,
As o'er the darkening fields with lingering steps they departed,
Urged by their household cares, and the weary feet of their chil-
    dren.   505
Down sank the great red sun, and in golden, glimmering vapors
Veiled the light of his face, like the Prophet[2] descending from
    Sinai.
Sweetly over the village the bell of the Angelus sounded.

  Meanwhile amid the gloom, by the church Evangeline lingered.
All was silent within; and in vain at the door and the windows   510
Stood she, and listened and looked, until, overcome by emotion,
"Gabriel!" cried she aloud with tremulous voice; but no answer
Came from the graves of the dead, nor the gloomier grave of the
    living.

8. "Hail Mary"; the liturgical prayer
inspired by the words of the angel of
the Annunciation (Luke i: 26–27).
9. The prophet Elijah ascended to
heaven in a "chariot of fire" (II Kings
ii: 11).

1. Ambrosia was the mythical food of
the immortals; hence the derived meaning, "of exquisite taste and smell."
2. Moses. Descending from the Mount
of the covenant with God, he had to
veil the radiance of his face from men
(Exodus xxxiv: 29–35).

Slowly at length she returned to the tenantless house of her father.
Smouldered the fire on the hearth, on the board was the supper
    untasted, 515
Empty and drear was each room, and haunted with phantoms of
    terror.
Sadly echoed her step on the stair and the floor of her chamber.
In the dead of the night she heard the disconsolate rain fall
Loud on the withered leaves of the sycamore-tree by the window.
Keenly the lightning flashed; and the voice of the echoing thunder
Told her that God was in heaven, and governed the world he
    created! 521
Then she remembered the tale she had heard of the justice of
    Heaven;
Soothed was her troubled soul, and she peacefully slumbered till
    morning.

V

Four times the sun had risen and set; and now on the fifth day
Cheerily called the cock to the sleeping maids of the farm-house.
Soon o'er the yellow fields, in silent and mournful procession, 526
Came from the neighboring hamlets and farms the Acadian
    women,
Driving in ponderous wains their household goods to the sea-shore,
Pausing and looking back to gaze once more on their dwellings,
Ere they were shut from sight by the winding road and the wood-
    land. 530
Close at their sides their children ran, and urged on the oxen,
While in their little hands they clasped some fragments of play-
    things.

Thus to the Gaspereau's mouth they hurried; and there on the
    sea-beach
Piled in confusion lay the household goods of the peasants.
All day long between the shore and the ships did the boats ply; 535
All day long the wains came laboring down from the village.
Late in the afternoon, when the sun was near to his setting,
Echoed far o'er the fields came the roll of drums from the church-
    yard.
Thither the women and children thronged. On a sudden the church-
    doors
Opened, and forth came the guard, and marching in gloomy pro-
    cession 540
Followed the long-imprisoned, but patient, Acadian farmers.
Even as pilgrims, who journey afar from their homes and their
    country,
Sing as they go, and in singing forget they are weary and wayworn,

So with songs on their lips the Acadian peasants descended
Down from the church to the shore, amid their wives and their
    daughters.   545
Foremost the young men came; and, raising together their voices,
Sang with tremulous lips a chant of the Catholic Missions:—
"Sacred heart of the Saviour! O inexhaustible fountain!
Fill our hearts this day with strength and submission and patience!"
Then the old men, as they marched, and the women that stood by
    the wayside   550
Joined in the sacred psalm, and the birds in the sunshine above them
Mingled their notes therewith, like voices of spirits departed.

    Half-way down to the shore Evangeline waited in silence,
Not overcome with grief, but strong in the hour of affliction,—
Calmly and sadly she waited, until the procession approached her,
And she beheld the face of Gabriel pale with emotion.   556
Tears then filled her eyes, and, eagerly running to meet him,
Clasped she his hands, and laid her head on his shoulder, and
    whispered,—
"Gabriel, be of good cheer! for if we love one another   559
Nothing, in truth, can harm us, whatever mischances may happen!"
Smiling she spake these words; then suddenly paused, for her father
Saw she slowly advancing. Alas! how changed was his aspect!
Gone was the glow from his cheek, and the fire from his eye, and his
    footstep   563
Heavier seemed with the weight of the heavy heart in his bosom.
But with a smile and a sigh, she clasped his neck and embraced him,
Speaking words of endearment where words of comfort availed not.
Thus to the Gaspereau's mouth moved on that mournful procession.

    There disorder prevailed, and the tumult and stir of embarking.
Busily plied the freighted boats; and in the confusion
Wives were torn from their husbands, and mothers, too late, saw
    their children   570
Left on the land, extending their arms, with wildest entreaties.
So unto separate ships were Basil and Gabriel carried,
While in despair on the shore Evangeline stood with her father.
Half the task was not done when the sun went down, and the twilight
Deepened and darkened around; and in haste the refluent ocean   575
Fled away from the shore, and left the line of the sand-beach
Covered with waifs of the tide, with kelp and the slippery sea-weed.
Farther back in the midst of the household goods and the wagons,
Like to a gypsy camp, or a leaguer[3] after a battle,
All escape cut off by the sea, and the sentinels near them,   580
Lay encamped for the night the houseless Acadian farmers.

3. The camp of a besieged army.

Back to its nethermost caves retreated the bellowing ocean,
Dragging adown the beach the rattling pebbles, and leaving
Inland and far up the shore the stranded boats of the sailors.
Then, as the night descended, the herds returned from their pas-
tures;   585
Sweet was the moist still air with the odor of milk from their
udders;
Lowing they waited, and long, at the well-known bars of the farm-
yard,—
Waited and looked in vain for the voice and the hand of the milk-
maid.
Silence reigned in the streets; from the church no Angelus sounded,
Rose no smoke from the roofs, and gleamed no lights from the
windows.   590

But on the shores meanwhile the evening fires had been kindled,
Built of the drift-wood thrown on the sands from wrecks in the
tempest.
Round them shapes of gloom and sorrowful faces were gathered,
Voices of women were heard, and of men, and the crying of chil-
dren.
Onward from fire to fire, as from hearth to hearth in his parish, 595
Wandered the faithful priest, consoling and blessing and cheering,
Like unto shipwrecked Paul on Melita's desolate sea-shore.[4]
Thus he approached the place where Evangeline sat with her father,
And in the flickering light beheld the face of the old man,
Haggard and hollow and wan, and without either thought or emo-
tion,   600
E'en as the face of a clock from which the hands have been taken.
Vainly Evangeline strove with words and caresses to cheer him,
Vainly offered him food; yet he moved not, he looked not, he spake
not,
But, with a vacant stare, ever gazed at the flickering fire-light.
"Benedicite!"[5] murmured the priest, in tones of compassion. 605
More he fain would have said, but his heart was full, and his ac-
cents
Faltered and paused on his lips, as the feet of a child on a thres-
hold,
Hushed by the scene he beholds, and the awful presence of sorrow.
Silently, therefore, he laid his hand on the head of the maiden,
Raising his tearful eyes to the silent stars that above them   610
Moved on their way, unperturbed by the wrongs and sorrows of
mortals.
Then sat he down at her side, and they wept together in silence.

---

4. *Cf*. Acts xxviii: 1–10. Shipwrecked on Melita, Paul healed the sick is-landers.
5. Be thou blessed!

Suddenly rose from the south a light, as in autumn the blood-red
Moon climbs the crystal walls of heaven, and o'er the horizon
Titan-like stretches its hundred hands upon mountain and
    meadow,[6]   615
Seizing the rocks and the rivers, and piling huge shadows together.
Broader and ever broader it gleamed on the roofs of the village,
Gleamed on the sky and the sea, and the ships that lay in the road-
    stead.
Columns of shining smoke uprose, and flashes of flame were
Thrust through their folds and withdrawn, like the quivering hands
    of a martyr.   620
Then as the wind seized the gleeds[7] and the burning thatch, and,
    uplifting,
Whirled them aloft through the air, at once from a hundred house-
    tops
Started the sheeted smoke with flashes of flame intermingled.

  These things beheld in dismay the crowd on the shore and on
    shipboard.
Speechless at first they stood, then cried aloud in their anguish, 625
"We shall behold no more our homes in the village of Grand-Pré!"
Loud on a sudden the cocks began to crow in the farm-yards,
Thinking the day had dawned; and anon the lowing of cattle
Came on the evening breeze, by the barking of dogs interrupted.
Then rose a sound of dread, such as startles the sleeping encamp-
    ments   630
Far in the western prairies or forests that skirt the Nebraska,
When the wild horses affrighted sweep by with the speed of the
    whirlwind,
Or the loud bellowing herds of buffaloes rush to the river.
Such was the sound that arose on the night, as the herds and the
    horses
Broke through their folds and fences, and madly rushed o'er the
    meadows.   635

  Overwhelmed with the sight, yet speechless, the priest and the
    maiden
Gazed on the scene of terror that reddened and widened before
    them;
And as they turned at length to speak to their silent companion,
Lo! from his seat he had fallen, and stretched abroad on the sea-
    shore
Motionless lay his form, from which the soul had departed.   640
Slowly the priest uplifted the lifeless head, and the maiden

6. *Cf.* Briareus, a hundred-handed giant   Titans.
of classical mythology, who fought the   7. Glowing coals.

Knelt at her father's side, and wailed aloud in her terror.
Then in a swoon she sank, and lay with her head on his bosom.
Through the long night she lay in deep, oblivious slumber;
And when she awoke from the trance, she beheld a multitude near
    her.   645
Faces of friends she beheld, that were mournfully gazing upon her,
Pallid, with tearful eyes, and looks of saddest compassion.
Still the blaze of the burning village illumined the landscape,
Reddened the sky overhead, and gleamed on the faces around her,
And like the day of doom it seemed to her wavering senses.   650
Then a familiar voice she heard, as it said to the people,—
"Let us bury him here by the sea. When a happier season
Brings us again to our homes from the unknown land of our exile,
Then shall his sacred dust be piously laid in the churchyard."
Such were the words of the priest. And there in haste by the sea-
    side,   655
Having the glare of the burning village for funeral torches,
But without bell or book,[8] they buried the farmer of Grand-Pré.
And as the voice of the priest repeated the service of sorrow,
Lo! with a mournful sound, like the voice of a vast congregation,
Solemnly answered the sea, and mingled its roar with the dirges.
'Twas the returning tide, that afar from the waste of the ocean, 661
With the first dawn of the day, came heaving and hurrying land-
    ward.
Then recommenced once more the stir and noise of embarking;
And with the ebb of the tide the ships sailed out of the harbor,
Leaving behind them the dead on the shore, and the village in
    ruins.[9]   665

1845–1847   1847

The Building of the Ship[1]

"Build me straight, O worthy Master!
    Stanch and strong, a goodly vessel,

8. "Bell, book, and candle" was a proverbial allusion to the formal rites of
the Christian church; *cf.* Cervantes, *Don
Quixote*, I, iii, 4.
9. Here ends the first half of the poem.
Part II is somewhat less successful, in
consequence of its use of scenes less
familiar to Longfellow. Separated from
Gabriel, Evangeline travels with Father
Felician down the Mississippi, seeking
her betrothed among the Acadian exiles
of Louisiana. Gabriel has already returned northward; she has passed him
on the river. Basil, his father, guides
her over Gabriel's trail into the Ozarks
before setting his face again toward
Acadia. Evangeline, following reports of
Gabriel, journeys into the Michigan
forests and down into the Ohio country
until the trail ceases amid the confusions of the American Revolution.
Seeking sanctuary among the Quakers
of Philadelphia, she remains as a Sister
of Mercy. Thirty-eight years after the
beginning of the tale, during the yellow
fever epidemic of 1793, the lovers are
momentarily reunited, as the stricken
Gabriel dies in Evangeline's arms, in the
beautiful old Pennsylvania Hospital.
1. In November, 1849, "The Building
of the Ship" appeared as the "leading
piece" in *The Seaside and Fireside*

That shall laugh at all disaster,
And with wave and whirlwind wrestle!"

The merchant's word 5
Delighted the Master heard;
For his heart was in his work, and the heart
Giveth grace unto every Art.
A quiet smile played round his lips,
As the eddies and dimples of the tide 10
Play round the bows of ships,
That steadily at anchor ride.
And with a voice that was full of glee,
He answered, "Erelong we will launch
A vessel as goodly, and strong, and stanch, 15
As ever weathered a wintry sea!"
And first with nicest skill and art,
Perfect and finished in every part,
A little model the Master wrought,
Which should be to the larger plan 20
What the child is to the man,
Its counterpart in miniature;
That with a hand more swift and sure
The greater labor might be brought
To answer to his inward thought. 25
And as he labored, his mind ran o'er
The various ships that were built of yore,
And above them all, and strangest of all
Towered the Great Harry,[2] crank and tall,
Whose picture was hanging on the wall, 30
With bows and stern raised high in air,
And balconies hanging here and there,
And signal lanterns and flags afloat,
And eight round towers, like those that frown
From some old castle, looking down 35

(dated 1850). It was at once recognized as relating to the national disunity that had just reached its crisis with the Mexican War. The Compromise of 1850 had not yet effected an uneasy truce between the factions of North and South when the great Fanny Kemble read the poem, on February 12, to an audience "of more than three thousand" in Boston. It swept the country and remained an eloquent plea for the preservation of the Union. On a dark day of the Civil War, when Noah Brooks read it to President Lincoln, "his eyes filled with tears, and * * * he did not speak for some minutes, but finally said, with simplicity: 'It is a wonderful gift to be able to stir men like that.'" During World War II, Winston Churchill, in a speech referring to Allied unity, quoted part of the famous closing section. Longfellow acknowledged the inspiration of Schiller's *The Song of the Bell* for the form of this poem; certainly he was also inspired by his love of craftsmanship, and especially by his observation of the craft of the shipbuilder in the Portland Harbor of his boyhood.
2. Famous war vessel, built in 1488 by Henry VII, first Tudor King of England (1485–1509), whose marriage in 1486 united the warring Houses of Lancaster and York.

Upon the drawbridge and the moat.
And he said with a smile, "Our ship, I wis,
Shall be of another form than this!"
It was of another form, indeed;
Built for freight, and yet for speed,   40
A beautiful and gallant craft;
Broad in the beam, that the stress of the blast,
Pressing down upon sail and mast,
Might not the sharp bows overwhelm;
Broad in the beam, but sloping aft   45
With graceful curve and slow degrees,
That she might be docile to the helm,
And that the currents of parted seas,
Closing behind, with mighty force,
Might aid and not impede her course.   50

In the ship-yard stood the Master,
With the model of the vessel,
That should laugh at all disaster,
And with wave and whirlwind wrestle!

Covering many a rood of ground,   55
Lay the timber piled around;
Timber of chestnut, and elm, and oak,
And scattered here and there, with these,
The knarred[3] and crooked cedar knees;
Brought from regions far away,   60
From Pascagoula's sunny bay,[4]
And the banks of the roaring Roanoke![5]
Ah! what a wondrous thing it is
To note how many wheels of toil
One thought, one word, can set in motion!   65
There's not a ship that sails the ocean,
But every climate, every soil,
Must bring its tribute, great or small,
And help to build the wooden wall!

The sun was rising o'er the sea,
And long the level shadows lay,   70
As if they, too, the beams would be
Of some great, airy argosy,
Framed and launched in a single day.
That silent architect, the sun,   75

3. Gnarled, knotty.
4. Mouth of the Pascagoula River, at the eastern extremity of the gulf coast of Mississippi.
5. The Roanoke flows through Virginia and northern North Carolina, emptying in Albemarle Sound.

Had hewn and laid them every one,
Ere the work of man was yet begun.
Beside the Master, when he spoke,
A youth, against an anchor leaning,
Listened, to catch his slightest meaning,   80
Only the long waves, as they broke
In ripples on the pebbly beach,
Interrupted the old man's speech.

Beautiful they were, in sooth,
The old man and the fiery youth!   85
The old man, in whose busy brain
Many a ship that sailed the main
Was modelled o'er and o'er again;—
The fiery youth, who was to be
The heir of his dexterity,   90
The heir of his house, and his daughter's hand,
When he had built and launched from land
What the elder head had planned.

"Thus," said he, "will we build this ship!
Lay square the blocks upon the slip,   95
And follow well this plan of mine.
Choose the timbers with greatest care;
Of all that is unsound beware;
For only what is sound and strong
To this vessel shall belong.   100
Cedar of Maine and Georgia pine
Here together shall combine.
A goodly frame, and a goodly fame,
And the UNION be her name!
For the day that gives her to the sea   105
Shall give my daughter unto thee!"

The Master's word
Enraptured the young man heard;
And as he turned his face aside,
With a look of joy and a thrill of pride   110
Standing before
Her father's door,
He saw the form of his promised bride.
The sun shone on her golden hair,
And her cheek was glowing fresh and fair,   115
With the breath of morn and the soft sea air.
Like a beauteous barge was she,
Still at rest on the sandy beach,

Just beyond the billow's reach;
But he
Was the restless, seething, stormy sea!   120
Ah, how skilful grows the hand
That obeyeth Love's command!
It is the heart, and not the brain,
That to the highest doth attain,
And he who followeth Love's behest   125
Far excelleth all the rest!
Thus with the rising of the sun
Was the noble task begun,
And soon throughout the ship-yard's bounds   130
Were heard the intermingled sounds
Of axes and of mallets, plied
With vigorous arms on every side;
Plied so deftly and so well,
That, ere the shadows of evening fell,   135
The keel of oak for a noble ship,
Scarfed[6] and bolted, straight and strong,
Was lying ready, and stretched along
The blocks, well placed upon the slip.
Happy, thrice happy, every one   140
Who sees his labor well begun,
And not perplexed and multiplied,
By idly waiting for time and tide!

And when the hot, long day was o'er,
The young man at the Master's door   145
Sat with the maiden calm and still,
And within the porch, a little more
Removed beyond the evening chill,
The father sat, and told them tales
Of wrecks in the great September gales,   150
Of pirates coasting the Spanish Main,
And ships that never came back again,
The chance and change of a sailor's life,
Want and plenty, rest and strife,
His roving fancy, like the wind,   155
That nothing can stay and nothing can bind,
And the magic charm of foreign lands,
With shadows of palms, and shining sands,
Where the tumbling surf,
O'er the coral reefs of Madagascar,   160
Washes the feet of the swarthy Lascar,

6. Jointed. Two timbers bearing weight   scarfed by halved and overlapped ends
in a continuous line, as in a keel, are   spliced together by bolts.

As he lies alone and asleep on the turf.
And the trembling maiden held her breath
At the tales of that awful, pitiless sea,
With all its terror and mystery,   165
The dim, dark sea, so like unto Death,
That divides and yet unites mankind!
And whenever the old man paused, a gleam
From the bowl of his pipe would awhile illume
The silent group in the twilight gloom,   170
And thoughtful faces, as in a dream;
And for a moment one might mark
What had been hidden by the dark,
That the head of the maiden lay at rest,
Tenderly, on the young man's breast!   175
Day by day the vessel grew,
With timbers fashioned strong and true,
Stemson and keelson and sternson-knee,[7]
Till, framed with perfect symmetry,
A skeleton ship rose up to view!   180
And around the bows and along the side
The heavy hammers and mallets plied,
Till after many a week, at length,
Wonderful for form and strength,
Sublime in its enormous bulk,   185
Loomed aloft the shadowy hulk!
And around it columns of smoke, upwreathing,
Rose from the boiling, bubbling, seething
Caldron, that glowed,
And overflowed   190
With the black tar, heated for the sheathing.
And amid the clamors
Of clattering hammers,
He who listened heard now and then
The song of the Master and his men:—   195

"Build me straight, O worthy Master,
    Stanch and strong, a goodly vessel,
That shall laugh at all disaster,
    And with wave and whirlwind wrestle!"

With oaken brace and copper band,   200
Lay the rudder on the sand,
That, like a thought, should have control

7. In the fundamental "frame" of a ship, the keelson (kelson) is the principal longitudinal supporting member of the keel; the stemson is the upright support of the timbers at the bow; the sternson-knee is the after end (rear) of the keelson, fitted to support the upright sternpost.

Over the movement of the whole;
And near it the anchor, whose giant hand
Would reach down and grapple with the land,   205
And immovable and fast
Hold the great ship against the bellowing blast!
And at the bows an image stood,
By a cunning artist carved in wood,
With robes of white, that far behind   210
Seemed to be fluttering in the wind.
It was not shaped in a classic mould,
Not like a Nymph or Goddess of old,
Or Naiad rising from the water,
But modelled from the Master's daughter!   215
On many a dreary and misty night,
'Twill be seen by the rays of the signal light,
Speeding along through the rain and the dark,
Like a ghost in its snow-white sark,[8]
The pilot of some phantom bark,   220
Guiding the vessel, in its flight,
By a path none other knows aright!
Behold, at last,
Each tall and tapering mast
Is swung into its place;   225
Shrouds and stays
Holding it firm and fast![9]

Long ago,
In the deer-haunted forests of Maine,
When upon mountain and plain   230
Lay the snow,
They fell,—those lordly pines!
Those grand, majestic pines!
'Mid shouts and cheers
The jaded steers,   235
Panting beneath the goad,
Dragged down the weary, winding road
Those captive kings so straight and tall,
To be shorn of their streaming hair,
And naked and bare,   240
To feel the stress and the strain
Of the wind and the reeling main,
Whose roar

8. Shroud.
9. Longfellow carefully notes "that sometimes * * * vessels are launched fully sparred and rigged * * * in order to save time, and to make a show." He begs the exception "as better suited to my purpose than the general rule"; citing instances in New York, and in Maine at Portland and Ellsworth.

Would remind them forevermore
Of their native forests they should not see again.   245

And everywhere
The slender, graceful spars
Poise aloft in the air,
And at the mast-head,
White, blue, and red,   250
A flag unrolls the stripes and stars.
Ah! when the wanderer, lonely, friendless,
In foreign harbors shall behold
That flag unrolled,
'Twill be as a friendly hand   255
Stretched out from his native land,
Filling his heart with memories sweet and endless!

All is finished! and at length
Has come the bridal day
Of beauty and strength.   260
Today the vessel shall be launched!
With fleecy clouds the sky is blanched,
And o'er the bay,
Slowly, in all his splendors dight,
The great sun rises to behold the sight.   265
The ocean old,
Centuries old,
Strong as youth, and as uncontrolled,
Paces restless to and fro,
Up and down the sands of gold.   270
His beating heart is not at rest;
And far and wide,
With ceaseless flow,
His beard of snow
Heaves with the heaving of his breast.   275
He waits impatient for his bride.
There she stands,
With her foot upon the sands,
Decked with flags and streamers gay,
In honor of her marriage day,   280
Her snow-white signals fluttering, blending,
Round her like a veil descending,
Ready to be
The bride of the gray old sea.

On the deck another bride   285
Is standing by her lover's side.

Shadows from the flag and shrouds,
Like the shadows cast by clouds,
Broken by many a sudden fleck,
Fall around them on the deck.   290

The prayer is said,
The service read,
The joyous bridegroom bows his head;
And in tears the good old Master
Shakes the brown hand of his son,   295
Kisses his daughter's glowing cheek
In silence, for he cannot speak,
And ever faster
Down his own the tears begin to run.
The worthy pastor—   300
The shepherd of that wandering flock,
That has the ocean for its wold,
That has the vessel for its fold,
Leaping ever from rock to rock—
Spake, with accents mild and clear,   305
Words of warning, words of cheer,
But tedious to the bridegroom's ear.
He knew the chart
Of the sailor's heart,
All its pleasures and its griefs,   310
All its shallows and rocky reefs,
All those secret currents, that flow
With such resistless undertow,
And lift and drift, with terrible force,
The will from its moorings and its course.   315
Therefore he spake, and thus[1] said he:—
"Like unto ships far off at sea,
Outward or homeward bound, are we.

Before, behind, and all around,
Floats and swings the horizon's bound,   320
Seems at its distant rim to rise
And climb the crystal wall of the skies,
And then again to turn and sink,
As if we could slide from its outer brink.
Ah! it is not the sea,   325
It is not the sea that sinks and shelves,
But ourselves

---

1. Pastors of sailors' churches, endeared in the tradition of New England wooden ships and whaling, are typified by the famous Father Taylor of the Seamen's Bethel of Boston, whose sea-savored sermons are recalled in that below, as also in that of Melville's Father Mapple (*Moby Dick*, Chapter 9).

That rock and rise
With endless and uneasy motion,
Now touching the very skies,   330
Now sinking into the depths of ocean.
Ah! if our souls but poise and swing
Like the compass in its brazen ring,
Ever level and ever true
To the toil of the task we have to do,   335
We shall sail securely, and safely reach
The Fortunate Isles,[2] on whose shining beach
The sights we see, and the sounds we hear,
Will be those of joy and not of fear!"

Then the Master,   340
With a gesture of command,
Waved his hand;
And at the word,
Loud and sudden there was heard,
All around them and below,   345
The sound of hammers, blow on blow,
Knocking away the shores and spurs.[3]
And see! she stirs!
She starts,—she moves,—she seems to feel
The thrill of life along her keel,   350
And, spurning with her foot the ground,
With one exulting, joyous bound,
She leaps into the ocean's arms!

And lo! from the assembled crowd
There rose a shout, prolonged and loud,   355
That to the ocean seemed to say,
"Take her, O bridegroom, old and gray,
Take her to thy protecting arms,
With all her youth and all her charms!"

How beautiful she is! How fair   360
She lies within those arms, that press
Her form with many a soft caress
Of tenderness and watchful care!
Sail forth into the sea, O ship!
Through wind and wave, right onward steer!   365
The moistened eye, the trembling lip,
Are not the signs of doubt or fear.
Sail forth into the sea of life,

2. Established by Vergil's "fortunate isle" as journey's end, or paradise; *cf.* *Aeneid*, Book VI, l. 639.

3. Carpenter's terms for the props and braces that hold the vessel in the slip.

O gentle, loving, trusting wife,
And safe from all adversity   370
Upon the bosom of that sea
Thy comings and thy goings be!
For gentleness and love and trust
Prevail o'er angry wave and gust;
And in the wreck of noble lives   375
Something immortal still survives!

Thou, too, sail on, O Ship of State!
Sail on, O UNION, strong and great!
Humanity with all its fears,
With all the hopes of future years,   380
Is hanging breathless on thy fate!
We know what Master laid thy keel,
What Workmen wrought thy ribs of steel,
Who made each mast, and sail, and rope,
What anvils rang, what hammers beat,   385
In what a forge and what a heat
Were shaped the anchors of thy hope!
Fear not each sudden sound and shock,
'Tis of the wave and not the rock;
'Tis but the flapping of the sail,
And not a rent made by the gale!   390
In spite of rock and tempest's roar,
In spite of false lights on the shore,
Sail on, nor fear to breast the sea!
Our hearts, our hopes, are all with thee,   395
Our hearts, our hopes, our prayers, our tears,
Our faith triumphant o'er our fears,
Are all with thee,—are all with thee!

1849   [1849] 1850

The Jewish Cemetery at Newport[4]

How strange it seems! These Hebrews in their graves,
   Close by the street of this fair seaport town,
Silent beside the never-silent waves,
   At rest in all this moving up and down!

4. In his diary for July 9, 1852, at New-port, Rhode Island, the poet wrote: "Went this morning into the Jewish burying-ground * * * There are few graves; nearly all are low tombstones of marble with Hebrew inscriptions, and a few words added in English or Portu-guese. * * * It is a shady nook, at the corner of two dusty, frequented streets, with an iron fence and a granite gate-way * * * " The poem was written in the difficult stanza of Gray's "Elegy Written in a Country Churchyard." Longfellow's poem appeared in *Putnam's Monthly Magazine* for July, 1854, and was included in the "Birds of Passage" section of *The Courtship of Miles Standish* (1858).

The trees are white with dust, that o'er their sleep   5
    Wave their broad curtains in the southwind's breath,
While underneath these leafy tents they keep
    The long, mysterious Exodus of Death.[5]

And these sepulchral stones, so old and brown,
    That pave with level flags their burial-place,   10
Seem like the tablets of the Law, thrown down
    And broken by Moses at the mountain's base.[6]

The very names recorded here are strange,
    Of foreign accent, and of different climes;
Alvares and Rivera[7] interchange   15
    With Abraham and Jacob of old times.

"Blessed be God! for he created Death!"
    The mourners said, "and Death is rest and peace;"
Then added, in the certainty of faith,
    "And giveth Life that nevermore shall cease."   20

Closed are the portals of their Synagogue,
    No Psalms of David now the silence break,
No Rabbi reads the ancient Decalogue
    In the grand dialect the Prophets spake.

Gone are the living, but the dead remain,   25
    And not neglected; for a hand unseen,
Scattering its bounty, like a summer rain,
    Still keeps their graves and their remembrance green.

How came they here? What burst of Christian hate,
    What persecution, merciless and blind,   30
Drove o'er the sea—that desert desolate—
    These Ishmaels and Hagars of mankind?[8]

They lived in narrow streets and lanes obscure,
    Ghetto and Judenstrass,[9] in mirk and mire;
Taught in the school of patience to endure   35
    The life of anguish and the death of fire.

All their lives long, with the unleavened bread
    And bitter herbs of exile and its fears,
The wasting famine of the heart they fed,
    And slaked its thirst with marah[1] of their tears.   40

5. Exodus, second book of the Old Testament, records the migration of the Israelites from Egypt under Moses.
6. *Cf.* Exodus xxxii: 19.
7. The majority of the colonial Jewish families of New England were traders from Portugal or Spain.
8. Abraham's concubine, Hagar, and her son, Ishmael, were exiled when his aged wife, Sarah, bore Isaac (Genesis xvi and xxi).
9. Like "ghetto," *Judenstrass* (German, "street of Jews") refers to a restricted urban area designated for Jews.
1. Hebrew, "bitterness." Marah was a spring of bitter, undrinkable water found by the famishing Israelites in the wilderness. *Cf.* Exodus xv: 23–26.

Anathema maranatha![2] was the cry
  That rang from town to town, from street to street;
At every gate the accursed Mordecai[3]
  Was mocked and jeered, and spurned by Christian feet.

Pride and humiliation hand in hand
  Walked with them through the world where'er they went;   45
Trampled and beaten were they as the sand,
  And yet unshaken as the continent.

For in the background figures vague and vast
  Of patriarchs and of prophets rose sublime,   50
And all the great traditions of the Past
  They saw reflected in the coming time.

And thus forever with reverted look
  The mystic volume of the world they read,
Spelling it backward, like a Hebrew book,
  Till life became a Legend of the Dead.   55

But ah! what once has been shall be no more!
  The groaning earth in travail and in pain
Brings forth its races, but does not restore,
  And the dead nations never rise again.   60

1852   1854, 1858

My Lost Youth[4]

Often I think of the beautiful town
  That is seated by the sea;[5]
Often in thought go up and down
The pleasant streets of that dear old town,
  And my youth comes back to me.   5

2. *Cf.* I Corinthians xvi: 22. St. Paul's terms, *Anathema* (Greek, "devoted to destruction") *Maran 'atha* (Aramaic, "at the coming of the Lord"), were applied to all those who "love not the Lord Jesus Christ"; later they were applied specifically to the Jews.
3. Haman and his friends, jealous of the advancement of the Jew Mordecai, attempted to obtain a decree for the destruction of all Jews in the realm of the Persian king, Ahasuerus. See Esther iii.
4. Like "The Building of the Ship," this poem contains "a memory of Portland, —my native town, the city by the sea," as Longfellow noted in his diary on March 29, 1855. The next day, he continued, "Wrote the poem; and am rather

pleased with it, and with the bringing in of the two lines of the old Lapland song." He was referring to the two-line refrain ending each stanza. These words became so familiar that, as late as 1913, Robert Frost could call his first volume *A Boy's Will*, and be understood. Longfellow's poem appeared in *Putnam's Monthly Magazine* for August, 1855, and was included among the "other poems" of *The Courtship of Miles Standish* volume (1858).
5. In his diary Longfellow associates these words with those of Francesca in Dante's *Inferno*, v, 97–98: "Sieda la terra dove nato fui / Sulla marina." (The city where I was born is situated on the seashore.)

And a verse of a Lapland song
Is haunting my memory still:
"A boy's will is the wind's will,
And the thoughts of youth are long, long thoughts."[6]

I can see the shadowy lines of its trees,   10
And catch, in sudden gleams,
The sheen of the far-surrounding seas,
And islands that were the Hesprides[7]
  Of all my boyish dreams.
    And the burden of that old song,   15
    Its murmurs and whispers still:
  "A boy's will is the wind's will,
And the thoughts of youth are long, long thoughts."

I remember the black wharves and the slips,
And the sea-tides tossing free;
And Spanish sailors with bearded lips,   20
And the beauty and mystery of the ships,
  And the magic of the sea.
    And the voice of that wayward song
    Is singing and saying still: 25
  "A boy's will is the wind's will,
And the thoughts of youth are long, long thoughts."

I remember the bulwarks by the shore,
And the fort upon the hill;[8]
The sunrise gun, with its hollow roar,   30
The drum-beat repeated o'er and o'er,
  And the bugle wild and shrill.
    And the music of that old song
    Throbs in my memory still:
  "A boy's will is the wind's will,   35
And the thoughts of youth are long, long thoughts."

I remember the sea-fight far away,[9]
  How it thundered o'er the tide!

6. The Cambridge *Complete Poetical Works* reports the source of this refrain as John Scheffer's *History of Lapland* (Oxford, 1674), where occur the lines: "A Youth's desire is the desire of the wind, / All his essaies / Are long delaies, / No issue can they find."
7. The mythical garden of the golden apples which Gē (the earth) gave Hera, queen of the gods, on her marriage to Zeus.
8. Years before, in 1846, Longfellow noted in his diary a walk around "Munjoy's Hill and Fort St. Lawrence." There he "lay down in one of the embrasures and listened to the lashing, lulling sound of the sea just at my feet. * * * the harbor was full of white sails * * * Meditated a poem on the old Fort." But no poem resulted at that time.
9. "This was the engagement between the [American] *Enterprise* and [British] *Boxer* off the harbor of Portland, in which both captains were slain. They were buried side by side in the cemetery on Mountjoy [Munjoy Hill]" [Longfellow's note]. The *Enterprise* won this battle (1813), which Longfellow, a boy of six, may have seen; he is reported as witnessing the burial of the captains.

And the dead captains, as they lay
In their graves, o'erlooking the tranquil bay
  Where they in battle died.   40
    And the sound of that mournful song
    Goes through me with a thrill:
"A boy's will is the wind's will,
And the thoughts of youth are long, long thoughts."   45

I can see the breezy dome of groves,
  The shadows of Deering's Woods;
And the friendships old and the early loves
Come back with a Sabbath sound, as of doves
  In quiet neighborhoods.   50
    And the verse of that sweet old song,
    It flutters and murmurs still:
"A boys will is the wind's will,
And the thoughts of youth are long, long thoughts."

I remember the gleams and glooms that dart
  Across the school-boy's brain;   55
The song and the silence in the heart,
That in part are prophecies, and in part
  Are longings wild and vain.
    And the voice of that fitful song
    Sings on, and is never still: 60
"A boy's will is the wind's will,
And the thoughts of youth are long, long thoughts."

There are things of which I may not speak;
  There are dreams that cannot die;
There are thoughts that make the strong heart weak,   65
And bring a pallor into the cheek,
  And a mist before the eye.
    And the words of that fatal song
    Come over me like a chill:
"A boy's will is the wind's will,   70
And the thoughts of youth are long, long thoughts."

Strange to me now are the forms I meet
  When I visit the dear old town;
But the native air is pure and sweet,
And the trees that o'ershadow each well-known street,   75
  As they balance up and down,
    Are singing the beautiful song,
    Are sighing and whispering still:
"A boy's will is the wind's will,
And the thoughts of youth are long, long thoughts."   80

And Deering's Woods are fresh and fair,
   And with joy that is almost pain
My heart goes back to wander there,
And among the dreams of the days that were,   85
   I find my lost youth again.
     And the strange and beautiful song,
       The groves are repeating it still:
     "A boy's will is the wind's will,
And the thoughts of youth are long, long thoughts."   90

1855   1855, 1858

Divina Commedia[9]

I

Oft have I seen at some cathedral door
   A laborer, pausing in the dust and heat,
   Lay down his burden, and with reverent feet
   Enter, and cross himself, and on the floor
Kneel to repeat his paternoster[1] o'er;   5
   Far off the noises of the world retreat;
   The loud vociferations of the street
   Become an undistinguishable roar.
So, as I enter here from day to day,
   And leave my burden at this minster gate,   10
   Kneeling in prayer, and not ashamed to pray,
The tumult of the time disconsolate
   To inarticulate murmurs dies away,
   While the eternal ages watch and wait.

II

How strange the sculptures that adorn these towers!
   This crowd of statues, in whose folded sleeves
   Birds build their nests; while canopied with leaves
   Parvis[2] and portal bloom like trellised bowers,
And the vast minster seems a cross of flowers!   5
     But fiends and dragons on the gargoyled eaves[3]
     Watch the dead Christ between the living thieves,[4]

9. After his second wife was burned to death in 1861, Longfellow found relief in his translation of Dante's *Divine Comedy*. Volume I, *Inferno*, appeared in 1865, introduced by the first two sonnets. In the complete translation (1867), the six sonnets were distributed as introductory pieces, two for each volume. They appeared first, however, in the *Atlantic Monthly* for December, 1864 and November, 1866. As a sequence of sonnets they were first published in the volume *Flower-de-Luce*

(1867). In these masterpieces of sonnet literature, the poet's experience of Dante and his great religious poem is identified with the personal tragedy of his wife's death in the flames.
1. Translated "our Father"; *i.e.*, the Lord's Prayer.
2. A court, or a single portico, before a church.
3. The grotesques in Dante's *Inferno* are in this passage compared with those of cathedral sculpture.
4. Christ was crucified between two

And, underneath, the traitor Judas lowers!
Ah! from what agonies of heart and brain,
   What exultations trampling on despair,
   What tenderness, what tears, what hate of wrong,   10
What passionate outcry of a soul in pain,
   Uprose this poem of the earth and air,
   This mediæval miracle of song!

III

I enter, and I see thee in the gloom
   Of the long aisles, O poet saturnine![5]
   And strive to make my steps keep pace with thine.
The air is filled with some unknown perfume;
The congregation of the dead make room   5
   For thee to pass; the votive tapers shine;
   Like rooks that haunt Ravenna's[6] groves of pine
The hovering echoes fly from tomb to tomb.
From the confessionals I hear arise
   Rehearsals of forgotten tragedies,   10
   And lamentations from the crypts below;
And then a voice celestial that begins
   With the pathetic words, "Although your sins
   As scarlet be," and ends with "as the snow."[7]

IV

With snow-white veil and garments as of flame,
   She stands before thee, who so long ago
   Filled thy young heart with passion and the woe
From which thy song and all its splendors came;[8]
And while with stern rebuke she speaks thy name,   5
   The ice about thy heart melts as the snow
   On mountain heights, and in swift overflow
Comes gushing from thy lips in sobs of shame.
Thou makest full confession; and a gleam,
   As of the dawn on some dark forest cast,   10
   Seems on thy lifted forehead to increase;
Lethe and Eunoë[9]—the remembered dream
   And the forgotten sorrow—bring at last
   That perfect pardon which is perfect peace.

V

I lift mine eyes, and all the windows blaze
   With forms of Saints and holy men who died,

---

thieves, and was declared dead before they.

5. Referring to the grave and solemn tone of Dante.

6. Dante often expressed fondness for Ravenna, where he was buried.

7. *Cf.* Isaiah i: 18, and Dante, *Purgatorio*, xxxi, 98.

8. Dante experiences visionary union with the dead Beatrice, both in the *Purgatorio* and the *Paradiso*.

9. In the *Purgatorio*, Dante drinks the waters of two rivers: Lethe, providing forgetfulness; and Eunoë, giving memory of the good.

Here martyred and hereafter glorified;
And the great Rose[1] upon its leaves displays
Christ's Triumph, and the angelic roundelays,   5
With splendor upon splendor multiplied;
And Beatrice again at Dante's side
No more rebukes, but smiles her words of praise.[2]
And then the organ sounds, and unseen choirs
Sing the old Latin hymns of peace and love   10
And benedictions of the Holy Ghost;
And the melodious bells among the spires
O'er all the house-tops and through heaven above
Proclaim the elevation of the Host![3]

VI

O star of morning and of liberty![4]
O bringer of the light, whose splendor shines
Above the darkness of the Apennines,
Forerunner of the day that is to be!
The voices of the city and the sea,   5
The voices of the mountains and the pines,
Repeat thy song, till the familiar lines
Are footpaths for the thought of Italy!
Thy flame is blown abroad from all the heights,
Through all the nations, and a sound is heard,   10
As of a mighty wind, and men devout,
Strangers of Rome, and the new proselytes,
In their own language hear thy wondrous word,
And many are amazed and many doubt.

1864–1867   1865–1867

Chaucer

An old man in a lodge within a park;
The chamber walls depicted all around
With portraitures of huntsman, hawk, and hound,
And the hurt deer. He listeneth to the lark,
Whose song comes with the sunshine through the dark   5
Of painted glass in leaden lattice bound;
He listeneth and he laugheth at the sound,
Then writeth in a book like any clerk.[5]

1. In the *Paradiso*, xxxi, Dante's pilgrimage ends with his vision of the *rosa sempeterna*, in which the Virgin and the Trinity appear, surrounded by the saints in a paradise shaped like the petals of a great rose.
2. *Cf. Paradiso*, xxx.
3. The consecrated bread of the sacrament of the Lord's Supper (Eucharist),

held up or "elevated" at the climax of this ritual.
4. The familiar concept of Dante as morning star of a new democratic freedom, especially for Italy.
5. A scholar. *Cf.* Chaucer's "Clerk of Oxenford," one of the most appealing characters of the *Canterbury Tales*.

He is the poet of the dawn, who wrote
   The Canterbury Tales, and his old age   10
   Made beautiful with song; and as I read
I hear the crowing cock, I hear the note
   Of lark and linnet, and from every page
   Rise odors of ploughed field or flowery mead.

1873   1875

Milton

I pace the sounding sea-beach and behold
   How the voluminous billows roll and run,
   Upheaving and subsiding, while the sun
Shines through their sheeted emerald far unrolled
And the ninth wave, slow gathering fold by fold   5
   All its loose-flowing garments into one,
   Plunges upon the shore, and floods the dun
Pale reach of sands, and changes them to gold.
So in majestic cadence rise and fall
   The mighty undulations of thy song,
   O sightless Bard, England's Mæonides![6]   10
And ever and anon, high over all
   Uplifted, a ninth wave superb and strong,
   Floods all the soul with its melodious seas.

1873   1875

Keats

The young Endymion sleeps Endymion's sleep;[7]
   The shepherd-boy whose tale was left half told!
   The solemn grove uplifts its shield of gold
   To the red rising moon, and loud and deep
The nightingale is singing from the steep;   5
   It is midsummer, but the air is cold;
   Can it be death? Alas, beside the fold
A shepherd's pipe lies shattered near his sheep.
Lo! in the moonlight gleams a marble white,
   On which I read: "Here lieth one whose name   10
   Was writ in water."[8] And was this the meed

6. Homer, by tradition the son of Maeon, hence "Mæonides"; Milton, like Homer, was blind. See *Paradise Lost*, Book III, ll. 18–50.
7. Keats is often fancifully identified with the hero of his *Endymion*, a shepherd lad of Greek mythology, beloved of Selene (the moon), who cast eternal sleep upon him that he might be unaware of her caresses.
8. Keats composed this as his own epitaph (writing "lies," not "lieth"), and directed that it be inscribed on his tombstone.

Of his sweet singing? Rather let me write:
"The smoking flax before it burst to flame
Was quenched by death, and broken the bruised reed."[9]

1873   1875

Morituri Salutamus[1]

POEM FOR THE FIFTIETH ANNIVERSARY OF THE CLASS OF 1825
IN BOWDOIN COLLEGE

Tempora labuntur, tacitisque senescimus annis,
Et fugiunt freno non remorante dies.
—OVID, FASTORUM, Lib. vi[2]

"O Cæsar, we who are about to die
Salute you!" was the gladiators' cry
In the arena, standing face to face
With death and with the Roman populace.

O ye familiar scenes,—ye groves of pine,   5
That once were mine and are no longer mine,—
Thou river, widening through the meadows green
To the vast sea, so near and yet unseen,—
Ye halls, in whose seclusion and repose
Phantoms of fame, like exhalations, rose   10
And vanished,—we who are about to die,
Salute you; earth and air and sea and sky,
And the Imperial Sun that scatters down
His sovereign splendors upon grove and town.

Ye do not answer us! ye do not hear!   15
We are forgotten; and in your austere
And calm indifference, ye little care
Whether we come or go, or whence or where.
What passing generations fill these halls,
What passing voices echo from these walls,   20
Ye heed not; we are only as the blast,
A moment heard, and then forever past.

Not so the teachers who in earlier days
Led our bewildered feet through learning's maze;
They answer us—alas! what have I said?   25

9. "A bruised reed shall he not break, and the smoking flax shall he not quench" (Isaiah xlii: 3).
1. This title, translated in the first two lines of the poem, refers to the traditional salutation of the gladiator to the Roman emperor on entering the arena. Longfellow apparently derived the general idea of the poem from a picture of gladiators painted by Gérôme, bearing the Latin legend, slightly different in construction, *Ave, Caesar, Imperator, Morituri te Salutant*. Longfellow read the poem to the anniversary audience in a Brunswick church, and published it in *The Masque of Pandora* (1875).
2. "Time slips away, and we grow old with these silent years, and the days fly by with no curb to delay them."

What greetings come there from the voiceless dead?
What salutation, welcome, or reply?
What pressure from the hands that lifeless lie?
They are no longer here; they all are gone
Into the land of shadows,—all save one.   30
Honor and reverence, and the good repute
That follows faithful service as its fruit,
Be unto him, whom living we salute.

The great Italian poet,[3] when he made
His dreadful journey to the realms of shade,   35
Met there the old instructor of his youth,
And cried in tones of pity and of ruth:
"Oh, never from the memory of my heart
Your dear, paternal image shall depart,
Who while on earth, ere yet by death surprised,   40
Taught me how mortals are immortalized;
How grateful am I for that patient care
All my life long my language shall declare."

To-day we make the poet's words our own,
And utter them in plaintive undertone;   45
Nor to the living only be they said,
But to the other living called the dead,
Whose dear, paternal images appear
Not wrapped in gloom, but robed in sunshine here;
Whose simple lives, complete and without flaw,   50
Were part and parcel of great Nature's law;
Who said not to their Lord, as if afraid,
"Here is thy talent[4] in a napkin laid,"
But labored in their sphere, as men who live
In the delight that work alone can give.   55
Peace be to them; eternal peace and rest,
And the fulfilment of the great behest:
"Ye have been faithful over a few things,
Over ten cities shall ye reign as kings."[5]
And ye who fill the places we once filled,   60
And follow in the furrows that we tilled,
Young men, whose generous hearts are beating high,
We who are old, and are about to die,
Salute you; hail you; take your hands in ours,
And crown you with our welcome as with flowers!   65

3. Dante, in the *Inferno* (v, 82–87), imagines meeting among the souls of the dead his old advisor, Brunetto Latini, and thanks him for his instruction in the words translated in this stanza. Longfellow pays this compliment to Professor Alphaeus Spring Packard.
4. A parable of Jesus. *Cf.* Matthew xxv: 14–29.
5. A parable of Jesus. *Cf.* Luke xix: 11–17.

How beautiful is youth! how bright it gleams
With its illusions, aspirations, dreams!
Book of Beginnings, Story without End,
Each maid a heroine, and each man a friend!
Aladdin's Lamp, and Fortunatus' Purse,[6]   70
That holds the treasures of the universe!
All possibilities are in its hands,
No danger daunts it, and no foe withstands;
In its sublime audacity of faith,
"Be thou removed!" it to the mountain saith,[7]   75
And with ambitious feet, secure and proud,
Ascends the ladder leaning on the cloud!

As ancient Priam[8] at the Scæan gate
Sat on the walls of Troy in regal state
With the old men, too old and weak to fight,   80
Chirping like grasshoppers in their delight
To see the embattled hosts, with spear and shield,
Of Trojans and Achaians in the field;
So from the snowy summits of our years
We see you in the plain, as each appears,   85
And question of you; asking, "Who is he
That towers above the others? Which may be
Atreides, Menelaus, Odysseus,
Ajax the great, or bold Idomeneus?"

Let him not boast who puts his armor on   90
As he who puts it off, the battle done.[9]
Study yourselves; and most of all note well
Wherein kind Nature meant you to excel.
Not every blossom ripens into fruit;
Minerva, the inventress of the flute,   95
Flung it aside, when she her face surveyed
Distorted in a fountain as she played;
The unlucky Marsyas found it, and his fate
Was one to make the bravest hesitate.[1]
Write on your doors the saying wise and old,   100
"Be bold! be bold!" and everywhere, "Be bold;
Be not too bold!"[2] Yet better the excess

---

6. In *Old Fortunatus* (1606), a play by
Thomas Dekker, Fortunatus receives
from the goddess of fortune an inexhaustible purse, but dies of his consequent follies.
7. *Cf.* I Corinthians xiii: 2.
8. King of Troy. *Cf. Iliad*, Book III, l.
174, for the beginning of the episode
described below.
9. *Cf.* I Kings xx: 11.

1. Marsyas, a satyr, discovered that the
flute, of its own accord, emitted ravish-
ing music; hence he challenged Apollo,
god of music, to a contest. The gods
decided in favor of Apollo, and Marsyas
was flayed alive as a presumptuous
cheat.
2. The inscription over the door of the
last room in the castle of love (Spenser,
The Faërie Queene, Book III, Canto xi,
stanza 54).

Than the defect; better the more than less;
Better like Hector in the field to die,
Than like a perfumed Paris turn and fly.[3]   105

And now, my classmates; ye remaining few
That number not the half of those we knew,
Ye, against whose familiar names not yet
The fatal asterisk[4] of death is set,
Ye I salute! The horologe of Time   110
Strikes the half century with a solemn chime,
And summons us together once again,
The joy of meeting not unmixed with pain.

Where are the others? Voices from the deep
Caverns of darkness answer me: "They sleep!"   115
I name no names; instinctively I feel
Each at some well-remembered grave will kneel,
And from the inscription wipe the weeds and moss,
For every heart best knoweth its own loss.
I see their scattered gravestones gleaming white   120
Through the pale dusk of the impending night;
O'er all alike the impartial sunset throws
Its golden lilies mingled with the rose;
We give to each a tender thought, and pass
Out of the graveyards with their tangled grass,   125
Unto these scenes frequented by our feet
When we were young, and life was fresh and sweet.

What shall I say to you? What can I say
Better than silence is? When I survey
This throng of faces turned to meet my own,   130
Friendly and fair, and yet to me unknown,
Transformed the very landscape seems to be;
It is the same, yet not the same to me.
So many memories crowd upon my brain,
So many ghosts are in the wooded plain,   135
I fain would steal away, with noiseless tread,
As from a house where some one lieth dead.
I cannot go;—I pause;—I hesitate;
My feet reluctant linger at the gate;
As one who struggles in a troubled dream   140
To speak and cannot, to myself I seem.

3. The death of the Trojan Hector in combat with Achilles is a tragic climax of the *Iliad* (Book XXII); Paris, lover of Helen, escapes the vengeance of her husband, Menelaus, only by the intervention of Venus in a "cloud of perfumes" (Book III, ll. 419–459).
4. The conventional mark beside the names of deceased members of a group.

Vanish the dream! Vanish the idle fears!
Vanish the rolling mists of fifty years!
Whatever time or space may intervene,
I will not be a stranger in this scene.   145
Here every doubt, all indecision, ends;
Hail, my companions, comrades, classmates, friends!

Ah me! the fifty years since last we met
Seem to me fifty folios bound and set
By Time, the great transcriber, on his shelves,   150
Wherein are written the histories of ourselves.
What tragedies, what comedies, are there;
What joy and grief, what rapture and despair!
What chronicle of triumph and defeat,
Of struggle, and temptation, and retreat!   155
What record of regrets, and doubts, and fears!
What pages blotted, blistered by our tears!
What lovely landscapes on the margin shine,
What sweet, angelic faces, what divine
And holy images of love and trust,   160
Undimmed by age, unsoiled by damp or dust!
Whose hand shall dare to open and explore
These volumes, closed and clasped forevermore?
Not mine. With reverential feet I pass;
I hear a voice that cries, "Alas! alas!   165
Whatever hath been written shall remain,
Not to be erased nor written o'er again;
The unwritten only still belongs to thee:
Take heed, and ponder well what that shall be."

As children frightened by a thunder-cloud   170
Are reassured if someone reads aloud
A tale of wonder, with enchantment fraught,
Or wild adventure, that diverts their thought,
Let me endeavor with a tale to chase
The gathering shadows of the time and place,   175
And banish what we all too deeply feel
Wholly to say, or wholly to conceal.

In mediæval Rome,[5] I know not where,
There stood an image with its arm in air,
And on its lifted finger, shining clear,   180
A golden ring with the device, "Strike here!"
Greatly the people wondered, though none guessed

---

5. The tale is number cvii of *Gesta Romanorum*, a medieval collection of Latin moralized stories which served as a source book for Chaucer, Shakespeare, and others.

The meaning that these words but half expressed,
Until a learned clerk, who at noonday
With downcast eyes was passing on his way, 185
Paused, and observed the spot, and marked it well,
Whereon the shadow of the finger fell;
And, coming back at midnight, delved, and found
A secret stairway leading underground.
Down this he passed into a spacious hall, 190
Lit by a flaming jewel on the wall;
And opposite, in threatening attitude,
With bow and shaft a brazen statue stood.
Upon its forehead, like a coronet,
Were these mysterious words of menace set: 195
"That which I am, I am; my fatal aim
None can escape, not even yon luminous flame!"

Midway the hall was a fair table placed,
With cloth of gold, and golden cups enchased
With rubies, and the plates and knives were gold, 200
And gold the breads and viands manifold.
Around it, silent, motionless, and sad,
Were seated gallant knights in armor clad,
And ladies beautiful with plume and zone,
But they were stone, their hearts within were stone; 205
And the vast hall was filled in every part
With silent crowds, stony in face and heart.

Long at the scene, bewildered and amazed
The trembling clerk in speechless wonder gazed;
Then from the table, by his greed made bold, 210
He seized a goblet and a knife of gold,
And suddenly from their seats the guests upsprang,
The vaulted ceiling with loud clamors rang,
The archer sped his arrow, at their call,
Shattering the lambent jewel on the wall, 215
And all was dark around and overhead;—
Stark on the floor the luckless clerk lay dead!

The writer of this legend then records
Its ghostly application in these words:
The image is the Adversary old, 220
Whose beckoning finger points to realms of gold;
Our lusts and passions are the downward stair
That leads the soul from a diviner air;
The archer, Death; the flaming jewel, Life;
Terrestrial goods, the goblet and the knife; 225

The knights and ladies, all whose flesh and bone
By avarice had been hardened into stone;
The clerk, the scholar whom the love of pelf
Tempts from his books and from his nobler self.

The scholar and the world! The endless strife,   230
The discord in the harmonies of life!
The love of learning, the sequestered nooks,
And all the sweet serenity of books;
The market-place, the eager love of gain,
Whose aim is vanity, and whose end is pain!   235

But why, you ask me, should this tale be told
To men grown old, or who are growing old?
It is too late! Ah, nothing is too late
Till the tired heart shall cease to palpitate.
Cato[6] learned Greek at eighty; Sophocles   240
Wrote his grand Œdipus, and Simonides
Bore off the prize of verse from his compeers,
When each had numbered more than four-score years,
And Theophrastus, at fourscore and ten,
Had but begun his "Characters of Men."   245
Chaucer, at Woodstock with the nightingales,
At sixty wrote the Canterbury Tales;[7]
Goethe at Weimar, toiling to the last,
Completed Faust when eighty years were past.[8]
These are indeed exceptions; but they show   250
How far the gulf-stream of our youth may flow
Into the arctic regions of our lives,
Where little else than life itself survives.

As the barometer foretells the storm
While still the skies are clear, the weather warm   255
So something in us, as old age draws near,
Betrays the pressure of the atmosphere.
The nimble mercury, ere we are aware,
Descends the elastic ladder of the air;
The telltale blood in artery and vein   260
Sinks from its higher levels in the brain;
Whatever poet, orator, or sage

6. Cato the Censor (234–149 B.C.) was a Roman statesman and puritan; Sophocles (495–405 B.C.), Greek tragedian, wrote his last masterpiece, *Oedipus Coloneus*, two or three years before his death; Simonides of Ceos (*fl.* 514 B.C.), was a famous lyrist of the Greek court; and Theophrastus (died *ca.* 287 B.C.) succeeded Aristotle as a philosopher.

7. Modern scholarship has altered the dates for Chaucer. Chaucer died at sixty, having laid aside the *Canterbury Tales* five years earlier, after twenty-two years of sporadic writing. Note Longfellow's sonnet to Chaucer, above.
8. The complete *Faust* was not ready for press until 1832, the year of Goethe s death at eighty-three; Part I was written in 1794 and published in 1808.

May say of it, old age is still old age.
It is the waning, not the crescent moon;
The dusk of evening, not the blaze of noon;
It is not strength, but weakness; not desire,
But its surcease; not the fierce heat of fire,
The burning and consuming element,
But that of ashes and of embers spent,
In which some living sparks we still discern,
Enough to warm, but not enough to burn.

What then? Shall we sit idly down and say
The night hath come; it is no longer day?
The night hath not yet come; we are not quite
Cut off from labor by the failing light;
Something remains for us to do or dare;
Even the oldest tree some fruit may bear;
Not Œdipus Coloneus, or Greek Ode,
Or tales of pilgrims that one morning rode
Out of the gateway of the Tabard Inn,[9]
But other something, would we but begin;
For age is opportunity no less
Than youth itself, though in another dress,
And as the evening twilight fades away
The sky is filled with stars, invisible by day.

1874   1875

Nature[1]

As a fond mother, when the day is o'er,
  Leads by the hand her little child to bed,
  Half willing, half reluctant to be led,
And leave his broken playthings on the floor,
Still gazing at them through the open door,
  Nor wholly reassured and comforted
  By promises of others in their stead,
Which, though more splendid, may not please him more;
So Nature deals with us, and takes away
  Our playthings one by one, and by the hand
Leads us to rest so gently, that we go
  Scarce knowing if we wish to go or stay,
Being too full of sleep to understand
How far the unknown transcends the what we know.

1875

9. So Chaucer's pilgrims rode.
1. This sonnet, famous for its fusion of
simplicity with profound sentiment, appeared in the volume *The Masque of
Pandora* (1875).

The Tide Rises, the Tide Falls

The tide rises, the tide falls,
The twilight darkens, the curlew calls;[2]
Along the sea-sands damp and brown
The traveller hastens toward the town,
    And the tide rises, the tide falls.   5

Darkness settles on roofs and walls,
But the sea, the sea in the darkness calls;
The little waves, with their soft, white hands,
Efface the footprints in the sands,
    And the tide rises, the tide falls.   10

The morning breaks; the steeds in their stalls
Stamp and neigh, as the hostler calls;
The day returns, but nevermore
Returns the traveller to the shore,
    And the tide rises, the tide falls.   15

1879   1880

The Cross of Snow

In the long, sleepless watches of the night,
    A gentle face—the face of one[3] long dead—
Looks at me from the wall, where round its head
The night-lamp casts a halo of pale light.
Here in this room she died; and soul more white   5
    Never through martyrdom of fire was led
To its repose; nor can in books be read
The legend of a life more benedight.
There is a mountain in the distant West
    That, sun-defying, in its deep ravines   10
Displays a cross of snow upon its side.
Such is the cross I wear upon my breast
    These eighteen years, through all the changing scenes
And seasons, changeless since the day she died.

1879   1886

2. The cry of the curlew along the shore must suggest evening for anyone with a seashore boyhood. This allegory of the evening of life, simple, yet strong, and deeply felt, stands high among Longfellow's many treatments of the theme at this time, such as "Morituri Salutamus," "Nature," and the two poems that follow. Appropriately, this poem appeared in the volume *Ultima Thule* (1880).

3. Longfellow's second wife, Frances Appleton, who burned to death in 1861. The poem, unpublished, was discovered among the poet's papers, bearing the date July 10, 1879. Samuel Longfellow printed it in the second volume of the *Life* of his brother (1886).

Ultima Thule

DEDICATION: TO G. W. G.[4]

With favoring winds, o'er sunlit seas,
We sailed for the Hesperides,[5]
The land where golden apples grow;
But that, ah! that was long ago.

How far since then the ocean streams   5
Have swept us from the land of dreams,
That land of fiction and of truth,
The lost Atlantis[6] of our youth!

Whither, ah, whither? are not these
The tempest-haunted Orcades,[7]   10
Where sea-gulls scream, and breakers roar,
And wreck and sea-weed line the shore?

Ultima Thule! Utmost Isle!
Here in thy harbors for awhile
We lower our sails, awhile we rest   15
From the unending endless quest.

1879   1880

From Kavanagh: A Tale

Chapter XX. [*The Question of a National Literature*][8]

* * * Mr. Churchill, also, had had his profile,[9] and those of his
wife and children, taken, in a very humble style, by Mr. Bantam,

4. The volume *Ultima Thule* (1880),
was dedicated, in this poem, to George
Washington Greene, a friend with whom,
in young manhood, Longfellow had
shared confessions of goals and aspirations in life. Ultima Thule, to ancient
navigators, suggested the northernmost
limits of the habitable world, the ultimate journey's end.
5. The Hesperides were the "blessed
Isles" of Greek myth, where the golden
apples grew which Ge (the earth) gave
to Hera as a wedding gift.
6. A fabulous land of wealth and happiness which, the ancients believed, had
sunk into the sea.
7. A variant text gives "Hebrides"; like
the Orcades these are islands off the
Scottish coast, and were, to the ancient
Greeks, "tempest-haunted."
8. The background of the following
selection is the persistent controversy,
during the first half of the nineteenth
century, concerning American "national"
literature. Longfellow was soon recog-

nized as the most successful of American poets in the treatment of the
American scene, but with increasing
consistency he stood out against those
who wished to confine the American
writer to "American" subjects and locale. He asserted, and in his poems of
European background he demonstrated,
that "American" denoted the stamp of
the American character, rather than
provincial restrictions as to the selection of materials and themes. The subject still has considerable liveliness in
American criticism. *Kavanagh* (1849)
from which this selection is taken, has
not impressed readers as an important
volume among Longfellow's works. It
is a somewhat superficial romance, conveyed in a succession of sketches. The
leading character, Mr. Churchill, is the
schoolmaster of Fairmeadow, a Massachusetts village.
9. A silhouette, or outline drawing in
solid color.

whose advertisement he had noticed on his way to school nearly a year before. His own was considered the best, as a work of art. The face was cut out entirely; the color of the coat velvet; the shirt-collar very high and white; and the top of his head ornamented with a crest of hair turning up in front, though his own turned down,— which slight deviation from nature was explained and justified by the painter as a license allowable in art.

One evening, as he was sitting down to begin, for at least the hundredth time, the great Romance,—subject of so many resolves and so much remorse, so often determined upon but never begun,— a loud knock at the street-door, which stood wide open, announced a visitor. Unluckily, the study-door was likewise open; and consequently, being in full view, he found it impossible to refuse himself; nor, in fact, would have done so, had all the doors been shut and bolted,—the art of refusing one's self being at that time but imperfectly understood in Fairmeadow. Accordingly, the visitor was shown in.

He announced himself as Mr. Hathaway. Passing through the village, he could not deny himself the pleasure of calling on Mr. Churchill, whom he knew by his writings in the periodicals, though not personally. He wished, moreover, to secure the co-operation of one, already so favorably known to the literary world, in a new Magazine he was about to establish, in order to raise the character of American literature, which, in his opinion, the existing reviews and magazines had entirely failed to accomplish.[1] A daily increasing want of something better was felt by the public; and the time had come for the establishment of such a periodical as he proposed. After explaining, in rather a florid and exuberant manner, his plans and prospects, he entered more at large into the subject of American literature, which it was his design to foster and patronize.

"I think, Mr. Churchill," said he, "that we want a national literature commensurate with our mountains and rivers,—commensurate with Niagara, and the Alleghanies, and the Great Lakes!"

"Oh!"

"We want a national epic that shall correspond to the size of the country; that shall be to all other epics what Banvard's Panorama of the Mississippi[2] is to all other paintings,—the largest in the world."

"Ah!"

"We want a national drama in which scope enough shall be given to our gigantic ideas, and to the unparalleled activity and progress of our people!"

---

1. This is a parody of the appeal and program of many magazines launched during these years.
2. John Banvard (1815–1891) in 1840 painted this panorama—a canvas advertised as being three miles long, slowly unrolled for spectators. This popular spectacle was the source for Longfellow's Mississippi scenery in *Evangeline*.

"Of course."

"In a word, we want a national literature altogether shaggy and unshorn, that shall shake the earth, like a herd of buffaloes thundering over the prairies!"

"Precisely," interrupted Mr. Churchill; "but excuse me!—are you not confounding things that have no analogy? Great has a very different meaning when applied to a river, and when applied to a literature. Large and shallow may perhaps be applied to both. Literature is rather an image of the spiritual world, than of the physical, is it not?—of the internal, rather than the external. Mountains, lakes, and rivers are, after all, only its scenery and decorations, not its substance and essence. A man will not necessarily be a great poet because he lives near a great mountain. Nor, being a poet, will he necessarily write better poems than another, because he lives nearer Niagara."

"But, Mr. Churchill, you do not certainly mean to deny the influence of scenery on the mind?"

"No, only to deny that it can create genius. At best, it can only develop it. Switzerland has produced no extraordinary poet; nor, as far as I know, have the Andes, or the Himalaya mountains, or the Mountains of the Moon in Africa."

"But, at all events," urged Mr. Hathaway, "let us have our literature national. If it is not national, it is nothing."

"On the contrary, it may be a great deal. Nationality is a good thing to a certain extent, but universality is better. All that is best in the great poets of all countries is not what is national in them, but what is universal. Their roots are in their native soil; but their branches wave in the unpatriotic air, that speaks the same language unto all men, and their leaves shine with the illimitable light that pervades all lands. Let us throw all the windows open; let us admit the light and air on all sides; that we may look towards the four corners of the heavens, and not always in the same direction."

"But you admit nationality to be a good thing?"

"Yes, if not carried too far; still, I confess, it rather limits one's views of truth. I prefer what is natural. Mere nationality is often ridiculous. Every one smiles when he hears the Icelandic proverb, 'Iceland is the best land the sun shines upon.' Let us be natural, and we shall be national enough. Besides, our literature can be strictly national only so far as our character and modes of thought differ from those of other nations. Now, as we are very like the English,—are, in fact, English under a different sky,—I do not see how our literature can be very different from theirs. Westward from hand to hand we pass the lighted torch, but it was lighted at the old domestic fireside of England."

"Then you think our literature is never to be anything but an imitation of the English?"

"Not at all. It is not an imitation, but, as some one has said, a continuation."

"It seems to me that you take a very narrow view of the subject."

"On the contrary, a very broad one. No literature is complete until the language in which it is written is dead. We may well be proud of our task and of our position. Let us see if we can build in any way worthy of our forefathers."

"But I insist on originality."

"Yes; but without spasms and convulsions. Authors must not, like Chinese soldiers, expect to win victories by turning somersets in the air."

"Well, really, the prospect from your point of view is not very brilliant. Pray, what do you think of our national literature?"

"Simply, that a national literature is not the growth of a day. Centuries must contribute their dew and sunshine to it. Our own is gowing slowly but surely, striking its roots downward and its branches upward, as is natural; and I do not wish, for the sake of what some people call originality, to invert it, and try to make it grow with its roots in the air. And as for having it so savage and wild as you want it, I have only to say, that all literature, as well as all art, is the result of culture and intellectual refinement."

"Ah! we do not want art and refinement; we want genius,—untutored, wild, original, free."

"But, if this genius is to find any expression, it must employ art, for art is the external expression of our thoughts. Many have genius, but, wanting art, are forever dumb. The two must go together to form the great poet, painter, or sculptor."

"In that sense, very well."

"I was about to say also that I thought our literature would finally not be wanting in a kind of universality. As the blood of all nations is mingling with our own, so will their thoughts and feelings finally mingle in our literature. We shall draw from the Germans, tenderness; from the Spaniards, passion; from the French, vivacity, —to mingle more and more with our English solid sense. And this will give us universality, so much to be desired."

1849

JOHN GREENLEAF WHITTIER
(1807–1892)

Longfellow became a poet of the people by choice and by nature, but Whittier was fitted for that rôle also by all the circumstances of his early experience and family tradition. The Whittiers had farmed along the Merrimack, almost within sight of the sea, since the days of Thomas Whittier, who in 1648 cleared the farmstead near Haverhill, Massachusetts, where the poet was born in 1807. The family immortalized in *Snow-Bound* was frugal by necessity, but also by conviction, for the Quaker way of life, to which the Whittiers were devoted, was one of simplicity, piety, and social responsibility. Although Whittier's opportunities were severely limited, the responsibility for study and expression was a Quaker tradition; the imagination of the young poet was nourished on the impassioned mysticism and moral earnestness of the classic journals of early Friends, on the Bible and *Pilgrim's Progress*, and on the few books that chance brought to a country farmhouse. Less by chance than by destiny, as it seems, the schoolmaster, Joshua Coffin, lent the boy the poetry of Robert Burns, whose lyric expression of the common life confirmed Whittier's natural bent as a writer. Burns's influence is everywhere apparent in Whittier's poems, although the American was fundamentally incapable of his Scottish master's discipline, wit, and racy earthiness.

At nineteen he had a poem accepted for publication. The Newburyport *Press*, in which it appeared, was edited by William Lloyd Garrison, soon to become the editor of the *Liberator*, the foremost journal of abolitionism. Garrison, who became Whittier's lifelong friend and associate in emancipation propaganda, encouraged the lad to think of himself as a writer. He abandoned the trade of cobbler, which he was learning, and returned to school. He spent a year at Haverhill Academy, taught school, worked for a Boston publisher, and held obscure editorial positions while his articles and poems appeared with increasing frequency in a variety of publications. His first volume, *Legends of New England* (1831) was prose; a poem published the next year, *Moll Pitcher*, had a story with some elements of interest, but after revising it for the volume of 1840 the poet wisely excluded it from further collections. This was the fate of a large proportion of his early poems. He had great facility, genuine feeling, and an engaging earnestness but little training for his task. As a result, his early poems are amateurish, and while a few were revised, the great majority were abandoned to the obscurity of the periodicals or early volumes in which they appeared.

Meanwhile his general activities had given him a position, if not actual prominence, in the journalism of reform. *Justice and Expediency* (1833) was a notable antislavery tract, coinciding with his election as delegate to the National Anti-Slavery Convention in Philadelphia. Such participation led to his election, in 1835, to the Massachusetts legislature, where he served one term, while drawing a small additional income as editor of the Haverhill *Gazette*. In 1836 he moved down the Merrimack to nearby Amesbury, where, in 1840, he chose the permanent residence which has become a shrine to his memory. Meanwhile his best energies and writing had been devoted to the antislavery cause. In 1835, he and the British abolitionist, George Thompson, mobbed on a lecture tour in Concord, New Hampshire, drove their carriage through a hail of bullets, miraculously escaping with their lives. In 1837 he went to Philadelphia to write for an abolition paper, which he edited as *The Pennsylvania Freeman* for two years before returning to Amesbury.

In this quiet town the remainder of his life was centered. He maintained intermittent editorial connections with the local *Transcript*, and was contributing editor for several more distant publications, notably the antislavery *National Era* in Washington. He continued, for the next quarter of a century, to be more generally known as a propagandist of reform than as a poet, although actually he had now found his own independent voice. A new Whittier, master of a firm and simple eloquence, appeared with increasing frequency in such volumes as *Ballads and Other Poems* (1844), *Voices of Freedom* (1846), *Songs of Labor* (1850), *The Chapel of the Hermits and Other Poems* (1853), *The Panorama and Other Poems* (1856), and *Home Ballads and Poems* (1860).

His fellow literary men recognized his maturity in this period, and he was inevitably included in the group associated with Lowell, Holmes, and others, in the founding of the *Atlantic*

Monthly in 1857. But although his poems were published in a collected edition in London (1850) and in Boston (1857), it was not until his masterpiece, *Snow-Bound*, appeared in 1866 that his countrymen at large recognized his value, and rewarded him with a sufficient sale to make his situation comfortable. It was now possible to see his earlier work in better perspective, and to distinguish, in the mass of his periodical poetry, the solid core of his true expression. The *Poetical Works* of 1869 was a success, and the remainder of Whittier's life was marked by mounting if modest prosperity.

His personal life was now beset by problems, reflected in the increasing religious fervor and thoughtfulness of his lyrics. He had never married, devoting his slender means to his family at Amesbury, and the death of his mother and two sisters occurred between 1857 and 1864. His health, which had never been vigorous, was in steady decline after a severe illness during the winter of 1867–1868. The end of the Civil War was a profound relief, as the thanksgiving of "Laus Deo" indicates, but emancipation, together with the success of other reforms, suddenly canceled the incentives for the bulk of his writing.

In the next score of years, however, he published twelve volumes of poems, some of the best of them in *The Tent on the Beach* (1867), *Among the Hills* (1869), *The Pennsylvania Pilgrim* (1872), and his last volume, *At Sundown* (1890). His seventieth birthday, in 1877, was celebrated at the famous dinner given him by the *Atlantic Monthly*, which was attended by almost every living American author of note from the generation of Bryant to that of Mark Twain and received much public attention both here and abroad. His eightieth birthday was marked by a national celebration in recognition of his unique expression of the common American life of an age that was then forever passing away. Five years later, in 1892, he died at Amesbury.

It would be injudicious to rank Whittier among the great poets, yet it is certain that his genuine values will survive the neglect of recent decades, during which there has been a tendency to undervalue poetry written in the familiar style. Whittier too often marred a poem by sentimentality, but such poems as "Telling the Bees" and "Abraham Davenport" prove him also the master of simplicity. Impassioned simplicity combines with the precise and sharply etched representation of a character or scene in many poems, even those of considerable extent. *The Pennsylvania Pilgrim*, a remarkable reconstruction of the early settlement of the German plain folk under Pastorius in colonial Philadelphia, and that more remarkable idyll, *Snow-Bound*, deserve comparison with Goldsmith's *The Deserted Village* or Burns's "The Cotter's Saturday Night." Many of Whittier's contemporary satires and occasional poems have lost their interest for a later age, no longer concerned with the same problems or events, but *Snow-Bound* makes a timeless appeal to a nation now nostalgic for its country boyhood. Equally timeless are his fine hymns and religious lyrics, not only because they remind us of our innocence, but also because, in their piety and their glowing faith, they assuage our present need.

The standard edition is *The Writings of John Greenleaf Whittier*, Riverside Edition, 7 vols., 1888–1889; reissued, enlarged, as the Standard Library Edition, 7 vols., 1894. The complete one-volume Cambridge Edition, *The Complete Poetical Works of John Greenleaf Whittier*, 1894, is still the best generally available edition.

The standard biography is Samuel T. Pickard, *Life and Letters of John Greenleaf Whittier*, 2 vols., 1894, revised 1907. The same author published *Whittier-Land*, a useful study, in 1904. G. R. Carpenter's *Whittier*, American Men of Letters Series, 1903, is a good introduction. More recent studies of value are Whitman Bennett, *Whittier: Bard of Freedom*, 1941; and John A. Pollard, *John Greenleaf Whittier: Friend of Man*, 1949.

Massachusetts to Virginia[1]

The blast from Freedom's Northern hills, upon its Southern way,
Bears greeting to Virginia from Massachusetts Bay:
No word of haughty challenging, nor battle bugle's peal,
Nor steady tread of marching files, nor clang of horsemen's steel,

1. The immediate circumstances of this protest against the fugitive-slave laws were explained in a note here reproduced as revised by the poet for his collected *Writings* (1888): "Written on reading an account of the proceedings of the citizens of Norfolk, Va., in reference to George Latimer, the alleged fugitive slave, who was seized in Boston without warrant at the request of James B. Grey, of Norfolk, claiming to be his master. The case caused great excitement North and South, and led to the presentation of a petition to Congress,

No trains of deep-mouthed cannon along our highways go;   5
Around our silent arsenals untrodden lies the snow;
And to the land-breeze of our ports, upon their errands far,
A thousand sails of commerce swell, but none are spread for war.

We hear thy threats, Virginia! thy stormy words and high
Swell harshly on the Southern winds which melt along our sky;   10
Yet not one brown, hard hand foregoes its honest labor here,
No hewer of our mountain oaks suspends his axe in fear.

Wild are the waves which lash the reefs along St. George's
      bank;[2]
Cold on the shores of Labrador the fog lies white and dank;
Through storm, and wave, and blinding mist, stout are the hearts
      which man   15
The fishing-smacks of Marblehead, the sea-boats of Cape Ann.

The cold north light and wintry sun glare on their icy forms,
Bent grimly o'er their straining lines or wrestling with the storms;
Free as the winds they drive before, rough as the waves they
      roam,
They laugh to scorn the slaver's threat against their rocky home.   20

What means the Old Dominion? Hath she forgot the day
When o'er her conquered valleys swept the Briton's steel array?
How, side by side with sons of hers, the Massachusetts men
Encountered Tarleton's charge of fire, and stout Cornwallis, then?

Forgets she how the Bay State, in answer to the call   25
Of her old House of Burgesses, spoke out from Faneuil Hall?
When, echoing back her Henry's cry,[3] came pulsing on each breath
Of Northern winds the thrilling sounds of "Liberty or Death!"

What asks the Old Dominion? If now her sons have proved
False to their fathers' memory, false to the faith they loved;   30
If she can scoff at Freedom, and its great charter[4] spurn,
Must we of Massachusetts from truth and duty turn?

signed by more than fifty thousand citizens of Massachusetts, calling for such laws and proposed amendments to the Constitution as should relieve the Commonwealth from all further participation in the crime of oppression. George Latimer himself was finally given free papers for the sum of four hundred dollars." There are some minor variations among the published texts. Whittier's final version (1888) is given below. The poem first appeared anonymously in *The Liberator* for January 27, 1843, and was first collected in *Lays of My Home and Other Poems* (1843).
2. The principal fishing grounds for Massachusetts (*cf.* Marblehead and Cape Anne, l. 16), these famous Atlantic banks are south of Labrador (l. 14).
3. Patrick Henry was a member of the colonial House of Burgesses (l. 26) in Virginia. The reference is to his famous "liberty or death" speech in the Virginia Convention (March 23, 1775). Faneuil Hall in Boston was also the scene of many historic public meetings during the Revolution.
4. The Declaration of Independence, proclaiming "that all men are created equal," was initiated by a resolution of the Virginia delegation; and Jefferson, a Virginian, wrote the first draft.

We hunt your bondmen, flying from Slavery's hateful hell;
Our voices, at your bidding, take up the bloodhound's yell;
We gather, at your summons, above our fathers' graves,   35
From Freedom's holy altar-horns[5] to tear your wretched slaves!

Thank God! not yet so vilely can Massachusetts bow;
The spirit of her early time is with her even now;
Dream not because her Pilgrim blood moves slow and calm and
    cool,
She thus can stoop her chainless neck, a sister's slave and tool!   40

All that a sister State should do, all that a free State may,
Heart, hand, and purse we proffer, as in our early day;
But that one dark loathsome burden ye must stagger with alone,
And reap the bitter harvest which ye yourselves have sown!

Hold, while ye may, your struggling slaves, and burden God's free
    air   45
With woman's shriek beneath the lash, and manhood's wild despair;
Cling closer to the "cleaving curse"[6] that writes upon your plains
The blasting of Almighty wrath against a land of chains.

Still shame your gallant ancestry, the cavaliers of old,
By watching round the shambles where human flesh is sold;   50
Gloat o'er the new-born child, and count his market value, when
The maddened mother's cry of woe shall pierce the slaver's den!

Lower than plummet soundeth,[7] sink the Virginia name;
Plant, if ye will, your fathers' graves with rankest weeds of shame;
Be, if ye will, the scandal of God's fair universe;   55
We wash our hands forever of your sin and shame and curse.

A voice from lips whereon the coal from Freedom's shrine hath
    been,
Thrilled, as but yesterday, the hearts of Berkshire's mountain men:
The echoes of that solemn voice are sadly lingering still
In all our sunny valleys, on every wind-swept hill.   60

And when the prowling man-thief came hunting for his prey[8]
Beneath the very shadow of Bunker's shaft of gray,
How, through the free lips of the son, the father's warning spoke;
How, from its bonds of trade and sect, the Pilgrim city broke!

A hundred thousand right arms were lifted up on high,   65
A hundred thousand voices sent back their loud reply;

5. The Hebrew altar horns afforded
sanctuary. *Cf.* I Kings i: 50 and ii: 28.
6. Some apologists for slavery argued
that Negroes were Cain's descendants,
who bore a curse "cleaving" them from
mankind. *Cf.* Genesis iv: 11–12.

7. *Cf.* Shakespeare, *The Tempest*, Act
III, Scene 3, l. 101.
8. There was a considerable profit in
the recapture and return of fugitive
slaves.

Through the thronged towns of Essex[9] the startling summons rang,
And up from bench and loom and wheel her young mechanics
    sprang!

The voice of free, broad Middlesex, of thousands as of one,
The shaft of Bunker calling to that of Lexington;   70
From Norfolk's ancient villages, from Plymouth's rocky bound
To where Nantucket feels the arms of ocean close her round;

From rich and rural Worcester, where through the calm repose
Of cultured vales and fringing woods the gentle Nashua flows,[1]
To where Wachuset's[2] wintry blasts the mountain larches stir,   75
Swelled up to Heaven the thrilling cry of "God save Latimer!"

And sandy Barnstable rose up, wet with the salt sea spray;
And Bristol sent her answering shout down Narragansett Bay!
Along the broad Connecticut old Hampden felt the thrill,
And the cheer of Hampshire's woodmen swept down from Holyoke
    Hill.[3]   80

The voice of Massachusetts! Of her free sons and daughters,
Deep calling unto deep aloud, the sound of many waters![4]
Against the burden of that voice what tyrant power shall stand?
No fetters in the Bay State! No slave upon her land!

Look to it well, Virginians! In calmness we have borne,   85
In answer to our faith and trust, your insult and your scorn;
You've spurned our kindest counsels; you've hunted for our lives;
And shaken round our hearths and homes your manacles and gyves!

We wage no war, we lift no arm, we fling no torch within
The fire-damps of the quaking mine beneath your soil of sin;   90
We leave ye with your bondmen, to wrestle, while ye can,
With the strong upward tendencies and god-like soul of man!

But for us and for our children, the vow which we have given
For freedom and humanity is registered in heaven;
No slave-hunt in our borders,—no pirate on our strand!   95
No fetters in the Bay State,—no slave upon our land!

                                                                    1843

---

9. The names of Massachusetts counties (ll. 58–86), from the western Berkshires to Cape Cod, indicate the large area over which, on January 2, 1843, public meetings concertedly protested the Latimer incident. Whittier's poem was read at Ipswich in Essex.

1. The Nashua flows north through Worcester county, emptying into the Merrimack in Vermont.

2. Mount Wachusett, Worcester County north-central Massachusetts.

3. The Connecticut River bisects both Hampden and Hampshire, passing Holyoke Hill in the latter county.

4. *Cf.* Psalms xlii: 7; Ezekiel xliii: 2.

Ichabod[5]

So fallen! so lost! the light withdrawn
    Which once he wore!
The glory from his gray hairs gone
    Forevermore!

Revile him not, the Tempter hath
    A snare for all;
And pitying tears, not scorn and wrath,
    Befit his fall!

Oh, dumb be passion's stormy rage,
    When he who might
Have lighted up and led his age,
    Falls back in night.

Scorn! would the angels laugh, to mark
    A bright soul driven,
Fiend-goaded, down the endless dark,
    From hope and heaven!

Let not the land once proud of him
    Insult him now,
Nor brand with deeper shame his dim,
    Dishonored brow.

But let its humbled sons, instead,
    From sea to lake,
A long lament, as for the dead,
    In sadness make.

Of all we loved and honored, naught
    Save power remains;
A fallen angel's pride of thought,
    Still strong in chains.

All else is gone; from those great eyes
    The soul has fled:

5

10

15

20

25

30

5. Hebrew, "without glory"; see I Samuel iv: 21. The poet wrote the following note for the collected *Writings* (1888): "This poem was the outcome of the surprise and grief and forecast of evil consequences which I felt on reading the seventh of March speech of Daniel Webster in support of the 'compromise' and the Fugitive Slave Bill. No partisan or personal enmity dictated it. On the contrary my admiration of the splendid personality and intellectual power of the great Senator was never stronger than when I laid down his speech, and, in one of the saddest moments of my life, penned my protest." Many then agreed with Whittier that the greatly beloved statesman had fallen from glory. However, his compromise with the moderate slavery views of Clay, in order to defeat the radical Calhoun, is sympathetically viewed by many later historians. Webster died in 1852. Thirty years later, in "The Lost Occasion," Whittier admitted that Webster erred on the side of logic. "Ichabod" first appeared in *The National Era* for May 2, 1850, was collected the same year in *Songs of Labor*, and was retained in later collections.

When faith is lost, when honor dies,
  The man is dead!

Then pay the reverence of old days
  To his dead fame;
Walk backward, with averted gaze,   35
  And hide the shame!

                                          1850

The Shoemakers[6]

Ho! workers of the old time styled
  The Gentle Craft[7] of Leather!
Young brothers of the ancient guild,
  Stand forth once more together!
Call out again your long array,   5
  In the olden merry manner!
Once more, on gay St. Crispin's[8] day,
  Fling out your blazoned banner!

Rap, rap! upon the well-worn stone
  How falls the polished hammer!   10
Rap, rap! the measured sound has grown
  A quick and merry clamor.
Now shape the sole! now deftly curl
  The glossy vamp around it,
And bless the while the bright-eyed girl[9]   15
  Whose gentle fingers bound it!

For you, along the Spanish main
  A hundred keels are ploughing;
For you, the Indian on the plain
  His lasso-coil is throwing;   20
For you, deep glens with hemlock dark
  The woodman's fire is lighting;
For you, upon the oak's gray bark,
  The woodman's axe is smiting.

6. "The Shoemakers" appeared in the *United States Magazine and Democratic Review* for July, 1845, and was collected in *Songs of Labor* (1850), together with poems on other crafts, such as "The Ship-Builders," "The Drovers," "The Fishermen," and the like. The poet himself was an apprentice shoemaker in his nineteenth year, and among farmers the repair of shoes at home was quite common.
7. In the Middle Ages, the British guilds called shoemaking "the gentle craft."

Thomas Deloney (1543–1600) kept the phrase alive by using it as title of a novel (1597).
8. The brothers Crispin and Crispinian, third-century shoemakers and Christian missionaries in Gaul, were martyred and became patron saints of the shoemakers; their festival is celebrated on October 25.
9. By 1840 the influx of young women into the New England factories had become a humanitarian concern.

For you, from Carolina's pine   25
    The rosin-gum is stealing;
For you, the dark-eyed Florentine
    Her silken skein is reeling;
For you, the dizzy goatherd roams
    His rugged Alpine ledges;   30
For you, round all her shepherd homes
    Bloom England's thorny hedges.

The foremost still, by day or night,
    On moated mound or heather,
Where'er the need of trampled right   35
    Brought toiling men together;
Where the free burghers from the wall
    Defied the mail-clad master,
Than yours at Freedom's trumpet-call,
    No craftsmen rallied faster.   40

Let foplings sneer, let fools deride,
    Ye heed no idle scorner;
Free hands and hearts are still your pride,
    And duty done, your honor.
Ye dare to trust, for honest fame,   45
    The jury Time empanels,
And leave to truth each noble name
    Which glorifies your annals.

Thy songs, Hans Sachs,[1] are living yet,
    In strong and hearty German;   50
And Bloomfield's[2] lay, and Gifford's wit,
    And patriot fame of Sherman;
Still from his book, a mystic seer,
    The soul of Behmen teaches,
And England's priesthood shakes to hear   55
    Of Fox's leathern breeches.

The foot is yours; where'er it falls,
    It treads your well-wrought leather,
On earthen floor, in marble halls,
    On carpet, or on heather.   60
Still there the sweetest charm is found
    Of matron grace or vestal's,

1. The great German cobbler-poet (1494–1576). *Cf.* Longfellow's "Nuremberg."
2. All these, in early life, were shoemakers: Robert Bloomfield (1766–1823), English nature poet; William Gifford (1756–1826), English poet and critic; Roger Sherman (1721–1793), a signer of the Declaration of Independence; Jakob Böhme (or Behmen; 1575–1624) German mystic; and George Fox (1624–1691) founder of the Society of Friends (Quakers).

As Hebe's[3] foot bore nectar round
    Among the old celestials!

Rap, rap!—your stout and bluff brogan,   65
    With footsteps slow and weary,
May wander where the sky's blue span
    Shuts down upon the prairie.
On Beauty's foot your slippers glance,
    By Saratoga's[4] fountains,   70
Or twinkle down the summer dance
    Beneath the Crystal Mountains!

The red brick to the mason's hand,
    The brown earth to the tiller's,
The shoe in yours shall wealth command,   75
    Like fairy Cinderella's!
As they who shunned the houschold maid
    Beheld the crown upon her,
So all shall see your toil repaid
    With hearth and home and honor.   80

Then let the toast be freely quaffed,
    In water cool and brimming,—
"All honor to the good old Craft,
    Its merry men and women!"
Call out again your long array,   85
    In the old time's pleasant manner:
Once more, on gay St. Crispin's day,
    Fling out his blazoned banner!

                        1845, 1850

First-Day Thoughts[5]

In calm and cool and silence, once again
   I find my old accustomed place among
My brethren,[6] where, perchance, no human tongue
Shall utter words; where never hymn is sung,
Nor deep-toned organ blown, nor censer swung,   5
Nor dim light falling through the pictured pane!

3. In Greek myth, the cupbearer of the gods on Olympus.
4. Saratoga Springs, New York, then a fashionable summer resort.
5. "First Day" is Sunday. The Quakers designated the days of the week by number, to avoid reference to the pagan gods for which the days are named. "First-Day Thoughts" was originally published in *The Chapel of the Hermits and Other Poems* (1853).
6. Friends' worship emphasized fellowship, and utilized communal silence instead of music, hymns, images, and stained glass (ll. 3–6). The object of worship was the direct revelation of God to the individual—the perception of the "inward light" (ll. 7–10).

There, syllabled by silence, let me hear
The still small voice which reached the prophet's ear;
Read in my heart a still diviner law
Than Israel's leader[7] on his tables saw!   10
There let me strive with each besetting sin,
    Recall my wandering fancies, and restrain
    The sore disquiet of a restless brain;
    And, as the path of duty is made plain,
May grace be given that I may walk therein,   15
    Not like the hireling, for his selfish gain,
With backward glances and reluctant tread,
Making a merit of his coward dread,
    But, cheerful, in the light around me thrown,
    Walking as one to pleasant service led;   20
    Doing God's will as if it were my own,
Yet trusting not in mine, but in his strength alone!

                                                            1853

Burns

ON RECEIVING A SPRIG OF HEATHER IN BLOSSOM[8]

No more these simple flowers belong
    To Scottish maid and lover;
Sown in the common soil of song,
    They bloom the wide world over.

In smiles and tears, in sun and showers,   5
    The minstrel and the heather,
The deathless singer and the flowers
    He sang of live together.

Wild heather-bells and Robert Burns!
    The moorland flower and peasant!   10
How, at their mention, memory turns
    Her pages old and pleasant!

The gray sky wears again its gold
    And purple of adorning,
And manhood's noonday shadows hold   15
    The dews of boyhood's morning.

The dews that washed the dust and soil
    From off the wings of pleasure,

---

7. Moses. For the "tables" of the laws, *cf.* Exodus xxxi: 18, and xx, *passim.*
8. In "Burns," Whittier acknowledges a deep personal indebtedness, while showing how the great Scottish poet overwhelmingly won the heart of "moral" America, in spite of "unco guid" disapproval of his moral license. The poem first appeared in *The Panorama and Other Poems* (1856).

The sky, that flecked the ground of toil
    With golden threads of leisure.   20

I call to mind the summer day,
    The early harvest mowing,[9]
The sky with sun and clouds at play,
    And flowers with breezes blowing.

I hear the blackbird in the corn,   25
    The locust in the haying;
And, like the fabled hunter's horn,
    Old tunes my heart is playing.

How oft that day, with fond delay,
    I sought the maple's shadow,   30
And sang with Burns the hours away,
    Forgetful of the meadow!

Bees hummed, birds twittered, overhead
    I heard the squirrels leaping,
The good dog listened while I read,   35
    And wagged his tail in keeping.

I watched him while in sportive mood
    I read "The Twa Dogs'" story,[1]
And half believed he understood
    The poet's allegory.   40

Sweet day, sweet songs! The golden hours
    Grew brighter for that singing,
From brook and bird and meadow flowers
    A dearer welcome bringing.

New light on home-seen Nature beamed,   45
    New glory over Woman;[2]
And daily life and duty seemed
    No longer poor and common.

I woke to find the simple truth
    Of fact and feeling better   50
Than all the dreams that held my youth
    A still repining debtor:

That Nature gives her handmaid, Art,
    The themes of sweet discoursing;

---

9. Whittier discovered Burns's poems as a farm boy of fourteen. Before he was twenty-one, his first published prose piece, on Robert Burns, appeared in the Haverhill *Gazette* (November 8, 1828).

1. Burns's "allegory" of that name is a dialogue between a rich man's dog and his own.
2. *Cf.* Burns's "Highland Mary," "John Anderson, My Jo," and others.

The tender idyls of the heart
  In every tongue rehearsing.   55

Why dream of lands of gold and pearl,
  Of loving knight and lady,
When farmer boy and barefoot girl
  Were wandering there already?   60

I saw through all familiar things
  The romance underlying;
The joys and griefs that plume the wings
  Of Fancy skyward flying.

I saw the same blithe day return,   65
  The same sweet fall of even,
That rose on wooded Craigie-burn,
  And sank on crystal Devon.[3]

I matched with Scotland's heathery hills
  The sweetbrier and the clover;   70
With Ayr[4] and Doon,[5] my native rills,
  Their wood hymns chanting over.

O'er rank and pomp, as he had seen,
  I saw the Man uprising;
No longer common or unclean,   75
  The child of God's baptizing!

With clearer eyes I saw the worth
  Of life among the lowly;
The Bible at his Cotter's hearth[6]
  Had made my own more holy.   80

And if at times an evil strain,
  To lawless love appealing,
Broke in upon the sweet refrain
  Of pure and healthful feeling,

It died upon the eye and ear,   85
  No inward answer gaining;
No heart had I to see or hear
  The discord and the staining.

Let those who never erred forget
  His worth, in vain bewailings;[7]   90

3. *Cf.* Burns's "Craigieburn Wood"
and "The Banks of Devon."
4. Burns's "The Brigs of Ayr" opens
with a reference to "The simple Bard,
rough at the rustic plough," which applies as well to Whittier in boyhood as
to Burns.
5. *Cf.* Burns's "The Banks o' Doon."
6. *Cf.* Burns's "The Cotter's Saturday
Night," stanzas 12–17.
7. *Cf.* Burns's "Address to the Unco
Guid," stanza 1.

Sweet Soul of Song! I own my debt
Uncancelled by his failings!

Lament who will the ribald line
Which tells his lapse from duty,
How kissed the maddening lips of wine   95
Or wanton ones of beauty;

But think, while falls that shade between
The erring one and Heaven,
That he who loved like Magdalen,[8]
Like her may be forgiven.   100

Not his the song whose thunderous chime
Eternal echoes render;
The mournful Tuscan's[9] haunted rhyme,
And Milton's starry splendor!

But who his human heart has laid   105
To Nature's bosom nearer?
Who sweetened toil like him, or paid
To love a tribute dearer?

Through all his tuneful art, how strong
The human feeling gushes!   110
The very moonlight of his song
Is warm with smiles and blushes!

Give lettered pomp to teeth of Time,
So "Bonnie Doon" but tarry;
Blot out the Epic's stately rhyme,   115
But spare his "Highland Mary"!

1856

The Barefoot Boy[1]

Blessings on thee, little man,
Barefoot boy, with cheek of tan!
With thy turned-up pantaloons,
And thy merry whistled tunes;
With thy red lip, redder still   5
Kissed by strawberries on the hill;
With the sunshine on thy face,

---

8. *Cf.* Luke vii: 37–47.
9. *I.e.*, Dante, born in Florence, Italy, ancient capital of Tuscany.
1. One of Whittier's best-loved poems in his own day, "The Barefoot Boy" again reflects the influence of Robert Burns. The poem appeared along with "Burns" in *The Panorama and Other Poems* (1856).

Through thy torn brim's jaunty grace;
From my heart I give thee joy,—
I was once a barefoot boy!   10
Prince thou art,—the grown-up man
Only is republican.
Let the million-dollared ride!
Barefoot, trudging at his side,
Thou hast more than he can buy   15
In the reach of ear and eye,—
Outward sunshine, inward joy:
Blessings on thee, barefoot boy!

Oh for boyhood's painless play,
Sleep that wakes in laughing day,   20
Health that mocks the doctor's rules,
Knowledge never learned of schools,
Of the wild bee's morning chase,
Of the wild-flower's time and place,
Flight of fowl and habitude   25
Of the tenants of the wood;
How the tortoise bears his shell,
How the woodchuck digs his cell,
And the ground-mole sinks his well;
How the robin feeds her young,   30
How the oriole's nest is hung;
Where the whitest lilies blow,
Where the freshest berries grow,
Where the ground-nut trails its vine,
Where the wood-grape's clusters shine;   35
Of the black wasp's cunning way,
Mason of his walls of clay,
And the architectural plans
Of gray hornet artisans!
For, eschewing books and tasks,   40
Nature answers all he asks;
Hand in hand with her he walks,
Face to face with her he talks,
Part and parcel of her joy,—
Blessings on the barefoot boy!   45

Oh for boyhood's time of June,
Crowding years in one brief moon,
When all things I heard or saw,
Me, their master, waited for.
I was rich in flowers and trees,   50
Humming-birds and honey-bees;

For my sport the squirrel played,
Plied the snouted mole his spade;
For my taste the blackberry cone
Purpled over hedge and stone;   55
Laughed the brook for my delight
Through the day and through the night,
Whispering at the garden wall,
Talked with me from fall to fall;
Mine the sand-rimmed pickerel pond,   60
Mine the walnut slopes beyond,
Mine, on bending orchard trees,
Apples of Hesperides![2]
Still as my horizon grew,
Larger grew my riches too;   65
All the world I saw or knew
Seemed a complex Chinese toy,
Fashioned for a barefoot boy!

Oh for festal dainties spread,
Like my bowl of milk and bread;   70
Pewter spoon and bowl of wood,
On the door-stone, gray and rude!
O'er me, like a regal tent,
Cloudy-ribbed, the sunset bent,
Purple-curtained, fringed with gold,   75
Looped in many a wind-swung fold;
While for music came the play
Of the pied frogs' orchestra;
And, to light the noisy choir,
Lit the fly his lamp of fire.   80
I was monarch: pomp and joy
Waited on the barefoot boy!

Cheerily, then, my little man,
Live and laugh, as boyhood can!
Though the flinty slopes be hard,   85
Stubble-speared the new-mown sward,
Every morn shall lead thee through
Fresh baptisms of the dew;
Every evening from thy feet
Shall the cool wind kiss the heat: 90
All too soon these feet must hide
In the prison cells of pride,
Lose the freedom of the sod,

2. In Greek myth, the garden at the western limit of the universe, where a dragon guarded the golden apples presented as a wedding gift to Hera, queen of heaven.

Like a colt's for work be shod,
Made to tread the mills of toil,   95
Up and down in ceaseless moil:
Happy if their track be found
Never on forbidden ground;
Happy if they sink not in
Quick and treacherous sands of sin.   100
Ah! that thou couldst know thy joy,
Ere it passes, barefoot boy!

1856

Skipper Ireson's Ride[3]

Of all the rides since the birth of time,
Told in story or sung in rhyme,—
On Apuleius's[4] Golden Ass,
Or one-eyed Calender's[5] horse of brass,
Witch astride of a human back,   5
Islam's prophet[6] on Al-Borák,—
The strangest ride that ever was sped
Was Ireson's, out from Marblehead!
    Old Floyd Ireson, for his hard heart,
    Tarred and fathered and carried in a cart   10
    By the women of Marblehead!

Body of turkey, head of owl,
Wings a-droop like a rained-on fowl,
Feathered and ruffled in every part,

3. Whittier declared that this ballad "was founded solely on a fragment of rhyme which I heard from one of my early schoolmates, a native of Marblehead." The "fragment" was the refrain sung by the women; and there was a story current about Skipper Ireson which, Whittier supposed, "dated back at least a century." The poet wrote a rough draft in 1828, nearly thirty years before he published the poem. However, his record of the events was "pure fancy," as he took pains to declare in his note for his edition of 1888. There he approves the recent *History of Marblehead*, by Samuel Roads (1879), which places the incident in 1808, names the historical Ireson "Benjamin," not "Floyd," and asserts that Ireson was not responsible for neglecting "a sinking wreck." His guilty crew, by false accusations, diverted the consequences from themselves to Ireson. Roads says that the victim, contrary to legend, was carried in a dory, not a cart, and that men, not women, were the principal avengers. The poem appeared in the *Atlantic Monthly*, in December, 1857. Lowell, the first editor of the *Atlantic Monthly*, "familiar with Marblehead and its dialect," suggested changes making the "burthen" more "provincial" (letter to Whittier, Nov. 4, 1857; in Pickard, *Life and Letters*, Vol. II, pp. 406–407). It was collected in *Home Ballads and Poems* (1860).
4. Second-century Roman rhetorician; in his *Golden Ass* (or *Metamorphoses*) the transformation of a man to an ass is made the vehicle for comic criticism.
5. A calender is a mendicant dervish, or friar. In the *Arabian Nights* tale ("The Story of the Third Calender," called "The Story of the Third Royal Mendicant" in later translations), he did not ride the "horse of brass" whose rider he killed, but his consequent enchanted journey cost him his eye.
6. Mohammed. In one legend, he was conveyed to the highest heaven by a supernatural winged creature named Al-Borák.

Skipper Ireson stood in the cart. 15
Scores of women, old and young,
Strong of muscle, and glib of tongue,
Pushed and pulled up the rocky lane,
Shouting and singing the shrill refrain:
   "Here's Flud Oirson, fur his horrd horrt, 20
    Torr'd an' futherr'd an' corr'd in a corrt
     By the women o' Morble'ead!"[7]

Wrinkled scolds with hands on hips,
Girls in bloom of cheek and lips,
Wild-eyed, free-limbed, such as chase 25
Bacchus[8] round some antique vase,
Brief of skirt, with ankles bare,
Loose of kerchief and loose of hair,
With conch-shells blowing and fish-horns' twang,
Over and over the Maenads sang: 30
   "Here's Flud Oirson, fur his horrd horrt,
    Torr'd an' futherr'd an' corr'd in a corrt
     By the women o' Morble'ead!"

Small pity for him!—He sailed away
From a leaking ship in Chaleur Bay,[9]— 35
Sailed away from a sinking wreck,
With his own town's-people on her deck!
"Lay by! lay by!" they called to him.
Back he answered, "Sink or swim!
Brag of your catch of fish again!" 40
And off he sailed through the fog and rain!
   Old Floyd Ireson, for his hard heart,
    Tarred and feathered and carried in a cart
     By the women of Marblehead!

Fathoms deep in dark Chaleur 45
That wreck shall lie forevermore.
Mother and sister, wife and maid,
Looked from the rocks of Marblehead
Over the moaning and rainy sea,—
Looked for the coming that might not be! 50
What did the winds and the sea-birds say
Of the cruel captain who sailed away—?
   Old Floyd Ireson, for his hard heart,

---

7. Following the advice of Lowell, his editor, Whittier used the Marblehead dialect for the refrain in stanzas 2, 3, 6, and 7, after establishing the standard English in stanza 1.

8. Roman god of wine, generally shown as attended by wild, frenetic girls called Bacchantes or Maenads (l. 30).
9. In the Gulf of St. Lawrence.

Tarred and feathered and carried in a cart
By the women of Marblehead!   55

Through the street, on either side,
Up flew windows, doors swung wide;
Sharp-tongued spinsters, old wives gray,
Treble lent the fish-horn's bray.
Sea-worn grandsires, cripple-bound,   60
Hulks of old sailors run aground,
Shook head, and fist, and hat, and cane,
And cracked with curses the hoarse refrain:
   "Here's Flud Oirson, fur his horrd horrt,
   Torr'd an' futherr'd an' corr'd in a corrt   65
      By the women o' Morble'ead!"

Sweetly along the Salem road
Bloom of orchard and lilac showed.
Little the wicked skipper knew
Of the fields so green and the sky so blue.   70
Riding there in his sorry trim,
Like an Indian idol glum and grim,
Scarcely he seemed the sound to hear
Of voices shouting, far and near:
   "Here's Flud Oirson, fur his horrd horrt,   75
   Torr'd an' futherr'd an' corr'd in a corrt
      By the women o' Morble'ead!"

"Hear me, neighbors!" at last he cried,—
"What to me is this noisy ride?
What is the shame that clothes the skin   80
To the nameless horror that lives within?
Waking or sleeping, I see a wreck,
And hear a cry from a reeling deck!
Hate me and curse me,—I only dread
The hand of God and the face of the dead!"   85
   Said old Floyd Ireson, for his hard heart,
   Tarred and feathered and carried in a cart
      By the women of Marblehead!

Then the wife of the skipper lost at sea
Said, "God has touched him! why should we!"   90
Said an old wife mourning her only son,
"Cut the rogue's tether and let him run!"
So with soft relentings and rude excuse,
Half scorn, half pity, they cut him loose,
And gave him a cloak to hide him in,   95
And left him alone with his shame and sin.

Poor Floyd Ireson, for his hard heart,
Tarred and feathered and carried in a cart
By the women of Marblehead!

1857, 1860

Telling the Bees[1]

Here is the place; right over the hill
  Runs the path I took;
You can see the gap in the old wall still,
  And the stepping-stones in the shallow brook.

There is the house, with the gate red-barred,   5
  And the poplars tall;
And the barn's brown length, and the cattle-yard,
  And the white horns tossing above the wall.

There are the beehives ranged in the sun;
  And down by the brink   10
Of the brook are her poor flowers, weed-o'errun,
  Pansy and daffodil, rose and pink.

A year has gone, as the tortoise goes,
  Heavy and slow;
And the same rose blows, and the same sun glows,   15
  And the same brook sings of a year ago.

There's the same sweet clover-smell in the breeze;
  And the June sun warm
Tangles his wings of fire in the trees,
  Setting, as then, over Fernside farm.   20

I mind me how with a lover's care
  From my Sunday coat
I brushed off the burrs, and smoothed my hair,
  And cooled at the brookside my brow and throat.

Since we parted, a month had passed,—   25
  To love, a year;

1. First collected in *Home Ballads and Other Poems* (1860) after appearing in the *Atlantic Monthly* for April, 1858. On submitting it to Lowell, Whittier admitted the fear that its "simplicity" might occasion disparagement. Actually, it is his purest ballad, free of didacticism, and simply faithful to the Whittier homestead, "Fernside farm." However, it was not his sister Mary who had died there the year before, but his mother. In the volume, the poet added the following explanatory note: "A remarkable custom, brought from the Old Country, formerly prevailed in the rural districts of New England. On the death of a member of the family, the bees were at once informed of the event, and their hives dressed in mourning. This ceremonial was supposed to be necessary to prevent the swarms from leaving their hives and seeking a new home."

Down through the beeches I looked at last
   On the little red gate and the well-sweep near.

I can see it all now,—the slantwise rain
   Of light through the leaves,   30
The sundown's blaze on her window-pane,
   The bloom of her roses under the eaves.

Just the same as a month before,—
   The house and the trees,
The barn's brown gable, the vine by the door,—   35
   Nothing changed but the hives of bees.

Before them, under the garden wall,
   Forward and back,
Went drearily singing the chore-girl small,
   Draping each hive with a shred of black.   40

Trembling, I listened: the summer sun
   Had the chill of snow;
For I knew she was telling the bees of one
   Gone on the journey we all must go!

Then I said to myself, "My Mary weeps   45
   For the dead to-day:
Haply her blind old grandsire sleeps
   The fret and the pain of his age away."

But her dog whined low; on the doorway sill,
   With his cane to his chin,
The old man sat; and the chore-girl still   50
   Sung to the bees stealing out and in.

And the song she was singing ever since
   In my ear sounds on:—
"Stay at home, pretty bees, fly not hence!   55
   Mistress Mary is dead and gone!"

                        1858, 1860

Laus Deo[2]

It is done!
Clang of bell and roar of gun

---

2. The title, familiar in the Latin Vulgate Bible, is translated as "Praise be to God." The prefatory note, as amplified in the collected *Writings* of 1888, reads as follows: "On hearing the bells ring on the passage of the constitutional amendment abolishing slavery. The resolution was adopted by Congress, January 31, 1865. The ratification by the requisite number of states was announced December 18, 1865."

Send the tidings up and down.
How the belfries rock and reel!
How the great guns, peal on peal,   5
Fling the joy from town to town![3]

Ring, O bells!
Every stroke exulting tells
Of the burial hour of crime.
Loud and long, that all may hear,   10
Ring for every listening ear
Of Eternity and Time!

Let us kneel:
God's own voice is in that peal,
And this spot is holy ground.[4]   15
Lord, forgive us! What are we,
That our eyes this glory see,
That our ears have heard this sound!

For the Lord
On the whirlwind is abroad;   20
In the earthquake He has spoken;
He has smitten with His thunder[5]
The iron walls asunder,
And the gates of brass are broken!

Loud and long   25
Lift the old exulting song;
Sing with Miriam by the sea,
He has cast the mighty down;
Horse and rider sink and drown;
'He hath triumphed gloriously!'[6]   30

Did we dare,
In our agony of prayer,[7]
Ask for more than He has done?
When was ever his right hand
Over any time or land   35
Stretched as now beneath the sun?[8]

How they pale,
Ancient myth and song and tale,

---

3. Whittier "sat in the Friends' meeting-house in Amesbury, and listened to
the bells and cannon." As he later told
Lucy Larcom, the poem "wrote itself,
or rather sang itself, while the bells
rang" (Pickard, *Life and Letters*, Vol.
II, pp. 488–489).
4. *Cf.* Exodus iii: 3–6.

5. *Cf.* Job xxxvii: 2–12.
6. *Cf.* Exodus xv: 21–22.
7. *Cf.* Luke xxii: 39–44.
8. Isaiah repeatedly used this figure, for
both God's wrath and God's mercy.
Compare Isaiah v: 25 with xiv: 27, and
see ix: 12–13 and x: 4.

In this wonder of our days,
  When the cruel rod of war
    Blossoms white with righteous law,[9]
And the wrath of man is praise!

    Blotted out!
  All within and all about
Shall a fresher life begin;   45
    Freer breathe the universe
    As it rolls its heavy curse
On the dead and buried sin!

      It is done!
  In the circuit of the sun   50
Shall the sound thereof go forth.
    It shall bid the sad rejoice,
    It shall give the dumb a voice,
It shall belt with joy the earth![1]

      Ring and swing,   55
  Bells of joy! On morning's wing
Sound the song of praise abroad!
    With a sound of broken chains
    Tell the nations that He reigns,
Who alone is Lord and God![2]   60

                                                           1865

Snow-Bound

A WINTER IDYL[3]

TO THE MEMORY OF THE HOUSEHOLD[4] IT DESCRIBES

THIS POEM IS DEDICATED BY THE AUTHOR

"As the Spirits of Darkness be stronger in the dark, so good Spirits which be Angels of Light, are augmented not only by the Divine Light of the Sun, but also by our common VVood Fire: and as the Celestial Fire drives away dark spirits so also this our Fire of VVood doth the same."—COR. AGRIPPA, OCCULT PHILOSOPHY, Book I. ch. v.[5]

9. A double reference to Aaron's rod: of war (*cf.* Exodus vii: 8–17), and of law (*cf.* Numbers xvii: 8–10).
1. *Cf.* Isaiah xxxv: 4–8.
2. *Cf.* Psalms xlvi, echoed in this stanza.
3. *Snow-Bound* was published as a small volume in 1866. The first issue was several times reprinted, and gave the author his first considerable income from any publication. New editions were repeatedly demanded, numbering at least twenty-one before 1930, although the poem had been incorporated in the collected *Writings* in 1888. The poet's lengthy introduction is here sub-

stantially represented in the notes to the text of the poem.
4. "The inmates of the family at the Whittier homestead, who are referred to in the poem, were my father, mother, my brother and two sisters, and my uncle and aunt both unmarried. In addition, there was the district schoolmaster who boarded with us" [Whittier's introduction].
5. Whittier explained in his introduction that he still possessed this strange "wizard's conjuring book," dated 1651 (*cf.* l. 270). It had belonged to a local "sorcerer" known to his mother. Its author, as he quotes from the title page,

> "Announced by all the trumpets of the sky,
> Arrives the snow; and, driving o'er the fields,
> Seems nowhere to alight; the whited air
> Hides hills and woods, the river and the heaven,
> And veils the farm-house at the garden's end.
> The sled and traveller stopped, the courier's feet
> Delayed, all friends shut out, the housemates sit
> Around the radiant fireplace, enclosed
> In a tumultuous privacy of storm."
> —EMERSON, THE SNOW-STORM.

The sun that brief December day
Rose cheerless over hills of gray,
And, darkly circled, gave at noon
A sadder light than waning moon.
Slow tracing down the thickening sky   5
Its mute and ominous prophecy,
A portent seeming less than threat,
It sank from sight before it set.
A chill no coat, however stout,
Of homespun stuff could quite shut out,   10
A hard, dull bitterness of cold,
That checked, mid-vein, the circling race
Of life-blood in the sharpened face,
The coming of the snow-storm told.
The wind blew east; we heard the roar   15
Of Ocean on his wintry shore,
And felt the strong pulse throbbing there
Beat with low rhythm our inland air.

Meanwhile we did our nightly chores,—
Brought in the wood from out of doors,   20
Littered the stalls, and from the mows
Raked down the herd's-grass[6] for the cows:
Heard the horse whinnying for his corn;
And, sharply clashing horn on horn,
Impatient down the stanchion rows   25
The cattle shake their walnut bows;[7]
While, peering from his early perch
Upon the scaffold's pole of birch
The cock his crested helmet bent
And down his querulous challenge sent.   30

Unwarmed by any sunset light
The gray day darkened into night,

was "Henry Cornelius Agrippa, Knight,
Doctor of Both Laws (*etc*)." Presumably this was a work of Cornelius Heinrich Agrippa (1486–1535), German
physician and writer on the occult.

6. Either timothy or redtop, both
esteemed as fodder.
7. "Stanchions" are upright posts, used
in a barn for tethering cattle; "bows,"
wooden yokes, facilitated tethering and
hauling; *cf.* "oxbow."

A night made hoary with the swarm
And whirl-dance of the blinding storm,
As zigzag, wavering to and fro
Crossed and recrossed the wingèd snow: 35
And ere the early bedtime came
The white drift piled the window-frame,
And through the glass the clothes-line posts
Looked in like tall and sheeted ghosts.   40

So all night long the storm roared on:
The morning broke without a sun;
In tiny spherule traced with lines
Of Nature's geometric signs,
In starry flake, and pellicle,   45
All day the hoary meteor fell;
And, when the second morning shone,
We looked upon a world unknown,
On nothing we could call our own.
Around the glistening wonder bent   50
The blue walls of the firmament,
No cloud above, no earth below,—
A universe of sky and snow!
The old familiar sights of ours
Took marvellous shapes; strange domes and towers 55
Rose up where sty or corn-crib stood,
Or garden-wall, or belt of wood;
A smooth white mound the brush-pile showed,
A fenceless drift that once was road;
The bridle-post an old man sat   60
With loose-flung coat and high cocked hat;
The well-curb had a Chinese roof;
And even the long sweep, high aloof,
In its slant splendor, seemed to tell
Of Pisa's leaning miracle.   65

A prompt, decisive man, no breath
Our father wasted: "Boys, a path!"
Well pleased, (for when did farmer boy
Count such a summons less than joy?)
Our buskins[8] on our feet we drew;   70
With mittened hands, and caps drawn low,
To guard our necks and ears from snow,
We cut the solid whiteness through.
And, where the drift was deepest, made
A tunnel walled and overlaid   75

8. Leather boots.

With dazzling crystal: we had read
Of rare Aladdin's wondrous cave,
And to our own his name we gave,
With many a wish the luck were ours
To test his lamp's supernal powers.   80
We reached the barn with merry din,
And roused the prisoned brutes within.
The old horse thrust his long head out,
And grave with wonder gazed about;
The cock his lusty greeting said,   85
And forth his speckled harem led;
The oxen lashed their tails, and hooked,
And mild reproach of hunger looked;
The hornèd patriarch of the sheep,
Like Egypt's Amun[9] roused from sleep,   90
Shook his sage head with gesture mute,
And emphasized with stamp of foot.

All day the gusty north-wind bore
The loosening drift its breath before;
Low circling round its southern zone,   95
The sun through dazzling snow-mist shone.
No church-bell lent its Christian tone
To the savage air, no social smoke
Curled over woods of snow-hung oak.
A solitude made more intense   100
By dreary-voicèd elements,
The shrieking of the mindless wind,
The moaning tree-boughs swaying blind,
And on the glass the unmeaning beat
Of ghostly finger-tips of sleet.   105
Beyond the circle of our hearth
No welcome sound of toil or mirth
Unbound the spell, and testified
Of human life and thought outside.
We minded[1] that the sharpest ear   110
The buried brooklet could not hear,
The music of whose liquid lip
Had been to us companionship,
And, in our lonely life, had grown
To have an almost human tone.   115

As night drew on, and, from the crest
Of wooded knolls that ridged the west,

9. Ammon; an Egyptian divinity who   sacred animal.
assumed the form of a ram (l. 89), his   1. Knew.

The sun, a snow-blown traveller, sank
From sight beneath the smothering bank,
We piled, with care, our nightly stack   120
Of wood against the chimney-back,—
The oaken log, green, huge, and thick,
And on its top the stout back-stick;
The knotty forestick laid apart,
And filled between with curious art   125
The ragged brush; then, hovering near,
We watched the first red blaze appear,
Heard the sharp crackle, caught the gleam
On whitewashed wall and sagging beam,
Until the old, rude-furnished room   130
Burst, flower-like, into rosy bloom;
While radiant with a mimic flame
Outside the sparkling drift became,
And through the bare-boughed lilac-tree
Our own warm hearth seemed blazing free.   135
The crane and pendent trammels[2] showed,
The Turks' heads on the andirons glowed;
While childish fancy, prompt to tell
The meaning of the miracle,
Whispered the old rhyme: "*Under the tree,*   140
When fire outdoors burns merrily,
There the witches are making tea."

The moon above the eastern wood
Shone at its full; the hill-range stood
Transfigured in the silver flood,   145
Its blown snows flashing cold and keen,
Dead white, save where some sharp ravine
Took shadow, or the sombre green
Of hemlocks turned to pitchy black
Against the whiteness at their back.   150
For such a world and such a night
Most fitting that unwarming light,
Which only seemed where'er it fell
To make the coldness visible.

Shut in from all the world without,   155
We sat the clean-winged hearth about,
Content to let the north-wind roar
In baffled rage at pane and door,
While the red logs before us beat

2. In a fireplace, the cooking pot was suspended by trammels (pothooks) from the crane, a long metal arm.

The frost-line back with tropic heat;   160
And ever, when a louder blast
Shook beam and rafter as it passed,
The merrier up its roaring draught
The great throat of the chimney laughed;
The house-dog on his paws outspread   165
Laid to the fire his drowsy head,
The cat's dark silhouette on the wall
A couchant tiger's seemed to fall;
And, for the winter fireside meet,
Between the andirons' straddling feet,   170
The mug of cider simmered slow,
The apples sputtered in a row,
And, close at hand, the basket stood
With nuts from brown October's wood.

What matter how the night behaved?   175
What matter how the north-wind raved?
Blow high, blow low, not all its snow
Could quench our hearth-fire's ruddy glow.
O Time and Change!—with hair as gray
As was my sire's that winter day,   180
How strange it seems, with so much gone
Of life and love, to still live on!
Ah, brother![3] only I and thou
Are left of all that circle now,—
The dear home faces whereupon   185
That fitful firelight paled and shone.
Henceforth, listen as we will,
The voices of that hearth are still;
Look where we may, the wide earth o'er
Those lighted faces smile no more.   190
We tread the paths their feet have worn,
    We sit beneath their orchard trees,
    We hear, like them, the hum of bees
And rustle of the bladed corn;
We turn the pages that they read,   195
    Their written words we linger o'er,
But in the sun they cast no shade,
No voice is heard, no sign is made,
    No step is on the conscious floor!
Yet Love will dream, and Faith will trust,   200
(Since He who knows our need is just,)
That somehow, somewhere, meet we must.
    Alas for him who never sees

3. Matthew Franklin Whittier (1812–1883).

The stars shine through his cypress-trees!
Who, hopeless, lays his dead away,   205
Nor looks to see the breaking day
Across the mournful marbles play!
Who hath not learned, in hours of faith,
    The truth to flesh and sense unknown,
That Life is ever lord of Death,   210
    And Love can never lose its own!

We sped the time with stories old,[4]
Wrought puzzles out, and riddles told,
Or stammered from our school-book lore
"The Chief of Gambia's golden shore."[5]   215
How often since, when all the land
Was clay in Slavery's shaping hand,
As if a far-blown trumpet stirred
The languorous sin-sick air, I heard:
"Does not the voice of reason cry,   220
    Claim the first right which Nature gave,
From the red scourge of bondage fly,
    Nor deign to live a burdened slave!"
Our father[6] rode again his ride
On Memphremagog's[7] wooded side;   225
Sat down again to moose and samp[8]
In trapper's hut and Indian camp;
Lived o'er the old idyllic ease
Beneath St. François'[9] hemlock-trees;
Again for him the moonlight shone   230
On Norman cap and bodiced zone;
Again he heard the violin play
Which led the village dance away.
And mingled in its merry whirl
The grandam and the laughing girl.   235
Or, nearer home, our steps he led

4. "In my boyhood, in our lonely farm-house, we had scanty sources of information; few books and only a small weekly newspaper. Our only annual was the Almanac. Under such circumstances story-telling was a necessary resource in the long winter evenings" [Whittier's introduction].
5. Whittier's note identifies the "school-book" as Caleb Bingham's *The American Primer*, and the poem as "The African Chief," of which this line was the first in the third stanza. The lines in italics (ll. 220–224) reproduce the fourth stanza of the poem, which was written, in fifteen stanzas, by Sarah

Wentworth Morton (1759–1846).
6. John Whittier (1760–1830). In the introduction, Whittier wrote: "My father when a young man had traversed the wilderness to Canada, and could tell us of his adventures with Indians and wild beasts, and of his sojourn in the French villages."
7. A lake on the border between Vermont and Canada, originally a French possession.
8. An Indian corn-meal mush or coarse hominy.
9. North of Lake Memphremagog (l. 225) in Quebec Province are a hamlet, a stream, and a lake named St. Francis.

Where Salisbury's[1] level marshes spread
   Mile-wide as flies the laden bee;
Where merry mowers, hale and strong,
Swept, scythe on scythe, their swaths along   240
   The low green prairies of the sea.
We shared the fishing off Boar's Head
   And round the rocky Isles of Shoals
   The hake-broil on the drift-wood coals;
The chowder on the sand-beach made,   245
Dipped by the hungry, steaming hot
With spoons of clam-shell from the pot.
We heard the tales of witchcraft old,
   And dream and sign and marvel told
To sleepy listeners as they lay   250
Stretched idly on the salted hay,
Adrift along the winding shores,
When favoring breezes deigned to blow
The square sail of the gundelow
And idle lay the useless oars.   255

Our mother,[2] while she turned her wheel
Or run the new-knit stocking-heel,
Told how the Indian hordes came down
At midnight on Cocheco[3] town,
And how her own great-uncle bore   260
His cruel scalp-mark to fourscore.
Recalling, in her fitting phrase,
   So rich and picturesque and free,
   (The common unrhymed poetry
Of simple life and country ways,)   265
The story of her early days,—
She made us welcome to her home;
Old hearths grew wide to give us room;
We stole with her a frightened look
At the gray wizard's conjuring-book,   270
The fame whereof went far and wide
Through all the simple country-side;
We heard the hawks at twilight play,

1. A town east of the Haverhill farm-stead, near the mouth of the Merrimack. Just north, on the New Hampshire coast (see ll. 242–243), are the promontory of Little Boar's Head, and offshore, the Isles of Shoals.
2. Abigail Hussey Whittier (1781–1857). "My mother, who was born in the Indian-haunted region of Somersworth, New Hampshire, between Dover and Portsmouth, told us of the inroads of the savages, and the narrow escape of her ancestors. She described strange people who lived on the Piscataqua and Cocheco, among whom was Bantam the sorcerer" [Whittier's introduction].
3. Site of an Indian raid, on the Cocheco River, above Portsmouth, New Hampshire.

The boat-horn on Piscataqua,[4]
The loon's weird laughter far away;   275
We fished her little trout-brook, knew
What flowers in wood and meadow grew,
What sunny hillsides autumn-brown
She climbed to shake the ripe nuts down,
Saw where in sheltered cove and bay   280
The ducks' black squadron anchored lay,
And heard the wild-geese calling loud
Beneath the gray November cloud.

Then, haply, with a look more grave,
And soberer tone, some tale she gave   285
From painful Sewel's ancient tome,[5]
Beloved in every Quaker home,
Of faith fire-winged by martyrdom,
Or Chalkley's Journal,[6] old and quaint,—
Gentlest of skippers, rare sea-saint!—   290
Who, when the dreary calms prevailed,
And water-butt and bread-cask failed,
And cruel, hungry eyes pursued
His portly presence mad for food,
With dark hints muttered under breath   295
Of casting lots for life or death,
Offered, if Heaven withheld supplies,
To be himself the sacrifice.
Then, suddenly, as if to save
The good man from his living grave,   300
A ripple on the water grew,
A school of porpoise flashed in view.
"Take, eat,"[7] he said, "and be content;
These fishes in my stead are sent
By Him who gave the tangled ram   305
To spare the child of Abraham."[8]

Our uncle,[9] innocent of books,
Was rich in lore of fields and brooks,
The ancient teachers never dumb

---

4. A river on the Maine–New Hampshire border.
5. William Sewel (sometimes Sewell), a Dutch Quaker; his *History of the Rise, Increase, and Progress of the People called Quakers* (in Dutch, 1717; in English, 1725) became a source book among Friends.
6. Thomas Chalkley (1675–1741), Quaker shipmaster and missionary, settled in Philadelphia in 1701 and there published his *Journal* (1747) from which Whittier quotes, in a note to this poem, the more tempered account of this incident (ll. 291–306).
7. *Cf.* the bread and wine of the Eucharist (Matthew xxvi: 26–27).
8. *Cf.* Genesis xxii: 7–14.
9. Moses Whittier (died 1824). "My uncle was ready with his record of hunting and fishing and, it must be confessed, with stories which he at least half believed, of witch-craft and apparitions" [Whittier's introduction].

Of Nature's unhoused lyceum.   310
In moons and tides and weather wise,
He read the clouds as prophecies,
And foul or fair could well divine,
By many an occult hint and sign,
Holding the cunning-warded keys   315
To all the woodcraft mysteries;
Himself to Nature's heart so near
That all her voices in his ear
Of beast or bird had meanings clear,
Like Apollonius[1] of old,   320
Who knew the tales the sparrows told,
Or Hermes,[2] who interpreted
What the sage cranes of Nilus said;
A simple, guileless, childlike man,
Content to live where life began;   325
Strong only on his native grounds,
The little world of sights and sounds
Whose girdle was the parish bounds,
Whereof his fondly partial pride
The common features magnified,   330
As Surrey hills to mountains grew
In White of Selborne's[3] loving view,—
He told how teal and loon he shot,
And how the eagle's eggs he got,
The feats on pond and river done,   335
The prodigies of rod and gun;
Till, warming with the tales he told,
Forgotten was the outside cold,
The bitter wind unheeded blew,
From ripening corn the pigeons flew,   340
The partridge drummed i' the wood, the mink
Went fishing down the river-bank;
In fields with bean or clover gay,
The woodchuck, like a hermit gray,
      Peered from the doorway of his cell;   345
The muskrat plied the mason's trade,
And tier by tier his mud-walls laid;
And from the shagbark overhead
   The grizzled squirrel dropped his shell.

1. Apollonius of Tyre, Greek philosopher of the first century, said to be a mystical worker of miracles.
2. A mythical personage, alleged author of the age-old *Hermetic Books* of Egyptian magic, influential in medieval alchemy and modern occult lore.
3. Gilbert White (1720–1793), English naturalist and clergyman of Selborne; published *The Natural History and Antiquities of Selborne* (1789), a classic in its field.

Next, the dear aunt,[4] whose smile of cheer 350
And voice in dreams I see and hear,—
The sweetest woman ever Fate
Perverse denied a household mate,
Who, lonely, homeless, not the less
Found peace in love's unselfishness, 355
And welcome wheresoe'er she went,
A calm and gracious element,
Whose presence seemed the sweet income
And womanly atmosphere of home,—
Called up her girlhood memories, 360
The huskings and the apple-bees,
The sleigh-rides and the summer sails,
Weaving through all the poor details
And homespun warp of circumstance
A golden woof-thread of romance. 365
For well she kept her genial mood
And simple faith of maidenhood;
Before her still a cloud-land lay,
The mirage loomed across her way;
The morning dew, that dries so soon 370
With others, glistened at her noon;
Through years of toil and soil and care,
From glossy tress to thin gray hair,
All unprofaned she held apart
The virgin fancies of the heart. 375
Be shame to him of woman born
Who hath for such but thought of scorn.

There, too, our elder sister[5] plied
Her evening task the stand beside;
A full, rich nature, free to trust,
Truthful and almost sternly just, 380
Impulsive, earnest, prompt to act,
And make her generous thought a fact,
Keeping with many a light disguise
The secret of self-sacrifice.
O heart sore-tried! thou hast the best, 385
That Heaven itself could give thee,—rest,
Rest from all bitter thoughts and things!
    How many a poor one's blessing went
    With thee beneath the low green tent
Whose curtain never outward swings! 390

4. His mother's sister, Mercy Evans   5. Mary Caldwell Whittier (1806–
Hussey, who died in 1846.   1861).

As one who held herself a part
Of all she saw, and let her heart
  Against the household bosom lean,
Upon the motley-braided mat   395
Our youngest and our dearest[6] sat,
Lifting her large, sweet, asking eyes,
  Now bathed in the unfading green
And holy peace of Paradise.
Oh, looking from some heavenly hill,   400
  Or from the shade of saintly palms,
  Or silver reach of river calms,
Do those large eyes behold me still?
With me one little year ago:—
The chill weight of the winter snow   405
  For months upon her grave has lain;
And now, when summer south-winds blow
  And brier and harebell bloom again,
I tread the pleasant paths we trod,
I see the violet-sprinkled sod   410
Whereon she leaned, too frail and weak
The hillside flowers she loved to seek,
Yet following me where'er I went
With dark eyes full of love's content.
The birds are glad; the brier-rose fills   415
The air with sweetness; all the hills
Stretch green to June's unclouded sky;
But still I wait with ear and eye
For something gone which should be nigh,
A loss in all familiar things,   420
In flower that blooms, and bird that sings.
And yet, dear heart! remembering thee,
  Am I not richer than of old?
Safe in thy immortality,
  What change can reach the wealth I hold?   425
  What chance can mar the pearl and gold
Thy love hath left in trust with me?
And while in life's late afternoon,
  Where cool and long the shadows grow,
I walk to meet the night that soon   430
  Shall shape and shadow overflow,
I cannot feel that thou art far,
Since near at need the angels are;
And when the sunset gates unbar,

6. Whittier's younger sister, Elizabeth Hussey Whittier, had died "one little year ago" (1864), aged forty-eight. For some idea of their close companionship, see Pickard, *Life and Letters*, Vol. I, pp. 29–31.

Shall I not see thee waiting stand,
And, white against the evening star,   435
  The welcome of thy beckoning hand?

Brisk wielder of the birch and rule,
The master of the district school[7]
Held at the fire his favored place,   440
Its warm glow lit a laughing face
Fresh-hued and fair, where scarce appeared
  The uncertain prophecy of beard.
He teased the mitten-blinded cat,
Played cross-pins[8] on my uncle's hat,   445
Sang songs, and told us what befalls
In classic Dartmouth's college halls.
Born the wild Northern hills among,
From whence his yeoman father wrung
By patient toil subsistence scant,   450
Not competence and yet not want,
He early gained the power to pay
His cheerful, self-reliant way;
Could doff at ease his scholar's gown
To peddle wares from town to town;   455
Or through the long vacation's reach
In lonely lowland districts teach,
Where all the droll experience found
At stranger hearths in boarding round,
The moonlit skater's keen delight,   460
The sleigh-drive through the frosty night,
The rustic-party, with its rough
Accompaniment of blind-man's-buff,
And whirling-plate, and forfeits paid,
His winter task a pastime made.   465
Happy the snow-locked homes wherein
He tuned his merry violin,
Or played the athlete in the barn,
Or held the good dame's winding-yarn,
Or mirth-provoking versions told   470
Of classic legends rare and old,
Wherein the scenes of Greece and Rome
Had all the commonplace of home,
And little seemed at best the odds
'Twixt Yankee pedlers and old gods;   475
Where Pindus-born Arachthus[9] took

7. The schoolmaster here immortalized
was George Haskell (1799–1876).
8. A game with pins, somewhat like
modern jackstraws.

9. The river Arachthus, storied in Greek
legend, rose in the Pindus range separating Epirus and Thessaly.

She sat among us, at the best,
A not unfeared, half-welcome guest,[2]   520
Rebuking with her cultured phrase
Our homeliness of words and ways.
A certain pard-like, treacherous grace
Swayed the lithe limbs and dropped the lash,
Lent the white teeth their dazzling flash;   525
And under low brows, black with night,
Rayed out at times a dangerous light;
The sharp heat-lightnings of her face
Presaging ill to him whom Fate
Condemned to share her love or hate.   530
A woman tropical, intense
In thought and act, in soul and sense,
She blended in a like degree
The vixen and the devotee,
Revealing with each freak or feint   535
    The temper of Petruchio's Kate,[3]
The raptures of Siena's saint.[4]
Her tapering hand and rounded wrist
Had facile power to form a fist;
The warm, dark languish of her eyes   540
Was never safe from wrath's surprise.
Brows saintly calm and lips devout
Knew every change of scowl and pout;
And the sweet voice had notes more high
And shrill for social battle-cry.   545

Since then what old cathedral town
Has missed her pilgrim staff and gown,
What convent-gate has held its lock
Against the challenge of her knock!
Through Smyrna's plague-hushed thoroughfares,   550
Up sea-set Malta's rocky stairs,
Gray olive slopes of hills that hem
    Thy tombs and shrines, Jerusalem,

2. "Harriet Livermore, daughter of Judge Livermore, of New Hampshire, a young woman of fine natural ability, enthusiastic, eccentric, with slight control over her violent temper, which sometimes made her religious profession doubtful. She was equally ready to exhort in school-house prayer-meetings and dance in a Washington ball-room, while her father was a member of Congress. She early embraced the doctrine of the Second Advent, and felt it her duty to proclaim the Lord's speedy coming. With this message she crossed the Atlantic and spent the greater part of a long life travelling over Europe and Asia * * * a friend of mine found her, when quite an old woman, wandering in Syria with a tribe of Arabs, who with the oriental notion that madness is inspiration, accepted her as their prophetess and leader" [Whittier's introduction].
3. *Cf.* Petruchio and Katharina, in Shakespeare's *Taming of the Shrew.*
4. St. Catherine of Siena (1347–1380), whose ecstatic revelations influenced two popes.

Or startling on her desert throne
The crazy Queen of Lebanon[5]   555
With claims fantastic as her own,
Her tireless feet have held their way;
And still, unrestful, bowed, and gray,
She watches under Eastern skies,
    With hope each day renewed and fresh,   560
    The Lord's quick coming in the flesh,
Whereof she dreams and prophesies!

Where'er her troubled path may be,
    The Lord's sweet pity with her go!
The outward wayward life we see,   565
    The hidden springs we may not know.
Nor is it given us to discern
    What threads the fatal sisters spun,
    Through what ancestral years has run
The sorrow with the woman born,   570
What forged her cruel chain of moods,
What set her feet in solitudes,
    And held the love within her mute,
What mingled madness in the blood,
    A life-long discord and annoy,   575
    Water of tears with oil of joy,
And hid within the folded bud
    Perversities of flower and fruit.
It is not ours to separate
    The tangled skein of will and fate,   580
To show what metes and bounds should stand
Upon the soul's debatable land,
And between choice and Providence
Divide the circle of events;
But He who knows our frame is just,   585
Merciful and compassionate,
And full of sweet assurances
And hope for all the language is,
That He remembereth we are dust![6]

At last the great logs, crumbling low,   590

5. Lady Hester Lucy Stanhope (1776–1839). *Cf.* Harriet Livermore, above, l. 520. Whittier's introduction states that "Harriet Livermore * * * lived some time with Lady Hester Stanhope, a woman as fantastic and strained as herself, on the slope of Mt. Lebanon, but finally quarrelled with her in regard to two white horses with red marks on their backs which suggested the idea of sad-dles, on which her titled hostess expected to ride into Jerusalem with the Lord." Of Lady Stanhope, Whittier had read in *Eothen* (1844), the eastern travel sketches of A. W. Kinglake, the English historian, who found her in the rôle of "prophetess" among the Druses of Lebanon, whom she had incited against the Arabs and British.
6. *Cf.* Psalms ciii: 9–14.

Sent out a dull and duller glow,
The bull's-eye watch that hung in view,
Ticking its weary circuit through,
Pointed with mutely warning sign
Its black hand to the hour of nine.   595
That sign the pleasant circle broke:
My uncle ceased his pipe to smoke,
Knocked from its bowl the refuse gray,
And laid it tenderly away;
Then roused himself to safely cover   600
The dull red brands with ashes over.
And while, with care, our mother laid
The work aside, her steps she stayed
One moment, seeking to express
Her grateful sense of happiness   605
For food and shelter, warmth and health,
And love's contentment more than wealth,
With simple wishes (not the weak,
Vain prayers which no fulfilment seek,
But such as warm the generous heart,   610
O'er-prompt to do with Heaven its part)
That none might lack, that bitter night,
For bread and clothing, warmth and light.

Within our beds awhile we heard
The wind that round the gables roared,   615
With now and then a ruder shock,
Which made our very bedsteads rock.
We heard the loosened clapboards tost,
The board-nails snapping in the frost;
And on us, through the unplastered wall,   620
Felt the light sifted snow-flakes fall.
But sleep stole on, as sleep will do
When hearts are light and life is new;
Faint and more faint the murmurs grew,
Till in the summer-land of dreams   625
They softened to the sound of streams,
Low stir of leaves, and dip of oars,
And lapsing waves on quiet shores.

Next morn we wakened with the shout
Of merry voices high and clear;   630
And saw the teamsters drawing near
To break the drifted highways out.
Down the long hillside treading slow
We saw the half-buried oxen go,

Shaking the snow from heads uptost,   635
Their straining nostrils white with frost.
Before our door the straggling train
Drew up, an added team to gain.
The elders threshed their hands a-cold,
    Passed, with the cider-mug, their jokes   640
    From lip to lip; the younger folks
Down the loose snow-banks, wrestling, rolled,
Then toiled again the cavalcade
    O'er windy hill, through clogged ravine,
    And woodland paths that wound between   645
Low drooping pine-boughs winter-weighed.
From every barn a team afoot,
At every house a new recruit,
Where, drawn by Nature's subtlest law,
Haply the watchful young men saw   650
Sweet doorway pictures of the curls
And curious eyes of merry girls,
Lifting their hands in mock defence
Against the snow-ball's compliments,
And reading in each missive tost   655
The charm with Eden never lost.

We heard once more the sleigh-bells' sound;
    And, following where the teamsters led,
The wise old Doctor[7] went his round,
Just pausing at our door to say,   660
In the brief autocratic way
Of one who, prompt at Duty's call,
Was free to urge her claim on all,
    That some poor neighbor sick abed
At night our mother's aid would need.   665
For, one in generous thought and deed,
    What mattered in the sufferer's sight
    The Quaker matron's inward light,
The Doctor's mail of Calvin's creed?
All hearts confess the saints elect   670
    Who, twain in faith, in love agree,
And melt not in an acid sect
    The Christian pearl of charity!

So days went on: a week had passed
Since the great world was heard from last.   675

7. Dr. Elias Weld, the family physician,   miles from us," and lent the young
lived at "the Rocks Village, about two   Whittier his books.

The Almanac we studied o'er,
Read and reread our little store
Of books and pamphlets, scarce a score;
One harmless novel, mostly hid
From younger eyes, a book forbid,   680
And poetry, (or good or bad,
A single book was all we had,)
Where Ellwood's[8] meek, drab-skirted Muse,
    A stranger to the heathen Nine,
    Sang, with a somewhat nasal whine,   685
The wars of David and the Jews.
At last the floundering carrier bore
The village paper to our door.
Lo! broadening outward as we read,
To warmer zones the horizon spread;   690
In panoramic length unrolled
We saw the marvels that it told.
Before us passed the painted Creeks,[9]
    And daft McGregor[1] on his raids
    In Costa Rica's everglades.   695
And up Taygetos winding slow
Rode Ypsilanti's Mainote Greeks,[2]
A Turk's head at each saddle-bow!
Welcome to us its week-old news,
Its corner for the rustic Muse,   700
    Its monthly gauge of snow and rain,
Its record, mingling in a breath
The wedding bell and dirge of death:
Jest, anecdote, and love-lorn tale,
The latest culprit sent to jail;   705
Its hue and cry of stolen and lost,
Its vendue[3] sales and goods at cost,
    And traffic calling loud for gain.
We felt the stir of hall and street,
The pulse of life that round us beat;   710
The chill embargo of the snow
Was melted in the genial glow;
Wide swung again our ice-locked door,
And all the world was ours once more!

---

8. Thomas Ellwood (1639–1714). Whittier here describes the *Davideis* (1712) of this young Quaker friend of John Milton, whose later life is valuably reflected in Ellwood's autobiography.
9. The raids of Creek Indians in Alabama, quelled by Andrew Jackson (1814).

1. The adventurer Gregor McGregor attempted to establish a filibuster colony in Costa Rica (1819).
2. General Prince Alexander Ypsilanti (1792–1828) in 1820 led the Greek army of independence against the Turks, winning a notable engagement at Mount Taygetos in the Peloponnesos.
3. French loan word for "auction."

Clasp, Angel of the backward look   715
   And folded wings of ashen gray
   And voice of echoes far away,
The brazen covers of thy book;
The weird palimpsest old and vast,
Wherein thou hid'st the spectral past;   720
Where, closely mingling, pale and glow
The characters of joy and woe;
The monographs of outlived years,
Or smile-illumed or dim with tears,
   Green hills of life that slope to death,   725
And haunts of home, whose vistaed trees
Shade off to mournful cypresses
   With the white amaranths[4] underneath.
Even while I look, I can but heed
   The restless sands' incessant fall,   730
Importunate hours that hours succeed,
Each clamorous with its own sharp need,
   And duty keeping pace with all.
Shut down and clasp the heavy lids;
I hear again the voice that bids   735
The dreamer leave his dream midway
For larger hopes and graver fears:
Life greatens in these later years,
The century's aloe[5] flowers today!

Yet, haply, in some lull of life,   740
Some Truce of God which breaks its strife,
The worldling's eyes shall gather dew,
   Dreaming in throngful city ways
Of winter joys his boyhood knew;
And dear and early friends—the few   745
Who yet remain—shall pause to view
   These Flemish pictures[6] of old days;
Sit with me by the homestead hearth,
And stretch the hands of memory forth
   To warm them at the wood-fire's blaze!   750
And thanks untraced to lips unknown
Shall greet me like the odors blown
From unseen meadows newly mown,
Or lilies floating in some pond,
Wood-fringed, the wayside gaze beyond;   755

---

4. In poetic literature, an imaginary unfading flower.
5. A species of plants, or their extracts,
renowned for bitterness; used in em-
balming the body of Jesus (*cf.* John

xix: 39–40).
6. Flemish and Dutch masters, especially in the seventeenth century, developed a powerful *genre* painting of
homely and domestic subjects.

The traveller owns the grateful sense
Of sweetness near, he knows not whence,
And, pausing, takes with forehead bare
The benediction of the air.

1866

Abraham Davenport[7]

In the old days (a custom laid aside
With breeches and cocked hats) the people sent
Their wisest men to make the public laws.
And so, from a brown homestead, where the Sound
Drinks the small tribute of the Mianas,   5
Waved over by the woods of Rippowams,
And hallowed by pure lives and tranquil deaths,
Stamford[8] sent up to the councils of the State
Wisdom and grace in Abraham Davenport.

'Twas on a May-day of the far old year
Seventeen hundred eighty, that there fell   10
Over the bloom and sweet life of the Spring,
Over the fresh earth and the heaven of noon,
A horror of great darkness, like the night
In day of which the Norland sagas tell,—
The Twilight of the Gods.[9] The low-hung sky   15
Was black with ominous clouds, save where its rim
Was fringed with a dull glow, like that which climbs
The crater's sides from the red hell below.
Birds ceased to sing, and all the barn-yard fowls   20
Roosted; the cattle at the pasture bars
Lowed, and looked homeward; bats on leathern wings
Flitted abroad; the sounds of labor died;
Men prayed, and women wept; all ears grew sharp
To hear the doom-blast of the trumpet[1] shatter   25
The black sky, that the dreadful face of Christ
Might look from the rent clouds, not as He looked

<hr />

7. "Abraham Davenport," noted for its dramatic simplicity and its characterization, is also Whittier's best accomplishment in blank verse. The incident is discussed in the poet's note: "The famous Dark Day of New England, May 19, 1780, was a physical puzzle for many years to our ancestors. * * * The incident of Colonel Abraham Davenport's sturdy protest is a matter of history." The poem first appeared in the *Atlantic Monthly* for May, 1866, and was collected in *The Tent on the Beach* (1867).

8. The locale of the story is the extreme western extension of Connecticut, where the Miamus and the Rippowams (now the Mill) empty into Long Island Sound.

9. The Norse and Germanic myths of the *Götterdämmerung;* the last judgment and destruction.

1. For the trumpet of Judgment Day, see I Corinthians xv: 52–53; but *cf.* Revelation xx.

A loving guest at Bethany,[2] but stern
As Justice and inexorable Law.

Meanwhile in the old State House, dim as ghosts,   30
Sat the lawgivers of Connecticut,
Trembling beneath their legislative robes.
"It is the Lord's Great Day! Let us adjourn,"
Some said; and then, as if with one accord,
All eyes were turned to Abraham Davenport.   35
He rose, slow cleaving with his steady voice
The intolerable hush. "This well may be
The Day of Judgment which the world awaits;
But be it so or not, I only know
My present duty, and my Lord's command   40
To occupy till He come.[3] So at the post
Where He hath set me in His providence,
I choose, for one, to meet Him face to face,—
No faithless servant frightened from my task,
But ready when the Lord of the harvest[4] calls;   45
And therefore, with all reverence, I would say,
Let God do His work, we will see to ours.
Bring in the candles." And they brought them in.

Then by the flaring lights the Speaker read,
Albeit with husky voice and shaking hands,   50
An act to amend an act to regulate
The shad and alewive[5] fisheries. Whereupon
Wisely and well spake Abraham Davenport,
Straight to the question, with no figures of speech
Save the ten Arab signs,[6] yet not without   55
The shrewd dry humor natural to the man:
His awe-struck colleagues listening all the while,
Between the pauses of his argument,
To hear the thunder of the wrath of God
Break from the hollow trumpet of the cloud.   60

And there he stands in memory to this day,
Erect, self-poised, a rugged face, half seen
Against the background of unnatural dark,
A witness to the ages as they pass,
That simple duty hath no place for fear.   65

1866, 1867

2. At Bethany, a guest of Simon the
Leper, Jesus was attended by the woman
with the precious ointment. *Cf.* Matthew xxvi: 6–13.

3. *Cf.* Luke xix: 13.
4. *Cf.* Luke x: 2.
5. A food fish of the herring family.
6. Arabic numerals, or figures.

The Eternal Goodness[7]

O friends! with whom my feet have trod
    The quiet aisles of prayer,
Glad witness to your zeal for God
    And love of man I bear.

I trace your lines of argument;   5
    Your logic linked and strong
I weigh as one who dreads dissent,
    And fears a doubt as wrong.

But still my human hands are weak
    To hold your iron creeds: 10
Against the words ye bid me speak
    My heart within me pleads.

Who fathoms the Eternal Thought?
    Who talks of scheme and plan?
The Lord is God! He needeth not   15
    The poor device of man.

I walk with bare, hushed feet the ground
    Ye tread with boldness shod;
I dare not fix with mete and bound
    The love and power of God.   20

Ye praise His justice; even such
    His pitying love I deem:
Ye seek a king; I fain would touch
    The robe that hath no seam.

Ye see the curse which overbroods   25
    A world of pain and loss;
I hear our Lord's beatitudes[8]
    And prayer upon the cross.[9]

More than your schoolmen teach, within
    Myself, alas! I know:
Too dark ye cannot paint the sin,   30
    Too small the merit show.

---

7. In spite of its simple form—the "common meter" of hymnology—"The Eternal Goodness" is a reasoned statement of the theology of a Quaker liberal of that time. Against the "iron creeds" of fundamentalist Calvinism, or the God of "justice" and wrath, Whittier sets the God of mercy and pity. The "closed revelation" of the scriptures is to be understood by the immediate revelation of the "inward light." The entire hymn has been set to music several times. Nine shorter hymns are reported as derived from it, two of them quite familiar. The poem first appeared in *The Independent* for March 16, 1865. It was collected in *The Tent on the Beach* (1867).

8. A part of Christ's Sermon on the Mount; see Matthew v: 1–12.

9. *Cf.* Luke xxiii: 34: "Father, forgive them, for they know not what they do."

I bow my forehead to the dust,
　　I veil mine eyes for shame,
And urge, in trembling self-distrust,　　　　35
　　A prayer without a claim.

I see the wrong that round me lies,
　　I feel the guilt within;
I hear, with groan and travail-cries,
　　The world confess its sin.　　　　40

Yet, in the maddening maze of things,
　　And tossed by storm and flood,
To one fixed trust my spirit clings;
　　I know that God is good!

Not mine to look where cherubim　　　　45
　　And seraphs may not see,
But nothing can be good in Him
　　Which evil is in me.

The wrong that pains my soul below
　　I dare not throne above,　　　　50
I know not of His hate,—I know
　　His goodness and His love.

I dimly guess from blessings known
　　Of greater out of sight,
And, with the chastened Psalmist,[1] own　　　　55
　　His judgments too are right.

I long for household voices gone,
　　For vanished smiles I long,
But God hath led my dear ones on,
　　And He can do no wrong.　　　　60

I know not what the future hath
　　Of marvel or surprise,
Assured alone that life and death
　　His mercy underlies.

And if my heart and flesh are weak[2]　　　　65
　　To bear an untried pain,
The bruisèd reed He will not break,[3]
　　But strengthen and sustain.

No offering of my own I have,
　　Nor works my faith to prove;　　　　70

1. David; for the next line, cf. Psalms
xix: 7–9.
2. Cf. Matthew xxvi: 41.

3. Cf. Matthew xii: 20, quoting Isaiah
xlii: 3.

I can but give the gifts He gave,
    And plead His love for love.

And so beside the Silent Sea
    I wait the muffled oar;
No harm from Him can come to me   75
    On ocean or on shore.

I know not where His islands lift
    Their fronded palms in air;
I only know I cannot drift
    Beyond His love and care.   80

O brothers! if my faith is vain,
    If hopes like these betray,
Pray for me that my feet may gain
    The sure and safer way.

And Thou, O Lord! by whom are seen   85
    Thy creatures as they be,
Forgive me if too close I lean
    My human heart on Thee!

                            1865, 1867

Centennial Hymn[4]

I

Our fathers' God! from out whose hand
The centuries fall like grains of sand,
We meet to-day, united, free,
And loyal to our land and Thee,
To thank Thee for the era done,   5
And trust Thee for the opening one.

II

Here,[5] where of old, by Thy design,
The fathers spake that word of Thine
Whose echo is the glad refrain
Of rended bolt and falling chain,   10
To grace our festal time, from all
The zones of earth our guests we call.

---

4. "Written for the opening of the International Exhibition, Philadelphia, May 10, 1876. The music for the hymn was written by John K. Paine, and may be found in the *Atlantic Monthly* for June, 1876" [Whittier's note]. The poem first appeared as a broadside distributed at the exposition, and was collected in *The Vision of Echard and Other Poems* (1878).

5. Philadelphia, where in 1776 the "fathers" by proclaiming human liberty in the Declaration of Independence fulfilled the Divine Will. This concept of special destiny became an active force in American policy.

III

Be with us while the New World greets
The Old World thronging all its streets,[6]
Unveiling all the triumphs won   15
By art or toil beneath the sun;
And unto common good ordain
This rivalship of hand and brain.

IV

Thou, who hast here in concord furled
The war flags of a gathered world,[7]   20
Beneath our Western skies fulfil
The Orient's mission of good-will,
And freighted with love's Golden Fleece,
Send back its Argonauts of peace.[8]

V

For art and labor met in truce,   25
For beauty made the bride of use,
We thank Thee; but, withal, we crave
The austere virtues strong to save,
The honor proof to place or gold,
The manhood never bought nor sold!   30

VI

Oh make Thou us, through centuries long,
In peace secure, in justice strong;
Around our gift of freedom draw
The safeguards of Thy righteous law:
And, cast in some diviner mould,   35
Let the new cycle shame the old!

1876, 1878

The Bartholdi Statue[9]

The land, that, from the rule of kings,
In freeing us, itself made free,

6. The Philadelphia exposition was conceived as an international exhibition of arts and industries.
7. With the ending of the Franco-Prussian War in 1871 the peace of Europe seemed assured (*cf.* stanza iv). The aggressive empire of Napoleon III had been succeeded by the Republic; the rivalries of Austria and Italy had given way to internal consolidation in each kingdom. Besides these, China and Japan, referred to in ll. 21–22, were represented at the exposition.

8. In Greek legend, the Golden Fleece, a treasure guarded by a dragon, was recovered by Jason and his band of Argonauts.
9. Frédéric Auguste Bartholdi (1834–1904) was the designer of the Statue of Liberty, given by the French people to the United States in commemoration of the centennial anniversary of American independence. It was dedicated in October, 1886. The poem was published in *The Independent* for October 28, 1886, and collected in the *Writings* (1888).

Our Old World Sister, to us brings
  Her sculptured Dream of Liberty:

Unlike the shapes on Egypt's sands   5
  Uplifted by the toil-worn slave,
On Freedom's soil with freemen's hands
  We rear the symbol free hands gave.

O France, the beautiful! to thee
  Once more a debt of love we owe: 10
In peace beneath thy Colors Three,
  We hail a later Rochambeau![1]

Rise, stately Symbol! holding forth
  Thy light and hope to all who sit
In chains and darkness! Belt the earth   15
  With watch-fires from thy torch uplit!

Reveal the primal mandate still
  Which Chaos heard and ceased to be,
Trace on mid-air th' Eternal Will
  In signs of fire: "Let man be free!"   20

Shine far, shine free, a guiding light
  To Reason's ways and Virtue's aim,
A lightning-flash the wretch to smite
  Who shields his license with thy name!

1886, 1888

Burning Drift-Wood[2]

Before my drift-wood fire I sit,
  And see, with every waif I burn,
Old dreams and fancies coloring it,
  And folly's unlaid ghosts return.

O ships of mine, whose swift keels cleft   5
  The enchanted sea on which they sailed,
Are these poor fragments only left
  Of vain desires and hopes that failed?

Did I not watch from them the light
  Of sunset on my towers in Spain,   10

1. Comte de Rochambeau (1725–1807), general in command of a French force sent to the aid of the Americans, assisted Washington in the defeat of Cornwallis at Yorktown (1781) while a French fleet prevented British escape by sea, thus ending the Revolutionary War.

2. This poem appeared in Whittier's last volume, *At Sundown* (1890).

And see, far off, uploom in sight
  The Fortunate Isles I might not gain?

Did sudden lift of fog reveal
  Arcadia's vales of song and spring,
And did I pass, with grazing keel,   15
  The rocks whereon the sirens sing?

Have I not drifted hard upon
  The unmapped regions lost to man,
The cloud-pitched tents of Prester John,[3]
  The palace domes of Kubla Khan?[4]   20

Did land winds blow from jasmine flowers,
  Where Youth the ageless Fountain fills?
Did Love make sign from rose blown bowers,
  And gold from Eldorado's[5] hills?

Alas! the gallant ships that sailed   25
  On blind Adventure's errand sent,
Howe'er they laid their courses, failed
  To reach the haven of Content.

And of my ventures, those alone
  Which Love had freighted, safely sped,   30
Seeking a good beyond my own,
  By clear-eyed Duty piloted.

O mariners, hoping still to meet
  The luck Arabian voyagers met,
And find in Bagdad's moonlit street,   35
  Haroun al Raschid[6] walking yet,

Take with you, on your Sea of Dreams,
  The fair, fond fancies dear to youth.
I turn from all that only seems,
  And seek the sober grounds of truth.   40

What matter that it is not May,
  That birds have flown, and trees are bare,
That darker grows the shortening day,
  And colder blows the wintry air!

The wrecks of passion and desire,   45
  The castles I no more rebuild,

3. A legendary priest and king of the Middle Ages, supposed to be ruler of a land in eastern Africa; celebrated in English lays and ballads.
4. The words echo Coleridge's poem on Kubla Khan (1216–1294), fabulous founder of a Mongol dynasty in western China.
5. "The golden"; a legendary South American kingdom, abounding in treasure.
6. In the *Arabian Nights*, the fabulous caliph of Bagdad.

May fitly feed my drift-wood fire,
  And warm the hands that age has chilled.

Whatever perished with my ships,
  I only know the best remains;
A song of praise is on my lips   50
  For losses which are now my gains.

Heap high my hearth! No worth is lost;
  No wisdom with the folly dies.
Burn on, poor shreds, your holocaust   55
  Shall be my evening sacrifice!

Far more than all I dared to dream,
  Unsought before my door I see;
On wings of fire and steeds of steam
  The world's great wonders come to me,   60

And holier signs, unmarked before,
  Of Love to seek and Power to save,—
The righting of the wronged and poor,
  The man evolving from the slave;

And life, no longer chance or fate,   65
  Safe in the gracious Fatherhood.
I fold o'er-wearied hands and wait,
  In full assurance of the good.

And well the waiting time must be,
  Though brief or long its granted days,   70
If Faith and Hope and Charity[7]
  Sit by my evening hearth-fire's blaze.

And with them, friends whom Heaven has spared,
  Whose love my heart has comforted,
And, sharing all my joys, has shared   75
  My tender memories of the dead,—

Dear souls who left us lonely here,
  Bound on their last, long voyage, to whom
We, day by day, are drawing near,
  Where every bark has sailing room.   80

I know the solemn monotone
  Of waters calling unto me;
I know from whence the airs have blown
  That whisper of the Eternal Sea.

As low my fires of drift-wood burn,   85
  I hear that sea's deep sounds increase,

7. *Cf.* I Corinthians xiii: 13.

And, fair in sunset light, discern
Its mirage-lifted Isles of Peace.

1890

OLIVER WENDELL HOLMES
(1809–1894)

Holmes's reading made a full man; his sense of responsibility made a man ever ready for the play of ideas which he regarded as inseparable from living; his scientific training made him an exact and formidable opponent; his wit was at once an instrument and a recreation; his sense of humor and love of fun gave a kindly and human dimension to his criticism of life.

These characteristics of his personality and his writing were a natural reflection of the New England "renaissance," of the highly cultured society into which he was born, in Cambridge, Massachusetts, in 1809. He was graduated from Harvard with the class of 1829, which he later celebrated annually for many years, in the best poems ever lavished upon such a subject. In 1830, while studying law at Harvard, he initiated the effective movement to prevent the scrapping of the gallant ship *Constitution*, by composing his famous poem "Old Ironsides," written impromptu with the competence of the born writer. In the next two years, magazine readers saw the first two of his *Autocrat* papers, thereafter not to be resumed for a quarter of a century although he frequently contributed to the periodicals during his busy years of professional activity.

That profession was medicine, which he began to study in 1830 in Boston. In 1835 he went to Paris, where the new emphasis on experimental techniques was revolutionizing medical science. Here Holmes laid the foundations for his later pioneering in microscopy, but his devotion to science was not so great as to prevent him from spending holidays on long rambles about Europe. He returned to Harvard in 1836 to take his degree in medicine, and that year he also published *Poems*, his first volume.

Although he acknowledged that he had "a right to be grateful to his ancestors," what he inherited was a tradition, not a fortune. He soon found that he was not happy in the practice of medicine, and turned to the teaching of medical science. After serving as professor of anatomy at Dartmouth (1838–1840), he returned to general practice in Boston upon his marriage in 1840; but in 1847 he found his true vocation in the appointment as Parkman Professor of Anatomy and Physiology in Harvard Medical School. Among his scientific publications, the most notable had been an analysis of the shortcomings of homeopathy, and, in 1843, a study of "The Contagiousness of Puerperal Fever," a contribution to the reduction of the fearful mortality rate then connected with childbirth. However, his professional reputation was won not by research, of which he did his share, but by his high accomplishments as a clinician and a medical educator. He was dean of Harvard Medical School from 1847 to 1853, and until his retirement, as emeritus professor, in 1882, he continued to contribute to the broad development of medical education.

Literature, however, remained his avocation. His periodical contributions were included, along with new poems, in the *Poems* of 1846 and 1849, the former published in London, where he began to be recognized for his light verse. In 1852 he first collected his *Poetical Works*. In 1854 he published the *Songs of the Class of 1829*, to be reissued with additions for many years.

In 1857, he, and other members of the Saturday Club, founded the *Atlantic Monthly*, which he named. His famous *Autocrat of the Breakfast-Table* appeared in it serially, beginning with the first number, and established the familiar tone which that justly celebrated magazine preserved for many years. The *Autocrat* was published as a volume in 1858. Thereafter this wise and whimsical table talk, which ranks with the best "conversations" of literature, continued to appear in the *Atlantic*, and was collected in *The Professor at the Breakfast-Table* (1860), *The Poet at the Breakfast-Table* (1872), and *Over the Teacups* (1891).

By contrast, the novels of Holmes are unimpressive, especially as narratives. Yet many readers have found compensation in the witty commentary, the sociological criticism, and the psychological explication of *Elsie Venner* (1861), *The Guardian Angel* (1867), and *A Mortal Antipathy* (1885). For all their shortcomings in fictional technique, these were pioneering experiments in the analysis of elements then becoming familiar to the clinicians of mental science, such as prenatal influence, hereditary traits, and mental trauma or fixations, in their relations to the problems of moral responsibility. Here Holmes arrayed the resources of his science against the Calvinistic orthodoxy that he attacked on various levels—including the ridiculous, in "The Deacon's Masterpiece."

Meanwhile many of his poems were published, chiefly in the *Atlantic*, and later in the volumes of 1862, 1875, 1880, 1883 (a collected *Poetical Works*), and 1888. In spite of the real merit of some of his reflective lyrics, his recognition as a poet, here and abroad, was based on the unquestioned success of his comic verse, his gracious occasional poems, his urbane and witty light verse and *vers de société*. By its nature, humorous and light verse must seem casual and easy, and in view of its relative impermanence as compared with serious poetry, the survival of Holmes's work with the best of this *genre* is evidence of his genius.

No short sketch can do justice to the many-sided activities of this small dynamo. He was scientist and teacher, poet, essayist, and novelist. He could have had a career as a serious lecturer; he became a favorite after-dinner speaker. He wrote three biographical volumes—*Motley* (1879); *Emerson*, for the American Men of Letters series (1885); and *Henry Jacob Biglow* (1891). He gave numerous professional lectures, assisted in founding the American Medical Association, and wrote his quota of medical articles and books. Retired from his professorship at seventy-three, he at once undertook the three-year task of revising and annotating his works. He turned the observations of a foreign journey into *Our Hundred Days in Europe* (1887). If he was conservative with respect to the humanitarian cultural tradition, he was also a radical and courageous opponent of all meaningless survivals or current shams. He broke with both the Calvinistic and Unitarian traditions of New England. Within his Brahmin "caste," as he called it, he attacked the snobbish respect for wealth, privilege, and idleness. In his novels he employed a new frankness which only his adroit

expression made acceptable to his time. While laughing at feminism, he supported the admission of women to medical schools. He advocated such unpopular advances in medical practice as anesthesia and antisepsis. He energetically and cheerfully outlived the entire illustrious generation of his contemporary authors, and died in 1894, just past eighty-five.

The standard text is the Riverside Edition, *The Writings of Oliver Wendell Holmes*, 13 vols., 1891–1892, reproduced in the Standard Library Edition, 1892, to which were added in 1896 the two volumes of Morse's *Life and Letters* (listed below). The poems below are taken from *The Complete Poetical Works of Oliver Wendell Holmes*, Cambridge Edition, 1 vol., edited by H. E. Scudder, 1895, still available, and the best text. The notes by Holmes reproduced in this volume are from his revised *Poetical Works* of 1883. *The Autocrat of the Breakfast-Table*, often reprinted, was critically edited by Franklin T. Baker, 1928. *Oliver Wendell Holmes: Representative Selections*, edited by S. I. Hayakawa and H. M. Jones, American Writers Series, 1939, is excellent for its selections, introduction, and bibliography.

For biography and criticism, see J. T. Morse, *Life and Letters of Oliver Wendell Holmes*, 2 vols., 1896; M. A. DeWolfe Howe, *Holmes of the Breakfast-Table*, 1939; Eleanor M. Tilton, *Amiable Autocrat*, 1947; and the introduction to the volume of *Representative Selections* edited by Hayakawa and Jones (listed above).

Old Ironsides[1]

Ay, tear her tattered ensign down!
Long has it waved on high,

[1]. In 1830, just graduated from Harvard and re-enrolled as a law student, Holmes saw in the Boston *Daily Advertiser* the announcement that the frigate *Constitution* was to be demolished. "Old Ironsides," then lying in Boston's Charlestown Navy Yard, a veteran of Decatur's fleet in the Barbary Wars, had decisively vanquished the renowned British *Guerrière* (August 19, 1812) in the last British war, and

was an object of national reverence. Holmes's stirring poem appeared in the *Advertiser* two days later (September 16, 1830), was widely reprinted, and circulated in broadside form in Washington. The poem is credited with having saved the ship, which was reconditioned; it certainly established young Holmes as a writer, and became part of the literature of the schoolroom for a century. In *Poems*, 1836, the author's

And many an eye has danced to see
  That banner in the sky;
Beneath it rung the battle shout,
  And burst the cannon's roar;—   5
The meteor of the ocean air
  Shall sweep the clouds no more.

Her deck, once red with heroes' blood,
  Where knelt the vanquished foe,
When winds were hurrying o'er the flood,   10
  And waves were white below,
No more shall feel the victor's tread,
  Or know the conquered knee;—
The harpies of the shore shall pluck   15
  The eagle of the sea!

Oh, better that her shattered hulk
  Should sink beneath the wave;
Her thunders shook the mighty deep,
  And there should be her grave;   20
Nail to the mast her holy flag,
  Set every threadbare sail,
And give her to the god of storms,
  The lightning and the gale!

1830, 1836

The Height of the Ridiculous[2]

I wrote some lines once on a time
  In wondrous merry mood,
And thought, as usual, men would say
  They were exceeding good.

They were so queer, so very queer,   5
  I laughed as I would die;
Albeit, in the general way,
  A sober man am I.

I called my servant, and he came;
  How kind it was of him   10
To mind a slender man like me,
  He of the mighty limb!

first collection, the poem appeared as
part of "Poetry: A Metrical Essay,"
which he had just read before the Harvard Phi Beta Kappa; after several re-
printings it appeared independently,
with its present title, in *Poems*, 1862.
2. Published July, 1830, in the *Colle-
gian*, a Harvard undergraduate humorous magazine, and collected in *Poems*,
1836.

"These to the printer," I exclaimed,
 And, in my humorous way,
I added (as a trifling jest),   15
 "There'll be the devil to pay."

He took the paper, and I watched,
 And saw him peep within;
At the first line he read, his face
 Was all upon the grin.   20

He read the next; the grin grew broad,
 And shot from ear to ear;
He read the third; a chuckling noise
 I now began to hear.

The fourth; he broke into a roar;   25
 The fifth; his waistband split;
The sixth; he burst five buttons off,
 And tumbled in a fit.

Ten days and nights, with sleepless eye,
 I watched that wretched man,   30
And since, I never dare to write
 As funny as I can.

1830, 1836

My Aunt[3]

My aunt! my dear unmarried aunt!
 Long years have o'er her flown;
Yet still she strains the aching clasp
 That binds her virgin zone;[4]
I know it hurts her,—though she looks   5
 As cheerful as she can;
Her waist is ampler than her life,
 For life is but a span.

My aunt! my poor deluded aunt!
 Her hair is almost gray;   10
Why will she train that winter curl
 In such a spring-like way?
How can she lay her glasses down,
 And say she reads as well,
When through a double convex lens   15
 She just makes out to spell?

3. Published in the *New England Magazine* for October, 1831; reprinted in the *Harbinger* volume of 1833; collected in *Poems,* 1836.
4. A broad ornamental girdle or belt.

Her father—grandpapa! forgive
    This erring lip its smiles—
Vowed she should make the finest girl
    Within a hundred miles;
He sent her to a stylish school;   20
    'T was in her thirteenth June;
And with her, as the rules required,
    "Two towels and a spoon."

They braced my aunt against a board,   25
    To make her straight and tall;
They laced her up, they starved her down,
    To make her light and small;
They pinched her feet, they singed her hair,
    They screwed it up with pins;—
Oh, never mortal suffered more   30
    In penance for her sins.

So, when my precious aunt was done,
    My grandsire brought her back
(By daylight, lest some rabid youth
    Might follow on the track);   35
"Ah!" said my grandsire, as he shook
    Some powder in his pan,[5]
"What could this lovely creature do
    Against a desperate man!"
                       40

Alas! nor chariot, nor barouche,[6]
    Nor bandit cavalcade,
Tore from the trembling father's arms
    His all-accomplished maid.
For her how happy had it been!
    And Heaven had spared to me   45
To see one sad, ungathered rose
    On my ancestral tree.

                            1831, 1836

The Chambered Nautilus[7]

This is the ship of pearl, which, poets feign,
    Sails the unshadowed main,—

5. In ancient breech-loading muskets and pistols, the hollow in the lock that received the priming powder.
6. Types of four-wheeled carriages then fashionable: the chariot light and open; the barouche with a folding top, facing seats, and a driver's seat in front.

7. The pearly nautilus is a cephalopod of the South Pacific and Indian oceans, which builds a spiral shell, adding a chamber each year, and was thought by the Greeks to be capable of sailing by erecting a membrane (ll. 3–5). Of this poem, Holmes wrote George Ticknor

The venturous bark that flings
On the sweet summer wind its purpled wings
In gulfs enchanted, where the Siren sings,   5
     And coral reefs lie bare,
Where the cold sea-maids rise to sun their streaming hair.

Its webs of living gauze no more unfurl;
     Wrecked is the ship of pearl!
     And every chambered cell,   10
Where its dim dreaming life was wont to dwell,
As the frail tenant shaped his growing shell,
     Before thee lies revealed,—
Its irised ceiling rent, its sunless crypt unsealed!

Year after year beheld the silent toil   15
     That spread his lustrous coil;
     Still, as the spiral grew,
He left the past year's dwelling for the new,
Stole with soft step its shining archway through,
     Built up its idle door,   20
Stretched in his last-found home, and knew the old no more.

Thanks for the heavenly message brought by thee,
     Child of the wandering sea,
     Cast from her lap, forlorn!
From thy dead lips a clearer note is born   25
Than ever Triton blew from wreathèd horn![8]
     While on mine ear it rings,
Through the deep caves of thought I hear a voice that sings:—

Build thee more stately mansions, O my soul,
     As the swift seasons roll!   30
     Leave thy low-vaulted past!
Let each new temple, nobler than the last,
Shut thee from heaven with a dome more vast,
     Till thou at length art free,
Leaving thine outgrown shell by life's unresting sea!   35

1858

(Morse, *Life and Letters*, Vol. II, p. 278), "I am as willing to submit this to criticism as any I have written, in form as well as in substance, and I have not seen any English verse of just the same pattern." In substance, it develops a religious idea persistent in his revolt against such concepts as original depravity, predestination, and grace, in the Calvinist tradition. Here the lowly shellfish and man are bound, by the same law of progress, to strive for constantly higher attainments. *Cf.* the anti-Calvinism of "The Living Temple" and "The Deacon's Masterpiece." This poem was part of *The Autocrat of the Breakfast-Table*, first published in the February, 1858 installment in the *Atlantic Monthly* and in the volume of the *Autocrat* later in that year. It was collected in *Songs in Many Keys* (1862).
8. *Cf.* Wordsworth's sonnet "The World Is Too Much with Us," l. 14: "Or hear old Triton blow his wreathèd horn."

The Living Temple[9]

Not in the world of light alone,
Where God has built his blazing throne
Nor yet alone in earth below,
With belted seas that come and go,
And endless isles of sunlit green,   5
Is all thy Maker's glory seen:
Look in upon thy wondrous frame,—
Eternal wisdom still the same!

The smooth, soft air with pulse-like waves
Flows murmuring through its hidden caves,   10
Whose streams of brightening purple rush,
Fired with a new and livelier blush,
While all their burden of decay
The ebbing current steals away,
And red with Nature's flame they start   15
From the warm fountains of the heart.

No rest that throbbing slave may ask,
Forever quivering o'er his task,
While far and wide a crimson jet
Leaps forth to fill the woven net   20
Which in unnumbered crossing tides
The flood of burning life divides,
Then, kindling each decaying part,
Creeps back to find the throbbing heart.

But warmed with that unchanging flame   25
Behold the outward moving frame,
Its living marbles jointed strong
With glistening band and silvery throng,
And linked to reason's guiding reins
By myriad rings in trembling chains,   30
Each graven with the threaded zone
Which claims it as the master's own.

See how yon beam of seeming white
Is braided out of seven-hued light,[1]
Yet in those lucid globes no ray   35

9. "The Living Temple," which Holmes calls "an anatomist's hymn" in the *Autocrat*, represents another phase of his revolt against Puritanism, which defamed the body as the vessel of man's corruption. Note how the poet's imagination transforms the otherwise gruesome discoveries of the anatomist's scalpel. The poem was published in the volume of *The Autocrat of the Breakfast-Table* (1858), after appearing in the *Atlantic Monthly* installment of the *Autocrat* for May, 1858. It appeared separately among the poems of *Songs in Many Keys* (1862).
1. *I.e.*, the seven colors of the visible spectrum into which white light is dispersed in a rainbow or a crystal.

Seventeen hundred and fifty-five.
Georgius Secundus[3] was then alive,—
Snuffy old drone from the German hive.
That was the year when Lisbon-town
Saw the earth open and gulp her down,[4]
And Braddock's[5] army was done so brown,
Left without a scalp to its crown.
It was on the terrible Earthquake-day
That the Deacon finished the one-hoss shay.[6]

Now in building of chaises, I tell you what,
There is always *somewhere* a weakest spot,—
In hub, tire, felloe,[7] in spring or thill,[8]
In panel, or crossbar, or floor, or sill,
In screw, bolt, thoroughbrace,[9]—lurking still,
Find it somewhere you must and will,—
Above or below, or within or without,—
And that's the reason, beyond a doubt,
That a chaise *breaks down*, but doesn't *wear out*.

But the Deacon swore (as deacons do,
With an "I dew vum," or an "I tell *yeou*")
He would build one shay to beat the taown
'N' the keounty 'n' all the kentry raoun';
It should be so built that it *could n'* break daown:
"Fur," said the Deacon, "'t 's mighty plain
Thut the weakes' place mus' stan' the strain;
'N' the way t' fix it, uz I maintain,
                    Is only jest
T' make that place uz strong uz the rest."

So the Deacon inquired of the village folk
Where he could find the strongest oak,
That couldn't be split nor bent nor broke,—
That was for spokes and floor and sills;
He sent for lancewood to make the thills;
The crossbars were ash, from the straightest trees,
The panels of white-wood, that cuts like cheese,
But lasts like iron for things like these;
The hubs of logs from the "Settler's ellum,"—

10

15

20

25

30

35

40

45

3. George II, king of England from 1727 to 1760, was German-born.
4. The devastating earthquake in Lisbon in 1755 evoked theological argument concerning God's agency.
5. General Edward Braddock (1695–1755), British commander in the last of the French and Indian Wars, was killed in action.

6. Actually it was in 1754, not 1755, that Edwards published *The Freedom of the Will.*
7. The exterior wooden rim of a wheel.
8. The thills of a carriage are the two slender shafts between which the horse is harnessed.
9. A stout leather support by which the body of the carriage was slung to the springs.

Last of its timber,—they couldn't sell 'em,
Never an axe had seen their chips,
And the wedges flew from between their lips,
Their blunt ends frizzled like celery-tips;
Step and prop-iron, bolt and screw, 50
Spring, tire, axle, and linchpin[1] too,
Steel of the finest, bright and blue;
Thoroughbrace bison-skin, thick and wide;
Boot, top, dasher, from tough old hide
Found in the pit when the tanner died. 55
That was the way he "put her through."
"There!" said the Deacon, "naow she'll dew!"

Do! I tell you, I rather guess
She was a wonder, and nothing less!
Colts grew horses, beards turned gray, 60
Deacon and deaconess dropped away,
Children and grandchildren—where were they?
But there stood the stout old one-hoss shay
As fresh as on Lisbon-earthquake-day!

EIGHTEEN HUNDRED;—it came and found 65
The Deacon's masterpiece strong and sound.
Eighteen hundred increased by ten;—
"Hahnsum kerridge" they called it then.
Eighteen hundred and twenty came;—
Running as usual; much the same. 70
Thirty and forty at last arrive,
And then come fifty, and FIFTY-FIVE.

Little of all we value here
Wakes on the morn of its hundredth year
Without both feeling and looking queer. 75
In fact, there's nothing that keeps its youth,
So far as I know, but a tree and truth.
(This is a moral that runs at large;
Take it.—You're welcome.—No extra charge.)

FIRST OF NOVEMBER,—the earthquake-day,— 80
There are traces of age in the one-hoss shay,
A general flavor of mild decay,
But nothing local, as one may say.
There couldn't be,—for the Deacon's art
Had made it so like in every part 85
That there wasn't a chance for one to start.

---

1. A linchpin, like a modern cotter pin, was inserted through the end of the axletree to retain the wheel on its bearing.

For the wheels were just as strong as the thills,
And the floor was just as strong as the sills,
And the panels just as strong as the floor,
And the whipple-tree² neither less nor more,
And the back crossbar as strong as the fore,
And spring and axle and hub *encore*.
And yet, *as a whole*, it is past a doubt
In another hour it will be *worn out!* 90

First of November, 'Fifty-five! 95
This morning the parson takes a drive.
Now, small boys, get out of the way!
Here comes the wonderful one-hoss shay,
Drawn by a rat-tailed, ewe-necked bay.
"Huddup!" said the parson.—Off went they. 100
The parson was working his Sunday's text,—
Had got to *fifthly*, and stopped perplexed
At what the—Moses—was coming next.
All at once the horse stood still,
Close by the meet'n'-house on the hill. 105
First a shiver, and then a thrill,
Then something decidedly like a spill,—
And the parson was sitting upon a rock,
At half past nine by the meet'n'-house clock,—
Just the hour of the Earthquake shock! 110
What do you think the parson found,
When he got up and stared around?
The poor old chaise in a heap or mound,
As if it had been to the mill and ground!
You see, of course, if you're not a dunce, 115
How it went to pieces all at once,—
All at once, and nothing first,—
Just as bubbles do when they burst.

End of the wonderful one-hoss shay.
Logic is logic. That's all I say. 120

1858

Dorothy Q.³

A FAMILY PORTRAIT

Grandmother's mother: her age, I guess,
Thirteen summers, or something less;

---

2. A bar pivoted on the frame behind the horse, to which the traces, or side harness, are fastened.

3. "Dorothy was the daughter of Judge Edmund Quincy, and the niece of Josiah Quincy, junior, the young poet and ora-

Girlish bust, but womanly air;
Smooth, square forehead with uprolled hair;
Lips that lover has never kissed;   5
Taper fingers and slender wrist;
Hanging sleeves of stiff brocade;
So they painted the little maid.

On her hand a parrot green
Sits unmoving and broods serene.   10
Hold up the canvas full in view,—
Look! there's a rent the light shines through,
Dark with a century's fringe of dust,—
That was a Red-Coat's rapier-thrust![4]
Such is the tale the lady old,   15
Dorothy's daughter's daughter, told.

Who the painter was none may tell,—
One whose best was not over well;
Hard and dry, it must be confessed,
Flat as a rose that has long been pressed;   20
Yet in her cheek the hues are bright,
Dainty colors of red and white,
And in her slender shape are seen
Hint and promise of stately mien.

Look not on her with eyes of scorn,—   25
Dorothy Q. was a lady born!
Ay! since the galloping Normans came,
England's annals have known her name;[1]
And still to the three-hilled rebel town[2]
Dear is that ancient name's renown,   30
For many a civic wreath they won,
The youthful sire and the gray-haired son.

O Damsel Dorothy! Dorothy Q.!
Strange is the gift that I owe to you;
Such a gift as never a king   35
Save to daughter or son might bring,—
All my tenure of heart and hand,
All my title to house and land;

tor who died just before the American
Revolution, of which he was one of the
most eloquent and effective promoters"
[Holmes's note]. This Dorothy was the
poet's maternal great-grandmother; her
girlish portrait was associated with his
childhood interest in the legends of his
family. The poem appeared in the *Atlantic Monthly* for January, 1871, and
was collected in *Songs of Many Seasons*
(1875).

4. "The British officer had aimed at the
right eye and just missed it" [unpub-
lished manuscript note, Tilton, *Amiable
Autocrat*, p. 6].
1. The Norman invasion (1066) brought
such French names as Quincy into English genealogies.
2. Colonial Boston was built on three
hills; Tremont Street preserves that
memory in its name, once given to the
city itself.

Mother and sister and child and wife
And joy and sorrow and death and life! 40

What if a hundred years ago
Those close-shut lips had answered No,
When forth the tremulous question came
That cost the maiden her Norman name,
And under the folds that look so still 45
The bodice swelled with the bosom's thrill?
Should I be I, or would it be
One tenth another, to nine tenths me?

Soft is the breath of a maiden's YES:
Not the light gossamer stirs with less; 50
But never a cable that holds so fast
Through all the battles of wave and blast,
And never an echo of speech or song
That lives in the babbling air so long!
There were tones in the voice that whispered then 55
You may hear to-day in a hundred men.

O lady and lover, how faint and far
Your images hover,—and here we are,
Solid and stirring in flesh and bone,—
Edward's and Dorothy's—all their own,— 60
A goodly record for Time to show
Of a syllable spoken so long ago!—
Shall I bless you, Dorothy, or forgive
For the tender whisper that bade me live?

It shall be a blessing, my little maid! 65
I will heal the stab of the Red-Coat's blade,[3]
And freshen the gold of the tarnished frame,
And gild with a rhyme your household name;
So you shall smile on us brave and bright
As first you greeted the morning's light, 70
And live untroubled by woes and fears
Through a second youth of a hundred years.

1871, 1875

Nearing the Snow-Line[4]

Slow toiling upward from the misty vale,
     I leave the bright enamelled zones below;
     No more for me their beauteous bloom shall glow,

3. "The canvas of the painting was so much decayed that it had to be replaced by a new one, in doing which the rapier thrust was of course filled up" [Holmes's note].

4. First published in the *Atlantic Monthly* for January, 1870; collected in *Songs of Many Seasons* (1875).

Their lingering sweetness load the morning gale;
Few are the slender flowerets, scentless, pale,　　　　　5
　　That on their ice-clad stems all trembling blow
　　Along the margin of unmelting snow;
Yet with unsaddened voice thy verge I hail,
　　White realm of peace above the flowering line;
Welcome thy frozen domes, thy rocky spires!　　　　10
　　O'er thee undimmed the moon-girt planets shine,
On thy majestic altars fade the fires
That filled the air with smoke of vain desires,
　　And all the unclouded blue of heaven is thine!

　　　　　　　　　　　　　　　　1870, 1875

At the Saturday Club[5]

This is our place of meeting; opposite
That towered and pillared building: look at it;
King's Chapel in the Second George's day,
Rebellion stole its regal name away,—
Stone Chapel sounded better; but at last　　　　　5
The poisoned name of our provincial past
Had lost its ancient venom; then once more
Stone Chapel was King's Chapel as before.
(So let rechristened North Street, when it can,
Bring back the days of Marlborough and Queen Anne!)　10
　Next the old church your wandering eye will meet—
A granite pile that stares upon the street—
Our civic temple; slanderous tongues have said
Its shape was modelled from St. Botolph's head,[6]
Lofty, but narrow; jealous passers-by　　　　　15
Say Boston always held her head too high.
　Turn half-way round, and let your look survey
The white façade that gleams across the way,—
The many-windowed building, tall and wide,
The palace-inn[7] that shows its northern side　　　20
In grateful shadow when the sunbeams beat
The granite wall in summer's scorching heat.
　This is the place; whether its name you spell

5. The Saturday Club, begun in 1855, met informally on the fourth Saturday of each month, and became famous as the rendezvous of the leading intellectuals of Boston's renaissance. The poem appeared in the *Atlantic Monthly* for January, 1884, and was collected in *Before the Curfew* (1888).
6. St. Botolph (died 680), an English Benedictine, built his monastery at the English town of Boston (from "Botolph's-tun"). From this port John Cotton, in 1633, brought a party of Puritans, and the name Boston, to Massachusetts. In the English town, St. Botolph's church has a tall, ancient tower, square-topped and ugly; hence Holmes's reference to the "head."
7. The Parker House, a famous hotel, where the Saturday Club met.

Tavern, or caravansera, or hotel.
Would I could steal its echoes! you should find
Such store of vanished pleasures brought to mind:
Such feasts! the laughs of many a jocund hour
That shook the mortar from King George's tower;
Such guests! What famous names its record boasts,
Whose owners wander in the mob of ghosts!
Such stories! Every beam and plank is filled
With juicy wit the joyous talkers spilled,
Ready to ooze, as once the mountain pine
The floors are laid with oozed its turpentine!

A month had flitted since The Club had met;
The day came round; I found the table set,
The waiters lounging round the marble stairs,
Empty as yet the double row of chairs.
I was a full half hour before the rest,
Alone, the banquet-chamber's single guest.
So from the table's side a chair I took,
And having neither company nor book
To keep me waking, by degrees there crept
A torpor over me,—in short, I slept.

Loosed from its chain, along the wreck-strown track
Of the dead years my soul goes travelling back;
My ghosts take on their robes of flesh; it seems
Dreaming is life; nay, life less than dreams,
So real are the shapes that meet my eyes.
They bring no sense of wonder, no surprise,
No hint of other than an earth-born source;
All seems plain daylight, everything of course.

How dim the colors are, how poor and faint
This palette of weak words with which I paint!
Here sit my friends; if I could fix them so
As to my eyes they seem, my page would glow
Like a queen's missal, warm as if the brush
Of Titian or Velasquez brought the flush
Of life into their features. *Ay de mi!*[8]
If syllables were pigments, you should see
Such breathing portraitures as never man
Found in the Pitti or the Vatican.[9]

Here sits our POET,[1] Laureate, if you will.
Long has he worn the wreath, and wears it still.

8. Spanish exclamation; equivalent to
"Ah me!"
9. Famous Italian collections of renaissance paintings, located, respectively, in
Florence and Rome.

1. Longfellow, "Laureate" because his
bust (l. 65) had been given a place in
the Poets' Corner of Westminster Abbey,
London.

Dead? Nay, not so; and yet they say his bust   65
Looks down on marbles covering royal dust,
Kings by the Grace of God, or Nature's grace;
Dead! No! Alive! I see him in his place,
Full-featured, with the bloom that heaven denies
Her children, pinched by cold New England skies,   70
Too often, while the nursery's happier few
Win from a summer cloud its roseate hue.
Kind, soft-voiced, gentle, in his eye there shines
The ray serene that filled Evangeline's.

    Modest he seems, not shy; content to wait   75
Amid the noisy clamor of debate
The looked-for moment when a peaceful word
Smooths the rough ripples louder tongues have stirred.
In every tone I mark his tender grace
And all his poems hinted in his face;   80
What tranquil joy his friendly presence gives!
How could I think him dead? He lives! He lives!

    There, at the table's further end I see
In his old place our Poet's *vis-à-vis*,[2]
The great PROFESSOR,[3] strong, broad-shouldered, square,   85
In life's rich noontide, joyous, debonair.
His social hour no leaden care alloys,
His laugh rings loud and mirthful as a boy's,—
That lusty laugh the Puritan forgot,—
What ear has heard it and remembers not?   90
How often, halting at some wide crevasse
Amid the windings of his Alpine pass,
High up the cliffs, the climbing mountaineer,
Listening the far-off avalanche to hear,
Silent, and leaning on his steel-shod staff,   95
Has heard that cheery voice, that ringing laugh,
From the rude cabin whose nomadic walls
Creep with the moving glacier as it crawls!
    How does vast Nature lead her living train
In ordered sequence through that spacious brain,   100
As in the primal hour when Adam named
The new-born tribes that young creation claimed!—
How will her realm be darkened, losing thee,
Her darling, whom we call *our* AGASSIZ!

2. French phrase meaning "face-to-face."
3. Jean Louis Agassiz (1807–1873), Swiss naturalist, became famous at Paris and in 1848 became a professor at Harvard. Although a scientific empiricist, he actively opposed pessimism in the interpretation of Darwin, as Holmes also did.

But who is he whose massive frame belies 105
The maiden shyness of his downcast eyes?[4]
Who broods in silence till, by questions pressed,
Some answer struggles from his laboring breast?
An artist Nature meant to dwell apart,
Locked in his studio with a human heart, 110
Tracking its caverned passions to their lair,
And all its throbbing mysteries laying bare.
　Count it no marvel that he broods alone
Over the heart he studies,—'tis his own;
So in his page, whatever shape it wear, 115
The Essex wizard's shadowed self is there.—
The great ROMANCER, hid beneath his veil
Like the stern preacher of his sombre tale;
Virile in strength, yet bashful as a girl,
Prouder than Hester, sensitive as Pearl.[5] 120

　From his mild throng of worshippers released,
Our Concord Delphi sends its chosen priest,[6]
Prophet or poet, mystic, sage, or seer,
By every title always welcome here.
Why that ethereal spirit's frame describe? 125
You know the race-marks of the Brahmin tribe,—
The spare, slight form, the sloping shoulder's droop,
The calm, scholastic mien, the clerkly stoop,
The lines of thought the sharpened features wear,
Carved by the edge of keen New England air. 130
　List! for he speaks! As when a king would choose
The jewels for his bride, he might refuse
This diamond for its flaw,—find that less bright
Than those, its fellows, and a pearl less white
Than fits her snowy neck, and yet at last, 135
The fairest gems are chosen, and made fast
In golden fetters; so, with light delays
He seeks the fittest word to fill his phrase;
Nor vain nor idle his fastidious quest,
His chosen word is sure to prove the best. 140
　Where in the realm of thought, whose air is song,
Does he, the Buddha of the West, belong?
He seems a wingèd Franklin, sweetly wise,
Born to unlock the secrets of the skies;
And which the nobler calling,—if 'tis fair 145
Terrestrial with celestial to compare,—

4. Hawthorne, "the great Romancer"　6. Emerson. Delphi, in Greece, was the
(l. 117).　site of the mythical oracle of Apollo.
5. *Cf. The Scarlet Letter.*

To guide the storm-cloud's elemental flame,
Or walk the chambers whence the lightning came,
Amidst the sources of its subtile fire,
And steal their effluence for his lips and lyre?   150
  If lost at times in vague aerial flights,
None treads with firmer footstep when he lights;
A soaring nature, ballasted with sense,
Wisdom without her wrinkles or pretence,
In every Bible he has faith to read,   155
And every altar helps to shape his creed.
Ask you what name this prisoned spirit bears
While with ourselves this fleeting breath it shares?
Till angels greet him with a sweeter one
In heaven, on earth we call him EMERSON.   160

  I start; I wake; the vision is withdrawn;
Its figures fading like the stars at dawn;
Crossed from the roll of life their cherished names,
And memory's pictures fading in their frames;
Yet life is lovelier for these transient gleams   165
Of buried friendships; blest is he who dreams!

1884, 1888

From The Autocrat of the Breakfast-Table[7]

I

I was just going to say, when I was interrupted,[8] that one of the many ways of classifying minds is under the heads of arithmetical and algebraical intellects. All economical and practical wisdom is an extension or variation of the following arithmetical formula: $2 + 2 = 4$. Every philosophical proposition has the more general character of the expression $a + b = c$. We are mere operatives, empirics, and egotists, until we learn to think in letters instead of figures.

They all stared. There is a divinity student lately come among us to whom I commonly address remarks like the above, allowing him to take a certain share in the conversation, so far as assent or

7. *The Autocrat of the Breakfast-Table* resulted from Lowell's insistence that, if he undertook the editorship of the projected *Atlantic Monthly,* Holmes would agree to become a regular contributor. Installments of the *Autocrat* began with the first number of the magazine, November, 1857, and concluded with the issue for October, 1858. These were a mature development of the "table-talk" that Holmes had long before published under the same title in

the *New England Magazine* (November, 1831, January, 1832). The *Autocrat* and succeeding collections represent at its best the patrician cultivation and Augustan wit that flourished with the New England renaissance, and perpetuated a long tradition in the "genteel" culture of the United States.
8. *I.e.,* twenty-five years ago, when he published the early *Autocrat* essays in the *New England Magazine.*

pertinent questions are involved. He abused his liberty on this occasion by presuming to say that Leibnitz[9] had the same observation.—No, sir, I replied, he has not. But he said a mighty good thing about mathematics, that sounds something like it, and you found it, *not in the original*, but quoted by Dr. Thomas Reid.[1] I will tell the company what he did say, one of these days.

—If I belong to a Society of Mutual Admiration?—I blush to say that I do not at this present moment. I once did, however. It was the first association to which I ever heard the term applied; a body of scientific young men in a great foreign city[2] who admired their teacher, and to some extent each other. Many of them deserved it; they have become famous since. It amuses me to hear the talk of one of those beings described by Thackeray—

"Letters four do form his name"[3]—

about a social development which belongs to the very noblest stage of civilization. All generous companies of artists, authors, philanthropists, men of science, are, or ought to be, Societies of Mutual Admiration. A man of genius, or any kind of superiority, is not debarred from admiring the same quality in another, nor the other from returning his admiration. They may even associate together and continue to think highly of each other. And so of a dozen such men, if any one place is fortunate enough to hold so many. The being referred to above assumes several false premises. First, that men of talent necessarily hate each other. Secondly, that intimate knowledge or habitual association destroys our admiration of persons whom we esteemed highly at a distance. Thirdly, that a circle of clever fellows, who meet together to dine and have a good

9. Gottfried Wilhelm von Leibnitz (1646–1716), German philosopher and mathematician. He contributed to the science of calculus, hence the appropriateness of this allusion.

1. Founder of the Scottish school of "common-sense," optimistic toward the self-determining powers of the human mind.

2. "The 'body of scientific young men in a great foreign city' was the Société d'Observation Médicale, of Paris, of which M. Louis was president, and MM. Barth, Grisotte, and our own Dr. Bowditch were members. They agreed in admiring their justly-honored president, and thought highly of some of their associates, who have since made good their promise of distinction.

"About the time when these papers were published, the Saturday Club was founded, or, rather, found itself in existence, without any organization, almost without parentage. It was natural enough that such men as Emerson, Longfellow, Agassiz, Peirce, with Haw-

thorne, Motley, Sumner, when within reach, and others who would be good company for them, should meet and dine together * * * If some of them had not admired each other they would have been exceptions in the world of letters and science. The club deserves being remembered for having no constitution or by-laws, for making no speeches, coming and going at will without remark, and acting out, though it did not proclaim the motto, 'Shall I not take mine ease in mine inn?' There was and is nothing of the Bohemian element about this club, but it has had many good times and not a little good talking" [Holmes's note].

3. Consider "snob," or "liar," or both, as the four-letter word in this context (Thackeray wrote *The Book of Snobs*). The line of verse, however, is quoted from Coleridge's "Fire, Famine, and Slaughter" (1798), a satire on Sir William Pitt, prime minister of England, whose name has four letters.

time, have signed a constitutional compact to glorify themselves and to put down him and the fraction of the human race not belonging to their number. Fourthly, that it is an outrage that he is not asked to join them.

Here the company laughed a good deal, and the old gentleman who sits opposite said: "That's it! that's it!"

I continued, for I was in the talking vein. As to clever people's hating each other, I think *a little* extra talent does sometimes make people jealous. They become irritated by perpetual attempts and failures, and it hurts their tempers and dispositions. Unpretending mediocrity is good, and genius is glorious; but a weak flavor of genius in an essentially common person is detestable. It spoils the grand neutrality of a commonplace character, as the rinsings of an unwashed wine-glass spoil a draught of fair water. No wonder the poor fellow we spoke of, who always belongs to this class of slightly flavored mediocrities, is puzzled and vexed by the strange sight of a dozen men of capacity working and playing together in harmony. He and his fellows are always fighting. With them familiarity naturally breeds contempt. If they ever praise each other's bad drawings, or broken-winded novels, or spavined verses, nobody ever supposed it was from admiration; it was simply a contract between themselves and a publisher or dealer.

If the Mutuals have really nothing among them worth admiring, that alters the question. But if they are men with noble powers and qualities, let me tell you that, next to youthful love and family affections, there is no human sentiment better than that which unites the Societies of Mutual Admiration. And what would literature or art be without such associations? Who can tell what we owe to the Mutual Admiration Society of which Shakespeare, and Ben Jonson, and Beaumont and Fletcher were members?[4] Or to that of which Addison and Steele formed the centre,[5] and which gave us the Spectator? Or to that where Johnson,[6] and Goldsmith, and Burke, and Reynolds, and Beauclerk, and Boswell, most admiring among all admirers, met together? Was there any great harm in the fact that the Irvings and Paulding[7] wrote in company? or any unpardonable cabal in the literary union of Verplanck and Bryant and Sands,[8] and as many more as they chose to associate with them?

4. This group met for fellowship in the Mermaid Tavern, London.

5. Joseph Addison (1672–1719) and Sir Richard Steele (1672–1729), great English essayists of the *Spectator* papers, together with Swift and other London wits were associated in the Kit-Cat Club.

6. Samuel Johnson (1709–1784) was the center of this coterie, known as "The Club"; *cf.* Boswell's *Johnson*.

7. Washington Irving collaborated with his older brothers, Peter and William, and with James K. Paulding in the *Salmagundi* essays, earliest work of the "Knickerbocker" coterie of New Yorkers.

8. The poet Bryant collaborated with Gulian Verplanck and Robert C. Sands, fellow "Knickerbockers," in *The Talisman* (1827–1830), a gift book.

The poor creature does not know what he is talking about when he abuses this noblest of institutions. Let him inspect its mysteries through the knot-hole he has secured, but not use that orifice as a medium for his popgun. Such a society is the crown of a literary metropolis; if a town has not material for it, and spirit and good feeling enough to organize it, it is a mere caravansary, fit for a man of genius to lodge in, but not to live in. Foolish people hate and dread and envy such an association of men of varied powers and influence, because it is lofty, serene, impregnable, and, by the necessity of the case, exclusive. Wise ones are prouder of the title M. S. M. A. than of all their other honors put together.

—All generous minds have a horror of what are commonly called "facts." They are the brute beasts of the intellectual domain. Who does not know fellows that always have an ill-conditioned fact or two which they lead after them into decent company like so many bulldogs, ready to let them slip at every ingenious suggestion, or convenient generalization, or pleasant fancy? I allow no "facts" at this table. What! Because bread is good and wholesome, and necessary and nourishing, shall you thrust a crumb into my windpipe while I am talking? Do not these muscles of mine represent a hundred loaves of bread? and is not my thought the abstract of ten thousand of these crumbs of truth with which you would choke off my speech?

[The above remark must be conditioned and qualified for the vulgar mind. The reader will, of course, understand the precise amount of seasoning which must be added to it before he adopts it as one of the axioms of his life. The speaker disclaims all responsibility for its abuse in incompetent hands.]

This business of conversation is a very serious matter. There are men whom it weakens one to talk with an hour more than a day's fasting would do. Mark this which I am going to say, for it is as good as a working professional man's advice, and costs you nothing: It is better to lose a pint of blood from your veins than to have a nerve tapped. Nobody measures your nervous force as it runs away, nor bandages your brain and marrow after the operation.

There are men of *esprit*[9] who are excessively exhausting to some people. They are the talkers who have what may be called *jerky* minds. Their thoughts do not run in the natural order of sequence. They say bright things on all possible subjects, but their zigzags rack you to death. After a jolting half-hour with one of these jerky companions, talking with a dull friend affords great relief. It is like taking the cat in your lap after holding a squirrel.

What a comfort a dull but kindly person is, to be sure, at times! A ground-glass shade over a gas-lamp does not bring more solace to

9. French, meaning "spirited wit."

our dazzled eyes than such a one to our minds.

"Do not dull people bore you?" said one of the lady-boarders,— the same who sent me her autograph-book last week with a request for a few original stanzas, not remembering that "The Pactolian" pays me five dollars a line for every thing I write in its columns.

"Madam," said I (she and the century were in their teens together), "all men are bores, except when we want them. There never was but one man whom I would trust with my latch-key."

"Who might that favored person be?"

"Zimmermann."[1]

—The men of genius that I fancy most, have erectile heads like the cobra-di-capello.[2] You remember what they tell of William Pinkney,[3] the great pleader; how in his eloquent paroxysms the veins of his neck would swell and his face flush and his eyes glitter, until he seemed on the verge of apoplexy. The hydraulic arrangements for supplying the brain with blood are only second in importance to its own organization. The bulbous-headed fellows who steam well when they are at work are the men that draw big audiences and give us marrowy books and pictures. It is a good sign to have one's feet grow cold when he is writing. A great writer and speaker once told me that he often wrote with his feet in hot water; but for this, *all* his blood would have run into his head, as the mercury sometimes withdraws into the ball of a thermometer.

—You don't suppose that my remarks made at this table are like so many postage-stamps, do you,—each to be only once uttered? If you do, you are mistaken. He must be a poor creature who does not often repeat himself. Imagine the author of the excellent piece of advice, "Know thyself,"[4] never alluding to that sentiment again during the course of a protracted existence! Why, the truths a man carries about with him are his tools; and do you think a carpenter is bound to use the same plane but once to smooth a knotty board with, or to hang up his hammer after it has driven its first nail? I shall never repeat a conversation, but an idea often. I shall use the same types when I like, but not commonly the same stereotypes. A thought is often original, though you have uttered it a hundred times. It has come to you over a new route, by a new and express train of associations.

Sometimes, but rarely, one may be caught making the same speech twice over, and yet be held blameless. Thus, a certain lec-

1. "*The Treatise on Solitude* is not so frequently seen lying about on library tables as in our younger days. I remember that I always respected the title and let the book alone" [Holmes's note]. The Swiss Johann Georg von Zimmermann (1728–1795) wrote these popular meditations.

2. The hooded cobra of Asia, when aroused, distends its skin into a hood about its erected head.

3. William Pinkney (1764–1822), lawyer, statesman, and foreign minister; famous for his orations.

4. Proverbial wisdom anciently reported among the utterances of the Greek Solon (died 559 B.C.).

turer, after performing in an inland city, where dwells a *Littératrice* of note, was invited to meet her and others over the social teacup. She pleasantly referred to his many wanderings in his new occupation. "Yes," he replied, "I am like the Huma,[5] the bird that never lights, being always in the cars, as he is always on the wing."—Years elapsed. The lecturer visited the same place once more for the same purpose. Another social cup after the lecture, and a second meeting with the distinguished lady. "You are constantly going from place to place," she said.—"Yes," he answered, "I am like the Huma,"—and finished the sentence as before.

What horrors, when it flashed over him that he had made this fine speech, word for word, twice over! Yet it was not true, as the lady might perhaps have fairly inferred, that he had embellished his conversation with the Huma daily during that whole interval of years. On the contrary, he had never once thought of the odious fowl until the recurrence of precisely the same circumstances brought up precisely the same idea. He ought to have been proud of the accuracy of his mental adjustments. Given certain factors, and a sound brain should always evolve the same fixed product with the certainty of Babbage's[6] calculating machine.

—What a satire, by the way, is that machine on the mere mathematician! A Frankenstein-monster,[7] a thing without brains and without heart, too stupid to make a blunder; which turns out results like a corn-sheller, and never grows any wiser or better, though it grind a thousand bushels of them!

I have an immense respect for a man of talents *plus* "the mathematics." But the calculating power alone should seem to be the least human of qualities, and to have the smallest amount of reason in it; since a machine can be made to do the work of three or four calculators, and better than any one of them. Sometimes I have been troubled that I had not a deeper intuitive apprehension of the relations of numbers. But the triumph of the ciphering hand-organ has consoled me. I always fancy I can hear the wheels clicking in a calculator's brain. The power of dealing with numbers is a kind of "detached lever" arrangement, which may be put into a mighty poor watch. I suppose it is about as common as the power of moving the ears voluntarily, which is a moderately rare endowment.

—Little localized powers, and little narrow streaks of specialized

5. "It was an agreeable incident of two consecutive visits to Hartford, Conn., that I met there the late Mrs. Sigourney. The second meeting recalled the first, and with it the allusion to the Huma, which bird is the subject of a short poem by another New England authoress, which may be found in Mr. Griswold's collection" [Holmes's note]. Lydia Huntley Sigourney, the *Littératrice* (see above) or authoress, was a lugubrious poet; the Huma first appears in Thomas Moore's *Lalla Rookh* (1817).

6. Charles Babbage (1792–1871), English mathematician and mechanical genius.

7. In Mary Shelley's *Frankenstein* (1818), the protagonist animates a monster, but fails to give it spiritual intelligence.

knowledge, are things men are very apt to be conceited about. Nature is very wise; but for this encouraging principle how many small talents and little accomplishments would be neglected! Talk about conceit as much as you like, it is to human character what salt is to the ocean; it keeps it sweet, and renders it endurable. Say rather it is like the natural unguent of the sea-fowl's plumage, which enables him to shed the rain that falls on him and the wave in which he dips. When one has had *all* his conceit taken out of him, when he has lost *all* his illusions, his feathers will soon soak through, and he will fly no more.

"So you admire conceited people, do you?" said the young lady who has come to the city to be finished off for—the duties of life.

I am afraid you do not study logic at your school, my dear. It does not follow that I wish to be pickled in brine because I like a salt-water plunge at Nahant.[8] I say that conceit is just as natural a thing to human minds as a centre is to a circle. But little-minded people's thoughts move in such small circles that five minutes' conversation gives you an arc long enough to determine their whole curve. An arc in the movement of a large intellect does not sensibly differ from a straight line. Even if it have the third vowel as its centre, it does not soon betray it. The highest thought, that is, is the most seemingly impersonal; it does not obviously imply any individual centre.

Audacious self-esteem, with good ground for it, is always imposing. What resplendent beauty that must have been which could have authorized Phyrne to "peel"[9] in the way she did! What fine speeches are those two: "*Non omnis moriar*,"[1] and "I have taken all knowledge to be my province"![2] Even in common people, conceit has the virtue of making them cheerful; the man who thinks his wife, his baby, his house, his horse, his dog, and himself severally unequalled, is almost sure to be a good-humored person, though liable to be tedious at times.

—What are the great faults of conversation? Want of ideas, want of words, want of manners, are the principal ones, I suppose you think. I don't doubt it, but I will tell you what I have found spoil more good talks than anything else;—long arguments on special points between people who differ on the fundamental principles upon which these points depend. No men can have satisfactory relations with each other until they have agreed on certain *ultimata* of belief not to be disturbed in ordinary conversation, and unless they have sense enough to trace the secondary questions depending

8. On the seashore near Boston.
9. Phryne, a fourth century Athenian courtesan of fabulous beauty, the reputed model for Praxiteles' "Aphrodite"; during a festival for Poseidon, god of the Mediterranean, she publicly disrobed and entered the sea.
1. *Cf.* Horace, *Odes*, III, xxx, l. 6: "I shall not altogether die."
2. From a letter written by Francis Bacon to Lord Burghley in 1592.

upon these ultimate beliefs to their source. In short, just as a written constitution is essential to the best social order, so a code of finalities is a necessary condition of profitable talk between two persons. Talking is like playing on the harp; there is as much in laying the hand on the strings to stop their vibrations as in twanging them to bring out their music.

—Do you mean to say the pun-question[3] is not clearly settled in your minds? Let me lay down the law upon the subject. Life and language are alike sacred. Homicide and *verbicide*—that is, violent treatment of a word with fatal results to its legitimate meaning, which is its life—are alike forbidden. Manslaughter, which is the meaning of the one, is the same as man's laughter, which is the end of the other. A pun is *primâ facie*[4] an insult to the person you are talking with. It implies utter indifference to or sublime contempt for his remarks, no matter how serious. I speak of total depravity, and one says all that is written on the subject is deep raving. I have committed my self-respect by talking with such a person. I should like to commit him, but cannot, because he is a nuisance. Or I speak of geological convulsions, and he asks me what was the cosine of Noah's ark; also, whether the Deluge was not a deal huger than any modern inundation.

A pun does not commonly justify a blow in return. But if a blow were given for such a cause, and death ensued, the jury would be judges both of the facts and of the pun, and might, if the latter were of an aggravated character, return a verdict of justifiable homicide. Thus, in a case lately decided before Miller, J.,[5] Doe presented Roe a subscription paper, and urged the claims of suffering humanity. Roe replied by asking, When charity was like a top? It was in evidence that Doe preserved a dignified silence. Roe then said, "When it begins to hum." Doe then—and not till then—struck Roe, and his head happening to hit a bound volume of the Monthly Rag-Bag and Stolen Miscellany, intense mortification ensued with a fatal result. The chief laid down his notions of the law to his brother justices, who unanimously replied, "Jest so." The chief rejoined, that no man should jest so without being punished for it, and charged for the prisoner, who was acquitted, and the pun ordered to be burned by the sheriff. The bound volume was forfeited as a deodand,[6] but not claimed.

People that make puns are like wanton boys that put coppers on the railroad tracks. They amuse themselves and other children, but

3. In the following paragraphs, Holmes's argument against puns is punctured by his own.
4. On first appearance; *i.e.*, by nature.
5. In legal parlance, "Miller, Judge"; but Holmes refers also to Joe Miller (1684–1738), famous English come-

dian, whose popular survival was occasioned by successive editions, over two centuries, of *Joe Miller's Jest-Book*.
6. Literally, "given to God"; a forfeit to the crown or church for charitable use.

their little trick may upset a freight train of conversation for the sake of a battered witticism.

I will thank you, B. F., to bring down two books, of which I will mark the places on this slip of paper. (While he is gone, I may say that this boy, our landlady's youngest, is called BENJAMIN FRANKLIN, after the celebrated philosopher of that name. A highly merited compliment.)

I wished to refer to two eminent authorities. Now be so good as to listen. The great moralist[7] says: "To trifle with the vocabulary which is the vehicle of social intercourse is to tamper with the currency of human intelligence. He who would violate the sanctities of his mother tongue would invade the recesses of the paternal till without remorse, and repeat the banquet of Saturn[8] without an indigestion."

And, once more, listen to the historian.[9] "The Puritans hated puns. The Bishops were notoriously addicted to them. The Lords Temporal carried them to the verge of license. Majesty itself must have its Royal quibble. 'Ye be burly, my Lord of Burleigh,' said Queen Elizabeth, 'but ye shall make less stir in our realm than my Lord of Leicester.' The gravest wisdom and the highest breeding lent their sanction to the practice. Lord Bacon playfully declared himself a descendant of 'Og, the King of Bashan.[1] Sir Philip Sidney, with his last breath, reproached the soldier who brought him water, for wasting a casque full upon a dying man. A courtier, who saw Othello performed at the Globe Theatre, remarked, that the blackamoor was a brute, and not a man. 'Thou hast reason,' replied a great Lord, 'according to Plato[2] his saying; for this be a two-legged animal *with* feathers.' The fatal habit became universal. The language was corrupted. The infection spread to the national conscience. Political double-dealings naturally grew out of verbal double meanings. The teeth of the new dragon were sown by the Cadmus[3] who introduced the alphabet of equivocation. What was levity in the time of the Tudors grew to regicide and revolution in the age of the Stuarts."

Who was that boarder that just whispered something about the Macaulay-flowers of literature?—There was a dead silence.—I said calmly, I shall henceforth consider any interruption by a pun as a hint to change my boarding-house. Do not plead my example. If I have used any such, it has been only as a Spartan father would

---

7. Several critics have detected a parody of Dr. Samuel Johnson in the following pretended quotation.
8. One of the myths of Saturn has him consuming all but one of his children.
9. As above, what follows is a parody, this time of the historian T. B. Macaulay (*cf.* the following paragraph).
1. *Cf.* Deuteronomy iii: 1.

2. Diogenes Laertius said: "Plato * * * defined man to be a two-legged animal without feathers"; but here Othello is ridiculously endowed *with* feathers, since he smothered Desdemona in her bed.
3. The Cadmus of Greek myth killed a dragon and sowed its teeth, reaping a crop of warriors who slew each other.

show up a drunken helot.[4] We have done with them.

—If a logical mind ever found out anything with its logic?—I should say that its most frequent work was to build a *pons asinorum*[5] over chasms which shrewd people can bestride without such a structure. You can hire logic, in the shape of a lawyer, to prove anything that you want to prove. You can buy treatises to show that Napoleon never lived, and that no battle of Bunker-hill was ever fought. The great minds are those with a wide span,[6] which couple truths related to, but far removed from, each other. Logicians carry the surveyor's chain over the track of which these are the true explorers. I value a man mainly for his primary relations with truth, as I understand truth,—not for any secondary artifice in handling his ideas. Some of the sharpest men in argument are notoriously unsound in judgment. I should not trust the counsel of a clever debater, any more than that of a good chess-player. Either may of course advise wisely, but not necessarily because he wrangles or plays well.

The old gentleman who sits opposite got his hand up, as a pointer lifts his forefoot, at the expression, "his relations with truth, as I understand truth," and when I had done, sniffed audibly, and said I talked like a transcendentalist. For his part, common sense was good enough for him.

Precisely so, my dear sir, I replied; common sense, *as you understand it*. We all have to assume a standard of judgment in our own minds, either of things or persons. A man who is willing to take another's opinion has to exercise his judgment in the choice of whom to follow, which is often as nice a matter as to judge of things for one's self. On the whole, I had rather judge men's minds by comparing their thoughts with my own, than judge of thoughts by knowing who utter them. I must do one or the other. It does not follow, of course, that I may not recognize another man's thoughts as broader and deeper than my own; but that does not necessarily change my opinion, otherwise this would be at the mercy of every superior mind that held a different one. How many of our most cherished beliefs are like those drinking-glasses of the ancient pattern, that serve us well so long as we keep them in our hand, but spill all if we attempt to set them down! I have sometimes compared conversation to the Italian game of *mora*, in which one player lifts his hand with so many fingers extended, and the other gives the number if he can. I show my thought, another his; if they agree, well; if they differ, we find the largest common factor, if we can,

4. Spartan servant or slave.
5. *Bridge of the asses*; an early stage in learning, difficult for beginners, traditionally associated with Euclid's fifth proposition.

6. "There is something like this in J. H. Newman's *Grammar of Assent*. See *Characteristics*, arranged by W. S. Lilly, p. 81." [Holmes's note].

but at any rate avoid disputing about remainders and fractions, which is to real talk what tuning an instrument is to playing on it.

—What if, instead of talking this morning, I should read you a copy of verses, with critical remarks by the author? Any of the company can retire that like.

ALBUM VERSES

When Eve had led her lord away,
    And Cain had killed his brother,
The stars and flowers, the poets say,
    Agreed with one another,

To cheat the cunning tempter's art,
    And teach the race its duty,
By keeping on its wicked heart
    Their eyes of light and beauty.

A million sleepless lids, they say,
    Will be at least a warning;
And so the flowers would watch by day,
    The stars from eve to morning.

On hill and prairie, field and lawn,
    Their dewy eyes upturning,
The flowers still watch from reddening dawn
    Till western skies are burning.

Alas! each hour of daylight tells
    A tale of shame so crushing,
That some turn white as sea-bleached shells,
    And some are always blushing.

But when the patient stars look down
    On all their light discovers,
The traitor's smile, the murderer's frown,
    The lips of lying lovers,

They try to shut their saddening eyes,
    And in the vain endeavor
We see them twinkling in the skies,
    And so they wink forever.

What do *you* think of these verses, my friends?—Is that piece an impromptu? said my landlady's daughter. (Aet. 19 +. Tender-eyed blonde. Long ringlets. Cameo pin. Gold pencil-case on a chain. Locket. Bracelet. Album. Autograph book. Accordeon. Reads Byron, Tupper, and Sylvanus Cobb, Junior,[7] while her mother makes the

---

7. Martin Farquhar Tupper (1810–1889) published many editions of his versified moral maxims, *Proverbial Philosophy* (1838); Sylvanus Cobb, Jr.

puddings. Says "Yes?" when you tell her anything.)—*Oui et non, ma petite,*—Yes and no, my child. Five of the seven verses were written off-hand; the other two took a week,—that is, were hanging round the desk in a ragged, forlorn, unrhymed condition as long as that. All poets will tell you just such stories. *C'est le* DERNIER *pas qui coute.*[8] Don't you know how hard it is for some people to get out of a room after their visit is really over? They want to be off, and you want to have them off, but they don't know how to manage it. One would think they had been built in your parlor or study, and were waiting to be launched. I have contrived a sort of ceremonial inclined plane for such visitors, which being lubricated with certain smooth phrases, I back them down, metaphorically speaking, stern-foremost, into their "native element," the great ocean of outdoors. Well, now, there are poems as hard to get rid of as these rural visitors. They come in glibly, use up all the serviceable rhymes, *day, ray, beauty, duty, skies, eyes, other, brother, mountain, fountain,* and the like; and so they go on until you think it is time for the wind-up, and the wind-up won't come on any terms. So they lie about until you get sick of the sight of them, and end by thrusting some cold scrap of a final couplet upon them, and turning them out of doors. I suspect a good many "impromptus" could tell just such a story as the above.—Here turning to our landlady, I used an illustration which pleased the company much at the time, and has since been highly commended. "Madam," I said, "you can pour three gills and three quarters of honey from that pint jug, if it is full, in less than one minute; but, Madam, you could not empty that last quarter of a gill, though you were turned into a marble Hebe,[9] and held the vessel upside down for a thousand years."

One gets tired to death of the old, old rhymes, such as you see in that copy of verses,—which I don't mean to abuse, or to praise either. I always feel as if I were a cobbler, putting new top-leathers to an old pair of bootsoles and bodies, when I am fitting sentiments to these venerable jingles.

>   .   .   .   .   .   .   youth
>   .   .   .   .   .   .   morning
>   .   .   .   .   .   .   truth
>   .   .   .   .   .   .   warning.

Nine tenths of the "Juvenile Poems" written spring out of the above musical and suggestive coincidences.

"Yes?" said our landlady's daughter.

I did not address the following remark to her, and I trust, from her limited range of reading, she will never see it; I said it softly to

(1823–1887) is credited with literally thousands of sentimental stories.

8. Usually, in the French proverb, "it is the *first* step that costs"; Holmes makes it the *last*.

9. Mythological cupbearer to the gods.

my next neighbor.

When a young female wears a flat circular side-curl, gummed on each temple,—when she walks with a male, not arm in arm, but his arm against the back of hers,—and when she says "Yes?" with the note of interrogation, you are generally safe in asking her what wages she gets, and who the "feller" was you saw her with.

"What are you whispering?" said the daughter of the house, moistening her lips, as she spoke, in a very engaging manner.

"I was only laying down a principle of social diagnosis."

"Yes?"

—It is curious to see how the same wants and tastes find the same implements and modes of expression in all times and places. The young ladies of Otaheite, as you may see in Cook's Voyages,[1] had a sort of crinoline arrangement fully equal in radius to the largest spread of our own lady-baskets. When I fling a Bay-State shawl over my shoulders, I am only taking a lesson from the climate which the Indian had learned before me. A *blanket*-shawl we call it, and not a plaid; and we wear it like the aborigines, and not like the Highlanders.

—We are the Romans of the modern world,—the great assimilating people. Conflicts and conquests are of course necessary accidents with us, as with our prototypes. And so we come to their style of weapon. Our army sword is the short, stiff, pointed *gladius* of the Romans; and the American bowie-knife is the same tool, modified to meet the daily wants of civil society. I announce at this table an axiom not to be found in Montesquieu[2] or the journals of Congress:—

The race that shortens its weapons lengthens its boundaries.

Corollary. It was the Polish *lance* that left Poland at last with nothing of her own to bound.

"Dropped from her nerveless grasp the *shattered spear!*"

What business had Sarmatia[3] to be fighting for liberty with a fifteen-foot pole between her and the breasts of her enemies? If she had but clutched the old Roman and young American weapon, and come to close quarters, there might have been a chance for her; but it would have spoiled the best passage in "The Pleasures of Hope."[4]

—Self-made men?—Well, yes. Of course every body likes and respects self-made men. It is a great deal better to be made in that way than not to be made at all. Are any of you younger people old enough to remember that Irishman's house on the marsh at Cam-

1. James Cook (1728–1779), English Pacific explorer, visited Otaheite, now Tahiti, in 1769. In the recent republication of his *Voyages* (1821), the pictures showed the Tahitian "young ladies" garmented, as Holmes suggests.
2. French baron and political philosopher (1689–1755), whose *Causes of the Grandeur and Decline of the Romans* (1734) is in Holmes's mind.
3. Ancient name of Poland.
4. The poem quoted above, by Thomas Campbell (1777–1844), a Scottish romantic poet.

bridgeport, which house he built from drain to chimney-top with his own hands? It took him a good many years to build it, and one could see that it was a little out of plumb, and a little wavy in outline, and a little queer and uncertain in general aspect. A regular hand could certainly have built a better house; but it was a very good house for a "self-made" carpenter's house, and people praised it, and said how remarkably well the Irishman had succeeded. They never thought of praising the fine blocks of houses a little farther on.

Your self-made man, whittled into shape with his own jack-knife, deserves more credit, if that is all, than the regular engine-turned article, shaped by the most approved pattern, and French-polished by society and travel. But as to saying that one is every way the equal of the other, that is another matter. The right of strict social discrimination of all things and persons, according to their merits, native or acquired, is one of the most precious republican privileges. I take the liberty to exercise it when I say that, *other things being equal*, in most relations of life I prefer a man of family.

What do I mean by a man of family?—O, I'll give you a general idea of what I mean. Let us give him a first-rate fit out; it costs us nothing.

Four or five generations of gentlemen and gentlewomen; among them a member of his Majesty's Council for the Province, a Governor or so, one or two Doctors of Divinity, a member of Congress, not later than the time of long boots with tassels.

Family portraits.[5] The member of the Council, by Smibert.[6] The

5. "The full-length pictures by Copley I was thinking of are such as may be seen in the Memorial Hall of Harvard University, but many are to be met with in different parts of New England, sometimes in the possession of the poor descendants of the rich gentlefolks in lace ruffles and glistening satins, grandees and grand dames of the ante-Revolutionary period. I remember one poor old gentleman who had nothing left of his family possessions but the full-length portraits of his ancestors, the Counsellor and his lady, saying, with a gleam of the pleasantry which had come down from the days of Mather Byles, and 'Balch the Hatter,' and Sigourney, that he fared not so badly after all, for he had a pair of *canvasbacks* every day through the whole year.

"The mention of these names, all of which are mere traditions to myself and my contemporaries, reminds me of the long succession of wits and humorists whose companionship has been the delight of their generation, and who leave nothing on record by which they will be remembered; Yoricks who set the table in a roar, story-tellers who gave us scenes of life in monologue better than the stilted presentments of the stage, and those always welcome friends with social interior furnishings, whose smile provoked the wit of others and whose rich, musical laughter was its abundant reward. Who among us in my earlier days ever told a story or carolled a rippling *chanson* so gayly, so easily, so charmingly as John Sullivan, whose memory is like the breath of a long bygone summer? Mr. Arthur Gilman has left his monument in the stately structures he planned; Mr. James T. Fields in the pleasant volumes full of precious recollections; but twenty or thirty years from now old men will tell their boys that the Yankee story-teller died with the first, and that the chief of our literary reminiscents, whose ideal portrait gallery reached from Wordsworth to Swinburne, left us when the second bowed his head and 'fell on sleep,' no longer to delight the guests whom his hospitality gathered around him with the pictures to which his lips gave life and action" [Holmes's note].

6. John Smibert (1688–1751), Scottish-born portrait painter, in Boston, after 1728; designed Faneuil Hall.

great merchant-uncle, by Copley,[7] full length, sitting in his arm-chair, in a velvet cap and flowered robe, with a globe by him, to show the range of his commercial transactions, and letters with large red seals lying round, one directed conspicuously to The Honorable, etc., etc. Greatgrandmother, by the same artist; brown satin, lace very fine, hands superlative; grand old lady, stiffish, but imposing. Her mother, artist unknown; flat, angular, hanging sleeves; parrot on fist. A pair of Stuarts,[8] viz., 1. A superb, full-blown, mediæval gentleman, with a fiery dash of Tory blood in his veins, tempered down with that of a fine old rebel grandmother, and warmed up with the best of old India Madeira; his face is one flame of ruddy sunshine; his ruffled shirt rushes out of his bosom with an impetuous generosity, as if it would drag his heart after it; and his smile is good for twenty thousand dollars to the Hospital, besides ample bequests to all relatives and dependants. 2. Lady of the same; remarkable cap; high waist, as in time of Empire;[9] bust *a la Josephine*; wisps of curls, like celery-tips, at sides of forehead; complexion clear and warm, like rose-cordial. As for the miniatures by Malbone,[1] we don't count them in the gallery.

Books, too, with the names of old college-students in them,—family names;—you will find them at the head of their respective classes in the days when students took rank on the catalogue from their parents' condition. Elzevirs,[2] with the Latinized appelations of youthful progenitors, and *Hic liber est meus*[3] on the title-page. A set of Hogarth's[4] original plates. Pope, original edition, 15 volumes,[5] London, 1717. Barrow on the lower shelves, in folio. Tillotson[6] on the upper, in a little dark platoon of octo-decimos.

Some family silver; a string of wedding and funeral rings; the arms of the family curiously blazoned; the same in worsted, by a maiden aunt.

If the man of family has an old place to keep these things in, furnished with claw-footed chairs and black mahogany tables, and tall bevel-edged mirrors, and stately upright cabinets, his outfit is complete.

---

7. John Singleton Copley (1738–1815), best known for the portraits he painted in Boston before 1774, when, a Tory, he emigrated to England.

8. Gilbert Stuart (1755–1828), famous for his portraits of American leaders, especially several of George Washington.

9. The French First Empire under Napoleon (1805–1814); Napoleon divorced Empress Josephine, the style-maker here, in 1809.

1. Edward Greene Malbone (1777–1807), American miniature painter who left Boston for Charleston, South Carolina.

2. Louis Elzevir (1540–1617) began printing at Leyden, Holland about 1570; for nearly two centuries the family published masterpieces of printing and binding.

3. "This is my book."

4. William Hogarth (1697–1764), British painter-engraver, whose work is still famous for its satiric realism and skill.

5. First collected edition (1717) of the early *Works* of Alexander Pope.

6. The Englishmen Isaac Barrow (1630–1677) and John Tillotson (1630–1694) were influential in America: the former was a mathematician and ecclesiastical logician; the latter, a master of a simple homiletics.

No, my friends, I go (always, other things being equal) for the man who inherits family traditions and the cumulative humanities of at least four or five generations. Above all things, as a child, he should have tumbled about in a library. All men are afraid of books, who have not handled them from infancy. Do you suppose our dear *didascalos*[7] over there ever read *Poli Synopsis*, or consulted *Castelli Lexicon*,[8] while he was growing up to their stature? Not he; but virtue passed through the hem of their parchment and leather garments whenever he touched them,[9] as the precious drugs sweated through the bat's handle in the Arabian story. I tell you he is at home wherever he smells the invigorating fragrance of Russia leather.[1] No self-made man feels so. One may, it is true, have all the antecedents I have spoken of, and yet be a boor or a shabby fellow. One may have none of them, and yet be fit for councils and courts. Then let them change places. Our social arrangement has this great beauty, that its strata shift up and down as they change specific gravity, without being clogged by layers of prescription. But I still insist on my democratic liberty of choice, and I go for the man with the gallery of family portraits against the one with the twenty-five cent daguerreotype, unless I find out that the last is the better of the two.

—I should have felt more nervous about the late comet, if I had thought the world was ripe.[2] But it is very green yet, if I am not mistaken; and besides, there is a great deal of coal to use up, which I cannot bring myself to think was made for nothing. If certain things, which seem to me essential to a millennium, had come to pass, I should have been frightened; but they haven't. Perhaps you would like to hear my

LATTER-DAY WARNINGS

When legislators keep the law,
    When banks dispense with bolts and locks,
  When berries, whortle—rasp—and straw—
    Grow bigger *downwards* through the box,—

When he that selleth house or land
    Shows leak in roof or flaw in right,—

7. " 'Our dear *didascalos*' [teacher] was meant for Professor James Russell Lowell, now Minister to England. It requires the union of exceptional native gifts and generations of training to bring the 'natural man' of New England to the completeness of scholarly manhood, such as that which adds new distinction to the name he bears, already remarkable * * * " [Holmes's note].
8. Matthew Poole (1625–1679) published in Latin the scholarly *Synopses of Sacred Scriptures* * * * (London, 1669–1676). Another standard scholarly work was Bartolommeo Castelli's *Lexicon of Graeco-Roman Medicine* (1713).
9. *Cf.* Luke vi: 17–19; Mark v: 25–30.
1. *I.e.*, fine bindings.
2. It was an ancient superstitition that comets portended the destruction of the earth. Donati's comet, on a two-thousand-year cycle, had just for the first time been observed (1858).

When haberdashers choose the stand
    Whose window hath the broadest light,—

When preachers tell us all they think,
    And party leaders all they mean,—
When what we pay for, that we drink,
    From real grape and coffee-bean,—

When lawyers take what they would give,
    And doctors give what they would take,—
When city fathers eat to live,
    Save when they fast for conscience' sake,—

When one that hath a horse on sale
    Shall bring his merit to the proof,
Without a lie for every nail
    That holds the iron on the hoof,—

When in the usual place for rips
    Our gloves are stitched with special care,
And guarded well the whalebone tips
    When first umbrellas need repair,—

When Cuba's weeds have quite forgot
    The power of suction to resist,
And claret-bottles harbor not
    Such dimples as would hold your fist,—

When publishers no longer steal,
    And pay for what they stole before,—
When the first locomotive's wheel
    Rolls through the Hoosac tunnel's bore;[3]—

Till then let Cumming[4] blaze away,
    And Miller's[5] saints blow up the globe;
But when you see that blessed day,
    Then order your ascension robe!

The company seemed to like the verses, and I promised them to read others occasionally, if they had a mind to hear them. Of course they would not expect it every morning. Neither must the reader suppose that all these things I have reported were said at any one breakfast-time. I have not taken the trouble to date them, as

3. "This hoped for, but long despaired of, event, occurred on the 9th of February, 1875. * * * " [Holmes's note, 1883]. The Hoosac Tunnel is on the Boston and Maine railroad east of North Adams, Massachusetts.
4. Alfred Cumming, first United States territorial governor of Utah, in May, 1857, had taken his office under protec-

tion of United States troops because of the presumed hostility of the Mormon settlers.
5. Followers of William Miller (1782–1849), the Millerites, undaunted by the failure of the millennium to arrive as predicted by Miller, continued after his death to make new predictions.

Raspail,[6] *père*, used to date every proof he sent to the printer; but they were scattered over several breakfasts; and I have said a good many more things since, which I shall very possibly print some time or other, if I am urged to do it by judicious friends.

I finished off with reading some verses of my friend the Professor, of whom you may perhaps hear more by and by.[7] The Professor read them, he told me, at a farewell meeting, where the youngest of our great historians[8] met a few of his many friends at their invitation.

Yes, we knew we must lose him,—though friendship may claim
To blend her green leaves with the laurels of fame;
Though fondly, at parting, we call him our own,
'Tis the whisper of love when the bugle has blown.

As the rider who rests with the spur on his heel,—
As the guardsman who sleeps in his corselet of steel,—
As the archer who stands with his shaft on the string,
He stoops from his toil to the garland we bring.

What pictures yet slumber unborn in his loom
Till their warriors shall breathe and their beauties shall bloom,
While the tapestry lengthens the life-glowing dyes
That caught from our sunsets the stain of their skies!

In the alcoves of death, in the charnels of time,
Where flit the gaunt spectres of passion and crime,
There are triumphs untold, there are martyrs unsung,
There are heroes yet silent to speak with his tongue!

Let us hear the proud story which time has bequeathed
From lips that are warm with the freedom they breathed!
Let him summon its tyrants and tell us their doom,
Though he sweep the black past like Van Tromp[9] with his broom!

*   *   *   *

The dream flashes by, for the west-winds awake
On pampas, on prairie, o'er mountain and lake,
To bathe the swift bark, like a sea-girdled shrine,
With incense they stole from the rose and the pine.

6. François Vincent Raspail (1794–1878), French scientist, was banished for revolutionary activities in 1848.
7. The Professor, like the Autocrat, an *alter ego* for Holmes. The installments of *The Professor at the Breakfast-Table* appeared in 1859–1860.
8. "'The youngest of our great historians,' referred to in the poem, was John Lothrop Motley. His career in authorship was as successful as it was noble, and his works are among the chief ornaments of our national literature. Are Republics still ungrateful, as of old?" [Holmes's note, 1883]. Before his death in 1877, he had established himself as the historian of the Dutch nation. In 1879, Holmes published a memoir of Motley.
9. The Dutch Admiral Cornelius Van Tromp hoisted a broom on his flagship after his victories in 1673 had "swept from the sea" his Franco-British enemies.

So fill a bright cup with the sunlight that gushed
When the dead summer's jewels were trampled and crushed:
THE TRUE KNIGHT OF LEARNING,—the world holds him dear,—
Love bless him, Joy crown him, God speed his career!

1857, 1858

From Elsie Venner[1]

Chapter I: The Brahmin Caste of New England

There is nothing in New England corresponding at all to the
feudal aristocracies of the Old World. Whether it be owing to the
stock from which we were derived, or to the practical working of
our institutions, or to the abrogation of the technical "law of
honor," which draws a sharp line between the personally responsible
class of "gentlemen" and the unnamed multitude of those who are
not expected to risk their lives for an abstraction,—whatever be the
cause, we have no such aristocracy here as that which grew up out
of the military systems of the Middle Ages.

What we mean by "aristocracy" is merely the richer part of the
community, that live in the tallest houses, drive real carriages, (not
"kerridges,") kid-glove their hands, and French-bonnet their ladies'
heads, give parties where the persons who call them by the above
title are not invited, and have a provokingly easy way of dressing,
walking, talking, and nodding to people, as if they felt entirely at
home, and would not be embarrassed in the least, if they met the
Governor, or even the President of the United States, face to face.
Some of these great folks are really well-bred, some of them are only
purse-proud and assuming,—but they form a class, and are named
as above in the common speech.

It is in the nature of large fortunes to diminish rapidly, when
subdivided and distributed. A million is the unit of wealth, now
and here in America. It splits into four handsome properties; each
of these into four good inheritances; these, again, into scanty com-
petences for four ancient maidens,—with whom it is best the family
should die out, unless it can begin again as its great-grandfather
did. Now a million is a kind of golden cheese, which represents in
a compendious form the summer's growth of a fat meadow of craft

1. The following extract from *Elsie
Venner* is reproduced here not in connection with the novel, of which it is
the first chapter, but because it deserves
attention as an essay characteristically
supporting the patrician concept of cultural inheritance as providing more de-
pendably for intellectual leadership than
the equalitarian tradition. Whether
leadership comes best by family inheritance or by spontaneous generation
of individual talents is still a question.
Elsie Venner—a literary failure, like all
of Holmes's novels—was serially published in the *Atlantic Monthly* as *The
Professor's Story* between January, 1860
and April, 1861. The volume was published in 1861.

or commerce; and as this kind of meadow rarely bears more than one crop, it is pretty certain that sons and grandsons will not get another golden cheese out of it, whether they milk the same cows or turn in new ones. In other words, the millionocracy, considered in a large way, is not at all an affair of persons and families, but a perpetual fact of money with a variable human element, which a philosopher might leave out of consideration without falling into serious error. Of course, this trivial and fugitive fact of personal wealth does not create a permanent class, unless some special means are taken to arrest the process of disintegration in the third generation. This is so rarely done, at least successfully, that one need not live a very long life to see most of the rich families he knew in childhood more or less reduced, and the millions shifted into the hands of the country-boys who were sweeping stores and carrying parcels when the now decayed gentry were driving their chariots, eating their venison over silver chafing-dishes, drinking Madeira chilled in embossed coolers, wearing their hair in powder, and casing their legs in long boots with silken tassels.

There is, however, in New England, an aristocracy, if you choose to call it so, which has a far greater character of permanence. It has grown to be a *caste*,—not in any odious sense,—but, by the repetition of the same influences, generation after generation, it has acquired a distinct organization and physiognomy, which not to recognize is mere stupidity, and not to be willing to describe would show a distrust of the good-nature and intelligence of our readers, who like to have us see all we can and tell all we see.

If you will look carefully at any class of students in one of our colleges, you will have no difficulty in selecting specimens of two different aspects of youthful manhood. Of course I shall choose extreme cases to illustrate the contrast between them. In the first, the figure is perhaps robust, but often otherwise,—inelegant, partly from careless attitudes, partly from ill-dressing,—the face is uncouth in feature, or at least common,—the mouth coarse and unformed,—the eye unsympathetic, even if bright,—the movements of the face are clumsy, like those of the limbs,—the voice is unmusical,—and the enunciation as if the words were coarse castings, instead of fine carvings. The youth of the other aspect is commonly slender,—his face is smooth, and apt to be pallid,—his features are regular and of a certain delicacy,—his eye is bright and quick,—his lips play over the thought he utters as a pianist's fingers dance over their music,—and his whole air, though it may be timid, and even awkward, has nothing clownish. If you are a teacher, you know what to expect from each of these young men. With equal willingness, the first will be slow at learning; the second will take to his books as a pointer or a setter to his field-work.

The first youth is the common country-boy, whose race has been bred to bodily labor. Nature has adapted the family organization to the kind of life it has lived. The hands and feet by constant use have got more than their share of development,—the organs of thought and expression less than their share. The finer instincts are latent and must be developed. A youth of this kind is raw material in its first stage of elaboration. You must not expect too much of any such. Many of them have force of will and character, and become distinguished in practical life; but very few of them ever become great scholars. A scholar is, in a large proportion of cases, the son of scholars or scholarly persons.

That is exactly what the other young man is. He comes of the *Brahmin caste of New England.* This is the harmless, inoffensive, untitled aristocracy referred to, and which many readers will at once acknowledge. There are races of scholars among us, in which aptitude for learning, and all these marks of it I have spoken of, are congenital and hereditary. Their names are always on some college catalogue or other. They break out every generation or two in some learned labor which calls them up after they seem to have died out. At last some newer name takes their place, it may be,— but you inquire a little and you find it is the blood of the Edwardses or the Chauncys or the Ellerys or some of the old historic scholars, disguised under the altered name of a female descendant.

There probably is not an experienced instructor anywhere in our Northern States who will not recognize at once the truth of this general distinction. But the reader who has never been a teacher will very probably object, that some of our most illustrious public men have come direct from the homespun-clad class of the people, —and he may, perhaps, even find a noted scholar or two whose parents were masters of the English alphabet, but of no other.

It is not fair to pit a few chosen families against the great multitude of those who are continually working their way up into the intellectual classes. The results which are habitually reached by hereditary training are occasionally brought about without it. There are natural filters as well as artificial ones; and though the great rivers are commonly more or less turbid, if you will look long enough, you may find a spring that sparkles as no water does which drips through your apparatus of sands and sponges. So there are families which refine themselves into intellectual aptitude without having had much opportunity for intellectual acquirements. A series of felicitous crosses develops an improved strain of blood, and reaches its maximum perfection at last in the large uncombed youth who goes to college and startles the hereditary class-leaders by striding past them all. That is Nature's republicanism; thank God for it, but do not let it make you illogical. The race of the hereditary scholar has exchanged a certain portion of its animal vigor for its new instincts, and it is hard to lead men without a good deal of animal vigor. The scholar who comes by Nature's special grace from an unworn stock of broad-chested sires and deep-bosomed mothers must always overmatch an equal intelligence with a compromised and lowered vitality. A man's breathing and digestive apparatus (one is tempted to add *muscular*) are just as important to him on the floor of the Senate as his thinking organs. You broke down in your great speech, did you? Yes, your grandfather had an attack of dyspepsia in '82, after working too hard on his famous Election Sermon. All this does not touch the main fact: our scholars come chiefly from a privileged order, just as our best fruits come from well-known grafts,—though now and then a seedling apple, like the Northern Spy, or a seedling pear, like the Seckel, springs from a nameless ancestry and grows to be the pride of all the gardens in the land. * * *

1860, 1861

JAMES RUSSELL LOWELL
(1819–1891)

James Russell Lowell conscientiously represented the patrician ideal of those who demand responsible leadership in return for democracy's highest benefits. As a spokesman for this tradition, he was less the Brahmin than Holmes, and had higher expectations of the people as a whole. Elmwood, his birthplace, the ancestral home in Cambridge, Massachusetts, remained throughout his life the hub of his versatile activities. Gifted, tireless, and by temperament both the humanitarian and the humanist, he gave himself zealously to social reform and the antislavery movement; he made a career as poet, critic, editor, and Harvard professor; and without seeking office, he participated in public leadership from the level of local politics to that of the national party councils and foreign diplomacy. Small wonder if his literary critics have been unable to discover a convincing unity in the brilliant but disparate accomplishments of his pen.

The son of a Unitarian clergyman of old family but somewhat limited means, Lowell was graduated in 1838 from Harvard College, and in 1840 from the Law School. The year before, he had sold his first poem, and he soon found the magazines, especially the popular *Graham's*, friendly to his verse and critical articles. Within two years he had collected the poems of *A Year's Life* (1841), and left the practice of law in favor of literature.

In 1843, with Robert Carter, he established and edited *The Pioneer*. Reflecting its founder's belief that a periodical of high literary quality could survive without concessions to mass appeal, the magazine lived only three months, but it foreshadowed the famous *Atlantic Monthly*, of which Lowell became the first editor in 1857. His second collection, *Poems*, appeared in 1844. That year he married Maria White, whose devotion to abolition and to humanitarian causes perhaps strengthened his own. They settled in Philadelphia, where Lowell had been called as editorial writer for *The Pennsylvania Freeman*, an antislavery periodical. He began also to contribute articles against slavery to the *National Anti-Slavery Standard* and other periodicals, including the London *Daily News*. A collection of his literary essays, *Conversations on Some of the Old Poets*, appeared in 1845, and was reprinted in London.

Now well established as a writer, he returned to Elmwood in 1846, to experience a virtual triumph that summer when the first of *The Biglow Papers* appeared in the Boston *Courier* (June 17, 1846). The series grew to nine numbers, and gained enormous popularity for its audacious opposition to the Mexican War, which free-soil readers regarded as an elaborate conspiracy among southern politicians for the extension of slave territory by conquest. The success of these letters was as much literary as political. Hosea Biglow's shrewd and homespun wit was enormously amusing, and

his "letters" represented the first successful effort to employ the Yankee dialect and humor—an established comic tradition—in satirical poetry of genuine excellence. The series was issued as a volume in 1848, at the conclusion of the war. In 1862, at a moment of northern despondency in the Civil War, Hosea Biglow again appeared, now as a stalwart defender of northern policy and a sharp-witted satirist of the Confederacy.

The year 1848 was truly Lowell's *annus mirabilis*. Then only twenty-nine, he collected his two-volume *Poems: Second Series*, and published *The Biglow Papers* and two new masterpieces, *The Vision of Sir Launfal* and *A Fable for Critics*. The former marks the high point of Lowell's earlier romanticism. An ethical romance inspired by the Arthurian legends, it taught that Holiness and the Grail do not wait at the end of chivalric adventure, but are found in the heart and in the wooden cup of charity. The poem remained a favorite for nearly a century, and its "Prelude" is still one of the most familiar of American poems of nature. A *Fable for Critics* was a daring publication for a young author, impishly dissecting the leading authors of the day, including reverend seniors such as Bryant and Cooper. Only an accepted member of the family, and one armed with Lowell's wit, urbane good nature, and sense of justice, could have accomplished it without disaster. Disarmingly and shrewdly, he hung up his own portrait as one "who's striving Parnassus to climb / With a whole bale of *isms*" on his back. Many of his comments still have value as impressionistic sketches, and their wit, at least, remains untarnished.

When his literary fame was at its greatest, Lowell reached a crucial turning point of his life. Between 1847 and 1853, death took three of his four children, and in 1853, the beloved and frail Maria White. He published travel sketches resulting from a trip abroad in 1851–1852 and gave a few lectures, but the creative fire was banked for a time.

In 1855, he was appointed to succeed Longfellow as Smith Professor of Modern Languages at Harvard, and he served with distinction in this capacity, particularly as a brilliant lecturer, until 1872. He joined with the founders of the *Atlantic Monthly* in 1857, and as editor during its first five years, he helped to shape its policy. This activity, and his remarriage in 1857, brought again a widening of his circle of literary association and interest. The events of the Civil War restored him to literary prominence with the resumption of *The Biglow Papers* which appeared at intervals in the *Atlantic Monthly* between January, 1862, and May, 1866, and were published as a collected *Second Series* in 1867.

In 1864 he became joint editor, with Charles E. Norton, of the *North American Review*, and he maintained this distinguished connection until he resigned his professorship at Harvard. At this time he made his reputation as a memorial poet, delivering, on public occasions, such lofty and stirring odes as

the "Commemoration Ode" (1865), and, in 1875, the "Concord Centennial Ode" and "Under the Old Elm." His poetry was becoming noticeably more restrained and formal in spirit, but also more thoughtful. During this period, he published two volumes of poems—*Under the Willows* (1869) and *The Cathedral* (1869, dated 1870)—and collections of his critical and familiar essays—*Among My Books* (1870; *Second Series*, 1876), and *My Study Windows* (1871). His literary criticism was now recognized at home and abroad, and on his trip to England (1872–1874) he was widely celebrated, and awarded honorary degrees at Oxford and Cambridge.

On his return, Lowell again took an active part in politics, particularly as a public speaker. He was a delegate to the Republican national convention in 1876, and sailed as American ambassador to Spain in July, 1877. In 1880 he became ambassador to Great Britain, where, as a cultural representative of the United States, his services were widely recognized. Among the several important speeches during his five years in this post, the most notable was "Democracy," delivered at Birmingham in 1884.

In the six years following his retirement from diplomacy, Lowell lived quietly at Elmwood, except for brief trips abroad in 1888 and 1889. He collected his essays and speeches: *Democracy and Other Addresses* (1887), *Political Essays* (1888), and *Latest Literary Essays* (1891). *The Old English Dramatists* was posthumously published in 1892. He collected the poems of *Heartsease and Rue* (1888). He edited his collected works in ten volumes. On August 21, 1891, he died at Elmwood. He was enormously gifted, but his meteoric writings do not suggest the inward order of a great author. However, the selections below are still alive, and lively records of the culture that produced them.

The standard text is the Riverside Edition, on which the selections in this volume are based. It was published as *The Writings of James Russell Lowell*, 10 vols., edited by James Russell Lowell, 1890. To this were added Vol. XI, *Latest Literary Essays and Addresses* * * * , 1891, and Vol. XII, *The Old English Dramatists*, 1892. The *Letters* * * * , 2 vols., edited by Charles E. Norton, appeared in 1894;

and the *Life*, 2 vols., by H. E. Scudder, in 1901; the texts of the Riverside Edition, together with these supplementary volumes, were reprinted under the editorial supervision of Charles E. Norton as the Elmwood Edition, 16 vols., 1904. Norton's *Letters* * * * was extended to 3 vols. in 1904. The best one-volume collection is *The Complete Poetical Works of James Russell Lowell*, Cambridge Edition, edited by H. E. Scudder, 1897, with valuable notes. A good one-volume selection of the prose and poetry, in the American Writers Series, was edited by H. H. Clark and Norman Foerster, 1949. M. A. DeWolfe Howe edited *New Letters of James Russell Lowell*, 1932. Thelma M. Smith edited *The Uncollected Poetry of James Russell Lowell*, 1950.

The standard biography is H. E. Scudder, *James Russell Lowell: A Biography*, 2 vols., 1901, included in the Elmwood Edition. Also useful are E. E. Hale, Jr., *James Russell Lowell and His Friends*, 1899; Ferris Greenslet, *James Russell Lowell: His Life and Work*, 1905; and Richmond C. Beatty, *James Russell Lowell*, 1942, the most recent appraisal.

Prelude

to THE VISION OF SIR LAUNFAL[1]

Over his keys the musing organist,
 Beginning doubtfully and far away,
First lets his fingers wander as they list,
 And builds a bridge from Dreamland for his lay:
Then, as the touch of his loved instrument   5
 Gives hope and fervor, nearer draws his theme,
First guessed by faint auroral flushes sent
 Along the wavering vista of his dream.

1. "According to the mythology of the Romancers, the San Greal, or Holy Grail, was the cup out of which Jesus partook of the Last Supper with his disciples. * * * It was incumbent upon those who had charge of it to be chaste in thought, word, and deed; but one of the keepers having broken this condition, the Holy Grail disappeared. From that time it was a favorite enterprise of the knights of Arthur's court to go in search of it. * * * The plot (if I may give that name to anything so slight) of the following poem is my own, and, to serve its purpose, I have enlarged the circle of competition in search of the miraculous cup in such a manner as to include, not only other persons than the heroes of the Round Table, but also a period of time subsequent to the

supposed date of King Arthur's reign" [Lowell's note]. The "slight" plot is a dream allegory of Sir Launfal's youthful departure in summer on his mission, his scornful dismissal of a leprous beggar at the castle gates, and his disillusioned and empty-handed return in the winter of his old age. He meets the beggar again, but in humble pity he offers a crust of bread and a cup of water. The beggar, radiantly transformed into a vision of Christ, reminds him that "Who gives himself with his alms feeds three, / Himself, his hungering neighbor, and me." The poem was first published as a volume in 1848, and reissued several times before inclusion in *The Vision of Sir Launfal, the Cathedral, and Favorite Poems* (1876).

Not only around our infancy
Doth heaven with all its splendors lie;[2]
Daily, with souls that cringe and plot, 10
We Sinais[3] climb and know it not.

Over our manhood bend the skies;
  Against our fallen and traitor lives
The great winds utter prophecies; 15
  With our faint hearts the mountain strives;
Its arms outstretched, the druid wood
  Waits with its benedicite;[4]
And to our age's drowsy blood
  Still shouts the inspiring sea. 20

Earth gets its price for what Earth gives us;
  The beggar is taxed for a corner to die in,
The priest hath his fee who comes and shrives us,
  We bargain for the graves we lie in;
At the devil's booth are all things sold,
Each ounce of dross costs its ounce of gold; 25
  For a cap and bells our lives we pay,
Bubbles we buy with a whole soul's tasking:[5]
  'Tis heaven alone that is given away,
'Tis only God may be had for the asking;
No price is set on the lavish summer; 30
June may be had by the poorest comer.

And what is so rare as a day in June?
  Then, if ever, come perfect days;
Then Heaven tries earth if it be in tune,
  And over it softly her warm ear lays: 35
Whether we look, or whether we listen,
We hear life murmur, or see it glisten;
Every clod feels a stir of might,
  An instinct within it that reaches and towers,
And, groping blindly above it for light, 40
  Climbs to a soul in grass and flowers;
The flush of life may well be seen
  Thrilling back over hills and valleys;
The cowslip startles in meadows green,
  The buttercup catches the sun in its chalice, 45

2. *Cf.* Wordsworth's "Ode, Intimations of Immortality from Recollections of Early Childhood," stanza v.
3. At Mount Sinai, Moses, leader of the Israelites, surrounded by the glory of God, received the Ten Commandments. *Cf.* Exodus xxiv: 15–18.

4. *I.e.*, the ancient forests of pagan ("druid") times now invoke a Christian blessing ("benedicite").
5. In ll. 27–28, the poet refers to the traditional accessories of the jester or fool, the "cap and bells" and the "bubbles" (baubles).

And there's never a leaf nor a blade too mean
    To be some happy creature's palace;
The little bird sits at his door in the sun,
    Atilt like a blossom among the leaves,   50
And lets his illumined being o'errun
    With the deluge of summer it receives;
His mate feels the eggs beneath her wings,
And the heart in her dumb breast flutters and sings;
He sings to the wide world, and she to her nest,—   55
In the nice ear of Nature which song is the best?

Now is the high-tide of the year,
    And whatever of life hath ebbed away
Comes flooding back with a ripply cheer,
    Into every bare inlet and creek and bay;   60
Now the heart is so full that a drop overfills it,
We are happy now because God wills it;
No matter how barren the past may have been,
'Tis enough for us now that the leaves are green;
We sit in the warm shade and feel right well   65
How the sap creeps up and the blossoms swell;
We may shut our eyes, but we cannot help knowing
That skies are clear and grass is growing;
The breeze comes whispering in our ear,
That dandelions are blossoming near,   70
    That maize has sprouted, that streams are flowing,
That the river is bluer than the sky,
That the robin is plastering his house hard by;
And if the breeze kept the good news back,
For other couriers we should not lack;   75
    We could guess it all by yon heifer's lowing,—
And hark! how clear bold chanticleer,
Warmed with the new wine of the year,
    Tells all in his lusty crowing!

Joy comes, grief goes, we know not how;   80
Everything is happy now,
    Everything is upward striving;
'Tis as easy now for the heart to be true
As for grass to be green or skies to be blue,—
    'Tis the natural way of living: 85
Who knows whither the clouds have fled?
    In the unscarred heaven they leave no wake;
And the eyes forget the tears they have shed,
    The heart forgets its sorrow and ache;
The soul partakes the season's youth,   90

And the sulphurous rifts of passion and woe
Lie deep 'neath a silence pure and smooth,
Like burnt-out craters healed with snow.

1848

From A Fable for Critics[6]

READER! *walk up at once (it will soon be too late) and buy at a
perfectly ruinous rate*

A

FABLE FOR CRITICS;

OR, BETTER,

(*I like, as a thing that the reader's first fancy may strike,
an old-fashioned title-page,
such as presents a tabular view of the volume's contents,*)

A GLANCE

AT A FEW OF OUR LITERARY PROGENIES
(*Mrs. Malaprop's word*)[7]

FROM

THE TUB OF DIOGENES;[8]

A VOCAL AND MUSICAL MEDLEY,

THAT IS,

A SERIES OF JOKES

BY A WONDERFUL QUIZ

*who accompanies himself with a rub-a-dub-dub, full of spirit and
grace, on the top of the tub.*

Set forth in October, the 21st day, In the year '48, G. P. Putnam,
Broadway.

It being the commonest mode of procedure, I premise a few candid
remarks

6. Lowell's delight in this *jeu d'esprit*, as he termed it, has been shared by his readers since it first appeared in 1848. Loosely modeled after other critical essays in verse (Alexander Pope's *Dunciad*, Leigh Hunt's *Feast of the Poets*), the *Fable* avoids extravagant satire or praise, aiming rather at witty criticism of contemporary American writers. The setting of the title page, and the preface "To the Reader," were carefully designed by Lowell to disguise the fact that they, too, are verse, suggesting the tone of casual humor of the entire book. Speaking of its composition several years later, Lowell said that the *Fable* was extemporized and sent off in daily installments to his friend Charles F. Briggs in New York, to whom he dedicated and gave the book. However, from letters passing between him and Briggs, it appears that he sent off some six hundred lines in the fall, and followed them with successive installments over a period of months, until August, 1848. The title page of the first edition gave the date as "October, the 21st day, in the year '48"; but the book actually came from the press on the twenty-fifth of the month.

7. Mrs. Malaprop, in Sheridan's *The Rivals* (1775), had a genius for misusing words.

8. Diogenes (412?–323 B.C.), Gr Cynic philosopher, according t᷍ tion, lived in a tub, and ⁄ ridiculed conventional ᷍

To the Reader:—

This trifle, begun to please only myself and my own private fancy, was laid on the shelf. But some friends, who had seen it, induced me, by dint of saying they liked it, to put it in print. That is, having come to that very conclusion, I asked their advice when 't would make no confusion. For (though in the gentlest of ways) they had hinted it was scarce worth the while, I should doubtless have printed it.

I began it, intending a Fable, a frail, slender thing, rhyme-ywinged, with a sting in its tail. But, by addings and alterings not previously planned, digressions chance-hatched, like birds' eggs in the sand, and dawdlings to suit every whimsey's demand (always freeing the bird which I held in my hand, for the two perched, perhaps out of reach, in the tree),—it grew by degrees to the size which you see. I was like the old woman that carried the calf, and my neighbors, like hers, no doubt, wonder and laugh; and when, my strained arms with their grown burthen full, I call it my Fable, they call it a bull.

Having scrawled at full gallop (as far as that goes) in a style that is neither good verse nor bad prose, and being a person whom nobody knows, some people will say I am rather more free with my readers than it is becoming to be, that I seem to expect them to wait on my leisure in following wherever I wander at pleasure, that, in short, I take more than a young author's lawful ease, and laugh in a queer way so like Mephistopheles,[9] that the public will doubt, as they grope through my rhythm, if in truth I am making fun *of* them or *with* them.

So the excellent Public is hereby assured that the sale of my book is already secured. For there is not a poet throughout the whole land but will purchase a copy or two out of hand, in the fond expectation of being amused in it, by seeing his betters cut up and abused in it. Now, I find, by a pretty exact calculation, there are something like ten thousand bards in the nation, of that special variety whom the Review and Magazine critics call *lofty* and *true*, and about thirty thousand (*this* tribe is increasing) of the kinds who are termed *full of promise* and *pleasing*. The Public will see by a glance at this schedule, that they cannot expect me to be oversedulous about courting *them*, since it seems I have got enough fuel made sure of for boiling my pot.

As for such of our poets as find not their names mentioned once in my pages, with praises or blames, let them send in their cards, without further delay, to my friend G. P. Putnam, Esquire, in Broadway, where a list will be kept with the strictest regard to the

9. One of the seven devils in the medieval hierarchy of the fallen archangels, second only to Lucifer, became the heartless and mocking villain of Christopher Marlowe's *Tragedy of Dr. Faustus* and Goethe's *Faust*.

day and the hour of receiving the card. Then, taking them up as I chance to have time (that is, if their names can be twisted in rhyme), I will honestly give each his PROPER POSITION, at the rate of ONE AUTHOR to each NEW EDITION. Thus a PREMIUM is offered sufficiently HIGH (as the magazines say when they tell their best lie) to induce bards to CLUB their resources and buy the balance of every edition, until they have all of them fairly been run through the mill.

One word to such readers (judicious and wise) as read books with something behind the mere eyes, of whom in the country, perhaps, there are two, including myself, gentle reader, and you. All the characters sketched in this slight *jeu d'esprit*,[1] though, it may be, they seem here and there, rather free, and drawn from a somewhat too cynical stand-point, are *meant* to be faithful, and that is the grand point, and none but an owl would feel sore at a rub from a jester who tells you, without any subterfuge, that he sits in Diogenes' tub.

* * *

"There comes Emerson first, whose rich words, every one,
Are like gold nails[2] in temples to hang trophies on,
Whose prose is grand verse, while his verse, the Lord knows,
Is some of it pr—No, 'tis not even prose;
I'm speaking of metres; some poems have welled   5
From those rare depths of soul that have ne'er been excelled;
They're not epics, but that doesn't matter a pin,
In creating, the only hard thing's to begin;
A grass-blade's no easier to make than an oak;
If you've once found the way, you've achieved the grand stroke; 10
In the worst of his poems are mines of rich matter,
But thrown in a heap with a crash and a clatter;
Now it is not one thing nor another alone
Makes a poem, but rather the general tone,
The something pervading, uniting the whole, 15
The before unconceived, unconceivable soul,
So that just in removing this trifle or that, you
Take away, as it were, a chief limb of the statue;
Roots, wood, bark, and leaves singly perfect may be,
But, clapt hodge-podge together, they don't make a tree. 20

"But, to come back to Emerson (whom, by the way,
I believe we left waiting),—his is, we may say,
A Greek head on right Yankee shoulders, whose range

1. French, meaning "a witty jest."   of the wise are * * * as ˉ
2. *Cf.* Ecclesiastes xii: 11; "The words   by the masters of ass˄

Has Olympus for one pole, for t'other the Exchange;[3]
He seems, to my thinking (although I'm afraid   25
The comparison must, long ere this, have been made),
A Plotinus-Montaigne,[4] where the Egyptian's gold mist
And the Gascon's shrewd wit cheek-by-jowl coexist;
All admire, and yet scarcely six converts he's got
To I don't (nor they either) exactly know what;   30
For though he builds glorious temples, 'tis odd
He leaves never a doorway to get in a god.
'Tis refreshing to old-fashioned people like me
To meet such a primitive Pagan as he,
In whose mind all creation is duly respected   35
As parts of himself—just a little projected;
And who's willing to worship the stars and the sun,
A convert to—nothing but Emerson.
So perfect a balance there is in his head,
That he talks of things sometimes as if they were dead;   40
Life, nature, love, God, and affairs of that sort,
He looks at as merely ideas; in short,
As if they were fossils stuck round in a cabinet,
Of such vast extent that our earth's a mere dab in it;
Composed just as he is inclined to conjecture her,   45
Namely, one part pure earth, ninety-nine parts pure lecturer;
You are filled with delight at his clear demonstration,
Each figure, word, gesture, just fits the occasion,
With the quiet precision of science he'll sort 'em,
But you can't help suspecting the whole a *post mortem*.   50

    "There are persons, mole-blind to the soul's make and style,
Who insist on a likeness 'twixt him and Carlyle;[5]
To compare him with Plato[6] would be vastly fairer,
Carlyle's the more burly, but E. is the rarer;
He sees fewer objects, but clearlier, truelier,   55
If C.'s as original, E.'s more peculiar;
That he's more of a man you might say of the one,
Of the other he's more of an Emerson;
C.'s the Titan, as shaggy of mind as of limb,—
E. the clear-eyed Olympian, rapid and slim;   60
The one's two thirds Norseman, the other half Greek,
Where the one's most abounding, the other's to seek;
C.'s generals require to be seen in the mass,—

---

3. The contrast between the practical
and the idealistic aspects of Emerson's
nature is suggested by these opposites—
the home of the gods of Greece and the
stock exchange.
4. Plotinus (205–270), a Roman Neo-
ᵗonic philosopher born in Egypt;

Michel Eyquem de Montaigne (1533–
1592), French essayist, known for his
skeptical and sophisticated wit.
5. Thomas Carlyle (1795–1881), English essayist and historian.
6. Plato (427–347 B.C.), Greek philosopher.

E.'s specialties gain if enlarged by the glass;
C. gives nature and God his own fits of the blues, 65
And rims common-sense things with mystical hues,—
E. sits in a mystery calm and intense,
And looks coolly around him with sharp common-sense;
C. shows you how every-day matters unite
With the dim transdiurnal recesses of night,— 70
While E., in a plain, preternatural way,
Makes mysteries matters of mere every day;
C. draws all his characters quite *à la* Fuseli,[7]—
Not sketching their bundles of muscles and thews illy,
He paints with a brush so untamed and profuse 75
They seem nothing but bundles of muscles and thews;
E. is rather like Flaxman,[8] lines strait and severe,
And a colorless outline, but full, round, and clear;—
To the men he thinks worthy he frankly accords
The design of a white marble statue in words. 80
C. labors to get at the centre, and then
Take a reckoning from there of his actions and men;
E. calmly assumes the said centre as granted,
And, given himself, has whatever is wanted.

"He has imitators in scores, who omit 85
No part of the man but his wisdom and wit,—
Who go carefully o'er the sky-blue of his brain,
And when he has skimmed it once, skim it again;
If at all they resemble him, you may be sure it is
Because their shoals mirror his mists and obscurities, 90
As a mud-puddle seems deep as heaven for a minute,
While a cloud that floats o'er is reflected within it.

* * *

"There is Bryant, as quiet, as cool, and as dignified,
As a smooth, silent iceberg, that never is ignified,
Save when by reflection 'tis kindled o' nights 95
With a semblance of flame by the chill Northern Lights.
He may rank (Griswold[9] says so) first bard of your nation
(There's no doubt that he stands in supreme iceolation),
Your topmost Parnassus[1] he may set his heel on,
But no warm applauses come, peal following peal on,— 100

7. Johann Heinrich Füessli (1742–1825), German-Swiss engraver and painter, whose illustrations for Milton's *Paradise Lost* are extravagant in anatomical detail.
8. John Flaxman (1755–1826), English sculptor and draftsman, whose drawings illustrating Homer's and Dante's works are in the classic pattern.

9. Rufus Wilmot Griswold (1815–1857), editor of the then popular *Poets and Poetry of America* (1842).
1. Parnassus, mountain in Greece, sacred to Apollo, the god of music and poetry, according to Greek myth the one mountain whose summit reached above the waves in the Flood.

He's too smooth and too polished to hang any zeal on:
Unqualified merits, I'll grant, if you choose, he has 'em,
But he lacks the one merit of kindling enthusiasm;
If he stir you at all, it is just, on my soul,
Like being stirred up with the very North Pole.   105

"He is very nice reading in summer, but *inter
Nos*,[2] we don't want *extra* freezing in winter;
Take him up in the depth of July, my advice is,
When you feel an Egyptian devotion to ices.[3]
But, deduct all you can, there's enough that's right good in him,
He has a true soul for field, river, and wood in him;   111
And his heart, in the midst of brick walls, or where'er it is,
Glows, softens, and thrills with the tenderest charities—
To you mortals that delve in this trade-ridden planet?
No, to old Berkshire's hills, with their limestone and granite.   115
If you're one who *in loco* (add *foco* here) *desipis*,[4]
You will get of his outermost heart (as I guess) a piece;
But you'd get deeper down if you came as a precipice,
And would break the last seal of its inwardest fountain,
If you only could palm yourself off for a mountain.   120
Mr. Quivis,[5] or somebody quite as discerning,
Some scholar who's hourly expecting his learning,
Calls B. the American Wordsworth; but Wordsworth
May be rated at more than your whole tuneful herd's worth.
No, don't be absurd, he's an excellent Bryant;   125
But, my friends, you'll endanger the life of your client,
By attempting to stretch him up into a giant:
If you choose to compare him, I think there are two per-
-sons fit for a parallel—Thomson and Cowper;[6]
I don't mean exactly,—there's something of each,   130
There's T.'s love of nature, C.'s penchant to preach;
Just mix up their minds so that C.'s spice of craziness
Shall balance and neutralize T.'s turn for laziness,
And it gives you a brain cool, quite frictionless, quiet,
Whose internal police nips the buds of all riot,—   135
A brain like a permanent strait-jacket put on

2. Latin, meaning "among ourselves,"
or "between us." Lowell makes a play
on this and *extra* [*nos*].
3. A play on the name of Isis, Egyptian
goddess.
4. *I.e.*, foolish in or about a certain
place. By adding *foco* ("at one's fireside"), Lowell also puns about a New
York Democratic faction supported by
Bryant. The "loco-focos" brought
matches to a party caucus in case their
opponents turned off the gaslights.
5. "Mr. Anyone" or "Whoever-he-is."

6. James Thomson (1700–1748), author of *The Seasons* (1730), graphic in
its description of nature, and *The Castle
of Indolence* (1748); William Cowper
(1731–1800), author of *Olney Hymns*
(1779) and *The Task* (1785), and
mentally unstable. Lowell added the following note: "To demonstrate quickly
and easily how per- / versely absurd 'tis
to sound this name *Cowper*, / As people in general call him named *super*, /
I remark that he rhymes it himself with
horse-trooper."

The heart that strives vainly to burst off a button,—
A brain which, without being slow or mechanic,
Does more than a larger less drilled, more volcanic;
He's a Cowper condensed, with no craziness bitten,   140
And the advantage that Wordsworth before him had written.

    "But, my dear little bardlings, don't prick up your ears
Nor suppose I would rank you and Bryant as peers;
If I call him an iceberg, I don't mean to say
There is nothing in that which is grand in its way;   145
He is almost the one of your poets that knows
How much grace, strength, and dignity lie in Repose;
If he sometimes fall short, he is too wise to mar
His thought's modest fulness by going too far;
'Twould be well if your authors should all make a trial   150
Of what virtue there is in severe self-denial,
And measure their writings by Hesiod's[7] staff,
Which teaches that all has less value than half.

    "There is Whittier, whose swelling and vehement heart
Strains the strait-breasted drab of the Quaker apart,   155
And reveals the live Man, still supreme and erect,
Underneath the bemummying wrappers of sect;
There was ne'er a man born who had more of the swing
Of the true lyric bard and all that kind of thing;
And his failures arise (though he seem not to know it)   160
From the very same cause that has made him a poet,—
A fervor of mind which knows no separation
'Twixt simple excitement and pure inspiration,
As my Pythoness[8] erst sometimes erred from not knowing
If 'twere I or mere wind through her tripod was blowing; 165
Let his mind once get head in its favorite direction
And the torrent of verse bursts the dams of reflection,
While, borne with the rush of the metre along,
The poet may chance to go right or go wrong,
Content with the whirl and delirium of song;   170
Then his grammar's not always correct, nor his rhymes,
And he's prone to repeat his own lyrics sometimes,
Not his best, though, for those are struck off at white-heats
When the heart in his breast like a trip-hammer beats,
And can ne'er be repeated again any more   175
Than they could have been carefully plotted before:
Like old what's-his-name[9] there at the battle of Hastings

7. Greek didactic poet of the eighth century B.C.
8. The priestess of the oracle at Delphi, named the Pythia, inhaled the vapors of the chasm while seated on a tripod (l. 165) and uttered the supposedly inspired prophecies.
9. Taillefer, an armed and mounted

(Who, however, gave more than mere rhythmical bastings),
Our Quaker leads off metaphorical fights
For reform and whatever they call human rights,   180
Both singing and striking in front of the war,
And hitting his foes with the mallet of Thor;
Anne haec, one exclaims, on beholding his knocks,
Vestis filii tui,[1] O leather-clad Fox?[2]
Can that be thy son, in the battle's mid din,   185
Preaching brotherly love and then driving it in
To the brain of the tough old Goliath[3] of sin,
With the smoothest of pebbles from Castaly's spring[4]
Impressed on his hard moral sense with a sling?

"All honor and praise to the right-hearted bard   190
Who was true to The Voice when such service was hard,
Who himself was so free he dared sing for the slave
When to look but a protest in silence was brave;
All honor and praise to the women and men
Who spoke out for the dumb and the downtrodden then!   195
It needs not to name them, already for each
I see History preparing the statue and niche;
They were harsh, but shall *you* be so shocked at hard words
Who have beaten your pruning-hooks up into swords,
Whose rewards and hurrahs men are surer to gain   200
By the reaping of men and of women than grain?
Why should *you* stand aghast at their fierce wordy war, if
Your scalp one another for Bank or for Tariff?[5]
Your calling them cut-throats and knaves all day long
Doesn't prove that the use of hard language is wrong;   205
While the World's heart beats quicker to think of such men
As signed Tyranny's doom with a bloody steel-pen,
While on Fourth-of-Julys beardless orators fright one
With hints at Harmodius and Aristogeiton,[6]
You need not look shy at your sisters and brothers   210
Who stab with sharp words for the freedom of others;—
No, a wreath, twine a wreath for the loyal and true
Who, for sake of the many, dared stand with the few,

minstrel, who led the charge of William's Norman horsemen at the battle of Hastings (October 14, 1066), singing the *Song of Roland,* and fell before the English forces.

1. *Anne haec * * * Vestis filii tui. Cf.* Genesis xxxvii: 32: "Is this thy son's coat, or not," asked by Joseph's brothers of his father Jacob.

2. George Fox (1624–1691), founder of the Society of Friends, was famous for his leather breeches.

3. The Philistine giant, slain by a stone from David's slingshot. *Cf.* I Samuel xvii: 49.

4. A fountain on Mount Parnassus, sacred to Apollo, god of poetry and music.

5. Two of the primary political issues of the time were the status of the Bank of the United States and the question of whether the tariff should be high or low.

6. Harmodius and Aristogeiton (died 514 B.C.), assassins of the Athenian tyrant Hipparchus, honored as heroes after their execution.

Not of blood-spattered laurel for enemies braved,
But of broad, peaceful oak-leaves for citizens saved!   215

* * *

"There is Hawthorne, with genius so shrinking and rare
That you hardly at first see the strength that is there;
A frame so robust, with a nature so sweet,
So earnest, so graceful, so lithe and so fleet,
Is worth a descent from Olympus to meet;   220
'Tis as if a rough oak that for ages had stood,
With his gnarled bony branches like ribs of the wood,
Should bloom, after cycles of struggle and scathe,
With a single anemone trembly and rathe;
His strength is so tender, his wildness so meek,   225
That a suitable parallel sets one to seek,—
He's a John Bunyan Fouqué, a Puritan Tieck;[7]
When Nature was shaping him, clay was not granted
For making so full-sized a man as she wanted,
So, to fill out her model, a little she spared   230
From some finer-grained stuff for a woman prepared,
And she could not have hit a more excellent plan
For making him fully and perfectly man.

* * *

"Here's Cooper, who's written six volumes to show
He's as good as a lord: well, let's grant that he's so;   235
If a person prefer that description of praise,
Why, a coronet's certainly cheaper than bays;
But he need take no pains to convince us he's not
(As his enemies say) the American Scott.[8]
Choose any twelve men, and let C. read aloud   240
That one of his novels of which he's most proud,
And I'd lay any bet that, without ever quitting
Their box, they'd be all, to a man, for acquitting.
He has drawn you one character, though, that is new,
One wildflower he's plucked that is wet with the dew   245
Of this fresh Western world, and, the thing not to mince,
He has done naught but copy it ill ever since;
His Indians, with proper respect be it said,
Are just Natty Bumppo[9] daubed over with red,

7. Lowell here exemplifies the antithetical combination of moral severity and romantic imagining which he finds in Hawthorne—John Bunyan (1628–1688) was the Puritan author of *Pilgrim's Progress* (1678); Friedrich Heinrich Karl La Motte-Fouqué (1777–1843) was the German author of romantic *Undine* (1811); and Ludwig Tieck (1773–1853) was a romantic German novelist and dramatist.
8. Lowell refers above (l. 235) to the alleged aristocratic bias of Cooper's writings on American democracy; and here, to the extravagant rating of his novels with those of the British romancer Sir Walter Scott (1771–1832).
9. The indefatigable and resourceful hero of the *Leather-Stocking Tales*.

And his very Long Toms[1] are the same useful Nat,   250
Rigged up in duck pants and a sou'-wester hat,
(Though once in a Coffin, a good chance was found
To have slipt the old fellow away underground).
All his other men-figures are clothes upon sticks,
The *dernière chemise*[2] of a man in a fix,   255
(As a captain besieged, when his garrison's small,
Sets up caps upon poles to be seen o'er the wall);
And the women he draws from one model don't vary,
All sappy as maples and flat as a prairie.
When a character's wanted, he goes to the task   260
As a cooper would do in composing a cask;
He picks out the staves, of their qualities heedful,
Just hoops them together as tight as is needful,
And, if the best fortune should crown the attempt, he
Has made at the most something wooden and empty.   265

"Don't suppose I would underrate Cooper's abilities;
If I thought you'd do that, I should feel very ill at ease;
The men who have given to *one* character life
And objective existence are not very rife;
You may number them all, both prose-writers and singers,   270
Without overrunning the bounds of your fingers,
And Natty won't go to oblivion quicker
Than Adams the parson or Primrose the vicar.[3]

"There is one thing in Cooper I like, too, and that is
That on manners he lectures his countrymen gratis,   275
Not precisely so either, because, for a rarity,
He is paid for his tickets in unpopularity.
Now he may overcharge his American pictures,
But you'll grant there's a good deal of truth in his strictures;
And I honor the man who is willing to sink   280
Half his present repute for the freedom to think,
And, when he has thought, be his cause strong or weak,
Will risk t'other half for the freedom to speak,
Caring naught for what vengeance the mob has in store,
Let that mob be the upper ten thousand or lower.   285

"There are truths you Americans need to be told,
And it never'll refute them to swagger and scold;
John Bull, looking o'er the Atlantic, in choler
At your aptness for trade, says you worship the dollar;

---

1. Long Tom Coffin, the American
sailor in *The Pilot* (1823).
2. Last shirt.
3. Parson Adams in Henry Fielding's
Joseph Andrews (1742), and Dr. Primrose in Oliver Goldsmith's *Vicar of
Wakefield* (1766), both memorably
realistic characters.

But to scorn such eye-dollar-try's what very few do, 290
And John goes to that church as often as you do.
No matter what John says, don't try to outcrow him,
'Tis enough to go quietly on and outgrow him;
Like most fathers, Bull hates to see Number One
Displacing himself in the mind of his son, 295
And detests the same faults in himself he'd neglected
When he sees them again in his child's glass reflected;
To love one another you're too like by half.
If he is a bull, you're a pretty stout calf,
And tear your own pasture for naught but to show 300
What a nice pair of horns you're beginning to grow.

"There are one or two things I should just like to hint,
For you don't often get the truth told you in print;
The most of you (this is what strikes all beholders)
Have a mental and physical stoop in the shoulders; 305
Though you ought to be free as the winds and the waves,
You've the gait and the manners of run-away slaves;
Though you brag of your New World, you don't half believe in it,
And as much of the Old as is possible weave in it;
Your goddess of freedom, a tight, buxom girl, 310
With lips like a cherry and teeth like a pearl,
With eyes bold as Herë's,[4] and hair floating free,
And full of the sun as the spray of the sea,
Who can sing at a husking or romp at a shearing,
Who can trip through the forests alone without fearing, 315
Who can drive home the cows with a song through the grass,
Keeps glancing aside into Europe's cracked glass,
Hides her red hands in gloves, pinches up her lithe waist,
And makes herself wretched with transmarine taste;
She loses her fresh country charm when she takes 320
Any mirror except her own rivers and lakes.

"You steal Englishmen's books[5] and think Englishmen's thought,
With their salt on her tail your wild eagle is caught;
Your literature suits its each whisper and motion
To what will be thought of it over the ocean; 325
The cast clothes of Europe your statesmanship tries
And mumbles again the old blarneys and lies;—
Forget Europe wholly, your veins throb with blood,
To which the dull current in hers is but mud;
Let her sneer, let her say your experiment fails, 330
In her voice there's a tremble e'en now while she rails,

4. Herë, or Hera, Olympian goddess and the wife of Zeus.

5. At this time foreign authors could not copyright their works in the United States.

And your shore will soon be in the nature of things
Covered thick with gilt driftwood of castaway kings,
Where alone, as it were in a Longfellow's Waif[6]
Her fugitive pieces will find themselves safe.   335
O my friends, thank your God, if you have one, that he
'Twixt the Old World and you set the gulf of a sea;
Be strong-backed, brown-handed, upright as your pines,
By the scale of a hemisphere shape your designs,
Be true to yourselves and this new nineteenth age,   340
As a statue by Powers, or a picture by Page,[7]
Plow, sail, forge, build, carve, paint, all things make new,
To your own New-World instincts contrive to be true,
Keep your ears open wide to the Future's first call,
Be whatever you will, but yourselves first of all,   345
Stand fronting the dawn on Toil's heaven-scaling peaks,
And become my new race of more practical Greeks.—
Hem! your likeness at present, I shudder to tell o't,
Is that you have your slaves, and the Greek had his helot."[8]

* * *

"There comes Poe, with his raven, like Barnaby Rudge,[9]   350
Three-fifths of him genius and two-fifths sheer fudge,
Who talks like a book of iambs and pentameters,
In a way to make people of common sense damn metres,
Who has written some things quite the best of their kind,
But the heart somehow seems all squeezed out by the mind,   355
Who— But hey-day! What's this? Messieurs Mathews[1] and Poe,
You mustn't fling mud-balls at Longfellow so,
Does it make a man worse that his character's such
As to make his friends love him (as you think) too much?
Why, there is not a bard at this moment alive   360
More willing than he that his fellows should thrive;
While you are abusing him thus, even now
He would help either one of you out of a slough;
You may say that he's smooth and all that till you're hoarse,
But remember that elegance also is force;   365
After polishing granite as much as you will,
The heart keeps its tough old persistency still;
Deduct all you can, *that* still keeps you at bay;

6. An anthology of poetry published by Longfellow (1845).
7. Hiram Powers (1805–1873), sculptor of Webster, Calhoun, and Jackson; and William Page (1811–1885), painter of American historical scenes.
8. A Spartan serf, or bondsman, whose condition was superior to the American slave's only in that he could not be sold and could be freed by the state.
9. The central character in Dickens' *Barnaby Rudge* (1841) owned a raven.
1. Cornelius Mathews (1817–1889), editor, novelist, and magazine writer who, like Poe, criticized Longfellow's poetic form and subject matter.

Why, he'll live till men weary of Collins and Gray.[2]
I'm not over-fond of Greek metres in English,[3]   370
To me rhyme's a gain, so it be not too jinglish,
And your modern hexameter verses are no more
Like Greek ones than sleek Mr. Pope[4] is like Homer;
As the roar of the sea to the coo of a pigeon is,
So, compared to your moderns, sounds old Melesigenes;[5]   375
I may be too partial, the reason, perhaps, o't is
That I've heard the old blind man[6] recite his own rhapsodies,
And my ear with that music impregnate may be,
Like the poor exiled shell with the soul of the sea,
Or as one can't bear Strauss[7] when his nature is cloven   380
To its deeps within deeps by the stroke of Beethoven;[8]
But, set that aside, and 'tis truth that I speak,
Had Theocritus[9] written in English, not Greek,
I believe that his exquisite sense would scarce change a line
In that rare, tender, virgin-like pastoral Evangeline.   385
That's not ancient nor modern, its place is apart
Where time has no sway, in the realm of pure Art,
'Tis a shrine of retreat from Earth's hubbub and strife
As quiet and chaste as the author's own life.

* * *

"What! Irving? thrice welcome, warm heart and fine brain,   390
You bring back the happiest spirit from Spain,[1]
And the gravest sweet humor, that ever were there
Since Cervantes[2a] met death in his gentle despair;
Nay, don't be embarrassed, nor look so beseeching,
I sha'n't run directly against my own preaching,   395
And, having just laughed at their Raphaels and Dantes,
Go to setting you up beside matchless Cervantes;
But allow me to speak what I honestly feel,—
To a true poet-heart add the fun of Dick Steele,
Throw in all of Addison,[3a] *minus* the chill,   400

2. William Collins (1721–1759), author of odes and elegies; Thomas Gray (1716–1771), author of "Elegy written in a Country Churchyard" (1751).
3. Referring to Longfellow's use of the hexameter in *Evangeline*.
4. Alexander Pope (1688–1744) used the heroic couplet in his translation of the *Iliad* (1715–1720), achieving the spirit more of eighteenth-century terseness than of Homeric grandeur.
5. *I.e.*, Melos-born, referring to Homer; his birthplace is actually uncertain.
6. Homer.
7. Johann Strauss (1804–1849), composer of waltzes and polkas.
8. Ludwig van Beethoven (1770–

1827), composer of symphonies and concertos.
9. Greek pastoral poet (third century B.C.).
1. Washington Irving's *Alhambra* (1832) and histories were America's literary introduction to Spain.
2a. Miguel de Cervantes Saavedra (1547–1616), whose *Don Quixote* (1605, 1615) and other works gently ridiculed and romanticized Spanish life.
3a. Sir Richard Steele (1672–1729), essayist and dramatist, and Joseph Addison (1672–1719), writer and statesman, who collaborated on the most famous of the early eighteenth-century periodicals, the *Spectator*.

With the whole of that partnership's stock and good-will,
Mix well, and while stirring, hum o'er, as a spell,
The fine *old* English Gentleman,[4] simmer it well,
Sweeten just to your own private liking, then strain,   405
That only the finest and clearest remain,
Let it stand out of doors till a soul it receives
From the warm lazy sun loitering down through green leaves,
And you'll find a choice nature, not wholly deserving
A name either English or Yankee,—just Irving."   410

* * *

"There's Holmes, who is matchless among you for wit;
A Leyden-jar[5] always full-charged, from which flit
The electrical tingles of hit after hit;
In long poems 'tis painful sometimes, and invites
A thought of the way the new Telegraph[6] writes,   415
Which pricks down its little sharp sentences spitefully
As if you got more than you'd title to rightfully,
And you find yourself hoping its wild father Lightning
Would flame in for a second and give you a fright'ning.
He has perfect sway of what I call a sham metre,   420
But many admire it, the English pentameter,
And Campbell,[7] I think, wrote most commonly worse,
With less nerve, swing, and fire in the same kind of verse,
Nor e'er achieved aught in't so worthy of praise
As the tribute of Holmes to the grand *Marseillaise*.[8]   425
You went crazy last year over Bulwer's New Timon;[9]—
Why, if B., to the day of his dying, should rhyme on,
Heaping verses on verses and tomes upon tomes,
He could ne'er reach the best point and vigor of Holmes.
His are just the fine hands, too, to weave you a lyric   430
Full of fancy, fun, feeling, or spiced with satiric
In a measure so kindly you doubt if the toes
That are trodden upon are your own or your foes'.

"There is Lowell, who's striving Parnassus to climb
With a whole bale of *isms* tied together with rhyme,   435
He might get on alone, spite of brambles and boulders,
But he can't with that bundle he has on his shoulders,

4. "The English Country Gentleman," an essay by Irving from *Bracebridge Hall*.
5. One of the earliest forms of electrical condensers.
6. The Morse code, demonstrated by its inventor, Samuel F. B. Morse (1791–1872), in 1844, supplanted older forms of telegraphic communication with its system of dots and dashes.
7. Thomas Campbell (1777–1844),

British poet, whose patriotic verses resemble in style Holmes's early attempts.
8. *Cf*. Holmes's "Poetry: A Metrical Essay * * * 1836," II, v, in which the patriot watched as "the morning gales / Swept through the world the war-song of the Marseilles!"
9. *The New Timon: A Romance of London* (1846), by Edward George Earle Lytton Bulwer-Lytton (1803–1873).

The top of the hill he will ne'er come nigh reaching
Till he learns the distinction 'twix singing and preaching;
His lyre has some chords that would ring pretty well,   440
But he'd rather by half make a drum of the shell,
And rattle away till he's old as Methusalem,[1]
At the head of a march to the last new Jerusalem."

* * *

1848

The Present Crisis[2]

When a deed is done for Freedom, through the broad earth's
    aching breast
Runs a thrill of joy prophetic, trembling on from east to west,
And the slave, where'er he cowers, feels the soul within him climb
To the awful verge of manhood, as the energy sublime
Of a century bursts full-blossomed on the thorny stem of Time.   5

Through the walls of hut and palace shoots the instantaneous
    throe,
When the travail of the Ages wrings earth's systems to and fro;
At the birth of each new Era, with a recognizing start,
Nation wildly looks at nation, standing with mute lips apart,
And glad Truth's yet mightier man-child leaps beneath the Future's
    heart.   10

So the Evil's triumph sendeth, with a terror and a chill,
Under continent to continent, the sense of coming ill,
And the slave, where'er he cowers, feels his sympathies with God
In hot tear-drops ebbing earthward, to be drunk up by the sod,
Till a corpse crawls round unburied, delving in the nobler clod.   15

For mankind are one in spirit, and an instinct bears along,
Round the earth's electric circle, the swift flash of right or wrong;
Whether conscious or unconscious, yet Humanity's vast frame
Through its ocean-sundered fibres feels the gush of joy or shame;—
In the gain or loss of one race all the rest have equal claim.   20

Once to every man and nation comes the moment to decide,
In the strife of Truth with Falsehood, for the good or evil side;

1. *Cf.* Genesis v: 27: "And all the days
of Methuselah were nine hundred sixty
and nine years * * * "
2. Evoked by the controversy as to
whether Texas should be annexed, permitting further extension of slavery,
Lowell's passionate plea for the remembrance of the spirit of freedom of the
Pilgrims was first published in the Boston *Courier* for December 11, 1844, and
was collected in *Poems: Second Series*
(1848). Beyond its timely comment on
slavery the poem extends its purpose to
urge the overthrow of evil and the ultimate victory of Humanity; for this
reason, it was for many years a familiar
clarion of American democratic faith on
public occasions.

Some great cause, God's new Messiah, offering each the bloom or
 blight,
Parts the goats upon the left hand, and the sheep upon the right,[3]
And the choice goes by forever 'twixt that darkness and that light.

Hast thou chosen, O my people, on whose party thou shalt stand,
Ere the Doom from its worn sandals shakes the dust against our
 land?[4]   27
Though the cause of Evil prosper, yet 'tis Truth alone is strong,
And, albeit she wander outcast now, I see around her throng
Troops of beautiful, tall angels, to enshield her from all wrong. 30

Backward look across the ages and the beacon-moments see,
That, like peaks of some sunk continent, jut through Oblivion's sea;
Not an ear in court or market for the low foreboding cry
Of those Crises, God's stern winnowers, from whose feet earth's
 chaff must fly;
Never shows the choice momentous till the judgment hath passed
 by.   35

Careless seems the great Avenger;[5] history's pages but record
One death-grapple in the darkness 'twixt old systems and the Word;[6]
Truth forever on the scaffold, Wrong forever on the throne,—
Yet that scaffold sways the future, and, behind the dim unknown,
Standeth God within the shadow, keeping watch above his own.   40

We see dimly in the Present what is small and what is great,
Slow of faith how weak an arm may turn the iron helm of fate,
But the soul is still oracular; amid the market's din,
List the ominous stern whisper from the Delphic cave[7] within,—
"They enslave their children's children who make compromise with
 sin."   45

Slavery, the earth-born Cyclops,[8] fellest of the giant brood,
Sons of brutish Force and Darkness, who have drenched the earth
 with blood,
Famished in his self-made desert, blinded by our purer day,
Gropes in yet unblasted regions for his miserable prey;—
Shall we guide his gory fingers where our helpless children play? 50

Then to side with Truth is noble when we share her wretched crust,
Ere her cause bring fame and profit, and 'tis prosperous to be just;
Then it is the brave man chooses, while the coward stands aside,

---

3. *Cf.* Matthew xxv: 31–33.
4. *Cf.* Luke ix: 5.
5. *I.e.*, God. *Cf.* I Thessalonians iv: 6.
6. *I.e.*, Christ, as the personification of
the word of God. *Cf.* John i: 14.
7. The grotto on Mount Parnassus from
which arose the mystical vapor inhaled
by the priestess who then prophesied.
8. In mythology, the one-eyed Cyclopes
were the offspring of Heaven and Earth,
representing the terrors of lightning and
thunder—or disaster.

Doubting in his abject spirit, till his Lord is crucified,
And the multitude make virtue of the faith they had denied.   55

Count me o'er earth's chosen heroes,—they were souls that stood
    alone,
While the men they agonized for hurled the contumelious stone,
Stood serene, and down the future saw the golden beam incline
To the side of perfect justice, mastered by their faith divine,
By one man's plain truth to manhood and to God's supreme design.

By the light of burning heretics Christ's bleeding feet I track,   61
Toiling up new Calvaries ever with the cross that turns not back,
And these mounts of anguish number how each generation learned
One new word of that grand *Credo* which in prophet-hearts hath
    burned
Since the first man stood God-conquered with his face to heaven
    upturned.
       65

For Humanity sweeps onward: where to-day the martyr stands,
On the morrow crouches Judas[9] with the silver in his hands;
Far in front the cross stands ready and the crackling fagots burn,
While the hooting mob of yesterday in silent awe return
To glean up the scattered ashes into History's golden urn.   70

'Tis as easy to be heroes as to sit the idle slaves
Of a legendary virtue carved upon our fathers' graves,
Worshippers of light ancestral make the present light a crime;—
Was the Mayflower launched by cowards, steered by men behind
    their time?
Turn those tracks toward Past or Future, that make Plymouth
    Rock sublime?
       75

They were men of present valor, stalwart old iconoclasts,
Unconvinced by axe or gibbet that all virtue was the Past's;
But we make their truth our falsehood, thinking that hath made us
    free,
Hoarding it in mouldly parchments, while our tender spirits flee
The rude grasp of that great Impulse which drove them across the
    sea.
       80

They have rights who dare maintain them; we are traitors to our
    sires,
Smothering in their holy ashes Freedom's new-lit altar fires;
Shall we make their creed our jailer? Shall we, in our haste to slay,
From the tombs of the old prophets steal the funeral lamps away
To light up the martyr-fagots round the prophets of to-day?   85

9. Judas, one of the twelve disciples, who betrayed Christ for thirty pieces of silver.
Cf. Matthew xxvii: 3.

New occasions teach new duties; Time makes ancient good un-
 couth;
They must upward still, and onward, who would keep abreast of
 Truth;
Lo, before us gleam her camp-fires! we ourselves must Pilgrims be,
Launch our Mayflower, and steer boldly through the desperate
 winter sea,   89
Nor attempt the Future's portal with the Past's blood-rusted key.

              1844, 1848

From The Biglow Papers, First Series[1]

No. I: A Letter

FROM MR. EZEKIEL BIGLOW OF JAALAM TO THE HON. JOSEPH T.
BUCKINGHAM, EDITOR OF THE BOSTON COURIER, ENCLOSING A
POEM OF HIS SON, MR. HOSEA BIGLOW

              JAYLEM, june 1846.

MISTER EDDYTER:—
 Our Hosea wuz down to Boston last week, and he see a crucTin
Sarjunt[2] a struttin round as popler as a hen with 1 chicking, with 2
fellers a drummin and fifin arter him like all nater. the sarjunt he
thout Hosea hed n't gut his i teeth cut cos he looked a kindo's
though he'd jest com down,[3] so he cal'lated to hook him in, but
Hosy wood n't take none o' his sarse[4] for all he hed much as 20
Rooster's tales stuck onto his hat and eenamost enuf brass a-bobbin
up and down on his shoulders and figureed onto his coat and trousis,

1. On June 17, 1846, in the Boston
Courier, there appeared a letter to the
editor, supposedly from an up-country
farmer enclosing a poem written by his
son after a disturbing trip to Boston.
In so unassuming and disguised a manner, Lowell began *The Biglow Papers*,
unsurpassed in American literature for
political and social satire, the authentic
use of Yankee idiom, and the skillful
blending of sincerity and broad humor.
Provoked by the poet's belief that the
Mexican War was a threat to domestic
unity and a political maneuver to extend slavery territory, the poems appeared in the Boston *Courier* and the
National Anti-Slavery Standard before
their publication as *The Biglow Papers*
in 1848. "Edited" by the pedantic "Rev.
Homer Wilbur," who blithely wrote his
own press notices, affixed a scholarly
title page and strewed Latin quotations through the volume, the poems
indicate the New England character of
Hosea Biglow—"homely common-sense
vivified and heated by conscience"—
and of Birdofredum Sawin, the "un-

moral" foil for Hosea, not here represented.
 The early years of the Civil War
brought Biglow and Sawin into print
again, as staunch and caustic supporters
of the Union, in the *Atlantic Monthly*,
and in 1862 *The Biglow Papers, Second
Series* was published in England. In the
introduction to the American edition of
1867, Lowell described the genesis of
the *Papers*, adding a masterly defense
and explanation of the Yankee dialect.
The notes signed "H.W." are those of
the supposititious editor, "Homer Wilbur."
2. President Polk, authorized by an
act of May 13, 1846, called out fifty
thousand volunteers, and in Massachusetts, as elsewhere, the recruiting
sergeants used every inducement to meet
their quota.
3. *I.e.*, "just come down from the country."
4. "*sarse*: abuse, impertinence" [Low-
ell's note; like other definitions that
follow, this is taken from the glossary
of the 1848 edition].

let alone wut nater hed sot in his featers, to make a 6 pounder out on.

wal, Hosea he com home considerabal riled, and arter I'd gone to bed I heern Him a-thrashin round like a short-tailed Bull in fli-time. The old Woman ses she to me ses she, Zekle, ses she, our Hosee's gut the chollery or suthin anuther ses she, don't you Bee skeered, ses I, he's oney amakin pottery[5] ses i, he's ollers on hand at that ere busynes like Da & martin,[6] and shure enuf, cum mornin, Hosy he cum down stares full chizzle,[7] hare on eend and cote tales flyin, and sot rite of to go reed his varses to Parson Wilbur bein he hain't aney grate shows o' book larnin himself, bimeby he cum back and sed the parson wuz dreffle tickled with 'em as i hoop you will Be, and said they wuz True grit.

Hosea ses 't ain't hardly fair to call 'em his'n now, cos the parson kind o' slicked off sum o' the last varses, but he told Hosee he did n't want to put his ore in to tetch to the Rest on 'em, bein they wuz verry well As thay wuz, and then Hosy ses he sed suthin an-uther about Simplex Mundishes[8] or sum sech feller, but I guess Hosea kind o' did n't hear him, for I never hearn o' nobody o' that name in this villadge, and I've lived here man and boy 76 year cum next tater diggin, and thair ain't no wheres a kitting spryer 'n I be.

If you print 'em I wish you'd jest let folks know who hosy's father is, cos my ant Keziah used to say it's nater to be curus ses she, she ain't livin though and he's a likely kind o' lad.

                                                          EZEKIEL BIGLOW.

> Thrash away, you'll *hev* to rattle
>   On them kittle-drums o' yourn,—
> 't ain't a knowin' kind o' cattle
>   Thet is ketched with mouldy corn;
> Put in stiff, you fifer feller,
>   Let folks see how spry you be,—   5
> Guess you'll toot till you are yeller
>   'fore you git ahold o' me!
>
> Thet air flag's a leetle rotten,
>   Hope it ain't your Sunday's best;
> Fact! it takes a sight o' cotton[9]   10
>   To stuff out a soger's[1] chest:
> Sence we farmers hev to pay fer 't,
>   Ef you must wear humps like these,

5. *"Aut insanit, aut versos facit.—H.W."* ["Either he is mad, or he is making poetry."]

6. Makers of shoe blacking, Day and Martin advertised their product in verse.

7. *I.e.*, full of grit; determined.

8. Hosea's misunderstanding of the parson's criticism: *simplex mundis*, "simpleton of the world."

9. A reference to the staple of southern economy.

1. *"sogerin',* soldiering: a barbarous amusement common among men in the savage state." [Lowell's note.]

S'posin' you should try salt hay fer 't,   15
    It would du ez slick ez grease.

'T would n't suit them Southun fellers,
    They're a dreffle graspin' set,
We must ollers blow the bellers
    Wen they want their irons het;   20
May be it's all right ez preachin',
    But *my* narves it kind o' grates,
Wen I see the overreachin'
    O' them nigger-drivin' States.

Them thet rule us, them slave-traders,   25
    Hain't they cut a thunderin' swarth
(Helped by Yankee renegaders),
    Thru the vartu o' the North!
We begin to think it's nater
    To take sarse an' not be riled;—   30
Who 'd expect to see a tater
    All on eend at bein' biled?

Ez fer war, I call it murder,—
    There you hev it plain an' flat;
I don't want to go no furder   35
    Than my Testyment fer that;
God hez sed so plump an' fairly,
    It's ez long ez it is broad,
An' you've gut to git up airly
    Ef you want to take in God.   40

'T ain't your eppyletts an' feathers
    Make the thing a grain more right;
't ain't afollerin' your bell-wethers[2]
    Will excuse ye in His sight;
Ef you take a sword an' dror it,   45
    An' go stick a feller thru,
Guv'ment ain't to answer for it,
    God'll send the bill to you.

Wut's the use o' meetin'-goin'
    Every Sabbath, wet or dry,   50
Ef it's right to go amowin'
    Feller-men like oats an' rye?
I dunno but wut it's pooty
    Trainin' round in bobtail coats,—
But it's curus Christian dooty   55
    This 'ere cuttin' folk's throats.

2. The male sheep with a bell on his neck, leading the flock.

They may talk o' Freedom's airy[3]
   Tell they're pupple in the face,—
It's a grand gret cemetary
   Fer the barthrights of our race;   60
They jest want this Californy
   So's to lug new slave-states in[4]
To abuse ye, an' to scorn ye,
   An' to plunder ye like sin.

Ain't it cute to see a Yankee   65
   Take sech everlastin' pains,
All to git the Devil's thankee
   Helpin' on 'em weld their chains?
Wy, it's jest ez clear ez figgers,
   Clear ez one an' one make two,   70
Chaps thet make black slaves o' niggers
   Want to make wite slaves o' you.

Tell ye jest the eend I've come to
   Arter cipherin' plaguy smart,
An' it makes a handy sum, tu,   75
   Any gump[5] could larn by heart;
Laborin' man an' laborin' woman
   Hev one glory an' one shame.
Ev'ythin' thet's done inhuman
   Injers all on 'em the same.   80

'T aint by turnin' out to hack folks
   You're agoin' to git your right,
Nor by lookin' down on black folks
   Coz you're put upon by wite;
Slavery ain't o' nary color,   85
   't ain't the hide thet makes it wus;
All it keers fer in a feller
   's jest to make him fill its pus.[6]

Want to tackle *me* in, du ye?
   I expect you'll hev to wait;
Wen cold lead puts daylight thru ye   90
   You'll begin to kal'late;[7]
S'pose the crows wun't fall to pickin'
   All the carkiss from your bones,
Coz you helped to give a lickin'   95
   To them poor half-Spanish drones?

3. "*airy:* area" [Lowell's note].
4. The Compromise of 1850 settled the doubt as to California's status by admitting her as a free state.
5. "*gump:* a foolish fellow, a dullard" [Lowell's note].
6. "*pus:* purse" [Lowell's note].
7. Calculate; *i.e.,* consider.

Jest go home an' ask our Nancy
    Wether I'd be sech a goose
Ez to jine ye,—guess you'd fancy
    The etarnal bung wuz loose!   100
She wants me fer home consumption,
    Let alone the hay's to mow,—
Ef you're arter folks o' gumption,
    You've a darned long row to hoe.

Take them editors thet's crowin'   105
    Like a cockerel three months old,—
Don't ketch any on 'em going',
    Though they *be* so blasted bold;
Ain't they a prime lot o' fellers?
    'Fore they think on 't guess they'll sprout   110
(Like a peach thet's got the yellers),[8]
    With the meanness bustin' out.

Wal, go 'long to help 'em stealin'
    Bigger pens to cram with slaves,
Help the men thet's ollers dealin'   115
    Insults on your fathers' graves;
Help the strong to grind the feeble,
    Help the many agin' the few,
Help the men thet call your people
    Witewashed slaves an' peddlin' crew!   120

Massachusetts, God forgive her,
    She's akneelin' with the rest,[9]
She, thet ough' to ha' clung ferever
    In her grand old eagle-nest;
She thet ough' to stand so fearless   125
    W'ile the wracks are round her hurled,
Holdin' up a beacon peerless
    To the oppressed of all the world!

Hain't they sold your colored seamen?
    Hain't they made your env'ys w'iz?[1]   130
W*ut*'ll make ye act like freemen?
    W*ut*'ll git your dander riz?
Come, I'll tell ye wut I'm thinkin'
    Is our dooty in this fix,

8. A disease of peach trees resulting in no fruit.
9. The seven representatives from Massachusetts had voted for the bill recognizing a state of war with Mexico on May 11, 1846, and allocating funds for military use.

1. Samuel Hoar and George Hubbard had been sent south to protest the capture and sale of free colored citizens of Massachusetts; as "env'ys," or envoys, they had been made to "w'iz" (whiz), *i.e.*, to leave the South.

They'd ha' done 't ez quick ez winkin'   135
    In the days o' seventy-six.

Clang the bells in every steeple,
    Call all true men to disown
The tradoocers of our people,
    The enslavers o' their own;   140
Let our dear old Bay State proudly
    Put the trumpet to her mouth,
Let her ring this messidge loudly
    In the ears of all the South:—

"I'll return ye good fer evil   145
    Much ez we frail mortils can,
But I wun't go help the Devil
    Makin' man the cus o' man;
Call me coward, call me traitor,
    Jest ez suits your mean idees,—   150
Here I stand a tyrant-hater,
    An' the friend o' God an' Peace!"

Ef I'd *my* way I hed ruther
    We should go to work an' part,
They take one way, we take t'other,   155
    Guess it would n't break my heart;
Man hed ough' to put asunder
    Them thet God has noways jined;
An' I should n't gretly wonder
    Ef there's thousands o' my mind.   160

[The first recruiting sergeant on record I conceive to have been that individual[2] who is mentioned in the Book of Job as *going to and fro in the earth, and walking up and down in it.* Bishop Latimer will have him to have been a bishop,[3] but to me that other calling would appear more congenial. The sect of Cainites[4] is not yet extinct, who esteemed the first-born of Adam to be the most worthy, not only because of that privilege of primogeniture, but inasmuch as he was able to overcome and slay his younger brother. That was a wise saying of the famous Marquis Pescara[5] to the Papal Legate, that *it was impossible for men to serve Mars and Christ at the same time.* Yet in time past the profession of arms was judged

2. *I.e.*, Satan.
3. Hugh Latimer, bishop of Worcester (1485?–1555), defender of the English Reformation, martyred with Nicholas Ridley in the reign of Queen Mary. In his famous sermon "Of the Plough" (January 17, 1548), he ascribed to the English bishops the characteristics of

Satan here referred to (*cf.* Job i: 7).
4. A second-century sect honoring characters represented as evil in the Old Testament.
5. Fernando Francisco de Ávalos, marqués de Pescara (1489–1525), Spanish commander in chief of Charles V.

to be κατ' ἐξοχήν[6] that of a gentleman, nor does this opinion want for strenuous upholders even in our day. Must we suppose, then, that the profession of Christianity was only intended for losels, or, at best, to afford an opening for plebeian ambition? Or shall we hold with that nicely metaphysical Pomeranian, Captain Vratz, who was Count Königsmark's chief instrument in the murder of Mr. Thynne,[7] that the Scheme of Salvation has been arranged with an especial eye to the necessities of the upper classes, and that "God would consider *a gentleman* and deal with him suitably to the condition and profession he had placed him in"? It may be said of us all, *Exemplo plus quam ratione vivimus.*[8]—H. W.]

No. III: What Mr. Robinson Thinks[9]

[A few remarks on the following verses will not be out of place. The satire in them was not meant to have any personal, but only a general, application. Of the gentleman upon whose letter they were intended as a commentary Mr. Biglow had never heard, till he saw the letter itself. The position of the satirist is oftentimes one which he would not have chosen, had the election been left to himself. In attacking bad principles, he is obliged to select some individual who has made himself their exponent, and in whom they are impersonate, to the end that what he says may not, through ambiguity, be dissipated *tenues in auras.*[1] For what says Seneca? *Longum iter per praecepta, breve et efficace per exempla.*[2] A bad principle is comparatively harmless while it continues to be an abstraction, nor can the general mind comprehend it fully till it is printed in that large type which all men can read at sight, namely, the life and character, the sayings and doings, of particular persons. It is one of the cunningest fetches of Satan, that he never exposes himself directly to our arrows, but, still dodging behind this neighbor or that acquaintance, compels us to wound him through them, if at all. He holds our affections as hostages, the while he patches up a

---

6. Particularly.
7. Captain Vratz was a follower of a Swedish nobleman, Count John Philip Königsmarck, who was in love with the fifteen-year-old Elizabeth, heiress of the Percy estates and wife of Thomas Thynne. Foiled in attempts to engage Thynne in a duel, Vratz and two companions ambushed and mortally wounded him on February 12, 1682. The subsequent trial, a sensation in England, resulted in the conviction and execution of Vratz and a suspiciously easy exoneration of Königsmarck, who had powerful friends at court.
8. We live more by example than by reason.
9. The campaign for governor in Massachusetts in 1847 occasioned Hosea's third excursion into satiric verse, pub-

lished first in the Boston *Courier* for November 2, 1847. John P. Robinson, a Whig leader, upset party expectations by announcing that he was supporting General Caleb Cushing ("Gineral C"), commander of Massachusetts' troops in the Mexican War, who ran for governor on the Democratic ticket. George N. Briggs ("Guvener B"), elected Whig governor in 1844, easily defeated his opponent in the predominantly anti-Democratic state. Homer Wilbur's detached apology for Hosea's satire only points up its vitriol.
1. Into thin air.
2. "It is a long way by means of precept, but a short and sure one by example"—one of the maxims of Lucius Annaeus Seneca (4 B.C.?–65 A.D.), Roman dramatist and philosopher.

truce with our conscience.

Meanwhile, let us not forget that the aim of the true satirist is not to be severe upon persons, but only upon falsehood, and, as Truth and Falsehood start from the same point, and sometimes even go along together for a little way, his business is to follow the path of the latter after it diverges, and to show her floundering in the bog at the end of it. Truth is quite beyond the reach of satire. There is so brave a simplicity in her, that she can no more be made ridiculous than an oak or a pine. The danger of the satirist is, that continual use may deaden his sensibility to the force of language. He becomes more and more liable to strike harder than he knows or intends. He may be careful to put on his boxing-gloves, and yet forget that, the older they grow, the more plainly may the knuckles inside be felt. Moreover, in the heat of contest, the eye is insensibly drawn to the crown of victory, whose tawdry tinsel glitters through that dust of the ring which obscures Truth's wreath of simple leaves. I have sometimes thought that my young friend, Mr. Biglow, needed a monitory hand laid on his arm,—*aliquid sufflaminandus erat*.[3] I have never thought it good husbandry to water the tender plants of reform with *aqua fortis*,[4] yet where so much is to do in the beds, he were a sorry gardener who should wage a whole day's war with an iron scuffle on those ill weeds that make the garden-walks of life unsightly, when a sprinkle of Attic salt will wither them up. *Est ars etiam maledicendi*,[5] says Scaliger, and truly it is a hard thing to say where the graceful gentleness of the lamb merges in downright sheepishness. We may conclude with worthy and wise Dr. Fuller,[6] that "one may be a lamb in private wrongs, but in hearing general affronts to goodness they are asses which are not lions."— H. W.]

> Guvener B. is a sensible man;
>   He stays to his home an' looks arter his folks;
> He draws his furrer[7] ez straight ez he can,
>   An' into nobody's tater-patch pokes;
>   But John P.
>   Robinson he
>   Sez he wunt vote fer Guvener B.   5
>
> My! aint it terrible? Wut shall we du?
>   We can't never choose him o' course,—thet 's flat;
> Guess we shall hev to come round, (don't you?)
>   An' go in fer thunder an' guns, an' all that;   10

3. He should be repressed a bit.
4. Nitric acid.
5. "There is art even in cursing"— comment of Julius Caesar Scaliger (1494–1558), Italian scholar and physician.
6. Thomas Fuller (1608–1661), English clergyman, for a brief time chaplain to Charles II.
7. "*furrer*, furrow. Metaphorically, *to draw a straight furrow* is to live uprightly or decorously" [Lowell's note].

Fer John P.
Robinson he
Sez he wunt vote fer Guvener B.

Gineral C. is a dreffle smart man:[8]   15
He's ben on all sides thet give places or pelf;
But consistency still wuz a part of his plan,—
He's ben true to *one* party,—an' thet is himself;—
So John P.
Robinson he   20
Sez he shall vote fer Gineral C.

Gineral C. he goes in fer the war;
He don't vally principle more 'n an old cud;
Wut did God make us raytional creeturs fer,
But glory an' gunpowder, plunder an' blood?   25
So John P.
Robinson he
Sez he shall vote fer Gineral C.

We were gittin' on nicely up here to our village,
With good old idees o' wut's right an' wut aint,   30
We kind o' thought Christ went agin war an' pillage,
An' thet eppyletts worn't the best mark of a saint;
But John P.
Robinson he
Sez this kind o' thing 's an exploded idee.   35

The side of our country must ollers be took,
An' Presidunt Polk,[9] you know, *he* is our country.
An' the angel thet writes all our sins in a book
Puts the *debit* to him, an' to us the *per contry;*[1]
An' John P.   40
Robinson he
Sez this is his view o' the thing to a T.

Parson Wilbur he calls all these argimunts lies;
Sez they're nothin' on airth but jest *fee, faw fum;*
An' thet all this big talk of our destinies   45
Is half on it ign'ance, an' t' other half rum;
But John P.
Robinson he
Sez it aint no sech thing; an', of course, so must we.

8. Caleb Cushing, one of the few northern supporters of Polk's foreign policies,
objected to slavery on moral grounds
but believed that the South had some
constitutional justification for its position—an attitude that was naturally

antagonistic to antislavery forces.
9. James K. Polk (1795–1849), whose
presidential policies on the Mexican
War were generally unpopular with the
Whigs.
1. Per contra, "just the opposite."

Parson Wilbur sez *he* never heerd in his life   50
Thet th' Apostles rigged out in their swaller-tail coats,
An' marched round in front of a drum an' a fife,
To git some on 'em office, an' some on 'em votes;
    But John P.
      Robinson he   55
Sez they didn't know everythin' down in Judee.[2]

Wal, it's a marcy we've gut folks to tell us
The rights an' the wrongs o' these matters, I vow,—
God sends country lawyers, an' other wise fellers,
To start the world's team wen it gits in a slough;   60
    Fer John P.
      Robinson he
Sez the world'll go right, ef he hollers out Gee![3]

[The attentive reader will doubtless have perceived in the fore-going poem an allusion to that pernicious sentiment,—"Our country, right or wrong."[4] It is an abuse of language to call a certain portion of land, much more, certain personages, elevated for the time being to high station, our country. I would not sever nor loosen a single one of those ties by which we are united to the spot of our birth, nor minish by a tittle[5] the respect due to the Magistrate. I love our own Bay State too well to do the one, and as for the other, I have myself for nigh forty years exercised, however unworthily, the function of Justice of the Peace, having been called thereto by the unsolicited kindness of that most excellent man and upright patriot, Caleb Strong.[6] *Patriae fumus igne alieno luculentior*[7] is best qualified with this,—*Ubi libertas, ibi patria.*[8] We are inhabitants of two worlds, and owe a double, but not a divided, allegiance. In virtue of our clay, this little ball of earth exacts a certain loyalty of us, while, in our capacity as spirits, we are admitted citizens of an invisible and holier fatherland. There is a patriotism of the soul whose claim absolves us from our other and terrene fealty. Our true country is that ideal realm which we represent to ourselves under the names of religion, duty, and the like. Our terrestrial organizations are but far-off approaches to so fair a model,

2. Judea, southern section of Palestine, where most of the public activities of Jesus and his disciples occurred.
3. The command given to a horse to make it turn right.
4. "Our country! In her intercourse with foreign nations may she always be in the right; but our country, right or wrong!" the famous toast of Stephen Decatur (1779–1820), successful American naval commander in the conflict with Algerian pirates (1815).
5. *I.e.*, "diminish by a tittle" (the

small accent mark in Hebrew); hence, "to lessen by the smallest possible degree."
6. Caleb Strong (1745–1819), governor of Massachusetts during the War of 1812; as a Federalist, he was opposed to that war for the same reasons that Homer Wilbur offers against this one.
7. The smoke of our own country is better than the fire of an alien land.
8. Where liberty is, there is my country.

and all they are verily traitors who resist not any attempt to divert them from this their original intendment. When, therefore, one would have us to fling up our caps and shout with the multitude,— *"Our country, however bounded!"* he demands of us that we sacrifice the larger to the less, the higher to the lower, and that we yield to the imaginary claims of a few acres of soil our duty and privilege as liegemen of Truth. Our true country is bounded on the north and the south, on the east and the west, by Justice, and when she oversteps that invisible boundary-line by so much as a hair's-breadth, she ceases to be our mother, and chooses rather to be looked upon *quasi noverca*.[9] That is a hard choice when our earthly love of country calls upon us to tread one path and our duty points us to another. We must make as noble and becoming an election as did Penelope between Icarius and Ulysses. Veiling our faces, we must take silently the hand of Duty to follow her.[1] * * * H. W.]

No. V: The Debate in the Sennit[2]

SOT TO NURSERY RHYME

To Mr. Buckenam

MR. EDITER,

As i wuz kinder prunin round, in a little nussry sot out a year or 2 a go, the Dbait in the sennit cum inter my mine An so i took & Sot it to wut I call a nussry rime. I hev made sum onnable Gentlemun speak thut dident speak in a Kind uv Poetikul lie sense the secson is dreffle backerd up This way

ewers as ushul

HOSEA BIGLOW.

"Here we stan' on the Constitution, by thunder!
  It's a fact o' wich ther's bushils o' proofs;
Fer how could we trample on 't so, I wonder,
  Ef't worn't thet it 's ollers under our hoofs?"
    Sez John C. Calhoun,[3] sez he;   5

9. As a stepmother.
1. Penelope, daughter of Icarius and wife of Ulysses, the hero of the *Odyssey*, silently replied to her father's plea to stay with him rather than to depart with her husband by lowering her veil to indicate her responsibility as a wife.
2. In April, 1848, Captain Drayton and his mate, Sayres, tried to kidnap seventy-seven slaves from Washington, but the slaves were recaptured and returned to the South. Drayton and Sayres, barely escaping from an angry mob, were convicted and given long prison terms, and were not pardoned until 1852, by President Fillmore. On April 20, 1848, Senator Hale of New Hampshire introduced a resolution urging sympathy for the slaves, but met with a storm of abuse from southern senators, particularly Calhoun and Foote. The debate served to point up the conflicting interpretations of the Constitution by the North and the South. Throughout the poem, Lowell satirizes the arguments for slavery: that it was biblically sanctioned, that it protected northern economy, that a breakup of the Union would result in revolution of the working classes. The poem first appeared in the Boston *Courier* for May 3, 1848.
3. John C. Calhoun (1782–1850), senator from South Carolina and architect of the states'-rights doctrine which led to southern secession.

"Human rights haint no more
Right to come on this floor,
No more'n the man in the moon," sez he.

"The North haint no kind o' bisness with nothin',
    An' you've no idee how much bother it saves;   10
We aint none riled by their frettin' an' frothin',
    We're *used* to layin' the string on our slaves,"
      Sez John C. Calhoun, sez he;—
        Sez Mister Foote,[4]
        "I should like to shoot   15
The holl gang, by the gret horn spoon!" sez he.

"Freedom's Keystone is Slavery, thet ther 's no doubt on,
    It 's sutthin' thet 's—wha' d 'ye call it?—divine,—
An' the slaves thet we ollers *make* the most out on
    Air them north o' Mason an' Dixon's line,"   20
      Sez John C. Calhoun, sez he;—
        "Fer all thet," sez Mangum,[5]
        " 'T would be better to hang 'em,
An' so git red on 'em soon," sez he.

"The mass ough' to labor an' we lay on soffies,   25
    Thet 's the reason I want to spread Freedom's aree;
It puts all the cunninest on us in office,
    An' reelises our Maker's orig'nal idee,"
      Sez John C. Calhoun, sez he;—
        "Thet 's ez plain," sez Cass,[6]   30
        "Ez thet some one 's an ass,
It 's ez clear ez the sun is at noon," sez he.

"Now don't go to say I'm the friend of oppression,
    But keep all your spare breath fer coolin' your broth,
Fer I ollers hev strove (at least thet 's my impression)   35
    To make cussed free with the rights o' the North,"
      Sez John C. Calhoun, sez he;
        "Yes," sez Davis[7] o' Miss.,
        "The perfection o' bliss
Is in skinnin' thet same old coon," sez he.   40

"Slavery's a thing thet depends on complexion,
    It's God's law thet fetters on black skins don't chafe;
Ef brains wuz to settle it (horrid reflection!)

---

4. Henry S. Foote (1804–1880), senator from Mississippi, one of the most rabid attackers of Senator Hale's proposal.
5. W. P. Mangum (1792–1861), senator from North Carolina.

6. Lewis Cass (1782–1866), senator from Michigan, whose antislavery sympathies were not strong enough to suit ardent abolitionists.
7. Jefferson Davis (1808–1889), senator from Mississippi, later president of the Confederacy.

Wich of our onnable body 'd be safe?"
　Sez John C. Calhoun, sez he;—　　　　　　　45
　　Sez Mister Hannegan,[8]
　　Afore he began agin,
　"Thet exception is quite oppertoon," sez he.

"Gen'nle Cass, Sir, you need n't be twitchin' your collar,
　Your merit's quite clear by the dust on your knees,[9]　50
At the North we don't make no distinctions o' color;
　You can all take a lick at our shoes wen you please,"
　　Sez John C. Calhoun, sez he;—
　　Sez Mister Jarnagin,[1]
　　"They wun't hev to larn agin,　　　　　　55
　They all on 'em know the old toon," sez he.

"The slavery question aint no ways bewilderin',
　North an' South hev one int'rest, it's plain to a glance;
No'thern men, like us patriarchs, don't sell their children,
　But they *du* sell themselves, ef they git a good chance,"　60
　　Sez John C. Calhoun, sez he;—
　　Sez Atherton[2] here,
　　"This is gittin' severe,
　I wish I could dive like a loon," sez he.

"It 'll break up the Union, this talk about freedom,　　65
　An' your fact'ry gals (soon ez we split) 'll make head,
An' gittin' some Miss chief or other to lead 'em,
　'll go to work raisin' permiscoous Ned,"
　　Sez John C. Calhoun, sez he;—
　　"Yes, the North," sez Colquitt,[3]　　　　70
　　"Ef we Southerners all quit,
　Would go down like a busted balloon," sez he.

"Jest look wut is doin', wut annyky 's brewin'
　In the beautiful clime o' the olive an' vine,
All the wise aristoxy 's atumblin' to ruin,　　　　75
　An' the sankylots[4] drorin' an' drinkin' their wine,"
　　Sez John C. Calhoun, sez he;—
　　"Yes," sez Johnson,[5] "in France
　　They 're beginnin' to dance
　Beëlzebub's[6] own rigadoon," sez he.　　　　80

8. Edward A. Hannegan (1807–1859),
Democratic senator from Indiana, sympathetic toward Polk's expansionist
policies.
9. A snide reference to Cass's piety,
evidenced by the dirt on his knees from
kneeling in prayer.
1. Spencer Jarnagin (died 1851), senator from Tennessee.

2. Charles G. Atherton (1804–1853),
senator from New Hampshire.
3. W. T. Colquitt (1799–1855), senator from Georgia.
4. *sans culottes*, without the short
breeches worn by gentlemen; hence an
epithet for the French revolutionaries.
5. Reverdy Johnson (1796–1876),
senator from Maryland.
6. *I.e.*, Satan.

"The South 's safe enough, it don't feel a mite skeery,
    Our slaves in their darkness an' dut air tu blest
Not to welcome with proud hallylugers[7] the cry
    Wen our eagle kicks yourn from the naytional nest,"
      Sez John C. Calhoun, sez he;—   85
      "Oh," sez Westcott o' Florida,
      "Wut treason is horrider
    Then our priv'leges tryin' to proon?" sez he.

"It 's coz they 're so happy, thet, wen crazy sarpints
    Stick their nose in our bizness, we git so darned riled; 90
We think it 's our dooty to give pooty sharp hints,
    Thet the last crumb of Edin on airth sha' n't be spiled,"
      Sez John C. Calhoun, sez he;—
      "Ah," sez Dixon H. Lewis,[8]
      "It perfectly true is   95
    Thet slavery 's airth's grettest boon," sez he.

                        1848

From The Biglow Papers, Second Series
From the Introduction

THE COURTIN'[9]

God makes sech nights, all white an' still
    Fur'z you can look or listen,
Moonshine an' snow on field an' hill,
    All silence an' all glisten.

Zekle crep' up quite unbeknown   5
    An' peeked in thru' the winder,

7. Hallelujahs.
8. Senator from Alabama from 1844 until his death in 1848.
9. Originally a poem of only forty-four lines in *The Biglow Papers, First Series* (1848), it was extended as Lowell here explains in the introduction to the *Second Series* (1867): "The only attempt I had ever made at anything like a pastoral (if that may be called an attempt which was the result almost of pure accident) was in 'The Courtin'.' While the Introduction to the First Series was going through the press, I received word from the printer that there was a blank page left which must be filled. I sat down at once and improvised another fictitious 'notice of the press,' in which, because verse would fill up space more cheaply than prose, I inserted an extract from a supposed ballad of Mr. Biglow. I kept no copy of it, and the printer, as directed, cut it off when the gap was filled. Presently I began to receive letters asking for the rest of it, sometimes for the *balance* of it. I had none, but to answer such demands, I patched a conclusion upon it in a later edition. Those who had only the first continued to importune me. Afterward, being asked to write it out as an autograph for the Baltimore Sanitary Commission Fair, I added other verses, into some of which I infused a little more sentiment in a homely way, and after a fashion completed it by sketching in the characters and making a connected story. Most likely I have spoiled it, but I shall put it at the end of this Introduction, to answer once for all those kindly importunings."

An' there sot Huldy all alone,
   'ith no one nigh to hender.

A fireplace filled the room's one side
   With half a cord o' wood in—
There warn't no stoves (tell comfort died)
   To bake ye to a puddin'.

The wa'nut logs shot sparkles out
   Towards the pootiest, bless her,
An' leetle flames danced all about
   The chiny on the dresser.

Agin the chimbley crook-necks[1] hung,
   An' in amongst 'em rusted
The ole queen's-arm[2] thet gran'ther Young
   Fetched back f'om Concord busted.

The very room, coz she was in,
   Seemed warm f'om floor to ceilin',
An' she looked full ez rosy agin
   Ez the apples she was peelin'.

'Twas kin' o' kingdom-come to look
   On sech a blessed cretur,
A dogrose blushin' to a brook
   Ain't modester nor sweeter.

He was six foot o' man, A 1,
   Clear grit an' human natur',
None couldn't quicker pitch a ton
   Nor dror a furrer straighter.

He'd sparked it with full twenty gals,
   Hed squired 'em, danced 'em, druv 'em,
Fust this one, an' then thet, by spells—
   All is, he couldn't love 'em.

But long o' her his veins 'ould run
   All crinkly like curled maple,
The side she breshed felt full o' sun
   Ez a south slope in Ap'il.

She thought no v'ice hed sech a swing
   Ez hisn in the choir;
My! when he made Ole Hunderd[3] ring,
   She *knowed* the Lord was nigher.

---

1. Gourds.
2. Revolutionary musket.

3. A psalm tune named from its use with the One Hundredth Psalm.

An' she'd blush scarlit, right in prayer,   45
   When her new meetin'-bunnet
Felt somehow thru' its crown a pair
   O' blue eyes sot upun it.

Thet night, I tell ye, she looked *some!*
   She seemed to 've gut a new soul,   50
For she felt sartin-sure he'd come,
   Down to her very shoe-sole.

She heered a foot, an' knowed it tu,
   A-raspin' on the scraper,—
All ways to once her feelin's flew   55
   Like sparks in burnt-up paper.

He kin' o' l'itered on the mat,
   Some doubtfle o' the sekle,[4]
His heart kep' goin' pity-pat,
   But hern went pity Zekle.   60

An' yit she gin her cheer a jerk
   Ez though she wished him furder,
An' on her apples kep' to work,
   Parin' away like murder.

"You want to see my Pa, I s'pose?"   65
   "Wal . . . no . . . I come dasignin' "—
"To see my Ma? She's sprinklin' clo'es
   Agin to-morrer's i'nin'."

To say why gals acts so or so,
   Or don't, 'ould be persumin';   70
Mebby to mean *yes* an' say *no*
   Comes nateral to women.

He stood a spell on one foot fust,
   Then stood a spell on t'other,
An' on which one he felt the wust   75
   He couldn't ha' told ye nuther.

Says he, "I'd better call agin!"
   Says she, "Think likely, Mister:"
Thet last word pricked him like a pin,
   An' . . . Wal, he up an' kist her.   80

When Ma bimeby upon 'em slips,
   Huldy sot pale ez ashes,
All kin' o' smily roun' the lips
   An' teary roun' the lashes.

4. Sequel, or outcome of his visit.

For she was jes' the quiet kind   85
  Whose naturs never vary,
Like streams that keep a summer mind
  Snowhid in Jenooary.

The blood clost roun' her heart felt glued
  Too tight for all expressin',   90
Tell mother see how metters stood,
  An' gin 'em both her blessin'.

Then her red come back like the tide
  Down to the Bay o' Fundy,
An' all I know is they was cried   95
  In meetin'[5] come nex' Sunday.

From *No. II: Mason and Slidell: A Yankee Idyll*[6]

JONATHAN TO JOHN

It don't seem hardly right, John
  When both my hands was full,
To stump me to a fight, John,—
  Your cousin, tu, John Bull!
    Ole Uncle S. sez he, "I guess   5
    We know it now," sez he,
"The lion's paw is all the law,
    Accordin' to J. B.,
  Thet's fit for you an' me!"

You wonder why we're hot, John?   10
  Your mark wuz on the guns,
The neutral guns, thet shot, John,
  Our brothers an' our sons:
    Ole Uncle S. sez he, "I guess
    There's human blood," sez he,   15
  "By fits an' starts, in Yankee hearts,

5. The wedding banns were "cried" or announced in church.
6. The *Trent* affair, the occasion of the first threat of European intervention in the Civil War, involved two Confederate agents, James M. Mason and John Slidell, who were forcibly removed from the British ship *Trent* on November 8, 1861, by Charles Wilkes, Union captain of the U.S.S. *San Jacinto*, to prevent them from accomplishing their diplomatic mission to London. Only the efforts of English and Union statesmen kept the furor in the press from erupting into a declaration of war over this breach of international neutrality. President Lincoln was persuaded to release the prisoners, who were sent on to their destination. The event actually served to strengthen English determination to remain neutral.

In his letter to the editors of the *Atlantic Monthly*, where the poem first appeared in February, 1862, Homer Wilbur sets forth the American distress over the affair, followed by a poem of Hosea's in the form of an allegory between Concord Bridge (representing anger at England) and the Bunker Hill Monument (representing conciliation toward England), and then concludes with "Jonathan to John" (America to England), given here. The entire work was first separately reprinted in Boston (1862), and was included in *The Biglow Papers, Second Series* (1867).

Though 't may surprise J. B.
More'n it would you an' me."

Ef *I* turned mad dogs loose, John,
 On *your* front-parlor stairs,   20
Would it jest meet your views, John,
 To wait an' sue their heirs?
  Ole Uncle S. sez he, "I guess,
   I on'y guess," sez he,
"Thet ef Vattel[7] on *his* toes fell,   25
   'T would kind o' rile J. B.,
   Ez wal ez you an' me!"

Who made the law thet hurts, John,
 Heads I *win*,—*ditto tails?*
"J. B." was on his shirts, John,   30
 Onless my memory fails.
  Ole Uncle S. sez he, "I guess,
   (I'm good at thet)," sez he,
"Thet sauce for goose ain't *jest* the juice
   For ganders with J. B.,   35
   No more 'n with you or me!"

When your rights was our wrongs, John,
 You did n't stop for fuss,—
Britanny's trident prongs, John,
 Was good 'nough law for us.[8]   40
  Ole Uncle S. sez he, "I guess,
   Though physic's good," sez he,
"It doesn't foller thet he can swaller
   Prescriptions signed 'J. B.,'
   Put up by you an' me!"   45

We own the ocean, tu, John:
 You mus' n' take it hard,
Ef we can't think with you, John,
 It's jest your own back-yard.
  Ole Uncle S. sez he, "I guess,   50
   Ef *thet* 's his claim," sez he,
"The fencin'-stuff'll cost enough

7. Emmerich von Vattel (1714–1767), Swiss jurist, whose *Droit des Gens* * * * (1758) argued that natural law was above legislation, providing a justification for liberal revolution.
8. A reference to the incident of the British seizure of the American *Caroline* in the Canadian insurrection of 1837. The American ship, in defiance of President Van Buren's insistence on neutrality, was used to convey armed American sympathizers across the Niagara River; English forces fired the ship in American waters, but five years later, in the Webster-Ashburton Treaty (1842), Britain made amends for the incident. The "trident prongs" here denote British naval law.

To bust up friend J. B.,
Ez wal ez you an' me!"

Why talk so dreffle big, John,   55
    Of honor when it meant
You didn't care a fig, John,
    But jest for *ten per cent?*[9]
        Ole Uncle S. sez he, "I guess
        He's like the rest," sez he: 60
"When all is done, it's number one
        Thet's nearest to J. B.,
        Ez wal ez t' you an' me!"

We give the critters back, John,
    Cos Abram thought 't was right;[1]   65
It warn't your bullyin' clack, John,
    Provokin' us to fight.
        Ole Uncle S. sez he, "I guess
        We've a hard row," sez he,
"To hoe jest now; but thet, somehow,   70
        May happen to J. B.,
        Ez wal ez you an' me!"

We ain't so weak an' poor, John,
    With twenty million people,
An' close to every door, John,   75
    A school-house an' a steeple.
        Ole Uncle S. sez he, "I guess
        It is a fact," sez he,
"The surest plan to make a Man
        Is, think him so, J. B.,   80
        Ez much ez you or me!"

Our folks believe in Law, John;
    An' it's for her sake, now,
They've left the axe an' saw, John,
    The anvil an' the plough.   85
        Ole Uncle S. sez he, "I guess,
        Ef 't warn't for law," sez he,
"There 'd be one shindy from here to Indy;
        An' thet don't suit J. B.
        (When 't ain't 'twix you an' me!)"   90

We know we've got a cause, John,
    Thet's honest, just, an' true;
We thought 't would win applause, John,

9. *I.e.,* the presumed English profit   1. The "critters" are Mason and Sli-
from selling war materiel to the South.   dell; "Abram" is Abraham Lincoln.

Ef nowheres else, from you.
    Ole Uncle S. sez he, "I guess
       His love of right," sez he,   95
"Hangs by a rotten fibre o' cotton:
    There's natur' in J. B.,
       Ez wal 'z you an' me!"

The South says, "*Poor folks down!*" John,   100
  An' "*All men up!*" say we,—
White, yaller, black, an' brown, John:
    Now which is your idee?
      Ole Uncle S. sez he, "I guess,
       John preaches wal," sez he;   105
"But, sermon thru, an' come to *du*,
    Why, there's the old J. B.
      A crowdin' you an' me!"

Shall it be love, or hate, John?
  It's you thet's to decide;   110
Ain't *your* bonds held by Fate, John,
    Like all the world's beside?
      Ole Uncle S. sez he, "I guess
       Wise men forgive," sez he,
"But not forgit; an' some time yit   115
    Thet truth may strike J. B.,
      Ez wal ez you an' me!"

God means to make this land, John,
  Clear thru, from sea to sea,
Believe and understand, John,   120
    The *wuth* o' bein' free.
      Ole Uncle S. sez he, "I guess,
       God's price is high," sez he;
"But nothin' else than wut He sells
    Wears long, an thet J. B.   125
      May larn, like you an' me!"

1867

Ode Recited at the Harvard Commemoration[2]

JULY 21, 1865

I

Weak-winged is song,
Nor aims at that clear-ethered height

2. Lowell read this poem to a group of
friends and alumni of Harvard College
on July 21, 1865, to honor the Harvard
men, living and dead, who had fought

Whither the brave deed climbs for light:
   We seem to do them wrong,
Bringing our robin's-leaf to deck their hearse 5
Who in warm life-blood wrote their nobler verse,
Our trivial song to honor those who come
With ears attuned to strenuous trump and drum,
And shaped in squadron-strophes their desire,
Live battle-odes whose lines were steel and fire: 10
   Yet sometimes feathered words are strong,
A gracious memory to buoy up and save
From Lethe's[3] dreamless ooze, the common grave
   Of the unventurous throng.

II

Today our Reverend Mother[4] welcomes back 15
   Her wisest Scholars, those who understood
The deeper teaching of her mystic tome,
   And offered their fresh lives to make it good:
      No lore of Greece or Rome,
No science peddling with the names of things, 20
Or reading stars to find inglorious fates,
      Can lift our life with wings
Far from Death's idle gulf that for the many waits,
      And lengthen out our dates
With that clear fame whose memory sings 25
In manly hearts to come, and nerves them and dilates:
Nor such thy teaching, Mother of us all!
      Not such the trumpet-call
      Of thy diviner mood,
      That could thy sons entice 30
From happy homes and toils, the fruitful nest
Of those half-virtues which the world calls best,
      Into War's tumult rude;

in the recently concluded Civil War. Three of his nephews had died in the conflict, and his personal involvement had been intensified by his hatred of war, evident in *The Biglow Papers, First Series,* and his resentment of slavery, reflected in the *Second Series.* In this poem he finds some consolation in the sober joy of peace and victory: "O Beautiful! my Country! ours once more!" He wrote to a friend: "The poem was written with a vehement speed, which I thought I had lost in the skirts of my professor's gown. Till within two days of the celebration I was hopelessly dumb, and then it all came with a rush, literally making me lean * * * and so nervous that I was weeks in getting over it." The form of

the poem, which is a so-called Pindaric ode, was chosen by the poet because of the suitability of the varied verse structure for reading aloud. The sixth strophe, on Lincoln, not in the original reading, was added immediately afterward. Privately printed at Cambridge in 1865, the poem appeared in the *Atlantic Monthly* for September, 1865, and was reprinted in *Harvard Memorial Biographies* (1866), *Under the Willows* (1869), and *Three Memorial Poems* (1877).

3. A river of Hades whose waters when drunk provided forgetfulness of the past life.

4. *I.e.,* Harvard College, their Alma Mater.

But rather far that stern device
The sponsors chose that round thy cradle stood   35
   In the dim, unventured wood,
   The VERITAS[5] that lurks beneath
   The letter's unprolific sheath,
Life of whate'er makes life worth living,
Seed-grain of high emprise, immortal food,   40
One heavenly thing whereof earth hath the giving.

III

Many loved Truth, and lavished life's best oil
   Amid the dust of books to find her,
Content at last, for guerdon of their toil,
   With the cast mantle she hath left behind her.   45
     Many in sad faith sought for her,
     Many with crossed hands sighed for her;
     But these, our brothers, fought for her,
     At life's dear peril wrought for her,
     So loved her that they died for her,   50
     Tasting the raptured fleetness
     Of her divine completeness:
     Their higher instinct knew
Those love her best who to themselves are true,
And what they dare to dream of, dare to do;   55
     They followed her and found her
     Where all may hope to find,
Not in the ashes of the burnt-out mind,
But beautiful, with danger's sweetness round her.
     Where faith made whole with deed   60
     Breathes its awakening breath
     Into the lifeless creed,
     They saw her plumed and mailed,
     With sweet, stern face unveiled,
And all-repaying eyes, look proud on them in death.   65

IV

Our slender life runs rippling by, and glides
   Into the silent hollow of the past;
     What is there that abides
   To make the next age better for the last?
     Is earth too poor to give us   70
   Something to live for here that shall outlive us?
     Some more substantial boon
Than such as flows and ebbs with Fortune's fickle moon?
     The little that we see
     From doubt is never free;   75

5. "Veritas" ("Truth") on the seal of Harvard College.

The little that we do
Is but half-nobly true;
With our laborious hiving
What men call treasure, and the gods call dross,
Life seems a jest of Fate's contriving,   80
Only secure in every one's conniving,
A long account of nothings paid with loss,
Where we poor puppets, jerked by unseen wires,
After our little hour of strut and rave,
With all our pasteboard passions and desires,   85
Loves, hates, ambitions, and immortal fires,
Are tossed pell-mell together in the grave.
But stay! no age was e'er degenerate,
Unless men held it at too cheap a rate,
For in our likeness still we shape our fate.   90
Ah, there is something here
Unfathomed by the cynic's sneer,
Something that gives our feeble light
A high immunity from Night,
Something that leaps life's narrow bars   95
To claim its birthright with the hosts of heaven;
A seed of sunshine that can leaven
Our earthly dullness with the beams of stars,
And glorify our clay
With light from fountains elder than the Day;   100
A conscience more divine than we,
A gladness fed with secret tears,
A vexing, forward-reaching sense
Of some more noble permanence;
A light across the sea,   105
Which haunts the soul and will not let it be,
Still beaconing from the heights of undegenerate years.

v

Whither leads the path
To ampler fates that leads?
Not down through flowery meads,   110
To reap an aftermath
Of youth's vainglorious weeds,
But up the steep, amid the wrath
And shock of deadly-hostile creeds,
Where the world's best hope and stay   115
By battle's flashes gropes a desperate way,
And every turf the fierce foot clings to bleeds.
Peace hath her not ignoble wreath,
Ere yet the sharp, decisive word

Light the black lips of cannon, and the sword   120
   Dreams in its easeful sheath;
But some day the live coal behind the thought,
   Whether from Baäl's stone[6] obscene,
     Or from the shrine serene
     Of God's pure altar brought,   125
Bursts up in flame; the war of tongue and pen
Learns with what deadly purpose it was fraught,
And, helpless in the fiery passion caught,
Shakes all the pillared state with shock of men:
Some day the soft Ideal that we wooed   130
Confronts us fiercely, foe-beset, pursued,
And cries reproachful: "Was it, then, my praise,
And not myself was loved? Prove now thy truth;
I claim of thee the promise of thy youth;
Give me thy life, or cower in empty phrase,   135
The victim of thy genius, not its mate!"
   Life may be given in many ways,
    And loyalty to Truth be sealed
As bravely in the closet as the field,
    So bountiful is Fate;   140
    But then to stand beside her,
    When craven churls deride her,
To front a lie in arms and not to yield,
   This shows, methinks, God's plan
   And measure of a stalwart man,   145
   Limbed like the old heroic breeds,
   Who stands self-poised on manhood's solid earth,
  Not forced to frame excuses for his birth,
Fed from within with all the strength he needs.

VI

Such was he, our Martyr-Chief,[7]   150
   Whom late the Nation he had led,
   With ashes on her head,
Wept with the passion of an angry grief:
Forgive me, if from present things I turn
To speak what in my heart will beat and burn,   155
And hang my wreath on his world-honored urn.
   Nature, they say, doth dote,
   And cannot make a man
   Save on some worn-out plan,
   Repeating us by rote: 160
For him her Old-World moulds aside she threw,

6. *Cf.* I Kings xviii for the contest be-   of the pagan deity Baäl.
tween Elijah and the idolatrous priests   7. Lincoln.

And choosing sweet clay from the breast
    Of the unexhausted West,
With stuff untainted shaped a hero new,
Wise, steadfast,, in the strength of God, and true.   165
    How beautiful to see
Once more a shepherd of mankind indeed,
Who loved his charge, but never loved to lead;
One whose meek flock the people joyed to be,
    Not lured by any cheat of birth,   170
    But by his clear-grained human worth,
And brave old wisdom of sincerity!
    They knew that outward grace is dust;
    They could not choose but trust
In that sure-footed mind's unfaltering skill,   175
    And supple-tempered will
That bent like perfect steel to spring again and thrust.
    His was no lonely mountain-peak of mind,
    Thrusting to thin air o'er our cloudy bars,
    A sea-mark now, now lost in vapors blind;   180
    Broad prairie rather, genial, level-lined,
    Fruitful and friendly for all human kind,
Yet also nigh to heaven and loved of loftiest stars.
        Nothing of Europe here,
Or, then, of Europe fronting mornward still,   185
    Ere any names of Serf and Peer
    Could Nature's equal scheme deface
    And thwart her genial will;
    Here was a type of the true elder race,
And one of Plutarch's men[8] talked with us face to face.   190
    I praise him not; it were too late;
And some innative weakness there must be
In him who condescends to victory
Such as the Present gives, and cannot wait,
    Safe in himself as in a fate.   195
        So always firmly he:
        He knew to bide his time,
        And can his fame abide,
Still patient in his simple faith sublime,
        Till the wise years decide.   200
    Great captains, with their guns and drums,
        Disturb our judgment for the hour,
        But at last silence comes;
These all are gone, and, standing like a tower,

8. Lowell compares Lincoln to one of the heroes of ancient history memorial- ized by Plutarch (46?–120) in his *Parallel Lives.*

Our children shall behold his fame. 205
  The kindly-earnest, brave, foreseeing man,
Sagacious, patient, dreading praise, not blame,
  New birth of our new soil, the first American.

VII

Long as man's hope insatiate can discern
    Or only guess some more inspiring goal 210
    Outside of Self, enduring as the pole,
  Along whose course the flying axles burn
  Of spirits bravely-pitched, earth's manlier brood;
    Long as below we cannot find
    The meed that stills the inexorable mind; 215
    So long this faith to some ideal Good,
  Under whatever mortal names it masks,
  Freedom, Law, Country, this ethereal mood
That thanks the Fates for their severer tasks,
    Feeling its challenged pulses leap, 220
    While others skulk in subterfuges cheap,
And, set in Danger's van, has all the boon it asks,
    Shall win man's praise and woman's love,
    Shall be a wisdom that we set above
All other skills and gifts to culture dear, 225
    A virtue round whose forehead we inwreathe
    Laurels that with a living passion breathe
When other crowns grow, while we twine them, sear.
    What brings us thronging these high rites to pay,
And seal these hours the noblest of our year, 230
    Save that our brothers found this better way?

VIII

We sit here in the Promised Land
  That flows with Freedom's honey and milk;[9]
  But 'twas they won it, sword in hand,
Making the nettle danger soft for us as silk. 235
    We welcome back our bravest and our best;—
    Ah me! not all! some come not with the rest,
Who went forth brave and bright as any here!
I strive to mix some gladness with my strain,
        But the sad strings complain, 240
        And will not please the ear:
I sweep them for a pæan, but they wane
        Again and yet again
Into a dirge, and die away, in pain.
In these brave ranks I only see the gaps, 245
Thinking of dear ones whom the dumb turf wraps,

9. *Cf.* Exodus iii: 8.

Dark to the triumph which they died to gain:
    Fitlier may others greet the living,
    For me the past is unforgiving;
        I with uncovered head   250
        Salute the sacred dead,
Who went, and who return not.—Say not so!
'Tis not the grapes of Canaan[1] that repay,
But the high faith that failed not by the way;
Virtue treads paths that end not in the grave;   255
No ban of endless night exiles the brave;
        And to the saner mind
We rather seem the dead that stayed behind.
Blow, trumpets, all your exultations blow!
For never shall their aureoled presence lack: 260
I see them muster in a gleaming row,
With ever-youthful brows that nobler show;
We find in our dull road their shining track;
        In every nobler mood
We feel the orient of their spirit glow,   265
Part of our life's unalterable good,
Of all our saintlier aspiration;
        They come transfigured back,
Secure from change in their high-hearted ways,
Beautiful evermore, and with the rays   270
Of morn on their white Shields of Expectation!

               IX

        But is there hope to save
    Even this ethereal essence from the grave?
    What ever 'scaped Oblivion's subtle wrong
Save a few clarion names, or golden threads of song?   275
        Before my musing eye
     The mighty ones of old sweep by,
    Disvoicèd now and insubstantial things,
As noisy once as we; poor ghosts of kings,
Shadows of empire wholly gone to dust,   280
And many races, nameless long ago,
To darkness driven by that imperious gust
Of ever-rushing Time that here doth blow:
O visionary world, condition strange,
    Where naught abiding is but only Change,   285
Where the deep-bolted stars themselves still shift and range!
    Shall we to more continuance make pretence?
Renown builds tombs; a life-estate is Wit;
        And, bit by bit,
The cunning years steal all from us but woe;   290

1. *Cf.* Numbers xiii: 23–27.

Leaves are we, whose decays no harvest sow.
      But, when we vanish hence,
Shall they lie forceless in the dark below,
Save to make green their little length of sods,
Or deepen pansies for a year or two,   295
Who now to us are shining-sweet as gods?
Was dying all they had the skill to do?
That were not fruitless: but the Soul resents
Such short-lived service, as if blind events
Ruled without her, or earth could so endure;   300
She claims a more divine investiture
Of longer tenure than Fame's airy rents;
Whate'er she touches doth her nature share;
Her inspiration haunts the ennobled air,
      Gives eyes to mountains blind,   305
Ears to the deaf earth, voices to the wind,
And her clear trump sings succor everywhere
By lonely bivouacs to the wakeful mind;
For soul inherits all that soul could dare:
      Yea, Manhood hath a wider span   310
And larger privilege of life than man.
The single deed, the private sacrifice,
So radiant now through proudly-hidden tears,
Is covered up erelong from mortal eyes
With thoughtless drift of the deciduous years;   315
But that high privilege that makes all men peers,
That leap of heart whereby a people rise
      Up to a noble anger's height,
And, flamed on by the Fates, not shrink, but grow more bright,
      That swift validity in noble veins,   320
Of choosing danger and disdaining shame,
      Of being set on flame
By the pure fire that flies all contact base
But wraps its chosen with angelic might,
      These are imperishable gains,   325
Sure as the sun, medicinal as light,
These hold great futures in their lusty reins
And certify to earth a new imperial race.

                         x
      Who now shall sneer?
      Who dare again to say we trace   330
      Our lines to a plebeian race?
      Roundhead and Cavalier![2]

2. Roundheads were Puritan followers of Cromwell in the English civil war, founders of Massachusetts; and Cava- liers were supporters of Charles I, representative of the early settlers of Virginia.

Dumb are those names erewhile in battle loud;
Dream-footed as the shadow of a cloud,
    They flit across the ear: ₃₃₅
That is best blood that hath most iron in 't,
To edge resolve with, pouring without stint
    For what makes manhood dear.
    Tell us not of Plantagenets,
Hapsburgs, and Guelfs,[3] whose thin bloods crawl   ₃₄₀
Down from some victor in a border-brawl!
    How poor their outworn coronets,
Matched with one leaf of that plain civic wreath
Our brave for honor's blazon shall bequeath,
    Through whose desert a rescued Nation sets   ₃₄₅
Her heel on treason, and the trumpet hears
Shout victory, tingling Europe's sullen ears
    With vain resentments and more vain regrets!

XI

    Not in anger, not in pride,
    Pure from passion's mixture rude   ₃₅₀
    Ever to base earth allied,
    But with far-heard gratitude,
    Still with heart and voice renewed,
    To heroes living and dear martyrs dead,
The strain should close that consecrates our brave.   ₃₅₅
    Lift the heart and lift the head!
        Lofty be its mood and grave,
        Not without a martial ring,
        Not without a prouder tread
        And a peal of exultation: ₃₆₀
        Little right has he to sing
        Through whose heart in such an hour
        Beats no march of conscious power,
        Sweeps no tumult of elation!
        'Tis no Man we celebrate,   ₃₆₅
        By his country's victories great,
    A hero half, and half the whim of Fate,
    But the pith and marrow of a Nation
    Drawing force from all her men,
    Highest, humblest, weakest, all,   ₃₇₀
    For her time of need, and then
    Pulsing it again through them,

3. Plantagenets, the ruling house of England (1154–1399); Hapsburgs, the rulers of the Holy Roman Empire from the middle of the fifteenth to the eighteenth centuries; Guelphs, the papal party in Italy in the thirteenth and fourteenth centuries; all here symbols of the intrigue and the disastrous wars that left Europe in political chaos.

Till the basest can no longer cower,
Feeling his soul spring up divinely tall,
Touched but in passing by her mantle-hem.   375
Come back, then, noble pride, for 'tis her dower!
    How could poet ever tower,
    If his passions, hopes, and fears,
    If his triumphs and his tears,
    Kept not measure with his people?   380
Boom, cannon, boom to all the winds and waves!
Clash out, glad bells, from every rocking steeple!
Banners, advance with triumph, bend your staves!
    And from every mountain-peak
    Let beacon-fire to answering beacon speak,   385
Katahdin tell Monadnock, Whiteface[4] he,
And so leap on in light from sea to sea,
        Till the glad news be sent
        Across a kindling continent,
Making earth feel more firm and air breathe braver: 390
"Be proud! for she is saved, and all have helped to save her!
    She that lifts up the manhood of the poor,
    She of the open soul and open door,
    With room about her hearth for all mankind!
    The fire is dreadful in her eyes no more;   395
    From her bold front the helm she doth unbind,
    Sends all her handmaid armies back to spin,
    And bids her navies, that so lately hurled
    Their crashing battle, hold their thunders in,
Swimming like birds of calm along the unharmful shore.   400
    No challenge sends she to the elder world,
    That looked askance and hated;[5] a light scorn
    Plays o'er her mouth, as round her mighty knees
    She calls her children back, and waits the morn
Of nobler day, enthroned between her subject seas."   405

           XII

Bow down, dear Land, for thou hast found release!
    Thy God, in these distempered days,
    Hath taught thee the sure wisdom of His ways,
And through thine enemies hath wrought thy peace!
    Bow down in prayer and praise!   410
No poorest in thy borders but may now
Lift to the juster skies a man's enfranchised brow.
O Beautiful! my Country! ours once more!

4. Mountains in Maine, New Hampshire, and New York.

5. A reference to the unpopularity of
the Union cause in some circles in England and France.

Smoothing thy gold of war-dishevelled hair
O'er such sweet brows as never other wore,   415
    And letting thy set lips,
    Freed from wrath's pale eclipse,
The rosy edges of their smile lay bare,
What words divine of lover or of poet
Could tell our love and make thee know it,   420
Among the Nations bright beyond compare?
    What were our lives without thee?
    What all our lives to save thee?
    We reck not what we gave thee;
    We will not dare to doubt thee,   425
But ask whatever else, and we will dare!

1865   1865

The Cathedral[6]

Far through the memory shines a happy day,
Cloudless of care, down-shod to every sense,
And simply perfect from its own resource,
As to a bee the new campanula's
Illuminate seclusion swung in air.   5
Such days are not the prey of setting suns,
Nor ever blurred with mist of after-thought;
Like words made magical by poets dead,
Wherein the music of all meaning is
The sense hath garnered or the soul divined,   10
They mingle with our life's ethereal part,
Sweetening and gathering sweetness evermore,
By Beauty's franchise disenthralled of time.

I can recall, nay, they are present still,
Parts of myself, the perfume of my mind,   15
Days that seem farther off than Homer's now

6. During his stay in France in 1855, Lowell visited the cathedral of Chartres. The emotion and spirituality of that experience culminated fourteen years later in the poem entitled "A Day at Chartres," published in the *Atlantic Monthly* in January, 1870 and separately, as *The Cathedral*, for the Christmas trade of 1869, in a volume dated 1870. There were some changes in successive editions of the poem (notably the excision of nineteen lines uncomplimentary to two English "tourists"). The present text is that of the Riverside Edition (1890). Lowell remarked that no other poem had so engrossed his thought and capabilities. Reminiscent of Tennyson's *In Memoriam*, with its clear statement that the nineteenth century is "no age to get cathedrals built," this poem still expresses an optimistic hope that the giant of democracy may yet develop new definitions of the old faith. Unsparing in his criticism of the imitativeness of much New World religious practice, Lowell is temporarily swept back to old allegiances in the medieval mysticism which was responsible for Chartres, yet he is confident that the inevitable changes in human history mean no change in God.

Ere yet the child had loudened to the boy,
And I, recluse from playmates, found perforce
Companionship in things that not denied
Nor granted wholly; as is Nature's wont, 20
Who, safe in uncontaminate reserve,
Lets us mistake our longing for her love,
And mocks with various echo of ourselves.

These first sweet frauds upon our consciousness,
That blend the sensual with its imaged world, 25
These virginal cognitions, gifts of morn,
Ere life grow noisy, and slower-footed thought
Can overtake the rapture of the sense,
To thrust between ourselves and what we feel,
Have something in them secretly divine. 30
Vainly the eye, once schooled to serve the brain,
With pains deliberate studies to renew
The ideal vision: second-thoughts are prose;
For Beauty's acme hath a term as brief
As the wave's poise before it break in pearl. 35
Our own breath dims the mirror of the sense,
Looking too long and closely: at a flash
We snatch the essential grace of meaning out,
And that first passion beggars all behind,
Heirs of a tamer transport prepossessed. 40
Who, seeing once, has truly seen again
The gray vague of unsympathizing sea
That dragged his Fancy from her moorings back
To shores inhospitable of eldest time,
Till blank foreboding of earth-gendered power, 45
Pitiless seignories in the elements,
Omnipotences blind that darkling smite,
Misgave him, and repaganized the world?
Yet, by some subtler touch of sympathy,
These primal apprehensions, dimly stirred, 50
Perplex the eye with pictures from within.
This hath made poets dream of lives foregone
In worlds fantastical, more fair than ours;
So Memory cheats us, glimpsing half-revealed.
Even as I write she tries her wonted spell 55
In that continuous redbreast boding rain:
The bird I hear sings not from yonder elm;
But the flown ecstasy my childhood heard
Is vocal in my mind, renewed by him,
Haply made sweeter by the accumulate thrill 60

That threads my undivided life and steals
A pathos from the years and graves between.

I know not how it is with other men,
Whom I but guess, deciphering myself;
For me, once felt is so felt nevermore.   65
The fleeting relish at sensation's brim
Had in it the best ferment of the wine.
One spring I knew as never any since:
All night the surges of the warm southwest
Boomed intermittent through the shuddering elms,   70
And brought a morning from the Gulf adrift,
Omnipotent with sunshine, whose quick charm
Startled with crocuses the sullen turf
And wiled the bluebird to his whiff of song:
One summer hour abides, what time I perched,   75
Dappled with noonday, under simmering leaves,
And pulled the pulpy oxhearts, while aloof
An oriole clattered and the robins shrilled,
Denouncing me an alien and a thief:
One morn of autumn lords it o'er the rest,   80
When in the lane I watched the ash-leaves fall,
Balancing softly earthward without wind,
Or twirling with directer impulse down
On those fallen yesterday, now barbed with frost,
While I grew pensive with the pensive year: 85
And once I learned how marvellous winter was,
When past the fence-rails, downy-gray with rime,
I creaked adventurous o'er the spangled crust
That made familiar fields seem far and strange
As those stark wastes that whiten endlessly   90
In ghastly solitude about the pole,
And gleam relentless to the unsetting sun:
Instant the candid chambers of my brain
Were painted with these sovran images;
And later visions seem but copies pale   95
From those unfading frescoes of the past,
Which I, young savage, in my age of flint,
Gazed at, and dimly felt a power in me
Parted from Nature by the joy in her
That doubtfully revealed me to myself.   100
Thenceforward I must stand outside the gate;
And paradise was paradise the more,
Known once and barred against satiety.

What we call Nature, all outside ourselves,
Is but our own conceit of what we see,   105
Our own reaction upon what we feel;
The world's a woman to our shifting mood,
Feeling with us, or making due pretence;
And therefore we the more persuade ourselves
To make all things our thought's confederates,   110
Conniving with us in whate'er we dream.
So when our Fancy seeks analogies,
Though she have hidden what she after finds,
She loves to cheat herself with feigned surprise.
I find my own complexion everywhere: 115
No rose, I doubt, was ever, like the first,
A marvel to the bush it dawned upon,
The rapture of its life made visible,
The mystery of its yearning realized,
As the first babe to the first woman born;   120
No falcon ever felt delight of wings
As when, an eyas, from the stolid cliff
Loosing himself, he followed his high heart
To swim on sunshine, masterless as wind;
And I believe the brown Earth takes delight   125
In the new snowdrop looking back at her,
To think that by some vernal alchemy
It could transmute her darkness into pearl;
What is the buxom peony after that,
With its coarse constancy of hoyden blush?   130
What the full summer to that wonder new?

But, if in nothing else, in us there is
A sense fastidious hardly reconciled
To the poor makeshifts of life's scenery,
Where the same slide must double all its parts,   135
Shoved in for Tarsus and hitched back for Tyre.[7]
I blame not in the soul this daintiness,
Rasher of surfeit than a humming-bird,
In things indifferent by sense purveyed;
It argues her an immortality   140
And dateless incomes of experience,
This unthrift housekeeping that will not brook
A dish warmed-over at the feast of life,
And finds Twice stale, served with whatever sauce.
Nor matters much how it may go with me   145

7. Tarsus and Tyre were ancient cities of Asia Minor.

Who dwell in Grub Street[8] and am proud to drudge
Where men, my betters, wet their crust with tears:
Use can make sweet the peach's shady side,
That only by reflection tastes of sun.

But she, my Princess, who will sometimes deign   150
My garret to illumine till the walls,
Narrow and dingy, scrawled with hackneyed thought
(Poor Richard slowly elbowing Plato out),[9]
Dilate and drape themselves with tapestries
Nausikaa[1] might have stooped o'er, while, between,   155
Mirrors, effaced in their own clearness, send
Her only image on through deepening deeps
With endless repercussion of delight,—
Bringer of life, witching each sense to soul,
That sometimes almost gives me to believe   160
I might have been a poet, gives at least
A brain desaxonized, an ear that makes
Music where none is, and a keener pang
Of exquisite surmise outleaping thought,—
Her will I pamper in her luxury: 165
No crumpled rose-leaf of too careless choice
Shall bring a northern nightmare to her dreams,
Vexing with sense of exile; hers shall be
The inviolate firstlings of experience,
Vibrations felt but once and felt lifelong: 170
Oh, more than half-way turn that Grecian front
Upon me, while with self-rebuke I spell,
On the plain fillet that confines thy hair
In conscious bounds of seeming unconstraint,
The Naught in overplus, thy race's badge!   175

One feast for her I secretly designed
In that Old World so strangely beautiful
To us the disinherited of eld,—
A day at Chartres, with no soul beside
To roil with pedant prate my joy serene   180
And make the minster shy of confidence.
I went, and, with the Saxon's pious care,
First ordered dinner at the pea-green inn,
The flies and I its only customers.

8. A London street described by Samuel Johnson as a habitation of literary hacks.
9. Franklin's *Poor Richard* almanacs were filled with aphorisms whose homely sentiments were more appealing to the unlearned American farmer than Plato's lofty wisdom.
1. Nausicaä, daughter of the king of Phaeacia, befriended Ulysses after he surprised her and her servants washing and airing the royal clothing and tapestries.

Eluding these, I loitered through the town,   185
With hope to take my minster unawares
In its grave solitude of memory.
A pretty burgh, and such as Fancy loves
For bygone grandeurs, faintly rumorous now
Upon the mind's horizon, as of storm   190
Brooding its dreamy thunders far aloof,
That mingle with our mood, but not disturb.
Its once grim bulwarks, tamed to lovers' walks,
Look down unwatchful on the sliding Eure,[2]
Whose listless leisure suits the quiet place,   195
Lisping among his shallows homelike sounds
At Concord and by Bankside heard before.
Chance led me to a public pleasure-ground,
Where I grew kindly with the merry groups,
And blessed the Frenchman for his simple art   200
Of being domestic in the light of day.
His language has no word, we growl, for Home;
But he can find a fireside in the sun,
Play with his child, make love, and shriek his mind,
By throngs of strangers undisprivacied.   205
He makes his life a public gallery,
Nor feels himself till what he feels comes back
In manifold reflection from without;
While we, each pore alert with consciousness,
Hide our best selves as we had stolen them,   210
And each bystander a detective were,
Keen-eyed for every chink of undisguise.

So, musing o'er the problem which was best,—
A life wide-windowed, shining all abroad,
Or curtains drawn to shield from sight profane   215
The rites we pay to the mysterious I,—
With outward senses furloughed and head bowed
I followed some fine instinct in my feet,
Till, to unbend me from the loom of thought,
Looking up suddenly, I found mine eyes   220
Confronted with the minster's vast repose.
Silent and gray as forest-leaguered cliff
Left inland by the ocean's slow retreat,
That hears afar the breeze-borne rote and longs,
Remembering shocks of surf that clomb and fell,   225
Spume-sliding down the baffled decuman,[3]
It rose before me, patiently remote

2. A river flowing through Chartres; a   3. The tenth wave.
minor tributary of the Seine.

From the great tides of life it breasted once,
Hearing the noise of men as in a dream.
I stood before the triple northern port,   230
Where dedicated shapes of saints and kings,
Stern faces bleared with immemorial watch,
Looked down benignly grave and seemed to say,
Ye come and go incessant; we remain
Safe in the hallowed quiets of the past;   235
Be reverent, ye who flit and are forgot,
Of faith so nobly realized as this.
I seem to have heard it said by learnëd folk
Who drench you with æsthetics till you feel
As if all beauty were a ghastly bore,   240
The faucet to let loose a wash of words,
That Gothic is not Grecian, therefore worse;
But, being convinced by much experiment
How little inventiveness there is in man,
Grave copier of copies, I give thanks   245
For a new relish, careless to inquire
My pleasure's pedigree, if so it please,
Nobly, I mean, nor renegade to art.
The Grecian gluts me with its perfectness,
Unanswerable as Euclid,[4] self-contained,   250
The one thing finished in this hasty world,
Forever finished, though the barbarous pit,
Fanatical on hearsay, stamp and shout
As if a miracle could be encored.
But ah! this other, this that never ends,   255
Still climbing, luring fancy still to climb,
As full of morals half-divined as life,
Graceful, grotesque, with ever new surprise
Of hazardous caprices sure to please,
Heavy as nightmare, airy-light as fern,   260
Imagination's very self in stone!
With one long sigh of infinite release
From pedantries past, present, or to come,
I looked, and owned myself a happy Goth.
Your blood is mine, ye architects of dream,   265
Builders of aspiration incomplete,
So more consummate, souls self-confident,
Who felt your own thought worthy of record
In monumental pomp! No Grecian drop
Rebukes these veins that leap with kindred thrill,   270
After long exile, to the mother-tongue.

4. The father of geometry (*fl.* 300 b.c.).

Ovid[5] in Pontus, puling for his Rome
Of men in invirile and disnatured dames
That poison sucked from the Attic bloom decayed,
Shrank with a shudder from the blue-eyed race   275
Whose force rough-handed should renew the world,
And from the dregs of Romulus[6] express
Such wine as Dante poured, or he who blew
Roland's[7] vain blast, or sang the Campeador[8]
In verse that clanks like armor in the charge,   280
Homeric juice, though brimmed in Odin's[9] horn.
And they could build, if not the columned fane
That from the height gleamed seaward many-hued,
Something more friendly with their ruder skies:
The gray spire, molten now in driving mist,   285
Now lulled with the incommunicable blue;
The carvings touched to meanings new with snow,
Or commented with fleeting grace of shade;
The statues, motley as man's memory,
Partial as that, so mixed of true and false,   290
History and legend meeting with a kiss
Across this bound-mark where their realms confine;
The painted windows, freaking gloom with glow,
Dusking the sunshine which they seem to cheer,
Meet symbol of the senses and the soul,   295
And the whole pile, grim with the Northman's thought
Of life and death, and doom, life's equal fee,—
These were before me: and I gazed abashed,
Child of an age that lectures, not creates,
Plastering our swallow-nests on the awful Past,   300
And twittering round the work of larger men,
As we had builded what we but deface.
Far up the great bells wallowed in delight,
Tossing their clangors o'er the heedless town,
To call the worshippers who never came,   305
Or women mostly, in loath twos and threes.
I entered, reverent of whatever shrine
Guards piety and solace for my kind
Or gives the soul a moment's truce of God,
And shared decorous in the ancient rite   310
My sterner fathers held idolatrous.
The service over, I was tranced in thought:

5. Publius Ovidius Naso (43 B.C.–17
A.D.?), Roman poet who eulogized the
heroes of Rome.
6. Romulus and his twin brother Re-
mus were the legendary founders of
Rome.

7. Hero of the *Song of Roland*, killed
at Roncesvalles, 778 A.D.
8. Cid Campeador ("Lord Conqueror"),
national hero of the Spanish Moorish
wars (died 1099).
9. Chief god of Norse mythology.

Solemn the deepening vaults, and most to me,
Fresh from the fragile realm of deal and paint,
Or brick mock-pious with a marble front;   315
Solemn the lift of high-embowered roof,
The clustered stems that spread in boughs disleaved,
Through which the organ blew a dream of storm,
Though not more potent to sublime with awe
And shut the heart up in tranquillity,   320
Than aisles to me familiar that o'erarch
The conscious silences of brooding woods,
Centurial shadows, cloisters of the elk:
Yet here was sense of undefined regret,
Irreparable loss, uncertain what: 325
Was all this grandeur but anachronism,
A shell divorced of its informing life,
Where the priest housed him like a hermit-crab,
An alien to that faith of elder days
That gathered round it this fair shape of stone?   330
Is old Religion but a spectre now,
Haunting the solitude of darkened minds,
Mocked out of memory by the sceptic day?
Is there no corner safe from peeping Doubt,
Since Gutenberg[1] made thought cosmopolite   335
And stretched electric threads from mind to mind?
Nay, did Faith build this wonder? or did Fear,
That makes a fetish and misnames it God
(Blockish or metaphysic, matters not),
Contrive this coop to shut its tyrant in,   340
Appeased with playthings, that he might not harm?

I turned and saw a beldame on her knees;
With eyes astray, she told mechanic beads
Before some shrine of saintly womanhood,
Bribed intercessor with the far-off Judge: 345
Such my first thought, by kindlier soon rebuked,
Pleading for whatsoever touches life
With upward impulse: be He nowhere else,
God is in all that liberates and lifts,
In all that humbles, sweetens, and consoles: 350
Blessèd the natures shored on every side
With landmarks of hereditary thought!
Thrice happy they that wander not lifelong
Beyond near succor of the household faith,

1. Johannes Gutenberg (1400?–1468), German inventor of printing from movable type.

The guarded fold that shelters, not confines!   355
Their steps find patience in familiar paths,
Printed with hope by loved feet gone before
Of parent, child, or lover, glorified
By simple magic of dividing Time.
My lids were moistened as the woman knelt,   360
And—was it will, or some vibration faint
Of sacred Nature, deeper than the will?—
My heart occultly felt itself in hers,
Through mutual intercession gently leagued.

Or was it not mere sympathy of brain?   365
A sweetness intellectually conceived
In simpler creeds to me impossible?
A juggle of that pity for ourselves
In others, which puts on such pretty masks
And snares self-love with bait of charity?   370
Something of all it might be, or of none:
Yet for a moment I was snatched away
And had the evidence of things not seen;
For one rapt moment; then it all came back,
This age that blots out life with question-marks,   375
This nineteenth century with its knife and glass
That make thought physical, and thrust far off
The Heaven, so neighborly with man of old,
To voids sparse-sown with alienated stars.
'Tis irrecoverable, that ancient faith,   380
Homely and wholesome, suited to the time,
With rod or candy for child-minded men:
No theologic tube, with lens on lens
Of syllogism transparent, brings it near,—
At best resolving some new nebula,   385
Or blurring some fixed-star of hope to mist.
Science was Faith once; Faith were Science now,
Would she but lay her bow and arrows by
And arm her with the weapons of the time.
Nothing that keeps thought out is safe from thought.   390
For there's no virgin-fort but self-respect,
And Truth defensive hath lost hold on God.
Shall we treat Him as if He were a child
That knew not His own purpose? nor dare trust
The Rock of Ages to their chemic tests,   395
Lest some day the all-sustaining base divine
Should fail from under us, dissolved in gas?

The armèd eye that with a glance discerns
In a dry blood-speck between ox and man,
Stares helpless at this miracle called life,   400
This shaping potency behind the egg,
This circulation swift of deity,
Where suns and systems inconspicuous float
As the poor blood-disks in our mortal veins.
Each age must worship its own thought of God,   405
More or less earthy, clarifying still
With subsidence continuous of the dregs;
Nor saint nor sage could fix immutably
The fluent image of the unstable Best,
Still changing in their very hands that wrought: 410
To-day's eternal truth To-morrow proved
Frail as frost-landscapes on a window-pane.
Meanwhile Thou smiledst, inaccessible,
At Thought's own substance made a cage for Thought,
And Truth locked fast with her own master-key;   415
Nor didst Thou reck what image man might make
Of his own shadow on the flowing world;
The climbing instinct was enough for Thee.
Or wast Thou, then, an ebbing tide that left
Strewn with dead miracle those eldest shores,   420
For men to dry, and dryly lecture on,
Thyself thenceforth incapable of flood?
Idle who hopes with prophets to be snatched
By virtue in their mantles left below;
Shall the soul live on other men's report,   425
Herself a pleasing fable of herself?
Man cannot be God's outlaw if he would,
Nor so abscond him in the caves of sense
But Nature still shall search some crevice out
With messages of splendor from that Source   430
Which, dive he, soar he, baffles still and lures.
This life were bruitish did we not sometimes
Have intimation clear of wider scope,
Hints of occasion infinite, to keep
The soul alert with noble discontent   435
And onward yearnings of unstilled desire;
Fruitless, except we now and then divined
A mystery of Purpose, gleaming through
The secular confusions of the world,
Whose will we darkly accomplish, doing ours.   440
No man can think nor in himself perceive,

Sometimes at waking, in the street sometimes,
Or on the hillside, always unforewarned,
A grace of being, finer than himself,
That beckons and is gone,—a larger life   445
Upon his own impinging, with swift glimpse
Of spacious circles luminous with mind,
To which the ethereal substance of his own
Seems but gross cloud to make that visible,
Touched to a sudden glory round the edge.   450
Who that hath known these visitations fleet
Would strive to make them trite and ritual?
I, that still pray at morning and at eve,
Loving those roots that feed us from the past,
And prizing more than Plato things I learned   455
At that best academe, a mother's knee,
Thrice in my life perhaps have truly prayed,
Thrice, stirred below my conscious self, have felt
That perfect disenthralment which is God;
Nor know I which to hold worst enemy,   460
Him who on speculation's windy waste
Would turn me loose, stript of the raiment warm
By Faith contrived against our nakedness,
Or him who, cruel-kind, would fain obscure,
With painted saints and paraphrase of God,   465
The soul's east-window of divine surprise.
Where others worship I but look and long;
For, though not recreant to my fathers' faith,
Its forms to me are weariness, and most
That drony vacuum of compulsory prayer,   470
Still pumping phrases for the Ineffable,
Though all the valves of memory gasp and wheeze.
Words that have drawn transcendent meanings up
From the best passion of all bygone time,
Steeped through with tears of triumph and remorse,   475
Sweet with all sainthood, cleansed in martyr-fires,
Can they, so consecrate and so inspired,
By repetition wane to vexing wind?
Alas! we cannot draw habitual breath
In the thin air of life's supremer heights,   480
We cannot make each meal a sacrament,
Nor with our tailors be disbodied souls,—
We men, too conscious of earth's comedy,
Who see two sides, with our posed selves debate,
And only for great stakes can be sublime!   485

Let us be thankful when, as I do here,
We can read Bethel[2] on a pile of stones,
And, seeing where God *has* been, trust in Him.

Brave Peter Fischer[3] there in Nuremberg,
Moulding Saint Sebald's miracles in bronze,   490
Put saint and stander-by in that quaint garb
Familiar to him in his daily walk,
Not doubting God could grant a miracle
Then and in Nuremberg, if so He would;
But never artist for three hundred years   495
Hath dared the contradiction ludicrous
Of supernatural in modern clothes.
Perhaps the deeper faith that is to come
Will see God rather in the strenuous doubt,
Than in the creed held as an infant's hand   500
Holds purposeless whatso is placed therein.

Say it is drift, not progress, none the less,
With the old sextant of the fathers' creed,
We shape our courses by new-risen stars,
And, still lip-loyal to what once was truth,   505
Smuggle new meanings under ancient names,
Unconscious perverts of the Jesuit, Time.
Change is the mask that all Continuance wears
To keep us youngsters harmlessly amused;
Meanwhile, some ailing or more watchful child,   510
Sitting apart, sees the old eyes gleam out,
Stern, and yet soft with humorous pity too.
Whilere, men burnt men for a doubtful point,
As if the mind were quenchable with fire,
And Faith danced round them with her war-paint on,   515
Devoutly savage as an Iroquois;
Now Calvin and Servetus[4] at one board
Snuff in grave sympathy a milder roast,
And o'er their claret settle Comte[5] unread.
Fagot and stake were desperately sincere: 520
Our cooler martyrdoms are done in types;

2. Hebrew, meaning "house of God"; the scene of Jacob's vision of the angels ascending and descending the mystical ladder (*cf.* Genesis xxviii: 12), where he built an altar of stones to commemorate the event.

3. Peter Vischer (1460–1529), one of a family of sculptors and brass founders, whose shrine of St. Sebald is an ornate structure containing the sarcophagus of the saint.

4. John Calvin (1509–1564), French theologian of the Reformation, prosecuted Michael Servetus (1511–1553), Spanish theologian, for his doctrinal heresies and was responsible for his death at the stake.

5. Auguste Comte (1798–1857), French mathematician and philosopher, founder of positivism, whose denial of metaphysics would have been vehemently opposed by both Calvin and Servetus.

And flames that shine in controversial eyes
Burn out no brains but his who kindles them.
This is no age to get cathedrals built:
Did God, then, wait for one in Bethlehem?   525
Worst is not yet: lo, where his coming looms,
Of Earth's anarchic children latest born,
Democracy, a Titan who hath learned
To laugh at Jove's old-fashioned thunderbolts,—
Could he not also forge them, if he would?   530
He, better skilled, with solvents merciless,
Loosened in air and borne on every wind,
Saps unperceived: the calm Olympian height
Of ancient order feels its bases yield,
And pale gods glance for help to gods as pale.   535
What will be left of good or worshipful,
Of spiritual secrets, mysteries,
Of fair Religion's guarded heritage,
Heirlooms of soul, passed downward unprofaned
From eldest Ind? This Western giant coarse,   540
Scorning refinements which he lacks himself,
Loves not nor heeds the ancestral hierarchies,
Each rank dependent on the next above
In orderly gradation fixed as fate.
King by mere manhood, nor allowing aught   545
Of holier unction than the sweat of toil;
In his own strength sufficient; called to solve,
On the rough edges of society,
Problems long sacred to the choicer few,
And improvise what elsewhere men receive   550
As gifts of Deity; tough foundling reared
Where every man's his own Melchisedek,[6]
How make him reverent of a King of kings?
Or Judge self-make, executor of laws
By him not first discussed and voted on?   555
For him no tree of knowledge is forbid,
Or sweeter if forbid. How save the ark,[7]
Or holy of holies, unprofaned a day
From his unscrupulous curiosity
That handles everything as if to buy,   560
Tossing aside what fabrics delicate
Suit not the rough-and-tumble of his ways?
What hope for those fine-nerved humanities
That made earth gracious once with gentler arts,

6. A type of the priest-king prefiguring Christ; *cf.* Genesis xiv: 18–20, and Hebrews v: 6.

7. *I.e.*, the ark of the covenant, which rested in the inner chamber of the Jewish tabernacle.

Now the rude hands have caught the trick of thought 565
And claim an equal suffrage with the brain?

The born disciple of an elder time,
(To me sufficient, friendlier than the new,)
Who in my blood feel motions of the Past,
I thank benignant Nature most for this,— 570
A force of sympathy, or call it lack
Of character firm-planted, loosing me
From the pent chamber of habitual self
To dwell enlarged in alien modes of thought,
Haply distasteful, wholesomer for that, 575
And through imagination to possess,
As they were mine, the lives of other men.
This growth original of virgin soil,
By fascination felt in opposites,
Pleases and shocks, entices and perturbs. 580
In this brown-fisted rough, this shirt-sleeved Cid,
This backwoods Charlemagne[8] of empires new,
Whose blundering heel instinctively finds out
The goutier foot of speechless dignities,
Who, meeting Cæsar's self, would slap his back, 585
Call him "Old Horse," and challenge to a drink,
My lungs draw braver air, my breast dilates
With ampler manhood, and I front both worlds,
Of sense and spirit, as my natural fiefs,
To shape and then reshape them as I will. 590
It was the first man's charter; why not mine?
How forfeit? when deposed in other hands?

Thou shudder'st, Ovid? Dost in him forebode
A new avatar of the large-limbed Goth,
To break, or seem to break, tradition's clew, 595
And chase to dreamland back thy gods dethroned?
I think man's soul dwells nearer to the east,
Nearer to morning's fountains than the sun;
Herself the source whence all tradition sprang,
Herself at once both labyrinth and clew. 600
The miracle fades out of history,
But faith and wonder and the primal earth
Are born into the world with every child.
Shall this self-maker with the prying eyes,
This creature disenchanted of respect 605
By the New World's new fiend, Publicity,
Whose testing thumb leaves everywhere its smutch,

8. King of the Franks and emperor of the Emperor of the Romans founded
the West, who by his crowning in 800 as the Holy Roman Empire.

Not one day feel within himself the need
Of loyalty to better than himself,
That shall ennoble him with the upward look? 610
Shall he not catch the Voice that wanders earth,
With spiritual summons, dreamed or heard,
As sometimes, just ere sleep seals up the sense,
We hear our mother call from deeps of Time,
And, waking, find it vision,—none the less 615
The benediction bides, old skies return,
And that unreal thing, preëminent,
Makes air and dream of all we see and feel?
Shall he divine no strength unmade of votes,
Inward, impregnable, found soon as sought, 620
Not cognizable of sense, o'er sense supreme?
Else were he desolate as none before.
His holy places may not be of stone,
Nor made with hands, yet fairer far than aught
By artist feigned or pious ardor reared, 625
Fit altars for who guards inviolate
God's chosen seat, the sacred form of man.
Doubtless his church will be no hospital
For superannuate forms and mumping shams,
No parlor where men issue policies 630
Of life-assurance on the Eternal Mind,
Nor his religion but an ambulance
To fetch life's wounded and malingerers in,
Scorned by the strong; yet he, unconscious heir
To the influence sweet of Athens and of Rome, 635
And old Judæa's gift of secret fire,
Spite of himself shall surely learn to know
And worship some ideal of himself,
Some divine thing, large-hearted, brotherly,
Not nice in trifles, a soft creditor, 640
Pleased with his world, and hating only cant.
And, if his Church be doubtful, it is sure
That, in a world, made for whatever else,
Not made for mere enjoyment, in a world
Of toil but half-requited, or, at best, 645
Paid in some futile currency of breath,
A world of incompleteness, sorrow swift
And consolation laggard, whatsoe'er
The form of building or the creed professed,
The Cross, bold type of shame to homage turned, 650
Of an unfinished life that sways the world,
Shall tower as sovereign emblem over all.

The kobold Thought moves with us when we shift
Our dwelling to escape him; perched aloft
On the first load of household-stuff we went;   655
For, where the mind goes, goes old furniture.
I, who to Chartres came to feed my eye
And give to Fancy one clear holiday,
Scarce saw the minster for the thoughts it stirred
Buzzing o'er past and future with vain quest.   660
Here once there stood a homely wooden church,
Which slow devotion nobly changed for this
That echoes vaguely to my modern steps.
By suffrage universal it was built,
As practiced then, for all the country came   665
From far as Rouen, to give votes for God,
Each vote a block of stone securely laid
Obedient to the master's deep-mused plan.
Will what our ballots rear, responsible
To no grave forethought, stand so long as this?   670
Delight like this the eye of after days
Brightening with pride that here, at least, were men
Who meant and did the noblest thing they knew?
Can our religion cope with deeds like this?
We, too, build Gothic contract-shams, because   675
Our deacons have discovered that it pays,
And pews sell better under vaulted roofs
Of plaster painted like an Indian squaw.
Shall not that Western Goth, of whom we spoke,
So fiercely practical, so keen of eye,   680
Find out, some day, that nothing pays but God,
Served whether on the smoke-shut battle-field,
In work obscure done honestly, or vote
For truth unpopular, or faith maintained
To ruinous convictions, or good deeds   685
Wrought for good's sake, mindless of heaven or hell?
Shall he not learn that all prosperity,
Whose bases stretch not deeper than the sense,
Is but a trick of this world's atmosphere,
A desert-born mirage of spire and dome,   690
Or find too late, the Past's long lesson missed,
That dust the prophets shake from off their feet
Grows heavy to drag down both tower and wall?
I know not; but, sustained by sure belief
That man still rises level with the height   695
Of noblest opportunities, or makes
Such, if the time supply not, I can wait.

I gaze round on the windows, pride of France,
Each the bright gift of some mechanic guild
Who loved their city and thought gold well spent   700
To make her beautiful with piety;
I pause, transfigured by some stripe of bloom,
And my mind throngs with shining auguries,
Circle on circle, bright as seraphim,
With golden trumpets, silent, that await   705
The signal to blow news of good to men.

Then the revulsion came that always comes
After these dizzy elations of the mind:
And with a passionate pang of doubt I cried,
"O mountain-born, sweet with snow-filtered air   710
From uncontaminate wells of ether drawn
And never-broken secrecies of sky,
Freedom, with anguish won, misprized till lost,
They keep thee not who from thy sacred eyes
Catch the consuming lust of sensual good   715
And the brute's license of unfettered will.
Far from the popular shout and venal breath
Of Cleon[9] blowing the mob's baser mind
To bubbles of wind-piloted conceit,
Thou shrinkest, gathering up thy skirts, to hide   720
In fortresses of solitary thought
And private virtue strong in self-restraint.
Must we too forfeit thee misunderstood,
Content with names, nor inly wise to know
That best things perish of their own excess,   725
And quality o'er-driven becomes defect?
Nay, is it thou indeed that we have glimpsed,
Or rather such illusion as of old
Through Athens glided menadlike and Rome,
A shape of vapor, mother of vain dreams   730
And mutinous traditions, specious plea
Of the glaived tyrant and long-memoried priest?"

I walked forth saddened; for all thought is sad,
And leaves a bitterish savor in the brain,
Tonic, it may be, not delectable,   735
And turned, reluctant, for a parting look
At those old weather-pitted images
Of bygone struggle, now so sternly calm.
About their shoulders sparrows had built nests,

9. Athenian political leader (died 422), whose reputation as a ruthless demagogue
is due to his enemy Aristophanes.

And fluttered, chirping, from gray perch to perch,   740
Now on a mitre poising, now a crown,
Irreverently happy. While I thought
How confident they were, what careless hearts
Flew on those lightsome wings and shared the sun,
A larger shadow crossed; and looking up,   745
I saw where, nesting in the hoary towers,
The sparrow-hawk slid forth on noiseless air,
With sidelong head that watched the joy below,
Grim Norman baron o'er this clan of Kelts.
Enduring Nature, force conservative,   750
Indifferent to our noisy whims! Men prate
Of all heads to an equal grade cashiered
On level with the dullest, and expect
(Sick of no worse distemper than themselves)
A wondrous cure-all in equality;   755
They reason that To-morrow must be wise
Because To-day was not, nor Yesterday,
As if good days were shapen of themselves,
Not of the very lifeblood of men's souls;
Meanwhile, long-suffering, imperturbable,   760
Thou quietly complet'st thy syllogism,
And from the premise sparrow here below
Draw'st sure conclusion of the hawk above,
Pleased with the soft-billed songster, pleased no less
With the fierce beak of natures aquiline.   765

Thou beautiful Old Time, now hid away
In the Past's valley of Avilion,[1]
Haply, like Arthur, till thy wound be healed,
Then to reclaim the sword and crown again!
Thrice beautiful to us; perchance less fair   770
To who possessed thee, as a mountain seems
To dwellers round its bases but a heap
Of barren obstacle that lairs the storm
And the avalanche's silent bolt holds back
Leashed with a hair,—meanwhile some far-off clown,   775
Hereditary delver of the plain,
Sees it an unmoved vision of repose,
Nest of the morning, and conjectures there
The dance of streams to idle shepherds' pipes,
And fairer habitations softly hung   780
On breezy slopes, or hid in valleys cool,

1. Avalon, the happy afterworld in Cel- the three queens and whence he was to
tic myth, or the mythical island where   return as a national savior (*cf.* Malory's
the mortally wounded Arthur, legendary   *Morte d'Arthur*).
king of ancient Britain, was taken by

For happier men. No mortal ever dreams
That the scant isthmus he encamps upon
Between two oceans, one, the Stormy, passed,
And one, the Peaceful, yet to venture on,   785
Has been that future whereto prophets yearned
For the fulfilment of Earth's cheated hope,
Shall be that past which nerveless poets moan
As the lost opportunity of song.
O Power, more near my life than life itself   790
(Or what seems life to us in sense immured),
Even as the roots, shut in the darksome earth,
Share in the tree-top's joyance, and conceive
Of sunshine and wide air and wingèd things
By sympathy of nature, so do I   795
Have evidence of Thee so far above,
Yet in and of me! Rather Thou the root
Invisibly sustaining, hid in light,
Not darkness, or in darkness made by us.
If sometimes I must hear good men debate   800
Of other witness of Thyself than Thou,
As if there needed any help of ours
To nurse Thy flickering life, that else must cease,
Blown out, as 't were a candle, by men's breath,
My soul shall not be taken in their snare,   805
To change her inward surety for their doubt
Muffled from sight in formal robes of proof:
While she can only feel herself through Thee,
I fear not Thy withdrawal; more I fear,
Seeing, to know Thee not, hoodwinked with dreams   810
Of signs and wonders, while, unnoticed, Thou,
Walking Thy garden still, commun'st with men,
Missed in the commonplace of miracle.

[1869] 1870

Democracy[2]

He must be a born leader or misleader of men, or must have been
sent into the world unfurnished with that modulating and restrain-

---

2. The appointment of Lowell at the
age of sixty-one as United States minister to Great Britain represented no
sinecure for a man grown old in his nation's literary and political service; he
had served with distinction in the same
capacity in Spain for the three previous
years, and the Court of St. James welcomed the cultured, witty, and devoted

American diplomat, whose popularity in
England led to many invitations to
represent his country at private and public functions. In the fall of 1884, he
was invited to become the president of
the Birmingham and Midland Institute,
an educational institution for working
people at Birmingham. He delivered his
inaugural address on October 6, 1884.

ing balance-wheel which we call a sense of humor, who, in old age, has as strong a confidence in his opinions and in the necessity of bringing the universe into conformity with them as he had in youth. In a world the very condition of whose being is that it should be in a perpetual flux, where all seems mirage, and the one abiding thing is the effort to distinguish realities from appearances, the elderly man must be indeed of a singularly tough and valid fibre who is certain that he has any clarified residuum of experience, any assured verdict of reflection, that deserves to be called an opinion, or who, even if he had, feels that he is justified in holding mankind by the button while he is expounding it. And in a world of daily—nay, almost hourly—journalism, where every clever man, every man who thinks himself clever, or whom anybody else thinks clever, is called upon to deliver his judgment point-blank and at the word of command on every conceivable subject of human thought, or, on what sometimes seems to him very much the same thing, on every inconceivable display of human want of thought, there is such a spendthrift waste of all those commonplaces which furnish the permitted staple of public discourse that there is little chance of beguiling a new tune out of the one-stringed instrument on which we have been thrumming so long. In this desperate necessity one is often tempted to think that, if all the words of the dictionary were tumbled down in a heap and then all those fortuitous juxtapositions and combinations that made tolerable sense were picked out and pieced together, we might find among them some poignant suggestions toward novelty of thought or expression. But, alas! it is only the great poets who seem to have this unsolicited profusion of unexpected and incalculable phrase, this infinite variety of topic. For everybody else everything has been said before, and said over again after. He who has read his Aristotle will be apt to think that observation has on most points of general applicability said its last word, and he who has mounted the tower of Plato to look abroad from it will never hope to climb another with so lofty a vantage of speculation. Where it is so simple if not so easy a thing to hold one's peace, why add to the general confusion of tongues? There is something disheartening, too, in being expected to fill up not less than a certain measure of time, as if the mind were an hour-glass, that need only be shaken and set on one end or the other, as the case may be, to run its allotted sixty minutes with decorous exactitude. I recollect being once told by the late eminent naturalist, Agassiz,[3] that when he was to deliver his first lecture as professor (at Zürich, I believe) he had grave doubts of his ability to occupy

The printing of the speech was made in London before Lowell left for Birmingham, and it was reprinted in *Democracy and Other Addresses* (1887).

3. Louis Agassiz (1807–1873), Swiss-born naturalist, Harvard professor and friend of Lowell; *cf.* his "Ode to Agassiz."

the prescribed three quarters of an hour. He was speaking without notes, and glancing anxiously from time to time at the watch that lay before him on the desk. "When I had spoken a half hour," he said, "I had told them everything I knew in the world, everything! Then I began to repeat myself," he added, roguishly, "and I have done nothing else ever since." Beneath the humorous exaggeration of the story I seemed to see the face of a very serious and improving moral. And yet if one were to say only what he had to say and then stopped, his audience would feel defrauded of their honest measure. Let us take courage by the example of the French, whose exportation of Bordeaux wines increases as the area of their land in vineyards is diminished.

To me, somewhat hopelessly revolving these things, the undelayable year has rolled round, and I find myself called upon to say something in this place, where so many wiser men have spoken before me. Precluded, in my quality of national guest, by motives of taste and discretion, from dealing with any question of immediate and domestic concern, it seemed to me wisest, or at any rate most prudent, to choose a topic of comparatively abstract interest, and to ask your indulgence for a few somewhat generalized remarks on a matter concerning which I had some experimental knowledge, derived from the use of such eyes and ears as Nature had been pleased to endow me withal, and such report as I had been able to win from them. The subject which most readily suggested itself was the spirit and the working of those conceptions of life and polity which are lumped together, whether for reproach or commendation, under the name of Democracy. By temperament and education of a conservative turn, I saw the last years of that quaint Arcadia[4] which French travellers saw with delighted amazement a century ago, and have watched the change (to me a sad one) from an agricultural to a proletary population. The testimony of Balaam[5] should carry some conviction. I have grown to manhood and am now growing old with the growth of this system of government in my native land, have watched its advances, or what some would call its encroachments, gradual and irresistible as those of a glacier, have been an ear-witness to the forebodings of wise and good and timid men, and have lived to see those forebodings belied by the course of events, which is apt to show itself humorously careless of the reputation of prophets. I recollect hearing a sagacious old gentleman say in 1840 that the doing away with the property qualification for suffrage twenty years before had been the ruin of the State of Massachusetts; that it had put public credit and private estate alike at the mercy of demagogues. I lived to see that Commonwealth

4. *I.e.*, the idealized concept of the agricultural and rural America of the eighteenth century.

5. *Cf.* Numbers xxii: 34.

twenty odd years later paying the interest on her bonds in gold, though it cost her sometimes nearly three for one to keep her faith, and that while suffering an unparalleled drain of men and treasure in helping to sustain the unity and self-respect of the nation.

If universal suffrage has worked ill in our larger cities, as it certainly has, this has been mainly because the hands that wielded it were untrained to its use. There the election of a majority of the trustees of the public money is controlled by the most ignorant and vicious of a population which has come to us from abroad, wholly unpracticed in self-government and incapable of assimilation by American habits and methods. But the finances of our towns, where the native tradition is still dominant and whose affairs are discussed and settled in a public assembly of the people, have been in general honestly and prudently administered. Even in manufacturing towns, where a majority of the voters live by their daily wages, it is not so often the recklessness as the moderation of public expenditure that surprises an old-fashioned observer. "The beggar is in the saddle at last," cries Proverbial Wisdom. "Why, in the name of all former experience, doesn't he ride to the Devil?" Because in the very act of mounting he ceased to be a beggar and became part owner of the piece of property he bestrides. The last thing we need be anxious about is property. It always has friends or the means of making them. If riches have wings to fly away from their owner, they have wings also to escape danger.

I hear America sometimes playfully accused of sending you all your storms, and am in the habit of parrying the charge by alleging that we are enabled to do this because, in virtue of our protective system, we can afford to make better bad weather than anybody else. And what wiser use could we make of it than to export it in return for the paupers which some European countries are good enough to send over to us who have not attained to the same skill in the manufacture of them? But bad weather is not the worst thing that is laid at our door. A French gentleman, not long ago, forgetting Burke's[6] monition of how unwise it is to draw an indictment against a whole people, has charged us with the responsibility of whatever he finds disagreeable in the morals or manners of his countrymen. If M. Zola[7] or some other competent witness would only go into the box and tell us what those morals and manners were before our example corrupted them! But I confess that I find little to interest and less to edify me in these international bandyings of "You're another."

I shall address myself to a single point only in the long list of

6. Edmund Burke (1729–1797), British statesman favoring moderation with the American colonies; *cf.* his speech *Conciliation with America* (1775).

7. Émile Zola (1840–1902), French naturalistic novelist who blamed excesses of the French Revolution in part on American example.

offences of which we are more or less gravely accused, because that really includes all the rest. It is that we are infecting the Old World with what seems to be thought the entirely new disease of Democracy. It is generally people who are in what are called easy circumstances who can afford the leisure to treat themselves to a handsome complaint, and these experience an immediate alleviation when once they have found a sonorous Greek name to abuse it by. There is something consolatory also, something flattering to their sense of personal dignity, and to that conceit of singularity which is the natural recoil from our uneasy consciousness of being commonplace, in thinking ourselves victims of a malady by which no one had ever suffered before. Accordingly they find it simpler to class under one comprehensive heading whatever they find offensive to their nerves, their tastes, their interests, or what they suppose to be their opinions, and christen it Democracy, much as physicians label every obscure disease gout, or as cross-grained fellows lay their ill-temper to the weather. But is it really a new ailment, and, if it be, is America answerable for it? Even if she were, would it account for the phylloxera, and hoof-and-mouth disease, and bad harvests, and bad English, and the German bands, and the Boers, and all the other discomforts with which these later days have vexed the souls of them that go in chariots?[8] Yet I have seen the evil example of Democracy in America cited as the source and origin of things quite as heterogeneous and quite as little connected with it by any sequence of cause and effect. Surely this ferment is nothing new. It has been at work for centuries, and we are more conscious of it only because in this age of publicity, where the newspapers offer a rostrum to whoever has a grievance, or fancies that he has, the bubbles and scum thrown up by it are more noticeable on the surface than in those dumb ages when there was a cover of silence and suppression on the cauldron. Bernardo Navagero,[9] speaking of the Provinces of Lower Austria in 1546, tells us that "in them there are five sorts of persons, Clergy, Barons, Nobles, Burghers, and Peasants. Of these last no account is made, because they have no voice in the Diet."

Nor was it among the people that subversive or mistaken doctrines had their rise. A Father of the Church[1] said that property was theft many centuries before Proudhon[2] was born. Bourdaloue[3] reaffirmed it. Montesquieu[4] was the inventor of national work-

---

8. *I.e.*, the highborn.
9. Italian cardinal and diplomat (1507–1565) from whose *Relazioni* * * * Lowell draws this quotation.
1. St. Ambrose (340–397), bishop of Milan.
2. Pierre Joseph Proudhon (1809–1865), French journalist and politician, active in the socialist movement; one

of his tenets was that possession of property was theft.
3. Louis Bourdaloue (1632–1704), French Jesuit professor and preacher.
4. Charles de Secondat, Baron de la Brède et de Montesquieu (1689–1755), French political philosopher whose *L'Esprit des Lois* (1748) had political influence in Europe and America.

shops, and of the theory that the State owed every man a living. Nay, was not the Church herself the first organized Democracy? A few centuries ago the chief end of man was to keep his soul alive, and then the little kernel of leaven that sets the gases at work was religious, and produced the Reformation. Even in that, far-sighted persons like the Emperor Charles V[5] saw the germ of political and social revolution. Now that the chief end of man seems to have become the keeping of the body alive, and as comfortably alive as possible, the leaven also has become wholly political and social. But there had also been social upheavals before the Reformation and contemporaneously with it, especially among men of Teutonic race. The Reformation gave outlet and direction to an unrest already existing. Formerly the immense majority of men—our brothers— knew only their sufferings, their wants, and their desires. They are beginning now to know their opportunity and their power. All persons who see deeper than their plates are rather inclined to thank God for it than to bewail it, for the sores of Lazarus have a poison in them against which Dives[6] has no antidote.

There can be no doubt that the spectacle of a great and prosperous Democracy on the other side of the Atlantic must react powerfully on the aspirations and political theories of men in the Old World who do not find things to their mind; but, whether for good or evil, it should not be overlooked that the acorn from which it sprang was ripened on the British oak. Every successive swarm that has gone out from this *officina gentium*[7] has, when left to its own instincts—may I not call them hereditary instincts?—assumed a more or less thoroughly democratic form. This would seem to show, what I believe to be the fact, that the British Constitution, under whatever disguises of prudence or decorum, is essentially democratic. England, indeed, may be called a monarchy with democratic tendencies, the United States a democracy with conservative instincts. People are continually saying that America is in the air, and I am glad to think it is, since this means only that a clearer conception of human claims and human duties is beginning to be prevalent. The discontent with the existing order of things, however, pervaded the atmosphere wherever the conditions were favorable, long before Columbus, seeking the back door of Asia, found himself knocking at the front door of America. I say wherever the conditions were favorable, for it is certain that the germs of disease do not stick or find a prosperous field for their development and noxious activity unless where the simplest sanitary precautions have been neglected. "For this effect defective comes by cause," as

5. Charles V (1500–1558), emperor of the Holy Roman Empire.
6. *Cf.* Luke xvi: 19–25, the parable of the beggar and the rich man (Dives), whose distress and comfort were reversed after death.
7. Laboratory of nations.

Polonius[8] said long ago. It is only by instigation of the wrongs of men that what are called the Rights of Man become turbulent and dangerous. It is then only that they syllogize unwelcome truths. It is not the insurrections of ignorance that are dangerous, but the revolts of intelligence:—

> The wicked and the weak rebel in vain,
> Slaves by their own compulsion.[9]

Had the governing classes in France during the last century paid as much heed to their proper business as to their pleasures or manners, the guillotine need never have severed that spinal-marrow of orderly and secular tradition through which in a normally constituted state the brain sympathizes with the extremities and sends will and impulsion thither. It is only when the reasonable and practicable are denied that men demand the unreasonable and impracticable; only when the possible is made difficult that they fancy the impossible to be easy. Fairy tales are made out of the dreams of the poor. No; the sentiment which lies at the root of democracy is nothing new. I am speaking always of a sentiment, a spirit, and not of a form of government; for this was but the outgrowth of the other and not its cause. This sentiment is merely an expression of the natural wish of people to have a hand, if need be a controlling hand, in the management of their own affairs. What is new is that they are more and more gaining that control, and learning more and more how to be worthy of it. What we used to call the tendency or drift—what we are being taught to call more wisely the evolution of things—has for some time been setting steadily in this direction. There is no good in arguing with the inevitable. The only argument available with an east wind is to put on your overcoat. And in this case, also, the prudent will prepare themselves to encounter what they cannot prevent. Some people advise us to put on the brakes, as if the movement of which we are conscious were that of a railway train running down an incline. But a metaphor is no argument, though it be sometimes the gunpowder to drive one home and imbed it in the memory. Our disquiet comes of what nurses and other experienced persons call growing-pains, and need not seriously alarm us. They are what every generation before us— certainly every generation since the invention of printing—has gone through with more or less good fortune. To the door of every generation there comes a knocking, and unless the household, like the Thane of Cawdor and his wife,[1] have been doing some deed without out a name, they need not shudder. It turns out at worst to be a

---

8. *Cf.* Shakespeare's *Hamlet* Act II, Scene 2.
9. From Samuel Taylor Coleridge's "France: An Ode." The first line should

read: "The Sensual and the Dark rebel in vain."
1. Lord and Lady Macbeth in Shakespeare's tragedy.

poor relation who wishes to come in out of the cold. The porter always grumbles and is slow to open. "Who's there, in the name of Beelzebub?"[2] he mutters. Not a change for the better in our human housekeeping has ever taken place that wise and good men have not opposed it,—have not prophesied with the alderman that the world would wake up to find its throat cut in consequence of it. The world, on the contrary, wakes up, rubs its eyes, yawns, stretches itself, and goes about its business as if nothing had happened. Suppression of the slave trade, abolition of slavery, trade unions,—at all of these excellent people shook their heads despondingly, and murmured "Ichabod."[3] But the trade unions are now debating instead of conspiring, and we all read their discussions with comfort and hope, sure that they are learning the business of citizenship and the difficulties of practical legislation.

One of the most curious of these frenzies of exclusion was that against the emancipation of the Jews. All share in the government of the world was denied for centuries to perhaps the ablest, certainly the most tenacious, race that had ever lived in it—the race to whom we owed our religion and the purest spiritual stimulus and consolation to be found in all literature—a race in which ability seems as natural and hereditary as the curve of their noses, and whose blood, furtively mingling with the bluest bloods in Europe, has quickened them with its own indomitable impulsion. We drove them into a corner, but they had their revenge, as the wronged are always sure to have it sooner or later. They made their corner the counter and banking-house of the world, and thence they rule it and us with the ignobler sceptre of finance. Your grandfathers mobbed Priestley[4] only that you might set up his statue and make Birmingham the headquarters of English Unitarianism. We hear it said sometimes that this is an age of transition, as if that made matters clearer; but can any one point us to an age that was not? If he could, he would show us an age of stagnation. The question for us, as it has been for all before us, is to make the transition gradual and easy, to see that our points are right so that the train may not come to grief. For we should remember that nothing is more natural for people whose education has been neglected than to spell evolution with an initial "r." A great man struggling with the storms of fate has been called a sublime spectacle; but surely a great man wrestling with these new forces that have come into the world, mastering them and controlling them to beneficent ends, would be a yet sublimer. Here is not a danger, and if there were it would be only a better school of manhood, a nobler scope for ambition. I have

2. *Cf.* Macbeth Act II, Scene 3.
3. Hebrew for "inglorious." *Cf.* I Samuel iv: 21.

4. English chemist and political liberal (1733–1804), whose home was ransacked by a mob in Birmingham in 1791.

hinted that what people are afraid of in democracy is less the thing itself than what they conceive to be its necessary adjuncts and consequences. It is supposed to reduce all mankind to a dead level of mediocrity in character and culture, to vulgarize men's conceptions of life, and therefore their code of morals, manners, and conduct— to endanger the rights of property and possession. But I believe that the real gravamen of the charges lies in the habit it has of making itself generally disagreeable by asking the Powers that Be at the most inconvenient moment whether they are the powers that ought to be. If the powers that be are in a condition to give a satisfactory answer to this inevitable question, they need feel in no way discomfited by it.

Few people take the trouble of trying to find out what democracy really is. Yet this would be a great help, for it is our lawless and uncertain thoughts, it is the indefiniteness of our impressions, that fill darkness, whether mental or physical, with spectres and hobgoblins. Democracy is nothing more than an experiment in government, more likely to succeed in a new soil, but likely to be tried in all soils, which must stand or fall on its own merits as others have done before it. For there is no trick of perpetual motion in politics any more than in mechanics. President Lincoln defined democracy to be "the government of the people by the people for the people." This is a sufficiently compact statement of it as a political arrangement. Theodore Parker[5] said that "Democracy meant not 'I'm as good as you are,' but 'You're as good as I am.'" And this is the ethical conception of it, necessary as a complement of the other; a conception which, could it be made actual and practical, would easily solve all the riddles that the old sphinx of political and social economy who sits by the roadside has been proposing to mankind from the beginning, and which mankind have shown such a singular talent for answering wrongly. In this sense Christ was the first true democrat that ever breathed, as the old dramatist Dekker[6] said he was the first true gentleman. The characters may be easily doubled, so strong is the likeness between them. A beautiful and profound parable of the Persian poet Jellaladeen[7] tells us that "One knocked at the Beloved's door, and a voice asked from within 'Who is there?' and he answered 'It is I.' Then the voice said, 'This house will not hold me and thee'; and the door was not opened. Then went the lover into the desert and fasted and prayed in solitude, and after a year he returned and knocked again at the door; and again the voice asked 'Who is there?' and he said 'It is thyself'; and the door was opened to him." But that is idealism, you will say, and this is an only too practical

5. Boston Unitarian minister and abolitionist (1810–1860).
6. Thomas Dekker (1570?–1641?), English dramatist, who spoke thus of
Christ in his *Honest Whore* (1604).
7. Jalal-uddin Rumi (1207–1272), Persian poet, author of the *Mesveni*, a collection of moral fables.

world. I grant it; but I am one of those who believe that the real will never find an irremovable basis till it rests on the ideal. It used to be thought that a democracy was possible only in a small territory, and this is doubtless true of a democracy strictly defined, for in such all the citizens decide directly upon every question of public concern in a general assembly. An example still survives in the tiny Swiss canton of Appenzell. But this immediate intervention of the people in their own affairs is not of the essence of democracy; it is not necessary, nor indeed, in most cases, practicable. Democracies to which Mr. Lincoln's definition would fairly enough apply have existed, and now exist, in which, though the supreme authority reside in the people, yet they can act only indirectly on the national policy. This generation has seen democracy with an imperial figurehead,[8] and in all that have ever existed the body politic has never embraced all the inhabitants included within its territory: the right to share in the direction of affairs has been confined to citizens, and citizenship has been further restricted by various limitations, sometimes of property, sometimes of nativity, and always of age and sex.

The framers of the American Constitution were far from wishing or intending to found a democracy in the strict sense of the word, though, as was inevitable, every expansion of the scheme of government they elaborated has been in a democratical direction. But this has been generally the slow result of growth, and not the sudden innovation of theory; in fact, they had a profound disbelief in theory, and knew better than to commit the folly of breaking with the past. They were not seduced by the French fallacy that a new system of government could be ordered like a new suit of clothes. They would as soon have thought of ordering a new suit of flesh and skin. It is only on the roaring loom of time that the stuff is woven for such a vesture of their thought and experience as they were meditating. They recognized fully the value of tradition and habit as the great allies of permanence and stability. They all had that distaste for innovation which belonged to their race, and many of them a distrust of human nature derived from their creed. The day of sentiment was over, and no dithyrambic affirmations or finedrawn analyses of the Rights of Man would serve their present turn. This was a practical question, and they addressed themselves to it as men of knowledge and judgment should. Their problem was how to adapt English principles and precedents to the new conditions of American life, and they solved it with singular discretion. They put as many obstacles as they could contrive, not in the way of the people's will, but of their whim. With few excep-

8. Louis Napoleon (1808–1873), the elected emperor of France, who set up a so-called democratic empire in 1852.

tions they probably admitted the logic of the then accepted syllogism,—democracy, anarchy, despotism. But this formula was framed upon the experience of small cities shut up to stew within their narrow walls, where the number of citizens made but an inconsiderable fraction of the inhabitants, where every passion was reverberated from house to house and from man to man with gathering rumor till every impulse became gregarious and therefore inconsiderate, and every popular assembly needed but an infusion of eloquent sophistry to turn it into a mob, all the more dangerous because sanctified with the formality of law.[9]

Fortunately their case was wholly different. They were to legislate for a widely scattered population and for States already practised in the discipline of a partial independence. They had an unequalled opportunity and enormous advantages. The material they had to work upon was already democratical by instinct and habitude. It was tempered to their hands by more than a century's schooling in self-government. They had but to give permanent and conservative form to a ductile mass. In giving impulse and direction to their new institutions, especially in supplying them with checks and balances, they had a great help and safeguard in their federal organization. The different, sometimes conflicting, interests and social systems of the several States made existence as a Union and coalescence into a nation conditional on a constant practice of moderation and compromise. The very elements of disintegration were the best guides in political training. Their children learned the lesson of compromise only too well, and it was the application of it to a question of fundamental morals that cost us our civil war. We learned once for all that compromise makes a good umbrella but a poor roof; that it is a temporary expedient, often wise in party politics, almost sure to be unwise in statesmanship.

Has not the trial of democracy in America proved, on the whole, successful? If it had not, would the Old World be vexed with any fears of its proving contagious? This trial would have been less severe could it have been made with a people homogeneous in race, language, and traditions, whereas the United States have been called on to absorb and assimilate enormous masses of foreign population, heterogeneous in all these respects, and drawn mainly from that class which might fairly say that the world was not their friend, nor the world's law. The previous condition too often justified the traditional Irishman, who, landing in New York and asked what his politics were, inquired if there was a Government there, and on being told that there was, retorted, "Thin I'm agin it!" We have taken from Europe the poorest, the most ignorant, the most

9. "The effect of the electric telegraph in reproducing this trooping of emotion and perhaps of opinion is yet to be measured. The effect of Darwinism as a disintegrator of humanitarianism is also to be reckoned with" [Lowell's note].

turbulent of her people, and have made them over into good citizens, who have added to our wealth, and who are ready to die in defence of a country and of institutions which they know to be worth dying for. The exceptions have been (and they are lamentable exceptions) where these hordes of ignorance and poverty have coagulated in great cities. But the social system is yet to seek which has not to look the same terrible wolf in the eyes. On the other hand, at this very moment Irish peasants are buying up the worn-out farms of Massachusetts, and making them productive again by the same virtues of industry and thrift that once made them profitable to the English ancestors of the men who are deserting them. To have achieved even these prosaic results (if you choose to call them so), and that out of materials the most discordant,—I might say the most recalcitrant,—argues a certain beneficent virtue in the system that could do it, and is not to be accounted for by mere luck. Carlyle said scornfully that America meant only roast turkey every day for everybody.[1] He forgot that States, as Bacon[2] said of wars, go on their bellies. As for the security of property, it should be tolerably well secured in a country where every other man hopes to be rich, even though the only property qualification be the ownership of two hands that add to the general wealth. Is it not the best security for anything to interest the largest possible number of persons in its preservation and the smallest in its division? In point of fact, far-seeing men count the increasing power of wealth and its combinations as one of the chief dangers with which the institutions of the United States are threatened in the not distant future. The right of individual property is no doubt the very corner-stone of civilization as hitherto understood, but I am a little impatient of being told that property is entitled to exceptional consideration because it bears all burdens of the State. It bears those, indeed, which can most easily be borne, but poverty pays with its person the chief expenses of war, pestilence, and famine. Wealth should not forget this, for poverty is beginning to think of it now and then. Let me not be misunderstood. I see as clearly as any man possibly can, and rate as highly, the value of wealth, and of hereditary wealth, as the security of refinement, the feeder of all those arts that ennoble and beautify life, and as making a country worth living in. Many an ancestral hall here in England has been a nursery of that culture which has been of example and benefit to all. Old gold has a civilizing virtue which new gold must grow old to be capable of secreting.

I should not think of coming before you to defend or to criticise

1. From *Latter Day Pamphlets*, No. 1 (1850), by Thomas Carlyle (1795–1881).

2. Sir Francis Bacon (1561–1626), English philosopher. *Cf.* his essay "Of the True Greatness of Kingdomes and Estates."

any form of government. All have their virtues, all their defects, and all have illustrated one period or another in the history of the race, with signal services to humanity and culture. There is not one that could stand a cynical cross-examination by an experienced criminal lawyer, except that of a perfectly wise and perfectly good despot, such as the world has never seen, except in that white-haired king of Browning's, who

> Lived long ago
> In the morning of the world,
> When Earth was nearer Heaven than now.[3]

The English race, if they did not invent government by discussion, have at least carried it nearest to perfection in practice. It seems a very safe and reasonable contrivance for occupying the attention of the country, and is certainly a better way of settling questions than by push of pike. Yet, if one should ask it why it should not rather be called government by gabble, it would have to fumble in its pocket a good while before it found the change for a convincing reply. As matters stand, too, it is beginning to be doubtful whether Parliament and Congress sit at Westminster and Washington or in the editors' rooms of the leading journals, so thoroughly is everything debated before the authorized and responsible debaters get on their legs. And what shall we say of government by a majority of voices? To a person who in the last century would have called himself an Impartial Observer, a numerical preponderance seems, on the whole, as clumsy a way of arriving at truth as could well be devised, but experience has apparently shown it to be a convenient arrangement for determining what may be expedient or advisable or practicable at any given moment. Truth, after all, wears a different face to everybody, and it would be too tedious to wait till all were agreed. She is said to lie at the bottom of a well, for the very reason, perhaps, that whoever looks down in search of her sees his own image at the bottom, and is persuaded not only that he has seen the goddess, but that she is far better-looking than he had imagined.

The arguments against universal suffrage are equally unanswerable. "What," we exclaim, "shall Tom, Dick, and Harry have as much weight in the scale as I?" Of course, nothing could be more absurd. And yet universal suffrage has not been the instrument of greater unwisdom than contrivances of a more select description. Assemblies could be mentioned composed entirely of Masters of Arts and Doctors in Divinity which have sometimes shown traces of human passion or prejudice in their votes. Have the Serene Highnesses and Enlightened Classes carried on the business of

3. From *Pippa Passes*, third song, by Robert Browning.

Mankind so well, then, that there is no use in trying a less costly method? The democratic theory is that those Constitutions are likely to prove steadiest which have the broadest base, that the right to vote makes a safety-valve of every voter, and that the best way of teaching a man how to vote is to give him the chance of practice. For the question is no longer the academic one, "Is it wise to give every man the ballot?" but rather the practical one, "Is it prudent to deprive whole classes of it any longer?" It may be conjectured that it is cheaper in the long run to lift men up than to hold them down, and that the ballot in their hands is less dangerous to society than a sense of wrong in their heads. At any rate this is the dilemma to which the drift of opinion has been for some time sweeping us, and in politics a dilemma is a more unmanageable thing to hold by the horns than a wolf by the ears. It is said that the right of suffrage is not valued when it is indiscriminately bestowed, and there may be some truth in this, for I have observed that what men prize most is a privilege, even if it be that of chief mourner at a funeral. But is there not danger that it will be valued at more than its worth if denied, and that some illegitimate way will be sought to make up for the want of it? Men who have a voice in public affairs are at once affiliated with one or other of the great parties between which society is divided, merge their individual hopes and opinions in its safer, because more generalized, hopes and opinions, are disciplined by its tactics, and acquire, to a certain degree, the orderly qualities of an army. They no longer belong to a class, but to a body corporate. Of one thing, at least, we may be certain, that, under whatever method of helping things to go wrong man's wit can contrive, those who have the divine right to govern will be found to govern in the end, and that the highest privilege to which the majority of mankind can aspire is that of being governed by those wiser than they. Universal suffrage has in the United States sometimes been made the instrument of inconsiderate changes, under the notion of reform, and this from a misconception of the true meaning of popular government. One of these has been the substitution in many of the States of popular election for official selection in the choice of judges. The same system applied to military officers was the source of much evil during our civil war, and, I believe, had to be abandoned. But it has been also true that on all great questions of national policy a reserve of prudence and discretion has been brought out at the critical moment to turn the scale in favor of a wiser decision. An appeal to the reason of the people has never been known to fail in the long run. It is, perhaps, true that, by effacing the principle of passive obedience, democracy, ill understood, has slackened the spring of that ductility to discipline which is essential to "the unity and married calm of States." But I feel assured that experience and necessity will cure this evil, as they have shown their power to cure others. And under what frame of policy have evils ever been remedied till they became intolerable, and shook men out of their indolent indifference through their fears?

We are told that the inevitable result of democracy is to sap the foundations of personal independence, to weaken the principle of authority, to lessen the respect due to eminence, whether in station, virtue, or genius. If these things were so, society could not hold together. Perhaps the best forcing-house of robust individuality would be where public opinion is inclined to be most overbearing, as he must be of heroic temper who should walk along Piccadilly at the height of the season in a soft hat. As for authority, it is one of the symptoms of the time that the religious reverence for it is declining everywhere, but this is due partly to the fact that state-craft is no longer looked upon as a mystery, but as a business, and partly to the decay of superstition, by which I mean the habit of respecting what we are told to respect rather than what is respectable in itself. There is more rough and tumble in the American democracy than is altogether agreeable to people of sensitive nerves and refined habits, and the people take their political duties lightly and laughingly, as is, perhaps, neither unnatural nor unbecoming in a young giant. Democracies can no more jump away from their own shadows than the rest of us can. They no doubt sometimes make mistakes and pay honor to men who do not deserve it. But they do this because they believe them worthy of it, and though it be true that the idol is the measure of the worshipper, yet the worship has in it the germ of a nobler religion. But is it democracies alone that fall into these errors? I, who have seen it proposed to erect a statue to Hudson,[4] the railway king, and have heard Louis Napoleon hailed as the saviour of society by men who certainly had no democratic associations or leanings, am not ready to think so. But democracies have likewise their finer instincts. I have also seen the wisest statesman and most pregnant speaker of our generation, a man of humble birth and ungainly manners, of little culture beyond what his own genius supplied, become more absolute in power than any monarch of modern times through the reverence of his countrymen for his honesty, his wisdom, his sincerity, his faith in God and man, and the nobly humane simplicity of his character. And I remember another whom popular respect enveloped as with a halo, the least vulgar of men, the most austerely genial, and the most independent of opinion. Wherever he went he never met a stranger, but everywhere neighbors and friends proud of him as their ornament and

4. George Hudson (1800–1871), English railway promoter. Lowell was voicing general disapproval of the proposal to honor him by erecting a statue.

decoration. Institutions which could bear and breed such men as Lincoln and Emerson had surely some energy for good. No, amid all the fruitless turmoil and miscarriage of the world, if there be one thing steadfast and of favorable omen, one thing to make optimism distrust its own obscure distrust, it is the rooted instinct in men to admire what is better and more beautiful than themselves. The touchstone of political and social institutions is their ability to supply them with worthy objects of this sentiment, which is the very tap-root of civilization and progress. There would seem to be no readier way of feeding it with the elements of growth and vigor than such an organization of society as will enable men to respect themselves, and so to justify them in respecting others.

Such a result is quite possible under other conditions than those of an avowedly democratical Constitution. For I take it that the real essence of democracy was fairly enough defined by the First Napoleon when he said that the French Revolution meant "la carrière ouverte aux talents"[5]—a clear pathway for merit of whatever kind. I should be inclined to paraphrase this by calling democracy that form of society, no matter what its political classification, in which every man had a chance and knew that he had it. If a man can climb, and feels himself encouraged to climb, from a coalpit to the highest position for which he is fitted, he can well afford to be indifferent what name is given to the government under which he lives. The Bailli of Mirabeau,[6] uncle of the more famous tribune of that name, wrote in 1771: "The English are, in my opinion, a hundred times more agitated and more unfortunate than the very Algerines themselves, because they do not know and will not know till the destruction of their over-swollen power, which I believe very near, whether they are monarchy, aristocracy, or democracy, and wish to play the part of all three." England has not been obliging enough to fulfil the Bailli's prophecy, and perhaps it was this very carelessness about the name, and concern about the substance of popular government, this skill in getting the best out of things as they are, in utilizing all the motives which influence men, and in giving one direction to many impulses, that has been a principal factor of her greatness and power. Perhaps it is fortunate to have an unwritten Constitution, for men are prone to be tinkering the work of their own hands, whereas they are more willing to let time and circumstance mend or modify what time and circumstance have made. All free governments, whatever their name, are in reality governments by public opinion, and it is on the quality of this public opinion that their prosperity depends. It is, therefore, their

5. Opportunity is open to those with talents.

6. Jean Antoine Riquetti, Bailli de Mirabeau (1666–1737), uncle of Honoré Gabriel Riquetti, Comte de Mirabeau (1749–1791), leading statesman of the French Revolution.

first duty to purify the element from which they draw the breath of life. With the growth of democracy grows also the fear, if not the danger, that this atmosphere may be corrupted with poisonous exhalations from lower and more malarious levels, and the question of sanitation becomes more instant and pressing. Democracy in its best sense is merely the letting in of light and air. Lord Sherbrooke,[7] with his usual epigrammatic terseness, bids you educate your future rulers. But would this alone be a sufficient safeguard? To educate the intelligence is to enlarge the horizon of its desires and wants. And it is well that this should be so. But the enterprise must go deeper and prepare the way for satisfying those desires and wants in so far as they are legitimate. What is really ominous of danger to the existing order of things is not democracy (which, properly understood, is a conservative force), but the Socialism which may find a fulcrum in it. If we cannot equalize conditions and fortunes any more than we can equalize the brains of men—and a very sagacious person has said that "where two men ride on a horse one must ride behind"—we can yet, perhaps, do something to correct those methods and influences that lead to enormous inequalities, and to prevent their growing more enormous. It is all very well to pooh-pooh Mr. George[8] and to prove him mistaken in his political economy. I do not believe that land should be divided because the quantity of it is limited by nature. Of what may this not be said? A *fortiori*,[9] we might on the same principle insist on a division of human wit, for I have observed that the quantity of this has been even more inconveniently limited. Mr. George himself has an inequitably large share of it. But he is right in his impelling motive; right, also, I am convinced, in insisting that humanity makes a part, by far the most important part, of political economy; and in thinking man to be of more concern and more convincing than the longest column of figures in the world. For unless you include human nature in your addition, your total is sure to be wrong and your deductions from it fallacious. Communism means barbarism, but Socialism means, or wishes to mean, co-operation and community of interests, sympathy, the giving to the hands not so large a share as to the brains, but a larger share than hitherto in the wealth they must combine to produce—means, in short, the practical application of Christianity to life, and has in it the secret of an orderly and benign reconstruction. State Socialism would cut off the very roots in personal character—self-help, forethought, and frugality—which nourish and sustain the trunk and branches of every vigorous Commonwealth.

7. Robert Lowe, Viscount Sherbrooke (1811–1892), liberal English statesman.

8. Henry George (1839–1897), economist, advocate of the single tax, whose most famous work is *Progress and Poverty* (1879).

9. With greater force.

HENRY TIMROD
(1828–1867)

Henry Timrod's enduring value for today's reader rests upon a small sheaf of poems written during the Civil War. However, among southern poets before the war, Poe alone surpassed Timrod in power, emotional clarity, and craftsmanship. The war matured Timrod and gave him his most compelling subject, but its rigors also hastened his death at the age of not quite thirty-nine.

Charleston, South Carolina, where Timrod was born in 1828, was then a southern literary capital, but its other poets, best represented by William Gilmore Simms and Paul Hamilton Hayne, were somewhat pallid and sentimental regionalists. Timrod, like these, was devoted to South Carolina and to his city, whose scenes and life gave substance to his poems, yet his loyalties were large, and he opposed secession until the war was inevitable. Humanist and humanitarian, he wrote in the perspective of a long tradition that incorporated both his beloved Latin classics and the work of such contemporaries as James Russell Lowell, with whose poems of the war his own may be justly compared. As Professor Hubbell has suggested (*The Last Years of Henry Timrod*), the range of his poetry during the few years of his life is such that, had he lived beyond the war, he might have been remembered as something more than the "Laureate of the Confederacy."

Unlike Paul Hamilton Hayne,

his schoolmate and lifelong friend, Timrod was not born into the patrician tradition that flourished in Charleston. He was the grandson of an immigrant German tailor; and his father was a bookbinder and bookseller who won fleeting attention for his poetry before his death when Henry was only ten. The boy attended an excellent private school and spent a year at the University of Georgia. The first serious breakdown of his health, together with financial difficulties, terminated his university life, although he continued for years to cherish the hope of becoming a college professor, in preparation for which he studied the classics, a labor of love, and read widely in general literature. Meanwhile, in somewhat better health, he read for the law in the office of a distinguished Charleston attorney, and then became a family tutor at three great plantations successively before entering journalism at the age of thirty.

His poems had been appearing sporadically in southern magazines since 1848, when he began sending verses to the *Southern Literary Messenger*. When Hayne became editor of the new *Russell's Magazine* in 1857, Timrod was an accepted member of the Charleston coterie that supported it. In 1860 his *Poems*, the only volume that he published, appeared in Boston. As compared with his poems of the next six years, these seem, as a whole, frail and immature.

For a few months in 1861–1862 he served in the Confederate army, but he was discharged because of ill-health. For the same reason he had to relinquish his assignment as war correspondent for the Charleston *Mercury*.

In 1864, when southern journalism was already ruined by the war, he married the "Katie" of his poems, having recently become editor of the Columbia *South Carolinian*, for a pittance. When Sherman's army, at the conclusion of the war, marched "from Atlanta to the sea," sacking and burning Columbia on February 17, 1865, Timrod was ruined. A sister, his brother-in-law, and his infant son had all died within two years, when, early in 1866, answering an inquiry of Hayne about his condition, he replied, "I can embody it all in a few words: *beggary, starvation, death, bitter grief, utter want of hope!*" Eighteen months later, on October 6,

1867, he died of tuberculosis and perhaps lack of proper food and care. His war poems, however, were still alive in southern memory, and not unknown in the North, when Hayne edited the first collection of Timrod's poems in 1873.

Timrod published only one volume, his *Poems*, 1860. After his death a collection was made by Paul Hamilton Hayne, in *The Poems of Henry Timrod*, 1873, the source of the texts below. A Memorial Edition, *Poems of Henry Timrod*, 1899, contained additional poems. *The Uncollected Poems of Henry Timrod*, edited by Guy A. Cardwell, 1942, increased the number of the collected poems. E. W. Parks edited *The Essays of Henry Timrod*, 1942, especially valuable in assembling the poet's critical essays. E. W. Parks also provided a good selection of the prose and verse, with bibliography and critical comment, in *Southern Poets*, American Writers Series, 1936.

Hayne's edition contains the first authoritative biographical sketch; see also the introductions to the other editions named. Biographical studies are G. A. Wauchope, *Henry Timrod: Man and Poet*, 1915; H. T. Thompson, *Henry Timrod: Laureate of the Confederacy*, 1928; and J. B. Hubbell, *The Last Years of Henry Timrod: 1864–1867*, 1941, containing valuable correspondence and fugitive prose.

Sonnet: I Scarcely Grieve[1]

I scarcely grieve, O Nature! at the lot
That pent my life within a city's bounds,
And shut me from thy sweetest sights and sounds.
Perhaps I had not learned, if some lone cot
Had nursed a dreamy childhood, what the mart   5
Taught me amid its turmoil; so my youth
Had missed full many a stern but wholesome truth.
Here, too, O Nature! in this haunt of Art,
Thy power is on me, and I own thy thrall.
There is no unimpressive spot on earth!   10
The beauty of the stars is over all,

1. Timrod's love of the sonnet form is strikingly revealed in his essay "The Character and Scope of the Sonnet," in *Russell's Magazine* for May, 1857, which may be found in Parks's edition of the *Essays*. There, and in the sonnets themselves, one discovers Timrod's devotion and indebtedness to Wordsworth. "I Scarcely Grieve," although it speaks with Timrod's voice and experience, recalls Wordsworth's sonnet "Composed upon Westminster Bridge."

And Day and Darkness visit every hearth.
Clouds do not scorn us: yonder factory's smoke
Looked like a golden mist when morning broke.

1860, 1873

Sonnet: Most Men Know Love

Most men know love but as a part of life;
They hide it in some corner of the breast,
Even from themselves; and only when they rest
In the brief pauses of that daily strife,
Wherewith the world might else be not so rife,   5
They draw it forth (as one draws forth a toy
To soothe some ardent, kiss-exacting boy)
And hold it up to sister, child, or wife.
Ah me! why may not love and life be one?
Why walk we thus alone, when by our side,   10
Love, like a visible God, might be our guide?
How would the marts grow noble! and the street,
Worn like a dungeon-floor by weary feet,
Seem then a golden court-way of the Sun!

1873

The Cotton Boll[2]

While I recline
At ease beneath
This immemorial pine,
Small sphere!
(By dusky fingers brought this morning here   5
And shown with boastful smiles),
I turn thy cloven sheath,
Through which the soft white fibers peer,
That, with their gossamer bands,
Unite, like love, the sea-divided lands;   10
And slowly, thread by thread,
Draw forth the folded strands,
Than which the trembling line,
By whose frail help yon startled spider fled

2. Timrod wrote two excellent odes on the Civil War, but "The Cotton Boll" is more disciplined in spirit and form than its companion piece, "Ethnogenesis." Although Lowell's "Commemoration Ode" has rather more formality, the two gifted poets, divided by war, reveal the same humanitarian impulses. "The Cotton Boll" first appeared in the Charleston *Mercury* for September 3, 1861, and was collected in *The Poems of Henry Timrod* (1873).

Down the tall spear-grass from his swinging bed,   15
Is scarce more fine;
And as the tangled skein
Unravels in my hands,
Betwixt me and the noonday light,
A veil seems lifted, and for miles and miles   20
The landscape broadens on my sight,
As, in the little boll, there lurked a spell
Like that which, in the ocean shell,
With mystic sound,
Breaks down the narrow walls that hem us round,   25
And turns some city lane
Into the restless main,
With all his capes and isles!

Yonder bird,
Which floats, as if at rest,
In those blue tracts above the thunder, where   30
No vapors cloud the stainless air,
And never sound is heard,
Unless at such rare time
When, from the City of the Blest,[3]
Rings down some golden chime,   35
Sees not from his high place
So vast a cirque of summer space
As widens round me in one mighty field,
Which, rimmed by seas and sands,
Doth hail its earliest daylight in the beams   40
Of gray Atlantic dawns;
And, broad as realms made up of many lands,
Is lost afar
Behind the crimson hills and purple lawns   45
Of sunset, among plains which roll their streams
Against the Evening Star!

And lo!
To the remotest point of sight,
Although I gaze upon no waste of snow,
The endless field is white;   50
And the whole landscape glows,
For many a shining league away,
With such accumulated light
As Polar lands would flash beneath a tropic day!
Nor lack there (for the vision grows,   55
And the small charm within my hands—

3. *I.e.*, the heavenly city, or "new Jerusalem" (Revelation xxi, xxii); represented as the "City of the Blest" also
by Dante, *Paradiso*, xxiv.

More potent even than the fabled one,
Which oped whatever golden mystery
Lay hid in fairy wood or magic vale,   60
The curious ointment of the Arabian tale[4]—
Beyond all mortal sense
Doth stretch my sight's horizon, and I see,
Beneath its simple influence,
As if with Uriel's[5] crown,   65
I stood in some great temple of the Sun,
And looked, as Uriel, down!)
Nor lack there pastures rich and fields all green
With all the common gifts of God,
For temperate airs and torrid sheen   70
Weave Edens of the sod;
Through lands which look one sea of billowy gold
Broad rivers wind their devious ways;
A hundred isles in their embraces fold
A hundred luminous bays;   75
And through yon purple haze
Vast mountains lift their plumed peaks cloud-crowned;
And, save where up their sides the plowman creeps,
An unhewn forest girds them grandly round,
In whose dark shades a future navy sleeps!   80
Ye Stars, which, though unseen, yet with me gaze
Upon this loveliest fragment of the earth!
Thou Sun, that kindlest all thy gentlest rays
Above it, as to light a favorite hearth!
Ye Clouds, that in your temples in the West   85
See nothing brighter than its humblest flowers!
And you, ye Winds, that on the ocean's breast
Are kissed to coolness ere ye reach its bowers!
Bear witness with me in my song of praise,
And tell the world that, since the world began,   90
No fairer land hath fired a poet's lays,
Or given a home to man!

But these are charms already widely blown!
His be the meed whose pencil's trace
Hath touched our very swamps with grace,   95
And round whose tuneful way
All Southern laurels bloom;
The Poet of "The Woodlands,"[6] unto whom

4. The *Arabian Nights,* in which various charms of this sort appear; *e.g.,* the "open sesame" of Ali Baba.
5. An archangel. *Cf.* Milton's light-crowned "Regent of the Sun" (*Paradise Lost,* Book III, ll. 621–724). "Uriel" is Hebrew for "light of God."
6. William Gilmore Simms (1806–1870), popular South Carolina poet and novelist, lived at "The Woodlands."

Alike are known
The flute's low breathing and the trumpet's tone,   100
And the soft west wind's sighs;
But who shall utter all the debt,
O land wherein all powers are met
That bind a people's heart,
The world doth owe thee at this day,   105
And which it never can repay,
Yet scarcely deigns to own!
Where sleeps the poet who shall fitly sing
The source wherefrom doth spring
That mighty commerce which, confined   110
To the mean channels of no selfish mart,
Goes out to every shore
Of this broad earth, and throngs the sea with ships
That bear no thunders; hushes hungry lips
In alien lands;   115
Joins with a delicate web remotest strands;
And gladdening rich and poor,
Doth gild Parisian domes,
Or feed the cottage-smoke of English homes,
And only bounds its blessings by mankind!   120
In offices like these, thy mission lies,
My Country! and it shall not end
As long as rain shall fall and Heaven bend
In blue above thee; though thy foes be hard
And cruel as their weapons, it shall guard   125
Thy hearth-stones as a bulwark; make thee great
In white and bloodless state;
And haply, as the years increase—
Still working through its humbler reach
With that large wisdom which the ages teach—   130
Revive the half-dead dream of universal peace!
As men who labor in that mine
Of Cornwall, hollowed out beneath the bed
Of ocean, when a storm rolls overhead,
Hear the dull booming of the world of brine   135
Above them, and a mighty muffled roar
Of winds and waters, yet toil calmly on,
And split the rock, and pile the massive ore,
Or carve a niche, or shape the archèd roof;
So I, as calmly, weave my woof   140
Of song, chanting the days to come,
Unsilenced, though the quiet summer air
Stirs with the bruit of battles, and each dawn

Wakes from its starry silence to the hum
Of many gathering armies. Still,   145
In that we sometimes hear,
Upon the Northern winds, the voice of woe
Not wholly drowned in triumph, though I know
The end must crown us, and a few brief years
Dry all our tears,   150
I may not sing too gladly. To thy will
Resigned, O Lord! we cannot all forget
That there is much even Victory must regret.
And, therefore, not too long
From the great burthen of our country's wrong   155
Delay our just release!
And, if it may be, save
These sacred fields of peace
From stain of patriot or of hostile blood!
Oh, help us, Lord! to roll the crimson flood   160
Back on its course, and while our banners wing
Northward, strike with us! till the Goth[7] shall cling
To his own blasted altar-stones, and crave
Mercy; and we shall grant it, and dictate
The lenient future of his fate   165
There, where some rotting ships and crumbling quays
Shall one day mark the Port which ruled the Western seas.

1861, 1873

Charleston[8]

Calm as that second summer which precedes
     The first fall of the snow,
In the broad sunlight of heroic deeds
     The City bides the foe.

As yet, behind their ramparts stern and proud,   5
     Her bolted thunders sleep—
Dark Sumter like a battlemented cloud
     Looms o'er the solemn deep.

No Calpe[9] frowns from lofty cliff or scar
     To guard the holy strand;   10

7. Romans regarded the Goths, a Teutonic people who invaded the Empire, as barbarians from the north.
8. First published in the Charleston *Mercury* for December 13, 1862. Stanzas 2 and 3 reflect the initial confidence of the Confederates resulting from their control of the strategic port of Charleston. Within a month after her secession (December 20, 1860), South Carolina had occupied Fort Moultrie without a struggle; fortified Castle Pinckney and the shore positions; and on April 13, 1861, forced the federal evacuation of Fort Sumter, thus securing the entrance of war materiel.
9. Gibraltar.

But Moultrie holds in leash her dogs of war
    Above the level sand.

And down the dunes a thousand guns lie couched
    Unseen beside the flood,
Like tigers in some Orient jungle crouched,   15
    That wait and watch for blood.

Meanwhile, through streets still echoing with trade,
    Walk grave and thoughtful men
Whose hands may one day wield the patriot's blade
    As lightly as the pen.   20

And maidens with such eyes as would grow dim
    Over a bleeding hound
Seem each one to have caught the strength of him
    Whose sword she sadly bound.

Thus girt without and garrisoned at home,   25
    Day patient following day,
Old Charleston looks from roof and spire and dome
    Across her tranquil bay.

Ships through a hundred foes, from Saxon lands[1]
    And spicy Indian ports   30
Bring Saxon steel and iron to her hands
    And Summer to her courts.

But still, along yon dim Atlantic line
    The only hostile smoke
Creeps like a harmless mist above the brine   35
    From some frail, floating oak.

Shall the Spring dawn, and she, still clad in smiles
    And with an unscathed brow,
Rest in the strong arms of her palm-crowned isles
    As fair and free as now?   40

We know not: in the temple of the Fates
    God has inscribed her doom;
And, all untroubled in her faith, she waits
    The triumph or the tomb.

1862, 1873

1. Chiefly England, which secretly supported and supplied the southerners in the earlier years of the war.

Spring

Spring, with that nameless pathos in the air
Which dwells with all things fair,
Spring, with her golden suns and silver rain,
Is with us once again.

Out in the lonely woods the jasmine burns   5
Its fragrant lamps, and turns
Into a royal court with green festoons
The banks of dark lagoons.

In the deep heart of every forest tree
The blood is all aglee,   10
And there's a look about the leafless bowers
As if they dreamed of flowers.

Yet still on every side we trace the hand
Of Winter in the land,
Save where the maple reddens on the lawn,   15
Flushed by the season's dawn;

Or where, like those strange semblances we find
That age to childhood bind,
The elm puts on, as if in Nature's scorn,
The brown of Autumn corn.   20

As yet the turf is dark, although you know
That, not a span below,
A thousand germs are groping through the gloom,
And soon will burst their tomb.

Already, here and there, on frailest stems   25
Appear some azure gems,
Small as might deck, upon a gala day,
The forehead of a fay.

In gardens you may note amid the dearth
The crocus breaking earth;   30
And near the snowdrop's tender white and green,
The violet in its screen.

But many gleams and shadows need must pass
Along the budding grass,
And weeks go by, before the enamored South   35
Shall kiss the rose's mouth.

Still there's a sense of blossoms yet unborn
In the sweet airs of morn;

One almost looks to see the very street
Grow purple at his feet.   40

At times a fragrant breeze comes floating by,
And brings, you know not why,
A feeling as when eager crowds await
Before a palace gate

Some wondrous pageant; and you scarce would start,   45
If from a beech's heart,
A blue-eyed Dryad, stepping forth, should say,
"Behold me! I am May!"

Ah! who would couple thoughts of war and crime
With such a blessèd time!   50
Who in the west wind's aromatic breath
Could hear the call of Death!

Yet not more surely shall the Spring awake
The voice of wood and brake,
Then she shall rouse, for all her tranquil charms,   55
A million men to arms.

There shall be deeper hues upon her plains
Than all her sunlit rains,
And every gladdening influence around,
Can summon from the ground.   60

Oh! standing on this desecrated mould,
Methinks that I behold,
Lifting her bloody daisies up to God,
Spring kneeling on the sod,

And calling, with the voice of all her rills,   65
Upon the ancient hills
To fall and crush the tyrants and the slaves
Who turn her meads to graves.

1863   1873

The Unknown Dead[2]

The rain is plashing on my sill,
But all the winds of Heaven are still;
And so it falls with that dull sound
Which thrills us in the church-yard ground,
When the first spadeful drops like lead   5

2. First published in the *Southern Il-*   collected in *The Poems of Henry Tim-*
lustrated News for July 4, 1863, and   *rod* (1873).

Upon the coffin of the dead.
Beyond my streaming window-pane,
I cannot see the neighboring vane,
Yet from its old familiar tower
The bell comes, muffled, through the shower.   10
What strange and unsuspected link
Of feeling touched, has made me think—
While with a vacant soul and eye
I watch that gray and stony sky—
Of nameless graves on battle-plains   15
Washed by a single winter's rains,
Where, some beneath Virginian hills,
And some by green Atlantic rills,
Some by the waters of the West,
A myriad unknown heroes rest.   20
Ah! not the chiefs, who, dying, see
Their flags in front of victory,
Or, at their life-blood's noble cost
Pay for a battle nobly lost,
Claim from their monumental beds   25
The bitterest tears a nation sheds.
Beneath yon lonely mound—the spot
By all save some fond few forgot—
Like the true martyrs of the fight
Which strikes for freedom and for right.   30
Of them, their patriot zeal and pride,
The lofty faith that with them died,
No grateful page shall farther tell
Than that so many bravely fell;
And we can only dimly guess   35
What worlds of all this world's distress,
What utter woe, despair, and dearth,
Their fate has brought to many a hearth.
Just such a sky as this should weep
Above them, always, where they sleep;   40
Yet, haply, at this very hour,
Their graves are like a lover's bower;
And Nature's self, with eyes unwet,
Oblivious of the crimson debt
To which she owes her April grace,   45
Laughs gayly o'er their burial-place.

1863, 1873

Ode

Sung at the occasion of decorating the graves of the Confederate dead, at Magnolia Cemetery, Charleston, S. C., June 16, 1866.[3]

Sleep sweetly in your humble graves,
   Sleep, martyrs of a fallen cause;
Though yet no marble column craves
   The pilgrim here to pause.

In seeds of laurel in the earth,   5
   The blossom of your fame is blown,
And somewhere, waiting for its birth,
   The shaft is in the stone!

Meanwhile, behalf the tardy years
   Which keep in trust your storied tombs,   10
Behold! your sisters bring their tears,
   And these memorial blooms.

Small tributes! but your shades will smile
   More proudly on those wreaths today,
Than when some cannon-molded pile   15
   Shall overlook this Bay.

Stoop, angels, hither from the skies!
   There is no holier spot of ground
Than where defeated valor lies,
   By mourning beauty crowned!   20

                                                            1866, 1873

3. The poem was published in the Charleston *Courier*, June 18, 1866, and in a revised version, July 23, 1866, not noted until 1933 (G. P. Voigt, "New Light on Timrod's Memorial Ode," *American Literature*, IV, January, 1933, 395–396). Collected in Hayne's edition (1873) and in Emerson's *Parnassus* (1874), it became Timrod's most familiar poem.

ABRAHAM LINCOLN
(1809–1865)

In the affections of his countrymen, Lincoln has become a legend, and the actual events of his life are also common knowledge. His parents, Thomas and Nancy Hanks Lincoln, were virtually illiterate pioneers, and their child of destiny was born, on February 12, 1809, in a backwoods log cabin in Hardin County, Kentucky. Two years later, the Lincolns were tilling thirty acres of cleared land in the forest at Knob Creek, below Louisville. When the boy was only seven, the family trekked north across the Ohio into southern Indiana, taking squatter-rights on woodland again. There young Lincoln grew to manhood. His mother, a mystical and sensitive woman who influenced him deeply, died when he was nine. Her place was soon taken by Sarah Bush, practical and courageous, who encouraged his innate genius and ambition. Educational opportunities were limited—the boy spent no more than a year altogether in several schoolhouses—but he read and reread the few good books that he could obtain, such as the Bible and *Pilgrim's Progress, Robinson Crusoe,* Aesop's *Fables,* Weems's *Washington,* and Grimshaw's *History of the United States.* At nineteen he worked his way to New Orleans on a Mississippi flatboat.

When Lincoln was twenty-one, he accompanied the still-impoverished family westward, to Decatur, Illinois; but when, the next spring, Tom Lincoln decided upon a further move, to Coles County, the young frontiersman decided that he must strike out for himself. He agreed to take a flatboat loaded with merchandise to New Orleans. Returning, Abe Lincoln brought history to the Sangamon country by settling at New Salem, near Springfield, Illinois. There the force of his homespun integrity gradually brought him into local prominence. From hired hand and rail splitter he rose to be storekeeper and postmaster of New Salem. He read whatever

he could find, and studied law. An unsuccessful candidate in 1832 for election to the legislature, he went off to the five-weeks' Black Hawk War with a company of volunteers who elected him as captain.

In 1834, running as a Whig, he won election to the Illinois legislature, and went up to Springfield on borrowed money, wearing a pair of new blue jeans. There his political moderation began to take form. He supported the opposition of his party to Jackson's financial policies, and he agreed with free-soilers that the federal authority legally extended to the control of slavery in the territories; however, on constitutional grounds, he had to oppose abolition in the states. But abolition was not yet a genuine political issue, and he was re-elected for four consecutive terms (1834–1842). In 1836 he left New Salem, and opened his law office in Springfield. There, in 1842, he returned to private practice, and married Mary Todd.

During the next few years, as a circuit-riding lawyer, he won a modest prosperity and a considerable reputation. In 1847 the Illinois Whigs sent him to Congress, just as the brief Mexican War drew to its close. The question of slavery in the newly won territories divided the Whigs in such border states as Illinois. Lincoln consistently opposed the extension of slavery, and joined those who sought to embarrass Polk, the Democratic president, as instigator of a slave-state war. Lincoln knew at the time that by taking this stand he would alienate voters of all parties in Illinois, and he was not nominated in 1849.

Again in private practice in Springfield, this time with William H. Herndon as his partner, he enjoyed great success as a lawyer, and continued to participate in politics, though apparently with no high ambitions. In 1854 he was again elected to the state legislature, but his opposition to the principle of squatter sovereignty embodied in Douglas's Kansas-Nebraska Bill sent him stump speaking, and he resigned from the legislature in 1855 to run for the Senate. He was defeated, but threw the votes of his supporters in such a manner as to elect an opponent of Douglas.

In 1856, after the disruption of the southern Whigs by these controversies, Lincoln joined the newly formed Republican party, and in 1858 he was the candidate for the Senate against the Democrat, Stephen A. Douglas. At the party convention he made the famous declaration that "A house divided against itself cannot stand," in a speech which, then and later, was heard through the land. In his seven debates with Douglas during the campaign, he demonstrated his cool logic, his devastating humor, and his firm moderation as an enemy of slavery who opposed both the abolition and the extension of slavery on consistent constitutional principles. Although he lost the election, he was clearly a man who might lead the Republicans to national victory; yet it seems that he then had no such idea himself.

In the speech at Cooper Union in 1860 he repeated more formally the principles which he had developed in the heat of the debates. Now that secession was openly advocated in the South, the preservation of the Union was the paramount issue; and this, he thought, could best be assured by strict adherence to the provisions of the Constitution, in respect to both the states and the territorial areas. Three months later the Republican party named him as their candidate. He defeated the candidates of the split Democratic party in November and was inaugurated on March 4, 1861.

The remainder of Lincoln's history is that of the Civil War. A few of the events which best reveal him are reflected in the selections in this volume. Unprepared by previous experience, he became, within two years, the master of complex and gigantic events, the principle strategist of the northern cause, and, as it seemed, the tragic embodiment of the nation's suffering, North and South. His second inauguration occurred on March 4, 1865. On April 9, Lee surrendered the remnant of the Army of Virginia to Grant at Appomattox. On the night of Good Friday, April 14, just six weeks after his inauguration, Lincoln was assassinated by John Wilkes Booth in Ford's Theatre, Washington. He died early the next morning.

Much might be said of Lincoln's place in literature, but that seems unnecessary. He spoke always from the heart of the people, with speech at once lofty and common; what he had to say seems to embody the best that they have learned of human compassion and nobility; and his words have been received and treasured around the earth as the language of humanity itself.

Among the collections of Lincoln's writings the most comprehensive is *The Collected Works of Abraham Lincoln*, 9 vols., edited by Roy P. Basler and others, 1953. Standard, though less comprehensive, is *The Complete Works of Abraham Lincoln*, 2 vols., edited by John G. Nicolay and John Hay, 1894; enlarged, 12 vols., 1905. One-volume selections are *Abraham Lincoln: His Speeches and Writings*, edited by Roy P. Basler, 1946, containing an excellent

critical introduction; and *Selections from Lincoln*, 1927.

John G. Nicolay and John Hay wrote the comprehensive biography, *Abraham Lincoln: A History*, 10 vols., 1890. Carl Sandburg's *Abraham Lincoln: The Prairie Years*, 2 vols., 1926, and *Abraham Lincoln: The War Years*, 4 vols., 1939, are classics. Satisfactory one-volume biographies are those by Lord Charnwood, 1917; and Albert J. Beveridge, 1928. Paul M. Angle compiled *The Lincoln Reader*, 1947, comprising selections from various biographies, chronologically arranged. See also James G. Randall, *Lincoln the President*, 1945; and Benjamin P. Thomas, *Abraham Lincoln*, 1952, the best and most available brief general treatment.

Speech at Cooper Union,[1] New York

MR. PRESIDENT AND FELLOW CITIZENS OF NEW YORK:

The facts with which I shall deal this evening are mainly old and familiar; nor is there anything new in the general use I shall make of them. If there shall be any novelty, it will be in the mode of presenting the facts, and the inferences and observations following that presentation. In his speech last autumn at Columbus, Ohio, as reported in the New York *Times*, Senator Douglas[2] said:

"Our fathers, when they framed the government under which we live, understood this question just as well, and even better, than we do now."

I fully indorse this, and I adopt it as a text for this discourse. I so adopt it because it furnishes a precise and an agreed starting-point for a discussion between Republicans and that wing of the Democracy headed by Senator Douglas.[3] It simply leaves the inquiry: What was the understanding those fathers had of the question mentioned?

1. Stephen A. Douglas, the "Little Giant" of the Democratic coalition of Illinois, won the 1858 senatorial election; but Lincoln, candidate of the newborn Republicans, emerged as a figure of national stature in their famous campaign debates. Eastern Republicans wanted to hear this "rail splitter," whose unquestioned opposition to slavery was rendered politically "moderate" by his insistence on remedies within the Constitution, the laws, and the Union. Invited to give a "political lecture" in Henry Ward Beecher's famous Brooklyn church, he decided to destroy Douglas's argument that the authors of the Constitution had made allowances for slavery. His sponsors, New York Republicans opposing Seward's nomination, changed the meeting place to Cooper Institute (later Union), where, on the night of February 27, 1860, fifteen

thousand listeners braved a heavy snow to hear this remarkable speech. On the platform were the mighty Horace Greeley of the *Tribune*, and William Cullen Bryant, of the New York *Evening Post*, who introduced the speaker. Lincoln's initial embarrassment is well known; but his mastery of his facts clarified the concept of constitutionalism as an antislavery policy, and paved the way for his selection as the Republican presidential candidate some months later.
2. This was not one of the seven Lincoln-Douglas debates, but a later Douglas speech, in September, 1859, in support of Democratic candidates in Ohio.
3. An appeal for the support of Douglas Democrats, a coalition of southern moderates who opposed secession and northerners who had made concessions in the cause of unity.

What is the frame of government under which we live? The answer must be, "The Constitution of the United States." That Constitution consists of the original, framed in 1787, and under which the present government first went into operation, and twelve subsequently framed amendments, the first ten of which were framed in 1789.

Who were our fathers that framed the Constitution? I suppose the "thirty-nine" who signed the original instrument may be fairly called our fathers who framed that part of the present government. It is almost exactly true to say they framed it, and it is altogether true to say they fairly represented the opinion and sentiment of the whole nation at that time. Their names, being familiar to nearly all, and accessible to quite all, need not now be repeated.

I take these "thirty-nine," for the present, as being "our fathers who framed the government under which we live." What is the question which, according to the text, those fathers understood "just as well, and even better, than we do now"?

It is this: Does the proper division of local from federal authority, or anything in the Constitution, forbid our federal government to control as to slavery in our federal territories?[4]

Upon this Senator Douglas holds the affirmative, and Republicans the negative. This affirmation and denial form an issue; and this issue—this question—is precisely what the text declares our fathers understood "better than we." Let us now inquire whether the "thirty-nine," or any of them, ever acted upon this question; and if they did, how they acted upon it—how they expressed that better understanding. In 1784, three years before the Constitution, the United States then owning the Northwestern Territory,[5] and no other, the Congress of the Confederation had before them the question of prohibiting slavery in that territory, and four of the "thirty-nine" who afterward framed the Constitution were in that Congress, and voted on that question. Of these, Roger Sherman, Thomas Mifflin, and Hugh Williamson voted for the prohibition; thus showing that, in their understanding, no line dividing local from federal authority, nor anything else, properly forbade the federal government to control as to slavery in federal territory. The other of the four, James McHenry, voted against the prohibition, showing that for some cause he thought it improper to vote for it.

In 1787, still before the Constitution, but while the convention

4. The principle of state sovereignty had been generally conceded in respect to slavery in the established states; hence proslavery interests persistently denied that the federal authority over new territories included the control of slavery.

5. Bounded by Pennsylvania and by the Ohio and Mississippi rivers, the Northwest Territory comprised Ohio, Indiana, Illinois, Michigan, Wisconsin, and part of Minnesota. It was won from the British during the Revolution and ceded to the United States by the Treaty of Paris (1783).

was in session framing it, and while the Northwestern Territory still was the only territory owned by the United States, the same question of prohibiting slavery in the territory again came before the Congress of the Confederation; and two more of the "thirty-nine" who afterward signed the Constitution were in that Congress, and voted on the question. They were William Blount and William Few; and they both voted for the prohibition—thus showing that in their understanding no line dividing local from federal authority, nor anything else, properly forbade the federal government to control as to slavery in federal territory. This time the prohibition became a law, being part of what is now well known as the Ordinance[6] of '87.

The question of federal control of slavery in the territories seems not to have been directly before the convention which framed the original Constitution; and hence it is not recorded that the "thirty-nine," or any of them, while engaged on that instrument, expressed any opinion on that precise question.

In 1789, by the first Congress which sat under the Constitution, an act was passed to enforce the Ordinance of '87, including the prohibition of slavery in the Northwestern Territory. The bill for this act was reported by one of the "thirty-nine"—Thomas Fitzsimmons, then a member of the House of Representatives from Pennsylvania. It went through all its stages without a word of opposition, and finally passed both branches without ayes and nays, which is equivalent to a unanimous passage. In this Congress there were sixteen of the thirty-nine fathers who framed the original Constitution. They were John Langdon, Nicholas Gilman, William S. Johnson, Roger Sherman, Robert Morris, Thomas Fitzsimmons, William Few, Abraham Baldwin, Rufus King, William Paterson, George Clymer, Richard Bassett, George Read, Pierce Butler, Daniel Carroll, and James Madison.

This shows that, in their understanding, no line dividing local from federal authority, nor anything in the Constitution, properly forbade Congress to prohibit slavery in the federal territory; else both their fidelity to correct principle, and their oath to support the Constitution would have constrained them to oppose the prohibition.

Again, George Washington, another of the "thirty-nine," was then President of the United States, and as such approved and signed the bill, thus completing its validity as a law, and thus showing that, in his understanding, no line dividing local from federal authority, nor anything in the Constitution, forbade the federal government to control as to slavery in federal territory.

6. The Ordinance of 1787 provided for government in the new territory, ultimate representation of the settlers, and the inviolability of contract, while banning slavery.

No great while after the adoption of the original Constitution, North Carolina ceded to the federal government the country now constituting the state of Tennessee;[7] and a few years later Georgia ceded that which now constitutes the states of Mississippi and Alabama.[8] In both deeds of cession it was made a condition by the ceding states that the federal government should not prohibit slavery in the ceded country. Besides this, slavery was then actually in the ceded country. Under these circumstances, Congress, on taking charge of these countries, did not absolutely prohibit slavery within them. But they did interfere with it—take control of it—even there, to a certain extent. In 1798 Congress organized the territory of Mississippi. In the act of organization they prohibited the bringing of slaves into the territory from any place without the United States, by fine, and giving freedom to slaves so brought. This act passed both branches of Congress without yeas and nays. In that Congress were three of the "thirty-nine" who framed the original Constitution. They were John Langdon, George Read, and Abraham Baldwin. They all probably voted for it. Certainly they would have placed their opposition to it upon record if, in their understanding, any line dividing local from federal authority, or anything in the Constitution, properly forbade the federal government to control as to slavery in federal territory.

In 1803 the federal government purchased the Louisiana country. Our former territorial acquisitions came from certain of our own states; but this Louisiana country was acquired from a foreign nation. In 1804 Congress gave a territorial organization to that part of it which now constitutes the state of Louisiana. New Orleans, lying within that part, was an old and comparatively large city. There were other considerable towns and settlements, and slavery was extensively and thoroughly intermingled with the people. Congress did not, in the Territorial Act, prohibit slavery; but they did interfere with it—take control of it—in a more marked and extensive way than they did in the case of Mississippi. The substance of the provision therein made in relation to slaves was:

1st. That no slave should be imported into the territory from foreign parts.

2d. That no slave should be carried into it who had been imported into the United States since the first day of May, 1798.

3d. That no slave should be carried into it, except by the owner, and for his own use as a settler; the penalty in all the cases being a fine upon the violator of the law, and freedom to the slave.

This act also was passed without ayes or nays. In the Congress

---

7. By this transaction, Tennessee became a federal territory in 1790, a state in 1796.

8. Georgia's cession of 1802 relinquished the inland territories of Alabama and Mississippi; the coastal areas were acquired from Spain in 1817.

which passed it there were two of the "thirty-nine." They were Abraham Baldwin and Jonathan Dayton. As stated in the case of Mississippi, it is probable that both voted for it. They would not have allowed it to pass without recording their opposition to it, if, in their understanding, it violated either the line properly dividing local from federal authority, or any provision of the constitution.

In 1819–20 came and passed the Missouri question.[9] Many votes were taken, by yeas and nays, in both branches of Congress, upon the various phases of the general question. Two of the "thirty-nine" —Rufus King and Charles Pinckney—were members of that Congress. Mr. King steadily voted for slavery prohibition and against all compromises, while Mr. Pinckney as steadily voted against slavery prohibition and against all compromises. By this, Mr. King showed that, in his understanding, no line dividing local from federal authority, nor anything in the Constitution, was violated by Congress prohibiting slavery in federal territory; while Mr. Pinckney, by his votes, showed that, in his understanding, there was some sufficient reason for opposing such prohibition in that case.

The cases I have mentioned are the only acts of the "thirty-nine," or of any of them, upon the direct issue, which I have been able to discover.

To enumerate the persons who thus acted as being four in 1784, two in 1787, seventeen in 1789, three in 1798, two in 1804, and two in 1819–20, there would be thirty of them. But this would be counting John Langdon, Roger Sherman, William Few, Rufus King, and George Read each twice, and Abraham Baldwin three times. The true number of those of the "thirty-nine" whom I have shown to have acted upon the question which, by the text, they understood better than we, is twenty-three, leaving sixteen not shown to have acted upon it in any way.

Here, then, we have twenty-three out of our thirty-nine fathers "who framed the government under which we live," who have, upon their official responsibility and their corporal oaths, acted upon the very question which the text affirms they "understood just as well, and even better than we do now"; and twenty-one of them—a clear majority of the whole "thirty-nine"—so acting upon it as to make them guilty of gross political impropriety and willful perjury if, in their understanding, any proper division between local and federal authority, or anything in the Constitution they had made themselves, and sworn to support, forbade the federal government to control as to slavery in the federal territories. Thus the twenty-one acted; and, as actions speak louder than words, so actions under such responsibility speak still louder.

9. Missouri's petition for statehood in 1818 produced months of debate over slavery, ending in Henry Clay's Missouri Compromise (1820) by which Maine was admitted as free, Missouri as slave, soil.

Two of the twenty-three voted against congressional prohibition of slavery in the federal territories, in the instances in which they acted upon the question. But for what reasons they so voted is not known. They may have done so because they thought a proper division of local from federal authority, or some provision or principle of the Constitution, stood in the way; or they may, without any such question, have voted against the prohibition on what appeared to them to be sufficient grounds of expediency. No one who has sworn to support the Constitution can conscientiously vote for what he understands to be an unconstitutional measure, however expedient he may think it; but one may and ought to vote against a measure which he deems constitutional if, at the same time, he deems it inexpedient. It, therefore, would be unsafe to set down even the two who voted against the prohibition as having done so because, in their understanding, any proper division of local from federal authority, or anything in the Constitution, forbade the federal government to control as to slavery in federal territory.

The remaining sixteen of the "thirty-nine," so far as I have discovered, have left no record of their understanding upon the direct question of federal control of slavery in the federal territories. But there is much reason to believe that their understanding upon that question would not have appeared different from that of their twenty-three compeers, had it been manifested at all.

For the purpose of adhering rigidly to the text, I have purposely omitted whatever understanding may have been manifested by any person, however distinguished, other than the thirty-nine fathers who framed the original Constitution; and, for the same reason, I have also omitted whatever understanding may have been manifested by any of the "thirty-nine" even on any other phase of the general question of slavery. If we should look into their acts and declarations on those other phases, as the foreign slave-trade, and the morality and policy of slavery generally, it would appear to us that on the direct question of federal control of slavery in federal territories, the sixteen, if they had acted at all, would probably have acted just as the twenty-three did. Among that sixteen were several of the most noted anti-slavery men of those times—as Dr. Franklin, Alexander Hamilton, and Gouverneur Morris—while there was not one now known to have been otherwise, unless it may be John Rutledge, of South Carolina.

The sum of the whole is that of our thirty-nine fathers who framed the original Constitution, twenty-one—a clear majority of the whole—certainly understood that no proper division of local from federal authority, nor any part of the Constitution, forbade the federal government to control slavery in the federal territories; while all the rest had probably the same understanding. Such, unquestionably, was the understanding of our fathers who framed the original Constitution; and the text affirms that they understood the question "better than we."

But, so far, I have been considering the understanding of the question manifested by the framers of the original Constitution. In and by the original instrument, a mode was provided for amending it; and, as I have already stated, the present frame of "the government under which we live" consists of that original, and twelve amendatory articles framed and adopted since. Those who now insist that federal control of slavery in federal territories violates the Constitution, point us to the provisions which they suppose it thus violates; and, as I understand, they all fix upon provisions in these amendatory articles, and not in the original instrument. The Supreme Court, in the Dred Scott case,[1] plant themselves upon the Fifth Amendment, which provides that no person shall be deprived of "life, liberty, or property without due process of law"; while Senator Douglas and his peculiar adherents plant themselves upon the Tenth Amendment, providing that "the powers not delegated to the United States by the Constitution" "are reserved to the states respectively, or to the people."

Now, it so happens that these amendments were framed by the first Congress which sat under the Constitution—the identical Congress which passed the act, already mentioned, enforcing the prohibition of slavery in the Northwestern Territory. Not only was it the same Congress, but they were the identical, same individual men who, at the same session, and at the same time within the session, had under consideration, and in progress toward maturity, these constitutional amendments, and this act prohibiting slavery in all the territory the nation then owned. The constitutional amendments were introduced before, and passed after, the act enforcing the Ordinance of '87; so that, during the whole pendency of the act to enforce the ordinance, the constitutional amendments were also pending.

The seventy-six members of that Congress, including sixteen of the framers of the original Constitution, as before stated, were pre-eminently our fathers who framed that part of "the government under which we live" which is now claimed as forbidding the federal government to control slavery in the federal territories.

Is it not a little presumptuous in anyone[2] at this day to affirm

1. Dred Scott, a slave, had been taken to the free soil of Illinois in 1834 and Wisconsin Territory in 1836 and then returned to Missouri. In 1846 he brought suit in the Missouri state courts for freedom on the ground that his former residence on free soil made him free. Upon losing in the state courts, he brought suit in federal courts in 1854. The decision of the Supreme Court, not rendered until 1857, denied Scott's claim because he was not a "citizen," but his master's property, assured by the "due process" clause of the Fifth Amendment.

2. *I.e.*, Douglas, here Lincoln's political target.

that the two things which that Congress deliberately framed, and carried to maturity at the same time, are absolutely inconsistent with each other? And does not such affirmation become impudently absurd when coupled with the other affirmation, from the same mouth, that those who did the two things alleged to be inconsistent, understood whether they really were inconsistent better than we— better than he who affirms that they are inconsistent?

It is surely safe to assume that the thirty-nine framers of the original Constitution, and the seventy-six members of the Congress which framed the amendments thereto, taken together, do certainly include those who may be fairly called "our fathers who framed the government under which we live." And so assuming, I defy any man to show that any one of them ever, in his whole life, declared that, in his understanding, any proper division of local from federal authority, or any part of the Constitution, forbade the federal government to control as to slavery in the federal territories. I go a step further. I defy anyone to show that any living man in the whole world ever did, prior to the beginning of the present century (and I might almost say prior to the beginning of the last half of the present century), declare that, in his understanding, any proper division of local from federal authority, or any part of the Constitution, forbade the federal government to control as to slavery in the federal territories. To those who now so declare I give not only "our fathers who framed the government under which we live," but with them all other living men within the century in which it was framed, among whom to search, and they shall not be able to find the evidence of a single man agreeing with them.

Now, and here, let me guard a little against being misunderstood. I do not mean to say we are bound to follow implicitly in whatever our fathers did. To do so would be to discard all the lights of current experience—to reject all progress, all improvement. What I do say is that if we would supplant the opinions and policy of our fathers in any case, we should do so upon evidence so conclusive, and argument so clear, that even their great authority, fairly considered and weighed, cannot stand; and most surely not in a case whereof we ourselves declare they understood the question better than we.

If any man at this day sincerely believes that a proper division of local from federal authority, or any part of the Constitution, forbids the federal government to control as to slavery in the federal territories, he is right to say so, and to enforce his position by all truthful evidence and fair argument which he can. But he has no right to mislead others who have less access to history, and less leisure to study it, into the false belief that "our fathers who framed the government under which we live" were of the same opinion—

thus substituting falsehood and deception for truthful evidence and fair argument. If any man at this day sincerely believes "our fathers who framed the government under which we live" used and applied principles, in other cases, which ought to have led them to understand that a proper division of local from federal authority, or some part of the Constitution, forbids the federal government to control as to slavery in the federal territories, he is right to say so. But he should, at the same time, brave the responsibility of declaring that, in his opinion, he understands their principles better than they did themselves; and especially should he not shirk that responsibility by asserting that they "understood the question just as well, and even better, than we do now."

But enough! Let all who believe that "our fathers who framed the government under which we live understood this question just as well, and even better, than we do now," speak as they spoke, and act as they acted upon it. This is all Republicans ask—all Republicans desire—in relation to slavery. As those fathers marked it, so let it be again marked, as an evil not to be extended, but to be tolerated and protected only because of and so far as its actual presence among us makes that toleration and protection a necessity. Let all the guaranties those fathers gave it be not grudgingly, but fully and fairly, maintained. For this Republicans contend, and with this, so far as I know or believe, they will be content.

And now, if they would listen—as I suppose they will not—I would address a few words to the Southern people.

I would say to them: You consider yourselves a reasonable and a just people; and I consider that in the general qualities of reason and justice you are not inferior to any other people. Still, when you speak of us Republicans, you do so only to denounce us as reptiles, or, at the best, as no better than outlaws. You will grant a hearing to pirates or murderers, but nothing like it to "Black Republicans." In all your contentions with one another, each of you deems an unconditional condemnation of "Black Republicanism" as the first thing to be attended to. Indeed, such condemnation of us seems to be an indispensable prerequisite—license, so to speak—among you to be admitted or permitted to speak at all. Now can you or not be prevailed upon to pause and to consider whether this is quite just to us, or even to yourselves? Bring forward your charges and specifications, and then be patient long enough to hear us deny or justify.

You say we are sectional. We deny it. That makes an issue; and the burden of proof is upon you. You produce your proof; and what is it? Why, that our party had no existence in your section—gets no votes in your section. The fact is substantially true; but does it prove the issue? If it does, then in case we should, without change of principle, begin to get votes in your section, we should thereby cease to be sectional. You cannot escape this conclusion; and yet, are you willing to abide by it? If you are, you will probably soon find that we have ceased to be sectional, for we shall get votes in your section this very year. You will then begin to discover, as the truth plainly is, that your proof does not touch the issue. The fact that we get no votes in your section is a fact of your making, and not of ours. And if there be fault in that fact, that fault is primarily yours, and remains so until you show that we repel you by some wrong principle or practice. If we do repel you by any wrong principle or practice, the fault is ours; but this brings you to where you ought to have started—to a discussion of the right or wrong of our principle. If our principle, put in practice, would wrong your section for the benefit of ours, or for any other object, then our principle, and we with it, are sectional, and are justly opposed and denounced as such. Meet us, then, on the question of whether our principle, put in practice, would wrong your section; and so meet us as if it were possible that something may be said on our side. Do you accept the challenge? No! Then you really believe that the principle which "our fathers who framed the government under which we live" thought so clearly right as to adopt it, and indorse it again and again, upon their official oaths, is in fact so clearly wrong as to demand your condemnation without a moment's consideration.

Some of you delight to flaunt in our faces the warning against sectional parties given by Washington in his Farewell Address.[3] Less than eight years before Washington gave that warning, he had, as President of the United States, approved and signed an act of Congress enforcing the prohibition of slavery in the Northwestern Territory, which act embodied the policy of the government upon that subject up to and at the very moment he penned that warning; and about one year after he penned it, he wrote Lafayette that he considered that prohibition a wise measure, expressing in the same connection his hope that we should at some time have a confederacy of free states.

Bearing this in mind, and seeing that sectionalism has since arisen upon this same subject, is that warning a weapon in your hands against us, or in our hands against you? Could Washington himself speak, would he cast the blame of that sectionalism upon us, who sustain his policy, or upon you, who repudiate it? We respect that warning of Washington, and we commend it to you, together with his example pointing to the right application of it.

But you say you are conservative—eminently conservative—while we are revolutionary, destructive, or something of the sort. What is

3. Washington, in his Farewell Address (September 17, 1796), particularly emphasized the dangerous "fury of party spirit, [or] a belief that there is any real difference of local interests and views."

conservatism? Is it not adherence to the old and tried, against the new and untried? We stick to, contend for, the identical old policy on the point in controversy which was adopted by "our fathers who framed the government under which we live"; while you with one accord reject, and scout, and spit upon that old policy, and insist upon substituting something new. True, you disagree among yourselves as to what that substitute shall be. You are divided on new propositions and plans, but you are unanimous in rejecting and denouncing the old policy of the fathers. Some of you are for reviving the foreign slave-trade; some for a congressional slave-code for the territories; some for Congress forbidding the territories to prohibit slavery within their limits; some for maintaining slavery in the territories through the judiciary; some for the "gur-reat pur-rinciple" that "if one man would enslave another, no third man should object," fantastically called "popular sovereignty"; but never a man among you is in favor of federal prohibition of slavery in federal territories, according to the practice of "our fathers who framed the government under which we live." Not one of all your various plans can show a precedent or an advocate in the century within which our government originated. Consider, then, whether your claim of conservatism for yourselves, and your charge of destructiveness against us, are based on the most clear and stable foundations.

Again, you say we have made the slavery question more prominent than it formerly was. We deny it. We admit that it is more prominent, but we deny that we made it so. It was not we, but you, who discarded the old policy of the fathers. We resisted, and still resist, your innovation; and thence comes the greater prominence of the question. Would you have that question reduced to its former proportions? Go back to that old policy. What has been will be again, under the same conditions. If you would have the peace of the old times, readopt the precepts and policy of the old times.

You charge that we stir up insurrections among your slaves. We deny it; and what is your proof? Harper's Ferry! John Brown!![4] John Brown was no Republican; and you have failed to implicate a single Republican in his Harper's Ferry enterprise. If any member of our party is guilty in that matter, you know it, or you do not know it. If you do know it, you are inexcusable for not designating the man and proving the fact. If you do not know it, you are inexcusable for asserting it, and especially for persisting in the assertion after you have tried and failed to make the proof. You need not be told that persisting in a charge which one does not know to be true, is simply malicious slander.

4. John Brown, an obsessed abolitionist from "bloody Kansas," captured the United States armory at Harpers Ferry, Virginia on October 16, 1859. Ten of his men were killed in a counterattack by the army, and Brown was executed on December 2, 1859.

Some of you admit that no Republican designedly aided or encouraged the Harper's Ferry affair, but still insist that our doctrines and declarations necessarily lead to such results. We do not believe it. We know we hold no doctrine, and make no declaration, which were not held to and made by "our fathers who framed the government under which we live." You never dealt fairly by us in relation to this affair. When it occurred, some important state elections were near at hand, and you were in evident glee with the belief that, by charging the blame upon us, you could get an advantage of us in those elections. The elections came, and your expectations were not quite fulfilled. Every Republican man knew that, as to himself at least, your charge was a slander, and he was not much inclined by it to cast his vote in your favor. Republican doctrines and declarations are accompanied with a continual protest against any interference with your slaves, or with you about your slaves. Surely, this does not encourage them to revolt. True, we do, in common with "our fathers who framed the government under which we live," declare our belief that slavery is wrong; but the slaves do not hear us declare even this. For anything we say or do, the slaves would scarcely know there is a Republican party. I believe they would not, in fact, generally know it but for your misrepresentations of us in their hearing. In your political contests among yourselves, each faction charges the other with sympathy with Black Republicanism; and then, to give point to the charge, defines Black Republicanism to simply be insurrection, blood, and thunder among the slaves.

Slave insurrections are no more common now than they were before the Republican party was organized. What induced the Southampton insurrection,[5] twenty-eight years ago, in which at least three times as many lives were lost as at Harper's Ferry? You can scarcely stretch your very elastic fancy to the conclusion that Southampton was "got up by Black Republicanism." In the present state of things in the United States, I do not think a general, or even a very extensive, slave insurrection is possible. The indispensable concert of action cannot be attained. The slaves have no means of rapid communication; nor can incendiary freemen, black or white, supply it. The explosive materials are everywhere in parcels; but there neither are, nor can be supplied, the indispensable connecting trains.

Much is said by Southern people about the affection of slaves for their masters and mistresses; and a part of it, at least, is true. A plot for an uprising could scarcely be devised and communicated to twenty individuals before some one of them, to save the life of a

5. Probably seventy of both races lost their lives in the insurrection led by the slave Nat Turner, in Southampton County, Virginia, in 1831.

favorite master or mistress, would divulge it. This is the rule; and the slave revolution in Haiti[6] was not an exception to it, but a case occurring under peculiar circumstances. The gunpowder plot[7] of British history, though not connected with slaves, was more in point. In that case, only about twenty were admitted to the secret; and yet one of them, in his anxiety to save a friend, betrayed the plot to that friend, and, by consequence, averted the calamity. Occasional poisonings from the kitchen, and open or stealthy assassinations in the field, and local revolts extending to a score or so, will continue to occur as the natural results of slavery; but no general insurrection of slaves, as I think, can happen in this country for a long time. Whoever much fears, or much hopes, for such an event, will be alike disappointed.

In the language of Mr. Jefferson, uttered many years ago, "It is still in our power to direct the process of emancipation and deportation peaceably, and in such slow degrees, as that the evil will wear off insensibly; and their places be, *pari passu*,[8] filled up by free white laborers. If, on the contrary, it is left to force itself on, human nature must shudder at the prospect held up."

Mr. Jefferson did not mean to say, nor do I, that the power of emancipation is in the federal government. He spoke of Virginia; and, as to the power of emancipation, I speak of the slave-holding states only. The federal government, however, as we insist, has the power of restraining the extension of the institution—the power to insure that a slave insurrection shall never occur on any American soil which is now free from slavery.

John Brown's effort was peculiar. It was not a slave insurrection. It was an attempt by white men to get up a revolt among slaves, in which the slaves refused to participate. In fact, it was so absurd that the slaves, with all their ignorance, saw plainly enough it could not succeed. That affair, in its philosophy, corresponds with the many attempts, related in history, at the assassination of kings and emperors. An enthusiast broods over the oppression of a people till he fancies himself commissioned by Heaven to liberate them. He ventures the attempt, which ends in little else than his own execution. Orsini's attempt[9] on Louis Napoleon, and John Brown's attempt at Harper's Ferry, were, in their philosophy, precisely the same. The eagerness to cast blame on old England in the one case,

6. In 1791; the first insurrection of Toussaint L'Ouverture, Negro liberator of Haiti.

7. Guy Fawkes was exposed and circumvented in a plot to blow up the British Parliament and Court on November 5, 1605.

8. At an equal ratio. See Jefferson's *Autobiography*. Lincoln also regarded the competition of the Negro, slave or free, as prejudicial for white labor, and by 1862 he was advocating foreign colonization of emancipated slaves (Thomas, *Abraham Lincoln*, p. 362).

9. Felice Orsini (1819–1858), revolutionist of the Young Italy party, had recently been executed for attempting to assassinate Napoleon III with a bomb that killed ten others.

and on New England in the other, does not disprove the sameness of the two things.

And how much would it avail you, if you could, by the use of John Brown, Helper's book,[1] and the like, break up the Republican organization? Human action can be modified to some extent, but human nature cannot be changed. There is a judgment and a feeling against slavery in this nation, which cast at least a million and a half of votes. You cannot destroy that judgment and feeling —that sentiment—by breaking up the political organization which rallies around it. You can scarcely scatter and disperse an army which has been formed into order in the face of your heaviest fire; but if you could, how much would you gain by forcing the sentiment which created it out of the peaceful channel of the ballot box into some other channel? What would that other channel probably be? Would the number of John Browns be lessened or enlarged by the operation?

But you will break up the Union rather than submit to a denial of your constitutional rights.

That has a somewhat reckless sound; but it would be palliated, if not fully justified, were we proposing, by the mere force of numbers, to deprive you of some right plainly written down in the Constitution. But we are proposing no such thing.

When you make these declarations you have a specific and well-understood allusion to an assumed constitutional right of yours to take slaves into the federal territories, and to hold them there as property. But no such right is specifically written in the Constitution. That instrument is literally silent about any such right. We, on the contrary, deny that such a right has any existence in the Constitution, even by implication.

Your purpose, then, plainly stated, is that you will destroy the government, unless you be allowed to construe and force the Constitution as you please, on all points in dispute between you and us. You will rule or ruin[2] in all events.

This, plainly stated, is your language. Perhaps you will say the Supreme Court has decided the disputed constitutional question in your favor. Not quite so.[3] But waiving the lawyer's distinction between *dictum* and decision, the court has decided the question for you in a sort of way. The court has substantially said it is your

1. Hinton R. Helper, *The Impending Crisis of the South: How to Meet It* (1857). Slaveholding aristocrats were outraged because it called on southern "poor whites" to resist slavery as unfair competition.

2. This classic phrase of political polemics was originated by John Dryden (1631–1700). See *Absalom and Achitophel*, l. 174: "Resolv'd to ruin or to rule the state."

3. So Douglas argued. In the following sentence Lincoln notes in passing that Justice Taney's remarks on federal control of slavery in the territories had no legal force, because they did not concern the precise issue of the case, but were a mere *dictum*. The legal decision —on the issue at law—was merely that Dred Scott, as a slave, did not possess the right of a citizen to sue in any court.

constitutional right to take slaves into the federal territories, and to hold them there as property. When I say the decision was made in a sort of way, I mean it was made in a divided court, by a bare majority of the judges, and they not quite agreeing with one another in the reason for making it; that it is so made as that its avowed supporters disagree with one another about its meaning, and that it was mainly based upon a mistaken statement of fact—the statement in the opinion that "the right of property in a slave is distinctly and expressly affirmed in the Constitution."

An inspection of the Constitution will show that the right of property in a slave is not "distinctly and expressly affirmed" in it. Bear in mind, the judges do not pledge their judicial opinion that such right is impliedly affirmed in the Constitution; but they pledge their veracity that it is "distinctly and expressly" affirmed there—"distinctly," that is, not mingled with anything else— "expressly," that is, in words meaning just that, without the aid of any inference, and susceptible of no other meaning.

If they had only pledged their judicial opinion that such right is affirmed in the instrument by implication, it would be open to others to show that neither the word "slave" nor "slavery" is to be found in the Constitution, nor the word "property" even, in any connection with language alluding to the things slave, or slavery; and that wherever in that instrument the slave is alluded to, he is called a "person"; and wherever his master's legal right in relation to him is alluded to, it is spoken of as "service or labor which may be due"—as a debt payable in service or labor. Also it would be open to show, by contemporaneous history, that this mode of alluding to slaves and slavery, instead of speaking of them, was employed on purpose to exclude from the Constitution the idea that there could be property in man.

To show all this is easy and certain.

When this obvious mistake of the judges shall be brought to their notice, is it not reasonable to expect that they will withdraw the mistaken statement, and reconsider the conclusion based upon it?

And then it is to be remembered that "our fathers who framed the government under which we live"—the men who made the Constitution—decided this same constitutional question in our favor long ago: decided it without division among themselves when making the decision; without division among themselves about the meaning of it after it was made, and, so far as any evidence is left, without basing it upon any mistaken statement of facts.

Under all these circumstances, do you really feel yourselves justified to break up this government unless such a court decision as yours is, shall be at once submitted to as a conclusive and final rule of political action? But you will not abide the election of a Republican President! In that supposed event, you say, you will destroy the Union; and then, you say, the great crime of having destroyed it will be upon us! That is cool. A highwayman holds a pistol to my ear, and mutters through his teeth, "Stand and deliver, or I shall kill you, and then you will be a murderer!"

To be sure, what the robber demanded of me—my money—was my own; and I had a clear right to keep it; but it was no more my own than my vote is my own; and the threat of death to me, to extort my money, and the threat of destruction to the Union, to extort my vote, can scarcely be distinguished in principle.

A few words now to Republicans. It is exceedingly desirable that all parts of this great confederacy shall be at peace, and in harmony one with another. Let us Republicans do our part to have it so. Even though much provoked, let us do nothing through passion and ill temper. Even though the Southern people will not so much as listen to us, let us calmly consider their demands, and yield to them if, in our deliberate view of our duty, we possibly can. Judging by all they say and do, and by the subject and nature of their controversy with us, let us determine, if we can, what will satisfy them.

Will they be satisfied if the territories be unconditionally surrendered to them? We know they will not. In all their present complaints against us, the territories are scarcely mentioned. Invasions and insurrections are the rage now. Will it satisfy them if, in the future, we have nothing to do with invasions and insurrections? We know it will not. We so know, because we know we never had anything to do with invasions and insurrections; and yet this total abstaining does not exempt us from the charge and the denunciation.

The question recurs, What will satisfy them? Simply this: we must not only let them alone, but we must somehow convince them that we do let them alone. This, we know by experience, is no easy task. We have been so trying to convince them from the very beginning of our organization, but with no success. In all our platforms and speeches we have constantly protested our purpose to let them alone; but this has had no tendency to convince them. Alike unavailing to convince them is the fact that they have never detected a man of us in any attempt to disturb them.

These natural and apparently adequate means all failing, what will convince them? This, and this only: cease to call slavery wrong, and join them in calling it right. And this must be done thoroughly —done in acts as well as in words. Silence will not be tolerated— we must place ourselves avowedly with them. Senator Douglas's new sedition law must be enacted and enforced, suppressing all declarations that slavery is wrong, whether made in politics, in presses, in pulpits, or in private. We must arrest and return their fugitive slaves with greedy pleasure. We must pull down our free-state constitutions. The whole atmosphere must be disinfected from all taint of opposition to slavery, before they will cease to believe that all their troubles proceed from us.

I am quite aware they do not state their case precisely in this way. Most of them would probably say to us, "Let us alone; do nothing to us, and say what you please about slavery." But we do let them alone—have never disturbed them—so that, after all, it is what we say which dissatisfies them. They will continue to accuse us of doing, until we cease saying.

I am also aware they have not as yet in terms demanded the overthrow of our free-state constitutions. Yet those constitutions declare the wrong of slavery with more solemn emphasis than do all other sayings against it; and when all these other sayings shall have been silenced, the overthrow of these constitutions will be demanded, and nothing be left to resist the demand. It is nothing to the contrary that they do not demand the whole of this just now. Demanding what they do, and for the reason they do, they can voluntarily stop nowhere short of this consummation. Holding, as they do, that slavery is morally right and socially elevating, they cannot cease to demand a full national recognition of it as a legal right and a social blessing.

Nor can we justifiably withhold this on any ground save our conviction that slavery is wrong. If slavery is right, all words, acts, laws, and constitutions against it are themselves wrong, and should be silenced and swept away. If it is right, we cannot justly object to its nationality—its universality; if it is wrong, they cannot justly insist upon its extension—its enlargement. All they ask we could readily grant, if we thought slavery right; all we ask they could as readily grant, if they thought it wrong. Their thinking it right and our thinking it wrong is the precise fact upon which depends the whole controversy. Thinking it right, as they do, they are not to blame for desiring its full recognition as being right; but thinking it wrong, as we do, can we yield to them? Can we cast our votes with their view, and against our own? In view of our moral, social, and political responsibilities, can we do this?

Wrong as we think slavery is, we can yet afford to let it alone where it is, because that much is due to the necessity arising from its actual presence in the nation; but can we, while our votes will prevent it, allow it to spread into the national territories, and to overrun us here in these free states?

If our sense of duty forbids this, then let us stand by our duty fearlessly and effectively. Let us be diverted by none of those sophistical contrivances wherewith we are so industriously plied and belabored—contrivances such as groping for some middle ground between the right and the wrong; vain as the search for a man who should be neither a living man nor a dead man; such as a policy of "don't care"[4] on a question about which all true men do care; such as Union appeals beseeching true Union men to yield to Disunionists, reversing the divine rule, and calling, not the sinners, but the righteous to repentance;[5] such as invocations to Washington, imploring men to unsay what Washington said and undo what Washington did.

Neither let us be slandered from our duty by false accusations against us, nor frightened from it by menaces of destruction to the government, nor of dungeons to ourselves. Let us have faith that right makes might, and in that faith let us to the end dare to do our duty as we understand it.

First Inaugural Address[6]

Fellow Citizens of the United States:

In compliance with a custom as old as the government itself, I appear before you to address you briefly, and to take in your presence the oath prescribed by the Constitution of the United States to be taken by the President "before he enters on the execution of his office."

I do not consider it necessary at present for me to discuss those matters of administration about which there is no special anxiety or excitement.

Apprehension seems to exist among the people of the Southern states that by the accession of a Republican administration their property and their peace and personal security are to be endangered.[7] There has never been any reasonable cause for such apprehension. Indeed, the most ample evidence to the contrary has all

4. Referring to the position Douglas was forced to adopt in his 1858 debates with Lincoln: "I don't care whether slavery is voted down, or voted up."
5. *Cf.* Matthew ix: 13.
6. Lincoln's inauguration on March 4, 1861, coincided with a national crisis, reflected in his passionate appeal for friendship and unity between the North and the South. Since his election on November 6, 1860, South Carolina had seceded from the Union (December 20), calling for the withdrawal of federal garrisons from forts Moultrie and Sumter in Charleston Harbor. Similar ordinances had been swiftly passed by Mississippi, Florida, Alabama, Georgia, Louisiana, and Texas, in spite of the passing of an emergency amendment (never ratified) affirming the constitutionality of slavery in the slave states. Yet Lincoln's speech "was as indulgent

as he could make it without renouncing constitutional duties" (Thomas, *Abraham Lincoln*, p. 247). The last paragraph, emphasizing this spirit of conciliation, was based on an idea submitted by Seward as an addition to the original draft. Lincoln "transformed the Secretary's graceless sentences into a moving and exalted plea" (Thomas, *Abraham Lincoln*, p. 248). The President spoke from a platform outside the uncompleted Capitol building—the huge bronze statue of Freedom, destined for the dome, still symbolically recumbent on the ground nearby.
7. Lincoln's "house divided" speech at the Illinois state Republican convention of June 16, 1858 had been widely quoted; he realized that he must now offset the effect of his earlier dictum that "this government cannot endure permanently half slave and half free."

the while existed and been open to their inspection. It is found in nearly all the published speeches of him who now addresses you. I do but quote from one of those speeches when I declare that "I have no purpose, directly or indirectly, to interfere with the institution of slavery in the states where it exists. I believe I have no lawful right to do so, and I have no inclination to do so."[8] Those who nominated and elected me did so with full knowledge that I had made this and many similar declarations, and had never recanted them. And, more than this, they placed in the platform for my acceptance, and as a law to themselves and to me, the clear and emphatic resolution which I now read:

"*Resolved*, That the maintenance inviolate of the rights of the states, and especially the right of each state to order and control its own domestic institutions according to its own judgment exclusively, is essential to that balance of power on which the perfection and endurance of our political fabric depend; and we denounce the lawless invasion by armed force of the soil of any state or territory, no matter under what pretext, as among the gravest of crimes."

I now reiterate these sentiments; and, in doing so, I only press upon the public attention the most conclusive evidence of which the case is susceptible, that the property, peace, and security of no section are to be in any wise endangered by the now incoming administration. I add, too, that all the protection which, consistently with the Constitution and the laws, can be given, will be cheerfully given to all the states when lawfully demanded for whatever cause —as cheerfully to one section as to another.

There is much controversy about the delivering up of fugitives from service or labor. The clause I now read is as plainly written in the Constitution as any other of its provisions:

"No person held to service or labor in one state, under the laws thereof, escaping into another, shall in consequence of any law or regulation therein be discharged from such service or labor, but shall be delivered up on claim of the party to whom such service or labor may be due."

It is scarcely questioned that this provision was intended by those who made it for the reclaiming of what we call fugitive slaves; and the intention of the lawgiver is the law. All members of Congress swear their support to the whole Constitution—to this provision as much as to any other. To the proposition, then, that slaves whose cases come within the terms of this clause "shall be delivered up," their oaths are unanimous. Now, if they would make the effort in good temper, could they not with nearly equal unanimity frame and pass a law by means of which to keep good that unanimous oath?

8. Referring to the amendment, just passed by Congress, reaffirming the constitutional guarantee of slavery in states where it already existed.

There is some difference of opinion whether this clause should be enforced by national or by state authority; but surely that difference is not a very material one. If the slave is to be surrendered, it can be of but little consequence to him or to others by which authority it is done. And should anyone in any case be content that his oath shall go unkept on a merely unsubstantial controversy as to how it shall be kept?

Again, in any law upon this subject, ought not all the safeguards of liberty known in civilized and humane jurisprudence to be introduced, so that a free man be not, in any case, surrendered as a slave? And might it not be well at the same time to provide by law for the enforcement of that clause in the Constitution which guarantees that "the citizens of each state shall be entitled to all privileges and immunities of citizens in the several states"?

I take the official oath today with no mental reservations, and with no purpose to construe the Constitution or laws by any hypercritical rules. And while I do not choose now to specify particular acts of Congress as proper to be enforced, I do suggest that it will be much safer for all, both in official and private stations, to conform to and abide by all those acts which stand unrepealed, than to violate any of them, trusting to find immunity in having them held to be unconstitutional.

It is seventy-two years since the first inauguration of a president under our national Constitution. During that period fifteen different and greatly distinguished citizens have, in succession, administered the executive branch of the government. They have conducted it through many perils, and generally with great success. Yet, with all this scope of precedent, I now enter upon the same task for the brief constitutional term of four years under great and peculiar difficulty. A disruption of the federal Union, heretofore only menaced, is now formidably attempted.[9]

I hold that, in contemplation of universal law and of the Constitution, the union of these states is perpetual.[1] Perpetuity is implied, if not expressed, in the fundamental law of all national governments. It is safe to assert that no government proper ever had a provision in its organic law for its own termination. Continue to execute all the express provisions of our national Constitution, and the Union will endure forever—it being impossible to destroy it except by some action not provided for in the instrument itself.

Again, if the United States be not a government proper, but an association of states in the nature of contract merely, can it, as a

9. The secession of seven states.
1. It was Lincoln's strategy to regard the secession ordinances as unconstitutional, and hence of no effect. The seceded states could reconsider, or the federal authorities could deal with the southern uprising as a civil disorder within the Union. See the argument that follows.

contract, be peaceably unmade by less than all the parties who made it? One party to a contract may violate it—break it, so to speak; but does it not require all to lawfully rescind it?

Descending from these general principles, we find the proposition that in legal contemplation the Union is perpetual confirmed by the history of the Union itself. The Union is much older than the Constitution. It was formed, in fact, by the Articles of Association in 1774. It was matured and continued by the Declaration of Independence in 1776. It was further matured, and the faith of all the then thirteen states expressly plighted and engaged that it should be perpetual, by the Articles of Confederation in 1778. And, finally, in 1787 one of the declared objects for ordaining and establishing the Constitution was "to form a more perfect Union."

But if the destruction of the Union by one or by a part only of the states be lawfully possible, the Union is less perfect than before the Constitution, having lost the vital element of perpetuity.

It follows from these views that no state upon its own mere motion can lawfully get out of the Union; that resolves and ordinances to that effect are legally void; and that acts of violence, within any state or states, against the authority of the United States, are insurrectionary or revolutionary, according to circumstances.

I therefore consider that, in view of the Constitution and the laws, the Union is unbroken; and to the extent of my ability I shall take care, as the Constitution itself expressly enjoins upon me, that the laws of the Union be faithfully executed in all the states.[2] Doing this I deem to be only a simple duty on my part; and I shall perform it so far as practicable, unless my rightful masters, the American people, shall withhold the requisite means, or in some authoritative manner direct the contrary. I trust this will not be regarded as a menace, but only as the declared purpose of the Union that it will constitutionally defend and maintain itself.

In doing this there needs to be no bloodshed or violence; and there shall be none, unless it be forced upon the national authority. The power confided to me will be used to hold, occupy, and possess the property and places belonging to the government, and to collect the duties and imposts; but beyond what may be necessary for these objects, there will be no invasion, no using of force against or among the people anywhere. Where hostility to the United States, in any interior locality, shall be so great and universal as to prevent competent resident citizens from holding the federal offices, there will be no attempt to force obnoxious strangers among the people for that object. While the strict legal right may exist in the government to enforce the exercise of these offices, the attempt to do so

2. Hence even the seceded states, while subject to the police power of the national government, were still assured of all the guarantees of the Constitution.

would be so irritating, and so nearly impracticable withal, that I deem it better to forego for the time the uses of such offices.

The mails, unless repelled, will continue to be furnished in all parts of the Union. So far as possible, the people everywhere shall have that sense of perfect security which is most favorable to calm thought and reflection. The course here indicated will be followed unless current events and experience shall show a modification or change to be proper; and in every case and exigency my best discretion will be exercised according to circumstances actually existing, and with a view and a hope of a peaceful solution of the national troubles, and the restoration of fraternal sympathies and affections.

That there are persons in one section or another who seek to destroy the Union at all events, and are glad of any pretext to do it, I will neither affirm nor deny; but if there be such, I need address no word to them. To those, however, who really love the Union may I not speak?

Before entering upon so grave a matter as the destruction of our national fabric, with all its benefits, its memories, and its hopes, would it not be wise to ascertain precisely why we do it? Will you hazard so desperate a step while there is any possibility that any portion of the ills you fly from have no real existence? Will you, while the certain ills you fly to are greater than all the real ones you fly from—will you risk the commission of so fearful a mistake?

All profess to be content in the Union if all constitutional rights can be maintained. Is it true, then, that any right, plainly written in the Constitution, has been denied? I think not. Happily the human mind is so constituted that no party can reach to the audacity of doing this. Think, if you can, of a single instance in which a plainly written provision of the Constitution has ever been denied. If by the mere force of numbers a majority should deprive a minority of any clearly written constitutional right, it might, in a moral point of view, justify revolution—certainly would if such a right were a vital one. But such is not our case. All the vital rights of minorities and of individuals are so plainly assured to them by affirmations and negations, guaranties and prohibitions, in the Constitution, that controversies never arise concerning them. But no organic law can ever be framed with a provision specifically applicable to every question which may occur in practical administration. No foresight can anticipate, nor any document of reasonable length contain, express provisions for all possible questions. Shall fugitives from labor be surrendered by national or by state authority? The Constitution does not expressly say. *May* Congress prohibit slavery in the territories? The Constitution does not expressly say. *Must* Congress protect slavery in the territories? The Constitution does not expressly say.

From questions of this class spring all our constitutional controversies, and we divide upon them into majorities and minorities. If the minority will not acquiesce, the majority must, or the government must cease. There is no other alternative; for continuing the government is acquiescence on one side or the other.

If a minority in such case will secede rather than acquiesce, they make a precedent which in turn will divide and ruin them; for a minority of their own will secede from them whenever a majority refuses to be controlled by such minority. For instance, why may not any portion of a new confederacy a year or two hence arbitrarily secede again, precisely as portions of the present Union now claim to secede from it? All who cherish disunion sentiments are now being educated to the exact temper of doing this.

Is there such perfect identity of interests among the states to compose a new Union, as to produce harmony only, and prevent renewed secession?

Plainly, the central idea of secession is the essence of anarchy. A majority held in restraint by constitutional checks and limitations, and always changing easily with deliberate changes of popular opinions and sentiments, is the only true sovereign of a free people. Whoever rejects it does, of necessity, fly to anarchy or to despotism. Unanimity is impossible; the rule of a minority, as a permanent arrangement, is wholly inadmissible; so that, rejecting the majority principle, anarchy or despotism in some form is all that is left.

I do not forget the position, assumed by some, that constitutional questions are to be decided by the Supreme Court; nor do I deny that such decisions must be binding, in any case, upon the parties to a suit, as to the object of that suit, while they are also entitled to very high respect and consideration in all parallel cases by all other departments of the government. And while it is obviously possible that such decision may be erroneous in any given case, still the evil effect following it, being limited to that particular case, with the chance that it may be overruled and never become a precedent for other cases, can better be borne than could the evils of a different practice. At the same time, the candid citizen must confess that if the policy of the government, upon vital questions affecting the whole people, is to be irrevocably fixed by decisions of the Supreme Court, the instant they are made, in ordinary litigation between parties in personal actions, the people will have ceased to be their own rulers, having to that extent practically resigned their government into the hands of that eminent tribunal. Nor is there in this view any assault upon the court or the judges. It is a duty from which they may not shrink to decide cases properly brought before them, and it is no fault of theirs if others seek to turn their decisions to political purposes.

One section of our country believes slavery is right, and ought to be extended, while the other believes it is wrong, and ought not to be extended. This is the only substantial dispute. The fugitive-slave clause of the Constitution, and the law for the suppression of the foreign slave-trade, are each as well enforced, perhaps, as any law can ever be in a community where the moral sense of the people imperfectly supports the law itself. The great body of the people abide by the dry legal obligation in both cases, and a few break over in each. This, I think, cannot be perfectly cured; and it would be worse in both cases after the separation of the sections than before. The foreign slave-trade, now imperfectly suppressed, would be ultimately revived, without restriction, in one section, while fugitive slaves, now only partially surrendered, would not be surrendered at all by the other.

Physically speaking, we cannot separate. We cannot remove our respective sections from each other, nor build an impassable wall between them. A husband and wife may be divorced, and go out of the presence and beyond the reach of each other; but the different parts of our country cannot do this. They cannot but remain face to face; and intercourse, either amicable or hostile, must continue between them. Is it possible, then, to make that intercourse more advantageous or more satisfactory after separation than before? Can aliens make treaties easier than friends can make laws? Can treaties be more faithfully enforced between aliens than laws can among friends? Suppose you go to war, you cannot fight always; and when, after much loss on both sides, and no gain on either, you cease fighting, the identical old questions as to terms of intercourse are again upon you.

This country, with its institutions, belongs to the people who inhabit it. Whenever they shall grow weary of the existing government, they can exercise their constitutional right of amending it, or their revolutionary right to dismember or overthrow it. I cannot be ignorant of the fact that many worthy and patriotic citizens are desirous of having the national Constitution amended. While I make no recommendation of amendments, I fully recognize the rightful authority of the people over the whole subject, to be exercised in either of the modes prescribed in the instrument itself; and I should, under existing circumstances, favor rather than oppose a fair opportunity being afforded the people to act upon it. I will venture to add that to me the convention mode seems preferable, in that it allows amendments to originate with the people themselves, instead of only permitting them to take or reject propositions originated by others not especially chosen for the purpose, and which might not be precisely such as they would wish to either accept or refuse. I understand a proposed amendment to the Constitution—

which amendment, however, I have not seen—has passed Congress, to the effect that the federal government shall never interfere with the domestic institutions of the states, including that of persons held to service. To avoid misconstruction of what I have said, I depart from my purpose not to speak of particular amendments so far as to say that, holding such a provision to now be implied constitutional law, I have no objection to its being made express and irrevocable.[3]

The chief magistrate derives all his authority from the people, and they have conferred none upon him to fix terms for the separation of the states. The people themselves can do this also if they choose; but the Executive, as such, has nothing to do with it. His duty is to administer the present government, as it came to his hands, and to transmit it, unimpaired by him, to his successor.

Why should there not be a patient confidence in the ultimate justice of the people? Is there any better or equal hope in the world? In our present differences is either party without faith of being in the right? If the Almighty Ruler of Nations, with His eternal truth and justice, be on your side of the North, or on yours of the South, that truth and that justice will surely prevail by the judgment of this great tribunal of the American people.

By the frame of the government under which we live, this same people have wisely given their public servants but little power for mischief; and have, with equal wisdom, provided for the return of that little to their own hands at very short intervals. While the people retain their virtue and vigilance, no administration, by any extreme of wickedness or folly, can very seriously injure the government in the short space of four years.

My countrymen, one and all, think calmly and well upon this whole subject. Nothing valuable can be lost by taking time. If there be an object to hurry any of you in hot haste to a step which you would never take deliberately, that object will be frustrated by taking time; but no good object can be frustrated by it. Such of you as are now dissatisfied, still have the old Constitution unimpaired, and, on the sensitive point, the laws of your own framing under it; while the new administration will have no immediate power, if it would, to change either. If it were admitted that you who are dissatisfied hold the right side in the dispute, there still is no single good reason for precipitate action. Intelligence, patriotism, Christianity, and a firm reliance on Him who has never yet forsaken this favored land, are still competent to adjust in the best way all our present difficulty.

In your hands, my dissatisfied fellow countrymen, and not in

3. A second reference to his recognition of the emergency amendment. This sentence was a last-minute interpolation, made to emphasize his conciliatory attitude toward the South.

mine, is the momentous issue of civil war. The government will not assail you. You can have no conflict without being yourselves the aggressors. You have no oath registered in heaven to destroy the government, while I shall have the most solemn one to "preserve, protect, and defend it."[4]

I am loath to close. We are not enemies, but friends. We must not be enemies. Though passion may have strained, it must not break our bonds of affection. The mystic chords of memory, stretching from every battlefield and patriot grave to every living heart and hearthstone all over this broad land, will yet swell the chorus of the Union when again touched, as surely they will be, by the better angels of our nature.

Reply to Horace Greeley[5]

EXECUTIVE MANSION,
WASHINGTON, August 22, 1862

HON. HORACE GREELEY.

DEAR SIR:—I have just read yours of the 19th, addressed to myself through the New York *Tribune*. If there be in it any statements or assumptions of fact which I may know to be erroneous, I do not, now and here, controvert them.[6] If there be in it any inferences which I may believe to be falsely drawn, I do not, now and here, argue against them. If there be perceptible in it an impatient and dictatorial tone, I waive it in deference to an old friend, whose heart I have always supposed to be right.

As to the policy I "seem to be pursuing," as you say, I have not meant to leave any one in doubt.

I would save the Union. I would save it the shortest way under the Constitution. The sooner the national authority can be restored, the nearer the Union will be "the Union as it was." If there be those who would not save the Union unless they could at the same time save slavery, I do not agree with them. If there be those who

---

4. Lincoln's original draft ended here.
5. Horace Greeley (1811–1872), the powerful editor of the New York *Tribune*, an ardent free-soiler and abolitionist, had supported Lincoln from the beginning, and sponsored his appearance in New York for the address at Cooper Union. However, in the summer of 1862 he shared the opinion of many northerners who criticized Lincoln's hesitation to emancipate the slaves—an act which he long postponed in accordance with the spirit of his first-inaugural message. Greeley's open letter to Lincoln, entitled "A Prayer of Twenty Millions," appeared in the *Tribune* on August 19, 1862. A month earlier, on July 22, Lin- coln had already shown his cabinet a first draft of the Emancipation Proclamation, but he was withholding it until a decisive improvement in the military fortunes of the North might give it proper emphasis. Meanwhile he replied to Greeley as here shown; the letter appeared in the *National Intelligencer* for August 23, 1862. A month later, on September 22, 1862, after Lee's army had been forced to withdraw at Antietam (September 17), Lincoln issued his famous Proclamation.
6. *I.e.*, public policy forbade his revealing that he had already written the Emancipation Proclamation.

would not save the Union unless they could at the same time destroy slavery, I do not agree with them. My paramount object in this struggle is to save the Union, and is not either to save or to destroy slavery. If I could save the Union without freeing any slave, I would do it; and if I could save it by freeing all the slaves, I would do it; and if I could save it by freeing some and leaving others alone, I would also do that. What I do about slavery and the colored race, I do because I believe it helps to save the Union; and what I forbear, I forbear because I do not believe it would help to save the Union. I shall do less whenever I shall believe what I am doing hurts the cause; and I shall do more whenever I shall believe doing more will help the cause. I shall try to correct errors when shown to be errors, and I shall adopt new views so fast as they shall appear to be true views. I have here stated my purpose according to my view of official duty, and I intend no modification of my oft-expressed personal wish that all men, everywhere, could be free.

Yours,

A. LINCOLN.

Letter to General Joseph Hooker[7]

January 26, 1863

MAJOR-GENERAL HOOKER.

GENERAL. I have placed you at the head of the Army of the Potomac. Of course I have done this upon what appear to me to be sufficient reasons, and yet I think it best for you to know that there are some things in regard to which I am not quite satisfied with you. I believe you to be a brave and skillful soldier, which of course I like. I also believe you do not mix politics with your profession, in which you are right. You have confidence in yourself, which is a valuable if not an indispensable quality. You are ambitious, which, within reasonable bounds, does good rather than harm; but I think that during General Burnside's command of the army you have taken counsel of your ambition and thwarted him as much as you could, in which you did a great wrong to the country and to a most

7. Lincoln's letter to Hooker reflects the darkest Union crisis in the Civil War. During 1862, the inactivity of General McClellan, commanding the major Army of the Potomac, stretched northern nerves to the limit. He was succeeded by Burnside, who combined a gallant aggressiveness with dangerous recklessness. The battle at Fredericksburg, December 13, resulting in disastrous carnage, aggravated the wave of despair and criticism, in which subordinate generals participated. General Hooker, after Fredericksburg, had openly advocated a "dictatorship." Lincoln also knew that he talked too much, drank heavily, and resisted authority; but he had justly earned in combat the nickname of Fighting Joe, he was a good strategist, and the troops idolized him. In elevating him to chief command, Lincoln handed him this frank letter, one of the most remarkable in military annals. Later, failing to defeat Lee at Chancellorsville (May 4, 1863), Hooker gallantly resigned his command, and was succeeded by Meade.

Address at the Dedication of the Gettysburg National Cemetery[1]

Four score and seven years ago our fathers brought forth on this continent, a new nation, conceived in Liberty, and dedicated to the proposition that all men are created equal.

Now we are engaged in a great civil war; testing whether that nation, or any nation so conceived and so dedicated, can long endure. We are met on a great battlefield of that war. We have come to dedicate a portion of that field as a final resting-place for those who here gave their lives that that nation might live. It is altogether fitting and proper that we should do this.

But, in a larger sense, we cannot dedicate—we cannot consecrate—we cannot hallow—this ground. The brave men, living and dead, who struggled here have consecrated it, far above our poor power to add or detract. The world will little note, nor long remember, what we say here, but it can never forget what they did here. It is for us the living, rather, to be dedicated here to the unfinished work which they who fought here have thus far so nobly advanced. It is rather for us to be here dedicated to the great task remaining before us—that from these honored dead we take increased devotion to that cause for which they gave the last full measure of devotion; that we here highly resolve that these dead shall not have died in vain; that this nation, under God,[2] shall have a new birth of freedom; and that government of the people, by the people, for the people,[3] shall not perish from the earth.

1. The thousands of dead were hastily buried at Gettysburg, but part of the battlefield was at once set apart as a national memorial where the slain could be reverently enshrined. Within three months, dedication ceremonies were announced, and numerous government dignitaries invited to attend. Edward Everett, honored statesman and orator, was chosen as the speaker. Although Lincoln had been invited to say a few appropriate words, it was not supposed that he could spare the time from his duties as president and commander in chief. Yet he had privately wanted such an opportunity to tell the plain people, simply, what was the true spiritual and democratic meaning of the war. Belatedly he accepted, and had the opportunity to compose only a first draft of his remarks before leaving Washington. The next morning in Gettysburg, he made a revised draft. On November 19, 1863, at least fifteen thousand peo-

ple listened while Everett recited, for two hours, a memorized address, a fine example of the formal oratory of his day. Then Lincoln stood before the throng, and in two minutes, scarcely glancing at the single page in his hand, spoke the two hundred and sixty words which succeeding generations were to repeat as their own rededication to the democratic love of mankind.

2. The words "under God," not in the earlier manuscript, came to Lincoln's lips as he spoke, and were included in copies of the speech that he later made. (See Thomas, *Abraham Lincoln*, p. 402).

3. Whether Lincoln knew it or not, Theodore Parker, Boston clergyman and abolition leader, in an antislavery address in 1850 had characterized democracy as "a government of all the people, by all the people, for all the people."

Second Inaugural Address[4]

FELLOW-COUNTRYMEN:

At this second appearing to take the oath of the presidential office, there is less occasion for an extended address than there was at the first. Then a statement, somewhat in detail, of a course to be pursued, seemed fitting and proper. Now, at the expiration of four years, during which public declarations have been constantly called forth on every point and phase of the great contest which still absorbs the attention and engrosses the energies of the nation, little that is new could be presented. The progress of our arms, upon which all else chiefly depends, is as well known to the public as to myself; and it is, I trust, reasonably satisfactory and encouraging to all. With high hope for the future, no prediction in regard to it is ventured.

On the occasion corresponding to this four years ago, all thoughts were anxiously directed to an impending civil war. All dreaded it—all sought to avert it. While the inaugural address was being delivered from this place, devoted altogether to saving the Union without war, insurgent agents were in the city seeking to destroy it without war—seeking to dissolve the Union, and divide effects, by negotiation. Both parties deprecated war; but one of them would make war rather than let the nation survive; and the other would accept war rather than let it perish. And the war came.

One-eighth of the whole population were colored slaves, not distributed generally over the Union, but localized in the Southern part of it. These slaves constituted a peculiar and powerful interest. All knew that this interest was, somehow, the cause of the war. To strengthen, perpetuate, and extend this interest was the object for which the insurgents would rend the Union, even by war; while the government claimed no right to do more than to restrict the territorial enlargement of it.

Neither party expected for the war the magnitude or the duration which it has already attained. Neither anticipated that the cause of the conflict might cease with, or even before, the conflict itself

4. At Lincoln's second inaugural, on March 4, 1865, the defeat of the Confederacy was assured. Within the previous six months, Sherman had swept victoriously from Atlanta to the sea and northward again, Sheridan had cleared the Shenandoah and Thomas the Tennessee country, Grant had the remnant of the Army of Virginia cornered in the defense of Richmond, and Lincoln had received the first Confederate peace delegation. These events were reflected in the words of the grave leader, haggard and careworn at the virtual moment of triumph, as he stood in a portico of the Capitol to deliver his inaugural address, the bronze statue of Freedom, which had been prone four years before, now mounted on the completed dome above his head. To the throng that surrounded him he uttered, in his noble last sentence, the words of forgiveness and love toward the vanquished that have re-echoed around the world, and may live forever. Six weeks later, on Easter eve, he lay dead of the assassin's bullet.

should cease.[5] Each looked for an easier triumph, and a result less fundamental and astounding. Both read the same Bible, and pray to the same God; and each invokes his aid against the other. It may seem strange that any men should dare to ask a just God's assistance in wringing their bread from the sweat of other men's faces; but let us judge not, that we be not judged.[6] The prayers of both could not be answered—that of neither has been answered fully.

The Almighty has his own purposes. "Woe unto the world because of offences! for it must needs be that offences come; but woe to that man by whom the offence cometh."[7] If we shall suppose that American slavery is one of those offences which, in the providence of God, must needs come, but which, having continued through his appointed time, he now wills to remove, and that he gives to both North and South this terrible war, as the woe due to those by whom the offence came, shall we discern therein any departure from those divine attributes which the believers in a living God always ascribe to him? Fondly do we hope—fervently do we pray—that this mighty scourge of war may speedily pass away. Yet, if God wills that it continue until all the wealth piled by the bondman's two hundred and fifty years of unrequited toil shall be sunk, and until every drop of blood drawn with the lash shall be paid by another drawn with the sword, as was said three thousand years ago, so still it must be said, "The judgments of the Lord are true and righteous altogether."[8]

With malice toward none; with charity for all; with firmness in the right, as God gives us to see the right, let us strive on to finish the work we are in; to bind up the nation's wounds; to care for him who shall have borne the battle, and for his widow, and his orphan —to do all which may achieve and cherish a just and lasting peace among ourselves, and with all nations.

5. *I.e.*, that the slaves would already have been freed, by the Emancipation Proclamation, effective January 1, 1863.

6. *Cf.* Matthew vii: 1.
7. *Cf.* Matthew xviii: 7.
8. *Cf.* Psalms xix: 9.

An American Chronology

This chronology is intended to provide a background for the introductory essays and to enable the reader to see the individual selections in the anthology in relation to their times.

Entries fall into three categories, each listed in a separate paragraph under the given date:

(L) Significant literary works and events.
(A) Representative works and events in the other arts.
(H) Concurrent events in political, social, and intellectual history.

In each category foreign works are indicated by an asterisk (*). The first time a writer's or artist's name appears it is given in full, together with dates of birth and death. Thereafter, unless there is a chance of confusion, it appears in the surname form alone. In only a few instances does the same name appear twice in the second category (A), for the aim is to be suggestive rather than inclusive.

1588

(L) *Thomas Hariot (1560–1621), *A Briefe and True Report of the New Found Land of Virginia*, first English book describing the new world.

1606

(H) London and Plymouth Companies chartered in London for colonization.

1607

(H) Jamestown, Virginia, founded by the London Company. Scrooby Pilgrims leave England for Amsterdam, Holland.

1608

(L) John Smith (1580?–1652), *A True Relation*.

1609

(H) Henry Hudson discovers Hudson River for the Dutch; claims New Netherland. Champlain explores Lake Champlain for French. "Starving time" in Jamestown. Galileo perfects a telescope.

1611

(L) *King James version of the Bible.

1612

(L) Smith, *A Map of Virginia*.
(H) John Rolfe cultivates tobacco in Virginia.

1616

(L) Smith, *A Description of New England*.

1619

(H) Representative government begins with convening of the Virginia House of Burgesses on July 30. Negro slaves introduced in Virginia.

1620

(H) Pilgrims settle Plymouth Colony, Massachusetts. *Mayflower* Compact (November 11), first American agreement for self-government. *Bacon, *Novum Organum*, formulation of the inductive method of science.

1621

(L) *Mourt's Relation*, presumably

by William Bradford (1590–1657) and
Edward Winslow (1595–1655). *John
Donne (1573–1631), *Sermons* (1622–
1630).

(H) Dutch found New Amsterdam
(New York).

1623

(L) * Shakespeare, first folio edition
of *Plays*.

(H) Bradford at Plymouth proclaims
first Thanksgiving Day.

1624

(L) Smith, *Generall Historie of Virginia*.

1625

(H) Thomas Morton and Captain
Wollaston settle Merry Mount in Massachusetts and resist the Puritans.
Charles I reigns in England (1625–
1649). Age of Cavalier-Puritan conflict
in England (1625–1660).

1629

(H) Massachusetts Bay Company
chartered in London. Minuit authorizes
patroon system of landed estates.

1630

(L) Bradford begins to record the
history "Of Plimoth Plantation" (continued until 1651). Smith, *True Travels*.
John Winthrop (1588–1640) begins his
Journal.

(H) First large group of Puritan
settlers reach Massachusetts Bay in
the *Arabella* and establish Boston.

1636

(H) Harvard College founded. Roger
Williams founds settlement at Providence, Rhode Island.

1637

(L) Thomas Morton (1590?–1647),
New English Canaan.

(H) Pequot War with the Indians,
Connecticut. Anne Hutchinson's doctrine of intuitional faith precipitates the
antinomian controversy in Massachusetts, and she is banished. *René Descartes (1596–1650), *Discourse on Method*, expounds rationalistic philosophy.

1639

(H) First American printing press,
operated by Stephen Daye, in Cambridge, Massachusetts. Fundamental
Orders of Connecticut, first document
creating constitutional government in
area now part of U. S. Roger Williams
establishes first Baptist church in
America at Providence.

1640

(L) The *Bay Psalm Book* (*The
Whole Book of Psalms*), first book
printed in English colonies (Cambridge,
Massachusetts).

(H) Population of all English colonies, *ca.* 27,950; of New England,
ca. 21,200. Puritan Revolution in
England (1640–1660).

1643

(H) New England Confederation
(1643–1684). Massachusetts population estimated at 16,000. Roger Williams (1603?–1683), *A Key into
the Language of America*, on the
language of the Indians.

1644

(H) Williams, *The Bloudy Tenent
of Persecution for Cause of Conscience*.

1647

(H) Massachusetts passes first
public-school law. John Cotton (1584–
1652), *The Bloudy Tenent Washed
and Made White * * * *.

1650

(L) Anne Bradstreet (1612?–1672),
*The Tenth Muse Lately Sprung Up in
America*.

(H) Colonial population estimated
at 51,700. *Jeremy Taylor (1613–
1667), *Holy Living*, English Puritan
piety.

1651

(H) British Navigation Act exploits
colonial commerce and causes discontent. *Thomas Hobbes (1588–1679),
Leviathan, defends monarchy.

1660

(H) Colonial population estimated
at 84,800. English literature of the
witchcraft controversy (1660–1688).
Restoration of Stuart monarchy in
England; Charles II reigns (1660–
1685).

1661

(H) John Eliot's translation of the
New Testament into Algonquin. Reign
of Louis XIV of France (1661–1715).

1662

(L) Michael Wigglesworth (1631–
1705), *The Day of Doom*. *Thomas
Fuller (1608–1661), *Worthies of England*.

1667

(L) * Milton, *Paradise Lost*. * Molière (1622–1673), *Tartuffe*. *Jean Baptiste Racine (1639–1699), *Andromaque*.

1669

(L) John Eliot (1604–1690), *The
Indian Primer*.

1670

(H) English settle Charleston, South
Carolina. Colonial population estimated
at 114,500.

1671

(L) Edward Taylor (1645?–1729),
one of the first American poets, goes to
Westfield as minister.

1674

(L) Samuel Sewall (1652–1730)
begins his *Diary* (1674–1729).

1675

(H) King Philip's War, caused by

raids under Chief Metacomet (died 1676), begins; it resulted in destruction of Massachusetts tribal life by 1678.

1676

(H) Nathaniel Bacon's Rebellion, a popular agrarian uprising in Virginia.

1678

(L) Bradstreet, *Poems*. *John Bunyan (1628–1688), *Pilgrim's Progress*, Part I.

1681

(L) *Dryden, *Absalom and Achitophel*.

(H) La Salle's exploration of Mississippi (1681–1687) extends French claims. Pennsylvania granted to William Penn as Proprietor. William Penn (1644–1718), *Some Account of the Province of Pensilvania in America*.

1682

(H) Penn establishes Philadelphia as the seat of Pennsylvania; issues his Frame of Government assuring popular representation and toleration; receives Delaware from the Duke of York. Reign of Peter the Great (1682–1725).

1683

(L) *The New England Primer;* conjectured dates for the first edition range from 1683 to 1690.

1684

(L) Increase Mather (1639–1723), *An Essay for the Recording of Illustrious Providences*.

(H) Massachusetts loses charter and is declared a royal colony.

1685

(H) Duke of York accedes to the throne as James II (reigns 1685–1688); relinquishes Proprietorship of New York, which becomes a royal colony. Revocation of Edict of Nantes ends toleration for French Protestants; large numbers of Huguenots emigrate to American colonies. *John Locke (1632–1704), *Two Treatises on Government*.

1687

(H) Anglican Church established in Boston. *Sir Isaac Newton (1642–1727), *Principia* (in full, *Philosophiae Naturalis Principia Mathematica*), the foundation of a new physics.

1688

(H) Glorious Revolution in England unseats James II and the Catholic power; William and Mary reign (1689–1694; after death of Mary, William continuing as ruler, 1694–1702).

1689

(H) Cotton Mather leads Boston Uprising, and William of Orange restores former charters. British Tolera-

tion Acts extend freedom of worship. King William's War with the French, resulting from Louis XIV's support of the deposed James II, causes bloody battles with French and Indian raiders (1689–1697).

1692

(H) Trials for witchcraft in Salem, Massachusetts.

1693

(L) Cotton Mather (1663–1728), *Wonders of the Invisible World*.

(H) William and Mary College founded at Williamsburg, Virginia.

1699

(H) French settle Louisiana. Williamsburg becomes capital of Virginia (to 1779).

1700

(L) *William Congreve (1670–1729), *The Way of the World*. *Height of British neoclassicism.

(H) Colonial population estimated at 275,000. Sewall, *The Selling of Joseph*, antislavery tract.

1701

(H) Yale College founded.

1702

(L) Cotton Mather, *Magnalia Christi Americana*. *Daniel Defoe (1661?–1731), *The Shortest Way with Dissenters*.

(H) Queen Anne reigns in England (1702–1714). Queen Anne's War (War of the Spanish Succession, 1701–1713) produces border warfare with French and Indian forces.

1704

(L) Sarah Kemble Knight (1666–1727) begins *Journal*.

(H) *Boston News-Letter*, first established newspaper in the U. S. (1704–1776).

1706

(H) British Navigation Act restricts colonial trade in rice, naval stores, and molasses.

1710

(L) Cotton Mather, *Bonifacius*, or *Essays to Do Good*.

(H) Colonial population estimated at 375,500. *Bishop George Berkeley (1685–1753), *Principles of Human Knowledge*, influences New England idealism.

1714

(H) George I reigns in England (1714–1727), establishing Hanoverian line (to Victoria).

1717

(H) Mississippi Bubble (1717–1720), French speculation for the rapid development of Louisiana, which culminated in financial disaster.

1719

(L) *Defoe, Robinson Crusoe.* *Isaac Watts (1674–1748), *Psalms and Hymns.*

(H) German Dunkers (Church of the Brethren) settle in Philadelphia under leadership of Peter Beck. Herculaneum and Pompeii rediscovered: classical revival.

1720

(H) Colonial population estimated at 474,400.

1721

(H) Smallpox inoculation first introduced in colonies. James Franklin edits the *New England Courant* (1721–1726).

1722

(L) Benjamin Franklin (1706–1790), *Dogood Papers.*

(A) *Johann Sebastian Bach (1685–1750), *The Well-Tempered Clavier,* Part I.

(H) Extension of restrictions under Navigation Act.

1723

(H) Franklin arrives in Philadelphia.

1724

(L) Cotton Mather, *Parentator,* biography of Increase Mather.

1726

(L) *Jonathan Swift (1667–1745), *Gulliver's Travels.*

1727

(H) Franklin founds the Junto, first formal cultural association in the colonies. George II reigns in England (1727–1760).

1728

(A) *James Gibbs (1682–1754), *Book of Architecture* influential in the colonies.

(H) *Pennsylvania Gazette* (1728–1815), owned and edited by Franklin (1729–1766). William Byrd surveys the line between Virginia and North Carolina.

1730

(A) *William Hogarth (1697–1764), *Rake's Progress.*

(H) Byrd begins Westover, Charles City County. Colonial population estimated at 655,000. Methodist Society founded at Oxford.

1731

(H) In Philadelphia, Franklin promotes the first subscription library.

1732

(H) Conrad Beissel's Dunker community of Pennsylvania Germans at Ephrata, Pennsylvania. First American almshouse erected in Philadelphia. Linnaeus (1707–1778), *System of Nature.*

1733

(L) William Byrd (1674–1744), *Journey to the Land of Eden.* Franklin founds *Poor Richard's Almanack* (1733–1758). *Pope, *An Essay on Man.*

(H) Oglethorpe establishes settlement in Georgia. Molasses Act levies heavy duty on colonial imports of rum, sugar, and molasses, a large factor in American trade. Richmond, Virginia, established.

1734

(H) The "Great Awakening" (1734–1750) begins with Jonathan Edwards' Northampton revival.

1735

(H) Peter Zenger's acquittal in New York ends first American trial concerning the free press. Visit to America of John and Charles Wesley influences the "Great Awakening" (Methodist revivalism began 1739).

1738

(H) George Whitefield's first visit to America accelerates the "Great Awakening."

1739

(H) *David Hume (1711–1776), *Treatise of Human Nature.*

1740

(L) *Samuel Richardson (1689–1761), *Pamela, or Virtue Rewarded.*

(H) The Charity School chartered at Philadelphia (soon called the Academy, and later the University of Pennsylvania). Colonial population estimated at 889,000.

1741

(L) *The General Magazine* founded by Franklin at Philadelphia.

1742

(L) *Henry Fielding (1707–1754), *Joseph Andrews,* picaresque novel.

(A) *George Frideric Handel (1685–1759), *Messiah.*

1744

(H) American Philosophical Society organized in Philadelphia. King George's War (War of the Austrian Succession) again produces French and Indian border massacres (1744–1748).

1745

(H) Franklin invents his stove.

1746

(H) Founding of the College of New Jersey (Princeton).

1748

(H) First Lutheran synod in America formed in Philadelphia. *Hume, *An Enquiry Concerning Human Understanding.* *Montesquieu (1689–1755), *The Spirit of Laws.*

1749

(L) *Fielding, *Tom Jones.*

(A) First regular theatrical company begins performances in Philadelphia.

(H) First Ohio Company chartered. *Emanuel Swedenborg (1688–1772), Arcana Celesta.*

1750

(L) *Transition toward romanticism in British literature (1750–1798).

(H) Colonial population estimated at 1,207,000.

1751

(L) *Thomas Gray (1716–1771), Elegy Written in a Country Churchyard.*

(H) Georgia becomes a royal colony. Franklin, *Experiments and Observations on Electricity.*

1752

(H) Pennsylvania Hospital, the first founded in the colonies, established in Philadelphia. First fire-insurance company founded in Philadelphia. Franklin's lightning-rod experiment.

1753

(H) Colonial postal system organized.

1754

(L) Jonathan Edwards (1703–1758), *Freedom of the Will.*

(H) Albany Congress accepts Franklin's plan for a colonial union against French and Indian attack, but it is rejected in colonial assemblies. French and Indian War (New World counterpart of the Seven Years' War, 1756–1763), during which the British capture Louisbourg, Fort Duquesne (Pittsburgh), Ticonderoga, Quebec, Montreal. King's College (later Columbia) founded.

1755

(L) *Samuel Johnson (1709–1784), A Dictionary of the English Language.*

(H) British deport French Acadians.

1757

(H) Franklin becomes Pennsylvania's representative in England.

1759

(L) *Laurence Sterne (1713–1768), Tristram Shandy,* Volumes I and II. *Voltaire, Candide.*

(A) Peter Harrison (1716–1775) commences Touro Synagogue, Newport, Rhode Island.

1760

(L) *James Macpherson (1736–1796), Ossian.* *Jean Jacques Rousseau (1712–1778), Julie, or The New Heloise.*

(H) George III reigns in England (1760–1820). Colonial population estimated at 1,610,000.

1762

(H) France cedes Louisiana to Spain.

Rousseau, Social Contract, theory of the social contract in government.

1763

(H) Treaty of Paris concludes Seven Years' War; French cede to the British their territories in Canada and Great Lakes Basin, and Florida. Pontiac's Uprising; disastrous Indian attacks from Detroit to western Virginia. Mason and Dixon line surveyed (1763–1767).

1764

(H) Rhode Island College (Brown University) founded. James Otis (1725–1783), *Rights of the British Colonies.*

1765

(A) Ezra Waite, Miles Brewton House, Charleston, South Carolina.

(H) British Quartering Act and Stamp Act. Stamp Act Congress issues Declaration of Rights and declares against "taxation without representation." James Watt invents the steam engine.

1766

(L) *Oliver Goldsmith (1728–1744), The Vicar of Wakefield.*

(H) Stamp Act repealed. Queen's College (Rutgers) founded. First permanent theater in colonies erected in Philadelphia.

1767

(A) John Singleton Copley (1738–1815), portrait of Nicholas Boylston. Thomas Jefferson (1743–1826), Monticello (altered and enlarged to 1809).

(H) Townshend Acts, levying colonial import taxes on such staples as tea, meet violent resistance. James Hargreaves invents spinning jenny.

1768

(L) John Dickinson (1732–1808), *Letters from a Farmer in Pennsylvania.*

1769

(A) *Robert Adam (1728–1792) with his brothers James and William builds Adelphi section of London (Georgian style in architecture).

(H) At San Diego, Fra Junipero Serra founds the first of nine missions in California (the first European settlement in Upper California), inaugurating the mission-culture there. Dartmouth College founded. Watauga Association begins settlement of Tennessee. Daniel Boone explores Kentucky (1769–1771).

1770

(H) Boston Massacre resulting from resistance of citizens to British troops sent to Boston to enforce the Townshend Acts. Acts repealed except for levy on tea. Colonial population estimated at 2,205,000.

1771

(L) Franklin begins his *Autobiography.* Philip Freneau (1752–1832) and Hugh Henry Brackenridge (1748–

1816), *A Poem on the Rising Glory of America.*

(A) Judah Woodruff (1720–1799), Congregational Meeting-House, Farmington, Connecticut.

(H) Violent uprising of North Carolina Regulators protesting excessive taxation of poor farmers and restrictions against nonconformists. *First edition of the *Encyclopedia Britannica.*

1772

(L) John Trumbull (1750–1831), *The Progress of Dullness.*

(H) In Boston, Samuel Adams forms the first Committee of Correspondence, an anti-British underground.

1773

(L) Franklin, "An Edict by the King of Prussia" and "Rules by Which a Great Empire May Be Reduced to a Small One."

(A) William Buckland (1734–1774?), Hammond House, Annapolis.

(H) Boston Tea Party, destruction of tea subject to duty under Townshend Acts; tea ship burned at Annapolis.

1774

(L) Francis Hopkinson (1737–1791), *A Pretty Story.* Thomas Jefferson (1743–1826), *Summary of the Rights of British America.* John Woolman (1720–1772), *Journal.* *Chesterfield (1694–1773), *Letters to His Son.*

(H) First Continental Congress convened in Philadelphia by Committee of Correspondence. Joseph Priestley discovers oxygen.

1775

(L) Trumbull, *McFingal.* *Richard Brinsley Sheridan (1751–1816), *The Rivals.*

(H) *Edmund Burke (1729–1797), makes his speech in Parliament, *On Conciliation with America.* American Revolution (1775–1783). Battles of Lexington, Concord (April); Second Continental Congress (May); Arnold and Allen take Ticonderoga (May); Washington assumes command (June); Bunker Hill (June); patriots unsuccessfully invade Canada. Daniel Boone cuts wilderness road through Cumberland Gap. First Anti-Slavery Society meets in Philadelphia.

1776

(L) Thomas Paine (1737–1809), *Common Sense* and the first of the *Crisis* pamphlets.

(H) British evacuate Boston (March); Congress authorizes Declaration of Independence (July); British take New York (Battle of Long Island, August); Washington retreats into Pennsylvania, crosses Delaware to take Trenton (December); British take Newport, Rhode Island (December). French begin secret aid to the Americans. Virginia Declaration of Rights, important source of the Bill of Rights of the Constitution (Amendments I–X). Spain settles San Francisco, builds Mission and Presidio. Delaware ends importation of slaves. Phi Beta Kappa founded at William and Mary College. *Adam Smith (1723–1790), *The Wealth of Nations.*

1777

(H) Americans win at Bennington, Oriskany (August), and force Burgoyne's surrender (Saratoga, October); British defeat Washington at Brandywine, take Philadelphia (September); Washington winters at Valley Forge. Congress approves Articles of Confederation for ratification, adopts national flag. Vermont abolishes slavery and adopts manhood suffrage.

1778

(A) *Jean Antoine Houdon (1741–1828), bust of Voltaire.

(H) France recognizes American independence; forms Franco-American Alliance (February); British evacuate Philadelphia (June), begin southern campaign, capture Savannah (December); George Rogers Clark begins western offensive, takes Kaskaskia (July). Indian-Tory massacres of patriots, Wyoming Valley, Pennsylvania (July), Cherry Valley, New York (November). Articles of Confederation approved (fully ratified 1781).

1779

(L) Brackenridge founds the *United States Magazine* (twelve monthly issues).

(H) Clark takes Vincennes (February); Anthony Wayne captures Stony Point (July); John Paul Jones, commanding *Bonhomme Richard,* captures *Serapis* (September); British evacuate Newport (October), but win victories in Georgia. Virginia disestablishes Anglican Church.

1780

(H) American Academy of Arts and Sciences chartered in Boston. British take Charleston, South Carolina (May), and win at Camden, South Carolina (August), but lose at King's Mountain, North Carolina (October). John André's capture and Benedict Arnold's treason. French send General Rochambeau and troops. Pennsylvania votes gradual emancipation. Transylvania College founded in Kentucky, first college west of the Alleghenies. Population estimated at 2,781,000.

1781

(L) Freneau, *The British Prison Ship.*

(H) Cornwallis successful in North Carolina campaign (January–March); in September is trapped at Yorktown, Virginia, between the army of Washington and Rochambeau and the French fleet under de Grasse; surrenders October 19, ending the war. Articles of Confederation in effect; Confederation era until 1789. Robert Morris becomes superintendent of finance. *Immanuel Kant (1724–1804), *Critique of Pure Reason*, transcendental philosophy.

1782

(L) St. Jean de Crèvecœur (1735–1813), *Letters from an American Farmer*.

(H) The Aitken Bible, first complete English Bible printed in America.

1783

(L) Noah Webster (1758–1843) publishes his *Spelling Book*.

(H) In Treaty of Paris, England recognizes American independence. Massachusetts Supreme Court decision rules slavery unconstitutional. Protestant Episcopal Church organized.

1784

(L) Jefferson writes *Notes on the State of Virginia* (1784–1785).

(H) Abortive effort to organize state of Franklin in Tennessee. Emancipation adopted in New Hampshire, Rhode Island, Connecticut. Methodist Episcopal Church organized. Ethan Allen (1738–1789), *Reason the Only Oracle of Man*. Jedediah Morse (1761–1826), *Geography Made Easy*, first geography in the U. S.

1785

(L) Timothy Dwight (1732–1819), *The Conquest of Canaan*. Friendly Club begun at Hartford by the Connecticut Wits about 1785 (to *ca.* 1807).

(H) University of Georgia founded. The *Grand Turk*, owned by Elias Hasket Derby of Salem, Massachusetts, makes the first round trip between Salem and China.

1786

(L) Freneau, *Poems*. *Robert Burns (1759–1796), *Poems, Chiefly in the Scottish Dialect*.

(H) Virginia Statute of Religious Freedom. Shays's Rebellion, Massachusetts insurrection against severe debtor laws.

1787

(L) Joel Barlow (1754–1812), *The Vision of Columbus*. *The Federalist* (1787–1788). Royall Tyler (1757–1826), *The Contrast*, first American comedy on the stage.

(A) *Wolfgang Amadeus Mozart (1756–1791), *Don Giovanni*.

(H) Constitutional Convention in Philadelphia (May–September); Delaware first to ratify (December). Northwest Ordinance (Ordinance of 1787) organizes territory north of Ohio and forbids slavery there. First prison-reform society founded in Philadelphia. First communal Shaker society founded

near Albany, New York. John Fitch launches his first steamboat.

1788

(L) Dwight, *The Triumph of Infidelity*.

(A) Francis Hopkinson (1737–1791), *Seven Songs for the Harpsichord or Forte Piano*, first American music.

(H) Struggle for ratification of Constitution; adopted June 21 with nine ratifications.

1789

(L) William Hill Brown (1765–1793), *The Power of Sympathy*, first American novel published in the U. S. Noah Webster, *Dissertation on the English Language*. *William Blake (1757–1827), *Songs of Innocence*.

(H) Government under the Constitution. Federalist era (1789–1801). First presidential election (January); George Washington inaugurated as president (April); cabinet system initiated. University of North Carolina founded. French Revolution begins. *Gazette of the United States*, Hamiltonian newspaper (New York, 1789; Philadelphia, 1790–1847).

1790

(H) Philadelphia capital of the U. S. (1790–1800). First Catholic bishop for U. S. Alexander Hamilton (1753?–1804), *Report on Manufactures*. U. S. population is 3,929,214 according to first census. *Burke's *Reflections on the Revolution in France* provokes Paine's rejoinder.

1791

(L) William Bartram (1739–1823), *Travels * * *. Paine, *The Rights of Man*. *James Boswell (1740–1795), *The Life of Samuel Johnson*.

(A) Major Pierre Charles L'Enfant (1754–1825) plans city of Washington. *Joseph Haydn (1732–1809), *Surprise* symphony (No. 94).

(H) Bill of Rights (Amendments I–X) added to Constitution. Congress charters first Bank of the United States. Vermont becomes fourteenth state. Williams College founded.

1792

(L) Brackenridge begins publication of *Modern Chivalry* (1792–1815).

(A) James Hoban (1762?–1831), the White House, Washington. (Hoban also designed the new White House, 1815–1829, after the first was destroyed by the British.) *Benjamin West succeeds Sir Joshua Reynolds as president of the Royal Academy.

(H) Congress establishes U. S. Mint in Philadelphia; authorizes standard for gold and silver coinage. New York Stock Exchange formed. Statehood for Kentucky.

1793

(H) First national Fugitive Slave Law. American neutrality proclaimed in wars of French Revolution; Citizen Genêt attempts to secure American aid. Eli Whitney invents cotton gin.

1794

(L) Dwight, *Greenfield Hill*. Paine, *The Age of Reason*. Susanna Rowson (1762–1824), *Charlotte Temple*. *William Godwin (1756–1836), *Caleb Williams*, sociological novel.

(H) Joseph Priestley, British liberal and physicist, settles in Philadelphia. American Neutrality Act accelerates American foreign trade; Jay's treaty with Britain secures American commercial rights. Anthony Wayne subdues hostile Ohio Indians of Northwest Territory (Greenville Treaty, 1795). Washington quells Whiskey Rebellion against excise tax in Pennsylvania. Yellow-fever epidemic strikes Philadelphia.

1795

(L) Freneau, *Poems*.

(A) Rembrandt Peale (1778–1860), portrait of Washington from life. Gilbert Stuart (1755–1828), "Vaughan" portrait of Washington.

(H) Pinckney Treaty with Spain defines boundaries of Florida and Louisiana, and guarantees U. S. navigation of the Mississippi.

1796

(L) Barlow, *Hasty Pudding*.

(H) Washington gives his Farewell Address. Tennessee becomes a state. Edward Jenner begins vaccination.

1797

(H) John Adams (Federalist), president (1797–1801); Thomas Jefferson (Democratic-Republican), vice-president.

1798

(L) Charles Brockden Brown (1771–1810), *Wieland*. *William Wordsworth (1770–1850) and Samuel Taylor Coleridge (1772–1834), *Lyrical Ballads* begins high tide of British romanticism. *Johann Wolfgang von Goethe (1749–1832), *Hermann and Dorothea*.

(H) Alien and Sedition Acts provide Federalist curb on opinions of pro-French Democratic-Republicans; Kentucky and Virginia Resolutions (drafted by Jefferson and Madison) challenge such laws in the first important assertion of state sovereignty. French demand bribe in diplomatic negotiations of XYZ Affair; "undeclared war" with France (1798–1800). Whitney's firearms manufacture provides first use of interchangeable parts. *Thomas Robert Malthus (1766–1834), *Essay on Population*.

1799

(L) Brown, *Ormond, Arthur Mervyn, Edgar Huntly*.

(A) Benjamin Henry Latrobe (1764–1820), Bank of Pennsylvania, Philadelphia, heralds Greek revival.

(H) New York adopts gradual emancipation.

1800

(A) Latrobe's design for Sedgley, Philadelphia, mansion initiates Gothic influence in U. S. architecture.

(H) Washington, D. C., becomes capital of U. S. France and U. S. end conflict but cancel alliance of 1778. Spain cedes Louisiana to France. The Federalist Adams defeated by Democratic-Republicans; Jefferson and Aaron Burr tied in electoral votes; House of Representatives elects Jefferson. U. S. population, 5,308,483. Alessandro Volta invents voltaic pile. Library of Congress founded. Mason L. Weems (1759–1825), *Life of Washington*.

1801

(L) Joseph Dennie founds *The Port Folio* (1801–1827). *Chateaubriand (1768–1848), *Atala*, romanticizes the American Indian.

(H) Thomas Jefferson (Democratic-Republican), president (1801–1809). John Marshall, chief justice (1801–1835). Tripolitan Wars (1801–1805): U. S. successfully resists piracy of the Barbary States. New York *Evening Post* founded.

1802

(A) Samuel McIntire (1757–1811), Pierce-Nichols House, Salem, Massachusetts.

(H) U. S. Military Academy founded at West Point.

1803

(H) Ohio admitted to statehood. Purchase of Louisiana territory from France increases national domain by 140 per cent. Supreme Court decision, in *Marbury v. Madison*, establishes right of the Court to nullify congressional legislation on constitutional grounds.

1804

(L) *J. C. F. von Schiller (1759–1805), *Wilhelm Tell*.

(A) *Ludwig van Beethoven (1770–1827), *Eroica* symphony (No. 3).

(H) New Jersey adopts gradual emancipation. Burr fatally wounds Hamilton in duel. Lewis and Clark explore the Northwest to the Pacific (1804–1806). Jefferson re-elected president. Napoleon becomes emperor of France. John Marshall (1755–1835), *The Life of George Washington* (1804–1807).

1805

(L) Boston Athenaeum founded.

1806

(L) Noah Webster, *Compendious Dictionary*.

(H) Nonimportation Act passed in

retaliation for British infringements upon American shipping.

1807

(L) Barlow, *The Columbiad*. William (1766–1821) and Washington (1783–1859) Irving and J. K. Paulding (1778–1860) begin *Salmagundi* papers (1807–1808).

(H) Embargo Act passed in protest against British and French interference with the commerce of neutrals in the Napoleonic Wars. Importation of slaves to the U. S. forbidden after January 1, 1808; England likewise abolishes all slave trade. Robert Fulton, with the *Clermont*, demonstrates commercial practicality of steamboats. Vermont decrees separation of church and state. *Georg Wilhelm Friedrich Hegel (1770–1831), *Phenomenology of Mind*.

1808

(L) *Goethe, *Faust*, Part I.

1809

(L) Washington Irving, *History of New York* "by Diedrich Knickerbocker."

(H) James Madison (Democratic-Republican), president (1809–1817), elected with the backing of Jefferson. Nonintercourse Act forbids commerce with the belligerents Great Britain and France in protest against violations of neutrality.

1810

(H) Madison proclaims annexation of West Florida. Construction of Cumberland Road authorized. Protestant denominations found first American missionary organization, Board of Commissioners for Foreign Missions. U. S. population, 7,239,881.

1811

(L) *Jane Austen (1775–1817), *Sense and Sensibility*.

(H) Democratic-Republican majority refuses to renew charter of the Bank of the United States, an instrument of Hamiltonian government finance. First steamboats appear on Mississippi. W. H. Harrison's forces resist insurrection of Indians under Tecumseh at Tippecanoe, Indiana. John J. Astor locates first fur-trading post in Oregon, at Astoria.

1812

(H) War of 1812, against Great Britain, in defense of rights of neutral American shipping (1812–1815). Americans forced to surrender Detroit; fail in efforts to invade Canada, defeated at Queenstown Heights; but the U.S.S. *Constitution* ("Old Ironsides") defeats the British *Guerrière*. Madison re-elected president. Napoleon invades Russia. Benjamin Rush (1745–1813), *Medical Inquiries and Observations upon the Diseases of the Mind*.

1813

(L) *Austen, *Pride and Prejudice*.

(H) British blockade American coast; Americans take Mobile, raid Canadian border; Perry wins naval victory on Lake Erie.

1814

(L) *Sir Walter Scott (1771–1832), *Waverley*, inaugurates the vogue of the romantic historical novel.

(H) Americans recapture Detroit; fight drawn battle at Lundy's Lane; check British invasion at Lake Champlain. British take Washington and burn White House, but are repulsed at Baltimore. Francis Scott Key writes "The Star-Spangled Banner" during British bombardment of Fort McHenry. War ended by Treaty of Ghent (December). Andrew Jackson defeats the Creek Indians at Talladega and Horsehoe Bend. Delegates from Massachusetts, Rhode Island, and Connecticut at the Hartford Convention oppose policies of Jefferson and Madison, and consider secession. Complete cotton mill established at Waltham, Massachusetts, by Francis Cabot Lowell.

1815

(L) Freneau, *Poems. North American Review* founded (1815–1950).

(A) Charles Bulfinch (1763–1844), University Hall, Harvard.

(H) Battle of New Orleans (January) fought before arrival of news of war's end. Battle of Waterloo. Congress of Vienna.

1816

(H) Congress again charters a Bank of the United States to carry part of the national debt incurred by War of 1812. Congress adopts a tariff policy based on protection of American industry. American Colonization Society founded for resettlement of Negroes in Africa. First American savings bank established in Boston. American Bible Society founded. Black Ball Line begins regular transatlantic service by sailing packet between New York and Liverpool.

1817

(L) William Cullen Bryant (1794–1878) publishes "Thanatopsis." *Coleridge, *Biographia Literaria*, romantic criticism. *Mary Wollstonecraft Shelley (1797–1851), *Frankenstein*, "Gothic" novel of terror.

(H) James Monroe (Democratic-Republican), president (1817–1825). Rush-Bagot Agreement with Great Britain demilitarizes the Great Lakes and Canadian border, initiating permanent peace with British Empire. Construction begins on Erie Canal; John Stevens secures first American railway charter. Seminole uprising in Florida. Mississippi admitted to statehood. University of Michigan founded. *David Ricardo (1772–1823), *Political Economy and Taxation.*

1818

(L) Bryant publishes "To a Waterfowl." *John Keats (1795–1821), *Endymion.*

(H) Seminole uprising quelled by Jackson. Illinois admitted to statehood. Anglo-American treaty provides joint occupation of Oregon territory. Cumberland Road opened to Wheeling, first national road to the West.

1819

(L) Irving, *The Sketch Book of Geoffrey Crayon, Gent.* *George Gordon, Lord Byron (1788–1824), *Don Juan,* Cantos I and II, a pattern of the "Byronic."

(H) Financial panic, followed by depression (1819–1821). Alabama admitted to statehood. Treaty with Spain provides for purchase of Florida (ratified 1821). Dartmouth College Case settled; Daniel Webster wins decision preventing a state from abrogating legal contracts. University of Virginia founded. *Arthur Schopenhauer (1788–1860), *The World as Will and Idea,* romantic pessimism.

1820

(L) James Fenimore Cooper (1789–1851), publishes his first novel, *Precaution.* *Charles Lamb (1775–1834), *Essays of Elia.* *Scott, *Ivanhoe.* *Percy Bysshe Shelley (1792–1822), *Prometheus Unbound.*

(H) Monroe re-elected president. Missouri Compromise, admitting Missouri as a slave state (1821), Maine as a free state (1820), initiates the struggle for balance of power between North and South. Land Law liberalized for sale of national lands—"hundred-dollar farms" (eighty acres). U. S. population, 9,638,453. Reign of George IV of England (1820–1830).

1821

(L) Bryant, *Poems.* Cooper, *The Spy. Saturday Evening Post* founded. *Scott, *Kenilworth.*

(H) Florida annexed. Moses Austin secures from Mexico large grant of land in Texas; numerous American colonists settle across the border; Santa Fe Trail becomes important trade route from Missouri to New Mexico. Russian proclamation claims control of Pacific coast north of 51°. *John Stuart Mill (1806–1873), *Political Economy.*

1822

(L) Irving, *Bracebridge Hall.*
(A) *Franz Schubert (1797–1828), *Unfinished* symphony (No. 8).

(H) U. S. recognizes independence of Latin-American countries. Liberia founded.

1823

(L) Cooper, *The Pioneers* and *The Pilot.*

(H) The Monroe Doctrine of "America for Americans" expresses U. S. reaction to Russian colonial expectations and the proclamation by the Holy Alliance nullifying Latin-American republics.

1824

(L) Irving, *Tales of a Traveller.*

(H) Jedediah Smith opens Oregon Trail as trade route. Russian-U. S. treaty sets 54° 40′ as Alaska boundary. Justice Marshall, in *Gibbons v. Ogden,* confirms federal control of interstate commerce. War of Greek Independence (1824–1830) stirs democratic sympathy and American unofficial participation. Simón Bolívar liberates South America. George Stephenson develops locomotive.

1825

(L) Daniel Webster's Bunker Hill oration. The appearance of the annual gift book (1825–1850) encourages short fiction and poetry. *Aleksander Pushkin (1799–1837), *Boris Godunov.*

(A) Beginning of the vogue of Italian opera in the U. S.

(H) House breaks electoral deadlock of 1824; names John Quincy Adams (Democratic-Republican) as president (1825–1829). Erie Canal opened. Robert Owen founds the socialist New Harmony Community (1825–1828) in Indiana. Organization of American Tract Society, American Sunday School Union, American Unitarian Association.

1826

(L) Cooper, *Last of the Mohicans. Graham's Magazine* founded (1826–1858).

(H) Josiah Holbrook's American Lyceum (for adult education) launched in Millbury, Massachusetts; three thousand lyceum centers in operation by 1834. American Home Missionary Society founded for work among Indians and frontier communities.

1827

(L) Cooper, *The Prairie.* Edgar Allan Poe (1809–1849), *Tamerlane and Other Poems.* *Heinrich Heine (1797–1856), *Songs.*

(H) The political issue of protective tariff, favoring northern manufactures at the expense of the South; southerners call tariff of 1828 a "tariff of abominations"; industrialists hold High Tariff Convention at Harrisburg.

1828

(L) Cooper, *Red Rover.* Nathaniel Hawthorne (1804–1864) publishes his first novel, *Fanshawe.* Irving, *Columbus.* Noah Webster, *An American Dictionary of the English Language.*

(A) *Hector Berlioz (1803–1869), *Symphonie Fantastique*.

(H) Construction of Baltimore and Ohio Railroad begins. Workingmen's Party formed in Philadelphia for political action.

1829

(L) Irving, *Conquest of Granada*. Poe, *Al Araaf, Tamerlane, and Minor Poems*. Samuel Kettell (1800–1855) publishes the first American anthology, *Specimens of American Poetry*.

(A) *Gioacchino Antonio Rossini (1792–1868), *William Tell*.

(H) Andrew Jackson (Democratic-Republican), president (1829–1837). First American missionary sent to China.

1830

(L) Oliver Wendell Holmes (1809–1894) publishes "Old Ironsides." Seba Smith (1792–1868) begins "Jack Downing" letters. *Godey's Lady's Book* founded (1830–1898). *Victor Hugo (1802–1885), *Hernani*, causes classicist-romanticist riots.

(H) Daniel Webster delivers his famous reply to Hayne. President Jackson's toast: "The Federal Union—it must be preserved." Joseph Smith (1805–1844), publishes *The Book of Mormon;* Mormons (Church of Latter-Day Saints) organized. Congress acts to move Indian tribes to territory west of the Mississippi. Peter Cooper builds "Tom Thumb," first American locomotive. U. S. population, 12,866,020. First railroad (Liverpool to Manchester) opened. Reign of William IV in England (1830–1837). July Revolution in France. James Audubon (1785–1851), *Birds of America* (1830–1838). *Auguste Comte (1798–1857), *Course of Positive Philosophy* (1830–1842). *Charles Lyell (1797–1875), *Principles of Geology*, emphasizes mechanistic view of nature.

1831

(L) Poe, *Poems*. *Hugo, *Notre Dame de Paris*. *Stendhal (1783–1842), *The Red and the Black*.

(H) Peggy Eaton affair disrupts Jackson's cabinet. First national political convention in U. S. (Anti-Masonic Party). New England Anti-Slavery Society founded; Nat Turner leads bloody insurrection of slaves in Southampton County, Virginia. William Lloyd Garrison founds *The Liberator* (1831–1865).

1832

(L) Bryant, *Poems*. Irving, *The Alhambra*. John Pendleton Kennedy (1795–1870), *Swallow Barn*.

(A) Lowell Mason (1792–1872) founds Boston Academy of Music.

(H) Jackson vetoes recharter of Bank of the United States. Extreme protectionist tariff of 1832; Nullification Ordinance of South Carolina declares that a state has sovereignty to resist the federal government; Congress passes Force Bill authorizing use of force to back federal law. Jackson (Democrat) re-elected, defeating Henry Clay (Whig). Black Hawk War: resistance of Sauk and Fox Indians to westward resettlement. First clipper ship launched at Baltimore. Fast wooden clippers, chiefly from New England, lead Pacific and California shipping until 1860. Cholera epidemic in New York. *Mrs. Frances Trollope (1780–1863), *Domestic Manners of the Americans*, disparages American institutions.

1833

(L) Henry Wadsworth Longfellow (1807–1882) publishes his first book, *Outre-Mer*. Seba Smith collects *The Life and Writings of Major Jack Downing*. *Knickerbocker Magazine* founded (1833–1865). *Honoré de Balzac (1799–1850), *Eugénie Grandet*. *Thomas Carlyle (1795–1881), *Sartor Resartus*, influences American transcendentalists.

(A) Thomas U. Walter (1804–1887), Girard College, Philadelphia.

(H) Compromise Tariff of 1833 provides for gradual reduction of protection; South Carolina rescinds Nullification Ordinance. Jackson begins withdrawal of federal deposits from Bank of the United States; redeposits in favored local banks. Massachusetts separates church and state (last state to do so). New York *Sun*, first penny newspaper, inaugurates large-scale popular journalism. American Anti-Slavery Society founded. First tax-supported free public library (Peterboro, New Hampshire). Oberlin College founded (admits women and Negroes); Haverford College founded. Slavery outlawed in British Empire.

1834

(L) George Bancroft (1800–1891) begins his *History of the United States* (1834–1876). *Life of David Crockett*, ascribed to Crockett (1786–1836). *Southern Literary Messenger* founded (1834–1864). *Bulwer-Lytton (1803–1873), *Last Days of Pompeii*.

(H) Cyrus H. McCormick patents the reaper.

1835

(L) Irving, *A Tour on the Prairies*. Augustus Baldwin Longstreet (1790–1870), *Georgia Scenes*. William Gilmore Simms (1806–1870), *The Yemassee*. First appearance of the "Crockett Almanacs" (1835–1856).

(H) National debt liquidated. Slavery tension increases; Charleston citizens raid the mails, burn abolition literature; local postmasters directed to refrain from delivering such material; Garrison suffers mob violence in Boston. Beginning of Second Seminole War (1835–1842); Indian troubles in Florida ended by deportation. Lyman Beecher's activities inaugurate period of anti-Catholic agitation. "Loco-Focos" (1835–1840), radical Democrats, anti-monopoly and prolabor. New York *Herald* founded.

1836

(L) Ralph Waldo Emerson (1803–1882), *Nature,* provides the first major formulation of American transcendentalism. First meetings of the Transcendental Club (1836–1844).

(H) Texas declares itself a republic, independent of Mexico. Battles of the Alamo (March), San Jacinto (April). Mount Holyoke founded (first women's college). Samuel Colt (1814–1862) patents six-shooter.

1837

(L) Cooper, *Gleanings in Europe* (1837–1838). Emerson delivers address at Harvard, "The American Scholar." Hawthorne, *Twice-Told Tales. United States Magazine and Democratic Review* founded (1837–1849). *Burton's Gentleman's Magazine* founded (1837–1840). *Charles Dickens (1812–1870), Oliver Twist,* initiates his vogue in America. *Nikolai Gogol (1809–1852), Dead Souls.*

(H) Martin Van Buren (Democrat), president (1837–1841). Beginning of financial panic and depression (1837–1843). U. S. recognizes independence of Texas. Michigan admitted to statehood. Samuel F. B. Morse exhibits telegraph instrument he has invented. Massachusetts sets up first board of education, with Horace Mann as secretary, and he begins campaign for universal free public education. Nativist (anti-Catholic) riots in Massachusetts. Abolitionist editor E. P. Lovejoy killed by mob in Alton, Illinois. Reign of Victoria in England (1837–1901).

1838

(L) Cooper, *The American Democrat.* Emerson delivers his "Divinity School Address." John Greenleaf Whittier (1807–1892), *Ballads and Anti-Slavery Poems.* *Harriet Martineau (1802–1876), Retrospect of Western Travel,* a favorable account of the U. S. *Alexis de Tocqueville (1805–1859), Travels in America,* American translation of the French (published in 1835), an impartial analysis, now classic.

(H) Underground Railroad established for escaped slaves.

1839

(A) *Frédéric François Chopin (1810–1849), Préludes (Op. 28).*

(H) Aroostook War: boundary dis-

putes between settlers of Maine and New Brunswick; boundary fixed by treaty in 1842. Charles Goodyear discovers process for vulcanizing rubber. Daguerreotype invented: beginnings of photography. Henry R. Schoolcraft (1793–1864), *Algic Researches* (on the Indians).

1840

(L) Cooper, *The Pathfinder.* Poe first collects his stories as *Tales of the Grotesque and Arabesque.* The transcendental group inaugurates *The Dial* (1840–1844).

(H) Ten-hour day proclaimed for federal workers. Rising political power of the Whig party. Beginning of potato famine in Ireland results in large Irish immigration to U. S.; rapid growth of the Catholic Church in America; Catholic population now 5 per cent of total. U. S. population, 17,069,453.

1841

(L) Cooper, *The Deerslayer.* Emerson, *Essays.* James Russell Lowell (1819–1891), *A Year's Life.* Poe, "Murders in the Rue Morgue." *Robert Browning (1812–1889), Pippa Passes.* *Carlyle, Heroes and Hero-Worship.*

(A) Fanny Elssler's tour introduces ballet in U. S.

(H) William Henry Harrison (Whig), president (1841). On his death, Vice-President John Tyler succeeds (1841–1845). Preëmption Act helps small settler and squatter to secure public lands in the West. Development of experimental communities: Brook Farm (1841–1847); Fruitlands (1842–1843); Hopedale (1842–1856); Fourierist North American Phalanx (1843–1854). New York *Tribune* founded. George Catlin (1796–1872), *Manners and Customs of the North American Indians.* *Schopenhauer, The Two Ground-Problems of Ethics.*

1842

(L) Longfellow, *Ballads and Other Poems.* Rufus Wilmot Griswold (1815–1857) first publishes anthology, *Poets and Poetry of America.* *Dickens visits the U. S. and publishes American Notes,* then a controversial account.

(A) New York Philharmonic Society organized. Christy's Minstrels established.

(H) Dorr Rebellion, Rhode Island (for broader suffrage). Supreme Court, in *Prigg v. Pennsylvania,* absolves the states from responsibility to recapture fugitive slaves. Massachusetts Supreme Court supports right of workers to organize. Dr. W. C. Long uses ether as an anesthetic. P. T. Barnum opens his American Museum.

1843

(L) Poe, *The Prose Tales of Edgar A. Poe.* William Hickling Prescott (1796–1859), *Conquest of Mexico.* Daniel Webster delivers second Bunker Hill oration.

(A) James Renwick (1818–1895), Grace Church, New York.

(H) John C. Frémont leads expedition across Sierras to California.

1844

(L) Cooper, *Afloat and Ashore.* Emerson, *Essays, Second Series.* Whittier, *Voices of Freedom.* *Alexandre Dumas père (1803–1870), *The Three Musketeers.*

(A) John W. Griffiths (1809?–1882) designs clipper ship *Rainbow.* *Richard Wagner (1813–1883), *Tannhäuser.*

(H) Morse's telegraph in commercial use. Hunker-Barnburner split in northern Democratic party (1844–1852), on free-soil issue; Baptists split over slavery.

1845

(L) Cooper, *Satanstoe.* Margaret Fuller (1810–1850), *Woman in the Nineteenth Century.* Johnson Jones Hooper (1815–1862), *Some Adventures of Captain Simon Suggs.* Poe, *The Raven and Other Poems* and *Tales of E. A. Poe.*

(H) James K. Polk (Democrat), president (1845–1849). Texas annexed; comes in as a state; statehood for Florida. Methodists split on slavery. U. S. Naval Academy founded. Immigration now averages 172,000 per year.

1846

(L) Hawthorne, *Mosses from an Old Manse.* Holmes, *Poems.* Herman Melville (1819–1891), *Typee.* Poe, "The Philosophy of Composition."

(A) Richard Upjohn (1802–1878), Trinity Church, New York.

(H) War with Mexico (1846–1848). Bear Flag War in California: insurrection of American settlers against Mexican government. Mormons start westward migration. Oregon Treaty with Great Britain; treaty with Colombia provides for transit of Panama. Wilmot Proviso, ruling against slavery in new territories, unsuccessful in the House, becomes principle of Free-Soil party. Independent U. S. Treasury permanently established. Iowa admitted as state. Elias Howe patents sewing machine; Robert Hoe invents rotary press; Dr. W. T. G. Morton publicly demonstrates ether anesthesia. Famine in Ireland.

1847

(L) Emerson, *Poems.* Longfellow, *Evangeline.* Melville, *Omoo.* Prescott, *Conquest of Peru.* Griswold, *Prose Writers of America,* a collection. *Charlotte Brontë (1816–1855), *Jane Eyre.* *Emily Brontë (1818–1848), *Wuther-*

ing Heights. *Alfred, Lord Tennyson (1809–1892), *The Princess.* *William Makepeace Thackeray (1811–1863), *Vanity Fair.*

(H) Mexican War: Battle of Buena Vista; Scott lands at Vera Cruz, defeats Mexicans at Cerro Gordo, takes Mexico City (September), ending war. Mormons settle in Utah. Oneida (New York) Community. New Hampshire ten-hour factory law. Louis Agassiz (1807–1873), *Introduction to Natural History,* emphasizes empirical attitudes.

1848

(L) Lowell collects the first series of *The Biglow Papers* (1846–1848); publishes *A Fable for Critics* and *The Vision of Sir Launfal.* Poe, *Eureka.* *Thomas Babington Macaulay (1800–1859) begins publication of *A History of England.* *Dante Gabriel Rossetti (1828–1882) promotes the Pre-Raphaelites.

(A) Stephen Collins Foster (1826–1864), first collection, *Songs of the Sable Harmonists.*

(H) Peace treaty with Mexico: U. S. acquires vast territory including New Mexico and California. Gold discovered in California. Wisconsin admitted to statehood; University of Wisconsin founded. Associated Press established. American Association for the Advancement of Science founded. First Women's Rights Convention, at Seneca Falls, New York, issues Declaration of Rights. Democratic revolutions in Italy, France, Germany, Hungary (1848–1852): American unofficial participation and increase in immigration from these countries. *Karl Marx (1818–1883) and Friedrich Engels (1820–1895), *Communist Manifesto.*

1849

(L) Longfellow, *Kavanagh.* Melville, *Mardi* and *Redburn.* Francis Parkman (1823–1893), *The California and Oregon Trail.* Henry David Thoreau (1817–1862), *A Week on the Concord and Merrimack Rivers;* "Civil Disobedience" appears in a collection of various writers. *Dickens, *David Copperfield.* *Thackeray, *Pendennis.*

(H) Zachary Taylor (Whig), president (1849–1850). California gold rush begins.

1850

(L) Emerson, *Representative Men.* Hawthorne, *The Scarlet Letter.* Melville, *White Jacket.* Whittier, *Songs of Labor and Other Poems;* "Ichabod" published in response to Webster's Seventh of March Speech. *Wordsworth, *The Prelude.*

(H) John C. Calhoun, Fourth of March Speech; Daniel Webster, Seventh of March Speech. President Taylor dies; Millard Fillmore succeeds him as president (1850–1853). Federal land grants for railroads initiated. Immigration rate reaches 300,000 per year. Compromise of 1850: Congress admits California as free state, New Mexico and Utah as territories which will determine the slavery issue by popular vote on achieving statehood; Fugitive Slave Law strengthened. Secession debated in Tennessee and Georgia. U. S. population 23,191,876.

1851

(L) Hawthorne, *The House of the Seven Gables*. Melville, *Moby Dick*.

(A) Donald McKay (1810–1880) designs clipper ship *Flying Cloud*.

(H) Maine passes first prohibition law. Y.M.C.A. organized in U. S. Louis Kossuth's visit to U. S. (1851–1852) stirs American sympathy for Hungarian independence. Schoolcraft, *Historical * * * Information Respecting * * * the Indian Tribes * * * (1851–1857)*. *The New York Times* founded.

1852

(L) Melville, *Pierre*. Harriet Beecher Stowe (1811–1896), *Uncle Tom's Cabin*. *Thackeray publishes *Henry Esmond*, and lectures in U. S.

(H) Massachusetts passes first compulsory school law. Second Empire, under Napoleon III (1852–1870).

1853

(L) Joseph Glover Baldwin (1815–1864), *Flush Times of Alabama and Mississippi*.

(H) Franklin Pierce (Democrat), president (1853–1857). Gadsden Purchase from Mexico adds to territory of New Mexico and Arizona. Elisha Kent Kane's Arctic expedition. Rail connection between New York and Chicago established. Elisha Graves Otis invents the first safe elevator, making the skyscraper practicable.

1854

(L) Timothy Shay Arthur (1809–1885), *Ten Nights in a Barroom*. Thoreau, *Walden*.

(H) Commodore M. C. Perry in Japan secures agreement to open Japanese ports to Western trade. First Japanese-American treaty (ratified 1855). Kansas-Nebraska Bill extends "squatter sovereignty" to those territories in determining status of slavery, resulting in competition for settlement by northern and southern forces. Republican party initiated by meeting (Ripon, Wisconsin) in opposition to Kansas-Nebraska Bill. Know-Nothing party, consisting of anti-Catholic nativists, carries Massachusetts. Crimean War (1854–1856; Charge of the Light Brigade, 1854).

1855

(L) Irving, *Life of George Washington* (1855–1859). Longfellow, *The Song of Hiawatha*. Melville, "Benito Cereno" and *Israel Potter*. Simms, *The Forayers*. Walt Whitman (1819–1892), *Leaves of Grass*. E. A. Duyckinck (1816–1878) and G. L. Duyckinck (1823–1863), *Cyclopaedia of American Literature*. Saturday Club founded in Boston. *Tennyson, *Maud*. *Thackeray's *The Newcomes* and *The Virginians* (1857) contain American materials.

(A) George Inness (1825–1894), "The Lackawanna Valley."

(H) Rival governments and violence in "bloody Kansas"; New England Emigrant Aid Company pours antislavery settlers into Lawrence, Kansas. Immigration now averages 260,000 per year.

1856

(L) Emerson, *English Traits*. Melville, *Piazza Tales* and *The Confidence Man*. Simms, *Eutaw*. Stowe, *Dred*.

(H) Republican party nationally organized. Proslavery forces sack Lawrence, Kansas; John Brown murders proslavery men at Osawatomie; President Pierce declares martial law. Antislavery leader Charles Sumner assaulted and seriously injured on Senate floor by Preston Smith Brooks of South Carolina. John Lothrop Motley (1814–1877), *Rise of the Dutch Republic*.

1857

(L) *Atlantic Monthly* founded. *Harper's Weekly* (1857–1916). *Charles Baudelaire (1821–1867), *The Flowers of Evil*. *Gustave Flaubert (1821–1880), *Madame Bovary*.

(A) Currier and Ives begin publishing prints.

(H) James Buchanan (Democrat), president (1857–1861). Dred Scott decision in Supreme Court supports property rights of slaveowners, intensifies antislavery feeling. Panic of 1857.

1858

(L) Holmes, *The Autocrat of the Breakfast-Table*. Longfellow, *The Courtship of Miles Standish*. *William Morris (1834–1896), *The Defence of Guenevere*.

(H) Lincoln debates Douglas, his opponent for the Senate, on issues of the slavery question; wins national attention. Presbyterians split over slavery. Statehood for Minnesota. First Atlantic cable, unsuccessful. G. H. Pullman develops sleeping car. Gail Borden evaporates milk commercially. A national baseball league organized.

1859

(L) Dion Boucicault (1820?–1890), *The Octoroon*, produced. *Dickens, *A Tale of Two Cities*. *George Eliot (1819–1880), *Adam Bede*. *Edward Fitzgerald (1809–1883) translates the *Rubaiyat of Omar Khayyam*. *Tennyson, *Idylls of the King*.

(A) *Jean François Millet (1814–1875), "The Angelus."

(H) Oregon becomes a state. Colorado gold rush begins. Comstock silver lode discovered in Nevada. Oil struck at Titusville, Pennsylvania. First chain stores established. John Brown raids Harpers Ferry arsenal; his execution augments abolitionist sentiment. *Charles Darwin (1809–1882), The Origin of Species, formulates the theory of evolution.

1860

(L) Emerson, The Conduct of Life. Hawthorne, The Marble Faun. Holmes, The Professor at the Breakfast-Table. Henry Timrod (1828–1867), Poems. Whitman, Leaves of Grass (third edition). Whittier, Home Ballads and Poems. *Dickens, Great Expectations. *Eliot, The Mill on the Floss.

(H) Pony Express established (1860–1861). South Carolina secedes following election of Lincoln as president. U. S. population, 31,443,321; slave population, 3,952,801.

1861

(L) Holmes, Elsie Venner. Frederick L. Olmsted (1822–1903), The Cotton Kingdom. *Eliot, Silas Marner. *Charles Reade (1814–1884), The Cloister and the Hearth.

(A) *Honoré Daumier (1808–1879), "The Washwoman."

(H) Abraham Lincoln (Republican), president (1861–1865). Kansas admitted as a free state (January). Civil War (1861–1865): secession of Mississippi, Florida, Alabama, Georgia, Louisiana, Texas, Virginia, Tennessee, Arkansas, North Carolina; Confederate States formed with Jefferson Davis as president; Confederates take Fort Sumter (April 14); southern ports blockaded; Confederates win at Bull Run (July); seizure of Confederate agents, James Murray Mason and John Slidell, aboard H.M.S. Trent; British intervention for the South narrowly averted. Emancipation of Russian serfs.

1862

(L) Charles Farrar Browne (1834–1867), Artemus Ward: His Book. Julia Ward Howe (1819–1910), "Battle Hymn of the Republic." *Ivan Turgenev (1818–1883), Fathers and Sons.

(H) Lee commands Confederate army; Monitor and Merrimac fight first battle between ironclad vessels; Grant in the West stopped at Shiloh (April); New Orleans taken (May); McClellan's Peninsular Campaign fails to take Richmond; Confederates win at Bull Run (August) but are repulsed at Antietam (September); northern advance on Richmond checked at Fredericksburg (December). Preliminary Emancipation Proclamation (Septem-

ber) to take effect January, 1863. Department of Agriculture formed; Homestead Act provides 160 acres of free western lands for settlers; Morrill Act authorizes land-grant colleges; beginning of flood of immigrants from Germany, Sweden, Norway, Denmark to the northwest U. S. *Herbert Spencer (1820–1903), System of Synthetic Philosophy: First Principles.

1863

(L) Hawthorne, Our Old Home. Edward Everett Hale (1822–1909), The Man Without a Country. Lincoln delivers the Gettysburg Address. Longfellow, Tales of a Wayside Inn. Thoreau, Excursions.

(A) *Édouard Manet (1832–1883), "Olympia."

(H) Stonewall Jackson dies in Confederate victory at Chancellorsville (May); Lee's northern campaign crushed at Gettysburg (July); South split by Grant's capture of Vicksburg (July), Union successes in Tennessee, Louisiana. *Thomas Henry Huxley (1825–1895), Man's Place in Nature.

1864

(L) David Ross Locke (1833–1888), Nasby Papers. Thoreau, The Maine Woods. *John Henry, Cardinal Newman (1801–1890), Apologia Pro Vita Sua. *Tennyson, Enoch Arden. *Tolstoi (1828–1910), War and Peace.

(H) Grant commands Union armies (March), suffers great losses in Battle of the Wilderness (May); Sherman takes Atlanta (July), marches to the sea, taking Savannah (December). Nevada admitted as state. Lincoln reelected president. Emergence of Tweed Ring in New York, first large-scale municipal corruption (1864–1871). Federal Immigration Bureau established; Congress provides for legal importation of contract labor.

1865

(L) Lowell delivers the "Commemoration Ode." Henry Wheeler Shaw (1818–1885), Josh Billings. Thoreau, Cape Cod. Whitman, Drum Taps. *Matthew Arnold (1822–1888), Essays in Criticism. *John Ruskin (1819–1900), Sesame and Lilies. *Algernon Charles Swinburne (1837–1909), Atalanta in Calydon.

(A) James McNeill Whistler (1834–1903), "An Arrangement in Gray and Black" (portrait of his mother).

(H) Lee surrenders to Grant at Appomattox (April 9). Lincoln assassinated (April 14). Andrew Johnson, president (1865–1869). Lincoln's moderate reconstruction plan rejected by Congress. Amendment XIII ends slavery (December). Ku Klux Klan local units organized. Cornell University founded. The Nation founded.

1866

(L) Whittier, *Snow-Bound. The Galaxy* founded (1866–1878). *Feodor Dostoievski (1821–1881), *Crime and Punishment.*

(H) Freedman's Bureau and first of the Civil Rights Acts give Negroes protection and citizenship. Atlantic cable completed. Grand Army of the Republic organized. New York *World* founded.

1867

(L) John Burroughs (1837–1921), *Notes on Walt Whitman.* Samuel Langhorne Clemens ("Mark Twain," 1835–1910), *The Celebrated Jumping Frog of Calaveras County and Other Sketches.* John W. De Forest (1826–1906), *Miss Ravenel's Conversion from Secession to Loyalty.* Emerson, *May Day and Other Poems.* G. W. Harris (1814–1869), *Sut Lovingood Yarns.* Bret Harte (1836–1902), *Condensed Novels.* Sidney Lanier (1842–1881), *Tiger-Lilies.* Longfellow completes translation of Dante's *Divine Comedy* (1865–1867). Lowell collects *The Biglow Papers, Second Series.* Whittier, *The Tent on the Beach.*

(H) Congress passes severe Reconstruction and Tenure of Office Acts. Alaska purchased from Russia for $7,200,000. Midway Islands annexed. Statehood for Nebraska. First national Grange (Patrons of Husbandry). Ku Klux Klan nationally organized. Immigration now averages 232,000 per year. *Marx, *Capital.*

1868

(L) Louisa May Alcott (1832–1888), *Little Women* (1868–1869). Harte, "The Luck of Roaring Camp," periodical publication. *Lippincott's Magazine* founded (1866–1916). *Overland Monthly* founded in San Francisco (1868–1875, 1883–1933). *Browning, *The Ring and the Book.*

(H) Johnson declares mild executive policy for Reconstruction; opposed by radical Republicans; impeached, narrowly acquitted. Amendment XIV provides constitutional guarantee of Negro citizenship, strict conditions for readmission of states and southern officials; paves way for military occupation and "carpetbag" government in South. Burlingame Treaty permits Chinese immigration. C. L. Sholes and others patent first practicable typewriter.

1869

(L) Clemens, *The Innocents Abroad.* Harte "Tennessee's Partner," periodical publication. *R. D. Blackmore (1825–1900), *Lorna Doone.* *Edmond (1822–1896) and Jules (1830–1870) de Goncourt, *Germinie Lacerteux,* first naturalistic novel.

(A) Matthew Brady (1823?–1896), *National Photographic Collection of War Views.* Winslow Homer (1836–1910), "Long Branch."

(H) Ulysses S. Grant (Republican), president (1869–1877). Black Friday (September 24): attempt of James Fisk and Jay Gould to corner gold; subsequent financial panic. Union Pacific Railroad completed. Suez Canal opened. Organization of Knights of Labor, first national union of all crafts, influential until 1886. Organization of Prohibition party, two woman-suffrage associations; Wyoming Territory grants woman suffrage (the first). Westinghouse locomotive air brake patented. First intercollegiate football game (Rutgers defeats Princeton).

1870

(L) Thomas Bailey Aldrich (1836–1907), *The Story of a Bad Boy.* Bryant, *Iliad* (translation). Emerson, *Society and Solitude.* Harte achieves national attention with *The Luck of Roaring Camp and Other Sketches* and "Plain Language from Truthful James"; beginning of the local-color movement. *Scribner's Monthly* founded. *Dante Gabriel Rossetti, *Poems.*

(H) Amendment XV guarantees suffrage to Negroes; states required to ratify before being readmitted; first Negro congressmen elected. Standard Oil Company incorporated. U. S. population, 38,818,449. Franco-Prussian War; William I becomes German emperor. Vatican council proclaims papal infallibility. *Thomas Henry Huxley, *Lay Sermons.*

1871

(L) Bryant, *Odyssey* (translation). Edward Eggleston (1837–1902), *The Hoosier Schoolmaster.* Harte, *East and West Poems.* John Hay (1838–1905), *Pike County Ballads.* Lowell, *My Study Windows.* Joaquin Miller (1839–1913), *Songs of the Sierras.* Whitman, *Democratic Vistas* and *Passage to India.*

(H) Treaty of Washington secures indemnity from Britain for having supplied Confederates with ships. Tweed Ring exposed in New York; Tweed indicted (convicted 1873). Great Chicago fire. Metropolitan Museum of Art opened. Smith College founded. Barnum opens his circus. Paris Commune. Unification of Italy accomplished. Stanley and Livingston in Africa. Josiah Willard Gibbs becomes professor of mathematical physics at Yale. *Darwin, *The Descent of Man.*

1872

(L) Clemens, *Roughing It.* Holmes, *The Poet at the Breakfast-Table.* William Dean Howells (1837–1920), *Their Wedding Journey* (his first novel).

*Samuel Butler (1835–1902), *Erewhon*.

(A) Henry Hobson Richardson (1838–1886) commences Trinity Church, Boston.

(H) *Congressional Record* established. Grant re-elected. Crédit Mobilier scandal discloses bribing of congressmen by exploiters of government railroad subsidies. Cheap sale of natural resources to private interests: Mining Act (1872), Coal Act (1873), Timber and Stone Act (1878). Montgomery Ward pioneers mail-order business. American Public Health Association formed. Eadweard Muybridge shows first pictures of objects in motion.

1873

(L) Samuel Langhorne Clemens and Charles Dudley Warner (1829–1900), *The Gilded Age*. Howells, *A Chance Acquaintance*. Henry Timrod (1828–1867), *Poems*. *Arthur Rimbaud (1854–1891), *A Season in Hell*.

(H) Failure of Jay Cooke and other speculators; panic followed by depression (1873–1879). J. E. Glidden's barbed wire ends the period of open cattle ranges, transforms ranching in West. Dynamo developed. The Great Bonanza, silver discovery in Nevada. Anthony Comstock secures antiobscenity statutes and becomes special agent of the Post Office Department.

1874

(L) Eggleston, *The Circuit Rider*. *Thomas Hardy (1840–1928), *Far from the Madding Crowd*. *Paul Verlaine (1844–1896), *Romances sans Paroles*.

(A) *Edvard Grieg (1843–1907), *Peer Gynt Suite No. 2*. *Johann Strauss, Jr. (1825–1899), *Die Fledermaus*.

(H) Massachusetts ten-hour law for women and children. Chatauqua movement launched (adult education). W.C.T.U. organized. Tennis introduced from England. John Fiske (1842–1901), *Outlines of Cosmic Philosophy*.

1875

(L) Emerson, *Letters and Social Aims*. Henry James (1843–1916), *A Passionate Pilgrim and Other Tales* (his first collection). *Tolstoi, *Anna Karenina*.

(A) Daniel Chester French (1850–1931), "The Minute Man," Concord, Massachusetts.

(H) Greenback party opposes redemption of paper money in specie; cheap money becomes political question. Gold discovered in Black Hills. Hawaiian reciprocity treaty stimulates sugar trade. Wellesley College founded. Immigration now averages 282,000 per year. Mary Baker Eddy (1821–1910), *Science and Health*.

1876

(L) Clemens, *The Adventures of Tom Sawyer*. Henry James, *Roderick Hudson*. Melville, *Clarel*. Whitman publishes Centennial Edition of *Leaves of Grass*. *Stéphane Mallarmé (1842–1898), *The Afternoon of a Faun*.

(A) *Pierre Auguste Renoir (1841–1919), "Le Bal du Moulin de la Galette."

(H) Philadelphia Centennial Exposition stimulates appreciation of American resources. Statehood for Colorado. George A. Custer and his expeditionary force annihilated at Little Big Horn, Montana Territory. Disputed Hayes-Tilden election; electoral vote contradictory; Samuel J. Tilden (Democrat) with popular majority. Granger laws for state control of railroad and finance monopolies; Supreme Court decisions support farm interests. Alexander Graham Bell demonstrates telephone. Johns Hopkins University opens first real graduate school in U. S. Founding of American Library Association, Johns Hopkins University. Internal-combustion engine invented. Felix Adler founds New York Society for Ethical Culture.

Bibliography

The introductory essays for the authors and texts represented in this work provide fundamental bibliographies. A library collection for reference purposes should contain at least the following works: *The Literature of the American People*, edited by Arthur Hobson Quinn and others; *Literary History of the United States*, three volumes, edited by R. E. Spiller and others; *The Oxford Companion to American Literature*, by J. D. Hart, valuable for authoritative brief references to authors and subjects; and *Harvard Guide to American History*, edited by O. Handlin and others, a comprehensive bibliography of American history, literature, and society. The bibliography which follows is a brief classified list of standard works of reference and history in the fields represented by the literature collected in the present volumes.

REFERENCE WORKS AND BIBLIOGRAPHIES

Adams, J. T., and Coleman, R. V., Editors. *Dictionary of American History*. Six vols., 1940.

Craigie, W. A., and Hulbert, J. R., Editors. *Dictionary of American English on Historical Principles*. Four vols., 1938–1944.

Dictionary of American Biography. Johnson, Allen, and Malone, Dumas, Editors. Twenty-two vols., 1928–1944. Supplements in preparation.

Handlin, O., Schlesinger, A. M., Morison, S. E., and others, Editors. *Harvard Guide to American History*. 1954. (Includes history, fine arts, literature, philosophy, and social sciences.)

Hart, J. D., *The Oxford Companion to American Literature*. Revised, 1948. (Author, title, and subject entries.)

International Index to Periodicals. Annual, 1907– . (Includes foreign-language periodicals and scholarly journals.)

Johnson, Merle. *Merle Johnson's American First Editions*. Revised and enlarged by Jacob Blanck, 1942.

Kunitz, S. J., and Haycraft, Howard, Editors. *American Authors, 1600–1900*. 1944. (A biographical dictionary.)

Kunitz, S. J., and Haycraft, Howard, Editors. *Twentieth Century Authors*. 1942. (A biographical dictionary.)

Leary, Lewis, Editor. *Articles on American Literature Appearing in Current Periodicals, 1920–1945*. 1947. (The best guide to scholarly articles on authors and literary subjects.)

Millet, F. B. *Contemporary American Authors: A Critical Survey and 219 Bio-bibliographies*. 1940.

Morris, R. B., Editor. *Encyclopedia of American History*. 1953.

Mott, F. L. *American Journalism: A History of Newspapers in the United States through 250 Years, 1690 to 1940*. 1941. Revised, 1950.

Mott, F. L. *A History of American Magazines*. Three vols., 1938.

Nineteenth Century Readers' Guide to Periodical Literature: 1890–1899; with Supplemental Indexing 1900–1922. 1944. (For entries later than 1899 also consult *Readers' Guide . . . .*)

Poole's Index to Periodical Literature. Annual, 1802–1881. Supplements, 1882–1907. (*Cf. Readers' Guide . . . .*)

Quinn, Arthur Hobson, Editor. *The Literature of the American People*. 1951. (Extensive bibliographies by chapters.)

Readers' Guide to Periodical Literature. Annual, 1900–   . (Especially useful for the location of articles and literature in nonprofessional magazines.)

Sabin, Joseph, and others. *A Dictionary of Books Relating to America from its Discovery to the Present Time*. Twenty-nine vols., 1868–1936.

Seligman, E. R. A., and Johnson, Allen, Editors. *Encyclopaedia of the Social Sciences*. Fifteen vols., 1931–1935.

Spiller, R. E., and others, Editors. *Literary History of the United States*. 1948. Vol. III, Bibliography. Thomas H. Johnson, Editor.

Trent, W. P., Erskine, John, Sherman, S. P., and Van Doren, Carl, Editors. *Cambridge History of American Literature*. Four vols., 1917–1921. (Good bibliography to 1918.)

Who's Who in America. Biennial, 1899–   .

Who Was Who In America. Vol. I, 1897–1942, 1942; Vol. II, 1943–1950, 1950.

LITERARY HISTORY

American Writers Series. Clark, H. H., General Editor. 1934–   . (Each volume contains representative selections of a major author, with a bibliography and critical introduction. Twenty-eight volumes have been published.)

Beach, J. W. *American Fiction: 1920–1940*. 1941. (Major authors only.)

Blair, Walter. *Native American Humor* (1800–1900). 1937.

Bogan, Louise. *Achievement in American Poetry, 1900–1950*. 1951.

Canby, H. S. *Classic Americans: A Study of Eminent American Writers from Irving to Whitman*. 1931.

Cowie, Alexander. *The Rise of the American Novel*. 1c48. (Principally eighteenth- and nineteenth-century novelists.)

Geismar, Maxwell. *The Last of the Provincials*. 1947. (Modern fiction.)

Geismar, Maxwell. *Writers in Crisis: The American Novel Between Two Wars*. 1942. (Major novelists, 1920–1940.)

Gregory, Horace, and Zalurenska, Marya. *A History of American Poetry, 1900–1940*. 1946.

Hubbell, Jay B. *The South in American Literature, 1607–1900*. 1954.

Kazin, Alfred. *On Native Grounds: An Interpretation of Modern American Prose Literature*. 1942.

Krutch, J. W. *The American Drama Since 1918: An Informal History*. 1939.

Leisy, E. E. *The American Historical Novel*. 1950.

Matthiessen, F. O. *American Renaissance: Art and Expression in the Age of Emerson and Whitman*. 1941.

Mencken, H. L. *The American Language: An Inquiry into the Development of English in the United States*. 1919. Revised to 1936. Supplement I, 1945; Supplement II, 1948.

Miller, Perry. *The New England Mind: The Seventeenth Century*. 1939.

Murdock, K. B. *Literature and Theology in Colonial New England.* 1949.

O'Connor, W. V. *An Age of Criticism, 1900–1950.* 1952.

Parrington, V. L. *Main Currents in American Thought: An Interpretation of American Literature from the Beginnings to 1920.* Three vols., 1927–1930.

Pattee, F. L. *A History of American Literature Since 1870.* 1915.

Quinn, Arthur Hobson. *American Fiction: An Historical and Critical Survey.* 1936. (Comprehensive to date of publication.)

Quinn, Arthur Hobson. *A History of the American Drama: From the Beginning to the Civil War.* 1923. Revised, 1943.

Quinn, Arthur Hobson. *A History of the American Drama: From the Civil War to the Present Day.* Two vols., 1927. Reissued in one vol., 1936.

Quinn, Arthur Hobson, Murdock, K. B., Godhes, Clarence, and Whicher, G. F. *The Literature of the American People.* 1951.

Rourke, Constance. *American Humor: A Study of the National Character.* 1931.

Smith, H. N. *Virgin Land: The American West as Symbol and Myth.* 1950.

Spiller, R. E., Thorp, W., Johnson, T. H., and Canby, H. S., Editors. *Literary History of the United States.* Three vols., 1948. Revised, one vol., 1953.

Taylor, W. F. *The Economic Novel in America.* 1942.

Tyler, M. C. *A History of American Literature during the Colonial Period, 1607–1765.* Two vols., 1878. Revised, 1897. One vol., 1949.

Tyler, M. C. *The Literary History of the American Revolution, 1763–1783.* Two vols., 1897. Reissued, one vol., 1941.

POLITICAL AND SOCIAL HISTORY

Adams, J. T. *Provincial Society, 1690–1763.* 1927.

Allen, F. L. *The Big Change: America Transforms Itself, 1900–1950.* 1952.

Allen, F. L. *Only Yesterday.* 1931. (Social history of the 1920's.)

Beard, C. A., and Beard, M. R. *The Rise of American Civilization.* Four vols., 1927–1942.

Billington, R. A. *Westward Expansion: A History of the American Frontier.* 1949.

Bowers, C. G. *Jefferson and Hamilton: The Struggle for Democracy in America.* 1925.

Buck, Paul H. *The Road to Reunion, 1865–1900.* 1937.

Chronicles of America Series. Johnson, Allen, General Editor. Fifty vols., 1918–1921. Six supplementary vols., Nevins, Allan, Editor, 1950–1951. (Brief histories of each period, authoritative in general.)

Dorfman, Joseph. *The Economic Mind in American Civilization.* Three vols., 1946–1949. (Through World War I.)

Faulkner, H. U. *The Quest for Social Justice, 1898–1914.* 1931.

Fish, C. R. *The Rise of the Common Man, 1830–1850.* 1927.

Greene, E. B. *The Revolutionary Generation, 1763–1790.* 1943.

Hesseltine, W. B. *A History of the South.* Revised, 1943.

Krout, J. A., and Fox, D. R. *The Completion of Independence, 1790–1830.* 1944.

Morison, S. E., and Commager, H. S. *The Growth of the American Republic.* Two vols., revised, 1950. (Excellent brief general history.)

Myrdal, Gunnar. *An American Dilemma: The Negro Problem and Modern Democracy.* Two vols., 1944.

Nevins, Allan. *The Emergence of Modern America. 1865–1878.* 1927.

Nichols, R. F. *The Disruption of American Democracy.* 1948. (Politics and the Civil War.)

Paxson, F. L. The History of the American Frontier, 1763–1893. 1924.

Schlesinger, A. M. The Rise of the City, 1878–1898. 1933.

Schlesinger, A. M., Jr. The Age of Jackson. 1945.

Slosson, W. P. The Great Crusade and After, 1914–1928. 1930.

Stephenson, W. H., and Coulter, E. M., Editors. A History of the South. Six vols., 1948–1953. To be completed in four more vols.

Sullivan, Mark. Our Times. Six vols., 1926–1935.

Tocqueville, Alexis de Democracy in America. Two vols., London, 1835. Bradley, Phillips, Editor, two vols., 1942.

Van Doren, Carl. The Great Rehearsal: The Story of the Making and Ratifying of the Constitution of the United States. 1948.

Wecter, Dixon. The Age of the Great Depression, 1929–1941. 1948.

Wish, Harvey. Contemporary America: The National Scene Since 1900. Second ed., 1948.

Wish, Harvey. Society and Thought in America. Two vols., 1950–1952.

Wright, L. B. The Atlantic Frontier: Colonial American Civilization, 1607–1763. 1948.

INTELLECTUAL AND CULTURAL HISTORY

Barker, Virgil. American Painting, History and Interpretation. 1950.

Cargill, Oscar. Intellectual America: Ideas on the March. 1941.

Cash, W. J. The Mind of the South. 1941.

Commager, H. S. The American Mind: An Interpretation of American Thought and Character Since the 1880's. 1950.

Curti, Merle. The Growth of American Thought. 1943. (American philosophy and ideas.)

Gabriel, R. H. The Course of American Democratic Thought: An Intellectual History since 1815. 1940.

Hofstadter, Richard. Social Darwinism in American Thought, 1860–1915. 1944.

Howard, J. T. Our American Music: Three Hundred Years of It. 1931. Third ed., 1946.

Jackson, G. P. White and Negro Spirituals: Their Life Span and Kinship. 1943.

LaFollette, Susanne. Art in America from Colonial Times to the Present Day. 1929.

Larkin, O. W. Art and Life in America. 1949.

Riley, I. W. American Thought from Puritanism to Pragmatism and Beyond. Second ed., 1923.

Schneider, H. W. History of American Philosophy. 1946.

Schneider, H. W. The Puritan Mind. 1930.

Tallmadge, T. E. The Story of Architecture in America. Revised, 1936.

Index